THE ETHICS AND CONDUCT OF LAWYERS IN ENGLAND AND WALES

This is the third edition of the leading textbook on legal ethics and the regulation of the legal profession in England and Wales. As such it maps the complex regulatory environment in which the legal profession in England and Wales now operates. It opens with a critical overview of professional ideals, organisation, power and culture and an examination of the mechanisms of professions, exercised through governance, regulation, discipline and education. The core of the book explores the conflict between duties owed to clients (loyalty and confidentiality) and wider duties (to the profession, third parties and society). The final part applies lawyers' ethics to dispute resolution and settlement (litigation, negotiation, advocacy and alternative dispute settlement). Now laid out in a more accessible format and written in a more approachable style, the book is ideal reading for those teaching and learning in the field of legal ethics.

The Ethics and Conduct of Lawyers in England and Wales

Third Edition

Andrew Boon

·HART·
PUBLISHING
OXFORD AND PORTLAND, OREGON
2014

Published in the United Kingdom by Hart Publishing Ltd
16C Worcester Place, Oxford, OX1 2JW
Telephone: +44 (0)1865 517530
Fax: +44 (0)1865 510710
E-mail: mail@hartpub.co.uk
Website: http://www.hartpub.co.uk

Published in North America (US and Canada) by
Hart Publishing
c/o International Specialized Book Services
920 NE 58th Avenue, Suite 300
Portland, OR 97213-3786
USA
Tel: +1 503 287 3093 or toll-free: (1) 800 944 6190
Fax: +1 503 280 8832
E-mail: orders@isbs.com
Website: http://www.isbs.com

First edition, 1999; second edition, 2007

Hart Publishing is an imprint of Bloomsbury Publishing plc.

British Library Cataloguing in Publication Data
Data Available

ISBN: 978-1-84946-669-1

Typeset by Compuscript Ltd, Shannon
Printed and bound in Great Britain by
CPI Group (UK) Ltd, Croydon CR0 4YY

In memory of
Professor Jenny Levin
12 May 1940–3 March 2013

Preface

This edition of this book was a long time in the making. Jenny Levin and I had planned to produce a third edition much sooner. In the event, Jenny's poor health meant that we delayed. In spring 2012 Jenny was feeling much better. We had a planning meeting and worked out how to proceed. Unfortunately, Jenny felt poorly in the autumn and died in March 2013. One of Jenny's many great achievements was her contribution to the Law Society group that produced the Solicitors' Code of Conduct 2007. This was the first statement of solicitors' ethics to claim that title and it looks as if it may be the last. A summary of Jenny's other considerable contributions to the discipline of law and legal practice was published by the Legal Action Group.[1]

The six years since the previous edition have seen seismic changes in the legal services market in England and Wales. The Legal Services Board began providing 'oversight regulation' to the legal professions, or 'authorised providers' of legal services. The professions themselves are no longer self-regulators. There are also new 'players' in the market, business organisations providing services on a different model, but employing lawyers. These Alternative Business Structures have arrived as a result of the Legal Services Act 2007. They are intended by government to provide competition in a market previously dominated by professional concerns.

These changes in the legal services market in England and Wales arguably put the jurisdiction at the forefront of experimentation in legal services regulation. Since the previous edition both solicitors and barristers have responded to the numerous demands of the Legal Services Act. They set up separate regulatory arms so, strictly, the professions are no longer directly responsible for regulation. They publish regulatory 'handbooks' that cover organisations as well as individuals. As part of this format, new codes of conduct have been published for both barristers and solicitors.

It is appropriate to consider whether it is still appropriate to talk of 'ethics and conduct', as opposed to the regulation of the legal profession. The title was retained for this edition because the book looks at the evolution of professional ethics rather than just its current incarnation. This edition emphasises how the historical legacy is manifest in regulation, including in the latest codes. In laying out the material I have attempted to separate legislative, judicial and regulatory influences and stated the position as it stands at the beginning of March 2014.

Andy Boon
Gray's Inn,
London

---

[1] S Hughes, *Obituary: Professor Jenny Levin 12 May 1940–3 March 2013.* See more at: www.lag.org.uk/magazine/2013/05/obituary-professor-jenny-levin-12-may-1940-3-march-2013.aspx#sthash.tqf23d94.dpuf.

Acknowledgements

I am grateful to colleagues at City Law School, City University London for comments on drafts. These include Susan Blake (negotiation and ADR), Andrew Choo (privilege), Peter Hungerford-Welch (criminal procedure) and Stuart Sime (civil litigation). I am also grateful to Alex Roy, formerly of the Legal Service Board but now at the Financial Conduct Authority (Part 2) and to Rachael Marsh of LawWorks (Service). All of these colleagues have provided valuable editorial comment on the text. Some have even provided additional material and drafting suggestions. Any errors, naturally, are my own.

Thanks to Emily Allbon and others at the City Law School Library for their assistance. Thanks also to my daughter Frankie, for advice on how the book might be made more useful to students. As ever, I am grateful to those at Hart Publishing who worked on this edition. Special thanks are due to Richard Hart for his encouragement and support, and for his advice on the current edition, to Rachel Turner, especially for organising the cover and special thanks to Rob Crossley for his diligent copy editing.

Contents

Table of Cases

Table of UK Legislation

Table of European Union Legislation

Table of International Instruments

Table of Secondary Legislation and Quasi-Statutory Codes

PART I

PROFESSIONAL ETHICS

Ideals

'Well, I don't want to be a lawyer mama, I don't want to lie'.[1]

I. Introduction

Occupations develop ideas about the right way to do the work they do. In the case of lawyers, this involves reconciling some apparently incompatible aspirations. A popular view is that they profess virtue, for example acting with integrity, while making money from helping murderers, tax avoiders or polluters to evade justice. This chapter deals with the issue of how that can be justified. It will explain how moral ambiguity is intrinsic to the job that lawyers do by considering the nature of the lawyer's role.

Later in the chapter the issue of whether the professional ethics of lawyers can or should be consistent with principles of 'ordinary morality' is considered. These issues are approached by exploring the implications of the commitment to the 'rule of law'. This shapes the roles of judges and lawyers in the Western democracies. It takes on a particular character in an adversarial system. The chapter examines the so-called 'standard conception' of the lawyer's role, together with criticisms of its moral orientation. It concludes with a defence of how the role of lawyer is interpreted in England and Wales.

II. Professional Ethics and Conduct

Ethics is a branch of philosophy concerned with how people make good and right decisions on the issues confronting them. Different ethical theories suggest distinct ways of thinking about making such decisions. Deontology is concerned with whether

---

[1] J Lennon, 'Don't Want to be a Soldier' from *Imagine* (Parlophone, 1971).

there is a duty to behave in a particular way.[2] Consequentialism advocates that one must consider outcomes before deciding on a course of action. Virtue ethics suggests that good character is essential to ethical decision-making. Principlism suggests that ethical decisions should be based on four basic ethical principles.[3]

In practice, decision-making tends to be intuitive. Most people do not consciously apply ethical theory. They may, however, take into account considerations that reflect one or more of these ethical theories. If making decisions is a complex process, it is more so if one is a lawyer. Considerations informing ethical decision-making for ordinary people apply differently to members of professions. Professionals have a distinct social role to perform. Consequently, they are placed in different relationships to clients, to individual third parties and to society as a whole. As a part of this process they are inducted into the nuances of decision-making in their field of practice.

A. Professions

For present purposes, professions are defined as occupations which the state has endowed with a degree of freedom in running their affairs. They are given this autonomy because they control an esoteric field of knowledge of vital concern to the functioning of a healthy society. This freedom includes having a degree of control over how services in their field of expertise are delivered. The actions of professionals are guided by values that underpin the role they perform.

Members of professions enjoy a high level of autonomy in guiding clients in making important decisions. In return for their freedom, professionals commit themselves to upholding high standards of behaviour. They are placed in an unusual position of trust and responsibility in relation to others. Accumulated practical experience helps them to choose the right course of action in difficult situations.

B. Professional Values

Values are standards influencing choices between courses of action.[4] They tend to fall into one of three groups: moral values such as fairness, justice and truth; pragmatic values such as thrift, efficiency and health; and aesthetic values such as beauty, softness and warmth. A value system is a collection of consistent and coherent values ranked according to importance. Professional value systems include a mixture of moral and pragmatic values. The core professional values of lawyers can be elusive,

[2] Derived from the Ancient Greek *deon*, meaning binding duty (J Pearsall and B Trumble (eds), *The Oxford English Reference Dictionary* (Oxford, New York, Oxford University Press, 1995); and see D Luban, 'Freedom and Constraint in Legal Ethics: Some Mid-Course Corrections to Lawyers and Justice' (1990) 49 *Maryland Law Review* 424, at 424–28).
[3] TL Beauchamp and JF Childress, *Principles of Biomedical Ethics*, 4th edn (New York, Oxford, Oxford University Press, 2001) at 12.
[4] N Rescher, *Introduction to Value Theory* (New Jersey, Prentice Hall, 1969) at 2.

or even controversial.[5] They may be unarticulated, reflect differences of opinion or change over time.

Three examples of lawyers' values illustrate shades of difference and emphasis. In 2003, a President of the Law Society opined that independence, integrity and confidentiality were the core values for solicitors.[6] In 2007, another President of The Law Society said that solicitors should possess the 'level of honesty, integrity and professionalism expected by the public and members of the profession'.[7] The Code of the International Bar Association emphasises 'the highest standards of honesty and integrity',[8] serving 'the interests of justice', observing the law, maintaining ethical standards[9] and maintaining sufficient independence to allow barristers to give their clients unbiased advice.[10]

i. Core Values

a. Client Goods

Professional values reflect client goods, such as a right to self-determination, privacy and protection from harm. These may also be limited by professional self-interest, such as the need to obey the law and keep personal feelings separate from work decisions. The realisation of these values has practical implications. For example, a profession may be committed to the value of client autonomy. In that case, it would promote client self-determination by ensuring that clients make their own moral choices. This would mean training professionals to present options for clients and facilitate client decisions.

b. Neutrality

Neutrality represents the value of disinterestedness. This enables professionals to take a detached view and to reconcile a pull on their loyalties in more than one direction. The value of neutrality is essential to any judicial role, but is relevant to lawyers in general. The idea of equality before the law means that lawyers must be able to represent morally indefensible individuals without compromising their own personal integrity.

c. Public Service

An aspiration to service is not confined to lawyers. In *Bhagavad Gita*, Lord Krishna says that '[o]ne must perform his prescribed duties as a vocation, keeping in sight the public good'.[11] The key professional value of legal professions in common law countries is the idea of a professional role as 'service'. Today this generally means working

---

[5] D Nicolson and J Webb, *Professional Legal Ethics* (Oxford, Oxford University Press, 1999) 13–21.

[6] P Williamson, 'When Core Values Matter' *Young Solicitors Group Magazine* Issue 21, July 2003, at 8.

[7] SRA, *Guidelines on the Assessment of Suitability and Character* (2007).

[8] *International Bar News* (1995) Summer, at 23, r 1.

[9] ibid, r 2.

[10] ibid, r 8.

[11] OP Dwivedi, 'Ethics for Public Sector Administrators: Education and Training' in RM Thomas (ed), *Teaching Ethics: Government Ethics* (London, HMSO, 1996) 339, at 345.

for the good of the community, being more interested in the work, or vocation, than in the extrinsic reward, money or prestige, it offers.[12] This is consistent with the traditional role of professions in providing alternatives to 'the tidal pull of the profit motive'.[13]

While there are different conceptions of what it might mean to be a 'good lawyer',[14] most are linked to intrinsic rather than extrinsic motivation. This is implicit in Alasdair MacIntyre's analogy between professional virtue and the game of chess.[15] A player who cheats at chess may succeed, acquiring the external goods of fame, fortune or prestige, but will not achieve the internal goods of the game. These come only to those who play honestly, according to the rules, *and* with knowledge and skill. MacIntyre argues that the 'internal goods' of a practice can only be achieved by 'subordinating ourselves within the practice in our relationship to other practitioners'.[16] A young professional is inculcated into the practices of a community performing a role well for its own sake. But it does not explain what defines the role. For this we need to look at the good that the role serves.

d. Justice

The status of professions is often attributed to a key good that they deliver to society. Just as the medical profession delivers health, lawyers deliver justice. There are many different meanings of justice and lawyers are associated with procedural justice of a kind delivered by courts. There is no reason why lawyers' notion of justice should be limited in this way. Lawyers' concept of justice could be defined to include responsibilities to fairness, to the accessibility of legal services or to striving for social justice.

C. Professional Virtues

Whereas values are standards set by a society or individual, virtues are aspirational qualities for individuals. Professionals aspire to 'an ideal defining a standard of good conduct, virtuous character, and a commitment, therefore, to excellence going beyond the norm of morality ordinarily governing relations among persons'.[17] Professionals also embrace values that it is not necessary for ordinary people to achieve. An advocate, for example, has to be brave to stand up in court. Professions often express their values as the virtues they expect to find in their members. Therefore, honesty is both a value and a virtue.

---

[12] R Pound, *The Lawyer from Antiquity to Modern Times: With Particular Reference to The Development of Bar Associations in the United States* (St Paul, Minn, West Publishing, 1953).
[13] WM Sullivan, 'Calling a Career: The Tensions of Modern Professional Life' in A Flores (ed), *Professional Ideals* (Belmont, CA, Wadsworth Publishing, 1988) at 41.
[14] AT Kronman, *The Lost Lawyer: Failing Ideals of the Legal Profession* (Harvard, Belknap Press, 1993) at 367.
[15] AD MacIntyre, *After Virtue: A Study in Moral Theory* (London, Duckworth, 1985) at 127.
[16] ibid, at 191.
[17] A Flores, *What Kind of Person Should a Professional Be?'* in A Flores (ed), *Professional Ideals* (1988) (n 13) at 1.

D. Conduct

Professions typically set and police standards for education, training and work. These standards are often systematised and reproduced as a code of conduct. This takes some of the effort out of ethical decision-making, but there are a number of reasons why codes do not resolve all problems. Professional codes cannot answer every question arising in professional work. The rules in different parts of a code of conduct may conflict, leaving doubt about which should prevail. Applying a rule may produce an outcome that a professional considers to be unethical. In these instances, professionals are presented with an ethical dilemma. Where rules do not provide an obvious and satisfactory answer, they may resort to underlying values to reach an ethical decision.

III. Systems and Roles

A. Professional Roles

Legal roles reflect economic systems. Considering why industrial capitalism developed in Europe and not in other regions of the world, Max Weber pointed to the roles played by social structure, religion and law.[18] In most capitalist countries, the practice of law is dominated by business. Nevertheless, the social good of justice has huge symbolic importance. The Western liberal democracies are committed to human emancipation from exploitation, inequality and oppression, and to institutions promoting justice, equality and participation.[19] In order that citizens can enjoy these goods, access to justice must usually be supported by the state.

European legal systems contributed to the development of the modern state by developing rational legal rules. These were deliberately made free of religious and other traditional values or direct political interference and were universally applied. Weber called systems of control by autonomous rules 'legalism'. Constitutional regimes require judges to protect human and property rights.[20] Independent lawyers monitor judges and prevent all but the most arguable cases reaching court. The legal system defines the work and tasks lawyers perform, which becomes integrated into a social role.[21] In Western societies, lawyers' roles are defined by the rule of law.

---

[18] M Weber, *Economy and Society* (G Roth and W Wittich, eds) (Oakland, CA, University of California Press, 1968) and for critical summaries, see DM Trubek, 'Max Weber on Law and the Rise of Capitalism' (1972) 3 *Wisconsin Law Review* 720 and M Albrow, 'Legal Positivism and Bourgeois Materialism: Max Weber's View of the Sociology of Law' (1975) 2 *British Journal of Law and Society* 14.

[19] A Giddens, *Modernity and Self-Identity: Self and Society in the Late Modern Age* (Cambridge, Polity Press, 1991) at 212.

[20] GC Hazard and A Dondi, *Legal Ethics: A Comparative Study* (Stanford, CA, Stanford University Press, 2004) at 92–93.

[21] F Znaniecki, *Social Relations and Social Roles* (San Francisco, CA, Chandler Publishing Co, 1965).

B. The Rule of Law

i. Origins and Contemporary Significance

The rule of law means that no person or institution is above the law. This idea has ancient origins beginning, as far as is known, with Aristotle's assertion that the rule of law is preferable to the rule of man.[22] In England, this meant controlling the absolute power of the monarchy, starting with Magna Carta in 1215. The rule of law continues to be evoked in legal cases and in legislation. The Constitutional Reform Act 2005,[23] a significant piece of constitutional legislation, requires that the Lord Chancellor swear an oath to uphold the rule of law and judicial independence.[24] Because the rule of law is used as a rhetorical device, some legal theorists regard the concept as devalued and meaningless.[25] Comparative study suggests, however, that it is of fundamental importance both in Europe and the common law jurisdictions based on the system in England and Wales.[26]

ii. Different Conceptions of the Rule of Law

Tamanaha identifies three formal versions of the rule of law.[27] These describe the source and form of legality, moving from 'thin', or minimalist, versions through to 'thicker versions', which add to the requirements of the previous form. The thin version, 'rule *by* law', means that government does not act arbitrarily but acts in accordance with its own laws. The next stage, formal legality, requires that law is also general, prospective, clear and certain. Finally, in the 'thick' version, formal legality is linked to democracy, whereby the governed are ruled by laws they have contributed to making. Formal equality before the law guarantees that everyone is treated alike. This is not the same as substantive equality, which could only be achieved by equalising intrinsic inequalities.

While formal versions of the rule of law describe legal processes, none say anything about the content of law. Governments, even democratic ones, could therefore make repressive or discriminatory laws that satisfy formal versions of the rule of law. This had led to suggested substantive additions to formal versions. The 'thin' substantive model protects the right to property, contract, privacy and autonomy. The mid-range position asserts the individual's right to dignity or justice. The 'thick' version of the rule of law promises equality, welfare and preservation of community. The last of these, by asserting an overtly political agenda of social reform, is arguably a step too far in describing the reality of the rule of law in Western society. Here, the rule of

---

[22] Aristotle, *Politics*, Bk III, 1286, 78, cited by BZ Tamanaha, *On the Rule of Law: History, Politics, Theory* (Cambridge, Cambridge University Press, 2004) at 9.

[23] Constitutional Reform Act 2005, s 1(a).

[24] Constitutional Reform Act 2005, s 17(1).

[25] EE Sward, 'Values, Ideology, and the Evolution of the Adversary System' (1989) 4(2) *Indiana Law Journal* 301.

[26] Hazard and Dondi, *Legal Ethics* (n 20).

[27] Tamanaha, *On the Rule of Law* (n 22).

law reflects the commitment to personal liberty. This version is linked to the triumph of liberalism in the late-seventeenth and eighteenth centuries following centuries of religious and political conflict.

iii. Liberalism and Formal Legality

In Britain, the dominant version of liberalism emphasised the right of every individual to pursue their notion of the good in their own way, provided it did not impinge on the rights of others to do likewise.[28] This does not mean that law is socially fair or moral. In fact, liberalism supports capitalists and businesses by protecting them from the democratic will of the majority. A legal system that tolerates social injustice is the price of preferring formal legality over 'thick' substantive versions of the rule of law. Notwithstanding that the system may be tilted in favour of the wealthy and privileged, formal legality offers advantages to individual citizens and minorities.

The protection afforded capitalism by the rule of law also protects ethnic, religious and sexual freedom. It allows dissenters to predict how government will respond to their actions and to know that the law will offer them a fair hearing. This predictability also has some disadvantages. To effectively fulfil its function, the legal system is rule bound. This inflexibility can have negative consequences, such as the possibility that guilty offenders go free. The absence of moral content in this version of the rule of law means that the consequences of its operation, and the role of agents such as lawyers, must be judged from 'the standpoint of justice and the good of the community'.[29]

Although there are different formulations, there is some agreement on the requirements of the formal version of the rule of law. The eminent political theorist, Joseph Raz, proposed that laws should be produced by open processes. They must be clear, accessible, predictable and prospective, not retroactive. The courts must be accessible to ordinary people, the principles of natural justice should be observed and the independence of the judiciary must be guaranteed. The courts should have the power of judicial review and they must be able to control law enforcement and any other agencies that might pervert the law. The rule of law is, however, a contested concept, including in England and Wales.

The notable judge and jurist, Tom Bingham, former Master of the Rolls, Lord Chief Justice and Senior Law Lord, bases his concept of the rule of law on that of AV Dicey.[30] Bingham goes further than both Dicey and Raz, however, adding requirements for adequate protection for human rights.[31] He quotes the European Commission, which treats 'democratization, the rule of law, respect for human rights and good governance as inseparably linked'.[32] He also regards compliance by the state with obligations arising under international law as part of the rule of law. This is an

---

[28] ibid, citing JS Mill, *On Liberty and Other Writings* (Cambridge, Cambridge University Press, 1989) at 16.

[29] Tamanaha (n 22) at 141.

[30] AV Dicey, *Introduction to the Law of the Constitution* (Indianapolis, Liberty Fund, 1982).

[31] T Bingham, *The Rule of Law* (London, Allen Lane, 2010).

[32] ibid, at 67.

example of a senior judge pressing for the addition of elements of 'thicker' versions to the formal version of the rule of law.

iv. The Control of State Power

In the Western democracies, the rule of law guarantees freedom by limiting the power of the state.[33] This gives rise to different kinds of liberty. First, through elections, all citizens play a role in determining the laws that govern them (political liberty). Secondly, government officials are bound to act in accordance with law that is declared in advance (legal liberty). Thirdly, a core of individual rights, for example, civil liberties, is treated as inviolable and protected by law (personal liberty).

The final mechanism for restricting the power of the state involves the different functions being allocated to different units. This provides checks and balances on the exercise of power. Horizontally, there is the constitutional separation of powers between executive, legislature and judiciary. Vertically, central and local government have distinct spheres of political influence. This dispersal of power contributes to the institutional preservation of liberty. Courts, therefore, protect political, legal and personal liberty.

C. The Common Law and Adversarial System

Common law systems, which originate in England and Wales, place emphasis on treating like cases alike. The decisions of superior courts in previous cases are binding on inferior courts. The reason for the binding decision is wrapped up in the judgment and a high level of skill is required to identify the material facts and the binding rationale. In common law countries, the dominant mode of dispute resolution is adversarial. In England and Wales, the adversarial trial arose in the medieval era when centralised courts replaced blood feuds, trial by combat and appeals to divine judgement by judicial authority.[34]

The adversarial trial has a number of distinctive features. The judge in court takes a relatively passive role, acting almost as an umpire, while lawyers take a leading role in questioning witnesses. Having heard all the factual evidence and the representatives' arguments on law, the judge delivers a verdict covering findings of fact and law. In serious criminal cases, juries are directed on the law by the judge and reach a verdict based on their finding of fact. This contrasts sharply with the tradition in continental Europe, where the inquisitorial system gives judges greater control of proceedings.

It is sometimes argued that the adversarial trial remains pre-eminent because it is the best way to test evidence. The presentation of conflicting theories and evidence tests factual accounts effectively. Indeed, cross-examination, where an advocate questions opposing witnesses, has been described as the 'greatest legal engine ever invented

---

[33] See further Tamanaha (n 22) ch 3.
[34] Sward, 'Values, Ideology' (n 25) at 321.

for the discovery of truth'.[35] It can also be argued that the formality of the adversarial process protects legal values[36] and that the impersonal nature of adversarial processes offers the best protection of individual dignity and autonomy.

IV. The Judicial Role

The adversarial system fits perfectly with the rule of law based on formal legality. It underpins the structural independence of lawyers and judges from the machinery of the state and provides a platform for the institutional separation of powers[37] and the rule of law.[38] From this position, the judiciary and legal profession are strongly placed to control government powers and restrict government immunities.[39]

A. Judges

Locke conceived of a social contract based on the state's promise to respect individual autonomy in return for the citizen's observance of positive law.[40] Restraints such as bills or declarations of rights are only flimsy protections against state power. Judges have a primary responsibility for limiting the state. They must follow the example of Chief Justice Coke who, in 1610, asserted that James I had no extra-legal or personal prerogative. Even a king could not judge cases personally because he was not versed in the 'artificial reason and judgement of the law'.[41] Confidence that judges can fulfil this constitutional role, without being influenced by other organs of state, hinges on the separation of state powers.

---

[35] JH Wigmore, *Evidence in Trials at Common Law* (Boston, MA, Little Brown, 1974) at 32.

[36] R Cotterrell, *Law's Community: Legal Theory in Sociological Perspective* (Oxford, Clarendon Press, 1995) at 156.

[37] See generally TC Halliday and L Karpik, *Lawyers and the Rise of Western Political Liberalism* (Oxford, Clarendon Press, 1997).

[38] TC Halliday and L Karpik, 'Politics Matter: A Comparative Theory of Lawyers in the Making of Political Liberalism' in Halliday and Karpik, ibid, at 15, 21 and 30.

[39] N MacCormick, 'The Ethics of Legalism' (1989) 2(2) *Ratio Juris* 184.

[40] J Locke, *Second Treatise of Government* (Indianapolis, Hackett, 1980).

[41] *The case of Proclamations* (1610) and see D Sugarman, 'Bourgeois Collectivism, Professional Power and the Boundaries of the State: The Private and Public Life of the Law Society 1825 to 1914' (1996) 3(1/2) *International Journal of the Legal Profession* 81, at 83–84.

B. The Judicial Role

i. Maintaining the Separation of Powers

The traditional conception of the division of constitutional roles under the doctrine of the separation of powers was expressed by Lord Mustill in 1995:

> Parliament has a legally unchallengeable right to make whatever laws it thinks right. The executive carries on the administration of the country in accordance with the powers conferred on it by law. The courts interpret the laws and see that they are obeyed.[42]

Prior to the Constitutional Reform Act 2005 there was considerable doubt that the structure of the state supported the effective separation of powers.[43] The Act addressed the central criticisms, most notably by confining the Lord Chancellor to an executive role, transferring his judicial functions to the Lord Chief Justice and relocating the highest appeal court from the House of Lords to a new Supreme Court.

Under the Constitutional Reform Act the Lord Chief Justice became President of the Courts of England and Wales, with the exception of the Supreme Court.[44] The Lord Chief Justice was given statutory authority to lay before Parliament any representations about the judiciary or administration of justice.[45] In another act of separation, a Judicial Appointments Commission was created[46] replacing the process whereby the Lord Chancellor selected judges following confidential and informal consultations.[47] Although the Lord Chancellor was no longer required to be a lawyer,[48] the Act imposed an obligation on him to support the effectiveness of the court system[49] and uphold the independence of the judiciary.[50]

The elaborate measures introduced by the Constitutional Reform Act were intended to safeguard the judicial role in checking the activity of the other constitutional powers. Any conflict between the judiciary and legislature would ultimately involve the Supreme Court, established in 2009 to assume the judicial function of the senior appeal court in the UK.[51] This step removed judges who had formerly sat as life peers in the House of Lords from the legislature, with the intention of increasing transparency and the appearance of independence of the superior civil court of appeal.[52] With this in mind, the Supreme Court was sited near to, but outside of Parliament, with one of the Justices as President.[53] Supreme Court Justices were to be appointed by the

---

[42] *R v Secretary of State for the Home Department, ex p Fire Brigades Union* [1995] 2 AC 513, at 567.

[43] K Malleson, *The New Judiciary: The Effects of Expansion and Activism* (Aldershot, Ashgate, 1999) at 44–47.

[44] Constitutional Reform Act 2005, ss 7 and 7(4).

[45] ibid, s 3(1) and ss 5(1) and 5(5)(a).

[46] ibid, s 61.

[47] Formally, the appointment is made by the monarch; ibid, s 14(a).

[48] ibid, s 15 and sch 4.

[49] ibid, s 10.

[50] ibid, s 3(1).

[51] ibid, s 40 and sch 9.

[52] Department for Constitutional Affairs, *Constitutional Reform: A Supreme Court or the United Kingdom* (London, DCA, July 2003).

[53] Constitutional Reform Act 2005, s 23(5).

President and Deputy President and a representative of one of the judicial appointment committees for the three jurisdictions in the UK.

The close relationship of the executive and legislature places responsibility on the judiciary to resist erosion of the separation of powers. The physical separation of judicial institutions from government and administration provides some insulation from day to day pressure or influence. It is also argued that the judiciary must control the administration and financing of courts if they are to be truly independent of government. In 2012, the Supreme Court judges asserted the principle of independence in resisting draft legislation allowing the chief executive of the court to be appointed by a government minister.[54]

The Justices are to a large degree self-regulating, the President having statutory power to create Supreme Court rules.[55] The true test of the judiciary's success in maintaining the separation of powers arguably lies in its record on holding the executive and Parliament to account. The scope of this role can be summarised as the defence of the rule of law.

ii. Formulation and Defence of the Rule of Law

a. Controlling Abuse of State Power

The judiciary has, both historically and more recently, invoked the rule of law when controlling government. An early example of court control of state power occurred in 1765, in *Entick v Carrington*.[56] The defendant was authorised by the Secretary of State to conduct a search of the plaintiff's property for papers evidencing seditious libel. In an action for trespass the defendant claimed that he

> held himself bound by his oath to pay an implicit obedience to the commands of the secretary of state; that in common cases he was contented to seize the printed impressions of the papers mentioned in the warrants; but when he received directions to search further, or to make a more general seizure, his rule was to sweep all.

The court said that, if, the power was so broad 'one should naturally expect that the law to warrant it should be clear in proportion as the power is exorbitant... If it is law, it will be found in our books. If it is not to be found there, it is not law'. The court decided that there was no authority to 'sweep all' and the defendant was liable in trespass to the plaintiff. The responsibility to check the executive survives in modern jurisprudence. In *R v Secretary for State of the Home Dept, ex p Fire Brigades Union*,[57] Lord Mustill said that '[t]he task of the courts is to ensure that powers are lawfully exercised by those to whom they are entrusted, not to take those powers into their own hands and exercise them afresh'.[58]

---

[54] O Bowcott and R Syal, 'Judges take on ministers over supreme court' *The Guardian* 17 December 2012. The Constitutional Reform Act 2005, s 48(2) gave the power of appointment to the Lord Chancellor.
[55] Constitutional Reform Act 2005, s 45.
[56] *Entick v Carrington* (1765) 19 Howell's State Trials 1029.
[57] *R v Secretary for State of the Home Dept, ex p Fire Brigades Union* [1995] 2 AC 513.
[58] ibid, at 560–61.

Ministers and public officials may only act prospectively, so government cannot deprive citizens of accrued rights.[59] In *Congreve v Home Office*,[60] for example, the claimant was one of many viewers who tried to avoid an increase in the television licence fee by purchasing a new licence before the old one expired. The government tried to revoke all such renewals. The Court of Appeal held that it was an improper exercise of the Minister's discretionary power to revoke a licence validly obtained.

The courts also ensure that the powers of the state are used fairly. In *R v Rimmington*,[61] a defendant's private joke, sending some salt in a letter to a friend containing a cheque, backfired. He was charged with public nuisance when the postal sorting office mistook it for anthrax. Overturning the conviction, Lord Bingham said that conduct forbidden by law should be clearly indicated, so that a person is capable of knowing what is wrong before he does it. No one should be punished for doing something which was not a criminal offence when it was done.

The courts also ensure that government does not interfere in the exercise of powers it has delegated to others. In *Secretary of State for Education and Science v Tameside Metropolitan Borough Council*,[62] the government tried to stop a new Conservative local council from adapting the former Labour council's plan for comprehensive schools by retaining grammar schools. The House of Lords held that it had no power to do so, unless the proposed conduct was that 'which no sensible authority acting with due appreciation of its responsibilities would have decided to adopt'.[63] These cases illustrate the ways in which courts have defined the powers of the state by invoking the rule of law. In those occurring over the last 30 years, the mechanism of judicial review has usually been used to hold the executive to account.

b. Failure to Exercise Adequate Control

There are examples of where the judiciary has not been sufficiently vigilant in protecting rights and the state has abused its power. In *McIlkenny v Chief Constable of the West Midlands*,[64] for example, men convicted of a terrorist bombing had claimed that confessions were extracted by torture. While the men were serving prison terms, the Court of Appeal halted their civil action for assault against the police because, it said, the allegations were too serious to be believable. The men were, much later, exonerated.

In *Gillan v United Kingdom*,[65] police stopped a couple under anti-terrorism legislation. One was wishing to protest against an arms fair, and the other was a journalist intending to film the demonstration. Both were detained and the journalist was ordered to stop filming. The courts unanimously upheld the right to stop and search, which were used to interfere with the right to protest. The European Court of Human

---

[59] *Phillips v Eyre* (1870–71) LR 6 QB 1.
[60] *Congreve v Home Office* [1976] 1 All ER 697, CA.
[61] *R v Rimmington* [2005] UKHL 63.
[62] *Secretary of State for Education and Science v Tameside Metropolitan Borough Council* [1977] AC 1014.
[63] ibid, per Lord Diplock at 1064.
[64] *McIlkenny v Chief Constable of the West Midlands* [1980] 2 WLR 689.
[65] *Gillan v United Kingdom* (2010) 50 EHRR 45.

Rights held that the detentions violated the right to respect for private life under the European Convention on Human Rights 1950, Article 8.

c. Subverting the Rule of Law

Allegations that judges are sometimes political in their role have re-surfaced recently in relation to the Profumo scandal. In 1963 John Profumo resigned as a Conservative Minister over lies he told to the House of Commons about a brief affair with Christine Keeler, an alleged call-girl. A recent book by Geoffrey Robertson QC suggests that the prosecution of a friend of Keeler, Stephen Ward, for living off earnings of prostitution was a politically motivated witch hunt.[66]

The prosecution of Ward was allegedly driven by the Home Secretary, with the active support of senior judges, in a spirit of 'Christian solidarity'. The prosecution apparently knew, but did not reveal, that Keeler, on whose evidence Ward's conviction hinged, was a liar. Ward killed himself on the last day of the trial. The fact that the narrative of the rule of law is not always positive underlines how important, and potentially fragile, it can be.

d. Control of the Legislature

Despite occasional tension between the judiciary and the executive, there is less conflict between judiciary and legislature. The judiciary tends to cast itself in a partnership role, ensuring that legislative intent is realised. In fact, if a test of judicial independence lies in the right to invalidate legislation, the Supreme Court has lesser powers compared with superior courts in other advanced states. It can overturn secondary legislation it finds to be ultra vires, but not primary legislation. In interpreting legislation, however, the rule of law is a powerful tool in divining the intention of the legislature.

In *R v Secretary of State for the Home Department*, for example, Lord Steyn said that 'unless there is the clearest provision to the contrary, Parliament must be presumed not to legislate contrary to the rule of law. And the rule of law enforces minimum standards of fairness, both substantive and procedural'.[67] This principle is illustrated in *Ghaidan v Godin-Mendoza*,[68] where the House of Lords reinterpreted the Rent Act 1977 in such a way as to protect homosexual couples. It was said that to do otherwise would be discriminatory and that 'discriminatory law undermines the rule of law because it is the antithesis of fairness'.[69]

In common with some other courts, the Supreme Court can make a declaration that primary legislation is incompatible with the Human Rights Act 1988.[70] While this does not invalidate the legislation, Parliament usually does, but is not required to, make amendments to it.[71] Despite the restrictions on judicial power, the Human

---

[66] G Roberston, *Stephen Ward was Innocent OK?: The Case for Overturning his Conviction* (London, Biteback Publishing, 2013).

[67] *R v Secretary of State for the Home Department, ex p Pierson* [1998] AC 539, at 581.

[68] *Ghaidan v Godin-Mendoza* [2004] UKHL 30.

[69] ibid, per Lord Nicholls at 565, [9].

[70] Human Rights Act 1988, s 4.

[71] ibid, s 10.

Rights Act represents a 'higher law' than the domestic law. Judges have been active in upholding the rights of suspected terrorists against executive action and legislative provisions.[72] In future the judiciary may regard it as its duty to defy legislation on the issue.[73]

The combined effect of the Human Rights Act and the Constitutional Reform Act is to strengthen the legitimacy and authority of the judiciary. These Acts could ultimately lead to a codified constitution in which the judiciary is given formal powers to override legislation that does not conform to defined constitutional principles. In the meantime, the limit of judicial power is unclear. Could, for example, the Supreme Court strike down action that conflicts with the rule of law, such as legislation that removes a sphere of executive action from judicial review? [74]

In *Jackson and others v Attorney General*,[75] the House of Lords cast doubt on whether parliamentary sovereignty was an absolute constitutional principle. Some of their Lordships said that it was a doctrine of the common law that could be changed by the judges. As to whether there is a supreme principle, Lord Hope said that '[t]he rule of law enforced by the courts is the ultimate controlling factor on which our constitution is based'.[76]

The absence of formal powers under the Constitutional Reform Act means that the scope of judicial responsibility for defending the rule of law against the legislature is unclear. Lord Bingham found evidence both in favour of the supremacy of Parliament; for example, the Human Rights Act makes clear that the courts cannot declare legislation in breach of the Act because that would breach sovereignty. He also saw evidence of the supremacy of the rule of law in the decision of the House of Lords in *R v Secretary of State for Transport, ex p Factortame Ltd (No 2)* to 'disapply' UK legislation applying to part-time employees because it violated an EU directive.[77]

The *Factortame* decision briefly invited the conclusion that the House of Lords was setting itself up as a constitutional court.[78] In common with most commentators, however, Bingham concludes that parliamentary sovereignty always prevails. This means that the British Parliament can legislate to infringe the rule of law or human rights. To do so would, however, invite conflict with the judges and could precipitate a constitutional crisis.[79]

---

[72] *A and Z and others v Secretary of State for the Home Dept*, for example, led to replacement of the Anti-Terrorism, Crime and Security Act 2001 with the Prevention of Terrorism Act 2005.

[73] V Bogdanor, *The New British Constitution* (Oxford, Hart Publishing, 2009) at 72–74.

[74] House of Lords Select Committee on the Constitution, *Fifth Report of Session 2005–06: Constitutional Reform Act 2005* (HL 2005–06, 83) at para 43.

[75] *Jackson and others v Attorney General* [2005] UKHL 56.

[76] ibid, at [120] (cited in Bogdanor, *The New British Constitution* (n 73) at 82).

[77] *R v Secretary of State for Transport, ex p Factortame Ltd (No 2)* [1990] 3 WLR 818.

[78] Bogdanor (n 73) at 57.

[79] ibid, at 83.

iii.   Maintaining Public Trust in the System of Justice

The judiciary has primary responsibility for maintaining public trust in the system of justice. This responsibility has at least two dimensions, reflected in the code of ethics, the Supreme Court Guide[80] (the 'Guide') adopted by the senior court, which is similar to that applying to judges in other UK courts.[81] The first dimension is to uphold the designated constitutional role. The statement in the Guide that the 'judiciary of the United Kingdom have been independent of the government since at least the early 18th century'[82] can be seen as a claim for legitimacy for the judicial role in maintaining and defending the rule of law. The second dimension of maintaining public trust in the justice system is the demonstration of proper conduct in the handling of day to day matters in the courts.

C. Judicial Ethics

The ethics of a judge under a system based on the formal version of the rule of law is based on the six 'values' of the Bangalore Principles of Judicial Conduct. This code is endorsed by the United Nations Human Rights Commission in 2003 and was published with a commentary in 2007. It set out widely accepted standards for the conduct of judges. They are judicial independence, impartiality, integrity, propriety, competence and diligence.

i. Independence

The independence of judges is seen as fundamental to good government[83] and, according to the Supreme Court Code, 'a prerequisite to the rule of law and a fundamental guarantee of a fair trial'.[84] There is potential overlap between the requirements of independence and impartiality. Separation from the other organs of state may best be seen as a collective dimension of the condition of judicial independence. This could mean, for example, that judges should not be trained by the state, work with state officials or be too aligned with state institutions.

Freedom of thought, of a kind necessary to bring an open and unbiased mind to hearing cases and making decisions, is the personal dimension of independence.[85] Both kinds of independence are required for judicial decision-making. It is presumably this distinction referred to by the Guide when it states that '[a] judge shall therefore

---

[80] *United Kingdom Supreme Court Guide to Judicial Conduct* (2009).

[81] *Guide for Judges in England and Wales* (March 2008).

[82] *Guide to Judicial Conduct* (n 80) at para 2(1).

[83] 'Commonwealth Principles on the Accountability of the Relationship between the Three Branches of Government' (2004) 96(1) *Commonwealth Legal Education* 7, Principle IV.

[84] *Guide to Judicial Conduct* (n 80) at para 1(2)i.

[85] This distinction is made in the Canadian case *Valente* (1983), cited by Malleson, *The New Judiciary* (n 43) at 44.

uphold and exemplify judicial independence in both its individual and institutional aspects'.[86] This section addresses the institutional aspect of independence.

The independence of the judiciary from executive influence is underpinned by the Constitutional Reform Act 2005. The Act explicitly provides that '[t]he Lord Chancellor, other Ministers of the Crown and all with responsibility for matters relating to the judiciary or otherwise to the administration of justice must uphold the continued independence of the judiciary'.[87] It continues by providing that 'the Lord Chancellor and other Ministers of the Crown must not seek to influence particular judicial decisions through any special access to the judiciary'.[88] The Lord Chancellor must have regard to the need to defend judicial independence.[89]

The House of Lords Select Committee on the Constitution speculated on whether this duty went far enough. The Select Committee mischievously asked whether the duty not to influence applied to 'Ministers who publicly ask for judges to be tough on suspected terrorists, or who threaten the courts with the prospect of amending legislation if they do not give effect to government policy?' It also wondered '[h]ow substantial is the duty placed by Section 3(6) on the Lord Chancellor to have regard to... the need to defend that independence?',[90] whether it went go beyond the duty to uphold judicial independence and, if so, how.

ii. Impartiality

a. The Impartial Disposition

Independence from state control is necessary before a judge can be said to be impartial, but it is not sufficient. Impartiality reflects the attitude to a particular case of a specific tribunal. To achieve this, judges must be independently minded, rationale, dispassionate and able to ignore every other opinion. It is fundamentally important in delivering the protection of minority rights and interests that are the promises of liberalism. Judges must be able to assume a neutral disposition towards an issue, uninfluenced by their own beliefs, the establishment or popular opinion. Therefore, the Guide provides that:

> The Justices must be immune to the effects of publicity, whether favourable or unfavourable. But that does not mean ignoring the profound effect which their decisions are likely to have, not only on the parties before the Court, but also upon the wider public whose concerns may well be forcibly expressed in the media.[91]

To this end, Supreme Court Justices swear a judicial oath, stating: 'I will do right to all manner of people after the laws and usages of this Realm, without fear or favour,

---

[86] *Guide to Judicial Conduct* (n 80) at para 1(2)1.
[87] Constitutional Reform Act 2005, s 3(1).
[88] ibid, s 3(5).
[89] ibid, s 3(6)(1).
[90] House of Lords Select Committee on the Constitution, *Fifth Report of Session 2005–06: Constitutional Reform Act 2005* (n 74) at para 43.
[91] *Guide to Judicial Conduct* (n 80) at para 2(4).

affection or ill-will'.[92] The apparently clear promise of the judicial oath is not as easy to deliver as first appears.

b. The Scope for Judicial Law-making

A system of formal legality demands that judges are not just rational, neutral and dispassionate. They must be predictable. The theory of the rule of law pre-supposes that law is fixed and certain and that judges merely apply the rules to reach their decisions. In the 1930s the legal realist movement demonstrated that judges brought their own values to judicial decision-making. Recognition that law was malleable in the hands of judges led to suggestions that the rule of law was a sham.

Critics on the left, like Roberto Unger,[93] echoed the critique of those on the right, like Dicey and Hayek,[94] that the growth of social welfare legislation demanded more interpretation by judges. Applying open-ended concepts, such as fairness or reasonableness, would lead different judges to diverse conclusions. This undermined law's certainty and precision, that is, its determinacy. According to the critics there could be no rule of law without predictability of outcome. British judges did conform to a conventional, passive role until the mid-1950s. Thereafter, it began to be acknowledged that judges filled in the legislative gaps left by Parliament.[95] By the 1990s the growth of judicial review had given rise to a culture of 'judicial activism' whereby judges began to act as policy-makers.

c. Judicial Activism

Tamanaha argues that the increased space for judicial interpretation is potentially dangerous; 'if judges are seated on the bench who have few qualms about exploiting the indeterminacy of law to favour personal of political objectives, the law is defenceless'.[96] The main hope that judges will faithfully apply the law lies in their commitment to a legal tradition in which the rule of law is central. This development was arguably fuelled by the use of courts to create law in controversial areas, like abortion, rather than to legislate. In reviewing executive action, judges might 'refuse to countenance behaviour that threatens either basic human rights or the rule of law'.[97] A crisis point occurred in the 1990s when Tory politicians suspected that political opponents among the judiciary were using the power of review to block reform.

In 1998 Lord Woolf sought to defuse a situation in which the judiciary was seen to be acting against the state. He asserted that it was the constitutional role of the judiciary to ensure that effective checks operated in the constitution.[98] In fact, judicial activism may be a global trend, but, in the UK, the degree of activity seems to

---

[92] ibid, at para 2(2).
[93] R Unger, *Law in Modern Society* (New York, Free Press, 1976).
[94] FA Hayek, *The Political Ideal of the Rule of Law* (Cairo, National Bank of Egypt, 1955).
[95] Lord Reid 'The Judge as Lawmaker' (1972–73) *Journal of the Society of the Public Teachers of Law* 22; and Malleson (n 43).
[96] Tamanaha (n 22) at 90.
[97] *ex p Bennett* [1994] 1 AC 42, at 62, cited by Malleson (n 43) at 11.
[98] H Woolf, 'Judicial Review—The Tensions between the Executive and the Judiciary' (1998) 114 *Law Quarterly Review* 579.

respond to increases in administrative activity.[99] Lord Woolf later conceded that, when parliamentary opposition to the Thatcher and Major Governments was weak, the judges' scrutiny of executive action was more rigorous.[100] Latterly, perceptions of judicial activism may well be fuelled by parliamentary attempts to devise standards for controlling the executive.[101] This inevitably provides material and scope for judicial interpretation.

It is currently unclear how the judiciary should defend the rule of law while maintaining impartiality. Which issues are constitutional and which political? The Prime Minister's recent proposal to exclude some categories of judicial review,[102] and make all such cases more difficult to bring,[103] is a case in point. Judges are increasingly likely to speak out on issues such as human rights. For example, Lord Neuberger, President of the Supreme Court, attacked the home secretary for criticising judges' decisions against the government in human rights cases.[104] The use of judicial review to control the executive has made the issue of political affiliations more relevant.[105]

d. Political Affiliation

In addition to impartially applying the law, it is arguable that judges must be seen to be impartial.[106] They should maintain a neutral persona and be free of bias towards or against any cause, group or party to a case.[107] This behaviour is critically important to maintaining faith and confidence in the rule of law. If 'the rule of law, not man', is to be meaningful, judges must embody the law, demonstrating the qualities inherent in the legal system. To avoid the appearance of bias it is often regarded as important that wider affiliations and political sympathies are concealed.[108]

The courts in England and Wales have adopted a fairly closed approach to the issue of judicial bias. A rare exception was *Re Pinochet (No 2)*, in which the House of Lords overturned its own judgment on the grounds that there was an appearance of bias.[109] The case concerned attempts to extradite a politician accused of human rights abuses in Chile. Their Lordships overturned their own decision that Pinochet was not entitled to immunity. The grounds were that one of them was a member of Amnesty International, which organisation had been given permission to intervene in the case.

---

[99]   Malleson (n 43) at 19.

[100] 'The Rise and Rise of Judicial Review' *BBC* 2008 (http://news.bbc.co.uk/1/hi/programmes/law_in_action/7289243.stm).

[101] T Zwart, 'Overseeing the Executive: Is the Legislature Reclaiming Lost Territory from the Courts?' in S Rose-Ackerman and PL Lindseth, *Comparative Administrative Law* (Cheltenham, Edward Elgar Publishing, 2010).

[102] P Wintour and O Boycott, 'David Cameron plans broad clampdown on judicial review rights' *The Guardian* 19 November 2012.

[103] T Dyke 'Why Cameron has got it wrong on judicial review reform' *The Lawyer* 29 January 2013.

[104] O Bowcott 'Judge defends court role over terror suspects' *The Guardian* 5 March 2013.

[105] J Rozenberg, *Trials of Strength: The Battle Between Ministers and Judges over Who Makes the Law* (London, Richard Cohen Books, 1997).

[106] *R v Sussex Justices, ex p MaCarthy* [1924] KB 256, per Lord Hewart at 259.

[107] K Malleson, 'Safeguarding Judicial Impartiality' (2002) 22(1) *Legal Studies* 53.

[108] *Guide to Judicial Conduct* (n 80) at para 3(3).

[109] *R v Bow Street Metropolitan Stipendiary Magistrate Ex parte Pinochet Ugarte (Re Pinochet (No 2))* [1999] UKHL 52.

After *Re Pinochet (No 2)*, the House of Lords moved to close down the possibility of a surge of similar applications.

In *Locabail (UK) Ltd v Bayfield Properties Ltd*, the House of Lords restricted the potential for disqualification of judges to cases where there is a real likelihood or danger of bias.[110] This apparently closed the door on disqualification for appearance of bias, potentially making it more difficult to detect or correct for the risk of bias. It arguably led attention away from the possibility of individual challenges for judicial bias and towards measures to ensure greater diversity in the judiciary.[111] This aim was advanced by the creation of the Judicial Appointments Commission.

e. Transparency

The suppression of affiliations may sometimes be insufficient to allay suspicion of bias, particularly when membership of an organisation seems inconsistent with the proper administration of justice. An example is membership of the freemasons, a semi-secret society in which members pledge to assist fellow masons. There is suspicion that judges who are freemasons may be unable to judge other freemasons fairly. A step towards transparency on the issue was taken in 1997, when the Home Affairs Select Committee demanded to know which judges were freemasons. The judiciary objected strongly and a compromise was adopted in 1998 whereby new judges declared membership on a register. This practice was abandoned in 2009 after successful appeals by Italian judges to the European Court of Human Rights against an obligation to declare freemasonry.[112] It is difficult to see how this is consistent with the avoidance of perceived bias.

iii. Integrity and Propriety

The Guide provides that judges must not accept gifts, lend their prestige to advance private interest or reveal any information gained through judicial activity in any other context.[113] The Guide goes on to state more generally, that judges

> will try to avoid situations which might reasonably lower respect for their judicial office, or cast doubt upon their impartiality as judges, or expose them to charges of hypocrisy. They will try to conduct themselves in a way which is consistent with the dignity of their office.[114]

It is particularly important that judges convey a polite and neutral demeanour in carrying out their official role. The Guide provides that:

> In Court, the Justices will seek to be courteous, patient, tolerant and punctual and to respect the dignity of all. They will strive to ensure that no one in Court is exposed to any display of bias or prejudice on grounds such as race, colour, sex, religion, national origin, disability, age, marital status, sexual orientation, social and economic status and other like causes. Care

---

[110] *Locabail (UK) Ltd v Bayfield Properties Ltd* [2000] 2 WLR 870, at 885.
[111] Malleson, 'Safeguarding Judicial Impartiality' (n 107) at 70.
[112] H Pidd, 'Freemasons shake off ruling on judiciary' *The Guardian* 5 November 2009.
[113] *Guide to Judicial Conduct* (n 80) at paras 4(4), 5(3) and 5(4).
[114] ibid, at para 4(2).

will be taken that arrangements made for and during a hearing do not put people with a disability at a disadvantage.[115]

In the few cases in which judges fail to meet these standards they may be removed from the case.[116]

Difficult situations inevitably arise when judges consistently fail to meet prescribed standards. In order that judges are in a position to exercise effective control over government they cannot be vulnerable to pressure or removable on a whim. They are therefore protected from civil action in respect of 'any act done by him in his judicial capacity, even though he acted oppressively and maliciously, to the prejudice of the plaintiff and to the perversion of justice'.[117]

Judges have secure tenure. They are required to retire at the age of 75, or 70 if first appointed to a judicial office after 31 March 1995. Justices may only be removed from office on address by both Houses of Parliament.[118] The Lord Chancellor has power to dismiss more junior judges and tribunal chairs after following prescribed procedures. Judicial office holders can however be warned, reprimanded or suspended (under prescribed circumstances) by the Lord Chief Justice.[119] Removal from protected judicial offices can only take place after a hearing by a specially convened tribunal.[120] The office of the Judicial Appointments and Conduct Ombudsman investigates complaints against judges.[121]

In addition to enjoying secure tenure, judges also enjoy immunity from actions in tort or other civil proceeding arising from acts in their judicial role.[122] This right can be traced to the immunity claimed to derive from the divine rights of monarchs. Recently, it has been argued that such immunity should be available only on a qualified basis.[123] The argument is that, in principle, judges should be potentially liable for the tort of misfeasance in public office for judicial acts motivated by corruption.

iv. Competence and Diligence

The Lord Chief Justice is responsible for the training, guidance and deployment of judges. In addition to undertaking any prescribed training, judges have personal responsibility for keeping up to date with practice in their areas of work.[124] The duty of diligence demands steady and careful application to the task at hand.

---

[115] *Guide to Judicial Conduct* (n 80) at para 4(3).
[116] *El Farargy v El Farargy* [2007] EWCA Civ 1149, [2007] All ER (D) 248.
[117] *Anderson v Gorrie* [1895] 1 QB 668.
[118] Constitutional Reform Act 2005, s 33.
[119] ibid, s 108.
[120] ibid, ss 133–35.
[121] ibid, s 62.
[122] *Sirros v Moore* [1975] QB 118, per Lord Denning at 134.
[123] J Murphy, 'Rethinking Tortious Immunity for Judicial Acts' (2013) 33(3) *Legal Studies* 455.
[124] *Guide to Judicial Conduct* (n 80) at para 6.

V. The Lawyer's Role

Weber perceived that legal systems were determined not only by political and cultural factors, but by the needs and preferences of stakeholders such as lawyers. He saw a professional group of lawyers as a key factor in the development of a rational system. Weber argued that values only become rules when adopted in the intellectual system devised by such groups. After the rules have been formulated, professional lawyers are necessary in order to maintain the unique skills and modes of thought that characterise the system. To Weber the independence of lawyers from political and other influence were essential to the autonomy, generality and universality of law as a system.

A. Lawyers and the Rule of Law

Lord Bingham considered an independent legal profession to be 'scarcely less important' to maintaining the rule of law than an independent judiciary.[125] This was partly because the production of independent judges committed to legality depends on the existence of a profession committed to the same goals. In addition to being schooled in the traditions of legality, lawyers have a separate and distinct duty to the rule of law that is intrinsic in their role. Therefore, the ascendancy of the rule of law assumes 'a legal profession sufficiently autonomous to invoke the authority of an independent judiciary'.[126]

Because judges in the common law tradition take the role of a neutral umpire, it falls to lawyers to present the case for the parties. This offers lawyers a role as 'the fearless advocate who champions a client threatened with loss of life and liberty by government oppression'.[127] This role places in ethical balance the legal profession's two basic affiliations; to clients and to the judiciary. These affiliations are reflected, in the case of clients, by the key ethical obligations of loyalty and confidentiality and, in the case of the judiciary by the duty of candour to the court.

B. The Standard Conception of the Lawyer's Role

The standard conception of the lawyer's role is a model proposed and developed by academics, mainly moral philosophers, in the US.[128] It is based on an interpretation of the American Bar Association model code, case law and other materials. The standard

---

[125] Bingham, *The Rule of Law* (n 31) at 92.
[126] Hazard and Dondi (n 20) at 1.
[127] GC Hazard Jr, 'The Future of Legal Ethics' (1991) 100 *Yale Law Journal* 1239, at 1243; M Bayles, *Professional Ethics* (Belmont, CA, Wadsworth Publishing, 1981) at 18–19.
[128] See eg ML Schwartz 'The Professionalism and Accountability of Lawyers' (1978) *California Law Review* 66; WH Simon, 'The Ideology of Advocacy: Procedural Justice and Professional Ethics' (1978)

conception provides a clear and simple description of how the role of lawyers in society is manifest in responsibilities towards prospective clients and actual clients. While it is contentious, even in the US, it is an important starting point for analysis. Most discussions of professional legal ethics assume the relevance of the standard conception.

The standard conception comprises two overarching principles, neutrality and partisanship. The principle of neutrality demands that lawyers present cases on behalf of unpopular causes or those they disagree with morally. The principle of partisanship demands that they follow their client's instructions so far as the law allows, even if this produces unjust outcomes. The first two principles of the standard conception are supported by a third, the principle of non-accountability. This suggests that, provided lawyers observe the principles of partisanship and neutrality, they are absolved of personal moral responsibility for the consequences of actions on behalf of clients. This is on the grounds that the role they perform is itself good.[129]

i. The Principle of Neutrality

The purest practical expression of the obligation of neutrality is a duty not to select clients. The importance of this principle flows from the imperative of representation. Neutrality ensures that every accused person has a champion because lawyers can act for unpopular clients without being associated with their cause. This increases social goods such as civil liberties and human rights. Success in individual cases, albeit for unpopular causes, produces a culture of rights which promotes the general welfare of society as a whole. This demonstrates the reality of the liberal promise to tolerate difference.

The second element of neutrality requires that lawyers are emotionally detached from their client's purposes. They focus on the legal merits of the case, offer dispassionate advice and resist emotional involvement with the client.[130] They should be indifferent regarding the final outcome of litigation because, otherwise, they may become excessively zealous and self-righteous or over-involved in their client's cause.[131] This may be contrary to their clients' interests. The mind that is independent of ties and conflicting interests can see the whole picture objectively and is more likely to offer wise advice.[132]

ii. The Principle of Partisanship

Partisanship fulfils the liberal promise to respect individual rights, and the dignity of the individual, by providing a 'champion against a hostile world'.[133] The need for

---

Wisconsin Law Review 29; D Luban, *Lawyers and Justice: An Ethical Study* (Princeton, NJ, Princeton University Press, 1988).

[129] See esp Schwartz, ibid, and Luban, ibid.
[130] TJ Johnson, *Professions & Power*, (London, MacMillan, 1972) at 36; V Denti, 'Public Lawyers, Political Trials and the Neutrality of the Legal Profession' (1981) 1 *Israel Law Review* 20.
[131] RE Rosen, 'On the Social Significance of Critical Lawyering' (2000) 3 *Legal Ethics* 169, at 170.
[132] Kronman, *Lost Lawyer* (n 14) at 144.
[133] M Freedman, 'Are there Public Interest Limits on Lawyers' Advocacy?' (1977) 2 *Journal of the Legal Profession* 47.

such a champion is acute where the individual is pitted against the power of the state, as in criminal cases. It can be just as important in areas like immigration or asylum. It is often argued that citizens should mistrust the power of the state because of the many ways in which it can be abused. Therefore, critics argue, partisanship demands that lawyers do not seek a fair result, or try to find the truth, or explore compromise between the parties.

According to some of the US literature, lawyers are there to defend a client's rights, even when they consider their goals to be unjustified, and regardless of harm to others.[134] They must not compromise their zeal in cases that challenge the establishment or a powerful force. In fact, powerful opponents demand more of lawyers, because the lawyer ensures equality of arms. In the early-nineteenth century, for example, a leading advocate threatened to discredit the king and 'throw the kingdom into confusion' for his client's sake.[135]

The partisan disposition, which guards against lawyers' co-optation by third parties against their clients' interests, is reflected in the most fundamental principles of lawyers' ethics, such as confidentiality. In the eighteenth-century case, *Annesley v Anglesey*, for example, it was said that (i) a 'gentleman of character' does not disclose his client's secrets; (ii) an attorney identifies with his client, and it would be 'contrary to the rules of natural justice and equity' for an individual to betray himself; and (iii) attorneys are necessary for the conduct of business, and business would be destroyed if attorneys were to disclose their communications with their clients.[136]

iii. The Principle of Non-accountability

An important restraint on the principle of partisanship is the requirement that the client's goal must not be an illegal purpose and does not require illegal means. Some critics of the standard conception suggest that an obligation to pursue client goals all the way up to the limit of the law, justifies acts that are legal but morally dubious.[137] This might include taking advantage of loopholes in the law, mistakes by the other side or grey areas in legal ethics.

Such renderings of the standard conception create a morally ambiguous role for lawyers. Neutrality, an obligation not to refuse clients, gives lawyers cases that they do not believe in, and partisanship forces them to vigorously pursue ends they do not agree with. The perception that lawyers are no more than 'guns for hire' can generate a cynical and sometimes hostile public opinion, particularly when a lawyer helps free a criminal or achieve a corporation's anti-social purpose.

---

[134] See esp M Freedman, 'Professional Responsibility of the Criminal Defence Lawyer: The Three Hardest Questions' (1966) 64 *Michigan Law Review* 1469; J Leubsdorf, 'Three Models of Professional Reform' (1982) 67 *Cornell Law Review* 1021.

[135] See further ch 19: 'Advocacy'.

[136] *Annesley v Anglesey* 17 How St Tr 1140, 1223–26, 1241 (Ex, 1743); JT Noonan, 'The Purposes of Advocacy and the Limits of Confidentiality' (1966) 64 *Michigan Law Review* 1485.

[137] G Postema, 'Moral Responsibility in Professional Ethics' (1980) 55 *NY University Law Review* 63.

C. The Critique of the Standard Conception

Academics in key common law jurisdictions have criticised the standard conception on a number of grounds. They argue that it requires lawyers to follow clients' immoral instructions, provided they are within the law. Consequently, the professional role requires them to represent a position they do not believe to be true, which is deceitful. The critics then argue that the standard conception requires that lawyers act in their client's interests, using tactical delay if necessary, which is tantamount to cheating.[138] This denies lawyers their right to exercise ethical discretion and may produce outcomes that some see as immoral.

Critics of the standard conception further argue that lawyers' ethics extend the rationale for such consequences from the criminal trial, where there may be some justification, to other contexts, where there is no justification. They suggest that the immorality at the heart of professional role distorts lawyers' ethical judgement, so that they are not attuned to behaving ethically.

Academics arguing for change in the professional ethics of lawyers suggest that the standard conception of the lawyers' role is not justified by the social role lawyers perform.[139] Not only is it intrinsically wrong for a profession to compromise professional values, like honesty and integrity, it is unprincipled to justify this position based on a reading of the role in relation to the adversary system, which they label 'the adversary system excuse'.[140]

The neutral disposition projects lawyers as amoral manipulators of legal rules;[141] shallow and unprincipled. The pursuit of clients' causes, right or wrong, seems at odds with wider social purposes and the common good. This places the underlying ethos of lawyers at odds with that of other professions, including those in fields involving personal conflict.[142] Some compelling and high profile examples are often quoted to support the proposition that the standard conception leads lawyers to undertake unethical actions.

When governments are contemplating illegal activity, for example, torturing insurgents, breaking into the offices of political opponents or embarking on war, government lawyers provide cover for the actions. When corporations are at the middle of financial or other scandals, lawyers are often criticised for complicity. Lawyers' ethics based on the standard conception are blamed for these situations, because of the imperatives of neutrality and partisanship and the corollary of non-accountability for consequences. When a scandal breaks, around government or corporation, critics

---

[138] D Markovits, *A Modern Legal Ethics: Adversary Advocacy in a Democratic Age* (Princeton, NJ, Princeton University Press, 2009).

[139] See eg in the UK, Nicolson and Webb, *Professional Legal Ethics* (n 5) at 215–18 and Nicolson and Webb 'Public Rules and Private Values: Fractured Profession(alism)s and Institutional Ethics' (2005) 12 *International Journal of the Legal Profession* 165, and, in Canada, A Hutchinson, 'Taking it Personally: Legal Ethics and Client Selection' (1998) 1(2) *Legal Ethics* 168.

[140] D Luban, 'The Adversary System Excuse' in D Luban (ed), *The Good Lawyer: Lawyers' Roles and Lawyers' Ethics* (Totowa, NJ, Rowman & Allenheld, 1983) 83.

[141] ED Cohen, 'Pure Legal Advocates and Moral Agents: Two Concepts of a Lawyer in an Adversarial System' in A Flores (ed), *Professional Ideals* (Belmont, CA, Wadsworth Publishing, 1988) at 87.

[142] D Rueschemeyer, 'Doctors and Lawyers: A Comment on the Theory of the Professions' (1964–65) 1 *Canadian Review of Sociology and Anthropology* 17.

ask, 'where were the lawyers?' The answer is that lawyers were often at the centre of the decision-making process.

Finally, there is concern that a role built on the standard conception harms lawyers themselves. Feminist and critical scholars argue that training lawyers to equate logic with reason, leads them to deny the value of feeling and imagination and to become cold and uncaring. The obsession with formal rationality is said to have a negative impact on personality.[143] Training to adopt the neutral disposition means that lawyers and judges block out an empathetic response to the human issues raised by legal problems.[144]

The dissonance between personal values and professional roles, it is said, induces 'role conflict', allegedly leaving lawyers suffering from 'debilitating psychic tension'.[145] This has been blamed for unusually high levels of drink and drug abuse among lawyers in the United States.[146]

D. Alternatives to the Standard Conception

Having characterised the standard conception as requiring morally problematic behaviour its critics in the US offer one from a range of solutions. William Simon advocates that lawyers have moral autonomy in making ethical decisions.[147] They should have 'discretion to disobey' when partisanship produces immoral consequences. Luban calls for 'moral activism', whereby lawyers should act as if the 'adversary system excuse' was not available to them.[148] Postema argues that lawyers' professional role does not exclude personal morality.[149] Rather, they should exercise 'engaged moral judgement' in deciding what it is legitimate to do for clients.

The critics do not deny that there is a professional role, but see it as what Postema calls a 'recourse role'. This means that lawyers have the recourse of not acting in accordance with role in a few extreme situations. The role expands or contracts depending on the underlying institutional objectives the role is designed to serve, with lawyers having discretion to disobey their code of ethics when the rule contradicts the objectives of the role.[150]

Some critics of the standard conception have advocated degrees of de-professionalisation of roles. These range from Simon's consideration of the abandonment of a neutral professional role to making it an institutional rather than a personal

---

[143] But see T Campbell, 'The Point of Legal Positivism' (1998–99) 9 *The King's College Law Journal* 63.

[144] LH Henderson, 'Legality and Empathy' (1986/87) 85 *Michigan Law Review* 1574; TM Massaro 'Empathy, Legal Storytelling, and the Rule of Law: New Words, Old Wounds?' (1988/89) 87 *Michigan Law Review* 2099.

[145] LE Fisher, 'Truth as a Double-Edged Sword: Deception, Moral Paradox, and the Ethics of Advocacy' (1989) 14 *The Journal of the Legal Profession* 89.

[146] P Goodrich, 'Law-Induced Anxiety: Legists, Anti-Lawyers and the Boredom of Legality' (2000) 9(1) *Social and Legal Studies* 143; and see Nicolson and Webb (n 5) at 175.

[147] W Simon, 'Ethical Discretion in Lawyering' (1988) 101 *Harvard Law Review* 1083.

[148] Luban, 'The Adversary System Excuse' (n 140); and D Cotterrell, 'In Defence of Contextually Sensitive Moral Activism' (2004) 7(2) *Legal Ethics* 269.

[149] Postema 'Moral Responsibility in Professional Ethics' (n 137) at 83; RS Tur, 'The Doctor's Defense' (2002) 69 *The Mountsinai Journal of Medicine* 317, at 327.

[150] S Kadish and M Kadish, *Discretion to Disobey* (Stanford University Press, CA, 1973) at 31.

responsibility. In a fully de-professionalised market, where legal services are treated like any other service, lawyers could negotiate with clients what level of service and commitment they would provide. Many people might think this a step too far in avoiding lawyers having to perform a morally ambiguous role.

The standard conception is not a purely American construct. English academics have levelled similar criticisms to those of their US counterparts against lawyers in England and Wales. Nicolson and Webb suggest that English lawyers are subject to similar obligations as US lawyers and are similarly compromised ethically.[151] Regarding partisanship, they follow Simon, arguing that lawyers should have discretion on moral questions. On neutrality, they suggest that unpopular clients should be able to select from panels of lawyers provided by the profession.[152]

E. How Far is the Standard Conception Relevant to England and Wales?

Much of the discussion of the morality of lawyers' roles is based on examples that do not apply in England and Wales. A common situation is that of an advocate told by a client that he is guilty of rape, but who conducts brutal cross-examination of the victim. This is an emotive example and one that is not sanctioned by the rules in England and Wales. Nevertheless, much theoretical discussion of legal ethics proceeds as if this practice represents the norm.[153] Therefore, before considering whether the standard conception of the lawyer's role can be justified, it is necessary to consider whether the standard conception is an accurate representation of lawyers' ethics.

i. The Standard Conception in Lawyers' Codes of Conduct

a. Neutrality

The codes of conduct of lawyers in England and Wales suggest a limited engagement with the standard conception. A famous example of neutrality in practice is the obligation of English barristers to accept any brief or instructions in any field in which they profess to practise. This so-called 'cab rank rule' goes beyond an obligation not to discriminate. It suggests responsibility to accept briefs in the order that they are received. Solicitors, however, are not subject to any such obligation, even as advocates, although they must not discriminate unlawfully, including in the selection of clients.[154] This is by no means the same as moral neutrality.

---

[151] Nicolson and Webb (n 5) at 46–49.

[152] See also Nicolson, 'Afterword: In Defence of Contextually Sensitive Moral Activism' (n 148) at 27.

[153] Luban, *Lawyers and Justice* (n 128) at 150, S Galoob, 'How do Roles Generate Reason? A Method of Legal Ethics' (2012) 15(1) *Legal Ethics* 1, at 6 and see ch 17: 'Advocacy'.

[154] SRA, *Code of Conduct 2011*, Indicative Behaviour 2.5. (www.sra.org.uk/solicitors/handbook/code/content.page).

b. Partisanship

In the US, partisanship is usually identified with requirements to represent clients 'zealously, within the bounds of the law'[155] and to 'not intentionally fail to seek the lawful objectives' of clients.[156] Similar obligations to client loyalty are found in the English codes, but no similar commitment to promoting client autonomy. For example, the version of partisanship in the Bar Code of Conduct is to 'promote fearlessly and by all proper and lawful means the client's best interests'.[157] While the fierce language is suggestive of partisanship, pursuing a client's best interests falls well short of an obligation to carry out the client's lawful preferences. Indeed, barristers must not limit their own discretion in deciding how the client's best interests are served.[158]

The Solicitors' Code of Conduct also talks in terms of acting in clients' best interests.[159] Both codes therefore follow the professional principle identified in the Legal Services Act, of acting in the best interests of their clients. While this is not necessarily inconsistent with partisanship, it does not require it. The codes therefore present a weak version of partisanship at best. In fact, the obligation is consistent with lawyers acting in accordance with what they perceive to be the client's best interests. This is consistent with acting in a paternalistic way and is therefore ethically problematic.[160]

c. Overriding Duty to the Administration of Justice

Language that appears to limit partisanship permeates the codes. The Solicitors' Code of Conduct stresses that any conflict between principles should be resolved in a way that 'serves the public interest in the particular circumstances, especially the public interest in the proper administration of justice'.[161] It stresses that solicitors should 'uphold the rule of law and the proper administration of justice, act with integrity and not allow your independence to be compromised'.[162] The preamble to the Code preserves solicitors' discretion in interpreting the provisions, thereby providing considerable latitude to avoid immoral action. The Bar Code contains similar admonitions against dishonesty or discreditable behaviour, actions prejudicial to the administration of justice and conduct likely to diminish public confidence in the legal profession.[163]

The opportunities to subvert justice are greater in an adversarial process than in other judicial systems. Lawyers' obligations to clients are, however, balanced by a wider duty to legality. In the case of advocates, this obligation is expressed as a duty to the court, which is defined by specific rules. They must be careful not to coach their clients on the law before hearing their story. They must be careful not to influence witnesses, leading to presentation of distorted evidence.[164] They must not deliberately mislead

---

[155] American Bar Association, *Model Code of Professional Responsibility 1969*, Canon 7.

[156] ibid, Disciplinary Rule 7-101(A)(1).

[157] *Bar Code of Conduct 2014*, rC15(1).

[158] ibid, rC15(4).

[159] SRA, *Code of Conduct 2011*, Principle 4.

[160] See further ch 9: 'Loyalty'.

[161] SRA, *Code of Conduct 2011*, The Principles.

[162] ibid, r 1.

[163] BSB, *Bar Code of Conduct 2014*, gC25.

[164] See GL Wells and EF Loftus (eds), *Eyewitness Testimony:* (Cambridge, MA, Harvard University Press, 1996) and Sward (n 25) at 312.

the judge. The wider duties of lawyers have been reinforced by the Legal Services Act 2007. It specifies professional principles requiring any person appearing before a court or conducting litigation to act 'with independence in the interests of justice'.[165]

The evidence of the English codes of conduct suggests that an attenuated version of the standard conception operates in England and Wales. There is a strong commitment to neutrality by the Bar, but not the solicitors' profession. There is no commitment to partisanship to compare with that originally derived from the American Bar Association Model Rules in either the barristers' or solicitors' codes. Further, as in the US, codes of conduct generally provide scope for lawyers to avoid acts they consider immoral.[166]

ii. The Standard Conception in Lawyers' Behaviour

Studies of how lawyers' actually behave contradict the idea that neutrality is a significant problem in legal practice. Most lawyers are involved in transactional work, where the conflicts presented by partisanship and neutrality rarely arise. Litigation is probably the area where neutrality could cause some moral conflict. Because lawyers specialise, as criminal defence advocates or as prosecutors, they can act consistently with their personal values most of the time.[167] Indeed, studies of how US lawyers behave in practice show that, away from metropolitan centres, they often refuse to act for unpopular defendants for fear of inciting local hostility.[168]

Studies of lawyers' behaviour do not support the idea that extreme partisanship is prevalent among practitioners, even at the Bar.[169] The standard conception is a 'straw man' erected for the sake of academic debate. In fact, lawyers often try to mediate their client's more extreme demands and, depending on the type of case, seek 'reasonable solutions'.[170] Just as non-contentious work is more voluminous than litigation, a fully-fledged adversarial trial is but a small part of litigation. Analysis of what most lawyers actually do suggests that the problem of 'role conflict' may be overstated by critics of the standard conception.

F. Defence of the Standard Conception of Lawyers' Role

Charles Fried tried to justify a partisan disposition in lawyers on the ground that the lawyer and client relationship is akin to friendship. This approach was based on the proposition that ordinary morality accepts that people do things for friends that they

---

[165] Legal Services Act 2007, s 1(3)(d).

[166] T Schneyer, 'Moral Philosophy's Standard Misconception of Legal Ethics' (1984) *Wisconsin Law Review* 1529.

[167] Rosen, 'On the Social Significance of Critical Lawyering' (n 131); A Boon 'Cause Lawyers and the Alternative Ethical Paradigm: Ideology and Transgression' (2004) 7 *Legal Ethics* 250.

[168] Schneyer, 'Moral Philosophy's Standard Misconception' (n 166).

[169] D Pannick, *Advocates* (Oxford, Oxford University Press 1992) at 105.

[170] S Macaulay, 'Lawyers and Consumer Protection Laws (1979) 14 *Law and Society Review* 115.

would not do for anyone else.[171] This argument, that a lawyer is a 'special purpose friend', was heavily criticised, not least because the analogy is difficult to sustain.[172] Unswerving loyalty is reserved for people we are very close to, not given to acquaintances and strangers for money. Lawyers have little opportunity to develop genuine concern for clients as people so as to justify treating them in the same way as family members or close friends.

Recently, supporters of the conventional legal role have tended to suggest that lawyers' obligation of partisanship depends on the circumstances of representation.[173] In criminal defence, for example, partisanship is given freer reign, within the constraints imposed by the system. Partisanship dictates that a lawyer can make the state prove its case even when the client is guilty, yet the system requires that no perjured evidence is presented. Lawyers' loyalty to client wishes is therefore conditional at best.

Although the obligation of partisanship is strong in criminal law, in civil litigation it is weaker. In family disputes, for example, lawyers should not inflame the situation or assert a case that is not legally defensible. In transaction work, lawyers should arguably be more co-operative and more aware of public interest considerations. Like judges, lawyers have an underlying obligation to support the rule of law. This includes a responsibility not to exploit the indeterminacy of law.[174]

The main argument in justification of the standard conception is that it is better than any alternative. Giving lawyers 'moral autonomy', as suggested by Simon, may be seen as unrealistic, impractical and an abrogation of regulatory responsibility.[175] If the standard conception is the only viable way of representing clients in a way that respects the rule of law, we are left with the issue of how to justify the lawyer's role morally.

G. Limiting Partisanship

Recently, a new wave of scholars has sought to divest the standard conception of the lawyer's role of the negative connotations alleged by its critics. Markovits argues that lawyers must be neutral and partisan if society is to derive the political benefit that resolving disputes through the legal system offers.[176] Dare argues that the obligation of partisanship only entitles clients to a level of commitment he calls 'mere zeal', rather than 'hyper zeal'.[177] Mere zeal, Dare suggests, is desirable whereas hyper-zeal is to blame for the worst excesses of lawyer behaviour.

---

[171] C Fried, 'The Lawyer as Friend: The Moral Foundations of the Lawyer-Client Relation' (1976) 85 *Yale Law Journal* 1060.

[172] EA Dauer and AA Leff, 'Comment on Fried's Lawyer as Friend' (1976) 85 *Yale Law Journal* 573.

[173] T Dare, *The Counsel of Rogues? A Defence of the Standard Conception of the Lawyer's Role* (Farnham, Ashgate Publishing Ltd, 2009).

[174] Tamanaha (n 22); WB Wendel, *Lawyers and Fidelity to Law* (Princeton and Oxford, Princeton University Press, 2010).

[175] Hazard and Dondi (n 20) at 173; MJ Osiel, 'Lawyers as Monopolists, Aristocrats and Entrepreneurs' (1990) 103 *Harvard Law Review* 2009, at 2016; L Sheinman, 'Looking for Legal Ethics' (1997) 4 *International Journal of the Legal Profession* 139.

[176] Markovits, *A Modern Legal Ethic* (n 138).

[177] T Dare, 'Mere Zeal, Hyper-Zeal and the Ethical Obligations of Lawyers' (2004) 7(1) *Legal Ethics* 24.

Wendel argues that it is not fidelity to clients that is the underlying justification of the lawyer's role, but fidelity to law.[178] The key change to the partisan obligation envisaged by the notion of fidelity to law is that lawyers' ethical duties are performed by providing that which clients are entitled to in law, rather than by delivering every advantage that the law allows. This involves respecting the determinacy of law, where the law is clear, by providing clear advice. Lawyers involved in corporate and government wrongdoing have often failed to carry out their role properly, for example, by suggesting that there are no clear rules against state torture.[179] This undermines formal legality and is therefore, according to this analysis, unethical.

Wendel's position regarding neutrality is less satisfactory and somewhat inconsistent with his general argument and his limitation on partisanship. In client selection he conceives a moral permission to represent unpopular clients rather than a moral obligation. He does, however, advocate that decisions to refuse clients be based on legal rather than moral values. This appears to offer lawyers a way of subverting their social role.

The idea of fidelity to law is located in the political system and its goals. It is consistent with the dominant version of the rule of law, formal legality. It is not the same as justice, meaning fair outcomes, but with fair processes. This approach recognises that lawyers need not strive for outcomes unacceptable to ordinary morality. This rationale for partisanship and neutrality limits the potential for immoral consequences alleged to arise from the standard conception of the lawyer's role. This is a more elevated notion of a professional role for lawyers,[180] at least contrasted with the image of the 'hired gun'.

H. Is a Professional Role for Lawyers Justified?

Partisanship is an unavoidable disposition for lawyers where clients' interests conflict with those of another person. The degree of partisan commitment or neutrality that is essential to the adversary process is, however, debatable. More extreme partisan behaviour may be reserved for lawyers acting for those threatened by the oppressive power of the state, for example, in criminal proceedings. The purpose of criminal justice is not merely to ensure a fair trial, but to secure order, suppress crime and reduce fear of crime.[181] Civil justice has rather different goals and a more co-operative ethos may be appropriate.[182] Whether different levels of dedication to client goals can be satisfactorily represented in universal principles of conduct is debatable.

Even within an adversarial system, therefore, legal roles find justification in the need 'to administer and to facilitate the operation of law'.[183] Ethical neutrality is the correct disposition for lawyers in modern, diverse, competitive societies because

---

[178] Wendel, *Lawyers and Fidelity to Law* (n 174).

[179] ibid, at 182–84.

[180] ibid, at 50.

[181] R Young and A Sanders, 'The Ethics of Prosecution Lawyers' (2004) 7(2) *Legal Ethics* 190.

[182] L Webley, 'Divorce Solicitors and Ethical Approaches—the Best Interests of the Client and/or the Best Interests of the Family?' (2004) 7(2) *Legal Ethics* 231.

[183] TW Giegerich, 'The Lawyer's Moral Paradox' (1979) 6 *Duke Law Journal* 1335.

neutrality facilitates pluralism.[184] Neutrality needs to underpin institutions and practices and procedures for selecting officials, judges and governments. Abrogating neutrality weakens the justification for partisanship. If all people are not entitled to partisan advice, why should a few people have that right? While lawyers' freedom to refuse clients is defensible, it is not very practical.[185] The logic of a system based on formal legality and a society of plural values is that all citizens should have representation in principle, even if their cause is not one that a particular lawyer approves of.

VI. Conclusion

Legal or professional ethics as a subject is often treated either as a discussion of codes of conduct or of personal morality. Neither approach is entirely satisfactory. Simon argues that 'the essence of the professional judgement of the lawyer is in his educated ability to relate the general body and philosophy of the law to the specific legal problems of the client'.[186] This involves a creative judgement that is informed by complex considerations. The challenge of such decisions is the essential appeal of professionalism.

Professional ethics ought to ensure that the practice of law achieves the social good of justice. On the one hand, lawyers work within an adversarial court system that prioritises individual rights. On the other, they aspire to high values and to personal virtue. The adversarial system itself may exacerbate tensions in the lawyer's role by placing the interests of clients and the demands of the system in sharper conflict than do other systems. This brings the ethic of lawyers into potential conflict with personal virtues such as honesty and integrity, leading some to argue for the alignment of professional ethics with wider social values.

The call for lawyers to observe 'ordinary morality' raises fundamental questions about the legal role. Is the lawyer's ultimate duty to protect clients from 'the oppressive power of the state'[187] or simply 'to administer and to facilitate the operation of law'?[188] The answer, it seems, is that lawyers must do both these things to some extent. This gives them licence to represent the guilty and to provide the best defence available within the rules governing the particular situation. Lawyers' obligations in an adversarial system are finely balanced. They must pursue their client's rights assertively and single-mindedly, but within the limits and consistent with the purposes of the law.

[184] Dare, 'Mere Zeal' (n 177).
[185] Postema (n 137) at 81.
[186] W Simon, 'The Trouble with Legal Ethics' (1991) 41(1) *Journal of Legal Ethics* 65.
[187] J Weinstein, 'On the Teaching of Legal Ethics' (1972) 72 *Columbia Law Review* 452; JF Sutton and JS Dzienowski, *Cases and Materials on the Professional Responsibility of Lawyers* (St Paul, MN, West Publishing, 1989) at 3.
[188] Giegerich, 'The Lawyer's Moral Paradox' (n 183).

Bringing lawyers' ethical decisions into line with 'ordinary' moral values would legitimise client cherry picking and encourage half-hearted representation. Lawyers could impose their own view of legal merit on their client. This would be both paternalistic and elitist, and at odds with the liberal philosophy of emancipation that underpins the rule of law. Clients are entitled to have cases determined according to objective standards rather than the subjective standards of their lawyer's conscience.

One of the issues posed in legal ethics in recent years is whether lawyers can live a 'good life' on this basis.[189] This means, in classical terms, can they live according to independent moral principles while fulfilling their professional role. Some critics of the standard conception of the legal role argue that it mandates lying and cheating and so cannot be consistent with a good life. Others argue that the standard conception, properly understood, is perfectly consistent with a life of virtue because of the good the role performs and the limitations it imposes on improper professional conduct.[190]

---

[189] Bayles, *Professional Ethics* (n 127) at 11.
[190] J Oakley and D Cocking, *Virtue Ethics and Professional Roles* (Cambridge, Cambridge University Press, 2001).

2

Culture

'When lawyers fall out! It would make a great ITV series. You'd see CCTV coverage of them hitting each other viciously with their pink-ribboned "bundles" before going back to the robing room for a laugh and a smoke. That's the way I feel about Tony Blair and Michael Howard. I picture them slapping each other on the back in private, having long forgotten whose client had just gone down for 15 years'.[1]

I. Introduction

Investigations of ethics may start with codes of conduct, but it is the culture of professions that explain the origins of practices and norms, and why they endure. The professional structure provides status for individuals and organisations and develops common understanding of purpose.[2] The mysteries of these structures are hidden in the history of lawyers in England and Wales. Much of the detail of early professional organisation is unrecorded, but some records remain. The origins and history of the English legal profession is still clearly visible in its current structures and organisation.

The culture of the English legal profession developed with the idea of a 'balanced constitution' guaranteeing core rights. These rights were assumed to be based on customary law, freedom guaranteed by law and a judiciary that was independent of the state. The notion of the 'independence' of lawyers is based on these assumptions. They are integral to the self-perception of the legal professions, particularly the Bar. This chapter begins with an examination of the meaning of culture before considering how the distinctive cultures of the legal professions evolved.

---

[1] S Hoggart, 'Grandest grandee sets gold standard for rage' *Guardian* 29 April 2004, at 2.
[2] E Friedson, 'The Theory of Professions: State of the Art' in R Dingwall and P Lewis (eds), *The Sociology of the Professions* (London, The Macmillan Press Ltd, 1983).

II. Theories of Culture

A. Definition

A simple, sociological definition of culture is the way of life of a society.[3] Culture is comprised of symbols, language, values, beliefs and norms. It is represented by artefacts, symbols and institutions and passed on in places of work, recreation and worship.[4] In fact, culture can be seen as 'conventional understandings made manifest as act and artefact'.[5] Language is also one of the main vehicles of culture, conveying ideas, attitudes and values. One of the main means by which culture is transmitted is by socialisation of junior members into the behaviour and rituals of the group.

Socialisation is a term used in the social sciences to describe the processes ensuring social and cultural continuity. The main vehicles of socialisation are families and other institutions. A society may comprise groups with distinctive values and norms. These often create an ideology, a body of ideas reflecting the group's needs and aspirations, as part of their culture. These ideas are often deeply felt and perceived to be true. Ideology is 'both interested and distorted, but also practical and lived'.[6] Groups that are distinctive in society usually have an ideology that justifies or explains their distinction and which the group tries to persuade others to accept.

B. Occupational Culture

Durkheim considered it natural that people with work interests in common would form communities of interest; a 'restricted group, having its special characteristics ... in the midst of general society'.[7] Larson suggests that occupations which require special skill and a special work context tend to develop marks of distinctiveness, dressing, talking, behaving, that tend to identify members to each other and to outsiders.[8] Community was an important attribute of occupations because education occurred naturally among people working on common tasks in proximity. Occupational groups therefore served as agents of moral education.

---

[3] A Giddens, *Sociology*, 3rd edn (Cambridge, Polity Press, 1997) at 18.
[4] H Becker, *Doing Things Together: Selected Papers* (Evanston, Northwestern University Press, 1986); C Geertz, 'Thick Description: Toward and Interpretative Theory of Culture' in C Geertz (ed), *The Interpretation of Cultures* (New York, Basic Books, 1973).
[5] R Redfield, *The Folk Culture of Yucatan* (Chicago, University of Chicago Press, 1941) at 132.
[6] J Laws (ed), *Power, Action and Belief: A New Sociology of Knowledge?* (London and Boston, Routledge and Kegan Paul, 1986) at 4.
[7] E Durkheim, *The Division of Labour in Society* (G Simpson, trans) (New York, Free Press, 1893/1933) at 14.
[8] MS Larson, *The Rise of Professionalism: Monopolies of Competence and Sheltered Markets* (New Jersey, Transaction Publishers, 2013) at 228.

Larson proposes that professional culture accommodates medieval notions of craft and community to industrial capitalism. Professions promoted the values of science in social and economic reform and in professional ethics.[9] Professional socialisation takes standards determined by the elite and attempts to make them part of the individual's *subjectivity*. There is an element of social control inherent in being subject to 'a calling' or vocation.[10]

Durkheim also considered that occupational culture had something to offer wider society. In one of his early texts on professions he observed that deliberation, reflection and a critical spirit in public affairs promoted the health of democracy.[11] To Durkheim, professions epitomised this intellectual orientation. This, he thought, would provide an important counterbalance to the drift of the modern state towards domination by the market and by state bureaucracy.

C. Legal Culture

Western legal professions tend to be inherently conservative. Law has a naturally bourgeois orientation. The legal system reflects the class structure of society and lawyers tend to represent the propertied classes in that system. So for example, lawyers tend to defend the ideology of legalism and procedure over substantive theories of justice.[12] Even so, the idea that there is a distinctive legal culture is controversial.[13]

Friedman describes legal culture as having an external dimension, popular attitudes towards law and legal institutions, and an internal dimension, the perspective of lawyers.[14] The external dimension is shaped by the projection of law in contemporary media, how it is understood and experienced[15] and the internal dimension by the sources and practices of legal reasoning and the values, ideologies and politics that maintain lawyers as a distinct professional group.

The criticism that legal culture is inseparable from general culture has some truth, since all fields of activity absorb wider social, political and economic influences.[16] Cotterrell prefers the term 'legal ideology' to legal culture, which he describes as the ideas, beliefs, values and attitudes embedded in and shaped by practice, particularly the practices of developing, interpreting and applying legal doctrine.[17]

It is certainly true that, over the 700 years of evolution of legal professions in England and Wales, a distinct ideology was created. It supports and is supported by complex professional norms. Some of these may be regarded either as rich

---

[9] ibid, at 58.

[10] ibid, at 227.

[11] Durkheim, *Professional Ethics and Civic Morals* (London, Routledge, 1992) at 89.

[12] Larson (n 8) at 168–69.

[13] D Nelken (ed), *Comparing Legal Cultures* (Aldershot, Dartmouth Publishing Company, 1996).

[14] LM Friedman, *The Legal System: A Social Science Perspective* (New York, Russell Sage Foundation, 1975).

[15] R Cotterrell, 'Law in Culture' (2004) 17 *Ratio Juris* 1.

[16] GC Hazard, 'The Future of Legal Ethics' (1991) 100 *Yale Law Journal* 1239, at 1241.

[17] R Cotterrell, *Law's Community: Legal Theory in Sociological Perspective* (Oxford, Clarendon Press, 1995) at 36; R Cotterrell, 'The Concept of Legal Culture' in Nelken, *Comparing Legal Cultures* (n 13) at 13.

traditions or as redundant myths, much like 'taboo' rules in anthropological studies.[18] In practice, many norms continue to have some force, certainly enough to affect the way lawyers interpret their role. It is arguable, therefore, that the work, institutions, community and values of the legal profession differ sufficiently from the mainstream to constitute a distinctive culture.[19]

To understand the present situation of the legal profession it really is necessary to explore its past. This shows how lawyers emerged as an occupation and how they transformed in successive ages. It illustrates how the concept of legal work was constructed, how the professional community evolved and how it achieved a position of special privilege among occupations. It will also show how the current institutions, culture and ethics of the legal profession grew out of its history.

III. Early History of Lawyers 1300–1700

Before the middle of the twelfth century, England was a country without lawyers. God was believed to be the judge of guilt or innocence and clergy were involved in proof, for example, the performance of oaths.[20] The church courts developed a division between advocates, who were trained at university, and proctors, who prepared cases and were not allowed to take on business without the assistance of advocates.

In the middle of the twelfth century civil courts developed. Their level of procedural sophistication generally lagged behind that of the church courts. Civil litigants were accompanied to court by relatives, friends or employees, who were allowed to speak on behalf of the parties.[21] The hire of full-time advocates began in the reign Henry II (1154–1189).

Henry divided the country into circuits visited by travelling justices. He established the Court of Common Pleas, or Common Bench, which heard cases between subjects not involving the monarch. The establishment of national courts laid the foundations for the common law. Full-time judges, a system of national law and growing technicality in procedure created the conditions for legal representation in the courts.

---

[18] AD MacIntyre, *After Virtue: A Study in Moral Theory* (London, Duckworth, 1985) at 112.
[19] Cotterrell, 'Law in Culture' (n 15).
[20] EE Sward, 'Values, Ideology, and the Evolution of the Adversary System' (1989) 4(2) *Indiana Law Journal* 301.
[21] ibid, at 10.

A. Work

i. Occupations

a. Serjeants at Law

The earliest full-time lawyers identifiable from records were called serjeants. In the thirteenth century they were termed narrators[22] ('one who tells a story') and they may have been no more than translators or helpers rather than the oral presenter of cases to judges. At some point this role became more formal. Nevertheless, records of early cases show that clients had the right to 'disavow', or disclaim, the serjeant's presentation of their case. This may have followed from the fact that early advocates were often servants of those they represented or were seen as such. It is likely that, in time, they advised, and spoke for, wealthier litigants.

In the first part of Henry III's reign the serjeants were a small group. Indeed, in 1239, a nobleman had to rely on an employee to speak for him because the king had instructed all the serjeants of the Common Bench.[23] The numbers of serjeants expanded rapidly during the second part of Henry's reign. Brand estimates that there were 12 serjeants in the Common Bench around 1278 and between 19 and 23 by 1289.[24] By the later Middle Ages, serjeants were equal in rank to knights. As the dominant lawyers in the early period, serjeants were the group from which judges were chosen.

b. Attorneys

Apart from the serjeants, the most significant group of civil lawyers in the Middle Ages were the attorneys. In the 1160s an attorney, perhaps an employee or family member, might speak on behalf of litigants in court with little formality. This was a great benefit to landowners and heads of ecclesiastical bodies which did not then have to appear personally. From 1182, a record was made on the court roll when an attorney appeared instead of a litigant.[25] This suggests an attempt to regulate the use of attorneys.

Court records show that some attorneys appeared so frequently and for such diverse parties, that they must have been operating full-time. By 1260 at least eight such attorneys worked in the Common Bench.[26] This number had grown to 102 by 1280 and to 200 by 1300. By the reign of Edward I (1272–1307) the appearance of attorneys was so frequent they had become an occupation.

By around 1300, attorneys were treated by the courts as the channel of communication with litigants. They were also undertaking a number of other tasks, such as issuing writs on behalf of clients. A significant right acquired by attorneys was to be

---

[22] ibid, at 94; R Pound, *The Lawyer from Antiquity to Modern Times: With Particular Reference to The Development of Bar Associations in the United States* (St Paul, MN, West Publishing, 1953) esp at 78.
[23] P Brand, *The Origins of the English Legal Profession* (Oxford, Blackwell Publishers, 1992) at 55.
[24] ibid, at 70–71.
[25] ibid, at 44.
[26] ibid, at 65.

able to disavow what a serjeant had said on behalf of the client.[27] This was important, because errors in the formulation of the claim were often fatal. Before responding to the case against them defendants routinely asked whether a serjeant's clients avowed the count, or pleading of the case.

c. Barristers

By the early-1300s apprentices were recruited to train as serjeants. By the fourteenth century senior apprentices were allowed to practise as advocates in their own right outside the Common Bench. It is from these senior apprentices, rather than the serjeants, that barristers evolved.[28] In 1596 Francis Bacon, then a barrister of Gray's Inn, persuaded Elizabeth I to appoint him Queen's Counsel Extraordinary, a rank superior to serjeant. Subsequent monarchs also appointed small numbers of Queen's Counsel, all of whom enjoyed this seniority over serjeants.

d. Others

By the sixteenth century a range of occupations, including doctors, proctors, pleaders, conveyancers and solicitors, fulfilled different legal jobs. Pleaders and conveyancers approximated to barristers.[29] Solicitors may have originally been servants of the litigants or of the attorneys conducting the litigation. They may later have carried out litigation tasks that an attorney could not carry out. They were recognised as a category of legal personnel by the end of the seventeenth century and were treated similarly to attorneys.[30]

ii. Roles

Serjeants had higher status than attorneys, but many serjeants spent varying amounts of time as attorneys before elevation to the Common Bench.[31] By 1300 there were about 30 serjeants in the Common Bench. These also appeared in other courts which might have their own complement of locally based serjeants. Records from provincial courts in the 1300s suggest that professional serjeants and attorneys operated at fair courts, seigniorial courts and hundred courts.[32]

In the sixteenth and seventeenth centuries, lawyers were men of business not restricted to legal tasks. As the only trained managerial group they were frequently involved in public administration.[33] During the latter part of the sixteenth century and the seventeenth century the roles of barristers and attorneys became more distinct. Barristers, who exercised the advocacy role, ceased to have direct client contact

---

[27] ibid, at 87.

[28] ibid, at 158.

[29] W Holdsworth, *A History of English Law*, vol VI (London, Methuen, 1924) at 432, Pound, *The Lawyer from Antiquity to Modern Times* (n 22) at 107.

[30] Holdsworth, *A History of English Law*, vol VI (n 29) at 448–50.

[31] Brand, *The Origins of the English Legal Profession* (n 23) at 113.

[32] ibid, at 85.

[33] M Burrage, *Revolution and the Making of the Contemporary Legal Profession: England, France and the United States* (Oxford, Oxford University Press, 2006) at 391.

by the end of the reign of Elizabeth I.[34] Attorneys had close contact with clients and focused on conducting litigation. The process of specialisation was reinforced by the move to written pleadings, which tended to be prepared by attorneys.

B. Regulation

i. Canon Lawyers

Between 1274 and 1307 canon lawyers were subject to ethical requirements and could be suspended from practice.[35] From at least 1237, canon law advocates took an admission oath, swearing that they would serve clients faithfully and not unjustly delay opponents with 'right on their side'.[36] This does not seem to have been universal and some local bishops imposed additional responsibilities, like not knowingly acting in unjust causes. The second Council of Lyon (1274) imposed a general requirement of an annual oath on all lawyers in church courts in Western Europe.

A particular concern in the late-thirteenth century was litigation concerning marriage, where pursuit of an unjust cause could result in excommunication. Advocates appearing in matrimonial cases where judgment was given for the other side could be suspended. The leading ecclesiastical courts in London had a detailed code of conduct for lawyers from 1295 covering, for example, presentation of false evidence, and containing a list of punishments.[37]

ii. Civil Lawyers

The reign of Edward I witnessed the first treatment of lawyers as a group expected to observe high standards and exhibit ethical behaviour. The consistent numbers of serjeants at the Common Bench recorded towards the end of Edward I's reign suggests that control of admission was exercised. An ordinance of 1292 controlled numbers of attorneys in the Common Bench. This may be because shortage of work encouraged lawyers to commit champerty, sharing the spoils of litigation.[38]

The first legislation concerned with the behaviour of lawyers was the Statute of Westminster (1275). Chapter 29 of the Act governed the penalty of a serjeant or pleader committing deceit, providing for the imprisonment for a term of one year and a day and disbarment.[39] The Act refers to 'deceit or collusion', terminology suggesting concern about lawyers being guilty of champerty, but also of 'ambidexterity'; receiving money from the other side.[40] More detailed norms were actually developed by the courts.

---

[34] Holdsworth (n 29) at 440.
[35] Brand (n 23) at 148–49.
[36] ibid, at 146.
[37] ibid, at 153.
[38] Brand (n 23) at 115 and see ch 12: 'Fees'.
[39] ibid, at 120.
[40] ibid, at 122.

From 1280 London courts had a code of conduct applying to all lawyers practising in city courts. Serjeants practising in the courts swore an oath to uphold the dignity of the city courts by, for example, not impugning decisions.[41] The evidence is that, outside London, courts often did not recognise distinctive lawyer norms. There are, for example, many examples of jurors in local courts, who made accusations of misconduct against lawyers, alleging that lawyers spoke 'as willingly for the true party as the false'.[42] This shows that there was no recognition, at least in parts of the country, that lawyers were morally neutral.

Historical records contain many more examples of disciplinary action against attorneys than serjeants around the end of the thirteenth century.[43] This is probably because attorneys were more numerous. The cases against them cover a wide range of behaviour. The main duty of the attorney for a plaintiff was to limit delay and to seize on any procedural default by the defendant. They were punished for failing to perform diligently but also for misleading the court and tricking opponents or wasting the court and jurors' time. The standard punishment was that provided for by the Statute of Westminster; imprisonment for a year and a day. In serious cases, as with serjeants, this was sometimes followed by suspension or permanent disbarment.

From these instances it can be seen that standards of behaviour were largely imposed by the courts on early lawyers. The disciplinary sanctions, such as suspension and disbarment were, however, of the kind that are nowadays associated with professional disciplinary processes. Also, when attorneys were brought before the court for breaches of discipline the jury was often composed of other attorneys. Distinctive 'professional' norms were evolving in the City of London and the king's court, the Common Bench at Westminster.

C. Community

i. Institutions

The regulation of early lawyers was largely by the monarch and through the courts. Legislation controlled the practice of both serjeants and attorneys. The possibility of regulation by the community of peers began to be realised with concentrations of lawyers at the Inns of Court. Lawyers probably worked in and around the Temple as advisers to the order of the Knights Templar.

The Crown obtained the land of the Temple on the dissolution of the Order of the Templars in 1312.[44] The Inns probably evolved from the accommodation provided for lawyers and law students from about 1340. The Inn of Inner Temple was established by 1388, probably expanded in around 1609, when the Crown granted the former

---

[41] ibid.

[42] ibid, at 141.

[43] See generally ibid, at 128–36.

[44] W Holdsworth, *A History of English Law*, vol II, 3rd edn (London, Methuen, 1922/23) at 501.

Templar land to the lawyers.[45] The Inner Temple was the largest Inn, with Gray's Inn, in Elizabethan times.

There were separate Inns for serjeants, for apprentices and for attorneys. While the Inns of Court provided a common location, a unified bar was not evident. This is because of differences in the practice of different courts, with serjeants having a monopoly in Common Pleas, the apprentices in law a monopoly before the other royal courts and the doctors a monopoly before ecclesiastical and admiralty courts.[46] This encouraged distinctive group identities. It is known, for example, that serjeants addressed each other as 'brother'.[47]

Between the fourteenth and sixteenth centuries, records mention the current four Inns of Court, Inner Temple, Temple, Gray's and Lincoln's, situated in the Holborn area on the fringes of the City of London. By Elizabethan times, there were around 3,500 inhabitants of Inner Temple and Gray's alone. From the 1500s several Inns of Court tried to exclude attorneys or to bar apprentices or students who worked as attorneys in vacations.[48] From the middle of the sixteenth century they were formally excluded from most of the Inns of Court and confined to the subordinate Chancery Inns, which were eventually dissolved.[49]

The chambers let to groups of barristers in the Inns created tight-knit communities. The physical identity of the Inn, the requirement of belonging to an Inn before training for the Bar commenced and the tradition of communal dinners reinforced the idea of a group identity. It also provided a framework for effective informal discipline. Although the Inns of Court, and later the Senate of the Inns of Court, and the Bar Mess of the six Circuits had responsibility for discipline, the Bar often relied on more informal mechanisms, such as reporting infractions to the heads of chambers.

Attempts to exclude attorneys from the Inns came to a head in the seventeenth century.[50] By that time, attorneys entitled to conduct litigation, who were probably better educated than other attorneys, were entitled to belong to an Inn. In 1614 the benchers of the Inns declared even these attorneys 'but ministerial persons and of an inferior nature'.[51] In fact, despite attempted purges, many attorneys did not go, or returned to the Inns. The significant fact is, however, that the Inns took no responsibility for them. The exclusion of the attorneys from membership of an Inn reinforced the superior status of the Bar in a divided legal profession.[52]

---

[45] ibid.
[46] Burrage, *Revolution and the Making of the Contemporary Legal Profession* (n 33) ch 4.
[47] Pound (n 22) at 13.
[48] Burrage (n 33) at 396.
[49] Holdsworth (n 29) at 440–41.
[50] ibid, at 448
[51] Burrage (n 33) at 396.
[52] WR Prest, *The Rise of the Barristers: A Social History of the Bar* 1590–1640 (Oxford, Clarendon Press, 1986) at 9.

ii. Organisation

a. The Bar

The fact that the Bar ultimately emerged as the strongest group of lawyers and a prototype profession is largely due to the Inns of Court. By the mid-sixteenth century apprentices were required to be called both to the Bar and to the bench of their Inn by giving a reading. This entitled an apprentice to be an utter barrister and, after about ten years performing work similar to that of an attorney, an advocate. The power of admittance distinguished the Inns. Serjeants and the doctors were admitted by the monarch and the Archbishop of Canterbury respectively.

b. Attorneys

Unlike the barristers, attorneys had weak organisation and little standing of their own. This is partly because they were a more diverse group. Like the different types of advocate, they were located in different courts with different practices and rules. They were also divided by the many different non-advocacy roles they performed. Additionally, the Chancery Inns of the attorneys did not develop the powers that the Inns of Court had over admission. Therefore, while the Inns of Court were beginning to control the conduct of barristers, attorneys continued to be subject to the jurisdiction of the courts in which they served.

Eventually, attorneys appearing in royal courts were required to obtain a royal grant. It is probably for this reason that attorneys were treated as officers of the court.[53] Later, they were regulated by the same ordinance as pleaders, though prevented from acting as such.[54] By 1403 judges had power to admit and remove attorneys. Despite direct control by the courts, there were frequent concerns about the conduct and discipline of attorneys. During the seventeenth century judges repeatedly called for them to be admitted to the Inns of Court. Burrage concludes that at one time or another 'every agency of English government, and every available regulatory device, was deployed against them, but if public dissatisfaction is any guide, enterprising attorneys outwitted and eluded them all'.[55]

iii. Education and Training

In Edward 1's reign some Common Bench serjeants knew some canon law, perhaps having attended university. By 1278 lectures in common law litigation were given, probably at Westminster and aimed at intending attorneys.[56] In the 1280s the records suggest attendance by apprentices in the court of the Common Bench. It appears that they may have been responsible for notes of cases, possibly made for their own use or for instruction.

---

[53] Holdsworth, *A History of English Law*, vol II (n 44) at 318.
[54] TFT Plucknet, *A Concise History of the Common Law* (Boston, Little Brown, 1956) 315–31.
[55] Burrage (n 33) at 407.
[56] Brand (n 23) at 117.

There also appears to have been regular use of *questiones disputate*, statements of facts, followed by questions of law and relevant arguments for both sides.

As courts began to refuse attorneys audience in the seventeenth century,[57] the Inns insisted that practice as an advocate was deferred. By 1640, however, the high demand for lawyers meant that this could not be enforced. Call to the Bar began to operate as an immediate licence to practise. With this relaxation, the hierarchy of the Inns, the masters, benchers and readers, began to impose formal educational requirements on the Utter-Barristers and the inner barristers or students.[58] By the late-sixteenth century the Inns had a relatively advanced educational role, although it is difficult to know how rigorous this was.[59] Indeed, at different times in the Bar's history, the discipline and education of the Inns was lax.

D. Ethics

Examples of current professional ethics emerge in early records. A case against a serjeant, William of Wells, suggests a duty of client loyalty was well established by 1282.[60] William acted for the men of West Petherton in an action against the lord of the manor. He was subsequently sued by the men for transferring his services to the lord without their permission. His defence was that they had paid only one instalment of the agreed fee before telling him they did not need him. He also argued that he had not helped their opponent. This shows, first, that a serjeant could not leave a client's service before the end of a case unless he was not paid or the client discharged him. Even then, he was not entitled to act for the other side unless given permission to do so.

In 1292, another serjeant was acting for a plaintiff against a defendant for whom he had previously acted in related litigation. The court decided that the serjeant must act for the defendant, his first client, because he knew 'his secrets'.[61] Another case of the same period suggests that a duty not to mislead the court also existed, although serjeants were not guilty of breach when following the instructions of attorneys. Nor were attorneys guilty of misleading the court when following the instructions of clients.[62] In the sixteenth century, attorneys were granted immunity from giving evidence about client confidences.

Attorneys were regarded as officers of the court and ostensibly subject to tighter control than barristers.[63] This was partly because the main courts had their own staffs of attorneys and required that attorneys were separately admitted to each. It was not until the 1730s that lawyers began to be involved in criminal trials, on both sides, and to cross-examine witnesses.[64] At about the same time, rules of evidence were formulated and juries became sole judges of fact.

---

[57] Burrage (n 33) at 392.
[58] Holdsworth (n 29) at 431 and 486.
[59] Burrage (n 33) at 392–96.
[60] Brand (n 23) at 123–24.
[61] ibid, at 124.
[62] ibid, at 125.
[63] Holdsworth (n 29) at 433.
[64] Burrage (n 33) at 450.

From the sixteenth century, barristers took retainers from magnates and corporations.[65] By the 1640s however, the Bar had resolved 'to act in the public interest,
to represent all comers, not to tout or enter into improper contracts with particular
solicitors for the supply of business'.[66] By the second half of the seventeenth century,
barristers eradicated direct relationships with lay clients. Receiving instructions only
from attorneys, and looking to them for payment of fees, obviated the need to hold
clients' money. Arrangements for briefs, including fees, were negotiated by barristers'
clerks, elevating barristers above 'trade'.

E. Ethos

i. Independence

The independence of the Inns was repeatedly tested during Tudor times, by the
attempts of monarchs and parliament to enforce conformity to either Catholic or
Protestant religions. There is evidence of some resistance to these efforts. Government
manifested uncertainty as to its right to control the Inns, which ignored direct requests
by monarchs. For example, despite a royal grant of the land occupied by Inner and
Middle temple in 1608, the benchers refused or ignored subsequent and repeated
requests by James I to form a militia.[67]

Before the English Civil War (1642–51) the Inns of Court had considerable power
but ill-defined rights and prerogatives. During the Protectorate (1653–59) which followed the execution of Charles I, the whole structure of law and the legal profession
was subject to intense pressure for radical change. In fact, very little change occurred.
A proposed reform of the Inns of Court was avoided by the ending of the Protectorate
and the restoration of Charles II to the throne in 1660.[68] Charles II encouraged the
Inns to purge parliamentarians implicated in his father's execution, but achieved little
other direct reform of lawyers.

Charles II was responsible for a campaign which is seen to have considerable significance for the subsequent power of the Bar and later professions. With the aim of
gaining greater control of his kingdom, the king began a campaign of reviewing and
revoking the charters of self-governing bodies, 'little republics', such as municipal
corporations, using a writ of *quo warranto*.[69] This writ began a procedure asking by
what authority a person or body held an office or privilege or a corporation its charter. Although the Inns of Court were not chartered, they were viewed in the same light
as other 'little republics'.

On his death, Charles' campaign against the little republics was continued by his
brother James II. As James' reign was threatened by internal dissent he began to reverse
his policy on charters, but it was too late to gain support and he was deposed. William

---

[65] D Sugarman, 'Simple Images and Complex Realities: English Lawyers and Their Relationship to
Business and Politics, 1750–1950' (1993) 11 *Law and History Review* 257, at 268.

[66] Burrage (n 33) at 398.

[67] ibid at 402.

[68] ibid, at 409–34.

[69] ibid, at 440.

of Orange acceded to the throne in what became known as the 'Glorious Revolution' of 1688. He guaranteed the rule of law and the security of chartered bodies. This promise never became law, leaving many chartered bodies, and the Inns of Court, in an ambiguous constitutional position.[70]

The independence of the Inns was tested almost immediately by the increase in the numbers of King's Counsel. Charles II made many such appointments to act against the little republics.[71] Appointees were often benchers of the Inns, possibly as a way of gaining influence over the Bar, or were made benchers on appointment. Early in William III's reign, King's Counsel who were not benchers demanded, but were refused, this privilege.[72] The dismissal of their claims by the courts established the right of the Inns to determine their own composition. It also sowed the seeds of a claim for the Bar's constitutional independence from the state.

IV. The Modern Era 1700–1969

A. Context

In the early-1700s the term 'profession' began to be used to describe learned and self-governing occupations.[73] By this time, the Bar, through the Inns, had control over admission, imposed educational requirements and controlled a well-defined field of expertise. It was a prototype of a profession in the Anglo-American tradition. At the beginning of the 1700s, the serjeants at law were in decline, but none of the other groups of lawyers had established control of a field of practice expertise to rival that of the Bar. This would change during the nineteenth century with the professionalisation of solicitors.

During the nineteenth century a burgeoning urban middle class produced an increased demand for technical services. The process of solicitor professionalisation coincided with the birth of industrial capitalism. The client base was limited by a small middle class and the fact that the poor could not afford legal services.[74] Capitalism also led to the development of the corporate form and large organisations. These are characterised by bureaucracies driven by an ideology of efficiency and expert decision-making.

---

[70] ibid, at 446–47.
[71] ibid, at 442–43.
[72] ibid, at 647.
[73] ibid, at 450.
[74] Larson (n 8) ch 1.

B. Community

i. *Institutions*

a. Serjeants at Law

The order of serjeants was eventually abandoned and no more were appointed after the Judicature Act of 1873.

b. Barristers

Towards the end of the nineteenth century the Inns began to develop collective institutions. In 1852 the Inns of Court established the Council of Legal Education, a body containing members of each Inn. This established five professorships to provide lectures which student had to attend as a condition of call. In 1883, a mass meeting of the junior bar complained about the failure of benchers to support a campaign against procedural reform. As a result a Bar Committee was formed to promote the interests of the junior bar. Although the Bar Committee continued in opposition to the benchers, it evolved into the Bar Council in 1895.

c. Attorneys

While the Bar rose in reputation and esteem, the standards and behaviour among other lawyers attracted criticism. An Act of 1729 responded to anxieties about the proliferation of lower branches, both attorneys and solicitors, by imposing training requirements on prospective attorneys. They would be required to serve five-year articles to an attorney who could only take two clerks at a time. They would also take an oath and be admitted and enrolled by a court on qualifying.[75]

In 1739, 28 elite London attorneys and solicitors established the Society of Gentleman Practisers in the Courts of Law and Equity ('The Gentleman Practisers'), partly in order to try and improve the situation.[76] The Gentleman Practisers declared their support for the 1729 Act and resolved to police it against 'unworthy' attorneys.[77] This promise was not effectively carried out because of the weak infrastructure of regulation for attorneys and the lack of resources of the Gentlemen Practisers. It did however serve as a declaration of serious intent.

The Gentleman Practisers belatedly recognised the importance of community in pursuing their aims. In the early-1800s they decided to erect a headquarters. In 1831 a Royal Charter was granted to 'The Society of Attorneys, Solicitors, Proctors and others not being Barristers, practising in the Courts of Law and Equity of the United Kingdom'. Although the cost of membership was originally pitched at a price beyond the reach of ordinary practitioners, the society swiftly lifted artificial restrictions on membership so

---

[75] ibid, 84; Burrage (n 33) at 456.

[76] D Sugarman, 'Bourgeois Collectivism, Professional Power and the Boundaries of the State: The Private and Public Life of the Law Society 1825 to 1914' (1996) 3(1/2) *International Journal of the Legal Profession* 81.

[77] Larson (n 8) at 11.

that it could speak with the authority of a broad base. It assumed responsibility for all legal professions, including attorneys, under the title 'solicitor'. The society is still constituted under replacement charter granted in 1845 but did not change its name to the Law Society until 1903.[78]

The Law Society is said to have copied three major policies of professionalisation from the Bar; controlling entry and training, monopoly and self-government. Unlike the Bar, which operated from the Inns of Court, the Law Society, organised nationally, needed statutory support in order to implement these policies.[79] In order to claim this support the Law Society needed to establish a professional community, identify a solid core of work and establish more effective control of members. A fourth policy, a priority in fact, was to identify a physical location and establish an identity for the aspiring profession.

The Law Society raised funds, by members' subscriptions, to erect an impressive home, the Law Society Hall, in Chancery Lane, which it entered in 1832.[80] This was in the middle of the area surrounded by the Inns of Court and next to the Supreme Court. The Hall had its own library, meeting rooms, dining rooms, a large members' room and an atmosphere like a gentleman's club. The Victorian vogue for public bodies linking learning, science and the public interest through public lectures was also influential.

Following the formation of the Law Society, the legal profession became two branches, barristers and solicitors. Membership of the Law Society reflected tension between elite, litigation-focused London solicitors and non-elite London and provincial conveyancing-focused solicitors. In 1870 only 10 per cent of provincial solicitors were members of the Law Society, despite being two-thirds of the profession.[81]

d. Legal Executives

Other groups carrying out legal work, scriveners, trade mark attorneys and notaries for example, were neither solicitors nor barristers. Legal executives, unqualified clerks employed in solicitors' offices, were numerically significant from the nineteenth century. The more experienced clerks were designated as managers of other clerks, becoming known as managing clerks. In 1892 the Solicitors Managing Clerks' Association was formed. From the 1950s and 1960s the Law Society chose to strengthen the Solicitors Managing Clerks' Association, and improve the career structure for clerks, rather than relax its examination standards. It supported the formation of the Institute of Legal Executives (ILEX), a company limited by guarantee, in 1963. ILEX was granted a royal charter in October 2011. In January 2012 it was re-launched as the Chartered Institute of Legal Executives.

---

[78] P Reeves, 'Case History—A look back to the 18th century to find the origins of the Law Society and the changes over 150 years' (92) *Law Society Gazette* 22 February 1995.

[79] ibid, at 51.

[80] Sugarman, 'The Private and Public Life of the Law Society' (n 76) at 91.

[81] G Hanlon, *Lawyers, the State and the Market: Professionalism Revisited* (Basingstoke, Palgrave Macmillan, 1999) at 60.

C. Work

i. Occupations

a. Barristers

The status of judges and of the Bar increased following the Glorious Revolution. The Bar was treated by the state as self-governing and barristers began to assert their independence as practitioners. By 1720 a barrister, on being called, was ranked by the College of Arms above a gentleman and equal with an esquire.[82] Although the Bar was rooted in London, it served circuits around the country, and barristers followed judges around the circuits. The Circuit Mess and its Grand Council were given disciplinary powers over the travelling bar.[83]

The formation of the Law Society put on a more solid footing the Bar's preference for specialisation in advocacy. There was only occasional conflict between barristers and solicitors over the higher status advocacy. This was most notable over the jurisdiction of the County Courts, where solicitors had rights of audience. For 100 years, from the 1820s onwards, the Bar tried to ensure that only low value claims could be brought in the County Courts. It also strove to retain control of divorce work.[84] In other ways the Bar actively tried to give up work. It continued to avoid dealing with clients direct, preferring to appear only for clients introduced by solicitors.

b. Solicitors

The Law Society was half-hearted in competing with the Bar for higher court advocacy. This was probably because solicitors held a lucrative statutory monopoly of their own; the right to conduct the legal transfer of land, or conveyancing. This was gained almost by accident by the Gentlemen Practisers in the late-1700s. In 1785 Pitt the Younger imposed a tax on the annual practising certificates of solicitors and attorneys. In 1803 this was doubled to finance the Napoleonic Wars. The Gentleman Practisers were appeased by the insertion of a clause in the Act limiting the right to conduct conveyancing to practising certificate holders.[85]

In addition to conveyancing, solicitors had two other significant monopolies. As a result of barristers' aversion to dealing with clients direct, solicitors launched and conducted litigation, which also gave them control of the investigation process. They were therefore best placed to brief barristers, when they needed either specialist advice or advocacy in higher courts. Barristers, for their part, only accepted instructions from solicitors.

Dealing with the most important client affairs, from litigation to land transfer, gave solicitors a commanding position over the wider field of business. The solicitors' limited monopolies provided a foundation for servicing a growing demand for legal services in the second half of the nineteenth century. The solicitors held a powerful

---

[82] Burrage (n 33) at 448.
[83] Pound (n 22) at 12.
[84] Burrage (n 33) at 479–81.
[85] ibid, at 459; Sugarman (n 76) at 89.

position through historic associations with aristocratic members and patrons[86] and a wide client base. Firms and individuals had considerable social and political connections, through lawyer politicians, lobbying and other work for clients.[87] Solicitors did not exploit their dominance of business as effectively as they might have done, largely because of the profitability of conveyancing.

Between 1910 and 1970 conveyancing equalised salaries across the solicitors' profession.[88] This was comfort brought at the expense of over-reliance. By the 1960s, conveyancing and legal aid represented almost 50 per cent of solicitors' work.[89] Solicitors missed an opportunity to dominate insolvency practice and accountancy, which was based in solicitors' firms in the nineteenth century. During the twentieth century, accountancy firms grew profitable more quickly than solicitors' firms. The folly of this was demonstrated when, in the late-twentieth century, accountancy firms threatened to dominate the market for business advice.[90]

c. Legal Executives

Managing clerks worked in the same areas as solicitors and were notionally under their supervision. Many clerks achieved considerable reputations as lawyers in their own right. Because of the historic relationship with solicitors, however, legal executives had no exclusive monopolies over work.

ii. Regulation

a. Solicitors

Self-regulation was the last of the three professionalising strategies achieved by the Law Society. Such moves were often a reaction to concerns about the behaviour of solicitors or a public scandal. By 1834, the Law Society initiated its first disciplinary proceedings and began to collect and publish 'best practice' on issues of etiquette and costs,[91] often supporting a hard line over solicitor infractions.[92] By the Solicitors Acts of 1888, 1910 and 1919 the Law Society's disciplinary committee was given powers of discipline, including suspension and removal from the roll. The Law Society also supported harsh penalties for solicitors, such as those under the Larceny Act 1901. One solicitor was sentenced to four years' penal servitude despite having returned money taken from client account.

In 1906, the Law Society promoted a bill to ensure that solicitors could not use client money for their own purposes. The following year it gained power to refuse practising certificates to bankrupt solicitors and investigate their accounts. It also

---

[86] TJ Johnson, *Professions and Power* (London and Basingstoke, Macmillan Press Ltd, 1972).
[87] Sugarman, 'Simple Images and Complex Realities' (n 65) at 281–84.
[88] Hanlon, *Lawyers, the State and the Market* (n 81) at 72.
[89] C Glasser, 'The Legal Profession in the 1990's: Images of Change' (1990) 10(1) *Legal Studies* 1, at 4.
[90] Hanlon (n 81) at 52.
[91] Cruikshank, 'Building a Profession' 100 (25) *Law Society Gazette* 32; and see M Burrage, 'From a Gentleman's to a Public Profession' (1996) *International Journal of the Legal Profession* 45, at 94.
[92] Cruikshank, 'Building a Profession' (n 91).

established a fund to protect clients against the consequences of misappropriation.[93] In 1933, rules were introduced requiring solicitors to keep client money separate from their own. Other powers of self-governance followed. In 1941, the Law Society completed its structures of self-regulation when it acquired powers to inspect the accounts of practitioners and with the creation of the compensation fund.[94]

The Law Society adopted meritocratic criteria for entry. It introduced an examination in 1836. In the 1860s, it introduced an intermediate examination, taken during the five-year articles. In 1877, legislation gave the Law Society authority to take over the control of these examinations from the judges,[95] giving it control over admissions. In 1906, it introduced an examination in accounts and bookkeeping. Numbers entering the profession were, however, controlled by the examination process. At the beginning of World War Two, for example, the pass rate for each examination was only 50 per cent.[96]

Entry was also restricted by substantial indirect costs, for example, the premium clerks paid to established practitioners for training, or articles of clerkship. This could run to several hundreds of pounds in 1903 when average industrial earnings were only £60 per annum.[97] Clerks also had to pay stamp duty of £80 and received no pay for five years.

b. Barristers

By the mid-eighteenth century legal education in the Inns and in the universities was perfunctory. This was partly because class, not legal education, was a decisive criterion for the selection of barristers. At the beginning of the nineteenth century barristers were upper class and co-opted by their peers. Entry to an Inn was at the benchers' discretion. Candidates had to keep five terms, eat six dinners in each and have references from two barristers. The number of terms for university graduates was reduced to three, during which they only had to take three dinners per term. All candidates then served two years' pupillage, after which they opened their own chambers. This was an extremely selective and expensive process. University degrees were rare and the whole process took 10 years. During this time fees and expenses were a constant drain on resources. There was no legal component to degrees, nor formal training in law in the Inns.[98]

In 1872, the Inns of Court were pressured to follow the Law Society's example and adopt examinations for entry. Examinations were more meritocratic and appeared to justify the claim to expertise that could not be assessed by outsiders.[99] Following its formation in 1895 the Bar Council assumed responsibility for laying down rules of etiquette, such as that requiring that a barrister be briefed by a solicitor.[100] It also developed a disciplinary role over the whole Bar. Although the Bar became more centralised, the Inns continued to have substantial responsibilities. It was not until 1966,

---

[93] Burrage (n 33) at 510.
[94] ibid, at 50.
[95] Reeves, 'Origins of the Law Society' (n 78).
[96] RL Abel, 'The Decline of Professionalism?' (1986) 49 *Modern Law Review* 1.
[97] Cruikshank (n 91).
[98] Abel, 'The Decline of Professionalism?' (n 96).
[99] Larson (n 8) at 92.
[100] Burrage (n 33) at 500–01.

for example, that the four Inns delegated the authority of each Inn over training to a Senate of the Inns of Court.

c. Legal Executives

The objects clause contained in the memorandum and articles of Association of ILEX included the regulation of members by ensuring compliance with published standards. The Institute controls its own admission process by examination, although exemptions and a fast track are available for law graduates. ILEX was authorised to discipline its members and hearings began around 1968. Members who work for solicitors' firms can also be made subject to an order of the Solicitors Disciplinary Tribunal controlling their employment by solicitors.[101]

D. Ethos

i. Independence

The independence of the Bar remained relatively undisturbed during the nineteenth century and most of the twentieth century. Assisted by its unparalleled influence in law reform, the Law Society achieved a similar standing and independence over the same period. Close ties with government began in the 1830s, when the Law Society established a committee containing solicitor MPs to lobby on proposed legislation. Since the civil service was relatively small, this evolved into involvement in legislative drafting. In 1838 the Law Society was invited to draft the Solicitors Act 1844.[102]

The Solicitors Act 1844 created the office of Registrar of Attorneys and delegated the role to the Law Society. Consultation by the Attorney General on other legislative measures followed. The Law Society subsequently prepared the Acts of 1860 and 1870. A solicitor, Edward Wilkes Field, led the effort to concentrate the dispersed London courts and the Royal Courts of Justice on the Strand, just behind the Law Society Hall, were completed in 1882.[103] By the end of the nineteenth century, the Law Society had developed a relationship of trust with government.[104] This reached new heights in 1948 when it was allowed to manage significant public funds under the new legal aid scheme.[105] Solicitors were a key group in formulating, articulating and binding together the great middle class revolution of the nineteenth century.[106]

By the latter half of the nineteenth century the elite London firms had extensive social networks and strategies for establishing embedded relations with major clients, such as banks. The partners in leading firms sent their sons to elite schools and universities where they could befriend the sons of banking families and other big businesses.

---

[101] Solicitors Act 1974, s 43.
[102] Sugarman (n 76) at 97 and 101.
[103] Reeves (n 78); and see Sugarman (n 76) at 93–94, 96.
[104] Sugarman (n 76) at 105.
[105] Burrage (n 33) at 511.
[106] ibid, at 288.

It was common to send one son to the Bar and take one into the firm.[107] The elite
London-based commercial firms dominated the Law Society and used their extensive
social networks for its benefit.

The formidable front presented by the professional bodies may explain how they
resisted change, such as fusion into one occupation, which had long been mooted.[108]
Abel-Smith and Stevens considered that the legal profession, which they describe as
eighteenth-century institutions with an eighteenth-century outlook, must have benefitted from weighty lawyer representation in government, or the patronage of the
Lord Chancellor or the judges.[109] This may well be the case, although Burrage argues
that the professions' independence were part of the political settlement accompanying
the Glorious Revolution in 1688.

The terms upon which William and Mary acceded to the throne guaranteed the
rights of Parliament and the Bar, and hence the legal profession.[110] While the Law
Society grew in influence, it also adopted positions opposing the state. In the 1880s,
for example, it advanced solicitors as a counterweight to state authoritarianism, or
'officialism', the growth of the state bureaucratic machinery and 'state socialism'.[111]
In the early-twentieth century the Law Society was part of a broad coalition supporting conservative, *laissez faire* politics and resisting state encroachment on civil
society.[112]

ii. Public Service

During the nineteenth century the lack of a highly developed civil service forced the
state to co-opt bodies like the Law Society to administer government. This led to
dependence and 'the blurring of the public and private spheres'.[113] In the earlier-
twentieth century occupational expertise continued to guarantee a measure of self-
determination. It was believed that expert occupations defined the public interest in
their sphere of operation and that the state would not interfere in the absence of an
overwhelming public interest.[114] This was accepted across society as a natural social
order, in part because it guaranteed the autonomy of a range of social institutions.

The industrial age disrupted the status structure of the medieval period. The established hierarchy of trades was replaced by employment within a division of labour in
factories. Larson suggests that professions sought to distance themselves from capitalist production by incorporating into their ideology *residues* of the pre-capitalist era.
She identifies these in three anti-market principles. First, work is valued for its intrinsic reward, rather than for the income it provides, and is seen as a calling or vocation.
Second, is the idea that services are universally available, which reflects the notion

[107] Hanlon (n 81) at 75.
[108] Cruikshank (n 91).
[109] B Abel-Smith and R Stevens, *Lawyers and the Courts: A Sociological Study of the English Legal System 1750-1965* (Cambridge, MA, Harvard University Press,1967)
[110] Burrage (n 33) at 549.
[111] Sugarman (n 76) at 111.
[112] Hanlon (n 81).
[113] ibid, at 119–20.
[114] Burrage (n 33) at 550.

of community responsibility and gentlemanly disinterest. Third, the aristocratic idea that rank carries responsibilities, or *noblesse oblige*.

In the capitalist phase, the professions re-organised their works and markets to establish a market monopoly based on expertise.[115] They claimed exclusive competence to determine how legal tasks were performed. This represented an attempt to make the professionals, as producers, into a commodity that markets could understand. It required standardisation of 'the product' to ensure the uniformity of 'producers', and hence the standardisation of training. It also unified the professions. The establishment of a rational and scientific language and knowledge supported the appearance of neutrality and legitimated the professional monopoly.

Prior to the Second World War professions served a fairly exclusive market. Hanlon suggests that solicitors had as little to do with the poor as possible. The Law Society co-operated in a limited legal aid system for divorce in 1926, but resisted most other welfare-orientated proposals.[116] They did, however, prioritise respectability, being perceived as gentlemen, over money. In the period following the Second World War, the British Government created a welfare state. This involved regulating the free market and a guarantee of social citizenship based on better health care, education, access to justice etc. The professional groups which controlled these resources called for ever-increasing expenditure. Between the 1930s and 1970 government spending grew from 30 per cent to 50 per cent of national income.

Much of the growth in national spending was in welfare, and specifically legal aid, which grew in scope to cover legal advice in the 1950s. As a consequence, lawyers were given greater control of state funding than any other professional group. The Law Society policy was to collaborate with this expansion provided lawyers remained in charge and it did not affect their interests. The Law Society opposed the expansion of civil legal aid eligibility during this period because it thought it could earn more from middle classes paying privately.[117] It was complicit in a failure to expand criminal legal aid in the 1960s because of a perceived threat to its respectability.[118]

The expansion of the legal profession from the 1960s, supported by legal aid, entailed a shift in professional ideology. Hanlon argues that the legal profession eventually entered a 'bargain with the state' to deliver social democracy as a right of citizenship.[119] This embrace of 'social service professionalism', he argues, led to the adoption of characteristics such as an ideology of public service, lack of interest in money and control over clients.

---

[115] Larson (n 8) at 13.
[116] T Goriely, 'Law for the Poor: The Relationship Between Advice Agencies and Solicitors in the Development of Poverty Law' (1996) 3(1/2) *International Journal of the Legal Profession* 215, at 216; Hanlon (n 81) at 67.
[117] Hanlon (n 81) at 69.
[118] ibid, at 70.
[119] ibid, at 83.

V. Legal Professional Culture

The account of the development of the legal profession outlined in this chapter concludes at 1970. The period arguably represents a high-water mark of distinctive cultures in the barristers' and solicitors' professions. This section attempts to identify key elements of professional culture at that time in the identities, communities and values of lawyers.

A. Identity

i. Constitutional Role

By 1970 the legal roles of barristers and solicitors were well established. Barristers were advocates and consultants to solicitors. Solicitors had diverse practices, typically organised around conveyancing, litigation and various legal tasks supporting business. The core areas of work, advocacy, litigation and conveyancing, were protected by statutory monopolies. Burrage argues that it was widely assumed that the Bar enjoyed constitutional protection, under guarantees given by William of Orange following the 'Glorious Revolution' of 1688.[120]

The Bar had a tradition that placed their expertise at the heart of an ideology of the rule of law:

> Lawyers supplied the ideological rationales for the great 'bourgeois' revolutions of England, France and America by converting the specialized, technical, languages of law into a general discourse of liberty and rights. The common law, for example, was turned from a collection of writs and specialized sciences of pleading and property interests into a repository of public law maxims and fundamental law, the constitutional rights of freeborn Englishmen, and eventually of all men everywhere.[121]

The idea that lawyers were key guarantors of the rule of law was linked with the adversarial ethic in litigation. This required a highly trained elite, able to reconcile client loyalty and wider responsibilities to the administration of justice. Solicitors, by a different route, had achieved a position of trust and security within the state, but they did not have a claim to a position of similar constitutional significance.

---

[120] Burrage (n 33) at 60–64; Sugarman (n 76) at 84.
[121] RW Gordon, 'The Role of Lawyers in Producing the Rule of Law: Some Critical Reflections' (2010) 11 *Theoretical Inquiries in Law* 441, at 446.

ii. Separation

Between the seventeenth and eighteenth centuries the work performed by barristers and attorneys was less important than differences in qualification, discipline, class background and education.[122] The education of barristers was by mooting, discussion, reading and reporting, while that of attorneys was by 'apprenticeship' to a practitioner.[123] This difference, between a theoretical and a practical education, reflected the attorneys' emphasis on procedure and the barristers' emphasis on legal doctrine and courtroom skills.[124] Call to the Bar was often regarded as preparation for entering the House of Commons by children of the nobility and gentry.[125] By the eighteenth century aristocratic entry had declined at the Bar. Barristers were predominantly, and attorneys almost exclusively, drawn from the gentry and 'middling wealthy'.[126]

Government first proposed fusion of barristers and solicitors into one profession during the period of reconstruction following the First World War. The idea was that solicitors would later transfer to the Bar if they wished to specialise in advocacy. The professions resisted and government backed down. A minority opinion of the Evershed Committee in 1953 proposed that fusion was in the public interest, but the idea was not pursued.

The division of roles between solicitor and barrister gave rise to different ethical priorities, most obvious in the lawyer and client relationship. Solicitors handled clients on a day to day basis and were under direct pressure. Barristers might only see lay clients once before a court hearing, even in serious cases, making it easier to observe a primary loyalty to the court. Numerous rules in the Bar Code supported the barrister's role as a specialist advocate. For example, a barrister could not conduct a case in court if he had previously investigated or collected evidence for that case, unless he reasonably believed that the investigation and collection of that evidence was unlikely to be challenged.[127]

The expertise of solicitors in the process of settlement was complementary to the advocacy expertise of barristers, thus supporting different roles and ethical priorities. For example, advocates argue wholeheartedly one side of the case whereas negotiators must see both sides to compromise.[128] Solicitors were ambivalent about measures that might diminish the Bar, and fusion of the branches of the profession, because they relied on the Bar to provide specialist advocates in any area.[129]

---

[122] Holdsworth (n 29) at 433.
[123] Holdsworth (n 44) at 506.
[124] Holdsworth (n 29) at 437.
[125] Cruikshank (n 91).
[126] D Sugarman '"A Haven for the Privileged": Recruitment into the Profession of Attorney in England, 1709–1792' (1986) 11 *Social History* 197.
[127] Bar Council, *Bar Code 1981*, at para 401(b)(iii).
[128] J Flood, A Boon, A Whyte, E Skordaki, R Abbey and A Ash, *Reconfiguring the Market for Advocacy Services: A Case Study of London and Four Fields of Practice* (London, University of Westminster, 1996) at 99.
[129] ibid, at 58.

iii. Status

The status of professions is determined by their public standing and recognition, and by their relationship to other occupations in the field. Higher status professions define not only their own field of practice but also those of subordinate groups. This is obvious in a work-place like a hospital, where physicians define the work of nurses, technicians and therapists.[130] The relationship between the Bar and the solicitors was not quite like this. The barristers' higher court advocacy monopoly and the solicitors' conveyancing monopoly were treated as a 'settlement' between the professions. The work of legal executives was, however, defined by solicitors. In the twentieth century, the Bar continued to be regarded as the superior branch of the legal profession, because of its consultancy role and relationship with the judiciary. Judges were appointed from senior advocates and were therefore, barristers. Many judges kept their chambers in an Inn.

Judges and barristers were invested with status and mystique by the highly distinctive artefacts of their role, the court clothes, wigs and gowns. Wigs were considered a regency affectation even in the 1700s,[131] but, in 1970, the wearing of full court regalia was rigorously enforced by judges.

In 1973 the Bar and the Law Society made a statement affirming their equality,[132] but most solicitors' professional relationship with barristers tended to be subservient, particularly in litigation.[133] This was not true of the large commercial solicitors' firms, which had the considerable advantage of controlling the gateway to lucrative commercial work. Nevertheless, reliance on barristers was such that solicitors could plead reliance on counsel as a defence to negligence actions.[134]

B. Communities

i. Collegiality

Larson contends that professions adopted a pre-industrial notion of community from the craft guilds. These communities are based on the idea of collegiality, which Durkheim traced to the Roman *collegia*.[135] *Collegia* were craft organisations membership of which carried duties and privileges and provided a focus of loyalty for members said to rival loyalty to their own families. The mediaeval European guilds were similar. Such groups may collect dues from members, have distinctive feasting rituals, claim 'ties of brotherhood'[136] and engage in common employment or pursuits. He described the primary motivation of such organisations as:

---

[130] E Freidson, *Professionalism: The Third Logic* (Oxford, Blackwell Publishers, 2001) at 48.
[131] Croake James [J Paterson], *Curiosities of the Law and Lawyers* (London, Low, Marston, Searle and Rivington, 1882).
[132] Burrage, 'From a Gentleman's to a Public Profession' (n 91) at 59.
[133] JO Orojo, *Conduct and Etiquette for Legal Practitioners* (London, Sweet & Maxwell, 1979) at 5.
[134] *Manor Electronics v Dickson* (1990) 140 *New Law Journal* 590.
[135] Durkheim, *Professional Ethics and Civic Morals* (n 11) at 19.
[136] ibid, at 21.

[J]ust to associate, for the sole pleasure of mixing with their fellows and of no longer feeling lost in the midst of adversaries, as well as for the pleasure of communing together, that is, in short, of being able to lead their lives with the same moral aim.[137]

Pound observed that early professional constitutions had the aim of cultivating 'a spirit of friendship and good will toward each other'.[138] Collegiality, he wrote, 'enables them to contest with their professional brethren all day in the forum, and meet outside on the friendliest terms and with respect for those with whom they have been engaged in the strife of litigation'.[139] Larson argues that '[c]ommunity and ethicality are indissolubly related. In fact, profession is more often defined as *an occupation that tends to be colleague-orientated*, rather than client-orientated'.[140]

In modern usage, 'collegiality' describes both a model of occupational control, of which professionalism is an example,[141] and a work relationship. Ihara, for example, defines collegiality as support and co-operation between colleagues, a reciprocal respect for colleagues' ability to further professional ends through their knowledge and skills, a commitment to common professional values and goals, a willingness to have confidence in colleagues as responsible autonomous agents, a sense of 'connectedness', or sharing with others the bond of being part of a larger independent whole.[142]

Larson argues professional culture includes a sense of craft and of work as self-identity and self-realisation. Collegiality supports the idea of foregoing short-term interests for the common good.[143] Intrinsic motivation towards work, doing it for its own sake, resists pressure towards commercialisation and instrumentalism.[144] Professional socialisation and culture, status and distinction are all incentives to conformity, small compensations for the lack of material rewards.[145]

The English Bar has an archetypal collegial structure. Arthurs, for example, observes that:

> For the Canadian legal profession, the real (or imagined) culture of the English bar is the point of reference (not to say reverence) ... Indeed, if there is any legal profession whose culture can be identified with some precision, it is surely this one. Accordingly, in the case of the English bar, culture can be seen as an important vehicle for the transmission of values and the regulation of behaviour.[146]

The key features of Bar collegiality were the organisation of independent practitioners in chambers, contained within Inns, providing physical proximity and identity.

---

[137] ibid, at 25.

[138] Pound (n 22) at 15.

[139] ibid, at 127.

[140] Larson (n 8) at 226 (italics in original)

[141] Johnson, *Professions and Power* (n 36) at 45.

[142] CK Ihara, 'Collegiality as a Professional Virtue' in A Flores (ed), *Professional Ideals* (Belmont, CA, Wadsworth Publishing, 1988) at 56.

[143] PF Camenisch, 'On Being a Professional: Morally Speaking' in Flores, ibid, at 14.

[144] Larson (n 8) at 62.

[145] RL Nelson, DM Trubeck and RL Solomon, 'New Problems and New Paradigms in Studies of the Legal Profession' in *Lawyers' Ideals/Lawyers' Practices: Transformations in the American Legal Profession* (Ithaca, NY, Cornell University Press, 1992) 1, at 17.

[146] HW Arthurs 'Lawyering in Canada in the 21st Century' (1996) *Windsor Yearbook of Access to Justice* 202, at 223.

By 1970, despite several small metropolitan locations, the Bar was still centred on London. Inns played an effective role in Bar life, for example, by helping to maintain discrete but effective discipline. The General Council of the Bar, while responsible for policy, was controlled by the Inns.

The Inns preserve Bar rituals collectively and individually within each Inn. An example of a collective ritual is dining in the Inn during the period before admission. This was originally introduced to establish residence in an Inn, and was then made a standard requirement across the Inns.[147] An example of an individual ritual is that Middle Templars sign the roll of members called to the bar on a hatch cover from Sir Francis Drake's ship, *The Golden Hind*. Dining was an increasingly controversial requirement, particularly when Bar students were allowed to study outside London.

The Inns eventually found an ingenious compromise to the dining requirement. Students are now required to complete 12 'units' in order to be called to the Bar.[148] These are known as qualifying sessions and are defined as 'educational and collegiate activities arranged by or on behalf of the Inn for the purpose of preparing junior barristers for practice'. These sessions typically include 'dining sessions', with senior practitioners, but they need not be so. It is more common now for these sessions to have relevant talks and training workshops. Even these limited requirements are sometimes resented.[149]

Solicitors had more difficulty in establishing a collegial profession. The national dispersal of solicitors' firms created more physical distance between solicitors and between and between local law societies and the Law Society. Nevertheless, a common education programme, and relatively few sites from which it was delivered, supported a sense of belonging to common group.

The effectiveness of The Law Society as the representative of all solicitors was evidenced by relatively few challenges to its authority from members.[150] In the 1960s, however, a National House Owners Society was established to encourage people to do their own conveyancing. Sections of the profession criticised the Law Society for failing to defend the conveyancing monopoly effectively. This led to the establishment of a short-lived competitor, the British Legal Association.[151]

ii. Hierarchy

The picture of professions as communities of equals is ideological.[152] Professions have internal badges of status; hierarchies that may not relate to wider status hierarchies.[153] In fact, the Bar is distinctive in having a formal hierarchy[154] with judges, Queen's

---

[147] Pound (n 22) at 109.
[148] BSB, 'Joining an Inn' (www.barstandardsboard.org.uk/qualifying-as-a-barrister/bar-professional-training-course/how-to-apply-for-the-bptc/joining-an-inn/).
[149] A Aldridge, 'Barristers' dinners – a bit of fun or one upper-class indulgence too many?' *The Guardian* 12 May 2011.
[150] Larson (n 8) at 227.
[151] Hanlon (n 81) at 79.
[152] Larson (n 8) at 205.
[153] ibid, at 226.
[154] Glasser, 'The Legal Profession in the 1990's' (n 89).

Counsel, benchers, readers and heads of the Inns. The Law Society, with fewer official degrees of hierarchy, has a more conventional internal elite in the long established and high status London firms. Both branches also have officers answering to elected councils and a president rotated annually. These elites dictate standards accepted by all in return for the esteem bestowed by association with elite reference groups.[155]

iii. Education

Larson observed that appointment to elites, such as professions, is sponsored by existing members in the UK.[156] Barristers used ascribed characteristics, the kind of person who could become a barrister, well into the twentieth century, while solicitors were seen to use formal or achieved qualities.[157] By the 1970s the legal professions were offering increased numbers from the aspiring middle classes the prospect of raising their status through work.

Accessibility was improved by the abandonment of practical for academic qualification. Education had become more meritocratic and anonymous, being based on qualification and examinations. Linking educational programmes to universities initially helped professions to control the production of expertise.[158] As the solicitors replaced apprenticeship with formal educational programmes, they could not control the numbers entering the profession as effectively.

C. Values

Larson argues that English legal professionalism fused gentlemen's values with business values to produce the professional ethic. The legal professions held many values in common, for example, a duty of client loyalty reflected in obligations of fidelity and confidentiality. They also represent some values that are quite distinct from each other.

i. Bar Neutrality

The Bar's commitment to neutrality is stronger than that of solicitors. This is consistent with barristers' role as consultants in legal matters, whereby they had a professional client, a solicitor, and a lay client. It is perhaps for this reason that barristers were able to remain very detached from client wishes. Indeed, barristers have been observed to sometimes take an almost judicial role, refusing unmeritorious claims and promoting settlement where they consider this advisable.[159]

---

[155] Larson (n 8) at 227.
[156] ibid, at 79.
[157] RL Abel, *The Legal Profession in England and Wales* (Oxford, Basil Blackwell, 1988).
[158] Larson (n 8) ch 2, esp at 17.
[159] Burrage (n 33) at 483.

The 'cab rank rule' is the expression of the Bar's commitment to neutrality. The rule is so called because barristers must accept briefs in the order they arrive. The Bar's Code of Conduct required barristers, as advocates, to accept a case, unless they had a valid, accepted reason for not doing so.[160] A separate rule required them to accept any brief to appear before a court in which they profess to practise.[161] Having accepted that brief, barristers could not withdraw from a case except in specified circumstances[162] and subject to specific requirements for return of the brief.[163]

The justifications for the 'cab rank rule' are, first, that it ensures that the smallest solicitors' firm can instruct the best barrister on behalf of any client. This maximises equal access to justice. Secondly, it ensures representation, because advocates cannot be identified with their clients in the minds of members of the public. Rather than offering convoluted justifications of how they can represent murderers and rapists, barristers can say that their professional rules require them to do so. This is consistent with the presumption of innocence, but it also reduces, in the words of Geoffrey Robertson QC, 'the excrement through the letter box'.[164]

There are examples where advocates have attracted criticism by agreeing to act.[165] Robertson alleges that the Bar Council prevented English barristers defending the accused in the Nuremberg Trails, that 21 QCs turned down briefs for the Old Bailey bombers in 1974 and that he was advised by a judge not to do so for risk of 'joining the alternative bar'.[166] Nevertheless, the cab rank rule is emblematic for the Bar. Solicitors have never been subject to an obligation to accept any client. Some solicitors say that they would not act for certain types of client and argue that the principle behind the cab rank rule is outmoded.[167] When solicitors acquired higher rights, the argument that solicitor advocates should adopt the cab rank rule was not accepted. Nevertheless, the cab rank rule has been compared favourably with other jurisdictions, like the USA, where there is no equivalent rule.[168]

ii. Solicitor Honour, Independence and Integrity

The original values of The Law Society were shaped by the example of the Bar and a concern with status and social standing.[169] The forerunner of the Law Society, The Society of Gentlemen Practisers, formed in 1739, expressed this in its aim of

> supporting the honour and independence of the profession [and the] moral elevation of its members, [who] being placed under the constant observation of the whole body, the least

---

[160] Bar Council, *Bar Code 1981*, at para 601.
[161] ibid, at para 602.
[162] ibid, at para 609.
[163] ibid, at para 610.
[164] G Robertson, *The Justice Game* (London, Chatto and Windus, 1998) at 377.
[165] D Pannick *Advocates* (Oxford, Oxford University Press 1992) at 143.
[166] Robertson, *The Justice Game* (n 164) at 379.
[167] G Bindman, 'Lies lawyers and ethics' *The Times* 1 May 2001.
[168] R Cranston, 'Legal Ethics and Professional Responsibility' in R Cranston (ed), *Legal Ethics and Professional Responsibility* (Oxford, Clarendon Press, 1995) 1, at 28–29.
[169] Burrage (n 91) at 89–90, Sugarman (n 76) at 88, Pound (n 22) at 105.

tendency to ungentlemanly conduct or dishonourable or illiberal practice will be immediately noticed and checked.[170]

The solicitors' leaders sought a protected market for a narrow range of preferred, high status work within a framework of institutional independence.

When provincial solicitors sought County Court rights of audience in the nineteenth century, the Council of the Law Society rejected the proposal because 'gentlemen did not frequent the county court'.[171] They promoted the image of the professional as a 'the solitary, disciplined, highly educated, and deeply ethical practitioner dealing with clients one by one'.[172] Sole practitioners were seen as the most ethically powerful lawyer. [173] Only they could make autonomous decisions on representation, most other lawyers being constrained by the policy and bureaucracy of organisations.

The picture of responsibility and reliability was continued into the organisational form for solicitors. Each partner had personal responsibility for all partnership debts.[174] Solicitors presented themselves as reliable men of business. Goriely suggests that solicitors consistently avoided low grade work, even if it promised to be profitable,[175] but were often forced to accept it by the threat of competition. She suggests that a pattern developed. First, the Law Society denied the need for legal services in the particular area. Secondly, having accepted a need, it devised a plan but did nothing about it. Thirdly, the advice sector developed the area of work and involved local solicitors. Fourthly, the profession defended the market that had been established.

VI. Pressures on Legal Professional Culture since 1970

A. Trends

i. Co-operation to Competition

In a protected market professions can agree set prices that offer a profit but are fair to consumers. This avoids consumers needing to 'shop around'. They can expect that, wherever, they go, they will get the same service at the same cost. This is consistent with the idea of collegiality because it supports stable markets and reduces friction between providers. The risk is that providers do not critically examine the value of the service provided, with the result that the price is set too high.

---

[170] Burrage, ibid, at 49.

[171] Sugarman (n 76) at 98 and 109.

[172] CO Houle, *Continuing Learning in the Professions* (San Francisco, Jossey-Bass, 1980) at i.

[173] L Sheinman, 'Looking for Legal Ethics' (1997) 4 *International Journal of the Legal Profession* 139, at 151.

[174] R Greenwood and CR Hinings, 'Understanding Radical Organisational Change: Bringing Together the Old and the New Institutionalism' (1996) 21 *Academy of Management Review* 1022, at 1027.

[175] Goriely, 'Law for the Poor' (n 116) at 216.

The 1970s marked the start of a period of dramatic changes to the monopolies and regulation of the legal profession. These are described in more detail in the next chapter. There were, however, a number of challenges to the established culture of the legal profession that materialised or intensified from the 1970s onwards. These were stimulated by political, economic and social factors. One of the most powerful was the growth of a more consumerist society. Consumerism favours competition as a means of reducing the cost of goods and services.

It was feared that competition could have a negative impact on standards in the legal profession. At the lower end of the market it might drive down the cost of legal services but encourage cutting corners, poor service standards and dishonesty. At the higher end of the market it might put lawyers under more pressure from clients to behave unethically.[176] It also has an impact on policy in professions. This was most obvious is relation to advertising.

ii. Autonomy to Bureaucracy

Durkheim speculated that a strong occupational culture is achieved by modest scale of operations.[177] He said that

> when the group is small, the individual and the society are not far apart; the whole is barely distinguishable from the part, and each individual can therefore discern the interests of the whole at first hand, along with the links that bind the interests of the whole to those of each one.[178]

Professional association with sole practice drives them to professional association beyond the workplace. Professions promote trust in the independence and neutrality of individuals and are therefore been seen as anti-bureaucratic. Professional institutions, such as the Bar, conformed to this pattern.

The organisations in which lawyers work have generally increased in size, a fact that almost inevitably increases levels of bureaucracy. This challenges notions of professionalism based on independence and autonomy. As organisations get bigger, levels of authority are introduced and processes are rationalised so as to reduce the scope of individual discretion.[179] There is a concern that the professional mind-set, which is autonomous and independent, may be unsuited to work in bureaucratic organisations.[180]

---

[176] LR Patterson 'On Analyzing the Law of Legal Ethics: An American Perspective' (1981) 16(1) *Israel Law Review* 28, from 31; CE Reason and C Chappell, 'Crooked Lawyers: Towards a Political Economy of Deviance in the Profession' in T Fleming (ed), *The New Criminologies in Canada: Status, Crime and Control* (Toronto, Oxford University Press, 1985) at 212.
[177] Durkheim (n 11).
[178] ibid, at 15.
[179] Larson (n 8) at 198.
[180] E Freidson and B Rhea, 'Processes of Control in a Company of Equals' in E Freidson and J Lorber (eds), *Medical Men and their Work* (Hawthorne, NY, Walter de Gruyter, 1971) at 185; Larson (n 8) at 190.

iii. Homogeneity to Heterogeneity

In social science, homogeneity refers to the uniformity of the composition or character of a society or group. Heterogeneity refers to differences, for example, in the ethnicity, class or gender of a group. It is often assumed that a strong occupational culture is fostered by social homogeneity. Until the 1970s the legal profession was relatively socially homogenous.

From the 1970s onwards, differences between the backgrounds and personal characteristics of entrants to the legal profession, between different kinds of lawyers and between the organisations in which they worked, were magnified. Therefore, if a profession is heterogeneous, and culture is considered important, there may need to be more effective socialisation, for example, through education and training.

iv. Generalisation to Specialisation

Professionals are usually credited with broad vision of their clients' problems. They can see beyond immediate or presenting issues. They also have sufficient expertise to handle a wide range of problems personally, without passing them to a colleague. This preserves the integrity of the professional relationship and client confidentiality. Competition and a larger scale of operations usually generate pressure for increased specialisation, undermining the personal relationship between professional and client. Specialisation also contributes to de-skilling. No one performs the whole transaction, and this can increase the risk of error. This may explain why cost cutting in conveyancing work has caused a massive increase in claims for negligence.[181] Finally, specialisation also generates greater differences between specialist groups, potentially leading to divergence on values and ethical issues.

B. Impacts

i. Professional Policy

a. Scale Fees

An example of a move for co-operation to competition lay in conveyancing scale fees. Until 1972, the fees charged by all solicitors were set as a fixed percentage of a transaction. Abandonment of the scale led many solicitors to charge less. By 1995, conveyancing accounted for about 10 per cent of solicitors' gross fee income, but nearly 55 per cent of claims to the Solicitors' Indemnity Fund and Compensation Fund.[182]

---

[181] Glasser (n 89); S Domberger and A Sherr, 'The Impact of Competition on Pricing and Quality of Legal Services' (1989) 9 *International Review of Law and Economics* 41.

[182] 'Conveyancing and the case for reform' *The Lawyer* 12 December 1995. (www.thelawyer.com/conveyancing-and-the-case-for-reform/83791.article)

Various attempts to restore scale fees were unsuccessful, generally because of lack of government support. In 2012, the legal services complaints ombudsman noted that conveyancing was the second most complained about area. The reason, he said, was that the 'increasingly commoditised automated and competitive' conveyancing market has resulted in traditional high street firms evolving or being displaced into 'conveyancing factories'.[183]

b. Advertising

Professions often ban individual advertising on the grounds that it is undignified for professionals to seek out clients. Hazard claims that lifting the advertising ban in the US 'changed the image of lawyers from professionals who deplored self-laudation into that of aggressive self-promoters'.[184] Stopping practitioners claiming individual distinction forces them to channel their effort into collective control and promotion.[185] This supports professional collegiality and community and encourages the modest demeanour associated with professionalism. Individual advertising symbolised the distinction between professions and business and was deplored as unprofessional conduct.[186] In 1979, Orojo asserted that '[i]mproper attraction of business will include all those acts which tend to give an unfair advantage in obtaining legal business, because such acts lower the prestige of the profession and, therefore, constitute unprofessional conduct'.[187]

One of the casualties of increased competition in the legal services market since the 1970s was a longstanding ban on advertising. Fearing competition from licensed conveyancers, solicitors allowed advertising, subject to restrictions, in 1984. Since then, most lawyers have produced promotional brochures.[188] By 1990, even the Bar capitulated to advertising, albeit heavily controlled.[189]

Advertising, particularly in the trade sections of local papers, resulted in a loss of mystique. They were possibly not even the most tasteless examples. One divorce specialist generated national news coverage with national advertisements, aimed at City-based clients, reading 'Ditch the bitch' and 'All men are bastards'.[190] The issue is now ever present, with concern about whether television advertising compromises professional gravitas.[191] European competition law supports ever deeper incursions into advertising restrictions.[192]

---

[183] C Baksi, 'Ombudsman warns of dangers from "conveyancing factories"' *Law Society Gazette* 11 December 2012.

[184] Hazard, 'The Future of Legal Ethics' (n 16) at 1243.

[185] D Rueschemeyer 'Doctors and Lawyers: A Comment on the Theory of the Professions' (1964–65) *Canadian Review of Sociology and Anthropology* 17.

[186] VW Boulton, A guide to Conduct and Etiquette at the Bar, 6th edn (London, Butterworths, 1978) at 55.

[187] JO Orojo, *Conduct and Etiquette for Legal Practitioners* (London, Sweet & Maxwell, 1979).

[188] J Flood, 'Megalawyering in the Global Order: The Cultural, Social and Economic Transformation of Global Legal Practice' (1996) 3(1/2) *International Journal of the Legal Profession* 169.

[189] General Council of the Bar, *Practice Management for the Bar—Standards and Guidelines for Barristers and Chambers* (1995).

[190] F Callister, 'Split Decisions' *The Lawyer* 4 June 2001, at 17.

[191] S Ward, 'As seen on TV' 97 (36) *Law Society Gazette* 21 September 2000, at 26.

[192] P Stanley, 'European briefing' *Solicitors Journal* 1 June 2001.

c. Membership

Entry

In the first half of the twentieth century both barristers and solicitors managed the qualification process directly, with the result that numbers of practitioners in both branches did not increase. In the 1960s and 1970s the production of lawyers increased dramatically. In the 1851 census there were 2,088 barristers and 11,684 solicitors.[193] In 1950 the combined professions numbered 20,000, in 1980 42,000 and in 1990 61,000.[194] This began with the Bar encouraging graduates, and then preferring them. The Law Society initially allowed entry by graduates with two years' articles instead of the standard five.

When the university degree became the main route in the early 1970s, the Law Society eventually abandoned five-year articles. Favouring graduates laid the foundation for expansion of the profession. From the 1970s the provision of law degrees increased. Before World War Two three-quarters of law students were enrolled at five elite colleges, including Oxford and Cambridge. By 1980 they accounted for less than 20 per cent.[195] Between 1961 and 1986 the numbers of lawyers in England and Wales increased by 147 per cent, compared with 129 per cent in the US and 253 per cent in Canada.[196] Burrage suggested that this presented a challenge to the Law Society:

> The solicitors' branch is becoming a more public profession than its predecessors ... more educated and heterogeneous, less concerned with its corporate honour, more market-oriented and competitive, with others and amongst themselves, and therefore less secure ... all these things make it more unruly and fractious, more unethical and disloyal.[197]

During the 1970s the Bar reduced barriers to entry, such as fees on joining an Inn, on call and on entering pupillage. It also introduced a one-year vocational course with examinations and pupillage in 1959.[198] This left obtaining pupillage and a tenancy in chambers as the only formal barrier to practise as a barrister. Similarly, solicitors needed to serve a training contract before they could qualify. For barristers there was also the considerable problem of obtaining briefs, and hence experience, during the early years of practice whereas solicitors received a salary. There was additional pressure on training places, with decisions more likely to be challenged on the ground of discrimination.

In terms of the market, growth of the profession was partly fuelled by the wide availability of legal aid.[199] The Bar, in particular, almost doubled in size, on the back of public funding. Many junior barristers received between a half and 90 per cent of their income from legal aid.[200] As the availability of legal aid reduced from the 1990s there was considerable pressure from within the Bar to restrict entry to the vocational stage, to reduce pressure on the Bar to supply more pupillages. The Office of Fair

[193] Larson (n 8).
[194] DS Clark, 'Legal Professions and Law Firms' in DS Clark (ed), *Comparative Law and Society* (Cheltenham, Edward Elgar Publishing Ltd, 2012).
[195] Abel (n 96) at 10.
[196] M Galanter, 'Law Abounding: Legalisation Around the North Atlantic' (1992) 55(1) *The Modern Law Review* 1, at 4.
[197] Burrage (n 91) at 75.
[198] Abel (n 96) at 7.
[199] ibid; Glasser (n 89).
[200] Abel (n 96).

Trading, a non-ministerial government department established in 1973 to promote competition, insisted that there be no artificial restriction on the number of those taking the vocational courses.

Diversity

Increased numbers entering the profession reduced homogeneity and increased diversity of both of the main branches of the legal profession in terms of sex, race, ethnicity and class. The most marked change was in relation to the sex of entrants. The first women were not called to the Bar[201] or admitted as solicitors[202] until 1922, following the Sex Disqualification (Removal) Act 1919. Initially, numbers of women were low compared with other professions, but began to increase from the 1970s. By the 1990s around half of law graduates were women, and significant numbers entered the legal profession.

Masculine and Feminine Ethics

Most of the discussion has centred on the theory that men and women use different moral languages and approaches in solving problems.[203] This was posed as a problem for the cultural norms of legal professionalism. 'Instrumental rationality, ambition, competitiveness, aggression' were seen to be masculine dispositions. They were said to contrast with feminine preferences for 'empathy, care or compassion'.[204] Research by Gilligan suggested that men approached problems as an issue of 'rights', ignoring the impact of decisions.[205] Women, she found, were more empathetic, seeking solutions that 'avoid pain' by meeting the needs of all those affected by a problem and attempting to minimise disruption of relationships. Gilligan's subjects were not lawyers, so her conclusions take no account of the effect of legal socialisation.[206]

Menkel-Meadow saw in this distinction between an 'ethic of rights' and 'ethic of care' the potential for a shift in practical legal problem solving. This would be away from adversarial and confrontational approaches towards more mediational dispute resolution methods, participatory lawyering and non-trial based methods of dispute resolution.[207] It is difficult to verify such developments empirically because of problems studying practice environments.[208] The predominance of women in legal

---

[201] H Hallett, 'My legal hero: Dr Ivy Williams' *The Guardian* 10 February 2011.

[202] MJ Mossman, *The First Women Lawyers* (Oxford, Hart Publishing, 2006); The Law Society, 'Our Heritage' (www.lawsociety.org.uk/communities/women-lawyers-division/our-heritage/).

[203] C Gilligan, *In a Different Voice* (Cambridge MA and London, Harvard University Press, 1982).

[204] R Collier, '"Nutty Professors", "Men in Suits" and "New Entrepreneurs": Corporeality, Subjectivity and Change in the Law School and Legal Practice' (1998) 7 *Social and Legal Studies* 2.

[205] Gilligan, *In A Different Voice* (n 203).

[206] JM Hedegard, 'The Impact of legal Education: An In-Depth Examination of Career-relevant Interests, Attitudes, and Personality Traits Among First-Year Law Students' (1979) 4 *American Bar Foundation Research Journal* 791.

[207] C Maughan and J Webb, *Lawyering Skills and the Legal Process* (London, Butterworths, 1995) 116–20.

[208] See B Danet, KB Hoffman and NC Kermish, 'Obstacles to the Study of Lawyer Client Interaction: The Biography of a Failure' (1980) 14 *Law and Society Review* 905.

workplaces does not necessarily produce less hierarchical management styles and greater integration between work and family lives.[209]

C. The Market for Legal Services

i. Scale and Difference

Even though there were differences between different kinds of lawyers, these became more obvious and extreme after the 1970s. Some of these differences concerned the type of work lawyers performed and the values associated with it. Differences were accentuated by the scale of operations. Competition fuelled a move to larger and more bureaucratic organisations.

a. Large Firms

In the 1970s professional assumptions about an appropriate scale of operations were significantly threatened by large law firms. Even among the elite London solicitors' firms, small partnerships were the norm until the mid-1950s. In 1937, Linklaters was the largest City partnership with 11 partners and Freshfields usually had three.[210] The Companies Act 1967 removed the ceiling partnership numbers, set at twenty. This paved the way for mega-firms with hundreds of partners. These firms not only dominated the national market in corporate and commercial law work, they quickly became the largest international firms in the world.

   The change in the size of large firms coincided with other social and economic transitions. Until the 1960s UK businesses were largely personal empires and business was run on personal relations. The leading partners in elite solicitors firms often had personal and family relationships with banking and business moguls spanning generations. During the 1960s business became more corporate, bureaucratic and professionally managed. Consequently, in the 1970s and 1980s, businesses became more demanding and more likely to treat professional services like a commodity.[211]

   Large firms tend to be highly focused on corporate and commercial work for large businesses. They surrendered lucrative private client work, like personal trusts and tax advice, to smaller firms.[212] Consequently, many lawyers in large firms have little contact with the concerns of individuals, even wealthy ones. When a similar trend appeared in the US, Llewellyn feared that such a retreat into corporate specialisation might produce expert practitioners with a technocratic outlook, narrow vision and a 'trained incapacity for social responsibility'.[213] Llewellyn argued that 'the practice of corporation law not only works for business men towards business ends, but develops within itself a

---

[209] C Menkel-Meadow, 'Portia Redux: Another Look at Gender Feminism, and Legal Ethics' in C Sampford (ed), *Legal Ethics and Legal Practice: Contemporary Issues* (Oxford, Clarendon Press, 1995) 24, at 34 and see ch 16: 'Employment'.
[210] Sugarman (n 65) at 265 and 266.
[211] Hanlon (n 81) at 80.
[212] J Currie, 'Reversal of fortune' *The Lawyer* 8 July 2002.
[213] K Llewellyn, 'The Bar Specialises: With What results?' (1933) *The Annals of the American Academy* 177.

business point of view toward the work to be done, toward the value of the work to the community'.[214] While Llewellyn's fears may seem extreme, many US academics suggest that large firm lawyers have different values from lawyers in more conventional firms.[215] Gordon argued that commercial firms are tainted by commercialism, to the detriment of 'their lofty professionalism'.[216]

The large London-based firms now dominate legal indicators such as partnership size, numbers of training places and gross fees. Increased size almost inevitably results in increased rationalisation, specialisation, hierarchy, meritocracy and market orientation.[217] Johnson argued that 'practitioners subject to corporate patronage ... will exhibit beliefs, attitudes ideologies which diverge from and sometimes conflict with those exhibited by practitioners subjected to meditative or collegiate forms of control.'[218] The atmosphere of such firms is more like a business than the 'gentlemen's clubs' of old.[219] They have centralised and bureaucratic management structures and their size supports specialist functions like finance, marketing, personnel, library, information technology and training, all performed by non-lawyers.[220]

Large firms are also said to be less collegial, and more entrepreneurial, competitive and meritocratic.[221] As regards pay, for example, traditional solicitors' firms have a flat structure where managerial tasks are shared and fee earners do similar work.[222] The traditional 'lockstep' system for partnership pay, rewarding experience, seniority and length of service, reinforces collegiality. The large firms favour differential pay policies that reward effort, billing, client attraction and client retention. Large firms also changed the relationship between solicitors and barristers. Barristers were expected to be 'part of the team' and were instructed with compatibility in mind.[223] Elite commercial chambers were driven to offer larger and larger pupillage salaries to compete with City solicitors for sought after trainees.

b. Cause Lawyers

Solicitors' firms offering services in areas such as family law, welfare and criminal are identified by an umbrella term, 'cause lawyers'.[224] Their primary interest is often

---

[214] ibid.

[215] M Galanter and T Palay, 'Public Service Implications of Evolving Law Firm Size and Structure' in RA Katzmann, *The Law Firm and the Public Good* (Washington, DC, The Brookings Institution, 1995) at 19.

[216] R Gordon,'The Independence of Lawyers' (1988) 68 *Boston University Law Review* 63; and see HF Stone, 'The Public Influence of the Bar' (1934) 48 *Harvard Law Review* 1; M Regan, *Eat What You Kill: The Fall of a Wall Street Lawyer* (Ann Arbor, MI, University of Michigan Press, 2006).

[217] KI Eisler, *Shark Tank: Greed, Politics and the Collapse of Finley Kumble, One of America's Largest Law Firms* (New York, Plume, 1990).

[218] Johnson (n 3) at 16–17 and 90.

[219] C Stanley, 'Enterprising Lawyers: Changes in the Market for Legal Services' (1991) 25(1) *Law Teacher* 44.

[220] EH Greenebaum, 'Development of Law Firm Training Programs: Coping with a Turbulent Environment' (1996) 3(3) *International Journal of the Legal Profession* 315, at 322.

[221] E Lazega, *The Collegial Phenomenon: The Social Mechanisms of Cooperation Among Peers in a Corporate Law Partnership* (New York, Oxford University Press, 2001).

[222] L Bishop, 'Regulating the Market for Legal Services in England: Enforced Separation of Function and Restrictions on Forms of Enterprise' (1989) 53 *Modern Law Review* 326.

[223] Greenebaum 'Development of Law Firm Training Programs' (n 220) at 321.

[224] A Boon, 'Cause Lawyers and the Alternative Ethical Paradigm: Ideology and Transgression' (2004) 7 *Legal Ethics* 250.

securing the interests of a specific underprivileged group, or cause. Despite sharing egalitarian values internally, cause lawyers present different public faces. Radical lawyers are likely to have a client base of organisations seeking to change basic social structures. Their own organisational culture may appear fairly conventional. Critical lawyers, however, work to undermine hierarchical social, family and workplace relationships and this will almost inevitably be reflected in their organisational cultural values.[225] They fit the professional profile in that they were not overtly driven by profit, but they contradict notions of professional neutrality. Most do not countenance acting for certain kinds of client. Christian Khan, solicitors, for example, reputedly refused to act for the National Front, Hitler's deputy and Saddam Hussein.[226]

c. Employed Lawyers

English legal professionalism is based on private practice.[227] Lawyers had often worked outside but, since the 1970s, numbers working in corporations, the civil service, local government, Crown Prosecution Service and law centres have grown significantly. The numbers of employed lawyers increased from around 3000 in 1966 to 15,000 in 1996.[228] Employed lawyers are typically restricted to working internally on their employer's matters. There are circumstances where they can also act for members of the public. These are occasionally mentioned in the codes. For example, a solicitor employed by an insurance company as an employed solicitor could, under the 2007 Code, act for an insured person, provided the latter gives specific consent, the claim comes within the small claims limit in the County Court, the case is not allocated to the fast or multi-track and does not concern personal injuries.[229]

In addition to the scale, bureaucracy and values of the organisations in which employed lawyers typically work, additional questions are posed for legal professional culture. Was it important that government-employed prosecutors were independent of the state or should they help the court to reach a wise decision?[230] What duty were employers owed as 'clients' and how did the obligation of confidentiality apply? Should private practice and employed lawyers be subject to the same ethics codes,[231] and if so, would exceptions be created for incompatible principles, like the cab rank rule?[232] In 1995, the Bar Council removed the rule which prevented employed barristers from being elected chair or vice chair of the Bar. This addressed the perception that employed barristers were inferior and enabled the Bar Council to claim that it represented all barristers equally.

---

[225] S Scheingold and A Bloom, 'Transgressive Cause Lawyering: Practice Sites and the Politicization of the Professional' (1998) 5 *International Journal of the Legal Profession* 209, at 220.

[226] N Hanson, 'Matter of principle' *Law Society Gazette* 19 August 2004.

[227] RL Abel, *The Legal Profession in England and Wales* (Oxford, Basil Blackwell, 1988) at 306.

[228] Lady Marre CBE, *A Time for Change: Report of the Committee on the Future of the Legal Profession* (London, General Council of the Bar and Council of the Law Society, 1988) para 6.8 and paras 5.24–5.25.

[229] SRA, *Solicitors' Code of Conduct 2007*, r 13.06(2).

[230] M Taruffo, 'The Lawyer's Role and the Models of Civil Process' (1981) 16 *Israel Law Review* 5.

[231] 'Employed Barristers Eligible for Office' *New Law Journal* 3 February 1995, at 134.

[232] But see Bar Council, *Bar Code 1981*, as amended, at para 604.

ii. Specialisation

Competition forced solicitors, from the mega-firms to the legal aid firms, to adopt more hierarchical and bureaucratic structures, managerial approaches and to handle work in a more routinised way.[233] As solicitors focused on narrower fields of work they were confident in these areas. Consequently, they were more inclined to compete with barristers for work such as drafting pleadings, appearing in interlocutory hearings in chambers and advising.[234] Many barristers also began to specialise more narrowly. By 1990, 70 per cent of the solicitors' branch claimed to be moderate or extreme specialists[235] and barristers and chambers reduced the areas of work offered leading to smaller numbers of lawyers regarded as competent to do work in certain fields.

Specialisation encouraged the formation of groups promoting sectional interests. For example, medical negligence defence lawyers set up a group (Healthcare Lawyers Association) to give them a 'balancing voice' in legal debates traditionally dominated by plaintiff groups.[236] It also led to promotion of specialist competence for discrete areas of practice.

Recognising the move towards specialisation, the Law Society introduced specialist panels for a number of areas. The personal injury panel was introduced in 1992 and there were five panels at 31 July 1996. Medical Negligence had 100 panel members, Children 1,597, Personal Injury 2,233, Planning 197 and Mental Health Review Tribunals 367. Panels for Local Government, Licensed Insolvency Practitioners, Rights of Audience in Higher Courts and Qualified to Conduct Discrete Investment Business followed.[237] By 2005 many panels were operating accreditation schemes and 18 per cent of solicitors belonged to one or more. There was a possibility that some of these groups would generate practice norms at odds with the established consensus.[238] In some cases the Law Society's panels issued their own codes or recommended the codes of associated bodies.[239]

Some groups combined the role of specialist interest group and specialist panel. In the early-1990s the Association of Personal Injury Lawyers (APIL) was formed. APIL was an association for solicitors and barristers representing personal injury plaintiffs. It was dedicated to the improvement of services provided for victims of accidents and disease. The objectives of the Association were to promote and develop expertise in the practice of personal injury law, campaign for improvements in the law,

[233] R Lee, 'From Profession to Business: The Rise and Rise of the City Law Firm' in P Thomas (ed), *Tomorrow's Lawyers* (Oxford, Blackwell, 1992) at 31; T Goriely, 'Debating the Quality of Legal Services: Differing Models of the Good Lawyer' (1994) 1 *International Journal of the Legal Profession* 159, at 163, citing L Bridges, B Sufrin, J Whetton and R White, *Legal Services in Birmingham* (Birmingham, Birmingham University, 1975).
[234] R Hill, 'Higher Aspirations' *Solicitors Journal* 14 April 1995, at 340.
[235] G Chambers and S Harwood, *Solicitors in England and Wales: Practice Organisation and Perceptions, First Report* (London, Research and Policy Planning Group, The Law Society, 1990) at 150.
[236] N Hilborne, 'New Voice for Defendants' Solicitors' *Law Society Gazette* 13 November 1996, at 1.
[237] See further A Sherr and L Webley, 'Legal Ethics in England and Wales' (1997) 4 *International Journal of the Legal Profession* 109.
[238] T Schneyer, 'Professionalism as Politics: The Making of a Modern Legal Ethics Code' in Nelson, Trubeck and Solomon, *Lawyers' Ideals/Lawyers' Practices* (n 145) at 95.
[239] See ch 20: 'Alternative Dispute Resolution'.

gain wider redress for personal injury, promote safety and alert the public to hazards wherever they arise.

In 1996, APIL published its own code of conduct for members.[240] While it was relatively short, and drew substantially on the Law Society Guide, an initial draft went beyond the Law Society's own regulations. It proposed prohibiting members from paying referral fees, a measure designed to prevent 'ambulance chasing'. Although complaints by members led to amendment,[241] this suggested that specialisation could begin to expose differences among different interest groups within professions.

D. The Legal System

i. *The Adversarial Ethic*

a. Partisanship

The adversarial ethic in both criminal and civil litigation was subject to criticism in the 1990s. In criminal litigation it was found that criminal defence solicitors sometimes provided inadequate defence to those appearing before Magistrates' Courts. Too often they assumed clients were guilty and offered less than zealous representation.[242] This heightened concerns about the risk of miscarriages of justice that were prevalent across jurisdictions. The Australian judge, Mr Justice Kirby, noted that miscarriages of justice arise 'from the way in which operators of the present system at every level allow it to be manipulated, pre-trial, at trial and on appeal, with too much attention to rules and procedures and insufficient concern about the risk of injustice.'[243]

Lawyers in civil proceedings were criticised for being too adversarial, leading litigation to be costly, complex and slow. New Civil Procedure Rules, introduced in 1999, increased judicial control of litigation, promoting the use of alternative methods of dispute resolution, like mediation.[244] Pre-action protocols were introduced to prevent proceedings being issued before defendants had a chance to settle claims. These innovations were intended to reduce lawyer control of the civil litigation process.

b. Neutrality and the Cab Rank Rule

Both solicitors and barristers were dismayed by continuing reductions in legal aid rates. There was continuing pressure from barristers to make an exception to the cab rank rule, because legal aid fees were not seen to be 'adequate in all cases'.[245] The Bar Code provided that a barrister was not obliged to accept instructions other than

---

[240] See APIL Code of Conduct 1996.

[241] C Fogarty and A Laferla, 'Protests Force APIL to Relax Ambulance-Chasing Clause' *The Lawyer* 21 January 1997.

[242] M McConville, J Hodgson, L Bridges and A Pavlovic, *Standing Accused: The Organisation and Practices of Criminal Defence Lawyers in Britain* (Oxford, Clarendon Press, 1994).

[243] M Kirby, *Miscarriages of Justice: Our Lamentable Failure?* (a public lecture delivered by Michael Kirby on 4 June 1991 (London, Inns of Court School of Law 1991)) at 6.

[244] See ch 20: 'Alternative Dispute Resolution'.

[245] J Malpas, 'Bar Council to Confront Cab Rank Rule' *The Lawyer* 16 July 1996.

for 'a fee which is proper' according to the case and the barrister's experience and expenses.[246] Legal aid fees in general were deemed by the same rule to be 'a proper professional fee' unless the Bar Council or the Bar in general meeting determined otherwise. In November 2003, the Bar Council resolved that 'graduated fees' for criminal work were deemed not to be proper fees.[247]

The issue of the relevance of the cab rank rule was brought to a head when the BSB sought Legal Services Board (LSB) approval of a rule change to accommodate new standard contract terms. It proposed excluding the cab rank rule from any arrangement outside those or other published terms. The LSB conducted a consultation and granted approval.[248] In 2012, expressing concern at the competitive implications of such exclusion, the LSB commissioned a report to help it understand 'the impact of the Bar Standards Board 'cab rank rule' on the regulatory objectives set out in Part 1 of the Legal Services Act 2007'.[249]

The authors of the report on the cab rank rule suggested that it was redundant.[250] They pointed to the number of exceptions to the rule and the lack of evidence that it is 'significant or efficacious'.[251] They also suggested that the underlying rationale, that being identified with a client's moral position would deny representation to unsympathetic litigants, was no longer relevant. According to the consultants, the modern legal market is one where finance denies representation, not despicability of personality.[252] This, they said, was a problem that the rule specifically evaded.

The conclusion that the Bar would abandon the rule under this critique, proved premature.[253] The LSB report provoked a strong reaction. Separate responses were made by the Bar Council[254] and Bar Standards Board[255] and both were, in different ways, unusually critical and trenchant. The report prepared for the BSB contains an appendix detailing nearly 60 alleged errors in the consultants' report. It accused the LSB consultants of using a defective approach, having flawed reasoning and weak or non-existent premises. This made its conclusions 'unjustified and incorrect' and 'no basis whatsoever' for the abolition of the rule.[256]

The Bar Council's response focused on judicial endorsement of the importance of the cab rank rule. Sir Sydney Kentridge pointed out that the absence of enforcement could be taken as evidence of compliance, rather than redundancy.[257] In the absence

---

[246] Bar Council, *Bar Code 1981*, as amended, 2004 version, r 604.
[247] BSB, 'Undeeming of Graduated Fees' (www.barstandardsboard.org.uk/code-guidance/undeeming-of-criminal-graduated-fees/).
[248] Rule 604(h) became operative on 31 January 2013
[249] LSB, *Research specification*, para 1 (https://research.legalservicesboard.org.uk/wp-content/media/Research-Specification-Cab-rank-rule.pdf).
[250] J Flood and M Hvvid, 'The Cab Rank Rule: Its Meaning and Purpose in the New Legal Services Market' (https://research.legalservicesboard.org.uk/wp-content/media/Cab-Rank-Rule_final-2013.pdf).
[251] ibid, at 39.
[252] ibid.
[253] C Baksi, 'Taxi for the cab rank rule' *Law Society Gazette* 22 January 2013 (www.lawgazette.co.uk/news/taxi-cab-rank-rule).
[254] S Kentridge, *The Cab Rank Rule: A Response to the Report Commissioned by the Legal Services Board* (http://live.barcouncil.netxtra.net/media/203452/sir_sydney_kentridge_crr_response.pdf).
[255] M Mclaren, C Ulyatt and C Knowles, 'The "Cab Rank Rule": a Fresh View' (www.barstandardsboard.org.uk/media/1460590/bsb_cab_rank_rule_paper_28_2_13_v6__final_.pdf).
[256] ibid, at 48.
[257] Kentridge, *The Cab Rank Rule* (n 254) at 12.

of evidence, he said, the burden should fall on those advocating change to show that abolition of the cab rank rule would have no adverse effect. Kentridge concluded that the LSB's consultants thought the rule is not significant or efficacious because

> they do not see the Bar as an honourable profession whose members generally obey the rules of the profession, and do not seek to evade them. Indeed, throughout the report one finds not merely hostility to the rule but hostility to the Bar and sneers at its ethical pretensions.[258]

Kentridge also hinted at complicity between the LSB consultants and the LSB, noting that the LSB website presenting the report endorsed the consultants' observation that terrorists are attractive clients because of the publicity they provide barristers.[259] The intensity of the response to the attack on the cab rank rule is remarkable. It shows the strength of feeling at the Bar about some of the criticism, explicit and implicit, of its traditions and record. It also reflects the clash of regulatory cultures, considered further in part two. The issue threatens to be controversial into the future. Most recently, the Bar has excluded public access work from the cab rank rule, except for barristers with fewer than three years' call.[260]

VII. Conclusion

Professional culture combines professional traditions, symbols and norms reflecting the occupation's perceived social role. The culture of the lawyers in England and Wales reflects vestiges of a long history based on two legal professions; barristers and solicitors. These professions have separate areas of work, supported by different professional bodies. These share some aspirations, but have quite distinct cultures. They both aspire to the values of independence, autonomy and collegiality, but articulate these differently and to different degrees. They both aspired to perform particular kinds of 'high quality' work for elite sections of society.

After the Second World War and the advent of the welfare state, sectors of the legal profession, and the professional bodies, adopted a wider view of lawyers' roles in service of social democracy. While the solicitors' profession generally embraced an ethos of public service, the elite London commercial firms rapidly evolved in response to the growth of a neoliberal, capitalist state. Such contradictory change is an example of many ruptures in the self-image and ideology of the legal professions. Since the 1970s, the culture of the legal professions has been under pressure from change in society, in the funding of legal services and in the market.

Many lawyers are being forced to consider becoming part of a larger entity in order to be more competitive. The vision of the lawyer as an isolated and committed general

---

[258] ibid, at 30.
[259] ibid, at 14.
[260] 'Fresh cab-rank rule row as LSB approves public access reforms' *Legal Futures* 2 April 2013 (www.legalfutures.co.uk/latest-news/fresh-cab-rank-rule-row-lsb-approves-public-access-reforms).

practitioner, working alone or in a small partnership or chambers, increasingly, has less relevance. The profession is assailed by problems of scale, by diversity and by extreme specialisation. As the legal profession comes under increasing pressure to conform to a business mode of operation, as memberships diverge in terms of wealth and standing, the potential for common culture to bind lawyers together in a mutually supportive community is open to question.

3

Power

'In The Conflict of Faculties, Kant noted that the "higher disciplines"—theology, law and medicine—are clearly entrusted with a social function. In each of these disciplines, a serious crisis must generally occur in the contract by which this function has been delegated before the question of its basis comes to seem a real problem of social practice. This appears to be happening today'.[1]

I. Introduction

Professions hold a position in society through which they exercise certain kinds of power. Lawyers in England and Wales played a significant role in building the medieval state. Their role grew as courts moved to rational systems for resolving disputes based on evidence and rules of logic.[2] The increasing importance of lawyers coincided with the growth of capitalism and the evolution of the modern state system.[3] With industrialisation and democracy, lawyers assisted the efficient resolution of new types of dispute. These were created by changing economic systems and modes of enterprise and the emergence of an increasingly powerful middle class.[4] Societies lacking a legal profession often do not have a dominant middle class majority producing a sufficient volume of distinctive work.[5]

The social order did not offer English lawyers the same political influence as their US counterparts. Lawyers in the USA have been described as a 'natural aristocracy', mingling with democratic elements of society and serving as intermediaries between property and poverty.[6] Nevertheless, Max Weber noted that the English Bar had

---

[1] P Bordieu 'The Force of Law: Toward a Sociology of the Juridical Field' (1987) 38 *The Hastings Law Journal* 805, at 819.

[2] MJ Saks and R Van Duizend, *The Use of Scientific Evidence in Litigation* (Williamsburg, VA, National Centre for State Courts, 1983) at 5.

[3] D Rueschemeyer, 'Professions Cross-Nationally: From a Profession Centred to a State-Centred Approach' (1986) *American Bar Foundation Research Journal* 415.

[4] D Phillips, 'Some General Thoughts on the State of the Republic and the Obligation of the Legal Profession to it' from an address to a conference of the Fourth Judicial Court of the United States at Hot Springs, Virginia, 1969 (cited in JF Sutton and JS Dzienowski, *Cases and Materials on the Professional Responsibility of Lawyers* (St Paul, MN, West Publishing, 1989) at 12).

[5] LM Friedman, 'Lawyers in Cross Cultural Perspective' in R Abel and P Lewis (eds), *Lawyers in Society* (Berkeley, CA, University of California Press, 1995).

[6] GC Hazard, 'The Future of Legal Ethics' (1991) 100 *Yale Law Journal* 1239, at 1272.

'a measure of power which neither King nor Parliament could have easily brushed aside'.[7] Increasing industrial and commercial activity during the nineteenth and twentieth centuries afforded solicitors great business opportunities. They were able to fulfil a central role in the emergent capitalist state.

The historical legacy of the legal profession is its most prized professional privileges; independence from political influence and autonomy in conducting its own affairs. This supports the personal autonomy of legal professionals within a collegial setting. Lawyers are, to some extent, independent, even when part of an organisation. Power can also be enjoyed in ways that have no obvious economic pay-off. Professions enjoy a high level of authority compared with other occupations. Collectively and individually professionals enjoy special status and privilege.

The conditions for these different types of power are threatened by the situation of contemporary society. Lawyers are increasingly in conflict with economic and political interests that threaten the autonomous and formal system of law. Since the beginning of the twentieth century, professions have been accused of a conspiracy against the general public.[8] Professional monopoly, far from serving the public good, forces up the price of work and conceals incompetent service.[9] Professional ethics is seen as holding 'in uneasy juxtaposition the two faces of professionalism—the one monopolistic, even narcissistic, and the other benign, even altruistic'.[10]

Privileges of knowledge, wealth and social position are sometimes seen as the reason why high standards are expected of professionals. The term *noblesse oblige* referred to the obligations of the aristocracy. The idea is that privilege comes with responsibility, particularly in leadership. Therefore, nobles would be expected to be in the front line in battle. This connection, between privilege and responsibility, has been cited as a possible basis for professional ethical responsibility.[11] If this is so, professional ethics are, arguably, contingent on professional power.

II. Theories of Professional Power

A. Professionalism and Alternatives

Hughes refers to professionalisation as a process of 'obtaining a mandate to select, train, initiate and define the nature of services provided, obtaining a monopoly,

---

[7] M Weber, 'Economy and Law (Sociology of Law)' in G Roth and C Wittich (eds), *Economy and Society* (Berkeley, CA, University of California Press, 1978) at 794.

[8] GB Shaw, *The Doctor's Dilemma* (Harmondsworth, Penguin Books Ltd, 1911) Act 1; see also I Illich, *Disabling Professions* (London, Marron Boyars, 1977).

[9] R Moorhead, A Sherr and A Paterson, 'What Clients Know: Client Perspectives and Legal Competence' (2003) 10 *International Journal of the Legal Profession* 5; R Moorhead, A Sherr and A Paterson 'Contesting Professionalism: Legal Aid and Non Lawyers in England and Wales' (2003) 37 *Law and Society Review* 765.

[10] TC Halliday, *Beyond Monopoly: Lawyers, State Crises, and Professional Empowerment* (Chicago, London, University of Chicago Press, 1987) at 3.

[11] D Nicholson and J Webb, *Professional Legal Ethics: Critical Interrogations* (Oxford, Oxford University Press, 1999).

providing a philosophy for society at large concerning the whole area of thought, value and action involved directly or even remotely in their work'.[12] Larson provided a historical analysis of the ways in which professions in England and the US organised themselves to attain power.[13] Of the various sociological theories seeking to explain professions, those based on the idea that professionalism is the result of social conflict between occupations[14] are now in the ascendancy.[15]

Larson also draws attention to the key role played by expert knowledge in professionalisation. Most vocations comprise technicality, that part of the work that can be standardised as education, and 'indetermination', the secret and mysterious component that combines personal skills, qualities and inspiration. High status professions typically have a high element of indetermination. Establishing knowledge and technique occurs in overlapping stages; the creation of a scientific and transferable base; focus on how technique achieves results; explaining the social function of the activity.[16] The second stage is highly ideological. During the process the production of theoretical and practical knowledge becomes distinct. Theoretical knowledge has higher status and so greater importance is attached to its mastery.[17] The theoretical domain is the province of universities and the practical that of trade schools.

Larson argued that the 'professional project' is to secure upward social mobility by exploiting the relationship between professional control and the market. Professions initially serve the economic role of connecting education to delivery of a service in a market place. They then shift to the ideological function of justifying closure of both the market and access to the occupation. Monopoly provision is achieved by controlling the production of the producers of those services.[18]

Abbott argues that the success of professions depends on appeals to the different audiences for three *jurisdictions*, workplace, public and legal.[19] The workplace defines professional work, first, in interactions with clients and then by negotiation of *settlements* with other occupations who do or might perform these tasks.[20] Public jurisdiction concerns the profession's authority in the field. This is determined by outsiders' perceptions, as shaped by codes of conduct, reports by the professional body, advertising and education.[21] Establishing legal jurisdiction involves convincing government of the need for control of the market.

---

[12] EC Hughes, *Men and Their Work* (London, Collier Macmillan, 1958) at 159.

[13] MS Larson, *The Rise of Professionalism: A Sociological Analysis* (Berkeley, CA, University of California Press, 1977).

[14] TJ Johnson, *Professions and Power* (London and Basingstoke, Macmillan Press Ltd, 1972) at 12–14 and RL Abel, *The Legal Profession in England and Wales* (Oxford, Basil Blackwell, 1988) at 5–6, 26–30 and 28–29.

[15] A Giddens, *Sociology*, 5th edn (Cambridge, Polity, 2006).

[16] H Jamois and B Peloille, 'Changes in the French University-Hospital System' in J Jackson (ed), *Professions and Professionalisation* (Cambridge, Cambridge University Press, 1970) at 117; and see Johnson, *Professions and Power* (n 14) at 57 and Larson, *The Rise of Professionalism* (n 13) at 42. This calls into question the whole notion of 'profession'; see P Bordieu and L Wacquant, *An Invitation to Reflexive Sociology* (Chicago, University of Chicago Press, 1992) at 242.

[17] Larson (n 13) at 44.

[18] Johnson (n 14) ch 2; Abel, *The Legal Profession in England and Wales* (n 14) at 4.

[19] A Abbott, *The System of Professions: An Essay on the Expert Division of Labour* (Chicago, University of Chicago Press, 1988).

[20] ibid.

[21] ibid, at 196.

Johnson identifies forms of control of occupational expertise by groups or institutions.[22] His typology comprises collegiate control (professionalism), patronage (control by consumers) and mediation (control, for example, by the state). Johnson's typology of control overlaps with Freidson's three 'logics' for managing the sale and distribution of services.[23] The first of these is perfect competition, where innovation is encouraged and prices kept low. The second is corporate bureaucracy, where efficient management produces reliable products at reasonable cost. The third is, professionalism, where expert workers are dedicated to doing good work, both for their own satisfaction and for the benefit of others, rather than for their personal financial advantage.

Although professionalism is an imperfect way of controlling important knowledge, the alternatives have weaknesses. For example, patronage systems allow powerful clients to define their own needs and the services they require, but offer insufficient curbs on improper behaviour by the patron's lawyers. Additionally, patronage control does nothing to provide legal assistance to the less powerful. Of the other alternatives, communal control, whereby consumer organisations control occupations, or state mediation, would be inflexible. Such systems would suppress initiative and occupational responsibility, encouraging legal occupations to act in their own economic interest.[24]

B. Professionalism and Ethics

What elevates professional practice to a privileged position among occupations is that it has an element of 'indeterminacy', or uncertainty, demanding the application of professional judgement.[25] Indeterminacy gives professional work a craft dimension which, together with professional prestige and status, creates a social and economic distance between lawyers and their clients. The fact that clients are generally unable to judge whether the legal service they receive is good or bad requires the professional to control the situation in the client's interest. Ethics institutionalises the fiduciary relationship between professional and client. If it works, it is a rational market solution.[26]

Larson argues that professional authority is highest when producers are relatively scarce and clients are unorganised. This creates a high risk of abuse and exploitation, which is counterbalanced by adopting an ethical orientation and a spirit of service.[27] Professions therefore share several features with business, such as an institutional pattern of rationality, but represent the anti-market principles of monopoly and public service. Abbott, Abel and others suggest that failure of market control will cause professions to retreat from ethical commitments.[28] The overproduction of producers

---

[22] Johnson (n 14).

[23] E Freidson, *Professionalism: The Third Logic* (Oxford, Blackwell Publishers, 2001).

[24] Johnson (n 14) at 46, 65 and 86.

[25] Johnson (n 14) at 43; H Jamous and B Pelloille, 'Changes in the French University Hospital System' in JA Jackson (ed), *Professions and Professionalization* (London, Cambridge University Press, 1970).

[26] D Rueschemeyer, 'Doctors and Lawyers: A Comment on the Theory of the Professions' (1964–65) 1 *Canadian Review of Sociology and Anthropology* 17.

[27] Larson (n 13) at 48–49.

[28] ibid; RL Abel, 'The Decline of Professionalism?' (1986) 49 *Modern Law Review* 1; Abbott, *The System of Professions* (n 19).

causes the price of services to fall. Reduced profitability undermines the attractiveness of professional roles. Ethics become an additional business overhead that cannot be afforded. It is now necessary to consider whether such a process, one of de-professionalisation, is occurring.

III. Legal Professionalism in the Late-Modern Period 1970–2007

A. Context

Abel argued that the legal profession lost control of the market for legal services, by failing to control, first, the production *of* producers and, second, production *by* producers. Abel identified three types of control over production by producers; the defence of monopoly against competitors, restrictive practices restricting internal competition and manipulation of client demand. Most of the changes in these forms of control occurred or accelerated during the period 1970 to 2007.

During the twentieth century legal services became an important political issue. Following the Second World War there was a massive expansion in demand for legal services. This was attributable to changing patterns of ownership (including personal ownership of real property or national ownership of industry), the increased regulation of social life and the development of technology. The growth in the personal resources of the employed, and the advent of legal aid, brought the services of lawyers within the scope of more people.

As demand for legal services forced up the numbers of lawyers, the legal profession took on low status work. The Law Society accepted that this was inevitable when the Lord Chancellor threatened giving waivers to solicitors to work in advice agencies following the Legal Aid and Advice Act 1972.[29] In the late-1980s the decline in residential conveyancing forced more solicitors into legal aid work,[30] particularly the newly introduced Magistrates' Courts duty solicitor scheme.[31]

Many lawyers were not rich. In 1972, the median income of the 4,000 strong Bar was £2,300 a year and 30 per cent earned less than £1,000.[32] Nevertheless, the perception that lawyers provided a social benefit became more contentious. Civil servants, academic research, media and consumer groups undermined professional claims to act in the public interest. As more people used legal services, public awareness and attitudes to professions became more critical in many Western countries.[33]

---

[29] E Cruikshank, 'Surviving Hard Times' (2003) 100 *Law Society Gazette* 22.
[30] M Hope, *Expenditure on Legal Services* (London, Lord Chancellor's Department, 1997) at 7.
[31] Cruikshank, 'Surviving Hard Times' (n 29).
[32] ibid.
[33] M Galanter, 'Law Abounding: Legalisation Around the North Atlantic' (1992) 55(1) *Modern Law Review* 1, at 3.

Increased claims consciousness[34] led consumers to challenge the necessity for professional interventions, their cost and effectiveness. The Marre Report noted, somewhat regretfully, that

> [m]ore members of the public are now inclined to complain about poor quality or costly services... are no longer deferential to those who provide professional services ... consumers are less willing to accept uncritically the authority which used to be attached to professional people.[35]

In 1995, a survey of consumer attitudes in the UK suggested that people saw the legal system as 'out of date, slow, too complicated and easy to twist'.[36] Only a quarter of respondents believed that the legal system was something to be proud of.

Middle income groups, ineligible for legal aid but not rich enough to fund litigation, were the most likely to be dissatisfied with the legal help available to them. The growth of the market for legal services made the issue of access and the cost of legal services an electoral issue. The provision of legal aid, funding work arising particularly from increases in the levels of crime, family breakdown and debt, gave the state a financial interest in the cost of legal services.[37] This, it was predicted, could lead to demands for more state control as a regulator and purchaser of legal services.[38]

By far the most significant factor influencing the profession was, however, the election of the Conservative Government led by Margaret Thatcher in 1979. The years preceding Thatcher had seen many small changes in the courts and legal markets. There had been considerable debate over bigger changes, such as fusion of the professions, and the Labour Government was sufficiently concerned to create a Royal Commission under Lord Benson in 1975. Benson reported in 1979,[39] but largely favoured the status quo. He recommended remarkably few significant changes to the existing arrangements in education, rights of audience or the organisation of the existing professions.[40]

Why had the legal professions survived virtually unchanged for 300 years and why did the tide suddenly turn? Burrage argues that the arrangements under which the legal profession flourished reflected a desire for a pluralistic civil society. This idea was supported by a social consensus through turbulent social periods from the sixteenth century onwards. The legal professions were, in effect, a bulwark against revolution. They occupied young men when they might otherwise have been inclined to ferment strife. They were a counterweight to the individualism that pervaded England, arguably throughout the medieval period.[41]

By the Thatcher period several factors had changed.[42] From the 1960s the swelling of the professions with practitioners who had taken the university route created

---

[34] WF Felstiner, RL Abel and A Sarat, 'The Emergence and Transformation of Disputes: Naming, Blaming, Claiming ...' (1980–81) 15 *Law and Society* 631.

[35] Lady Marre CBE, *A Time for Change: Report of the Committee on the Future of the Legal Profession* (London, General Council of the Bar and Council of the Law Society, 1988) (Marre Report) at para 3.52.

[36] National Consumer Council, *Seeking Civil Justice* (London, NCC, 1995) at 8.

[37] Marre Report, *A Time for Change* (n 35) at paras 3.14–3.31.

[38] RL Abel, 'Between Market and State: The Legal Profession in Turmoil' (1989) 52(3) *Modern Law Review* 285.

[39] The Royal Commission on Legal Services Final Report (1979) Cmnd. 7648 (Benson).

[40] M Burrage, *Revolution and the Making of the Contemporary Legal Profession: England, France and the United States* (Oxford, Oxford University Press, 2006) at 552–53.

[41] ibid, at 636–37.

[42] ibid, at 554–56.

a different environment. The increasing numbers of academics led to more research and an increasingly critical perspective on the profession. From the 1970s there was increased interest from new pressure groups, such as Legal Action Group and the Consumers' Association. There was also increased attention from civil servants in the Lord Chancellor's Office in the 1970s and the Office of Fair Trading in the 1980s. Added to these factors were the personalities of the main protagonists, Thatcher herself, a barrister who had been rejected by a number of chambers, and Lord Mackay, a Scottish lawyer and therefore outside the English legal establishment.

The Thatcher Government had a reformist agenda for the whole of society, underpinned by a neoliberal political philosophy. The aim was to benefit consumers of goods and services at home and restore the United Kingdom as a trading nation in an increasingly competitive, globalised economy.[43] The strategy was to encourage economic liberalisation, promoting free trade and open markets. There would be privatisation of state-run industry and deregulation in the economic sphere.

Under the Conservative Government's plans, public sector and public expenditure would decrease while many of its roles would be increasingly fulfilled by the private sector. The state would confront vested interests seen as anti-competitive forces. This included trade unions and the 'little republics', like the Bar, which hindered both the dominance of the state and the operation of markets. The neoliberal policy was tempered but largely continued by the Labour Government of Tony Blair elected in 1997.

B. Community

There have been times since the 1970s when huge additional numbers undergoing legal training could not be accommodated in the conventional professions. Considerable bottlenecks at the pupillage and training contract stages left many aspiring lawyers unable to take the first step in private practice. Many entered employment 'in-house' in government service and corporations or as para-legal workers. These lawyers were potential competitors for private practitioners and potential opponents of the private legal professions.

C. Work

i. Monopolies

a. Conveyancing

The first inroad into professional monopoly was the solicitors' control of land transfers. Land transfer contributed a large part of solicitors' income. The Solicitors' Remuneration Act 1881 caused unrealistically high conveyancing fees, leading to the Law of Property Act 1925 and a simpler system. This was supported by the Law

---

[43] M Burrage, 'Mrs. Thatcher Against the "Little Republics": Ideology, Precedents, and Reaction' in TC Halliday and L Karpik (eds), *Lawyers and the Rise of Western Political Liberalism* (Oxford, Clarendon Press, 1997) 124, at 148.

Society, which secured concessions ensuring that there were still fees to be made from land transfer.[44]

By 1968, 55.6 per cent of solicitors' income, but only 40.8 per cent of expenses, came from conveyancing. Levels of charges were investigated by the competition authorities in 1966, 1970 and 1974. The abolition of conveyancing scale fees in 1973, combined with a property slump, produced competition between solicitors and lower charges. Consumer pressure for lower conveyancing fees grew with the increase in owner occupation.[45] In the 1980s, the cost of land transfer was seen as an impediment to the Thatcher Government's policy of selling council houses. Owner-occupied dwellings increased from around 7 million in 1961 to over 14 million in 1986.[46]

In 1985, legislation created the Licensed Conveyancer, to conduct 'the disposition or acquisition of estates or interests in land'.[47] A year later, the Lord Chancellor was given statutory power to recognise building societies and other institutions as providers of conveyancing services.[48] The Council for Licensed Conveyancers, created by statute,[49] had power to make training rules,[50] award licences[51] and make codes of conduct and discipline.[52]

The numbers of licensed conveyancers were not great but their anticipated arrival in 1986 stimulated unprecedented competition between solicitors. Between 1983 and 1986 solicitors reduced their conveyancing fees by around 25 to 30 per cent.[53] Conveyancing remained one of the main areas of solicitors' work. Even by 1990, high street firms derived more than half of their income from that source.[54]

The success on conveyancing greatly encouraged the Thatcher Government, but further progress against the legal monopoly was halted in the early years of the Thatcher Governments by Lord Hailsham, the Lord Chancellor between 1979 and 1987. Hailsham had long periods of practice as a barrister and was sympathetic to professions and their 'arcane ethics'. He believed that the independence of the judiciary would be threatened by weakening the legal profession and considered this more important than *laissez faire*.[55] Hailsham's departure began a period in which successive governments, Tory and Labour, began an assault on lawyers' legal jurisdiction. The next target was advocacy.

---

[44]   E Cruikshank, 'Building a Profession' (2003) 100 *Law Society Gazette* 32.
[45]   C Glasser, 'The Legal Profession in the 1990's: Images of Change' (1990) 10(1) *Legal Studies* 1.
[46]   Marre Report (n 35) at paras 3.16–3.17.
[47]   Administration of Justice Act 1985, s 11(3).
[48]   Building Societies Act 1986, s 124 and sch 21.
[49]   Administration of Justice Act 1985, s 12.
[50]   ibid, s 13.
[51]   ibid, s 15.
[52]   ibid, s 20(1).
[53]   S Domberger and A Sherr, 'Competition in Conveyancing: An Analysis of Solicitors' Charges' (1987) 8(3) *Fiscal Studies* 17; A Sherr, 'Coming of Age' (1994) 1(1) *International Journal of the Legal Profession* 3; Abel (n 14) at 292.
[54]   Glasser, 'The Legal Profession in the 1990's: Images of Change' (n 45).
[55]   Abel (n 14) at 14.

b. Advocacy and Litigation

Until 1990 solicitors had automatic rights to appear as advocates in Magistrates' Courts and County Courts on qualification. In 1979 the Benson Report rejected the idea of solicitor advocacy in higher courts. In 1984, the threat to conveyancing caused the Law Society to reopen the debate with a call for solicitors to have the same advocacy rights as barristers. A joint committee with the Bar under Lady Marre failed to agree a resolution that might satisfy government. In 1989 a Green Paper proposed the creation of another occupation, called 'licensed advocates'.[56] The subsequent White Paper diluted the radical agenda of the Green Papers, partly because of unprecedented and concerted pressure by senior judges.

The Courts and Legal Services Act 1990 provided for authorised bodies to accredit their members in the exercise of advocacy rights. This opened the way for solicitors to acquire 'higher rights of audience' and to compete with barristers for advocacy in the High Court and senior appeal courts. It also created opportunities for others to break the settlement between solicitors and barristers and the established status hierarchy. Announcing new rights of audience for legal executives the Lord Chancellor, Lord Irvine, welcomed the Institute of Legal Executives as a 'fully-fledged part of the profession'.[57]

Competition between solicitors and barristers over advocacy spilled over into disputes over cultural symbols. Solicitors feared that barristers' wigs and gowns conferred competitive advantage. This led to these symbols being used less in some courts, and proposals that judges not wear wigs in civil trials.[58] Solicitors argued that they should have the benefit of court attire, 'to command respect and authority and bestow on the wearer gravitas and anonymity'.[59] From 2 January 2008 solicitors have been able to wear wigs in court when barristers are allowed to do so.[60]

The Courts and Legal Services Act 1990 provided for authorised bodies other than the Law Society to accredit their members to conduct litigation. As a result the Bar established 'direct professional access' to barristers for occupational groups, such as patent agents, parliamentary agents, local authority and employed lawyers, in 1990. This was extended incrementally until a public access scheme allowed any person to instruct a barrister direct from 2004.[61]

ii. Funding

The Legal Advice and Assistance Act 1949 led to a universal system of legal aid from 1950.[62] The scheme was administered by the Law Society and provided by private

---

[56] Lord Chancellor's Department, *The Work and Organisation of the Legal Profession* (Cmnd 570, 1989).

[57] AM Francis, 'Legal Executives and the Phantom of Legal Professionalism: the Rise and Rise of the Third Branch of the Profession?' (2002) 9 *International Journal of the Legal Profession* 5.

[58] R Burns, 'When will we be rid of this hairy affectation?' *The Times* 11 May 2004; C Dyer 'Civil court judges prepare to cast aside their wigs after 300 years' *The Guardian* 5 January 2007, at 5.

[59] S Allen, 'Solicitor-advocate begins wig campaign' *Law Society Gazette* 15 February 2001, at 3.

[60] N Goswami, 'Solicitors get permission to wear wigs' *The Lawyer* 21 December 2007.

[61] J Flood and A Whyte, 'Straight There, No Detours: Direct Access to Barristers (2009) 16(2) *International Journal of the Legal Profession* 131, at 133.

[62] See further DCA, *A Fairer Deal for Legal Aid* (Cmnd 6591, 2005) chs 1 and 2.

practitioners. In 1987 administration of the Legal Aid Scheme was transferred from the Law Society to a Legal Aid Board, known as the Legal Services Commission (LSC) since 2000 and Legal Aid Agency from 2013. This was a foretaste of conflict between government and the profession over legal aid. In the 1980s and 1990s a spiralling legal aid bill forced government to cut eligibility rates for civil legal aid. This threatened the post-war promise of access to justice.

In response to government calls for greater efficiency the Marre Report asserted that, when justice is in question, there can be little compromise with cost.[63] Government nevertheless implemented a strategy for reducing legal aid expenditure. Legal aid franchising aimed to ensure that legal aid cases were handled within a tight costs framework. The system was piloted in 1992, rolled out in 1994, then made universal in 1998. Block contracts were issued for delivery of a number of cases for fixed prices. Potential franchisees were assessed for quality standards and office systems, sometimes over-zealously,[64] and delivery was monitored. Alternative sources of funding were introduced to replace legal aid. Conditional fee arrangements, popularly known as 'no win, no fee', initially replaced legal aid for most personal injury claims and subsequently in a wider range of cases.

The escalating cost of criminal legal aid in particular, possibly caused by government changes to the system,[65] led to a review by Lord Carter of Coles. In 2006, Carter recommended a move away from administratively set rates for criminal legal aid work in favour of best value tendering for block contracts. Providers under a range of contracts for civil work were offered a unified contract with the LSC providing fixed and graduated legal aid fees in replacement of hourly rates.[66] The Constitutional Affairs Select Committee expressed reservations about the scope and pace of the reforms and the threat to the quality of complex work and to the supplier base generally.[67] These concerns were dismissed by the government.[68]

The civil contract was to be subject to unilateral change by the LSC. The Court of Appeal subsequently restricted the LSC's power to unilaterally amend the contract,[69] a relatively minor impediment to the reforms. Around 10 per cent of solicitors' firms accepted the unified contract with the LSC. A spokesman for one leading London legal aid firm said 'This is an abusive contract with a future of slavery and gradual strangulation and decline. So far as I am concerned we're out of it'.[70] In the face of

---

[63] Marre Report (n 35) at para 6.9.

[64] P Rohan, 'High Court rules LSC legal aid embargo was unlawful' *Law Society Gazette* 9 August 2001, at 5.

[65] E Cape and R Moorhead, *Demand Induced Supply? Identifying Cost Drivers in Criminal Defence Work* (www.lsrc.org.uk/publications.htm).

[66] Lord Carter of Coles, *Legal Aid: A Market-based Approach to Reform* (London, Lord Chancellor's Department, 2006).

[67] R Miller, 'The Rush to Reform' (2007) 157 *New Law Journal* 645; M Zander, 'Carter's Wake' (2007) 157 *New Law Journal* 872.

[68] Ministry of Justice, *Implementing Legal Aid Reform: Government Response to the Constitutional Affairs Select Committee Report* (Cm 7158, 2007).

[69] *Law Society v Legal Services Commission* [2007] EWCA Civ 1264.

[70] C Dyer, 'Poor likely to suffer in fees dispute as some legal aid firms hold out' *The Guardian* 2 April 2007.

opposition from the legal profession the LSC withdrew proposals for competitive tendering under a standard crime contract in 2009.[71]

Reduction of the legal aid bill continues. In April 2013 further areas were taken outside the scope of civil legal aid.[72] In the same year, the government consulted on proposals to introduce competitive tendering for criminal legal aid, with a price cap set at 17.5 per cent below previous rates.[73] This, it was predicted, would reduce the number of contracts issued from 1600 to 400. As part of the proposals criminal defendants would lose the right to choose their solicitor. This sparked bitter opposition from lawyers complaining about loss of access to justice. The government's response was that 'the legal sector' should not be immune from the government's programme of 'austerity'.[74]

iii. Competitors

In addition to reducing professional monopoly, government reduced its reliance on the private professions and stimulated competition with them in other ways. This is a common way by which states expand access to professional services.[75] A potential competitor was the advice agency network. The first Law Centre was established in the UK in 1970,[76] joining an established network of Citizens' Advice Bureaux (CABs). Although the Law Society was originally suspicious of CABs, by the 1990s they were regarded as a complementary service.[77]

One way for the government to encourage competition was to allow advice agencies to bid for legal aid franchises. They were therefore allowed to compete with solicitors to conduct fixed numbers of civil cases at set prices.[78] Another was to create a more efficient network for providing legal advice, the Community Legal Service.[79] This was an umbrella for existing provision in Citizens' Advice Bureaux and Law Centres coordinated by the internet.

As alternatives to using private practitioners to prosecute crime, government created the Crown Prosecution Service. This employed lawyers on a salary to handle criminal prosecution. An experimental Criminal Defence Service was instigated in several areas of the country, with the express aim of 'benchmarking' costs by comparing public and private provision.[80] This proved to be only a limited success and the service survives at only eight centres.

---

[71] A Mutasa and R Miller, 'Criminal legal aid procurement' *Law Society Gazette* 11 March 2013.

[72] Legal Aid, Sentencing and Punishment of Offenders (LASPO) Act 2012.

[73] Ministry of Justice, *Transforming Legal Aid: Delivering a More Credible and Efficient System* (Consultation paper CP14/2013) (London, Ministry of Justice, 2013).

[74] O Bowcott, 'QCs join protesters against coalition's raid on legal aid' *The Guardian* 5 June 2013.

[75] Johnson (n 14) at 79.

[76] See National Consumer Council, *Ordinary Justice: Legal Services and Courts in England and Wales: A Consumer View* (London, HMSO, 1989); and Galanter, 'Law Abounding' (n 33) at 12.

[77] Marre Report (n 35) at ch 9.

[78] Lord Chancellor's Department, *Legal Aid: Targeting Need* (Cmnd 2854, 1995); and see E Gilvarry, 'Mackay Taken by Fundholding' *Law Society Gazette* 7 September 1994, at 3 and '550 Firms Offered Franchises' *Solicitors Journal* 29 July 1994, at 755.

[79] Access to Justice Act 1999.

[80] Lord Chancellor's Department, *Modernising Justice* (Cm 4155, 1998) at paras 6.18–6.19.

iv. Restrictive Practices and the 'Divided Profession'

In the 1970s a Royal Commission, chaired by Lord Benson, was asked to 'examine the structure, organisation, training and regulation of the legal profession and to recommend those changes that would be desirable to the interests of justice'. The Benson Report concluded that 'a two-branch profession was more likely than a fused one to ensure the high quality of advocacy'. Benson's proposals led to the creation of the Lord Chancellor's Advisory Committee on Legal Education and Conduct (ACLEC). In the 1990s, ACLEC recommended common vocational training for solicitors and barristers, but this came to nothing. While the Bar has always vehemently resisted fusion of solicitors and barristers in a single profession, a report by the Law Society in 1987 actually proposed it.[81]

In 1989 three Green Papers proposed radical changes in in the legal services market. The main Green Paper stated that barriers between solicitors and barristers should be reduced and all other restrictive practices, measures that reduced market competition within the professions, would need to be justified. Other proposals included the introduction of conditional fees and lifting restrictions on lending institutions doing conveyancing work.[82]

The Competition Act 1998 prohibited 'agreements between undertakings, decisions by associations of undertakings or concerted practices which may affect trade within the United Kingdom or have as their object or effect the prevention, restriction or distortion of competition'.[83] The legal profession, having not sought exemption from the Chapter I prohibition in relation to any of their rules, was caught by the Act. The providers of legal services were 'undertakings', their professional associations 'associations of undertakings' and their codes of conduct 'decisions by an association of undertakings'.

In 2000 the Office of Fair Trading (OFT) reviewed professional arrangements in law, accountancy and architecture under the Fair Trading Act 1973, section 2. The report, *Competition in Professions*, identified rules, practices and customs with anticompetitive effects and put the onus of proof on their proponents to 'demonstrate strong justifications for them in terms of consumer benefit'.[84] The professions concerned were asked to make changes in the identified areas within a reasonable time, or within a year, in default of which the OFT threatened to use its own powers to remove the restrictions.[85]

The Law Society was invited to defend restrictions on multi-disciplinary practice,[86] employed solicitors acting for third parties,[87] seeking business by telephone and comparative fee advertising[88] and receiving payment for referrals.[89] It was told to

---

[81] The Law Society, *Lawyers and the Courts: Time for Change* (London, The Law Society, 1987); Cruikshank (n 29).
[82] Lord Chancellor's Department, *The Work and Organisation of the Legal Profession* (n 56).
[83] Competition Act 1998, ch I.
[84] Director General of Fair Trading, *Competition in Professions* (OFT 328) (2001) at paras 3 and 11.
[85] ibid, at para 50.
[86] Solicitors' Practice Rules 1990, rr 4 and 7.
[87] Employed Solicitors' Code 1990 and Solicitors' Practice Rules 1990, r 4.
[88] Solicitors' Publicity Code 1990.
[89] Solicitors' Practice Rules 1990, r 3.

stop issuing fee guidance for conducting probate work. The Law Society successfully argued against the cold-calling of non-business clients[90] but otherwise set about amending or reviewing its rules. The OFT was inclined to allow it to continue its 'programme of reform ... so long as self-deregulation is proceeding effectively, public action is not immediately necessary'.[91]

The General Council of the Bar was told to remove restrictions on barristers forming partnerships, barristers having direct access to clients, advertising, including fees, success rates and comparisons with other barristers, and employed barristers conducting litigation. The report also suggested that the separate roles of solicitors and barristers may add unnecessarily to costs,[92] that the QC system was of dubious value to consumers,[93] and that there should be an extension of professional privilege to accountants providing tax advice.[94]

The Bar's response to the OFT proposals was prepared by a committee led by Sir Sydney Kentridge.[95] The Kentridge Report accepted that barristers should be allowed to accept instructions direct from clients and to advertise fee comparisons. It argued, however, that advertising success would provide a disincentive to accepting difficult cases, that winning cases did not correlate with 'success' and that such rates would be misleading.[96] It also rejected the proposals that barristers should be able enter partnership or conduct litigation. It asserted that the QC system was of value to consumers, and would provide useful information of quality if direct access was permitted. Addressing another OFT suggestion for promoting competition, Kentridge argued that there was no justification for expanding legal professional privilege to non-lawyers.

The OFT was persuaded by some of the professions' arguments. It admitted there was force in the Bar's arguments against advertising success rates and announced that it did not intend to pursue the point.[97] It rejected the Bar's arguments against allowing barristers to conduct litigation and promised further detailed consideration of the arguments against partnership.[98] The OFT did not accept that handling clients' money would impinge on barristers' capacity to specialise in, and maintain excellence at, advocacy,[99] or that partnership would limit choice, increase overheads and undermine the cab rank rule. It did not accept that a split profession was in the public interest.

---

[90] Office of Fair Trading, *Competition in Professions: Progress Statement* (OFT 385) (April 2002) at para 3.15.
[91] ibid, at para 3.18.
[92] OFT 328 (2001) (n 84) at para 49.
[93] ibid, at para 46.
[94] ibid, at para 47.
[95] Sir S Kentridge (chair), *Competition in Professions* (General Council of the Bar, January 2002).
[96] Kentridge Committee Report (n 95) at para 5.3.
[97] OFT 385 (n 90) at para 3.24.
[98] M Gerrard, 'Lifting the bar to progress' *Law Society Gazette* 19 September 2002, at 26.
[99] OFT 385 (n 90) at paras 3.25–3.31.

D. Regulation

A general loss of confidence in the Law Society's complaint handling procedures, and professional self-regulation in general, was encouraged by the 'Glanville Davies affair'. This was characterised as an inept response to a charge of profiteering against a member of the Law Society Council. The client concerned had complained repeatedly to the Law Society between 1976 and 1982 and ultimately took private action. A bill of £197,000 was reduced to £67,000 by the court. The solicitor escaped censure and was allowed to quietly resign from Council.

As a result of the debacle the Law Society narrowly avoided losing its power to investigate complaints against members. The affair helped to create the climate for the 1989 Green Papers[100] and the Courts and Legal Services Act. This proposed that an Advisory Committee on Legal Education would acquire responsibility for professional conduct issues. The new Lord Chancellor's Advisory Committee on Legal Education and Conduct (ACLEC)[101] was dominated by lay persons and its 15 members were appointed by the Lord Chancellor.

The Law Society's response to the Green Papers proposing these changes objected that 'the proposals represent a dangerous accumulation of power in the hands of a government minister … the government should not take control over the very profession that has a duty to act for the citizen against government power and state prosecution'.[102] The response of the judges and House of Lords was equally hostile. The Courts and Legal Services Act 1990 was radical in terms of what had gone before, but not as radical as proposed in the Green Papers.

While the Courts and Legal Services Act undoubtedly intruded on the legal profession's self-regulatory powers, it also preserved areas of independence. For example, the Legal Services Ombudsman established by section 21 did not have powers to investigate matters which were being or had been determined by the Solicitors Disciplinary Tribunal or the Disciplinary Tribunal of the Council of the Inns of Court. Similarly, the role of ACLEC was limited to 'assisting in the maintenance and development of standards in the education, training and conduct of those offering legal services'.[103] The ACLEC was therefore less powerful than envisaged by the Green Paper. Its creation did, however, mean that professional education and conduct would be subjected to more formal and public review processes than before.

Prior to the Act, the procedures, statutory rules and regulations governing solicitors were drafted by Law Society committees and approved by the Council prior to approval by the Master of the Rolls under section 31 of the Solicitors Act 1974. Rules and regulations relating to incorporated practices were approved under procedures set out in the Administration of Justice Act 1985, section 9, prior to their submission to the Master of the Rolls for approval under the 1974 Act. Most of the practice rules were based on common law case outcomes and were amended by the Law Society

---

[100] Burrage, *Revolution and the Making of the Contemporary Legal Profession* (n 39) at 69.
[101] Lord Chancellor's Department, *The Work and Organisation of the Legal Profession* (n 55).
[102] The Law Society, *Striking the Balance: The Final Response of the Council of the Law Society on the Green Papers* (London, The Law Society, 1989) at para 1.4.
[103] Courts and Legal Services Act 1990, s 20(1).

Council to conform to case law.[104] There was no requirement to involve other Senior Judges, the Office of Fair Trading, or the Lord Chancellor in the regulatory process.

After the Act, proposed rule changes were scrutinised by the ACLEC, composed as prescribed by the Act,[105] then approved by the Lord Chancellor. ACLEC issued several reports on aspects of legal education and areas of conduct, but did not have a significant impact. It was soon abandoned in 1999 amid government's apparent disillusionment with the pace of progress. Responsibility for advising on legal education rests with the Legal Services Consultative Panel based at the Ministry of Justice. The Lord Chancellor's powers of approval for regulatory changes remained.

E. Independence

The independence of the legal professions declined markedly in the period 1969–2007. Abel argued that the period marks the beginning of the end of legal professionalism in England and Wales. The professions lost control of the 'production of producers' to the universities and of exclusive statutory monopolies of their key areas of work. Government actively sought to promote market competition by encouraging alternative providers of legal services.

Burrage argues that the 1989 Green Paper was significant because it articulated government's view that there were no boundaries to state power over the professions.[106] The Green Papers were framed in the now familiar language of competition; legal services were a market, legal professions were an industry and clients were consumers or customers. The Courts and Legal Services Act only began to implement a deprofessionalising agenda. This process was continued by the Legal Services Act 2007.

IV. The Legal Services Act 2007

A. Context

Government abandoned some of the proposals of the 1989 Green Papers, for example, that barristers should be able to form partnerships, in enacting the Courts and Legal Services Act.[107] Other issues, like allowing lawyers, accountants and others to practise together in multi-disciplinary partnerships had not been tackled. In 2003 the Department of Constitutional Affairs published a report that concluded that the regulatory framework for legal services was 'outdated, inflexible, over-complex and

---

[104] Response from Law Society to request for information.
[105] Courts and Legal Services Act 1990, ss 19(1), 19(2) and (3).
[106] Burrage (n 39) at 562.
[107] Lord Chancellor's Department, *The Work and Organisation of the Legal Profession* (n 55).

insufficiently accountable or transparent'.[108] Sir David Clementi, who was then asked to undertake a review of the regulatory framework for legal services, added to this list that they were 'inconsistent'.[109]

The Clementi Review encouraged opponents of the legal profession. The National Consumer Council (NCC), for example, which assesses goods and services against criteria such as access, choice, information, quality and value for money, safety and representation,[110] was a consistent critic.[111] The NCC had achieved success with previous suggested regulatory reform. It particularly advocated having a consumer voice in professional regulation[112] and the expansion of the advice sector through legal aid funding.[113] The NCC continued to be an agent for reform of the profession throughout the period leading to the enactment of the Legal Services Act 2007 (LSA 2007). In 2006 it produced a survey showing public confidence in solicitors at 'rock bottom'.[114]

Clementi's consultation paper, issued in March 2004, floated the idea that the regulatory functions of the professional bodies, entry standards, rule-making, monitoring and enforcement, complaints and discipline, should be placed with a single regulator, leaving them with only representative functions on behalf of their members. He favoured, however, a 'half-way house', whereby the professional bodies would separate their representative and regulatory functions and an oversight regulator would monitor and approve regulatory changes made by the professions.

The NCC welcomed the Legal Services Bill, demanding that the proposals for independent complaints handling were not watered down. The government accepted the recommendations of the Clementi Report proposing a compromise regulatory structure. This involved separation of the representative and regulatory functions of the professions and increased lay representation on their regulatory committees. The Law Society broadly welcomed the changes, which were much less stringent than predicted at the start of the process.[115] It warned, however, that the government must not be allowed to make its own appointments to positions of power over the profession or change regulatory objectives through secondary legislation.[116]

---

[108] DCA, *Competition and Regulation in the Legal Services Market* (London, DCA, 2003) at para 70.

[109] D Clementi, 'Review of the Regulatory Framework for Legal Services in England and Wales: A Consultation Paper' (2004); and see R Baldwin, K Malleson, M Cave and S Spicer, *Scoping Study for the Regulatory Review of Legal Services* (London, Lord Chanceloor's Department, 2003) at 16.

[110] See further C Ervine, *Settling Consumer Disputes: A Review of Alternative Dispute Resolution* (London, NCC, 1993).

[111] See eg the following National Consumer Council (NCC) publications: *Making Good Solicitors: The Place of Communication Skills in their Training'* (London, NCC, 1989); *Professional Competence in Legal Services: What is it and how do you Measure it?'* (London, NCC, 1990); *Eligibility for Civil Legal Aid: Response to the Lord Chancellor's Department* (London, NCC, 1991); *Out of Court: A Consumer View of Three Low-Cost Arbitration Schemes* (London, NCC, 1991); *Court Without Advice: Duty Court-Based Advice and Representation Schemes* (London, NCC, 1992); and *Seeking Civil Justice: A Survey of People's Needs and Experiences* (London, NCC, 1995).

[112] NCC, *Ordinary Justice* (London, HMSO, 1989) at 3.

[113] NCC, *Civil Justice and Legal Aid* (London, NCC, 1995).

[114] 'Legal profession set to improve' *Which* July 2006, at 71.

[115] Law Society press release, 'Clementi review let loose' 1 August 2003; Law Society press release, 'Balancing Act' 21 November 2003.

[116] ibid.

The LSA 2007 was an opportunity to finally curtail the power of the legal professions and bring lawyers under state control. This would have been a radical move, sure to excite enormous opposition. It would also have been inconsistent with the philosophy of the small state and the policy of competition. Perhaps for these reasons, the LSA 2007 preserved the professions while considerably constraining their activities. This may have been seen as an interim step towards de-professionalisation.

B. Main Provisions

i. Introduction of Alternative Business Structures

The theme of competition was evident in the consultation leading up to the LSA 2007.[117] The introduction of Alternative Business Structures (ABS) was one of the radical features of the LSA 2007. This was a move that had not been recommended by Clementi, but was intended by government to be the final step in providing competition to lawyer owned and run legal businesses. ABS were conceived as organisations employing lawyers and delivering legal services, yet owned and managed by non-lawyers. Nor were potential regulators of ABS confined to established professions. They could even include the LSB itself if no other regulator came forward.

ii. Regulatory Objectives

The LSA 2007 imposed a statutory duty on approved regulators of lawyers to observe and to comply with eight regulatory objectives. These objectives, together with the 'professional principles', which must be promoted under one of the regulatory objectives, provide a framework for the professional role of lawyers. Support for the rule of law is the second regulatory objective. Otherwise, these duties attempt to place in balance the interests of producers (lawyers) and consumers (clients).

The interests of the profession are protected by subjecting the LSB to duties to support the constitutional principle of the rule of law and encourage a strong legal profession. The interests of consumers are protected by the objectives of improving access to justice, promoting the interests of consumers and encouraging competition in the legal services market. The last of these is assumed to benefit consumers by forcing down the price of legal services. The professional principles identified by the LSA 2007 represent the main principles of lawyers' ethics evolved over the previous centuries.

---

[117] DCA, *The Future of Legal Services—Putting Consumers First* (Cm 6679, 2005).

V. A Future for Professionalism?

In 1986 Abel noted the declining level of control that the legal profession exercised over the market for their services.[118] This has continued, although the profession is still responsible for legal education, regulation, including codes of conduct, and discipline. Regulation is exercised through separate and independent 'regulatory arms' and overseen by a government agency, the Legal Services Board. This change in the basis of professional power may not be permanent. It seems unlikely, however, that barristers and solicitors will ever recover the secure market positions they once enjoyed or that the professional bodies of the legal profession will re-establish their former authority.

A. Predicting Changes in Key Elements of Professionalism

The advantage that professionalism has over other forms of control of expert knowledge lies in the exercise of discretion. Professionalism encourages discrimination in the application of knowledge in different situations. There is potential that reform of the legal services market may yet go further and that professional control of legal knowledge will be further diminished. The limits of change will depend on a number of factors, including the nature of legal knowledge, the maintenance of professional authority and the relationship with the state.

i. Control of Legal Knowledge

a. Demystification of Knowledge and Skill

Control of a distinctive field of knowledge is the rationale of professionalism.[119] Constituted as a university discipline, knowledge acquires status[120] and mystique.[121] Law, while firmly established in the academy, is unusual in the field of professional knowledge in having a social scientific rather than pure science base. Law's lack of a scientific base makes it particularly vulnerable to deconstruction. In the US the legal realists theorised a gap between legal knowledge and law in action which has been supported by socio-legal scholarship. Practical legal analysis inevitably involves extra-legal

---

[118] Abel, 'The Decline of Professionalism?' (n 28).

[119] E Freidson, *Professional Powers: A Study of the Institutionalization of Formal Knowledge* (Chicago, University of Chicago Press, 1986).

[120] RA Barnett, RA Becher and NM Cork, 'Models of Professional Preparation: Pharmacy, Nursing and Teacher Education' (1987) 12(1) *Studies in Higher Education* 51, at 61.

[121] MJ Osiel, 'Lawyers as Monopolists, Aristocrats and Entrepreneurs' (1990) 103 *Harvard Law Review* 2009, at 2023.

factors.[122] Legal monopolies may be vulnerable because technical legal knowledge and skills can be acquired without exceptional intellect or a taxing education.

In the 1990s both barristers and solicitors began to teach legal skills on their professional courses. Even the skill of advocacy, declared by earlier generations of barristers to be achievable only through experience, underwent demystification.[123] Solicitors declared there to be 'no magic to advocacy'[124] and litigants were advised to represent themselves in court.[125] Peer review claimed to be able to accurately assess legal competence.[126] This opened the way for new methods of external control of lawyers, from controlling the flow of work to legal aid providers to assessing the competence of advocates.[127] The argument that legal work was indeterminate, and depended on the exercise of discretion, has been weakened.[128]

b. Technologies

In the future, information systems and technology will perform tasks now performed by lawyers.[129] A commoditised legal product is defined by Susskind as an 'online solution made available for direct use by the end user, often on a DIY basis'.[130] Susskind suggests that the commoditisation of legal services is inevitable, as firms are led, by market forces and technological innovation, through a sequential process of standardisation, systemisation and packaging.

Even if law firms do not commodify legal services, Alternative Business Structures will be more motivated to use technology to cut cost. The role of ABS in bringing commoditised legal products to the market is an aspiration of the LSA 2007 and an outcome predicted by the LSB.[131] The intention is that lawyers will cease to dominate the interface between citizens and the law.[132]

Susskind predicts that there will be a change in lawyers' core business, with a stronger emphasis on dispute resolution and problem solving. Consequently, there will be fewer lawyers. They will be creating or supporting the delivery of commoditised legal packages. He also predicts that legal roles will change. Lawyers will engage in more management, legal risk or general counselling and project management. Even large firms, Susskind suggests, will be forced to reduce the ratio of assistants to partners, as clients will refuse to pay top rates for routine work. In Susskind's analysis, few areas of 'bespoke service', traditional legal practice, will survive.

---

[122] SS Silbey, '"Let Them Eat Cake": Globalization, Postmodern Colonialism, and the Possibilities of Justice' (1997) 31(2) *Law and Society Review* 207, at 231.

[123] HM Kritzer, *Legal Advocacy: Lawyers and Nonlawyers at Work* (Ann Arbor, University of Michigan Press, 1998).

[124] J Edwards, 'Revolution: Solicitors March on Bar's Territory' (1995) *Legal Business* March, at 46.

[125] M Randle, 'The DIY Defence' *The Guardian* 26 September 1995.

[126] A Sherr and S Thomson, 'Professional Competence: Some Work in Progress' (2006) 49 *Socio-Legal Newsletter* 8.

[127] See discussion of the Quality Assurance for Advocacy Scheme in ch 19: 'Advocacy'.

[128] Johnson (n 14) at 47; Abel (n 14) at 10.

[129] R Susskind, *The Future of Law: Facing the Challenges of Information Technology* (Oxford, Clarendon Press, 1998).

[130] R Susskind, *The End of Lawyers?: Rethinking the Nature of Legal Services* (Oxford, New York, Oxford University Press, 2008) at 32.

[131] LSB, *Business Plan 2009/10*, at para 12.

[132] Susskind, *The End of Lawyers?* (n 130).

The Bar, the epitome of bespoke service and custom work, may be best suited to survive the commoditisation of legal services. This depends on the value placed on specialist consultancy and advocacy services in a market where large firms provide these services 'in-house'. It is possible that the highly profitable commercial, chancery, tax and intellectual property sets might survive in the traditional model. Common law sets or those doing publicly funded work will have to adapt to the new market or they will go out of business. In any event, the control that the legal profession exercises over legal expertise will lie in education and training. There will be relatively weak control over practice in many legal workplaces.

c. Re-forming Communities

A technological revolution in the delivery of legal services will lead to changes in traditional units of delivery. It might be anticipated that law firms will withdraw from established areas of practice, like legal aid, and that lawyers working for ABS will fill the gap. The barrier between solicitors and barristers and the relationship between them will change. Solicitors are necessary to barristers as referrers of cases, whereas barristers are less necessary as pleaders or advocates. Barristers are therefore more likely to form barrister organisations or join larger solicitors' firms, or other entities, which are better able to afford in-house advocates.

This re-formulation of work boundaries might have implications for training or for the way professions are organised. It seems likely however that many familiar kinds of legal work will survive. It is very difficult to remove the exercise of discretion from non-routine legal work.[133] There are many human processes that cannot be readily replaced. Wealthier clients will probably be prepared to pay for customised service. Ultimately, it is difficult to predict with precision those areas of legal work where lawyers can be replaced by computers and legal technicians.

ii. Professional Ideology

a. De-professionalisation

De-professionalisation typically refers to loss of control over the knowledge base and decline in the notion of service. These two factors are connected. If the legal profession does not offer an attractive career structure, it may lose its appeal as a destination for top graduates. In order to maintain recruitment to the profession it may be necessary to reduce time spent in education and training. If a long, generalist education is not considered necessary for all legal tasks, workers connected with these roles will lose status and could be excluded from professional membership. In these circumstances it is likely that the idea that the work is conducted in a spirit of service will diminish. This, in turn, is likely to increase the appeal of trade unionism, leading to increases in strike action by groups affected by low rates of legal aid.[134]

---

[133] Law Society press release, 'Legal profession must be truly independent' 23 January 2006.
[134] C Dyer, 'Lawyers threaten strike over low pay' *The Guardian* 6 June 2005.

Criminal barristers at the lower end of the scale had not seen their rates rise since 1997. In 2005, a strike by criminal barristers was averted by the promise of a review of legal aid payments by Lord Carter of Coles.[135] The Carter Report noted that England and Wales had the highest per capita spending on criminal legal aid in the world. Attributing this to payment by the hour, he proposed fixed fees for all cases except the most complex.[136] Carter's proposals also sought to encourage the more efficient solicitors' firms, reducing the numbers doing criminal legal aid work. He concluded that 'good quality, fully employed advocates, regardless of experience, can make a reasonable income from criminal defence work'.[137]

While changes were made to the distribution of legal aid to lawyers, cuts continued to be made in the overall budget. A threatened cut of a further 30 per cent resulted in a half-day strike of criminal defence barristers in January 2014. A war of words between the Criminal Bar Association and the Ministry of Justice ensued, with competing claims about the levels of income available to criminal barristers.[138] The government said that criminal barristers' average annual earnings from legal aid were £86,000 and six barristers had received around £500,000 from legal aid during 2013.[139] Similar data released before the Carter Review had shown that, in 2004–05, one barrister had been paid £1.18 million from legal aid and the next 10 highest made more than £600,000 each.

The action of criminal lawyers in striking is open to interpretation. It can be presented as action in defence of the right to legal representation. The emphasis on salaries, for example, was explained by concern that barristers would desert criminal defence and that talented and able people would not be drawn to the Criminal Bar. The refusal to appear in cases where briefs had been delivered is an apparent breach of the Bar Code. It weakens the case for professionalisation of lawyers based on rule of law arguments.

b. Weakening of Professional Ideology

Perkin suggests that, from the nineteenth century, there has been a wider movement towards professional society, constituting the third great revolution of social relations.[140] A wide range of specialised occupations have selected members by merit and developed trained expertise. They have excluded the unqualified and used human capital, the value of education, training and experience, to command an increased share of resources. As a result, Perkin argues, the professional ideal, trained expertise and selection by merit, as judged by similarly educated experts, now permeates society. It is part of the vision of the ideal citizen.

Kritzer argues that formal professions like law, which combine elements of expert knowledge with self-regulation, are losing their uniqueness and being eclipsed by what

---

[135] C Dyer, 'Shakeup in legal aid will put end to £1m-a-year earnings' *The Guardian* 10 February 2006, at 16.

[136] Lord Carter of Coles *Legal Aid: A Market-based Approach to Reform* (London, Lord Chancellor's Department, 2006).

[137] Ibid, para 159.

[138] O Bowcott, 'Lawyers walk out in protest against legal aid budget cuts' *The Guardian* 6 January 2014.

[139] O Bowcott, P Walker and L O'Carroll, 'Lawyers' walkout empties criminal courts' *The Guardian* 7 January 2014.

[140] H Perkin, *The Rise of Professional Society: England Since 1880* (London, Routledge, 1989).

he calls 'general professions', occupations with expert knowledge but no additional privileges.[141] This transformation is reflected in sociological analysis of professionalism, which focuses on issues of professional identities, competence and responsibility.[142] Because of these transformations, society, it could be argued, has absorbed the benefit of professional values and no longer needs professions.

c. Counter-ideology

Freidson suggests that critical attacks on professions often involve empty rhetoric.[143] Public policy towards professions is driven as much by ideology as by necessity or evidence.[144] The counter-ideology of competition does not answer the question of how expert knowledge should be controlled. Yet, competition has its own logic. As Abel observes 'arguments against it quickly become unconvincing, and producers and consumers who gain from competition strenuously resist the re-imposition of restraints'.[145] Competition tends to concentrate resources. The size of organisations increases, producing an oligopoly, a situation where an industry has a small number of sellers, actually reducing competition.

iii. Relations with the State

a. Competition with the State

A profession's relations with the state reflect the circumstances of its creation. Where the state creates professions, the civil service becomes the cultural and social exemplar of occupational and social success. Where professions emerge independently, 'from below', they become the exemplar of success. Legal professions, independent, corporately and privately organised occupations, emerged from below in Anglo-American society.

The circumstances in which the English professions developed placed them in competition with elements of the state, such as the civil service. Professional power and privilege is ultimately within the power of the state to grant or withhold. Abbot shows that, even in the 1880s the state created government offices and procedures that would deliver legal services without the need for lawyers.[146] Thus, he concludes, while US lawyers competed with major corporations over the legal market, the chief competitor of English lawyers was always the state.

[141] H Kritzer, 'The Professions are Dead, Long Live the Professions: Legal Practice in a Post Professional World' (1999) 33(3) *Law and Society Review* 713.
[142] J Evetts, 'The Sociological Analysis of Professionalism: Occupational Change in the Modern World' (2003) 18(2) *International Sociology* 395.
[143] Freidson, *Professionalism: The Third Logic* (n 23) at 14.
[144] ibid.
[145] Abel, 'Between Market and State' (n 38) at 291.
[146] Abbott (n 19) at 218.

b. The Regulative Bargain

Professional relations with the state can be interpreted as a 'regulative bargain'. Under this bargain, the state devolves power to a profession provided it acts in the public interest.[147] If the power is abused, the state may alter or avoid the contract. Therefore, Paterson construed the removal of the conveyancing monopoly as state retaliation for over-pricing.[148] If this was as re-negotiation of the regulative bargain between the state and solicitors, successive Acts of Parliament suggest that the state continues to seek new solutions to the problem of controlling legal expertise.

The idea that professions are altruistic communities working for the common good and swimming against the tide of materialism, fell out of favour with functionalist sociological theories.[149] Rather, it was assumed that professions operated in their own financial self-interest. Burrage doubts this interpretation. He contends that the historic behaviour of the legal profession is consistent with its own notion of the public good. This is focused on 'honour and status rather than money and markets'.[150] Burrage sees the Bar's efforts to exclude solicitors from high value claims in the County Court as a defence of a principled division of labour.[151] It certainly was not seeking financial advantage when it channelled representation of the capitalist classes to solicitors.

Some more recent evidence of the impact of monopoly is less positive for professions. The decline in conveyancing charges in anticipation of competition does suggest that they were set too high. It was often said, however, that solicitors used conveyancing to subsidise other services, like litigation, which were more difficult to make pay. Leaving aside the example of conveyancing, solicitors seemed little concerned about the market. Evidence that legal charges are evidence of monopoly profits is elusive. A report by economists prepared for the LSB found no evidence of overcharging.[152] One of the factors that restricted development of the public defender service was that it was found to be no cheaper than using private lawyers.[153]

c. Government Agendas

Hanlon suggests that the neoliberal agenda of the Thatcher regime was to break the professions' commitment to social democracy and in the process change work practices, socialisation processes and ideology.[154] The 1989 Green Papers and subsequent

---

[147] D Cooper, T Puxty, K Robson and H Wilmot, *Regulating the UK Accountancy Profession* (ESRC Research Conference, Policy Studies Institute) cited in Department for Education and Skills, *Literature Review in Relation to 'Gateways to the Professions'* (London, DfES, 2005) fn 5.

[148] AA Paterson, 'Professionalism and the Legal Services Market' (1996) 3(1–2) *International Journal of the Legal Profession* 137.

[149] RM Rich, 'Sociological Paradigms and the Sociology of Law: A Historical Analysis' in C Reasons and RM Rich (eds), *The Sociology of Law: A Conflict Perspective* (Toronto, Butterworths, 1978) 147.

[150] Burrage (n 39) at 484.

[151] ibid.

[152] D Decker and G Yarrow, *Understanding the Economic Rationale for Legal Services Regulation* (London, Legal Services Board, 2010) at 44–49.

[153] L Bridges, E Cape, P Fenn, A Mitchell, R Moorhead and A Sherr, *Evaluation of Public Defenders Service* (London, Legal Services Commission, 2007).

[154] G Hanlon, *Lawyers, the State and the Market: Professionalism Revisited* (Basingstoke, Macmillan Business, 1999) at 84.

legislation signals government frustration with the legal professions' resistance of government agendas for legal services. It is possible, however, that there was never a clear agenda in relation to the legal profession. What has transpired is a process of exploration of the possibility of replacing private lawyers in the delivery of legal services for the poor. The latest stage, the LSA 2007, promotes legal corporations, in the form of ABS, over professions. This may be because corporations are a more natural fit with the consumer state.

Under recent governments the public sector has been increasingly dominated by the private sector.[155] In relation to professions this change is reflected in the declining success of welfare professions, like social work, and the increasing power and wealth of corporations. This exposes the schism in the legal profession, between the commercial lawyers, linked to the corporate sector, and the legal aid lawyers linked to the public sector.[156] The implication of this is that the professions could break up, reconfigure along different lines and pursue different survival strategies. An alternative is to seek a new engagement with the state.

d. State Mediation

State mediation can define client needs or determine how they will be provided. Johnson suggests that the state may mediate professionalism with a minimum of encroachment upon an existing system of professionalism and that this may support, for a time at least, existing institutions.[157] This may suggest that current reform is transitional. Government appears increasingly sceptical of the rationale for the established professions, but, contradictorily, often sees professionalism as the solution to abuse of power in relationships with consumers.[158] Freidson considers that the 'worst and not unlikely possibility is that professionals will be slowly transformed into especially privileged technical workers'.[159]

iv. Authority

a. Power to Influence

Authority is subtly different from power. Power is the ability to make something happen. Authority refers to legitimacy, the basis of the right to exercise power. Expert knowledge is the key to professional power. In the context of the present discussion, authority refers to the exercise of power by legal professions through their professional bodies. This culturally legitimised organisation of power[160] enables the profession to

---

[155] Perkin, *The Rise of Professional Society* (n 138).

[156] ibid, at 14.

[157] Johnson (n 14).

[158] M O'Hara, 'Licensing and code of ethics urged to stamp out rogue estate agents' *The Guardian* 29 April 2004, at 7.

[159] EA Freidson, *Profession of Medicine: A Study of the Sociology of Applied Knowledge* (Chicago, University of Chicago Press, 1988) at 209.

[160] RK Merton, *Social Theory and Social Structure* (New York, The Free Press, 1957).

influence policy, for example, in law reform work.[161] The profession claims occasional success in influencing government policy on legal issues, for example, on mental health[162] and fraud trials.[163]

The fact that legal knowledge is primarily normative, unlike the natural and biological sciences,[164] means that legal experts are more easily contested by those of other disciplines, like sociology or economics. Professional authority is also contingent; its legitimacy depends on how it is exercised. Therefore, the campaign waged by dentists for the fluoridisation of water, even though this would decrease their work, increased the dental profession's legitimacy.[165] Conversely, trying to influence public policy to the profession's advantage undermines legitimacy. Lawyers protesting against cuts in legal aid, for example, can be presented as self-interest, even though it is also an issue of access to justice, in which lawyers have a legitimate interest.

There is no doubt that professional authority has been weakened in the neoliberal state. Not only has the traditional establishment been marginalised by the emphasis on competitive markets, corporations have gained greater power and prominence. The separation of regulatory and representative functions may also undermine legitimacy of the representative arms of the professional bodies. As the very term 'representative' suggests, their role is seen as special pleading on behalf of members. The proliferation of ABS in providing legal services will dilute and weaken the authority of professional bodies.

b. Professional Legitimacy

Halliday argues that the degree of legitimacy of the professional view depends on the conjunction of its authority in relation to particular types of issues and the sphere of influence in which it is operating. The legal professions have had considerable legitimacy in their areas of technical expertise, for example, the conduct of litigation, and in their primary institutional sphere, the operation of the legal system. In addition to their areas of expert authority and spheres of primary influence, professions also have spheres of secondary influence.

In secondary areas of authority, the weakness of Law's disciplinary base becomes an advantage. Normative professions, like Law, have 'a broad mandate to range extensively over moral terrain'.[166] Lawyers colonise secondary institutional spheres like politics, where they have always been disproportionately represented, and where the legal point of view is often influential.[167]

---

[161] R Cranston, 'Legal Ethics and Professional Responsibility' in R Cranston (ed), *Legal Ethics and Professional Responsibility* (Oxford, Clarendon Press, 1995) 1.

[162] Law Society press release, 'Huge success in long-running Law Society campaign' 23 March 2006.

[163] Law Society press release, 'Government climb down over abolishing juries in fraud trials' 14 March 2006.

[164] TC Halliday, *Beyond Monopoly: Lawyers, State Crises, and Professional Empowerment* (Chicago and London, University of Chicago Press, 1987) at 32.

[165] D Koehn, *The Ground of Professional Ethics* (London and New York, Routledge, 1994) at 178.

[166] Halliday, *Beyond Monopoly* (n 164) at 36.

[167] ibid, at 41–47.

c. Fora

Promoting a professional agenda may be hampered by a relative absence of platforms for divergent views. According to Perkin, in the successful capitalist countries, France and Germany for example, stakeholding is built into the structure of society. Business stakeholders co-operate and elites balance their own interests with the public good. English society had no entrenched system of stakeholding. When Labour Governments in the late 1990s sought to make the professions stakeholders in its 'third way' between right-wing economic policies and left-wing social reform, its overtures were resisted. It may be that what the state really requires is for the legal professions to engage with the technical and social revolutions of late modernity, essentially to modernise using competitive rather than professional logic.

B. Neo-professionalism?

There are a number of possible responses to the decline of legal professionalism, depending on the nature of surviving professional institutions. Freidson predicts that professional economic and political institutions will survive, but that the independence of professions to choose the direction of development of their knowledge, and the uses to which it is put, will decline.[168] How can the legal profession respond?

i. Protection of the Constitutional Role of Lawyers

The framing of the LSA 2007 makes it clear that the notion that lawyers have a constitutional role in protection of the rule of law and administration of justice still has some traction. If, for example, the state were to go further in making lawyers government employees, there could be a threat to the quality of justice and a threat to civil liberties.

A chair of the American Bar Association has warned that innovations such as block contracting and public defenders will eventually lead to deterioration in the quality of representation to the poor.[169] Lawyers employed directly by the state might be less trusted to take action to limit state power, like control of data from the internet. These considerations provide a position for the maintenance of a core of independent professional control.

ii. Entrepreneurialism

The legal professions have a position of considerable advantage in the market for legal services. They have experience of a wide range of business, exclusive rights to undertake key activities, such as litigation, and the trust of consumers. They will be able to use this expertise as a platform to capture new areas of work. Having done so, they will be able to build a de facto monopoly and, in some areas, build a case for legal

---

[168] Freidson (n 23).
[169] 'Poor may be disadvantaged by legal aid block contracts' *The Lawyer* 10 August 1996.

monopoly. Opportunities to identify new areas of work are likely to arise in a number of areas, including on the international stage.

Ramsay identifies a range of factors which influence demand for legal services.[170] These include the increasing need to regulate the relations of individuals and corporations; the organisation of legal business, for example, by creating or reinforcing monopolies; internationalisation of legal work bringing together geographically remote parties; population diversity requiring normative ordering, changing demographics, wealth levels, levels of complexity in life; increasing bureaucratisation of society and growth in the range and use of administrative remedies; changes in production of goods and services; transactions affecting the allocation of resources; complexity in business transactions and financial innovation and changing technologies.

iii. Internal (Organisational) Closure

Failure to achieve social closure of the market can be overcome in the short term by internal closure within firms themselves.[171] By stratification within the legal services market, organisational closure, professional elites can preserve their position at the expense of junior members and at the expense of collegiality. While such strategies may preserve the power of elites, the legitimacy and influence of professions will suffer.

iv. Professional Bodies

Professional bodies have a vital role in the new occupational order, not least in marshalling the argument for professional jurisdiction over the market for legal services. Professions have to organise the various resources required for such a struggle of ideas, particularly rhetorical resources.[172] In the short term it is not likely that professional bodies will be replaced by other organisations charged with training lawyers. Although education is largely the responsibility of separate educational establishments, professional bodies determine the curriculum, providing a vital link with practitioner knowledge.

Corporations tend to generate knowledge in their own economic interest rather than for the common good. Professions, as collegial organisations, also generate knowledge of general public utility. They 'ceaselessly scan their environments for any changes in their knowledge base or in client needs that bear on the positional interests of anyone in their entrenched position of power'.[173] Sometimes this activity is self-interested, as when the Law Society warns of the risks run by those instructing

---

[170] IM Ramsay, 'What Do Lawyers Do? Reflections on the Market for Lawyers' (1993) 21 *International Journal of the Sociology of Law* 355; and see Abel (n 14) at 20.

[171] D Muzio and S Ackroyd, 'On the Consequences of Defensive Professionalism: Recent Changes in the Legal Labour Process' (2005) 32 *Journal of Law and Society* 615.

[172] R Abel, *English Lawyers Between Market and State: The Politics of Professionalism* (Oxford, New York, Oxford University Press, 2003).

[173] D Sciulli, 'Continental Sociology of Professions Today: Conceptual Contributions' (2005) 53 *Current Sociology* 915, at 936.

unregulated advisors, like will writers and claims farmers.[174] Nevertheless, it is a kind of activity that is generally beneficial to society.

VI. Conclusion

Until recently the legal professions and lawyers in England and Wales enjoyed considerable autonomy. The legal professional bodies were self-regulating and there was little competition in the legal services market. Lawyers largely controlled important areas of work, such as litigation, subject only to the rules of court. This freedom arose partly because independent legal professions were regarded as an important counterweight to state power. Lawyers helped to control the state through the courts. Professionalised occupations encouraged the kind of active citizenship necessary to counterbalance the risk of impersonal state encroachment on the rights of the individual. This dynamic relationship between the state and occupational groups was seen as vital to maintaining individual freedom.[175]

In the 1980s, the re-emergence of market capitalism brought a new focus on competition in monopolistic industries, including the legal services market. Particular targets were routine but important consumer matters, such as the cost of conveyancing. A more significant issue was litigation. To be meaningful, the rule of law demands swift and economic resolution of civil disputes. Historically, the adversarial system was seen as inefficient. During the 1990s, a declining proportion of the population was eligible for legal aid. This forced the issue of access to justice up the political agenda.

Government strategy has been to force down legal costs by reducing the market privileges of the legal professions. From the 1980s more competition was introduced in the legal services market. One strategy was to create new groups, such as licensed conveyancers, and another was to increase competition between the existing legal professions. The LSA 2007 forced professions to separate their representative and regulatory functions. Regulatory activity was placed under an 'oversight regulator', the Legal Services Board. The LSB instigates challenges to professional regulation and approves changes to their rules and regulations. These cumulative restrictions on the legal professions mark a significant diminution of professional power since the 1980s.

Despite the incremental loss of the trappings of professional power, monopoly and self-regulation, workplace jurisdiction, the key to professional power, remains. Aspects of this jurisdiction, the aggressive international performance of English firms for example, is something government does not want to lose. Such considerations may bring the state into a new compromise with the legal profession. Independence is the new warrant of legal professionalism, although continued sponsorship of professional power undoubtedly depends on the profession's guarantee of ethical behaviour. Lawyers will be required to deliver legal services more efficiently, while balancing effectively client demands and the social harm involved in fulfilling them.

---

[174] Law Society press release, 'The risk of unregulated advisors' 19 January 2006.
[175] Durkheim, *Professional Ethics and Civic Morals* (London, Routledge, 1992).

4

Organisation

'Arising from the proposal that lawyers with different professional qualifications should be permitted to work together as equals, the first and most important issue is to ensure that there is a high level of ethical standards within the legal practice'.[1]

I. Introduction

Professionals are identified by belonging to a professional body, which typically has responsibility for regulating the standards of members. For example, in England and Wales barristers are members of the General Council of the Bar, solicitors are members of the Law Society and legal executives are members of the Chartered Institute of Legal Executives. The professional body is not, however, directly concerned with delivering legal services. The way in which this is done usually reflects the available possibilities, for example the forms of organisation that members of the profession can join. The choice of organisational form is affected by tradition and by considerations of efficiency.

It is often assumed that close proximity and close relationships promote adherence to common norms and standards. Organisational diversity is therefore seen as a threat to professional cohesion. Until recently there was great similarity in the way that solicitors and barristers organised their practices. The major difference between the everyday lives of practitioners in each profession was one of scale. Even this had an impact. Writing of the USA in the 1950s, Pound commented on the threats to professionalism posed by the 'increasing bigness of things in which individual responsibility as a member of a profession is diminished or even lost, the exploitation of young lawyers producing pressures to organise in trade unions and the desire of the service state to replace professional services with administrative bureaux'.[2]

---

[1] D Clementi, *Review of the Regulatory Framework for Legal Services in England and Wales—Final Report* (London, DCA, 2004) at paras 25, 111.
[2] R Pound, *The Lawyer from Antiquity to Modern Times: With Particular Reference to The Development of Bar Associations in the United States* (St Paul, MN, West Publishing, 1953) at 354.

One of the many things for which the Legal Services Act 2007 (LSA 2007) was notable was the promotion of new organisational forms, called Alternative Business Structures (ABS). These were promoted as a means of injecting more competition into the legal services market in the interests of consumers. The main feature of ABS is that they allow lawyers to work in organisations that are owned and managed by non-lawyers. This strikes at the professional arrangements most open to question; the monopolies of provision that the state recognises. Lawyers' work has been organised around these monopolies and to a large extent they dictated organisational form. In order to understand the changing organisation of the legal profession it is important to consider the erosion of professional monopolies.

II. The Legal Services Market

At the time the LSA 2007 was enacted the legal services market was worth about £20 billion a year, approximately 2 per cent of Gross Domestic Product. The number of lawyers per head of population had risen from one per 1,000 people to one per 400 over the previous 20 years, partly because the numbers of women practicing as solicitors increased to equal the numbers of men. The number of law firms had, however, declined by one-tenth, to 9000, largely as a result of mergers. This consolidation was driven by declining fee levels and rising costs. Nevertheless, it was arguable that there were too many firms, meaning that high quality, represented by increasing numbers of legal professionals, was spread too thin, and the overhead of collective legal practice was too high.[3]

There were around 145,500 practising lawyers in England and Wales in 2011. They comprised 120,202 solicitors, 15,204 barristers, 7907 members of the Chartered Institute of Legal Executives, 1071 licensed conveyancers, 639 trade mark attorneys, 1687 patent attorneys, 858 notaries and 565 law costs draftsmen.[4] The number of people engaged in providing legal services may be far greater. This is because some areas of work, immigration and asylum for example, are performed by lawyers and non-lawyers and the non-lawyers do not appear in these figures.

A large number of people performing legal tasks under the supervision of qualified lawyers, para-legal workers, for example, do not register in official figures for the numbers of lawyers in the legal services market. The number of 'legal associate professionals' increased from 24,000 to over 50,000 between 2001 and 2009,[5] bringing the total numbers providing what could be legal services to around 200,000. These figures are

---

[3] S Mayson, *Legal Services Reforms: Catalyst, Cataclysm or Catastrophe?* (London, Legal Services Policy Institute, 2007).

[4] www.legalservicesboard.org.uk/can_we_help/faqs/.

[5] UK Commission for Employment, *Skills for Jobs: Today and Tomorrow. The National Strategic Skills Audit for England 2010.*

very uncertain. Some areas of work have an ambiguous status as 'legal work'. Advice giving, for example, may or may not have a legal dimension.

III. Traditional Organisation of Legal Practice

A. The Monopolies of Solicitors and Barristers

The main monopoly of barristers, advocacy in the higher courts, was traditionally regulated by the courts and was not the subject of statutory regulation. Advocacy rights, including those of barristers, are now governed by the Courts and Legal Services Act 1990, as amended by the Access to Justice Act 1999. Practising barristers remain the only group with automatic rights of audience on qualification (including the right to prepare documents in relation to litigation) in all courts. The Solicitors Regulation Authority (SRA) consulted on the proposition that solicitors should automatically have full advocacy rights on qualification, but did not pursue the issue.[6] For the present therefore, all professionals wishing to exercise rights of audience in higher courts, except barristers, must acquire an advocacy qualification in accordance with the Act.[7]

Solicitors have always shared advocacy in lower and other courts with barristers. Members of other approved bodies such as the Institute of Legal Executives (ILEX) and other more specialised groups such as Patent Agents and Costs Draftsmen also have rights.[8] ILEX members, for example, can obtain advocacy rights in the Magistrates' and County Courts. They can do some criminal work such as committal hearings, bail applications, trials in the Magistrates' and Youth Courts. Advocacy and the preparation of documents for litigation can be done for gain only by 'authorised litigators'.[9] This right can be conferred by an authorised body such as the Law Society, Bar Council, ILEX and the Institute of Patent Agents. Whereas authorised litigators owe a duty to the court to act independently and in the interests of justice,[10] this does not apply to other professionals involved in preparation for litigation.

The monopolies exclusive to practising solicitors were formerly laid down in the Solicitors Act 1974, as amended. The Act refers to the 'reserved services' of conveyancing, probate, preparation for litigation, lower court advocacy and various notarial acts.[11] In some of these fields, solicitors gradually shared the work with other authorised

---

[6] SRA, *Higher Rights of Audience* (11 July 2007) (www.sra.org.uk/sra/consultations/higher-rights-of-audience-january-2007.page).

[7] See further ch 19: 'Advocacy'.

[8] 157 *New Law Journal* 25 May 2007, at 718.

[9] Courts and Legal Services Act 1990, s 28.

[10] ibid, s 28(2A).

[11] Solicitors Act 1974, ss 22 and 23, and see LSA 2007, s12 and sch 2.

practitioners. So, while only solicitors could prepare transfers of and documents relating to land for registration with the Land Registry for gain, this work is now also available to licensed conveyancers. Anyone can do their own legal work in these areas, and a third party could help them provided they did not charge a fee.

Under the Solicitors Act, only solicitors could prepare documents relating to grants of probate or letters of administration. This monopoly was first extended to barristers and then, from November 2004, to banks, insurance companies, members of ILEX and licensed conveyancers. Surprisingly, the provision of legal advice was never a monopoly of the legal profession. Anyone can advise members of the public, either free or for a fee, without being registered, or subject to the regulation of a professional body or to any rules about methods of practice.

B. Professional Status

While the areas in which lawyers have statutory monopolies may seem relatively restricted, their professional status is also protected by statute. Therefore, it is an offence for an unqualified person to act as a solicitor, 'wilfully pretend to be' a solicitor or imply that he or she is a solicitor.[12] The Bar and Law Society ensure that the statutory demarcation of roles is legally enforced. In *Agassi v Robinson*,[13] a case relating to costs, both professional bodies intervened, winning a declaration that a client briefing a barrister directly was a litigant in person.

As a consequence of the ruling, the client could not obtain an order for the costs in relation to the services of his accountants who, quite properly under the Bar's direct access rules, briefed the barrister on the client's behalf. This was because the accountants were not authorised litigators. Any other decision, as Lord Justice Dyson said, would 'allow a litigant in person [to] be able to recover the ... fees of any person who provides general assistance in litigation' and this in turn would allow 'ample scope for any unqualified and unregulated person to provide general assistance in litigation secure in the knowledge that the litigant in person, if successful, would recover the cost of that assistance as a disbursement'.[14]

IV. Practitioners

A range of different groups are entitled to practise law. These include those authorised directly by the approved regulators.

---

[12] Solicitors Act 1974, ss 20 and 21, as amended.
[13] *Agassi v Robinson* [2006] 1 All ER 900 (CA).
[14] ibid, at [81].

A. Barristers

i. *Right to Practise*

a. Non-practising Barristers

Barristers can only practise as such if called to the Bar by one of the Inns. They must have satisfied the Bar's educational requirements and joined an Inn. Those who have completed the Bar Vocational Course (BVC) and have been called to the Bar are entitled to use the title barrister even though they have not completed pupillage. In these circumstances they have not completed their training, cannot acquire a practising certificate and therefore cannot practise as barristers.

In 1995, in order to deal with the apparent anomaly that barristers could be 'called' but not entitled to practise, the Bar ratified the policy that call should be deferred until the completion of either the first or second sixth months of pupillage. This was to alert the public to the fact that a non-practising barrister had not completed pupillage, was not subject to Continuing Professional Development requirements and might not be insured against professional negligence.

Implementation of deferral of call was stalled amid fears of a challenge on the ground of discrimination. Subsequently there was further debate on the possible negative impact of deferring call on the flow of students from overseas common law jurisdictions to the BVC. Many jurisdictions recognise call to the English Bar as a part of their own qualification regimes. It was on this ground that a number of specialist Bar associations objected to deferral of call.[15] The loss of overseas students qualified as English barristers would, it was feared, diminish the influence of the English Bar overseas.[16]

A review of the regulation of legal services cited the tortuous deliberations over deferral of call as illustrating the over-complexity of the Bar's regulatory structure.[17] Finally, the Bar Standards Board reversed the decision to defer call, suggesting that it would be an inappropriate and disproportionate response to the risk of consumer confusion.[18] Consequently, non-practising barristers may undertake legal work on the same basis as a layperson, but must make clear that they are non-practising barristers.[19] They must also make clear the implications of their status for their regulation.

b. Employed Bar

Approximately 2500 barristers are employed by organisations, such as solicitors' firms, commercial companies or government agencies. Employed barristers can hold practising certificates but can only provide legal services to members of the public

---

[15] The Commercial Bar Association, London Common Law and Commercial Bar Association and the Chancery Bar Association.

[16] D Matthews, *Deferral of Call: A Review* (London, Bar Council Education and Training Committee, 2005).

[17] Clementi, *Review of the Regulatory Framework for Legal Services in England and Wales: Final Report* (n 1) at para 22.

[18] BSB, *Deferral of Call: Report of Provisional Conclusions* (June 2007) at para 50.

[19] BSB, *Bar Code of Conduct 2014*, rC144.

as permitted by the Code of Conduct. So, for example, barristers employed by specific organisations, such as the Legal Services Commission, can supply services to criminal defendants and those employed in advice centres can supply legal services to the centre's clients.[20] Barristers employed in non-authorised bodies, organisations like companies, can only supply legal services to specified others, including fellow employees or other organisations.[21] Barristers employed by authorised (non-BSB) bodies, such as solicitors' firms, can provide legal services to the clients of the firm.[22]

c. Private Practice

Business Units
The majority of barristers occupy chambers in one of the four Inns of Court (Gray's Inn, Lincoln's Inn, Inner Temple or Middle Temple) within a mile of the High Court on Strand in Central London. Many metropolitan centres outside London support small local bars. Before 1987, chambers in London had to be situated in an Inn. Pressure on space led to the abandonment of this rule and many chambers are now based outside the Inns. Further, barristers of over three years' call can practise from their home and about 250 do this. Since 2005 barristers must hold a current practising certificate. They must also be insured for professional negligence through the Bar Mutual Indemnity Fund (BMIF) in accordance with terms approved by the Bar Council from time to time. Finally, since 1997 they must comply with requirements for post-qualification continuing education.

The traditional mode of practice for barristers was designed to protect independence. According to the old Bar Code of Conduct, barristers in private practice must be, 'completely independent in conduct and professional standing as sole practitioners … to act as consultants instructed by solicitors and other approved persons'.[23] They could not offer their services to the public through partnerships or limited companies. Groups of barristers do, however, combine in chambers. Members of chambers share the cost of rent, of employing staff, such as clerks, secretaries and book-keepers, and of other services such as marketing and staff training. For the present this is the dominant form of practice.

The day to day running of chambers is typically organised by a chief clerk. These share a percentage of each barrister's brief fees and can command large incomes.[24] They can be powerful figures because they allocate work between members. Nowadays, in addition to a senior barrister, or head of chambers, with general management responsibilities, many chambers also employ a chambers manager, possibly instead of a clerk. Barristers, whether in London or the provinces, must be a member of an Inn. These connections provide access to library and other facilities and encourage a collegial ethos. Provincial barristers are also encouraged to join one of the six circuits in England and Wales, but this is not compulsory.

---

[20] ibid, B7. Scope of practice as an employed barrister (non authorised body) rS39.7 and 8.
[21] ibid, rS39.3.
[22] ibid, B6. Scope of practice as a manager of an authorised (non-BSB) body or as an employed barrister (authorised non-BSB body) rS36.
[23] Bar Council, *Bar Code of Conduct 1981*, at paras 104(a)(i) and (ii).
[24] J Flood, *Barristers' Clerks: The Law's Middlemen* (Manchester, Manchester University Press, 1983).

A set may contain several Queen's Counsel (QCs) but the majority of its members will be junior counsel, that is, career barristers who have not yet been appointed QC. Each set of chambers is normally headed by a QC but this is not compulsory. In addition there will be some pupil barristers in training and maybe some 'squatters' and door tenants who have the right to practise but who are not formally members of the chambers and do not contribute to the running costs. There are about 300 sets of chambers with an average membership of t30, although some chambers have over 100.

Hierarchy
The Bar has a clearly defined professional hierarchy. Barristers are identified by their year of call. After a decade or more of practice barristers can apply for 'silk', that is to become Queen's Counsel (QC). Many, but not all senior practitioners, apply for silk and most senior judges were, and still are, recruited from the ranks of QCs, as are government counsel. Judges often maintain membership of chambers and remain active in both their chambers and Inns of Court.

QCs are instructed in more difficult or serious cases and receive higher fees. They can insist on the appointment of a junior, a non-QC barrister, who drafts the papers for the case. The process for appointing QCs used to be obscure, depending in part on 'secret soundings' amongst the judiciary. It offended all the normal recruitment or promotion policies common in industry or the public service. The Law Society was vociferously against the system which discriminated against solicitor advocates. The Lord Chancellor set up a committee to look into the issue, chaired by Sir Leonard Peach, which reported in 2001.[25] In 2003 the Lord Chancellor announced that the system would cease and the appointment of QCs was suspended. It was then decided to allow the QC title to continue but that appointment to it would be subject to a merit-based system of open competition.

From July 2005 the system for appointing QCs changed. Applicants must now apply anonymously and include references from judges and clients. Applications are made to the Ministry of Justice and are considered by an interview panel consisting of a lay chair, three other laypersons, two solicitors and barristers and one retired judge. They work to an agreed set of competences and have the advice of an HR professional. The cost of the new system is to be met by the fees paid by the applicants. The first appointments under this system were made in July 2006. The numbers of female applicants (68) almost doubled over those applying in 2003 (39). The success rate of female applicants also doubled, from under a quarter in 2003 to nearly half.[26] Ten applicants from ethnic minorities and four solicitors were also appointed.

Receiving Work
A major restriction on the way that barristers could offer their services to the public was the rule that they could be briefed only by solicitors, not instructed by clients directly. The rule was introduced in 1888 in contentious matters apparently as part

[25] See for an account of the controversy up to 2002, R Abel, *English Lawyers Between Market and State* (Oxford, Oxford University Press, 2003) at 190.
[26] See (2006) 156 *New Law Journal* 1186.

of a settlement accepting barristers' advocacy monopoly in the higher courts. It was extended to most other matters in 1955. The restriction had an ethical justification. It sought to ensure that clients received advice from a lawyer whose view was not clouded by a continuing personal or business relationship.

As the respective monopolies of barristers and solicitors were eroded throughout the 1980s and 1990s, so was the barristers' role as consultants. Direct professional access to barristers was first permitted by the Bar Council in 1989 when members of certain professions, such as accountants and surveyors, were permitted to brief barristers without using solicitors as intermediaries. This mechanism, which was known as Bar Direct, was gradually extended to other professions or employees of public bodies throughout the 1990s.

In 2004 a more general direct access to barristers by members of the public was introduced. The move was a response to a report from the OFT in which the old rule was criticised as an unjustifiable restrictive practice.[27] It was accepted by the Bar Council as a response to its own Kentridge Report.[28] Access was restricted to barristers of over three years' call who had completed a one-day training course covering record keeping and money laundering rules. The Public Access Rules provide that members of the public can instruct barristers directly. This means that clients need not instruct a solicitor in order to have access barristers' services. Clients carry out the routine work of the case themselves rather than paying a solicitor to do it.

Direct access barristers must be registered as such with the Bar Council. Certain cases, involving immigration, asylum, family proceedings and crime, are excluded from the scheme. Barristers are not bound by the cab rank rule when approached under the schemes. This means that they can refuse clients provided they do not discriminate unlawfully. Barristers must refuse a case if it is in the interests of the client or of justice that a solicitor should be instructed.

There are in fact many obstacles in the way of direct access. For example, barristers cannot hold client monies, cannot conduct the preliminaries of litigation such as writing letters to the other side and cannot issue proceedings or serve documents. Barristers are therefore not on the court record as being the client's representative. If the client is unable to do these tasks as a litigant in person, or get them done by someone else, barristers cannot take the case on.

Where the client is capable of taking simple steps or is only interested in getting a legal opinion, direct access could prove to be the speediest and most economical route. The barrister can draft documents, such as letters before action or offers to settle, for the client to send. Direct access represents a major departure from the Bar's traditional method of working. It may even prove to be a decisive step towards fusion of the professions. There will undoubtedly be further pressure to reduce the restrictions.

---

[27] Licensed Access Recognition Regulations and Licensed Access Rules 2004.
[28] Sir S Kentridge (chair), *Competition in Professions* (General Council of the Bar, January 2002).

B. Solicitors

i. Right to Practise

It is an offence for a person to practise or hold out that they are a solicitor without a practising certificate under the Solicitors Act 1974, sections 20 and 21. In order to obtain a practising certificate, solicitors must provide details of insurance. Such insurance used to be arranged by the Law Society itself but since 2001 has been provided under approved commercial schemes.[29] Under the old rules solicitors also had to prove compliance with continuing education requirements.[30] This is no longer required by the new rules,[31] although specified Continuing Professional Development is still required under the relevant regulations.[32]

The practising certificate fee must be set in order to cover only those costs approved by the Lord Chancellor, such as regulation, training and developing and disseminating professional guidance. Some law reform work related to the profession and human rights work can also be included in fixing the cost of the practising certificate.[33] The cost of practising certificates has risen sharply in recent years to cover the increasing cost of regulation.

Solicitors who have qualified, but do not have a practising certificate, may call themselves solicitors but not act as such for reward. There is not the same degree of concern over the non-practising profession as at the bar, since solicitors are not admitted to the roll of solicitors until they have complied with the training regulations,[34] including completing the prescribed two year training period.

a. Private Practice

The majority of solicitors are in private practice. Of the 128,778 solicitors with practising certificates on 31 July 2013 nearly 88,000 were private practitioners.[35] This is a continuation of a trend of an increase in total numbers at a rate of about 4 per cent per annum. In 2007 there were 104,543 solicitors with practising certificates and over 77 per cent worked in private practice. In 2009, it was 115,475 with 73.7 per cent in private practice.

b. Employed Solicitors

Solicitors may practise as an employee of an organisation provided they work only for that employer.[36] They can be held out as a solicitor or provide reserved legal services

---

[29] Solicitors' Indemnity Insurance Rules 2001.

[30] SRA, *Solicitors' Code of Conduct 2007*, rr 20.01 and 20.03.

[31] SRA Practising Regulations 2011 (www.sra.org.uk/solicitors/handbook/practisingregulations/content. page).

[32] SRA Training Regulations 2011, pt 3: CPD Regulations (www.sra.org.uk/solicitors/handbook/cpd/ content.page). (to be replaced in July 2014)

[33] Access to Justice Act 1999, s 46(2)(b).

[34] SRA Admission Regulations 2011, reg 4(1).

[35] The Law Society, *Trends in the Solicitors' Profession Annual Statistics Report 2012: Summary Figures* (London, The Law Society, 2013).

[36] SRA Practice Framework Rules 2011, r 1.1(e) and see r 4.

for which they are authorised if they hold a practising certificate.[37] In 2012, 23,577 solicitors holding practising certificates were in the employed sector. An increasing proportion of all solicitors holding practising certificates were employed solicitors. Between 1999 and 2009 the proportion grew from 19.5 per cent to 26.3 per cent.[38] Over half were employed in commerce and industry and just under a third in government service.[39]

There are a large number of exceptions to the rule that they can only work for their employer. These cover, for example, acting for work colleagues, or bodies related to the employer, like subsidiaries.[40] In general, the conduct rules that apply to private practice solicitors apply to in-house solicitors. Different rules may apply when an in-house solicitor is acting for his employer or for a client other than his employer.

ii. Size and Spread of Organisations

The vast majority of law firms are relatively small. In 2009, 85.3 per cent of firms had four or fewer partners.[41] In 2009 2 per cent of firms had 26 or more partners. They employed 31.3 per cent of all principals and 41.8 per cent of all solicitors in private practice. Sole practices accounted for 40.7 per cent of firms, yet employed only 7.9 per cent of all private practitioners.

The largest firms, those with 81 or more partners, had on average, 2.19 assistant/ associate solicitors per partner. This compared with between 0.7 and 1.62 in the smaller and medium-sized firms. The trend is towards solicitors' firms growing larger. Between 2011 and 2012, the number of small firms, those with between one and four partners, decreased by 2 per cent. Over a similar period, the numbers of both medium and large firms increased by around 5 per cent each.[42]

iii. Traditional Business Model of Private Practice

The traditional business unit of solicitors was a partnership, or firm, in which equity partners shared profits as laid out in the partnership deed. Partnership was the preferred form of organisation for two reasons. First, equity partners were jointly and severally liable for the firm's debts to the extent of their private resources. Unlimited liability was a position that was thought to encourage responsibility. Secondly, solicitors could not share professional fees with anyone other than another solicitor. Therefore, all partners must be solicitors. This was thought to guarantee the independence of the solicitor from external influence.

---

[37] ibid, r 9.
[38] B Cole, N Fletcher, T Chittenden and J Cox, *Trends in the Solicitors' Profession Annual Statistical Report 2009* (London, The Law Society, 2009).
[39] The Law Society, *Trends in the Solicitors' Profession Annual Statistics Report 2012: Summary Figures* (n 35).
[40] SRA Practice Framework Rules 2011, r 4.
[41] Cole et al, *Trends in the Solicitors' Profession* (n 38).
[42] The Law Society, *Trends in the Solicitors Profession 2012* (London, The Law Society, 2013) at 20.

The partnership arrangement supported diverse forms of organisation, from sole practitioners to extremely large international firms. Any categorisation of this wide diversity involves a degree of generalisation, but there are some recognisable ways in which firms organise and engage with a client base. Some basic types were identified in the 1990s among firms typically engaged in criminal defence work.[43] The descriptions used there, classical, managerial, political and routine, are a useful starting point for describing firms operating in other fields. There are other terms commonly used to describe types of law firm, for example, large firms, often operating in the corporate/commercial field, high street firms and boutique firms. All of these terms are very broad descriptions. They sometimes confuse organisational form and market orientation. For example, a high street firm could be either a classical or political firm. Therefore, the features of these different firm types may overlap.

a. Classical

The classical firm model describes a traditional partnership. The firm is often organised in departments each headed by a partner. The firm tends to represent local businesses and so has repeat clients. Solicitors often handle a relatively low volume of high value cases. The solicitors are therefore able to be centrally engaged in all the legal tasks, research, interviewing clients and advocacy. In addition, the solicitor inducts trainees and non-qualified staff and allocates and supervises their work. Solicitors expect to graduate to partnership and stay with the firm throughout their careers. A senior partner usually holds the title managing partner and spends some time dealing with partnership matters. The role is often rotating. There is a low turnover of staff and the atmosphere of the firm is collegial. Such firms are often cohesive and stable. They are found in large numbers, particularly in provincial centres.

b. Managerial/Routine

Firms with a strong managerial ethos are likely to specialise in particular areas of work, like crime, family law or immigration. They may handle a lot of relatively small value matters. They have responded to the need for efficiency by introducing strong managerial structures, introducing systems and procedures aimed at reducing administration and delay. This has the effect of introducing routines for time recording and billing, training and the delegation of work. Work in such firms can be physically demanding, repetitive and unending. There may be high staff turnover leading to instability and variable service to clients. Staff may be initially attracted to these firms by the public service dimension of the work, but have relatively poor working conditions and relatively low pay.

c. Political

The political firm is organised around personal commitment to kinds of work, like criminal defence, civil liberties or human rights, and particular types of clients, like

---

[43] M McConville, J Hodgson, L Bridges and A Pavlovic, *Standing Accused: The Organisation and Practices of Criminal Defence Lawyers in Britain* (Oxford, Clarendon Press, 1994) ch 2.

terrorists, whose cases test the law in these areas. Firm members may empathise with poor and disadvantaged clients in their disputes with the state, corporations or employers.[44] This kind of work has recently been called 'cause lawyering', because the law is used politically to highlight injustice and bring about political change. These firms attract highly motivated staff committed to providing quality services. They are keen to test and change the law by pursuing test cases. Some such firms specialise in disaster litigation, such as that arising from road or rail accidents, class actions concerning drugs or tobacco or political cases involving clients alleged to be involved in terrorism.

d. Large Firms

In the United States large firms serving business clients were a feature of the legal landscape since the before the turn of the century. They became a form of business in their own right stressing high quality service and demanding large staff, a high degree of organisation, a high overhead and more intense specialisation. The 'law factory' emerged with the mass of work performed by the ablest products of the best law schools. From these, the most dedicated and entrepreneurial were selected for partnership.[45] The partners lent their name to the work but were principally business getters and the repository of the goodwill of the corporate clientele.[46]

In the UK, partnerships of solicitors were not permitted to exceed 20 until the passing of the Companies Act 1967.[47] Since then, the increasing numbers of large firms, and the concentration of legal resources within them, has been one of the most significant developments in the legal professions of the United States, Canada and Britain. They have grown faster than the profession as a whole and receive a larger proportion of the money spent on legal services, mainly from business clients.[48] Between 1984 and 1986, the number of firms with more than 11 partners increased by 8 per cent and the number of principals in those firms by 12 per cent.[49] In the UK, the 100 largest firms represent nearly 1 per cent of all solicitors' firms but account for half the turnover of all private practitioner solicitors.

The opportunity for expansion of firms was fuelled by the 'Thatcher revolution' of financial services in the 1980s. This led to the 'big bang' in the City of London which created substantial work for solicitors' firms,[50] which coincided with the abandonment of fee regulation in England and Wales.[51] The expertise in large-scale financial work paved

---

[44] S Sheingold and A Sarat (eds), *Cause Lawyering: Political Commitments and Professional Responsibilities* (New York, Oxford University Press, 1998).

[45] M Galanter and T Palay, *Tournament of Lawyers: Transformation of the Big Law Firm* (Chicago, University of Chicago Press, 1991).

[46] K Llewelyn, 'The Bar Specialises: With What Results?' (1933) *The Annals of the American Academy* 176.

[47] Companies Act 1967, s 120(1)(a).

[48] M Galanter, 'Law Abounding: Legalisation Around the North Atlantic' (1992) 55 *Modern Law Review* 1.

[49] Lady Marre CBE, *A Time for Change: Report of the Committee on the Future of the Legal Profession* (London, General Council of the Bar and Council of the Law Society, 1988) at para 5.22.

[50] J Flood, 'Megalaw in the UK: Professionalism or Corporatism?: A Preliminary Report' (1989) 64 *Indiana Law Journal* 569.

[51] See E Skordaki and D Walker, *Regulating and Charging for Legal Services: An International Comparison* Research Study No 12 (London, Research and Policy Planning Unit, The Law Society, 1994) at para 3.6.

the way for City of London firms to grow, by merger and otherwise. The largest firms rapidly grew to comprise hundreds of partners and thousands of lawyers. They generate sufficient profit to pay some partners in excess of £1million per annum.[52] Massive scale allowed English solicitors' firms to dominate a growing international market for corporate and commercial legal services. This prospect led to the merger of Coward Chance and Clifford Turner, creating Clifford Chance. At the time, in 1988, the firm had 168 partners, 386 assistants and 123 articled clerks. It now has 589 partners[53] and is one of the largest law firms in the world. The resources of large firms stood in stark contrast to those of most other solicitors. A dichotomy, already established in the USA, emerged between wealthy firms serving corporate/commercial clients and smaller 'general practice' firms handling lower value work on behalf of individual clients.[54] Within a short time, large firms transformed views of the possibilities for handling legal work and perceptions of the legal profession.

The City firms are organised around four broad categories of work: corporate and commercial, property, litigation and tax, but their principal focus is corporate and commercial work.[55] The de-nationalisation of publicly owned companies created new areas of work and built expertise. Ambiguous drafting and the discretionary decisions of new regulators for these industries created fresh legal problems to solve.[56] City firms provided expertise in solving complex problems on a massive scale, being adept at 'custom work', solving the multitude of problems raised by complex commercial transactions.[57] Their approach is often multi-disciplinary, involving large teams of lawyers, accountants, economists and architects. The firms, and the individuals working within them, were 'becoming more corporate, more specialist, more competitively aware, and more orientated to economic productivity'.[58]

The dominance of large firms had a range of impacts on the legal services market. Among the positive influences, large firms offer a democratic and meritocratic environment for employees, reflecting prevailing standards in the public sector.[59] They therefore provide better opportunities for the advancement of women and ethnic minorities. They boost national productivity with their work for international clients and can also afford to take a lead in activity in providing free legal services to meet the legal need among disadvantaged sections of the population. Less positively, large firm

---

[52] www.thelawyer.com/pictures/web/s/p/x/uk200_1_p114.jpg.

[53] 'Clifford Chance appoints 20 new partners' 29 April 2013 (www.cliffordchance.com/news/news/2013/04/clifford_chance_appoints20newpartners.html).

[54] J Heinz and E Laumann, *Chicago Lawyers: The Social Structure of the Bar* (New York, Russell Sage Foundation, 1982).

[55] Flood, 'Megalaw in the UK' (n 50).

[56] C Stanley, 'Enterprising Lawyers: Changes in the Market for Legal Services' (1991) 25(1) *Law Teacher* 44.

[57] Skordaki and Walker, *Regulating and Charging for Legal Services* (n 51) at paras 2.5.4, 2.9.1 and 2.10.1; M Galanter 'Mega-Law and Mega-Lawyering in the Contemporary United States' in R Dingwall and P Lewis (eds), *The Sociology of the Professions: Doctors, Lawyers and Others* (New York, The Macmillan Press, 1983) at 166.

[58] EH Greenebaum, 'Development of Law Firm Training Programs: Coping with a Turbulent Environment' (1996) 3(3) *International Journal of the Legal Profession* 315, at 322.

[59] WW Powell, 'Fields of Practice' (1996) 21 *Law and Social Inquiry* 956.

trainee salaries and benefits cannot be matched by High Street practices, so that large numbers of the most able applicants are recruited to the service of corporate clients.[60]

e. High Street Firms

High street firms are those found on most main roads in metropolitan suburbs, towns and villages. They may comprise a sole practitioner with supporting staff or a firm organised on the classical model with a large number of lawyers. They specialise in services responding to local markets, but are also diverse and versatile. They are the most numerous kinds of firm.

f. Boutique Firms

Boutique firms represent a high degree of specialisation, often in areas considered niche markets. As originally conceived they conducted high value work, intellectual property or medical law, for example. These firms tend to be smaller than typical large and medium firms and less likely to draw their clientele from a local area. The development of technology assists these firms as they are not now dependent on any particular locality for their business. There is, for example a firm that specialises in dental law whose clients come from all over the country although their office is in Nantwich.[61]

Specialist firms were encouraged to bid for publicly funded work by the introduction of contracting for legally aided work in 2000. They needed to demonstrate to the Legal Services Commission, which awarded block contracts, that they were specialised and organised to cope with work at reasonable volume. Therefore, 'boutique firms' might also describe firms doing lower value work, child care, immigration, crime or family. Such firms can be organised on the lines of the classical, managerial or political models.

iv. Distribution

It is difficult to be categorical about the spread of types of firm, but size of firm gives a rough indication of probable type of firm. In 2007 there were 8,926 solicitors' firms. Although 46.3 per cent of these firms were sole practitioners, such firms employed only 8.2 per cent of solicitors. Only 1.3 per cent of firms had over 26 partners, but they employed 39 per cent of solicitors. Around 25 firms, mostly in London, had more than 81 partners.[62]

---

[60] *The Guardian* 23 August 2007, at 28. See also MJ Powell, *From Patrician to Professional Elite: The Transformation of the New York City Bar Association* (New York, Russell Sage, 1989)

[61] The Dental Law Partnership (www.dentallaw.co.uk).

[62] B Cole, *Trends in the Solicitors Profession: Annual Statistical Report 2006* (London, The Law Society, 2006) (http://www.lawsociety.org.uk/representation/research-trends/annual-statistical-report/documents/annual-statistical-report-2006-(pdf-333kb)/).

v. Challenges to the Partnership Model

Before the advent of large firms, solicitors' firms were subject to considerable restraints in developing their practices and competing with other businesses offering similar services. The principle that solicitor partners must accept personal responsibility for his or her work also meant that no corporate business structure or limited liability could be used. This made considerably less sense when the restriction on size of partnership was lifted. Firms with hundreds of partners rendered the idea that they could personally control every aspect of their business implausible. Requiring consensus between partners would mean that effective decision-making was impeded. Further inroads into the idea that partnership was a necessary mode of business organisation for solicitors were made by the introduction of rules permitting limited liability and by rules permitting fee sharing with non-lawyers.

a. New Business Forms for Solicitors

The Limited Liability Partnership Act 2000 resulted from pressure by large accounting firms seeking the flexibility of partnership and benefits of limited liability. Solicitors were allowed to incorporate in 2001, allowing them limited liability, like other business persons, but subject to various safeguards in relation to client liability insurance to compensate for the loss of personal liability.[63] This protected their personal property from being used to pay business debts. Complex rules provided that only practising solicitors could be a partner, shareholder or director of solicitors' limited companies.[64] All solicitors' firms needed at least one principal or director of at least three years' standing. This person was responsible for the work of the practice and compliance with the regulations.[65]

When they were introduced, it was anticipated that about one-third of the top 100 firms would convert to limited liability partnerships by 2005,[66] but LLPs were less popular than predicted. In 2007, of the 8926 solicitors firm in England and Wales, 941 were incorporated and 1288 had formed limited liability partnerships.[67]

b. Exception to the Ban on Fee Sharing

An exception to the ban on fee sharing was introduced in the Solicitors' Code of Conduct 2007.[68] This made it easier for firms to raise working capital or acquire services such as computing packages. The rule permitted solicitors to make fee sharing arrangements with non-solicitors provided the arrangement was solely to facilitate the introduction of capital or the provision of services. It did not allow the fee sharer to constrain the solicitor's professional judgement in dealing with clients. Solicitors had

---

[63] Limited Liability Partnership Act 2000, ss 1(4) and (5).
[64] *Solicitors' Code of Conduct 2007*, rr 14.03 and 14. 04.
[65] ibid, rr 5.01 and 5.02. All the principals or directors of the firm are so responsible.
[66] *Law Society Gazette* 29 April 2004.
[67] See *Law Society Gazette* 5 April, at 1 and 17 May 2007, at 16.
[68] Although originally introduced in February 2004.

to ensure that the arrangement did not in fact create a partnership and that there was no breach of the rules against payment for the referral of business.[69]

The SRA is likely to be concerned if fee sharing agreements provide more than 15 per cent of a firm's gross fees. Contributions above that level might be seen to compromise the firm's independence. The fear is that a firm might change the way it deals with clients in order to suit the fee-sharers' interest in maximising profits. The Law Society may also be concerned to constrain profit sharing of this kind because, without these rules, it would be possible for *any* business to offer the full range of legal services to the public to the detriment of traditional solicitors' practice.

c. Restrictions on Linked Businesses

A solicitor's firm, whether a partnership or incorporated, could only carry on the business of providing 'professional services such as were provided by individuals practising as solicitors'[70] and could only provide legal services to the public through a regulated solicitors' practice. They could not, therefore, offer legal services and estate agency or accountancy services unless they did it through a separate business.[71] The aim of this rule was to ensure that the two businesses were kept separate and that the public were not misled into thinking that the regulator was responsible for the non-solicitor business simply because it is owned or managed by a qualified solicitor.

Where a solicitor owned an estate agency, clients referred to the solicitor's practice from that agency had to be informed personally and in writing of the interest of the solicitor in the two businesses and consent to the firm acting. These rules were designed to avoid restricting a client's choice of solicitor. It might also avoid a potential conflict of interest between the client and the solicitor, for example, where the convey-ancing solicitor is tempted to conceal from the client adverse results from searches or defects in title in order not to prejudice claiming an estate agent's commission.

There was some concern as to the adequacy of the rules on separate businesses to protect clients from conflicts of interest. This concern was fuelled by the growth of solicitor-owned claims companies following relaxation of the rules on claiming conditional fees in personal injury actions in 2001. Claims companies needed a tie-in with solicitors because they could advise and prepare cases but not conduct litigation. The Law Society found some difficulty monitoring these sometimes complex relation-ships. Claims companies must now be registered under the Compensation Act 2006, which makes it an offence for a solicitor to have dealings with an unregistered claims company. Solicitors have been warned by the SRA that dealing with an unregulated claims company is a disciplinary offence as well as carrying the risk of criminal pros-ecution.[72] Paying claims companies for personal injury and fatal injury claims is now banned.[73]

---

[69] SRA, *Solicitors' Code of Conduct 2007*, r 8.02.
[70] ibid, r 14.02.
[71] ibid, r 21.01.
[72] (2007) 157 *New Law Journal* 567.
[73] See ch 12: 'Fees'.

C. Legal Executives

There are around 22,000 Legal Executives in England and Wales. They originated in the nineteenth century as experienced, non-qualified lawyers who supervised junior clerks in solicitors' firms. Known originally as managing clerks, they evolved into lawyers sitting examinations set by their own professional body. Members qualified by a combination of evening classes and practical experience in solicitors' firms. Although they were restricted to working for solicitors, and could not practise in their own right, many legal executives developed high levels of expertise in specific areas, becoming recognised as leading practitioners in their area.

D. Licensed Conveyancers

Licensed conveyancers were established by statute, with an independent professional body, the Council for Licensed Conveyancers (CLC).[74] Their main role is to prepare documents for property transfer, in the same way as solicitors. They tend to work for solicitors' firms, banks or property developers, but can form their own partnerships after three years' employment. There are about 200 independent licensed conveyance firms. Unlike solicitors, licensed conveyancers can act on both sides of a transaction, despite the risk of conflict of interest, and need not disclose to clients that they have paid referral fees for work. Following calls from the Law Society for the banning of referral fees in 2009, the Legal Services Board commissioned analyses of the impact of referral fees. It concluded a ban was not justified provided there were requirements for disclosure. This was the position taken by the CLC in a consultation closing in March 2013.[75]

E. Patent Attorneys

The relatively small number of specialist patent attorneys work on protecting and enforcing intellectual property rights in, for example, industrial designs and copyright. The work includes registering patents and trade marks. They tend to work either in-house for corporations or government departments or in firms of patent attorneys. Law qualifications are not required to begin practising. The main requirement is a science or engineering degree. Legal skills of drafting, analysis and logical thought tend to be acquired on the job. The Chartered Institute of Patent Attorneys offers examinations leading to entry on the Register of Patent Agents.[76] The business is increasingly international and knowledge of French and German is encouraged.[77]

---

[74] Administration of Justice Act 1985, pt II.
[75] CLC Referral Arrangements: Disclosure and Publication Provisions (3 December 2012).
[76] www.saccomann.com/routes-to-qualification-within-the-ip-sector.
[77] www.cipa.org.uk/pages/about-careers.

F. Trade Mark Attorneys

There are around 50 firms registered as trade mark attorneys in the UK, although some of these are solicitors' firms.[78] At least half have an office on London. The Institute of Trade Mark Attorneys offer examinations for entry to the Register of Trade Mark Agents and those with some legal qualifications may be given exemption from some of the papers.

G. Law Costs Draftsmen

A Law Costs Draftsman prepares the more complicated legal bills for other legal professionals. This service is provided to other professionals, mainly solicitors. A Costs Draftsman can also be instructed by litigants in person who can recover fees in respect of advice given.[79] The professional body, currently called the Association of Costs Lawyers, was founded in 1977. Costs lawyers may attend the procedure, called taxation, whereby the court approves the costs of a representative, such as a solicitor, awarded against a party in litigation. Qualified costs lawyers can appear as advocates in such proceedings.

H. Notaries

Notaries are primarily concerned with the authentication and certification of signatures and documents for use abroad. The Notaries Society, founded in 1882 and incorporated in 1907, is a membership body with no disciplinary functions. Admission as a notary follows a two-year part-time course covering similar ground as law degrees.[80] Substantial exemptions are given to law degree holders and solicitors and barristers with five years' experience.

I. European and Foreign Lawyers

Legal practitioners do not have to be British nationals or qualified in England and Wales to offer legal advice. As a result of an EU directive in 1989, qualified lawyers from EU Member States could practise under the designation accorded lawyers, for example, solicitor or barrister, in another Member State having passed an aptitude test.[81] A further directive in 1998 provided that qualified lawyers should be able to achieve integration after a period of professional practice in the host Member State

---

[78] www.legal500.com/c/london/tmt-technology-media-and-telecoms/trade-mark-attorneys.
[79] Civil Procedure Rules 1998.
[80] The Notaries (Qualification) Rules 1998.
[81] Council Directive 89/48/EEC of 21 December 1988 on a general system for the recognition of higher-education diplomas awarded on completion of professional education and training of at least three years' duration (OJ L19/16 1989).

under their host-country professional titles or else continue to practise under their home-country professional titles.[82]

Acceptance of European lawyers was necessary to meet the requirements of EU policy on free movement of labour. In fact, it also responded to the fact that the EU internal market increasingly called for lawyers who operated across national borders. A similar rationale applies to foreign lawyers, who also have limited rights to practise in England and Wales without re-qualifying. Lawyers from the EU have general access to all areas of practice reserved to solicitors and barristers, but with some restrictions. They must appear in courts with a local lawyer. They cannot handle conveyancing and probate if these activities are reserved to a separate profession in their home state. Non-EU foreign lawyers do not have general rights of audience or rights to conduct litigation. They may apply to the chair of the Bar Council for permission to appear in the English courts in matters from their home jurisdiction.

Subject to the restrictions on areas of practice, overseas lawyers can practise English law, as well as the law of their own country, as sole practitioners, as a Registered European Lawyer (REL). This status is only required of lawyers practising in the UK under the title of another European Union or European Economic Area jurisdiction, or Switzerland, and under conditions of citizenship. They may also practise in a partnership of foreign lawyers, as an assistant or consultant in a law firm, in partnership with English solicitors and REL, but only if registered with the SRA as a Registered Foreign Lawyer (RFL) or as a REL. They can also practise in employment with English solicitors or as in-house lawyers.

Overseas lawyers wishing to practise with no restrictions can qualify for the appropriate profession in England and Wales. This usually involves passing a series of tests on aspects of English Law, together with Professional Conduct and Accounts. They can then call themselves the relevant English professional, but must meet any additional requirements to offer financial, immigration and asylum advice. There is a schedule of foreign legal professions recognised by the SRA as appropriate managers of recognised bodies.[83]

J. Unauthorised Persons

Analysis of SRA data shows that in 2009/10 around 40 per cent of fee earners in SRA-regulated firms were not solicitors. In legal aid firms, diversity surveys show around two out of five fee earners are non-solicitors.[84] These figures cannot be explained by the presence of legal executives and suggest large numbers of para-legal fee earners.

---

[82] The Establishment Directive 98/5/EC of the European Parliament and of the Council of 16 February 1998 to facilitate practice of the profession of lawyer on a permanent basis in a Member State other than that in which the qualification was obtained (OJ L209)

[83] www.sra.org.uk/sra/regulatory-framework/professions-approved-by-SRA-for-RFL-status.page.

[84] LSB, *Market Impacts of the Legal Services Act: Interim Baseline Report* (April 2012) at para D.12.7 (www.legalservicesboard.org.uk/what_we_do/Research/Publications/pdf/market_impacts_of_the_legal_services_act_interim_baseline_report.pdf).

V. The Legal Services Act 2007

The LSA 2007 was intended to have a major impact on the operation of the legal services market, from the right to conduct reserved activities through to regulation. It pursued the longstanding aim of successive governments to subject the established legal professions to greater competition. It provided a framework in which eradication of distinctions between different kinds of lawyers could be accelerated, including by allowing them to share legal businesses between themselves and with outsiders. This chapter deals only the organisational dimensions of this process, including the introduction of new business forms, Legal Disciplinary Practice and Alternative Business Structures, and consequential changes in regulation.

A. Background to the Act

Much of the focus before the LSA 2007 was on multi-disciplinary practices, organisations providing flexible, 'one-stop shops' for clients requiring a variety of professional services. In 1979, the influential Benson Report concluded that multi-disciplinary practices (MDPs) were not in the public interest.[85] In 1990 the Courts and Legal Services Act permitted the Law Society to retain restrictions on solicitors entering unincorporated associations with other professionals like barristers.[86] The rules of the professional bodies continued to prohibit such entities. The decades preceding the LSA 2007 were dominated by discussion of the merits of MDPs.

The Bar shared the Law Society's concerns about loss of professional independence within MDPs,[87] but was also anxious about other potential losses if the proposals went through. These included loss of independent barristers to MDPs, loss of cross-monitoring of the work of solicitors and barristers by each, loss of small local solicitors' practices through unfair competition with larger units[88] and loss of the public benefit of the 'cab rank' rule.[89]

A cautionary note on the risks of MDPs was sounded by the Enron scandal. Enron was a US based, multi-national company providing tax advice and auditing services. It was one of the top five companies in its field. In 2001 it filed for bankruptcy leaving massive debts and around $11 billion in shareholder losses. Enron's in-house lawyers

[85] Lord Chancellor's Department, *Report of the Royal Commission on Legal Services* (Cmnd 7648, 1979) at 401.
[86] Courts and Legal Services Act, s 66(2).
[87] The Law Society, *Striking the Balance: The Provisional Views of the Council of the Law Society on the Green Paper* (London, The Law Society, 1989) at 4 and 17.
[88] The General Council of the Bar, *The Quality of Justice: The Bar's Response* (London, Butterworths, 1989) at para 2.35.
[89] ibid, at para 2.57.

and accountants facilitated the dishonest and ultimately illegal activities of the managers of the business. These professionals maximised returns from the business yet deceived the investing public as to the company's true financial position. This raised some doubt about whether professionals embedded in non-lawyer organisations would demonstrate the necessary integrity or independence required to guard against massive financial catastrophe.

The Law Society's resistance was probably eroded by the apparent inevitability of multi-disciplinary practice. In 1993 Arthur Anderson, a multi-national accounting firm, established a law practice of 100 lawyers operating alongside a separate accounting business, with a projected income of £22 million.[90] This arrangement avoided the Law Society's ban on fee splitting by the maintenance of separate accounts.[91] Perhaps, recognising the inevitable arrival of MDPs, and the risk that they would be dominated by accountancy firms, the Law Society formally ended its opposition to lawyer MDPs.[92]

Shortly after the turn of the century, two reports sought elimination of restrictions on competition within the legal professions.[93] The government appointed Sir David Clementi to carry out a review of the legal services market, including the restrictive nature of business structures. Clementi reported that some lawyers saw a conflict between lawyers as professionals and lawyers as business people. He disagreed, arguing that 'access to justice requires not only that the legal advice given is sound, but also the presence of business skills necessary to provide a cost-effective service in a consumer-friendly way'.[94]

Clementi was not unsympathetic to the legal profession. He concluded that the professional self-regulation had 'produced a strong and independently minded profession, operating in most cases to high standards, able to compete successfully internationally' and was therefore disinclined to 'start from scratch'.[95] Clementi was sympathetic to the idea of MDPs, but preferred Legal Disciplinary Practices (LDPs) offering only legal services.[96] Clementi envisaged that the management of such firms could be separate from the persons who owned it, but lawyers, Clementi thought, should be in the majority. He suggested that the problem of having employees not bound by client confidentiality rules could be addressed by denying them access to client files.

[90] *The Lawyer* 27 May 1997, at 18.

[91] Solicitors' Practice Rules 1990, r 7.

[92] 'Medium Sized City Partners Accept Need for MDPs' *The Lawyer* 11 February 1997, at 48; S Parker, 'Introduction to Legal Ethics and Legal Practice' in S Parker and C Sampford (eds), *Legal Ethics and Legal Practice* (Oxford, Clarendon Press, 1995) at 1.

[93] Director General of Fair Trading, *Competition in Professions* (OFT 328) (London, OFT, 2001); DCA, *Competition and Regulation in the Legal Services Market – A Report Following the Consultation 'In the Public Interest?'* (2003).

[94] Clementi Report (n 1) at 5.

[95] ibid, ch 2, at para 32.

[96] ibid.

B. Major Changes Introduced by the Act

i. Regulatory Objectives

Four of the eight regulatory principles set out in the LSA 2007 are particularly relevant to the organisation of legal services. They are:

——   improving access to justice;
——   protecting and promoting the interests of consumers of legal services;
——   promoting competition in the provision of legal services; and
——   encouraging an independent, strong, diverse and effective legal profession.

These objectives were to be achieved by general liberalisation of the market and increased competition. Some objectives were furthered directly by sections of the Act. Promoting competition to the legal services market was to be achieved by allowing non-lawyer ownership and management of organisations providing legal services. This apparently furthered the first two principles. The responsiveness of regulation to the new environment was to be promoted by a new Legal Services Board (LSB).[97] The interests of consumers were to be promoted by a Consumer Panel.[98] The LSB would be bound to consider any representations made by the panel.[99] The assumption of the Act appears to be that a strong and effective legal profession will be achieved in the crucible of competition.

ii. Approved Regulators of Authorised Persons

The LSA 2007 introduced a restructuring of the legal services market while preserving the identity of the legal professions. Legal professionals became 'authorised persons' under the Act, defined by their right to undertake the six 'reserved legal activities'; advocacy, conduct of litigation, work on reserved instruments, probate work, notarial work and administration of oaths.[100] Those entitled to carry on these activities are authorised, or exempt, in relation to that activity.[101] Schedule 3 provides a list of such persons, for example, a person granted a right of audience by the court in a particular matter. The regulated persons were placed under a statutory duty to comply with the regulatory arrangements of the approved regulator.[102]

    The professional bodies became approved regulators in relation to the reserved legal activities they could authorise their members to undertake.[103] However the LSA 2007 required that they ensure that the regulatory function operated independently of influence by the professional body.[104] The professions therefore established

---

[97] LSA 2007, s 2.
[98] ibid, s 8.
[99] ibid, s 10(1).
[100] ibid, s 12(1) and sch 2.
[101] ibid, s 13(2).
[102] ibid, s 176.
[103] ibid, s 20.
[104] ibid, ss 27–31 and ch 5.

regulatory arms. For example, the General Council of the Bar established the Bar Standards Board (BSB), the Law Society the Solicitors Regulation Authority (SRA) and the Chartered Institute of Legal Executives ILEX professional standards (IPS). The LSB was given responsibility to assist in the development of standards in regulation by the approved regulators and education and training.[105]

iii.   Approved Regulators as Licensing Authority for Licensable Bodies (ABS)

The LSA 2007 provides that an entity may be licensed to carry out a reserved legal activity by an approved licensing authority.[106] Such an entity is one where a manager or person with an interest in it, or who controls at least 10 per cent of the voting rights in it,[107] is a non-authorised person.[108] The LSB or an approved regulator may license such bodies to carry out reserved legal activities. A licensed body is one governed by Part 5 of the Act, under which Alternative Business Structures (ABS) are permitted.[109] Of the approved regulators only the SRA and the Council for Licensed Conveyancers are approved regulators for ABS.

iv.   New Business Structures

The Act modified Clementi's recommendations on organisations by introducing ABS[110] as well as LDPs. LDPs could comprise a combination of approved persons supported by non-lawyers such as IT experts or management personnel. The services offered must, however, be *exclusively* legal services. All the different kinds of lawyers could be equally involved in the management of the firm and participate in its profits. Non-lawyers could own or control up to 25 per cent of capital in the business. Non-lawyers could also be managers in the business, subject to proof of suitable character. From September 2011, firms appointing non-lawyer managers needed to apply to become an ABS.

ABS are the same as LDPs in that they can consist of lawyers of all types, and non-lawyers, offering all legal services, reserved and unreserved, but different in that they can offer related services, such as insurance or surveying. They can also be wholly owned and managed by non-lawyers. Non-authorised employees and managers of licensed bodies are under a statutory duty not to do anything that contributes to a breach of duty by authorised persons or licensed bodies.[111] The LSA 2007 also places the Head of Legal Practice of a licensed body under a duty to do all that is reasonably practicable to ensure compliance with their duty to observe the rules of their regulator

---

[105] ibid, s 4.
[106] ibid, s 18(1).
[107] ibid, s 72(2).
[108] ibid, s 72.
[109] ibid, s 71(2).
[110] ibid, pt 5, s 71 onwards.
[111] ibid, s 90.

and to inform the regulator of breaches.[112] The Head of Finance and Administration is under a similar duty in relation to compliance with accounts rules.[113]

ABS might offer a 'one-stop shop' for selected services financed and managed by non-lawyers. The illustration was of a supermarket offering standardised legal services, dubbed Tesco-law. Tesco, in fact, launched an online service in June 2004 offering to make and store wills and give advice on a variety of legal issues including Do-It-Yourself divorce, rights at work and starting a business. This operation required no change in the practising rules as none of the work was within the reserved categories of legal services.[114]

A number of organisations, including the motoring organisation, the RAC, and Halifax Bank prepared to expand to take advantage of the Act.[115] The proposals were said to be advantageous to consumers and lawyers. The benefit for consumers was that they would improve choice, reduce prices, improve services and provide better access to justice. The advantage for legal businesses was greater access to capital and finance, greater flexibility and, for individual lawyers, more choice of working environment.

Some essentially legal work, immigration advice, claims management and insolvency, for example, is not regulated under the LSA 2007 but by other statutes. Others, will writing for example, are not regulated by any statute but may be indirectly regulated because the person carrying out the work is licensed by professional body.[116]

The LSA 2007 contained no conditions governing ABSs, leaving the details of the regime to be worked out by the LSB established by the Act. The LSB could grant the licences necessary to regulate ABS or establish a regulatory regime itself if no regulator came forward. In fact, the Law Society's regulatory arm, the SRA, was granted the right to license ABS. LDPs were licensed from 2009 and ABS from October 2011 when a common code of practice covering solicitors in private practice and in employing organisations like LDPs and ABS came into force.

VI. Impact of the Legal Services Act 2007 on the Legal Services Market

A. Legal Disciplinary Practices

LDPs became operative under regulation by the SRA from March 2009 but were required to become ABS between October 2011 and October 2012.[117] They were

---

[112] ibid, s 91.

[113] ibid, s 92.

[114] See (2004) 154 *New Law Journal* 947.

[115] See (2006) 156 *New Law Journal* 694 and (2007) 157 *New Law Journal* 134; *Law Society Gazette* 2 November 2006.

[116] S Mayson and O Marley, *Reserved Legal Activities: History and Rationale* (London, Legal Services Institute, 2010).

[117] SRA, *The Architecture of Change Part 2: The SRA's New Handbook* (2010) at para 50.

owned and managed by a combination of different types of lawyer. No more than 25 per cent of the managers (or shareholding) in an SRA-regulated LDP can be non-lawyers, and only non-lawyers who are managers can own a shareholding. By September 2009, 105 LDPs had been established, containing 125 non-solicitor partners.[118] Of these, 98 were claimed as Chartered Legal Executive lawyers, the largest single group, licensed conveyancers, legal executives, accountants and a patent attorney.[119] In November 2009, the Bar Standards Board allowed barristers to join LDPs.[120]

B. Alternative Business Structures

One of the intended consequences of LSA 2007 was bringing more commoditised legal products to the legal services market.[121] ABS are predicted to accelerate the domination of the private client market by commoditised solutions.[122] This is because non-lawyer capital will be more motivated to build technological infrastructure and less inhibited by the professional assumptions of lawyers. ABS may encourage more self-help among consumers. Eventually, even corporate work may be susceptible to 'un-bundling'. While solicitors' firms could apply to be ABS it was not known how many would do so. The main advantage for such firms would be the acquisition of management expertise or extra capital to expand the business or make it more efficient.

Within a short time the SRA had granted 29 licences and the Council for Licensed Conveyancers, the other approved regulator for ABS, had granted nine.[123] Among the leaders in offering ABS was Cooperative Legal Services Limited. The Co-operative Group Ltd, originally a grocery business which had expanded into different commercial areas, established a legal services division in 2006. Co-operative Legal Services was one of the first four ABS to be approved by the SRA in March 2012 and is a flagship for such entities. It offers legal services in conveyancing, employment law, family law, personal injury and probate and estate administration. At the end of 2012 it entered the top hundred law firms by turnover and announced plans to establish five regional hubs across England and hire 3000 additional staff. Other big brand retailers waited in a queue for licences.

The advantages of ABS include familiarity to customers, brand confidence and loyalty. Added to these market advantages is the power of large-scale advertising, capacity to invest in new technologies and economies of scale. There have been a

---

[118] C Baksi, 'Barristers and the Legal Services Act: Will the bar modernise in time? Does it even need to?' *Law Society Gazette* 24 September 2009 (www.lawgazette.co.uk/features/barristers-and-the-legal-services-act-will-the-bar-modernise-in-time-does-even-need-to).

[119] 'Future Rights of Legal Executives' The Chartered Legal Executive Journal's 2010 Student Supplement.

[120] C Baksi, 'Bar Standards Board sanctions legal disciplinary practices' *Law Society Gazette* 26 November 2009 (www.lawgazette.co.uk/news/bar-standards-board-sanctions-legal-disciplinary-practices).

[121] Legal Services Board, *LSB Business Plan* 2009/10 (London, Legal Services Board, 2009) at para 12 (www.legalservicesboard.org.uk/news_publications/publications/pdf/business_plan_2009_10.pdf).

[122] R Susskind, *The End of Lawyers?: Rethinking the Nature of Legal Services* (Oxford, Oxford University Press, 2008).

[123] N Rose, 'Future of Law: Big Brands and Alternative Business Structures' *The Guardian* 12 October 2012.

range of reactions from traditional legal businesses. Some surprisingly small outfits had applied to become ABS so that family members could be partners, investors or managers in the business. Quality Solicitors, a marketing collective of 250 small firms designed to maximise the benefit of television advertising, aims to take on ABS by building its own brand.

Most ABS, unless they are converted solicitors' firms, typically did not offer comprehensive services. Many solicitors were nevertheless gloomy about the future of private practice in the wake of declining legal aid and increasing competition. Barristers were also unenthusiastic. By June 2010, nine months after LDPs were authorised, only 10 barristers were known to have become partners.[124] A sluggish market for advocacy led more than a third of barristers to anticipate joining an entity in the next five years.[125] Barrister only entities were favoured by 23 per cent, ABS by 21 per cent and LDPs by 17 per cent. These data provided the Bar with food for thought. Surveys of law students, however, revealed scepticism about working in ABS, even though starting salaries were competitive with similar work in the private sector.[126]

In June 2012, the BSB announced that it intended to apply to become a regulator of advocacy-focused ABS, LDPs and Barrister Only Entities, but not MDPs.[127] BSB-regulated entities and self-employed barristers would be permitted to conduct litigation and provide the same services as the self-employed Bar. Under the proposals, owners of BSB-regulated entities would also be managers, with a 25 per cent limit on non-lawyer owners or managers of Alternative Business Structures. The majority of owners or managers of ABSs regulated by the BSB would be barristers or other advocates with higher rights of audience. BSB-regulated entities and self-employed barristers would not be permitted to hold client money and all managers of BSB-regulated entities (barristers, solicitors and non-lawyers) would be subject to the same conduct rules.

In 2013, research conducted for the LSB on changes in the legal services market since the LSA 2007 found the median amount of income generated per fee earner had fallen from £87,000 in 2010/11 to £85,000 in 2012/13.[128] Turnover per fee earner was less among firms with a higher proportion of local clients. This was linked to less face-to-face delivery of services. Research found ABS firms were concentrated in the personal injury sector, taking up 20 per cent of the market share, split between new entrants and existing firms who converted to ABS status.

In 2010/11, there were 378 LDPs, 491 in 2011/12 and 429 in 2012/13, with 39 having closed and 23 LDPs converting to ABS.[129] However, while this group of firms never represented more than 5 per cent of all firms, they accounted for 14 per cent of market share in 2012/13. Firms who were LDPs in 2012/13 were statistically more likely to have seen an increase in turnover in the previous three years; 57 per cent compared to

---

[124] 'Barristers slow to join LDPs' *Legal Futures* 2 June 2010 (www.legalfutures.co.uk/latest-news/barristers-slow-to-join-ldps).

[125] 'More than a third of barristers keen to join new business structures, BSB survey finds' *Legal Futures* 12 July 2010 (www.legalfutures.co.uk/regulation/barristers/third-of-barristers-keen-to-join-new-business-structures-bsb-survey-finds.Legal Futures, 2010b).

[126] H Gannagé-Stewart, 'One year on, are students still unconvinced by ABSs?' *The Guardian* 12 November 2012.

[127] www.barstandardsboard.org.uk/regulatory-requirements/changes-to-regulation/entity-regulation/.

[128] J Hyde, 'ABSs "more productive" than traditional law firms says LSB' *Law Society Gazette* 22 October 2013.

[129] ibid.

49 per cent for all providers. Under transitional arrangements, all LDPs will convert to ABS.

In December 2013, the LSB approved the application of the Institute of Chartered Accountants of England and Wales (ICAEW) to become a regulator of probate activities. More activities are likely to follow as accountants, as predicted, enter the legal market.

C. Professional Monopolies and Competition

i. Monopoly

It continues to be an offence punishable by imprisonment and fine to carry on a reserved activity unless entitled to do so.[130] Therefore, ABS must use approved persons and ensure that any non-lawyer employees do not cause breaches of the rules applying to approved persons.[131] While a monopoly of legal work is preserved, there will be greater competition between law firms organised along traditional lines and new organisational forms like ABS. ABS are expected to cut the cost of delivering legal services by using unqualified staff for non-reserved activity such as advice giving, increasing the leverage of qualified to non-qualified staff working on reserved work and by greater use of technology.

ii. Competition

a. New Technology

It was predicted that new technologies could reduce the cost of legal services by standardisation, systemisation, packaging, and commoditisation of legal services for the benefit of consumers.[132] This has been demonstrated with the use of online, fixed costs regimes for litigation.[133] Lawyers were seen to be reluctant to embrace the full potential of disruptive legal technologies, such as document assembly or online dispute resolution, because they prefer delivering more satisfying 'bespoke services'. Given the choice, clients might prefer more efficient, less costly services delivered online. It is predicted that conventional legal businesses could eventually shrink to core activity like dispute resolution and problem solving.[134] This prediction does not recognise, for example, the complex reasons that corporations use large law firms, particularly for international business.[135]

Lawyers may fear that ABS will swallow up standard and lucrative legal work, leaving high street practices with only the low paid legal aid work, or the difficult

---

[130] Legal Service Act 2007, s14.
[131] Legal Service Act 2007, sch 11, paras 16 and s 90.
[132] R Susskind, *The End of Lawyers?* (n 122).
[133] See ch17: 'Litigation'.
[134] Susskind (n 122).
[135] J Flood, 'Lawyers as Sanctifiers: The Role of Elite Law Firms in International Business Transactions' (2007) 14(1) *Indiana Journal of Global Legal Studies* 35.

non-standard client who is also unable to pay fully for the service required. While firms in cities may be most at risk of direct competition it may that those in rural areas will also find some areas of work affected. The Carter Review suggested that 400 legal aid firms could disappear in competition with retail legal services. The actual figure could be more. It may be that only ABS, with the backing and philosophy of supermarkets, could provide the infrastructure and support to make legal aid pay.[136]

b. Business

The period since the enactment of the LSA 2007 coincides with a significant and deep economic recession. A large survey of solicitors found declining income among firms with repeat clients, suggesting negotiated reductions in fee levels.[137] Approximately a third of firms specialising in legal aid work anticipated withdrawing from one or more areas within three years. It is not known how many lawyer-led organisations will fail in the coming years or what that will do to numbers of lawyers overall or to recruitment to different kinds of organisation.

One way in which solicitors have geared up to compete with ABS is to pool resources. Quality Solicitorshas located representatives in WH Smith, a national retailer, launched the largest national advertising campaign by a legal provider and entered a partnership with US online legal services provider LegalZoom. In 2011 a private equity company purchased a controlling interest in the Quality Solicitors holding company.

c. Employment

ABS could prefer to use members of less prestigious professions in preference to solicitors and barristers. This could be achieved by using them for non-reserved activity or by deploying them, under supervision, for routine parts of reserved activity. One consequence is to create a more level playing field for lawyers outside the traditional professional elite. For example, Chartered Legal Executives are eligible to become partners in LDPs and ABS as well as advocates or judges. This may explain a 40 per cent growth of numbers of students taking Institute of Legal Executive Fellowships in 2010.[138] This is the best established 'alternative' legal qualification, which can be taken at the stage equivalent to 'A' level.

The result of this 'unbundling' of legal services is unpredictable. Using para-legals for aspects of complex transactions, for example, may result in fewer lawyers, but release those remaining for direct contact with clients.[139] More pessimistic analyses of the prospects for lawyers foresee pay reductions of up to a half for members of legal professions working in affected fields.[140]

---

[136] J Robins, 'Where does publicly-funded law fit into the new world of Tesco law?' *The Guardian* 21 September 2012.

[137] P Pleasance, NJ Balmer and R Moorhead, *A Time of Change: Solicitor's Firms in England and Wales* (London, Law Society, Legal Services Board, Ministry of Justice, 2012)

[138] J Rayner, 'Legal executive numbers grow' *Law Society Gazette* 27 January 2011 (www.lawgazette. co.uk/news/legal-executive-numbers-grow).

[139] C Griffiths, 'Addleshaws vows: no more drudge work for associates' (2011) 25(6) *The Lawyer* 1.

[140] R Rothwell, 'Profession facing job shake-out – Mayson' *Law Society Gazette* 20 March 2008 (www. lawgazette.co.uk/news/profession-facing-job-shake-out-mayson).

d. Regulatory Objectives

The provision of independent advocacy services by barristers has ensured that small firms can instruct the most eminent advocates for serious cases. This appears to be a good example of an efficient market. The effect of declining legal aid and erosion of barristers' monopoly of higher court advocacy has been loss of work, forcing many barristers to consider moving in-house. This means that they less independent and not available to the general public.[141]

If independent advocates were eventually to disappear, small firms unable to support advocates, and the general public, would lose an option for pursuing cases. The system would lose the benefit of barristers subject to the cab rank rule. Significant diminution of the pool of independent advocates would appear to be contrary to the regulatory objectives of promoting the public interest, improving access to justice and supporting the rule of law.

D. Regulation

The Law Society had longstanding regulatory powers over recognised bodies, but they were little used. The decision to pursue regulatory control of ABS led to the Code of Conduct 2007 being amended in 2009 to make this right explicit. The introduction of new business forms under the LSA 2007 necessitated a shift from the regulation of individuals to the regulation of entities, the organisations in which they work. Consequently, regulators of ABS exercise regulatory control of all those working in entities, professionals and non-professionals. An entity regulator, for example the SRA, could therefore be regulating an entity that may, or may not, include members of the profession of which it is also the approved regulator. These issues are considered in more detail in part two.

VII. Conclusion

The legal profession in England and Wales has traditionally organised around the delivery of reserved activities by either sole practice or partnership. Barristers were sole practitioners while members of one of the Inns of Court and usually of chambers. A large proportion of solicitors' firms have been owned by sole practitioners. Both forms have operated to exclude the possibility of non-lawyer ownership and management of the delivery of legal serves. Government policy has been to reduce the cost of legal services, in part, by increasing competition between existing legal providers and by bringing new providers into the legal services market.

---

[141] J Webb, 'Commentary' (2005) 8 *Legal Ethics* 185.

It remains to be seen what the impact of the Legal Services Act 2007 will be. The security of professional monopoly made parts of the English legal profession complacent, over-dependent on routine activity, such as conveyancing, and unwilling to innovate. Leaving solicitors to manage their own businesses may not have led to optimum number and size of business, a barrier to the market efficiency that government desired. It is also arguable that drastic action was necessary in order to achieve an efficient re-ordering of the legal services market. The Legal Services Act will increase the business orientation of lawyers. Whether it will also have an impact on ethical orientation is unknown.

PART II

PROFESSIONAL STRUCTURES

5

Governance

'Be strong, be supple; that is the way to rule'.[1]

I. Introduction

This chapter looks at the institutions and systems of governance of the legal professions. The traditional structure of professional bodies is complex. They typically employ a permanent executive, administrative and secretarial structure. This structure services a plethora of committees that formulate policies for approval by a council. Typically, the committee structure draws extensively on the professional membership. Member involvement in policy and regulation is a manifestation of collegiality and public service. This ensures that members are closely involved in procedures for developing standards and promoting ethical practice.

The Legal Services Act 2007 (LSA 2007) requires separation of the representative and regulatory arms of the professions. This has introduced a complex relationship affecting, among other things, governance of the profession. One feature of this relationship is that the representative side is not supposed to influence the policy and practice of the regulatory side, except as one of many stakeholders. The Legal Services Board is, however, supposed to influence regulation, in particular by making sure that the regulatory objectives are achieved. It is not, however, supposed to interfere with the representative side of the professional body.

---

[1] From 'Crouching Tiger, Hidden Dragon' (Dir: Ang Lee) (United China Vision Inc, 2000).

II. Principles of Governance

A. Principles

i. Theory

The literature on governance largely relates to corporations, but the principles of accountability and ethics developed are of general relevance.[2] All institutions are concerned with using their resources to solve conflicts and make decisions. Governance describes how organisations manage this process. It is concerned with how organisations are directed and controlled and where accountability and responsibility is located within them. Analysis of governance identifies who sets and implements rules, where the power to take action is located and how organisations are structured in order to manage change.

ii. Values

Good governance of organisations concerns recognising and complying with legal requirements, meeting organisational aims, making good, timely decisions, using funds effectively and transparently, providing good leadership and treating people fairly and equally.[3] To facilitate good governance the decision-making bodies of an organisation must understand their role, work to achieve the organisational purpose, individually and together, exercise effective control, behave with integrity and be open and accountable.

Governance is directly relevant to ethics. Values such as transparency, accountability and participation are as relevant to the ethics of professional organisations as they are to professional practitioners or firms. It is important for the credibility of the professional organisation as an ethical leader that those working for it behave ethically. Secondly, it is important that an organisation sets an example and builds the trust of the membership. It is damaging if the profession has progressive policies for members, but does not follow them internally. It is unrealistic to expect members to behave ethically if its leadership does not.

---

[2] See further RSF Eells, *The Meaning of Modern Business: An Introduction to the Philosophy of Large Corporate Enterprise* (New York, Columbia University Press, 1960); J Charkham, *Keeping Better Company: Corporate Governance Ten Years On* (Oxford, Oxford University Press, 2005);

[3] Good Governance, *A Code for the Voluntary and Community Sectors* (www.governancecode.org/about-the-code/#sthash.Y62Fyitj.dpuf).

iii. Activities

a. Structures

In the context of professions, governance refers to the activities of a governing body. In membership organisations, like professions, a governing body may not be full-time. A professional executive, or secretariat, usually operates with delegated powers. This enacts policies and takes action, like publishing documents or issuing press releases, on an everyday basis. Governance is usually managed through policies and processes generated by networks of special interest committees.

b. Role

Traditionally, professional bodies are the main means through which professions develop policy, offer leadership to members and seek to influence public policy. The importance of leadership in sustaining a professional ethic is described by Ravetz:

> For the effective enforcement of a professional ethic, it is not necessary that all members of the profession adhere to it with total commitment ... But ... there must be excellent leadership and good morale. The leadership is necessary to provide definition and application of the professional ethic in constantly changing circumstances; and morale is necessary if this leadership is to be effective. The ordinary members of the profession must respect the leaders according to their criteria of skill and success, and be prepared to accept their guidance and control. Also, they must have some degree of commitment to doing good work, so that a consensus can operate against those who betray the good name of the profession. Otherwise the enforcement of a professional ethic is impossible.[4]

c. Engagement

Small exclusive bodies can more effectively engage and mobilise their membership. Their problem is that they may lack legitimacy and, therefore, influence. A large and inclusive professional group confers a degree of legitimacy on the professional body, allowing it to speak with authority. The more inclusive professional membership becomes, the wider the range of views which must be represented. An organisation with a large membership may have legitimacy but will find it difficult to take effective collective action.

There is more risk with a large and diverse organisation that members pursue sectional advantage at the expense of the higher goals the profession may set itself. Effective leadership and consultation are important because the observance of rules depends on the support of members. This support is easier to achieve when the members share a common purpose and common values and have a lively interest in the development of the profession. Membership of professional bodies and local associations is perhaps indicative. For example, a survey of solicitors found that over

---

[4] JR Ravetz, 'Ethics in Scientific Activity' in A Flores (ed), *Professional Ideals* (Belmont, CA, Wadsworth Publishing, 1988) 147, at 153.

50 per cent of respondents were not involved with the Law Society or their local law societies.[5]

III. Governance of Legal Professions before the Legal Services Act 2007

A. Barristers

The Bar had a more complex governance structure than solicitors because of the control exercised by the ancient seats of governance, the Inns of Court. Following its formation in 1895, the General Council of the Bar assumed responsibility for laying down rules of etiquette, such as that requiring that a barrister be briefed by a solicitor.[6] It also developed a disciplinary role over the whole Bar. Although the Bar became more centralised, the Inns continued to have substantial responsibilities. It was not until 1966, for example, that the four inns delegated the authority of each Inn over training to a Senate of the Inns of Court.

The Inns comprised students, barristers and Masters of the Bench, or Benchers. The governing body of each Inn was typically comprised of judges and benchers. Much of what the Bar Council enacted by way of policy was negotiated with the Inns. The influence and residual power of the Inns before 2007 was strong, yet uncertain.

B. Solicitors

The basis of the constitutional governance of the Law Society was provided by the Royal Charter of 1845, although this provides that the title is 'The Society of Attorneys, Solicitors, Proctors, and others not being Barristers, practising in the Courts of Law and Equity of the United Kingdom'.[7] The charter provides that

> there shall be a Council of the Society, to be elected from the Members of the said Society and a President and a Vice-President of the Society to be elected from the Council[8]

The charter went on to provide that the original membership of the Council should consist of not more than 30, nor less than 20 members, but this was amended by

---

[5] 'Law Soc Damned by Members' (1997) 11(22) *The Lawyer* 1.

[6] M Burrage, *Revolution and the Making of the Contemporary Legal Profession: England, France and the United States* (Oxford, Oxford University Press, 2006) at 500–01.

[7] Law Society, The Charter of the Society 1845 (text of the original and supplemental charters referred to can be found at www.lawsociety.org.uk/about-us/our-constitution/).

[8] ibid, para VIII.

supplemental charters to an upper limit of 50^9 and then 120.[10] A further supplemental charter in 1903 changed the name to the Law Society.

In the debates regarding the legalisation of trade unions in the late-nineteenth century the Law Society increasingly saw its representative role as both legitimate and necessary. The Law Society's claim to represent all solicitors was evidenced by relatively few challenges to its authority from members.[11] Most were generated by conveyancing. During the periods 1840–50 and 1880–1914 tensions between the London-dominated Law Society and provincial solicitors became severe, particularly when the Law Society was thought not to be defending the conveyancing monopoly or other work sufficiently strongly. The ultimate humiliation occurred when country solicitors' opposition to a land transfer bill forced the government to back down even though the Law Society had already agreed its terms. Thereafter the Law Society was forced to become more vocal in protecting its members' interests.[12]

Various alliances of provincial law societies threatened the control of the Law Society but failed to gain a significant foothold.[13] In the 1960s a National House Owners Society was established to encourage people to do their own conveyancing. Sections of the profession criticised the Law Society for failing to defend the conveyancing monopoly effectively. This led to the establishment of a short-lived competitor, the British Legal Association.[14] As the Law Society increasingly promoted the idea that it advanced the public interest, it became diffident in defending the profession's interests against the government.

The strains of representing a diverse membership became severe in the 1990s. In the middle of the period Sugarman wrote that:

> [T]he strength and weakness of the Law Society (and the profession) has stemmed from its propensity to express several contradictory tendencies side by side: its claim to act in the general interests of society; its much asserted independence and relative autonomy from external influence, notably that of the state; its 'gentlemanly' character, in part sustained by the image of the barrister, its 'national' character; its claims to act as an effective pressure group and trade union on behalf of its membership; and its inherent dependence upon and imbrication within the state.[15]

In the 1990s the image of the Law Society as a consensual and collegial organisation began to crack.

In 1995 the election of the President of the Society was contested for the first time since 1954. In an acrimonious election campaign, Martin Mears was elected on a populist ticket to represent the interests of the 'ordinary' practitioner. His themes were the damage done to standards of conveyancing by the ending of the solicitors' monopoly, the oversupply of lawyers and the bureaucracy of the Law Society. Henry Hodge,

---

[9] Law Society, Supplemental Charter 1872.

[10] Law Society, Supplemental Charter 1954.

[11] MS Larson, *The Rise of Professionalism: Monopolies of Competence and Sheltered Markets* (New Jersey, Transaction Publishers, 2013) at 227.

[12] D Sugarman, 'Bourgeois Collectivism, Professional Power and the Boundaries of the State: The Private and Public Life of the Law Society 1825 to 1914' (1996) 3(1/2) *International Journal of the Legal Profession* 81.

[13] ibid, at 103.

[14] G Hanlon, *Lawyers, the State and the Market: Professionalism Revisited* (Basingstoke, Palgrave Macmillan, 1999) at 79.

[15] Sugarman, 'The Private and Public Life of the Law Society' (n 12) at 115.

the official Council candidate, was defeated by over 3000 votes.[16] Mears' period in office highlighted the tension between the elite and the rest of the profession. Almost immediately he proposed a reduction in powers of the Secretary General at a Council Meeting.[17] In October 1995 Mears excited adverse press reaction with attacks on the Equal Opportunities Commission and the Commission for Racial Equality.[18]

The challenge to the liberal establishment both within and outside the Law Society excited much disagreement about its role. After 40 years of uncontested elections for senior positions in the Law Society, there were four contested and acrimonious elections in the 1990s. Even this was not enough to mobilise solicitors as an active membership. Law Society elections traditionally had a poor turnout, but even in the 1995 presidential elections, only 23,000, of over 65,000 solicitors eligible, voted.[19] Solicitors, as a body, were at least partly to blame for the Law Society's position.

Many solicitors were torn between different conceptions of the Law Society's role. One view was that it should be a detached and authoritative professional body. Others thought it should be a campaigning organisation on behalf of members. The presidential polls suggested that many members favoured the Society being more of a 'trade union', a negotiator and lobbyist on behalf of solicitors. In 1989, a survey found that 32 per cent of solicitors thought that the Law Society was good at promoting the profession and 53 per cent that it was good at representing the profession. By 1997 only 8 per cent of solicitors in private practice felt that the Law Society promoted the profession to the public well and only 21 per cent that it effectively represented the views of the profession to decision-makers and Parliament.[20]

The issue that the polls revealed was the Law Society's irreconcilable roles. Some thought that the Law Society had become too strident. Solicitors were felt to have fallen in public esteem and many criticised the Law Society for this. The Law Society's reaction to the negative polls was to share the blame. A spokesperson for the Law Society said 'I fully accept that the Law Society must bat more strongly. Individual solicitors must do so too. The Law Society cannot single-handedly guard and promote the reputation of the profession'.[21] The problem, in part, was that the Law Society no longer had a cosy relationship of trust with government. It had to be more open in seeking its objectives.

The pressure on the Law Society to become more of a 'trade union' on behalf of solicitors was successful, but had negative consequences. One of its campaigns was against continuing cuts to legal aid. This was supported by expensive newspaper advertising implicitly critical of government policy. This was arguably within the scope of the Law Society's public role in defending the rule of law, although it could also be seen as promoting members' interests. The Lord Chancellor publicly rebuked the Law Society for 'scaremongering' on the legal aid issue.[22]

---

[16] *The Guardian* 11 April 1995.
[17] *The Independent* 11 September 1995.
[18] J Malpas, 'Mears' speech sparks uproar at conference' *The Lawyer* 10th October 1995, www.thelawyer.com/mears039-speech-sparks-uproar-at-conference/86036.article
[19] *The Times* 11 July 1995.
[20] 'Law Soc Damned by Members' (n 5).
[21] ibid.
[22] LCD press release, 'Lord Chancellor accuses Law Society of scaremongering' 23 April 1999.

The government moved quickly to control professions' use of funding for representative purposes. The Administration of Justice Act 1999 prevented use of monies raised from practising certificates for general purposes.[23] The measure appeared, at least to some parliamentarians, to reflect the government's irritation at the Law Society's campaign against legal aid cuts.[24] The Act was a precursor to the recommendations of the Clementi Review of legal services, launched a few years later, that the representative and regulatory roles of professions be exercised independently of each other. The resulting legislation, the LSA 2007, specified specific purposes for which monies raised by practising fees could be applied.[25]

The Law Society had reached a curious position. Its powers of self-regulation had been seriously curtailed. In relation to its remaining function, representation, the situation was ambiguous. On one hand, its ability to adequately represent diverse sectors of the solicitors' profession, particularly the international law firms, was doubted. On the other hand, it was the largest and most entrepreneurial legal services regulator. As such, it was potentially the dominant partner, if not the likely leader, in any prospective fusion of the solicitors' profession with the Bar and ILEX.[26]

IV. Development of the Codes of Conduct

In the early development of the legal professions the gathering of regulatory power was integral to governance of the profession generally. While memberships were led centrally they were controlled by evolving and centrally endorsed standards. These standards were eventually represented in codes of conduct devised by the governing bodies, latterly through expert committees. As extensive documents, however, codes are a fairly recent innovation.

The first formal code of ethics in the USA was adopted by the Alabama State Bar Association in 1887, which served as a model for the ABA's Canons of Professional Ethics in 1908.[27] The first code of conduct to claim that status in England and Wales is the Bar Code of Conduct 1981. The development of codes is only one example of the exercise of regulatory control of members described in the next chapter. The process is dealt with here because the development of the codes reflected on the

---

[23] Administration of Justice Act 1999, s 47.

[24] HC Deb 22 June 1999 vol 333 cols 1028–37; R Abel, *English Lawyers Between Market and State: The Politics of Professionalism* (Oxford, New York, Oxford University Press, 2003).

[25] LSA 2007, s 51(4).

[26] AM Francis, 'Out of Touch and out of Time: Lawyers, their Leaders and Collective Mobility within the Legal Profession' (2004) 24(3) *Legal Studies* 322; A Boon, J Flood and J Webb, 'Postmodern Professions?: The Fragmentation of Legal Education and the Legal Profession' (2005) 32(3) *Journal of Law and Society* 473.

[27] LR Patterson, 'On Analyzing the Law of Legal Ethics: An American Perspective' (1981) 16(1) *Israel Law Review* 28.

process of governance, but also because it became the public manifestation of regulatory power.

A. Solicitors' Codes of Conduct

i. The Solicitors' Practice Rules

The Law Society accepted powers to make regulations governing solicitors under the Solicitors Act 1933. The resulting rules, the Solicitors' Practice Rules 1936, were very brief, amounting to bans on touting, charging less than scale fees, sharing fees and entering agreements for referrals by claims farmers. The rules pre-empted regulation by the government in the wake a growing scandal surrounding the embezzlement of client funds by solicitors.[28] Accepting responsibility for standards enhanced the Law Society's credibility in the eyes of the government and improved its prospects of taking control of the infant legal aid scheme in 1949.[29]

After some changes and different versions, the Solicitors' Practice Rules 1990 were made under delegated powers conferred on the Law Society by the Solicitors Act 1974. The Practice Rules did not claim to constitute a complete code. They omitted any rules on confidentiality and conflict, a gap which was remedied only in 2005. They did, however, contain what have proved to be enduring core principles, set out in Practice Rule 1, as follows:

> A solicitor shall not do anything in the course of practising as a solicitor, or permit another person to do anything on his or her behalf, which compromises or impairs or is likely to compromise or impair any of the following:
> (a) the solicitor's independence or integrity;
> (b) a person's freedom to instruct a solicitor of his or her choice;
> (c) the solicitor's duty to act in the best interests of the client;
> (d) the good repute of the solicitor or of the solicitor's profession;
> (e) the solicitor's proper standard of work;
> (f) the solicitor's duty to the Court.[30]

The Law Society also made the Solicitors' Accounts Rules under their delegated powers. These were, and are, binding on practitioners.

Until 2007 the Law Society did not have a comprehensive and binding body of principles and rules and so might be said to have not had a code of conduct. The Solicitors' Conduct Rules 2007 repealed the Solicitors' Practice Rules from June 2007. They are still used as the basis for disciplinary charges against solicitors when offences occurred before 2007. The rules were also used as the basis of *The Guide to the Professional Conduct of Solicitors* which, until, 2007 provided something close to a code of conduct for solicitors.

---

[28] L Sheinman, 'Looking for Legal Ethics' (1997) 4 *International Journal of the Legal Profession* 139; C Maughan and J Webb, *Lawyering Skills and the Legal Process* (London, Butterworths, 1995) at 92, note 4.
[29] C Glasser, 'The Legal Profession in the 1990s: Images of Change' (1990) 10 *Legal Studies* 1.
[30] Solicitors' Practice Rules 1990, r 1.

ii. The Guide to the Professional Conduct of Solicitors

The Law Society's *A Guide to the Professional Conduct and Etiquette of Solicitors* was first published in 1960 and ran to eight editions. In later editions, the shorter title *The Guide to the Professional Conduct of Solicitors* (the Guide), was adopted. As a collection of rules, principles of conduct and regulation it grew with every edition. The Guide was a sometimes confusing amalgamation, as the Legal Services Ombudsman pointed out.[31] It described its principles as 'based on a common law ethical requirement'[32] but stated that they should not be 'confused with the requirements of the general law of contract or tort or ... criminal law'.[33] Of course, ethical considerations, broadly conceived, may form the basis of common law rules, but, in England and Wales at least, it is usually the other way round. Some of the non-statutory guidance was stated to be based on 'an interpretation of statutory rules'.[34]

Some of the content of the Guide had no legal status at all. Crawley and Bramall, who worked in the Professional Ethics Division of the Law Society, pleaded for a broad approach, arguing that '[t]he codes of conduct ... should not be treated as if they were tax statutes to be scrutinised for loopholes'.[35]

The Guide grew rapidly through later editions. The 1990 version contained 600 pages, whereas the 1999 edition was 860 pages. It never aspired to be a 'code' and was not capable of being fairly enforced. As the Law Society later acknowledged, the Guide had become 'a mix of mandatory and non-mandatory conduct requirements and best practice information which sometimes left the reader unable to identify the relevant regulatory obligations 'amongst a morass of material'.[36]

iii. The Solicitors' Code of Conduct 2007

In 1999 the Law Society set up a Regulation Review Working Party to make proposals for a comprehensive code of conduct for solicitors. The working party sought to comply with basic principles of rule-making, promulgated by the government's Better Regulation Task Force. These were that rules should be necessary, clear, fair, enforceable, proportionate, targeted and consistent. After extensive consultation the new rules were passed by the Law Society Council and submitted to the Lord Chancellor for the approval process. The Law Society was keen to stress that the rules were necessary, fair and enforceable.[37]

Approval was finally received at the end of 2006 and the rules came into force in July 2007 as the *Solicitors' Code of Conduct 2007* (the Code).[38] This was a legally

[31] Legal Services Ombudsman, *Annual Reports 1995* and *1996*.
[32] N Taylor (ed), *The Guide to the Professional Conduct of Solicitors*, 8th edn (London, The Law Society 1999) at para 1.03, note 3.
[33] ibid.
[34] ibid.
[35] A Crawley and C Brammall, 'Professional Rules, Codes and Principles Affecting Solicitors (or What has Professional Regulation to do with Ethics?)' in R Cranston (ed), *Legal Ethics and Professional Responsibility* (Oxford, Clarendon Press, 1995) 99, at 103.
[36] SRA, 'Introduction to the Solicitors' Code of Conduct 2007' at ix.
[37] See the Final Consultation, *Rules for the Twenty-First Century* (The Law Society, April 2004) at iii.
[38] SRA, *Solicitors' Code of Conduct 2007* (www.fassit.co.uk/pdf/solicitors-code-of-conduct-full.pdf).

binding code, delegated legislation in the form of Solicitors' Practice Rules made under powers contained in the Solicitors Act.[39] The Code was much shorter than the Guide and aimed to deal only with the fundamental principles governing practice as a solicitor. The rules did not replace the more detailed rules governing the organisation and management of solicitors' firms such as the Accounts, Investment Business or Incorporated Practice Rules. It did replace the 1990 Solicitors' Practice Rules and a range of specialist rules and codes.[40]

Whereas the Guide had grown to over 800 pages long by this point, the Code comprised slightly over 200 pages. The structure adopted in the Code began with a set of six 'core duties' intended as a statement of the basic ethical duties of solicitors. The core duties required solicitors to uphold the rule of law and administration of justice, act with integrity, not allow their independence to be compromised, act in the best interests of each client, provide a good standard of service to clients and not to behave in a way that is likely to diminish the trust the public places in you or the profession.

The core duties constituted Rule 1 and were binding. The working party had proposed 10 core duties, 'the ten commandments', but these were reduced to six somewhere along the prolonged approval process in the Department of Constitutional Affairs. The regulator was given power to waive many of the rules in individual circumstances, but not the core duties or the basic rules on conflict of interests or confidentiality.[41]

Deriving from the core duties were 25 sections setting out more detailed and binding practice rules. Attached to each rule was guidance which was not binding. However, as the introduction to the Code noted, 'Although the guidance is not mandatory, solicitors who do not follow the guidance may be required to demonstrate how they have nevertheless complied with the rule'. The guidance stated that a breach of a core duty could by itself constitute misconduct, but it is more likely that a breach would relate to one of the more detailed rules made under these 'over-arching principles'.

The effort of the Law Society to revise and enlarge the rules and principles of conduct was a welcome development. It involved consultation with the membership, and with sections of the profession on matters of drafting. This provided a benchmark for future efforts, which might have included more debate with the lay recipients of legal services. This could have made a significant contribution to the development of the professional ethics of lawyers, potentially increasing the legitimacy of self-regulation itself in the eyes of both the members of the Law Society and the public.

The relative brevity of the Code was a move towards encouraging solicitors to exercise their own discretion using the general ethical principles of core duties. Nevertheless, the Law Society published a Companion to the Code,[42] which aimed to help practitioners on issues covered in the Guide, but not in the Code. The Code was, after all, intended to be enforceable through disciplinary sanctions, an objective not

---

[39] Solicitors Act 1974, ss 31–34.

[40] Eg the Incorporated Practice Rules, the Overseas Practice Rules and the Solicitors' Anti-Discrimination Rules, the Employed Solicitors' Code, the Solicitors' Publicity Code and the Solicitors' Costs Information and Client Care Code.

[41] SRA, *Solicitors' Code of Conduct 2007*, rr 3.23, 4.06 and 22(2).

[42] P Camp, *Companion to the Solicitors' Code of Conduct 2007* (London, The Law Society, 2007).

generally a priority for those favouring ethical discretion.[43] It was, however, super-seded, following the LSA 2007, by a new code and a new approach to the regulation of solicitors.

B. Barristers' Codes of Conduct

i. Early Codes

The first attempt to publish a code of ethics for the Bar was in 1645 by John Cooke, the parliamentarian lawyer who prosecuted Charles I. This effort was doomed to obscurity with the restoration of Charles II and the execution of Cooke.[44] An 'etiquette' for the Bar was published in 1875,[45] but it did not prescribe standards and so did not have one of the essential features of a disciplinary code.

ii. Bar Code of Conduct 1981

The Royal Commission on Legal Services 1979 recommended that the Bar adopt written standards.[46] This resulted in publication of the *Code of Conduct for the Bar of England and Wales* (Bar Code of Conduct) in 1981. The eighth edition of the *Bar Code of Conduct* was published in 2004. The Bar Code of Conduct was not a statutory code, unlike the Solicitors' Code 2007, but was subject to the same approval process.[47] Insofar as the Bar Code replicates the common or statutory law, it is of course binding on both barristers and others.

The force of the Bar Code itself lay in the risk of disciplinary sanction. This could range from a small fine to being unable to practise at all, either because of a regulatory failure, for example a failure to acquire a valid practising certificate, or because of being struck off by the Disciplinary Tribunal for a major breach like a breach of confidentiality. Like the Law Society, the Bar Council had the power to waive any part of the Bar Code 'either conditionally or unconditionally'.[48]

The aim of the Bar Code of Conduct was to provide a basis for practice and also for enforcement of the rules by the appropriate disciplinary machinery. It was much shorter than the solicitors' code. This is not surprising since the Bar Code of Conduct arguably covers a less complicated range of activity. Barristers could not handle a client's business affairs, prepare for litigation or hold client money. Although not very long, the Code was rather wordy.

---

[43] For a survey of these approaches, see D Nicolson, 'Mapping Professional Ethics: The Form and Focus of the Codes' (1998) 1 *Legal Ethics* 51, at 66.

[44] G Robertson, *The Tyrannicide Brief* (London, Chatto & Windus, 2005).

[45] R Abel, *The Legal Profession in England and Wales* (Oxford, Basil Blackwell, 1988) at 133.

[46] Lord Chancellor's Department, *The Royal Commission on Legal Services Final Report* (Cmnd7648, 1979) (Benson Report) vol 1, at 310.

[47] Originally laid down in s 31 of the Courts and Legal Services Act 1990, as amended by the Access to Justice Act 1999 and now the LSA 2007.

[48] Bar Council, *Bar Code of Conduct 1981*, as amended, at para 108.

The Bar Code contained no overarching statement of the basic or core ethical principles. Part 1 of the Code stated that the general purpose of the Code is to provide requirements and rules and standards of conduct appropriate in the interests of justice and in particular:

> (a) in relation to self-employed barristers to provide common and enforceable rules and standards which require them: (i) to be completely independent in conduct and in professional standing as sole practitioners …; (ii) to act only as consultants instructed by solicitors and other approved persons (save where instructions can be properly dispensed with); (iii) to acknowledge a public obligation based on the paramount need for access to justice to act for any client in cases within their field of practice;

> (b) to make appropriate provision for employed barristers taking into account the fact that such barristers are employed to provide legal services to or on behalf of their employer.[49]

Part (iii) of paragraph (a) referred to the cab rank rule and barristers' obligation of neutrality. Paragraph (b) is, of course, a nod to the fact that employed barristers cannot comply with the cab rank rule. This was added following considerable debate within the Bar about whether employed barristers would be regulated by the Bar or subject to the Bar Code. In the event, the Bar adapted its code to recognise the position of employed barristers.

These general principles were augmented by Part III of the Bar Code which laid down some 'Fundamental Principles' for barristers. Barristers could not engage in conduct 'dishonest or otherwise discreditable to a barrister'. They could not do anything prejudicial to the administration of justice or that is 'likely to diminish public confidence in the legal profession or the administration of justice or otherwise bring the legal profession into disrepute'.[50] It was also stressed that the barrister had an overriding duty to the court and must not 'knowingly or recklessly mislead' it.

The details of the old Bar Code, like that of the old solicitors' rules and principles, then consisted of a mix of practising regulations with little if any ethical content and, such as those on confidentiality and conflict, those that did. For example Part III, after laying down the 'fundamental principles', went on to prescribe an odd mixture of duties and prohibitions ranging from the barrister's duty to the Legal Services Commission, the duty not to discriminate unlawfully, not to give or accept loans from clients or receive or handle money other than remuneration.

There were many annexes to the Bar Code dealing with detail of, for example, the barristers' contractual relationship with the solicitor, the direct access rules and the complaints procedure. Standards of Professional Work were dealt with in a separate section 3 added to the Code. This was not regarded as setting mandatory standards but was conceived of as advice. However failure to adhere to the advice could be cited in complaints or disciplinary proceedings. It was, in general, difficult to read and navigate the Bar Code and its Annexes and it was certainly not written in plain English or aimed at the lay reader.

---

[49] ibid, at para 104.
[50] ibid, at para 301.

V. The Clementi Proposals

In 2004, Sir David Clementi reported that the legal profession's governance structures were confusing.[51] He was particularly confused by the Bar. He thought that 'it would be hard for any reviewer to conclude that it is clear where regulatory authority, and hence responsibility, lies between the Bar Council and the Inns'.[52] Clementi also thought that professional organisation had advantages and was keen to preserve the legal profession's independence. He therefore recommended a 'half-way house' that retained professional organisation but provided for more independent regulation. First, he recommended that there should be 'an oversight regulator', taking over the role of the Lord Chancellor in approving of rules of conduct. Secondly, he recommended that professional regulation should operate independently of the professional bodies.

In 1996, on the issue of whether the Law Society should separate its representative and regulatory role, less than 30 per cent of the membership voted.[53] The Law Society finally made the move in January 2006 after a referendum of members. The referendum vote in favour of the Council's proposal was close. In favour were 7909, against 7175, a majority of only 734.[54] Around 123,000 solicitors were entitled to vote, so only 12.2 per cent did so. The Bar Standards Board was also established as an independent regulator of barristers in January 2006. The professions had therefore pre-empted the requirement for independent regulation recommended by Clementi. Nevertheless, in the LSA 2007, the government stuck with its decision to create a regulatory overseer of the legal professions.

VI. The Legal Services Act 2007 and Professional Governance: Oversight, Representation and Regulation

Although the LSA 2007 leaves the governance structures of the legal professional bodies intact, it fundamentally changes their powers of self-governance. The main change is in the self-regulatory capacity of the governing councils. These no longer have a direct responsibility for regulatory arrangements, which have been delegated to ancillary bodies. The governing councils of the professions have also been made

---

[51] D Clementi, *Review of the Regulatory Framework for Legal Services in England and Wales* (London, DCA, 2004) ch B, at para 23.
[52] ibid, ch B, at para 23.
[53] N Hilborne, 'Voters Reject Split Society' *Law Society Gazette* 16 October 1996, at 1.
[54] *Law Society Gazette* 15 September 2005, at 4.

answerable to the Legal Services Board (LSB).[55] The powers of the LSB impinge on the legal professions' former power in a number of ways.

VII. Oversight: The Legal Services Board

A. Constitution

The LSB consists of a chair appointed by the Lord Chancellor, a Chief Executive of the Board and at least seven, but not more than ten, other persons appointed by the Lord Chancellor.[56] The chair and a majority of members must be laypersons,[57] broadly defined so as to exclude people who are, or who ever have been, any kind of lawyer.[58] The Board may appoint staff and committees and delegate functions to either.[59]

B. Duties of the Legal Services Board

i. *Observing and Promoting the Regulatory Objectives*

The duty of the LSB is to promote the regulatory objectives. The eight regulatory objectives identified by the LSA 2007 are:

—— protecting and promoting the public interest;
—— supporting the constitutional principle of the rule of law;
—— improving access to justice;
—— protecting and promoting the interests of consumers of legal services;
—— promoting competition in the provision of legal services;
—— encouraging an independent, strong, diverse and effective legal profession;
—— increasing public understanding of the citizen's legal rights and duties;
—— promoting and maintaining adherence to the professional principles.[60]

The professional principles mentioned in the last statutory objective of the LSA 2007 require that persons authorised under the Act:

—— behave with independence and integrity;
—— maintain proper standards of work;
—— act in the best interests of their clients;

---

[55] LSA 2007, s 2.
[56] ibid, sch I, s 1(1).
[57] ibid, sch I, s 2(1).
[58] ibid, sch I, ss 2(4) and (5).
[59] ibid, sch I, ss 13–23.
[60] ibid, s 1(1).

—— act with independence in the interests of justice;
—— comply and observe their duty to the court when appearing as an advocate in court or conducting litigation; and
—— keep affairs of clients confidential.[61]

The regulatory objectives are somewhat contradictory. The elimination of professional distinctions in the pursuit of competition will undermine professional identity. Measures that are assumed to promote the interests of consumers, such as the authorisation of ABS, will drive many independent lawyers out of business. Therefore, the regulatory objectives can only sensibly be pursued by taking a balanced view with regard to the likely impact of decisions. Competition goals are likely to predominate unless there is a clear and unambiguous threat to other objectives and a demonstrable threat to the public interest.

C. Functions of the Legal Services Board

The LSA 2007 specifies a range of functions that the LSB must perform. In performing these functions it must keep in mind the regulatory objectives. The LSB aspires to base its pursuit of the objectives, and performance of the functions, on evidence. The LSB has produced and commissioned a range of research which it publishes on its website. The commitment to transparency is refreshing, even if research does not always support the claims made for it.

i. Exercising Regulatory Oversight

a. Making Rules

The LSB must make rules providing for the imposition of a levy on 'leviable bodies', which includes approved regulators, to cover the costs of the Board, the Office for Legal Complaints and the Lord Chancellor.[62]

b. Approving Rule Changes by Approved Regulators

The LSB must approve some changes to the rules of the Solicitors Disciplinary Tribunal (SDT).[63] It also has power to give directions to the SDT.[64]

c. Developing Standards

The LSB must assist in the maintenance and development of standards by approved regulators of persons authorised by them to carry reserved legal activities, and the education and training of persons so authorised.[65]

---

[61] ibid, s 1(3).
[62] ibid, ss 173(1) and (5).
[63] ibid, s 178.
[64] ibid, s 179.
[65] ibid, s 4.

d. Formulating Policy

The LSB has an explicit and implicit role in formulating policy for the operation of the legal services market. An example of the explicit responsibility of LSB is its statutory duty to prepare and issue statements of policy with respect to the exercise of its functions regarding performance targets and monitoring, directions to approved regulators, public censure, financial penalties, intervention directions, cancellation of the designation of a body as an approved regulator and the cancellation of a designation as a licensing authority.[66]

The LSB also has other specific responsibilities in relation to policy. It is only on the recommendation of the LSB,[67] for example, that the Lord Chancellor can make an order adding a legal activity[68] to the list of reserved legal activities; advocacy, conduct of litigation, work on reserved instruments, probate work, notarial work and administration of oaths.[69] Only the Lord Chancellor can remove a reserved activity from the list.[70]

The implicit role arises under the LSB's general remit to promote the regulatory objectives and to maintain and develop standards. Two bodies are recognised by the LSA 2007 as having a special role in influencing policy. They are the Consumer Panel and the Office of Fair Trading (OFT). The latter will be replaced by the Competition and Markets Authority (CMA) in April 2014, when it will take over the OFT's ancillary regulatory functions under the LSA 2007 and other legislation.[71] The LSB was required to establish a Consumer Panel to represent the interests of consumers.[72] The panel was to give a fair degree of representation to those using 'in connection with businesses carried on by them, services provided by persons who are authorised persons in relation to activities which are reserved legal activities'.[73] The LSB is bound to consider any representation made to it by the Consumer Panel and to give notice, with reasons, for disagreeing with any such representation.[74] The LSB can also request that the Consumer Panel carry out research for it, which the LSB must then consider.[75]

The CMA will report to the LSB any regulatory arrangement that it considers prevents, restricts or distorts competition to any significant extent.[76] The LSB must allow the relevant approved regulators 28 days to make representations on any such report. It must also inform the CMA of any action it proposes to take. If the CMA is not satisfied it can refer the matter to the Lord Chancellor Ultimately, the Lord Chancellor can direct the LSB to take action in respect of any matter raised in the LSB's report.[77]

---

[66] ibid, s 49(1).
[67] ibid, s 24(2).
[68] As defined by LSA 2007, s 12(3).
[69] ibid, s 12(1) and sch 2; see ch 4.
[70] ibid, s 26.
[71] Enterprise and Regulatory Reform Act 2014, Schedule 6.
[72] ibid, s 8(1).
[73] ibid, s 8(4).
[74] ibid, ss 10(1) and (2).
[75] ibid, s 11.
[76] ibid, s 57.
[77] ibid, s 61.

e. Giving Guidance

The Board has an important function in giving guidance:

(a) about the operation of this Act and of any order made under it;
(b) about the operation of any rules made by the Board under this Act;
(c) about any matter relating to the Board's functions;
(d) for the purpose of meeting the regulatory objectives;
(e) about the content of licensing rules;
(f) about any other matters about which it appears to the Board to be desirable to give guidance.[78]

The guidance may take any form and may be published generally. A recent example is a consultation containing draft guidance to regulators on education and training.[79]

f. Monitoring Approved Regulators

The LSA 2007 states that the LSB's 'principal role is the oversight of approved regulators'.[80] Therefore, most of the LSB's powers, as opposed to duties, are exercisable over approved regulators.

D. Powers of the Legal Services Board

The LSA 2007 gives the LSB specific powers. The most important powers relate to the oversight of approved regulators and the capacity to act as an approved regulator.

i. Obtaining Information from Approved Regulators

The LSB can require approved regulators to provide information or documents and summon a representative to attend to explain any information provided.[81]

ii. Sanctioning Approved Regulators

Where the act or omission of an approved regulator adversely impacts on regulatory objectives, the LSB may set performance targets for it, or direct it to set targets for itself.[82] These performance targets may come with conditions to which they must conform.[83]

---

[78] ibid, s 162(1).
[79] LSB, *Increasing Flexibility in Legal Education and Training: Consultation on Proposals for Draft Statutory Guidance to be Issued under Section 162 of the Legal Services Act 2013* (London, LSB, 2013). See further ch 6: 'Education'.
[80] LSA 2007, s 49(3).
[81] ibid, s 55.
[82] ibid, ss 31(1) and (2).
[83] ibid, s 3.

In more serious cases, the LSB may direct an approved regulator to mitigate any adverse impact on regulatory objectives or remedy or mitigate the effect of any breach of the requirements for separation of functions.[84] Such a direction is enforceable on application to the High Court.[85] If the LSB considers it appropriate, it can impose penalties, public censure, fines and intervene in the activities of an approved regulator.[86] Ultimately, it can recommend to the Lord Chancellor that the designation of an approved body be cancelled.[87]

iii. Acting as an Approved Regulator

The Lord Chancellor can designate the LSB an approved regulator of reserved activities where an approved regulator's designation is cancelled or a new legal activity becomes reserved.[88] The LSB can then carry out normal regulatory functions, such as making practice and conduct rules.[89] The LSB is also a licensing authority for licensed bodies, better known as Alternative Business Structures,[90] and can also designate approved regulators as licensing authorities in relation to one or more reserved legal activities.[91]

VIII. Representation: Approved Regulators

The LSA 2007 distinguishes between regulatory functions and representative functions of approved regulators.[92] Representative functions refer to the representation, or promotion, of the interests of persons regulated by the approved regulator. Regulatory functions refer to activity concerned with regulatory arrangements and making or altering those arrangements. This means, for example, that the approved regulator of solicitors is the Law Society, but any regulatory functions relating to solicitors must be carried out by its independent regulator, the Solicitors Regulatory Authority.

---

[84] ibid, ss 32(1) and (2).
[85] ibid, s 34.
[86] ibid, ss 35–43.
[87] ibid, s 45.
[88] ibid, ss 62 and 63.
[89] ibid, s 64(d).
[90] ibid, s 73
[91] ibid, s 74 and sch 10, pt 1.
[92] ibid, ss 27(1) and (2)

A. Solicitors

i. The Law Society

The representative functions of the Law Society are carried out by the Law Society through the Council of the Law Society and its boards and committees. Its everyday business is managed by a Chief Executive supported by a large secretariat including Directors of Communications, of Legal Policy and of Governmental Relations. These posts are primarily answerable to the Chief Executive, but all such employees are ultimately accountable to the Council of the Law Society.

a. Council of the Law Society

The policy of the Law Society is approved by a Council. The Council currently consists of 105 members, including five laypersons. The solicitor members are elected by the membership and most represent constituencies throughout England and Wales, along with some members representing specialist groups. There is a code of conduct for council members, which refers to the core principles of selflessness, integrity, account-ability, openness, honesty, leadership, equality and diversity and respect.[93] The code states that members are representatives of constituencies.[94] Their role, therefore, is to protect the interests of constituents and keep them informed.

The Council has powers granted under the Law Society's various charters. The original charter provided that the Council has responsibility for holding property, passing bye-laws and holding annual general meetings.[95] Supplemental charters added further powers. For example, a supplemental charter granted in 1954 conferred power for the Society to enter alliance with other societies in the British Commonwealth whose objects were analogous to those of the Society.[96]

The conduct of the Council is dictated by General Regulations[97] which can only be amended, suspended or revoked by the Council by a vote of two-thirds of the members present.[98] These provide that motions may be proposed by the chair, the Law Society boards, the Business and Oversight Board, the SRA Board and individual Council members.[99] The Council presides over a number of boards and committees, from which it receives reports and recommendations for policy.

b. Law Society Boards

The Law Society Council has a number of boards which act as committees of Council. They are the Business and Oversight Board, the Legal Affairs and Policy Board, the Management Board, the Membership Board, the Regulatory Affairs Board and the

[93] The Law Society, *Code of Conduct for Council Members* (London, The Law Society, April 2013).
[94] ibid, r 9.
[95] The 1845 Charter (n 7) at para XIII.
[96] The Supplemental Charter 1954 (n 10).
[97] The Law Society General Regulations 2013 (www.lawsociety.org.uk/about-us/our-constitution/).
[98] ibid, para 58.
[99] ibid, para 10(1).

Solicitors Regulation Authority Board.[100] The President, Vice President and Deputy Vice President are ex officio members of the Law Society boards. The Boards carry out functions of the Council as defined in their terms of reference[101] and can delegate these functions to sub-units or individuals. There are exceptions in relation to the SRA Board, which cannot delegate certain functions.[102]

In relation to the SRA Board, the Council retains power of approval of the amount proposed to be charged for practising certificates and as contributions to the compensation fund.[103] The General Regulations provide that the SRA Board shall comply with a direction by the Council, within the specified time, as to the exercise of any functions delegated to it if the Council considers it reasonably necessary in order to comply with, or avoid breaching, general rules or other legislative requirements imposed on the Society.[104]

c. Law Society Council Special Committees

The Law Society Council has a number of special committees. These are the Audit Committee, the Council Members' Conduct Committee, the Council Membership Committee, the Equality and Diversity Committee, the Remuneration Committee and the Scrutiny and Performance Review Committee. Except in narrow areas, the special committees are advisory only and generally exercise no delegated powers.[105]

The Council Members' Conduct Committee has the role of keeping under review, promoting and giving guidance on the Code of Conduct for Council Members and proposing amendments to Council. It also investigates and reports to the Council on complaints made about the conduct of Council members and non-Council members of boards. In doing so, it sits in panels of three or five of its members, as decided by the chair of the Committee.[106]

The Equality and Diversity Committee advises Council on diversity issues and monitoring progress towards the Society's commitment to eliminating discrimination in all its activities as a regulator and representative body. When the Committee makes a recommendation, the body to which it is directed must consider it and give reasons if it does not fully accept it.[107]

The Scrutiny and Performance Review Committee scrutinises decisions or action taken under delegated powers by the President or any of the Law Society boards and reports to the Council.[108] Decisions of the SRA Board and the Business and Oversight Board cannot, however, be reviewed under these general powers.

---

[100] ibid, para 15(1).
[101] ibid, para 16(1).
[102] See eg ibid, para 31(18) to make, amend and revoke rules, regulations and codes under any primary or secondary legislation relating to regulatory matters; para 31(20) to set and amend from time to time the level of fees and charges payable by any person or body in relation to the discharge of its functions; and para 31(21) regarding pay policy.
[103] ibid, paras 36 and 37.
[104] ibid, para 35.
[105] ibid, para 42.
[106] ibid, para 46.
[107] ibid, para 50.
[108] ibid, para 54(1).

B. Barristers

i. The General Council of the Bar

The representative body of barristers is the General Council of the Bar (known as the Bar Council). The Council was not set up by any statute, as was the Law Society, but its existence is recognised by statute.[109] Like the Law Society, the Bar Council has an administration and secretariat, headed by a Director of Representation and Policy, supporting the representative side.

a. General Council of the Bar (Bar Council) and the Inns of Court

The Constitution of the Bar Council provides that it is established to be the governing body of the Bar.[110] It is composed of a chair and officers, ex officio members such as the Attorney General, Solicitor General and Director of Public Prosecutions, and 102 'subscribers', elected and co-opted members, of which 39 from the self-employed Bar is the largest group.

The Annual General Meeting or an Extraordinary General Meeting of the Bar Council considers resolutions put forward by subscribers.[111] These meetings can only bind the executive or officers by a directive resolution.[112] Such action has to meet various conditions, including receiving two-thirds of the votes of those present.[113] The Council can delegate its power to committees, but the only committee identified by name is the General Management Committee.[114] This has delegated powers to carry out many of the actions provided for in the Constitution, such as conduct a ballot of the Bar.[115]

The functions of the General Management Committee are to implement general policy on all matters affecting the Bar, maintain the standards, honour and independence of the Bar, promote, preserve and improve the services and functions of the Bar and represent and act for the Bar generally, in its relations with others and in matters affecting the administration of justice.[116]

The Council's functions include formulating and implementing policies for regulation of all aspects of education and training for the Bar, considering all recommendations for changes to the Bar Training Regulations. However, the Constitution also provides for the creation of a Bar Standards Board to perform regulatory functions, under such constitution as the Bar Council shall from time to time decide.

---

[109] Courts and Legal Services Act 1990, s 31 (in relation to its power to make rules on rights of audience).
[110] Bar Council, *Introduction and Constitutions of the General Council of the Bar and of the General Council of the Inns of Court and of the Inns of Court and the Bar Educational Trust* (May 2011) (the Constitution) (www.barcouncil.org.uk/media/68152/bar_council_constitution_may_2011.pdf).
[111] Bar Council, Constitution, sch III, para 2.
[112] ibid, para 16.
[113] ibid, sch V.
[114] ibid, para 12(b).
[115] ibid, para 15(e).
[116] ibid, pt II.

b. The Inns of Court

The Bar's Constitution is interesting in that it explicitly preserves the separate positions of the Inns of Court while accommodating them collectively and individually. For example, the benchers of the Inns nominate 12 subscribers of the Bar Council.[117] The Constitution also requires the Bar Council to refer all matters affecting the assets or liabilities of the Inns, or that need to be implemented by the Inns, and to consider any observations and recommendations the Inns make.[118]

The Inns of Court also have a right to 'opt out' of the Bar Council. The introduction to the Constitution states that the Inns undertake to apply Bar Council policy, while acknowledging that they are not under any enforceable obligation in law to do so. This undertaking may be cancelled or amended on 12 months' notice.[119] The Constitution envisages that the reason for this would be that an Inn objects to a Bar Council policy. In that case the policy would not apply to it during the period of 12 months' notice.[120]

c. Council of the Inns of Court

The Council of the Inns of Court comprises the President, various ex officio members, including the chair and vice chair of the Bar Standards Board, and eight members of the Inns, two from each. The Council of the Inns of Court is the representative body of the Inns with power to bind them on any matter referred to them by the Bar Council or by an Inn.[121] It formulates the policies of the Inns, secures the implementation of Bar Council policy and appoints disciplinary tribunals.[122] The responsibility of the Inns Council to accept Bar Council policy is tightly defined. It may refer back general polices referred to it and, if it states that the policy is likely to be detrimental to the Inns or their members, can only be required to accept the policy when approved by two-thirds of the membership of the Bar Council.[123]

C. Others

The other approved regulators have similar arrangements to the main professions, although typically with a smaller management and employee base. For example, ILEX Professional Standards (IPS) regulates members of the Chartered Institute of Legal Executives (CILEx). It oversees the education, qualification and practice standards of Chartered Legal Executive lawyers and other CILEx members.

---

[117] ibid, pt II, para 2(b)iv.
[118] ibid, pt 2, para 4.
[119] ibid, pt 1.
[120] ibid, pt I, para 5.
[121] ibid, pt III, para 1.
[122] ibid, pt III.
[123] ibid, pt III, para 12.

IX. Regulation: Independent Regulatory Bodies

A. Regulatory Functions

The requirement of the LSA 2007 that regulatory functions are operated independently of representative bodies[124] led the professions to establish regulatory arms, for example, the Bar Standards Board (BSB), the Solicitors Regulatory Authority (SRA) and ILEX Professional Standards (IPS). Only if the regulatory and representative functions were adequately separated would the proposed Legal Services Board be able to approve the professions as frontline bodies exercising regulatory functions.

Regulatory functions are not defined by the LSA 2007. They are however implicit in the tasks an approved regulator has 'under or in relation to its regulatory arrangements, or in connection with the making or alteration of those arrangements'.[125] The section of the LSA 2007 setting out the regulatory arrangements of a body states that they need not be defined by any statute.[126] The section states that the regulatory arrangements of a body are:

a. its arrangements for authorising persons to carry on reserved legal activities;
b. its arrangements (if any) for authorising persons to provide immigration advice or immigration services;
c. its practice rules;
d. its conduct rules;
e. its disciplinary arrangements in relation to regulated persons (including its discipline rules);
f. its qualification regulations;
g. its indemnification arrangements;
h. its compensation arrangements;
i. any of its other rules or regulations (however they may be described), and any other arrangements, which apply to or in relation to regulated persons, other than those made for the purposes of any function the body has to represent or promote the interests of persons regulated by it; and
j. its licensing rules (if any), so far as not within paragraphs (a) to (i).

The Lord Chancellor can modify the functions of an approved regulator on the recommendation of the LSB.[127] Therefore, the regulatory functions of the approved regulators are largely defined by their regulatory objectives, their regulatory arrangements and by their powers under the LSA 2007.

---

[124] See LSA 2007, ss 27–31 and ch 5.
[125] ibid, s 27(1).
[126] ibid, s 21.
[127] ibid, s 69.

The LSB is required by the LSA 2007, section 30 to make rules to prevent the exercise of an approved regulator's regulatory functions being prejudiced by its representative functions. It must ensure that decisions relating to the exercise of an approved regulator's regulatory functions are taken independently from decisions relating to the exercise of its representative functions. The LSB sought to achieve this by creating Internal Governance Rules applicable to regulators.[128]

B. Regulatory Objectives

In discharging their regulatory functions, approved regulators are under a duty to promote, and act compatibly with, the same eight regulatory objectives as apply to the LSB.[129] Some of these regulatory objectives may be considered particularly relevant to the frontline regulator. They include protecting and promoting the interests of consumers of legal services, promoting competition in the provision of legal services and promoting and maintaining adherence to the professional principles. They must also have regard to principles under which regulatory activities should be transparent, accountable, proportionate, consistent and targeted only at cases in which action is needed. Approved regulators may, however, adopt any other principle appearing to represent the best regulatory practice.[130]

C. Regulatory Powers

The approved regulators can collect practising certificate fees approved by the LSB. The sums collected can only be applied for the permitted purposes. These include the regulation, accreditation, education and training of authorised persons or those wishing to become authorised persons, including maintaining and raising their professional standards and providing advice and support about practice management.[131]

Practising certificate fees can also be applied for activities that appear to cross the line between representation and regulation. These include participation in law reform, promotion of protection by law of human rights and fundamental freedoms and promotion of relations between the approved regulator and national bodies, governments or legal professions in other jurisdictions.[132]

---

[128] LSB, Internal Governance Rules 2009, as amended February 2014 (www.legalservicesboard.org.uk/Projects/pdf/internal_governance_rules%202009_final_km.pdf).
[129] LSA 2007, ss 2 and 8(2).
[130] ibid, s 28(3).
[131] ibid, s 51(4).
[132] ibid, ss 51(4) (c)–(f).

X. Regulatory Structures of Approved Regulators

A. The Solicitors Regulatory Authority

i. Executive

As noted in the previous section, the regulation of solicitors is the province of the Solicitors Regulatory Authority (SRA).[133] The SRA employs a Chief Executive, three executive directors, for Supervision, Authorisation, and Intelligence and Investigation, for Legal and Enforcement, and Post Enforcement and for Policy, Risk, Strategy, Communications, Standards and Researchand a Group Chief Operating Officer. Each executive directorate contains several teams dealing with constituent areas of activity. This large, professional organisation obviously enjoys a considerable degree of strategic and operational autonomy. Its work is overseen by the SRA Board, one of the boards subordinate to the Council of the Law Society.

ii. The SRA Board

a. Membership

The General Regulations of the Law Society provide that the chair of the SRA Board (SRB) shall not be a Council member, but may be either a solicitor or a lay person. There are then no fewer than six, and no more than eight, lay, non-Council members. There are no fewer than five, and no more than seven, solicitor non-Council members. All members are appointed by the Council following an open recruitment process taking into account guidelines issued by the Commissioner for Public Appointments.

The current regulations provide that the number of lay members of the SRB (including the chair if he or she is not a solicitor) shall always be one more than the number of solicitor-members (including the chair if he or she is a solicitor).[134]

These requirements were an early test of how the relationship between the LSB and professional bodies would work. There were originally nine solicitor and seven lay members of the SRB. In 2010 the LSB insisted that the Law Society achieve a lay majority, but the Law Society would only undertake to achieve this by 2013. In the event, after negotiations the LSB settled for parity.[135]

---

[133] So named from January 2007. Previously known as the Regulation Board.
[134] The Law Society General Regulations 2013, para 29.
[135] 'Law Society strikes deal with LSB to expand SRA board and produce solicitor/lay parity' *Legal Futures* 18 October 2010 (www.legalfutures.co.uk/regulation/solicitors/law-society-strikes-deal-with-lsb-to-expand-sra-board-and-produce-solicitorlay-parity).

The LSB recently published the result of a consultation on lay chairs. It concluded that

[a]fter five years of experience, it is our view that amending the Internal Governance Rules to require lay chairs [of regulators] is a wholly rational route to embedding and strengthening independence in legal services regulation. Further, we believe that additional restructuring of the appointments and reappointments process is needed as a proportionate route to secure that independence.[136]

b. Terms of Reference

The terms of reference of the SRB are defined by the Law Society's General Regulations in relation to regulated individuals and entities, including, for example, solicitors, licensed bodies and registered foreign lawyers.[137] In relation to such persons the SRA is able to exercise all powers and functions vested in the Law Society or the Council under the statutes defining its regulatory tasks, from the Solicitors Act 1974 onwards.[138] These include monitoring, regulatory, investigative, adjudication, disciplinary, intervention, enforcement, supervisory, admission, authorisation, licensing, civil litigation and cost recovery powers and functions.

The SRA's terms of reference include consenting to LSB recommendations on regulatory arrangements and making applications relating to the delegated regulatory functions. This does not include applications to regulate persons not presently regulated or to cease regulating persons or to changing the Society's position as an approved regulator. They also provide for the SRA to deal with all matters relating to the setting of standards for entry into the profession and the education and training of solicitors, including monitoring of training institutions and those providing authorised courses.[139]

c. Functions

The general functions of the SRA Board are defined in the General Regulations of the Law Society. They are to:

—— set the strategic objectives for the Society in its regulatory role, monitor performance against those objectives and prepare an operational plan and budget for presentation to the Business and Oversight Board;
—— take into account the recommendations of the Better Regulation Task Force in exercising its functions;
—— comply with such oversight and scrutiny arrangements as the Council shall lay down from time to time, following appropriate consultation with the Board;

---

[136] LSB Chairs of Regulatory Boards, *Summary of Responses to Consultation* (London, LSB, 2014) at para 2.
[137] The Law Society General Regulations 2013, paras 31(1) and (2).
[138] ibid, para 31(including Administration of Justice Act 1985, Courts and Legal Services Act 1990, Access to Justice Act 1999, LSA 2007, European Communities (Services of Lawyers) Order 1978 and European Communities (Lawyer's Practice) Regulations 2000).
[139] The Law Society General Regulations 2013, para 31(3).

—— ensure that the need to obtain value for money is recognised in all matters for which it is responsible;

—— ensure that the principles of equality and diversity are incorporated in every aspect of its work;

—— ensure that the principles of 'Turnbull' risk analysis are incorporated in every aspect of its work;

—— report to the Council when required by the Council to do so on the discharge of its functions, including (but without limitation) risk management and budgetary issues;

—— monitor expenditure against budget; and

—— monitor compliance with any external regulatory provisions or obligations which are applicable.[140]

d. Committees

The SRA presides over a range of committees reflecting the main areas of regulatory responsibility. These are Regulatory Risk, Education and Training, Finance and Resources and Standards. There are also two groups: Communications Group and Equality and Diversity Group.[141] Each committee and group has a remit defined by terms of reference.

The Standards Committee has the remit of advising and acting on behalf of the Board on matters concerning the development of an effective regulatory standards framework. It keeps the regulatory framework under review and reports to the Board, proposing changes where necessary. It has responsibility for supporting the development of the SRA Handbook and for the use of the Code of Conduct by the profession and the public.

The Regulatory Risk Committee has two broad areas within its remit: policy and quality assurance. In relation to policy, the committee advises the SRB on the delivery of risk-based and outcomes-focused regulation in Authorisation, Supervision and Enforcement activity. As part of this brief, it is required to keep under review thematic risks, co-ordinate investigations with potential public interest, strategic or systemic impact and strategic work on regulatory risk. In its quality assurance role, the Regulatory Risk Committee must implement operational arrangements to assure the quality of decision-making and the effectiveness, timeliness and proportionality of supervision and enforcement activity. It also advises the SRB on firm-based regulatory activity, including supervision, investigation and SDT and court proceedings.

---

[140] ibid, para 33.
[141] www.sra.org.uk/sra/how-we-work/board/committees.page.

B. The Bar Standards Board

Like the SRA, the BSB was created in anticipation of the changes to be brought forward in the LSA 2007. The Constitution of the Bar Standards Board emphasises that it is the regulatory arm of the Bar Council with no separate legal personality.[142] Staff in the BSB are organised into five departments: Professional Practice, Professional Conduct, Education and Training, Quality and Strategy and Communications.[143] The Heads of these departments report to the Director of the BSB. Most departments have between five and ten members. An exception is the Professional Conduct department which has around 30 staff. These are mainly involved in investigation of complaints and preparing cases against barristers who have breached the Code of Conduct.

i. Membership

The Board of the BSB comprises a chair, vice chair, five barrister members and eight lay members. The BSB Constitution commits the BSB to establish an appointments panel to make appointments and to act in accordance with the 'Nolan principles of public life' in making appointments to all its internal committees.[144] These principles are:

—— *Selflessness* – Holders of public office should act solely in terms of the public interest. They should not do so in order to gain financial or other benefits for themselves, their family or their friends.
—— *Integrity* – Holders of public office should not place themselves under any financial or other obligation to outside individuals or organisations that might seek to influence them in the performance of their official duties.
—— *Objectivity* – In carrying out public business, including making public appointments, awarding contracts, or recommending individuals for rewards and benefits, holders of public office should make choices on merit.
—— *Accountability* – Holders of public office are accountable for their decisions and actions to the public and must submit themselves to whatever scrutiny is appropriate to their office.
—— *Openness* – Holders of public office should be as open as possible about all the decisions and actions that they take. They should give reasons for their decisions and restrict information only when the wider public interest clearly demands.
—— *Honesty* – Holders of public office have a duty to declare any private interests relating to their public duties and to take steps to resolve any conflicts arising in a way that protects the public interest.
—— *Leadership* – Holders of public office should promote and support these principles by leadership and example.

---

[142] Constitution of the Bar Standards Board, as amended 12 November 2011, para 1 (www.barstandardsboard.org.uk/about-bar-standards-board/how-we-do-it/our-board/).
[143] ibid.
[144] ibid, para 12.

ii. Functions

The BSB is responsible for performing all regulatory functions and for determining what constitutes a regulatory function.[145] Regulatory functions are set out in its Constitution under paragraph 11, which outlines the duties of the BSB. They are to:

—— supervise and monitor the work and conduct of its committees, disciplinary tribunals and any other panels;

—— ensure that equal opportunity and diversity issues are taken into account in respect of regulatory functions;

—— liaise with the Bar Council, the Inns' Council, judges and other committees as appropriate;

—— prepare and keep under review a plan for the development and effective discharge of the regulatory functions of the Bar Council;

—— co-operate with the Bar Council over financial and other resources provided and comply with the relevant procedures and requirements of the Standing Orders of the Bar Council;

—— co-operate with the Bar Council in its monitoring of the BSB;

—— provide to the Bar Council all information and documents which it may reasonably request;

—— comply with reasonable requests for the chair of the Bar Council or his nominee to attend any BSB meetings; and

—— prepare an annual report to the Bar Council on its work for publication.[146]

iii. Powers of the BSB

The BSB's Constitution provides that it has power to do all things calculated to facilitate, or incidental or conducive to, to the performance of its functions or duties.[147] This includes regulating its own procedure, making rules and arrangements and establishing and regulating committees, sub-committees and panels. It can delegate any of its functions to any committee, sub-committee, panel, working party or other person or body. It can make representations to or be consulted by anyone appearing relevant to its functions. Finally, it can notify the LSB where it considers that its independence or effectiveness is being prejudiced.

iv. Committees

The BSB runs eight regulatory committees. These are Education and Training, Equality and Diversity, Governance, Risk and Audit, Planning, Resources and Performance, Professional Conduct, Qualifications, Quality Assurance and Assessment. The

---

[145] ibid, para 4.
[146] ibid, para 11.
[147] ibid, paras 13–15.

committees make recommendations to the BSB, sometimes in the form of detailed pieces of work for approval. Most of the committees are advised by a number of sub-committees covering different areas of their remit. For example, the Education and Training Committee has three sub-committees covering the Bar Vocational Course, Pupillage and Continuing Professional Development.

XI. Professional Bodies in the New Regulatory Framework

A. Control

i. Expertise

One of the fundamental tasks of professions is to articulate the membership's demands for autonomy in the way that they conduct their work. Some critics suggest that this is all that professional bodies achieve; that 'what is done is largely trivial or irrelevant, what needs to be done is left unaccomplished'.[148] One of the consequences of the separation of regulatory and representative functions is that it could lead to the separation of regulatory and subject expertise. At present, practitioner bodies, such as subject committees and the Law Society expert panels are on the representative side. SRA committees, meanwhile, are dominated by members with regulatory experience or commercial practice experience.

The regulatory body has expertise in regulation, while the representative side has practitioners with day to day practice expertise. It is the practitioners whose everyday experience of practice is the raw material that regulators need. Therefore, the mechanisms for gathering this expertise and translating it into regulatory standards need to be effective.

ii. Funding

The operating principle is that the revenue from compulsory charges on practitioners, such as practising certificate fees, should be used for regulating the profession, not for its political purposes. There are clear risks that some activity the Law Society may undertake, for example in relation to education, could be seen as regulatory activity.

---

[148] MD Bayles, *Professional Ethics*, 2nd edn (Belmont, CA, Wadsworth Publishing, 1989) at 8; JC Payne, 'The Weakness of Bar Associations' (1977) 2 *The Journal of the Legal Profession* 55.

iii. Regulation

The obvious impact of the new regulatory arrangements is on the breadth of control the Law Society and Bar Council exercise over regulation. The independent regulatory bodies operate under 'internal governance rules' made by the LSB. These rules set out requirements for ensuring that the exercise of regulatory functions and decisions made are taken independently of, and are not prejudiced by, the exercise of representative functions.[149] They must also establish communication between the approved regulator and the Consumer Panel that is unaffected by the representative function.[150]

The LSB is prohibited from interfering in the exercise of an approved regulator's representative functions, but can ensure that the approved regulator is not influenced by its representative body.[151] An opportunity to test this power arose in 2012. The Bar Council had spent many years preparing new standard terms of contract for instructing barristers. The BSB took over this work and subsequently sought approval for a new rule introducing the change. The rule change proposed that the cab rank rule, the obligation to accept work, would not apply where solicitors did not accept the new contract, or when they were on a list of defaulters on counsels' fees in other cases.

The LSB signalled two competition concerns with the rule changes to accommodate the new standard contract. The first concern was that restricting the application of the cab rank rule may interfere with the negotiation of brief fees. The second was whether a profession-wide measure against a law firm which was possibly in dispute with only one barrister, might be against consumer interests. The LSB then approved the rule change in July 2012, but expressed reservations about the process by which the rule had evolved.[152]

In June 2013 it was announced that the LSB was to investigate whether the BSB had allowed the Bar Council to compromise its independence by allowing it to influence its handling of the application.[153] In a report containing 50 pages of analysis and numerous appendices, the LSB reported on its investigation and considered what involvement the Bar Council had in drafting the document, whether there was an attempt to deceive the LSB about the role of the Bar Council and various other issues.[154]

The Bar Council admitted that, because the issue had been under consideration for many years before the requirement to separate regulation, it had provided advice to the BSB on the issue.[155] The LSB found that the Bar Council had 'enjoyed a substantial degree of autonomy over the drafting of the proposed changes'.[156] It concluded that, since the Bar Standards Board 'did not comply with the principle of regulatory

---

[149] LSA 2007, s 30.

[150] ibid, s 30(2).

[151] ibid, s 29.

[152] C Baksi, 'Warning over BSB's "cab rank" plans' *Law Society Gazette* 26 January 2012.

[153] J Hyde, 'Bar Council faces probe over cab rank "interference"' *Law Society Gazette* 5 June 2013.

[154] LSB, *Bar Council Investigation Report: Formal Investigation into the Bar Council's Involvement in the BSB Application to the LSB for Approval of Changes to the Code of Conduct in Relation to the 'Cab Rank Rule'* (www.legalservicesboard.org.uk/Projects/pdf/LSB_investigation_into_bar_council_influencing_of_the_BSB_%2825-11-13%29.pdf).

[155] ibid, at para 2.6.

[156] ibid, at para 2.15.

independence, we find that this failure had an adverse impact on protecting and promoting the public interest'.[157] This example provides an illustration of the sharp divide that must be maintained between representative and regulatory activity.

The professional bodies are now several steps removed from day to day control of regulation. The regulators are not allowed to use any expertise that they may have relating to the field of professional practice. The boards of the independent regulators oversee the operations of regulation by executives and set broad policy objectives. The role of the professional bodies is only to intervene if it appears that their regulatory arms will not meet statutory objectives. So, for example, despite the fact that the BSB is virtually an independent entity within the Bar Council, it is still the function of the Bar Council to change the practice rules.

B. Reconciliation

Increasing differentiation of the legal profession creates tensions between the so-called professional elites, whose interests tend to dominate professional bodies, and the bulk of the membership. There are increasing pressures for professional leaders to be made more accountable to the rank and file.[158] Inter-professional conflict is by no means new. Examples of these tensions have occurred throughout the history of the solicitors' branch. It may be that the separation of regulatory and representative functions will clarify these issues, and their implications for governance, for the legal profession.

C. Facilitation

While the representative side cannot actively participate in regulation, it can contribute in a number of ways to the development of professional standards. For example, it can monitor the expertise base and ensure that the regulator is aware of new developments, issues and problems. As a stakeholder, it can contribute to consultations. As a membership body it can complement regulatory activity. It can help members achieve and maintain competence, for example, by providing Continuing Professional Development and other supporting activity.

D. Participation

One of the key justifications of self-regulation is the 'ownership' of regulation that this engenders. Before the LSA 2007, the Law Society and Bar Council had very similar basic structures, including committee and management networks. The operation of committees depended on a large amount of time contributed by members of the

---

[157] ibid, at para 3.8.
[158] R Owen, 'The Governance of the Bar: Constitutional Reform' *Counsel* May/June 1997, at 3.

professional bodies. One issue is whether the new governance arrangements will gain participation from ordinary members. The downgrading of the professional bodies' impact on regulatory issues may negatively affect legal professionals' perception that devoting time to professional and public service type activity is a good use of their time.

There were mixed reactions to the new regulatory arrangements. Over 70 per cent of solicitors apparently believed that the LSB would have too much power over the profession.[159] Activity on behalf of professional bodies may therefore have been devalued. There may also have been fewer opportunities for participation for junior members of the professions. Lay membership, and lay majorities, for regulatory committees reduced scope for practitioner participation. Meritocratic selection procedures favour the appointment of experienced and senior members of the professions to the remaining practitioner places on committees.

E. Representation

One of the primary functions of professional bodies under the new regulatory regime is representation of members' interests. They can still seek to be joined as parties in court proceedings in matters affecting the profession. In this way they are able to make an impact on judicial decisions affecting their members' work. Now they have been shorn of powers of regulation, their powers of influence may also have suffered. In addition to their loss of authority, the loss of regulatory power also curtails the power to control directly reputational threat.

There are various examples of how regulatory power can be used to protect reputation. One occurred in the case of the solicitor who represented multi-murderer Frederick West. He proposed to write a book on his client's case. The Law Society, which was then in control of complaints, took the issue up and instituted disciplinary proceedings for breach of confidentiality. Another example occurred in relation to a proposed takeover of the Cooperative Wholesale Society. Here, it was alleged that the solicitors for a predator investor had acted on the basis of documents they knew were confidential and stolen.[160] Opportunities for the Law Society to make decisive interventions of these kinds have obviously diminished.

Before the LSA 2007, the professional bodies had developed their own research capability and become more 'conscious of the need to justify their policies publicly and to demonstrate how the public and professional interest may be reconciled'.[161] It continues to be part of the representative function to anticipate and to deal with reputational threats to the profession. It is unfortunate if the profession always seems to be responding to crises highlighted by others, rather than being proactive. The membership may, however, be less convinced that research activity is beneficial, particularly when it sometimes casts the professions in a negative light.

---

[159] *New Law Journal* 1 September 2006.
[160] See *The Lawyer* 6 May 1997.
[161] M Burrage, 'From a Gentleman's to a Public Profession' (1996) 3(1–2) *International Journal of the Legal Profession* 45, at 75.

XII. The Future of Professional Bodies

It is currently unclear where the experiment with regulation of the legal professions will end. Under current arrangements, the significance of professional bodies has been reduced to a largely representative role. This could be seen as a transition to a framework where a single regulator regulates lawyers directly, according to the activities they undertake rather than the profession in which they qualified. This might well produce different kinds of representative body, which may, or may not, look like the current professional bodies.

The future of the professional bodies may depend therefore, not only on what happens in the market for legal services, but on how they react to the changing in their circumstances. Professions will need to work harder and be more effective in advocating their own value to society. They will need to build the structures and mechanisms that can help them achieve this. In effect they need to create a new role in the limited space left to them by the LSA 2007.

XIII. Conclusion

During the nineteenth century the governance of the legal professions became increasingly centralised. The Law Society built a broad-based membership and managed to centralise power around its London base. In the case of the Bar, power shifted from the Inns to the Bar Council. Both institutions governed diverse professions using regulatory power as a means of imposing coherent ideologies on diverse memberships. The Solicitors Regulation Authority and Bar Standards Board now wield the considerable regulatory powers formerly used by the professions. Professional bodies now have the difficult task of carving out a meaningful role as representatives of their members.

The Legal Services Act 2007 reduced the regulatory power of professional bodies, largely confining professional bodies to representative tasks. Both the Bar Council and the Law Society have extremely diverse memberships. Within each there are powerful sectional interests, rendering representation a difficult task. As Burrage predicted, increasing diversity in the professions, and extreme differences in the status and circumstances of members, may well exacerbate problems of governance.[162]

Now that they are confined to a representative role, professional bodies face a stark choice. They may seek a traditional role, as authoritative voice for the occupation, or act more like a trade union, trying to improve the circumstances of less favoured sections of the membership. It is difficult for one body to perform both roles. Choosing either at the expense of the other is likely to leave a large part of the membership disaffected.

---

[162] ibid, at 73.

6

Education

'I always was of opinion that the placing a youth to study with an attorney was rather a prejudice than a help. We are all too apt by shifting on them our business, to encroach on that time which should be devoted to their studies. The only help a youth wants is to be directed what books to read, and in what order to read them'.[1]

I. Introduction

From the point of view of potential members, professions seem to offer unusually stable and orderly career paths.[2] The dual promise of education and rewarding work life provides an opportunity to transcend a mundane existence. As Larson observes, '[e]ducation, intelligence, persistent effort and social usefulness appear to grant professionals dignity and the possibility of full human development'.[3] In the sociology of professions, the legitimacy of monopoly requires that the opportunity to acquire professional competence and qualification is open to all.[4]

Until recent times, professional ethics had no part in legal education and training in England and Wales, even at the vocational stage. Its exclusion from the initial stage results in part from the historical relationship between the main stakeholders. Pressure has been growing for some time for a different legal education curriculum, and for a role for professional ethics within it. The latest in a long line of reports on the issue, prepared as part of the recent Legal Education and Training Review, leaves open whether and how this will be achieved.

---

[1] T Jefferson, Letter to Thomas Turpin, 5 February 1769, in *Papers of Thomas Jefferson* 1(24) (JP Boyd (ed), Princeton, Princeton University Press, 1950).
[2] MS Larson, *The Rise of Professionalism: Monopolies of Competence and Sheltered Markets* (New Jersey, Transaction Publishers, 2013) at 229.
[3] ibid, at 242.
[4] ibid, at 51.

II. Historical Context

A. Origins of Legal Education

For historical reasons the English legal profession has considerable authority in relation to the law curriculum.[5] Whereas, on the European continent, the universities created the modern law, in England it was created by the judiciary and the profession in the Inns of Court.[6] The medieval Bar required attendance at lectures and debates led by senior practitioners, participation in moots as a part of the dining tradition and taking notes in court as a condition of call.[7]

The fifteenth-century Inns of Court were collegiate, with conditions of life similar to those of modern Oxford or Cambridge universities. The Inns attracted many students who did not intend to practise. Holdsworth identified training to be a barrister as both a superb technical training in law and a social and moral education.[8] While subsequent periods of decline led to criticisms of low standards and unqualified practice, the Bar maintained control over education and training until modern times.

B. The Vocational Stage

i. Controlling Entry to the Legal Professions

In the nineteenth century the profession began to use educational requirements, particularly examinations, to control entry. The Law Society instituted examinations in 1836 to control unqualified practice. The Solicitors Act 1860 introduced a three-tier examination at the beginning, middle and end of articles. The preliminary examination included Latin. Formal training for the Bar began in 1852 when the Inns of Court standardised training by creating the Council of Legal Education but examinations were introduced in 1872. Passing an examination became compulsory in 1872 but the process leading to it was haphazard.[9]

Firm 'vocational stage' requirements developed in the twentieth century. By 1925 the Inns of Court School of Law (ICSL) was responsible for preparation for the Bar, under the Council of Legal Education. Full-time staff were not appointed until 1968. The Law Society acquired the private law tutors Gibson and Weldon in 1961

---

[5] See further A Boon and J Webb, 'Legal Education and Training in England and Wales: Back to the Future?' (2008) 58(1) *Journal of Legal Education* 79.
[6] B Hepple, 'The Renewal of the Liberal Law Degree' (1996) 55 *Cambridge Law Journal* 470.
[7] R Pound, *The Lawyer from Antiquity to Modern Times: With Particular Reference to the Development of Bar Associations in the United States* (St Paul, Minn, West Publishing, 1953) at 90.
[8] W Holdsworth, *A History of English Law*, vol II (London, Methuen and Co, 1924) at 509–10.
[9] E Cruikshank, 'Building a Profession' 100 (25) *Law Society's Gazette* 32.

and established the College of Law.[10] Students had to pass examinations in order to proceed to articles of clerkship. The Law Society offered both five-year articled clerks and university law graduates a course at the College ending in the examinations.

The use of educational requirements to control entry to the legal profession was often blatantly discriminatory. This is demonstrated by the efforts to ensure that women did not qualify as lawyers. In 1903, the Benchers of Gray's Inn refused to admit Bertha Cave as a law student. In 1913, the Court of Appeal held that the Law Society could refuse to register four female graduates for its examinations. In doing so the court cited medieval authority 'that the law will not suffer women to be attorneys, nor infants nor serfs'. [11]

After the First World War the Law Society revised its view. It supported the Sex Disqualification (Removal) Act 1919, following which a trickle of women entered the legal profession. Helena Normanton began practice as the first woman barrister and Carrie Morrison qualified as the first woman solicitor in 1922.[12] Numbers of women increased from the 1960s onwards. In the 1990s, women became a majority of law graduates and, gradually, the majority of those in training contracts.

ii. The Vocational Courses

The Bar and Law Society have historically prescribed different vocational courses for aspiring practitioners. By the 1970s all intending solicitors, students from university or those completing four-year articles, had to pass professional examinations. These were divided into Part I, to be taken by for non-graduates, and Part II to be taken by both graduates and non-graduates. Vocational preparation for professions generally seeks a balance between 'scientific knowledge' ('knowing that') with client interaction skills ('knowing how').[13] The early vocational courses were bastions of 'knowing that'. The nature of vocational education changed as the universities came to play a greater role in legal education and training.

Until the 1990s, the vocational courses adopted a similar doctrinal approach to degree courses. Different subjects were introduced such as Company Law for solicitors and Evidence for barristers, but often university subjects were repeated. From 1969 the Bar course was remodelled[14] and the Law Society Finals (LSF) course was made more practical in 1982. They still provided somewhat dubious preparation for practice. The 1982 LSF was based on preparation for the typical firm, a 'four partner firm in Oldham' but, by 1992, 70 per cent of trainees worked in large firms dealing with commercial law.[15] Neither of the vocational courses, at this stage, paid much

---

[10] E Cruikshank, 'Surviving Hard Times' 100(32) *Law Society Gazette* 29 August 2003, at 22.

[11] *Bebb v Law Society* [1914] 1 Ch 286; and see R Auchmuty, 'Whatever Happened to Miss Bebb? Bebb v The Law Society and Women's Legal History' (2011) 31(2) *Legal Studies* 175.

[12] Cruikshank, 'Building a Profession' (n 9).

[13] RA Barnett, RA Becher and NM Cork, 'Models of Professional Preparation: Pharmacy, Nursing and Teacher Education' (1987) 12(1) *Studies in Higher Education* 51, at 61.

[14] V Johnston and J Shapland, *Developing Vocational Legal Training for the Bar* (University of Sheffield, Faculty of Law, 1990) at 42–47.

[15] A Sherr, 'Professional Legal Training' (1992) 20 *Journal of Law & Society* 163, at 164.

attention to ethics, although the US, Canada and Australia had already incorporated clinical or skills components in the education and training of lawyers.

The vocational courses adopted something like their current form with the introduction of the Bar Vocational Course (BVC) in 1989 and the Legal Practice Course (LPC) in 1993. The new vocational courses were influenced by developments in other common law countries and the early signs of a new emphasis on skills in universities. The new vocational courses had broad aims, aspiring to provide students with such knowledge, skills and attitudes to prepare them for pupillage and future practice.

The new Bar course would 'emphasise the importance of being able to practice in a culturally diverse society, communicate effectively with everyone involved in the legal process, and of recognising the role of other professionals and their expertise'.[16] The new vocational courses focused on 'transactions', requiring students to work through realistic, simulated legal processes, drafting paperwork, interviewing each other as clients and so on. They also aspired to 'inculcate a professional approach to work and to develop in students a respect for the principles of professional conduct'.[17]

The curriculum of the vocational courses was built around the 'legal skills, of drafting, research, advocacy, interviewing and negotiation' (the DRAIN skills). The knowledge components of the courses for solicitors' and barristers' courses overlapped. Both barristers and solicitors studied Civil and Criminal Litigation for example. The BVC focused on Civil and Criminal Litigation and Evidence while the LPC had Business Law and Practice, Litigation and Evidence, Conveyancing and Wills and Probate. Both had a third term of option subjects. Professional ethics was one of a few 'pervasive' subjects on both courses. This often meant that it did not command much teaching time.

Although the new vocational courses gained general approval, continuing complaints from practitioners about the defective knowledge of pupils and trainees[18] forced the professional bodies to reintroduce more substantive material, reducing time for practical work.[19] In the more frank analyses, both skills and ethics became increasingly marginal on the courses.[20] The LPC was revised in 2009 to implement changes recommended by the Law Society Training Framework Review. The Bar course was re-launched as the Bar Professional Training Course following the report of the Wood Working Group.[21] The changes made are considered below.

C. University Legal Education

In the mid-1800s a select committee urged the development of law in the universities. Identifiable law programmes combining philosophy, theory, practice and reform,

---

[16] General Council of the Bar Validation Steering Committee, *Application Procedure to be Validated to Offer the Bar Vocational Course: Course Specialisation Guidelines* (London, General Council of the Bar, 1995) at 3, para 1.1.

[17] ibid, at para 1.1(2)(6).

[18] S Nathanson, 'The Real Problem with the Legal Practice Course' *New Law Journal* 24 May 2002.

[19] EH Greenebaum, 'How Professionals (Including Legal Educators) "Treat" Their Clients' (1987) 37 *Journal of Legal Education* 554.

[20] H Brayne, 'LPC Skills Assessments—A Year's Experience' (1994) 28 *Law Teacher* 227.

[21] BSB, *Review of the Bar Vocational Course: Report of the Working Group* (London, BSB, 2008).

emerged at Oxford, Cambridge and London towards the end of the nineteenth century.[22] The 'University route' into practice was established in 1756 when the Bar introduced a two-year exemption from the qualification period for entrants with a university degree. The aim was to attract higher status entrants. The Law Society followed this lead in 1821. In the 1960s the 'University route' overtook five-year articles of clerkship as the most popular way to qualify as a solicitor. The profession then abandoned the five-year route, having accepted the recommendation of the Ormrod Report that the legal profession should be a graduate entry occupation.[23]

The context of legal education began to change with the 1960s expansion of higher education and the creation of the polytechnics in the 1970s. In 1938 there were around 1,500 students studying law at university. In 1970 there were 5,000.[24] Substantial numbers of qualified lawyers and practitioners were recruited as academics, stimulating adoption of a more practical perspective. It also made possible the growth of so-called 'clinical', or practical approaches. These included students being involved in real cases at university law clinics, Citizens' Advice Bureaux and the like.

III. Current Education and Training Requirements

By 1980, legal education comprised a law degree, a one-year vocational course for either solicitors or barristers and a period of training. This was two-year articles for solicitors or one-year pupillage for barristers. This is currently the basic framework for education and training.

A. The Partnership Model

Compulsory education and training for lawyers currently has four stages. These are Initial stage, the Vocational stage, the Training stage and Continuing Professional Development (CPD), which continues after qualification. The initial stage comprises a three-year full-time law degree or a non-law degree followed by a one-year 'conversion course', called a graduate diploma in law. Alternatively entrants can qualify as a fellow of the Institute of Legal Executives and then take the solicitors' vocational course. The vocational stage is a one-year full-time course, followed by a period of work-based learning under the guidance of an approved practitioner.[25]

---

[22] M Partington, 'Academic Lawyers and "Legal Practice" in Britain: A Preliminary Reappraisal' (1988) 15 *Journal of Law and Society* 374.

[23] The Hon Mr Justice Ormrod (chair), *Report of the Committee on Legal Education* (Cmnd 4595, 1971) (the Ormrod Report).

[24] PA Thomas and GM Mungham, 'English Legal Education: A Commentary on the Ormrod Report' (1972) 7(1) *Valparaiso Law Review* 87, at 89.

[25] See ch 16: 'Employment'.

The structure provides progression from theory to practice, dividing delivery phases between universities (the initial or academic stage) and practitioners (the vocational stage). This is known as the 'partnership model' of professional preparation.[26] The model envisages that one of three modes of learning, inquiry, instruction and performance, dominates each stage.[27] Inquiry is the province of the academy, instruction the province of the professional school and performance, including the development of skills in a practical context, that of the employer. This last stage comprises one year's pupillage for barristers and a two-year traineeship for solicitors. Only practising solicitors and barristers are also subject to CPD requirements

B. The Initial Stage

i. Law Degrees and Conversion Courses

The core of a law degree that qualifies a holder to progress to the vocational stage (a qualifying degree) was traditionally agreed between the professional bodies and the collective representation of the University Law Schools. In its earlier incarnations it was known as the 'joint announcement' and described the outcomes achieved and material covered in undergraduate degrees.[28] Only students successfully passing a qualifying degree could enrol on a vocational course. The current version, a joint statement, describes the kinds of knowledge and general transferable skills required.[29] It also lists the core curriculum, the 'Seven Foundations of Legal Knowledge', which must be passed.

The Seven Foundations fill approximately one half of a three year degree. The subjects are contracts, torts, crime, land law, equity and trusts, public law and European law. European law was added in 1995 in recognition of its importance in shaping domestic law. Otherwise, the core is extremely difficult to change because of the diverse interests involved. The balance of degree courses is typically made up of locally prescribed core courses, such as legal method, and optional subjects. Graduate Diploma students squeeze the core subject matter of a law degree into one academic year.

ii. Non-degree Routes

There are two routes to qualifying as a solicitor through the CILEx fellowship route and the CILEx membership route. Both begin with exams set and authorised by the CILEx. These are taken while working under the supervision of a solicitor or CILEx Fellow. At this point, CILEx students join Law and GDL graduates taking an LPC

---

[26] Barnett, Becher and Cork, 'Models of Professional Preparation' (n 13).

[27] CO Houle, *Continuing Learning in the Professions* (London, Jossey-Bass Publishers, 1980).

[28] Law Society and the Council of Legal Education, 'Announcement on Qualifying Law Degrees' (January 1995) at 6.

[29] SRA, *Joint Statement on the Academic Stage of Training* (September 2002) sch 1. (www.sra.org.uk/students/academic-stage-joint-statement-bsb-law-society.page#schedule-1).

and training contract. The Legal Education and Training Review, which reported in 2013, recommended that more formal apprenticeship routes be available. These will provide alternative career paths into law for 16-year-olds, initially through a para-legal route.

C. The Vocational Stage

i. Legal Practice Course

The LPC is currently divided into two stages.[30] Stage 1 covers the essential practice areas of Business Law and Practice, Property Law and Practice, and Litigation, Professional Conduct and Regulation, Taxation, and Wills and Administration of Estates. Stage 2 is made up of three vocational electives and, having passed Stage 1, students can delay taking it if they wish. Providers are authorised to offer Stage 1, Stage 2 or both. The so-called 'legal skills', Practical Legal Research, Writing, Drafting, Interviewing and Advising, and Advocacy, must be demonstrated in both parts of the course.

The course is currently defined by the outcomes students are expected to achieve. These include researching and applying knowledge of the law, identifying clients' objectives and different means of achieving those objectives in the light of financial, commercial and personal priorities and constraints and the costs, benefits and risks involved in transactions or courses of action. They are required to understand the key ethical requirements contained in the SRA Principles of Regulation and Code of Conduct, understand where these may impact and be able to apply them in context. They must also reflect on their learning and identify their learning needs.

On completion of Stage 1, students should be able to identify and act in accordance with the core duties of professional conduct and professional ethics which are relevant to the course. The relevant area, Professional Conduct and Regulation, comprises Outcomes-Focused Regulation and the 10 principles of the Code of Conduct, Money Laundering, Financial Services and Solicitors' Accounts. Providers are expected to demonstrate that at least 8 per cent of students' notional learning hours relate to Professional Conduct and Regulation. Notional learning hours include all the hours a student may expect to devote to a course. A degree year comprises 1000 such hours, the LPC 1400.

Providers are given flexibility in assessment subject to some requirements.[31] For example, Business Law and Practice, Property Law and Practice and Litigation must all be assessed by a practice assessment lasting a minimum of three hours. Professional Conduct and Regulation must be assessed by a discrete assessment lasting for a minimum of two hours. It must also be assessed within each of the three core practice assessments, with at least 5 per cent of the marks required to be allocated to Professional Conduct and Regulation. The marks for these assessments are not

---

[30] SRA, *Legal Practice Course Outcomes 2011* (www.sra.org.uk/students/lpc.page).
[31] SRA, *Information for providers of Legal Practice Courses* (May 2012) (www.sra.org.uk/students/lpc.page).

aggregated. Students must pass the discrete assessment in Professional Conduct and Regulation in order to pass the subject.

ii. Bar Professional Training Course

The current course for intending barristers is the Bar Professional Training Course. This introduces students to the core skills labelled Case Work, Legal Research, General Written Skills, Opinion-writing, Interpersonal Skills, Conference Skills (interviewing clients), Resolution of Disputes Out of Court and Advocacy. These are often taught in the context of the main areas of knowledge: Civil Litigation and Remedies, Criminal Litigation and Sentencing, Evidence and Professional Ethics together with two optional subjects.

Students sit online tests in Civil Litigation, Evidence and Remedies, Criminal Litigation, Evidence and Sentencing and Professional Ethics. These are set by a Central Examinations Board composed of experienced legal practitioners and academics appointed by the BSB. The tests comprise a short answer questions (SAQ) section and a multiple choice question (MCQ) section.

D. The Training Stage

The training stage is a required component of the qualification regime. It has always occupied a place between education and employment. At various points it has contained explicit educational or training requirements, but, generally, inclusion of these in the training stage is minimal. It is seen more as a process of learning by observing experienced practitioners and 'learning by doing' with their guidance. Both branches allow trainees to undertake work for payment. Since the 1970s, it was common for trainee solicitors to be salaried and for pupil barristers to receive fees when undertaking low level advocacy. The training stage is dealt with in more detail in chapter sixteen, 'Employment'.

IV. Reforming Legal Education and Training from an Ethical Viewpoint

A. A Critique of the Present System

The US, Australia, New Zealand and Canada all require professional ethics to be studied at undergraduate level. England and Wales is now one of the few leading jurisdictions not to make some material on ethics a central part of the qualification process. There has been some disquiet about this situation for some time. There are various arguments for having such a requirement. Student understanding of legal roles is a foundation for understanding law and the legal process. This then provides a basis for considering career options and opportunities. It is therefore arguable that the early teaching of legal ethics is itself an ethical responsibility on providers of legal education.[32]

i. The Socialising Role of Education and Training

There are three strands to criticism of the existing system from an ethical standpoint. The first is that the focus on rule-handling techniques produces lawyers who are merely 'narrow, uncritical technicians'.[33] This may have a generally negative on students' moral reasoning.[34] It shifts attitudes and values towards a conservative view of legal roles, away from idealism towards instrumentalism. This instils in law students the values of individualism, competitiveness, legalism and authoritarianism.[35] The result is that they are too willing to accept uncritically established power relationships and values.[36]

The second strand of the criticism of the undergraduate law curriculum is that it indoctrinates students into a neutral orientation, stripping them of passion and rendering legal study conservative and sterile.[37] Imbued with formality, neutrality and objectivity, students reject the personal, and hence, bias, passion and commitment.[38] This is consistent with the conclusion that the evolution of the case method in the nineteenth century mirrored the rule of law.[39] It suggests that legal education makes a good job of instilling neutrality. Many academics advocate that lawyers should not be encouraged to be morally neutral, but that is a different issue.

The third criticism of a doctrinally focused legal education is that students struggle to understand the practical impact or potential of law for lawyers, clients or society. Students often change career intentions during degree courses, away from public service type work towards better paid areas of work. The impact of legal education therefore has a negative impact on those with ambitions to help the socially disadvantaged. It is not clear that this is entirely to do with financial prospects.

There is some evidence that legal study undermines idealism. Schleef found that during their studies, US degree students, irrespective of gender, shifted from extreme

---

[32] A Boon, 'Ethics in Legal Education and Training: Four Reports, Three Jurisdictions and a Prospectus' (2002) 5(1) *Legal Ethics* 34.

[33] Thomas and Mungham, 'English Legal Education' (n 24) at 94–95.

[34] TF Willging and TG Dunn, 'The Moral Development of the Law Student: Theory and Data on Legal Education' (1982) 32 *Journal of Legal Education* 306.

[35] C C Stanley, Training for the Hierarchy? Reflections on the British Experience of Legal Education', (1988) 22(2–3) *The Law Teacher* 78; J Webb, 'Ethics for Lawyers or Ethics for Citizens? New Directions for Legal Education' (1998) 25 *Journal of Law and Society* 134.

[36] Stanley, ibid.

[37] AC Hutchinson 'Beyond Black-Letterism: Ethics in Law and Legal Education' (1999) 33 *Law Teacher* 301.

[38] P Goodrich, 'Law-Induced Anxiety: Legists, Anti-Lawyers and the Boredom of Legality' (2000) 9(1) *Social and Legal Studies* 143, at 151; and P Schlag, *The Enchantment of Reason* (Durham, NC, Duke University Press 1998) at 126.

[39] D Sugarman, '"A Hatred of Disorder": Legal Science, Liberalism and Imperialism' in P Fitzpatrick (ed), *Dangerous Supplements: Resistance and Renewal in Jurisprudence* (London, Pluto Press, 1991) 36.

self-interest or altruism towards a mid-point consensus.[40] So, for example, Hedegard found that, during legal education, career intentions drift away from legal aid, public service or government work.[41] A desire to 'help the poor' transforms into support for zealous advocacy and pro bono representation. This could be considered important in an occupation professing public service orientation.[42]

There is limited evidence that induction into the Anglo-American legal professions gives, as Glasser claimed, entrants a high sense of 'calling'.[43] A study of those training in legal aid firms found that many were candidates for jobs in higher paid fields.[44] They were, however, strongly motivated towards legal aid work. A later part of a Law Society longitudinal study suggested that many entrants retained a desire for 'meaningful' public service work.[45] This may be manifest as participation in *pro bono publico* and similar work. It may also resurface a little later in legal careers as a desire for a change in career direction.

Analyses of motivation are problematic, if only because we often do not understand ourselves. The reliability of evidence may depend on context. Much of the material is from the US and is based on snapshots of a single cohort or longitudinal studies of one institution. Hedegard's study, for example, is of the law school at Brigham Young University, a Mormon college, whereas Schleef's was a small-scale longitudinal study. The English research was either qualitative studies based on interviews[46] or quantitative work based on a single university cohort.[47]

What these various studies suggest, however, is that legal education does impact on lawyers' values. It is arguable that, this being the case, ethics education should be more planned, transparent and open. During the process it may be useful to explore student understandings of the legal profession and its ethics. At present, as a body students hold somewhat populist views. In a world-wide survey, over 70 per cent of students agreed that lawyers have a lot of prestige, and over 60 per cent agreed

---

40 D Schleef, 'Empty Ethics and Reasonable Responsibility: Vocabularies of Motive Among Law and Business Students' (1997) 22 *Law and Social Inquiry* 619; and see J Taber, MT Grant, MT Huser, RB Norman, JR Sutton, CC Wong, LE Parker and C Picard, 'Gender, Legal Education, and the Legal Profession: An Empirical Study of Stanford Law Students and Graduates' (1988) 40 *Stanford Law Review* 1209.

41 JM Hedegard, 'The Impact of Legal Education: an In-Depth Examination of Career-relevant Interests, Attitudes, and Personality Traits Among First-Year Law Students' (1979) 4 *American Bar Foundation Research Journal* 791, at 805. See also S Homer and L Schwartz, 'Admitted but Not Accepted: Outsiders Take an Inside Look at Law School' (1989–90) *Berkeley Women's Law Journal* 1, at 42; R Granfield, *Making Elite Lawyers* (New York, Routledge, 1992); HS Erlanger and DA Klegon, 'Socialisation Effects of Professional School: The Law School Experience and Student Orientations to Public Interest Concerns' (1976) 13 *Law and Society Review* 11.

42 Schleef, 'Empty Ethics and Reasonable Responsibility' (n 40).

43 C Glasser, "The Legal Profession in the 1990's: Images of Change" (1990) 10(1) *Legal Studies* 1.

44 S Bacquet, A Boon, L Webley and A Whyte, 'Making Legal Aid Solicitors?: The Training Contract Grant Scheme' in A Buck, P Pleasence and NJ Balmer (eds), *Reaching Further: Innovation, Access and Quality in Legal Services* (London, The Stationery Office, 2009).

45 A Boon, 'From Public Service to Service Industry: the Impact of Socialisation and Work on the Motivation and Values of Lawyers' (2005) 12(2) *International Journal of the Legal Profession* 193.

46 ibid.

47 A Sherr and J Webb, 'Law Students, the External Market, and Socialisation: Do We Make them Turn to the City?' (1980) 16(2) *Journal of Law and Society* 225.

that they deserved high incomes, while less than 30 per cent agreed that they were trustworthy or ethical.[48]

ii. The Core or Foundation Subjects

a. Relevance of the Existing Core

It is arguable whether, if the core of legal study were a blank slate, the current subjects would be chosen to fill it. Whether two property subjects, Equity and Land, or both Public and European Law, would make the cut is open to question. The continuing relevance of the core subjects is therefore a significant issue. Criticising the Ormrod Report, Thomas and Mungham spoke of the core subjects being 'embalmed... whereas the nature of the practitioners' work has so altered as to make the very idea of core courses questionable'.[49] Changes in the 40 years since Ormrod make this criticism even more relevant.

There are often suggestions for new core subjects, but little consensus on those that must be added. With the passage of years since Ormrod, universities have developed different approaches to studying Law. Allowing more flexibility regarding the core of legal study would allow institutions to respond to different student markets and encourage innovation. It may be advisable to abandon the idea of prescribed foundations altogether. Universities could be told that at least half of law degrees must contain law and that this must include a specified proportion of legal ethics. There are arguments for and against prescribing what that ethics core should comprise.

b. Ethics in the Core

The view that the undergraduate stage should cover system and professional ethics enjoys wide support, including from influential individuals and bodies. Bob Hepple, who chaired the ACLEC, believed that 'the teaching of professional ethics and conduct cannot simply be left until the vocational courses'.[50] At an Anglo-American conference on ethics in legal education Lord Justice Potter argued that the undergraduate curriculum must include the ethics of law and the ethics of practising lawyers.[51] The Law Society's Training Framework Review Group was warm to the proposition, but not prescriptive.

The case for including professional ethics in the core of the initial stage hinges on three propositions. The first is that the chances of inculcating professional values increase with the time devoted to them. The second is that the process should start at the earliest time possible. The third is that the degree is a particularly important stage in professional formation. This is because the start of legal education is when

---

[48] M Asimow, S Greenfield, G Jorge, S Machura, G Osborn, P Robson, C Sharp and R Sockloskie, 'Perceptions of Lawyers—a Transnational Study of Student Views on the Image of Law and Lawyers' (2005) 12 *International Journal of the Legal Profession* 407.

[49] Thomas and Mungham (n 24) at 94.

[50] B Hepple, 'The Renewal of the Liberal Law Degree' (1996) 55 *Cambridge Law Journal* 470, at 484.

[51] Potter LJ, 'The Role of Ethics in Legal Education' in *Legal Education in the United Kingdom and the United States in the New Millennium* (Chicago, IL, American Bar Association, 2000) 33, at 43.

the process of learning and socialisation is most intense and when students have the opportunity to consider issues at relative leisure.

The experience of prescribing 'pervasive' ethics for the vocational courses, in many ways similar to prescribing outcomes, is instructive. On professional courses, professional ethics became marginal. Delivery was idiosyncratic and often banal. Until the Bar introduced central tests of ethics, assessment typically involved the dispersal of marks throughout the course for spotting conduct issues in substantive subjects. Ethical issues were often confused with 'good practice'.[52] Outcomes were uncertain at best.

The first argument against making ethics a core subject is that it would be at odds with the notion of the liberal law degree and the university ethos of inquiry. Subjects related in any way to legal practice are symbols of 'vocationalism'.[53] The second argument is that teaching professional conduct would involve 'indoctrination' into prescribed values. This, it is sometimes suggested, is antithetical to the aims of a liberal degree.

B. Designing Legal Ethics Courses

Course design is a process of choosing teaching and learning methods and course materials to achieve a purpose. The content of an ethics curriculum therefore reflects the priorities and aims of those designing it. The curriculum will promote certain values, either explicitly or implicitly. Content may also reflect the teaching and learning methods the course employs.

i. Aims

There are different possible reasons for introducing ethics to degree students. Purposes dictate the aims of the course and the nature of the curriculum. For example, professions may aspire to increase the prevalence of ethical behaviour in legal practice, government may seek to promote entrepreneurial behaviour and consumers of legal services to promote an ethic of public service. Students, however, may simply need reassurance that they are entering an ethical profession.

a. Promoting Compliance

Education begins the process by which professionals internalise values. The initial part of the process must involve establishing the fundamental importance and legitimacy of the values that are promoted.[54] In modern society people no longer simply accept rules. They often need to understand their rational basis. Compliance is achieved

---

[52] A Sherr, 'Lawyers and Clients: The First Meeting' (1986) 49 *Modern Law Review* 323, at 324.

[53] J Webb, 'Inventing the Good: Prospectus for Clinical Education and the Teaching of Legal Ethics in England' (1996) 30(3) *The Law Teacher* 270, at 271 and fnn 4 and 6.

[54] T Parsons, 'The Law and Social Control' in WM Evan (ed), *The Sociology of Law: A Social-Structural Perspective* (New York, London, The Free Press, 1980) at 60.

because rational behaviour is absorbed as part of the individual's self-identity. Values are absorbed over a period of time and often directly affect behaviour. In one study, Economics students were told that self-interest is natural and immediately became markedly more selfish.[55]

b. Promoting Understanding of Role

The legal role is complex and demanding. Students absorb a sense of what the functions of the profession are and of their individual role from the start of their studies.[56] There is a very good chance that most students are well advanced in their legal careers before they understand the full potential and responsibility of lawyers' social role. There are competing arguments about when they should be exposed to more detailed analysis. It is arguable that the process should be more conscious and more explicit at a much earlier stage if it is to make a beneficial impact.

c. Promoting Ethical Decision-making

Rest argues that four distinct capacities need to be present in making ethical decisions.[57] These are *recognition* of ethical issues, *judgement* in identifying ethical actions, *motivation* to act accordingly and *character* to see the action through. The difficulty of imparting these capacities through education and training rises sequentially. Recognition and judgement are relatively easily addressed, while building motivation and character are more difficult.

Recognition of ethical issues is a standard educational outcome that can be developed by problem questions and simulated exercises.[58] Judgement can be built though the same process, by discussion and by analysis of choices. Motivation to behave ethically may flow from development of the previous two capacities. It could be developed by positive reinforcement, for example, the approval of peers and the support of the wider profession. It might also be enhanced by awareness of the importance of ethical action and by the wider environment.

The most difficult to develop of the four capacities of ethical decision-making identified by Rest, is character. Character describes a person's very nature. It includes various elements, attributes, traits and qualities, such as integrity and courage. These constitute the moral strength of an individual. These dispositions are obviously very deep rooted by the time legal education and training begins. It might be argued that character can only be marginally affected by the process.

---

[55] M Ridley, *The Origin of Virtue* (Harmondsworth, Penguin, 1996) at 260.

[56] JB Weinstein, 'On the Teaching of Legal Ethics' (1972) 72 *Columbia Law Review* 452.

[57] J Rest, 'Background: Theory and Research' in J Rest and D Narvaez (eds), *Moral Development in the Professions: Psychology and Applied Ethics* (Hilsdale, NJ & Hove, Lawrence Erlbaum Associates, 1994); and see J Webb, 'Ethics for Lawyers or Ethics for Citizens? New Directions for Legal Education' (1998) 28 *Journal of Law and Society* 134, at 290–92.

[58] N Fletcher, *Equality, Diversity and the Legal Practice Course: Research Study 49* (London, The Law Society, 2004) at 58–60.

d. Promoting Moral Agency

Many academics have argued that ethical legal practice requires more than simply following rules of conduct. Simon argues that practitioners must be trained to act as moral agents rather than simply to follow the professional code.[59] This is especially so when professional norms become advisory, as with the 'indicative behaviours' of Outcomes Focused Regulation, rather than mandatory, as with conduct rules.

It has been argued that developing moral agency would require novel educational regimes. One proposal for such regime is based on a 'communitarian' ethical model operating 'holistically'. Communitarian models build on concepts such as reflexivity to develop understanding of the perspectives of others through dialogue.[60] Their aim is a 'negotiated ethic' offering greater congruence between professional ethics and personally held values.[61]

e. Promoting Higher Standards

There are limits to what education and training can demonstrably achieve. It may be possible to reduce complaints, for example, by attempting to build empathy with clients or focusing attention on effective client care. This may not affect the rates of disciplinary offending, which may be unconnected to ethical awareness.[62] Arthurs showed that 80 per cent of serious disciplinary proceedings in Canada involve lawyers who have been qualified for 11 years or more.[63] This suggests that factors other than education and training are at play. This is, however, no reason not to try to influence future behaviour.

f. Promoting Relevant Values

The values of legal education, like the legal system, reflect wider political, economic and social values. This is reflected in Kronman's assertion that US legal education should be underpinned by the ultimate value of democratic individualism.[64] There are various ways that the values implicit in liberal democracies, such as the US and UK, can be classified. Barber characterised the US political system as the co-existence of three dispositions, anarchism, realism and minimalism. These dispositions reflect responses to the possibility of political conflict.[65] Anarchism denies conflict, realism represses conflict and minimalism tolerates conflict.

Barber's analysis provides a sketch of the relationship between dispositions, values, and institutions. Americans, he says, are

> anarchist in their values (privacy, liberty, individualism, property, rights); realists in their
> means (power, law, coercive mediation and sovereign adjudication) and minimalists in their

---

[59] W Simon, 'The Trouble with Legal Ethics' (1991) 41 *Journal of Legal Education* 65; W Simon, 'The Ideology of Advocacy: Procedural Justice and Professional Ethics' (1978) 29 *Wisconsin Law Review* 30.
[60] SG Kupfer, 'Authentic Legal Practices' (1996) 10(1) *Georgetown Journal of Legal Ethics* 33, at 62–67.
[61] ibid.
[62] Weinstein, 'On the Teaching of Legal Ethics' (n 56).
[63] S Arthurs, 'Discipline in the Legal Profession in Ontario' (1970) 70 *Osgoode Hall Law Journal* 235.
[64] A Kronman, *The Lost Lawyer* (Cambridge, MA, Belknap Press, 1993).
[65] BR Barber, *Strong Democracy: Participatory Politics for a New Age* (Berkeley, CA, University of California Press, 2003).

political temper (tolerance, wariness of government, pluralism, and such institutionalizations of caution as separation of powers and judicial review).[66]

To a large degree this assessment applies equally, although probably not in the same way, to the UK.

The values currently promoted by legal study in England and Wales are not formally articulated and may not be well understood. This position contrasts with that in the US. A report by the American Bar Association task force (The MacCrate Commission), proposed four key professional objectives for legal education in American universities.[67] The objectives were providing competent representation, promoting justice, fairness and morality, maintaining and improving the profession and taking personal responsibility for one's own professional development. These objectives are consistent with Kronman's notion of democratic individualism. Their vocational flavour is explained by the fact that US law degrees are postgraduate and students are therefore more committed to legal careers.

There are many other contenders for the values that legal education should promote. Cownie emphasises broader educational values, singling out the capacity for critical self-examination.[68] Webb proposes integrity, loyalty and respect for others.[69] In Australia, Evans and Palermo suggest personal values such as honesty, and moral values such as truth and justice.[70] Arguments for articulating values are numerous. It is arguable that, otherwise, hidden and potentially harmful values prevail. Specifying values makes it possible to devise an appropriate curriculum. This facilitates monitoring success in imparting values and adjustment of strategies if necessary.

g. Promoting Development of Professional Ethical Regimes

One potential aim of a legal ethics curriculum that is rarely promoted by stakeholders is that of increasing individuals' propensity to promote changes in professional norms. The proposition is that professional rule-making would benefit from an environment that encourages local discussion and reflective judgement rather than conformity.[71] This is arguably necessary if professional ethics are to reflect the everyday experience of practitioners.

Experience in the US suggests that effective participation in discussions of professional responsibility is encouraged by a broad programme of initial education. It could include exposure to practical experience supported by suitable instruction.[72]

---

[66] ibid, at 5.

[67] R MacCrate, 'Preparing Lawyers to Participate Effectively in the Legal Profession' (1994) 44 *Journal of Legal Education* 89.

[68] F Cownie, 'Alternative Visions in Legal Education' (2004) 6 *Legal Ethics* 159, at 174.

[69] Webb, 'Ethics for Lawyers or Ethics for Citizens?' (n 57) at 142–44.

[70] A Evans and J Palermo, 'Australian Law Students' Perceptions of their Values: Interim Results in the First Year—2001—of a Three-Year Empirical Assessment' (2002) 5 *Legal Ethics* 103.

[71] RW Gordon and WH Simon, 'The Redemption of Professionalism' in RL Nelson, DM Trubeck and RL Solomon (eds), *Lawyer's Ideals/Lawyer's Practices* (Ithaca and London, Cornell University Press, 1992) 230, at 236–40.

[72] RL Doyel, 'The Clinical Lawyer School: Has Jerome Frank Prevailed?' (1983) 18 *New England Law Review* 578, at 597.

Debate should embrace professional policy issues, like access to justice.[73] Such discussions might replicate an ideal professional community, implying 'integration, shared symbolic experience and self-regulating activities groups and institutions'.[74] Such an environment should be dedicated to achieving the individual pursuits of rationality, autonomy and a greater social good.

ii. Perspective

Brownsword, an early supporter of teaching ethics on degree courses,[75] highlighted a range of possible approaches.[76] These reflect different theoretical positions: legal idealist, intersectionist, contextualist and liberal. As discussed above, the liberal position predominates in British universities. The liberal legal education does not prepare for a specific vocation, but produces cultivated individuals with a deep understanding of law and a critical view of social institutions informed by ethical perspectives.

Legal idealists see law itself as a moral enterprise. Methods of legal and moral argumentation are therefore inevitably linked. The legal idealist would explore the moral dimension of law, even though teaching from a positivist base is inevitable. The intersectionist identifies instances where legal and moral issues intersect and the elasticity of legal argumentation in such circumstances. Contextualists view Law in the economic, social, political or ethical circumstances in which legal problems arise.

Brownsword argued that the contextual or liberal approach might see the role of lawyers in delivering legal services as an essential part of understanding Law. The idealist and intersectionist approaches are more consistent with exploring the moral dimensions of Law 'pervasively', rather than as a subject. None of the approaches necessarily provides for students whose interests are primarily vocational. On encountering this pervasive ethics, they might object that they chose to study law, not moral philosophy.[77]

Another problem of perspective is highlighted by Arthurs.[78] He identifies two main views on professional ethics as a discrete academic subject; from the 'inside out' or from the 'outside in'. The 'inside out' approach involves studying ethics codes to master the norms of professional practice. This, the approach normally taken on vocational courses, Arthurs describes as naive and superficial, often the first response to the demand for an ethics curriculum. This view is supported by Bundy, who

---

[73] C Menkel-Meadow, 'The Legacy of Clinical Education: Theories about Lawyering' (1980) 29 *Cleveland State Law Review* 555, at 573.

[74] P Selznick, 'The Idea of a Communitarian Morality' (1987) 75 *California Law Review* 445, at 449; R Cotterrell, *Law's Community: Legal Theory in Sociological Perspective* (Oxford, Clarendon Press, 1995) esp at 246 and 332–37.

[75] R Brownsword, 'Ethics in Legal Education: Ticks, Crosses and Question Marks' (1987) 50 *Modern Law Review* 529 and 'Where are all the Law Schools Going?' (1996) 30 *The Law Teacher* 1.

[76] R Brownsword, 'High Roads and Low Roads, Mazes and Motorways' (1999) 33 *The Law Teacher* 269.

[77] ibid, at 281–83.

[78] HW Arthurs, 'Why Canadian Law Schools Do Not Teach Ethics' in K Economides (ed), *Ethical Challenges to Legal Education and Conduct* (Oxford, Hart Publishing, 1998) at 105.

described the first wave of US ethics courses as 'legalistic, stressing the external rather than the internal regulation of lawyers'.[79]

Viewing professions from 'the outside in' is a better fit with academic Law. This involves a more critical approach. Arthurs' concern is that showing the profession's record, warts and all, may normalise or legitimise unethical behaviour in the minds of students. This argument seems dubious. It seems arguably necessary to anticipate and confront problems with ethics, as well as ethical problems, if one is to effectively socialise a profession.

The conundrum that Arthurs poses raises the issue of whether lawyers should be prepared so as to enter the world as it is, or be prepared in such a way that they can change it.[80] The 'inside out' perspective reflects 'replicative models' of teaching ethics. This involves learning what the codes say, an approach that cannot promote change. The 'outside in' approach should promote discussion of the notion that professionalism is a worthy tradition deserving support.[81] It should also provide the perspective, language and tools to change the existing order and produce professionals equipped to lead change. It can therefore be seen as a 'transformative model' of ethical education.[82]

iii. Content

Where professional bodies specify ethics requirements for degree courses they usually ensure that the main professional duties, like duties of confidentiality and conflicts of interest, are covered. To these are sometimes added detail reflecting local concerns. For example, in Canada, the requirement that students have 'an awareness of the importance of professionalism in dealing with clients, other counsel, judges, court staff and members of the public', appears to be a response to a specific problem.[83] Educational schemes can also be broader than simply specifying specific conduct rules and general behaviour. Canadian students, for example, are required to understand 'the importance and value of serving and promoting the public interest in the administration of justice'.[84]

Whatever minimal requirements for the study of ethics are imposed by professions, the content of the programme of study can be broadened to complement an 'outside in' perspective. Students could, for example, explore professions as intermediate bodies in civil society and empirical evidence of workplace studies. They may then better understand the impact of stress, competition, authority, peer and time pressures.[85] Relevant materials might include authoritative documents, legislation, cases

---

[79] S Bundy, 'Ethics Education in the First Year: An Experiment' (1995) 58 *Law and Contemporary Issues* 19, at 31.

[80] K Economides, 'Learning the Law of Lawyering' (1999) 52 *Current Legal Problems* 392, at 410.

[81] C Parker, *Just Lawyers* (Oxford, Oxford University Press, 1999) at 171.

[82] A Goldsmith and G Powles, 'Lawyers Behaving Badly: Where Now in Legal Education for Acting Responsibly in Australia' in Economides (ed), *Ethical Challenges* (n 78) at 119.

[83] Federation of Law Societies of Canada, *Task Force on the Canadian Common Law Degree: Final Report* (2009) (www.slaw.ca/wp-content/uploads/2009/10/Task-Force-Final-Report.pdf).

[84] ibid.

[85] DL Rhode, 'Ethics by the Pervasive Method' (1992) 42 *Journal of Legal Education* 31.

and codes, socio-legal scholarship, empirical studies of different practice fields and interdisciplinary scholarship.

iv. Teaching and Learning Methods

a. Discrete and Pervasive Teaching

The issue of how to deliver the ethics curriculum has been a topic of debate. In the US, discussion focused on whether professional ethics should be a discrete subject, taught separately in its own right, or a 'pervasive' topic taught throughout law degrees. The problem with the pervasive method is that the treatment of ethics is not weighty or developed enough to be taken seriously. As Rhode says, 'there is no place in which students and institutions confront in any probing and systematic way, the central ethical concepts, institutional and political understandings and regulatory alternatives that underline all areas of professional ethics and regulation'.[86] In short, the probability is that ethics is not dealt with properly anywhere, and possibly not at all.

The risk with legal ethics being a subject is that it takes one of two equally unpromising directions. The first direction features a kind of 'moralising' that is seen as irrelevant to technical law. The second becomes a case of learning rules, with limited assistance to ethical development. In extreme cases the rule-based courses can be a training in 'unethics ... the careful delineation of precisely how far the lawyer can go without disbarment, with copious suggestions on how to do things lawyers ought not to be doing'.[87]

Integrating the subject and pervasive approaches may help to address some of the weaknesses inherent in the different approaches. In this way, 'system ethics' can be dealt with pervasively and professional ethics taught as a subject. This strategy provides a platform of knowledge and understanding of ethical responsibilities, but may have little impact on improving students' ethical judgement.

b. Communities of Practice

In the past 10 years, economy, effectiveness and efficiency reasons have driven employers to foster learning environments in the workplace. One approach has been to form groups, sometimes called communities of practice. This term was originally coined to explain situated learning, or how newcomers to professional communities learned about the social structure of communities from the periphery.[88] It is often used to describe group learning within cognate professional areas.[89] Such schemes could very easily be integrated into law firm operations as a part of daily routine. One case study describes how a department in a law firm analysed Employment Tribunal

---

[86] ibid, at 32.

[87] Rhode, 'Ethics by the Pervasive Method' (n 85).

[88] J Lave and E Wenger, *Situated Learning: Legitimate Peripheral Participation* (Cambridge, Cambridge University Press, 1991).

[89] N Hara (ed), *Communities of Practice: Fostering Peer-to-Peer Learning and Knowledge Information Sharing in the Workplace* (Berlin, Springer, 2009).

decisions and applied them to ongoing cases.[90] It would not be difficult to envisage such a model incorporating analysis of ethical issues.

v. Achieving Diverse Aims

Some methods of teaching and learning may be more successful than others in achieving educational aims. Most aims depend on some systematic programme of learning about appropriate values. There are however, aims of ethical programmes that are more ambitious but which may be considered essential. Prominent among such aims are promoting ethical decision-making and the capacity to engage in ethical debate.

a. Promoting Appropriate Values

Values are often part of a 'hidden curriculum'. A simple example relates to sensitivity to the perspective of others. This is seen as a necessary prerequisite of ethical action and is part of the aspiration of the legal profession to promote equal opportunity. The way in which courses are delivered explicitly and implicitly promotes values that promote such goals, such as appreciation of diversity. Law Society longitudinal research found that good integration was important to the success of group work[91] but that, in some institutions, students from different ethnic backgrounds only worked with each other.[92] This suggests that action is often necessary to promote taken for granted values.

b. Promoting Ethical Decision-making

Aristotle proposed that the capacities required for ethical action, particularly motivation and character, are most successfully developed when deployed habitually in role. One way of providing this kind of experience is though clinical legal education, with students working with real clients from an early stage in their legal education. In this environment, every step 'can be the object of the most painstaking planning, reflection and review'.[93]

One of the advantages of teaching ethics though the medium of clinical education is the opportunity it provides to perform a real-life role under supervision. This facilitates discussion of the difficulties, dilemmas and temptations that arise in legal practice. Exposure to these problems may be more successful in an educational setting than the workplace, where outcomes are less certain. This depends on the availability of teachers familiar with both current practice and ethical issues to ensure that experience is put

[90] J Gold, R Thorpe, J Woodall and E Sadler-Smith, 'Continuing Professional Development in the Legal Profession' (2007) 38(2) *Management Learning* 235.

[91] Fletcher (n 58) at 58–60.

[92] ibid, at 61.

[93] M Meltsner and G Shrag, 'Scenes from a Clinic' (1978) 127(1) *University of Pennsylvania Law Review* 1; R Barnhiler, 'The Clinical Method of Legal Education: Its Theory and Implementation' (1979) 30 *Journal of Legal Education* 67.

to best use.[94] Clinical instructors sometimes pass on bad habits or cynical attitudes to professional responsibility.[95]

Schon argued that professional students cannot be taught about professional practice but can be coached, seeing for themselves the relationship between means, methods and results.[96] His notion of 'reflective practice' is predicated on one-to-one coaching, whereby professional learners are inducted into the ways of thinking of practitioners. Stimulating reflection of this kind can be difficult in an educational setting.[97] Kupfer provides an engaging account of her attempt to do so through the clinical programme in a US law school.[98] She describes how the case work of students often produces stimulating material for ethical reflection, enabling them to make 'self-determined, responsible, self-reflective and critical judgements about themselves and their work'.[99]

c. Capacity to Debate Ethical Issues

The capacity to debate ethical issues is an essential prerequisite of practitioner involvement in developing professional norms. Kupfer argues that ethics programmes should enable students to critically scrutinise ethical norms and to argue the merits of different perspectives. This arguably requires the 'holistic' development of the law student, linking students' individual experience and values to their developing skills and knowledge.[100]

vi. Location

There has been considerable debate about the location of legal ethics within the phases of education and training. The decision depends on a number of factors, including the aims to be achieved and the level of commitment to them. Different aims could be allocated to different phases of the process. There are also practical considerations, such as the amount of time and the level of resources available. It may not be feasible, for example, to insist on clinical work or the creation of

---

[94] P Brest, 'The Responsibility of Law Schools: Educating Lawyers as Counsellors and Problem Solving' (1995) 58 *Law and Contemporary Problems* 5.

[95] RJ Condlin, 'Clinical Education in the Seventies: An Appraisal of the Decade' (1983) 33 *Journal of Legal Education* 604.

[96] DA Schon, *Educating the Reflective Practitioner: Toward a New Design for Teaching and Learning in the Professions* (London, Jossey-Bass Publishers, 1987) at 17; DA Schon, *The Reflective Practitioner: How Professionals Think in Action* (New York, Basic Books, 1983); A Boon, 'Skills in the Initial Stage of Legal Education: Theory and Practice for Transformation' in J Webb and C Maughan (eds), *Teaching Lawyers' Skills*, London, Butterworths, 1996).

[97] D Boud and D Walker, 'Promoting Reflection in Professional Courses: the Challenge of Context' (1998) 23 *Studies in Higher Education* 191.

[98] Kupfer, 'Authentic Legal Practices' (n 60).

[99] ibid.

[100] A Boon, 'History is Past Politics: A Critique of the Legal Skills Movement in England and Wales' (1998) 25 *Journal of Law and Society* 151; J Webb, 'Developing Ethical Lawyers: Can Legal Education Enhance Access to Justice?' (1999) 33 *The Law Teacher* 284.

communities of practice in the initial stage. It is feasible, however, to expect university students to reject plagiarism and other academic offences.[101]

An effective scheme for achieving the various aims of education and training in ethics should provide a continuum.[102] This would be a sequence of educational steps involving different types of experience. It would cover the whole process, including practice post-qualification. The initial stage would comprise a critical appraisal of professional ethics 'from the outside in'. This would consider legal ethics as a core subject, including consideration of the underlying rationale and values of the legal role. The vocational stage could then build on this foundation in practical settings, including simulation and clinical work.

The training and post-qualification phase of legal education would include analysis and critical reflection on the experience of practice. It would include Continuing Professional Development activity involving analysis of material related to the specific areas of practice engaged in. This may be based around the idea of a community of practice aimed at raising standards generally.

V. Stakeholders and their Interests

Twining observed that legal education is shaped by three entrenched spheres of influence, the universities, the Bar and the Law Society.[103] As far as law degrees are concerned this is certainly the case. The partnership model privileges two main stakeholders, the academy, comprising universities and other academic institutions, and the profession. Increasingly government and employers have become more active voices in legal education. This is partly because of the increasing importance of the university experience of students and the considerable investment required to build a legal career.

There is a generally a mismatch between those seeking legal careers and the opportunities available. In 2003, 10,000 students accepted places to study undergraduate Law courses in England and Wales. In 2008 numbers increased to nearly 20,000[104] with over 60 per cent female and around 15 per cent from overseas.[105] In the same year nearly 14,000 students graduated.[106] In 2009, 9,337 students enrolled on the LPC, a number that includes conversion course students. Of these, 83 per cent sat the examinations in

---

[101] Webb, ibid, at 296–97.

[102] Boon, 'Ethics in Legal Education and Training' (n 32).

[103] W Twining, *Blackstone's Tower: The English Law School* (London, Stevens and Sons/Sweet and Maxwell, 1994) ch 2.

[104] B Cole, N Fletcher, T Chittenden and J Cox, *Trends in the Solicitors' Profession Annual Statistical Report 2009* (London, The Law Society, 2009) at 29.

[105] ibid, at 30.

[106] ibid, at 31.

the summer or autumn. In 2009, there were just over 5000 traineeships available, down 500 on the previous year.

There were over 2000 validated places for the BVC in 2009 of which just over 1500 were filled.[107] The overall pass rate was over 80 per cent. Just over 2800 students registered on a pupillage portal opened by the Bar in 2009.[108] There were around 400 to 500 pupillages available.[109] This number had been fairly consistent since 2003–04 when the number of pupillages available fell to 572 from the high of 853 offered in 2000-01.[110] As these data show, many students at each stage of legal education and training do not make it to the next stage. The availability of training places is a particular bar to progress.

A. The Academy

Nearly every higher education institution in the UK offers Law courses. The academy is extremely diverse, comprising institutions of different vintage, often created in waves. A significant line divides the 'old' universities, from the polytechnic institutions. As a generalisation, 'old' universities adhere to the Ormrod view that the role of the liberal law degree is to educate rather than to train. Teaching staff tend to come through a doctoral research route. They assert the importance of providing a 'liberal' education, conceived of as the pursuit of knowledge for its own sake,[111] producing a good citizen rather than a good lawyer, an educated person rather than a good worker.[112] Polytechnics were formed with a view to providing more relevant, vocational degrees. Staff often had professional backgrounds and were sympathetic to a practical curriculum.

B. Government

i. Growing the Economy

Government has a direct financial interest in higher education through its funding of the system, including student loans. A recurring theme in higher education is concern about the contribution it makes to the economy. Since the 1980s, government perceptions that universities were academic 'ivory towers', began to drive policy. Universities came under pressure to pay more attention to the 'employability' of graduates. They

---

[107] J Sauboorah, *An Analysis of Full-time Students Enrolled on the 2009/10 BVC* (London, General Council of the Bar of England and Wales, 2011).

[108] C Carney, *A Comparison between the Backgrounds of Pupillage Portal Applicants in 2009 and Registered Pupils in 2011* (London, General Council of the Bar of England and Wales, 2012).

[109] C Carney, *An Analysis of Pupillages Advertised between 2009 and 2011* (London, General Council of the Bar of England and Wales, 2012).

[110] C Grimshaw, 'Bar Special: An Educated Risk' *Legal Week Student* 25 March 2005 (www.legalweek.com/legal-week/news/1168834/bar-special-an-educated-risk).

[111] A Bradney, *Conversations, Choices and Chances: The Liberal Law School in the Twenty-First Century* (Oxford, Hart Publishing, 2003) at 37.

[112] ibid, at 38–39.

were encouraged to form relationships with employers and explore their needs. Many Law Schools responded by creating clinical programmes for students.

ii. Accessibility of Professional Careers

Since the Ormrod Report, accessibility to professional careers has been a recurring issue. Government is concerned to promote open access and meritocratic entry by ensuring there are no artificial or unnecessary barriers to entry or progression. In 1979, the Royal Commission on Legal Services found that 54 per cent of university law students had fathers with professional or managerial positions and while only 16 per cent had working class fathers. This compared with 50 per cent and 30 per cent in the general university student population.[113] Those who attended independent schools were also disproportionately represented in the legal profession.

In 1994, the Law Society commissioned an important longitudinal study of entry to the legal profession. It found that most ethnic minorities were better represented on law degrees and conversion courses than the proportion they represented in that age group in the general population.[114] The same study found, however, that only 18 per cent of law students had working class backgrounds.[115] Whereas 6 per cent of pupils were at independent schools, 18 per cent of new university, 26 per cent of other university and 45 per cent of Oxbridge law students had been at independent schools at age of 14. One in five law students had a close relative in the legal profession. Among home students, this was a 10 times higher number than would be expected by chance.[116]

One of the concerns arising from the demography of the student body was diversity. In the 1990s there was growing awareness of problems of social mobility and equal opportunity in access to legal jobs. Even at a time when more part-time, mature and disadvantaged students obtained law degrees, these larger numbers were not represented in the profession. An associated issue was the motivation of potential lawyers. Would enough lawyers from privileged backgrounds want to work on public law and social welfare law issues?

C. Students

Students are an increasingly important body of stakeholders in legal education. Often, their influence is very indirectly applied through mechanisms such as the National Student Survey. This gives them an opportunity to comment on the education they have received. What they want or need is less obvious.

---

[113] Lord Chancellor's Department, *The Royal Commission on Legal Services Final Report* (Cmnd7648, 1979) (Benson Report).

[114] D Halpern, *Entry into the Legal Professions: The Law Student Cohort Study* (London, The Law Society, 1994) at 18–19.

[115] ibid, at 21.

[116] ibid, ch 5.

A small study of Warwick University students found that their motivations for studying law were mixed.[117] In descending order students sought interest in subject matter, desire for intellectual stimulation, desire for professional training, desire to practise law, prospects of above average income, enjoyment of debating and arguing, desire for independence, expectation of a stable, secure future and the prestige of the profession. This was consistent with a much larger US study which found that students chose law for its offer of future independence, varied work, handling others' affairs and interest in the subject matter.[118]

Students consistently ranked altruistic reasons, such as the opportunity for public service, quite low among their priorities. Stevens found that restructuring society or working with the underprivileged came around the middle of the range of student motivations. The Warwick students were drawn to public interest subjects but put off by the financial prospects. Students see careers in Government Legal Service, for example, as a form of public service in which financial benefits are surrendered in order to work for the public good.[119] Analysis of the motivation of entrants to the legal profession is confusing. It appears that students are keen to be involved in public interest law, but daunted by the career prospects.

i. Informing Student Choice

Career considerations are an important consideration for law undergraduates and most consider a legal career before applying to study Law.[120] The Law Society longitudinal study found that at age 16, more than 80 per cent of home law students had seriously considered a legal career, 50 per cent as a solicitor and 33 per cent as a barrister.[121] Security issues, apparently, subsequently affected their choice of legal profession. By their second year at university, those thinking about being a solicitor had jumped to 75 per cent of home undergraduates, while those considering the Bar had fallen to 14 per cent. It is not known whether these changes are based on sound information. In the event, only around 60 per cent of law graduates go into practice.

ii. Curriculum Needs

The Law Society longitudinal study found that undergraduates generally preferred a practical flavour to law degree studies. Law students seek degree courses that are consistent with their career aspirations. They prioritise technical mastery over broad goals such as personal development, understanding the social context of law, law reform and preparation as policy makers.[122]

---

[117] Sherr and Webb, 'Law Students, the External Market, and Socialisation (n 47) at 233.
[118] R Stevens, 'Law Schools and Law Students' (1973) 59 *Virginia Law Review* 551.
[119] J Currie, 'For Queen and Country' *Lawyer 2B* June 2002, at 50.
[120] Halpern, *Entry into the Legal Professions* (n 114) at 46.
[121] ibid, ch 7.
[122] Halpern (n 114) at 21; Sherr and Webb (n 47).

Surprisingly, the practically focused vocational courses always drew mixed reviews. There have always been a number of students who do not see the point of skills training in Law School or who resent paying substantial vocational course fees. Initial research into experience of the courses suggested widespread approval.[123] The majority of students welcomed the practical orientation of the vocational courses and the integration of skills and ethics. More than half of the barristers responding to the Bar study reported ethical difficulties encountered through naiveté.[124] The emphasis on dealing with clients, and other professionals, relieved their anxiety about what they may face in work.

iii. Careers

The fifth survey of the cohort study showed a close relationship between subject interest and intended work areas.[125] Students had a strong orientation to social welfare subjects including Personal Injury, Commercial Law, Family and Childcare, Criminal Law, European Community Law, Employment and Human Rights. Many students with interests in these areas did not intend to work in them because of poor pay, lack of status or too few jobs. Human rights and EU law had a disproportionately high level of interest compared with numbers of trainees who expected to find work. Commercial areas, including commercial property and business and commercial affairs, had low levels of interest compared with numbers expecting to work in them.[126]

iv. Employers

Until relatively recently legal employers' interest in legal education and training was limited to complaining that trainees have inadequate writing skills, research skills or knowledge of law. Loudest complaints came from large commercial solicitors' firms, which tended to pay prospective trainees' LPC fees. It was not surprising therefore when a group of elite law firms negotiated with three providers and the Law Society to validate a 'City LPC'.[127] The customised LPC delivered a curriculum suited to the practice of the sponsoring firms. In 2004 the 'City five' dropped two of the three providers, but agreements between individual firms and LPC for bespoke courses have continued. In 2006 a firm launched an LPC in collaboration with the College of Law for only 25 potential trainees studying over a single semester.[128]

---

[123] Johnston and Shapland, *Developing Vocational Legal Training for the Bar* (n 14).

[124] J Shapland and A Sorsby, *Starting Practice: Work and Training at the Junior Bar* (Sheffield, University of Sheffield, Faculty of Law, Institute for the Study of the Legal Professional, 1995).

[125] E Duff, M Shiner, A Boon and A Whyte, *Entry into the Legal Professions: The Law Student Cohort Study Year 6* (London, Law Society, 2000) 32–33 and 60.

[126] ibid; and see P McDonald 'The Class of "81"—A Glance at the Social Class Composition of Recruits to the Legal Profession' (1982) 9 *Journal of Law and Society* 267.

[127] A Mizzi, 'The City generation' *Law Society Gazette* 5 September 2002.

[128] J Parker, 'Fast train to London Bridge' *The Lawyer* 13 March 2006, at 16.

Competitor providers of the LPC described the notion of bespoke courses as divisive and unhealthy.[129] A more detached critic of the arrangement was Lord Woolf. He argued that isolating more able students from other entrants to the profession would negatively affect the quality of courses. Woolf also thought that separating students would undermine the important goal of 'lawyers emerging into practice regard[ing] themselves as one profession'.[130] One concern is that trainees on employer-sponsored courses might not receive their education in ethics from an independent source.

D. The Legal Professions

The legal profession's interest as a stakeholder in legal education includes convincing other stakeholders of its suitability as the guardian of the curriculum. It has generally taken a conservative view of its custodianship, apparently out of a desire to avoid confronting the academic lobby. The failure to make legal ethics a central curriculum requirement is striking. The US made professional ethics a mandatory element of law degrees in the 1980s[131] and Australia and Canada have since followed suit.[132] Various bodies, of different levels of authority, have recommended introducing some such requirement over the past 40 or so years.

VI. Official Reports on Legal Education and Training

Between 1970 and 1990 three major reports, by the Ormrod, Benson and Marre Committees, considered legal education. Although, they all touched on the issue of induction to the profession, none focused specifically on professional ethics as a subject. Inclusion of professional ethics as a subject in the initial stage was raised as an issue by the Lord Chancellor's Advisory Committee on Education and Conduct in the 1990s. Since then the topic has received many airings in other reports. The recent Legal Education and Training Review was expected to lead to legal ethics being introduced as an undergraduate subject. This section considers the evolution of thinking on the subject.

---

[129] G Charles, 'A revolution in legal education' *The Lawyer* 22 March 2004.
[130] A Mizzi, 'Lord Woolf criticises City law firms for launching "elite" training consortium' *Law Society Gazette* 22 June 2000.
[131] R MacCrate, 'Preparing Lawyers to Participate Effectively in the Legal Profession' (1994) 44 *Journal of Legal Education* 89.
[132] G Powles, 'Taking the Plunge: Integrating Legal Ethics in Australia' (1999) 33 *Law Teacher* 315; Federation of Law Societies of Canada Task Force on the Common Law Degree (2009) (www.flsc.ca/en/pdf/CommonLawDegreeReport.pdf).

A. The Ormrod Report

The Ormrod Committee was specifically established to consider the education of the legal profession in England and Wales, reporting in 1971.[133] It was Ormrod who endorsed the aim of higher education is producing 'not mere specialists but rather cultivated men and women'.[134] Ormrod welcomed the 'practically useful' on law degrees so long as it was 'taught in such a way as to promote the general powers of the mind'. Ormrod sought better integration of legal education to soundly equip future generations of lawyers. He defined the role of university education in this process as providing knowledge of law, application of abstract concepts to case facts and the relationship of law to the social and economic environment.

Ormrod also recommended increasing the practical content and keeping to a minimum the substantive content of the vocational stage. He favoured providing a stronger focus on continuing education after qualification. Ormrod addressed the problem of securing a more varied intake to the legal profession.[135] He focused on some very practical ethical issues, such as ensuring that potential entrants from diverse backgrounds were not deterred by the cost of qualifying as lawyers.[136]

The tone of future debates on ethics was set by Ormrod. He considered that the 'vision, range, depth, balance and rich humanity' of ethical practitioners would be fostered by the study of law as a liberal art,[137] with morality at its core.[138] Despite his mention of the 'ethos' of the profession, the issue of ethics was not specifically addressed by Ormrod. He acknowledged that lawyers needed to 'grasp... the ethos of the profession' but saw a problem in reconciling the demand for a 'learned' profession with instruction in the skills and techniques essential to legal practice.[139]

B. The Benson Report

In the late 1970s a Royal Commission under the chairmanship of Lord Justice Benson was asked to enquire into changes to 'the structure, organisation, training, regulation of and entry to the legal profession' that were desirable in the public interest.[140] The Benson Report, published in 1979 stated that:

> It is essential that throughout their training students should be impressed with the importance of maintaining ethical standards, rendering a high quality of personal service, maintaining a good relationship with clients, providing information about work in hand for clients, avoiding unnecessary delays, maintaining a high standard in briefs and preparation for trial, promptly

---

[133] Ormrod Report (n 23).

[134] Committee on Higher Education, *Report of the Committee on Higher Education* (Cmnd 2154, 1963) (The Robbins Report) at paras 24–26 and Ormrod Report (n 23) at para 106.

[135] Ormrod Report (n 23) at para 98.

[136] ibid, at para 185.

[137] K Llewellyn, 'The Study of Law as a Liberal Art' (1960) reprinted in *Jurisprudence: Realism in Theory and Practice* (Chicago, University of Chicago Press, 1962) at 376; Twining, *Blackstone's Tower* (n 103) ch 4.

[138] ibid, at 159–62.

[139] Ormrod Report (n 23) at para 100.

[140] Benson Report (n 113) vol 1, at vi.

rendering accounts with clear explanations and attending to other matters mentioned elsewhere in this report.[141]

Benson considered that the place to bring together theory and practice was at the vocational stage.[142]

C. The Marre Report

The Marre Committee was organised by the legal profession to resolve the dispute over advocacy, but undertook a wide review of regulation. The report endorsed the shift to a more practical legal education and proposed a split between skills suited to the academic and vocational stages. It proposed confining those skills with an ethical dimension, such as, 'an ability to help clients understand the options available to them so that they can make an informed choice of action or direction',[143] to the vocational stage. A general list also included 'an adequate knowledge of professional and ethical standards',[144] but this was not assigned to either stage.

D. Reports of the Lord Chancellor's Advisory Committee for Education and Conduct (ACLEC)

During the 1990s ethics moved higher up the agenda, due largely to the efforts of the Lord Chancellor's Advisory Committee on Education and Conduct (ACLEC). ACLEC was created to advise the Lord Chancellor on legal education and conduct under the Courts and Legal Services Act 1990. It issued a series of reports on education and training, beginning in 1996 with one covering the whole process.[145] This endorsed Twining's observation that the three, entrenched spheres of influence, the universities, the Bar and the Law Society, led to inertia in developing the curriculum.

ACLEC decried the rigid separation of the initial and vocational stages and proposed that legal education should develop students' capacities in five key areas. These were intellectual integrity and independence of mind, core knowledge, contextual knowledge, legal values and professional skills.[146] Contextual knowledge included 'appreciation of the law's ... moral ... contexts' and professional skills included 'learning to act like a lawyer'.[147] ACLEC envisaged that the initial stage would contribute to students' ethical education by paying more attention to 'the moral quality of law', with universities deciding what to teach provided they included 'a proper knowledge of ... legal

---

[141] ibid at para 39.47; and see vol 1, at para 3.40.
[142] ibid, vol 1, at 629, para 39.4.
[143] Lady Marre CBE, *A Time for Change: Report of the Committee on the Future of the Legal Profession* (London, General Council of the Bar and Council of the Law Society, 1988) (Marre Report) at para 12.21, no 18.
[144] ibid, at 12.21, no 15.
[145] ACLEC *First Report on Legal Education and Training* (London, ACLEC, 1996).
[146] ibid, at paras 2.3–2.8.
[147] ibid, at para 2.4

values and ethical standards'.[148] It envisaged that the profession's power to prescribe a compulsory core would be reduced.[149]

Although ACLEC advocated that legal education should imbue 'the standards and codes of professional conduct'[150] it proposed that the curriculum should go beyond 'a familiarisation with professional codes of conduct and the machinery for enforcing them'.[151] The report proposed that intending lawyers should 'fully appreciate the essential link between law and legal practice and the preservation of fundamental democratic values'.[152] This was said to entail commitments:

> [T]o the rule of law, to justice, fairness and high ethical standards, to acquiring and improving professional skills, to representing clients without fear or favour, to promoting equality of opportunity, and to ensuring that adequate legal services are provided to those that cannot afford to pay for them.[153]

ACLEC anticipated negative reaction to its proposals from university law schools.[154] In the event both the profession and universities were largely unreceptive.[155]

Similar indifference awaited ACLEC's proposals for the vocational stage. It proposed that barristers and solicitors should follow a licentiate programme common to both for half the vocational year. The licentiate was to involve an element called 'Professional Responsibility' including 'general principles, with projects in the context of criminal and civil procedure and evidence'.[156] Following the licentiate students would follow their own courses, and a Master's programme built around a rigorous basic education in common professional values. None of ACLEC's main proposals for legal education was adopted, and it was disbanded by the Lord Chancellor, perhaps because it was making insufficient progress.

E. Reviews by Professional Bodies

i. The Law Society

In 1998 the Law Society and Bar Council adopted the ACLEC view that the law degree should stand as an independent liberal education not tied to any specific vocation.[157] They also adopted a general move towards assessing 'transferable skills', rather than legal skills, in higher education.[158] They added a requirement that students should acquire knowledge 'of the social economic political, historical, philosophical,

---

[148] ibid, recommendations 4.2 and 4.4.4.
[149] ibid, at 4.4.5.
[150] ibid, at para 1.10 and 1.21.
[151] ibid, at para 1.19
[152] ibid, at para 1.5.
[153] ibid, at para 2.4.
[154] ibid, at para 2.5.
[155] 'Earthworks against ACLEC' *SPTL Reporter* Spring 1996.
[156] ACLEC *First Report on Legal Education and Training* (n 145) at para 5.14.
[157] The Law Society and the General Council of the Bar, *A Consultation Paper on the Revision of the Joint Announcement on Qualifying Law Degrees* (September 1998).
[158] J Bell, 'General Transferable Skills and the Law Curriculum' (1996) 2(2) *Contemporary Issues in Law* 1.

moral, ethical, cultural and comparative contexts in which law operates' to the joint announcement.

Despite the requirement that Law be studied in its 'ethical context', no specific content was prescribed. In the meantime, more common law countries were joining the US in requiring ethics in law degrees.[159] The Law Society consulted on a new training framework in 2001, proposing that ethics join knowledge and skills as core elements of solicitors' education and training 'from the cradle to the grave'.[160] Respondents to a consultation gave almost universal approval to this proposal.[161] The Law Society convened a group, the Training Framework Review Group (TFRG), to develop the concept.

a. Training Framework Review

The TFRG identified what newly qualified solicitors should know and be able to do when beginning as qualified practitioners. This knowledge and associated skills and capacities were named the Day One Outcomes ('outcomes'). The idea was that education and training should focus on assessing the outcomes, rather than courses or other processes. TFRG proposed that the conventional stages of the partnership model be abandoned. The only course requirement would be an honours degree, the common currency of European education and professional entry under the Bologna Declaration,[162] the European blueprint for harmonization of university degrees.

The review took place amid increasing controversy, particularly regarding the hindrance that the cost of legal education posed to those from poorer backgrounds.[163] It was proposed that students would not be required to attend a course before taking vocational examinations. A two-year period of work-based learning, completed under the supervision of a solicitor, would also be required. The training contract would, however, be abolished. Students would then be able to complete their training with a period of work-based learning in organisations other than a firm of solicitors.

The TFRG's proposals mapped onto the existing structure of legal education and training, although not perfectly.[164] The first of six groups of outcomes re-worked the 'Seven Foundations' of the initial stage. The second group, intellectual, analytical and problem-solving skills, underpins the whole of education and training. The LPC was represented in a third group comprising transactional and dispute resolution skills, and the fourth, legal, professional and client relationship knowledge and skills.

The fifth group of outcomes, personal development and work management skills, and the sixth group, professional values, behaviours, attitudes and ethics, overlap the LPC and work-based learning. None of the content was tied to a particular

---

[159] G Powles, 'Taking the Plunge: Integrating Legal Ethics in Australia' (1999) 33(3) *Law Teacher* 315.

[160] Law Society, *Consultation: Training Framework Review* (London, The Law Society, 2001).

[161] A Boon and J Webb, *Consultant's Report on the Training Framework Review Consultation* (London, The Law Society, 2002).

[162] J Webb, 'Academic Legal Education In Europe: Convergence And Diversity' (2002) 9 *International Journal of the Legal Profession* 139, at 142.

[163] C Sanders, '£40,000 bill before you get near the Bar' *Times Higher Education Supplement* 3 October 2003; NA Bastin, 'Why I think legal training has to change' *Times Higher Education Supplement* 3 October 2003, at 16; N Wikeley, 'The Law Degree and the BVC' *The Reporter* Spring 2004, at 23.

[164] The current version of the Day One Outcomes is on the SRA website (www.sra.org.uk.securedownload/file/229).

stage. Allowing a multiplicity of routes to qualification was an explicit aim of the framework. Therefore, degrees and conversion courses for non-law graduates might incorporate the 'vocational stage' outcomes, vocational courses might incorporate work-based learning and some of the larger firms might incorporate the 'vocational stage' outcomes in the period of work-based learning.[165]

This was not welcomed by providers of the LPC. Their courses were threatened by the intended flexibility. Nor were they welcomed by some firms, who feared declining standards.[166] The Chief Executive of the Law Society robustly defended the proposals, arguing that they would increase access to the profession.[167] It is not clear how the TFRG's proposals delivered the promise to make ethics central from cradle to grave.

The TFRG's first group of outcomes, echoing ACLEC, include 'the jurisdiction, authority and procedures of the legal institutions and the professions that initiate, develop and interpret the law' of 'the rules of professional conduct' and of the 'values and principles on which professional rules are constructed'. The fact that these outcomes map onto the initial stage, suggests that a substantial programme of ethics could become part of qualifying degrees, but how much time would be spent on each outcome, what activity might be involved or how the profession would check whether the outcomes are met were unresolved and acknowledged by the chair of TFRG to be problematic.[168]

The Seven Foundations could be revised to reduce the old content and introduce some new, but because of the lack of detail, even academics broadly supportive of the proposals reserved judgement.[169] Before the TFRG proposals, speculation about a possible ethics curriculum for the initial stage ranged from incorporating professional ethics[170] to a more gradual progress from 'general system ethics'.[171] The TFRG clarified this by proposing the legal profession, the rules of professional conduct and the values and principles on which professional rules are constructed, as material for the initial stage. Because of the open-ended nature of the framework, students would not have to cover this (or any) material in a degree. They could be exposed to some material at the vocational stage. This, though, was hardly 'ethics from cradle to grave'.

The TFRG established 'Day One outcomes' for solicitors, covering the range of things that they should know or be able to do on qualification. It also came close to breaking the stranglehold on access to the solicitors' profession imposed by the cost of the vocational stage. The TFRG concluded that students would only have to

---

[165] ibid, at para 38.

[166] C Sanders, 'Law Revamp Could Hit Coffers' *The Times Higher* February 2005; B Malkin, 'Market Slams Law Soc plans to Abolish Vocational Training' *Lawyer 2B* February 2005, at 1; N Johnson, 'The Training Framework Review—What's All The Fuss About?' (2005) 155 *New Law Journal* 341.

[167] C Sanders, 'Profile: Janet Paraskeva, Chief Executive, Law Society' *The Times Higher* February 2005.

[168] S Nelson, 'Reflections from the International Conference on Legal Ethics from Exeter' (2004) 7 *Legal Ethics* 159.

[169] J Webb and A Fancourt, 'The Law Society's Training Framework Review: On the Straight and Narrow or the Long and Winding Road' (2004) 38 *Law Teacher* 293; A Boon, J Flood and J Webb, 'Postmodern Professions?: The Fragmentation of Legal Education and the Legal Profession' (2005) 32(3) *Journal of Law and Society* 473.

[170] R O'Dair, 'Recent Developments in the Teaching of Legal Ethics–A UK Perspective' in Economides (n 78) at 151–52.

[171] J Webb, 'Conduct, Ethics and Experience in Vocational Legal Education: Opportunities Missed' in Economides (n 78) at 292.

achieve the outcomes, without having to attend courses. This proposal split the TFRG group but was carried by a majority.

In the result the radical implications of moving to outcomes were not achieved. The LPC was split into two stages so that the cost of the second, elective stage could be spread and possibly shared by employers. Most students continued, however, to take the course in a single block. The possible financial savings achievable with an outcomes approach was further diluted when the Law Society was persuaded in the final stages of the TFRG process to specify 'notional learning hours'. These currently stand at a minimum of 1100 hours for Stage 1 of the LPC and a further 300 hours to the study of Stage 2. That is 100 hours for each vocational elective.[172]

b. Consultants' Reports

Following the TFRG the Law Society commissioned a report from academic consultants Economides and Rogers on what part ethics should play in the curriculum.[173] The report recommended that ethics be introduced to the legal education process at the earliest stage possible, and that outcomes that would ensure 'commitment to legal values and the moral context of law' be introduced on law degrees.[174] The report did not propose content or method,[175] suggesting further work on 'how best to introduce ethics and professional responsibility'.[176]

The Law Society then commissioned a further consultant's report from Boon on the form the ethics curriculum would take if introduced at the initial stage.[177] This suggested that a suitable framework for degree level study would be:

> The study of the relationship between morality and Law, the values underpinning the legal system, and the regulation of the legal services market, including the institutions, professional roles and ethics of the judiciary and legal professions.

The overarching aims of the study of ethics, the report suggested, was to stimulate students to reflect on the nature of legal ethics, equip them to behave ethically and enable them to play an active role in the formation of professional ethics. Some objectives consistent with these aims were to:

—— further appreciation of the relationship between morality and law;
—— promote understanding of the role of the legal profession in supporting democracy and protecting justice and the rule of law;
—— provide opportunities for ethical decision-making;
—— promote understanding of the importance of values, including justice, honesty, integrity, critical self-reflection and respect for others; and
—— stimulate reflection on the ethical challenges of practice and lay a foundation for ethical behavior.

---

[172] SRA, *Legal Practice Course Outcomes 2011*, at 28 (www.sra.org.uk/students/lpc.page).
[173] K Economides and J Rogers, *Preparatory Ethics Training For Future Solicitors* (London, The Law Society, 2009).
[174] ibid, at 6–8.
[175] S Nelson, 'Reflections from the International Conference on Legal Ethics from Exeter' (2004) 7 *Legal Ethics* 159.
[176] Economides and Rogers, *Preparatory Ethics* (n 173) rec 1.
[177] A Boon, *Legal Ethics at the Initial Stage: A Model Curriculum* (London, The Law Society, 2010).

The report argued that 'if the Law Society is to be confident that the specified aims, objectives and learning outcomes are achieved, it is important that a core is delivered and examined discretely'.[178] The implications of this proposal were that if, for example, the idea of core subjects was retained, Legal Ethics would become a core subject. The Law Society adopted these proposals as its position on the issue. By this time, however, the power to implement them resided in the SRA.

ii. The Bar

a. The Bell Working Party

In 2004 a working group led by John Bell reviewed the education and training framework of the Bar. The remit of the Bell Working Party was to consider the vocational stage, which had been criticised for high cost against the low chance of pupilage and tenancy. The consultation paper the group produced proposed little substantive change. The review was overtaken by the creation of the Bar Standards Board and a BVC review chaired by Derek Wood QC.

b. Neuberger

When the BVC Working Group was in its early stages, a comprehensive report by the Entry to the Bar Working Party, chaired by Lord Neuberger of Abbotsbury, was published. This recommended improving access to careers at the Bar by the less privileged and raising standards of education and practice.[179] Among 57 wide-ranging recommendations, including for the introduction of a module on law and lawyers to the National Curriculum in schools, 14 related to the BVC.

Neuberger's proposals for the vocational course included retaining the length of the course and the policy of open entry, but arranging matters so that students knew in advance whether or not they had pupilage. The most radical proposals were the introduction of a national final examination and having the Bar Standards Board investigate the impact of introducing the requirement of at least an upper second class law degree for entry to the vocational stage. No recommendations specifically related to ethics.

c. The Wood Reports

Derek Wood QC led comprehensive reviews of the BVC, pupilage and post-qualification education, undertaken in sequence. The report on the vocational course recommended that it be retitled the Bar Professional Training Course (BPTC).[180] It recorded that the large gap between the numbers of students graduating from the BVC and the much smaller number of pupilages was a cause for 'considerable concern'.

---

[178] ibid, rec 18.
[179] Lord Neuberger of Abbotsbury, *Entry to the Bar Working Party* (2007) (www.barcouncil.org.uk/search/).
[180] BSB, *Review of the Bar Vocational Course: Report of the Working Party*.

Wood concluded that some students were 'so far lacking in the qualities needed for successful practice at the Bar' that they would have no chance of pupillage however many were available.[181] He recommended that numbers should not be artificially limited but that students should pass a centrally set aptitude test in analytical and critical reasoning and fluency in English in order to gain access to the course. Students should also pass centrally set assessment by multiple choice and short answer questions.

The Wood Report noted Neuberger's aspiration that able graduates were not deterred by cost from joining the Bar. It saw no way to reduce the length of the course or the overall cost of reading for the Bar. Wood was, however, concerned that the cost of qualifying, and the vocational course in particular, would dissuade all but the wealthy from trying. This would lead to a loss of able barristers. The cost of the course, and contribution from the profession, compared unfavorably to the situation in France. The report therefore concluded:

> [U]nless and until the profession collectively can find a solution to the cost of reading for the Bar, the problems of access, diversity and equality of opportunity will not be solved.[182]

The Wood Report on the BVC also recommended a number of adjustments to the curriculum. These included omitting Negotiation as a separately taught and assessed subject and introducing a new subject, Resolution of Disputes out of Court (including negotiation), as a new taught and assessed subject. One of the most important changes recommended was the introduction of Professional Ethics and Conduct as a separately taught subject.[183] Professional Ethics is one of the subjects on the BPTC assessed by centrally set multiple choice assessments, along with Criminal and Civil Litigation.[184]

VII. Legal Education and Training Review

A. Context

The Legal Education and Training Review (LETR) was said to be the only dedicated, system-wide examination of legal education and training undertaken since Lord Justice Ormrod in 1971 This ignored the review by ACLEC, but LETR was different because it was overseen by the BSB, SRA and ILEX Professional Standards. It is envisaged as three stages; a research stage, a review stage to consider any consequent changes to the regulators' education and training requirements and a consultation stage.

---

[181] ibid, Summary of Conclusions and Recommendations, rec 6.
[182] ibid, at 73.
[183] ibid, rec 16(1).
[184] ibid, rec 22.

Although the review was undertaken by professional bodies, the research stage for the LETR Report was produced by Law academics from different institutions led by Julian Webb who, at the time the review commenced, was Director of the UK Centre for Legal Education based at Warwick University. The report for the review stated that the exercise was precipitated by the liberalisation of legal services, the arrival of innovative delivery models, developments in technology, globalisation and consumerism.[185]

The report noted that, simultaneously, there were growing student numbers, escalating costs of qualification and difficulties in finding employment after qualification, resulting in calls for reform of the current system of legal education and training. There were cuts in the availability of civil legal aid and tightening criminal legal aid budgets. None of these factors were new. In fact, the review was promoted by the Legal Services Board, ostensibly to obtain an overview of how education and training fitted with 'market needs'.

The LSB may have foreseen a number of results of the LETR. These possibly included, for example, combined education training routes and increased accreditation to undertake reserved activities. Only one outcome was actually signalled by the BSB. Announcing the review, the LSB chairman said '(a)s a minimum, we will be looking at a changed and earlier emphasis on the teaching of professional ethics and wider responsibilities to the client'. The reference to an 'earlier emphasis' could only refer to degree level teaching. The LSB had signaled a need for an analysis based on the regulatory needs of the legal services market.

B. The LETR Report

i. Recommendations

The LETR did not recommend a move to activity-based authorisation, which would focus on regulation of specific reserved activities or other legal tasks. Rather, it suggested that the current entity-focused system was probably preferable.[186] The reason offered for this conclusion was the complexity of the present system of multiple regulators. The report did, however, support a limited step in the direction of activity-based regulation. It suggested removing advocacy and wills from the LPC and requiring specialist training to undertake these activities.

There were no major changes recommended in the current structure of legal education and training. Relatively minor amendments were proposed to the content. The report suggested the assessment of legal research, writing and critical thinking skills in the law degree and graduate diploma in law. The LETR's more radical suggestions were on access to the profession and for the para-legal sector. For example, it suggested restoring the apprenticeship route to qualification as a solicitor. It suggested tighter regulation of internships and work experience in order to combat discrimination and

---

[185] IPS, BSB and SRA, *The Future of Legal Services Education and Training Regulation in England and Wales* (June 2013) at v.
[186] ibid, at 175–81.

social disadvantage. It also suggested that para-legal law firms be allowed to operate where fully qualified practitioners were not necessary.

The LETR made a number of recommendations that had been made before and rejected others. For example, it followed the TFRG line that vocational training should be based on achieving the 'day one' outcomes rather than on the time served. Like ACLEC, it favoured a stronger focus on professional ethics throughout education and training. Also like ACLEC, it suggested creating a 'Legal Education Council' to oversee, co-ordinate and support innovation in legal education and training. Previous ideas the LETR did not favour included common training for solicitors and barristers and periodic re-accreditation of practitioners.

ii. Recommendations on Ethics

The LETR Report suggested the development of outcomes for legal ethics at all stages of legal education. A major surprise was that there were no major recommendations for teaching legal ethics. The report recommended that 'all approved regulators review the treatment of ethics and professionalism within their education and training regimes to ensure that the subject is addressed with the prominence and in the depth appropriate to the public profession of law'.[187] This is more remarkable since the report suggested that the 'perceived centrality of professionalism and ethics to practice across the regulated workforce is one of the clearest conclusions to be drawn from the LETR research'.[188]

In research conducted for the LETR Report, legal ethics was apparently rated 'important' or 'somewhat important' by over 90 per cent of respondents. It was also 'seen as a defining feature of professional service in the qualitative data'.[189] The report went on to say that the 'majority of respondents thought that an understanding of legal values, ethics and professionalism needs to be developed throughout legal services education and training'.[190] The first finding mentioned the need to 'strengthen requirements for education and training in legal ethics, values and professionalism',[191] but the proposals for achieving this were vague.

The report encouraged regulators to develop a broad approach to the subject, rather than a limited focus on conduct rules or principles. Recommendation 7 is that:

> The learning outcomes at initial stages of LSET should include reference (as appropriate) to the individual practitioner's role, to an understanding of the relationship between morality and law, the values underpinning the legal system, and the role of lawyers in relation to those values.[192]

It was not clear how this was to be achieved without relevant content being added to, or some other adjustment of, the Seven Foundations of Legal Knowledge. The LETR Report recommended that Legal Services Education and Training schemes

---

[187] ibid, at para 4.66.
[188] ibid, at para 7.10.
[189] ibid, at para 2.71.
[190] ibid, at para 4.67.
[191] ibid, at 9.
[192] ibid, rec 7 at 287.

should include 'appropriate learning outcomes' in respect of professional ethics.[193] This, unfortunately, threatens to repeat the mistake made when professional conduct was introduced as a 'pervasive' subject at the vocational stage.

The LETR Report noted that general support for a greater emphasis on ethics training 'did not amount to extensive support for ethics to become a separate Foundation subject'.[194] This was all the more puzzling because the LETR Report did not recommend abolition or adjustment of the Seven Foundations of Legal Knowledge. It added that this would not ' prevent a basis for the study of professional ethics being provided at the academic stage' noting that there is 'general support for all authorised persons receiving some education in legal values, as well as the technical 'law on lawyering'.[195]

The LETR Report implied that ethics training should continue post-qualification. It suggested that that there is 'a public interest (and a competitive interest) for regulated lawyers in demonstrating and maintaining the integrity and high ethical standards of legal services provision'.[196] It noted that the Professional Skills Course for trainee solicitors and the Bar New Practitioners Programme include ethics and that ILEX Professional Standards mandates coverage of ethics in the new CPD scheme for CILEx members. The SRA was said to be considering post-qualification requirements.

iii. Evaluation

The LETR Report had mixed reactions. It skated over many important areas and did not give a clear steer to the regulators. Whereas the brief for the research suggested an analysis of need, the report reflected the views of stakeholders. The consensus of respondents tended, as might be expected, to favour the status quo. The LETR Report, like many of its predecessors, was therefore relatively conservative. While those hoping for a radical shake-up were disappointed, many were relieved that there was plenty of space left to continue the discussion about the future of legal education. Perhaps most significantly, the regulators who had commissioned the report were given freedom to do more or less what they wanted.

VIII. The Future of Ethics in Legal Education and Training

The structure of legal education and training has remained virtually unchanged since the Ormrod Report in 1971. The ACLEC first floated the idea that undergraduate legal studies should contain some ethics in the 1990s. The professional bodies have toyed with the idea. The Law Society even commissioned two reports on the subject.

---

[193] ibid, rec 6.
[194] ibid, at para 2.73.
[195] ibid, at para 7.10.
[196] ibid, at para 5.91.

The first Law Society report thoroughly reviewed the arguments for the citing of ethics and repeated ACLEC's suggestion that outcomes be developed for the undergraduate stage.[197] The second Law Society report outlined a detailed prospectus for a subject and outlined why it was important that legal ethics become a core subject if the Seven Foundations were retained.[198] The LETR Report ignored both reports. Consequently, it did not take this particular debate further forward. In fact, it returned to square one, suggesting that outcomes be developed.

Both the partnership model and the concept of the liberal law degree were implicitly endorsed by the LETR research report. This left the regulators who sponsored the report, and the LSB, which promoted the review, with difficult decisions. Did they accept the conclusion that only minor systemic adjustments are needed, or embark on more radical plans? If the latter, did they accept the suggestion that some ethical outcomes be added to the joint announcement or look to make more fundamental changes?

The LSB appeared disinclined to accept the direction, process or pace of change implicit in the LETR Report. It issued a consultation in which it proposed issuing statutory guidance to all the approved regulators under the Legal Services Act 2007, section 162. This was intended to take the form of five outcomes the LSB considered would deliver greater flexibility in the education and training markets, with positive impacts on access, cost and flexibility. These were:

—— education and training requirements focus on what an individual must know, understand and be able to do at the point of authorisation;

—— providers of education and training have the flexibility to determine how best to deliver the outcomes required;

—— standards are set that find the right balance between what is required at entry and what can be fulfilled through ongoing competency requirements;

—— obligations in respect of education and training are balanced appropriately between the individual and entity both at the point of entry and ongoing; and

—— education and training regulations place no direct or indirect restrictions on the numbers entering the profession.[199]

At this point, the SRA had responded to the LETR Report with a policy statement and consultation. This conceded that regulation had previously been 'overly preoccupied with detailed educational design and inputs'.[200] It continued by promising that the SRA intended to 'move our attention from prescribing the educational "how" and to focus instead on assuring standards of competence against a framework which is fit for modern legal practice'. This referred to the proposed move towards flexible pathways to qualification where solicitors would only need to show 'the day-one skills, knowledge

---

[197] Economides and Rogers (n 73).

[198] Boon, *Legal Ethics at the Initial Stage* (n 177).

[199] LSB, *Increasing Flexibility in Legal Education and Training: Consultation on Proposals for Draft Statutory Guidance to be Issued under Section 162 of the Legal Services Act 2013* (London, LSB, 2013) at para 24.

[200] SRA, 'Training for Tomorrow' (www.sra.org.uk/sra/policy/training-for-tomorrow/resources/policy-statement.page).

and attributes that a new solicitor must possess'.[201] The other two commitments were related to continuing education and removing unnecessary regulation.

The SRA plan is, therefore, to permit much greater flexibility as to how competencies are acquired. This means that they will no longer be requiring law degrees, or their equivalent, LPC and training contract. The 'unnecessary regulation' refers to the regulations supporting these requirements. One example cited is the need for a certificate of completion of the academic stage before progressing to the vocational stage.

The consultation refers to the EU case *Morgenbesser v Consiglio dell'Ordine degli avvocati di Genova.*[202] This requires regulators to assess the competences of part-qualified EU national lawyers holistically, by evaluating their abilities, knowledge and competence when admitting EU nationals to English legal professions. This suggests the introduction of the qualified lawyer transfer regime, previously a much maligned necessity implemented in order to accommodate EU law.

The removal of qualifying requirements accommodates the LETR Report suggestion for development of higher level apprenticeship qualifications as a non-graduate pathway into regulated professions. The SRA welcomed such a development but considered it was for employers and education providers to propose the pathways. The SRA conceived its role in the process to be the provision of mechanisms for individuals seeking qualification through such routes to demonstrate that they meet a prescribed standard.[203]

One of the implications of the SRAs plans was a move to centralised assessment of standards at the point of qualification as a solicitor. No other system would meet the requirement of demonstrating consistent achievement of outcomes across the system. The SRA claimed that the assessment regimes established to test overseas lawyers knowledge of English law and procedure demonstrated that outcomes could be satisfied by a rigorous assessment-based process.

Both the BSB and IPS provided a less detailed indication of their intended actions following receipt of the LETR Report. The Bar referred to changes to education and training it had made as a consequence of the Wood Review. It indicated six areas for future work. These were to develop a competency framework, revise the training regulations, establish an outcomes-focused approach to Continuing Professional Development, publish relevant regulatory data, improve access routes to the profession and work with other regulators in looking at academic stage requirements.[204]

The ILEX Professional Standards response welcomed the endorsement of outcomes-focused assessment of competence, more constructive and meaningful ways to maintain competence through Continuing Professional Development, and support for thorough training in ethics and professionalism in the curriculum. It suggested that it would focus particularly on supporting diversity by providing alternative routes to qualification.[205]

---

[201] ibid.

[202] Case C-313/01 *Morgenbesser v Consiglio dell'Ordine degli avvocati di Genova* [2003] All ER (*D*) 190 (Nov).

[203] SRA, 'Training for Tomorrow' (n 200).

[204] BSB, *Education Stage Requirements* (www.barstandardsboard.org.uk/regulatory-requirements/changes-to-regulation/legal-education-and-training-review/education-strategy-framework/).

[205] ILEX Professional Standards, *Fit for the Future: IPS Responds to LETR* (www.cilex.org.uk/ips/ips_home/notice_board/ips_responds_to_letr.aspx).

All of the regulators therefore endorsed increased use of outcomes, although not necessarily in the same areas of work.

Any concrete scheme to revise education and training is likely to be controversial. It is difficult to see how outcomes currently achieved and assessed incrementally over up to seven years of education and training, can be adequately assessed at a single point pre-admission. A single, pre-qualification, day one outcome assessment would be controversial and administratively burdensome. More important, the quality of provision might be difficult to assure if the primary focus was on the outcome of a long education and training process. There would be a fear of providers offering shorter and shorter routes to qualification and a 'race to the bottom' in terms of quality.

Twining, usually a farsighted and progressive member of the university legal establishment, observed that most agreed that ethics and values should feature at all stages of legal education and training. How and when to do it is problematic, he said.[206] He argued that '[o]ne must distinguish conceptually between personal morality and public ethics, positivism/non-positivism, common law values, professional integrity, and disciplinary guidance, regulation and enforcement'.[207]

Twining argued that much of the relevant material could feature in theory and philosophy courses. His question, 'is this too radical?', was posed in relation to his suggestion that philosophy might benefit the vocational stage and CPD. It applies equally to almost any proposal for legal ethics in education and training. Unfortunately, such ideas occupy a different universe to those likely to be on offer. Requirements for ethics in education and training will probably become pragmatic and sketchy rather than aspirational.

IX. Conclusion

There is growing concern that the cost of legal vocational education skews the profession by discouraging the less well off. On recent evidence, there will continue to be pressure on the profession to justify or amend its requirements for practice. This will stimulate the trend to towards liberalisation of educational requirements for entry to the legal profession. There will be exploration of the potential for cheaper paths to qualification, potentially avoiding expensive courses and apprenticeship. Increasing diversity in professional membership, and potential differentiation of routes to qualification, may lead to calls for more effective socialisation of lawyers.

Despite recognition of the importance of professional ethics in official reports, including the recent report for the Legal Education and Training Review, the subject has not gained a significant foothold in the initial stage. It was introduced into the

---

[206] W Twining, *The Role of Academics in Legal Education and Training* (www.ucl.ac.uk/laws/academics/profiles/twining/2013-LETR-Report.pdf).
[207] ibid, at para 10, 3.

vocational stage as a pervasive subject in the early-1990s. There, on some accounts, it struggled to make much impact. The Bar recently established Professional Ethics as an independent, centrally assessed subject as a result of the Woods Review. It is doubtful, however, that it will continue to be accepted that professional issues be left to the vocational stage.

The prospect for creation of an undergraduate legal ethics curriculum is not promising. At the point when legal ethics appears ready to enter the mainstream, the recommendation, as in the LETR Report, is invariably to prescribe ethical outcomes. Outcomes have previously had relatively inconsequential impact on undergraduate study. At present, it seems likely that ethics outcomes will need to compete for curriculum time against the megalith of the core subjects. Whatever is implemented, at least within the template of the LETR Report, is therefore unlikely to have much impact on future lawyers.

7

Regulation

'But one who is intended coming to the profession might ask where is this code to be found, and how is to be learnt? The answer to the first question is in the traditions of the profession. The answer to the second is in the Schools of the profession, its ancient craft guilds, called the Inns of Court, where all matters of professional conduct are freely and daily discussed, and where the transgressor is answerable for his misconduct. It is, of course, incapable of being stated or written out in full like a Legal Code'.[1]

I. Introduction

The aim and process of regulation is the systematic attempt to restrict fluctuations in behaviour. In the case of professional ethics, this involves controlling professionals by requiring conformity to norms of behaviour. This task has traditionally been approached by developing a culture of compliance. This is supported by a variety of mechanisms including professional codes of conduct, education and disciplinary tribunals. Codes of conduct have been the repository of the legal profession's ethical commitments. They continue to be important as statements of the conduct lawyers should aspire to. The new regulatory system is, however, giving rise to new kinds of rules and new mechanisms of enforcement.

The regulatory regimes emerging after the Legal Services Act 2007 are directed at managing entities. Individuals continue to be subject to disciplinary procedures but the focus of regulation has changed. Regulatory responsibility is placed on organisations. Regulatory activity is much more focused on organisations. Regulatory sanctions have been developed that are appropriate to the organisational scale of operations. This has the effect of making organisations more responsible for the conduct of the individuals, including the professionals, they employ.

---

[1] M Hilbery, *Duty and Art in Advocacy* (London, Stevens and Sons Ltd, 1946) at 7.

II. Regulatory System before the Legal Services Act 2007

Self-regulation of legal services is traditional in common law countries.[2] The rationale is that consumers benefit from experts regulating their own markets in a spirit of public service, even if this also in the long-term interests of professions. The argument is that the security of the professional monopoly enables lawyers to genuinely consider the public good in the way they offer services.[3] Prior to the Legal Services Act 2007 the legal profession operated a system of self-regulation within which there were multiple mechanisms of regulation. These primarily involved regulation by the courts and regulation by the professions underpinned by codes of conduct.

A. Courts

Lawyers were, historically, controlled by the courts, both indirectly and directly. An example of indirect control is that the courts would not entertain solicitors' claims for payment for negligent work.[4] As regards direct controls, there is a general, inherent jurisdiction over solicitors preserved for the High Court, Crown Court and higher courts, by the Solicitors Act 1974.[5] According to Lord Justice Mummery,

> [t]he power is essentially a summary disciplinary one exercised by the court over its own officers to ensure their observance of an honourable standard of conduct and to punish derelictions from duty'. [It] is 'flexible and unfettered by any absolute rules and is to be exercised according to the facts of the particular case.[6]

The inherent power of the court is discretionary and infrequently used, because it is often difficult to deal with allegations justly on the spot as they arise. Orders can include an order that a solicitor pays compensation. This is an alternative to suing the lawyer in contract or tort and is therefore advantageous to the applicant.[7] Courts have power under the Civil Procedure Rules to manage and cap the costs of cases[8] or to make wasted costs orders against lawyers.[9] It is arguable that much of the inherent jurisdiction has been superseded by the rules of court, particularly those relating to wasted costs orders.[10]

---

[2] T Johnson, *Profession and Power* (London and Basingstoke, Macmillan, 1972).

[3] TC Halliday, *Beyond Monopoly: Lawyers, State Crises, and Professional Empowerment* (Chicago and London, University of Chicago Press, 1987).

[4] *Nicholas Drucker & Co v Pridie Brewster & Co* [2005] EWHC 2788.

[5] Solicitors Act 1974, s 50.

[6] *Taylor v Ribby Hall Leisure* [1997] 4 All ER 760 (CA) at 768–69.

[7] See *Myers v Elman* [1939] 4 All ER 484; *Udall v Capri Lighting Ltd* [1987] 3 All ER 262. See also AD Ipp, 'Lawyers' Duties to the Court' (1998) 114 *Law Quarterly Review* 63.

[8] Civil Procedure Rules 1998, as amended, r 44.2.

[9] ibid, r 44.11.

[10] See further ch 17: 'Litigation'.

Courts can also refer lawyers to one or more of their professional bodies. Judges used to refer minor misdemeanours to a barrister's head of chambers, but it is not clear how widespread this practice still is. It is probably more usual that, where a barrister fails in his duty to the court, the judge refers the matter to the Bar for disciplinary investigation. The court can also refer a solicitor to the Solicitors Regulation Authority.[11] There is no information as to how frequently these types of reference occur.

Courts also preside over court cases involving lawyers, often arising from the conduct of work. These can arise from either criminal or civil proceedings. Until relatively recently, the Bar enjoyed immunity from actions in contract and professional negligence related to advocacy. This was partly based on public policy grounds[12] and partly on the proposition that barristers did not enter into a contract to provide advocacy services when accepting a brief.

This contractual argument was eroded by the Courts and Legal Services Act 1990, section 61, which allowed barristers to make binding contracts. This was initially overridden by the Bar Code of Conduct, which was subsequently amended to allow barristers to make binding contracts with solicitors on specified terms of work.[13] In the meantime, advocates' immunity was not seriously challenged in any of the reviews of the legal profession taking place between 1969 and 1999 and was preserved by the Act.[14] On the contrary, the Courts and Legal Services Act 1990 extended any immunity to those acquiring advocacy rights under the Act (see section 62). In 2000, however, immunity was abolished by the House of Lords.

B. The Professional Code of Conduct

Traditionally, codes of conduct provide the rules governing professional behaviour. They are therefore one of the primary mechanisms of regulation. They symbolise a high degree of occupational professionalization.[15] They also operate as a mechanism for building professional empires. Pound refers to the attempts of the American Bar Association (ABA) to establish a common code for state Bar Associations as an example.[16] A strong influence on lawyers' codes of conduct is the courts. The bases of many of the rules of professional conduct are found in the ordinary law of contract, agency or trusts and much of the detail in the rules derives from court decisions on particular issues of conduct.

---

[11] *Goodwood Recoveries v Breen* [2006] 2 All ER 533.

[12] Upheld in *Rondel v Worsley* [1967] 1 AC 191. See also *Saif Ali v Mitchell* [1978] 3 All ER 1033; *Kelley v Corsten* [1997] 4 All ER 466; and *Atwell v Perry & Co* [1998] 4 All ER 65.

[13] Bar Council/BSB, *Code of Conduct of the Bar of England and Wales 1981*, 8th edn, as amended, Annex G2.

[14] *Hall v Simons* [2000] 3 All ER 673 (HL); and see M Seneviratne, 'The Rise and Fall of Advocates' Immunity' (2001) 21(4) *Legal Studies* 644.

[15] LH Newton, 'Lawgiving for Professional Life: Reflections on the Place of the Professional Code' in A Flores (ed), *Professional Ideals* (Belmont, CA, Wadsworth Publishing, 1988) at 47.

[16] R Pound, *The Lawyer from Antiquity to Modern Times: With Particular Reference to The Development of Bar Associations in the United States* (St Paul, MN, West Publishing, 1953) at 270–349.

i. Form

Codes of conduct are often composed of three distinct types of norm.[17] First, there are 'standards' set by the professional body, usually virtues such as honesty and competence. Secondly, 'principles' prescribe general responsibilities and allow a degree of discretion in interpretation and implementation. Thirdly, 'rules' prescribe specific conduct, leaving little room for interpretation. Disciplinary sanctions are normally imposed for breaches of rules rather than for breaches of standards or principles.

ii. Link to Discipline

Breaches of codes of conduct generally result in the professional being subject to professional disciplinary machinery. While, in theory, all breaches could result in disciplinary proceedings this tends not to happen.[18] Breaches may be regarded as technical or trivial and may not be pursued. Not all of the norms represented in a code of conduct are intended to have the same disciplinary force.

Professional codes sometimes contain aspirational rules. For example, breaking a rule requiring lawyers to do 40 hours of pro bono work a year, may not have disciplinary implications. It can sometimes be difficult to predict which rules will be taken seriously. The English professions have, for example, often invoked quite strong sanctions, like the refusal of a practising certificate, for failing to complete Continuing Professional Development requirements.

iii. Legal Status of the Codes of Conduct

It might be thought that the rules in the professional codes would be binding in the same way as any other delegated legislation. The courts, however, have not always followed this line. The fact that the Solicitors' Practice Rules prohibit a practice does not, by itself, mean that the practice is illegal.[19] In *Giles v Thompson*,[20] Lord Mustill stated that rules banning contingency fees were simply rules of professional conduct. This was supported by Lord Justice Millett in *Thai Trading Co v Taylor*,[21] who said that rules against contingency fees were based on a perception of public policy derived from judicial decisions. In effect, he also declared the relevant Solicitors' Practice Rule to be inapplicable.

In contrast, it was implied in *Garbutt v Edwards*[22] that the conduct rules were binding, but not necessarily all the guidance or supplementary codes issued under the rules. The rules appearing in the Guide, however, often went beyond the Solicitors' Practice

---

[17] MD Bayles, *Professional Ethics* (Belmont, CA, Wadsworth Publishing, 1981) at 22.
[18] R Cranston, *Legal Ethics and Professional Responsibility* (Oxford, Clarendon Press, 1995) at 1–6.
[19] See *Picton Jones & Co v Arcadia Developments Ltd* [1989] 1 EGLR 43 and *Thai Trading Co v Taylor* [1998] 3 All ER 65, at 69.
[20] *Giles v Thompson* [1993] 3 All ER 321.
[21] *Thai Trading Co v Taylor* [1998] 3 All ER 65.
[22] *Garbutt v Edwards* [2005] All ER (D) 316.

Rules. The same applied to the other codes that were developed. The Client Care Code of 1999 or the Solicitors' Publicity Code, for example, had a debatable legal status and could not be regarded as legally binding.[23] Nevertheless, the 1999 version of the Guide firmly noted that Law Society guidance was 'treated as authoritative' by various bodies, including 'the Solicitors' Disciplinary Tribunal and the Court'. [24] The legal status of the 2007 Rules was probably firmer, but they were not in place for long enough to attract significant judicial guidance.

Codes of conduct are often conceived of as the basis on which professionals offer services to the public. There may therefore be perceived to be an implicit obligation to obey explicit and unequivocal rules of the code of conduct. Surprisingly, this proposition is open to question. Writers in several disciplines criticise approaches which reduce ethical decision-making to simply following rules.[25] Approaches which place heavy reliance on lawyers exercising their own judgement and discretion[26] strengthen the lawyer's own 'ethical autonomy', but at a substantial risk to client autonomy.

iv. Making and Changing Rules of Conduct

Since it acquired rule-making powers in 1933, the Law Society's rules had to be approved by the Master of the Rolls. The Courts and Legal Services Act 1990 established the Lord Chancellor's Advisory Committee on Legal Education and Conduct (ACLEC).[27] The ACLEC, a body consisting of lawyers and laypersons, had to recommend approval of proposed rule changes relating to rights of audience and the conduct of litigation before approval by the Lord Chancellor and four designated judges. Government had wanted the Lord Chancellor alone to approve professional rules.[28]

By 1998, ACLEC was under attack from the Lord Chancellor. One of his concerns was the amount of time it took to obtain approval for change. The Access to Justice Act 1999 changed the rules to require the consent of the Lord Chancellor to any rule changes concerning audience rights and rights to conduct litigation. He also had the power to review rules he considered unduly restrictive, taking advice from the designated judges and the Legal Services Consultative Panel.[29] Consultation on rule changes was required, for example on competition issues, with the OFT and the Financial Services Authority (FSA).

---

[23] HWR Wade, *Administrative Law* (Oxford, Clarendon Press, 1994) at 857.

[24] R Taylor (ed), *The Guide to the Professional Conduct of Solicitors* (London, The Law Society, 1996) at para 1.03.

[25] J Ladd, 'Legalism and Medical Ethics' in Flores, *Professional Ideals* (n 15).

[26] W Simon, 'Ethical Discretion in Lawyering' (1988) 101 *Harvard Law Review* 1083.

[27] See further ch 3.

[28] A Crawley and C Brammall, 'Professional Rules, Codes and Principles Affecting Solicitors (or What has Professional Regulation to do with Ethics?)' in Cranston, *Legal Ethics and Professional Responsibility* (n 18) at 101.

[29] Lord Chancellor's Department, *Rights of Audience and Rights to Conduct Litigation: The Way Ahead* (Consultation Paper) (June 1998) ch 4.

C. Legal Services Ombudsman

Before 1991, solicitors were subject to the jurisdiction of an official called the Lay Observer. The post was established by statute[30] to deal with situations where complainants were dissatisfied with the profession's response. The Lay Observer was replaced with the Legal Services Ombudsman (LSO) by the Courts and Legal Services Act 1990. The remit of the LSO was to consider complaints about the way legal professional bodies, including the Council for Licensed Conveyancers, the Institute of Legal Executives, Bar Council and Law Society,[31] handled complaints against their members. The LSO was appointed by the Lord Chancellor and was required to be a qualified lawyer.[32]

Although the LSO's main task was to review complaints handling, he or she could also investigate the complaint itself. The Ombudsman could recommend that the professional body reconsider the complaint, initiate disciplinary proceedings against the member, pay compensation for the loss, distress or inconvenience caused by the way it dealt with the complaint or pay the complainant's costs. It could also recommend that the lawyer originally complained of pay compensation for loss, inconvenience or distress caused and the costs.[33]

On completing investigations, the LSO sent a written report to the complainant, the lawyer against whom the complaint was made and the relevant professional body. The LSO's report was a public document and absolutely privileged, in the same way as a legal judgment. A failure by the lawyer complained of, or the professional body, to do what the Ombudsman ordered within three months could result in that failure being publicised and a further order for costs. The Ombudsman's reports were not directly enforceable in any other way.

In 2004–05 the LSO reviewed 1,265 cases against solicitors. This represented just around 7 per cent of the total complaints made to the Law Society, an improvement on the figure of 10 per cent, which was common in the late-1990s. The LSO was dissatisfied with the way 38 per cent of these complaints were handled. Of 455 complaints against barristers, the LSO dealt with 174, but she was satisfied that nearly 79 per cent had been properly handled.[34]

In addition to reviewing complaints handling by the professional bodies, the LSO acquired the role of Legal Services Complaints Commissioner (LSCC), set up under the Access to Justice Act 1999, with powers to monitor and set targets for the Law Society complaints service. Despite the oversight of the LSO, most clients with a complaint about professional services were required to first use the procedures operated by the professions themselves.

---

[30] Administration of Justice Act 1985, s 3.
[31] Courts and Legal Services Act 1990, ss 21–26.
[32] ibid, s 21 and Administration of Justice Act 1999, ss 51 and 52.
[33] Courts and Legal Services Act 1990, s 23(2).
[34] LSO, *Annual Report of the Legal Services Ombudsman for England and Wales 2004–2005, Making Sure Your Voice is Heard* (July 2005) at 40.

D. Complaints

Complaints systems fall within broad definitions of regulation. The primary purpose may be to provide recompense to injured clients but they may also bring about changes in the parties complained about. One of the main ways by which the profession enforces its ethical and regulatory rules is by receiving, investigating and acting on complaints received from clients or, sometimes, from other solicitors or the courts. Complaints and disciplinary procedures run by the professions were accused of being slow and providing inadequate redress to the consumer.

i. Complaints about Solicitors

a. Firms' Internal Complaints Handling

The Law Society was keen that firms set up effective complaints systems in order to minimise the number of complaints. The OSS, the predecessor of the Complaints Service, dealt with some 12–20 complaints per 100 solicitors a year.[35] The requirement that firms have an internal complaints-handling system was first introduced in 1991. Solicitors were generally slow to comply. In 1997, 86 per cent of all firms stated that they had a formal complaints procedure, but in the case of single partner firms, only 66 per cent had complied. Only 29 per cent of solicitors had received any training in handling complaints.[36] The LSO Report noted that the Law Society's attempts to encourage proper complaints handling at firm level had largely failed.

Research into solicitors' firms' complaint systems concluded that it is 'probably a mistake to press solicitors to adopt systems which do not accord with their sense of professional obligation, and which, in the context of their particular practice, do not make economic sense'.[37] Research conducted for the Clementi Review noted that the requirements of the old Rule 15 (which preceded Rule 2 in the 2007 Code) were 'either derided or misunderstood by a sizable proportion of the profession'.[38] Firms responded by not complying or complying grudgingly. Some were said to use incomprehensible client care letters.

By the time the Solicitors' Code of Conduct 2007 was enacted, the requirement for firms to have in-house procedures for handling complaints was reinforced by rules. Every firm had to have a written complaints procedure for clients and ensure that complaints were handled 'promptly, fairly and effectively'.[39] Clients had to receive a letter setting out who to complain to in the firm, how complaints would be handled

[35] LSO, *Annual Report 2000–01*, at 4.
[36] Client Care Survey reported in the *Law Society Gazette* 25 June 1997, at 26.
[37] G Davis, C Christensen, S Day and J Worthington, 'The Client as Consumer' (1998) 5 *New Law Journal* 832,
[38] R Moorhead, 'Self Regulation and the Market for Legal Services' in S Holm and J Gunning (eds), *Ethics, Law and Society*, vol II (Aldershot, Ashgate, 2005) and see D Clementi, *Review of the Regulatory Framework for Legal Services in England and Wales—Final Report* (London, DCA, 2004) (Clementi Report) ch C, at para 59.
[39] SRA, *Solicitors' Code of Conduct 2007*, r 2.05.

and within what timescales. They had to be given a copy of the procedure on request. Solicitors were not allowed to charge for handling complaints.

b. Complaints Handling by External Bodies

The Solicitors' Complaints Bureau

Until 1986 complaints were dealt with directly by the Law Society. This led to the criticism that the process was more concerned to protect the profession rather than the public.[40] In 1986, the Society set up the semi-autonomous Solicitors' Complaints Bureau (SCB). This was accused of being insufficiently independent of the Law Society and also of being very slow. It would not deal with complaints of negligence as the Law Society considered that these should be dealt with by the courts. While it would deal with shoddy work, this was not defined in written professional standards and clients found it difficult to establish that work was shoddy. The line between negligent and shoddy work was difficult to draw.

Criticisms of the SCB extended to its communications, which were seen as legalistic and evasive. According to both the Lord Chancellor's Department and the National Consumer Council, the administration of complaints was not working.[41] In his 1996 Annual Report, the Legal Services Ombudsman (LSO) said that

> [i]n ... 1995 ... I expressed the view that, unless the professional bodies were able to deliver a higher level of consumer satisfaction with the way that complaints were dealt with, it was unlikely that self-regulatory complaints handling would survive into the next century.[42]

In the 1997 Annual Report the newly appointed LSO, Ann Abraham, warned that poor communication in dealing with complaints 'pervades the dealing of both practitioners and the professional bodies with clients and complainants [which] suggests a ... significant and deep-rooted introspection which fails to engage with the legitimate expectations of the contemporary consumer of legal services'.[43] Solicitors were not happy with the SCB, which they saw as favouring clients and as an expensive public relations disaster. The SCB cost £13,213 million in 1994–95, a rise of just over 23 per cent on the previous year.[44]

The Office for the Supervision of Solicitors

The SCB was replaced by the Office for the Supervision of Solicitors (OSS) in 1996. This was thought to be a last chance to retain a measure of self-regulation in the field of complaints. Complaints rose sharply at the end of 1997 and the delays in dealing with them once again became unacceptable.[45] The delays and the criticism, especially from the LSO, continued, leading to targets being set by the Lord Chancellor's Office. The OSS was asked to deal with 75 per cent of complaints within six months, but by November 2003 the OSS was 'falling well short of its agreed targets'.[46]

---

[40] M Davies, 'The Regulatory Crisis in the Solicitors' Profession' (2003) 6 *Legal Ethics* 185.
[41] LSO, *Annual Report 1995*, 147 *New Law Journal* March 1997.
[42] LSO, *Report of the Legal Services Ombudsman 1996* (London, HMSO, 1997).
[43] See article in *Legal Action*, August 1998, at 8.
[44] SCB, *Annual Report 1995*, at 17.
[45] *The Lawyer* 24 March 1998.
[46] LSO Interim Report, *Breaking the Cycle* (November 2003).

The Law Society attempted to remedy failings in the OSS by appointing its own lay Complaints Commissioner to audit the system, a post that lasted until 2005. As the LSO noted in her 2003–04 Report, reorganisations were welcome but 'insufficiently robust'.[47] The LSO was satisfied with the Law Society's handling of complaints in only 53 per cent of the cases brought to her. This was down from 67 per cent satisfaction in the previous year.

The penultimate complaints system operated by the Law Society before the Legal Services Act was the Consumer Complaints Service (CCS), created in April 2004. The quality of complaints handling had improved but the speed and quantity had declined since the previous year. The Law Society continued to fail all but one of the targets on time scales.[48] The immediate response of the government was to utilise a power, originally created by the Access to Justice Act 1999,[49] to appoint the LSO to the post of Legal Services Complaints Commissioner (LSCC). From February 2004 the LSO was charged with the task of reviewing the Law Society's performance, setting targets and imposing penalties (of up to £1million) if necessary.

In May 2006, the LSCC fined the Law Society £250,000 for failing to improve complaints handling sufficiently and for not having a plan to do so.[50] The chair of the Law Society's Consumer Complaints Board described this as being 'wholly unreasonable' and 'outrageously disproportionate'.[51] Eventually, £30,000 of the fine was remitted when a plan setting targets for the CCS was agreed.[52]

The Legal Complaints Service
In October 2004 Sir David Clementi said, 'I do not believe that the current system delivers sufficient independence from the legal practitioner, nor that it provides appropriate levels of consistency and clarity'.[53] Clementi recommended setting up an independent Office for Legal Complaints. The Law Society then separated its regulatory and representative functions, placing the latter under an independent Solicitors Regulation Board, now the Solicitors Regulation Authority (SRA).

In 2006, the Law Society set up a separate Consumer Complaints Board (CCB) under the Solicitors Act 1974 and the Law Society Charter. This was to be responsible for the Consumer Complaints Service. The final change, in 2007, was to rename the CCS the Legal Complaints Service (LCS). It pledged to keep both sides better informed on the progress of complaints and to go online from September 2007.

Towards the end of its life, the LCS was dealing with more than 18,500 complaints a year. In April 2007, the Board agreed with the LSO that at least 67 per cent of complaints should be closed within three months of receipt and no more than 65 files should be open for more than 12 months. The LSCC criticised complaints handling in the year 2006–07, being satisfied with the conduct of only 68 per cent of the 1680 cases referred to her. While this was an improvement over previous years, she considered the service was 'still well short of where a modern, customer focussed organisation

---

[47] LSO, *Annual Report 2003–04*, at 14.
[48] ibid, at 13.
[49] Access to Justice Act 1999, ss 51–52.
[50] C Dyer, 'Law Society fined over solicitor complaints' *The Guardian* 18 May 2006.
[51] ibid.
[52] *Law Society Gazette* 9 November 2006, at 3.
[53] DCA, *The Future of Legal Services: Putting Consumers First* (Cm 6679, 2005) ch C, at para 33.

should be'.[54] In June 2008, the LSC was fined £275,000 by the LSCC for having an inadequate complaints-handling plan.

ii. Complaints against Barristers

a. Bar Complaints Schemes

Until April 1997 there was no effective complaints system for barristers' clients. Abel noted that the majority of complaints since 1957 were dismissed before reaching the Senate.[55] In 1979, the Senate rejected a recommendation of the Royal Commission that it should interview all complainants, a measure that might have improved the success rate.[56] In so far as a system did exist, its function was to alert 'the Professional Conduct Committee to possible breaches of the Bar's code of conduct'.[57]

Suspicions about the Bar's receptiveness to complaints were reinforced by its treatment of those experiencing problems with advocacy. Because of the civil immunity from negligence claims until 2000, the Bar excluded advocacy from its complaints jurisdiction. Consumers obviously disliked the rule, but it also came under increasing criticism from lawyers and judges. For example, in *Kelley v Corston*, Lord Justice Judge commented,

> the immunity of the advocate is not founded on some special protection granted by the court to the legal profession to enable lawyers to avoid justified complaints by dissatisfied clients... The immunity arises in very limited circumstances when the general public interest prevails against even a meritorious claim.[58]

In other respects, the Bar did not encourage complainants. There was no indication in the Bar Code of Conduct as to what should be done if a client or solicitor wished to complain, although it did set out, in an appendix, details of the workings of the Professional Conduct Committee. About 400 complaints were received by this committee each year. After lengthy and often acrimonious negotiations[59] the Bar Council launched a new complaints system dealing both with matters of discipline and also with inadequate professional service. Heads of chambers had to ensure that chambers had a properly operated complaints procedure. Only complainants not satisfied after having used this system could use the Bar complaints system.

b. Professional Conduct and Compliance Committee

The 1997 reform introduced an improved but complex system with a Professional Conduct and Compliance Committee (PCCC). The procedure ran to 71 lengthy paragraphs with numerous sub and sub-sub clauses.[60] The Bar Council also appointed a lay Complaints Commissioner to vet all complaints and to send those that merited

---

[54] *Law Society Gazette* 21 June 2007, at 1.
[55] RL Abel, *The Legal Profession in England and Wales* (Oxford, Basil Blackwell, 1988).
[56] ibid, at 135–36.
[57] LSO, *Annual Report for England and Wales 1996* (n 42) at para 3.23.
[58] *Kelley v Corston* [1997] 4 All ER 466, at 471.
[59] M Zander, *Cases and Materials on the English Legal System*, 7th edn (London, Butterworths, 2006) at 578–79.
[60] Bar Council, *Bar Code of Conduct 1981*, as amended, Annex J.

referral to the PCCC. This then referred cases of inadequate professional service to an adjudicating panel chaired by the Complaints Commissioner. Complaints against barristers rose by 25 per cent after the introduction of the new system. Of the 551complaints made in 1997, 140 were referred to the PCCC.[61]

In 1998 the Complaints Commissioner published a report on the new system that reached rather mixed conclusions. It concluded that the Bar had a good system in which the strengths outweighed the weaknesses.[62] The report noted, however, that

> a very small percentage of barristers are disciplined as a result of criminal conviction. A slightly larger percentage apparently make mistakes through incompetence or cutting corners. Overwork or laziness leads to mishaps. Arrogance and self-importance result in rudery and bombast. Sometimes these can cause real disadvantage and distress.[63]

Complaints, and references for action, continued to rise after 2000. There were 667 complaints against barristers in 2004 and 877 in 2005. In 2006–07, 166 cases were referred from the Bar complaints system to the LSO. She was satisfied that 84 per cent of cases had been satisfactorily dealt with.[64] Remarkably, there was no significant increase of complaints following introduction of the direct access rules.

While the Bar complaint system was potentially confusing for non-lawyers, it seemed to work quite well. In 2004, the LSO found the Bar complaints machinery to be reasonably competent.[65] It only needed to be made more responsive to the needs of complainants, less complex, more independent and more accessible.[66] Even the Clementi Report joined the chorus of approval.[67]

c. The Professional Conduct and Complaints Committee of the Bar Standards Board

From 2006 complaints had to be made to the Bar Standards Board and dealt with by the Professional Conduct and Complaints Committee (PCCC). Matters of professional misconduct were referred to the Bar Disciplinary Tribunal. Up until March 2011, after which date consumer complaints had to be referred to a Legal Services Ombudsman, the PCCC considered whether there was a realistic prospect of a finding of inadequate professional service. If there was such a possibility, but no realistic prospect of a finding of professional misconduct, it could direct that the complaint be referred to an adjudication panel to be dealt with as a case of inadequate professional services alone.[68]

Adjudication panels comprised two lay persons and two barristers. They decided whether, on a balance of probabilities, a barrister had provided inadequate professional services. In terms of remedies the adjudication panel could direct the barrister to:

—— make a formal apology to the complainant for the inadequate service provided;
—— direct the barrister to repay or forego all or part of any fee rendered in respect of the inadequate service;

[61] *Law Society Gazette* 20 May 1998.
[62] V Cowan, 'Great Scott? Not Quite but Showing Promise' *The Lawyer* 9 June 1998, at 7.
[63] 'Barristers Accused of Arrogance and Self Importance' *The Lawyer* 19 May 1998.
[64] LSO, *Annual Report and Accounts 2006–07, Delivering Excellence* (June 2007) ch 5, at 40.
[65] LSO, *Annual Report 2003–04*, at 65–66.
[66] R Behrens, *A Strategic Review of Complaints and Disciplinary Processes* (London, BSB, July 2007); and see BSB, *Complaints and Disciplinary Processes Consultation Paper* (London, BSB, 2007).
[67] Clementi Report (n 38) ch C, at para 23.
[68] BSB, The Complaints Rules 2011, sch 2.

—— direct the barrister to pay compensation to the complainant in such sum as the panel shall direct not exceeding £15,000;
—— direct the barrister to complete Continuing Professional Development of such nature and duration as the panel shall direct and to provide satisfactory proof of compliance with this requirement to the Complaints Committee.

Where a barrister was directed to apologise to the complainant, the panel could direct that the apology was approved by the chair of the panel before being sent to the complainant. Appeals lay to a five-person panel containing two lay members and chaired by a QC.

Issues of professional misconduct had three possible outcomes, depending on severity. The first level involved holding an informal hearing before two barristers and one layperson. If the complaint was upheld the panel could order compensation of up to £15,000 to the client for any element of inadequate professional service involved. More serious cases of professional misconduct were dealt with by a Summary Procedure Panel consisting of a QC, a barrister and a layperson or by the Bar Disciplinary Tribunal (BDT).

d. The Professional Conduct Committee

When the Bar lost jurisdiction over consumer complaints, the PCCC was reconstituted as the Professional Conduct Committee (PCC). Its procedures are set out in Part 5 of the new BSB Handbook 2014 in the Complaint Regulations.[69] These give the PCC numerous powers, including the right to direct the investigation of complaints. It can determine whether any complaint discloses a potential breach of the Handbook, a potential case of professional misconduct or possibly satisfies the disqualification condition and, if so, deal with it accordingly.[70]

The rules provide that any complaint made against a BSB-regulated person, or against an individual working as an employee or manager of a BSB-authorised body, by or on behalf of a client must be referred without further consideration to the Legal Ombudsman.[71] This obviously reduces considerably the scope of the PCC's work. Where a breach of the Handbook justifies an administrative sanction, the PCC can impose small fines. The maximum level of fine that can be imposed is £1000 on a BSB-regulated individual and £1500 on a BSB-authorised body.[72] Appropriate cases can be referred to the BDT.[73]

E. Intervention

In addition to other regulatory powers the professions had power to directly intervene in the conduct of firms' and chambers' businesses. These powers are usually reserved for extreme cases, those where a legal practice poses a threat to its clients, the public or

---

[69] BSB, *Handbook 2014*, pt 5: 'Enforcement Regulations', A, 'The Complaints Regulations'.
[70] ibid, at rE2.
[71] ibid, at rE13.
[72] ibid, at rE52.
[73] ibid, at rE56.

the reputation of the profession. Whereas complaints systems were changed following the LSA 2007, powers of intervention remain solely with the regulators.

i. Solicitors

The Law Society, and subsequently the SRA, had powers to intervene in the conduct of the firm's business under the Solicitors Act 1974, section 35. The specified circumstances included those where the solicitor was suspected of dishonesty, adjudged bankrupt or sent to prison.[74] These powers could be used to prevent a firm from operating freely or at all. Documents could be possessed, finances frozen and monies due to the solicitor received if the Council passed a resolution.[75] Solicitors' practising certificates could be suspended where there was a suspicion of dishonesty.[76]

The Solicitors Act specified the circumstances calling these powers into operation. They included the need for urgent action to protect clients, where dishonesty was suspected, where the solicitor was bankrupt, had been imprisoned or otherwise incapacitated or where he or she was practising without a practising certificate.[77] When exercising powers of intervention, the regulator is bound to preserve the confidentiality of clients of the firm. It cannot even disclose information to an insurer seeking evidence of a partner's complicity in dishonesty, material which may affect its obligation to provide indemnity.[78]

Power of intervention in firms was exercisable where there was a breach of certain practice rules, in particular relating to the Solicitors' Indemnity Insurance or Accounts Rules. Although a client complaint about a solicitor was insufficient, undue delay in responding to a complaint investigation could trigger intervention. The SRA conducted some 50 to 60 interventions a year, the majority in sole practitioner firms.[79] Solicitors were given written notice of the intention to intervene and eight days in which to object.

The High Court could grant orders withdrawing intervention. In *Sheikh v Law Society*,[80] a solicitor had committed breaches of the Accounts Rules. She applied for withdrawal of intervention on the ground that there was no evidence of dishonesty and the breaches were not serious. At first instance she succeeded, but the Court of Appeal held that the court should be slow to substitute its own views for those of the Law Society. The Law Society should look at the whole situation, including the likelihood of future compliance, bearing in mind the potentially catastrophic consequences of intervention for solicitors and their clients.

---

[74] Solicitors Act 1974, sch 1: 'Intervention in a Solicitors Practice', 'Part I: Circumstances in which Society may Intervene'.

[75] ibid, sch 1: 'Intervention in a Solicitors Practice', 'Part II: Powers Exercisable on Intervention'.

[76] ibid, s 15(1A), as inserted by the CLSA 1990, s 91(2).

[77] ibid, sch 1, pt 1.

[78] *Quinn Direct Insurance Ltd v Law Society* [2010] EWCA Civ 805.

[79] M Davies, 'The Solicitors' Accounts Rules: How Safe is Clients' Money?' (2000) 3 *Legal Ethics* 49.

[80] *Sheikh v Law Society* [2005] 4 All ER 717 at first instance; [2006] EWCA Civ 1577, [2007] 3 All ER 183 on appeal. See also *Sritharan v Law Society* [2005] 4 All ER 1105.

ii. Barristers

The Bar had less developed powers of intervention than solicitors, probably because barristers did not handle client money. The Bar Standards Board did initiate a Chambers Monitoring Scheme in 2008 to assess compliance with the Code of Conduct. Chambers and sole practitioners were required to complete the questionnaire under the Code of Conduct.[81] Failure to complete and return the questionnaire could result in disciplinary action being taken by the BSB against the head of chambers. Low levels of non-compliance were reported.[82]

The Bar introduced an additional system in 2007, whereby poorly performing barristers could be referred to an advisory panel for help. Referrals came from solicitors, barristers or judges. This was not a part of either the complaints or disciplinary procedures. It was an intervention intended to provide assistance to struggling practitioners with a view to pre-empting a complaint.

III. Insurance

A. Solicitors

Apart from compensation orders made as a result of complaints, regulation provides compensation for clients for losses connected with the work done by their solicitors. This compensation comes from two other main sources. The first source is the solicitor's own indemnity insurance, maintenance of which is a requirement of practice. The second source is the Solicitors' Compensation Fund, which is currently run by the SRA. These systems of compensation were unaffected by the LSA 2007.

i. Indemnity Insurance

Indemnity insurance used to be organised by the Law Society, but the premiums were not appropriate to all types of practice. The main cause of claims is commercial and residential conveyancing, which represents 46 per cent of claims according to one insurer, whereas litigation gives rise to only 22 per cent of claims.[83] After much debate, it was decided that insurance should be negotiated on an individual firm basis. This proved a sensible decision. Competition pushed average premiums down, by 14 per cent in 2006 alone.[84]

---

[81] Bar Council, *Bar Code of Conduct 1981*, as amended, at para 905(a)(i).
[82] 'Chambers monitoring pilot' *Counsel* July 2013.
[83] Report of Zurich Professional (2005–06).
[84] *Law Society Gazette* 16 November 2006, at 1.

All solicitors, overseas lawyers and licensed bodies must maintain professional indemnity insurance or 'cease practice promptly'.[85] The insurance must be from a qualified insurer with cover of up to £1 million. Limited companies and limited liability partnerships must normally have additional cover of £2 million. The SRA Handbook 2011 contains an outcome in Chapter 1, that clients have the benefit of a firm's compulsory professional indemnity insurance. The outcome also contains a requirement that firms do not exclude or attempt to exclude liability below the minimum level of cover required by the SRA's Indemnity Insurance Rules.[86]

Where firms had failed to acquire insurance they had to apply to an 'assigned risk pool' (ARP).[87] This was funded by the qualifying insurers in proportion to their premium income to ensure that all firms were covered. Firms in the ARP were required to pay the premium set, and the costs of the SRA, and submit to monitoring by the SRA. If a firm failed to make an application to the ARP, but carried on practice without having obtained qualifying insurance, each principal in that firm committed a disciplinary offence.[88]

Only 17 firms were in the ARP in 2006. In 2010 this had grown to 259 firms.[89] The firms generally had fewer than four employees. They were concentrated in and around London, particularly the East and South East, and in Birmingham. Of the 188 firms providing details of specialisation, the main areas of work covered were immigration and conveyancing. In these firms 52 per cent had a Black and Minority Ethnic solicitor majority and 27 per cent had a White majority. The BME firms tended to have been established for a shorter period of time. Overall, 39 per cent of the firms had a claim outstanding.

The SRA, with the support of the Law Society, decided to close the ARP to new entrants by December 2013.[90] Existing members would be required to leave, except in limited circumstances.[91] Firms unable to obtain qualifying insurance were given a 90-day policy extension from their previous insurer, the 'extended indemnity period' (EIP). The EIP was a period of 30 days in which a firm could continue to practise and try to obtain qualifying insurance. After this time, firms entered a cessation period of 60 days in which they could only perform work in connection with existing instructions. The Law Society claims that abolishing the ARP, with the obligation to contribute to claims through the ARP, would encourage new and smaller insurers to offer solicitors insurance cover.

ii. Solicitors' Compensation Fund

The Solicitors' Compensation Fund (SCF) was established in 1942. It was originally a 'discretionary fund of last resort' to compensate victims of defaulting solicitors.[92] The

---

[85] SRA, Indemnity Insurance Rules 2012, r 4(1) and (2).
[86] SRA, *Handbook 2011*, Outcome 1.8.
[87] SRA, Indemnity Insurance Rules 2012, r 10(1).
[88] ibid, r 16(1).
[89] G Carpenter and O Wyman, *Law Society of England and Wales Assigned Risks Pool: Review of Law Firms* (New York, Marsh, 2010).
[90] www.lawsociety.org.uk/advice/articles/assigned-risks-pool/.
[91] SRA, Indemnity Insurance Rules 2012, r 12(1).
[92] E Skordaki and C Willis, *Default by Solicitors* (London, The Law Society, 1991).

power to make such payments is contained in the Solicitors Act 1974.[93] It now covers the defaults of all those regulated by the SRA, such as managers of authorised bodies, and their employees. Major claims were made on the fund in the 1980s in connection with mortgage fraud, fuelled by the collapse of the property market. The discretionary powers of the Law Society in compensating for such frauds were the subject of litigation in the case of *R v The Law Society, ex p Mortgage Express Ltd*.[94]

R v The Law Society was a test case, with claims by lenders of up to £25 million hinging on the outcome. The facts concerned inflated valuations made of properties about which the solicitor failed to warn a mortgage lender. As a result, when the borrowers defaulted, the lenders lost a considerable amount of money in trying to recoup loans from the sale of property. The Law Society's policy was to refuse compensation from the fund where the dishonest solicitor did not commit the fraud for his own benefit. This policy was upheld by the Court of Appeal. Lord Bingham considered that the profession was not called upon to make good *every* loss caused by a solicitor's dishonesty. He said that 'The Law Society has always ... made clear that they regard the fund as, first and foremost, a source from which to replace money which has been taken by dishonest solicitors for their own benefit'.[95]

Clients may also be unable to recover if their solicitor has been reckless or negligent in relation to the loss incurred. In *R v Law Society, ex p Ingram Foods*,[96] the applicants were found to be reckless. They had accepted an undertaking in relation to a $5 million deposit from a sole practitioner without any documentation or other checks. The Law Society was held to be entitled to reduce the compensation that would otherwise have been ordered by 100 per cent.

The principles established by the various cases in which claims were made against the SCF underpin the current operation of the fund. The SCF is currently administered by the SRA under the Solicitors' Compensation Fund Rules 2011.[97] This means that applications are entertained only where there is no other source of compensation from insurance or elsewhere. Contributions of about £300 per year currently are made to it by all practising solicitors holding client monies under the Solicitors Act 1974, section 36, and authorised bodies or licensed bodies under the LSA 2007.

The SCF makes grants to those who have suffered loss as a result of a solicitor's dishonesty or failure to account for money that is due. Claims must normally be made within 12 months of the date of the loss or the applicant's knowledge of it.[98] The claimant does not necessarily have to be a client of the defaulting solicitor, but dishonesty by the solicitor must be proven. This may be by establishing that there has been a conviction for fraud, or a civil finding of fraud, or by presenting evidence leading to the 'inevitable presumption' of theft.[99] Victims may also be required to pursue other remedies.[100]

---

[93] Solicitors Act 1974, s 36.
[94] *R v The Law Society, ex p Mortgage Express Ltd* [1997] 2 All ER 348.
[95] ibid, at 360.
[96] *R v Law Society, ex p Ingram Foods* [1997] 2 All ER 666.
[97] Solicitors' Compensation Fund Rules 2011 (www.sra.org.uk/solicitors/handbook/v1/compfund/content.page).
[98] ibid, r 11.
[99] ibid, sch, para 4.
[100] ibid, r 13.

Claimants must show one of two grounds of claim. First, they must show that they have suffered or are likely to suffer loss in consequence of the dishonesty of a defaulting practitioner or the employee or manager or owner of a defaulting practitioner.[101] Alternatively, they must show they suffered loss and hardship in consequence of a failure to account for money by the defaulting practitioner. Grants can also be made to practitioners who have suffered as a result of others' default, normally by way of loan.[102]

The maximum grant is normally £2 million,[103] although this limit is subject to waiver.[104] Where an applicant or their servant or agent has contributed to the loss as a result of his, her or its activities, omissions or behaviour whether before, during or after the event giving rise to the application, the SRA may reduce the amount of any grant or reject the application in its entirety.[105]

The majority of the defaulters whose clients are compensated from this fund are sole practitioners. Sole practitioners are more likely than other categories of firm to be guilty of fraud. This can be misleading however. Negligence actions are typically against three to five partner firms rather than sole practitioners. The largest claim against the Compensation Fund was in respect of a £13 million fraud committed by the senior partner of a 35-partner practice.[106] The indemnity fund will not provide compensation for fraud in multi-partner firms unless all the partners are involved in the fraud. Although defaulters do not appear to be a homogenous group, common factors include a history of submitting late accounts to the Law Society and personal problems at the time of the default.

The SRA has announced a 'root and branch review' of the compensation fund arrangements to be completed in autumn 2014.[107] The review will consider whether compensation is an essential part of protecting clients, what limits should be placed on entitlements, whether arrangements should distinguish between different types of legal services providers, whether calculation of contributions is appropriate, whether compensation arrangements are effective and efficient and whether there are gaps in client protection. The review will include research and public consultations.

B. Barristers

Barristers must be insured against claims for professional negligence with Bar Mutual Indemnity Fund (BMIF) in accordance with the terms approved by the Bar Council from time to time.[108] Barristers acting as self-employed barristers must be a member of the Bar Mutual Insurance Fund, unless they are a pupil covered by

---

[101] ibid, r 3(4).

[102] ibid, r 6.

[103] ibid, r 17.

[104] ibid, r 24.

[105] ibid, r 19.

[106] A Sherr and L Webley, 'Legal Ethics in England and Wales' (1997) 4 *International Journal of the Legal Profession* 109, at 130.

[107] SRA, *Compensation Arrangements Review* (www.sra.org.uk/sra/how-we-work/compensation-fund-review.page).

[108] BSB, *Bar Code*, at para 302.

his pupil supervisor's insurance or a Registered European Lawyer carrying separate insurance.[109] The new Bar code requires unregistered barristers to inform clients if they have no indemnity insurance.[110]

IV. Regulatory Infrastructure of the Legal Services Act 2007

A. Background

The Clementi Report criticised the way that practice rules were made by the professions. Clementi considered, for example, that the Bar Council and the Law Society were often held back by their members in making desirable changes to the rules. This, he thought, had restricted both competition and innovation in the professions. Changes, he observed, were often forced on the professions by outside pressures that they could no longer resist, such as the rules on direct access to the Bar. He concluded that 'issues such as changes in the practice rules should be examined, not against the wishes of the membership, but against the test of public interest'.[111]

Clementi did not recommend that all rule-making powers should be taken away from the professions. He felt that day to day rule-making should be left with them; they had the necessary knowledge and expertise to do it. Moreover, he considered it more likely that practitioners would be committed to high standards if the rules were formulated by their own profession. If they were formulated by another, such as government agencies, they might be regarded as a 'constraint to be circumvented'.[112]

The LSA 2007 contained proposals to change radically the complaints procedures. The disciplinary procedures of the professions, which Clementi considered work appropriately,[113] were untouched. By the time the Act was passed the Law Society and Bar Council had divested their regulatory powers. There were however, other significant changes to the regulatory infrastructure.

B. Legislative Infrastructure

In addition to requiring separation of the regulative and representative functions of professional bodies, the LSA 2007 required the introduction of other regulatory structures and requirements. The first change was the establishment of the oversight

---

[109] BSB, *Bar Handbook 2014*, rC77.
[110] ibid, rC144.
[111] Clementi Report (n 38) at para 13.
[112] ibid, at para 29.
[113] ibid, ch C, at para 84.

regulator, the Legal Services Board. The second was the authorisation of Alternative Business Structures and the creation of a framework for their operation. The third was the consolidation of complaints handling within a single organisation for the sector, the Office for Legal Complaints.

i. Legal Services Board and Approved Regulators

The Legal Services Board[114] and the approved regulators[115] must, so far as is reasonably practicable, act in a way which is compatible with the regulatory objectives. They must have regard to the principles under which regulatory activities should be transparent, accountable, proportionate, consistent and targeted only at cases in which action is needed. They must also be conscious of what appears to represent the best regulatory practice.

ii. Alternative Business Structures

a. Licensed Bodies

Alternative Business Structures (ABS) are defined as potentially licensed bodies under Part 5 of the LSA 2007. A body (B) is 'licensable' as a provider of one or more reserved legal activities if a non-authorised person is a manager of it or has an interest in it. It can also be licensable if another body (A) is a manager of or has an interest in B, and non-authorised persons control 10 per cent of the voting rights in A.[116] ABS are, therefore, vehicles for ownership and management of law firms by non-lawyers.

b. Licensing Authorities

Approved regulators[117] or the Legal Services Board (LSB)[118] can be designated as 'licensing authorities' for licensed bodies to deliver specified reserved activities. Licensing authorities must issue a policy statement approved by the LSB, stating how they will promote the regulatory objectives.[119] They must make licensing rules containing details of how licensable bodies will qualify for regulation by them. They must also specify regulatory arrangements, including conduct rules, discipline rules and practice rules, and indemnification and compensation arrangements.[120]

Licenses granted to licensable bodies must state the reserved activities that they are entitled to carry out and any conditions attached to the licence.[121] Conditions may include restrictions on the non-reserved activities, such as advice giving, which the

---

[114] LSA 2007, s 3.
[115] ibid, s 28.
[116] ibid, s 72.
[117] ibid, s 73.
[118] ibid, s 74.
[119] ibid, s 82.
[120] ibid, s 83(5).
[121] ibid, s 85.

licensed body may or may not carry on.[122] Licensing authorities do not necessarily have jurisdiction over all ABS activity. They only regulate reserved legal activity, non-reserved legal activity undertaken by the ABS and any non-legal activity that is subject to conditions imposed on the licence of the ABS.

Licensing authorities can suspend or revoke licences.[123] Designation of approved regulators can be cancelled by order of the Lord Chancellor on the recommendation of the LSB.[124]

c. Head of Legal Practice and Head of Finance and Administration

The LSA 2007 requires all licensed bodies to have a head of legal practice (HOLP) and head of finance and administration (HOFA). The HOLP is required to ensure compliance with the terms of the licence,[125] and the HOFA is required to ensure compliance with licensing rules relating to accounts.[126] Both are required to report breaches in their area of responsibility to the licensing authority.

d. Referral to Appropriate Regulator

Authorised persons are either authorised by an approved regulator to carry on a reserved activity or the manager or employee of such a person. Authorised persons working for a licensed body are referred to the approved regulator for breaches of that regulator's rules. The approved regulator would be either the regulator of the authorised person or the regulator of a non-reserved activity, as appropriate.[127] Licensing authorities can also refer employees or managers of licensed bodies, or HOLPs and HOFAs, to an appropriate regulator and to the LSB.[128] Licensing authorities can disqualify HOLPs or HOFAs or the managers or employees of licensed bodies for breaches of any duty to which they are subject. They may also be suspended where they 'substantially contribute to a significant breach of the terms of the licensed body's licence'.[129]

e. Breaches by Non-authorised Persons

Non-authorised persons, employees of the licensed body, including managers, or someone with an interest in it are also subjected to obligations under the LSA.[130] They must not do anything causing the body, or regulated persons within it, to breach duties to comply with the arrangements of the approved regulator.[131] They must also provide any information required by the licensing authority.[132] Failure to do so could

---

[122] ibid, s 85(7).
[123] ibid, s 101.
[124] ibid, ss 76–78.
[125] ibid, s 91.
[126] ibid, s 92.
[127] ibid, s 98(3).
[128] ibid, s 98(1).
[129] ibid, s 99.
[130] ibid, s 90.
[131] ibid, s 176.
[132] ibid, s 93.

result in an order made by the High Court.[133] These and other breaches could result in financial penalties imposed by the licensing authority.[134]

f. Financial Penalties

The LSA 2007 authorises licensing authorities to impose 'on a licensed body, or a manager or employee of a licensed body, a penalty of such amounts as it considers appropriate', up to a maximum prescribed by the LSB. [135] Appeals by licensed bodies to a designated appellate body are permitted on the grounds that the imposition of a penalty was unreasonable, or that the amount, or the time period allowed for payment, is unreasonable.[136] With the permission of the High Court, either party can appeal to that court on a point of law.[137]

g. Disqualification

A licensing authority can disqualify HOLPs, HOFAs or managers and employees of licensed bodies from undertaking those activities that are carried out in accordance with its licensing rules. The disqualification can cover one or more of those activities. In such cases, a disqualification condition, causing a breach of a duty to which they or the licensing body are subject, must be satisfied.[138] The licensing authority must also be satisfied that it is undesirable for the person to engage in those activities.[139]

iii. Office for Legal Complaints

a. The Legal Ombudsman

The LSA 2007 requires the establishment of an Office for Legal Complaints (OLC).[140] The OLC must prepare an annual report[141] and report to the LSB on any matter specified by it. The LSB may also set performance targets for the OLC. The OLC created a scheme for handling complaints which began operations in October 2010 under the title Legal Ombudsman. The Act provides for the appointment of a Chief Ombudsman who prepares an annual report and reports to the OLC.[142] The scheme is funded by a levy on approved regulators by the LSB.

---

[133] ibid, s 94(2).
[134] ibid, s 95.
[135] ibid, ss 95(1)–(3).
[136] ibid, s 96(2).
[137] ibid, s 96(6).
[138] ibid, s 99(3).
[139] ibid, s 99.
[140] ibid, s 114.
[141] ibid, s 118.
[142] ibid, ss 122–124.

b. Jurisdiction

Complaints can be received under the scheme either from individuals or, with the approval of the Lord Chancellor, from the OLC, LSB or the Consumer Panel.[143] They may be made against a person authorised in relation to a reserved activity, including ABS, whether or not the act or omission complained of relates to a reserved activity.[144] Such acts in the course of employment are treated as acts of the employer, whether or not they knew about them.[145] Complainants must have first used the complaints procedures required to be provided in relation to the respondent.[146]

c. Claims Handling

The office of the Legal Ombudsman has issued advice on bringing claims.[147] This is necessarily quite complex, and is a potential problem for some complainants. It provides that complaints be investigated and that the Ombudsman can hold hearings if necessary.[148] The Ombudsman can require production of any evidence that could be required in civil proceedings in the High Court.[149] The matter can exceptionally be referred to the court, either in whole or in part.[150]

d. Remedies

If the Legal Ombudsman finds in favour of complainants he can direct respondents to:

—— apologise;
—— pay compensation of a specified amount for loss suffered;
—— pay interest on that compensation from a specified time;
—— pay compensation of a specified amount for inconvenience/distress caused;
—— ensure (and pay for) putting right any specified error, omission or other deficiency;
—— take (and pay for) any specified action in the interests of the complainant;
—— pay a specified amount for costs the complainant incurred in pursuing the complaint; or
—— limit fees payable to them by the complainant to a specified amount.[151]

There is limit of £50,000 on the total value of compensation complainants can receive for loss suffered, inconvenience and distress caused, the reasonable cost of putting right any error, omission or other deficiency and the reasonable cost of any specified action in the interests of the complainant.[152]

---

[143] ibid, ss 28(3) and 130(6).
[144] ibid, s 128.
[145] ibid, s 131.
[146] ibid, s 126(1).
[147] Legal Ombudsman, Scheme Rules (February 2013) (www.legalombudsman.org.uk/downloads/documents/publications/Scheme-Rules.pdf).
[148] ibid, at paras 5.33–5.35.
[149] ibid, at para 5.22.
[150] ibid, at paras 5.8–5.11.
[151] ibid, at para 5.38.
[152] ibid, at para 5.43.

e. Complaints Revealing Misconduct

If the Legal Ombudsman considers that a complaint reveals misconduct, he may inform the approved regulator and tell the complainant that this is the case. The Legal Ombudsman may require that the approved regulator informs him of proposed action. Failure by that approved regulator to take action may be reported to the Legal Services Board.[153]

f. Costs

Because complainants are expected to act in person, costs orders against the lawyers complained about are rare.[154] They could, however, be ordered to pay a case fee of £400. Such orders are even less likely if the Legal Ombudsman is satisfied that the lawyers took all reasonable steps under their own complaints procedures to resolve the complaint.[155]

V. Wider Impact of the Legal Services Act on Regulation: Outcomes Focused Regulation

A. Background

The Legal Services Act did not make direct changes to regulation. The legal professions entered the post-LSA 2007 era with their education and training regimes, their codes of conduct and disciplinary arrangements intact. Nevertheless, the LSA 2007 did set in train events that drove significant changes in regulatory philosophy and, ultimately, led to the adoption of a new method of regulation for solicitors. This was initially known as Principles Focused Regulation, but is currently called Outcomes Focused Regulation (OFR). OFR is usually posed as an alternative to rule-based regulation of the kind associated with codes of conduct.

B. The Politics of OFR

i. Policy of the Legal Services Board

One of the driving motivations of the LSB was to establish ABS. This presented a number of problems, one of which was that ABS would be employing non-lawyers

---

[153] ibid, at para 5.59.
[154] ibid, at para 39.
[155] ibid, at paras 6.2 and 6.3.

alongside lawyers. Therefore, it would be necessary to ensure that non-professional staff did not interfere with the standards expected of legal businesses. This meant, for example, that legal professional privilege rules would need to apply to all those employed in in ABS.

An LSB consultation on ABS identified three, further 'key protections' to protect consumer interests, best professional principles and the public interest. The first was the need for a 'fit and proper test' for non-lawyer owners and managers of legal practices. The second was the appointment of HOLPs and HOFAs. The third was creating a forum where complaints about the 'non-legal' activities of ABS could be presented.

The LSB's pursuit of the regulatory objectives, and its obligation to promote the best regulatory practice, resulted in support for principles-based regulation (PBR) and risk-based regulation.[156] PBR formed part of a suite of regulatory approaches promoted as an alternative to the sort of rule-based regulation operated by professions. It was seen as an alternative to the 'nit-picking bureaucracy [of rule-based regulation] in which compliance with detailed provisions is more important than ... the overall outcome'.[157] PBR was tested in the financial services industry by the Financial Services Authority.

The financial services crash of 2007 caused the worst world-wide economic crises since the 1930s. This did not, apparently, undermine confidence in the idea of PBR, although it did lead to a change of name. The Financial Services Authority announced a new focus on 'outcomes focused regulation'.[158] This involved the same methods but applied with less of a 'light touch'. Indeed, there would be 'a greater depth of analytical rigour' and a commitment to 'proactively look to influence outcomes, not merely react to events'.[159] OFR in the financial services industry was to involve stronger emphasis on monitoring and inspection, involving more investigations and more 'intensive supervision'.

ii. The Law Society

Anticipating the challenge of regulating solicitors under the LSA 2007, the Law Society commissioned two reports on regulation in 2008. For the first, the former Tory politician and life peer, and chair of the financial services division of Beachcroft LLP, Lord Hunt of Wirral, was asked to consider ' the appropriate regulatory rules, monitoring and enforcement regime to ensure high standards of integrity and professionalism for solicitors and their firms in all sectors'.[160] The other report, from Nick

---

[156] LSB, *LSB Business Plan 2009/10* (London, Legal Services Board, 2009) at para. 30 (www.legalservicesboard.org.uk/news_publications/publications/pdf/business_plan_2009_10.pdf).

[157] J Black, 'The Rise, Fall and Fate of Principles Based Regulation' (2010) LSE Law, Society and Economy Working Papers (http://ssrn.com/abstract=1712862).

[158] H Wilson, 'Hector Sants calls time on FSA's light touch regulation' *The Telegraph* 12 March. 2010 (www.telegraph.co.uk/finance/newsbysector/banksandfinance/7431645/Hector-Sants-calls-time-on-FSAs-light-touch-regulation.html#).

[159] J Pain, 'FSA's Approach to Intensive Supervision' (FSA, 18 May 2010) (www.fsa.gov.uk/pages/Library/communication/Speeches/2010/1518_jp.shtml).

[160] Lord Hunt of Wirral, *The Hunt Review of the Regulation of Legal Services* (London, The Law Society, 2009).

Smedley, a former civil servant, was concerned with the regulation of corporate legal work as a sub-strand of the Hunt Review.

a. The Smedley Report

Smedley reported unrest among large firms about the way the fledgling SRA operated, claiming that it had no expertise and insufficient understanding of corporate or international legal work. This had led to 'a breakdown of trust and relationships between the sector and its regulator over recent years'.[161] In his view, simply scaling up the traditional model of regulation for large, corporate firms would not work. Smedley envisaged that 'effective regulation of the sector needs to be holistic, covering the development and refinement of appropriate practice rules, *ad hoc* regulatory guidance, training and so on'.[162]

In most cases, Smedley predicted, corporate firms would have low levels of complaint by clients to the SRA and could be reasonably assessed as a low risk. They have a low probability of regulatory failure, but with high impact when it occurs, a risk category suggesting regular, strategic systems level regulation. The appropriate regulatory regime for corporate firms, he concluded, taking into account their high motivation and high capacity, would involve a rule book of general principles and strategic supervision.[163] Smedley proposed a shift to 'principles-based regulation' for large firms.[164]

Smedley proposed creating a Corporate Regulation Group within the SRA, led by a Group Director recruited from the practice field or with strong regulatory experience in a comparable sector and with expertise supplemented by a Client and Practitioner Panel.[165] The Group would comprise Account Managers to visit firms, examine their business systems and issue low level sanctions as appropriate. Suspension or striking off, however, would continue to be exercised by the Solicitors Disciplinary Tribunal.

Investigations would be focused and short. They would quickly identify the issue, discuss shortfalls with senior partners, and require assurances on system-wide remedial action. Detailed forensic investigations would be reserved for cases of very serious and deliberate malpractice.[166] Smedley feared that, although the SRA accepted his recommendations for creating a specialist unit to handle large firms in principle, they would water them down in practice. He urged that, in that case, the Law Society should set up a separate regulator for corporate law firms.[167]

b. The Hunt Report

Lord Hunt was familiar with PBR and advocated it in his report. Hunt thought that a system of Authorised Internal Regulation (AIR), similar to the Smedley model, should be rolled out for all firms with compliance and governance processes that were

---

[161] N Smedley, *Review of the Regulation of Corporate Legal Work* (London, The Law Society, 2009) at iii.
[162] ibid, at para 3.22.
[163] ibid, at paras 2.30–2.32.
[164] ibid, at i.
[165] ibid, at 47, para 4.31.
[166] ibid at 42, para 4.12.
[167] ibid at 54, para 5.5.

sufficiently sophisticated and robust.[168] This would cover, initially, only the larger corporate firms.[169] Hunt also thought that the SRA should gather information on the risks posed by sectors and by different types of entity, and allocate the cost of regulation between all regulated parties, from individuals to entities.[170] Introducing his report in October 2009, Hunt welcomed many of Smedley's recommendations but sounded a note of caution on any regulatory measure that might divide the profession.

iii. The SRA

At the end of 2009, the chair of the LSB urged solicitors to seize the opportunity to change the profession.[171] The recently established SRA approached the issue of regulating solicitors having received a very strong steer. The LSB, and two consultant reports from the Law Society, had urged it to adopt PBR. Additionally, there seemed every prospect that the SRA would become a licensing authority for ABS.

The Law Society, an occasional supporter of multi-disciplinary practice, had decided this would be advisable, the President of the Law Society announcing that:

> We consider this to be good for solicitors, for the users of legal services and for UK plc. We are a global leader in selling legal services to the world.[172]

Had the SRA not stepped forward as a regulator of ABS, other approved regulators may have been tempted to, gaining a market advantage. If none had come forward, the LSB could have done so. It was assumed that regulation of ABS would require a broader approach than professional, rule-based regulation, which applied only to regulated persons.

Regulation of ABS, where regulated persons may be in the minority, and in minor positions, would require regulators to regulate the organisation or 'entity' as a whole, rather than just those individuals who happened to be regulated by an approved regulator. OFR appeared to offer a solution to this problem, because it looked to the outcomes achieved by the organisation rather than the behaviour of the individual. The SRA then had to decide whether to use more than one method of regulation. This would involve using the old, rule-based regulation method for regulating solicitors individually and the new organisation-based method for ABS. The alternative was to attempt a merger of the two methods. In the event it decided on merger.

In June 2009, the SRA consulted on its proposed new regulatory regime. It was in a confessional mood. It roundly criticised its existing procedures, stating that the lack of management information on firms prevented analysis of risk. It conceded that its approach to supervision was more focused on identifying detailed rule breaches than assessing the outcome for clients and the public interest. It agreed with criticism that its Ethics Helpline encouraged dependence, with staff spending excessive time advis-

---

[168] Hunt of Wirral, *The Hunt Review* (n 160) rec 41.

[169] ibid, rec 42.

[170] ibid, rec 38.

[171] D Edmonds, 'Seize the opportunity to change the profession' *The Lawyer* 7 December 2009.

[172] R Heslett, 'What alternative business structures mean for the legal profession' *The Guardian* 9 June 2010.

ing on detailed cases rather than empowering firms to decide, improving standards or protecting the interests of clients.[173]

The SRA consultation accepted a need to assist firms in achieving standards, to focus on risk management systems and on senior managers rather than on investigation of rule breaches. It welcomed new administrative sanctions, such as settlements agreed with offending organisations, rather than disciplinary sanctions.[174] This was an example of the shift of focus in regulation, away from the role and conduct of individual solicitors towards the role and performance of their employing organisations.

In March 2009, the SRA implemented rules bringing into effect 'firm-based regulation'. Thereafter, all legal practices, regardless of size, were to be regulated as a firm or 'recognised body' and subject to the SRA's Recognised Body Regulations (RBR). The composition and structure of recognised bodies, and a description of the services they could provide, was specified in the Solicitors' Code of Conduct 2007.[175] Until that point, these regulations had been used only for companies and limited liability partnerships. Afterwards, individuals could only provide services through recognised bodies. The RBR were amended to enable both entities and individuals within them to be charged a fee in their practising certificate. This was to be divided between regulation cost and a compensation fund contribution.[176]

In 2010, the SRA published three major consultations, the first seeking views on the intended move to Outcomes Focused Regulation,[177] the second outlining intentions for its practical implementation[178] and the third focusing on consequent changes to the Code of Conduct.[179] The promise was a 'proactive, risk-based and proportionate regulation' and a flexible regime for all types of legal service providers, creating a new handbook of regulatory requirements that would facilitate a 'flexible regime for all types of legal service providers, enabling them to create the right controls given their own individual business models, structures and client bases'.[180]

Despite the different statutory and practical bases for the regulation of first, recognised bodies and sole practitioners, and, second, ABS, the SRA considered that two regimes would create confusion for consumers and providers and would be expensive to operate.[181] It was therefore proposed, contrary to the recommendations of Smedley and Hunt, to apply the new regulatory system to all those regulated by the SRA, from sole practitioners to ABS.

In October 2010 the SRA published the results of the consultations to date and offered a last chance to comment on the emergent regime.[182] There were some objections, but most respondents were said to approve of the general direction of change.

---

[173] SRA, *An Agenda for Quality: a Discussion on how to Assure the Quality of the Delivery of Legal Services* (June 2009) at para 19.
[174] ibid, at paras 21–25.
[175] SRA, *Solicitors' Code of Conduct 2007*, r 14.
[176] Solicitors Act 1974, ss 79–80; Administration of Justice Act 1985; ss 9–9A; Legal Services Act 2007, sch 22, s 16.
[177] SRA, *Achieving the Right Outcomes* (January 2010).
[178] SRA, *The Architecture of Change: The SRA's New Handbook* (May 2010).
[179] SRA, *Outcome-focused Regulation: Transforming the SRA's Regulation of Legal Services* (May 2010).
[180] SRA, *The Architecture of Change* (n 178) at para 10.
[181] ibid, at paras 15, 17 and 18.
[182] SRA, *The Architecture of Change Part 2—the New SRA Handbook—Feedback and Further Consultation* (2010).

The Law Society raised some serious concerns about the abandonment of rules and the switch to OFR,[183] but the SRA brushed these aside. The SRA therefore adopted OFR despite the reservations of the Law Society, against Smedley's advice that the forerunner (PBR) only be used for corporate firms and Hunt's advice that a similar system be extended over time.

C. Implementation of OFR: The New Regulatory System

i. The Rule Book

Both Hunt and Smedley envisaged reduction in the volume of rules of conduct. Smedley proposed a single code of conduct with variations in respect of certain types of work.[184] When the SRA consulted in 2010, it stated that the new system would 'not mean the abolition of all detailed rules' but would offer a high level structure 'combining the flexibility of Outcomes Focused Regulation with the certainty of rules'.[185] It was anticipated that rules might be needed in 'high risk areas' involving a client's liberty or money. It was not clear until later consultations that OFR meant the end of rules in the conventional sense.

All regulatory requirements, Code, Accounts Rules, Licensing Rules etc, were consolidated in one handbook, published online. The idea was that new 'rule book' would lift the 'binding regulatory requirements' ('rules') to the level of principles and, would therefore be less detailed and prescriptive, not 'hinder innovation' and support providers in achieving 'good outcomes for consumers and the public interest'.[186] The new SRA code was timed to coincide with the introduction of ABS in 2011. The rules applied equally to individuals and entities. Therefore, when the SRA Code of Conduct refers to 'you' and 'your', this applies to individuals and firms collectively.

a. Principles

The Code identifies 10 principles, the first six taken from Rule 1 of the Solicitors' Conduct Rules 2007, the last four reflecting the new focus on regulation of businesses, or entities. They provide that regulated parties must:

1.   uphold the rule of law and the proper administration of justice;
2.   act with integrity;
3.   not allow your independence to be compromised;
4.   act in the best interests of each client;
5.   provide a proper standard of service to your clients;
6.   behave in a way that maintains the trust the public places in you and in the provision of legal services;

---

[183] ibid, at paras 73 and 83.
[184] SRA, *An Agenda for Quality* (2009) at 57, at para 6.1.
[185] SRA, *The Architecture of Change* (n 178) at para 25.
[186] ibid, at paras 1 and 17(a).

7. comply with your legal and regulatory obligations and deal with your regulators and ombudsmen in an open, timely and co-operative manner;
8. run your business/carry out your role in the business effectively and in accordance with proper governance and sound financial and risk management principles;
9. run your business/carry out your role in the business in a way that promotes equality and diversity and does not discriminate unlawfully in connection with the provision of legal services;
10. protect client money and assets.

b. Outcomes

The SRA Code comprises sections devoted to different topics, for example, client care, equality and diversity and conflicts of interest. Each section contains mandatory outcomes that must be achieved, by organisations and individuals. The mandatory nature of the outcomes is the element of the new rule book that most closely corresponds to conventional rules. Most outcomes are however, broader than rules would normally be. Curiously, some outcomes are expressed negatively, giving them something of the character of rules. For example, an outcome for publicity is that it must not be misleading.[187]

c. Indicative Behaviours

Indicative behaviours are not mandatory, because outcomes might be achieved by different routes.[188] Like some outcomes, some indicative behaviours are expressed negatively, giving them the character of rules. Take, for example, the indicative behaviours for publicity. The relevant outcome is that solicitors 'do not make unsolicited approaches in person or by telephone to members of the public in order to publicise your firm or in-house practice or another business'.[189]

The Code follows the outcome against unsolicited approaches with eight indicative behaviours, such as approaching people in the street, which would 'tend to show that you have not achieved these outcomes'.[190] The idea is that the firm may advance some reason why they had to approach people in the street. If, as seems likely, no reason for such approaches could be acceptable, this is the same as saying that not approaching people in the street for publicity reasons is a rule. Perhaps it would be fair to say that indicative behaviours are rebuttable presumptions about acceptable and unacceptable behaviour.

ii. Personnel

a. HOLPs and HOFAs/COLPs and COFAs

In its new regulatory framework, the SRA has taken the roles defined by the LSA 2007 (HOLP and HOFA) and renamed them compliance officer for legal practice

---

[187] SRA, *Code of Conduct* (2011), as amended, Outcome 8.1.
[188] SRA, *The Architecture of Change* (n 178) at 44,
[189] SRA, *Code of Conduct* (2011), as amended, Outcome 8.3.
[190] ibid, Indicative Behaviour 8.5–8.12.

(COLP) and compliance officer for finance and administration (COFA). It also required that all authorised bodies were required to nominate members for these roles. Therefore all law firms, including sole practitioners, were required to have posts that the Act only required ABS to have.

The SRA Authorisation Rules for Legal Services Bodies and Licensable Bodies outlines the requirements for the roles of COLP and COFA. Both must be an authorised person and either managers or employees of an authorised body. They must be registered with the SRA and able to prove that they have suitable skills. Therefore, a suitably qualified barrister could be a COLP. The primary obligation is that COLPs and COFAs must record any failures of a practice to comply with authorisation or statutory obligations, and make such records available to the SRA on request.

b. Suitability

In 2011 a Suitability Test was introduced to apply to those seeking admission or restoration to the roll as a solicitor and to legally qualified and non-legally qualified applicants for roles in authorised bodies as authorised role holders, that is a COLP or a COFA. Therefore, solicitors must show that they are of the required standard of character and suitability, while an authorised role holder must show that they are a fit and proper person.[191] The regulations include strict stipulations of behaviour that will debar applicants. There are 10 paragraphs, many lengthy, setting out prohibitions and factors weighing on suitability decisions.

The SRA states that it will refuse applications where the person has been convicted of certain criminal offences, for example, involving dishonesty, fraud, perjury or bribery.[192] It will refuse applications, except in exceptional circumstances, where applicants 'have been adjudged by an education establishment to have committed a deliberate assessment offence which amounts to plagiarism or cheating to gain an advantage for yourself or others'.[193] It may refuse applications for lesser infractions, for example where the applicant has received a caution by police.[194]

iii. Method

a. Relationships

OFR implicitly involves a move from reactive regulation, the prosecution of default, to a more proactive approach, looking at systems and anticipating problems. The Law Society's traditional method of investigating default, descending on a firm, probably after a tip-off, and going through the books with a fine toothcomb, will presumably be reserved for extreme cases under the new regime. What was promised was a more diagnostic approach, with routine visits to discuss issues. Standard visits to organisations might examine the evidence used for internal monitoring, results of audits and

---

[191] SRA, *SRA Suitability Test 2011*, Outcome SB1 and 2 (www.sra.org.uk/solicitors/handbook/suitabilitytest/content.page).
[192] ibid, at pt 1, para 1.1.
[193] ibid, at para 4.1.
[194] ibid, at para 1.3.

training or be thematic, for example, looking at client care or conflicts of interest. The focus would be discussion of issues and advice on how to deal with problems.

b. Sanctions

Under the new system, the SRA retains the right of intervention in solicitors' practices and to refer individual solicitors to the Solicitors Disciplinary Tribunal (SDT). The shift in regulatory focus from individual to corporate responsibility should, however, ensure that only the most serious cases follow that route. For many cases, particularly less serious cases, there may be greater use of administrative sanctions, fines and regulatory agreements. These are imposed on or negotiated with organisations direct, and can be administered without reference to the SDT (see further chapter eight).

VI. Advantages and Disadvantages of Outcomes Focused Regulation

A. Potential Advantages of OFR

There are potential advantages in the regulatory shift to OFR. Its advocates promise a stronger focus on areas of highest regulatory risk and on client protection and high standards of service. The substantive features of this kind of regulation can vary greatly. It generally involves focus on the suitability of the firms' management systems and controls for ensuring compliance with the regulatory outcomes, defined in qualitative or behavioural terms, desired by the regulator.

The processes employed under the new-style regulatory regimes usually include intense dialogue between involved actors covering the purpose and application of the principles. The burden of interpretation and responsibility for achieving outcomes is, however, on the regulated organisation. Helping organisations to deliver their outcomes, and achieving the overarching aims of the system, the regulatory principles of the LSA 2007, depends on the methods of regulation adopted by the regulator.[195]

i. Flexible and Proactive Regulation

a. Principles-based Regulation

A criticism of traditional, rule-based regulation is that it is not 'reflexive'; the rule is inflexible, there is no reflection back in the light of experience.[196] Ideal

---

[195] Black, 'The Rise, Fall and Fate of Principles Based Regulation' (n 157).
[196] D Nicolson and J Webb, *Professional Legal Ethics: Critical Interrogations* (Oxford, Oxford University Press, 1999) at 93.

processes might provide routine oversight of the impact of regulatory processes on practice, space for dialogue between regulator and regulated and scope to share successful strategies with the regulated community. Yet another consideration is facilitating international legal practice, for which detailed conduct rules might be inappropriate.[197]

b. Risk-based Regulation

Risk-based regulation is concerned with identifying risks in the regulatory environment and directing resources to controlling these risks. It appears to be more directed to the old method of regulation, where investigations were instigated after tip-offs. It could also involve identifying types of risks associated with particular kinds of organisation and focusing resources on those organisations.

c. Client Protection

Client protection was formerly concerned with compulsory insurance requirements for solicitors and the maintenance of an indemnity fund. Ethical observance among providers is also a dimension of client protection. Therefore, methods that develop attitudes and behaviour consistent with ethical compliance within organisations support the goal of client protection. Regulation can help to develop mechanisms for reviewing and propagating these methods.

d. Client Service

Client service has an ethical and business dimension. Both are supported by effective quality assurance within organisations. A more proactive relationship with providers of legal services provides opportunities to ensure that appropriate management systems are in place.[198] An example of this is complaints handling.

ii. Cultural Regulation

The methodology associated with OFR is inspection of quality assurance processes within organisations. This gives regulators an opportunity to encourage the development of internal structures and processes that promote, formalise and embed ethical behaviour. The New South Wales (NSW) regulator refers to this system as 'cultural regulation'.[199]

---

[197] RG Lee, 'Liberalisation of Legal Services in Europe: Progress and Prospects' (2010) 30(2) *Legal Studies* 186.

[198] C Parker, T Gordon and S Mark, 'Regulating Law Firm Ethics Management: an Empirical Assessment of an Innovation in Regulation of the Legal Profession in New South Wales' (2010) 37(3) *Journal of Law and Society* 466.

[199] S Mark, 'The Future is Here: Globalisation and the Regulation of the Legal Profession: Views from an Australian Regulator' (paper presented at ABA Conference, Chicago, 2009) at 14 (www.law.georgetown.edu/legalprofession/documents/May27-2009-StevenMark-Paper.pdf).

a. Managerial Accountability

Conventional ethics codes and disciplinary systems tend to be geared to holding individual practitioners to account. Disciplining managers before professional tribunals for organisational failures is difficult. Even where it is technically possible, as in the US, there are low numbers of reported cases.[200] The problem of holding managers to account for organisational failings is less of a problem in a system geared to regulating entities. The entity can be punished in the event of failure. Managerial accountability creates a strong incentive to ensure that systems are in place to support individuals in making ethical decisions.

b. Ethical Infrastructure

The term 'ethical infrastructure' was coined by Schneyer to describe organisational structures supporting ethical behaviour.[201] There is some evidence that organisations with good management and good values have a more positive impact on compliance than competent management and formal systems, even where there are plentiful resources.[202]

c. Self-assessment

Research into PBR in NSW attributed a significant decline in complaints against incorporated practices to a system of self-assessment. Practices were asked to rate their performance against indicative criteria, from fully to partially compliant, for the 'ten objectives of sound legal practice'.[203] For example, a criterion suggested for the first objective, 'competent work practices to avoid negligence', is that 'fee earners practice only in areas where they have appropriate competence and expertise'. Any gaps found in this self-assessment of good office practice and ethical behaviour are discussed with the regulator, the Office of the Legal Services Commissioner (OLSC).

The data collected from the NSW self-assessment regime assisted in developing a 'risk profile' and enabled targeting of high risk units. The OLSC conducted compliance audits of appropriate management systems. These 'practice reviews' looked at files and behaviour that had been highlighted in the self-assessment forms. Analysis of the complaints against such firms showed that completion of the self-assessment triggered improvement in complaints records. Self-assessment was a more powerful factor in improving performance than either incorporation or management systems.[204]

---

[200] E Chambliss and D Wilkins, 'A New Framework for Law Firm Discipline' (2003) 16 *Georgetown Journal of Legal Ethics* 335.

[201] T Schneyer, 'A Tale of Four Systems: Reflections on how Law Influences the "Ethical Infrastructure' of Law Firms' (1998) 39 *South Texas Law Review* 245.

[202] C Parker and VL Nielsen, 'Corporate Compliance Systems: Could they Make any Difference? (2009) 41(1) *Administration and Society* 3.

[203] Mark, 'The Future is Here' (n 199).

[204] Parker, Gordon and Mark, 'Regulating Law Firm Ethics Management' (n 198).

B. Potential Disadvantages of OFR

i. Scale and Proportionality

Early proponents of principles-based regulation promised that it would be 'light touch', more concerned with improving practices and raising standards than with punishing offenders after the event.[205] There would be high level principles governing practice and the quality of practice, rather than 'tick-box' compliance with rules.[206] This, of course, was when such systems were to be applied only with large firms.

Smedley expected his system of corporate regulation to apply only to the largest firms in terms of staffing and turnover, those dealing largely or exclusively with corporate clients (say, a minimum of 70 per cent of its client base). These were the firms who could be expected to have high level compliance and risk management systems in place, together with a designated senior Risk and Compliance Partner, or other partner carrying out a similar role.

Large organisations might experience the regulatory methodology accompanying OFR as 'light touch', because of their scale of operations. It is relatively easy to designate specific personnel to fulfil the different roles necessary for compliance. Smaller firms and sole practitioners could find the 'compliance machinery' onerous. The methodology of OFR therefore, potentially imposes disproportionate costs on small firms and sole practitioners.

ii. Resources

The effectiveness of monitoring depends to a large degree on the types of mechanisms employed. There is a premium on smart use of resources. The lesson from the financial services disaster was that 'light touch' regulation carries serious risks. OFR, like any other kind of regulation, requires both resources and teeth. When the FSA changed its regulation regime from PBR to OFR, the main difference was the addition of 350 new staff. This created a team of direct supervisors 1200 strong for regulation of 20,000 firms.

The SRA employs around 600 overall to control 10,000 firms and, now, various ABS. Of its overall complement, the SRA has a relatively small team focused on supervision of law firms. Additionally, unlike the FSA, the SRA operates two systems, the new regime of 'firm-based' regulation, which is supposed to be supportive and developmental, and the conventional structures of intervention and preparing disciplinary cases. This is unlike the FSA, which refers serious cases to the police.

---

[205] Smedley, *Review of the Regulation of Corporate Legal Work* (n 161) at 43, para 4.17.
[206] SRA, *The Architecture of Change* (2010).

iii.   Effectiveness

Proponents of PBR, the LSB, Hunt, Smedley and the SRA, all cite the regulation of corporate law firms in New South Wales as evidence that it works.[207] The key statistic is the fact that there was a reduction of complaints by two-thirds in the regulated group after the introduction of the new system.[208] The regulated group in NSW was, however, incorporated practices. These tend to be larger firms operating under ordinary company law and with no restrictions on share ownership.

It is notable that the NSW system operates alongside more familiar frameworks of discipline, which remain the method of regulation for unincorporated firms. Parker comments that

> the whole self-assessment regime only works because the lawyers responsible for filling it in fear individual disciplinary action if they do not do it properly—and because they under-stand that it is aimed at demonstrating that their firm has systems to make sure they are meeting the pre-existing rules[209]

Parker notes that there were not many true multi-disciplinary practices in NSW and data was not kept to enable analysis of their performance. Therefore, in general, the focus of regulation and discipline remained the individual, who was still subject to substantially the same professional code and disciplinary system that preceded the introduction of measures for incorporated practices. Evidence to support the effectiveness of PBR, or OFR, was therefore thin at best.[210]

C.   The Code of Conduct

i.   Rules or Outcomes?

Black distinguishes between formal and substantive PBR.[211] Formal PBR operates at the level of the rule book, where most ethics regimes supplement principles with guidance, explanations and rules.[212] The formal aspects of the PBR regime are gener-ally no clue to its substantive nature; detailed rules might co-exist with an approach that is 'light touch'. Abandoning rules altogether is, Black suggests, usually a mistake.

One of the most startling changes made under the OFR regime implemented by the SRA was the replacement of rules in the Code of Conduct by principles, outcomes and indicative behaviours. This high level of generality was thought necessary to cover the wide range of organisations, sectors and professions the SRA aspires to regu-late.[213] The risk is that the methodology will not be adequate to meet the challenge

---

[207] LSB, *LSB Business Plan 2009/10* (n 156) at para 36.
[208] Parker, Gordon and Mark (n 198).
[209] Note to author (2009).
[210] ibid.
[211] Black (n 157).
[212] ibid, at 5.
[213] LSB, *LSB Business Plan 2009/10* (n 156) at para 36.

of regulating diverse organisations. This may lead to inconsistent quality assurance processes and insufficiently robust standards.[214]

ii. Discipline

The traditional code is the basis of individual responsibility and disciplinary proceedings. One of its advantages is that professionals at risk of losing their careers can know the specific breaches they are accused of. This is more difficult when they have failed to achieve a very broad outcome and there are acknowledged to be different ways in which it could be achieved. Another risk of OFR, therefore, is that it creates uncertainty about professional standards and undermines the authority of and effectiveness of disciplinary machinery.

iii. Practitioner Compliance

Reasons why practitioners adhere to professional norms include a sense of common identity and solidarity with professional colleagues. The risk in shifting the focus of regulation, making organisations and 'compliance professionals' responsible for ethics, is the risk, anticipated by Clementi, that practitioners come to regard regulation as 'external', rather than their own professional responsibility.

VII. The Bar

A. The Scope of Regulation

The Bar did not need initially to embrace OFR because it did not follow the solicitors into the regulation of ABS. Eventually it announced that it would introduce entity regulation, probably covering 'barrister-only entities' and legal disciplinary partnerships. It would also apply to become a licensing authority for ABS from 2014.[215] In July 2013, the BSB confirmed its intention to be a 'niche regulator' of advocacy-focused businesses.[216] Barristers and BSB-authorised entities would be allowed to

---

[214] E Kinney, 'Private Accreditation as a Substitute for Direct Government Regulation in Public Health Insurance Programs: When is it Appropriate?' (1995) 57(4) *Law and Contemporary Problems* 47; M Casile and A Davis-Blake, 'When Accreditation Standards Change: Factors Affecting Differential Responsiveness of Public and Private Organizations' (2002) 45(1) *Academy of Management Journal* 180.

[215] D Bindman, 'BSB sets course for barrister partnerships in 2013 and ABS in 2014' *Legal Futures* 22 October 2012.

[216] 'New BSB Handbook to give barristers more freedom and flexibility' (www.barstandardsboard.org.uk/media-centre/press-releases/new-bsb-handbook-to-give-barristers-more-freedom-and-flexibility/).

apply for authorisation to conduct litigation, offering a 'one-stop shop' for litigation and advocacy services. This meant that clients would not have to conduct the administrative tasks of litigation when instructing public access barristers.

B. Regulatory Strategy

The new regime allows barristers to continue working as traditional, self-employed referral practitioners, or with others in firms, companies or other entities. Previous rules preventing self-employed barristers from sharing premises and forming associations with non-barristers were removed, allowing them to pool risks and resources. The BSB promised to adopt a 'new risk based approach to supervision and enforcement' from January 2014. This would focus energy and resources on the greatest areas of risk, involving ongoing assessment of the likelihood and potential impact of regulated parties not complying with regulatory requirements.

The BSB continued with many of the Bar's established methods for monitoring risk. For example, in 2012, 635 chambers were sent the monitoring questionnaire and 624 responded.[217] Of these, 83 per cent were compliant in all areas and given a low risk rating, 13 per cent received a medium risk rating and 4 per cent a high risk rating. All have since addressed areas of non-compliance. Of the 104 chambers that were non-compliant in one area or more, the most frequent problems were not having a written complaints procedure, not providing clients who were considering a complaint with a copy of a complaints procedure and not informing clients of the existence of the Legal Ombudsman.

The 2012 monitoring exercise found that sole practitioners are more likely to trigger enforcement action by not completing the questionnaire. In general, there was no pattern of failure; certain kinds of chambers were not consistently non-compliant. There was, for example, no evidence suggesting that small chambers were more likely than large chambers to be non-compliant. Sole practitioners were no more likely to be the subject of complaints than barristers in chambers. Some variables were consistent with general compliance. For example, chambers carrying out work under the Money Laundering Regulations were significantly more likely to comply with complaints-handling requirements.[218]

The new regulatory approach includes adjustments to the traditional approach to discipline, considered in more detail in the next chapter. They include the introduction of a new power of disqualification covering people working for BSB-authorised individuals or businesses. The BSB also proposed increasing the available sanctions for 'administrative action' from £300 to £3,000 for individuals and £5,000 for businesses. In such cases the BSB would apply the civil standard of proof.

---

[217] BSB, *Chambers Monitoring 2012 Report.* (www.barstandardsboard.org.uk/media/1456510/chambersmonitoring2012_report.pdf).
[218] ibid.

C. Bar Standards Board Handbook 2014

i. Background

The Bar Code had not been comprehensively reviewed since 1981. In June 2007, the Bar embarked on a three-year review of the Code, so as to be ready to respond to the LSA 2007. An initial consultation on revisions issued by the Bar Standards Board noted that the Code was drafted very legalistically and inconsistently, some rules being very detailed and others very general with little added guidance.[219] The BSB proposed adopting the core principles and plain English approach of the 2007 Solicitors' Code. The review tackled business structures, core principles, the cab rank rule and client care and concluded with complaints and discipline.

The BSB review led to the introduction of the BSB Handbook in 2014, replacing the Code of Conduct. Part 2 of the Handbook comprises a code of conduct. This introduces core duties and outcomes, but does not use indicative behaviours. Some rules have been retained in order to ensure clarity about what is expected of barristers. These tend to be less prescriptive than the former Code of Conduct and are supplemented by guidance. The new code aspires to provide more focus and guidance on what the outcome of a rule should be, rather than describing how to act in every situation.

ii. Organisation: Core Duties and Sections

Unlike its predecessor, the BSB Handbook 2014 contains a set of core duties applicable to all barristers, whether or not they hold current practising certificates. This means that they apply to unregistered barristers when they are providing legal services. The core duties are:

—— observing the duty to the court in the administration of justice (CD1);
—— acting in the best interests of each client (CD2);
—— acting with integrity and honesty (CD3);
—— maintaining independence (CD4);
—— behaving in a way which does not diminish the trust and confidence which the public places in the barrister or the profession (CD5);
—— keeping the affairs of each client confidential (CD6);
—— providing a competent standard of work and service to each client (CD7);
—— not discriminating improperly in relation to any person (CD8);
—— being open and co-operative with the regulator (CD9); and
—— managing your practice, and carrying out your role within it, competently and in such a way as to achieve compliance with legal and regulatory obligations (CD10).[220]

The outcomes precede each section of rules. The purpose of these was said to be an indication of the result of applying the conduct rules. The conduct rules were divided

---

[219] BSB, *Initial Consultation Paper on the Review of the Code of Conduct* (June 2007).
[220] BSB, *Handbook 2014*, pt 2: The Code of Conduct, B, 'The Core Duties'.

into five sections: You and the court; Your behaviour towards others; You and your client; You and your regulator; and You and your practice.

iii.   Rules, Guidance and Outcomes

The BSB application for approval to the LSB explained that the approach was to express all mandatory requirements as rules. The guidance provided further information or examples of behaviour that would breach the rules.[221] The rules are intended to be prescriptive only where this is necessary to achieve a desired outcome. In particular, barristers were given freedom to organise their business except insofar as the regulatory objectives, especially the interests of clients, might be adversely affected.

The BSB took a quite different approach to outcomes to the SRA. It explained that outcomes are not themselves mandatory rules, but factors which BSB-regulated persons should have in mind when considering how the core duties and rules should be applied in particular circumstances.[222] Barristers would need to consider outcomes when interpreting the rules. Whether or an outcome is achieved will be taken into account when considering alleged breaches of core duties and the rules. Misconduct charges and administrative sanctions would however continue to be based on breaches of core duties and rules, not outcomes.[223]

For the first time, the BSB's new Handbook contains guidance to the rules, which was previously provided separately on the BSB website. This is intended to serve several purposes. It assists in the interpretation of rules by explaining how they apply in certain circumstances. It draws attention to related rules or provides examples of behaviour leading to compliance with core duties and rules. If regulated persons fail to comply with guidance they may be under an additional burden. They will need to demonstrate how the core duty or rule has been met.

With the introduction of the new Handbook, the BSB is introducing powers of disqualification for lay employees of chambers and other regulated organisations. The Disciplinary Tribunal or Interim Panel would have the power to disqualify any non-authorised employees if they breach or cause others to breach the rules. It will be a breach of the Handbook for any person authorised by the BSB to employ the disqualified person without prior approval. The Head of Professional Practice at the Bar Standards Board anticipated that the power would be used relatively infrequently.

iv.   Changes Introduced by the BSB Handbook

The new BSB Handbook made a number of changes to the previous regime. It was initially approved and published with sections relating to entity regulation scored through, pending LSB approval. The rules recognised the new right of self-employed barristers to apply for practising certificate extensions to conduct

---

[221] BSB, *Amendments to the Bar Code of Conduct–New BSB Handbook: Final Application*, at para 2.15 (www.legalservicesboard.org.uk/Projects/statutory_decision_making/pdf/bsb_new_handbook_application.pdf.
[222] ibid, at para 2.10.
[223] ibid, at para 2.11.

litigation. This addressed the problem that clients of public access barristers had to act as self-representing litigants. Rules preventing self-employed barristers from sharing premises and forming associations with non-barristers were also removed.

Among the substantive rules, the cab rank rule was extended to non-advocacy work. It was also applied to instructions for work in England and Wales coming from lawyers in Scotland, Northern Ireland and from EEA Member States. The new Handbook retained provisions in the previous code prohibiting handling client money, paying referral fees and managing client affairs. Various aspects of the new Handbook related to discipline. The new code required barristers self-report and report others in relation to 'serious misconduct'. There was, however, an exemption for barristers providing advice through the Bar Council Ethics Helpline.

The Handbook introduced a disqualification power covering persons, whether barristers or employees of BSB-regulated persons, who breach, or cause an authorised person to breach, regulatory rules applying to them. A core duty to co-operate with the regulator came with an obligation on chambers to appoint a member responsible for liaising with the BSB. This replaced the duty on heads of chambers. All barristers are under a duty to ensure, commensurate with their role, that their chambers are administered competently.

VIII. The Future

It is perhaps still too early to say whether there will be discernible, long-term impacts of the new systems of regulation. The LSB claims that new business entities are more efficient in responding to initial complaints.[224] Its report said that, in 2012/13, ABS resolved 93 per cent of complaints received, LDPs 88 per cent and other organisations 83 per cent. ABS also resolved 11 complaints for every one referred to the Legal Ombudsman, LDPs five and other solicitors' firms four. The LSB notes that the proportion of private consumers which considered that the services they received were value for money had increased from 46 per cent to 56 per cent between 2009 and 2011.[225]

An ambiguous piece of information is the falling number of calls received by the SRA Professional Ethics Helpline over time (from nearly 67,000 in 2006/07 to just over 58,000 in 2010/11).[226] This fall could be explained in a number of ways. It could be that the Solicitors' Code of Conduct 2007 was clearer than what went before, reducing the need for guidance. It could be that solicitors became less concerned about ethics over the period. It could be that they were seeking alternative sources of

---

[224] J Hyde, 'ABSs "more productive" than traditional law firms says LSB' *Law Society Gazette* 22 October 2013.

[225] LSB, *Market Impacts of the Legal Services Act: Interim Baseline Report* (April 2012) at para B.8.4 (www.legalservicesboard.org.uk/what_we_do/Research/Publications/pdf/market_impacts_of_the_legal_ services_act_interim_baseline_report.pdf).

[226] ibid, at para C.11.4.

advice. It could be that solicitors were anticipating their increased freedom to make ethical choices.

It would be foolish to think that OFR marks the end point of experimentation with regulation of legal services. Recent research for the Legal Services Board suggests that policy in the legal services market is still be too 'regulatory' in orientation.[227] The SRA, on which the study was based, was said to have fair regulations for entry. These could, however, in their totality, deter new entrants to the market. In making decisions about whether prospective entrants to the market were fit and proper, the SRA was said to place too much emphasis on regulation to decrease risk to consumers, rather than on remedies for breach.[228]

In future, it is possible to envisage further rationalisation of the infrastructure of regulation. For example a single regulator may emerge, either from one of the existing 'front-line regulators' or in the form of a state agency. In this event, it is unlikely that the conventional professional groupings and codes of conduct would remain functional. In that event, regulation might be applied to groups in different ways using different regulatory strategies according to the type of activities undertaken and the type and level of risk.

There are various options for alternative kinds of regulation within the legal services market. First, there could be regulation of each reserved activity, for example, litigation, advocacy, probate. Secondly, there could be regulation of selected areas of legal specialisation, for example, corporate law, property law, intellectual property. Thirdly, there could be regulation of different classes of entity, for example, ABS, LLP, large firm or small firm. Finally, there could be regulation, as at present, of groups of lawyers, perhaps organised along new lines, for example, international lawyers, corporate lawyers, private client lawyers.

Another possibility is suggested by the research conducted for the LSB.[229] This proposes that the current, entity-based regulatory strategy is expensive. An individual and rule-based approach could allow easier entry to the legal services market and, therefore, greater competition. It recommends that consideration be given to placing greater emphasis on 'after the event' remedies, such as insurance and compensation, rather than proactive regulation strategies, such as training, guidance and monitoring. The logic of this approach is that, in the long term, standards would be flexible. Clients would get the protection, including the ethical standards, that they contract and pay for.

There are fashions in regulatory regime. The regulatory transformation of the legal profession occurred during a vogue for regulation using broad principles rather than rules. The legal profession has adopted outcomes-focused regimes without much resistance. It is far from clear that it is suitable for all kinds of legal practice, particularly smaller units, which may be more effectively regulated within a framework of rules. Contradictorily, codes of ethics remain the government's solution of choice

---

[227] S Rab, C Jenkins and G Yarrow, *Understanding Barriers to Entry, Exit and Changes to the Structure of Regulated Legal Firms* (Oxford, Regulatory Policy Institute, 2013).

[228] ibid at 86–92.

[229] ibid.

when scandals occur in the public facing organisations for which they are directly responsible.[230]

One of the most significant regulatory changes may be the change in the focus of regulation away from individuals to organisations. This can be seen as part of a deliberate attempt to manage a shift from occupational professionalism, where a group constructs its own occupational identity, to organisational professionalism.[231] In the latter form, a discourse constructed from above is used to promote and facilitate occupational change. This is driven by organisational objectives rather than occupational ones and achieved through hierarchical structures and managerialism. This ultimately limits the discretion of professionals, potentially squeezing out the service ethic from professional work.

IX. Conclusion

Historically, a range of controls have been used to regulate the legal profession. Codes of conduct provide the standards against which the behaviour of the individual was measured and reinforced the idea of individual responsibility. Ethical compliance depended on a twin strategy of training and deterrence. The deterrent effect of discipline depends on ethical infractions being detected through audit, or as a result of references from public authorities, such as courts, clients or other lawyers. The weakness of a system that operates on deterrence principles is that there is no systematic approach to finding breaches of the rules. Relying on information received is random at best and unlikely to detect certain kinds of infraction.

A new regime of regulation was introduced following the Legal Services Act 2007 (LSA 2007). It promised a version of self-regulation overseen by a public agency, the Legal Services Board. Partly in order to accommodate ABS, the SRA, the regulator of solicitors, adopted a scheme of Outcomes Focused Regulation. This was said to focus on regulatory risks and on securing compliance rather than on deterrence. More significantly, the new regulatory system marked a change from occupational professionalism. By focusing on entities rather than individuals it encourages organisations to adopt a more hierarchical and less collegial form.

---

[230] S Laville, 'May to publish police ethics code after Mitchell row' *The Guardian* 24 October 2014.
[231] J Evetts, 'The Management of Professionalism: a Contemporary Paradox' (2005) *Economic and Social Research Council* (www.tlrp.org/dspace/retrieve/1858/paper-evetts.pdf).

8

Discipline

'Bar Associations are notoriously reluctant to disbar or even suspend a member unless he has murdered a judge down town at high noon, in the presence of the entire Committee on Ethical Practices'.[1]

I. Introduction

Disciplinary powers over members are among the most basic and important forms of regulatory control. These powers can result in an offender being suspended from practice or even struck from the professional roll. They are generally used only for more serious breaches of discipline and not for cases of poor or negligent service. The numbers of cases dealt with by disciplinary panels is often small compared with the numbers of complaints. They are also important because, although they are the tip of a disciplinary iceberg, the decisions set the standard of observance for practitioners.

The ability of professions to command obedience, or to consciously socialise members to their norms, is itself an ethical issue. The decisions of professional disciplinary tribunals potentially deny a practitioner's autonomy and deprive them of their livelihood. It is important therefore, that the decision is fair and procedurally defensible. Disciplinary tribunals operate in addition to the normal civil and criminal legal processes that apply to everyone else. The profession has often claimed that, because of the overlap of general and professional jurisdictions, the public enjoy double protection and the profession endures double jeopardy.

[1] SJ Harris, quoted in M Teigh Bloom, *The Trouble with Lawyers* (New York, Simon and Schuster, 1968) at 157.

II. Theories of Professional Discipline

A. Causes of Disciplinary Infractions

There is relatively little material on lawyers' disciplinary offences, possibly due to the aura of secrecy formally surrounding disciplinary processes.[2] Professional discipline fits, however, within an extensive literature on 'white-collar crime', a term, coined by Sutherland in 1939.[3] This is highly relevant, despite being non-specific regarding occupations.[4] Even though lawyers often do not appear in ordinary courts as a result of disciplinary cases, and may not appear in criminological studies of white-collar crime, the circumstances and psychology of perpetrators are similar.[5] One recent piece of work on lawyer disciplinary processes, Abel's case studies of disciplinary tribunal cases, explores the inter-relation of three factors: the propensity of the individual for transgression, the nature of the organisation they belong to and the regulatory environment.

B. Offenders

i. Types of Offences

Various offences can lead to disciplinary proceedings. Some occur in a professional's private life and outside the context of legal work. These offences could include anything from assault to theft. They may be reported to the offender's professional body by judges or other interested parties. They may be prosecuted as disciplinary offences because the offender has brought the profession into disrepute. In such cases, the conduct may be so serious that serious sanctions, such as striking off, are considered. This is usually on the basis that the offence reveals a character flaw from which the public needs protection.

Of the disciplinary offences that occur at work, Abel focuses on three categories: neglect, fees and over-zealousness. Cases involving neglect of client matters, and various problems over fees, are common matters for disciplinary tribunals. Over-zealousness, undertaking illegal or unethical acts on behalf of clients, is less common but potentially more interesting. Disciplinary cases against over-zealous lawyers help

---

[2] RL Abel, *Lawyers in the Dock: Learning from Attorney Disciplinary Proceedings* (Oxford and New York, Oxford University Press, 2008) at 37.

[3] EH Sutherland, *White Collar Crime: The Uncut Version* (New Haven and London, Yale University Press, 1983).

[4] Abel, *Lawyers in the Dock* (n 2).

[5] L Levin, 'Bad Apples, Bad Lawyers and Bad Decision-making: Lessons from Psychology and from *Lawyers in the Dock*' (2009) 22 *Georgetown Journal of Legal Ethics* 1549.

to draw the boundary of client loyalty. Such offences are not, apparently, motivated by self-interest. This underlines the fact that there are very different motivations behind lawyers' disciplinary infractions.

ii. Motivation

It is difficult to research personal motivations in relation to crime. Some work is based on symbolic interactionism. This is a method which explores how reality is defined by patterns of communication, interpretation and adjustment between individuals. Research of this kind suggests that people often offer motivations that are 'neutralisation strategies', rationalisations of their behaviour.[6]

Coleman identified six neutralisation strategies which white-collar offenders use to justify their actions. They may claim positive motives, for example, cheating customers to pay employees. They may deny harming individuals or suggest that everyone else was doing the same thing. Or they may argue that the rules they infringed were an unjust or unwarranted interference in a free market.[7] These claims suggest a 'higher reason' for misbehaviour, or that what was done was not wrong.

Acquiring wealth is a common motive for deviance, but it is not always driven by greed. For many people, wealth and success are central goals of human existence.[8] Capitalism fuels inequality and a 'culture of competition'. For some, therefore, only 'the most capable and the hardest-working individuals emerge victorious'.[9] It is sometimes difficult to draw lines between entrepreneurship, commercial innovation and deviant economic activity. Privileged sections of society can sometimes feel that exploitation of others is justified because they have earned or deserve power.[10]

Wheeler argues that some people stop acquiring wealth at a certain level, while others see no limits.[11] People taking high risks may see themselves 'as pitting their wits against those of the system in some very high stakes games'.[12] Acquisition of wealth at these higher levels may 'take the form of a true pathology of personality—a person oblivious of the pattern though engaged in it'.[13]

Cases of neglect often arise because of the personal circumstances of lawyers. They might include illness, indebtedness and overwork. Often, 'incompetence shades into betrayal as it becomes pervasive, prolonged, and incorrigible'.[14] Neglect of responsibilities to clients can also be caused taking on too much work and being unable to

---

[6] JW Coleman, 'Competition and Motivation to White-Collar Crime' in N Shover and JP Wright, *Crimes of Privilege: Readings in White Collar Crime* (New York and Oxford, Oxford University Press, 2001).

[7] ibid, at 344–46.

[8] ibid, at 341.

[9] ibid, at 348.

[10] J Braithwaite, *Inequality, Crime and Public Policy* (London and Boston US, Routledge and Kegan Paul Ltd, 1979) ch 10.

[11] S Wheeler, 'The Problem of White–Collar Crime Motivation' in K Schlegel and D Weisburd, 'Introduction' to *White Collar Crime Reconsidered* (Boston, Northeastern University Press, 1992) at 108.

[12] ibid, at 113.

[13] ibid.

[14] Abel (n 2) at 8.

cover it all. These kinds of offences, and fee offences and other kinds of financial impropriety, tend to be caused by 'need or greed'.[15]

iii. Character

Psychology distinguishes between personality and character. Personality is the collection of traits a person presents to the outside world. It is relatively superficial. Character is represented in the deeper and usually hidden traits. These traits tend to be only revealed in specific, unusual circumstances. Therefore, someone may be straightforward, a personality trait suggesting honesty. Their dishonest character would only be revealed by, for example, not returning a purse found with money in it. Character traits are based on beliefs. These shared norms and values of social life are absorbed and accepted during primary socialisation within the family and by secondary socialisation by peer group, school and other agencies.[16] They may be difficult to change once they are set. That is why the criminology literature suggests that delinquency is probably the result of individual propensity. A recurring finding is that those involved in one type of illegitimate activity are often involved in others. Those convicted of white-collar crime often have previous arrests.[17]

Another important variable is age. This is the strongest demographic variable for offences of neglect. Maturity brings together opportunity, the main factor in deviance, with character failings and other pressures. This combination of factors is a potent cause of professional delinquency. In Canada, Arthurs also found that disbarred sole practitioners shared a profile.[18] They were typically 10-year qualified with average law school performance. At the time of committing a disciplinary offence they had life problems that were predictable for people of that age. These might include family problems, disputes over children, debt and business commitments. Many had also been the subject of previous disciplinary proceedings.

A common character trait demonstrated by some attorneys in Abel's case study was that, when charged, they stubbornly refused to change course. They made their situations worse with adversarial tactics and bluster. Abel suggests that 'they generalize the dependence of clients to argue that they are performing an essential service to society, which will suffer most if they are suspended or disbarred'.[19] They seemed to believe they were above the law.[20] Also, however, their legal background seemed to have blurred their behavioural boundaries; there was an arguable defence to every charge.

---

[15] ibid, at 492.

[16] T Parsons, 'The Normal American Family' in SM Farber (ed), *Man and Civilization: The Family's Search for Survival* (New York, McGraw Hill, 1965).

[17] Schlegel and Weisburd, 'Introduction' to *White Collar Crime Reconsidered* (n 11) at 362; and D Weisburd, E Chayet and E Waring, 'White Collar Crime and Criminal Careers: Some Preliminary Findings' (1990) 36(3) *Crime and Delinquency* 342. See also DJ Newman, 'White-Collar Crime: An Overview and Analysis' (1958) 23 *Law and Contemporary Problems* 737; T Hirschi and M Gottfredson, 'Causes of White Collar Crime' (1987) 25 *Criminology* 957.

[18] HW Arthurs, 'Why Canadian Law Schools Do Not Teach Ethics' in K Economides (ed), *Ethical Challenges to Legal Education and Conduct* (Oxford, Hart Publishing, 1998) at 105.

[19] ibid, at 494.

[20] ibid, at 495.

C. Organisations

i. Organisational Culture

Historically, the deterrent effect of discipline, in both criminal courts and professional tribunals, has been directed towards the individual rather than their employing organisation. This tends to ignore or downplay the impact that the organisation can have on individual delinquency. Humans have a tendency to assume that something is acceptable if others around them do it. Whistle-blowers are often exceptional. Failings are, therefore, often endemic in organisations. The criminology literature shows how new recruits to occupations are inducted into 'fiddles' as a form of protection for existing staff. There are numerous self-deceptions which perpetrators share in order to relieve themselves of moral responsibility.

Understanding of the role of organisations in professional deviance is underdeveloped in the literature. Sutherland's deliberately vague definition of 'white-collar crime' was 'crime committed by a person of respectability and high social status in the course of his occupation'.[21] His original text often describes the acts of relatively lowly employees. This is partly because he found that those who were prosecuted were often not in control of significant operations in organisations. This, he concluded, was not because they were less guilty, but because the powerful were less likely to be brought to book.

ii. Opportunity Structures

Sutherland asserts that deviance results from a coincidence of motivation and opportunity, the attractiveness of the latter being determined by prospective gains, potential risks, the compatibility with ideas, beliefs and rationalisations and any other available opportunities (the actor's opportunity structure).[22] Studies of organisations are important in understanding the opportunity structures for breaches of professional norms. They can show, for example, consumer exploitation by misuse of legitimate business techniques.[23]

iii. The Impact of Firm Size: Solo Practitioners, Small Firms and Large Firms

Whereas, in legal culture, sole practice is an idealised ethical form, research in many jurisdictions suggests that busy sole practitioners, acting for individuals in conveyancing, estates and litigation, are the most likely subjects of complaints and, often, disciplinary action. Abel's literature review indicated that sole practitioners and small

---

[21] Sutherland, *White Collar Crime* (n 3) at 9.
[22] Coleman, 'Competition and Motivation to White-Collar Crime' (n 6).
[23] RF Sparks, '"Crime as Business" and the Female Offender' in F Adler and RJ Simon (eds), *The Criminology of Deviant Women* (Boston, Houghton Mifflin Co, 1979) at 171.

firm lawyers are disproportionately represented in disciplinary cases.[24] The examples, he says, are usually small scale, repeated infractions, frequently resulting from ignorance, indifference or inattention. They are usually individual failures, 'unique and unrepeated'.[25]

Abel's study of six US disciplinary cases often involved solo practitioners in their middle to late career. They worked hard, often alone for long periods of time. Sole practitioners also have the perfect opportunity; they have no partners to advise or constrain them. Because they have no one to share burdens they are subject to unmanageable pressures. They may also have the space to develop a distorted mental picture of their relationship to their clients and their work.

Abel noted that his subjects often seemed to have the attitude that clients were lucky to have them, yet were ungrateful for their services. He speculated that solo practitioners can come to feel that, 'because they punish themselves, clients have no right to complain. But of course there is no connection'.[26] Abel's solo practitioners often found themselves charged because they did not have the resources, financial or emotional, to extricate themselves from difficult situations. The theory that sole practitioners tend to be charged because they lack power and resources fits somewhat with Sutherland's theory that it is the small fry in organisations who tend to be disciplined.

Firm size may also affect other aspects of opportunity structures, for example, the type of work performed. Carlin's study of the New York City Bar in the 1970s found that lawyers with lower status clientele, working in lower status courts, were more likely to violate ethical standards. Carlin attributed this to the instability of clientele and the temptation offered by personal gain.[27] Lower status lawyers also reported more frequent pressure from clients to breach ethics.

D. The Regulatory Environment

i. Ethical Consensus

The regulatory environment affects behaviour, and hence discipline, through the mechanisms of norms, education and training, detection and deterrence. In his study of the New York City Bar, Carlin analysed the acceptance of ethical norms by status of firm, dividing them into basic and elite norms. Basic norms proscribe behaviour that is generally socially unacceptable, for example, cheating and bribery. Elite, or paper, norms cover conduct acceptable in the wider community, such as advertising or accepting commissions for referring business, which are frowned upon by professional elites.

---

[24] Abel (n 2) at 54–55.
[25] ibid, at 32.
[26] ibid, at 521.
[27] ibid, at 264.

Carlin found that the different kinds of norm were differently accepted by lawyers, depending on the status of the field in which they operate.[28] A large majority of lawyers in all firms accepted certain basic standards, usually pertaining to lawyer client relations. Only high status lawyers, usually those in large firms, accepted norms going beyond wider social norms.

Based on his research, Carlin suggested that, where there is no consensus on ethical norms, there are three possible results. First, there can be random disagreement, where it was not possible to predict adherence to particular norms. Secondly, there might be plural standards, where different groups uphold different or opposing norms. Thirdly, there may be a norm hierarchy, where certain norms are universally upheld, but only a minority adhere to additional, more demanding norms.

ii. Regulatory Focus and Bias

In a diverse market of providers, as described by Carlin, regulators have a difficult task in calculating where to deploy maximum effort. Do they focus on large units and large transactions, where the consequences of breach are magnified? Or do they direct energies at smaller units, where the risk of infraction may be greater? Regulators must also decide when to prosecute offenders and when to take other action.

Explaining the prevalence of those with low social standing before courts and tribunals was the main purpose of Sutherland's exposure of white-collar crime. His aim was to challenge the myth that deviance was the preserve of the lower classes. He argued that the statistics could be explained by the failure to bring prosecutions against those from elite groups, or the failure of prosecutions that were brought. The perception that small firms and sole practitioners are especially prone to ethical breaches may be affected by regulator bias in favour of larger units.

In general, research suggests that action is less likely to be taken when the regulator and regulated parties are close in social background and when regulated units are relatively large.[29] Elite organisations may be treated differently by regulators, because it is a greater risk to take them on. It may also be because they respond swiftly and positively to threat by accepting responsibility, working hard to make amends and doing whatever else is necessary to stave off the threat of discipline.

iii. Disincentives to Prosecute

Regulators can try and produce better consensus on norms by ensuring good education and by socialisation, by reducing the negative impact of workplace culture, by effective detection and judicious use of deterrence. Disciplinary action is often a last resort, possibly for understandable reasons. A dominating aim of professions is to

---

[28] J Carlin, 'Lawyer's Ethics' in WM Evan (ed), *The Sociology of Law: A Socio-Structural Perspective* (London, The Free Press, Collier Macmillan, 1980) at 257.

[29] P Grabosky and J Braithwaite, *Of Manners Gentle: Enforcement Strategies of Australian Business Regulatory Agencies* (Melbourne, Oxford University Press, 1986) cited in R Baldwin, C Scott and C Hood, *A Reader on Regulation* (Oxford, Oxford University Press, 1998) at 19.

maintain public confidence. Dealing with complaints and discipline openly, publicly highlights professional inadequacies and threatens to undermine self-regulation.[30] It is therefore a rational strategy for professional bodies to use disciplinary sanctions in the clearest cases and in cases where offences are likely to become public anyway.[31] This suggests that professions have a conflict of interest in pursuing sanctions against members.

III. The Functions of Discipline

The system of discipline is not generally concerned with compensation for victims. It arguably has two main functions; protection of potential clients, that is, the public in general, and promoting compliance with professional rules and standards. This raises interesting cases about whether certain kinds of serious criminal behaviour, sexual deviance for example, should lead to serious disciplinary sanctions in addition to any criminal sanctions imposed by the courts.[32]

A. Protection

There are usually some members of a profession who are a public danger. There has to be some mechanism for removing them from practice. This is often done on the basis that it is necessary in order to protect consumers or clients, or that it is necessary in order to protect the profession's reputation and standards. This test is applicable to the issue of criminal convictions. If such convictions, for dangerous driving for example, do not suggest that a person is a risk in their professional capacity, disbarment should not necessarily follow. If conviction creates cause for doubt about whether the public is at risk, serious disciplinary sanctions should, logically, follow.

B. Exclusion

Professional discipline often involves the imposition of sanctions, which usually include exclusion or suspension from practice. This prevents consumers being subject to further risk of exposure to inadequate lawyers. It is also a demonstration of several useful tendencies. It shows that a profession takes its role in public protection

---

[30] Abel (n 2) at 30.
[31] M Burrage, 'From a Gentleman's to a Public Profession' (1996) *International Journal of the Legal Profession* 45, at 57.
[32] R Mortensen, 'The Lawyer as Parent: Sympathy, Care and Character in Lawyers' Ethics' (2009) 12(1) *Legal Ethics* 1.

seriously, does not protect members who fail to meet its standards and is not afraid to be decisive.

C. Compliance

The machinery of professional discipline is typically operated by fellow professionals. This emphasises collective responsibility for the conduct of all fellow practitioners. Disciplined practitioners are therefore conscious of having failed in their trust and in their calling. Therefore, in a properly socialised profession, discipline operates as an effective control mechanism beyond the tribunal itself. The disciplinary process can be as much part of professional punishment as any sanction imposed.[33]

Disciplinary processes form the backdrop of practice, encouraging compliance in subtle ways. For most people, the emotions of shame or guilt are powerful incentives to compliance. Foucault observed that

> [t]he web of discipline aims at generalising the *homo docilis* required by 'rational', 'efficient', 'technical society', an obedient, hard-working, conscience ridden useful creature pliable to all modern tactics of production and warfare ... discipline thrives on 'normalizing judgement'.[34]

If the aim of regulation is a profession observant of its rules, an effective disciplinary system is essential.

D. Deterrence

i. Avoiding Sanctions

The possibility of incurring a serious sanction, and suffering financial losses as a consequence, may operate as a deterrent to unethical behaviour. The imposition of a substantial fine or losing a licence to practise and being unable to work is an economic deterrence to professional transgression.

ii. Avoiding Guilt and Shame

Some cultures socialise individuals to experience guilt when they break social norms.[35] Others rely more on external sanctions inducing feelings of shame in the person subjected to them. The cultures of antiquity are identified as predominately shame

---

[33] See further L Haller, 'The Public Shaming of Lawyers' (2004) 10 *International Journal of the Legal Profession* 281.

[34] JG Merquoir, *Foucault* (London, Fontana Press, 1991) at 94. See also J Simons, *Foucault and the Political* (London and New York, Routledge, 1995) at 22 and 116–18; M Ridley, *The Origin of Virtue* (Harmondsworth, Penguin, 1996) at 183; D Nicolson and J Webb, *Professional Legal Ethics: Critical Interrogations* (Oxford, Oxford University Press, 1999) at 43–46.

[35] EA Posner, *Law & Social Norms* (Cambridge, MA, Harvard University Press, 2000) at 5.

cultures while those of Renaissance Europe, under Christian influence, tend to be guilt cultures.[36] The effectiveness of guilt as a control mechanism was undermined by the declining power of religion. In the Enlightenment, discovery, science and social processes created systems and institutions that questioned traditional habits, customs and authorities.

In the eighteenth century, the philosophy of Kant and, in the nineteenth century, that of Kierkegaard explored the philosophical foundations of morality.[37] Both emphasised the relationship of the self to the world. Kant argued that there was no source of good beyond the good will of the human subject. This compelled an individual to act from a duty to treat the rational agency of human beings as an end in itself and not as a means to other ends. Kierkegaard, likewise saw a sense of self as essentially subjective, grounded in self-reflection and introspection.

Later philosophers saw perceptions of morality as relative. There were, they argued, no universal answers to what is 'good', culturally, aesthetically or socially.[38] Nietzsche argued that moral judgements are no more than the means by which dominant social groups control others, 'a creation of individual will in search of power'.[39] This required fresh thought on 'the psychology of acting morally'.[40]

Industrialisation and capitalism continued to change people's sense of self. Giddens suggests that, in modern society, mastery of the self has overtaken the motivation to be 'moral'.[41] People construct their self-identity around a personal biographical narrative. In this way we, make sense of who we are and we avoid anxiety about personal adequacy.[42] There has been a growth in our sense of moral agency. We see ourselves as capable of making choices, taking responsibility for our behaviour and being able to give rational explanations for the way we act.

A feature of this transition from morality to self-identity is that shame has replaced guilt or fear as a motivation for compliance.[43] Shame operates in a very individual way. Psychological pressure to conform is only experienced when an individual feels that they have let themselves down by not conforming to their constructed self-identity. Therefore, it is arguable that, if we aim to effectively deter the disciplinary infractions of professionals, professional identity must be a part of self-identity.

---

[36] A Giddens, *Modernity and Self-Identity: Self and Society in the Late Modern Age* (Cambridge, Polity Press, 1991) at 202.

[37] J Hospers, *Human Conduct: Problems of Ethics* (Andover, Cengage Learning, 1995) ch 5; AD Macintyre, *After Virtue: A Study in Moral Theory* (London, Duckworth, 1985) at 47.

[38] Macintyre, *After Virtue* (n 37) at 32, AA Leff, 'Unspeakable Ethics, Unnatural Law' (1979) 6 *Duke Law Journal* 1229.

[39] Macintyre (n 37) at 258.

[40] D Nicolson, 'The Theoretical Turn in Professional Legal Ethics' (2004) 7 *Legal Ethics* 17, at 22.

[41] Giddens, *Modernity and Self-Identity* (n 36).

[42] ibid, at 65.

[43] ibid, at 153.

IV. Detection, Investigation and Preparation

A. Detection

Detection of possible professional infractions often occurs as a result of complaints from clients, criminal proceedings or tip-offs, including from other lawyers. They may also result from the actions of a whistle-blower; someone within a company who draws attention to illegal or immoral conduct by the company, its owners or employees.

The 1990 edition of the Guide contained an obligation to report serious misconduct by another solicitor, subject to client consent. It published data showing that 33 allegations of impropriety were made by solicitors against fellow solicitors in 1986 and 45 in 1987. Similar data did not appear in subsequent editions. Later editions of the Guide stated that solicitors were under a duty to report serious misconduct by another solicitor, subject to client consent.[44] This applied to serious misconduct within the firm the solicitor worked for.[45]

The Solicitors' Code of Conduct 2007 contained a similar reporting obligation to that previously appearing in the Guide.[46] The SRA Code of Conduct 2011 now places an obligation on solicitors to report, 'serious misconduct by any person or firm authorised by the SRA, or any employee, manager or owner of any such firm'.[47] The rider is no longer that clients must consent to such a report, but that the solicitor takes into account, where necessary, their duty of confidentiality.

B. Investigation

If allegations of misconduct are serious, an investigation can be launched. This is conducted by the Bar Standards Board in the case of barristers or the Solicitors Regulation Authority in the case of solicitors. In the case of solicitors there is the possibility of forensic investigation of accounts, files and the interviewing of partners and employees.

The task of an investigating authority is to decide whether there is sufficient evidence to conclude that a disciplinary offence has been committed. If so they can assess whether a reference to a disciplinary tribunal is necessary. This might include consideration of whether the lawyer is likely to repeat the conduct. The regulator can

---

[44] N Taylor (ed), *The Guide to the Professional Conduct of Solicitors*, 8th edn (London, The Law Society, 1999) Principle 19.04.

[45] ibid, guidance note 2.

[46] SRA, *Solicitors' Code of Conduct 2007*, rr 20.04(a) and (c).

[47] SRA, *Code of Conduct 2011*, as amended, Outcome 10.4.

decide to advise, reprimand or warn the lawyer about future conduct. Serious cases are referred to the Solicitors Disciplinary Tribunal or Bar Disciplinary Tribunal.

C. Preparation

Where the investigating authority decides that a case should be referred to a disciplinary tribunal, it usually prepares the case, undertaking such further investigation as necessary. This may include interviewing further witnesses.

V. Pre-qualification Disciplinary Processes

Discipline can be applied to those who are not qualified, for example, students. This kind of discipline is based on assumptions about character. It assumes that people can behave in such a way that indicates unsuitability for a profession before they even begin education and training. Therefore, sanctions may be imposed for criminal behaviour pre-dating training or for academic offences, such as plagiarism.

The SRA Training Regulations provide that the SRA can impose a number of sanctions when it is not satisfied as to the character and suitability of a potential entrant to become a solicitor.[48] These include cancelling the student's enrolment, prohibiting entry into a training contract, refusing to register a training contract, terminating a training contract, prohibiting attendance at a Legal Practice Course (LPC) and prohibiting attendance at a Professional Skills Course (PSC). The regulations provide rights of review, including the right to appeal to the High Court within three months of receiving notification of the decision.[49]

VI. Disciplinary Tribunals and Related Processes

There are a variety of ways in which discipline can be exercised. Qualified practitioners can be referred to a disciplinary tribunal constituted by the profession. There is, as we have seen, some overlap between complaints processes and disciplinary procedures in that disciplinary action may arise from a complaint. However, disciplinary action can arise independently of complaints from clients, for example, following a

---

[48] SRA Training Regulations 2011, pt 1: Qualification Regulations, reg 33.1.
[49] ibid, reg 33.5.

reference by a court or some other authority. It is therefore necessary to deal with disciplinary proceedings as a separate issue.

Professions have, traditionally, operated their own disciplinary tribunals. Practitioners are, typically, judged by their peers. This creates some suspicion of these processes.[50] It is important to consider what standards the tribunals are asked to apply. The traditional approach has been for disciplinary tribunals to consider the conduct from the perspective of the profession and its reputation. There are alternatives. For example, it would be possible for the tribunal to consider whether the behaviour is what the public should expect from a reasonably competent practitioner.

A. The Solicitors' Disciplinary Tribunal

The Law Society started to deal with discipline in 1888. The Solicitors Disciplinary Tribunal (SDT) was established under the Solicitors Act 1974, section 46. A useful review of practice in the 1990s can be found in a guide by a former President of the SDT.[51] Much of this practice is still relevant, despite changes in the constitution of the SDT.

i. Description

a. Constitution

The SDT is currently constituted under the Solicitors Act 1974, section 46.[52] The Tribunal previously made its own procedural rules with the consent of the Master of the Rolls. The former rules were the Solicitors (Disciplinary Proceedings) Rules 1994. The tribunal is currently regulated by the Solicitors (Disciplinary Proceedings) Rules 2007.[53] Changes to the rules of the SDT have to be approved by the Legal Services Board (LSB).[54] Much of the case law relevant to the work of the SDT was created under the old rules, but is still relevant.

The SDT is independent of, though funded by, the Law Society with an annual budget of around £3 million per annum.[55] It is run by Solicitors Disciplinary Tribunal Administration Limited (SDTA Ltd), a company limited by guarantee controlled by the SDT. The Legal Services Act 2007 (LSA 2007) requires the Tribunal to formulate a budget for each forthcoming year for approval by the LSB. The Law Society is required to pay the specified amount to SDTA Ltd.

---

[50] LC Levin, 'Building a Better Lawyer Discipline System: The Queensland Experience' (2006) 9(2) *Legal Ethics* 186, at 192.

[51] B Swift, *Proceedings Before the Solicitors' Disciplinary Tribunal* (London, The Law Society, 1996).

[52] Solicitors Act 1974, as amended by the Administration of Justice Act 1985 and the Courts and Legal Services Act 1990.

[53] The Solicitors (Disciplinary Proceedings) Rules 2007 (SI 2007/3588), r 3(2).

[54] LSA 2007, s 178.

[55] SDT, *Annual Report 2011–12*, 10 (www.solicitorstribunal.org.uk/Content/documents/Annual%20Report%20 2011-2012%20final.pdf).

b. Board

The Board of SDTA Ltd is made up of the Tribunal's President, who is chair of the Board, the lay and solicitor vice presidents, a non-executive director and, currently, the immediate past president. Board meetings are held regularly and are attended by the clerk to the Tribunal, who is also company secretary, its operations manager and its finance officer.

c. Membership

The President of the SDT holds office for three years and is elected from solicitor members by a simple majority. One solicitor and one lay vice president are elected from members for a period of three years.[56] The solicitor chair and the 21 legal members of the SDT are appointed by the Master of the Rolls[57] and 11 lay members are appointed by the Ministry of Justice. The Tribunal currently consists of 53 members, of whom 34 are solicitor members and 19 are lay members drawn from a variety of backgrounds. Solicitor members cannot also be members of the Council of The Law Society.

The Tribunal is staffed by the clerk, who must be a solicitor or barrister of 10 years' standing, together with a team of deputy clerks. Although the clerk is, indirectly, paid by the Law Society, the argument that this could lead to an appearance of bias or risk infringement of Article 6 Convention rights, is no impediment to the clerk advising the Tribunal or recording decisions.[58]

ii. Jurisdiction

a. Complainants

Anyone may apply to the Tribunal in relation to an allegation of misconduct unbefitting a solicitor, including that arising prior to admission.[59] Detailed analysis of cases in 2008 showed that just over 40 per cent resulted from inspections by the Law Society, usually triggered by information received.[60] In the next largest category, 23 per cent originated in a complaint lodged by, for example, a member of the public or a fellow solicitor, with a complaints body. The third largest category of cases, nearly 17 per cent, comprised matters referred by an agency like the Law Society. Seven per cent of cases were referred following a criminal conviction, nearly 7 per cent following an audit of the firm and 4 per cent following a 'tip-off'.[61]

Cases are usually brought by the SRA. Only the SRA may make the application where the issue relates to breaches of the rules. These include rules such as the accounts rules or those relating to practising certificates. Costs can only be awarded

---

[56] The Solicitors (Disciplinary Proceedings) Rules 2007, r 3(3).
[57] Solicitors Act 1974, s 46(1).
[58] *Virdi v the Law Society of England and Wales & Anor* [2010] EWCA Civ 100.
[59] *Re A Solicitor* (Co/2860196) May 1997 *Current Law* 421.
[60] A Boon, A Sherr and A Whyte, *The Disciplinary Processes of the Legal Profession* (unpublished research study).
[61] ibid.

in favour of the SRA, so it is usually in the interests of applicants to allow the SRA to take over the conduct of cases. The SDT can adjourn applications made by parties other than the SRA for up to three months to allow an investigation to take place.[62]

b. Respondents

An application can be made to the Tribunal in respect of any allegation or complaint made in respect of a solicitor, a recognised body, a registered European lawyer or a registered foreign lawyer.[63] A single solicitor member of the SDT decides whether there is a case to answer.[64]

Analysis of the 2008 cases showed that over 61 per cent of respondents admitted the allegations brought against them in their entirety. A further 17.2 per cent admitted them in part. Only 9 per cent totally denied all the allegations brought against them. In 20 per cent of cases the defence and mitigation related to the circumstances of firms, for example, loss of key staff, IT breakdown, financial and other work-related pressures. This category was closely followed by personal circumstances, such as the ill health of the claimant or a family member. Around 18 per cent of respondents claimed not to be aware of the relevant rules.

c. Employees

Applications can also be made by the Law Society for orders against employees of solicitors. If an employee is convicted of a criminal offence the SDT can ban him or her from employment by a solicitor or recognised body.[65] It can impose a similar sanction where an employee has been party to an act or default in relation to a legal practice which indicates that it would be undesirable for him to be involved in a legal practice, In such cases, the solicitor, recognised body, or registered European lawyer employing such person may be named as joint respondent.[66]

d. Applications for Restoration to the Roll or Termination of Suspension

Solicitors seeking restoration to the roll or termination of a period of suspension may also apply to the SDT.[67]

iii. Caseload

In the five SDT sessions reported between 2008 and 2012, the SDT heard an average of around 200 cases a year.[68] This represents less than 0.25 per cent of solicitors

---

[62] The Solicitors (Disciplinary Proceedings) Rules 2007, r 20.
[63] ibid, r 5(1).
[64] ibid, r 6.
[65] Solicitors' Practice Rules 1974, r 43(2).
[66] The Solicitors (Disciplinary Proceedings) Rules 2007, r 8.
[67] ibid, r 9.
[68] See SDT, *Annual Report 2011–12* (n 55).

holding practising certificates,[69] and bears little relation to the volume of complaints or the numbers that are upheld. Unfortunately, the annual reports of the SDT do not provide a detailed breakdown of different offences. In 2005–06 over half the cases related to breaches of the Solicitors' Accounts Rules or the misappropriation of client funds.[70]

Analysis of data from the 2008 calendar year showed that, at 13 per cent, Solicitors' Accounts Rules breaches remained the largest single category.[71] The next largest category involved failures surrounding information and advice giving, at nearly 11 per cent. This included, for example, cases of failure to disclose information or of providing false or misleading information. In nearly 10 per cent of cases, breaches of rule 1 (the basic principles) of Solicitors' Practice Rules were cited as the reason for bringing the case. These data were broadly similar to those in the SDT's annual report for 2008/09, where 5 per cent of cases involved improper use or misappropriation of client money.[72]

iv. Procedure

a. Hearings

Applications must be supported by a statement setting out the allegations, the facts and matters in support.[73] Three members, including one lay person, constitute a division and sit for each hearing or application.[74] Proceedings are usually public, formal and court-like. Procedure is set out in the Rules.

b. Evidence

The Tribunal has powers to compel attendance[75] and evidence is given on oath. The Civil Evidence Acts of 1968 and 1995 normally apply to proceedings. This means that the rules of evidence apply unless suspended by the SDT in its discretion.[76] Any written evidence can be accepted including statements of witnesses.[77]

A respondent is not required to give evidence, but inferences may be drawn from failure to do so. The President of the Queen's Bench Division recently said, obiter, 'ordinarily the public would expect a professional man to give an account of his actions'.[78] As a result, the SDT issued a practice direction that in future 'the Tribunal shall be entitled to take into account the position the respondent has decided to adopt as regards the giving of evidence when reaching its findings'.[79]

---

[69] Based on data taken from *The Law Society Annual Statistical Reports* (www.lawsociety.org.uk/aboutlawsociety/whatwedo/researchandtrends/statisticalreport.law).
[70] M Davies, 'The Solicitors' Accounts Rules: How Safe is Clients' Money?'(2000) 3 *Legal Ethics* 49.
[71] Boon, Sherr and Whyte, *The Disciplinary Processes of the Legal Profession* (n 60).
[72] SDT, *Annual Report 2008/09*;
[73] The Solicitors (Disciplinary Proceedings) Rules 2007, r 5(2).
[74] ibid, r 4.
[75] See Solicitors Act 1974, s 46(11).
[76] The Solicitors (Disciplinary Proceedings) Rules 2007, r 13(1).
[77] ibid, r 14.
[78] *Muhammed Iqbal v SRA* [2012] EWHC 3251, at [25]–[26].
[79] SDT, Practice Direction No 5, 'Inference to be Drawn where Respondent Does not Give Evidence' 4 February 2014.

c. Decisions

After a finding that all or any of the allegations in the application have been substantiated, a clerk informs the Tribunal of previous disciplinary proceedings where allegations were found to have been substantiated against the respondent. Respondents are entitled to make submissions supporting the mitigation of sanctions or costs.[80]

v. *Criteria*

a. Burden and Standard of Proof

The burden on the complainant is to prove the charges beyond reasonable doubt, the standard required in criminal proceedings.[81] The Tribunal will not normally reopen any finding of dishonesty already decided in a civil court or proceedings.[82]

b. Breach of Rules and 'Conduct Unbefitting a Solicitor'

The practice of the SDT suggests that there are two categories of case. One category covers breach of rules, either of the code of conduct or of more detailed rules covering specific activity. The second category, covering serious infringements possibly not covered by rules but which violate the spirit of the code, is known as 'conduct unbefitting a solicitor'. The criteria for unbefitting conduct follow the formula laid down in *Re A Solicitor*.[83] Mere negligence is not enough; conduct must be 'such as to be regarded as deplorable by his fellows in the profession' or 'a serious and reprehensible departure from the proper standards of a solicitor as a professional'.[84]

The old Law Society Guide was said to be 'a Highway Code' for solicitors,[85] but notions of what may constitute 'unbefitting conduct' may change. Normally an element of culpability is required but 'impecuniosity will not excuse failure to discharge a professional liability'.[86] Honest and genuine decisions by solicitors on questions of professional conduct do not give rise to a disciplinary offence. If the decision is one no reasonable solicitor could make, then the only conclusion is that the solicitor did not address the issue.[87] That is then a disciplinary matter.

vi. *Sanctions*

The Tribunal has the power to make 'such order as it thinks fit', including,

—— striking a solicitor off the roll;
—— suspension from practice indefinitely or for a fixed period;

---

[80] The Solicitors (Disciplinary Proceedings) Rules 2007 r 16(4).
[81] See *Re A Solicitor* [1992] 2 All ER 335; *Campbell v Hamlet* [2005] 3 All ER 1116.
[82] *Conlon v Simms* [2006] 2 All ER 1024.
[83] *Re A Solicitor* [1972] 2 All ER 811.
[84] Swift, *Proceedings Before the Solicitors' Disciplinary Tribunal* (n 51) at 12.
[85] ibid, at 13.
[86] ibid, at 17.
[87] *Connolly v Law Society* [2007] EWHC 1175 (Admin).

—— a fine
—— the imposition of conditions on the issue of a practising certificate;
—— exclusion from legal aid work permanently or for a fixed period;
—— the issue of a reprimand; or
—— an order for payment of costs.[88]

There is a rough tariff of penalties according to the significance of the offence, with striking of the roll of solicitors, which means they may no longer practise, the most serious.[89] It was established in *R (on the application of Camacho) v Law Society*[90] that previous practice, whereby the Tribunal had simply recommended that the Law Society impose conditions on practising certificates, was not adequate or in the public interest. It held that the SDT should impose the conditions and the Law Society had then to enforce them.[91]

a. Fines

Under the Solicitor Act 1974 the fine was up to £5,000 for each established allegation. Under 2013 guidance there is no limit to the level of fine. Historically fines were low. In 2002 a fine of £25,000 was exceptional. It was imposed on a solicitor who had written to leaseholders demanding ground rents of £6.50 and threatening forfeiture for the arrears and £250 for his costs. This was considered conduct unbecoming a solicitor by making an improper demand, seeking to take an unfair advantage, sending a misleading letter and seeking irrecoverable costs.[92]

b. Striking Off

As with white-collar criminal offences, moral wrongdoing is usually required where striking off the roll is considered.[93] This element is usually dishonesty. In *Bolton v The Law Society*,[94] the Court of Appeal noted that the most serious charges against solicitors involved dishonesty and 'in such cases the tribunal almost invariably, no matter how strong the mitigation, ordered that the solicitor be struck off'. A solicitor not disclosing to his partners that he had an interest in a claims management company[95] was deemed to be dishonesty worthy of striking off. This, it will be noted, involved minimal prejudice to clients or to the public. In that case the court held that all but trivial cases involving dishonesty should lead to striking off.[96]

Where no dishonesty was found 'it remained a matter of very great seriousness in a member of a profession whose reputation depended on trust. A striking off order might, but would not necessarily, follow'. The Tribunal should be concerned fundamentally to maintain the reputation of the profession as one in which every solicitor

---

[88] Solicitors Act 1974, s 47.
[89] Swift (n 51) at 80.
[90] *R (on the application of Camacho) v Law Society* [2004] 4 All ER 126.
[91] ibid, at [131e].
[92] R Colbey, 'Writing a letter before action' 152(8) *New Law Journal* 11 January 2002; see also L Haller, 'Disciplinary Fines: Deterence or Retribution? (2002) 5 *Legal Ethics* 152.
[93] S Green, *Lying, Cheating and Stealing: A Moral Theory of White-Collar Crime* (Oxford, Oxford University Press, 2006) at 396–40.
[94] *The Times* 8 December 1996.
[95] *SRA v Anthony Lawrence Clarke Dennison* [2012] EWCA Civ 421.
[96] ibid.

can be completely trusted. In addition to dishonesty and accounts offences, solicitors have also been struck off for grossly misleading clients, failing to honour undertakings, failing to comply with court orders and knowingly employing a struck off or suspended solicitor.

vii. Costs

The SDT may make such costs order as it thinks fit.[97] Often, the costs incurred are substantially higher than the fines, particularly in contested cases. The courts have indicated that the power to award costs against a regulator should not be used in the absence of proof of dishonesty or lack of good faith. According to Sir Igor Judge, '[f]or the Law Society to be exposed to the risk of an adverse costs order simply because properly brought proceedings were unsuccessful might have a chilling effect on the exercise of its regulatory obligations, to the public disadvantage'.[98]

viii. Appeals

The SDT's decisions can be appealed to the Divisional Court of the Queen's Bench Division or, in the case of applications for restoration to the roll, to the Master of the Rolls. The 2010 Annual Report suggests that, in that year, 16 appeals against the findings of the SDT were heard by the High Court. Of these nine were dismissed, four were allowed, one was partly upheld, one was withdrawn and one was resolved by agreement.

The 2011/12 report shows that 15 cases were appealed during the period of report, many decided by the SDT in previous years. Of these, three were appeals by the SRA. In two of these appeals, *Dennison* and *Rahman*, the SRA was successful in having a solicitor struck off on appeal when the SDT had imposed a lesser sanction. In three of the remaining 12 cases, the respondents' appeals were allowed.

ix. Overview

In relation to the detailed study of the 2008/09 data[99] the numbers of respondents was 279, because some cases involved multiple respondents. Of these, the SDT found the allegations wholly substantiated in 77 per cent of cases and partially substantiated in 15 per cent. Once a finding was made, the most common sanction was for a fine and costs to be awarded. Of the sample, around 37 per cent were fined and 94 per cent were held liable for costs. Nearly 2 per cent of charges were found to be wholly unsubstantiated. Of the remaining caseload, six applications by solicitors, for example, for restoration to the roll, were denied.

---

[97] The Solicitors (Disciplinary Proceedings) Rules 2007, r 18.
[98] *Baxendale Walker v Law Society* [2007] 3 All ER 330, at [39].
[99] Boon, Sherr and Whyte (n 60).

With regard to the severest sanctions, 17.2 per cent of respondents were struck off, around 15 per cent were suspended and 18 per cent were reprimanded. Cases of dishonesty usually led to striking solicitors off the roll, while breaches of the accounting rules involving substantial sums normally results in either striking off or suspension.

The total amount levied as fines has risen more or less consistently. Total fines levied in 2005–06 amounted to £257,500, compared with £433,000 in 2004–05 and £93,000 in 2003.[100] In 2005–06, 64 respondents were fined amounts between £500 and £15,000. In 2011–12, 102 solicitors were subject to orders for payment of fines, ranging from £500 to £30,000. The total levied was £765,000, down from £862,250 the previous year.[101] The average fine in 2011–12 was therefore between £7000–8000.

In the five yearly sessions between 2007 and 2012, an average of 66 solicitors were struck from the roll, up to 20 suspended indefinitely and up to 40 were suspended for fixed periods. Between 19 and 49 reprimands were issued each year during the period. In a small number of cases, sometimes less than 10, no sanction is imposed, apart, possibly, from a costs order. These data, with some variations, are reasonably consistent over time. To the extent that there are pattern, the period between 2000 and 2009 showed an increase in the use of fines and reprimands and a slight decrease in numbers struck off, particularly towards the end of the period.

B. Alternatives to Disciplinary Proceedings

i. Regulatory Sanctions

Under the LSA 2007, the SRA was empowered to make findings of breach of regulatory obligations or professional misconduct, and to impose sanctions, a written rebuke and penalty of up to £2000, without reference of cases to the SDT.[102] As a result the SRA Disciplinary Procedure Rules 2011 were adopted after consultation with the SDT and with the approval of the LSB.[103] These prescribe processes that overlap with those of the SDT, but without the formality usually attached to a disciplinary process.

Under the SRA Disciplinary Procedure Rules, sanctions can be imposed in a number of ways. In the first instance, the SRA may agree with a person under investigation that they will accept a penalty. If not, parties duly authorised by the SRA, either a single adjudicator or an adjudication panel, can impose a penalty.[104] In considering the matter, the SRA will apply the civil standard of proof (on a balance of probabilities) to decide whether charges are proven.[105]

---

[100] SDT, *Annual Report 2004–05* and *2005–06* (www.solicitorstribunal.org.uk).

[101] SDT, *Annual Report 2011–12*, at 18.

[102] Solicitors Act 1974, ss 31, 44D; Administration of Justice Act 1985, ss 79–80; LSA 2007, sch 11.

[103] SRA, Disciplinary Procedure Rules 2011 (dated 17 June 2011 commencing 6 October 2011 (www.sra. org.uk/solicitors/handbook/discproc/content.page).

[104] ibid, r 7.

[105] ibid, r 7(7).

a. Disqualification

The regulated person may be given a written rebuke or directed to pay a penalty. A person can also be disqualified from acting as a HOLP or HOFA, or being a manager or employee of a licensed body referred to the Tribunal.[106]

b. Fines

Regulated Persons
The SRA is empowered by the LSA 2007 to impose fines of up to £2000 on solicitors '[w]here [it is] satisfied that a firm or individual has failed to comply with the SRA Principles' without referring the case to the SDT.[107] This power does not apply to misconduct occurring wholly before 1 June 2010.

Alternative Business Structures
Regulators that discover breaches of rule while auditing ABS can levy fines on the entity and individuals.[108] The SRA, for example, can fine ABSs £250 million and individuals in ABSs up to £50 million. The SRA consultation proposes general criteria for determining the scale of fine imposed. These are:

—— proportionality to the harm done, to the misconduct in question and the means of the paying party;

—— deterrence of repetition of the misconduct by the regulated person and by other regulated persons;

—— elimination of any financial gain or benefit arising from the misconduct;

—— culpability of the regulated person in relation to intentions, recklessness or neglect;

—— aggravating factors, such as failing to correct any harm caused or failing to cooperate with the SRA;

—— mitigation, such as prompt correction of harm caused and preventative action on future problems.[109]

It is proposed to operate the criteria alongside a formula producing a baseline figure, probably between 10 per cent and 30 per cent of turnover of the entity being fined. Decisions to impose fines under the 'traditional' or the ABS regime are appealable to the SDT. Any fine is payable for the benefit of Her Majesty's Treasury.

There is obviously a significant inconsistency in the SRA's powers. It is able to levy fines on law firms of up to £2000 and on ABS up to £250 million. The SRA is concerned to eliminate the discrepancy by being able to levy the higher fines on solicitors' firms as well as on ABS.[110]

---

[106] ibid, r 2(1).

[107] www.sra.org.uk/consumers/solicitor-check/fines-and-rebukes.page.

[108] The Legal Services Act 2007 (Maximum Penalty for Licensing Authorities) Rules 2011, which came into force on 1 August 2011 (www.legislation.gov.uk/uksi/2011/1659/made).

[109] SRA, 'Indicative Guidance on Financial Penalties', at para 13. (www.sra.org.uk/sra/consultations/financial-penalties.page).

[110] ibid, at para 15 and see J Hyde, 'SRA ponders £250m fine limit for firms' *Law Society Gazette* 30 March 2012 (www.lawgazette.co.uk/news/sra-ponders-250m-fine-limit-firms).

ii. *Regulatory Agreements*

Before the introduction of the Disciplinary Procedure Rules 2011 the SRA used regulatory settlement agreements to resolve disciplinary issues direct with firms rather than referring them to the SDT. These are agreements made between the SRA and the individuals. The agreement covers acceptance of the charges and agreement to sanctions such as or reprimand and payment of costs. Under the Disciplinary Procedure Rules 2011, the scope of these agreements was extended to cover payments to clients and fines.[111] There are two main kinds of regulatory agreement; issue agreements and regulatory settlement agreements.[112]

a. Issue Agreements

Issue agreements are intended to resolve a point that arises during the course of an investigation, such as paying compensation to a client, without concluding the investigation.

b. Settlement Agreements

Settlement agreements conclude an investigation in which breaches of rules and regulations are discovered, possibly by imposing terms. Material breach of a Regulatory Settlement Agreement is likely to be treated as professional misconduct.[113] The settlement agreement may be published where the SRA considers this to be a proportionate outcome in all the circumstances.

Settlement agreements are in writing and agreed with the solicitor. They state the relevant facts and identify any failings admitted by the solicitor. The solicitor's admission statement must acknowledge that the statement is made voluntarily and that the statement and agreement will be published by the SRA. The settlement agreement will then identify action the solicitor has taken or has committed to take and any sanction imposed by the agreement. It will be published by the SRA unless the contrary is expressly stated otherwise in the agreement.[114]

Solicitors may mitigate offences by identifying and contacting clients or others affected by a failure, by refunding money due to them, reporting periodically to the SRA on the progress of any such action and submitting to monitoring by the SRA.[115] Solicitors may be offered quite serious practice controls as part of a settlement agreement, such as not engaging in a particular kind of work or closing their firm within a set period.[116]

Solicitors may also agree to their removal from the roll without a decision by the SDT providing that they sign an agreement attaching a witness statement, an 'admission statement', containing a statement of truth admitting allegations of misconduct

[111] www.sra.org.uk/consumers/solicitor-check/agreements.
[112] SRA, *Settlement of Regulatory and Disciplinary Cases* (30 November 2007) at para 8.
[113] ibid, at para 15.
[114] ibid, at para 12.
[115] ibid, at para 22.
[116] ibid, at para 24.

and facts relevant to those allegations.[117] The statement must also acknowledge any previous disciplinary or regulatory findings. It must acknowledge that serious disciplinary action could be taken by the SDT in the light of the admissions, and request removal from the roll to save costs, distress and further risk to the public.

A solicitor agreeing to removal from the roll under a settlement agreement must undertake not to seek restoration to the roll and not to work for a solicitors' practice without the written permission of the SRA. He must make full and frank disclosure to any prospective employer of the agreement with the SRA.

C. The Bar Disciplinary Tribunal

In 1988 Abel observed that complaints reaching the Bar Disciplinary Tribunal (BDT) led to disbarment in only 3 per cent and suspension in only one per cent of the total.[118] Since that time, numbers of cases heard by the BDT has remained relatively low. Data from a limited sample suggests, however, that the percentage of disbarment and suspension cases has now risen to over 30 per cent of total cases. This may be partly due to the fact that the BDT deals with larger numbers of barristers who are not practising as self-employed.

i. Constitution

Bar disciplinary tribunals are organised by an independent body called the Bar Tribunals and Adjudication Service (BTAS). They are governed by the Disciplinary Tribunal Regulations 2009, which can now be found in the BSB Handbook in Section B of the Enforcement Regulations (Part 5).[119]

ii. Membership

The BDT members are selected by Council of Inns of Court (COIC). Each panel consists of either a three-person or a five-person panel. A five-person panel is chaired by a judge, and has two practising barristers and two lay representatives nominated by the President of the Bar. A three-person panel is chaired by a QC or a judge with a lay member and a practising barrister.[120]

---

[117] ibid, at para 26.

[118] ibid, at para 136.

[119] BSB, *Handbook*, Enforcement Regulations, Section B (pt 5): The Disciplinary Tribunals Regulations 2009 (amended February 2012) (www.tbtas.org.uk/wp-content/uploads/2013/08/BSB-Handbook-January-2014.pdf).

[120] The Disciplinary Tribunals Regulations 2009, reg 2.

iii. Respondents

Detailed study of one year of data suggests that 50 per cent of the 73 barristers appearing before the BDT in 2008 were self-employed, while nearly 20 per cent were non-practising, 11 per cent employed and 4 per cent were unregistered barristers. Data was missing in 15 per cent of the 73 cases.[121] There was one QC of 40 years' call, 12 of these years as Silk, in the sample.

iv. Caseload

The 2008 data for barristers was only detailed in relation to the 27 cases which resulted in disbarment or suspension. This is because the Bar's policy is to remove details of all disciplinary hearings not resulting in disbarment or suspension after two years. The charges leading to these severe sanctions, all involved breaches of the barrister's Code of Conduct.[122] These were categorised as follows:

—— Dishonesty (no 8);
—— Discreditable/Disreputable conduct (no 7);
—— Practising without a certificate/Holding out as being a practising barrister (no 3);
—— Failure to complete continuous professional development (CPD) requirements (no 12);
—— Failure to pay an administrative fine, generally relating to CPD infractions (no 11);
—— Failure to respond to a complaint (no 14);
—— Failure to respond to notification/Request for information (no 6);
—— Failure to report, for example, bankruptcy, being struck off the solicitors' roll or a criminal conviction (no 6);
—— Failure to comply with directions/Pay costs (no 3);
—— Breach of pupillage regulations (no 13);
—— Incompetence (during conduct of a trial) (no 1).

This small sample suggests that breach of the CPD rules, including failure to pay a resulting administrative fine, was the most common case in the category treated as serious.

Dishonesty and other discreditable behaviour is the main serious reason barristers appear before the BDT. Though there were 13 offences in connection with pupillage regulations, these related to only three barristers.[123] They set up a bogus chambers in order to award pupillage to one of their number, circumventing the pupillage regulations.[124]

---

[121] Boon, Sherr and Whyte (n 60).
[122] Then it its seventh edition and now its eighth; see www.barstandardsboard.org.uk/regulatory-requirements/the-code-of-conduct.
[123] See eg Naeem Sajid Khan (www.barstandardsboard.org.uk/complaints-and-professional-conduct/disciplinary-tribunals-and-findings/disciplinary-findings/?DisciplineID=74827).
[124] BSB, *Pupillage Handbook* (September 2011) (www.barstandardsboard.org.uk/media/261792/pupillage_handbook20august202011lc.pdf).

v. *Procedure*

Charges are formulated by a barrister appointed by the BSB.[125] Defendants are entitled to receive a copy of the evidence of each witness intended to be called in support of the charge or charges, a list of the documents intended to be relied on by the BSB representative, details of any evidence that is still being sought and a statement of when it is believed that it will be practicable to supply that evidence to the defendant.[126]

A directions hearing is usually held to consider matters such as the need for an oral hearing, applications for separate hearings, applications to sever or strike out charges, attendance of witnesses and provision of the names of all witnesses to be called at the hearing.[127]

The Tribunal may still hear evidence from a witness where a statement has not been served provided it is of the opinion that the defendant is not materially prejudiced or on such terms as are necessary to ensure that no such prejudice occurs. The defendant can appear or give a written answer to the charge if he thinks fit.[128] He can represent himself or be represented by counsel, with or without the involvement of an instructing solicitor.

The hearing is subject to the rules of natural justice.[129] The Tribunal does, however, have discretion to hear any evidence, oral or written, whether direct or hearsay, and whether or not the same would be admissible in a court of law.[130] The hearing is normally in public but the Tribunal has discretion to hear a case in private.[131]

vi. *Criteria*

The standard of proof for professional misconduct in Bar Disciplinary Tribunals is the criminal standard of proof.[132] If the Tribunal is divided as to the verdict on any charge 'the burden of proof being on the BSB, the finding recorded on that charge shall be that which is the most favourable to the defendant'.[133]

vii. *Sanctions*

If the charge is found to be proved the main powers of the Tribunal are:

—— disbarment;
—— suspension for a prescribed period or until a condition is met;
—— a fine of up to £15,000;

---

[125] The Disciplinary Tribunals Regulations 2009, reg 5.
[126] ibid, reg 7.
[127] ibid, reg 8.
[128] ibid, reg 8(2)(c).
[129] ibid, reg 11(2).
[130] ibid, reg 11(2)(a).
[131] ibid, reg 12 (but this rarely happens, see Haller, 'The Public Shaming of Lawyers' (n 33) 298).
[132] ibid, reg 11(1).
[133] ibid, reg 18.

—— prohibition, either indefinitely or for a prescribed period and either unconditionally or subject to conditions, from accepting or carrying out any public access instructions;

—— order to complete continuing professional development of such nature and duration as the Tribunal shall direct and to provide satisfactory proof of compliance to the Professional Conduct Committee;

—— order to take and pass a professional conduct and ethics test by a stated date, failing which the defendant shall be suspended from practice until such test has been passed;

—— order to attend on a nominated person to be reprimanded or given advice as to his future conduct;

—— a reprimand by the treasurer of the barrister's Inn or by the Tribunal; and

—— advice from the Tribunal on future conduct.[134]

A three-person panel cannot disbar but can refer to a five person panel if necessary.[135] There are additional powers to cancel fees arising out of a proceedings relating to a legal aid case.[136]

viii. Costs

The Tribunal may make such order as to costs as it thinks fit.[137]

ix. Decisions

The reports of decisions, where there is an adverse finding against the respondent, are sent to a variety of persons and bodies, including the Bar Council. The Bar's disciplinary proceedings have been published since 2002 and new findings are published on the BSB's website within seven days of a decision.[138] Of the 75 cases decided before the BDT in 2008, the imposition of a fine, independently or in conjunction with another order, was the most common finding, followed by reprimands.

In 2008, there were 14 suspensions and 13 disbarments. There was an order of no further action in five cases and advice regarding future conduct in seven. There were 12 findings involving other orders. These included a requirement to attend on head of chambers or Leader of the Circuit (no 2), to pay for or complete continuing professional development (no 4) and to pay outstanding fines (no 4).

[134] ibid, reg 19.
[135] ibid, reg 19(4).
[136] ibid, reg 19(6)(a).
[137] ibid, reg 31.
[138] www.barstandardsboard.rroom.net/complaintsofprofessionalmisconduct/publisheddisciplinary findings.

x. Appeals

In cases where one or more charges of professional misconduct have been proved, an appeal may be lodged with the Visitors in accordance with the Hearings Before the Visitors Rules 2005.[139] The Visitors are High Court judges appointed by the Lord Chief Justice. One or three Visitors will hear the appeal, depending on the issue involved. This may be an appeal against conviction by the defendant and/or an appeal against sentence. Complainants other than the BSB have no right of appeal.[140]

xi. Overview

In 2012 a report by the COIC disciplinary tribunals and review group reported 'systemic failures' in the administration of the Tribunal system for disciplining barristers.[141] These failings included errors relating to the eligibility of tribunal members and the discovery of potential conflicts of interest. The Tribunal was administered by a single secretary from a small room in a set of chambers. This may have contributed to a detrimental impact on record keeping. The report made 82 recommendations for reform, including the establishment of a COIC Tribunals Service, covering both COIC disciplinary tribunals and the Inns Conduct Committee.

D. Alternative and Complementary Routes to the Bar Disciplinary Tribunal

i. Determination by Consent

Determination by Consent (DBC) is a procedure for dealing with complaints. Barristers' participation in the DBC process is voluntary. If they do not agree to the DBC process the matter may be referred directly to a Bar Disciplinary Tribunal.[142] Complaints subject to the DBC procedure are dealt with by the Professional Conduct Committee (the PCC) of the Bar Standards Board. If the case appears appropriate for the DBC process, a Case Officer of the Investigations and Hearings team will prepare a brief.

On the basis of the paperwork the PCC decides whether there has been a breach of the Code of Conduct and, if so, whether any sentence would be likely to involve suspension or disbarment. The defendant's case and mitigation, if any, is added to the paperwork. Provided there are no substantial disputes of fact which can only fairly be resolved by oral evidence being taken, the PCC will impose a sentence.

---

[139] The Disciplinary Tribunals Regulations 2009, reg 25.

[140] ibid, reg 25(5).

[141] C Baksi, 'Review slams "systemic failures" in bar's disciplinary system' *Law Society Gazette* 30 July 2012 (www.lawgazette.co.uk/news/review-slams-systemic-failures-bar-s-disciplinary-system).

[142] BSB, *Determination by Consent: Explanatory Note for Barristers* August 2009 (updated May 2012) (www.barstandardsboard.org.uk/media/1408127/dbc_explanatory_note_for_barristers_and_flowchart_-_updated_10.05.12.pdf).

The PCC can impose the following sanctions:

—— a fine of up to £5000 (for acts or omissions prior to 31 March 2009) or up to £15,000 (for acts or omissions that took place on or after 31 March 2009);
—— completion of additional CPD requirements;
—— reprimand;
—— attendance on a nominated person to be reprimanded; and/or
—— advice as to future conduct.

The PCC has no power to award costs.

Barristers give express written consent to continue with DBC at different points in the procedure. A barrister who has agreed to the procedure has a choice of accepting the PCC's finding, and sentence, or requesting a hearing before the BDT. There are risks in exercising this option; the BDT may suspend or disbar barristers and make orders for costs against them.

ii. The Bar Complaints Committee

The Bar Complaints Committee has complementary and overlapping functions with the Disciplinary Tribunal. It hears complaints from parties other than the BSB and directs cases of professional misconduct to the BDT. It also has additional powers and functions in relation to determining consumer complaints of inadequate professional service.[143] From 31 March 2011 the Bar ceased to have any jurisdiction over these complaints. From that date, any complaint made about a barrister by or on behalf of a client is referred without further consideration to the Legal Ombudsman, and the complainant notified of this.[144]

There is a residual jurisdiction in relation to non-consumer complaints, for example, those made by a solicitor or another barrister. These continue to be investigated by the Professional Conduct Department under the direction of the PCC.[145] The powers of the PCC include reference to the procedures of either the BDT or of DBC.[146] It can also refer complaints to a barrister's chambers,[147] or to the barrister's Inn, Circuit, employer or some other regulatory body, for resolution.[148] In suitable cases, the Interim Suspension Rules or the Fitness to Practise Regulations are implemented immediately.

iii. Interim Suspension

The interim suspension rules apply where a barrister is convicted of or charged with an indictable offence. They can also apply if the barrister is sanctioned by an approved

---

[143] The Complaints Rules 2011, r 8.
[144] ibid, r 14.
[145] ibid, r 28.
[146] ibid, r 32.
[147] ibid, r 15.
[148] ibid, r 22.

regulator for misconduct leading to suspension or termination of the right to practise in an authorised body.[149] In such cases the Complaints Committee considers whether to establish a five-person Suspension Panel and the barrister is given notice of a date of hearing within 14 to 21 days.[150]

The panel can invite the barrister to undertake to withdraw from practice, and accept no further instructions, pending disposal of the case by a disciplinary tribunal.[151] Following a hearing the panel may impose a period of interim suspension or interim prohibition from accepting or carrying out any public access instructions (either unconditionally or subject to conditions). The period of suspension may be up to six months pending the hearing before a Disciplinary Tribunal.[152]

No period of interim suspension can be imposed unless the panel considers that it is likely that a Disciplinary Tribunal would impose a sentence of disbarment, or suspension for more than 12 months, for professional misconduct. It must also be in the public interest that the defendant should be suspended. Interim prohibition from accepting public access instructions can be imposed where disbarment, a year's suspension or prohibition from accepting public access instructions is likely.[153]

iv. Declaration of Being Unfit to Practise

The Complaints Committee may request referral to a Medical Panel where circumstances suggest a barrister may be unfit to practise.[154] The Fitness to Practise Regulations potentially apply to barristers suffering from serious incapacity. Such incapacity must be due to a mental or physical condition, including addiction, that seriously impairs fitness to practise. Suspension, or the imposition of conditions, must be necessary to protect the public.[155]

Medical Panels consist of five members nominated by the President. They include a chair and two other barristers of at least seven years' call. The chair and at least one other barrister must be Queen's Counsel. The panel must also include a medical expert and a lay representative.[156] At the conclusion of a preliminary hearing the panel may give directions for a full hearing. The directions may include provision for examination of the barrister by an appointed medical adviser. The direction may include disclosure of medical records. Adverse inferences may be drawn from refusal to provide such records.

The Medical Panel may direct that the barrister be suspended from practice or prohibited from accepting or carrying out any public access instructions, either

---

[149] BSB, *Handbook 2014*, pt 5D: Enforcement Regulations, The Interim Suspension and Disqualification Regulations; BSB, *Handbook 2014*, pt 2: The Code of Conduct, CD 8 (http://handbook.barstandardsboard.org.uk/handbook/part-2/).
[150] BSB, The Interim Suspension and Disqualification Regulations, reg 9(b).
[151] ibid, reg 9(c).
[152] ibid, reg 15(b).
[153] ibid, reg 15(b)(2).
[154] BSB, *Handbook*, pt 5, Section E: Fitness to Practise Regulations, reg 8.
[155] ibid, reg 4(g).
[156] ibid, reg 5.

unconditionally or subject to conditions, for a specified period or indefinitely.[157] Other than in exceptional circumstances the period should not exceed three months. In lieu of imposing a period of suspension or prohibition the panel may accept a barrister's written undertaking. The undertaking may include a promise to suspend his practice, or not to accept or carry out any public access instructions, pending the conclusion of the full hearing.[158]

E. Planned Adjustments to Bar Disciplinary Processes

The Bar's new regulatory regime is in force from January 2014. The intention is to resolve more regulatory issues through supervision and monitoring and to promote compliance by use of administrative sanctions. Disciplinary proceedings will be reserved for those cases where an administrative sanction is not severe enough or where the public interest requires a formal process. The BSB will broaden the grounds for interim suspension and introduce the immediate suspension in exceptional cases. It will expand the rules on determination by consent, disciplinary tribunals and interim suspension to cover businesses as well as individuals. There will be an increase in the level of fines available to the BDT for breaches of the Handbook.

VII. Rehabilitation

A. Solicitors

Applications for restoration to the roll of solicitors are made to the SDT.[159] They must be supported by an affidavit setting out details of the original order of the Tribunal, the history of the applicant's employment since the order was made and the applicant's future intentions as to employment within the profession in the event that the application is successful. The main factors that are considered in applications for restoration to the roll are the length of time since striking off, the extent to which the offender has been rehabilitated and re-employment prospects. The tribunal must be satisfied that sufficient time has elapsed since striking off. It normally expects at least six years to have passed since the date of the original order.

The Tribunal approaches applications for restoration as a question of whether the applicant has established that he is now a fit and proper person to have his name

---

[157] ibid, reg 16.
[158] ibid, reg 16(g).
[159] SRA, Disciplinary Procedure Rules 2011 (Version 7) r 9(1)(a).

restored to the roll.[160] Evidence of rehabilitation would normally include employment, either in the solicitors' profession or in a position of trust in a legal environment. The tribunal might expect to see evidence that another solicitor would be willing to employ the applicant in connection with a legal practice. Rehabilitation might also be evidenced in other ways. The tribunal would expect to see a sustained effort to clear liability to the Solicitors' Compensation Fund, for example.

According to the SDT website, a criminal conviction involving dishonesty, or a finding of dishonesty by the Tribunal, is an all but insurmountable obstacle to a successful application for restoration.[161] It cites a statement by the Master of the Rolls in 1993 that solicitors seeking restoration must prove more than fitness to be a solicitor. They must also show that restoration would not adversely affect the good name and reputation of the solicitors' profession or be contrary to the interests of the public. It warns that the Tribunal should not and will not be swayed by evidence of hardship.

The Solicitors Act provides that no solicitor shall, except with written permission granted under the section, 'employ or remunerate in connection with his practice' any person who to his knowledge is struck off, suspended or bankrupt.[162] The SRA considers applications for permission, which are unlikely to be granted where the striking off involved dishonesty.[163] Permission will not cover activities reserved to solicitors and may be subject to other conditions. In cases of refusal, appeal is to the High Court, which may also impose conditions on employment.

Restoration to the roll is likely to be difficult to achieve when relevant employment is almost a prerequisite. Striking off often involves an element of dishonesty. Dishonesty is itself a significant barrier to restoration to the roll, but it is also a potential bar to employment in a solicitor's firm. It is surprising, therefore, that any solicitors are successful in being restored to the roll. Nevertheless, in the five years between 2007 and 2012, three applications to the SDT for restoration to the roll succeeded and 15 were refused.[164] Over the same period, three applications for defining or lifting terms of indefinite suspensions succeeded and five were refused.

B. Barristers

Barristers who seek to return to the bar following disbarment must apply to an Inn. As with all other candidates for admission, the Inn will consider whether the former barrister is a fit and proper person to be admitted. In some circumstances, for example, where there has been a criminal conviction or disciplinary misconduct,[165] the Inn must refer the matter to to the Inns' Conduct Committee to decide whether it can re-admit

---

[160] SDT, *Applications in Respect of Solicitors* (www.solicitorstribunal.org.uk/constitution-and-procedures/applications/).
[161] www.solicitorstribunal.org.uk/constitution-and-procedures/applications/.
[162] Solicitors Act 1974, s 41.
[163] SRA, *Suspension, Removal from the Roll* (www.sra.org.uk/solicitors/enforcement/practising-certificate-pc-conditions-suspension-removal-roll/suspension-removal-roll-appeal-employment.page).
[164] SDT, *Annual Report 2011–12*, 8.
[165] Bar Handbook 2014, Bar Training Rules, Part 4 Admission to the Inns of Court rQ17.

the barrister.[166] Barristers suspended under the Fitness to Practice Regulations can seek a review of their suspension on the grounds that their circumstances have changed.[167]

VIII. Disciplinary Processes and Regulatory Sanctions

The juxtaposition of traditional disciplinary systems and regulatory action is not new. Both the Bar Council and Law Society imposed various penalties and restrictions on members without applying full disciplinary processes. What is new under the post-LSA regulatory regime is that fines and other ad hoc sanctions are intended to be a more central item of the regulatory toolkit. The use of less formal methods of securing compliance poses questions about the way the two systems will articulate.

While the different approaches associated with each system are complementary, they can also be in conflict. This is demonstrated by the standard of proof required by the SDT (the criminal standard) and that adopted by the SRA in the exercise of its disciplinary powers (the civil standard). Now that the SRA can impose modest fines and even strike a solicitor from the roll, the issue of consistency is raised. Similar problems of consistency arise in relation to the sanctions applicable to regulated persons and ABS. There could be problems where a party appeals against a regulatory fine and a different standard is applied.

A. Rules and Principles

The LSB, and others, have encouraged the professions to adopt principles in place of rules when drafting regulatory standards. This shift reflects the 'more modern' style of regulation promoted by government. It is also arguable that principles are more flexible and adaptable to the diverse situations that regulators have to deal with. They can apply to organisations and individuals. Because of this flexibility, principles lack specificity. When individuals are charged with disciplinary offences it may be arguable that principles have been broken. It is for this reason, presumably, that the Bar, while adopting the Handbook terminology for their new regulations, retain the rule format in most areas.

One aspect of the argument between the LSB consultants on the cab rank rule and those responding on behalf of the Bar, related to this distinction between rules and principles. The LSB consultant concluded that

> [w]hile [the cab rank rule] can be lauded as a professional principle enshrining virtuous values, as a rule it is redundant. We can see no justification for the continuation of the cab

---

[166] ibid, rQ16.
[167] Bar Handbook 2014, Enforcement Regulations, Part 5: Reviews and Appeals.

rank rule as a rule in the modern, globalised legal services market. By all means the Bar can espouse it as laudable principle but it should not pretend that the rule is significant or efficacious.[168]

The proposition that the cab rank rule could be replaced by a principle evoked much discussion in the Bar's responses. The Bar Standards Board's respondents were confused by the suggestion. They pointed out that whether the cab rank rule became a principle would depend on the form regulatory standards took. If they took the form of rules, then the suggestion that an obligation become a principle might suggest that the intention was to weaken its force. If, however, a code was composed purely of principles, it would matter less. The 'cab rank principle' would then still be enforceable. In fact, they suggested, in a code such as the solicitors now had, principles were more likely to be enforced than outcomes.[169]

The Bar Council's respondent, Sir Sydney Kentridge QC, argued that, in their evaluation of the cab rank rule, the consultants 'ignore the force of professional tradition and in particular that this element in it is inculcated into every Bar student'. Kentridge's discussion cites Dworkin's distinction between rules, being applicable in an 'all or nothing fashion', and principles, 'requirements of justice or fairness or some other dimension of morality'.[170] On this basis he dismisses the idea that the rule could work as a principle because it would involve, 'down-grading the cab rank rule to a vaguely desirable principle'.[171]

The points made in the Bar consultants' reports are somewhat supported by the LSB consultant's report. It states that the Bar was unable to find any data on returned briefs or examples of enforcement as evidence that the rule is not significant. It does, however, refer to a 2006 case in which a barrister was fined £1,000 for breach of the cab rank rule. In that case the barrister, a regional chair of the Lawyer's Christian Fellowship, refused a brief on behalf of an immigrant who wanted to use his homosexuality as part of his grounds for asylum. The issue is whether, in the absence of such a rule, but the presence of a principle, such a fine could have been imposed.

Below the surface of the debate about the relevance of the cab rank rule lies an important issue about the nature and use of professional standards. The LSB consultants reveal cynicism regarding the effect of professional rules. They also display scepticism about the continuation of professional regulation by rule. They suggest that measures like the cab rank rule were the product of self-regulation and expressive of the 'regulatory bargain'. Now, they said, we have 'external regulation ... we can ask how many of the rules are still relevant'.[172] This suggests that the LSB consultants see the establishment of regulatory arms as a complete break with the tradition of

---

[168] J Flood and M Hvvid, *The Cab Rank Rule: Its Meaning and Purpose in the New Legal Services Market*, 39 (https://research.legalservicesboard.org.uk/wp-content/media/Cab-Rank-Rule_final-2013.pdf); C Baksi, 'Taxi for the cab rank rule' *Law Society Gazette* 22 January 2013 (www.lawgazette.co.uk/news/taxi-cab-rank-rule).

[169] M Mclaren, C Ulyatt and C Knowles, *The 'Cab Rank Rule': a Fresh View* (www.barstandardsboard.org.uk/media/1460590/bsb_cab_rank_rule_paper_28_2_13_v6__final_.pdf).

[170] Sir S Kentridge, *The Cab-rank Rule: A Response to the Report Commissioned by the Legal Services Board* (London, Bar Council, 2013) at 18. http://www.barcouncil.org.uk/media/203452/sir_sydney_kentridge_crr_response.pdf.

[171] ibid, at 20.

[172] Flood and Hvvid, *The Cab Rank Rule* (n 168) at 38.

self-regulation. It may also suggest that they see the LSB as the main player in shaping regulation, rather than simply being overseers of the system.

B. The Burden of Proof in Applying 'Regulatory' and 'Disciplinary' Sanctions

Although the circumstances in which the power to fine or strike off is different, the underlying principle is still relevant. For example, the SDT can impose an unlimited fine while the SRA can only impose a fine of up to £2000. There are no restrictions on the power of the SDT to strike off whereas the SRA can only do so with the agreement of the solicitor. The SDT needs to see evidence that satisfies it beyond reasonable doubt. The SRA only needs to be satisfied on a balance of probabilities. Are these different standards justified?

The adoption of the civil standard of proof was approved by the SRA Board and incorporated in the SRA Disciplinary Procedure Rules. The Board received a paper containing numerous reasons for the SRA adopting the civil standard in applying its regulatory powers. This raised a number of arguments that have been used since by advocates of the civil standard of proof. They can be broadly grouped under the heading of consumer benefit, proportionality, rigour and flexibility.

i. Case for the Civil Standard

The first argument concerned the impact on consumers of adopting the civil standard. If the SRA were to adopt the criminal standard, more cases would be rejected at an early stage because of lack of proof, or the disproportionate cost of collecting proof, to meet that standard. This would reduce public protection and increase frustration with regulation. The SRA and its predecessors had applied the civil standard of proof for many years in exercising regulatory functions, resolving cases more quickly and cost-effectively than the SDT and without significant difficulty or controversy.

The second argument downplayed the significance and impact of the new regulatory powers. They would only allow the SRA to impose fines of up to £2,000 and publish findings of misconduct resulting in a rebuke. The criminal standard of proof was not appropriate to these relatively minor findings of misconduct. In exercising its powers the SRA would not be putting anyone's liberty at stake. Further, there was a statutory appeal, as of right, to the SDT against findings that implied serious wrongdoing.

The third argument asserted the robustness of the civil standard of proof. Decisions having a major impact on lives, businesses and livelihoods are taken every day in civil cases applying the civil standard of proof. The civil standard can deal with serious allegations by what the case law refers to as a need for 'heightened examination', allowing the regulator to 'look closely into the facts grounding an allegation of fraud before accepting that it has been established'. It allows for 'appropriately careful consideration by the tribunal before it is satisfied of the matter which has to be established'.

The final argument related to the SRA's increased emphasis on 'regulation of firms and overall proportionality'. This, it was said, was likely to be facilitated by the new powers being exercisable using the civil standard. It appears that this was shorthand for suggesting that using the civil standard would fit better with OFR, and a focus on firms, rather than individuals.

ii. Case for the Criminal Standard

Most of the arguments for using the civil standard of proof in deciding whether to impose regulatory sanctions are an implicit criticism of using the criminal standard of proof in misconduct cases. The case for using the criminal standard largely rests on the case for consistency in the processes for reaching decisions. It therefore depends, to a large extent, on the use of the criminal standard for the most serious cases in the disciplinary tribunals.

The case for using the criminal standard in the disciplinary tribunals is based on the need to be fair to the accused. Professional practitioners facing charges of misconduct risk losing their reputations, incomes and careers. These consequences are at least as serious as those faced by defendants in criminal courts. In most disputes with professionals, the consequences for consumers are much less serious. The decision to impose a serious sanction on a professional person, the argument goes, should not be taken lightly. It should not be done for the convenience of achieving artificial compatibility between two regimes.

iii. Responses of the Professions

Before coming to a conclusion the SRA Board considered the prospect that the SDT would be applying a higher standard of proof in cases it decided. This would potentially include those cases appealed from SRA decisions taken applying the lower standard. In opting for the civil standard of proof in applying its new regulatory powers the SRA undertook not to use them in cases involving dishonesty. This could reduce the chances of inconsistency between SRA and SDT decisions. It will not, however, resolve all the issues raised by the operation of two distinct but interconnected systems, one focused on individuals and one on organisations.

The SRA Board considered the prospect that the LSB, SDT, SRA and the Law Society would all move to applying the civil standard. This seemed likely when it was revealed that CILEx had adopted the civil standard for disciplinary matters and that the BSB was considering it. The prospect receded when it became clear that the criminal standard would, in fact, be retained for both the SDT and BDT cases.

Retaining different burdens of proof for imposing 'regulatory' or 'disciplinary' sanctions presents problems. It may encourage appeals from SRA regulatory decisions when firms think that their reputation might suffer and the proof of infraction does not reach the criminal standard. The initial application by the SRA to adopt the civil standard in disciplinary matters was initially rejected in 2009 by the Lord Chancellor and the Master of the Rolls.

The Bar saw the difficulty in applying different standards of proof to the same facts. Responding to a consultation by another regulator it responded

> [w]hile there remains a line of thought that it may be appropriate to apply a different standard of proof to allegations that amount to criminal behaviour, the BSB recognises the practical problems in applying different standards according to the nature of the allegation/complaint.[173]

In 2011 the BSB was reported to again be considering a switch to a civil standard of proof in disciplinary matters.[174]

When the Bar came to implement its new regulatory regime it also ran into the difficulty of applying different standards of proof to serious and non-serious breaches. It announced that administrative sanctions would apply to breaches of rules that 'do not amount to professional misconduct' and that disciplinary action would be reserved for 'more serious professional misconduct'.[175] This appeared to leave professional misconduct that lay between 'non-serious' and 'more serious' uncovered by either administrative sanctions or disciplinary processes. It is in this grey area where jurisdictional problems are likely to arise.

C. Erosion of Distinctions between Disciplinary Charges

Before the Solicitors' Code of Conduct 2007, it was understood that misconduct fell into two categories. The first category was a breach of code or other regulation. The second category was 'unbefitting conduct'. It has been alleged that, since the new code was enacted, all breaches of the code have been prosecuted and the distinction between code breaches and 'unbefitting conduct' eroded.[176] This move was attributed to a desire to ensure that the Solicitors Conduct Rules 2007 created obligations to manage firms effectively.

The attempt to shift regulation from an individual to a corporate basis was apparently reflected in an increase in cases where the SRA charged solicitors for the acts of employees. In *Akodu v SRA*[177] the Divisional Court overturned a decision of the SDT finding a partner guilty of conduct unbefitting a solicitor for the act of an employee. The employee, a fee earner under his supervision, failed to inform a mortgagee, a lender client, of a reduction in the price paid for a property by the purchasing client. In the absence of any evidence of personal fault in *Akodu*, a finding of conduct unbefitting a solicitor could not be sustained purely on the basis that he had been a partner in the firm.

---

[173] Letter from BSB to the Immigration Services Commissioner dated 15 September 2011 (www.barstandardsboard.org.uk/media/1387123/20110915_letter_20to_20suzanne_20mccarthy.pdf).
[174] 'Criminal standard of proof in disciplinary matters "could expose clients of ABSs"' *Legal Futures* 21 March 2011 (www.legalfutures.co.uk/regulation/solicitors/criminal-standard-of-proof-in-disciplinary-matters-could-expose-clients-of-abss).
[175] BSB, 'New BSB Handbook to give barristers more freedom and flexibility' (www.barstandardsboard.org.uk/media-centre/press-releases/new-bsb-handbook-to-give-barristers-more-freedom-and-flexibility/).
[176] A Hopper and G Treverton-Jones, 'Rule Breaches and Professional Misconduct – Where to Draw the Line?' *Law Society Gazette* 1 April 2010.
[177] Akodu v SRA [2009] All ER (D) 180 (Nov).

Although the finding was quashed, the order that the appellant pay 40 per cent of the costs was upheld. This was because it could reasonably be said that he had brought the allegations on himself. The case illustrates a contemporary debate about the purpose and scope of disciplinary proceedings. On one hand, there are those who argue that discipline must deal with partners who do not manage others adequately.[178] On the other, it is arguable that, in principle, solicitors should not be brought before the SDT for employee infractions over which they had no control.[179]

The doctrines of strict and vicarious liability have never applied in disciplinary proceedings. They have always been concerned with personal professional responsibility. Perhaps the power of the SRA to impose sanctions might avoid such cases coming to the SDT in future.

D. Levels of Fine between 'Regulated Persons' and ABS

The difference in level of fines the SRA is able to level on regulated persons (£2000), on manager or employees of ABS (£50 million) and on ABS (£250 million), is huge. There will almost certainly be litigation should the SRA attempt to levy such fines at the higher end of the scale. The lack of fairness reflected in this discrepancy is likely to be an argument used by ABS in appealing such fines.

E. Forum Shopping

'Forum shopping' is a practice of litigants, initially identified in private international law, seeking to have a case heard in the jurisdiction or court most likely to provide a favourable judgment. ABS can choose any licensing authority to regulate them. This raises the possibility that they will choose regulatory regimes providing the most favourable terms, including the level of fine and the standard of proof required to show breach of licence.

In 2011 the Council for Licensed Conveyancers' (CLC) applied to become an ABS licensing authority. It proposed using the criminal standard of proof in serious cases, such as those alleging dishonesty. The Legal Services Consumer Panel (LSCP) warned that this would attract ABS looking for a less rigorous regulatory regime and could expose customers of CLC regulated ABS to risk.[180] The LSCP suggested that it was 'surprised' and 'disappointed' that the CLC had responded to 'informal enquiries' with a position paper confirming its adherence to the criminal standard.

---

[178] E Chambliss and D Wilkins 'A New Framework for Law Firm Discipline' (2003) 16 *Georgetown Journal of Legal Ethics* 335.

[179] Hopper and Treverton-Jones, 'Rule Breaches and Professional Misconduct' (n 176).

[180] 'Criminal standard of proof in disciplinary matters "could expose clients of ABSs"' *Legal Futures* 21 March 2011 (n 174).

F. Use of Regulatory Sanctions

i. Diminution of Impact

Abel points out that, in the case of professional disciplinary proceedings, the process is part of the punishment.[181] When sanctions are imposed as part of an administrative process they may not have the same impact. Fines, which have long been used as disciplinary sanctions, are an example of this. When imposed by disciplinary tribunals, fines can be seen as one of a range of penalties reflecting the seriousness of misconduct. Fines imposed by regulators might be seen as administrative matters and not a form of serious reprimand.

ii. Regulator Discretion

Whereas disciplinary processes are open, transparent and accountable, administrative processes may be less so. There is no external review of mechanisms such as regulatory settlement agreements. The regulated party has an incentive to agree to the sanction to avoid the disciplinary process. Thereafter, there can be no appeal about the process or fine. The availability of regulatory discretion raises issues about due process and fairness to regulated parties in terms of both the imposition and scale of sanction. For example, solicitors in large firms may be subject to settlement agreements whereas those in smaller firms may be brought before the SDT.[182]

IX. The Future of Professional Discipline

As in most areas of lawyers' work, the LSA 2007 has put in motion processes that call into question the traditional approach to professional discipline. There is potential for a turf war between the approved regulators and the disciplinary tribunals. These are constituted separately from regulators but typically receive cases prepared by them and hear appeals from their decisions on imposing regulatory sanctions.

As regulators expand their regulatory powers, the role of, and necessity for, the disciplinary tribunals will be called into question. It is possible that, in future, approved regulators could exercise all the powers currently exercised by disciplinary tribunals. A safety net would be provided by a right of appeal, either to an appeals tribunal or a court. An alternative would be for regulators to use a more limited range of sanctions and leave serious cases of misconduct to criminal courts. In this way, issues over using different standards of proof would be avoided.

---

[181] Abel (n 2) ch 8.
[182] A Boon and A Whyte, 'Icarus Falls: The Coal Health Scandal' (2012) 15(2) *Legal Ethics* 277.

If, as seems likely, some role for formal disciplinary proceedings is retained, there will continue to be tension between tribunals and regulators exercising similar disciplinary powers. This may be resolved or mitigated by the allocation of clear spheres of responsibility. Even so, further thought will need to be given to whether existing sanctions are effective, and when. It may also be desirable to consider the role of alternative disciplinary mechanisms, for example, apologies, in the disciplinary armoury.[183]

X. Conclusion

The machinery of professional discipline, whether internally or externally imposed, traditionally serves several purposes in securing compliance. It provides an exclusion mechanism for those who are a menace to the integrity of the profession, a deterrence mechanism for those who might be tempted to transgress and assurance to members of the profession that their mutual commitment to ethics is taken seriously. The disciplinary processes of the legal profession are relatively longstanding and well respected, but they are not immune from change.

Sir David Clementi's review of the legal services market directed no criticism at disciplinary tribunals, to which he proposed virtually no changes.[184] This is remarkable given the range and depth of his criticism, for example, of complaints procedures. Clementi may not, however, have anticipated the consequential changes the enactment of his proposals would have on the institutions of the profession. Professional discipline is one of the areas experiencing the stresses and strains of a new system. Disciplinary tribunals deal with relatively small numbers of extreme cases, but they play an important symbolic role.

There are several points of tension between the traditional and new systems of compliance operated by the legal professional regulators. The SDT is under pressure from the SRA to adopt the civil standard of proof, the balance of probabilities, which is what the SRA now applies in exercising its new powers of regulatory sanction. Grossly different levels of fine operate as sanctions, depending on different regulators and kinds of organisation. There is a possibility of forum shopping between different regulators for the best regulatory terms. It is ironic that Clementi considered the old system a confusing maze.

---

[183] F Bartlett, 'The Role of Apologies in Professional Discipline' (2011) 14(1) *Legal Ethics* 49.
[184] DCA, *The Future of Legal Services: Putting Consumers First* (Cm 6679, 2005).

PART III

CLIENTS

Loyalty

'I'll take fifty per cent efficiency to get one hundred per cent loyalty'.[1]

I. Introduction

The duty to clients is the foundation of the distinctive ethic of professions. It is composed of a number of separate and specific obligations, such as the avoidance of conflicts of interest and respect for client confidences. These duties are dealt with elsewhere in this part. This chapter focuses specifically on the foundation of the lawyer and client relationship, in the loyalty that the lawyer owes to the client. This involves further consideration of why even undeserving clients should receive loyalty, what this means in practical terms and where any limits to the obligation of loyalty lie. These issues are linked to the nature of the lawyer and client relationship and the issue of where ultimate control lies.

The relationship of all professional persons with their clients, or patients, has been the subject of considerable debate in the last 25 years or so. This attention may stem from changing perceptions of the nature of professional work and professional responsibility. In particular, there has been a move towards recognising that clients have a greater right to personal autonomy than once was the case. For lawyers, one of the core issues is the degree of control that they can exert over the client's matter and, critically, in making decisions. Such decisions potentially cover a range of matters, including making moral choices on the client's behalf.

In this chapter 'clients' describes present and former clients, that is, people who have, at some point, instructed a specific lawyer to act on their behalf. This does not include people, consumers, who may become clients. This is slightly at odds with the SRA Handbook, which defines a client as 'the *person* for whom you act and, where the context permits, includes prospective and former clients'.[2] The chapter does not cover the selection or refusal of clients, which is dealt with in the chapters on Third

---

[1] Samuel Goldwyn, Film Producer.
[2] SRA, *Code of Conduct 2011*, as amended, Glossary.

Parties. This chapter focuses on the foundations of the relationship between lawyers and those they have accepted as clients. It examines the duties that flow from the relationship, in theory, in law and in the codes.

II. Loyalty to Clients

The obligation of loyalty is often traced to the adversarial system. The argument is that adversarial justice protects client autonomy and dignity. Parties decide for them-selves what they wish to claim and how they wish to support their claims and the lawyer facilitates that exercise of autonomy. Lawyers ensure that the promise of client autonomy is realised by ensuring that clients' cases are presented in the way that they would present them, if they had the legal skills. It on this basis that lawyers claim not to be accountable morally when acting for their client, even if they would not neces-sarily do the same thing for themselves.

The balance between duties to clients and to the wider system varies considerably between countries as a result of various factors. The main differences between juris-dictions relate to conceptions of the judicial process and its purpose, to theories about justice and to ideologies relating to the role of the judge and the legal profession.[3] Nevertheless, most systems qualify loyalty to clients in some way. There is usually an expectation that lawyers will not compromise justice, that is, justice in the shape of formal legality. What is meant by loyalty to clients, and the limits to that loyalty, is defined in detail within each system.

III. The Lawyer and Client Relationship at Common Law

The relationship between lawyers and clients was defined over time by the common law. So, for example, a solicitor's authority to act on behalf of a client arises from what is traditionally called the 'retainer'. This term usually refers to short-term contracts of hire. Such an arrangement is called a retainer because it usually calls for a payment 'up front'. It is often used in relation to solicitors because it used to be a

---

[3] M Taruffo, 'The Lawyer's Role and the Models of Civil Process' (1981) 16 *Israel Law Review* 5.

common arrangement. The solicitor's authority extends only as far as the terms of the retainer specify, either expressly[4] or impliedly.[5]

In England and Wales the issue of the lawyer and client relationship is complicated by the existence of the 'split profession' and the allocation of responsibility between the professionals in such an arrangement. Barristers are instructed as consultants and specialist advocates and paid for by clients, albeit through solicitors. Nevertheless, the courts require that solicitors do not follow counsel's advice blindly but continue to exercise their own judgement, especially where counsel is obviously or seriously wrong.[6]

IV. Legal Basis of the Lawyer-Client Relationship

The lawyer and client relationship is often compared with different kinds of legal relationship. The main comparisons are with agency, contract and trusts.[7] All of these legal concepts resemble the legal relationship between lawyers and clients in some degree. None of them perfectly describes the lawyers' obligations arising in the relationship with clients. Each of them contributes elements to the legal conception of relations between lawyers and clients.

A. Three Prospective Legal Bases for the Lawyer and Client Relationship

i. Agency

An agent is someone who agrees to act on behalf of another, the principal, in relation to a specific business transaction with a third party. The agent usually has some special skill or experience in relation to the proposed transaction. The agency agreement defines the scope of the agent's authority. The agent has broad authority in conducting the task, but is held to a high standard of accountability. Third parties can assume that agents are acting within the scope of their authority. The agent can be liable to the principal for exceeding instructions or causing loss.

The lawyer and client relationship is similar to agency in structure, but different in detail.[8] The similarity is that the client directs the professional as to the broad remit

---

[4] *James v Ricknell* (1887) 20 QBD 164.
[5] *Wright v Pepin* [1954] 2 All ER 52.
[6] See *Locke v Camberwell Health Authority* [1991] 2 Med LR 249; *Davy-Chiesman v Davy-Chiesman* [1984] 1 All ER 321; and *Matrix Securities Ltd. v Theodore Goddard* [1997] 147 NLJR 1847. See also on wasted costs, *Tolstoy v Aldington* [1996] 2 All ER 556.
[7] See further M Bayles, *Professional Ethics* (Belmont, CA, Wadsworth Publishing, 1981).
[8] DA DeMott, 'The Lawyer as Agent' (1998) 67 *Fordham Law Review* 301.

of the task to be performed. The lawyer, like any agent, has considerable latitude as to how the task is achieved. Any constraints on the agent tend to be fixed by the general law or by custom and practice, relating mainly to the duty the agent owes to the principal. They operate so as to reinforce the fidelity of the agent to the client's prime objective. There are, however, two main problems with regarding the lawyer and client relationship as being one purely based on agency.

The first problem with basing the lawyer and client relationship on agency is that it is inconsistent with the way the relationship operates in practice, both in relation to clients and third parties. This is because the agency relationship permits a relatively wide implied authority to the agent. If it applied, lawyers could undertake actions or bind the client in ways that are incompatible with the role. Agency cannot easily be reconciled with the requirements of both the law and professional conduct codes. In particular, it is inconsistent with obligations to take into account the interests of justice and the duty to the court.

The second problem with the agency model is connected with this idea that lawyers should not merely follow instructions. The view that lawyers are simply agents encourages or reinforces an unethical view of legal practice. This is because an agent cannot presume to question the task given to them. The agency model would therefore require that lawyers abandon any evaluation of the client's objectives or the methods of achieving them. In the context of legal practice, the agency model is consistent with visions of the lawyer as a 'hired gun' or the client's mouthpiece.

ii. Contract

Under a contractual basis for the lawyer and client relationship, the parties would agree upon their respective rights and duties. This is arguably more flexible than agency in being able to accommodate ethical limits to the lawyer's conduct. These duties have to be implied into any contractual arrangement, because they are imposed by the law or by professional codes. Even though the lawyer and client relationship is often assumed to be a contractual agreement between them, some features of the situation are unusual.

A contract for legal assistance is unusual in that not all of the details are capable of being agreed in advance. Therefore, a lawyer must frequently return to the client for information or instructions on how to proceed. These deviations in the path of the relationship could change the original basis of agreement. It is also debatable whether what typically happens when a client instructs a lawyer is consistent with contract. There is often no negotiation of terms, nor issue of a standard term contract. Typically, the lawyer sends the client a letter confirming that they have received instructions. These are often referred to in very broad terms.

A contractual model of the lawyer and client relationship must accommodate the fact that different ethical obligations apply in different situations. The client may be vulnerable, ignorant or poor. This places them at a disadvantage in agreeing terms. Alternatively, a rich and powerful corporate client may dominate a lawyer by the threat of withdrawing their business. An ethic based on the contract therefore needs to anticipate either a high degree of client dependency or, alternatively, a high degree of client autonomy. Different ethical considerations may apply in each case.

iii. Trusts

A fiduciary relationship is one in which a person, the fiduciary, has been placed in a position of trust and confidence to manage and protect the property or money of another. In the law of trusts, trustees, persons holding or managing assets for others, are held to exacting standards. They must account for all assets and profits produced by trust property. There is a presumption that any profit made by the trustee from dealings arising from the trust, or from opportunities that are presented to the trustee through the trust, accrue as trust property. This responsibility can be seen as a price of the extremely broad scope of their power and autonomy. Those establishing a trust have limited control over the trustees' performance of their duties.

Trustees and agents are often subject to fiduciary obligations. This is usually because they are in the position of holding property, but also because of the scope of their powers. Trusts typically vest far more power over property in the fiduciaries than does agency, hence trustees' onerous obligations. The beneficiary or principal is expected to trust the fiduciary and the fiduciary is expected to justify that trust.

Lawyers could be subject to fiduciary duties, most obviously when they hold client money or property. Such duties may also derive from a duty of loyalty, and the duty of care. A fiduciary basis to the lawyer and client relationship would derive from the fact that, like trustees and agents, lawyers have broad discretion to act in clients' interests in a way that is not controlled by clients.

B. Unique Legal Basis of Lawyer and Client Relationship

The courts tend to treat the lawyer and client relationship as a contractual relationship carrying fiduciary responsibilities. This is illustrated by the decision of the House of Lords in *Hilton v Barker Booth & Eastwood*.[9] In that case a solicitor acted where there was a conflict of interest. The solicitor argued that an implied term of his contract with the client enabled him to modify his duty to disclose all relevant information to the client. This argument had in fact succeeded in the Court of Appeal but was rejected firmly by the Lords.

In the House of Lords, Lord Walker considered the solicitor's duty to the client was 'primarily contractual' but it was also a fiduciary relationship. The fiduciary relationship could be 'moulded and informed' by the terms of the contract but its fundamental basis could not be modified. This suggests that the lawyer and client relationship is legally unique. Courts may draw on similar legal concepts depending on the circumstances presented. They may also seek consistency with decisions in similar cases in other fields.

The SRA Handbook states that a solicitor's relationship with clients 'is a contractual one which carries with it legal, as well as conduct, obligations'.[10] It is, however, a unique legal construct.[11] While it is primarily based on contract, other legal concepts,

---

[9] *Hilton v Barker Booth & Eastwood* [2005] 1 All ER 651, esp [28] and [38].
[10] SRA, *Handbook*, ch 1: 'Client Care' (Prelude).
[11] JM Perillo 'The Law of Lawyers' Contracts is Different' (1998) 67(2) *Fordham Law Review* 443.

such as trusts, are imported into the relationship. Treatment by the courts also recognises the distinctive obligations that lawyers owe to clients and to the wider administration of justice.

A fiduciary basis places the lawyer under a duty to take special care to ensure that no advantage is taken of the client. This includes ensuring that there is no undue influence of the client.[12] In this way, lawyers are often placed under disadvantages by courts in relation to their agreements with clients than are other contracting parties. The fact that the lawyer and client relationship may have a fiduciary basis perhaps suggests an expectation of a higher level of consultation with clients than is suggested in the other bases. If the lawyer must act in the client's best interests, clearly the client has to be consulted. Therefore, as fiduciaries, lawyers would need to make every reasonable effort to inform clients and obtain authority to act. The day-to-day conduct of transactions is, however, a matter for the lawyer. All kinds of decision, which may or may not affect the client, including ethical decisions, may be taken on their behalf by the professional.

V. Control of the Lawyer and Client Relationship

A. Implications of the Legal Basis of the Lawyer and Client Relationship

The legal basis of the lawyer and client relationship raises a question about who is in control of the relationship. The issue of who is, theoretically and ultimately, in charge of the lawyer and client relationship is unclear in most jurisdictions.[13] This is a matter relevant to any situations where the lawyer and client disagree. It has particular bearing on the issue of who has the last word on any decision with a moral component.

B. Theoretical Models

Theoretical models describe different conceptions of the respective responsibilities of professionals and their clients. They may not be found in pure form in practice, but most lawyer and client relationships are based on these models or display some elements of them. The degree of control exercised by each side of the lawyer and client relationship varies according to which theoretical model of the relationship is subscribed to.

---

[12] For discussion of this model in the American context, see RD Dinerstein, 'Client-Centered Counselling: Reappraisal and Refinement' (1990) 32 *Arizona Law Review* 501.

[13] GC Hazard Jr and A Dondi, *Legal Ethics: A Comparative Study* (Stanford, CA, Stanford University Press, 2004) at 176–79.

Each model reflects different assumptions about the client's capacity to make decisions and moral choices. This might engender, at one end of the spectrum, perceptions of an almost child-like dependency. At the other end of the spectrum, clients may be treated as acting as independent moral agents. The models may also reflect different perceptions of the lawyer's responsibility for promoting clients' moral agency. Those dealt with here are paternalism, participation, autonomy and empowerment.

i. Paternalism

It can be argued that 'the parental' is an appropriate metaphor for the lawyer and client relationship.[14] The parental relationship envisages that the lawyer has superior knowledge, skills and experience of the matter in hand and therefore knows what is best for the client.[15] The conventional term for a lawyer and client relationship reflecting these assumptions is 'paternalistic'. Paternalism describes a policy or practice of treating or governing people in a fatherly manner. It is arguably a traditional professional mode for lawyers.

In a paternalistic relationship with clients lawyers may attend to their needs without the clients themselves having autonomous rights or specific responsibilities. It reflects the assumption that the most efficient way of proceeding with the matter in terms of both time and expense is for the lawyer to handle everything while troubling the client as little as possible. Paternalism can be identified with traditional notions of professionalism, whereby practitioners determine client needs and how to meet them.

This implication of the paternalist model is that, once clients have revealed their aims, lawyers should be left to take all strategic and tactical decisions. The issues involved are far too complicated for clients to understand, hence the need for lawyers. The considerable control that paternalism affords the lawyer over the client's affairs may provide circumstances for abuse. This is one reason why the spirit of public service is invoked in legal practice. It encourages lawyers to prioritise client interests over their own.

ii. Participation

The inequality in the lawyer and client relationship is usually attributed to the fact that the lawyer has superior knowledge and information about the client's situation and options. This is sometimes called a situation of 'information asymmetry'. In a lawyer and client relationship based on client participation, the imbalance in the relationship is reduced, if not equalised. It is redressed by the lawyer providing information and guidance on legal and non-legal options, enabling the client to participate in decision-making.

---

[14] R Mortensen, 'The Lawyer as Parent: Sympathy, Care and Character in Lawyers' Ethics' (2009) 12(1) *Legal Ethics* 1.
[15] D Nicholson and J Webb, *Professional Legal Ethics: Critical Interrogations* (Oxford, Oxford University Press, 1999) ch 5.

The participatory approach implies a continual dialogue between lawyer and client. In pure form, the progress of work is evaluated in the light of the client's aims and interests at each stage. New agreements are reached on the steps to be taken. In client-centred relationships, with shared decision-making responsibility and mutual participation by lawyer and client, neither lawyer nor client dominates.[16]

In the participatory model, clients control decision-making and lawyers are technical advisers and counsellors. In research conducted in the USA Rosenthal found that higher levels of participation by clients in their personal injury claims tended to increase the sums that they recovered in damages.[17] This suggests that, in addition to promoting autonomy, participatory professional relationships might have advantages in promoting client interests, certainly when compared to the paternalistic model.

iii. Autonomy

Western society has moved towards promoting autonomy in most professional fields. This is consistent with the contemporary emphasis on individual, personal autonomy as an overarching ethical good. The change can be illustrated by developments in the relationship between doctor and patient. In the medical field, for example, doctors often did not give patients full information about their condition on the ground that anxiety might make it worse.

Patient autonomy has, in the medical field led to increased emphasis on the need for patients' informed consent to treatment. Many jurisdictions have abandoned the *Bolam* test,[18] which stated that it was a matter for the doctor's professional judgement what a patient is told about their condition. Instead the 'prudent patient' test is preferred. Doctors must typically consider what a prudent patient, in the particular circumstances of the patient in question, needs to know about his medical condition in order to decide what treatment to follow.

In England and Wales, courts have edged towards imposing a duty on doctors to warn patients of all factors, including small risks, affecting their choice of treatment. In 1985, in *Sidaway v Bethlem*[19] the House of Lords held that a doctor was not negligent in failing to warn a patient of a 1 per cent risk of paraplegia attached to surgery. At the time of the operation, in 1974, he had followed a practice accepted as proper by a responsible body of medical opinion. Nevertheless, their Lordships endorsed the need for informed consent. They indicated that, where the degree of risk was substantial or the consequences particularly grave, the patient's right to make the decision himself outweighed even the respected body of medical opinion.

Since *Sidaway* the requirement for obtaining informed consent has become well established. In *Chester v Afshar*,[20] the majority of the House of Lords held that a patient was entitled to succeed when not warned of a 1 to 2 per cent risk of an

---

[16] Dinerstein, 'Client-Centered Counselling: Reappraisal and Refinement' (n 12) at 556.
[17] DE Rosenthal, *Lawyer and Client: Who's in Charge?* (New York, Russell Sage Foundation, 1974); and see A Gutmann, 'Can Lawyers be Taught Virtue' (1993) 45 *Stanford Law Review* 1759.
[18] *Bolam v Friern Hospital Management Committee* [1957] 1 WLR 582.
[19] *Sidaway v Governors of the Bethlem Royal Hospital* [1985] AC 871.
[20] *Chester v Afshar* [2004] UKHL 41, [2005] 1 AC 134.

operation going wrong. The minority dissented on the grounds that the information would have made no difference on the crucial issue of causation. Among the majority, Lord Steyn cited Ronald Dworkin in support of an individual's right to personal autonomy in controlling their medical treatment.[21] He quoted a section of text supporting the integrity of the individual and their autonomy in making their own choice. This

> allows us to lead our lives rather than be led along them, so that each of us can be, to the extent a scheme of rights can make this possible, what we have made of ourselves. We allow someone to choose death over radical amputation or a blood transfusion, if that is his informed wish, because we acknowledge his right to a life structured by his own values.[22]

His Lordship therefore asserted that the autonomy of the patient required that adults should consent, on a fully informed basis, to surgery. The doctor had violated the patient's right to choose and, if damages were not awarded, the surgeon's duty to seek consent would seem hollow.

The move away from paternalistic professional relationships is broader and more pervasive than the limited issue of consent to treatment. Professionals are encouraged to see clients, not as passive recipients of advice or assistance, but as consumers purchasing a service. This sensitivity to human individuality ensures that professionals do not subvert the client's personal values, take over, manage them or do what they do not want.[23]

iv. Empowerment

The final model describing the possible relationship between lawyer and client emphasises empowerment. It envisages that clients are encouraged and helped to be autonomous individuals. This could even involve helping them to use legal processes themselves. Clients might therefore handle as much of their matter themselves as they can, without the assistance of lawyers. This is a step beyond autonomous decision-making to autonomous action.

The empowerment model was formerly restricted to some forms of radical lawyering. It was associated with the so-called 'unbundling' of legal services into different components, some of which could be handled by lawyers. It has been predicted, by Susskind and others, that these options will move more mainstream with the increasing power of computer technology and the sophistication in software and internet solutions. Clients, it is predicted will, in future, be more easily able to purchase 'Do-it-yourself' law packages and *a la carte* law services.

It is arguable that aspects of the empowerment thesis have already been enacted. Initiatives securing direct client access to barristers have made a virtue of self-help. Because barristers are not able to hold client money, clients seeking assistance from barristers under the Bar Direct scheme must take steps such as issuing their own

[21] See R Dworkin, *Life's Dominion: An Argument About Abortion, Euthanasia, and Individual Freedom* (New York, Alfred A Knopf, 1993).
[22] ibid, at 224.
[23] D Koehn, *The Ground of Professional Ethics* (London and New York, Routledge, 1994) at 176.

proceedings. Although this may be a stopgap until more traditional arrangements are established, it is also an interesting experiment in empowerment.

C. Decision-making in the Model Relationships

In the models described, the key issue is responsibility for making decisions. It is not suggested that clients are responsible for making every decision in a matter. It is arguable however that they should set the objectives of the representation and make important decisions thereafter. Important issues may include those with a moral component. In these situations the operating model of the lawyer and client relationship determines who can take the decision and with what degree of responsibility for any moral choices made.[24] The implications of this can be worked through using an example of a situation that arises often in legal practice.

i. An Illustration

In litigation, it is common for there to be a procedure whereby a party who is sued notifies an intention to defend the claim. They then have a fixed period within which to file a defence. After the fixed period has expired, a claimant can usually enter judgment in default of defence. Failure to file may occur as a result of an oversight by the defendants or their lawyers.

To enter judgment in default of defence is to take advantage of technical failure by the defendant and nothing to do with the merit of the claim. Such judgments are often set aside by the court, usually at the defendant's cost, where a meritorious defence can be shown. The decision whether to enter judgment therefore has an ethical dimension. It used to be the case that solicitors acting for claimants would ask lawyers for a defendant whether they intended filing a defence before entering judgment. Although there was no rule on the matter, many solicitors considered it a 'professional courtesy' to warn another solicitor of such action. Where defendants had no lawyers, and were impecunious, a claimant's lawyer might be more inclined to simply enter judgment.

The practice of deciding how to respond to failure to file a defence without consulting the client illustrates the operation of the paternalistic model. Obtaining judgment in such circumstances might be justified on the grounds that it is the client's explicit objective to win the case. How it is done is within the scope of the lawyers' operational discretion. Not obtaining judgment could be justified on the grounds that, although it is within the scope of the lawyer's instructions to win the case, the lawyer is bound to behave honourably and with integrity. To enter judgment could be seen as underhand and therefore dishonourable. The paternalistic model would place responsibility for the decision squarely with the lawyer.

Both actions described had ethical implications on which the client could, and arguably should, have been consulted. Giving the defendant a chance to file a defence

---

[24] ED Cohen, 'Pure Legal Advocates and Moral Agents: Two Concepts of a Lawyer in an Adversary System' in A Flores (ed), *Professional Ideals* (Belmont, CA, Wadsworth Publishing Co, 1988) at 82.

without asking the client put the relationship with other solicitors above the client's. Consequently, the defendant's interests were also placed above the client's interests. Entering judgment without asking the client assumed that the client's only interest in the matter was succeeding in the claim. It ignored the client's right to decide an issue of principle. There may also have been commercial issues involved. Entering judgment in default may have business implications, for example, by undermining the client's reputation with other contractors.

Under the participatory model, the client would be consulted about the course of action to be taken where a defence is not filed in time. Any reputational issues arising from entering default judgment could be considered. There may even be a discussion of the morality of taking a judgment on a technicality, particularly if it was clear that there was an arguable defence. In such circumstances, the client may be dissuaded from deciding to enter judgment, at least until due warning is given. If lawyer and client disagree on a course of action following discussion, the participatory model does not provide a resolution. Whether or not the lawyer was prepared to enter judgment having advised against it would be a true measure of who controls the relationship.

The model of client autonomy suggests that the decision to enter judgment in default is unambiguously the client's to make. The lawyer might advise that such a step would invite terrible publicity. She may table numerous other pragmatic arguments showing how entering judgment would be against the client's best interests. She is, however, bound to follow the client's instructions, even if they are unwise. Even if she disagrees with the client's instructions, the lawyer operating under this model should carry them out.

The empowerment model provides a consumer with exactly the legal service that they want. This may or may not involve moral counselling or advice about the propriety of a course of action. It might be anticipated that clients want to know what the law allows. They do not necessarily want advice about moral choices. If the client does want such advice it might come at an additional cost. Having obtained any necessary paperwork, and advice on how to complete it, the client can attend court and enter judgment on their own behalf.

ii. Expected Trends

It is arguable that the trend in legal practice has moved away from paternalism, towards participatory lawyer client relationships, and, in some areas, beyond, into the model of client autonomy. This shift is consistent with increased emphasis on individual rights and on clients' rights as consumers. The implication is that lawyers should allow clients to reach their own decisions, exercising free will. The process is more likely to involve participatory decision-making on material and morally sensitive issues. The rest of legal representation, the nuts and bolts of how a matter is handled, arguably falls within the area of the lawyers' operational discretion.

Participatory decision-making involves lawyers providing sufficient information to allow clients to make informed decisions regarding their own interests. The supportive atmosphere of participatory relationships is intended to facilitate wise decisions by clients. Clients are assisted in exploring the legal, pragmatic and moral implications of particular courses of action. If a client intends to take a decision their lawyer considers immoral, the lawyer has a chance to dissuade them using moral and pragmatic arguments, such as the impact of negative publicity. In some cases, they may be unable to continue to act, for example, where the client's decision would involve the lawyer in a breach of conduct rules. Sometimes, morality and pragmatism overlap, for example, where there is a risk that a client's lie will be revealed in court.[25]

The difficult issue for the participatory model arises where clients, despite counselling, require action that their lawyer considers immoral. Lawyers might argue that they should not be passive in the relationship, that promoting client autonomy is not simply a question of doing what clients say. Within the participatory model, there may be scope for a lawyer to refuse to take action he has counselled against. Even this is not clear, however. It may arise where action is required that was not contemplated when the original instructions were accepted. Within the model of client autonomy the lawyer must refuse to take illegal actions on a client's behalf. There is, however, no right, or responsibility, to ensure that clients make ethically defensible decisions.

In the current cultural climate, participatory decision-making is compatible with contemporary social norms. It responds to clients as autonomous consumers, but also recognises the moral agency of lawyers. The opportunity to express and discuss moral choices, and possibly dissuade clients from immoral ones, offers lawyers a more satisfactory role than that of 'hired gun'. Since moral responsibility is notionally shared, lawyers arguably have a right to decline to take courses of action that, while legal, they consider immoral and beyond the scope of the original instructions. This may prevent the fragmentation of personality, or 'false self', sometimes associated with professional roles.[26]

VI. Model Lawyer and Client Relationships in Practice

A. The Complexity of Practice Settings

The model of lawyer and client relationship in operation may be affected by factors in the practice environment. These factors include the type of firm they belong to and the practice area in which they operate. These factors affect the kinds of client that lawyers habitually deal with and their expectations of the interaction. Two practice areas present examples of extreme possibilities. These are corporate and commercial work and cause lawyering. Different expectations operate in these areas regarding the

---

[25] A Boon, 'Assessing Competence to Conduct Civil Litigation: Key Tasks and Skills' in P Hassett and M Fitzgerald (eds), *Skills for Legal Functions II: Representation and Advice* (London, Institute of Advanced Legal Studies, 1992).
[26] A Giddens, *Modernity and Self-Identity: Self and Society in the Late Modern Age* (Cambridge, Polity Press, 1991).

outcome of representation. This may, in part, be due to the fact that different types of clients are found in these distinct spheres of operation.

i. 'One-shotters' and 'Repeat Players'

As regards clients, representing a child, a confused elderly person or a mental patient, for example, may encourage a more paternalistic approach than representing an adult able to exercise full choice. It is in these kinds of circumstances where the obligation to protect a client's best interests comes to the fore. Lawyers must do their best to determine what the client wants and to achieve what is consistent with their interests. In practice, however, other situations tend to fall at the paternalistic end of the spectrum of possibilities for the lawyer and client relationship. Clients with inexperience of legal matters may also encounter paternalistic lawyer and client relationships.

Clients who only consult lawyers in crisis moments in their lives, such as personal injury or divorce, have been labelled 'one-shotters'. Those who frequently instruct lawyers in similar matters are known as 'repeat players'.[27] One-shotters tend to be individuals with limited resources for lawyers, while repeat players tend to be institutions with more resources. The distinction affects the kinds of outcomes clients want and expect, the timescales they are willing to work to and the sums they are willing to expend.

Heinz and Laumann identified different patterns of lawyer behaviour in 'two hemispheres' of legal practice.[28] In one hemisphere lawyers serve organisational clients, such as corporations and institutions such as trade unions. In the other lawyers provide personal services to individuals and small businesses. Repeat players are more likely to appear in the first hemisphere and one-shotters in the second. This accentuates the very different nature of likely lawyer and client interactions. Dealing with either type of client can affect the time a lawyer might spend, for example, explaining matters. The nature of consultation may also vary between types of matter.

ii. Commercial and Corporate Clients

In large firms corporate and commercial work clients are typically repeat players. The client's representative may have considerable experience of the kind of matters dealt with. They can anticipate what is going to happen, give very detailed instructions and ask to be consulted on specified issues. In some cases commercial clients dominate their lawyers, seeking control of the decision-making process. In some circumstances clients may also demand unethical actions.

In the corporate and commercial sphere, lawyers may be subject to rules of conduct not generated by their profession. Lloyds of London, for example, produce a code

---

[27] M Galanter, 'Why the "Haves" Come Out Ahead: Speculations on the Limits of Legal Change' (1974) 9 *Law & Society Review* 95.

[28] J Heinz and E Laumann, *Chicago Lawyers: The Social Structure of the Bar* (Evanston, IL, Northwestern University Press, 1982).

regulating the relationship of Lloyds' Underwriters and their lawyers.[29] This code imposes obligations that go beyond the professional codes of lawyers. It provides that lawyers must justify their fees, provide advance notice of bills, standardise their advice and make greater use of Alternative Dispute Resolution.[30]

iii. 'Personal Plight' Clients

The situation in large firms corporate is very different work from the work of smaller, local firms. 'High street lawyers' are more likely to deal with clients in a situation of personal plight, for example, criminal or matrimonial matters. Such clients are more likely to be 'one-shotters'. Funding constraints may limit how much time can be spent with such clients. If they are funding matters themselves, the case may proceed in a disjointed fashion. Advice and assistance may be required episodically. Initial contact may be made by email and it may be difficult to obtain detailed instructions initially or as the matter progresses.

iv. Cause Lawyers

In two volumes edited by Sarat and Scheingold, the impact of cause lawyers was demonstrated to be a world-wide phenomenon.[31] Numerous case studies showed that some lawyers use litigation, and various other means, to advance social and political causes. So, for example, litigation might be used to establish precedents that might be beneficial to groups, to causes or to civil rights generally. One question that arose from these case studies was the extent to which lawyers were prepared to sacrifice loyalty to clients in order to advance the cause they believed in.

Causes can often be advanced by establishing precedents through the courts. It may be a long wait to find strong cases that will establish a legal principle. Client loyalty could be compromised if, when such a case is found, a defendant tries to 'buy off' the claimant with a generous settlement. The cause lawyer might advise acceptance, in the client's interest, or be tempted to advise rejection, in the interests of the cause. A lawyer who prioritises the cause he or she works to promote acts in breach of a duty to act in a client's best interests.

---

[29] *Law Society Gazette* 1 July 1998, at 9.
[30] See ch 20: 'Alternative Dispute Resolution'.
[31] A Sarat and S Scheingold (eds), *Cause Lawyering: Political Commitments and Professional Responsibilities* (New York, Oxford University Press, 1998); A Sarat and S Scheingold (eds), *Cause Lawyering and the State in a Global Era* (Oxford Socio-Legal Studies, 2001); A Sarat and S Scheingold, *Something to Believe in: Cause Lawyers and Social Movements* (Stanford, CA, Stanford University Press, 2004).

B. The Implications of Complexity for the Lawyer and Client Relationship

Examples of legal practice demonstrate that models of the lawyer and client relationship in use may reflect a number of factors. Levels of client consultation and client decision-making may depend on the model of legal practice, the needs, experience and abilities of the client in question, the nature of the work involved, the economic circumstances in which it is done and the wishes of the client.

Under a model of client autonomy a client may decide that they want very little to do with a matter. It may be agreed, or be implicit, that consultation will only occur when vital interests are affected, possibly only at the end of a transaction. The client may give their lawyer *carte blanche*. Ironically, the autonomous client can decide they prefer a remote relationship with their lawyers. In order to create a different situation, one where a particular model of the lawyer and client relationship was preferred, professional rules would need to impose very specific obligations.

VII. Models of the Lawyer and Client Relationship Reflected in the Courts, Legal Education and the Legal Services Act 2007

It is to be expected that an idea of the model of the lawyer and client relationship in use will be reflected in a number of professional sources. The obvious materials include court cases, professional codes of conduct and education and training curricula.

A. The Courts

The courts are generally unsympathetic to the paternalistic model of lawyer and client relationships. This is evident in antipathy towards lawyers who substitute their own moral choices for those of their clients. In *Griffiths v Dawson*,[32] for example, a solicitor failed to lodge an application to protect a wife's future right to a widow's pension. This would have held up the divorce. The solicitor considered this to be 'unsporting', in other words unfair and improper. It was held that a solicitor was negligent in such circumstances. He could not make a personal decision not to take such a vital step. In ordinary circumstances, the presumption is that decisions on important matters are taken by clients.

---

[32] *Griffiths v Dawson* [1993] FL 315.

B. The Lawyer and Client Relationship in Legal Education and Training

The representation of the lawyer and client relationship in education and training curricula has presented a somewhat lawyer-centred picture. In the current LPC regulations there are two relevant elements. These are concerned with interviewing and advice giving and follow-up. They are both directed to collecting information as a basis for providing advice. Both elements are rather prosaic. There is no reference to moral issues, or other signalling that a participative model of the lawyer and client relationship is envisaged.

In the interviewing element of the LPC outcomes, for example, the main criterion for effectiveness describes eliciting the relevant information, allowing the client to explain any concerns, anticipating the client's questions and having clear outcomes. In the advice element the students must identify possible courses of action, the legal and non-legal consequences of a course of action (including the costs, benefits and risks) and assist the client in reaching a decision.[33] This, at least, suggests that it is the client's decision to make.

The description of client interviewing and advice giving in the curriculum for the BPTC is similarly directed to gathering information and issuing advice.[34] The constituent elements of conducting a conference with a client are listening to what clients say, permitting them to raise concerns, listening to the client in a non-judgmental manner, empathising with and reassuring the client when appropriate, clarifying the relevant gaps and any ambiguities, selecting and using appropriate questioning techniques, eliciting the information required to advise the client and demonstrating a clear understanding of the client's account of the case or facts.

The BPTC standards related to advising a client similarly describe a process.[35] It requires setting out the strengths and weaknesses of the case, advising on the consequences of any course of action taken and what further steps should be taken. The student must then ensure that the client understands what has been discussed, obtain the client's full instructions and adhere to the instructions. There is not much clue from these standards as to the nature of the relationship, the importance of interests or the expectation of an ongoing, participative relationship. In fact, the tone is suggestive of a paternalistic relationship with clients.

C. Professional Principles of the LSA 2007

It is a regulatory objective of the Legal Services Act 2007 (LSA 2007) to promote and maintain adherence to the professional principles identified in the Act. These principles are directed at lawyers as authorised persons. They contain two references to clients. One is that authorised persons should act in the best interests of their clients

---

[33] SRA, Legal Practice Course Outcomes 2011 (www.sra.org.uk/students/lpc.page).
[34] BSB, *BPTC Handbook, Academic Year 2012–2013*, at 49 (www.barstandardsboard.org.uk/media/1435625/bptc_081112.pdf).
[35] ibid, at 50.

and the other is that the affairs of clients should be kept confidential. These principles scratch the surface of the complex duty that lawyers owe clients as elaborated in the codes of the legal professions.

VIII. Models of the Lawyer and Client Relationship Reflected in Professional Regulation

A. Clients in the Codes

Codes of conduct often convey a very clear, if sometimes contradictory, picture of the place of clients in professional priorities. Even the relative absence of clients from the code speaks volumes. The failure to mention clients, or to describe what responsibilities are owed to them, implicitly reserves a wide range of discretion to lawyers. This section considers the growth of specific professional responsibilities to clients through the codes of conduct.

B. Solicitors

i. A Brief History of 'Client Care'

Concerns about the nature of the lawyer and client relationship have tended to find expression in client care regimes. These detail requirements that lawyers must observe, usually at the beginning of the relationship. They tend to relate to the provision of information. This may have started as a defensive practice in terms of reducing the volume of complaints. It is generally more difficult for a client to allege that they have not been properly advised if a client care regime has been followed. As the regime developed, however, it began to promote more participative decision-making, at least at the beginning of the lawyer and client relationship.

The Solicitors' Practice Rules 1990 appeared to have little concern for the promotion of client satisfaction. They were concerned with standards of work rather than good relationships between lawyers and clients. It was already clear however, that more attention to client needs was required. In an experiment reported in 1986, intending solicitors' were found to have a number of 'failings' when conducting interviews.[36] One of the most significant was that they recorded what they had to do for the client in their notes, but did not share this information with the client. The research was conducted before the introduction of the Legal Practice Course, the interviewing component of which aimed to remedy problems identified in the research.

---

[36] A Sherr, 'Lawyers and Clients: The First Meeting' (1986) 49 *Modern Law Review* 323, at 330.

In the 1990s the Law Society was under pressure to raise standards of client care, partly as a result of scandals over costs.[37] Solicitors' legal aid work was under threat from the government's Legal Aid Efficiency Scrutiny[38] and plans for the development of legal aid contracting. The Green Paper, *Legal Services: A Framework for the Future*, published in 1989,[39] made it clear that the Law Society had to do something about standards of work and the treatment of complaints about bad service. The Law Society had a strong incentive to act on its own account. Reducing the number of dissatisfied clients would reduce pressure on a complaints system that was costly to run.

By the late-1990s, many solicitors had experience of stiffer requirements on client care. Firms seeking a legal aid contract had to demonstrate that they had systems for recording instructions, the requirements of clients and the advice given. They also had to comply with written standards on costs, confirming them in writing. Information about any costs liability had to be refreshed at least every six months. Firms on panels for insurance companies or trades unions usually had to comply with contractual standards for providing client information.

In 1999, the Law Society amended the Solicitors' Practice Rules 1990 by introducing Rule 15. This provided a rudimentary client care regime. Solicitors were required to give clients information about costs and other matters. They were also required to operate a complaints handling procedure. The detail was specified in a Solicitors' Costs Information and Client Care Code issued by the Council of the Law Society.[40] This was not a particularly successful innovation. The majority of solicitors did not comply with some or all of the requirements of Rule 15.[41]

The Solicitors' Code of Conduct 2007 provided a more developed and consistent framework for an open relationship between solicitors and clients. Any constraints on the relationship arising from the solicitor's relationship with a third party, such as a funder or introducer, had to be explained to the client. The name of the person handling the matter and his or her supervisor had to be given to the client in writing. The best information possible had to be provided to clients. How costs were to be met had to be discussed, as did the possible liability for the costs of the other side.[42]

The 2007 Code specified that information must be given on any payments the client would or might have had to make to others, so-called disbursements. Methods of payment had to be investigated, for example the availability of legal aid or insurance. All this information on costs had to be 'clear and confirmed in writing' under Rule 2.03(2). Conditional fee agreements (CFAs) were subject to additional requirements regarding provision of information.[43] Reflecting new procedural rules on proportionate costs, solicitors had to discuss with clients whether the potential outcomes of their

[37] O Hansen, 'The Lessons of the Peggy Wood Case' *Legal Action* October 1993, at 9.
[38] Lord Chancellor's Department, *Legal Aid Efficiency Report* (London, Lord Chancellor's Department, 1986).
[39] Lord Chancellor's Department, *Legal Services: A Framework for the Future* (London, HMSO, 1989).
[40] Council of The Law Society, *Solicitors' Costs Information and Client Care Code* (1990).
[41] C Christenson, S Day and J Worthington, '"Learned Profession?—the Stuff of Sherry Talk": The Response to Practice Rule 15?' (1999) 6(1) *International Journal of the Legal* Profession 27.
[42] SRA, *Solicitors' Code of Conduct 2007*, r 2.03.
[43] ibid, r 2.03 (2) and guidance. See further ch 12: 'Fees'.

case would justify the expense or risk involved, including the risk of having to pay the other side's costs.

The principle behind all the new provisions of the Solicitors' Code of Conduct 2007 was to ensure that solicitors were aware of clients' concerns and that clients had sufficient information to make informed choices. Solicitors had to 'identify clearly the client's objectives', provide the client with a clear explanation of the issues involved and the options available, agree on the next steps to be taken and keep the client informed of progress.[44] The Code introduced a requirement to agree an appropriate level of service and explain the responsibilities of both client and solicitor.

The 2007 rules made expectations more explicit and encouraged a greater flow of information between solicitor and client. There was also an attempt to improve communication between solicitors and clients. Guidance suggested that solicitors provided information 'in a clear and readily accessible form' and that 'over complex or lengthy terms of business letters covering many matters' may not be the most helpful way of doing it. These revisions evinced an intention to leave paternalistic assumptions behind and create more participatory lawyer and client relationships.

Previous experience of trying to implement a client care regime had obviously caused the Law Society Working Group to reflect on enforcement. The 2007 rules contained a warning that failure to comply with the client care requirements could lead to enforcement 'in a manner which is proportionate to the seriousness of the breach'.[45] In some cases this could include the solicitor's retainer becoming unenforceable.

ii. The Lawyer and Client Relationship in the SRA Handbook

The lawyer and client relationship described in the new SRA Handbook builds very substantially on the Solicitors' Code of Conduct 2007. Many of the principles, outcomes and indicative behaviours in the Handbook are recognisable as former rules or parts of rules. Of the 10 principles set out in the SRA Handbook, three directly relate to clients. These are acting in the best interests of each client,[46] providing a proper standard of service to clients[47] and protecting client money and assets.[48] Among the outcomes that must be achieved, one operates at a similar high level of generality. This is the outcome specifying that clients must be treated fairly.[49] The principles apply to solicitors, their employees and those in licensed bodies. These are referred to collectively as solicitors in this part.

The principles operating in favour of clients may be reinforced, or balanced, depending on perception, by some of the other principles applying to the regulated parties. These include upholding the rule of law and the proper administration of

---

[44] ibid, r 2.02.
[45] ibid, r 2, guidance paras 1 and 2.
[46] SRA, *Handbook 2011*, as amended, SRA Principles 2011, Principle 4. (www.sra.org.uk/solicitors/handbook/handbookprinciples/content.page).
[47] ibid, Principle 5.
[48] ibid, Principle 10.
[49] SRA, *Handbook 2011*, as amended, SRA, *Code of Conduct*, Outcome 1.1.

justice,[50] acting with integrity[51] and not allowing independence to be compromised.[52] The last two of these three could apply to protect client interests. They could also operate as counterweights to excessive client loyalty and as a reminder of wider duties to the system of justice.

The section of the SRA Handbook called 'You and Your Client' contains 16 outcomes that must be achieved. Many of these refer to the inception of the relationship and information that must be provided. Some refer to the nature of the relationship itself and the service provided. Finally, a few relate to the end of the relationship and the consequences if something has gone wrong. This section is organised around these stages rather than the sequence in which the outcomes are listed.

iii. Chronological Stages of the Relationship and Outcomes Attributable to each Stage

a. Inception

Many of the outcomes deal with matters that must be settled at the start of any matter. Clients must have the benefit of the solicitor's compulsory professional indemnity insurance and the exclusion of liability below the minimum level of cover required by the SRA Indemnity Insurance Rules is not permitted.[53] Clients should receive the best possible information at the time of engagement about the likely overall cost of their matter.[54] Solicitors can only to enter into fee agreements with clients that are legal, suitable for the client's needs and take account of the client's best interests.[55] This might include discussing whether the possible outcomes can justify the expense or risk involved, including the risk of paying another party's legal fees.[56]

Solicitors must inform clients whether and how their services are regulated and how this affects the protections available.[57] They must be informed in writing of their right to complain, and how complaints can be made to the firm, at the outset of the matter.[58] They must also be informed in writing, both at the time of engagement and on the written copy of the firm's complaints procedure, of their right to complain to the Legal Ombudsman (LeO) and the time frame for doing so.[59] Solicitors must also provide clients with the contact details of the LeO.

b. Conduct of the Ongoing Relationship

The SRA Handbook contain significant indicators of the way in which the lawyer and client relationship is currently conceived. An important outcome is that solicitors

---

[50] SRA, *Handbook 2011*, as amended, SRA Principles 2011, Principle 1.
[51] ibid, Principle 2.
[52] ibid, Principle 3.
[53] SRA, *Code of Conduct* 2011, Outcome 1.8.
[54] ibid, Outcome 1.13.
[55] ibid, Outcome 1.6.
[56] ibid, Indicative Behaviour 1.13.
[57] ibid, Outcome 1.7.
[58] ibid, Outcome 1.9.
[59] ibid, Outcome 1.10.

put clients in a position to make informed decisions about the services needed, the handling of their matter and the options available to them.[60] It may be significant, however, that the phrasing of the outcome suggests an initial rather than an ongoing obligation. Another outcome includes a requirement that the service provided 'takes account of their needs and circumstances'.[61] Yet another requires solicitors to 'agree an appropriate level of service with clients, for example the type and frequency of communications'.[62]

The various outcomes requiring consultation with clients, and client choice about the service provided, obviously require quite detailed discussion of options. This suggests commitment, at some level, to participatory decision-making. Another suggested outcome is that solicitors ensure that they 'have the resources, skills and procedures to carry out your clients' instructions'.[63] This suggests, albeit not definitively, a commitment to client autonomy in decision-making. Another outcome suggesting ongoing dialogue is the requirement to discuss costs, when appropriate, as the matter progresses.[64]

c. Conclusion of the Matter

The end of the matter might, but does not necessarily, mean the termination of the relationship. The client may well have other matters in progress, or, if they are a repeat player, intend to return at a later date. Several of the outcomes relate to events that may tend to occur at the end of the matter. For example, if a solicitor discovers any act or omission in the handling of the matter which could give rise to a claim by the client against the firm, the client must be informed.[65]

Clients must be informed of their right to challenge or complain about their bill and their liability to pay interest on an unpaid bill.[66] Any complaint by the client must be dealt with promptly, fairly, openly and effectively.[67] A proper account must be given to clients for any financial benefit received as a result of their instructions.[68]

iv. Complaints

Private plight and one-shotter clients dominate complaints data. In 2011/12, for example, there were over 75,000 contacts and 8420 cases accepted for investigation by the Legal Ombudsman (LeO).[69] Analysis of the LeO data by the Law Society shows

---

[60] ibid, Outcome 1.12.
[61] ibid, Outcome 1.5.
[62] ibid, Indicative Behaviour 1.1.
[63] ibid, Outcome 1.4.
[64] ibid, Outcome 1.13.
[65] ibid, Outcome 1.16.
[66] ibid, Outcome 1.14.
[67] ibid, Outcome 1.11.
[68] ibid, Outcome 1.15.
[69] Office for Legal Complaints, *Annual Report and Accounts 2011–12* (TSO, 2012).

that solicitors are the subject of 96 per cent of the active complaints.[70] Three areas of law accounted for just over half of all complaints handled by the LeO in 2011–12.

The largest areas in terms of complaints registered were family law (18 per cent), residential conveyancing (18 per cent) and wills and probate (14 per cent). These could be areas where lawyers are cutting costs in order to compete, with deleterious results for quality of service. The Law Society analysis found that of the 7455 active complaints about solicitors,[71] 40 per cent arose directly out of dysfunction in the lawyer and client relationship. They related to failure to advise (16.50 per cent), failure to follow instructions (15.70 per cent) and failure to keep the client informed (10 per cent).

C. Barristers

The longstanding Code of Conduct of the Bar of England and Wales (1981, as amended) was superseded in 2014 by the BSB Handbook. The new Code of Conduct, contained in the Handbook, preserves many of the former rules, and the orientation towards clients that they reflect. Both derive from the distinctive relationships that existed between barristers and what are referred to as 'professional clients' and 'lay clients'. Before considering the new Code of Conduct, it is instructive to examine the position set out in the previous code.

i. The Orientation of the Bar Code of Conduct 1981

The Bar Code of Conduct 1981 was originally written from the perspective of the role of a freelance advocate working through intermediaries.[72] These intermediaries were originally solicitors, but were expanded to include a wide range of other 'professional clients'. The Code therefore provided that self-employed barristers could only supply legal services if appointed or instructed by a court or if instructed by a professional client.[73] Consequently, barristers were not ordinarily permitted to undertake activity associated with service to clients. They could not, for example, undertake the management, administration or general conduct of a lay client's affairs or take any steps in conducting litigation.[74]

ii. Barrister and Client Duties Based on the Advocacy
and Consultancy Role

The focus in the Bar Code on the advocacy and consultancy role was reflected in restrictions on barristers conducting correspondence. They could only do so when

---

[70] The Law Society 'Complaints to the Legal Ombudsman' (13 December 2012) (www.lawsociety.org.uk/advice/articles/complaints-to-the-legal-ombudsman/).

[71] ibid.

[72] General Council of the Bar of England and Wales, *Code of Conduct 1981*.

[73] ibid, r 401(a).

[74] ibid, r 401(b).

satisfied that it was in the lay client's best interests and where there were adequate systems, experience and resources for managing appropriately such correspondence.[75] They also had to be satisfied that they had adequate insurance cover in the event that the lay client suffer any loss arising from the conduct of any such correspondence.

Given the focus on advocacy the Bar Code was heavily orientated towards the complex duties impinging on that role. The first rule in Part III of the Code, the Fundamental Principles, noted the barrister's overriding duty to the court to act with independence in the interests of justice. It stated that he '... must not deceive or know-ingly or recklessly mislead the Court'.[76] This emphasis may be telling. It suggests that the duty to the court was uppermost in the mind of the drafters of the Code and, conceivably, more important than responsibilities to client.

The rule stressing the overriding duty to the court was followed by a rule defin-ing the barrister's duty to clients. This required a barrister to 'promote and protect fearlessly and by all proper and lawful means the lay client's best interests and do so without regard to his own interests or to any consequences to himself or to any other person'.[77] The rule went on to clarify that 'any other person' means 'any colleague, professional client or other intermediary or another barrister, the barrister's employer or any Authorised Body of which the barrister may be an owner or manager'. The same rule clarified that barristers owed their primary duty as between the lay client and any other person to the lay client. They were not to permit any other person to limit their discretion as to how the interests of the lay client could best be served.[78]

This focus on the barrister's standards was reinforced by a further rule stating that '[a] barrister is individually and personally responsible for his own conduct and for his professional work: he must exercise his own personal judgement in all his professional activities'.[79] The view that barristers' loyalty to clients is subordinate to loyalty to judges is reflected by the attitudes of judges in court. They often regard the advocate's duty to the court as extending to the whole way in which the client's case is presented.

In carrying out their duty to the court, advocates were expected to preserve the court's time and to focus on the issues as efficiently and economically as possible. They were required to refuse to put questions demanded by their client which they consider unnecessary or irrelevant, and refuse to take false points however much their client may insist that they should do so: 'He is not bound by the wishes of his client in that respect, and the mere fact that he has declined to do what his client wishes will not expose him to any kind of liability'.[80]

The Fundamental Principles conveyed the notion that lay clients are important, but not, perhaps, the most important consideration for advocates. The invocation of the word 'fearlessly' conveys a zeal that is immediately contradicted by a qualification; the use of 'proper and lawful means'. Finally, the rules made it clear that barristers' discretion in deciding how lay clients' interests were served must not be fettered. This emphasis on the barrister's discretion, rather than the client's decision, reflected the

---

[75] ibid, r 401A.1.
[76] ibid, r 302.
[77] ibid, r 303(a).
[78] ibid, r 303(b).
[79] ibid, r 306.
[80] *Arthur Hall v Simons* [2000] 3 All ER 673, per Lord Hope at 715–25.

traditional view that control of the lawyer and client relationship in the courtroom resided in the professional, the barrister.

iii. Barrister and Client Relationships Based on the Advocacy and Consultancy Role

Apart from delineating the split loyalty between professional and lay clients and the court, the Bar Code 1981 did not focus on the nature of the lawyer and client relationship. Even the Written Standards of Work, to be found as Part III of the old Bar Code, said very little about the nature of relationships with clients. What was said tended to reinforce the impression, given by the Code, that barristers were in charge of the relationship.

   The old Bar Code repeatedly emphasised that barristers must not simply follow the instructions of their lay or professional client but exercise their own professional judgment. As an advocate, a barrister was 'personally responsible for the conduct and presentation of his case and must exercise personal judgment upon the substance and purpose of statements made and questions asked'.[81] When advising or preparing documents barristers were told that they must exercise personal judgment upon substance and purpose.[82] They could not devise facts which would assist in advancing a lay client's case.

   Barristers were required to be particularly careful in drafting a number of specified, formal court documents. These were originating process, pleading, affidavit, witness statement or notice of appeal. In these documents barristers could not state facts or make contentions not supported by the lay client. They were not permitted to make any contention which they did not consider to be properly arguable. They could not make any allegation of fraud unless there were clear instructions and 'reasonably credible material which as it stands establishes a prima facie case of fraud'.[83]

   The advice on client care in the Written Standards of Work for barristers was brief and to the point. A barrister was told to 'ensure that advice which he gives is practical, appropriate to the needs and circumstances of the particular client, and clearly and comprehensibly expressed'.[84] This, despite the nod to good communication, does little to counteract the impression, probably intended, that barristers should keep clients at arms' length.

iv. Barrister and Client Relationships in Licensed and Public Access Work

The general restrictions on barristers dealing directly with professional clients other than solicitors were relaxed with recognition of Licensed Access clients, members

---

[81] Bar Council, *Code of Conduct 1981, Written Standards of Work*, at para 5.10.
[82] ibid, at para 5.8.
[83] ibid, at para 5.8(c).
[84] ibid, at para 5.7.

of those professions or other organisations approved for such work. Restrictions on dealing with lay clients were also lifted. In these cases the barrister was required to comply with the Licensed Access Rules and the Public Access Rules respectively.

a. Licensed Access Work

Before accepting licensed access work the instructing organisation had to produce a current licence authorised by the BSB. [85] The barrister also had to ensure that the terms of work were established and confirmed with the client.[86]

b. Public Access Work

Before undertaking public access work barristers were required to '[b]e properly qualified by having more than three years' practising experience, by having undertaken and satisfactorily completed the appropriate training, and by registering with the Bar Council as a Public Access practitioner'.[87] They were then required to establish whether it would be in the best interests of the client or in the interests of justice for the lay client to instruct a solicitor or other professional client.[88]

Finally, before accepting public access clients, barristers had to take 'such steps as are reasonably necessary to ensure that the client is able to make an informed decision about whether to apply for legal aid or whether to proceed with public access'.[89] The barrister needed to keep the client's interest and the public interest in the arrangement continuing under constant review.[90]

Barristers accepting public access instructions were required to confirm to clients a number of matters, 'in writing, and in clear and readily understandable terms'. Barristers normally met the requirements by sending an adjusted copy of a model letter provided by the Bar. The confirmation covered the work they have agreed to perform, the fees to be charged for that work, and the basis on which they would be calculated, the barrister's contact arrangements and both the in-house and Bar complaints procedures.

Barristers were required to make it clear that they could not perform the functions of a solicitor or other authorised litigator, that barristers were sole practitioners, not members of firms, and did not take on any arranging role.[91] Another notable requirement on barristers conducting public access work was that they were required to warn their clients that they could be prevented from completing the work if professional duties conflicted.[92] They had to inform the client what they could expect of the barrister in such a situation.

---

[85] Bar Council, *Bar Code of Conduct 1981*, as amended, Annex F1: Licensed Access and Recognition Rules, r 4; and the Licensed Access Recognition Regulations.
[86] Licensed Access and Recognition Regulations, regs 6 and 7.
[87] Bar Council, *Bar Code of Conduct 1981*, as amended, Annex F2: Public Access Rules, r 2(i).
[88] Public Access Rules, r 2(ii).
[89] ibid, r 2(iii).
[90] ibid, r 4.
[91] ibid, rr 6(a)–(d).
[92] ibid, r 6(f).

v. *The BSB Handbook 2014 and the New Code of Conduct*

The new Bar Code follows the previous versions closely in defining the lawyer and client relationship. The core duties include a duty to act in the best interests of each client (CD2), to provide a competent standard of work and service to each client (CD7) and to keep the affairs of each client confidential (CD6). The obligations include promoting fearlessly and by all proper and lawful means the client's best interests.[93]

The obligation to promote the client's interest must be without regard to the barrister's own interests or to any consequences to them or to any other person, whether professional client, employer or any other person. Barristers must not let any of these parties limit their discretion as to how the interests of the client can best be served.[94] Nor can they accept instructions that seek to limit their ordinary authority or discretion in the conduct of proceedings in court'.[95]

In the new Conduct Rules, the duty to act in the best interests of each client continues to be subject to the duty to the court, to barristers' obligations to act with honesty, and integrity and the obligation to maintain their independence. Barristers are required to cease acting, and return instructions, if a client requires action that will breach the barrister's duty to the court.[96] The same consequence must follow if a client will not sanction the return of privileged documents to the other side.[97]

The sequence of the chapters may suggest an order of priorities. The first chapter of the new conduct rules is 'You and the Court', while 'You and Your Client' does not appear until Chapter 3, after 'Behaving Ethically'. There are 10 outcomes in Chapter 3. While some of these are conventional, providing a competent standard of work and service[98] or protecting and promoting client interests,[99] for example, others may anticipate more direct relationships with clients.

The outcomes to Chapter 3 of the BSB's new Conduct Rules specify that clients should 'know what to expect and understand the advice they are given'.[100] Care must be taken to ensure that the interests of vulnerable clients are taken into account and their needs are met.[101] Clients should understand who is responsible for work done for them,[102] be adequately informed as to the terms on which work is to be done[103] and should have confidence in those instructed.[104] They must be told how to bring a complaint and complaints must be dealt with promptly, fairly, openly and effectively.[105]

The new rules provide extended attention to barristers providing public access and licensed access services. There are three outcomes overall. First, barristers undertaking public access or licensed access work must have the necessary skills and experience

---

[93] BSB, *Handbook 2014*, pt 2, *The Code of Conduct*, rC15.1.
[94] ibid, rC15.4.
[95] ibid, rC21.5.
[96] ibid, rC25.1.
[97] ibid, rC25.2.
[98] ibid, oC10.
[99] ibid, oC11.
[100] ibid, oC13.
[101] ibid, oC14.
[102] ibid, oC20.
[103] ibid, oC18.
[104] ibid, oC15.
[105] ibid, oC19.

required to do the specific kind of work.[106] Secondly, they must maintain appropriate records of the work.[107] Thirdly, they can only accept public access work when it is in the client's interests that they do so and when the client fully understands what is expected of them.[108]

Few specific adjustments to the nature of the lawyer and client relationship are specified for when barristers depart the advocacy role for a more conventional relationship with clients. They must, however, consider whether work should be conducted under public access or legal aid and advise clients accordingly.[109] Unless the barrister is authorised to conduct litigation by the Bar Standards Board, the client must be warned that the barrister cannot be expected to perform the functions of a solicitor or other authorised litigator.[110]

D. Evaluation of the Lawyer and Client Relationship Revealed in the Codes of Conduct

It would be fair to say that the legal professions' initial attempts at codes of conduct reflected rather paternalistic notions about the lawyer and client. The latest version of the SRA Handbook has maintained the conception of a participatory model established in the client care regime. The rules reflect some recognition that solicitors are, for the most part, dealing with autonomous individuals wishing to make informed decisions about the services needed, the handing of their matter and the options available to them. The new code has not, however, moved the conceptual framework of the lawyer and client relationship forward.

The Bar Code and Written Standards of Work did not make the same concessions to the concept of client autonomy as do the solicitors' codes. This is despite the fact that barristers have become more involved in work involving direct client contact. The old Bar Code reflected a vision of the barrister, primarily as a defender of the proper administration of justice. They pursued their clients' goals but subject to a duty to the court. Much of the old Bar Code was devoted to specifying and delineating this conception of the role.

Perhaps because of the emphasis in the Bar Code on the barrister as an independent advocate, clients appeared almost as a subtext. The general tone of the Bar Code, certainly in defining the relationship between clients and the advocate, cast the barrister as a remote figure. The Code was unclear about the location of responsibility for decision-making, but appears to reserve a very substantial, but ultimately undefined, discretion to the barrister. This emphasis has largely been retained in the 2014 Code. There are outcomes concerned with clients knowing what to expect and understanding advice, and measures for vulnerable clients, but the locus of decision-making is unclear.

The Bar Code and supporting schedules convey a somewhat paternalistic impression. This is slightly at odds with some barristers' new role in conducting litigation. It is

---

[106] ibid, oC30.
[107] ibid, oC31.
[108] ibid, oC32.
[109] ibid, rC120.4.
[110] ibid, rC125.

debatable whether the professional detachment from clients that is arguably desirable in the advocacy role is also appropriate to a relationship involving direct client contact. It could be argued that paternalism is an inevitable element of professional relationships and that this is reflected in the new Bar Code. It is questionable whether this orientation to clients can survive. Consumer ideology will increasingly drive lawyers towards providing the service a client contracts for. It is debatable whether this is consistent with lawyers also being guardians of the administration of justice. Exploring this issue requires examination of the limits the codes place on what lawyers can do for clients.

IX. The Limits of Loyalty

Irrespective of who controls the lawyer and client relationship, the issue of the limits of lawyers' actions on behalf of clients remains. So far, this issue has been considered from the point of view of whose decisions hold sway in the lawyer and client relationship. It is now necessary to consider the nature and the extent of the obligation of loyalty. This involves consideration of whether a lawyer has an obligation to be partisan. This question arises irrespective of whether the lawyer is operating from paternalistic assumptions or trying to promote client autonomy.

A. Codes of Conduct

The obligation to be partisan is derived from the Model Rules and Canons of Ethics of the American Bar Association. The position on the lawyer and client relationship reflected in the English professional codes of conduct can be usefully contrasted with the rules and principles upon which the standard conception of the lawyer's role is derived. This section sets out the position in these codes before comparing and considering the implications of each.

B. The American Bar Association

i. Partisanship in The American Bar Association Canons of Professional Ethics and Model Code of Conduct

Some excesses of the obligation of partisanship were perceived to flow from the reference in the ABA code to the notion of 'zealous advocacy' on behalf of clients.[111] The

---

[111] See R J Condlin, 'Bargaining in the Dark: The Normative Incoherence of Lawyer Dispute Bargaining Role (1992) 51(1) *Maryland Law Review* 1, at 72.

term came from the ABA Canons of Professional Ethics, first adopted in 1908.[112] Canon 15 provided that a lawyer

> owes entire devotion to the interest of the client, warm zeal in the maintenance and defense of his rights and the exertion of his utmost learning and ability, to the end that nothing be taken or be withheld from him, save by the rules of law, legally applied.

This then appeared in the ABA Model Code of ethics as follows:

> The duty of a lawyer, both to his client1 and to the legal system, is to represent his client zealously, within the bounds of the law, which includes Disciplinary Rules and enforceable professional regulations.[113]

There is some debate about what the qualification 'within the bounds of the law' means. It might mean legal entitlements or it could mean everything a lawyer can extract from the other side. This is, to some extent, a matter of degree. In either case the obligation is to vindicate the client's legal claims irrespective of the justice of those claims. This disposition of lawyers, as much as the obligation of 'zealous advocacy' is, blamed for a legal culture leading to the 'discrepant moral reasoning' lawyers.[114] They are also the basis of the obligation of partisanship.

The 1980 ABA Model Code recognised a distinction between the duty owed to clients by lawyers acting as either advocate or adviser. It suggested that an advocate must resolve doubts about the bounds of the law in favour of clients. Lawyers acting as advisers could, however, give their professional opinion as to what the courts would be likely to decide was the applicable law.[115] Lawyers could then continue in the representation of a client even though the client elected to pursue a different course of conduct, provided they did not 'knowingly assist the client to engage in illegal conduct or to take a frivolous legal position'.[116]

The current ABA Model Code does not refer to zeal in the rules.[117] The preamble does state, however, that '[a]s advocate, a lawyer zealously asserts the client's position under the rules of the adversary system'.[118] The rule purporting to cover the allocation of authority between lawyer and client states that a lawyer shall abide by a client's decisions concerning the objectives of representation and consult with the client as to the means by which they are to be pursued.[119]

The concept of zeal has not been replaced by a direct alternative in the rules, although they do also require diligence.[120] To the extent that partisanship depends on the concept of zealous advocacy, the analysis must therefore be treated with caution.[121] The duty of zeal has also been quietly dropped from many state Bar

---

[112] American Bar Association, *Canons of Professional Ethics 1908*, Canon 15. (www.americanbar.org/content/dam/aba/migrated/cpr/mrpc/Canons_Ethics.authcheckdam.pdf).

[113] American Bar Association, *Model Code of Professional Responsibility 1980*, Canon 7, EC 7-1.

[114] R Wasserstrom, 'Lawyers as Professionals: Some Moral Issues' (1975–76) 5 *Human Rights* 1, at 15.

[115] American Bar Association, *Model Code of Professional Responsibility 1980*, Canon 7, EC 7-3.

[116] ibid, Canon 7, EC 7-5.

[117] American Bar Association, *Model Code of Professional Conduct 2004*.

[118] ibid, Preamble: 'A Lawyer's Responsibilities'.

[119] ibid, r 1.2.

[120] ibid, r 1.3.

[121] But for a recent application of the concept, see T Dare, 'Mere Zeal, Hyper-Zeal and the Ethical Obligations of Lawyers' (2004) 7(1) *Legal Ethics* 24.

codes.[122] This does not mean that partisanship is not a kind of default position for lawyers. The former model rules did, however, make it fairly clear that lawyers did not have to comply with instructions they disagreed with.

The ABA Model Code provided considerable clarity about expectations of lawyers' behaviour. It allowed them to pursue a client's wishes and preferences but apparently, did not require them to do so. The ABA Code provides a fairly clear example of what should happen when lawyers and clients disagree. The comment to Rule 1(2), dealing with the scope of representation and the allocation of authority, states that:

> On occasion, however, a lawyer and a client may disagree about the means to be used to accomplish the client's objectives. Clients normally defer to the special knowledge and skill of their lawyer with respect to the means to be used to accomplish their objectives, particularly with respect to technical, legal and tactical matters. Conversely, lawyers usually defer to the client regarding such questions as the expense to be incurred and concern for third persons who might be adversely affected.[123]

The comment went on to say that lawyers should try to persuade clients to their point of view, but if a mutually acceptable solution cannot be agreed to 'a fundamental disagreement with the client, the lawyer may withdraw from the representation'.[124]

The notion that partisanship justifies lawyers' extreme behaviour on behalf of clients appears to have lost ground. If lawyers can extricate themselves from their retainer on the grounds of a 'fundamental disagreement', they can do so on moral grounds. This leaves the pursuit of a client's lawful wishes and of partisanship generally, looking like options rather than obligations. At the same time, obligations of candour to the court and fairness to others have apparently gained ground in the USA.[125] Taken together, these trends suggest that lawyers' ethics in the US are moving away from a hard line on partisanship.

ii. Duties to Clients in the Current American Bar Association Model Code

The current American Bar Association Model Code of Conduct states that the lawyer should 'abide by a client's decisions concerning the objectives of the representation'.[126] This rule suggests that clients are ultimately in control of the relationship between lawyer and client. It is also close to suggesting that the model of the lawyer and client relationship in use is one of client autonomy. It will be noted, however, that clients only determine objectives. The rule does not specify who controls the means of achieving them. Such decisions could, ultimately, reside in the realm of the lawyer's discretion.

---

[122] PC Saunders, 'Whatever Happened to "Zealous Advocacy"?' (2011) 245(47) *New York Law Journal* 1.
[123] *ABA Model Rules of Professional Conduct 2004*, r 1(2), comment 2.
[124] ibid.
[125] See LR Patterson, 'The Limits of the Lawyer's Discretion and the Law of Legal Ethics: National Student Marketing Revisited' (1979) 6 *Duke Law Journal* 1251.
[126] American Bar Association, *Annotated Model Rules of Professional Conduct*, 6th edn (Center for Professional Responsibility, 2007) r 1.2.

The ABA Model Code provides another rule that appears to go further in promoting client autonomy. This provides that '[a] lawyer shall not intentionally fail to seek the lawful objectives of his client through reasonably available means permitted by law and the Disciplinary Rules'.[127] There are however qualifications to the apparently absolute control that an obligation to pursue lawful objectives gives clients. Lawyers can waive client rights, or fail to assert them, 'where permissible, and refuse to aid a client in conduct they believe to be unlawful, even though it is arguably legal'.[128]

C. The Lawyer and Client Relationship in England and Wales

i. Clients Best Interests

The professional principles of the LSA 2007 and the codes of the English legal professions, specify that lawyers in England and Wales act in clients' 'best interests'.[129] This neutral formulation emphasises the obligation to protect the client, but gives little indication of where responsibility for decision-making resides. Nor does it specify whose perception of the client's interest prevails. The 'best interests' formula is consistent with almost any model of the lawyer and client relationship.

ii. Partisanship in the Codes

a. Solicitors

The English profession does not carry the same semantic baggage as the US profession. The term 'zeal' has not been used in either the Law Society Guide or the Bar's Code of Conduct.[130] The old Guide stated that a solicitor was bound to exercise diligence in carrying out a client's instructions.[131] Bayles argues that '[a] responsibility of diligence or zeal is closely related to, but distinct from, that of competence. One can be supremely competent but not diligent, or diligent and zealous but incompetent'.[132] This interpretation is debatable. Diligence simply means conscientiousness, which does not have the same connotation as zeal. Zeal is an extreme level of engagement with a person or cause bordering on fervour.

In any event, not even the obligation of diligence was transferred to the Solicitors' Code of Conduct 2007. No similar description of the nature of solicitors' commitment to clients appears in the SRA Handbook. Nor is there a duty to seek a client's lawful objectives or anything similar. As discussed below, solicitors must not terminate their

---

[127] ibid, DR 7-101(A)1.
[128] ibid, DR 7-101(B).
[129] LSA 2007, s 1(3)(c).
[130] J Levin, *An Ethical Profession?* (Swansea University, 1994) at 23.
[131] R Taylor (ed), *The Guide to the Professional Conduct of Solicitors* (London, The Law Society, 1996) r 12.11.
[132] MD Bayles, 'Trust and the Professional-Client Relationship' in Flores (ed), *Professional Ideals* (n 24) 71.

instructions without good reason. Unlike the ABA Code, the SRA Handbook provides no guidance on whether a 'fundamental disagreement' with a client is a good reason.

b. Barristers

The Bar Code comes closer to the old US position on zealous advocacy with the obligation to promote a client's best interests 'fearlessly and by all proper lawful means'.[133] At first sight this is fierce language, but being fearless does not have the same partisan connotation as does zeal. Nor is fearlessness as client-centred, or as radical, as an obligation to pursue a client's lawful objectives. The use of all 'lawful means' does, however, suggest an obligation to pursue client objectives.

iii. The Limitation Imposed on Partisanship by Duties to Uphold the Rule of Law and the Administration of Justice

The codes in England and Wales have an explicit inclination towards preserving the integrity of the legal system. These are expressed as duties to upholding the rule of law and the administration of justice. Although this is probably intended as limit on partisanship, it is not clear how the limitation is intended to operate. It is therefore necessary to consider what upholding the rule of law and the administration of justice might mean.

It is presumed that the obligation to uphold the rule of law, in both the LSA 2007 and the SRA Handbook, refers to a commitment to formal legality. The obligation to uphold the rule of law involves upholding the rights of citizens. This is part of the traditional role of lawyers and the justification for partisanship in criminal defence. An obligation to uphold the rule of law does not therefore impinge on lawyers' loyalty to clients, except insofar as it also implies an obligation to observe the duty to the court.

Both of the main legal professions make significant commitments to upholding the administration of justice. The guidance to the core duties for solicitors, for example, states that any conflict in core duties must be determined according to the public interest, and 'especially the public interest in the administration of justice'.[134] The Bar Code is more circumspect in that the duty to the administration of justice is framed as a duty to the court. In the former code, barristers were told that they have an 'overriding duty to the court to act with independence in the interests of justice'.[135] This formula was assumed to reflect the focus on advocacy. In the present code, Core Duty 1, 'observing your duty to the court in the administration of justice',[136] makes this assumption explicit. This overrides any other core duty if, and to the extent, the two are inconsistent.[137]

---

[133] BSB, *Handbook 2014, Code of Conduct*, rC15.1.

[134] SRA, *Solicitors' Code of Conduct 2007*, Core Duties, guidance para 3 and see now SRA, *Code of Conduct 2011*, as amended, 'Introduction to the SRA Code of Conduct'.

[135] Bar Council, *Bar Code 1981*, as amended, 2004 edn, at para 302.

[136] BSB, *Bar Code of Conduct 2014*, CD1.

[137] ibid, gC1.

It is clear immediately that the principles of the SRA Code express a potentially broader limitation on pursuing clients' interests than the Bar Code does. Principle 1 of the SRA Code does not equate a duty to the administration of justice to a duty to the court. It is assumed, therefore, that for solicitors, upholding the administration of justice is wider than a duty to the court. This interpretation may be supported by an outcome in the SRA Handbook stating that solicitors must provide services to clients 'in a manner which protects their interests in their matter, subject to the proper administration of justice'.[138]

If the reference to solicitors' duty to the administration of justice is intended to limit client autonomy, it is not obvious how such a limitation operates. It may be intended to extend the scope of the conventional duty to the court in advocacy, to litigation. This is consistent with the LSA 2007. The outcome could imply responsibility for constraining malign or immoral client preferences, even if those preferences are legal. On the other hand, it may not. In short, if solicitors have some responsibility to the administration of justice beyond duties in litigation and advocacy, it is not clear what they are.

D. Comparing the Position of Clients under the ABA Model Code and the Codes in England and Wales

The US position, where it is clear that lawyers are expected to act on the basis of the instructions of the client, is inconsistent with paternalism. In fact, an issue in the US academic literature for some time is whether it should be lawyers' main function to facilitate client autonomy.[139] This does not mean that paternalism is completely absent in the US. Rhode suggests that paternalistic approaches are 'seldom preached but often practised'.[140] Nevertheless, as David Luban observes, as far as the Code is concerned, 'the American model is loyalty to the client's wishes and not his interests'.[141] Thus, a lawyer following the model rules promotes client autonomy even when the course of action involed is unwise in in the circumstances.

The professional codes in England convey no expectation of participatory decision-making or an obligation to promote client autonomy. If there were, it is likely that it would be made explicit in the rules. The obligation to act in the best interest of clients is consistent with either paternalistic or participative models. In order to discover a clients' best interests lawyers may need to explore their situations in a way that is consistent with the participatory model. This is the implication of the client care regime, which suggests an intention to promote participation. It is possible, however,

---

[138] SRA, *Handbook 2011*, as amended, SRA, *Code of Conduct 2011*, Outcome 1.2.

[139] SL Pepper, 'The Lawyer's Amoral Ethical Role' (1986) *American Bar Foundation Research Journal* 613 and reply by D Luban (1987) *American Bar Foundation Research Journal* 637; S Spiegel, 'Lawyering and Client Decision Making: Informed Consent and the Legal Profession' (1978) 128 *University of Pennsylvania Law Review* 41.

[140] D Rhode, *Professional Responsibility: Ethics by the Pervasive Method* (Little Brown, Boston, 1994) at 411.

[141] D Luban, 'The Sources of Legal Ethics' (1984) 48 *Rabels Zeitschift* 262.

to shower clients with information and to operate within a paternalistic framework thereafter.

There are two main risks in the operation of the paternalistic model of the lawyer and client relationship. First, it places a high premium on the altruistic motives of practitioners.[142] Enlightened self-interest, it is argued, predisposes professionals to act with integrity and in their clients' interests, because this serves their own collective, long-term commercial interests.[143] Secondly, under most of the models, professionals must hear a client's individual story before deciding what can be done for them. In an extreme paternalistic position, lawyers could assume, on the basis of inadequate information provided by clients, what their interests are.

X. Representing Clients to the Press

A. Context

Lawyers have a personal interest in public appearances. Some may see it as cheap advertising of their capability and eminence. Others adopt a wider role as 'men of affairs', promoting the business or other interests of their clients.[144] This work may include lobbying, presentational and educational work. Lawyers are often asked to comment on clients' newsworthy cases. Press statements can be made only with the consent of clients otherwise there may be a breach of confidence. Lawyers are generally allowed to give their clients' statements to the press. They may also comment on their client's position, or on the adequacy of the law in dealing with the client's particular problem. This is common in high profile criminal cases and also in test cases or other public interest litigation. This is an extension of lawyers' wider role as client representatives.

As far as clients are concerned, statements to the press may serve several purposes. They may be intended to reassure family and friends of their innocence, to mobilise public opinion in their favour, to correct adverse publicity generated by the press and police or even to begin the process of rehabilitating their reputation. No one expects a lawyer to give a statement to the press saying their client is guilty of an offence. The lawyer is expected to put their client's view on the matter. The proper administration of justice requires that such statements are controlled. It is obviously undesirable that proceedings are invaded by a media circus or that lawyers transfer the arguments of the courtroom to the steps of the court.

Anybody, including lawyers, may be in contempt of court when commenting about a case or defendant in a way that could prejudice a trial. Conduct may be treated as

---

[142] M Ridley, *The Origin of Virtue* (Harmondsworth, England, Penguin, 1997) esp ch 1.
[143] JR Ravetz, 'Ethics in Scientific Activity' in Flores (n 24) 147, at 152.
[144] As is illustrated in the case of *BCCI* ([2004] 3 All ER 168 (CA) and [2005] 1 AC 610 (HL)).

contempt of court as tending to interfere with the course of justice in particular legal proceedings.[145] The offence is strict liability, in that it can be committed regardless of intent.

Generally, a person is not guilty of contempt of court under the strict liability rule in respect of a fair and accurate report of legal proceedings held in public, published contemporaneously and in good faith.[146] The court can, however, prevent any comment.[147] It is therefore possible to be in contempt of court despite accurate comment and without apparently prejudicing a trail. In 2012, for example, nine people were prosecuted for contempt of court having tweeted the name of a rape victim.[148]

Subject to the rules on contempt, the courts have been fairly relaxed about lawyers exercising the right to make statements. Lord Woolf said in *Hodgson v Imperial Tobacco Ltd*, that

> [t]he professionalism and the sense of duty of lawyers who conduct litigation of this nature should mean that the courts are able to rely on the legal advisers to exercise great self-restraint when making comments to the press, while at the same time recognising the need for the media to be properly informed of what is happening in the proceedings.[149]

Lord Woolf did not recommend any greater restrictions than were already contained in the law on contempt of court.

Professions have a clear interest in controlling their members' appearances or communication with press. Inappropriate appearances or handling could result in damage to the reputation of the profession as a whole or compromise the impression of independence. Restraints might also be imposed in recognition of the substantial difference between what must be done for clients under the cloak of professionalism and the image of lawyers that should be presented to the public.

B. A Brief History of Controls

As with advertising, the legal profession viewed lawyers' relations with the media with suspicion. The Law Society's old guidance on press statements, contained in the 1999 Guide, was sparse. It provided that

> [a] solicitor who on the client's instructions gives a statement to the press must not become in contempt of court by publishing any statement which is calculated to interfere with the fair trial of a case which has not been concluded.[150]

The guidance to the 2007 Code, Rule 11 added little. It recommended that solicitors exercise their 'professional judgement' in deciding whether it is appropriate to make statements to the media, doing so in the client's best interests with his or her consent and with regard for the law of contempt.[151]

---

[145] Contempt of Court Act 1981, s 1.
[146] ibid, s 4(1).
[147] ibid, s 4(2).
[148] BBC News UK, 'Social media user warned over case comments' 4 December 2013.
[149] *Hodgson v Imperial Tobacco Ltd* [1998] 2 All ER 673.
[150] Taylor, *The Guide to the Professional Conduct of Solicitors* (n 131) at 381.
[151] SRA, *Solicitors' Code of Conduct 2007*, r 11, guidance para 10.

Solicitors were also subject to an overarching duty not to damage the reputation or integrity of the profession.[152] They are also subject to the tort of defamation when making press statements. In *Regan v Taylor*,[153] the complainant was the editor of a 'scurrilous' journal called *Scallywag*. The defendant was a solicitor who replied to a defamatory attack on his client in *Scallywag* with a response that was also defamatory. It was held that a solicitor was covered by qualified privilege in making statements on his client's behalf to the press provided the reply was relevant and proportionate.

The issue of press comment by lawyers in criminal cases was the subject of a report by the Lord Chancellor's Advisory Committee on Legal Education and Conduct (ACLEC) in 1997.[154] ACLEC considered that it was not adequate for the Law Society to rely solely on the law of contempt as a guide. This was because contempt of court required proof of intention and was subject to the criminal standard of proof. This was considered to be too high a standard against which to judge solicitors' comments to the press.

In criminal cases ACLEC considered that solicitors should not say anything that might prejudice the outcome of the proceedings. They should, however, be able to say anything on behalf of the client that the client could lawfully say. They could say, for example, 'My client denies any involvement with this charge and considers the evidence against him flimsy and unreliable'. ACLEC suggested a rule prohibiting advocates from expressing a personal opinion about the merits of a current case and extending that rule to solicitors generally. The prohibition would cover the period from charge to acquittal and the disposal of any appeal. It would not prevent comment beyond the merits of the case, such as any delay in prosecuting.

ACLEC sought to eliminate the risk that personal comments from lawyers 'detract from public recognition of the principle that these are matters to be decided by the courts and the courts alone'. They were also concerned that 'lawyers may come under pressure to express views [to the press] that they do not genuinely hold on the merits of their clients' cases'. ACLEC did not consider civil cases, but recommended that the profession adopt similar rules for all litigation. The report was not well received by either the professions or commentators.

As a result of ACLEC's report, the old Bar Code was amended to advise barristers that they must not express a personal opinion to the press or in any public statement on any 'anticipated or current proceedings or mediation' in which they are or expect to be briefed.[155] They could therefore represent their client's opinion or offer an explanation of the legal or factual issues involved in the case which did not include a personal opinion. This represented a relaxation of a prohibition on any comment on cases on which barristers were currently briefed. Moreover, the prohibition did not apply to educational or academic comment.

---

[152]   ibid, Core Duty 1.06, on which see ch 13.

[153]   *Regan v Taylor* The Times 15 March 2000 (CA).

[154]   *Lawyers' Comments to the Media* (London, Lord Chancellor's Advisory Committee on Legal Education and Conduct, May 1997). See further (1998) 2 *Legal Ethics* 109.

[155]   Bar Council, *Bar Code 1981*, as amended, at para 709.1.

C. The New Codes

The SRA Handbook 2011 does not mention speaking to the press in the chapter on publicity. One outcome does, however, require that 'your publicity in relation to your firm or in-house practice or for any other business is accurate and not misleading, and is not likely to diminish the trust the public places in you and in the provision of legal services'.[156]

The new Bar Code of Conduct does not include the former prohibition on practising barristers expressing a personal opinion in the media in relation to any future or current proceedings in which they are briefed.[157] The new code refers to the guidance given under the old code[158] which has been retained on the BSB website. Therefore, barristers must still not express an opinion on 'anticipated or current proceedings or mediation in which he is briefed or expects to appear'.[159] They must ensure that such comments do not undermine, and are not reasonably seen as undermining, their independence. Neither must they bring the profession or any other barrister into disrepute.

XI. Ceasing to Act

A. Background

Lawyers are generally restricted in deciding that they cannot act for a client. Both solicitors and barristers have required good reasons for withdrawal from a case. Under the Solicitors' Code of Conduct 2007 solicitors could not terminate the relationship unless for 'good reason and upon reasonable notice'.[160] Because of the difficulty that withdrawal of advocates causes the court, barristers were generally subject to tighter restrictions. Even so, barristers must cease to act if continuation would cause them professional embarrassment.[161] This phrase embodies all the reasons, such as lack of skill or time, which justify refusing the brief in the first place.[162]

Before the enactment of the new codes, solicitors could withdraw from representation when clients failed to make agreed payments on account, on the bankruptcy of either solicitor or client and mental incapacity. The circumstances where withdrawal is allowed included those where clients required a breach of professional duty or where there was a breakdown of confidence between lawyer and client. Solicitors, but not barristers, might argue that this included circumstances where the client was determined on a course of

[156] SRA, *Code of Conduct*, ch 8: 'Publicity', Outcome 8.1.
[157] BSB, *Code of Conduct 2014*, ch 2: 'Behaving Ethically' gC22.
[158] ibid.
[159] www.barstandardsboard.org.uk/code-guidance/media-comment-guidance-april-2013.
[160] SRA, *Solicitors Code of Conduct 2007*, r 2.01(2).
[161] Bar Council, *Bar Code 1981*, as amended, r 608.
[162] ibid, r 603.

conduct to which there were grave moral objections. Lawyers were not generally allowed to withdraw simply because the court made it difficult to do their best for their client.

Prior to the enactment of the new codes, the courts had already put some flesh on the bones of previous restrictions on withdrawal. In *R v Ulcay*,[163] a solicitor and barrister had been retained to represent a criminal defendant after previous representatives had withdrawn because of professional embarrassment. The court then refused an application for an adjournment to prepare the case. The court decided that the proper remedy was to appeal against the refusal rather than withdraw. Once the order was made, the lawyers owed a duty to the court to comply and 'soldier on'.

B. Ceasing to Act under the New Codes

If solicitors decide they can no longer act for the client the SRA Code provides they must comply with the law and the Code when terminating their instructions.[164] Solicitors may fail to achieve that outcome when they 'cease to act for a client without good reason and without providing reasonable notice'.[165]

One of the outcomes in the Bar Code 2014 is that '[i]nstructions are not accepted, refused, or returned in circumstances which adversely affect the administration of justice, access to justice or (so far as compatible with these) the best interests of the client'.[166] Another outcome provides that '[c]lients and BSB authorised persons and authorised (non-BSB) individuals and BSB regulated managers are clear about the circumstances in which instructions may not be accepted or may or must be returned'.[167]

There are 10 circumstances set out in the Bar Code that require a barrister not to accept instructions[168] and a similar number requiring their return.[169] Among the more interesting is the situation where the barrister feels that the

> instructions seek to limit your ordinary authority or discretion in the conduct of proceedings in court' or because of a threat to the barrister's professional independence caused by a connection with the client, with the court or a member of it, or otherwise.

Barristers are also severely restricted in returning instructions. The new Bar Code provides that barristers can cease to act on a matter and return instructions only if their professional conduct is called into question, the client consents or for other good reason such as illness or jury service.[170] The guidance provides that when considering whether or not barristers are required to return instructions in accordance with the

---

[163] *R v Ulcay* [2007] EWCA Crim 2379, [2008] All ER 547.
[164] SRA, *Code of Conduct*, ch 1: 'Client Care', Outcome 1.3.
[165] ibid, ch 1: 'Client Care', Indicative Behaviour 1.26.
[166] BSB, *Code of Conduct 2014*, ch 3: 'You and Your Client', oC16.
[167] ibid, ch3: 'You and Your Client', oC17.
[168] ibid, ch 3: 'You and Your Client', rC21.
[169] ibid, ch 3: 'You and Your Client', rC25–26.
[170] ibid, ch 3: 'You and Your Client', rC26.

rule, they should have regard to relevant case law.[171] The specific cases referred to relate to not using privileged information inadvertently disclosed by the other side.[172]

XII. Conclusion

The way in which the lawyer and client relationship is presented in codes of conduct suggests an underlying legal basis containing elements of agency, contract and trusts. These elements may exist in different proportions depending on the nature of clients and the nature of the problem. The basic relationship is, however, contractual. In England and Wales the codes describe the lawyer's duty as the pursuit of a client's best interests. There is no mention of pursuing a client's wishes or preferences. The English codes therefore have a potentially paternalistic flavour.

The dominant principle of lawyers' relations with clients has been characterised as loyalty, or in the terminology of US academics, partisanship. This construction was based on a reading of the ABA Model Code which emphasised a requirement of 'zeal' in pursuit of a client's lawful wishes. The obligation to pursue a client's lawful aims is a more explicit expression of what partisanship entails. This orientation is, arguably, more consistent with a consumerist society and the notion of client autonomy.

Current changes to the legal profession in England and Wales reflect a drive to replace the professional ethos of lawyers with a consumerist orientation. This will increase the premium placed on client wishes and client autonomy. The LSA 2007 and the new codes suggest an intention to balance this, by emphasising various overarching, system-orientated duties; the rule of law, the administration of justice, the public interest. None of these provides a clear and satisfactory basis for constraining lawyers' actions in clients' interests.

A development that might mark a compromise between the professional and consumer ideologies is participatory decision-making by lawyers and clients. This model of the lawyer and client relationship provides scope for ethical debate with clients about their aims and wishes. Such discourse allows clients autonomy while enabling lawyers to influence aims and outcomes. This is potentially an ideal ethical stance for lawyers. It allows them to present their authentic personalities in their relationship with clients. Ultimately, however, whether lawyers are bound to carry out their clients' lawful instructions is unclear. It seems likely that, in most situations, lawyers could refuse to follow clients' instructions where they fundamentally disagree with a course of action.

---

[171] ibid, ch 3: 'You and Your Client', gC86.
[172] *English & American Insurance Co Ltd & Others v Herbert Smith* [1988] FSR 232, ChD 1987, (1987) *New Law Journal* 148; and *Ablitt v Mills & Reeve (A Firm) and Another* Ch D Times 24 October 1995 (see further ch 13: 'Individual Third Parties').

10

Confidences

Legal advice is not confined to telling the client the law. It must include advice as to what should prudently and sensibly be done in the relevant context ... We want people to obey the law, enter into valid and effective transactions, settle their affairs responsibly when they separate or divorce, make wills which will withstand the challenge of the disappointed, and present their best case before all kinds of court, tribunal and inquiry in an honest and responsible manner.[1]

I. Introduction

Professionals generally promise to respect client confidences. The law also respects communications between lawyers and their clients as privileged. This means that lawyers cannot be forced to reveal client confidences, nor can privileged information be produced in court. The duty of confidence and the right of privilege are deemed beneficial to society. One reason is because they promote client autonomy. This is based on the proposition that everyone should be able to take wise counsel on their position. If clients do not believe that any information disclosed will be kept confidential, they may be selective in the information they divulge. Professionals may then not be in a position to give the best possible advice.

A right to confidence is also potentially harmful to society. It is an obligation that may implicate lawyers in harm to others. Lawyers may have been given information that could avert harm. They may suspect, for example, that a client intends to intimidate a witness. Most jurisdictions allow lawyers to breach confidence in order to prevent harm, but only in limited circumstances, usually related to preventing future harm. They must usually respect confidences where no harm is imminent. For example, a lawyer who has been told by a murderer what they did with the victim's body must respect that confidence.

Increased sensitivity about the risk of social harm has caused government to encroach on the principles of client confidentiality. Therefore, the state may require

---

[1] *Three Rivers District Council & Others v Governor and Company of the Bank of England (No 6)* [2004] 3 All ER 168 (CA) and [2005] 1 AC 610, per (HL) Baroness Hale at [62].

professionals to breach confidences where protection would be particularly harmful to society. Examples include money laundering and serious crime. Because of the importance of the principle of confidentiality, the circumstances for such disclosures must be carefully defined. A separate but related issue is the extent to which privilege should be recognised where some kind of harm may result.

II. Lawyer and Client Confidences at Common Law

A. Context

The common law of lawyer and client confidence sits within the general framework protecting confidential information. Confidentiality is implied in situations where it is expected to be assumed by those involved.[2] In the case of both solicitors and barristers, confidence attaches to the relationship with clients as 'a necessary and traditional incident'.[3] Confidentiality in the lawyer and client relationship has some distinctive features because of the nature of the legal role. This defines the lawyer and client relationship.

Actions by clients against lawyers for breach of confidence are relatively rare. An exception arises when the confidentiality owed to past clients clashes with the loyalty owed to present clients. The right to act for a client in the present whose interest conflicts with those of a past client is not absolute. There are some arguments that it should be. Even if the nature of the two matters may be different, the solicitor's knowledge of a former client could be relevant. The solicitor may know for example, that their former client is without resources, anxious and prone to panic. A person may be justified in thinking that the promise of loyalty is a little shallow when this knowledge could be turned upon them. That is, however, the position at common law.

B. The Right to Confidentiality of Former Clients

Out of a long line of antecedents, the case which provides a platform for the modern law was *Rakusen v Munday, Ellis and Clarke*.[4] In that case, the defendants were solicitors consulted by R, the claimant, who was considering launching proceedings against his former company. One of the defendant's two partners, M, had several consultations with R, but R subsequently instructed other solicitors. M's partner, C, was away at the time and knew nothing of the matter.

---

[2] *Gotha v Sothebys* [1988] 1 WLR 114.
[3] *Halsbury's Laws*, vol 8(1) at paras 452–53.
[4] *Rakusen v Ellis Munday and Clarke* [1912] 1 Ch 831.

R's litigation against his former company went to arbitration and C was appointed to appear as representative of the company. R's application for an injunction to restrain the defendant firm from acting in the arbitration was granted at first instance. The evidence was that M and C were in the habit of doing business separately and without any knowledge of each other's clients. Nevertheless, the judge held that a solicitor, once appointed, could not act against his former client in the same matter.

The Court of Appeal unanimously reversed the judgment, holding that the prohibition on acting was not absolute. A complete prohibition on acting in such circumstances might cause great difficulty in small towns where there was a limited choice of solicitor. Much was also made of the fact that M and C were 'solicitors of the highest position whose honour and integrity are beyond any imputation'. C had no knowledge of anything that had happened and, as an officer of the court, could be held to the highest standards.

Cozens Hardy MR said that, before restricting a client's freedom to instruct a solicitor 'we must be satisfied that real mischief and real prejudice will in all human probability result if the solicitor is allowed to act'. Lord Justice Buckley said that the court had jurisdiction to restrain the solicitor from giving the new client any assistance against the old client by reason of knowledge acquired as solicitor for the old client. If, to achieve that result, it was necessary to restrain the employment of the solicitor by the new client the injunction would be granted, 'but on no other ground could such an injunction be granted as against the client'.

C. Controlling Information: Walls, Barriers and Ethical Screens

Following the decision in *Rakusen v Munday, Ellis and Clarke* the preservation of a right to act against former clients became a problem of managing knowledge. In England and Wales, firms used a practice of insulating lawyers in situations where there would otherwise be a breach of confidentiality. An information barrier was established between new clients and past clients in situations where information relevant to the new matter existed and the interests of the clients conflicted. This information barrier was known as a 'Chinese wall', possibly a reference to the Great Wall of China. In some jurisdictions there have been objections to the term and the phrase information barrier, information screen or ethical screen are preferred.

In *Re A Firm of Solicitors*,[5] guidance was provided on how impermeable the screen should be. A large firm of City solicitors wished to represent a client bringing an action against a company which, some years previously, had been a client of the firm. The solicitors went to some trouble to erect a screen between the staff working on the current case and those who had worked on the previous case.

The Court of Appeal upheld the grant of an injunction prohibiting the firm from representing the new client. It acknowledged that there was no absolute prohibition on acting against a former client. A lawyer could not do so, however, if a reasonable man would reasonably anticipate a breach of confidentiality or some likelihood of

---

[5] *Re A Firm of Solicitors* [1992] 1 All ER 353 (CA). See also *Supasave Ltd v Coward Chance* [1991] 1 All ER 668; *David Lee & Co v Coward Chance* [1991] 1 All ER 668.

mischief. In this particular case, on the facts, an information barrier could not provide an effective guarantee against such a risk.

D. *Bolkiah v KPMG:* The Unqualified Importance of Confidentiality

Accepted practice for dealing with potential conflicts of interest between former and present clients was called into question by the landmark case, *Bolkiah v KPMG.*[6] Although the defendants were a firm of accountants it was held that the principles developed in the case applied to solicitors.

In *Bolkiah*, KPMG had acted as the auditors of an agency of the Government of Brunei. The agency was chaired by Prince Jefri. KPMG also acted for Prince Jefri in his own affairs. He paid them £4.6 million for advice on litigation in which he was involved. After Prince Jefri ceased to chair the government agency, the Government of Brunei asked KPMG to investigate the agency's affairs. KPMG had ceased to act for Prince Jefri two months previously. It wished to accept the government work.

Aware of the potential conflict of interest, KPMG sought to isolate the staff undertaking the government work from the rest of the firm. They sought to prevent access to any information about Prince Jefri by those staff. Unsurprisingly, Prince Jefri sought an injunction to prevent KPMG acting for the Brunei Government. He argued that the information barrier around the investigation could not adequately protect his confidentiality or his interests.

Giving judgment for Prince Jefri, Lord Millett found that there was no absolute duty preventing a firm acting in cases in circumstances where the interests of former clients might be prejudiced. If, however, a former client showed that the adviser held relevant confidential information adverse to their interests, the client had to consent to them acting. An ad hoc information screen was insufficient to prevent the possible leakage of such information. Lord Millett said, 'the duty to preserve confidential information is unqualified. It is a duty to keep the information confidential, not merely to take all reasonable steps to do so'.[7]

The case suggested that the courts expected much higher standards of protection for the information of former clients than had previously applied. This caused considerable concern among City firms. They considered that they had developed rigorous systems for dealing with the possibility of information leakage that threatened confidentiality.

E. The Interpretation and Application of *Bolkiah*

Despite the disquiet caused by *Bolkiah*, the courts limited its impact in subsequent cases. In *Koch Shipping v Richards Butler*,[8] for example, a solicitor employed by a firm representing the applicants to an arbitration left her employment and joined the law

---

[6] *Bolkiah v KPMG* [1999] 1 All ER 517.
[7] ibid, at 527.
[8] *Koch Shipping v Richards Butler* [2002] EWCA Civ 1280 (Comm). See also *GUS Consulting v Leboeuf Lamb Greene* [2006] EWHC 2527(Comm).

firm, Richards Butler, which was acting for the defendants. The applicants sought an injunction to prevent Richards Butler from acting on the ground that their new employee had confidential information about the applicant's case, which she did. The injunction was refused. The Court of Appeal accepted that an effective information screen had been erected between the employee and those working on the case.

It was material to the decision that the solicitor concerned was a woman of unchallenged integrity who had given an undertaking not to discuss the case with those handling it. She worked on a different floor of the firm's building. She was the sole employee with the confidential information. The case was therefore distinguishable from *Bolkiah*, which involved a team of accountants. Lord Justice Tuckey was anxious that clients should not be deprived of their chosen solicitors in the name of preserving confidentiality where 'the risk is no more than fanciful or theoretical'.

In *Marks & Spencer plc v Freshfields Bruckhaus Deringer*,[9] the claimants applied to prevent a large law firm, Freshfields, from acting for a former director, G, in a hostile takeover bid. Freshfields had acted for Marks and Spencer (M&S) in a great deal of its contentious commercial and employment work, and in particular on the renegotiation of a particularly valuable and important contract. Freshfields alleged that there was no conflict in relation to the actual transaction, namely the takeover bid, but that in any case they had erected an information barrier to deal with any potential leakage of confidential information.

At first instance the court granted M&S an injunction. It found that Freshfields held considerable confidential information on M&S and that no effective internal information barriers could be put into place to prevent leakage. Freshfields also pleaded that it would be difficult for G to find another solicitor sufficiently expert in the field able to act for him. This argument was rejected by the trial judge. Lawrence Collins J said 'I find it hard to accept ... that there will be no reasonably competent firm in the City able to help'.

Despite the ruling in favour of the claimant, *Marks & Spencer plc v Freshfields Bruckhaus Deringer* introduced a vital qualification to *Bolkiah*. At first instance, Collins J held that there had to be some reasonable relationship between the two matters for rules against conflict of interest to bite. The Court of Appeal agreed that a potential conflict arose between past and present clients only where there was a degree of relationship between the two matters. This limited the potential scope of the *Bolkiah* decision.

The position at common law had gradually returned to one where the courts looked at the substance of the situation. There was no blanket prohibition on acting; it all depended on the circumstances. In *GUS Consulting v Leboeuf Lamb Greene*, for example, it was decided that an ethical wall, put in place to isolate an arbitration team from knowledge its firm (L) held about a former client, was an effective device to prevent leakage of information.[10] There was unchallenged evidence of the members of L's arbitration team about their ignorance of, and lack of access to, the former client's information. There was an undertaking, offered by L, to instruct staff previously

---

[9]   *Marks & Spencer plc v Freshfields Bruckhaus Deringer* [2004] EWHC 1337 (Ch).
[10]   *Gus Consulting GmbH v Leboeuf Lamb Greene & Macrae* (also known as *CAIB InvestmentBank AG v Leboeuf*) [2006] EWCA Civ 683.

involved with the relevant matter not to discuss that work with members of the arbitration team or amongst themselves. There was also an undertaking to secure an information barrier. On the facts, the former client's information was safe. The court held that there was no real risk of disclosure or misuse of confidential information and no need to grant an injunction.

Lawyers' obligation to respect client confidences is reinforced by legal professional privilege. The doctrine of privilege does, however, recognise some exceptions to confidentiality. It is therefore necessary to explore the effect of legal professional privilege before examining the regulation of the obligation of confidentiality by the legal profession.

III. Legal Professional Privilege

Legal professional privilege is, in some respects, more restricted than the duty of confidentiality owed by a lawyer to a client. It only protects communications between the client and lawyer and, generally, only information given for the purpose of obtaining legal representation. Information is not protected when available from another source. Nor is it available where the purpose of the communication is to further a criminal purpose.

The effect of these limitations is that information cannot be placed under a cloak of privilege just because it has been given to a lawyer. Much criticism of confidentiality is directed at privilege, although this is not always clear. Recently, legal professional privilege has been under attack by governments eager to convict criminals or reduce money laundering or tax evasion.

A. Basis in Common Law and Statute

Legal professional privilege was developed as a rule of evidence. The original principles covered work done by the lawyer in giving legal advice to the client or in preparing for litigation. Neither lawyer nor client could be ordered to give evidence in court, or elsewhere, of communications between them. The sanctity of advice is also bolstered by statute. The Police and Criminal Evidence Act (PACE) 1984, section 58(1) provides that '[a] person arrested and held in custody in a police station or other premises shall be entitled, if he so requests, to consult a solicitor privately at any time'.

PACE also gave the privilege a statutory definition, applicable to both criminal and civil proceedings, in section 10(1). The section states that:

(1) Subject to subsection (2) below, in this Act 'items subject to legal privilege' means—
   (a) communications between a professional legal adviser and his client or any person representing his client made in connection with the giving of legal advice to the client;

(b)   communications between a professional legal adviser and his client or any person representing his client or between such an adviser or his client or any such representative and any other person made in connection with or in contemplation of legal proceedings and for the purposes of such proceedings; and

(c)   items enclosed with or referred to in such communications and made—

(i)   in connection with the giving of legal advice; or

(ii)   in connection with or in contemplation of legal proceedings and for the purposes of such proceedings, when they are in the possession of a person who is entitled to possession of them.

(2)   Items held with the intention of furthering a criminal purpose are not items subject to legal privilege.

The statutory definition is said to embody the common law.[11]

Privilege has acquired significance beyond its original scope. In *General Mediterranean Holdings v Patel*,[12] Toulson J stated that privilege was a fundamental basis of the administration of justice, which cannot be overridden by the general words of a statute. The House of Lords has held that legal privilege is a fundamental human right protected by Article 8 of the European Convention on Human Rights.[13] The case law is often ambiguous or confused and has not received extended analysis by either the judiciary or the legal profession.[14]

B.   Communications between a Lawyer and his Client (Legal Advice Privilege)

i.   Private Practitioners

It will be noted that, under PACE, all communications between solicitor and client are privileged if they concern giving legal advice, whether or not they relate to litigation. This is often known as legal advice privilege. An illustration of the operation of this professional privilege, and a justification for it, can be found in the House of Lords decision in *R v Derby Magistrates' Court, ex p B*.[15]

On arrest B admitted murdering a girl. Before trial, he retracted his confession and implicated the girl's stepfather. B was acquitted. He later admitted the offence again and then retracted the confession. Eventually, the stepfather was charged with the murder and B was called as a witness for the Crown. Counsel for the stepfather sought evidence from B, and his solicitor, of B's previous inconsistent instructions.[16]

At first instance disclosure was ordered on the balance of public interest. The public interest in ensuring that all relevant evidence was available to the defence was

---

[11]   *R v Bowden* [1999] 4 All ER 43 (CA) at 48.

[12]   *General Mediterranean Holdings v Patel* [1999] 3 All ER 673.

[13]   *R v Special Commissioners of Income Tax* [2002] UKHL 21; and see *R v Secretary of State for Home Dept, ex p Daly* [2001] UKHL 26 and C Tapper, 'Prosecution and Privilege' (1996) 1 *International Journal of Evidence and Proof* 5.

[14]   But see J Auburn, *Legal Professional Privilege* (Oxford, Hart Publishing, 2000).

[15]   *R v Derby Magistrates' Court, ex p B* [1995] 4 All ER 526.

[16]   Under the Criminal Procedure Act 1965, ss 4 and 5 and the principles laid down in *R v Barton* [1972] 2 All ER 1192 and *R v Ataou* [1988] QB 798.

held to outweigh the public interest in confidentiality. B no longer had any recognisable interest in the privilege. Having been acquitted of the murder he could not, at the time, be tried again. He was not likely to be prosecuted for perjury. It was held by the Lords, however, that B's statements were protected by professional privilege and so immune from production.

In a comprehensive judgment the Lord Chief Justice, Lord Taylor, examined the history of legal privilege. He concluded

> [t]he principle which runs through all these cases ... is that a man must be able to consult his lawyer in confidence, since otherwise he might hold back half the truth. The client must be sure that what he tells his lawyer in confidence will never be revealed without his consent.

The judgment in *R v Derby Magistrates' Court* raised legal advice privilege above a rule of evidence to 'a fundamental condition on which the administration of justice as a whole rests'. Lord Taylor concluded that legal advice privilege '*once established*' should be absolute. No exception should be allowed.[17] Were this not to be the law, solicitors would have to tell their clients that their confidence would be broken if 'in some future case the court was to hold that [they] no longer had "any recognisable interest" in asserting it'.[18] The idea that, once established, legal advice privilege is absolute has been accepted in a number of leading cases.[19]

Lord Nicholls, agreeing with Lord Taylor, considered that if a court could override privilege it 'would be faced with an essentially impossible task'. What criteria would it use? Would the public interest in the conviction of the guilty always override it? Would the need for evidence in a serious civil claim be a sufficient cause, 'say where a defendant is alleged to have defrauded hundreds of people of their pensions or life savings?'[20]

The broad scope potentially afforded to advice privilege potentially protects clients confessing crimes to their lawyer with a view to obtaining advice. Thus, in the exceptional cases, considered below, where the state seeks information by covert surveillance or other methods, there is no guarantee that the court will let it be used in evidence.

ii. In-house Lawyers

In-house lawyers are subject to the same codes as private practitioners in England and Wales. Doubts arise regarding the privileged status of in-house communications. There is a risk that, if legal advice privilege applies to in-house lawyers, corporations might use it to protect sensitive documents, and dubious activities, from scrutiny by the courts.

The English courts have treated the issue of the independence of in-house counsel as only one consideration in assessing whether in-house communications with lawyers

---

[17] *R v Derby Magistrates' Court, ex p B* (n 15) per Lord Taylor at 542d.

[18] ibid, at 541g.

[19] Eg the Privy Council *in B v Auckland District Law Society* [2004] 4 All ER 269, esp at 283. But see *Saunders v Punch Ltd* [1998] 1 All ER 234, at 244 and *Three Rivers DC v Bank of England* [2004] 3 All ER 168, at 182, [39].

[20] *R v Derby Magistrates' Court, ex p B* (n 15) per Lord Nicholls at 545.

were created in a relevant legal context. This approach is different from that in Australia and Europe, for example, where employment in-house negates any question of privilege.[21]

In England and Wales, communications between in-house lawyers and their employing companies have been treated as potentially attracting privilege, including in investigations by competition authorities, such as the former Office for Fair Trading. Some doubt is cast on this assumption by European competition law and the recent decision in *Akzo Nobel Ltd v European Commission*.[22] The case involved the investigation of possible anti-competitive practices at the appellant company and the seizure by the respondents of communications with in-house lawyers for which privilege was claimed.

The European Court of Justice held that privilege only extended to 'independent lawyers' committed to 'collaborating in the administration of justice'. In-house lawyers, because of their employed status and relationship with their client, were 'less able to deal effectively with any conflicts between his professional obligations and the aims of his client'.[23] The court held that the decision need not affect the policy of Member States in pursuing competition investigations. It does, however, create considerable uncertainty about the vulnerability of confidential communications with in-house lawyers. It also indicates the possibility of a longer-term drift in domestic law towards the European position.

iii. Non-lawyers Providing Legal Advice

In the current legal services market it is arguable that legal professional privilege should be available to non-legal professionals providing legal advice. This proposition was tested recently in the Supreme Court, in the case of *Prudential PLC and Prudential (Gibraltar) Ltd v Special Commissioner of Income Tax and Philip Pandolfo (HM Inspector of Taxes)*.[24] The appellants sought a declaration that legal professional privilege protected advice given on a tax avoidance scheme by its accountants.

The appellants argued that changes in the legal services market had rendered the reservation of privilege to lawyers an anomaly. It was noted that patent agents were once not regarded as lawyers and so their clients did not have common law privilege.[25] Given their intervening development and contemporary role, counsel argued, patent and trade mark attorneys were now regarded as lawyers. Lord Neuberger, however, noted that, Parliament had extended privilege to new groups in very specific instances. For example, patent attorneys acting to protect inventions, designs, technical information,

---

[21] L Bastin, 'Should "independence" of in-house counsel be a condition precedent to a claim of legal professional privilege in respect of communications between them and their employer clients?' (2011) 30(1) *Civil Justice Quarterly* 33.

[22] *Akzo Nobel Ltd and anor v European Commission* [2010] All ER (D) 72; and see *AM & S v Commission of the European Communities* [1983] 3 WLR 17.

[23] *Akzo Nobel Ltd and anor v European Commission*, ibid, at [40]–[45].

[24] *Prudential PLC and Prudential (Gibraltar) Ltd v Special Commissioner of Income Tax and Philip Pandolfo (HM Inspector of Taxes)* [2013] 2 AC 185.

[25] See *Wilden Pump Engineering Co v Fusfeld* [1985] FSR 159.

or trade marks, now enjoys statutory protection of communications as if they were 'acting as the client's solicitor'.[26]

By a majority the court decided that privilege applies only to qualified lawyers, solicitors and barristers, even where advice is legal advice which a professional person is qualified to give. In the leading judgment in the Supreme Court, Lord Neuberger said that Parliament has legislated to extend privilege in some cases. Therefore, extending common law privilege to non-legal professionals, such as accountants, was a matter for parliament. To decide otherwise, he said, would 'would be likely to lead to what is currently a clear and well understood principle becoming an unclear principle, involving uncertainty'.

iv. The Client

a. Individuals

In most circumstances it is clear who the client is. Special care has to be exercised, however, when the lawyer holds an ambiguous status. An example is when a lawyer is employed by A, a corporation, and is asked to advise another employee of A. Similarly, when a client's capacity is or may be in doubt, there may be an issue of whether a carer's communications with a lawyer on behalf of the client are covered.

b. Organisations

In *Three Rivers District Council & Others v Governor and Company of the Bank of England (No 6)*,[27] the issue arose as to whether communications between a Bank's employees or ex-employees, or officers or ex-officers and its solicitors, could qualify for legal advice privilege. The case concerned the collapse of the Bank of Credit and Commerce International SA (BCCI). The claimants were creditors of BCCI and the liquidators in its insolvency (A). They brought an action against the Bank of England, the respondents, for misfeasance in public office. This related to the supervision of BCCI before its collapse. The government appointed Lord Justice Bingham to conduct an inquiry into the supervision of BCCI.

On the announcement of the Bingham Inquiry, B had established the Bingham Inquiry Unit (BIU) to prepare its case. The Bank of England had retained Freshfields, solicitors to advise on dealings with the inquiry. The Court of Appeal held that only communications between Freshfields and the BIU could qualify. Communications between the lawyers and third parties could not. Since it was not relevant to the appeal, the House of Lords declined to express a view. Baroness Hale said that, in organisations, there are particular difficulties in identifying 'the client' to whose communications privilege should attach.[28]

---

[26] Copyright, Designs and Patents Act 1988, s 280.
[27] *Three Rivers District Council & Others v Governor and Company of the Bank of England (No 6)* [2004] 3 All ER 168 (CA) and [2005] 1 AC 610 (HL).
[28] *Three Rivers District Council & Others v Governor and Company of the Bank of England (No 6)* [2005] 1 AC 610 (HL) at [63].

v. Legal Advice

Legal advice privilege is not exclusively concerned with preparation for litigation but covers legal advice given to a client by a lawyer in all contexts, for example in making a will, drawing up contracts or undertaking conveyancing. It is in this context that the Court of Appeal attempted to rein in what was seen as an attempt to overextend the scope of this privilege in the *Three Rivers* case. In fact, the Court of Appeal and the House of Lords reached different conclusions on restricting the scope of legal advice privilege.

In order to succeed in a claim for losses suffered as a result of the BCCI collapse, depositors had to show an omission attributable to bad faith.[29] This would be all but impossible without access to internal documents. A, therefore, sought disclosure of documents created by the BIU for Freshfields. The Bank of England claimed legal professional privilege in respect of those documents.

In the Court of Appeal, Lord Phillips was critical of the wide scope afforded legal privilege. He said that

> [w]here ... litigation is not anticipated it is not easy to see why communications with a solicitor should be privileged. Legal advice privilege attaches to matters such as the conveyance of real property or the drawing up of a will. It is not clear why it should.[30]

He called for a review of the law.

The Court of Appeal held that legal professional privilege could only be claimed for communications between the Unit and the solicitors seeking or giving legal advice. In order to claim legal advice privilege the advice being sought from the lawyers had to be advice as to legal rights or liabilities. Advice as to how the Bank of England should present its case to the inquiry did not qualify for privilege.

On appeal to the House of Lords, A argued that legal advice privilege attached to communications between lawyer and client where the advice and assistance was of a kind that was part of the proper function of a lawyer to give. The Bank of England argued that legal advice privilege was an extension of litigation privilege and should be confined to advice on legal rights and obligations. It should, it was said, extend to advice and assistance in the presentation of a client's case to a public inquiry.

The House of Lords agreed with the Bank of England and allowed the appeal. It held that legal advice privilege attached to communications between the Unit and its solicitors. It covered the manner in which the Bank should appropriately present evidence and material to the Bingham Inquiry. Legal advice privilege was not, however, an extension of litigation privilege. Legal professional privilege was a single privilege. Its two sub-heads were legal advice privilege and litigation privilege.

The rationale for the decision was that solicitors, as 'men of affairs', provided clients with a wide variety of advice on their rights, liabilities and obligations. This was covered by legal advice privilege, and the advice given to the bank in this case

---

[29] See Banking Act 1987, s 1(4).
[30] *Three Rivers District Council & Others v Governor and Company of the Bank of England (No 6)* [2004] 3 All ER 168 (CA) at 182, [39].

was so covered. Legal advice included, said Lord Carswell 'advice as to what should prudently and sensibly be done in the relevant legal context'.[31]

Baroness Hale said the their Lordships endorsed the approach of the Court of Appeal in *Balabel v Air India*,[32] and the observation of Lord Justice Taylor,[33] that 'legal advice is not confined to telling the client the law; it must include advice as to what should prudently and sensibly be done in the relevant legal context'. She added,

> [t]here will always be borderline cases in which it is difficult to decide whether there is or is not a 'legal' context. But much will depend upon whether it is one in which it is reasonable for the client to consult the special professional knowledge and skills of a lawyer, so that the lawyer will be able to give the client sound advice as to what he should do, and just as importantly what he should not do, and how to do it.[34]

Lord Scott said,

> it is necessary in our society, a society in which the restraining and controlling framework is built upon a belief in the rule of law, that communication between clients and lawyers, whereby the clients are hoping for the assistance of the lawyers' skills in the management of their affairs, should be secure against the possibility of any scrutiny from others.[35]

Therefore, where information was found to be subject to legal professional privilege, it could not be set aside on the ground of some higher public interest.

vi. Non-legal Advice

The courts have adopted a wide definition of legal advice in interpreting the scope of legal advice privilege. Privilege extends to the client's instructions to the solicitor, instructions to a barrister and the barrister's opinion. It covers documents, and copies of them, created in order to obtain legal advice and those which indicate the advice being given.[36] It does not necessarily extend to client attendance notes. In *R (Howe) v South Durham Justices*,[37] privilege was claimed for an attendance note made by a solicitor at a trial in which his client was disqualified for driving offences. The note was required by the authorities in order to establish that the defendant in the present case was the same person, in which case he was driving while disqualified. The defendant claimed, inter alia, that the note was covered by privilege. The Divisional Court held that the note could be used purely for the sake of proving identity, provided any privileged material could be concealed.

The substance of 'legal advice' is interpreted broadly. For example in *Nederlandse Reassurantie Groep Holding NV v Bacon & Woodrow*,[38] assistance provided for the client included advice given by solicitors on the commercial wisdom of a proposed

---

[31] ibid, at [59].
[32] *Balabel v Air India* [1988] Ch 317.
[33] ibid, at 330.
[34] *Three Rivers District Council & Others v Governor and Company of the Bank of England (No 6)* [2005] 1 AC 610 (HL) at [62].
[35] ibid, per Lord Scott at [25] and [34].
[36] *Re Barings Plc* [1998] 1 All ER 673, per Sir Richard Scott VC.
[37] *R (Howe) v South Durham Justices* [2004] EWHC 362 (Admin).
[38] *Nederlandse Reassurantie Groep Holding NV v Bacon & Woodrow* [1995] 1 All ER 976.

transaction. This information was held to be covered by privilege provided it was given in the context of acting as a legal adviser. This is similar to the reasoning of the House of Lords in *Three Rivers*. 'Legal advice' is also given wide definition by extension of the privilege to employed lawyers and also to patent agents, licensed conveyancers and 'authorised advocates and litigators'.[39] In relation to EU competition investigations before the European Court of Justice, however, legal professional privilege does not extend to communications between employed lawyers and their employer clients.

C. Litigation Privilege

In *Three Rivers*, Lord Scott said that he favoured 'a new look at the justification for litigation privilege' in the light of the Civil Procedure Rules and the fact that civil litigation was 'in many respects no longer adversarial'. In fact, the courts seem to have been more inclined to apply the privilege beyond the conventional courts.

i. Parties to Litigation Privilege

Litigation privilege potentially covers communication between solicitors or barristers and third parties relating to litigation. This includes the work of in-house litigation solicitors in exactly the same way as if they were external lawyers.[40] Under the Courts and Legal Services Act, legal professional privilege was extended to a person who was not a barrister or solicitor at any time when that person was providing advocacy or litigation services as an authorised advocate or authorised litigator. It also covered those providing conveyancing services as an authorised practitioner or providing probate services as a probate practitioner. Under the section, any communication was, in any legal proceedings, privileged from disclosure as if the person in question were acting as his client's solicitor.[41]

ii. Venue and the Nature of Proceedings

The assumption that litigation privilege is restricted to proceedings or anticipated proceedings in a court of law was tested in *Tesco Stores Ltd v Office of Fair Trading*.[42] The applicants (T) appealed a decision by the Office of Fair Trading (OFT) to impose a fine for alleged practices designed to increase the price of cheese. T had interviewed a number of witnesses connected with the case and the OFT sought disclosure of their statements.

---

[39] Courts and Legal Services Act 1990, s 63.
[40] *Alfred Crompton Amusement Machines v Commissioners of Customs and Excise No 2* [1972] 2 QB 102, at 129.
[41] Courts and Legal Services Act 1990, s 63 (see now Legal Services Act 2007 s 190).
[42] *Tesco Stores Ltd v Office of Fair Trading* [2012] Comp AR 188.

The OFT argued that the process was an administrative procedure under the Competition Act 1998 and therefore not litigation. The Competition Appeal Tribunal found that the procedure was administrative, but that, by the time T began collecting statements, it had become adversarial. Litigation privilege could therefore apply. The decision suggests that it is the nature of the proceedings rather than the venue that determines whether litigation privilege applies.

iii. Documents Covered

Litigation privilege covers a wide range of documents, including reports compiled by an expert in preparation for litigation. Prior to PACE this was an area of inconsistency. The courts first declared that solicitors could not be required to produce or give evidence of the report[43] and then that they could.[44] This was apparently contrary to PACE, section 10 and was rightly criticised.[45] Although the position now seems settled in favour of privilege applying, protection is less than watertight. Circumstances will inevitably arise where the right to privilege will be tested. An expert preparing a report can be subpoenaed by the other side to give evidence, there being no property in a witness. It should be emphasised, therefore, that *Three Rivers, Derby Magistrates* and numerous other cases, state that the doctrine of privilege is absolute once established.

IV. Exceptions to Legal Advice Privilege

A. Furthering a Criminal Purpose

Neither form of privilege protects information generated with a view to furthering a criminal purpose.[46] In *Three Rivers*, Lord Nicholls was clearly concerned about the scope of this exception and its potential abuse by the state. Legislation such as the Regulation of Investigatory Powers Act 2000[47] (RIPA) gives a wide range of public bodies[48] powers to conduct surveillance and investigation. These include the right to intercept communications on a number of grounds. The reasons include national security, or for crime detection, prevention of disorder, public safety, protecting public health, or in the interests of the economic well-being of the United Kingdom.[49]

---

[43] *Harmony Shipping Co SA v Saudi Europe Line Ltd* [1979] 3 All ER 177.
[44] *R v Egdell* The Times 14 December 1988.
[45] JV McHale, 'Confidentiality, an Absolute Obligation' (1989) 52 *Modern Law Review* 715.
[46] *Kuwait Airways Corporation v Iraqi Airways Company* [2005] EWCA Civ 286
[47] Regulation of Investigatory Powers Act 2000.
[48] ibid, sch 1.
[49] ibid, s 5(3).

The concern with RIPA is not that information will be used in legal proceedings. In fact, public authorities are generally much too concerned about disclosing the extent of their surveillance capability to want to disclose evidence collected by covert methods in court. The concern is that the state generally respects the principle that lawyer and client communications are truly private.

In *Re McE*,[50] the House of Lords held, Lord Phillips dissenting, that RIPA allows covert surveillance of defendants and their lawyers. Under subsequent statutory instruments, the use of this authorisation was restricted to circumstances deemed 'exceptional and compelling', such as threats to national security or to life or limb.[51] These limitations are arguably much too broad, giving rise to the possibility of routine invasion of lawyer and client communications by authorities 'fishing' for information.[52]

Lawyers drew some comfort from the thought that such intrusions would be regarded as contrary to the European Convention of Human Rights, Articles 6 (right to fair trial) and 8 (right to privacy).[53] The European Court of Human Rights has, however, been inconsistent in its approach. In *Öcalan v Turkey*,[54] the complainant, Öcalan (O), was the leader of the Kurdistan Workers' Party, a separatist movement that had engaged in terrorist activities in Turkey. O complained that the secret recording of his conversations with his lawyer was a breach of his human rights. In a previous application, the court had held that the conditions of O's detention in Turkey were commensurate with the level of security required given the offences and the risks of either assassination or escape.

In the instant case, the European Court of Human Rights condoned the Turkish authorities secretly recording conversations between O and his lawyer on the grounds that this was 'strictly necessary to protect society against violence'.[55] The chair of The Law Society Human Rights Committee argued that '[t]his stance is open to misuse by governments and, while the protection of society from violence must be paramount, respect for privileged communications between lawyers and their clients is essential except in the most extreme circumstances'.[56] It remains to be seen how far the state respects the principle that information passing between lawyer and client remains secret.

---

[50] *Re McE* [2009] 1 AC 908.

[51] The Regulation of Investigatory Powers (Covert Human Intelligence Sources: Matters Subject to Legal Privilege) Order 2010 SI 2010/123 and The Regulation of Investigatory Powers (Extension of Authorisation Provisions: Legal Consultations) Order 2010 SI 2010/461.

[52] N Griffin and G Nardell, 'R.I.P. Legal Professional Privilege' *Counsel* May 2012, at 30.

[53] ibid.

[54] *Öcalan v Turkey* (2005) 41 EHRR 45.

[55] M Cross, 'Alarm as Strasbourg backs bugging of lawyers' client meetings' *Law Society Gazette* 24 March 2014.

[56] ibid.

B. Items Held with the Intention of Furthering a Criminal Purpose

Both the common law and statute deny legal advice privilege and litigation privilege to items held with the intention of furthering a criminal purpose.[57] The wording of the statute, PACE, is, however, curious. It states that '[i]tems held with the intention of furthering a criminal purpose are not items subject to legal privilege'.[58] The issue of whether a lawyer's intent to further a criminal purpose was actually necessary in order to compromise legal advice privilege was considered by the House of Lords in *Francis & Francis v Central Criminal Court*.[59]

In the case, G retained a solicitor to assist her in purchasing a house. Unknown to both G and the solicitor, the money for this purchase allegedly came from drug trafficking by a member of G's family. The police applied for an order requiring the solicitors to deliver up all the files in their possession relating to the transaction. The House of Lords agreed that the files fell within PACE, section 10(2). It did not matter that neither the solicitor, as holder of the records, nor G, intended to further a criminal purpose. As long as someone had a criminal intention in relation to the documents they fell within section 10(2).[60]

There must be prima facie, and probably strong, evidence of a criminal purpose. Such a purpose can include civil fraud or 'iniquity' which might not constitute a crime. In *Barclays Bank v Eustice*,[61] the relevant documents were created by solicitors for the 'dominant' purpose of prejudicing the interests of their client's bank, which was the client's creditor. There was strong evidence that the purpose of seeking legal advice was not to explain what had been done or to prepare a criminal defence. Rather, the purpose was to deceive others about the value of the relevant transactions.[62]

Lord Justice Schiemann regarded the deceitful purpose as being 'sufficiently iniquitous for public policy to require that communications between [the client] and his solicitor in relation to the setting up of these transactions be discoverable'.[63] The documents were not privileged in civil proceedings by the bank under the Insolvency Act 1986. How far this decision is consistent with the *Derby Magistrates* case is debatable. The cases were decided at about the same time and neither discussed the other. Any distinction is not, presumably, based on whether the case is civil or criminal, since their Lordships in the *Derby Magistrates* case clearly thought that the principle applied to both. The same view was taken in the Court of Appeal decision on money laundering, *Bowman v Fels*.[64]

In *Barclays Bank v Eustice*, Lord Justice Schiemann was more than happy to carry out what Lord Nicholls in the *Derby* case considered to be the 'impossible task' of

---

[57] *R v Cox & Railton* [1884] 14 QBD 153; PACE 1984, s 10(2).
[58] PACE 1984, s 10(2).
[59] *Francis & Francis v Central Criminal Court* [1989] AC 346.
[60] But see L Newbold, 'The Crime/Fraud Exception to the Legal Professional Privilege' (1990) 53 *Modern Law Review* 472.
[61] *Barclays Bank v Eustice* [1995] 4 All ER 511.
[62] ibid, at 524f.
[63] See also *Derby & Co Ltd v Weldon No 7* [1990] 3 All ER 161; *Re Konigsberg* [1989] 3 All ER 289.
[64] *Bowman v Fels* [2005] EWCA Civ 226, and see further ch 14: 'Collective Third Parties'.

evaluating the balance of public interest. Considering the policy arguments for and against denying privilege, Schiemann LJ said:

> I do not consider that the result of ... the order in the present case will be to discourage straightforward citizens from consulting their lawyers. Those lawyers should tell them that what is proposed is liable to be set aside and the straightforward citizen will then not do it and so the advice will never see the light of day. In so far as those wishing to engage in sharp practice are concerned, the effect of the present decision may well be to discourage them from going to their lawyers. This has the arguable public disadvantage that the lawyers might have dissuaded them from the sharp practice. However, it has the undoubted public advantage that the absence of lawyers will make it more difficult for them to carry out their sharp practice.[65]

The case was followed in *Nationwide Building Society v Various Solicitors*,[66] which held that procuring a loan by deception fell within the exception to professional privilege. It was sufficient that the solicitor's advice furthered the offence, even though the solicitor was unaware of the deception.

Restriction on the extent of privilege must extend to confidential information unlawfully acquired by the client. A case illustrating this involved the solicitors who advised Andrew Regan in his attempt to take over the Cooperative Wholesale Society in April 1997. Stolen documents, which were privileged, were allegedly used by the solicitors in preparing the predatory takeover. This was not only unethical but probably unlawful.[67]

In the light of notorious city frauds and sharp financial practices, such as those perpetrated by Robert Maxwell and BCCI in the UK and Enron in the USA, the restriction of privilege is a timely warning for city financiers and their solicitors. The public mood is unsympathetic to the use of legal advice privilege to cover up wrongdoing. The courts uneasily walk a line between exposing fraud and protecting privilege. This often involves denying full disclosure but ordering provision of key items of confidential information that a litigant ought not to object to disclosing.

An example of the approach of the courts to balancing privilege with the public interest in disclosure occurred in *JSC BTA Bank v Solodchenko*.[68] The defendant (S) had been sentenced to 18 months for contempt of court for failing to comply with disclosure requirements relating to an alleged international fraud. The applicant bank sought an order against S's solicitors (C) for disclosure of (i) S's contact details, (ii) details of S's assets, required in order to obtain a freezing order; and (iii) the source of funding to pay C's fees.

The court distinguished a client's right to claim legal professional privilege, which was absolute, and the right to protection of confidential information, which was capable of being overridden by other considerations. In the instant case, the balance fell in favour of ordering disclosure of S's contact details. This was because these were necessary if effect was to be given to a court order, that is, a committal order.[69] The court held that, although it had jurisdiction to order C to disclose information about

---

[65] *Barclays Bank v Eustice* [1995] 4 All ER 511, at 525c.
[66] *Nationwide Building Society v Various Solicitors* (1998) NLJR 241.
[67] *The Lawyer* 6 May 1997, at 7.
[68] *JSC BTA Bank v Solodchenko* [2011] EWHC 2163 (Ch).
[69] ibid, at [24]–[26] and [37]–[39].

S's assets, it was not appropriate to make such an order. In the circumstances it was overwhelmingly likely that any such information supplied by S to C would have been given for the purpose of obtaining legal advice and was, therefore, privileged.

C. Statutory Exceptions

Parliament can create legislative exceptions to the principle of privilege. The courts have held that, in order to create such exceptions, Parliament's intention must be clear. This was explained by Lord Hoffmann in *R v Secretary of State for the Home Department, ex p Simms*,[70] as follows:

> Parliamentary sovereignty means that Parliament can, if it chooses, legislate contrary to fundamental principles of human rights. The Human Rights Act 1998 will not detract from this power. The constraints upon its exercise by Parliament are ultimately political, not legal. But the principle of legality means that Parliament must squarely confront what it is doing and accept the political cost. Fundamental rights cannot be overriden by general or ambiguous words. This is because there is too great a risk that the full implications of their unqualified meaning may have passed unnoticed in the democratic process. In the absence of express language or necessary implication to the contrary, the courts therefore presume that even the most general words were intended to be subject to the basic rights of the individual. In this way the courts of the United Kingdom, though acknowledging the sovereignty of Parliament, apply principles of constitutionality little different from those which exist in countries where the power of the legislature is expressly limited by a constitutional document.[71]

Such exceptions, for example, those relating to money laundering, are covered below.[72]

D. Items Required by the Relevant Regulator

In *Parry-Jones v Law Society*,[73] the Law Society tested rules it had made to enforce compliance with the Solicitors' Accounts Rules and Solicitors' Trust Accounts Rules. The rules provided that the Law Society could require a solicitor to produce documents relating to his practice to an appointed investigator. Mr Parry-Jones objected to such a request on the ground that production would breach client confidentiality. He was refused an injunction to restrain the Law Society. In *R v Special Commissioner and Another, ex P Morgan Grenfell & Co Ltd*,[74] Lord Hoffmann said that the true justification for the decision was not that Mr Parry-Jones's clients had no legal privilege, nor that it had been overridden by the Law Society's rules, but that it would not be infringed.

---

[70] *R v Secretary of State for the Home Department, ex p Simms* [2000] 2 AC 115.
[71] ibid, at 131.
[72] Chapter 14: 'Collective Third Parties'.
[73] *Parry-Jones v Law Society* [1969] 1 Ch 1.
[74] *R v Special Commissioner and Another, ex P Morgan Grenfell & Co Ltd* [2003] 1 AC 563.

Lord Hoffmann said that The Law Society was not entitled to use information disclosed by the solicitor for any purpose other than the investigation. Otherwise the confidentiality of the clients had to be maintained. In his Lordship's opinion

> this limited disclosure did not breach the clients' Legal Professional Privilege or, to the extent that it technically did, was authorised by the Law Society's statutory powers. It does not seem to me to fall within the same principle as a case in which disclosure is sought for a use which involves the information being made public or used against the person entitled to the privilege.[75]

The current Bar Code of Conduct cites *R v Special Commissioner and Another, ex P Morgan Grenfell & Co Ltd* in support of Rule C64, under which barristers may be required to disclose documents for which clients could claim privilege.[76] This is a dubious claim. What Lord Hoffmann said about *Parry-Jones v Law Society* was partially based on the Law Society's statutory position, which is different from that of the Bar now. It was also obiter dicta. The guidance is probably right to suggest, however, that the requirement to report serious misconduct by others can be overridden by privilege.

E. 'Severable' Documents

A set of documents containing privileged and non-privileged sections that can be separated into distinct documents are 'severable documents'.[77] Where this separation is not possible the document is known as a 'composite document'. Solicitors preparing to give disclosure of documents in litigation must be careful to claim privilege for the sections of composite documents that they do not intend to disclose. Otherwise, they may waive the client's privilege and give the other party access to sections of the document that the client objects to producing. This is particularly the case with expert reports prepared for use in litigation.[78]

V. Exceptions to Litigation Privilege

A. Freedom of Information

The Freedom of Information Act 2000 gives the public a right of access to certain information held by public authorities. It therefore affects lawyers in public organisations. These include central and local government, the National Health Service, police

---

[75] ibid, per Lord Hoffmann at [32].
[76] BSB, *Bar Code of Conduct 2014*, gC93.
[77] *Great Atlantic Insurance v Home Insurance* [1981] 1 WLR 529, at 536.
[78] See 'Waiver of Litigation Privilege' (section V.C)

and education authorities. There are exemptions, classified as either absolute or qualified exemptions. Where the exemption is qualified a balance must be struck between the public interest in maintaining confidence and that in requiring disclosure. The Act treats information held under a legal duty of confidence as one of eight absolute exemptions. If disclosure would amount to an actionable breach of confidence then the information is treated as exempt.[79]

The Act also provides qualified exemption based on whether information falls into a particular class or whether particular types of harm might ensue from disclosure. One of the classes of exemption relates to information in respect of which a claim to legal professional privilege could be maintained.[80] There are various categories of harm which might also give rise to a claim of exemption. These include cases where disclosure might endanger the physical or mental health or safety of an individual[81] or prejudice commercial interests.[82]

Whether or not information subject to qualified exemption must be disclosed is determined by application of a public interest test. Therefore, potentially privileged material relating to a public authority must be revealed if the public interest in disclosure outweighs the public interest in keeping it confidential. This appears to be the only exception to legal professional privilege on the general ground of public interest recognised by the law. It must be emphasised that it applies only to information held by public bodies, not private lawyers' offices.

B. Children Act 1989

i. Dominant Public Policy in the Care and Welfare of Children

a. The Investigative Nature of Children Act Cases

The Children Act 1989 provides for securing the welfare of children and for allocating responsibility for their care between parents, local authorities and other bodies. It provides mechanisms for deciding who has responsibility for the child and for determining issues such as residence and contact. While the Act works from the premise that children are generally better off in their families, it promotes diligence in recognising and dealing with situations where this is not the case.

An issue in Children Act cases is the extent to which potentially confidential material connected with the child's arrangements or welfare is protected from disclosure. One reading of the vague and conflicting case law is that legal professional privilege does not apply in Children Act cases.[83] This is because Children Act proceedings have

---

[79] Freedom of Information Act 2000, s 41.
[80] ibid, s 42.
[81] ibid, s 38.
[82] ibid, s 43(2).
[83] J McEwan, 'The Uncertain Status of Privilege in Children Act Cases: Re L' (1996–97) 1 *International Journal of Evidence and Proof* 80; I Dennis, *The Law of Evidence*, 4th edn (London, Sweet and Maxwell, 2010) at 10.35.

been considered investigative rather than adversarial.[84] This line of thought makes two assumptions. The first is that the proceedings are not, in reality, experienced as adversarial by the parties, especially the parents. The second is that privilege is justified only in adversarial settings. These assumptions have been called into question by the cases.

b. Expert Reports

Another reason why Children Act cases are exceptional lies in treatment of expert reports. The general policy of the Children Act is that the welfare of the child is paramount. Litigation privilege has therefore been overridden in order that expert reports are made available to the parties and the court, including in subsequent proceedings. This policy is supported by the Family Proceedings Rules 1991, particularly Rule 4.23. The rule provides that, with the leave of the court, documents normally treated as confidential can be disclosed to all parties, *guardians ad litem* and welfare officers.

Starting with *Re A*[85] the courts have denied recognition of legal privilege to experts' reports in Children Act proceedings. The precise scope of the exception was not clear. In 1996 in *Re L* the House of Lords had an opportunity to consider the issue. The mother, a drug addict, had, through her solicitor, commissioned a report by a chemical pathologist on how her child had come to take methadone. The consultant evidently thought that it had been administered by the mother, whereas her story was that the child had swallowed it accidentally.

The report was disclosed to all parties in the care proceedings under the normal procedures. The police were not parties to the care proceedings. They heard of the existence of a report at a case conference. They sought a copy of the report with a view to instituting criminal proceedings against the mother. The mother claimed that the report was covered by legal professional privilege, and also the privilege against self-incrimination.

Lord Jauncy gave the sole judgment for the majority of the House of Lords in *Re L*. He recognised that the privilege attaching to solicitor and client communications was absolute, but he considered that reports by third parties for the purposes of litigation were not covered by privilege in care proceedings under the Children Act. This was because such proceedings were non-adversarial and investigative. Further, because the documents were not covered by privilege, there was no need to decide whether it was in the public interest to order their disclosure.[86]

ii. Significant Doubts

Re L was notable because the court was willing to ignore privilege for a purpose arguably unconnected with the purposes of the Children Act. A powerful dissenting judgment was given by Lord Nicholls, with which Lord Mustill agreed. Lord Nicholls' basic point was that the Children Act does not make clear whether and, if so, how

---

[84] *In Re L (A Minor) (Police Investigation: Privilege)* [1997] AC 16.
[85] *Re A* [1991] 2 FLR 473. See also *Essex CC v R* [1994] Fam 167; *Oxfordshire CC v M* [1994] Fam 151.
[86] *Re L* (n 84) per Lord Jauncy at 87j.

litigation privilege is abrogated. He considered that abrogation cannot be implied from the welfare principle in section 1. This principle, in any case, considerably predates the passing of the Act in 1989. It had not been suggested that the privilege did not apply before 1989.

If the Children Act had abrogated privilege, then the Family Proceedings Rules 1991, Rule 4.23, specifying disclosure of evidence, would not have been required. Lord Nicholls thought that privilege cannot be split into legal advice privilege and litigation privilege covering third party reports. Both are equally privileged. It is worth noting that the decision of the majority in *Re L* was contrary to the decision of the House of Lords in the *Derby Magistrates* case.

Lord Nicholls' dissent asserts the fundamental importance of the right of parties to family proceedings to a fair hearing. This includes the right to the same safeguards enjoyed by parties to other proceedings. He suggested that

> it must be doubtful whether a parent who is denied the opportunity to obtain legal advice in confidence is accorded the fair hearing to which he is entitled under Article 6(1), read in conjunction with Article 8, of the European Convention of Human Rights.[87]

iii. A Duty to Disclose without Order?

One consequence of *Re L* could be that a court order is not needed to secure disclosure. Their Lordships were not clear on this point. Lord Jauncy considered the issue of whether solicitors have a 'duty' to make a 'voluntary' disclosure of 'all matters likely to be material to the welfare of the child'.[88] He referred to cases suggesting that no court order is needed,[89] but did not find it necessary to decide the issue. He did say that 'this further development of the practice in cases where the welfare of children is involved [may well be] welcomed'.[90] These remarks did not seem to be confined to reports by third parties. They may have been intended to refer communications between solicitor and client also.

If it is argued that there is a duty to disclose in third party reports in Children Act cases, it is not clear what penalty applies for non-disclosure. Failure to disclose would be contempt of court only where a court order had been made. It is doubtful that failure by the solicitor or barrister to disclose without an order would amount to professional misconduct. Unnecessary disclosure could render lawyers vulnerable to action by clients. It is therefore safer for lawyers in Children Act cases to preserve confidentiality in the absence of a specific order. Clearly there are issues here which have not been explored by their Lordships in *Re L* and the law is in need of clarification.

---

[87] ibid, at 90h.
[88] ibid, at 86e.
[89] Eg *Re R* [1994] Fam 167; *Re DH* [1994] 1 FLR 679.
[90] *Re L* (n 84) at 97b.

iv. Professional Guidance

In the light of the uncertain case law, a solicitor must be cautious when acting for parents whose behaviour could be considered prejudicial to their child's welfare. Any report commissioned for litigation could be subject to disclosure in future Children Act proceedings. Lawyers should therefore obtain all existing medical reports and information before deciding to commission another report, and also ensure that the expert instructed is fully informed about the risk of disclosure.

In 1994 the Law Society advised solicitors to consider carefully with their client whether or not to commission an expert's report.[91] Although this guidance has been consistently updated, it does not currently include this advice.[92] The guidance to the 2007 Code noted a duty to reveal experts' reports, but also that 'the position in relation to the voluntary disclosure of other documents or solicitor client communication is uncertain'.[93] Reading between the lines, this guidance might be construed as advice not to commission reports unless absolutely unavoidable and not to disclose them unless ordered. The rest of the guidance was at odds with this interpretation.

Solicitors finding themselves in situations where they were under a duty to disclose a report adverse to their client were reminded of the general duty not to mislead the court. They were told to persuade the client to agree to disclosure on the ground that this would enable the solicitor to do a better job. The solicitor was effectively being advised to sell clients the idea that disclosure was usually in their interest. The notion that this is a disinterested perspective was somewhat undermined by a reminder that failure to reveal adverse information may result in the *solicitor* being subject to 'severe criticism' by the court.

In cases where clients would not authorise disclosure of adverse reports, and this would result in a breach of the obligation to the court, solicitors were advised to withdraw from the case. This advice did not reflect the ambiguity of the legal situation or a very supportive line on client autonomy. Whether the rule in *Re L* covers private, as well as public, proceedings involving children is also unclear. Certainly the justification for the *Re L* rule, that the proceedings are not adversarial, can also be used in private cases.

C. Waiver of Litigation Privilege

i. Scope of Disclosure

Litigation privilege in relation to documents can be waived by clients. Such waiver is difficult to control. Where part of the report of an expert witness is given to the other side, for example, the litigation privilege in all of the report is waived. In *Clough v*

---

[91] The Law Society, *Disclosure of Reports in Children's Cases* (London, The Law Society, 1994).

[92] The Law Society, *Attendance of Solicitors at Local Authority Children Act Meetings* (9 January 2013) (www.lawsociety.org.uk/advice/practice-notes/attendance-of-solicitors-at-local-authority-children-act-meetings/).

[93] SRA, *Solicitors' Code of Conduct 2007*, r 4.02, guidance, para 15.

Tameside and Glossop Health Authority,[94] Bracewell J stressed that her decision was also based on the need to make the litigation process more open, in the light of the Woolf Report. She noted that, '[a]lthough civil litigation is adversarial, it is not permissible to withhold relevant information, nor to delete nor amend the documents of a report before disclosure, as was submitted ... to be the practice of some firms of solicitors'.[95]

The principle that disclosure cannot be selective applies generally. Therefore, once privilege in a document is waived for one purpose, it cannot be retained for other purposes.[96] The client's reasons for trying to make a limited disclosure are irrelevant. Nor, when privilege in a report is waived, can privilege in any background material referred to in the report be retained. The possible exception to this general position is that waiver cannot be implied where documents are handed to the police in order to assist a criminal investigation.[97]

It may be possible to waive privilege over some documents but not others, but partial waiver must be fair. For example, where the documents relate to the same issue, and are not severable, then waiver of one may lead the court to order the discovery of the other. This is because 'to allow an individual item to be plucked out of context would be to risk injustice through its real weight or meaning being misunderstood'.[98] Merely mentioning a privileged document in a witness statement, however, does not automatically mean that privilege is waived.[99]

There is some confusion about the point in the proceedings that an opposing party is entitled to the additional related documents where there has been partial disclosure. Some authorities consider that additional documents are not discoverable until those originally waived have been used in court.[100] In *R v Secretary of State for Transport ex parte Factortame and Others (No 5)*,[101] however, Lord Justice Auld, held that, while the effect of partial disclosure depended on the facts of the case, additional discovery could be ordered as soon as the documents, in relation to which privilege was waived, were disclosed.

ii. Disclosure in Error

If documents are disclosed by accident or mistake there is no implied waiver. If solicitors acquire information from the other side which is clearly confidential and came to them by mistake, then the information must be returned[102] and cannot be used in litigation.[103] Where a solicitor, on a client's instructions, read documents obviously

---

[94] *Clough v Tameside and Glossop Health Authority* [1998] 2 All ER 971.
[95] ibid, at 977.
[96] *B v Auckland District Law Society* [2004] 4 All ER 269.
[97] *British Coal Corp v Dennis Rye Ltd* [1988] 3 All ER 816.
[98] *Nea Kateria Maritime Co Ltd v Atlantic and Great Lakes Steam-Ship Corp* [1981] Comm LR 138, per Mustill J.
[99] *Expandable v Rubin* [2008] EWCA Civ 59.
[100] C Passmore, 'The Dangers of Waiving Privilege' (1997) 147 *New Law Journal* 931.
[101] *R v Secretary of State for Transport ex parte Factortame and Others (No 5)* (1997) The Times, 11 September 1997, 9 Admin LR 591.
[102] *English & American Insurance Co Ltd v Herbert Smith* [1988] FSR 232.
[103] SRA, *Solicitors' Code of Conduct 2007*, r 4, guidance, para 21(c).

sent in error, he may be restrained by injunction from taking further part in the relevant proceedings.[104] The only possible circumstance in which the courts may make an exception to the strictness of this rule is where the mistake would not have been obvious to a reasonable solicitor.[105]

D. Waiver by Operation of Law

Waiver can sometimes result from the operation of law, independent of the express or implied consent of the client. In *R v Bowden*,[106] the defendant, B, acting on legal advice, refused to answer police questions. After the interview, B's solicitor made a statement setting out the grounds of this advice. At trial the Crown led evidence of B's refusal to answer questions, but not of the solicitor's statement. Defence counsel, seeking to avoid any adverse inference being drawn from B's refusal to answer questions, asked the interviewing police officer about the solicitor's statement. The judge accepted the Crown's argument that B had thereby waived privilege. B was cross-examined about what he had told his solicitor. B was convicted and appealed. The Court of Appeal upheld the decision that legal privilege was waived.

VI. Solicitors and Confidentiality

Solicitors' duty of confidentiality closely follows the common law. Any duty imposed by rules of conduct must be at least as rigorous, or onerous, as the rights recognised by the legal duty of confidence and by the privilege attaching to legal advice and litigation.

A. A Brief History of Regulating Confidentiality

i. Solicitors' Practice Rules 1990

The Solicitors' Practice Rules 1990 made no mention of confidentiality in either the Basic Principles or the rules. By 1999, the eighth edition of the Guide devoted a chapter to confidentiality with seven principles and several pages of guidance. The main principle was that '[a] solicitor is under a duty to keep confidential to his or her firm the affairs of clients and to ensure that the staff do the same'.[107]

---

[104] *Ablitt v Mills & Reeve (a firm)* (1995) The Times 25 October 1995.
[105] *Al Fayed v Metropolitan Police Commissioner* [2002] EWCA Civ 780.
[106] *R v Bowden* [1999] 4 All ER 43.
[107] N Taylor (ed), *The Guide to the Professional Conduct of Solicitors*, 8th edn (1999) Principle 16.01.

ii. The impact of Bolkiah

The implication of the decision in *Bolkiah*, that a potential conflict of interest between past and present clients could not be avoided by erecting information barriers, caused considerable concern. Acting for past and present clients with interests in the same subject matter was, at the time, treated as a conflict of interest. The relevant principle in the Guide to the Professional Conduct of Solicitors 1999 stated that 'a solicitor or a firm of solicitors should not accept instructions to act for two or more clients where there is a conflict or a significant risk of conflict between interests of those clients'.[108] This was buttressed by an explicit prohibition stating that 'if a solicitor or firm of solicitors has acquired relevant confidential information about an existing or former client during the course of acting for that client, the solicitor or the firm must not accept instructions to act against the client'.[109]

The House of Lords decision in *Bolkiah* was perfectly consistent with the Code of Conduct, but not with what was happening 'on the ground'. According to research published in 2002, over 60 per cent of City firms broke the old rules for commercial reasons. They believed that their corporate clients were happy with the practice.[110] It was argued that strict rules on 'past client confidentiality' would significantly restrict client choice. Anyone suing one of the top five clearing banks would find it virtually impossible to instruct one of the top firms.

The position was particularly worrying for large City law firms. They argued that conflicts should be 'managed', not prohibited. They claimed that the Law Society principles were unclear and unenforceable.[111] The City firms were not always as successful at 'managing' conflict as they claimed.[112] Nevertheless, it was said that top firms might resist the rules in order to keep business.[113] They proposed relaxation of the rules. This provoked opposition, especially from smaller firms. They considered that big firms were attempting to establish an effective monopoly over lucrative business such as corporate takeovers and licensing.

iii. The City of London Law Society Working Party on Conflict of Interest Rules

The publicity and attention given to the *Bolkiah* case meant it was unsafe for solicitors to carry on as they had before. The decision raised the issue of whether past client conflicts could be successfully managed and began a search for how. Different solutions were canvassed, including the possibility of exempting certain transactions

---

[108] ibid, Principle 15.01.

[109] ibid, Principle 15.02.

[110] J Griffiths-Baker, *Serving Two Masters: Conflicts of Interest in the Modern Law Firm* (Oxford, Hart Publishing, 2002) at 174. See also HM Cvea, '"Heard it through the Grapevine": Chinese Walls and Former Client Confidentiality in Law Firms' (2000) 59 *Cambridge Law Journal* 370.

[111] Griffiths-Baker, ibid, at 163–64.

[112] See *Marks & Spencer plc v Freshfields Bruckhaus Deringer* [2004] EWHC 1337 (Ch).

[113] See *The Lawyer*, 27 September 2004, at 1.

from conflict rules.[114] Partly as a result of *Bolkiah*, the Law Society invited the City of London Law Society to establish a working party on conflict of interest rules (hereafter 'the working party').

According to Chris Perrin, who chaired the working party, two factors drove the post-*Bolkiah* re-examination of past and present client conflict rules.[115] One was the practice of many corporate clients of instructing different large firms on different matters. This created a strong possibility that leading firms could be 'conflicted out', unable to accept instructions for any leading corporate client because they had previously acted for all of them.

The second factor was the growth of the overseas market. Lawyers working overseas encountered less restrictive conflict regimes in other countries, even in the EU. Lawyers in other countries could generally act against past clients provided the present matter was not related to the previous work. English solicitors therefore felt at a disadvantage because their domestic conduct regime required them to refuse instructions that overseas competitors could accept in the same circumstances.

Under pressure from the large firms the Law Society established the working party. This announced shortly after that Lord Millett's judgment was unclear, that on vital issues it was only obiter dicta and, if it was the law, it should be changed.[116] A further argument for change was the pan-European Council of Bar and Law Societies of Europe (CCBE) ethics code. These rules provided that conflicts were restricted to present matters. Under Practice Rule 15 this CCBE code governed the cross-border activities of English lawyers. Further, the European professions were committed towards working towards harmonisation of domestic ethics regimes around the CCBE code.[117]

iv. Proposed Rules for Dealing with Past and Present Client Situations

In 2000, the working party published a proposal that solicitors only be prevented from acting where past or present clients had an interest in the same or related matters. This had implications for the *Bolkiah* judgment. If Lord Millett's ruling applied to lawyers acting against former clients, as some academics argued,[118] any change to the position would have to be enacted as subordinate legislation.[119] Six weeks before the approval of new rules by the Law Society Council, *Marks & Spencer plc v Freshfields Bruckhaus Deringer* was decided. This opened the way for the Law Society to introduce the new rules.

---

[114] S Holland, S Heenan, M Harris, E Whewell and J Worthington, 'Conflicts of Interest: Time for a Change?' (2000) 3(2) *Legal Ethics* 132.

[115] C Perrin, 'Solicitors Conflicts of Interest: The Context and Significance of the New Rules' (2005) 58 *Amicus Curiae* 2.

[116] ibid.

[117] ibid.

[118] C Hollander and S Salzedo, *Conflicts of Interest and Chinese Walls* (London, Sweet and Maxwell, 2000) at 27.

[119] Perrin, 'Solicitors Conflicts of Interest' (n 115).

According to Perrin, the revised rules sought to be stricter than the emergent common law standard in two respects. First, the Law Society wanted solicitors to be obliged to disclose to a client any information relevant to a present matter, not just that from a relevant previous retainer. Second, a firm should not be able to try and manage a potential past and present client conflict merely by erecting information barriers. The Law Society considered it proper that the past client be informed beforehand so that they could challenge the arrangements proposed for protecting their confidentiality.[120]

v. The Solicitors' Practice (Confidentiality and Disclosure) Amendment Rule 2004

In addition to amending the rules on conflict of interest the working party also proposed amending the Solicitors' Practice Rules 1990 by adding a new sub-section, 16E, on confidentiality and disclosure.[121] The rules emphasised the pre-eminence of the duty of confidentiality, but also stated that '[y]ou must disclose all information relevant to your client's matter of which you are aware which is material to that client's matter regardless of the source of the information'.

This lawyer's duty to disclose was qualified by the rider 'unless there is a duty of confidentiality ... which always over-rides the duty to disclose'. The duty to disclose was also qualified by three exceptions. The first exception was circumstances where disclosure is prohibited by law. The second was where it is agreed expressly with the client that no duty to disclose arises or a different standard of disclosure applies. The third was 'where there is a serious belief that serious physical or mental injury will be caused to any person if information is disclosed to a client'.[122]

The rules went on to impose a duty not to risk breach of confidentiality to a previous client. The solicitor would have to consider whether acting for another client would involve use of information that might reasonably be expected to be material where that client has an interest adverse to the former client. Even here, solicitors would be able to act where proper arrangements could be made to secure confidentiality.[123] These arrangements included the present client knowing that the solicitors held information relevant to their matter that they could not disclose. Both clients were required to understand the relevant issues and consent to the conditions proposed for the solicitors continuing to act. Finally, it had to be reasonable to continue to act.[124] The possibility of continuing to act under existing instructions, but without the consent of a past client, was preserved. It was made subject to similar conditions, but subject also to the legal safeguards required at the time being in place.[125]

---

[120] ibid, at 5.
[121] The Solicitors' Practice (Confidentiality and Disclosure) Amendment Rule 2004.
[122] ibid, r 3.
[123] ibid, r 4.
[124] ibid, r 5.
[125] ibid, r 6.

Preservation of a right to continue acting without a past client's consent was justified by an example. If a firm is already acting for a new client and then discovers that it holds relevant confidential information about a former or existing client, then it may be possible to continue so to act even where the latter client does not consent to this. For example it may not be possible to obtain informed consent from the client whose confidential information needs protection. Indeed, to ask for such consent might in itself be a breach of the confidentiality of the new client. Equally, it may be an acceptable reason that the existing client is incapacitated and unable to consent. Neither the Rule nor the guidance mentions this possibility.

In circumstances where solicitors discovered that they held information on a former client relevant to a present matter, Rule 4.05 allowed a firm to continue acting. In order to do so, the new client had to understand and agree that the firm held information it could not disclose. Additionally, all safeguards required by law had to be in place. On whether it would be reasonable to so act, the guidance warned that only sophisticated clients, such as corporate bodies with in-house legal advisers, would be able to give informed consent.[126]

As a result of the 2004 rule amendment the problem of past and present client conflicts of interest was re-formulated as a problem of confidentiality. This changed the nature of the duty from a potentially absolute prohibition to a duty to preserve confidences. This distinction was preserved in the Solicitors' Code of Conduct 2007.

vi. The Solicitors' Code of Conduct 2007

The Solicitors' Code of Conduct 2007 continued the passage to the current outcomes on confidentiality. The Code incorporated the working party's rules on confidentiality in full. Additionally, in 2010, the SRA, under pressure from the City of London Law Society,[127] added a note to Rule 4, which dealt with confidentiality. This noted that the issue of past clients' information had previously been dealt with as a conflict of interests issue. It added that '[t]he rule does recognise that confidential information can be protected by the use of information barriers with the consent of the client and, in very limited circumstances, without that consent'.

The duty of confidentiality in the code was to 'keep the affairs of clients and former clients confidential except where disclosure is required or permitted by law or by your client'.[128] This protected existing clients, previous clients and deceased clients. It also covered prospective clients, for example, those interviewed but not acted for. It covered all information about clients, whether acquired by acting for them or from some other source.[129]

---

[126] SRA, *Solicitors Code of Conduct 2007*, r 4.05, guidance, para 35.
[127] J Loughrey, 'Large Law Firms, Sophisticated Clients and the Regulation of Conflicts of Interest' (2011) 14(2) *Legal Ethics* 215, at 218.
[128] SRA, *Solicitors Code of Conduct 2007* r 4(1).
[129] ibid, guidance to r 4.01, at para 4.

B. Confidentiality in the SRA Handbook and Code of Conduct

i. Principles, Outcomes and Indicative Behaviours

None of the principles of the SRA Code of Conduct 2011 deal explicitly with confidentiality. The obligation may however be implicit in the duty to act in the best interests of each client and to act with integrity. It is also important to consider the implications of the first principle, requiring that solicitors uphold the administration of justice. This is presumably the basis on which lawyers could break the duty of confidence to clients in order to comply with orders of the court.

There are five outcomes concerned with client confidentiality. These reflect the Law Society Working Party amendment to the Solicitors' Practice Rules 1990. The first and overarching outcome is that 'you keep the affairs of clients confidential unless disclosure is required, or permitted, by law or the client consents'.[130]

a. Affairs of Clients

The duty of confidentiality is extensive. It applies to all matters communicated in confidence by the client to the lawyer. It also covers all other information relating to the representation that the lawyer acquires, regardless of the source. In theory, confidentiality lasts throughout the representation and beyond. It endures even after the death of the client. The information can only be used to advance the client's interests and cannot be used to the detriment of the client.

b. Disclosure to Client of Pre-existing Knowledge of the Client and Matter

The second outcome on confidentiality is not about protecting the secrecy of what clients tell lawyers. Rather, it is about what lawyers must tell clients. Therefore, the outcome is that 'any individual who is advising a client makes that client aware of all information material to that retainer of which the individual has personal knowledge'.[131] Nor is the third outcome about confidentiality as such. Rather it states that 'you ensure that where your duty of confidentiality to one client comes into conflict with your duty of disclosure to another client, your duty of confidentiality takes precedence'.[132]

c. Disclosure Required or Permitted by Law

Exceptions to lawyer client privilege can also arise when there is an overriding public policy. Most jurisdictions permit and may require disclosure to prevent death or substantial bodily injury. Lawyers are often able to disclose information in order to prevent or rectify the consequences of a crime or fraud that injures the financial or property interests of another. The Law Society's 1999 Guide advised that where the solicitor is being 'used by the client to facilitate the commission of a crime or

---

[130] SRA, *SRA Code of Conduct 2011*, as amended, Outcome 4.1.
[131] ibid, Outcome 4.2.
[132] ibid, Outcome 4.3.

fraud' the solicitor is not bound by confidentiality.[133] This accords with the scope of privilege defined by PACE.

An unusual dilemma arises where a lawyer believes it is unethical to comply with a court order. The lawyer may be asked to produce client information or to testify regarding client communications. The lawyer may believe that they owe a superior ethical duty to maintain the confidence and even be prepared to risk prison to protect it. This would doubtless be considered antithetical to upholding the rule of law and proper administration of justice.

d. Client Consent to Disclosure

Confidentiality 'belongs' to the client and not the lawyer; only the client can waive it, either expressly or, sometimes, impliedly. For example, privilege can be inadvertently waived at trial by, for example, a failure to object to prevent testimony about the privileged communications. Under normal circumstances, clients must give informed consent to revealing confidential information or information protected by the privilege.

e. Exception to Requirements

The SRA Handbook countenances circumstances in which a solicitor could act for two clients whose interests are adverse, where confidential information is held on one of them and that client does not consent. This most likely situation to arise is where a prospective client (A) asks a solicitor to act in a matter and the solicitor realises that he holds information on a past client (B) that is relevant to A's matter.

In the circumstances of past client conflict, the obligation of disclosure to A is subordinate to the duty of confidentiality to B (see (b) above). Outcome 4.4 does not, however, operate to preclude a solicitor acting when the duties of confidentiality and disclosure conflict. It provides as follows:

> [Y]ou do not act for A in a matter where A has an interest adverse to B, and B is a client for whom you hold confidential information which is material to A in that matter, unless the confidential information can be protected by the use of safeguards, and:
> (a) you reasonably believe that A is aware of, and understands, the relevant issues and gives informed consent [and];
> (b) either:
>   (i) B gives informed consent and you agree with B the safeguards to protect B's information; or
>   (ii) where this is not possible, you put in place effective safeguards including information barriers which comply with the common law; and
>   it is reasonable in all the circumstances to act for A with such safeguards in place.

The outcome requires that the prospective client, A, gives informed consent. It also requires that the past client, B, does so. If B fails to consent to their former solicitor acting for A, this does not prevent the solicitor acting. In order to act, however, there must be adequate safeguards to protect B's information and it must be reasonable in

---

[133] *Law Society Guide to Professional Conduct of Solicitors*, 8th edn (1999) Principle 16.02, para 1, at 325.

all the circumstances to act. This is a rule of some complexity and it is considered first in the next section on the general context of exceptions.

VII. Exceptions to Solicitors' Duty of Confidentiality

The exceptions to confidentiality can be broadly divided into two groups. The first group covers situations where lawyers are required by law or by conduct rules to break confidence. The second group covers situations where they are may be permitted to do so. There are several exceptions to solicitors' duty of confidentiality either specified in the rules or in the general law. Additionally, the Law Society has reproduced guidance to the Solicitors' Code of Conduct 2007. This is not definitive but it is a useful pointer on some of the issues. It is interesting that the guidance is often designed to ensure that the solicitor does not create a situation where they need to breach confidentiality. As will be seen, such situations are not always avoidable.

A. Requirement to Break Confidence

i. Statutory Requirements to Report

Solicitors and others may be required by statute to breach client confidentiality where money laundering or terrorist activity is suspected.[134] In such cases information may still be protected by privilege.[135] This area is covered in more detail in chapter fourteen: 'Collective Third Parties'.

ii. Request by Lawful Authority

Some public authorities, for example tax authorities, are empowered to require disclosure of confidential information. When lawyers hold this information, requests may be directed at them. Solicitors are advised to check the source of the legal authority for the request, seek the client's specific consent and, if it is not given, to consider whether privileged information is protected from disclosure. They are advised to only provide such information as they are required by law to disclose.[136]

---

[134] SRA, *Solicitors Code of Conduct 2007*, guidance note 11.
[135] Terrorism Act 2000, as amended, ss 19(5)(a) and 21A(5)(b); and see Anti-Terrorism Practice Note issued by the Law Society, July 2007.
[136] *Solicitors Code of Conduct 2007*, guidance note 10.

Solicitors presented with court orders to produce documents are advised to discuss making an application to have the order set aside with the client.[137] They should insist upon receiving a witness summons or subpoena if asked to give evidence, so that, where appropriate, privilege can be claimed.[138] In cases involving publicly funded clients solicitors may be required to convey confidential and privileged information concerning the client to the Legal Aid authorities.[139]

iii. Joint Retainers

Problems may arise where a solicitor acts for two or more clients jointly, for example, for a husband and wife purchasing a property. Generally, the solicitor must share all information with both of the clients. Neither party can expect protection from the rules on confidentiality. There have been a number of cases confirming the duty of solicitors to inform a mortgagee of a change in the mortgagor's circumstances where both are being represented by the same solicitor.

Therefore, if the wife tells the solicitor that she will start divorce proceedings after completion of a property purchase, the solicitor will tell the wife that he must inform the husband. The information is relevant to the purchase and the solicitor acts jointly for both. If the information is irrelevant to the purchase, the confidence should not be broken.

When two clients jointly instruct a solicitor, and one of them has done so in the past, the duty to disclose relevant material to both clients still applies. The past client cannot claim confidentiality in respect of the other.[140] Therefore, if a solicitor knows damaging information about the past client that may affect the new client's view of a matter, they must be informed. Obviously, the existing client needs to be forewarned of this. Where there is a joint retainer, all joint clients must waive their rights before confidential information is given to a third party.[141]

iv. Insolvency and Bankruptcy

a. Insolvency

The task of identifying the client when instructed by an organisation becomes even more of a problem when a company goes into liquidation. The solicitor may perceive a problem when they have dealt with a particular director, particularly if the liquidator may be pursuing individual directors for breach of duty. It is not an exception to confidentiality, in theory at least, because liquidators assume the position of the company itself in relation to this information. They have extensive duties and powers to collect information about the company's business dealings. Therefore, solicitors for companies must provide all the information in their possession to the liquidator.

---

[137] ibid, guidance note 16.
[138] ibid, guidance note 17.
[139] ibid, guidance note 20.
[140] *Hilton v Barker Booth & Eastwood* [2005] UKHL 8.
[141] *Buttes Gas & Oil Co v Hammer No 3* [1981] QB 223, CA.

b. Bankruptcy

Where an individual client becomes bankrupt, there is an obligation to hand over all the bankrupt's property, including papers and records relating to his estate and affairs, to the trustee in bankruptcy. This can apply to confidential or privileged communications with a solicitor.[142] While the trustee in bankruptcy may be thought to be in a similar position to a liquidator, the analogy is imperfect. The bankrupt and the trustee rarely have identical interests. The rules in the Insolvency Act are therefore better thought of as producing an exception to confidentiality.

The combined impact of the principles of confidentiality on joint retainers and bankruptcy is illustrated in the case of *Re Konigsberg*.[143] Mr and Mrs Konigsberg jointly consulted a solicitor in order to transfer property from the husband to the wife. The husband subsequently became bankrupt and the trustee in bankruptcy sought to set aside the transfer as being a voluntary settlement. If this argument were upheld the transfer would be void as against the trustee under the Bankruptcy Act. Mrs Konigsberg objected to the solicitor giving evidence to the trustee on the ground that a communication between solicitor and client was covered by legal advice privilege.

It was held that the communication was properly available to both clients as the solicitor was jointly retained by them. The trustee in bankruptcy had to be treated as being in the same position as the bankrupt client and therefore no assertion of legal privilege could be made to prevent his receipt of the communication. A trustee in bankruptcy, said Peter Gibson J, 'is no ordinary third party'. All the assets of the bankrupt are vested in him and, as a successor in title he 'stands in the predecessor's shoes'.[144]

The likelihood that bankrupts have adverse interest to their trustee in bankruptcy is recognised in the advice given to solicitors. The guidance to Solicitors' Code of Conduct 2007 recognised the distinct interests of bankrupt and trustee in bankruptcy by advising that solicitors should ensure 'that any disclosure you make is strictly limited to what is required by the law'.[145]

B. Permission to Break Confidence

i. Client Consent

It is rare that clients consent to lawyers breaching their confidence. In these cases, the client may sanction disclosure even though this may appear to be against their own interests. This occurred after Rupert Murdoch told the House of Commons Committee for Culture, Media and Sport that the solicitors acting for his company, News International, had made a 'major mistake' in advising the company's internal

---

[142] Insolvency Act 1986, s 311.
[143] *Re Konigsberg* [1989] 3 All ER 289.
[144] ibid, at 297a.
[145] SRA, *Solicitors' Code of Conduct 2007*, r 4, guidance para 8.

investigation of allegations of telephone hacking by journalists.[146] The implication of Murdoch's statement was that the opportunity to uncover criminal activity had been missed by the firm.

The firm, Harbottle & Lewis, contacted the committee alleging it had been erroneously maligned. It was given permission by News International to give evidence to the committee and police about the instructions provided by the client. This, it transpired, involved reading some 2500 emails, looking for evidence implicating the editor of the paper in phone-hacking.[147] It did not therefore include looking for other kinds of criminal activity, such as making payments to police.

ii. Past and Present Clients

There is duty of complete disclosure to present clients of information known about their matter. This duty is potentially in conflict with the duty to preserve past client confidences, especially where the past client's information relates to the present matter. There are a number of conditions that must be satisfied before a past client can consent to a solicitors' acting for a present client in the same or a related matter.

Before a past client (B) can waive a right to prevent a firm acting for a proposed client (A), A must consent to the solicitor not making full disclosure. That consent must be informed. A must know that the firm holds relevant information that it cannot disclose and, before they consent, they need to have a reasonable idea of what that is. This must be done in such a way that it does not breach B's confidence. B must then consent to the firm acting for A and it must be possible to establish a satisfactory information barrier to protect B's information.

Where a conflict between the duty of confidentiality and that of disclosure arises *without* consent, solicitors might still be able to act for B. The relevant outcome covers situations where it is 'not possible' to obtain consent. This presumably does not mean 'it is not possible to obtain consent because the past client refuses it'. Rather, it envisages a situation where the past client cannot be contacted. Such a situation might occur where two firms merge and the client is either physically unable to consent or cannot be traced.

Finally, the outcome specifies that, even with consents and information barriers in place, it must be reasonable for the firm to act. There is no guidance on what this means. Possibly it is intended as a safeguard against a foolish client consenting against their own interests. In such circumstances, the solicitor must consider the degree of risk in any conflict between A and B's interests.

It is anticipated that circumstances that meet the solicitors' rules for acting in breach of past client confidentiality will be relatively rare. The potential client is unlikely to consent to their lawyer holding back information that could be useful, particularly when they cannot be given any clue what it is. If they do consent, their lawyer may have a hard job convincing a court that the client's consent was truly

---

[146] L O'Carroll, J Martinson and C Davies, 'Law firm fights Murdoch's mistake claim' *The Guardian* 21 July 2011.

[147] L O'Carroll, 'Phone hacking: Harbottle & Lewis lawyer "found no criminal activity"' *The Guardian* 9 September 2011.

informed.[148] The past client is unlikely to consent to the risk of leaks adversely affecting their interests. The expectation that the rule applies only to 'sophisticated' clients probably anticipates that commercial clients will take a long-term and reasonable view of clients switching lawyers. In a commercial environment, that may be optimistic.

iii. Prevention of Harm

Lawyers are usually allowed to disclose information that may prevent harm to third parties. This may anticipate the possibility that they could be sued for negligence if they failed to do so. This proposition is based on the US case, *Tarasoff v Regents of the University of California*.[149] In that case, a disturbed student stalked and killed a fellow student who had rejected his advances. A mental health professional, who was consulted by the killer and knew of the specific threat to the named victim, was held to have a duty to protect persons who were subject to a specific threat from their patients.

Provision for the possibility that solicitors might discover threats to third parties from clients was made previously in the solicitors' codes and guidance. For example, the guidance to the 2007 Code stated that solicitors may reveal confidential information if they 'believe it necessary to prevent the client or a third party from committing a crime that [they] reasonably believe is likely to result in serious bodily harm'.[150] It is notable that the exception is framed as a permission to break confidence. It was not a requirement that confidence is breached, even when serious harm is anticipated.

The formulation of the physical harm exception to confidentiality had three apparently essential requirements; activity constituting a crime, the likelihood of serious bodily harm to a third party and a reasonable belief on the part of the solicitor that this would occur. The guidance to the old rules was not totally clear on what degree of risk and what level of harm would justify breaking confidentiality. Would it be sufficient, for example, if bodily injury was not the purpose of a crime, for example armed robbery, but an incidental risk? What was fairly clear was that solicitors could not break confidence and reveal anticipated crimes which did *not* involve serious bodily harm.

The very specific conditions in which solicitors could breach confidentiality created a complex but consistent position. Solicitors were bound by confidentiality where the client revealed details about a criminal offence, however heinous, and about relevant past offences. Solicitors could not reveal material covered by legal privilege, even if it would prevent serious harm to another, such as an innocent person serving a term of imprisonment. This privilege does not, however, exist when withholding information amounts to furthering a criminal purpose.

The current SRA Handbook does not mention a prevention of harm exception in the chapter on confidentiality. It is, however, very likely to be accepted by regulators and tribunals as a 'live' exception. In fact, it is a surprise that it has only ever applied

---

[148] SE Mize, 'Should the Lawyer's Duty to Keep Confidences Override the Duty to Disclose Material Information to a Client' (2009) 12(2) *Legal Ethics* 171, at 205.

[149] *Tarasoff v Regents of the University of California* (1976) 131 Cal Rpter 14.

[150] SRA, *Solicitors Code of Conduct 2007*, r 4.02, guidance para 13.

to prospective criminal activity. This is at odds with the rules in some other jurisdictions. The US Model Rules, for example, also cover 'substantial injury to the financial interests or property of another'.[151] It is possible however, that wider types of harm such as these could be covered by disclosure in the public interest, considered below.

iv. Children under Threat

Many jurisdictions in the United States have 'reporting' statutes in relation to child abuse which require professionals, including lawyers, to break confidence and inform the authorities where they have reason to suspect child abuse. There are no such statutory provisions in this country. The 1999 guidance to solicitors stated that, '[o]nly in cases where the solicitor believes that the public interest in protecting children outweighs the public interest in maintaining the duty of confidentiality could the solicitor have a discretion to disclose confidential information'.

The Solicitors' Code of Conduct 2007 anticipated situations where child clients revealed continuing sexual or other physical abuse but refused to allow disclosure of such information. A report could, but did not have to, be made to Social Services or the police in these circumstances. The advice provided under the Code suggested that solicitors should 'consider whether the threat to the child's life or health, both mental and physical, is sufficiently serious to justify a breach of the duty of confidentiality'.[152] The balancing of 'sufficiently serious abuse' with a duty of confidence is very difficult. It suggests that even some 'serious' abuse is accepted. The formula may therefore suggest a presumption against reporting.

v. Disclosure in the Public Interest

Professional codes sometimes contain a public interest exception to a duty of confidentiality. Doctors, for example, can breach confidentiality under this head where secrecy would cause serious harm to anyone.[153] There is academic support for extending this type of obligation.[154] The possible impact of such an exception can be deduced from *W v Egdell*,[155] where protecting public safety prevailed over the public interest in confidentiality.

Doctor Egdell was instructed by solicitors for W, a patient detained under mental health legislation, to prepare a report on W. This was to be used by W's solicitor as evidence in a hearing before a Mental Health Review Tribunal (MHRT) considering W's release. The report opposed W's release from a mental hospital on the ground that he was a danger to the public. W abandoned his application to the MHRT in the light of this report and it was not revealed to the tribunal.

---

[151] ABA, *Model Rules of Professional Conduct*, r 1.6.
[152] SRA, *Solicitors Code of Conduct 2007*, guidance note 14.
[153] General Medical Council, *Confidentiality* (London, General Medical Council, 1995).
[154] D Nicolson and J Webb, *Professional Legal Ethics* (Oxford, Oxford University Press, 1999) at 263 and see ch 14: 'Collective Third Parties'.
[155] *W v Egdell* [1990] 1 All ER 835.

The doctor was concerned that the decision not to pursue the application for release mean that the relevant authorities were not aware how dangerous he considered W to be. He was particularly concerned that there was a process of automatic review under which the hospital might release W voluntarily. He therefore sent a copy of the report to the hospital and to the Secretary of State.

W applied for an injunction to restrain further disclosure of the report and also for damages for breach of confidence. It was accepted by counsel that legal professional privilege did not arise.[156] The question had been argued in the court below and Scott J had found that expert evidence is evidence of fact and therefore not subject to legal professional privilege.[157] The Court held that the public interest required disclosure of Egdell's report.

The principle underpinning *Egdell* is that a doctor who fears that a decision to release a prisoner will be made on the basis of inadequate information is justified in breaking a confidential relationship.[158] Whether such a principle applies also to lawyers, at least in quite the same way, is doubtful. First, in Egdell, the patient had a solicitor who strenuously opposed the doctor's right of disclosure, without criticism or comment from the court. What distinguishes the doctor and the lawyer in the situation is not, as has been argued, that the lawyer's ethics are more self-interested than the doctors' ethics.[159] It lies in the nature of the roles of the professionals in the particular situation, and specifically, the duty of loyalty of the lawyer.

The public interest is not mentioned in the 10 mandatory principles providing the framework of the present SRA Handbook. It is however mentioned in the notes to the Principles. Here, it says that '[w]here two or more Principles come into conflict, the Principle which takes precedence is the one which best serves the public interest in the particular circumstances'.[160] It is doubtful that public interest disclosure falls within duties to uphold the rule of law or the proper administration of justice. At the high level of generality at which the principles operate, it is more likely that avoiding third party harm is integral to acting with integrity or not allowing one's independence to be compromised.

It may be fanciful to read an obligation to avoid third party harm into the principles. If it were so, invoking the public interest would provide a considerable counterweight to client loyalty. It would open up a public interest exception going beyond the harm caused by commission of a crime. Imagine a situation where a client tells a solicitor that his litigation adversary's occupied building is seriously unsafe, but asks the solicitor not to reveal the information for tactical reasons. The *Derby Magistrates* case, with its robust 'no exceptions' approach to legal privilege, suggests that the solicitor must stay silent. A public interest exception may suggest the opposite.

---

[156] ibid, at 846b.
[157] But see McHale 'Confidentiality, an Absolute Obligation' (n 45) at 719.
[158] *W v Egdell* (n 155) per Bingham LJ at 852–53.
[159] K Wheat, 'Lawyers, Confidentiality and Public and Private Interests' (1998) 1(2) *Legal Ethics* 184.
[160] SRA, *Handbook 2011*, as amended, pt 1, para 2(2).

If the case of *Egdell* were applied to solicitors, then the courts might well accept the argument that,

> as a matter of public policy ... the solicitor ought to be entitled, without either being liable to action by his client or to a charge of professional misconduct, to take the necessary steps in the public interest to prevent death or serious injury.[161]

This, it seems, is an unlikely development for reasons already canvassed. Were it possible, of course, it assumes that a solicitor would wish to break his client's confidence in the public interest. It would be a significantly bigger step if they were under a positive obligation of disclosure in such circumstances.

The implications can be seen in the investigation of the allegations of 'phone-hacking' by *News of the World* journalists. A solicitor with Farrer and Co, well known as acting for the Queen, had represented Rupert Murdoch's company, News International, the parent company of the newspaper. He admitted to the House of Commons Select Committee for Culture, Media and Sport that he had realised that Parliament had been misled when told that telephone hacking was the act of a 'rogue reporter'.[162] He had not spoken out, he said, because of client confidentiality.

Had the evidence been given in court, the solicitor would have had to counsel his client against perjury and withdraw from the case if the issue was not rectified.[163] It is arguable that misleading Parliament is at least analogous. A clearer case for public interest disclosure may not be obvious, but, given the nature of the legal role, it is still debatable that respecting client confidentiality was the wrong decision.

C. Client Litigation against Solicitors

When clients sue their solicitors, complain or bring proceedings to the Solicitors Disciplinary Tribunal, confidentiality vanishes.[164] The solicitor can, but can choose not to, reveal confidential information from the client in order to establish a defence. The technical explanation is not that this is an exception to confidentiality or privilege, but that the client has impliedly waived both.[165] Confidentiality is not therefore waived where the solicitor initiated the proceedings against the client, as in an action for fees.

An example of the operation of these rules is *Lillicrap v Nalder & Son*.[166] The claimants were property developers for whom the defendant solicitors had acted in a number of purchases. In relation to one purchase, the claimant alleged that the solicitors had negligently failed to tell them of a right of way over the land. The solicitors admitted negligence but maintained that this did not cause loss. The claimants would have gone ahead with the purchase anyway.

---

[161] M Brindle and G Dehn, 'Confidence, Public Interest and the Lawyer' in R Cranston (ed), *Legal Ethics and Professional Responsibility* (Oxford, Clarendon Press, 1995) 122.
[162] J Robinson, 'Hacking lawyer was aware NI had misled parliament' *The Guardian* 20 October 2011.
[163] See ch 19: 'Advocacy'.
[164] SRA, *Solicitors' Code of Conduct 2007*, r 4, guidance para 19.
[165] N Taylor (ed), *The Guide to the Professional Conduct of Solicitors*, 7th edn (London, The Law Society, 1996).
[166] *Lillicrap v Nalder & Son* [1993] 1 All ER 724 CA.

The solicitors produced evidence that, in six other transactions in which they had acted, the claimants had bought property despite having been told of various risks. The claimants considered that this evidence was covered by legal privilege. On appeal it was held that, once the client had instituted proceedings against the solicitors, they had impliedly waived privilege in relation to all documents relevant to the suit.

VIII. Barristers and Confidentiality

A. Bar Code of Conduct 1981, as Amended

Under the old Bar Code, barristers were required to 'preserve the confidentiality of the lay client's affairs' and not reveal 'the contents of the papers in any instructions' or any other information entrusted to him without the prior consent of the lay client.[167] They were not to use confidential client information 'to the client's detriment or to his own or another client's advantage'. No possible exceptions were mentioned. The refusal of instructions because of a 'significant risk' of a breach of client confidentiality was one of the exceptions to the cab rank rule.[168]

B. The Code of Conduct of the Bar of England and Wales 2014

Core Duty 6 of the new Bar Code is that a barrister 'must keep the affairs of each client confidential'. This obligation is said to be 'central to the administration of justice'.[169] The treatment of confidentiality in the new code is subject to disclosures 'permitted or required by law or to which your client gives informed consent', which would not amount to a breach of CD6.[170] The treatment is slightly more extensive than it was in the previous code. It is more focused on advocacy than is the solicitors' code. Barristers are reminded that the duty to the court, and the requirement not to mislead the court, does not mean that they should compromise confidentiality.[171] There is also material on reconciling those duties in presenting cases to the court.[172] Self-employed barristers must make proper arrangements for managing conflicts of interest and the confidentiality of clients' affairs'.[173]

---

[167] Bar Council, *Bar Code of Conduct 1981*, as amended, at para 702.
[168] ibid, pt VI, para 603(f), and see also para 608.
[169] BSB, *Handbook 2014*, pt 2, The Code of Conduct, CD6.
[170] ibid, r C15.5.
[171] ibid, gC13.
[172] ibid, guidance to C1. And see ch 19: 'Advocacy'.
[173] ibid, rC89.5.

The new Bar Code of Conduct also addresses potential problems caused by knowledge of past clients' affairs. It provides that

> [y]ou must not accept instructions to act in a particular matter if there is a real risk that information confidential to another former or existing client, or any other person to whom you owe duties of confidence, may be relevant to the matter, such that if obliged to maintain confidentiality, you could not act in the best interests of the prospective client, and the former or existing client or person to whom you owe that duty does not give informed consent to disclosure of that confidential information.[174]

This rather wordy formula, which leaves it to a barrister to decide whether they can still represent a client, may not give past clients much comfort. The rule is more relaxed rule than that which applies to solicitors. This may be explained by the fact that barristers retain no document or formal record of previous clients' matters. It may also be because barristers tend not to be involved in business negotiations between clients.

IX. Conclusion

Confidentiality, supported by legal professional privilege, is the bedrock of the distinctive social role of lawyers and of legal ethics. Confidentiality and privilege are also valuable commodities; a package that only lawyers can deliver to clients. Aspects of the doctrine of legal professional privilege are under increasing attack. It is understandable that the courts have been willing to abrogate litigation privilege in proceedings relating to children. They are keen to detect abuse before deciding issues concerning a child's future. These incursions into privilege have been made on the ground that the proceedings are not adversarial.

Lack of adversarial context is a dangerous ground on which to assert that there is no justification for maintaining legal privilege. Lord Woolf's reform of civil litigation aimed at reducing the adversarial ethos. There is greater emphasis on disclosure, openness and co-operation. If the relevance of privilege is determined by the adversarial nature of proceedings, lawyers and clients would be in a constant state of uncertainty. Better therefore to proceed by way of clearly justified exceptions to the assumption of privilege.

The second justification for attacking privilege is the need to protect the public interest. Privilege may, in some cases, have to give way to the need to protect the welfare of a child or the prevention or detection of crimes. The obvious example is the speedy development of the money laundering legislation to cover all proceeds of crime. In effect, lawyers act as gatekeepers in order to assist in the detection of certain financial crime. This, however, apparently marks the limits of government's desire to constrain confidentiality in the public interest for the present.

---

[174] ibid, rC21.4.

Money laundering can be seen as a special case. Laundering is possible only if the launderer engages the services of a lawyer under the cloak of secrecy provided by professional privilege. The privilege is therefore being abused to allow the client to benefit from the proceeds of his or her unlawful acts and not simply to prepare a defence. The extension of an obligation to break confidence in other situations of potential harm would be a radical departure for lawyers. It would also, arguably, be in contradiction of the obligation to uphold the rule of law.

Preserving confidence and privilege hinges on trust in professionals. Society allows confidence to reign in the public interest, but at the cost of other public goods. This is an area where particularly high professional and ethical standards are required from lawyers when advising clients. To put it at its lowest level, the commercial interests of the profession demand ethical behaviour or this valuable commodity, legal professional privilege, will be lost. This, then, is perhaps a prime example of why the legal profession must maintain high values and ethicality.

11

Conflicts of Interest

'There can be no betrayal if there is no pre-existing trust'.[1]

I. Introduction

A central tenet of professional practice is that lawyers should promote the best interests of clients. One of the most basic protections, and manifestations, of loyalty to clients is the lawyer's duty to avoid conflicts of interest. Situations of conflict can arise between client interests and those of the lawyer or between the interests of two or more clients. Unlike rules on confidentiality, those on conflicts of interest have attracted only moderate academic criticism. Perhaps this is because unlike confidentiality, conflict rules only operate to the commercial disadvantage of lawyers. They require lawyers to forgo business rather than help them to acquire it.

Conflicts of interest are not uncontroversial. It is one of the areas in which there can be very different approaches to definition, and variations in treatment, between jurisdictions. Lawyers in England and Wales have occasionally pressed to relax the scope of rules against conflicts so that they can acquire or hold on to business. This has sometimes resulted in elaborate evasions and justifications. Rules designed to maximise conveyancing business are an example of this. To the lay observer there is a clear conflict of interest, but there is no absolute prohibition on lawyers acting for both sides in conveyancing.

II. Foundation

This idea that conflicts of interest must be avoided is often said to derive from the adversarial nature of common law systems. Adversarial systems require that each

---

[1] AC Grayling, *The Meaning of Things: Applying Philosophy to Life* (London, Weidenfeld and Nicholson, 2001) at 51.

party to a dispute has someone on their side whose duty it is 'to advocate its own case and to assault the case of the other' irrespective of the moral or other merits of that client or the case.[2] Whilst rules on conflict of interest and confidentiality are closely connected with the adversarial process, they can also be justified independently of it.

Rules against conflicts protect client autonomy. A lawyer is retained by a client in order to do what the client would have done for him or herself, given the necessary knowledge, skills or time. The lawyer provides access to the law, increasing the client's ability to engage with society.[3] The justification rooted in client autonomy applies just as much to non-contentious business, such as making wills or drafting contracts, as to contentious business. The need for the lawyer to act disinterestedly, in the interests of the client alone, is important in any context.

Conflict of interest is sometimes closely linked to confidentiality, as shown in the previous chapter in relation to the treatment of lawyers with an apparent conflict of interest between past and present clients. Unless clients can confide absolutely freely in the lawyer, confident that the information will not be used to their disadvantage, they cannot be sure that lawyers are willing to act for them as they would act for themselves. If clients cannot be sure who else their lawyer owes allegiance to, they cannot be sure how frank they can afford to be.

III. The Nature of Interests

A. Material and Personal Interests

In this chapter interests means benefits or advantages which a person may wish to assert, acquire, defend or promote. Typically interests have a material dimension, being valued as pecuniary assets. Material interests include sources of income, financial or property interests. Other interests may be purely personal, such as maintaining good family relations. Sometimes material and personal interests intersect. Examples include business relationships, or maintaining certain unpaid public offices. While these may not appear to have a material dimension, they may hold the key to pecuniary advantage.

Obligations to respect or defend people's interests assume that these are identifiable. Individuals may be able to identify and articulate what their interests are. Where a lawyer represents a child or an incompetent person it is clear that the person in front of them is the client, but who instructs the lawyer or decides what the best interests

---

[2] D Luban, *Lawyers and Justice: An Ethical Study* (Princeton and New Jersey, Princeton University Press, 1988) at xx and 57.

[3] SL Pepper, 'The Lawyer's Amoral Ethical Role: A Defense, A Problem, and Some Possibilities' (1986) 11(4) *American Bar Foundation Research Journal* 613 and the response by D Luban, 'The Lysistratian Prerogative: A Response to Stephen Pepper' (1986) 11(4) *American Bar Foundation Research Journal* 637.

of the client are? Institutions or corporations are made up of many individuals and interests and it may be less easy to identify them all or to prioritise them.[4]

The difficulty of determining organisational interests is illustrated by the example of the prosecution lawyer. Is the prosecutor's client the Crown or the Crown Prosecution Service? Are the interests of each organisation different? Do they share an 'interest' in maximising convictions or particular dispositions of cases? If not, what are their interests? Sir Herbert Stephen wrote that the role of the prosecutor was 'not to get a conviction without qualification, but to get a conviction only if justice requires it'. In similar vein, the CPS Statement of Purpose and Values (1993) required prosecutors to treat defendants 'fairly'.[5] Therefore, it is fair to say that the CPS has interests other than merely gaining convictions.

B. Moral Interests

It is arguable that lawyers have an interest in maintaining their personal moral standards. This interest may conflict with the interests of clients. A clash of moral standards between lawyer and client is not usually treated as a conflict of interests. Were it to be so, it could be a basis for a lawyer refusing representation. Generally however, lawyers are only able to escape their professional obligations when the client requires illegal conduct or conduct specifically forbidden by rules. A good example is the duty not to deceive the court.

IV. The Nature of Conflicts

A. Situations

There are four main situations presenting actual or potential conflicts of interest in the lawyer and client relationship. The first is conflict between the lawyer's and the client's interests. The second is a conflict between two present clients. The third is between the interests of a former client and a present client in the same matter. The fourth is between the interests of a former client and a present client in a different matter.

---

[4] WH Simon, 'Whom (or What) Does the Organisation's Lawyer Represent? An Anatomy of Intra-client Conflict' (2003) 91 *California Law Review* 59.

[5] A Ashworth, 'Ethics and Criminal Justice' in R Cranston (ed), *Legal Ethics and Professional Responsibility*, (Oxford, Clarendon Press, 1995) at 172.

B. Torn Loyalties

A conflict of interests creates a risk that someone with a duty towards another may suffer torn loyalties. It is not possible, for example, to perform fiduciary duties to two competing or disputing clients simultaneously. The possibility that a person's motivation to act in accordance with their duty may be undermined by a conflict is sufficient. Actual corruption of their motivation is not required. It is the risk of corruption that creates a conflict of interest, rather than actual corruption.

Between past and present clients there is no torn loyalty. The problems usually relate to the duty of confidentiality. The duty to disclose relevant information to a client is subject to the duty of confidentiality owed to all clients. If a lawyer holds information affecting the interests of a current client in a matter in which they are instructed, but cannot disclose it because of confidentiality, he used to be seen to have a conflict of interests. Except in limited circumstances, a lawyer should not continue to act for a client to whom he cannot disclose material information.

A contentious issue is whether a duty of loyalty continues in the same way as a duty of confidentiality. If, for example, a lawyer is asked to act for a competitor of a previous client, should that previous client expect loyalty as well as the preservation of their confidentiality? It may be that the lawyer does not know anything specific about the past client that must be protected as a confidence. He will, however, inevitably know general things about the past client's business that could be very helpful to a present client, particularly if they are a competitor of the past client. In general, therefore, there is an issue about whether lawyers should be prohibited from acting in such situations.

C. Material Conflicts

No human being can act in a way that totally or exclusively prioritises the interests of another. A lawyer's considerations include the need to run an efficient or profitable practice, balancing their own workload and managing relationships with partners and family. In reality, it is not possible to eliminate all these other considerations from the lawyer's mind when dealing with clients. It may not be desirable that they do so. It is naive for any professional, whether doctor, lawyer or social worker, to maintain that they *always* put the interests, or the best interests, of the patient, client or child first. On material issues, however, they must do so.

V. The Common Law Position

Injunctions are issued by the courts to prevent solicitors acting in conflict of interest situations. They tend to be granted, however, only where it can be shown that harm will be caused otherwise.[6] Courts often act to offer redress in conflict of interest situations, without necessarily recognising them as such. Many of the cases involve lawyers, although other professions, persons and institutions in conflict of interest situations add to the jurisprudence. The professional conduct rules reflect these decisions.

A. Conflict between the Lawyer's Interest and those of one or more Clients (Own Interest Conflicts)

At common law, solicitors would not be allowed to defend transactions with clients that were advantageous to the lawyer unless they could show that they had disclosed all the material facts.[7] Where they had done so, however, and it could be shown that the client had understood the terms of an arrangement, the solicitor would not be held to account.[8] Some court cases suggest that the legal profession was slow to recognise the danger of own interest conflicts. In the Peggy Wood case in 1993, the Law Society saw no conflict of interest where a solicitor arranged a loan between clients, even though the solicitor had a substantial interest in the loan company.[9]

B. Conflicts of Interest between Simultaneous Clients

i. Criminal Proceedings

In criminal defence, lawyers are generally precluded from acting for a party against the interests of a former client. The qualification is necessary because the criminal courts have not developed definitive rules. The case of *R v Ataou*,[10] illustrates the kind of situation that can arise and the risks of solicitors continuing to act for one of two former clients when their interests diverge.

In *Ataou*, three men were arrested in a car and charged with conspiracy to supply heroin. The appellant claimed he had nothing to do with the dealings of the other two in the case, but had merely been a visitor at the flat of one of them, a drug dealer, H. The appellant's solicitors acted for both the appellant and H. H pleaded guilty and gave evidence for the prosecution, contradicting the appellant's account. Because of the conflict of interest between them, H was invited to find other solicitors.

At the trial, H said that the appellant was involved in the conspiracy to supply heroin. During the course of H's evidence, a representative of the appellant's solicitors was looking through his file. He found an attendance note of a meeting with H, prepared by a former employee of the firm. The note recorded H's assertion that the appellant was not involved with any dealings concerning heroin.

---

[6] *David Lee Co Lincoln Limited v Coward Chance* [1991] Ch 259.
[7] *McMaster v Byrne* [1952] 1 All ER 1362.
[8] *Hanson v Lorenz Jones* [1986] NLJ Rep 1088.
[9] O Hansen, 'The Lessons of the Peggy Wood Case' *Legal Action* October 1993, at 19.
[10] *R v Ataou* [1988] 1 QB 798.

The appellant's counsel sought to cross-examine H on the basis of the alleged previous inconsistent statement. H claimed privilege and the judge ruled that cross-examination without H's consent would be a breach of privilege between client and solicitor. The appellant was convicted and appealed against the judge's ruling. The Court of Appeal allowed the appeal because the trial judge had not heard relevant arguments on the asserted privilege. This, however, is merely the context. The relevant part is the Court of Appeal's response to the disclosure of the attendance note.

The Court of Appeal deplored the handling of the situation by the solicitor's representative. By informing counsel of the note, the solicitors' representative had acted in complete disregard of the firm's duty of confidentiality to H, their former client. In delivering the judgment French J offered the opinion that

> the solicitors' profession should, we consider, be alert to prevent any similar problem arising in future, particularly where … counsel is assisted at the trial by a representative who is … [not] familiar with the rules of confidentiality governing the profession.

The case also illustrates how solicitors can be affected by a conflict of interest in a case while a barrister acting for the same client is not affected. The duty that the solicitors were under did not affect the appellant's whole team of representatives. The court found that counsel's duty was to make the argument of behalf his client, the appellant. He owed no duty to anyone else.

Surprisingly, in view of the lecture given to the lawyers in *Ataou*, the Court did not endorse a ban on acting for multiple defendants in the circumstances of the case. French J was only prepared to say that '[w]e consider it at least doubtful, in circumstances where conflict may arise at the trial between the interests of an existing and a former client, whether it is proper for a solicitor to continue to act for either client'. Presumably this reticence was necessary because of the possibility of circumstances where lawyers may be constrained in withdrawing. If, for example, a trial has reached an advanced stage, the balance of argument may be in favour of them continuing to act, despite a risk of conflict of interest.

Firmer guidance was given to lawyers on what to do in the circumstances found in *Ataou* in *Saminadhen v Khan*.[11] In that case Lord Donaldson said,

> I can conceive of no circumstances in which it would be proper for a solicitor who has acted for a defendant in criminal proceedings, the retainer having been terminated, to then act for a co-defendant where there is a cut-throat defence between the two defendants.

ii. Civil Litigation

a. Co-defendants

Civil litigation may appear to lack the dynamic that gives rise to conflicts of interest as dramatic as those in criminal litigation. It is, however, easy to imagine circumstances where defendant parties may have a common interest in defeating a claim, but divergent interests in how it is defended. Such circumstances might arise where

---

[11] *Saminadhen v Khan* [1992] 1 All ER 963.

an employer could be vicariously liable for an employee's negligence. In such circumstances, there are divergent interests in arguing against the finding of fault. Allocation of liability could determine which party is likely to pay damages. Similarly an owner and tenant of land may have a common interest in defeating the claim of a trespasser, but divergent interests in how the claim should be defended.

b. Class Actions

Class actions were common in early English law. They allowed several claimants, possibly with small claims, to band together, save costs and make it worth a lawyer's while to represent them. The class action died out in England in the nineteenth century. The circumstances of modern life suggest a need for class actions. Major disasters, such as air crashes, adverse reactions to drugs or environmental problems, can affect large groups of people, all or some of whom may want to seek compensation. Modern society also creates conditions that make class actions viable; wide and targeted communication means that hardly any member of a class is not contactable.

Although there is a case for the viability of class actions, the arguments for them are not all supportive. There may be conflicts of interest between the victims and also between them and their lawyers. Some victims may not be aware that litigation is underway or, if they are, will not understand what is happening. The majority of the victims may leave the matter to a small group of representative claimants or even to the lawyers alone.

The difficulties of managing class actions mean that they are relatively rare anywhere else than the US. There, a well-established procedure follows once proceedings are launched by individuals with common claims. The defendant is typically ordered to provide information allowing for the class to be identified and certified by the court. Despite some advantages for claimants, class actions in the US have a reputation for being abused. This is partly because of the rules, such as those requiring members of a class to 'opt out' and partly because of incentives for lawyers to litigate, like contingency fees.[12]

In England and Wales, mass actions demonstrated the problems of not having a developed system of class actions. Prior to the creation of new Civil Procedure Rules in 1998 two options existed. The first option was that the parties sued at the same time, leaving the court to join them as parties equally involved in the progress of the case. The second option involved some parties bringing the action as representatives of others. This avoided the need to join large numbers of people as claimants, but every person represented was bound by the outcome of the litigation.

Representative actions were comparatively rare. The more common multi-party group actions include litigation relating to injury caused by industrial operations, for example, asbestosis and mining, contraception, Dalkon Shield for example, and drugs, for example Opren.[13] A multi-party action against British Coal in respect of

---

[12] S Goldfein and J Keyte, 'European Commission Releases Proposals on Antitrust Class Actions' (2013) 250(11) *New York Law Journal* (www.skadden.com/sites/default/files/publications/070071321%20 Skadden.pdf).

[13] M Day and S Moore, 'Multi-party Actions: A Plaintiff View' in R Smith (ed), *Shaping the Future New Directions in Legal Services* (London, Legal Action Group, 1995) at 188.

miners' lung disease was relatively successful, leading to a compensation scheme being established.[14]

The Opren case concerned the alleged side-effects of the anti-arthritis drug. Two group actions, involving about 1500 claimants, were launched against the manufacturers, Eli Lilly & Co and were co-ordinated by a group of solicitors known as the Opren Action Group (OAG). The clients set up an Opren Action Committee (OAC), and the Law Society set up a register of solicitors acting for Opren victims.

The management of the Opren case was difficult, with underlying conflict between the different groups. It was further complicated by funding issues. The action was brought only by claimants entitled to legal aid, but the Court ordered that the costs of the action should be shared equally by all claimants, including those not legally aided.[15] The unaided parties naturally had a different attitude towards the risks of the litigation than the legally aided, the latter being unlikely to face any personal liability for the costs of the action.

A settlement was finally reached whereby a lump sum payment was agreed with the defendants and was distributed between the various claimants by the solicitors in OAG, subject to an appeal to a judge as arbitrator. It subsequently transpired that the solicitors did not discuss the terms of the settlement with OAC and, moreover, told their clients that if the settlement were not agreed they would cease to act.[16]

The Opren case illustrated the actual and potential conflicts inherent in class-based litigation. The case involved investigations and scientific research costing millions of pounds. Without acting as a class, the group would have been unable to get any redress, bearing in mind the complexity and costs of the litigation. The parties had to sacrifice some of the protection provided by conflict of interest rules in order to obtain benefits, in terms of finance and expertise. These inherent conflicts had to be appropriately managed if justice was to be done equally to all the parties.

Lord Woolf's Final Report on civil justice recommended special procedures for managing group actions. The Civil Procedure Rules 1998 reintroduced the possibility of class actions in England and Wales.[17] The rules allowed one or more persons with the same interest in a claim to begin or, at the order of the court, continue an action. This may be by, or against, one or more of the persons with the same interest as representatives of any other persons who have that interest.[18] The court may, on application or on its own motion, make a group litigation order. This will set up a register establishing the court and judge, the issues and the management of the case.

There were only two reported cases launched in the first 10 years of the operation of the rules. This low number of class actions may reflect the English courts' caution regarding aggregated claims, perhaps because of the scope of potential liability. Actions have failed where the claimant group cannot be clearly defined.[19] There has

---

[14] See *The Lawyer* 10 February 1998.

[15] *Davies v Eli Lilly & Co* [1987] 1 WLR 1136.

[16] G Dehn, 'Opren: Problems, Solutions and more Problems' (1989) 12 *Journal of Consumer Policy* 397.

[17] Civil Procedure Rules 1998, as amended, pt 19 III Group Litigation, rr 19.10–15 and the associated practice direction.

[18] ibid, pt 19.6.

[19] *Emerald Supplies Limited & Anor v British Airways* [2010] EWCA Civ 1284.

been limited use of similar mechanisms, such as group litigation orders and opt-in actions under the Competition Act 1998, section 47B.[20]

There is suspicion of class actions, certainly on the US model, across Europe. This aversion is such that policy-makers use terms like 'collective actions' and 'representative actions'.[21] Such actions are, however, suited to consumer class actions and have advantages as a means of facilitating competition policy. The opt-in model has severe limitations because, in most situations, it severely limits the scale of damages.

The European Competition Commissioner, Joaquín Almunia, signalled plans for Europe-wide measures to be published in 2011. The proposal finally appeared in 2013 with a view to implementing a directive for 2015–16. The particular focus is class actions in competition cases. The European Commission estimates that, in Europe alone, breaches of competition law amount to over 20 billion euros (£16.6 billion) a year of uncollected damages.[22] The proposals are not limited in to competition cases however.

Class actions raise issues of conflict of interest, both within and beyond an identified class. There is an obvious risk that individuals' interests will not be prioritised, for example, where a claim is pursued by a core group of activists. This risk has to be balanced against the possibility that individual claimants will not be bothered to pursue small claims. It seems inevitable that an opt-out regime, of the type that encourages class actions, will be introduced to the UK.[23] This is likely to be heavily policed by the courts, in order to prevent abuse of the litigation process by claimants and by lawyers. It is likely that court regulation, rather than conduct rules, will be the primary mechanism for regulating agents.

C. Transactions

i. Conveyancing

Solicitors acting for a purchaser in conveyancing transactions were frequently also instructed by the mortgage lender providing the loan to purchase the property. This is advantageous to the lender, since the solicitor is able to provide assurances on title and hold monies. In most circumstances this does not present a problem. Purchasers benefit because they might otherwise have to pay for another solicitor to represent the lender. They save the additional cost of a lawyer familiarising themselves with the

---

[20] P Boylan and D Bridge, 'Different Class: UK Representative Actions Suffer a Setback' (http://uk.practicallaw.com/7-504-0554?sd=plc).

[21] B Wardhaugh, 'Bogeyman, lunatics and fanatics: collective actions and the private enforcement of European law' (2014) 34(1) *Legal Studies* 1, at 2.

[22] BFY Chee, 'EU to pave way for class actions against cartels' *Reuters* (http://uk.reuters.com/article/2013/06/06/uk-eu-classactions-idUKBRE95514R20130606).

[23] Office of Fair Trading, *Private Actions in Competition Law: A Consultation on Options for Reform: The OFT's Response to the Government's Consultation* (London, OFT, 2012) at para 1.2; Department of Business, Innovation and Skills, *Private Actions in Competition Law: A Consultation on Options for Reform— Government Response* (London, BIS, 2013).

file. Representing both borrower and lender has caused considerable litigation against solicitors.

Lord Justice Peter Gibson noted in *National Home Loans Corporation v Giffen Couch & Archer*,[24] that

> the recession and the collapse of the housing market at the beginning of this decade, left mortgage lenders, who had vied with each other to obtain business in the 1980's, with defaulting mortgagors and substantial losses which they were unable to recover out of the security they had taken. This has led mortgage lenders to seek ways to recover their losses from others, and actions in negligence against their professional advisers have become only too common.[25]

Actions by lenders whose borrowers have defaulted on the repayments caused heavy calls upon the compensation fund. Several cases occurred before the rules were changed to restrict the terms of instructions from mortgage lenders. In the *National Home Loans Corporation* case, the loan company lent the borrower over £92,000 on the security of a home which was already subject to another mortgage. On default of repayment the property was sold for £70,000. The loan company sued for their loss.

The company and the borrowers had both been represented by the same firm of solicitors, Giffen Couch & Archer. The company maintained that the solicitors should have told them that the lenders were in arrears with their existing mortgage and had been threatened with legal proceedings. They succeeded at first instance. On appeal, however, it was held that, in the circumstances of the case, there was no duty on the solicitors to pass this information about the borrower to the lenders.

In the *National Home Loans Corporation* case, it was said that the solicitors' duties in acting for a mortgage lender depended heavily on what they were instructed to do, and were paid for, by the client. In this case they were instructed to report on title and to certify whether there had been a change in circumstances since the loan had been offered. They had to undertake a bankruptcy search. They were not asked to report on the personal credit-worthiness of the borrowers.

The *National Home Loans* case can be contrasted with that of *Mortgage Express v Bowerman*,[26] which held that there was a more extensive and onerous duty to report. In that case, a solicitor acting for both lender and borrower became aware that the lenders had been told that the value of the property was £220,000, whereas in fact the purchaser was buying it at £150,000. In the report on title to the lender the solicitor did not mention this discrepancy. The borrower eventually defaulted on the loan and the property was repossessed and sold for only £96,000.

It was held that the solicitors did have a duty to pass on information which had a bearing on the value of the lender's security. Their duty was not confined to advising on title alone. The instructions to the solicitors required them to undertake 'the

---

[24] *National Home Loans Corporation v Giffen Couch & Archer* [1997] 3 All ER 808.
[25] ibid, at 810.
[26] *Mortgage Express v Bowerman* [1996] 2 All ER 836 (CA). See also *Bristol & West BS v Fancy and Jackson and others* [1997] 4 All ER 582.

normal duties of a solicitor when acting for a mortgagee'.[27] Lord Bingham considered that

> if, in the course of investigating title, a solicitor discovers facts which a reasonably competent solicitor would realise might have a material bearing on the valuation of the lender's security, or some other ingredient of the lending decision, then it is his duty to point this out.[28]

ii. Spouses

Representing both parties to a marriage may seem natural, but their interests often diverge. A common situation is when the matrimonial home is charged, usually in order to raise finance for the family business. In the past, this was often run by the husband. A not uncommon circumstance was that the marriage breaks down and the business goes into liquidation, leaving the wife in a matrimonial home under threat of repossession. The courts have tended to leave the decision of whether to act for spouses to solicitors, even in situations where problems that can arise are well known. In *Royal Bank of Scotland v Etridge*,[29] the court said it was a matter of 'professional judgement' for a solicitor to decide whether to continue to represent both a husband and a wife where the home was to be charged.

In *Barclays Bank v Thomson*, the bank obtained a charge over the home, which was owned by the wife.[30] The solicitors acted for the husband's business, for the wife when the home was transferred into her name and for the bank in registering the charge. They were also asked by the bank to ensure that the wife fully understood the nature of the charge. In resisting a possession order when the loan repayments were in arrears, the wife attempted to negate the validity of the charge on the ground, inter alia, that she had not been properly advised by the solicitors of the extent of her potential liability under the charge.

It was argued in *Barclays Bank v Thomson* that the bank had constructive knowledge of this deficiency in the wife's knowledge because the solicitors were acting for them. The solicitor's fee was paid initially by the bank, but would be added to the borrower's total liability. The wife lost the case because the bank was entitled to rely on their solicitor's assurance that they had discharged their duty to the wife to warn her of the nature of the charge.

Significantly, there was no comment in the judgments of the Court of Appeal on the wisdom or the propriety of one firm of solicitors acting for all the parties, despite an obvious conflict of interests. The position may well have been very different had the action been against the solicitor or had the solicitor been asserting some right in the same circumstances. Similar outcomes were achieved in other cases of this kind.[31]

---

[27] It will be noted that no such general instruction had been included in the case of *National Home Loans Corporation v Giffen Couch & Archer* (n 24).

[28] *Mortgage Express v Bowerman* (n 26) at 842.

[29] *Royal Bank of Scotland v Etridge* [1998] 4 All ER 705.

[30] [1997] 4 All ER 816.

[31] *Banco Exterior Internacional v Mann* [1995] 1 ALL ER 936 and *Bank of Baroda v Rayarel* [1995] 2 FLR 376.

The lesson is that solicitors should not act for the wife in such circumstances where any conflict of interest is possible.

iii. General Transactions

The case of simultaneous client conflict is illustrated by the case of *Hilton v Barker Booth & Eastwood*.[32] Surprisingly, the case travelled to the House of Lords for a decision that many would consider uncontestable. The defendant solicitors had acted for B when he was convicted and imprisoned for fraud and in his bankruptcy proceedings. B subsequently contacted H, a small builder eager to get into property development. B suggested that H buy some commercial property from him. H agreed, and also agreed to sell on the property to B once it was developed. B had, at the same time, agreed to sell the property to a third party. The three contracts were all completed on the same day, the solicitors acting for both B and H, having lent the deposit to B.

All the background facts were unknown to H and the solicitors did not enlighten him. B failed to complete the contracts, resulting in financial disaster for H. H sued the solicitors for breach of contract. In the Court of Appeal he lost on the extraordinary basis that there was an implied term in his contract with his solicitors excusing them from revealing the confidential information they held on B. The House of Lords reversed the decision.

Giving the leading judgment in the House of Lords, Lord Walker said that he found the case 'particularly shocking'. The solicitors could not act for both parties in the circumstances, even if they had obtained informed consent, which they had not. The Court of Appeal's decision that the solicitors could rely on an implied term limiting their duty of disclosure to their client was, he said, 'contrary to common sense and justice' as well as being contrary to legal principle. Remarkably, neither the Court of Appeal nor the House of Lords suggested that the solicitors were guilty of a breach of professional conduct justifying disciplinary sanctions.

D. Conflict of Interests between Past and Present Clients in Different Matters

Clients may consider that there is a conflict of interests because, for example, they are business competitors with later clients of their former lawyers. The lawyers may hold general information related to a past client that does not appear relevant to a later matter for a different client, but is in fact useful to the present client's business. This may be detrimental to the interests of the past client. To permit such potential conflicts of interest undermines client confidence in the integrity of the profession. Different legal professions have taken different lines in balancing the important values of confidentiality and choice.

In the US, strict rules prohibit conflicts of interest between past and present clients. If a business competitor of a prospective client has used a law firm in the past, the

---

[32] *Hilton v Barker Booth & Eastwood* [2005] UKHL 8.

firm may be 'conflicted out' of acting for the prospective client. Commercial clients can use these rules against conflict cynically, as a litigation tactic.[33] This was noted as an emerging phenomenon in England in the Report of the Solicitors' Complaints Board for 1994. This brings policy considerations into the equation, for example, whether choice of lawyer should be fettered or whether there is adequate legal expertise in the market to deal with the problem at hand.

English case law has developed a less draconian approach to potential past and present client conflicts. Generally, it recognises a need to strike a balance between the need to protect client confidences on the one hand, and maintaining the freedom of clients to instruct lawyers of their choice on the other. Preventing lawyers from acting, especially where it is because a client's business competitor has used them in the past, represents a significant restriction of choice.

E. Conflict of Interests between Past and Present Clients in the Same or Related Matter

i. Firms

For most of the twentieth century it was assumed that the common law imposed no absolute ban on solicitors acting against previous clients, even in the same matter. The lesson of *Rakusen v Munday, Ellis and Clarke* (1912)[34] was that there is no inherent conflict of interest in acting against a former client. Any potential conflict relates to the information held about that client or his matter and whether it is relevant to the current matter. It was a matter of substance and of fact whether holding knowledge about a former client created a conflict of interest.

In *Rakusen*, C's ignorance of R's matter was crucial to him being allowed to act against the firm's former client. It is on this basis that it is possible for firms to act against their former client. The possibility is contingent on those involved in the present matter having no knowledge of the past matter. It also depends on it being possible to erect an information barrier to prevent them from acquiring that knowledge from their colleagues.

ii. Individual Lawyers

The risk of breaches of confidentiality greatly increased with the trend towards greater mobility among solicitors and mergers of firms. Solicitors may find that their new firm is acting against their own former clients. As might be expected, the firm must cease to act if there is likely to be a leakage of confidential information as a result of such moves. In *Re A Firm of Solicitors*,[35] a solicitor who had been employed

---

[33] See eg L Crocher, 'The Ethics of Moving to Disqualify Opposing Counsel for Conflict of Interest' (1979) 6 *Duke Law Journal* 1310.

[34] *Rakusen v Ellis Munday and Clarke* [1912] 1 Ch 831.

[35] *Re A Firm of Solicitors* [1995] 3 All ER 482.

by a firm acting for a claimant in patent litigation moved firms. Some two and a half years later the new firm was retained to act for the defendants in the patent litigation.

The individual solicitor had never been involved in the case against the defendants in his previous employment. Moreover, he managed to establish that he had no information relating to the previous litigation that could now be recalled, confidential or relevant, bearing in mind the lapse of time and the complexity of the issues. The application for an injunction to prevent the firm from acting was refused. The judge reaffirmed the principle that grounds for the court intervening was not a perception of possible impropriety. The jurisdiction was based on the protection of confidential information.

The judge acknowledged that the American-based claimants in the action were 'genuinely aghast' at the circumstances. In the US, there would be no question of the solicitor continuing to act. The court had to balance two conflicting principles, namely the protection of client confidence and the freedom of the client to instruct a solicitor of its choice. It held, however, that it was for the solicitor to prove that there was no reasonable prospect of a conflict between the two clients. It was not for the complainant to prove that there was a conflict. The court considered that the same rules applied to barristers.

The court accepted the principle that barristers are independent of other barristers in their chambers in *Laker Airways Inc v FLS Aerospace Ltd.*[36] It was held that no conflict of interest existed where an arbitrator was appointed from the same set of chambers as counsel for the defendant. Barristers were said to be sole practitioners working 'on their own papers for their own clients and sharing neither career nor remuneration'.[37] The breadth of such a ruling will probably not survive significant numbers of barristers joining corporate entities.

VI. Creating Conflict of Interest Rules

A code of professional ethics should advise and also seek to control any avoidable, unacceptable or unreasonable conflicts of interest between lawyers and their clients.[38] Rules should be realistic. This is especially important in the context of conflicts of interest because lawyers must refuse business where a conflict of interest arises. This potentially interferes with access to justice and the right of individuals to instruct their chosen lawyers.

Conflict rules must potentially cover the four kinds of conflict situation discussed in this chapter. These are conflicts between the interests of the lawyer and the client, conflicts between the interests of a present client and a past client or clients in the

---

[36] *Laker Airways Inc v FLS Aerospace Ltd* [2000] 1 WLR 113.
[37] ibid, at 125.
[38] C Wolfram, *Modern Legal Ethics* (St Paul, MN, West Publishing, 1986) at 313.

same and in different matters and conflicts between the interests of present clients. In the second and third of these situations the confidentiality of client information is an allied concern to conflict of interest.

A lawyer who knows something material about client A from past or present cases may inadvertently reveal that information to client B, to client A's detriment. This could harm their interests. What the lawyer knows about client A may, perhaps even subconsciously, affect the lawyer's performance for client B in a way that harms client A's interests.

Finally, it is necessary to recognise that clients may want to consent to a clear or possible conflict. This may be because they have a common interest and want to save costs. It is arguable that they should be allowed to consent to a risk of conflict of interest provided there are adequate safeguards.

VII. Brief History of Regulating Solicitors' Conflicts of Interest

A. Solicitors' Practice Rules 1990

The Solicitors' Practice Rules 1990 contained no general rule against conflict of interests, but did contain a rule about avoiding conflicts of interest in conveyancing, property selling and mortgage-related services.[39] This emphasis is probably explained by the fact that avoidance of conflicts of interest in general was, like confidentiality, considered 'a necessary and traditional incident' of the relationship. Otherwise, it might have been thought to be covered by the requirement, set out in the basic principles, to act in the best interests of clients.

i. The Solicitors' Practice (Conflict) Amendment Rules 2004

In the wake of *Bolkiah v KPMG*[40] the priority of the Law Society was to clarify practice on what were seen as past and present client conflicts of interest. This was not however, the only purpose. The Law Society had decided to thoroughly review all of its rules. Therefore, as part of this process, the City of London Law Society Working Party was asked to consider the whole area of conflicts.

The rules produced by the working party amended the Solicitors' Practice Rules 1990 by adding a new sub-section, 16D. This amendment underpins the current rules and practice. The key section on past and present client conflicts provided that firms could not act when owing 'separate duties to act in the best interests of two or more

---

[39] The Solicitors' Practice Rules 1990, as amended to 2001.
[40] *Bolkiah v KPMG* [1999] 1 All ER 517 and see ch 10: 'Confidences'.

clients in the same or related matters, and those duties conflict or... there is a significant risk that those duties may conflict'.[41] The rules also provided that 'a related matter will always include any matter which involves the same asset or liability'.[42]

Two exceptions were introduced to the ban on acting for two clients with interests in the same matter; the common interest exception and the competing for the same asset exception.

a. The Common Interest Exception

Where different clients had a substantially common interest in relation to a matter, or a particular aspect of it, the solicitor and firm could act for both.[43] The clients had to give their written, informed consent in relation to a matter in situations of conflict or possible conflict. For there to be common interest, a clear common purpose and a strong consensus on achieving it was needed. The solicitor had to consider whether equal weight could be given to the instructions of each client and keep that assessment under review.

The chair of the working group stated that the common interest situation might be relevant to several areas of work for City firms. These include acting for a borrower and a parent company guarantor on a financing, acting for arrangers on a note programme and, at the same time, for the trustees, acting for lenders on a syndicated loan and advising on an inter-creditor agreement between them and acting for joint venture partners in seeking to achieve a specific contract.[44] He envisaged that, in the event that differences arose, firms could agree arrangements to 'carve out' the problem area for handling by another firm.

b. The Competing for the Same Asset Exception

The rule amendment provided that two or more clients could give written consent to a firm acting where clients wish to compete for the same asset, which only one of them could attain.[45] This was subject to the proviso that there is no other conflict, or significant risk of conflict of interest between the parties. The chair of the working group explained that this exception is primarily aimed at two situations common in corporate practice: the public auction of a business and situations of company insolvency and financing.

The exemption of the public auction of a business reflected City practice. Private equity houses wished to retain certain financial advisers, accountants, lawyers or other consultants, and were usually content to accept that they would act for competing interests, provided suitable information barriers were in place. The exception permits a firm to act for competing bidders through to the point where a preferred bidder is chosen.[46]

---

[41] The Solicitors' Practice (Conflict) Amendment Rules 2004, r 2(b)(i).
[42] ibid, r 2(d).
[43] ibid, r 3(a).
[44] C Perrin, 'Solicitors Conflicts of Interest: The Context and Significance of the New Rules' (2005) 58 *Amicus Curiae* 2, at 6.
[45] The Solicitors' Practice (Conflict) Amendment Rules 2004, r 3(b).
[46] Perrin, 'Solicitors Conflicts of Interest' (n 44) at 6.

The other areas of work that the exception was expected to apply to concerned insolvency and refinancing. Firms could act for more than one client in competition for limited assets and potentially advise them how assets would be split in the event of the insolvency or restructuring of a company. The firm might also act for creditors on the preparation of an inter-creditor agreement, in cases where this did not fall within the 'common interest' exception. The Solicitors' Code of Conduct 2007 repealed the Solicitors' Practice Rules with effect from 1 July 2007.

B. The Solicitors' Code of Conduct 2007

The Solicitors' Code of Conduct 2007 provided an opportunity to consolidate the new rules on conflicts of interest into the code, with the accumulated guidance developed for the Guide. This was particularly useful in determining the scope of solicitor and own client conflicts of interest.

The Solicitors' Code of Conduct 2007, Rule 3.01 provided that solicitors must not act if a conflict of interest existed. The Rule continued to say that conflict of interest existed if:

(2)(a) you owe, or your firm owes, separate duties to act in the best interests of two or more clients in relation to the same or related matters, and those duties conflict, or there is a significant risk that those duties may conflict; or

(b) your duty to act in the best interests of any client in relation to a matter conflicts, or there is a significant risk that it may conflict, with your own interests in relation to that or a related matter.

(3) ... a related matter will always include any other matter which involves the same asset or liability.[47]

i. Solicitor and Own Client Conflicts

The obligation on solicitors not to act was limited by Rule 3.02(b) to situations where the solicitor thought there was a conflict in the same or related matter. This meant that a number of situations were debatable, either because the client's interests were not perceived to clash with the solicitor's or because the matters were not related.

a. Buying from and Selling to Clients

A conventional conflict of interest arises where the solicitor, or his firm, buys from or sells, or lends, to the client, or has a personal interest in any transaction which the client is undertaking. In these cases solicitors were required to reveal the interest to the client with 'complete frankness'.[48] The client had to receive independent advice from another solicitor or other professional adviser. The rule applied where another

[47] SRA, *Solicitors' Code of Conduct 2007*, rr 3.01 (1) and (2)(b).
[48] ibid, guidance to r 3, para 45.

member of the firm had an interest, providing the solicitor was aware of the fact and it impaired their ability to give independent and impartial advice'.[49]

b. Divided Loyalty

A lawyer's loyalty may be divided between contemporaneous clients, even though they do not have interests in the same cases. An example that is well established in the literature is where lawyers attach too much importance to relationships with opponent professionals or court officials. In such cases they may not pursue their own client's interests sufficiently vigorously.

An analogous situation is where lawyers receive repeat work from a client. A firm of solicitors, might, for example, have close ties with the local police, one of their partners being an ex-policeman. They might handle divorces and conveyances for officers working in the local police station. Arrested suspects who know of these circumstances and arrangements might wonder whether a solicitor advising them would advise a course of action that might upset those arrangements. However, it was not clear that this was an example of conflict of interest under the 2007 Code.

c. Publishing

An example of a situation of potential conflict arises when a solicitor proposes publishing details of a client's case. There could be financial advantages to both parties in this arrangement, but the situation is fraught with ethical issues. The lawyer could only write about the case with the client's agreement since they cannot reveal confidential information. In obtaining that consent the solicitor must ensure that the client has independent advice under the guidance noted below. The lawyer must then consider whether they can write honestly about the case, because of the obligation of integrity, and whether there are implications for the reputation of the profession generally.

A startling example of this situation arose in relation Frederick West, convicted of multiple murders in 1994. His solicitor was alleged to have been commissioned by a publisher to write a book about the case when it was concluded. The guidance stated that a solicitor should never enter into any arrangement relating to publication rights with the client prior to the conclusion of the matter.[50] This suggests there was no problem with agreeing publishing deals with clients once cases finished.

d. Personal Relationships

Lawyers are in a potential conflict of interest situation when in a personal relationship with clients. It raises the issue of whether either lawyer or client will be frank in their professional dealings when this might affect their personal relationship. The guidance to the 2007 Code stated that solicitors in a sexual relationship with a client must 'consider' whether this impaired the ability to act in the best interests of the client.[51]

---

[49] ibid, at para 48.
[50] ibid, at para 42.
[51] ibid, guidance to r 3, para 49.

The guidance appeared a little thin. It did not seem to reflect the spirit of Core Duty 1.04, to treat the interests of the client as paramount. It failed to deal adequately with the risk of abuse of power by lawyers in relationships with clients. If professionals claim higher standards than the norm, it might be expected that rules would preclude solicitors and barristers acting for their spouses, cohabitants or lovers or from starting relationships with existing clients. The advice also seemed to underestimate the risk that the reputation of all lawyers would be undermined if sordid allegations appeared in the press.

e. Holding an Office Creating a Risk of Conflict

The 2007 Rules stated that a solicitor must decline to act for a client where the solicitor, or a partner, employee or relative, held an office giving rise to a significant risk of a conflict of interest.[52] The guidance gave examples such as local councillor, judge, coroner and member of the police authority. Solicitors were told to consider whether the duties or interests of the public role conflicted with the ability to provide the client with independent advice.

The guidance gave examples of office holding that created risks of conflict of interest. They included a solicitor member of a Police Authority appearing as an advocate in prosecutions brought by the CPS in the Authority's area. It also included the example of a solicitor, being a recorder, deputy judge or registrar, not sitting in a court in which any member of his firm regularly practised.

Oddly, the advice against solicitors holding public office seemed to be based on Core Duty 1.06, not acting to damage the reputation or integrity of the profession, rather than concern to avoid conflict of client interest. This impression was reinforced by guidance stating that the solicitor should consider whether to act where there 'is likely to be a public perception that you, or your firm, have been able to obtain an unfair advantage for your client as a result of the office or appointment'.

f. Possible Liability of Solicitor to Client

The 2007 Code provided that, when solicitors discover a prospective claim against them, for example for negligence, clients must be informed and advised to take independent advice. When a claim was made, the Code continued, the solicitor must cease to act.[53]

ii. Contemporaneous Client Conflicts

a. Same or Related Matters

The formulation of the new conflict of interest rule provided scope for not finding conflicts of interest where they might be expected. For example, Rule 3.01(2)(a) only forbade acting where a conflict of interest between clients existed in the 'same or related matters'. It would be easy to imagine circumstances where lawyers might

---

[52] ibid, r 3.05 and guidance paras 64–66.
[53] ibid, guidance para 55, which also referred to r 20.07 for dealing with such claims.

not be able to do their best for two clients for whom they acted even if their current matters were not related.

The guidance recognised that the solicitor would have to make a judgement on what matters are related. For example, suppose a solicitor acts for a company in dispute with a garage over the cost of repairs to a car. If a potential bidder for the company then asks the solicitor to act for them, the work could be accepted. Although the car is an asset of the company being bid for, it is a very minor asset and the two issues are not related.[54] Solicitors were advised that they should get the views of their existing client if that can be done without a breach of confidentiality.

b. Exceptions

The Solicitors' Code of Conduct 2007 included the new exceptions to contemporaneous client conflict situations described in the previous section. The first of these was provision for acting for two or more clients where a conflict existed provided clients had substantially common interests and gave informed consent in writing.[55] The conflict must therefore be substantially less important to the clients than their common interest.

Under the common interest exemption solicitors could act for a number of family members in relation to family affairs, or a number of people setting up a company. It had to be reasonable to act in all the circumstances and care has to be taken to ensure that the clients are aware of the situation, capable of understanding it and not under any undue influence. Where this was in doubt, separate representation was recommended.[56] The solicitor had to show that the representation was reasonable, the test being whether 'one client is at risk of prejudice because of the lack of separate representation'.[57] Solicitors needed to be particularly careful where a couple re-mortgaged their home.[58]

Rule 3.02(2) permitted a firm (but not an individual solicitor) to act for consenting clients competing for the same asset where there is no other conflict between the parties. The solicitor had to be satisfied the parties were of full capacity and understood the issues. It also had to be reasonable to act. This exception was specifically intended to cover 'multi-party, complex commercial transactions where sophisticated users of legal services, who have a common purpose' want a single firm to act for two or more parties because this would speed up the transaction or make it more efficient.[59]

The 2007 Rules stated that solicitors acting for two or more clients when a dispute or conflict arose between them could act 'for one of the clients ... provided that the duty of confidentiality to the other client(s) is not put at risk'.[60] There was no guidance on which client to choose to continue to represent in these circumstances. Subsequently, encouraged by the City of London Law Society, the SRA consulted twice, in 2008 and 2009, on further relaxations of the rules.[61]

---

[54] ibid, guidance to r 3, para 4.
[55] ibid, r 3.02(1).
[56] ibid, guidance to r 3.02(1), para 7(a)(viii).
[57] ibid, at para 9.
[58] *Kenyon-Brown v Desmond Banks & Co* (1999) 149 NLJ 1832, CA.
[59] ibid, at para 7(a)(iv).
[60] ibid, r 3.03.
[61] J Loughrey, 'Large Law Firms, Sophisticated Clients and the Regulation of Conflicts of Interest' (2011) 14(2) *Legal Ethics* 215.

The SRA consultations on conflicts concerned two situations. One involved allowing representation of multiple clients with consent, except in litigation. The other proposal was to allow representation of new clients without the consent of past clients where no material information was held on the past client. The first of these was not pursued. As to the second, Rule 4, on confidentiality, was amended to allow use of information barriers to protect the information of past clients with their consent and, in very limited circumstances, without consent.[62]

VIII. The SRA Handbook 2011, as Amended

A. Relevant Principles

None of the 10 principles preceding the current outcomes in the SRA Handbook mention conflicts of the interests as such. The first four principles, it could be argued, underpin conflicts rules. These are the principles requiring solicitors to uphold the rule of law and the proper administration of justice, act with integrity, not allow their independence to be compromised and to act in the best interests of each client.

Chapter 3 of the SRA Code of Conduct is devoted entirely to conflicts of interest. It contains seven outcomes and 14 indicative behaviours. It identifies conflicts of interest potentially arising between solicitors and their current clients ('own interest conflict') and between two or more current clients ('client conflict'). Some outcomes apply to both types of situation, for example, the existence of effective systems and controls in place to enable identification and assessment of potential conflicts of interests.[63] Other outcomes apply to one or other of the situations.

B. Solicitor and Client Conflicts ('Own Interest Conflicts')

i. Definition

The SRA Handbook defines own interest conflicts of interest as

> any situation where your duty to act in the best interests of any client in relation to a matter conflicts, or there is a significant risk that it may conflict, with your own interests in relation to that or a related matter.[64]

In such cases the Handbook states that solicitors can never act where there is a conflict, or a significant risk of such a conflict.[65]

---

[62] Chapter 10: 'Confidences'.
[63] SRA, *Handbook 2011*, as amended, SRA Code of Conduct, ch 3, Outcome 3.1.
[64] SRA, *Handbook 2011*, Glossary.
[65] SRA, *Code of Conduct*, ch 3, Outcome 3.4.

ii. Examples

Obvious examples of a breach of the ban on solicitors acting in situations where their interests conflict with those of clients include selling to or buying from a client and lending to or borrowing from a client. In both situations, however, the situation can be resolved by the client obtaining independent legal advice.[66] It is not possible, however, to cure a conflict arising when a solicitor advises a client to invest in a business in which the solicitor has an interest. In such a situation it is considered to be impossible for the solicitor to give impartial advice.[67]

Indicative behaviours suggestive of conflicts of interest also appear in Chapter 1 of the SRA Handbook, on clients. These include 'refusing to act where your client proposes to make a gift of significant value to you or a member of your family, or a member of your firm or their family, unless the client takes independent legal advice'.[68] Another is the obligation to consider

> whether a conflict of interests has arisen or whether the client should be advised to obtain independent advice where the client notifies you of their intention to make a claim or if you discover an act or omission which might give rise to a claim.[69]

C. Client Conflicts

The Handbook defines a conflict of interest for the purposes of Chapter 3 of the SRA Code of Conduct as

> any situation where you owe separate duties to act in the best interests of two or more *clients* in relation to the same or related matters, and those duties conflict, or there is a significant risk that those duties may conflict.[70]

i. Exceptions to the Ban on Acting in Client Conflict Situations

In the chapter on conflicts of interest, the SRA Handbook states that, in circumstances where there is a significant risk of conflict between the interests of two or more clients, 'you must not act for all or both of them unless the matter falls within the scope of the limited exceptions set out at Outcomes 3.6 or 3.7'.[71]

The situations where the rules on conflict may be abrogated are where clients have a substantial common interest in the outcome and where they are competing for the same objective. In deciding whether to act in these limited circumstances, the overriding consideration will be the best interests of each of the clients concerned and,

---

[66] ibid, Indicative Behaviour 3.8.
[67] ibid, Indicative Behaviour 3.9.
[68] ibid, Indicative Behaviour 1.9.
[69] ibid, Indicative Behaviour 1.12.
[70] SRA, *Handbook*, Glossary.
[71] See also *SRA Code of Conduct*, ch 3, Outcome 3.5.

in particular, 'whether the benefits to the clients of you acting for all or both of the clients outweigh the risks'.[72]

a. Substantial Common Interest

Solicitors can potentially act in a situation of client conflict where the clients have a substantially common interest in relation to a matter or a particular aspect of it, provided they can comply with Outcome 3.6. They must have explained the relevant issues and risks to the clients and have a reasonable belief that the clients understand the issues and risks. All clients must give informed consent in writing to the solicitor acting. The solicitor must then be satisfied that it is reasonable for them to act for all the clients and that it is in their best interests. Finally, they must be satisfied that the benefits to the clients of acting outweigh the risks.[73]

There are some common situations of substantial common interest considered below, such as acting for mortgage lenders and borrowers in conveyancing transactions. A situation of substantially common interest does not exist where the clients' interests in the end result are different. One example is where a partner is buying out the interest of another partner in their joint business or where a seller is transferring a property to a buyer.[74]

b. Competing for the Same Objective

The second exception allowing a solicitor to represent clients in a potential conflict situation arises under Outcome 3.7. This covers situations where clients are competing for the same objective. In such circumstances, solicitors can act if they have explained the relevant issues to the clients and where they have a reasonable belief that the clients understand those issues and risks. The clients must then confirm in writing that they want the solicitors to act, knowing that they are competing with other clients for the same objective.

Clients competing for the same objective are likely to be undertaking an activity such as bidding for a franchise. Indeed, an indicative behaviour indicates that the outcomes directed at avoiding conflicts of interest are more likely to be met where clients are sophisticated users of legal services.[75] They are not likely to be met where a solicitor is acting for two private purchasers, for example, two buyers competing to buy a residential property.[76]

Even where solicitors can act for clients competing for the same objective the firm may need to provide safeguards. Unless the clients specifically agree otherwise, no individual within the firm can act for more than one client in the matter. Nor can one person be responsible for supervising the work of different individuals in relation to different clients in that matter. Finally, the solicitor must be satisfied that it is reasonable to act for all the clients and that the benefits to them outweigh the risks.[77]

---

[72] ibid, ch 3, Preamble.
[73] ibid, ch 3, Outcome 3.6.
[74] ibid, Indicative Behaviour 3.11.
[75] ibid, Indicative Behaviour 3.6.
[76] ibid, Indicative Behaviour 3.13.
[77] ibid, ch 3, Outcome 3.7.

ii. Factors in Deciding whether the Client Conflict Exceptions Apply

Where one on the two exceptions might apply, solicitors must consider whether the circumstances will allow them to be even-handed in dealing with both parties' interests. For example, where there is unequal bargaining power between the clients it may be impossible not to favour one or other client, either by acting to redress the balance or by not acting. The example given in the Code is acting for a seller and buyer where a builder is selling to a non-commercial client.[78] Similarly, it would be impossible to be even-handed if the circumstances require the solicitor to help negotiate the price between a buyer and seller of a property.[79]

iii. Systems for Detection

a. Proportionality

A new development in the SRA Handbook is the introduction of outcomes requiring systems and controls for identifying different types of conflict of interest. The systems for detecting both own interest conflicts and potential client conflicts must be appropriate to the size and complexity of the firm and the nature of the work undertaken.

b. Decision-making

When deciding whether to act in a situation of potential conflict with their own interests, solicitors must allow all relevant circumstances to be assessed. This includes consideration of whether the ability of the solicitor or anyone else in the firm is impaired by financial interests and personal relationships. It also requires examining the appointment of anyone at the firm, or their family members, to public office, commercial relationships or employment.[80]

In identifying client conflicts, the solicitor must consider differences in client interests and the solicitors' ability to give independent advice to the client. Solicitors also need to consider, where there is a need to negotiate between clients, whether there is imbalance in bargaining power between clients or whether one of the clients is vulnerable.[81] These are factors that would indicate that separate representation is warranted.

---

[78] ibid, ch 3, Indicative Behaviour 3.4.
[79] ibid, ch 3, Indicative Behaviour 3.3.
[80] ibid, ch 3, Outcome 3.2.
[81] ibid, ch 3, Outcome 3.3.

IX.   Potential Conflict of Interest Situations and the Codes

A. Litigation

The Criminal Defence Service Regulations encourage one solicitor to represent two or more co-defendants as it is more economical. Pressure is often put on solicitors by the court to act for more than one defendant in the same case. The circumstances of *R v Ataou*, considered above, do occur frequently in criminal cases. A solicitor represents co-defendants and initially there is no problem; both clients are telling the same story. Then, one client either changes his story and implicates the other, or says something which is inconsistent with the other's story. In such cases the solicitor should withdraw from representing both clients. Continuing to represent one involves a breach of the confidence of the other. Solicitors should not explain why they have withdrawn from representation, because that would be a breach of confidentiality.

Even in situations where there is no breach of confidence, it would be inconsistent for solicitors to act for co-defendants when one pleads guilty and the other not guilty to an offence based on the same facts. It would imply acceptance in one case that evidence was probative whereas in the other case the evidence was contested. Even when co-defendants clients plead guilty, conflicts of interest can arise when pleas in mitigation are considered and one defendant claims a lesser part in the offence. The 2007 Code took a stronger line than the common law, the guidance stating that solicitors should cease to act for one 'and possibly all' clients.[82] The Criminal Law Solicitors' Association resisted changes to the rule, pointing out the human rights implications for the defendant.[83]

The SRA Handbook is not particularly helpful on the issue of litigation conflicts of interest. There is one, relevant, indicative behaviour that suggests the outcomes will be met by 'declining to act for clients whose interests are in direct conflict, for example claimant and defendant in litigation'.[84] Outcome 3.3 is, however, generally relevant to more nuanced situations, such as joint criminal defence. Here, it would be necessary to consider factors such as different interests, a need to negotiate between the clients, imbalance in bargaining power between the clients and the vulnerability of any client,[85] in deciding whether to represent co-defendants.

The situation is less clear in a *Rakusen* situation, where a client consults, but does not instruct, a firm, which is then instructed by the other side in litigation. The outcomes on conflict are addressed to the individual solicitor (by use of the term 'you'), so it is

---

[82] SRA, *Solicitors' Code of Conduct 2007*, guidance to r 3, paras 24–36 covered the issue of co-defendants and conflict generally.

[83] *Law Society Gazette* 16 September 2004.

[84] *SRA Code of Conduct*, ch 3, Indicative Behaviour 3.2.

[85] ibid, ch 3, Outcome 3.3.

possible that firms may not be prohibited from acting. As in *Rakusen*, the issue could be treated as one of confidentiality only, in which case an information screen, between the lawyer previously consulted and the lawyer handling the matter, may be sufficient.

A contrary argument would have to be based on the indicative behaviour suggesting that solicitors should decline to act for those 'whose interests are in direct conflict, for example claimant and defendant in litigation'.[86] This clearly envisages a prohibition on one solicitor representing two clients involved in opposite sides of the same suit simultaneously. It would arguably not prevent what happened in *Rakusen*, because the solicitors were different solicitors in the same firm.

B. Acting for Organisations

In acting for a company, partnership or other organisation, a solicitor must be clear who gives the instructions. There is a danger that the solicitor might become involved in conflicts within the organisation, for example, between shareholders and the board of directors or between partners. There was no guidance in the 2007 Code, but a starting point for solicitors is to make sure that the board of directors has approved the instructions or authorised the instructor.

Where a solicitor has acted for the company, and for directors of the company as individuals, it is unlikely that he will be able to act for either party in a subsequent dispute between directors and shareholders. A solicitor who has acted for a partnership may act against a partner only if he or she had no confidential information relating to that partner, provided there is no conflict of interest.[87]

C. Conveyancing

The conflict of interest arising from acting for more than one party in the same or related conveyancing matters might be thought to be an obvious example of a conflict of interest. Ambivalence and anxiety over the issues are longstanding.[88] There are considerable pressures from within and beyond the profession to continue with conflict of interest rules that allow joint representation for conveyancing. There is also external pressure to relax the conflict of interest rules in this area.

Abolishing joint representation in conveyancing would lose solicitors business and fees and make conveyancing more expensive for clients. Thus, when the SRA consulted on the SRA Handbook 2011, the Legal Services Board Consumer Panel argued that conflict rules should be minimal, allowing conveyancers more freedom to act for both buyer and seller.[89] In the event, the SRA's new Handbook followed this path.

---

[86] ibid, ch 3, Indicative Behaviour 3.2.

[87] *Re A Solicitor* [1995] 3 All ER 482.

[88] For an account of the Rules, see L Sheinman, 'Ethical Practice or Practical Ethics? The Case of the Vendor Purchaser Rule' (2000) 3 *Legal Ethics* 27.

[89] 'Consumer panel: conveyancers should have more freedom to act for both buyer and seller' *Legal Futures* 5 August 2010 (www.legalfutures.co.uk/regulation/solicitors/consumer-panel-says-conveyancers-should-have-greater-freedom-to-act-for-both-buyer-and-seller).

It allowed firms to act where there is a non-substantive client conflict of interests, and subject to certain conditions, such as obtaining each client's informed consent. No specific outcomes refer to conveyancing situations, although several indicative behaviours do.

While the SRA abandoned the focus on conveyancing in the Code of Conduct, it treated conveyancing as a distinct arm of the enforcement strategy published in April 2011.[90] This noted that about 50 per cent of the value of professional indemnity claims arising against firms arose from conveyancing. There was a substantial increase in Fund payments, from £9.23 million in 2008 to £21.2 million for 2010. This was linked to the economic cycle and, through it, a downturn in the conveyancing market.

While the SRA Handbook 2011 trod lightly around conveyancing, the SRA promised that its enforcement strategy would be particularly vigilant in considering conveyancing practices. It would identify risks through the authorisation process, through information gathering processes, through the work of its Risk Centre and through thematic work focusing on conveyancing as an area of practice.

i. Acting for Buyer and Seller

Detailed rules on acting for buyer and seller dominated the Solicitors' Practice Rules 1990.[91] The length and complexity of the rules resulted from the fact that, in reality, these situations were riven with conflict, scope for unprofessional conduct and the risk of negligence claims. The Solicitors' Practice Rules on acting for both parties in conveyancing contexts were largely transferred into the 2007 Code.[92] The position was different depending on whether or not the transaction was one at 'arm's length'. In transactions not 'at arm's length' solicitors could act for both buyer and seller, provided there was no actual conflict or significant risk of it.[93] In transactions at arm's length more stringent requirements had to be met.

A transaction was at arm's length if it was between related persons, settlor and trustee, trustee and beneficiary, personal representatives and beneficiaries, sole traders and their companies and associated companies.[94] In transactions at arm's length, the solicitor could potentially act for both the buyer and the seller if one of three preliminary conditions were met. The preliminary condition was either that both parties were established clients, or that the consideration was less than £10,000, or that the parties were represented by different individuals at separate offices or practices.[95]

If one of the three preliminary conditions for acting for buyer and seller were met, additional requirements applied. The parties had to consent, in writing, to the joint representation and the solicitor could not be involved in negotiating the sale of the property, nor in representing the developer of the property.[96] Where the grounds

---

[90] SRA, 'Draft Supervision and Enforcement Strategy for Conveyancing' (www.sra.org.uk/sra/strategy/sub-strategies/supervision-enforcement-strategy.page).
[91] Solicitors' Practice Rules 1990, r 6.
[92] SRA, *Solicitors' Code of Conduct* 2007, rr 3.07–3.22.
[93] ibid, r 3.08.
[94] ibid, guidance to r 3.08, para 73.
[95] ibid, rr 3.09–10 and guidance from para 74.
[96] ibid, r 3.10.

for acting were that the solicitor had separate offices in different localities, different individuals, qualified to do conveyancing and normally working at each office, had to conduct or supervise the transaction. Further, no office of the firm (or an associated firm) was allowed to have referred either client to the office conducting the transactions.[97]

The chapter of the SRA Handbook concerned with conflicts of interest contains several indicative behaviours relating to conveyancing. Two indicative behaviours 'may tend to show that you have not achieved [the] outcomes.' The first is 'acting for a buyer (including a lessee) and seller (including a lessor) in a transaction relating to the transfer of land for value, the grant or assignment of a lease or some other interest in land for value'.[98] The second is acting for two buyers where there is a conflict of interests under Outcome 3.7 (competing for the same objective), for example where two buyers are competing for a residential property.[99]

The chapter on Conflicts of Interest also contains two relevant indicative behaviours suggesting that a firm is meeting the outcomes. The first of these is 'declining to act for clients where you may need to negotiate on matters of substance on their behalf, for example negotiating on price between a buyer and seller of a property'.[100] The second is 'declining to act where there is unequal bargaining power between the clients, for example acting for a seller and buyer where a builder is selling to a non-commercial client.[101]

The SRA enforcement strategy set out some risk situations where further work was promised. These were:

—— acting for a buyer and seller where there is a conflict or a significant risk of a conflict of interests. For example, acting for an elderly, vulnerable client selling their property to their child for whom you also act;
—— acting for a borrower and lender where the borrower client has provided inaccurate information to the lender to obtain a mortgage and the firm are aware of this; and
—— acting for a buyer and lender if the lender has a significant interest in the ABS conveyancing practice.

The SRA outcomes indicate problematic areas without stating how the problems can be met; it is for the solicitor to decide how to meet the outcomes. Since the outcomes for conflicts of interest are consistent with the old rules on conveyancing buyer and lender conflicts, it is very likely that solicitors will follow existing practice. It is not clear whether they can do so with confidence.

ii. Acting for Lender and Borrower

The property buyer, usually also a mortgagee, has a strong interest in minimising costs and progressing the transaction efficiently. It therefore makes sense that, in most

---

[97] ibid, rr 3.10(d)(i) and (ii).
[98] ibid, ch 3, Indicative Behaviour 3.14.
[99] ibid, ch 3, Indicative Behaviour 3.13.
[100] ibid, ch 3, Indicative Behaviour 3.3.
[101] ibid, ch 3, Indicative Behaviour 3.4.

situations, one solicitor can protect the buyer's interests in taking out the mortgage and the mortgagor's interests in securing the loan. There have, however, been historically high levels of default and mortgage fraud in cases where the solicitor acted for both lender and borrower.[102] This was remedied by the Law Society by permitting standard terms of instructions from lenders which restricted the work solicitors were supposed to do.

a. SRA Code of Conduct 2007

Under the Solicitors' Code of Conduct 2007, solicitors could only act for both a purchaser and a 'standard' mortgage lender.[103] A standard mortgage was one provided in the normal course of the lender's activities, where a significant part of the lender's activities consists of lending and where the mortgage was on standard terms.[104] All other mortgages were individual mortgages and each party had to have their own solicitor. This effectively restricted the possibility of solicitors acting for lender and borrower to situations where the lender was a building society or bank offering a mortgage on its standard terms. Solicitors were only allowed to accept instructions to act for a lender and borrower where no conflict of interest was involved.[105]

Rule 3.19 contained an extensive list of matters on which solicitors could accept instructions from the lender. The list of standard instructions contained in Rule 3.19 did not include the buyer's creditworthiness, thus clarifying expectations created by *National Home Loans Corporation v Giffen Couch & Archer.* They did not cover notifying the lender of the true value of the property. These were the matters which caused so many problems before the Rules were changed. They could, however, include a bankruptcy search.

The solicitor is, however, bound by confidentiality and so the information can be given to the lender only if the borrower consents. Legal professional privilege does not protect purchasers where their solicitors' advice was used to 'further iniquity' by procuring a loan by deception.[106] If the buyer-client refuses to allow the solicitor to reveal confidential information, which the lender has a right to receive, then the solicitor must presumably decline to act for either on grounds of professional embarrassment. This is not a very satisfactory situation for either client.

b. SRA Handbook 2011

Under the SRA Handbook, an indicative behaviour that shows a solicitor has complied with the outcomes reflects the position, reached by the previous rules, on acting for purchasers, as borrowers, and for mortgage lenders.[107] The instructions must relate to a mortgage of land where the mortgage is a standard mortgage of property to be used as the borrower's private residence. The mortgage must be one provided in the normal course of the lender's activities, where a significant part of the

---

[102]   *R v Law Society, ex p Mortgage Express Ltd* [1997] 2 All ER 348.
[103]   SRA, *Solicitors' Code of Conduct 2007*, r 3.17.
[104]   ibid.
[105]   ibid, r 3.16(2)(a).
[106]   *Nationwide Building Society v Various Solicitors* [1998] NLJR 241.
[107]   SRA, *Code of Conduct*, ch 3, Indicative Behaviour 3.7.

lender's activities consists of lending and the mortgage is on standard terms. The certificate of title required by the lender must be in the form approved by the Law Society and the Council of Mortgage Lenders. Finally, the solicitors must be satisfied that it is reasonable and in the clients' best interests for them to act. Seven other indicative behaviours relate to acting for more than one party in conveyancing transactions.

iii. Linked Businesses

Conveyancing is an area of legal work where there is plenty of scope for linked businesses and introduction mechanisms, all of which create potential conflicts of interest. There is no blanket ban on such activities, but clients do need to give informed consent to potential conflicts of interest. Under general principles, for example, solicitors must be transparent about any payments made for referrals of conveyancing business from estate agents.

Solicitors are able to hold an interest in an estate agency and conduct business as estate agents subject to SRA rules.[108] Clients must be informed of any interests held when matters are transferred between parts of the business. In these circumstances, clients may not see anything unusual in the situation and may not pay much attention to the terms they are agreeing to. It is therefore incumbent on solicitors to recognise, and guard against, the inherent conflict of interest.

D. Family Situations

i. Acting for Spouses

It was not always considered obvious, where both spouses have been clients, that a solicitor should not normally agree to act for one spouse against the other in matrimonial proceedings. This situation is quite likely to arise. Solicitors are may have acted for both spouses in the context of house purchase or making a will. The 1999 Guide advised that it would be 'prudent' to check, if it was proposed to continue acting for one party, whether the other party objected. As this would usually mean that the other party would have to find another solicitor, it is likely that they would. If the solicitor held confidential information, unknown to the spouse he was to represent, objection was a certainty. In such circumstances, it might be thought obvious that the solicitor should not act for either spouse.

It is not always the case that spouses want separate representation. Even in contested matrimonial matters the parties may sometimes seek a non-contentious divorce settlement. Under the Solicitors' Code of Conduct 2007 this was allowed if certain conditions were complied with.[109] There had to be a substantial common interest and fully informed written consent. Nevertheless, it is difficult to continue to act if, once

[108] SRA, Property Selling Rules 2011.
[109] SRA, *Solicitors' Code of Conduct 2007*, r 3.02(1)

the work is begun, conflicts do arise between the parties. Additionally, settlements may be vulnerable to allegations of bias or of undue influence.

Solicitors attempting to represent both parties in matrimonial proceedings may have to prove a lack of significant conflict, leading to considerable difficulties. The savings in costs arising from such joint representation could prove illusory.

ii. Acting for Children

a. Civil Proceedings

In representing children in civil proceedings, the solicitor must be clear who gives instructions. In ordinary civil litigation, such as personal injuries, a minor cannot initiate litigation except by a litigation friend.[110] A parent has the right to act as such a friend. It is for the litigation friend to instruct the solicitor in the best interests of the child and he or she must not have any interest adverse to that of the child.

Any settlement or compromise of a case involving a child requires the consent of the court. The solicitor acts for the litigation friend, but must be conscious of any conflict of interest between the child and the friend. The solution, if such a conflict does arise, is for the litigation friend to be removed by the court on the application of the solicitor or other interested person.[111]

b. Criminal Proceedings

In criminal proceedings, which can only involve children over 10 years old, it has never been suggested that the child client needs a litigation friend. It is up to the solicitor to ensure that the child understands the legal advice and then to take instructions. When a child is interviewed at a police station an 'appropriate adult' (AA) should be present to ensure that the child understands the process and generally to protect the child's interests. The AA can be a relative or, often, a member of the local Youth Offending team or a social worker.

The AA does not represent the child and does not have the right to give instructions or override the advice of the solicitor. If any conflict of interest arises, or there are differences of view as to what should be done in the case between the AA and the child, the solicitor must follow the instructions of the child. It may also be necessary to have the AA replaced. It is important that the AA should not be present at the child client's interviews with the solicitor. The AA has no duty of confidentiality and does not have the protection of professional privilege.

A solicitor representing a child who cannot give proper instructions, and who cannot get instructions from another source, must act in the best interests of the child. A solicitor in this position should avoid presenting the court with his or her own personal views on the best way to bring up children. In the absence of instructions from a litigation friend or a competent child, it is probably best that the solicitor relies on the court rather than his own opinions. Solicitors are not expert in the field of family welfare and their opinions may even be inappropriate or potentially harmful to the particular child or family.

---

[110] Civil Procedure Rules 1998, as amended, r 21.2, unless the court so orders under r 21.2(3).
[111] ibid, r 21.7 and *Re Taylor's Application* [1972] 2 All ER 873.

c. Family Proceedings

In family proceedings there is provision for a child to initiate or defend litigation without a litigation friend.[112] The solicitor must ascertain if the child has both a sufficient understanding of the issues, so that they can give true consent, and the ability to give instructions.[113] If this is the case, the solicitor can act directly for the child. If expert evidence of what is in the best interests of the child is required, a social worker from the Children and Family Court Advisory and Support Service (CAFCASS), a government agency charged with improving the welfare of children involved in family proceedings, can be instructed.

In *Re T*, it was held that a solicitor forming the view that the child is capable of instructing him, must accept those instructions.[114] The court stressed that while it is basically for the solicitor to determine whether a child is capable of giving instructions, nevertheless the court has the ultimate right to decide the issue, either on its own motion or on the application of another, because 'there are bound to be some cases... where a maverick assessment might be made by a solicitor'.[115]

The court can also appoint a CAFCASS officer as *guardian ad litem* of the child. Where it appears that it is in the interests of any child to be made a party to the proceedings, such an appointee will have authority to take part in the proceedings on the child's behalf.[116] A *guardian ad litem* or next friend can be removed by the court if it considers that the minor concerned has sufficient understanding to participate as a party in the proceedings. Children can also seek separate legal representation.

In *Mabon v Mabon*,[117] parents of six children separated, the three youngest leaving with the mother and the three elder, teenage boys staying with the father. A CAFCAS officer was appointed *guardian ad litem* and representative of all six children in the proceedings. The three eldest children consulted a solicitor and sought to be represented separately. At first instance the request was refused by the judge on multiple grounds, but mainly because he thought the older children were influenced by the father. He unfortunately summed up his position with the observation that separate representation would only provide 'perhaps the more articulate and elegant expression of what I already know'.[118]

The Court of Appeal noted that the European Convention on Human Rights, Article 8 provided that the child's right to private life demanded a respect for his personal autonomy. The child's right to family life included a procedural right of participation in the court's decision-making process. Lord Justice Wall stressed

the need for the boys on the facts of this particular case to emerge from the proceedings (whatever the result) with the knowledge that their position had been independently represented and their perspective fully advanced to the judge.[119]

---

[112] Children Act 1990, s 8.
[113] *Gillick v West Norfolk etc AHA and DSS* [1986] AC 112.
[114] *Re T* [1993] 4 All ER 518.
[115] ibid, per Waite LJ at 529.
[116] Under the Family Proceedings Rules 1991, r 9.2(A) (as amended).
[117] *Mabon v Mabon* [2005] 2 FCR 354.
[118] ibid, at para 44.
[119] ibid.

These cases reflect the difficulty of managing family cases sensibly, respecting the rights of children to their own voice and deciding whether it really is their own voice. The recognition that children have a right to have their views separately heard, whatever the source of those views, reflects a wider, but incomplete, shift within the legal system towards respecting the individual autonomy of children.[120]

E. Class Actions

Class actions are often characterised by a 'relative absence of client control',[121] which can leave the lawyers free to follow their own inclinations rather than the instructions of the client. This could lead to conflicts of interest between clients that are unidentified or concealed. This situation might be mitigated, if not totally avoided, by the involvement of professional bodies in proceedings. The Law Society co-ordination of multi-party action in the Opren case is a good example.

Solicitors involved in multi-party actions are asked to consult the Law Society's Multi-Party Information Scheme and a lead solicitor is appointed. Any judgments or orders are binding in relation to all the claims on the register at the time, unless the court orders otherwise. Lord Woolf thought that an application should be made to the court at the outset. This would allow a multi-party action to be certificated and for a managing judge to be appointed to control the proceedings. In multi-party actions the role of the informed client can be taken by an action group or, where there is no such group, by the appointment of a trustee to undertake this role. All settlements have to be approved by the court so as to ensure, in Lord Woolf's words, that 'the lawyers do not benefit themselves while obtaining minimal benefits for their clients'.

Lord Woolf recommended that the Bar and the Law Society 'give special attention to the ethical problems involved in multi-party litigation'[122] but, so far, this has not happened. Ethical guidance on the issue would meet a number of requirements. First, all parties would need to be fully informed, in writing, of the nature of the group action and the operating constraints. Secondly, because the relationship between lawyer and client in multi-party actions is unusual, the client would need to be fully apprised, from the outset, regarding what could be expected from the lawyer. Thirdly, ethical guidance would provide for regular progress reports, either in person or in writing, containing, when appropriate, information about the terms of proposed settlements and how individuals in the class would be affected.

F. Past and Present Clients

The previous chapter, on Confidentiality, dealt with situations in which solicitors act for clients when they hold confidential information for a past client that is relevant to

---

[120] A MacDonald, 'The Child's Voice in Private Law: Loud Enough?' (2009) 39 *Family Law* 40; N Hansen, 'Mabon v Mabon: a Decision Long Overdue?' (2005) 50 *Family Law Journal* 8.
[121] Lord Woolf, *Access to Justice: Final Report to the Lord Chancellor on the Civil Justice System in England and Wales* (London, HMSO, 1996) at 243, para 72.
[122] ibid, ch 17.

the present matter. This situation is now treated as an issue of confidentiality whereas, previously, it was treated as a conflict of interest issue. Acting against a former client on behalf of a new client is arguably a conflict of interest because it is a betrayal of the loyalty promised by the lawyer and client relationship.

Such situations are allowable under the current rules, where there is no conflict of interest going beyond a manageable issue of confidentiality. One of the difficulties for solicitors involves assessing whether there is any prejudice to the past client if they act. A number of different variables affect any decision about the ethicality of acting. These include the length of time between the matters, the degree of relation between them, the amount of information held on the previous client, the nature of that information, whether it widely known in the firm and so on.

X. Barristers' Conflicts of Interest

Under the old Bar Code the basic rule on conflict was expressed as an accepted exception to the cab rank rule. A barrister could reject instructions

> if there is or appears to be a conflict or a risk of conflict either between the interests of the barrister and some other person or between the interests of any one or more clients (unless all relevant persons consent to the barrister accepting instructions).[123]

Similarly, when representing multiple clients there appeared to be a conflict between them, the barrister was told to withdraw from the representation unless all parties consented.[124] There was little more guidance provided.

The new Code of Conduct contains an outcome that 'BSB authorised persons do not accept instructions from clients where there is a conflict between their own interests and the clients' or where there is a conflict between one or more clients except when permitted in the Handbook'.[125] The rules provide that

> [y]ou must not accept instructions and ... you must cease to act and return any instructions which you have accepted, if 'due to any previous instructions you are not able to fulfill your obligation to act in the best interests of the prospective client[126]

or

> there is a conflict of interest between the prospective client and one or more of your former or existing clients in respect of the particular matter unless all of the clients who have an interest in the particular matter give their informed consent to your acting in such circumstances'.[127]

---

[123] BSB/Bar Council, *Code of Conduct of the Bar of England and Wales* 1981, 8th edn, as amended (London, Bar Standards Board, 2004) pt VI, para 603(e).
[124] ibid, para 608.
[125] BSB, *Handbook 2014*, pt 2: The Code of Conduct, oC12.
[126] ibid, rC21.1.
[127] ibid, rC21.3.

As considered in the previous chapter, barristers must also refuse instructions if there is a 'real risk that information confidential to another former or existing client may prejudice the ability to act in the best interests of the prospective client, unless there is informed consent to disclosure of that confidential information'.[128] In general, the rules on conflicts and confidentiality are less onerous than those in the solicitors' Code. This is explained partly by the fact that barristers in the same chambers are considered to be independent of each other and partly because they are assumed to be able to act on different sides in the same case. Therefore, an area of potential regulation is closed off unless, of course, the implications of barristers operating collectively are considered.

The Bar Code does not address what it is about previous instructions that may prevent barristers fulfilling their obligation to act in the best interests of each client. This leaves the position regarding past and present client conflicts of interest in the same or related matters open. There are a number of possibilities. For example, it may be thought that barristers, as advocates, are generally unaffected by knowledge about previous clients. In that case, it would need to be something exceptional about the past case that invoked the rule. This position is unlikely because it would mean that barristers would not accept a duty of full disclosure to present clients.

Under the Code of Conduct in the new BSB Handbook, one of the new outcomes is that BSB authorised persons must not '... accept instructions from clients where there is a conflict between their own interests and the clients' or where there is a conflict between one or more clients except when permitted in this Handbook'.[129] Specific rules provide that barristers must not accept instructions to act in a matter if, due to any existing or previous instructions, they are not able to fulfil their obligation to act in the best interests of the prospective client, including where there is a conflict of interest.[130] An exception is provided where all of the clients who have an interest in the particular matter give their informed consent to the barrister acting in such circumstances.[131] The new Bar Code prohibits a barrister from acting where there are information conflicts between past and present clients.[132]

XI. The Future for Conflicts of Interest

There are numerous pressures to weaken conflict of interest rules. They emanate from self-interested professionals who want more business, from consumer advocates who argue that such rules are anti-competitive and from those seeking a less adversarial, more co-operative legal system.

---

[128] ibid, rC.21.4.
[129] ibid, oC12.
[130] ibid, rC21.1 and 2.
[131] ibid, rC21.3.
[132] See ibid, rC21.4 and ch 10: 'Confidences'.

Accepting that there will be situations of possible conflict when lawyers should be able to act, the question becomes one of who bears the onus of proof. On the basis of *In Re A Solicitor*, it is the lawyer who must establish that there is no risk. Even so, it is arguable that the rules against acting in conflict of interest situations are not strict enough. Private clients are normally most upset if 'their' solicitor acts for an opponent. The solicitor will obviously know them, their character and the way they are likely to act under stress. All of this information could be used against a former client.

A similar case could be made in relation to acting against an organisation that is an existing client or indeed was a former client. A general knowledge of the culture of a company or public authority and of the way they work will often be very useful in conducting litigation or negotiations with it. Information that is often not regarded as confidential can still be useful to an opponent.

There are situation in which lawyers and academics have argued for further relaxation of conflict rules. In the family context, for example, the rules against acting for both spouses may be seen to be unduly restrictive. Tur argues that 'some reformulation of the conflict-of-interest rules of professional conduct is highly desirable in order to permit family lawyers to act, where appropriate, for and in the best interests of the family rather than solely for one individual member'.[133] This would place the lawyer more in the role of a mediator rather than a representative.

Acting for a whole family might be allowed under Rule 3.02(1), but all the parties must consent and the consent must be fully informed. Tur's suggestion involves a change of culture whereby the appointment of a 'lawyer for the family', becomes more normal. Such a move would be consistent with the general move away from adversarial assumptions. It would make sense, financially and in the interests of the family, and could therefore be justified ethically. There are risks, however, in denying a representative to individual family members, especially those with the least power.

XII. Conclusion

An intuitive view of conflicts of interest is that a professional representative, having offered a duty of loyalty to one person, cannot later oppose that person on behalf of another. Some have argued that this is too broad and onerous a rule. It denies the possibility that it is in the client's best interest that a solicitor acts in a conflict of interest situation. It also creates the possibility that rules could be abused, tactically, to deny an opponent their lawyer of choice. Rather than adopt a strict ban on any possible conflict of interest, the English professions have preferred to base obligations on the duty of confidence rather than the duty of loyalty.

---

[133] RH Tur, 'Family Lawyering in Legal Ethics' in S Parker and C Sampford (eds), *Legal Ethics and Legal Practice: Contemporary Issues* (Oxford, Clarendon Press, 1995).

The litigation that has arisen in relation to the joint representation of buyer and seller or mortgagor and mortgagee, suggests a need for caution in further relaxation of conflict of interest rules. Joint representation in such situations allows solicitors to offer an efficient and less costly service in a non-contentious situation. Nevertheless, this relaxation caused numerous problems, prompting calls for tighter regulation. It may be asking too much of anyone that they represent different interests at the same time while being constantly alive to the possibility of a conflict of interest arising. No lawyer can guarantee that there will be no conflict of interest between the interests of the client and other interests. However, one of the most valuable services that lawyers offer, in contrast to many other commercial advisers, is disinterested and confidential advice. The client needs to know what this entails, that their advisers are sensitive to the risk of conflicts of interest and what the position is where a conflict can or does arise.

Sensitivity to potential conflicts of interest is particularly important where the lawyer is working outside the context of a one-to-one lawyer-client relationship. This can occur in representing an institution, or group, or undertaking mediation, conciliation or other non-conventional work. Another factor in favour of reducing the scope of conflict rules lies in the fact that civil procedures are less adversarial. It may be that the rules and principles on conflict of interest could be revisited in order to accommodate a more co-operative and facilitative ethos. It is therefore desirable to keep conflict rules under review, particularly with regard to practices and developments in other jurisdictions.

12

Fees

'There are three golden rules in the profession [criminal law] ... the first ... thoroughly terrify your client. Second, find out how much money he has and where it is. Third, get it. The merest duffer can usually succeed in following out the first two of these precepts, but to accomplish the third requires often a master's art. The ability actually to get one's hands on the coin is what differentiates the really great criminal lawyer from his inconspicuous brethren'.[1]

I. Introduction

Fees are the name for the professional charges lawyers seek from clients for providing their services. They reflect the amount necessary to cover overheads and produce a profit. Both of these elements can fluctuate, producing widely different fee rates. The charging of fees therefore cuts across the duty of loyalty, with the implicit obligation of transparency. It also involves an inherent conflict of interest; the more the lawyer charges the less money the client retains. The amount of money that must be paid, whether it is fair and whether the bill is understood by the client, goes to heart of issues of trust and loyalty and honesty. In most professional relationships, clients are unable to evaluate the amount or type of work that needs to be done.

Because client trust depends on fair billing, regulation of charging is a central regulatory issue. In the case of lawyers the position is complicated by the fact that the amount of work required may depend on factors beyond the lawyer's control, such as the behaviour of other parties. Further, in some situations, costs may be recoverable from the other side, reducing the fee payable by the client. Nevertheless, lawyers generally have an idea of the likely and possible costs and the fees clients may end up paying in different situations. They are better able than clients to balance the result of this calculation against the benefits of any proposed course of action.

---

[1] A Train, *The Confessions of Artemas Quibble* (New York, Scribners, 1926) at 77.

II. Fees and Costs

The terms 'fees' and 'costs' are potentially confusing. In this chapter the term 'fee' refers to the charge lawyers make to clients. Fees include a contribution to the lawyer's overheads and a profit element. They generally include chargeable expenses, disbursements, incurred on the client's behalf. One source of confusion is that sums paid to court, for example, to issue proceedings, are called court fees, but of course, to lawyers, these sums are disbursements.

'Costs' generally refers to the sums recoverable from the other side in litigation. This sum is based on the successful party's lawyer's fees,[2] but it may be less than the lawyer's bill to his own client. Sometimes, lawyers refer to expenses incurred on a client's behalf in non-contentious matters as costs. It is only when they deliver a bill that these costs are seen as fees. It is possible that a party can be responsible for another's costs in a non-contentious matter. This might occur for example when a borrower agrees to pay the costs of a mortgage lender's solicitors to check title.[3]

Who is responsible for payment of fees and costs is a fundamental issue in providing access to justice through the civil courts. Such access is a basic constitutional right. It can be abrogated only by express provision in an Act of Parliament. Therefore, an order by the Lord Chancellor withdrawing exemption from court fees to those on income support was declared ultra vires because there was no specific enabling provision in the relevant Act.[4]

In England and Wales legislation attempting to control lawyers' costs goes back to at least 1605.[5] Other countries have also taken measures to constrain charges. In the US, George W Bush made the issue part of his presidential campaign, saying that 'avarice among many plaintiffs' lawyers has clogged our civil courts'. Bush advocated a clients' bill of rights on the issue.[6] Controlling costs has generally proven difficult, partly because of the complexity of rules and the variety of contexts to which they must apply. Lord Justice Balcombe commented in *Symphony Group v Hodgson*,[7] that 'there is only one immutable rule in relation to costs, namely that there are no immutable rules'.

---

[2] SRA, *Handbook*, Glossary (www.sra.org.uk/solicitors/handbook/glossary/content.page).
[3] See ch 11: 'Conflicts of Interest'.
[4] *R v Lord Chancellor, ex p Witham* [1997] 2 All ER 779.
[5] M Cook, *Cook on Costs* (London, Butterworths, 2001–02) at 77.
[6] HM Kritzer, 'The Fracturing Legal Profession: the Case of Plaintiffs' Personal Injury Lawyers' (2001) 8 *International Journal of the Legal Profession* 225.
[7] *Symphony Group v Hodgson* [1993] 4 All ER 143.

III. Traditional Basis of Charging Fees

A. Solicitors

In 1843, conveyancing fees reflected the length of documents, a recipe for both verbosity and complexity.[8] This led to the introduction of a*d valorem* fees, which varied according to the value of the subject matter dealt with, for sales, purchases and mortgages.[9] These scale charges dated back to the Solicitors Remuneration Act 1881 and the Solicitors' Remuneration Order 1883. Practice Rules passed in 1936 prevented solicitors from acting at less than scale fees fixed by the court or prevailing in the area where they practised.[10] In the mid-1930s, solicitors' professional rules fixed fees to prevent undercutting.[11]

Scale fees, which might be thought to be aimed at maximizing income, were justified on the ground that undercutting encourages 'fee shopping' and low standards of work. These matters were considered a proper issue for professional codes of conduct. By 1963, nearly all local law societies had set their scale fees at the maximum allowed by the remuneration orders. Under pressure from consumers, the Law Society abolished the scale in 1972.[12] In 1996, some solicitors tried to restore fixed fees for conveyancing. The Law Society Council avoided what would have been a controversial and, some would say, anti-competitive move.[13]

Time charging, hourly fees paid for the actual work done, is now the usual basis of charging fees for solicitors. The fees element of the bill is based on the number of hours the lawyer spent working on the matter. The amount at which time is charged can vary dramatically according to different areas of work, type of firm and experience of lawyer. To the total produced by the number of hours worked is added an 'uplift'. This is usually a percentage based on the difficulty of the case. This uplift is referred to as 'care and conduct'. A solicitor's bill includes a list of disbursements, payments made to third parties on behalf of clients in connection with the case or transaction. They include items such as stamp duties, registration fees, court fees and witness fees.

---

[8] RL Abel, *The Legal Profession in England and Wales* (Oxford, Basil Blackwell, 1988) at 193.

[9] PF Evans, *The Solicitors Remuneration Act 1881 and the General Order Made in Pursuance Thereof* (London, William Maxwell and Sons, 1883).

[10] L Sheinman, 'Ethical Practice or Practical Ethics: The Case of the Vendor-Purchaser Rule' (2001) 3 *Legal Ethics* 27.

[11] ibid.

[12] Abel, *The Legal Profession in England and Wales* (n 8) 194.

[13] *The Lawyer* 19 March 1996, at 2.

B. Barristers

Barristers normally quote a fixed fee for a written advice or piece of drafting and a daily rate for court work. While this may be based on an estimate of how long a normal day will be, the fixed fee will still be charged if the judge sits longer than anticipated or rises early. They are paid by fixed fees in some civil work, especially family matters, and in legally aided criminal work. In general, however, barristers were not allowed to charge a fixed fee over a fixed period of time, irrespective of the amount of work done.[14]

Barristers have traditionally attempted to avoid the problems of conflict of interest inherent in fixing fees by denying any involvement in the issue. Their fees were negotiated by their clerks and are regarded as 'honoraria' which give rise to no legal liability on either side. This was used, inter alia, to justify the immunity of barristers for liability in negligence for court work,[15] since abolished.[16] Under the Courts and Legal Services Act 1990, section 61, barristers were given the power to enter into binding contracts. This was eventually reflected by the Bar Code of Conduct in an annex setting out the contractual terms of work between barristers and solicitors.[17]

IV. Controlling Fees and Costs

Lawyers do not have complete freedom to charge whatever they want. There are various mechanisms controlling fees. These include fees recoverable from the other side, for example in litigation, and those charged to clients. There are also mechanisms for controlling the costs recoverable from opponents in litigation. Controls over fees and over costs employ many of the same mechanisms. They are also related in other ways. For example, if a lawyer does not recover all his costs from an opponent, he may well attempt to recover any shortfall from his client.

A number of practices are identified with some well-known abuses of hourly billing systems. One of the most obvious is charging for work that has not been done. Others are less easy to detect yet familiar. 'Gouging', for example, refers to charging more than a reasonable price; it can occur when a lawyer settles any possible debate about a particular item in his own favour. 'Churning' refers to doing more work than is necessary given the nature or value of the case. Even sophisticated corporate clients may find this difficult to control. These issues cannot be left to the operation of the market, and mechanisms for external assessment of fees and costs therefore exist.

---

[14] Bar Council, *Bar Code of Conduct 1981*, as amended, at para 307.
[15] B Abel-Smith and L Stevens, *Lawyers and the Courts* (London, Heinemann Educational Books Ltd, 1967) at 231.
[16] *Hall v Simons* [2000] 3 All ER 673, HL.
[17] Bar Council, *Bar Code of Conduct 1981*, as amended, Annex G2.

A. The Basic System

The basic system for assessing costs paid, usually by the losing party, has been adjusted by a number of innovations. It is necessary to consider how the system works in principle. It usually assumes action by one or more of the parties challenging the lawyer's bill. This system involves detailed assessment after the event by specialist officers of the court. The process used to be, and often still is, called taxation of costs. The official name, introduced to make terminology more consumer friendly, is 'detailed assessment'.[18] In litigation, detailed assessment is available at the conclusion of a case, if costs are not agreed between the parties. Outside of the context of litigation, solicitors' bills can also be assessed by the court at the request of clients.

Determining an appropriate hourly rate tends to be fairly broad brush. The costs judge has a table of what is appropriate for a solicitor of particular seniority and needs a fairly good argument for approving or disapproving something outside that range. Therefore, for example, the court tends not to look at the actual overhead of a firm in determining whether an hourly rate is reasonable. Thus, it is immaterial that a lawyer is 'in-house' and has lower overheads than a lawyer in private practice.[19]

i. Assessment Requested by Opponent in Litigation

a. The Incidence of Costs

In the English system of litigation the fees of the winner's lawyers are usually paid by the loser.[20] This is on an indemnity basis, so, the costs cannot exceed those for which the successful party would have been liable to his lawyer. Therefore, if the winner incurred no costs, none can be recovered.[21] This principle is incorporated in the Civil Procedure Rules (CPR). The court has discretion to order payment of costs by one party to another, the amount of those costs and when they are to be paid.[22]

In deciding whether to make an order for the payment of costs by one of the parties to litigation, and the proportion of costs payable, the court has regard to all the circumstances. Circumstances do not include the means of the parties, but do include their conduct. This refers to whether they succeeded in all or part of the claim, whether they were reasonable in the way they framed their case and whether they followed the relevant court procedures.[23] The court also considers whether either party refused reasonable offers to settle.

---

[18] Civil Procedure Rules 1998, as amended.
[19] *Re Eastwood* [1975] Ch 112; *Re Arora* [2013] UKUT 0362 (LC).
[20] Civil Procedure Rules 1998, as amended, r 44.3(2)(a).
[21] *Gundry v Sainsbury* [1910] 1 KB 645.
[22] Senior Courts Act 1981, ss 51(1) and (3); Civil Procedure Rules 1998, as amended, r 44.2.
[23] Civil Procedure Rules 1998, as amended, r 44.5

b. Process

The main constraint on lawyers' costs in litigation in the English system is detailed assessment of costs by the court after the event.[24] The process is specified in the CPR and conducted by costs judges exercising all the powers of a court, except powers to sanction the behaviour of lawyers.[25] The party claiming costs submits a detailed and itemised bill. The court focuses on the costs that are specifically challenged and does not evaluate the solicitor's bill as a whole unless this is asked for. Party and party costs are assessed on either the standard basis or the indemnity basis. The standard basis of assessment is the usual or default position. The basic difference is that, in standard assessments, the costs must be proportionate to the matter in issue. On an indemnity basis, costs need not be proportionate. In both cases the costs must be reasonable, but, in assessments on the standard basis, any doubt as to reasonableness is resolved in favour of the paying party. When costs are assessed on the indemnity basis, any doubts are resolved in favour of the receiving party. Costs on an indemnity basis are awarded only where there has been some culpability or abuse of process by the paying party. The court decides which is applicable in a particular case.

c. Recovery

Lawyers may not be able to recover all of their costs from the other side. They may then seek to recover any shortfall from clients. This shortfall is sometimes called 'solicitor and own client costs'.

ii. Assessment Requested by Clients

This assessment of costs by the court can be applied for by the client in both contentious and non-contentious business.[26] In the assessment of solicitor and client costs, much depends on the terms of the retainer, particularly what the client instructed the solicitor to do. In general, these costs are assessed on an indemnity basis. If there is any doubt as to their reasonableness, it will be assumed they are reasonable if they were approved by the client, either expressly or impliedly.[27]

There are two main reasons why assessment of solicitor and client costs is rare. First, solicitors must tell clients of the availability of assessment only before suing for their costs. Secondly, clients must pay the costs of assessment unless the bill is reduced by more than one-fifth.[28] A third factor applies only to situations where there has already been a party and party assessment. These often act as a kind of protection for the winning client against additional charges. Few solicitors are happy to present their client with bills for work which a costs judge has decided was unnecessary, unless the client expressly required it.

---

[24] ibid, r 47.
[25] ibid, r 47.3.
[26] Solicitors Act 1974, ss 68 and 70.
[27] Civil Procedure Rules 1998, as amended, pt 48, r 48.8.
[28] Solicitors Act 1974, s 70(9).

The process of assessment by the court applies also to legally aided cases. The legally aided client can take part in this process if he or she has an interest in the outcome. Such an interest may arise if the client is liable for a contribution or because the client is affected by the statutory charge. The costs of the assessment will be covered by legal aid.

iii. Detailed Assessment of Costs Required by Third Parties

Third party funders of litigation are potentially liable for adverse costs up to the amount of the funding contributed.[29] A third party who has paid, or is liable for, the costs of an action can also apply for court assessment.

B. Control by Courts

Lord Woolf's Report *Access to Justice* (1995) aimed to reduce cost, delay and complexity in civil cases. In his interim report Woolf concluded that 'the present system provides higher benefits to lawyers than to their clients'.[30] He was sceptical that the profession was concerned about controlling costs. The Civil Procedure Act 1997 led to revision of rules of court and the introduction of the Civil Procedure Rules (CPR). The 'overriding objective' of the rules was enabling the court to deal with cases justly. This meant, as far as practicable, saving expense, putting the parties on an equal footing and dealing with cases proportionately bearing in mind costs and the financial position of the parties.[31] Proportionality meant relating costs to the amount of money involved, the importance of the case, the complexity of the issues and to the financial position of each party. The main measure for controlling costs was active case management by judges.

Several of the 12 specific tasks identified in the CPR as part of the judges' active case management role involved control of the amount of work done by lawyers.[32] Therefore, for example, the judge must decide promptly which issues need full investigation and adjudication and dispose summarily of the others.[33] The judge must also consider whether the likely benefit of taking a particular step justifies the cost of taking it.[34] These measures were supplemented by further amendment of the CPR following a review by Lord Justice Jackson of the costs of civil litigation in 2010.[35]

[29] Arkin v Borchard Lines Ltd and others [2005] EWCA Civ 655.
[30] Lord Woolf, *Access to Justice: Interim Report to the Lord Chancellor on the Civil Justice System in England and Wales* (London, Lord Chancellor's Department, 1995) at 13. See also P Abrams, A Boon and D O' Brien, 'Access to Justice: The Collision of Funding and Ethics' (1998) 3(1) *Contemporary Issues in Law* 59.
[31] Civil Procedure Rules 1998, as amended, r 1.1.
[32] ibid, r 1.4.
[33] ibid, r 1.4(c).
[34] ibid, r 1.4(h).
[35] The Right Honourable Lord Justice Jackson, *Review of Civil Litigation Costs* (Norwich, TSO, 2010).

i. Fixed Costs

In his review of civil procedure, Lord Woolf saw fixed fees as essential to the success of the proposed 'fast track' procedure for civil litigation cases. The imposition of a system of task-based fixed fees has been one of the main innovations since the introduction of the CPR. The system has been strongly identified with the development of automated, online claims portals. Since 2000 the CPR have increasingly introduced fixed costs especially for routine or minor steps in cases.[36]

In 2002 a web-based system was introduced for initiating claims. The automated claims portal with fixed fees was introduced for debts up to £100,000. This was followed by another portal for road traffic accident claims below £10,000 with fixed costs.[37] Following the Legal Aid and Punishment of Offenders Act (LASPO) 2012, the upper limit for such claims was increased to £25,000 and similar portals, with fixed costs regimes, were introduced for employers' liability and public liability personal injury cases.

ii. Costs Capping Orders

The courts have increasingly used principles in the CPR to cap costs. The use of protective costs orders at an early stage in civil proceedings is an example.[38] Cost capping orders were available for some time in judicial review proceedings. They were meant to enable charitable or campaigning bodies to bring judicial review proceedings without fear that costs would cripple claims. They were particularly useful if their lawyers were acting pro bono. In such cases, the issue had to be one of public importance that the applicant had no private interest in. It also had to be fair and reasonable to make the order.

The approach was approved by the House of Lords in *Campbell v MGN (No 2)*,[39] although it cannot be retrospective and must be applied for by the parties rather than on the initiative of the court.[40] The courts have been hesitant to extend the practice. In *R v Secretary of State for Trade*,[41] it was said that a costs capping order should be made only in exceptional circumstances. In *Knight v Beyond Properties Ltd*,[42] it was stated that, in order to contemplate such an order, there must be evidence of extravagance which cannot otherwise be controlled. Whether capping orders will become normal in future remains to be seen. Their use to curtail costs in cases where conditional fee agreements operate is considered further below.

---

[36] See eg Civil Procedure Rules 1998, as amended, pt 45.
[37] ibid, pt 45, r 2.5.
[38] A Zuckerman, 'Costs Capping in CFA Cases' (2005) 24 *Civil Justice Quarterly* 1.
[39] *Campbell v MGN (No 2)* [2005] 4 All ER 793, at 805.
[40] *Henry v BBC* [2005] EWHC 2503
[41] *R v Secretary of State for Trade* [2005] EWCA Civ 192.
[42] *Knight v Beyond Properties Ltd* [2006] EWHC 1242.

iii. Costs Budgeting

One of the main measures proposed by Lord Justice Jackson to increase judicial control over the increasing cost of civil litigation was cost budgeting. The CPR now require litigators to agree a realistic assessment of costs at the start of a case.[43] The court records such agreement or, if the budgets are not agreed, will review them and, after making any appropriate revisions, record that the budget falls within the range of reasonable and proportionate costs. If the budget changes for any reason during the case, revised budgets must be submitted.[44]

Early indications were that the rules would be strictly enforced. In *Sylvia Henry v News Group Newspapers Ltd*,[45] neither the court nor the other side had been informed at the correct time that the agreed costs budget had been exceeded. The successful claimant in a defamation claim was therefore denied costs of nearly £270,000 that would otherwise have been allowable.

The courts' strict line was continued in *Mitchell v News Group Newspapers Limited.*[46] The claimant (M) was a former cabinet minister who resigned following allegations arising from an altercation with police at the gates of Downing Street. M claimed damages in a libel action against *The Sun* newspaper for a story it ran in connection with the incident. M's solicitors failed to file their costs budget by the deadline. In fact they were seven days late, delivering the calculation just before the costs management conference. The excuse was that they were a small office, heavily affected by maternity leave, and had key staff engaged on another case. Their recoverable costs, estimated to run to £1 million, were capped by the trial judge at £2,000.

The Court of Appeal considered an application for relief of sanctions by Mitchell's solicitors.[47] It held that courts should normally grant relief for trivial non-compliance such as a failure of form rather than substance, or where a deadline is narrowly missed. If the default was not trivial, the burden of establishing a cause for relief was on the defaulting party. The Master of the Rolls outlined the reasons for which relief is likely to be granted. These were debilitating illness or an accident, developments causing the original period for compliance to become unreasonable and reasons outside of the party's control. They did not include overlooking a deadline or pressure of work. The imposition of the cap on the costs of the claimant's solicitors was therefore upheld.

In a subsequent decision it was held that this guidance had been interpreted in such a way as to produce harsh outcomes and a raft of satellite litigation.[48] The Court of Appeal therefore introduced a three stage test with the aim of producing greater consistency in decisions. In the first stage the court should consider the nature of the breach. If it was not serious, it would not normally be necessary to consider sanctions. In the second stage the court should consider the reason for the breach.

---

[43] The Supreme Court, Practice Direction 3e – Costs Management, at para 2.3, supplementing s II of CPR, pt 3.
[44] ibid, at para 2.6.
[45] *Sylvia Henry v News Group Newspapers Ltd* [2013] EWCA Civ 19.
[46] *Mitchell v News Group Newspapers Limited* [2013] EWHC 2355.
[47] *Mitchell v News Group Newspapers Limited* [2013] EWCA Civ 1537, [2014] 1 WLR 795.
[48] *Utilise TDS Limited v Davies* [2014] EWCA CA Civ 906.

Finally, whatever, the outcome of the other two stages, the court should consider all the circumstances in order to deal justly with an application for relief from sanctions.

iv. Interlocutory Costs Orders

Before 2000, the payment of costs awarded in interlocutory matters was postponed until the end of the case. At that stage the loser could face a bill inflated by purely tactical interlocutory proceedings. Lord Woolf considered that the award of such costs should not await the end of the case. He recommended that they be awarded at the conclusion of the interlocutory proceedings and paid forthwith.[49] This principle was embodied in Rule 44.7, which provides that orders for specified costs must be paid in 14 days.

The CPR Rule 44.8, also provides that 'the party's legal representative must notify that party in writing of the costs order no later than seven days after the legal representative receives notice of the order'. As Cook and Hurst remarked, this rule makes clients 'realize that their lawyers have lost a battle and they will have to put their hands in their pockets and part with their money at an early stage in the proceedings'.[50]

v. Wasted Costs Orders

The wasted costs jurisdiction is another method by which solicitors' and barristers' costs can be controlled at the behest of both their clients and the other side.[51] It is partly aimed at protecting third parties from inflated costs and is a jurisdiction that has greatly expanded in recent years. It is dealt with in detail in part five.[52]

C. Control by Clients and Funders

Corporate and commercial clients, and others with a degree of power in the lawyer and client relationship, frequently seek ways of controlling lawyers' costs. This section outlines one of the main methods, fixed fees. This kind of fixed fee could apply to a whole case or transaction (case-based fixed fees), or simply to parts of it (task-based fixed fees).

i. Imposition of Fixed Fees

Fixed fees operate as an alternative to the hourly charge. However long a particular task takes a lawyer, he is only be paid the fixed rate for that job. This is obviously

---

[49] See Lord Woolf, *Final Report to the Lord Chancellor on the civil justice system in England and Wales* (London, HM Stationery Office, 1996), ch 7, at para 30.

[50] M Cook and PT Hurst, *The New Civil Costs Regime* (London, Butterworths, 1999) at 23.

[51] Senior Courts Act 1981, s 51(6), as amended by the Courts and Legal Services Act 1990.

[52] Ch 17: 'Litigation'.

disadvantageous to lawyers, who may perform work at a loss. In 1993, the Law Society failed in an action for judicial review of the Lord Chancellor's decision to introduce standard fees in legally aided criminal cases. Many lawyers say that legally aided work has since become unprofitable. They claim that they can often only act in the best interests of clients if they are prepared to do unpaid work.

ii. Case-based Fixed Fees

Fixed fees are attractive to clients because they know in advance what they are committed to paying. From the early-1990s there was growing pressure on solicitors, from commercial clients, for fixed rather than hourly fees in other areas of work.[53] This was largely aimed at controlling overwork and overbilling,[54] which many institutions, including the judiciary, saw as endemic in the legal profession.[55] Large corporations often produce detailed codes regulating their relationship with their lawyers. These may require them to justify their fees and to give advance warning of bills.[56] Increasingly, in routine transactions, like conveyancing or making wills, a fixed fee is normal.

Fixed fees also appeal to third party institutions, like government agencies, funding litigation, for example, through legal aid. The Legal Services Commission controlled costs in civil cases by contracting solicitors to do a fixed number of case starts per year for a fixed yearly fee. In addition, the Civil Justice Council aims to negotiate set fees with the major players in certain types of litigation. For example, in personal injury cases agreements are being made with insurers, employers and lawyers relating to levels of success fee in conditional fee cases.[57]

iii. Task-based Fixed Fees

Task based fixed fees were introduced for legally aided criminal work, in the teeth of lawyer opposition, during the 1980s and 1990s. This idea has been extended by the introduction, by LASPO 2012, of the new funding code. This means that legal aid is more likely to be available only for targeted interventions in parts of the case. These could include only one activity, for example, of initial advice, assistance at court or advocacy.

---

[53] See eg *The Lawyer* 18 May 1993, at 12.
[54] See eg G Hanlon, 'A Profession in Transition' (1997) 60 *Modern Law Review* 798, at 813.
[55] See eg *The Guardian* 18 November 1996.
[56] 'Lloyds Underwriters are concerned about over-manning in solicitors' firms' *Law Society Gazette* 1 July 1998, at 9.
[57] See eg 154 *New Law Journal* 18 June 2004.

D. Regulation

i. *Brief Review of Attempts to Control Costs of Solicitors*

The regulation of fees and costs was historically based on an assumption of time charging and itemised billing. The Law Society, and later the SRA, offered a free review of bills under £50,000 until 1 March 2010.[58] The procedure was only available in non-contentious matters[59] resulting in the issue of a remuneration certificate stating the fair and reasonable charge for the work covered by the bill.

The right to seek a remuneration certificate did not apply where a non-contentious business agreement under the Solicitors Act 1974, section 57 existed.[60] This was an agreement made in writing between solicitor and client and signed by both. Clients could enter such an agreement without realising that they forfeited the right to use the remuneration certificate procedure. This situation was criticised by the Legal Services Ombudsman.[61]

Solicitors applied for the review, usually before suing the client for fees, in situations where they did not hold client money. Clients could also request a referral. A client requesting a remuneration certificate had to pay 50 per cent of the costs, plus VAT and disbursements in advance. This could be waived by the SRA. The client could not get a remuneration certificate after the expiry of the time limits, where the bill had already been paid or where a court ordered an assessment of the bill. Failure by the solicitor to comply with the certificate could result in disciplinary proceedings.

The remuneration certificate procedure was little used compared to the numbers who, in surveys, expressed concern about solicitors' costs. This may be because the procedure was not known to clients or because clients felt that the SRA was unlikely to disagree with solicitors. In fact, of approximately 2000 bills reviewed each year, about 60 per cent were reduced.

ii. *Current System*

From 1 March 2010 complaints about costs were directed to the Legal Ombudsman (LeO).[62] Many complaints do not require a detailed cost analysis, but those that do are referred to the Senior Courts Costs Office. Where the complaint is that the fees were excessive, LeO assesses whether the costs were reasonable overall. Lawyers are asked to explain anything questionable, such as unrelated, duplicated or disproportionate costs or discrepancies between estimates and final bills.

LeO can order the rectification of errors, omissions and deficiencies and require that costs are limited in amount. He can order the solicitor to make an apology or

---

[58] Solicitors' (Non-Contentious Business) Remuneration Order 1994 (which was repealed from that date).
[59] ibid.
[60] ibid, cl 9(c).
[61] Legal Services Ombudsman, *Annual Report* (1996) at 15.
[62] Legal Services Act 2007, s 137.

make a payment of compensation for distress or inconvenience. After two complaints have been made against a firm, LeO charges it a fee for subsequent complaints.

According to the LeO report, many of the complaints he handles about costs arise in relation to litigation and family matters. In these areas it may be difficult to give an accurate estimate at the start of the matter because costs are often dependent on the actions of the other side. LeO guidance on costs emphasises the importance of keeping clients updated, especially when the costs are likely to exceed an estimate or limit set by the client. Lawyers should also be clear, when a client requests work, that this is likely to take fees outside the original estimate and what additional work will cost.

V. Contingency Fees

A. Context

The term 'contingency fee' has many meanings. The basic idea is that the lawyer does not get paid unless the contingency occurs, but gets a higher fee than would be normal if it does. Usually, the contingency is the winning of the case in which the fee is chargeable. If no additional fee then becomes payable, the fee is a speculative fee, a different arrangement dealt with in the next section.

There is a long history of antipathy towards the use of contingency and speculative fees to support litigation. This was reflected in the rules of conduct of the legal profession. The recent relaxation of rules prohibiting contingency fees is intended to save public money, legal aid payments, while supporting access to justice. There are some concerns regarding the ethical risks surrounding contingency fees.

B. Public Policy against Stirring up Litigation

Hostility to contingency fees can be traced to longstanding rules aimed at discouraging third parties from supporting or stirring up litigation by maintaining or taking a share of proceeds of cases. Such practices were banned at least since the Statute of Westminster of 1275. Rejection of third party support is not universal. In the US, for example, contingency fees are a common way of supporting litigation. American texts on legal ethics marvel at 'the mysteries of the Macbethian witches of the common law who stirred the law of despised litigation; maintenance, champerty and barratry'.[63]

---

[63] CW Wolfram, *Modern Legal Ethics* (St Paul, MN, West Publishing Co, 1986) at 489; D Luban, 'Speculating on Justice: The Ethics and Jurisprudence of Contingency Fees' in S Parker and C Sampford (eds), *Legal Ethics and Legal Practice: Contemporary Issues* (Oxford, Clarendon Press, 1995) 89, at 114.

i. *Maintenance, Champerty and Barratry*

Maintenance describes the act of a third party becoming involved in, supporting and encouraging a law suit. Champerty is exacerbated maintenance, whereby the third party takes a share of any damages. Barratry is the act of bringing a vexatious case, one intended to harass and intimidate an opponent. The offences of maintenance, champerty and barratry made those encouraging litigation subject to sanctions, both in criminal law and in tort.

Lawyers were particularly affected by the rules against maintenance and champerty. The normal contingency fee arrangement in the US, where the lawyer is not paid if the case is lost but gets a percentage of the winnings if it is won, was prohibited in the UK under the common law relating to champerty.[64] Speculative fees, where a lawyer agrees to be paid only what the losing side is ordered to pay in costs, and arrangements whereby a client's fees are paid by third parties or by the lawyer, were prohibited by the common law prohibiting maintenance.[65]

The consequences of charging unlawful contingency fees were, first, that the lawyer could not recover the fee, or even disbursements, from the client.[66] Further, if the case was won, and the arrangement was discovered, there was no basis for ordering the losing party to pay costs. This was because, applying the indemnity principle, the claimant had no costs liability. If, however, the client had already paid money to the solicitor, it could not be reclaimed, the agreement being unenforceable rather than void or voidable.[67] Nor was the loss of a champertous fee insurable.[68] More serious for solicitors, that they could find themselves liable for the costs of the other side if the case was lost.[69]

The common law offences were nearly rendered obsolete by the professional ethics of lawyers in the nineteenth century. Rules prohibiting maintenance prevented conflicts of interest between lawyer and client and removed lawyers' disincentives to probity in court proceedings. The Criminal Law Act 1967 removed criminal and tortious liability for maintenance and champerty, but arrangements for the support of litigation were still unenforceable.[70] It is instructive to consider why maintenance and champerty were considered so dangerous and unprofessional that they justified such serious consequences.

ii. *The Ethics of Supporting Clients' Litigation*

Maintenance and champerty offend the ethical principle against lawyer and client conflicts of interest. If lawyers can support litigation, they owe allegiance to a party

---

[64] *Aratra Potato v Taylor Joynson Garrett* [1995] 4 All ER 695; *Factortame v Secretary of State (No 2)* [2002] 4 All ER 97.

[65] See *Hill v Archbold* [1968] 1 QB 686 and *Shah v Karanjia* [1993] 4 All ER 792.

[66] *Re Trepca Mines* [1963] Ch 199; *Wild v Simpson* [1919] 2 KB 544.

[67] *Aratra Potato Co v Taylor Joynson Garrett* [1995] 4 All ER 695.

[68] *Haseldine v Hosken* [1933] 1 KB 822.

[69] *McFarlane v EE Caledonia* [1995] 1 WLR 366.

[70] Criminal Law Act 1967, ss 13 and 14.

outside of the lawyer and client relationship; they have a potential personal conflict of interest. This can give rise to various temptations to sell the client short. For example, it may be in the client's interest to negotiate long and hard for maximum damages but, for the lawyer, any extra damages recovered by hard bargaining might not compensate for the extra hours put in to achieve it, particularly in small value cases.[71] Giving lawyers a personal interest in the outcome of a case also provides an incentive to engage in corruption or sharp practices, such as suborning perjury.

iii. Access to Justice

The principle that a third party should not support litigation brought by another was initially compromised on the grounds of providing access to justice. By the introduction of legal aid, the state rapidly became the largest maintainer of litigation of all. In England, some lawyers resisted the introduction of the legal aid scheme in the 1940s and 1950s on the ground that the independence of lawyers to act in their clients' best interests would be compromised by their responsibilities to the legal aid fund.[72] Later, proposals for block funding and franchising of legal aid proposed by the Conservative and Labour Governments led to similar concerns.[73]

As the century progressed, concern grew over the inadequacy of state funding to support access to justice. Organisations devoted to the task of encouraging and enabling others to take legal action were established. These included charitable organisations, pressure groups and bodies like insurance companies, motoring organisations and trades unions. Similar developments in the US, for example, the growth of trades' union organised legal expenses insurance plans, were resisted on the ground that it constituted maintenance. Nowadays, few people consider providing support for litigation to be unethical; access to justice is a more serious concern.

As eligibility rates for legal aid fell in the 1980 and 1990s, pressure to find alternative ways to enable ordinary people to bring litigation increased. The compromise was that lawyers would be able to support litigation in return for a success fee by entering a conditional fee agreement (CFA) with clients. Despite the widespread use of contingency type agreements, there remain concerns that such arrangements are vulnerable to exploitation by legal professionals. CFAs were ringed with strict requirements and lawyers who did not comply with them could find that their arrangement was struck down.

Maintenance and champerty continue to have great relevance, despite the new centrality of contingency type fees in delivering access to justice. Technically, only fee arrangements specifically allowed by statute escape the common rules of maintenance and champerty. Support for litigation that does not satisfy the relevant statutory

---

[71] HM Kritzer, *The Justice Broker: Lawyers and Ordinary Litigation* (New York, Oxford University Press, 1990) at 108; P Danzon, 'Contingent Fees for Personal Injury Litigation' (1983) 14(1) *Bell Journal of Economics* 213; L Schwartz and DB Mitchell, 'An Economic Analysis of the Contingent Fee in Personal Injuries Litigation' (1970) 22 *Stanford Law Review* 1125.

[72] B Abel-Smith and R Stevens, *Lawyers and the Courts: A Sociological Study of the English Legal System, 1750–1965* (London, Heinemann, 1967) ch 5, fn 343.

[73] Abrams, Boon and O'Brien, 'Access to Justice' (n 30).

or regulatory regimes may be unenforceable.[74] The practical effect of this is that defendants are not liable for the costs of claimants supported by such arrangements. Further, claimants may not be liable for the fees of their own lawyers. It is therefore necessary to consider the main types of permitted fee agreement.[75]

C. Conditional Fee Agreements

A government Green Paper, published in 1989, rejected US-style contingency fees based on lawyers receiving a percentage of damages. It argued that litigants would be unable to negotiate terms meaningfully with lawyers.[76] A variant, so-called 'conditional fees', were therefore created by the Courts and Legal Services Act 1990. These were, however, only finally implemented by the Conditional Fee Agreement Regulations 1995.

i. Scope

CFAs were initially available for actions for personal injury, to wind up companies or in bankruptcy proceedings and actions before the European Commission or Court of Human Rights. From July 1998 they were available for all litigation except criminal and matrimonial cases.[77] This coincided with the withdrawal of legal aid in personal injury cases, with the exception of medical negligence. The Courts and Legal Services Act 1990, section 58 did not extend the use of CFAs to arbitrations, but there is no public policy objection to extension to arbitration in cases similar to those covered by the Act.[78]

The Administration of Justice Act 1999 made a number of significant changes to the CFA regime. As regards scope there were two main changes. The first extended the use of CFAs to dispute resolution other than court proceedings. The second allowed for the use of Collective Conditional Fee Agreements (CCFAs) by membership organisations, such as trade unions.

A CCFA is an arrangement that does 'not refer to specific proceedings, but provides for fees to be paid on a common basis in relation to a class of proceedings ... or more than one class of proceedings'.[79] In order to facilitate these, the Act provided that the indemnity principle did not apply to the recovery of costs.[80] Many CCFA arrangements relate to personal injury. These claims continue to be the most significant in terms of volume for both CFAs and CCFAs.

In November 2008, Lord Justice Jackson was appointed to lead a fundamental review of the rules and principles governing the costs of civil litigation. The broad

---

[74] But see below *Thai Trading Co v Taylor* [1998] 3 All ER 65.
[75] See further M Cook (ed), *Butterworths Costs Service* (London, Butterworths, 2012) at Division E.
[76] Lord Chancellor's Department, *Contingency Fees* (Cm 571, 1989) at para 4.9.
[77] Conditional Fee Agreements Order 1998 (SI 1998/1860).
[78] *Bevan Ashford v Geoff Yeandle* [1999] Ch 239.
[79] Collective Conditional Fee Agreement Regulations 2000, (SI 2000/2988) reg 3(1)(b).
[80] But not implemented until 2003; AJA 1999 (Commencement No 10) Order 2003 (SI 2003/1241).

conclusion of his final report, published in January 2010,[81] was that some areas of civil litigation costs were disproportionate and impeded access to justice. Jackson proposed 'a coherent package of interlocking reforms, designed to control costs and promote access to justice'.[82] Some recommendations included further adjustment of the rules on CFAs. Others included the introduction of another kind of contingency fee, called a damages-based agreement, as an alternative to CFAs.

Lord Justice Jackson's proposals were taken forward in a variety of ways, coinciding with serious cuts in civil legal aid. Some measures required primary legislation and were implemented as part of LASPO 2012 in April 2013. Many involved amendment of the CPR. It is necessary to outline how these fee agreements operate in order to consider threats to the professional ethics of lawyers.

ii. Main Elements

From 1995, CFAs allowed solicitors to finance litigation, in return for payment, on satisfaction of a condition.[83] The normal terms provided for a success fee if the claim succeeded. When first introduced, CFAs would usually provide that clients would also pay their own lawyer's disbursements, win or lose. If the case was successful, most of the disbursements would be recoverable as part of a costs order. Therefore, under a CFA, a losing claimant may have to pay the defendant's costs and his lawyers disbursements. The risk of paying the defendant's costs could be covered by 'after the event insurance' (ATE insurance) which might also cover the client's own disbursements.

a. After the Event Insurance

The first and most commonly used insurance, provided by Accident Direct, was arranged by the Law Society. Clients paid a reasonably modest premium provided their solicitor agreed to insure all his personal injury cases with Accident Direct. The policy could also be used to cover the client's disbursements that were not paid by the other side on winning the case. In some cases, however, premiums were reported to be extremely high, up to half of projected damages.

b. Calculation of the Success Fee

In successful claims the regulations limited the success fee to a percentage up to 100 per cent of the normal fee, excluding disbursements. The ethical issue for the solicitor was being fair to the client. The percentage for calculating the success fee was supposed to reflect the degree of risk the case represented for the solicitor. Such calculations inevitably involve numerous variables involving the merits of the case and the strength of the evidence. The evaluation of each variable involved, potentially, a large number of assumptions.

---

[81] Jackson LJ, *Review of Civil Litigation Costs* (n 35).
[82] ibid, Foreword.
[83] Courts and Legal Services Act 1990, s 58A(6), as amended by the Access to Justice Act 1999, ss 27 and 28. See also M Napier and F Bawdon, *Conditional Fees, a Survival Guide* (London, The Law Society, 1995).

The complex calculation of CFA success fees depends entirely on the solicitor's experience and expertise. Precision is almost impossible.[84] The process is entirely impenetrable to clients, who have no basis of comparison. The difficulty of protecting clients was one of the reasons why the success fee chargeable was limited to 100 per cent of the solicitor's costs.

iii. Recoverability of Success Fees and ATE Insurance Premiums

There were two major costs issues to be confronted on the introduction of CFAs. The first was allocating responsibility for paying, first, the success fee and, secondly, the ATE insurance premiums, if the claimant won. Both of these involved costs over and above claimants' legal costs in an ordinary claim. It might therefore be considered unfair to make the defendant pay such fees. This unfairness was magnified in difficult cases. If the claim was high risk, such that the defendant was justified in defending it, the amount paid in costs as a success fee would increase.

Ambivalence on the impact of the additional costs of CFAs is reflected in almost constant changes in the detail of CFA arrangements since 2000.[85] The incidence of responsibility for the extra costs was different in the three main regimes for CFAs, particularly in relation to personal injury claims.

a. Initial Phase: Non-recovery of Success Fees and ATE Premiums

When introduced in 1995, success fee and insurance costs were not recoverable from the other side. Clients were hesitant about using the new conditional fees. They were complex and did not protect them against paying for disbursements.[86] Additionally, the cost of ATE insurance was also a disincentive to clients without moderate resources. Large numbers of people had dropped out of the scope of legal aid, but it was not clear that CFAs were sufficiently attractive to fill the gap. It seemed that access to justice might have taken a step backwards.

b. Second Phase: Recovery of Success Fees and ATE Premiums Allowed

The Access to Justice Act 1999 provided for recovery of success fees and ATE insurance premiums from defendants if the case was won. Rules were introduced for CFAs made after 1 April 1 2000. The successful CFA litigant was therefore protected from most costs. There was, however, a theoretical possibility that the lawyer would ask the client for any shortfall in actual costs compared with those recovered from defendants.[87] From 2003, a 'simplified CFA' could provide that the percentage of the success fee was levied on the recoverable costs, not on the costs chargeable to the client.[88]

---

[84] See further DJ Chalk, *Risk Assessment in Litigation: Conditional Fee Agreements, Insurance and Funding* (Haywards Heath, Tottel Publishing, 2007) at pt 9.

[85] See further Cook, *Butterworths Costs Service* (n 75).

[86] S Yarrow, *Just Rewards? The Outcome of Conditional Fee Arrangements* (London, Nuffield, 2001).

[87] Chalk, *Risk Assessment in Litigation* (n 84) ch 8.

[88] Conditional Fee Agreements (Miscellaneous Amendments) Regulations 2003 (SI 2003 No 3344).

The strategic balance in the CFA regime substantially changed in the second phase. New rules were introduced so as to be fair to defendants who might have to bear this additional liability. The defendant and Registry had to receive notice that a CFA was in place as soon as reasonably practicable after execution.[89] Defendants, for whom CFAs were rarely available or appropriate, often settled cases, however spurious and unlikely to succeed in court, because of the risk of having to pay additional costs of litigation.

The new arrangements certainly increased access to justice. Anyone, including the poor and those of moderate means, could litigate personal injury cases and other claims without worrying too much about cost. Clients could even take out loans to pay insurance premiums, albeit at the generally high rates of consumer loans. Lord Nicholls was seriously concerned that 'claimants now operate in a costs-free and risk-free zone'.[90] This raised the question of whether the arrangements were fair to defendants.

The control of claimants' costs in CFA cases had passed to losing defendants in assessment proceedings. This led to a considerable volume of satellite costs litigation where defendants queried not only the base costs but also the percentage uplift. To facilitate this, the CFA regulations required claimants to agree to disclose the level of the success fee. This overcame potential claims for privilege that clients might make. Although the courts attempted to indicate appropriate levels of success fees, 5 per cent in claims for passengers in road traffic cases for example, this did not prevent challenges. Even the courts had to acknowledge that the guidelines were reviewable.[91]

c. Third Phase: Non-recovery of Success Fees and ATE Premiums from Defendants Re-introduced in Personal Injury Cases

Lord Justice Jackson's review of the cost of civil litigation concluded that the recovery of success fees and ATE premiums was a major driver of disproportionate cost. He recommended that both ceased to be recoverable in personal injury claims, including those involving clinical negligence. The incidence of these costs would therefore revert to successful claimants. This burden, Jackson suggested, should be offset by a 10 per cent increase in general damages for pain, suffering and loss of amenity.[92] From 1 April 2013 new rules on CFAs came into force.[93] These required most clients entering into a CFA on or after that date to pay the success fee and any ATE premium from their damages.[94]

Claimants with mesothelioma claims, insolvency proceedings, publication and privacy proceedings and pre-commencement agreements would still be able to claim success fees.[95] The inability to claim ATE insurance premiums was offset by the introduction

---

[89] The Supreme Court, Practice Direction 13 – 'Costs', s 16.1 (Conditional Fee Agreements).

[90] *Callery v Gray* [2002] 3 All ER 417, at 422.

[91] D Chalk, 'Sounding the retreat' *Solicitors Journal* 20 September 2002, at 831.

[92] Jackson LJ, *Review of Civil Litigation Costs* (n 35) executive summary, at para 2.4.

[93] LASPO 2012, ss 44 and 46 and the Conditional Fee Agreements Order 2013 (SI 2013/689).

[94] Law Society, *Conditional Fee Agreements Guidance* (May 2013) (www.lawsociety.org.uk/advice/articles/new-model-conditional-fee-agreement/).

[95] Conditional Fee Agreements Order 2013, art 6; and see for a summary of impact of new rules, Lexis/Nexis, *CFA Special: the Confusing World of CFAs Explained* (www1.lexisnexis.co.uk/email_attachments/2013/_hosted/COLP/0313-043_COLP_Report_Mar_2013.pdf).

of qualified one way costs shifting (QOCS) for personal injury and clinical negligence claims. This means that orders for costs against a claimant can only be enforced, without the permission of the court, if the aggregate of such costs do not exceed the aggregate amount of damages awarded the claimant.[96] In the majority of cases, claimants will not be liable for the defendants' costs in the event that the claim is unsuccessful. The exception is where they refuse a reasonable offer of settlement before trial.[97]

The maximum success fee remains an uplift on basic costs of 100 per cent. There is, however, a cap on the amount deductible as a success fee from the claimant's damages in personal injury and clinical negligence claims. The cap on the recoverable success fee in personal injury claims heard at first instance is 25 per cent of general damages and past losses, less any benefits recoupable by the Department of Work and Pensions.[98] Whilst it is not clear from the legislation, the Law Society considers it is likely that the cap includes any success fee payable to counsel.[99]

iv. Lawyers Indemnifying Claimant's Liability for Defendant's Costs

It is likely that the removal of claims for success fees and ATE insurance premiums in the Jackson reforms will reduce the provision and availability of insurance. There are circumstances when, despite QOCS, personal injury victims may be liable to pay defendant's costs. This possibility arises, for example, where a claimant fails to accept what the court later considers a reasonable offer to settle. If they are not to face significant pressure to accept low offers of settlement they may still need indemnity against such a risk.

Reduced availability of ATE insurance and increasing cost of premiums will probably increase the pressure for lawyers to provide indemnity for client liability. In effect, lawyers in this situation are offering to replace the ATE contract of insurance. Arrangements where solicitors provide indemnities for defendants' costs are challengeable on the grounds that they are champertous and constitute an illegal insurance contract.

In one case it was found that upholding a CFA where the lawyer agreed to indemnify the client against paying a defendant's costs was contrary to public policy.[100] The Court was concerned that lawyers providing such an indemnity would have too much at stake on the outcome. This would be dangerous when they were in a position to influence the conduct of the litigation. In another case, such an arrangement was found not to be maintenance.[101] The costs judge considered that the professionalism of solicitors was sufficient guard against temptation to try and influence the outcome of a case unethically, even if they had a financial interest.

---

[96] Civil Procedure Rules 1998, as amended, r 44.14.

[97] ibid, pt 36.

[98] Conditional Fee Agreements Order 2013, art 5.

[99] The Law Society, *Conditional Fee Agreements Guidance* (London, the Law Society, May 2013) (www.lawsociety.org.uk/advice/articles/new-model-conditional-fee-agreement/).

[100] *Dix v Townend* (costs) [2008] EWHC 90117 (Sup Ct Costs Office).

[101] *Murray Lewis v Tennants Distribution Ltd* [2010] EWHC 90161 (Costs).

The uncertain position regarding solicitors providing clients with indemnity for defendants' costs was addressed in *Sibthorpe v Southwark LBC*.[102] The claim was for housing disrepairs worth £1300. The CFA provide for a 10 per cent success fee. It also provided that the claimant's solicitors would indemnify their client against the defendant's costs if insurance was not available. The Court of Appeal decided that this arrangement was not champerty because the indemnity was not a share of the outcome of litigation. It is likely, however, that there will be further challenges to such arrangements.

It seems that the position of lawyers who support litigation, outside of the strict statutory framework for CFAs and DBAs, is risky. While the courts seem satisfied that indemnities for costs do not constitute insurance contracts, the conclusion that they are not champertous is less secure. The courts have been generous in interpreting such arrangements, apparently aware that ATE insurance is disproportionately expensive for some types of claim and may not be available for others.[103] Nevertheless, solicitors entering such arrangements are at risk of not being paid and being responsible for paying the defendant's costs.

The position regarding solicitor indemnity for client costs liability reflects increasing tolerance of ethical risks. One of the possible impacts of the new regime appears to be acceptance of situations that would once have been seen as an unacceptable conflict of interest.

v. Regulation

a. Statutory Regime

The early CFA regime was managed by detailed regulations made under statute. Initially, the agreement had to state the percentage of uplift.[104] Regulations made in 2000 added requirements covering the contents of the agreement,[105] including reasons for setting the percentage uplift,[106] and specifying the information provided to clients.[107] The regulations required that legal representatives inform clients, before the agreement was made, of the circumstances in which costs would be payable by the client to the representative and how they would be assessed.

Solicitors were required to consider other potential sources of funding available to clients before agreeing a CFA with them. This included any 'before the event' insurance, such as household policies covering policy holders' legal expenses in the event of injury. They also had to explore the availability and appropriateness of other methods of financing an action.[108] The information provided to clients was required to be

---

[102] *Sibthorpe v Southwark LBC* [2011] EWCA Civ 25.
[103] DJ Chalk, 'Solicitor Client Costs Indemnities: Unregulated Insurance or Benign Assistance?' (2013) 1 *Journal of Business Law* 59.
[104] Courts and Legal Services Act 1990, s 58(4)(b).
[105] Conditional Fee Agreements Regulations 2000, reg 2.
[106] ibid, reg 3(1)a.
[107] Courts and Legal Services Act 1990, s 58(3)a.
[108] Conditional Fee Agreements Regulations 2000, reg 4(2).

given orally, whether or not it was also given in writing.[109] Many claimants did not understand the information and, since after 2000 they were not substantially at risk on costs, most were not interested.

b. Professional Regulation

Given the statutory and regulatory requirements imposed on CFAs, there seemed little need for additional regulation by the profession. Some changes to the conduct rules were implemented to reflect the new reality. In 1996, the Law Society's Practice Rule 8, which prevented solicitors charging a contingency fee in respect of contentious proceedings, was amended. The new wording was that contingency arrangements were prohibited 'save one permitted under statute or by the common law'.[110] Solicitors failing to observe these requirements might, in theory, face disciplinary charges. This was more likely if, for example, the circumstances caused a conflict of interest.

From November 2005, the government repealed the complex rules on CFAs implemented since 1995.[111] From that date, the Law Society was told to regulate CFAs. Those made after November 2005 were governed by the Solicitors' Code of Conduct. The 2007 Code included a specific rule,[112] but CFAs were not, as might be expected, smothered in professional practice rules. The Law Society was keen to promote their use, producing a model contract and detailed guide.

The guidance to solicitors added little. Solicitors acting under a CFA were required to give additional information to the client on costs. They had to be informed how they might be liable to pay their own solicitor. They also had to be told of the availability of any alternative funding mechanisms and of their right to seek assessment of those costs.

Guidance to solicitors did include a reminder of the statutory requirements for agreements to be in writing and that success fees could not be more than 100 per cent. It recommended that solicitors should not charge a success fee which exceeded 25 per cent of the amount recovered by the client. This was a limitation on the success fee, rather than the total fee recovered, which could exceed 25 per cent of the sum recovered. Ultimately, it was for the courts to confirm the success fee and much lower percentages were often imposed.

The Law Society's model contract used plain English to be comprehensible to the lay client, stating clearly hourly rates, liability for disbursements and the success fee. Clients terminating the agreement paid basic costs to the solicitor. The solicitor could terminate the agreement where the client failed to discharge his or her obligations. These were to give instructions, not to mislead the solicitor, to be co-operative, submit to any necessary medical or other examinations and to pay disbursements as the case proceeded. The solicitor could also terminate the agreement if the client rejected advice on settlement.

---

[109] ibid, reg 4(5).
[110] Solicitors Practice Rules' 1990, as amended, r 8(1).
[111] CFA Revocation Regulations 2005 (SI 2005 No 2305).
[112] SRA, *Solicitors' Code of Conduct 2007*, r 2.03.

The new guidance warns that breaches of the statutory requirements could render agreements unenforceable.[113] Under the previous regime, the courts decided that CFAs were unenforceable if there was a 'material' departure from the regulations. It was not necessary to show detriment to the CFA client in order to establish a material departure.[114] A failure to abide by the Code in providing costs estimates did not, however, mean that the contract between solicitor and client was unenforceable. Therefore, the indemnity principle in awarding costs still applied.[115]

Although costs orders against third parties were originally viewed as 'exceptional',[116] there were several bases for orders against third parties. Solicitors entering into CFAs can be liable for costs under the general discretion to award, or disallow, costs under the Senior Court Act 1981.[117] They could be liable in costs because they had management of the action or because they had maintained or financed it.[118] Further, costs orders could also be made against solicitors where the CFA with their client was invalid and unenforceable.[119]

An example of the courts controlling CFA costs occurred in the case of *King v Daily Telegraph Group*,[120] in which the claimant in a libel case had a fee agreement providing for a 100 per cent success fee. The likely costs would exceed £1 million, far in excess of any damages that would be awarded, estimated at £150,000. The defendant newspaper could not get their costs paid, even if they won, because the claimant had no money and no ATE insurance.

As the situation stood, the defendants in *King* would be better off financially by conceding the case than by winning it. As was pointed out by Lord Justice Brooke, the case was more valuable to the claimant's lawyers. If the claimant won, the lawyers stood to gain huge costs from the defendant. They had no incentive 'to advance their client's claim in a reasonable and proportionate manner'. In the judge's opinion, the solution was for the court to make an order capping the recoverable costs early in the proceedings. This would be by way of an order under CPR Rule 44.8 or by a retrospective costs assessment or wasted costs order.[121]

D. Damages-based Agreements

i. Legalisation

In England and Wales, it was possible to enter into a contingency fee arrangement, based on a percentage of sums recovered, for the conduct of various non-contentious

---

[113] Law Society, *Conditional Fee Agreements Guidance* (May 2013) at 3.
[114] *Samonini v London General Transport Services Ltd* [2005] EWHC 90001; *Garrett v Halton BC* [2006] EWCA Civ 1017 and *Crook v Birmingham CC* [2007] EWHC 1415.
[115] *Garbutt v Edwards* [2006]1 All ER 553.
[116] *Aiden Shipping Co Ltd v Interbulk Ltd* [1986] AC 965, per Lord Goff at 980 ff .
[117] Senior Court Act 1981, s 51.
[118] *Singh v Observer Ltd* [1989] 2 All ER 751; *Gupta v Comer* [1991] 1 All ER 289.
[119] *Myatt v NCB* [2007] 4 All ER 1094.
[120] *King v Daily Telegraph Group* [2005] 1 WLR 2282.
[121] ibid, at [105].

business. For example, a solicitor could charge for the collection of debts on a contingency basis, provided legal proceedings were not started. The ban on contingency fees in litigation by statute,[122] and by professional rules,[123] did not apply to cases before Employment Tribunals.[124]

Lord Justice Jackson recommended the wider introduction of contingency fees to increase the funding methods available to litigants. This was considered important as CFA success fees and ATE insurance premiums ceased to be recoverable from the losing party. From 1 April 2013 contingency fees, or damages-based agreements (DBAs), were permitted for litigation and arbitration proceedings in England and Wales.[125]

The terms on which DBAs can be entered are set out in regulations[126] allowing lawyers to conduct contentious work for a share of damages. DBAs may be available for some kinds of group litigation, but not for the class actions to be introduced for competition law claims. The percentage of damages the lawyer is allowed to take varies from case to case. In Employment Tribunal cases the existing 35 per cent cap continues to apply. Most other types of claim are subject to a 50 per cent cap, but personal injury and clinical negligence claims are subject to a 25 per cent cap.

The only sums recoverable from a successful client are the 'payment', the capped percentage recovery, and non-counsel disbursements. Counsel fees must be paid from the solicitor's profit costs. If there is no recovery the lawyer has no entitlement other than recovering non-counsel disbursements. Lawyers are not allowed to combine a DBA with other methods of payment, such as bills based on the hourly rate.[127] If lawyers act under a DBA the agreement must truly be 'no win no fee'.

The DBA Regulations do not specify that the contingency fee charged must reflect the degree of risk in supporting the proceedings. They do require that the reason for setting the amount of the payment at the level agreed be set out in the agreement.[128] In an employment matter, this must deal with whether the claim or proceedings is one of several similar claims or proceedings.

ii. Recoverability

The existence of a contingency fee arrangement will not increase the amount of the defendant's costs liability. Costs recoverable by a claimant are limited according to the 'Ontario model' operating in Canada. A successful claimant's costs are assessed conventionally, based on reasonable hours and rates and proportionality, reflecting the overall reasonableness of the costs to the matters in issue. If the contingency fee is higher than the costs assessed in this way, the claimant pays the shortfall from the damages.

---

[122] Solicitors Act 1974, s 59(2).
[123] SRA, *Solicitors' Code of Conduct 2007*, r 2.04.
[124] Courts and Legal Services Act 1990, s 58AA.
[125] LASPO 2012, s 45.
[126] The Damages-Based Agreements Regulations 2013 (SI 2013/609).
[127] ibid, reg 4.
[128] ibid, reg 3c.

The existence of a contingency fee arrangement may, however, operate to decrease the defendant's costs liability. This is because the claimant cannot recover more in costs than he is liable to pay its own lawyer. If the agreed contingency fee is lower than the figure arrived at through a traditional costs assessment, the defendant only has to pay the lower amount. If a claimant's DBA is unenforceable as a result of a breach of legislation or the regulations, the defendant is not liable for costs, even if liable for damages.

The DBA Working Group recommended that lawyers working under a DBA should not be liable for costs awarded against their client when cases are lost. The DBA Regulations do not make express provision for this, so, unless the lawyer agrees to indemnify the client, it is thought that they would not be liable.

E. Regulation

The terms and conditions of a DBA must specify the claim or proceedings or parts of them to which the agreement relates, the circumstances in which the representative's payment, expenses and costs, or part of them, are payable and the reason for setting the amount of the payment at the level agreed.[129] In an employment matter the reason for the level of payment must include whether the claim or proceedings is one of several similar claims or proceedings. Since no criteria have been set for determining appropriate percentages charged, it is anticipated that most lawyers will charge up to the cap.

As with CFAs, it is anticipated that breaches of the regulations by lawyers could lead to their DBAs being unenforceable against clients. These obligations are largely formal. Since no additional sums are recoverable from opponents, lawyers are under no obligation to notify opponents of the existence or terms of DBAs. One of the new potential conflicts of interest arising from DBAs is the fact that counsel fees are deducted from the lawyer's costs rather than being treated as a disbursement. This is an additional incentive for solicitors to settle outside of court rather than to incur the expense of trial.

F. Impact of Funding Arrangements

Under the new arrangements for CFAs, clients can agree to pay their lawyers a success fee and take out ATE insurance, but must bear the cost themselves. Since these costs cannot be recovered from the other side, CFAs may become less attractive, particularly in lower value claims. Unfortunately, because they have to give credit for costs recovered under DBAs but not CFAs, DBAs may also be unattractive to lawyers.[130] This, together with the familiarity of CFAs, means that they could continue to be the main source of litigation support. The arrival of DBAs adds a new dimension to the

---

[129] ibid, reg 3.
[130] K Underwood, 'The impossible rise of damages-based agreements' 157(22) *Solicitors Journal* 4 July 2013.

ethical decision-making of solicitors when advising clients. They must now be sure that they state clearly which funding arrangement is in the client's best interest. They must also consider whether their own, or perhaps another firm, would be prepared to offer the best terms.

Solicitors usually calculate whether to offer a client a funding arrangement on a case by case basis. When deciding whether to accept a case, firms have no obligation to consider an obligation to provide access to justice. To do this they would have to be required to consider their record in taking riskier cases. A method already exists for this purpose. When CFAs were introduced, the Law Society, concerned that solicitors were unused to calculating risk, provided Continuing Professional Development to prepare them. Risk calculations were supposed to be based on factors such as the merits and value of the claim, the likelihood of settlement, estimated costs involved and the likelihood of justification for success fees, including by considering the risk at different stages of a case. The purpose of this development was so that firms of solicitors could aim to break even in terms of cases won and lost.

Some solicitors could charge success fees without ever taking risky cases and suffering any losses. This creates doubt over the capacity of CFAs to promote access to justice on a par with legal aid. It is arguable that firms should aim to use success fees in winning cases to support losing cases. It would, however, be necessary to review a large number of cases in order to see whether this was achieved, or whether success fees were purely providing additional profit to lawyers. It is not possible for courts to consider the reasonableness of success fees in individual cases with reference to firms' overall caseload. Regulators could conduct such investigations, but even if they did, they could not, under present regulation, require lawyers to accept more risky cases.

VI. Speculative Fees and *Pro Bono Publico*

A. Speculative Fees

Speculative fees are defined as fees that are only payable if a case is won.[131] It is different from a contingency fee in that there is no increase for risk. In many cases, the risk may be small. Lawyers may know that either, clients will be in funds when they win or, more likely, that costs including the solicitor's fees, will be ordered against, and paid by, the losing party. In England, accepting a case on a speculative basis was regarded as unlawful maintenance, although it was permitted in Scotland.[132]

In addition to the distaste for maintenance, a lawyer agreeing to speculate on a case succeeding was probably suspected of 'ambulance chasing'. To modern eyes, the

---

[131] J Levin, 'Solicitors Acting Speculatively and Pro Bono' (1996) 15 *Civil Justice Quarterly* 44, at 47 and *Bevan Ashford v Yeandle* [1999] Ch 239.
[132] HL Debs 12 June 1995 Vol 564 col 1573.

contempt was undeserved. Lawyers may agree a speculative fee in a genuine effort to make a meritorious claim viable. Indeed, there were strong arguments for allowing speculative fees in some cases, for example, for clients who cannot get legal aid on financial grounds.[133]

It appeared that a breakthrough for speculative fees came with acceptance of conditional fees. Shortly after the introduction of CFAs, in *Thai Trading Co v Taylor*[134] the Court of Appeal held that there was no problem with a solicitor not charging a fee if a case was lost, provided that no extra fee was charged if the case was won. Lord Justice Millett said that a speculative fee should not 'be regarded as contrary to public policy today, if indeed it ever was'.[135]

The new clarity on speculative fees was short-lived. Subsequently, in *Awwad v Geraghty & Co (a firm)*, a solicitor (G) failed in a claim for speculative fees on the ground that it was a champertous arrangement. She had agreed with the client, A, to charge him a 'conditional normal fee', meaning her standard hourly fee, if successful, but only £90 per hour if he lost. A lost and refused to pay G.[136] The Court of Appeal said that conditional fee arrangements had become acceptable within certain statutory parameters, but, under common law, had always been illegal and unenforceable. Such an agreement was contrary to public policy and exposed lawyers to temptation. In effect, a speculative fee agreement was a CFA, but without any formal requirements. In any event, the current position is that the common law has not actually changed to allow speculative fees. In *Sibthorpe v Southwark LBC*,[137] the Court of Appeal confirmed *Awwad v Geraghty* and doubted *Thai Trading*. It may, nonetheless, be time for a change of public policy on the issue.[138]

B. *Pro Bono Publico*

Acting *pro bono publico* generally means offering legal services without any charge. Although it was once regarded as a form of maintenance, it is now positively encouraged by the Law Society and the Bar.[139] When lawyers were 'acting pro bono' the operation of the indemnity principle meant that, if their clients were successful, they would not get costs awarded against the other side. This was because the lawyer had agreed that there would be no costs.

---

[133] H Genn, *Hard Bargaining: Out of Court Settlement in Personal Injury Actions* (Oxford, Clarendon Press, 1987) and Levin, 'Solicitors Acting Speculatively and Pro Bono' (n 131).
[134] *Thai Trading Co v Taylor* [1998] 3 All ER 65.
[135] ibid, per Millett LJ at 788.
[136] *Awwad v Geraghty & Co (a firm)* [2001] QB 570.
[137] *Sibthorpe v Southwark LBC* [2011] EWCA Civ 25.
[138] *Kellar v Williams* [2004] UKPC 30.
[139] See ch 15: 'Service'.

i. Pro Bono Costs Orders

It would once have been anomalous to consider acting *pro bono publico* as part of a discussion of fees. It is, however, no longer so. From October 2008 courts in England and Wales were empowered to order a losing party to make a payment to a designated organisation, under section 194 of the Legal Services Act 2007. Pro bono costs orders were available where a case has been won with pro bono help, and the losing party would otherwise have escaped liability for costs simply because it had lost to a party that had been helped pro bono.

Pro bono costs orders were introduced at the same time as the establishment of an Access to Justice Foundation (AJF). AJF is a national charity established by the Advice Services Alliance, Bar Council, ILEX and Law Society. It provides grant funding to support pro bono and advice agencies and receives sums produced by pro bono costs orders. Initially, there was lack of awareness of the availability of costs orders among practitioners. Apparently, only £100,000 was raised by pro bono costs orders in 2012.[140] Anticipated difficulties in having costs taxed by the court may deter pro bono lawyers from seeking orders. This raises the question of whether such orders should be compulsory.[141]

ii. Costs Awarded against Party Aided Pro Bono Publico

There is probably a high chance that a party winning a case against a claimant aided pro bono public will not recover costs. This raises the question of whether legal costs awarded against a pro bono client should be recoverable from that party's lawyer. Some old cases mandated personal liability where the lawyers had not satisfied themselves that the client had a reasonable case. The law was clarified in *Tolstoy-Miloslavsky v Aldington*,[142] where it was held that the court had no jurisdiction to make a costs order against a solicitor solely on the ground that he acted without a fee.

In *Tolstoy*, the Court held that lawyers acting without expectation of a fee are not under an obligation to protect the other side from a hopeless case. They do not have to 'impose a pre-trial screen through which litigants must pass', before receiving free representation.[143] Therefore, a lawyer acting pro bono should only be held personally liable for the other side's costs under the wasted costs jurisdiction.[144] This risk arises in some cases irrespective of whether the lawyer acts without charge or for a fee.

---

[140] This figure was produced by the Low Commission, set up by Legal Action Group to consider support for the provision of legal advice.

[141] See www.accesstojusticefoundation.org.uk/downloads/Access_to_Justice_Foundation_leaflet.pdf.

[142] *Tolstoy-Miloslavsky v Aldington* [1996] 2 All ER 556.

[143] See also *Orchard v SE Electricity* [1987] QB 565, at 572.

[144] See ch 17: 'Litigation'.

VII. Conduct on Fees and Costs

In relation to fees, there is an inherent conflict of interest between lawyer and client. Given a knowledge imbalance in favour of lawyers, a few general principles suggest themselves. First, most obviously, the level of the fees cannot be left solely to market forces or individual agreement. Secondly, the client should give an informed and unpressured consent to any agreement made with the lawyer, whether at the beginning of the case or as it progresses.

The third general principle suggested for regulation of lawyer's fees is that clients should be aware of any actual or potential conflicts arising in relation to different funding mechanisms. Fourthly, clients should be regularly updated on their liability for fees and the amount owed. Fifthly, there should be effective, fair and accessible review procedures to identify any failure by the lawyer to abide by the above principles or to rectify overcharging.

A. A Brief History of Rules on Fees and Costs

Under the Solicitors Act 1974, non-contentious business agreements and agreements on costs in contentious matters had to be in writing.[145] Until 1991 there were no rules or specific legislation on what information solicitors had to provide on costs. In 1991 the Law Society promulgated Written Professional Standards on Information on Costs, to supplement the introduction of Rule 15 of the Solicitors' Practice Rules 1990.

The Law Society Guide 1999 provided a fairly brief 40 pages to the topic including all annexes. These contained little that could be described as general principles of an ethical nature. Significantly, the first 'general principle' dealt with in the relevant chapter was the power of solicitors to 'require' payments on account from clients.[146] The Bar Code said little about fees in relation to clients, except to state that a barrister may charge on any basis or by any method he thinks fit.[147]

The rules on costs developed through iterations of the Guide. It is quite possible that a breach of these rules would not have made a contract between solicitor and client on fees unenforceable.[148] In any event, it appears they were frequently disregarded.[149] The guidance was incorporated in the Solicitors' Code of Conduct 2007, as part of

---

[145] Solicitors Act, 1974 ss 57 and 59.

[146] *Guide to the Professional Conduct of Solicitors* (London, The Law Society, 1999) Principle 14.01.

[147] BSB, *Code of Conduct of the Bar of England and Wales*, 8th edn (London, Bar Standards Board, 2004) at para 405.

[148] *Garbutt v Edwards* [2006] 1 All ER 553

[149] Research and Policy Planning Unit, *Quality of Solicitors' Practice Management* Research Study No 10 (London, Law Society, RPPU, 1993); Legal Services Ombudsman *Annual Report* (1995); National Consumer Council Report, *Solicitors and Client Care* (London, NCC, 1994).

Rule 2 on client relations. Rule 2 required solicitors to let clients know the basis of their fees, when they could be increased and what payments had to be made to others.

Under the 2007 Code, solicitors had to provide clients with 'the best information possible about the likely overall cost of a matter both at the outset and, when appropriate, as the matter progresses'. They also had to explore how payment was to be made, and the availability of legal aid, insurance or other third party funding.[150] Information on costs had to be clear and confirmed in writing and regularly updated.[151] Solicitors had the burden of proving that it was inappropriate to meet all or some of the requirements in the circumstances, for example, for repeat work. The rules were legally binding on solicitors, unlike the previous guidance.

B. Fees under Outcomes Focused Regulation

i. Principles and Outcomes

None of the principles in the SRA Handbook are directly concerned with fees, although several may be said to be indirectly so. Of the 16 outcomes relating to clients in the Handbook, three relate directly to fees. The first outcome is that 'you only enter into fee agreements with your clients that are legal, and which you consider are suitable for the client's needs and take account of the client's best interests'.[152] The second is that 'clients receive the best possible information, both at the time of engagement and when appropriate as their matter progresses, about the likely overall cost of their matter'.[153] The third outcome on fees is that 'clients are informed of their right to challenge or complain about your bill and the circumstances in which they may be liable to pay interest on an unpaid bill'.[154]

ii. Indicative Behaviours

Approximately one-third of indicative behaviours in Chapter 1 are concerned with fees. In order to meet the outcomes, solicitors are advised to discuss whether the outcomes of the client's matter justify the expense and risk involved, including any risk of paying someone else's legal fees.[155] They should clearly explain their fees and any possible changes[156] and warn the client about any other payments for which they may be responsible.[157] At the conclusion of the matter, solicitors should ensure that

---

[150] *David Truex Solicitor v Kitchin* [2007] EWCA Civ 618.
[151] SRA, *Solicitors' Code of Conduct 2007*, r 2.03, guidance para 27.
[152] SRA, *Handbook 2011*, as amended; SRA, *Code of Conduct*, ch 1, Outcome 1.6.
[153] SRA, *Code of Conduct*, ch 1, Outcome 1.13.
[154] ibid, Outcome 1.14.
[155] ibid, ch 1, Indicative Behaviour 1.13.
[156] ibid, Indicative Behaviour 1.14.
[157] ibid, Indicative Behaviour 1.15.

disbursements included in their bills reflect the actual amount spent, or to be spent, on behalf of the client.[158]

Solicitors are also advised to discuss how the client will pay, considering the availability of sources of third party funding, such as a trade union.[159] They should provide information in a clear and accessible form, appropriate to the needs and circumstances of the client.[160] This might include details of any fee arrangements governed by statute, such as conditional fee agreements.[161] Where they act for a publicly funded client, they should explain how their publicly funded status affects costs.[162]

VIII. Third Party Receipts and Payments

Receipts of money from third parties are not fees in the conventional sense. They are however income, and can be used to reduce fees. Payments to third parties, as a reward for introducing clients, for example, are fees paid out by solicitors. In some circumstances such payments create a risk of conflicts of interest. Under the old Bar Code, barristers were forbidden from arrangements carrying these risks. They could not, for example, give or receive commissions or loans from clients or intermediaries or pay referral fees.[163]

A. Commissions

When a broker arranges an insurance policy, pension, the purchase of shares or similar transaction for a client, he or she is often paid a commission by the third party. Solicitors sometimes act as brokers of such transactions. If they are allowed to keep any commission payable, this seems to create a clear conflict of interests. The relevant interests are the duty of the solicitor to promote the client's best interests and the solicitor's interest in successfully selling something to the client. The risk in such a conflict is that, rather than looking for the best arrangement for the client, a solicitor may be tempted to promote that which pays the largest commission.

Under the Solicitors' Code of Conduct 2007, solicitors were allowed to keep commissions of under £20.[164] This rule was justified by the argument that the administrative work in accounting to the client would exceed the amount paid over. This was somewhat anomalous, and a deviation from the principle that a fiduciary shall

---

[158] ibid, Indicative Behaviour 1.21.
[159] ibid, Indicative Behaviour 1.16.
[160] ibid, Indicative Behaviour 1.19.
[161] ibid, Indicative Behaviour 1.17.
[162] ibid, Indicative Behaviour 1.18.
[163] Bar Council, *Bar Code of Conduct 1981*, as amended, at para 307.
[164] SRA, *Solicitors' Code of Conduct 2007*, r 2.06.

not take a secret profit. Clients had to be notified of commissions exceeding £20 and could agree that the firm kept it. Consent did not have to be in writing.[165]

The rules did not specify that clients should be advised to take independent advice where the commission was a significant amount. The guidance to Rule 3, on conflicts of interest, did, however, stress that a solicitor 'must insist that the client receives independent advice' in cases where a solicitor has a personal interest in a client's transaction.[166] This would seem to catch the receipt of commissions. In the previous edition we argued that these rules would only operate in the client's interests if the client's bill were reduced accordingly. We also suggested that allowing commissions to be retained was dangerous to the long-term interest of the profession.

In the current SRA Handbook, two principles might be thought to preclude solicitors from receiving commissions. These are Principle 3, not letting independence be compromised, and Principle 4, acting in the best interests of clients. In fact, commissions would now appear to be caught by an indicative behaviour in the chapter on clients. This provides that solicitors may show that they meet the outcomes by accounting for any financial benefit received as a result of acting for a client, either paying it to the client or offsetting it against their fees. They may keep such a benefit, however, if they can justify keeping it, have told the client the amount, or approximate amount of the benefit, and the client has agreed that they can keep it.[167]

Solicitors also have to be aware of Chapter 6, 'Your client and introductions to third parties', in the SRA Handbook. One of the outcomes in that chapter is that clients are fully informed of any financial or other interest the solicitor has in referring the client to another person or business.[168]

B. Referral Fees

i. Solicitors' Relationship with Third Party Introducers

Referral fees (or introducer fees) are sums paid, usually by solicitors, to a third party for introducing business. Such payments were prohibited until October 2004, when a limited exception was made to the code banning referral fees.[169] The rules on referrals exposed the difference in perception between advocates of professionalism and of consumerism. The traditional view was expressed in 1998 by Mr Justice Lightman, who commented that 'clients are not merchantable commodities to be bought and sold.'[170] The new approach was promoted by agencies such as the Office of Fair Trading (OFT). In 2001, an OFT report suggested that the Law Society ban on referral fees was obstructing the development of an online market for introductions, to the disadvantage of solicitors.[171]

---

[165] ibid, guidance to r 2.05, at para 59.
[166] ibid, r 3, guidance para 45.
[167] SRA, *Handbook 2011*, as amended; SRA, *Code of Conduct*, ch 1, Indicative Behaviour 1.20.
[168] SRA, *Handbook 2011*, as amended; SRA, *Code of Conduct*, ch 1, Outcome 6.2.
[169] Solicitors Introduction and Referral Code 1990, as amended (7 October 2004).
[170] *Mohamed v Alaga & Co* [1998] 2 All ER 720, at 724.
[171] Director General of Fair Trading, *Competition in Professions* (2001), Report 328, at 14.

The third parties usually associated with payment of referral fees are claims management companies. In 2006, claims companies were required to register and meet set conditions of operation.[172] Solicitors could not deal with unregistered companies. The exercise revealed that there were over 1,176 such companies, twice as many as previously thought. There were problems with 90 per cent of the applications for registration. The Regulator of Claims Companies was bound to pass to the SRA the names of any solicitors dealing with unregulated claims companies.[173]

Claims companies sold their own insurance packages and arranged loans through related companies at high interest rates to cover ATE insurance premiums. They employed their own expert witnesses who often paid a referral fee to the company for the privilege of being a paid court expert witness. They also received referral fees from solicitors on their lists in return for the clients where proceedings had to be commenced. Many of the claims they handled were of small value, and sometimes of doubtful merit, and the costs, in terms of legal fees and insurance expenses, often far outweighed the value of the claim to the client.

The payment of referral fees by solicitors potentially created many problems. Such arrangements set up a conflict of interest for the solicitor between the client and the third party who introduced them to the solicitor. The solicitor might be disinclined, for example, to advise clients that they need not pay introducer's charges. There is also a potential conflict of interest if solicitors attempt to recoup referral fees from their client.

Referral arrangements also create problems of transparency and trust. Problems emanated from the fact that claimants with small claims could find that the cost of ATE insurance exceeded the estimated value of the damages. Solicitors might fail to explain to their clients how they had come by their cases or the nature of the agreements they had made with claims companies. Some might try to recoup referral fees by charging high success fees or contingency fees in simple cases. Others might call such fees 'administration fees' and include them in the client's bill as a disbursement.

Many of the theoretical problems with referral fees lay behind the so-called miners' costs scandal. In this case, large numbers of firms received cases for presentation to a government compensation scheme for miners, deducting referral fees from miners' compensation. Some even operated their own referral businesses for the purpose. An investigation resulted in 115 solicitors in 25 firms being referred to the Solicitors Disciplinary Tribunal.[174] Three solicitors were struck off and three suspended for periods of between six months and four years.

ii. The TAG Litigation

The deep problems with referral fees were exposed in a number of challenges in extensive costs litigation by the insurers of unsuccessful defendants and by the insolvency

---

[172] Compensation Act 2006 and the Compensation (Regulating Claims Management Services) Order 2006 (SI 2006/3319).

[173] Law Society Gazette 21 June 2006 and 22 February 2007.

[174] See further A Boon and A Whyte, 'Icarus Falls: The Coal Health Scandal' (2012) 15(2) Legal Ethics 277, on which much of the rest of this section is based.

of two of the largest claims companies.[175] A key case is *Sharratt v London Central Bus Co (No 2)*,[176] in which a decision by a costs judge, Hurst J, was upheld by the Court of Appeal. The case involved a number of personal injury cases against the defendant handled by the claims firm The Accident Group (TAG).

Solicitors receiving the cases paid a TAG subsidiary company, Accident Investigation Ltd, housed in the same building as TAG, a fee of £310 plus VAT, for investigations. The fact that the same payment was made in every case suggested that this payment did not actually relate to work performed. Judge Hirst held that these payments were, in reality, a referral fee and therefore a payment proscribed by the professional conduct rules.

Another problem arising in the TAG and associated litigation related to solicitors delegating their duties. Under the prevailing regulations, clients had to be given extensive information on the nature of the CFA contract and their potential liabilities and alternative sources of funding investigated. In the TAG cases all this information and investigation was done by TAG and not the solicitor, who simply relied on TAG's employees doing the job properly.

It was decided in *Sharratt (No 1)* that solicitors could delegate the duty to inform the client to agents, but only if they were properly appointed and provided an explanation to the client as required under the regulations. It was unrealistic to think that this could be done by the unqualified agents of a claims company. From 2007 claims companies were required to abide by certain conditions. Solicitors were forbidden from dealing with unregulated companies, and the SRA frequently reminded them that to do so was a disciplinary matter.

iii. Banning Referral Fees in Personal Injury Cases

In his report on civil litigation costs, Lord Justice Jackson stated that:

> It is a regrettably common feature of civil litigation, in particular personal injuries litigation, that solicitors pay referral fees to claims management companies, before-the-event ('BTE') insurers and other organisations to 'buy' cases. Referral fees add to the costs of litigation, without adding any real value to it. I recommend that lawyers should not be permitted to pay referral fees in respect of personal injury cases'[177]

The Bar and Law Society supported a ban,[178] but the Legal Services Board claimed that 'sufficient evidence of consumer detriment, which would have been needed to

---

[175] See *Re Claims Direct Test Cases* [2003] EWCA Civ 136; *Callery v Gray* [2002] 3 All ER 417.
[176] *Sharratt v London Central Bus Co (No 2)* [2004] EWCA Civ 575. Details can also be found at the report of the *No 1* case, decided on a different point ([2003] EWCA Civ 718).
[177] Jackson LJ, *Review of Civil Litigation Costs* (n 35) executive summary, at para 2.5.
[178] R Rothwell, 'Society formally urges Clarke to ban referral fees' *Law Society Gazette* 4 July 2011 (www.lawgazette.co.uk/news/society-formally-urges-clarke-ban-referral-fees); 'Bar Council urges LSB to look again at referral fees' *Counsel* July 2011 (www.counselmagazine.co.uk/counsel-news/bar-council-urges-lsb-to-look-again-at-referral-fees.html).

merit a ban, has not been found'.[179] In September 2011, the government issued a press release announcing that it would adopt Jackson's recommendation.[180]

In April 2013 LASPO 2012, sections 56–60 made it a regulatory offence to pay or receive referral fees in prescribed legal business. Currently, this only covers cases of personal injury or death or in ancillary claims. The ban covers solicitors, claims management companies and insurers. A contract to make or to pay for a referral or an arrangement which is in breach of section 56 of LASPO is unenforceable.[181] Breaches of the ban are also subject to action by the regulators of these industries.

iv. Regulation of Solicitors' Referral Fees

a. Brief History of Regulation

The Solicitors Introduction and Referral Code 1990 stated that '[s]olicitors must not reward [introducers of clients] by the payment of commission or otherwise'.[182] Solicitors were also warned to be wary of being too reliant on limited sources of referral.[183] They were required to conduct six-monthly reviews to ensure that the code had been complied with[184] and consider, if they received more than 20 per cent of their income from referrals from a single source, whether that proportion should be reduced.[185] Solicitors were also obliged to draw these provisions to the attention of those introducing clients to them.[186]

In October 2004, the Introduction and Referral Code was amended by the addition of section 2A, containing seven paragraphs of additional rules.[187] These allowed payment of a referral fee provided 'immediately upon receiving the referral and before accepting instructions to act the solicitor provides the client with all relevant information concerning the referral and, in particular, the amount of any payment'.[188] Additionally, the solicitor had to be satisfied that the introducer had not breached any standards implicit in the practice rules, for example, on solicitors' advertising.[189] The ordinary rules did not apply to 'normal hospitality, proper disbursements or normal business expenses'.[190] This was intended to clear up doubt about the payment to third parties of their 'genuine expenses', such as charges for investigations properly made.

---

[179] LSB, *Referral Fees, Referral Arrangements and Fee Sharing: Decision Document* (May 2011) at 2.

[180] A Higgins, 'Referral Fees – the Business of Access to Justice' (2012) 32(1) *Legal Studies* 109; Ministry of Justice press release, 'Curbing Compensation Culture: Government to Ban Referral Fees' 9 September 2011.

[181] SRA, 'The Prohibition of Referral Fees in the Legal Aid, Sentencing and Punishment of Offenders Act 2012 (LASPO) Sections 56-60' (www.sra.org.uk/solicitors/code-of-conduct/guidance/guidance/Prohibition-of-referral-fees-in-LASPO-56-60.page).

[182] Solicitors Introduction and Referral Code 1990, at para 2(3) (see annex 11B, at 238 of *The Guide* 1999).

[183] ibid, at para 2(4).

[184] ibid, at para 2(10)(a).

[185] ibid, at para 2(11).

[186] ibid, at para 2(2).

[187] Solicitors Introduction and Referral Code 1990, as amended (7 October 2004).

[188] ibid, at para 2A(3).

[189] ibid, at paras 4(a) and (b).

[190] ibid, at para 2(A)(3).

Lord Falconer, the Lord Chancellor at the time of the 2004 amendment, was reported to dislike the new rules. When in 2006 the Practice Standards Unit visited 135 firms, only 6 per cent fully complied with them, and in 39 per cent of firms the breaches were major. In June 2007, the SRA reported that one-third of 52 firms inspected had signed referral agreements which 'required the solicitor to act contrary to the client's best interests and may also compromise their ability to act independently'.[191] The SRA launched a campaign on compliance. It threatened that referral fees would be banned if the rules were not obeyed.[192]

The Solicitors' Code of Conduct 2007 built on the foundations of past experience. The rules allowed solicitors to seek clients through potential professional connections such as commercial organisations or public bodies, including other solicitors or estate agents or insurance agents, provided certain conditions were satisfied.[193] These required a written agreement with the introducer, subject to SRA inspection, that it could not 'influence or constrain' the solicitor's advice to the client. Clients were to receive written details of the referral fee and the business arrangements between the solicitor and the introducer. The introducer and solicitor had to agree to abide by the rule, including publicity restrictions.

Advice about not depending on referrals was diluted in the 2007 Code. Solicitors were warned not to 'become so reliant on an introducer as a source of work that this affects the advice you give to your client'.[194] In monitoring volumes of work from particular sources, firms were to consider 'the amount and proportion of your firm's income' arising from a particular referrer.[195]

b. Current Regulation

In the SRA Handbook, fee sharing and referrals are covered in Chapter 9. The seven outcomes and 12 indicative behaviours are overlapping and slightly repetitious. The main outcomes are that solicitors must ensure that their independence and professional judgement are not prejudiced by virtue of any arrangement with another person[196] and that clients' interests are protected notwithstanding those arrangements.[197] Solicitors must ensure that financial arrangements with introducers are in writing.[198] They must be sure not to pay for referrals of persons the subject of criminal proceedings or receiving public funding.[199]

Clients must be informed of any fee sharing arrangement relevant to their matter.[200] They must be informed of any financial or other interest which an introducer has in

---

[191] *Law Society Gazette* 28 June 2007, at 1.
[192] P Holt, 'Cash for Services' *Law Society Gazette* 2 November 2006 and (2006) 156 *New Law Journal* 1859.
[193] SRA, *Solicitors' Code of Conduct* 2007, r 9.02.
[194] ibid, guidance to r 9 – Referrals of Business, at para 1.
[195] ibid.
[196] SRA, *Handbook 2011*, as amended; SRA, *Code of Conduct*, ch 1, Outcome 9.1.
[197] ibid, Outcome 9.2.
[198] ibid, Outcome 9.7.
[199] ibid, Outcome 9.6.
[200] ibid, Outcome 9.5.

referring the client to the solicitor.[201] The final outcome is that clients must be able to make informed decisions about how to pursue their matter.[202] In Chapter 1, also, one of the key indicative behaviours in relation to fees is 'explaining any arrangements, such as fee sharing or referral arrangements, which are relevant to the client's instructions'.[203]

The other indicative behaviours in Chapter 9 are consistent with the outcomes. For example, solicitors should be satisfied that referrals have not been acquired as a result of activities which are forbidden to SRA-regulated persons or contrary to the principles or Code.[204] Similar restrictions apply to making referrals to others. For example, in the SRA Handbook, Chapter 6 'Your client and introductions to third parties' one of the four outcomes is 'not being paid a prohibited referral fee'.[205]

v. Barristers and Referral Fees

Under the old Bar Code barristers were not allowed to 'make any payment ... to any person for the purpose of procuring professional instructions'.[206] Where self-employed barristers shared premises with other persons they were not allowed to have a 'general referral arrangement or understanding'.[207] They were required to keep available for inspection a record of any work or clients referred by any such persons, or referred to any such persons, and of the reasons for any referral.[208]

The current Bar Code of Conduct contains an outcome prohibiting the payment of any referral fees.[209] The notes for guidance on referral fees explain that making such payments is inconsistent with the core duties protecting clients' best interests, barristers' independence and trust and public trust and confidence in the profession. The guidance reminds barristers that the Legal Aid Agency's Unified Contract Standard Terms prohibit contract-holders from making or receiving any payment or other benefit for the referral or introduction of client, whether or not they know of or consent to, the payment.[210] It goes on the state that, in private or publicly funded cases, payment of referral fees to which clients have not consented can be criminal offences under the Bribery Act 2010.

---

[201] ibid, Outcome 9.4.
[202] ibid, Outcome 9.3.
[203] SRA, *Handbook 2011*, as amended; SRA, *Code of Conduct*, ch1, Indicative Behaviour 1.4.
[204] ibid, Indicative Behaviour 9.4.
[205] ibid, Outcome 6.4.
[206] Bar Council, *Bar Code of Conduct 1981*, as amended, at para 307(e).
[207] ibid, at para 403(2)(iv).
[208] ibid, at para 403.4.
[209] BSB, *Handbook 2014*, pt 2, The Code of Conduct, rC10.
[210] ibid, gC30.

IX. Looking after Client Funds

A. The Solicitors' Accounts Rules

Accounting rules are needed to protect client money. They are a manifestation of solicitors' duty to act in the best interests of the client. They prevent the solicitor acting fraudulently or making a secret profit from a fiduciary relationship. Looking after client funds was almost entirely based on binding rules made under the Solicitors Act 1974. These rules were then consolidated into the Solicitors' Accounts Rules 1998.

The rules on managing client funds traditionally occupied many pages in the professional rules. For example, they represented 260 pages of the 1999 edition of the Law Society Guide. The Account Rules were revised and re-presented as the SRA Account Rules for the purposes of the new SRA Handbook.[211] Unlike other parts of the Handbook, Accounts are not dealt with as outcomes, but as rules. The 52 rules and guidance are, however, shorter than in previous versions.

The overarching purpose of the rules is 'to keep client money safe'.[212] Responsibility for adhering to the Rules lies with all the principals or partners of a firm, the directors of recognised bodies or licensed bodies and the COFA of a firm, whether a manager or non-manager.[213] All must ensure compliance by everyone employed in the firm.

B. The Basic Accounting System

The system laid down by the Rules relies on the requirement to maintain two separate sets of accounts, the client account and the office account.[214] In addition, there must be a controlled trust account to hold money that the solicitor receives as a sole trustee. Separate accounts ensure that the bank, building society or the solicitor cannot use the monies in one account for the purposes of the others. It means, for example, that funds in a client account cannot be used to satisfy the debts or expenses of the firm. It also means that missing client money must be replaced at the solicitors' expense, even if a deficit results from a banking error.[215]

The Rules specify what constitutes client and office money.[216] This dictates which monies must go into the client account and which to the office account, and what withdrawals may legitimately take place from both. Any money held or received by the solicitor on account of his client must be paid without delay into the client account, unless the client instructs otherwise. This includes money paid by the client

---

[211] SRA Accounts Rules 2011 (www.sra.org.uk/solicitors/handbook/accountsrules/content.page).
[212] ibid, r 1.1.
[213] ibid, r 6.1.
[214] ibid, rr 12.1 and 13–16.
[215] ibid, r 7.
[216] ibid, r 12.

on account of costs.[217] Where a single cheque consists of a mixture of client and office monies, the payment may be divided into each account or, if not, all of it must be paid into the client account.

C. Compliance

Some of the Accounts Rules are directed to ensuring compliance. The SRA has the power to order that any books and files must be produced at any time and place for inspection.[218] This power overrides confidence and privilege between solicitor and client.[219] The SRA may give brief reasons for such inspections.[220] Secondly, annual accounts prepared by an accountant must be delivered to the SRA by the firm within six months of the end of the accounting period.[221]

The Solicitors Act 1974 provides that the Law Society can make rules for the filing of reports on solicitors' firms by accountants.[222] All reporting accountants must be registered auditors. Their terms of engagement, which must be in writing, must incorporate the SRA's standard terms. The accountant completes a standard form checklist as well as producing a report. This provides greater assurance that the audit work has actually been done.

The Solicitors Act 1974 requires an accountant to report two matters to the Law Society immediately. The first is any evidence of fraud or theft in relation to money held by a solicitor for a client, or for any other person in an account operated by the solicitor. The second is any information that may be of material significance in determining whether a solicitor is a fit and proper person to hold money for clients or other persons.[223] Breaches of accounts rules are the most common reasons for disciplinary complaints and penalties. The client who suffers as a result of any breach is protected by the Solicitors' Indemnity Fund, established under section 37 of the Solicitors Act 1974.

D. Interest on Client Accounts

The total amount in client account at any one time can be considerable, and interest will accrue on this balance. In *Brown v IRC*,[224] the Inland Revenue wanted to charge a solicitor tax on interest in client account. The Court said that a solicitor taking this interest is unlawfully profiting at the expense of clients. The Law Society, citing administrative difficulties produced by *Brown*, had section 33 inserted into the

---

[217] ibid, rr 17.2 and 17.3.
[218] ibid, r 31.1.
[219] ibid, guidance to r 31, note i.
[220] ibid, guidance to r 31, note iii.
[221] ibid, r 32.
[222] Solicitors Act 1974, s 34.
[223] ibid, s 34(9).
[224] *Brown v IRC* [1965] AC 244.

Solicitors Act 1974. This stated that, except as defined in the Rules, a solicitor is not liable to account to the client for interest on client accounts.[225]

The SRA Accounts Rules 2011 continue the trend, begun in the 1991 Rules, requiring that solicitors account to clients for any interest earned on deposits in separate, designated client accounts. They provide that solicitors must have a written policy on paying interest that they show to clients at the start of the retainer. Further, solicitors holding 'money in a client account for a client, or for a person funding all or part of their fees, or for a trust, must account for interest when it is fair and reasonable to do so in all the circumstances'.[226]

The SRA Accounts Rules state that they have an outcomes-focused approach 'allowing firms the flexibility to set their own interest policies in order to achieve a fair outcome for both the client and the firm'.[227] Extensive guidance delineates what might be seen as good practice and therefore 'fair and reasonable'. Some of the guidance is obvious yet extremely vague. For example, it states that 'it is likely to be appropriate for firms to account for all interest earned in some circumstances, for example, where substantial sums of money are held for lengthy periods of time'.[228] In other cases it is quite specific, for example, in suggesting that a firm's rules may specify that no interest is payable on small sums, for example, under £20.[229]

It is not known to what extent solicitors benefit financially from interest on client accounts. In 1984, the Consumer Council issued a discussion paper on the issue.[230] They estimated, conservatively, that it amounted to over £40 million a year at that time. Since 1984, the Rules have been tightened up in favour of clients, interest rates have declined and more use is now made of electronic money transfers. This means that less money is held in client accounts. Modern computing makes it possible and simple to calculate client interest and pay it to each individual client.[231] This is clearly in the client's best interest and it is not clear why the rules have not been amended to reflect this.

In some jurisdictions, Australia and Ontario, Canada, a proportion of interest on client accounts is paid into a foundation managed by the Law Society and devoted to supporting a wide variety of charitable and pro bono legal activities, such as educational scholarships, supporting law centres or libraries, research into the justice system and public interest advocacy centres. This was suggested for England and Wales by the Consumer Council in 1984.

More recently, Peter Goldsmith, the former Attorney General, proposed that client account interest be used to bolster pro bono legal services.[232] It was also targeted by the Conservative Government as part of plans to boost the legal aid fund following

---

[225] Solicitors Act 1974, s 33(3).
[226] SRA Accounts Rules 2011, r 22.1.
[227] ibid, guidance to r 22, note i(b).
[228] ibid, guidance to r 22, note i(f).
[229] ibid, guidance to r 22, note i(e).
[230] National Consumer Council, *Whose Interest?: Solicitors and their Clients' Accounts: A Discussion Paper* (London, NCC, 1984).
[231] A Evans, 'Professional Ethics North and South: Interest on Clients' Trust Funds and Lawyer Fraud. An Opportunity to Redeem Professionalism' (1996) 3(3) *International Journal of the Legal Profession* 281.
[232] N Rose, 'No accounting for taste' *Legal Futures* 18 November 2010.

the cutbacks made by LASPO 2012.[233] The Law Society took credit for dissuading the Ministry of Justice from pursuing this plan.[234]

X. Recovering from Clients

The financial relationship between solicitor and client is basically contractual. The contract can stipulate for payments on account, for example, and solicitors are free to sue if fees are not paid. Certain general rules relating to payment may be more significant than in other relationships. Two are particularly relevant. First, solicitors have a lien over papers and property held by them where fees are not paid. Secondly, solicitors may refuse to do further work until they have been paid. In general, the duty of confidentiality and legal privilege are not waived where the solicitor sues a client for fees.[235]

A. Transfer of Fees

Solicitors often ask for 'payments on account of costs' before beginning work on a case or matter. When a solicitor instructed in a contentious matter asks for a sum on account of costs, 'and the client refuses or fails within a reasonable time to make that payment' the solicitor can terminate the retainer on reasonable notice.[236] On the conclusion of a matter, or as agreed with the client, money can only be transferred from the firm's client account to the office account if the client or the paying party has been given or sent a bill of costs, or other written notification of the costs incurred.[237] Payments by clients 'on account of costs' remain client money until this has been done.[238]

B. Suing for Fees

A solicitor can only sue for costs having issued a bill. Under the Solicitors Act 1974 a valid bill for this purpose must be signed by the solicitor or an employee on his behalf, or enclosed with a signed letter. The bill must be delivered personally, sent by post or

---

[233] 'Government targets client account interest as it outlines £400m legal aid cuts' *Legal Futures* 15 November 2010.
[234] C Baksi, 'Clarke rules out raid on client account interest' *Law Society Gazette* 22 June 2011.
[235] See ch 11: 'Conflicts of Interest'.
[236] Solicitors Act 1974, s 65(2).
[237] SRA Accounts Rules 2011, r 17.2.
[238] ibid, r 17.4.

454   FEES

left at the client's business, dwelling house or last known place of abode.[239] No action can be brought until one month after the delivery of the bill of costs. Where the bill relates to contentious matters the solicitor must always seek the leave of the court.[240]

i. Contentious Business

Under the Act, bills in respect of contentious business may be either a gross sum or an itemised bill.[241] If the solicitor delivers a gross sum bill, clients have three months to require delivery of a detailed bill. The court may order assessment of a gross sum bill within one month from the service on that party of the writ or other originating process.[242] Clients can also request a solicitor and own client assessment under the Solicitors Act 1974, section 70 and Part 48 of the CPR. When the costs to be assessed are discounted by 20 per cent or more, the solicitor pays the costs of the assessment.

ii. Non-contentious Business

A committee of senior members of the government, judiciary and professions can make orders for the remuneration of non-contentious business. The former rule, requiring solicitors to obtain a remuneration certificate before suing, no longer applies.[243] It has been replaced by the right to complain and to seek assessment by the court. While solicitors have an obligation to advise clients of these rights, the procedure appears to offer clients less protection than that provided previously. There are special provisions relating to contentious business agreements.[244]

C. The Solicitor's Lien

In general, a client's failure to pay fees is a good reason to cease acting for the client, on reasonable notice.[245] Normally a solicitor must return all the client's papers at the end of a case. The solicitor's lien enables the solicitor to retain papers and property belonging to the client pending the payment of the bill.[246] The client must be informed about this at the outset of the case.[247] The lien does not arise until a properly itemised bill has been delivered to the client. It applies to all papers of the client held by the solicitor, not simply to those relating to the unpaid bill.[248]

[239] Solicitors Act 1974, s 69 as amended by the Legal Services Act 2007.
[240] ibid, s 61.
[241] ibid, s 64 as amended by the Legal Services Act 2007.
[242] ibid, s 64(3), as amended by the Legal Services Act 2007.
[243] Solicitors (Non-Contentious Business) Remuneration Order 2009 (SI 2009/1931).
[244] Solicitors Act 1974, ss 57(4) and 60(2), as amended by the Legal Services Act 2007.
[245] SRA, *Solicitors' Code of Conduct 2007*, r 2.01(2).
[246] ibid, r 2.11.
[247] ibid, r 2.03 (1)(e).
[248] *Law Society Gazette* answer to an ethics problem in August 1996.

The lien is not unique to solicitors; any person who has done work for another may retain the property on which the work has been done pending payment. However the power is particularly effective in the case of solicitors as they frequently have possession of large sums of client funds. Holding on to papers will also make it difficult for the client to instruct another solicitor.

The court has discretion to order a solicitor to deliver up any documents in his custody.[249] It will normally do this where the client needs the documents for continuing litigation. The order is usually conditional on the client giving an undertaking to restore the documents to the solicitor at the end of that litigation. Further conditions might be imposed by the court, depending on the circumstances of the case. For example, in *Ismail v Richards Butler*[250] the ex-client was required to provide further security for the payment of the outstanding bills.

XI. Conclusion

Ensuring effective and fair control over lawyers' charges is difficult, even for governments and corporate clients. Complaints on costs formed the majority of those formerly made to the Law Society and now made to the Legal Ombudsman Service. This is not surprising as there is an essential conflict of interest between a lawyer and client on the issue of the fee charged.

The high cost of litigation, which is contributed to by lawyers' fees, is a key political issue. Governments are charged with securing access to justice, but cannot meet the costs through legal aid. The pressure on the public purse of funding access to justice has two consequences. First, there is an imperative to introduce funding mechanisms that were formerly thought to present a high a risk of lawyer and client conflicts of interest. Secondly, there is increasing pressure for stronger control of lawyers' fees. These take the form of professional regulation and external measures to control costs, for example, by the courts. Both are likely to increase. Hence, there is likely to be greater use of wasted costs procedures, costs budgeting, costs capping and standard or fixed fees. This is because these procedures can be invoked by defendants or by the courts. They are not, therefore, solely the responsibility of clients to enforce.

---

[249] Solicitors Act 1974, s 68, as amended by the Legal Services Act 2007.
[250] *Ismail v Richards Butler* [1996] QB 711.

PART IV

WIDER OBLIGATIONS

13

Individual Third Parties

'The very structure of law, as it is created, practiced and enforced, assumes a duality, an otherness – the defendant, the opposing side, the client, those inside the law, and those outside'[1]

I. Introduction

Professionals are expected to be socially responsible. They cannot be oblivious to the impacts of their actions. Part of the trust placed in professionals assumes that they can justify the implicit public pledge to consider the good of other members of the community when helping clients.[2] Arguably, if the role is good, there will be a justifiable balance between the benefit a profession achieves for society, and the harm it does. A valid question for professional ethics, therefore, is whether the good of promoting client autonomy justifies the kinds of harm resulting to third parties.

Lawyers are subject to three basic but competing duties owed to different parties. These are loyalty to clients, candour towards the court and fairness towards third parties.[3] Obligations to others inevitably limit what can be done for clients. This is why third party obligations tend not to figure large in the codes of ethics of legal professions. Where they do appear, they tend to be negative obligations, rather than positive ones. Apart from the few, specific obligations to regard third party interests, other obligations to third parties are arguably reflected in overarching standards of behaviour, such as core duties.

Obligations deriving from very broad standards are, by their nature, difficult to specify. Therefore, an obligation to be honest or fair could be applied very narrowly, say, only to clients. It could also be interpreted broadly, so as to benefit third parties. In order to see what obligations third parties are owed, it is necessary to look at the practice of the courts or the rules of conduct. These sources suggest that there is no general principle covering third party obligations owed by lawyers. Rather, there are narrow areas in which obligations have been found to exist.

---

[1] C Menkel-Meadow, 'Is Altruism Possible in Lawyering' (1992) 8(2) *Georgia State University Law Review* 385, at 387.

[2] D Koehn, *The Ground of Professional Ethics* (London and New York, Routledge, 1994) ch 4.

[3] LR Patterson, 'On Analysing the Law of Legal Ethics: An American Perspective' (1981) 16(1) *Israel Law Review* 28, at 33.

Situations in which lawyers' duties to third parties have been recognised can be broken down into two categories; responsibilities assumed by lawyers and those imposed on lawyers. Imposed responsibilities tend to be collective. They include the duty not to mislead the court and not to participate in money laundering. These topics are dealt with in the next chapter. Responsibilities assumed by lawyers fall into two groups, collective responsibilities accepted by the profession and responsibilities assumed by individual lawyers.

An example of an assumed collective responsibility to third parties is, potentially, a duty owed to prospective clients, as opposed to actual clients. This is illustrated by the cab rank rule. An example of a duty assumed by individual lawyers is a promise to a third party in litigation or in a transaction. The promise may be intended to facilitate a transaction or court process. Such promises are usually proffered in the interests of clients, for example, to advance the efficiency and speed of legal business. Nevertheless, the third party is entitled to hold the lawyer to the promise.

II. Obligations to Prospective Clients

People who are seeking lawyers are essentially third parties until they have been accepted as clients. They are owed obligations and even defined as clients for some purposes, for example, in the current SRA Handbook, where the context permits.[4]

A. Supporting Free Choice of Lawyer

Lawyers, as professionals, are generally under a duty to decide honestly whether a prospective client's best interests are served by them acting. Supporting a free choice of lawyer therefore has several dimensions. It means providing information to help a client make the best choice of lawyers. It requires that the lawyer is not party to arrangements that fetter the prospective client's freedom to select a lawyer. It involves not applying any pressure or doing anything else inappropriate that may influence free choice. For this limited purpose, ensuring freedom in the choice of representation, prospective clients are third parties whose best interests must be protected by their prospective lawyers.

B. Barristers

There a number of exceptions to the barristers' strict rules on providing representation. Under the old Bar rules the 'cab rank rule' was always subject to specific exceptions relating to professional embarrassment.[5] For example, barristers were required

---

[4] SRA, *Handbook 2011*, as amended, Glossary.
[5] Bar Council, *Bar Code of Conduct 1981*, as amended, at para 603.

to refuse instructions if they were not competent to handle a matter or if they considered it in the client's best interests to go elsewhere.[6]

C. Solicitors

The old Rule 1 of the Solicitors' Practice Rules 1990 provided that a solicitor should 'do nothing to restrict a person's freedom to instruct the solicitor of their choice'. This was re-emphasised by Principle 11.01 in the 1999 Law Society Guide. The aim of the rule was to protect the client from improper influence by third parties, or even from influence by the solicitor.

The guidance to old Rule 1 provided an example of improper influence. It was that of a landlord client who required his solicitor to ask a tenant not to use solicitor Y because, in the past, Y had pointed out unfavourable terms in a lease to another tenant. Another example is where a solicitor is requested to include a term in a settlement agreement that the other side's solicitor should not act for other clients against his client in the future. The guidance noted that solicitors accepting these instructions would be in breach of Rule 1.

It was significant that no similar rule appeared in the core duties of the Solicitors' Code of Conduct 2007. The principle still applied to referrals, in relation to which the relevant rule stated that '[y]ou must not enter into any agreement or association which would restrict your freedom to recommend any particular firm'.[7] The reach of this rule was, however, considerably more restricted than the old Rule 1. The reason for this was probably recognition of the impracticality of the rule under certain conditions.

A case that demonstrated the limits of Rule 1 in supporting the principle of freedom of choice of solicitor concerned litigation against tobacco companies.[8] An action by lung cancer sufferers alleged that Imperial Tobacco knew of the association of tobacco with cancer long before they revealed it. The claimants entered a conditional fee agreement, but the costs escalated to the point that their solicitors could not afford to finance the case. The costs of Imperial Tobacco had apparently, by that stage, reached £7 million. The claimants were forced to settle.

Agreement was reached whereby the litigation ceased and the defendant company agreed not to ask for costs, provided the solicitors agreed not to represent any claimants against Imperial Tobacco in a similar matter for 10 years. This prevented the free choice of solicitor of future potential clients. The settlement was agreed by the court and approved by the Law Society. The solicitors acted in the overwhelming best interests of their existing clients, but could not also comply with Rule 1.

Practice also began to accommodate exceptions to the idea of freedom to choose solicitor. There were special regulations on choice of lawyer where legal expenses insurance was involved.[9] Companies were allowed to restrict their insured's freedom

---

[6] ibid, at para 606.
[7] SRA, *Solicitors' Code of Conduct 2007*, r 9.03.
[8] *Hodgson v Imperial Tobacco* [1998] 2 All ER 673.
[9] Insurance Companies (Legal Expenses Insurance) Regulations 1990 (SI 1990/1159). See H Blundell, 'Free to Choose?' (2004) *Journal of Personal Injury Law* 93.

of choice of solicitor to members of their panels, albeit in specified circumstances only.[10] Courts also recognised that over-strict interpretation of rules on conflict of interest could result in a denial of a free choice of solicitor.[11]

The nail in the coffin of Rule 1 was possibly the 2001 decision in *Sarwar v Alam*,[12] a case relating to legal expenses insurance. In the case, the Court of Appeal held that a strong public interest in maintaining a client's freedom to retain the solicitor of his choice, did not override all other considerations, such as cost. In accordance with the Civil Procedure Rules, costs should be reasonable and proportionate. That would usually imply a restriction on the choice of solicitor.

D. The SRA Handbook

None of the principles or any of the outcomes of the current code replicates the old Rule 1 on the freedom to choose solicitor. It is arguable that Principles 3 (not compromising independence), 4 (acting in client's best interests) and 6 (maintaining public trust) are relevant. It is, however, difficult to imagine that they would be sufficient alone to support an obligation to promote freedom of choice of solicitor. Any obligation must therefore be inferred from other outcomes and indicative behaviours.

The outcomes to Chapter 1, on Clients, includes one that is particularly relevant to promoting freedom of choice. It requires that solicitors 'have the resources, skills and procedures to carry out client instructions'.[13] This may of course work against freedom of choice of solicitor, in the sense that the rule might conflict with the client's decision. A client may be firmly committed to instructing a firm, but a lawyer working there may be bound to dissuade them because they think the firm lacks capacity to handle the matter. If the client insists, the lawyer may need to decline. The outcome is expressed in such a way that does not seem to admit the possibility of informed consent to lack of competence or capacity.

The same chapter contains two relevant indicative behaviours. One involves solicitors considering whether they should decline to act when unable to act in the client's best interests.[14] The other involves being cautious when acting for clients where there are reasonable grounds for believing that their instructions are affected by duress or undue influence.[15] The first of these overlaps with the outcome related to capacity. The second is directly relevant to the issue of freedom of choice; solicitors dealing with vulnerable clients must take extra care to ensure that their instructions reflect the client's preference, rather than that of a guardian or carer.

The idea that the common law, and professional ethics, requires a free choice of a solicitor, the view taken in 1990, is now only partly true. A problem may arise as a side issue, one of conflict of interest, for example, in which case conflicts rules would

---

[10] P Camp, *Companion to the Solicitors' Code of Conduct 2007* (London, The Law Society, 2007) at 7.
[11] *Koch Shipping v Richards Butler* [2002] 2 All ER (Comm) 957 and *Re A Firm of Solicitors* [1995] 3 All ER 482.
[12] *Sarwar v Alam* [2001] 4 All ER 541. See also *R v Legal Aid Board, ex p Duncan* [2000] COD 159 DC.
[13] SRA, *Handbook 2011*, as amended, SRA, *Code of Conduct 2011*, Outcome 1.4.
[14] ibid, Indicative Behaviour 1.7.
[15] ibid, Indicative Behaviour 1.28.

be enforced. In general though, the idea of freedom of choice has been overtaken by realities. Most people could only afford legal lawyers' fees through personal insurance, such as car insurance, or collective insurance, such as trade union personal injury schemes. A condition of cover was that they used lawyers nominated by the insurers or trade union.

Any obligation to promote freedom of choice of solicitor must now be conjured from abstract values, like promoting independence. These abstract values could justify a number of conclusions about whether a choice of lawyer is necessary in a given situation. Because of the vagueness of these principles, it is difficult to imagine circumstances in which the issue might become a disciplinary matter.

E. Refusing to Represent

The most basic obligation of a lawyer is to provide legal assistance, notwithstanding disapproval of their clients or of their moral positions. The legal role that flows from obedience to the rule of law is based on a theory of neutrality and non-accountability in client selection. Refusing clients appears to offend the principle of neutrality. The issue of when clients can be refused, and on what basis, therefore has theoretical as well as practical importance.

i. Barristers

Barristers have traditionally made neutrality in client selection a central pillar of their professional ethics. The eighth edition of the Bar Code of Conduct, like all of its predecessors, stated that self-employed barristers 'must comply with the "Cab-rank rule"' in any field in which they profess to practise in relation to work appropriate to their experience and seniority and irrespective of whether their client is paying privately or is publicly funded.[16]

The substance of the rule is that they must accept any brief or instructions on behalf of any person irrespective of the party, the nature of the case and 'any belief or opinion which he may have formed as to the character, reputation, cause, conduct, guilt or innocence of that person'. In addition to not acting where it is not in their prospective client's interests that they should, barristers did not need to comply with the cab rank rule unless a proper fee was payable.[17] Queen's Counsel was not obliged to act without junior counsel in situations where they considered it inappropriate to do so.[18]

Despite the exceptions, the existence of the cab rank rule does have practical implications for barristers, not least because it tends to be endorsed, and occasionally rigorously enforced, by the judges. In *Arthur Hall & Co v Simons*, Lord Steyn affirmed that it was a 'valuable professional rule' and Lord Hoffmann suggested it was a 'valuable

[16] Bar Council, *Bar Code of Conduct 1981*, as amended, at para 602.
[17] ibid, at para 604.
[18] ibid, at para 605.

professional ethic of the English Bar'. In *Ridehalgh v Horsefield and another*,[19] the Court of Appeal quashed a wasted costs order made against counsel because the judge had overlooked the obligations imposed on counsel by the cab rank rule. The absence of sufficient time for a barrister to prepare a defence was not regarded as a good excuse for not complying with the rule.[20]

Judicial endorsement of the cab rank rule, as essential to the proper administration of justice, has not prevented it from being controversial. A recent suggestion, in a report commissioned by the Legal Services Board (LSB), that the cab rank rule is symbolic, rather than substantive, evoked a robust response from the Bar and BSB. It is surprising therefore that the rationale of the cab rank rule does not figure more prominently in the new Bar Handbook. The new core duties do not mention the cab rank rule and provide only that barristers must not discriminate improperly in relation to any person.[21]

The cab rank rule itself is retained in the new Bar Code as an obligation on self-employed barristers to accept briefs irrespective of any 'belief or opinion which you may have formed as to the character, reputation, cause, conduct, guilt or innocence of the client'.[22] The BSB promises to extend the rule to all BSB-authorised bodies and authorised individuals working in them where instructions are given on a referral basis and seek the services of a named authorised individual.[23] Indeed, the rule has been strengthened by removal of power for the Bar Council to deem fees to be reasonable for the purposes of the Code.

ii. Solicitors

Solicitors have never had an equivalent of the cab rank rule. Therefore, the right of clients to freedom of choice of solicitor was rather meaningless; solicitors could decline representation. Many solicitors are probably, in fact, morally neutral in client selection, but some deny that they have an obligation not to discriminate on moral grounds.[24] Human rights lawyers, for example, might refuse to represent parties identified with committing human rights abuses.

Chapter 1 of the SRA Handbook ('Client Care') states that 'when deciding whether to act you comply with the law and the Code'.[25] Chapter 2 of the SRA Handbook ('Equality and Diversity') provides that solicitors must not discriminate unlawfully[26] and provide services in a way that respects client diversity.[27] They must make reasonable

[19] *Ridehalgh v Horsefield and another* [1994] Ch 205.
[20] *R v Ulcay and Toygun* [2007] ECWA Crim 2379, citing the above examples at [40].
[21] BSB, *Handbook 2014*, pt 2: *The Code of Conduct*, CD 8 (http://handbook.barstandardsboard.org.uk/handbook/part-2/).
[22] ibid, at r C29.
[23] Amendments to the Bar Code of Conduct–New BSB Handbook: Final Application (26 April 2013) at para 2.19 (www.legalservicesboard.org.uk/Projects/statutory_decision_making/pdf/bsb_new_handbook_application.pdf).
[24] A Boon, 'Cause Lawyers in a Cold Climate' in S Sheingold and A Sarat (eds), *Cause Lawyering and the State in a Global Era* (Oxford, Oxford University Press, 2001) at 143.
[25] BSB, *Handbook 2014*, pt 2: *The Code of Conduct*, Outcome 1.3.
[26] SRA, *Handbook 2011*, as amended, Outcome 2.1.
[27] ibid, Outcome 2.2.

adjustments to ensure that disabled clients are not at a substantial disadvantage compared to those who are not disabled.[28]

The key negative indicative behaviour is discriminating unlawfully when accepting or refusing instructions to act for a client.[29] This might involve having been found to have committed, or being treated as having committed, an unlawful act of discrimination by a court or tribunal of the UK.[30] Both the outcomes and indicative behaviours in the SRA Handbook only require that solicitors comply with the general law on discrimination when it comes to client selection. This means that solicitors must not refuse clients on grounds of race, colour, nationality or ethnic origins or on grounds of their religion or philosophical beliefs. Neither can they refuse clients on grounds of sex, disability or age.

III. The Future of Obligations to Prospective Clients

The traditional idea that the legal representative of choice is open to anyone may be gradually disappearing. Solicitors have abandoned the idea of an obligation to promote freedom of choice of solicitor. The Bar's commitment to the cab rank rule has survived an attack, but will be weakened, in practical terms, by the decline of legal aid and the Criminal Bar. There now appear to be three potential routes for the principle of client selection. The professions may continue to have different lines on client selection or they may fall into line on the issue, with the idea of neutrality in client selection adopted or rejected by both.

In their application to the LSB for approval of their new handbook, the BSB signalled the intention to engage the SRA in discussions on applying the cab rank rule to solicitors as well as barristers. This would, the BSB claimed, increase access to justice in the legal profession. If it were to be achieved, the BSB would consider extending the cab rank rule to its public access work.[31] It seems unlikely that the Law Society will be convinced of the need for neutrality in client selection, and even less likely that it could convince solicitors that it was necessary to introduce it.

There appears to be a particularly strong case for existing differences between solicitors and barristers on the issue of client selection being preserved and strengthened. One of the best arguments for a bar of independent advocates is that they are available to equalise arms between the smallest and largest solicitors in the land. It is therefore important that independent barristers are available to all, in a way that solicitors need not be. The differentiation argument may apply less convincingly to solicitors in rural areas, where the relative lack of choice is an argument against

---

[28] ibid, Outcome 2.3.
[29] ibid, Indicative Behaviour 2.5.
[30] ibid, Indicative Behaviour 2.4.
[31] Amendments to the Bar Code of Conduct (n 23) at para 2.19.

client selection. Nevertheless, there is a rational basis for a different approach between professions.

IV. Obligations to Identified Third Parties

Intellectually, it is easier to contemplate imposing an obligation on a person to care for someone they know than it is a stranger that they do not know. In this way, a lawyer might be seen to have moral responsibilities to identified third parties, non-clients. It is possible that they also have legal responsibility to those that they have harmed as a consequence of their activities.

There are three large areas of responsibility that lawyers must consider in carrying out their work. The first area of responsibility is to lay third parties, particularly those who are vulnerable or, even though not a client, rely on the lawyer's special skill or judgement or on a specific promise to do something. The second area of responsibility is to other professionals who need to be able to rely on certain standards of behaviour in order to carry out their own work. The third area of responsibility is to third party funders of litigation. Although these are not, strictly speaking, clients, they are also entitled to consideration from lawyers whom they pay to do work.

The legislature and the courts impose obligations to identified third parties in a numbers of ways, including through contracts, torts and trusts. The decisions shape the legal profession's perception of the duties lawyers might owe third parties and the nature of those duties. In each of the three areas of special responsibility for third parties, the legal background is outlined, including any potential liability, before the professional regulation of the area is considered.

V. Legal Responsibilities to Lay Third Parties

A. Specific Causes of Action and Remedies

i. Negligence

The notion that lawyers might have legal responsibilities other than to their client is relatively recent. This was because the harm a lawyer might cause to a third party tended to be financial loss. This was classified as 'pure economic loss', meaning it was independent of physical injury and visible only on a balance sheet. The courts of many jurisdictions were reluctant to allow recovery of damages for pure economic loss, for fear of opening up an uncontrollable vista of liability.

a. Negligent Misstatements

In England, the possibility of liability for pure economic loss in the service sector was opened up by the case of *Hedley Byrne v Heller*.[32] Here, financial loss was caused to a third party when a bank gave a reference confirming the financial stability of one of its customers. It was held by the House of Lords that a negligent, though honest, misrepresentation could give rise to an action for damages for financial losses it caused, even though no contract or fiduciary relationship existed.

The House of Lords conceived of the possibility of a duty of care on a party seeking information from a party possessed of a special skill. It held that a duty would be implied when the party seeking the reference trusted the other to exercise due care, and the party providing the reference knew or ought to have known that reliance was being placed on that skill and judgement.

The caution of the courts towards extending liability for pure financial loss in negligence is largely due to the spectre of indeterminate liability. In order to limit the number of people a defendant can be liable to compensate, the courts require that a third party claimant is distinguished by 'proximity'. In one of the leading cases on statements causing loss, it was said that a potential claimant must be (i) the person directly intended by the maker of the statement to act upon the statement; (ii) in a specific transaction of which the maker knows; and (iii) the statement must be relied on for the purpose for which it was made.[33]

b. Negligence Causing Loss to Beneficiaries

It was for some time thought that *Hedley Byrne* created a limited category of negligence limited to misstatements of opinion or fact. This was not thought to include statements or opinions on law, or advice, whether on law or fact, or acts or omissions. The decision was relevant to lawyers, but in a quite confined area of operations. In 1980, however, the developing tort of negligence took lawyers firmly within its compass in *Ross v Caunters*.[34]

In *Ross v Caunters*, a law firm sent a will for execution by their client without warning that the two required witnesses could not be spouses of beneficiaries. The husband of an intended beneficiary witnessed the will and it was held invalid for this reason. The intended beneficiary sued for a sum equal to the lost inheritance. The lawyers admitted negligence but denied that they owed the beneficiary any duty of care.

The argument for not holding the lawyers liable was not cast purely on the ground that the loss caused to the intended beneficiary was purely economic. It was argued that a solicitor could only be liable to his own client and only for breach of contract. If solicitors could not be liable in negligence to their clients, how could they be liable to anyone else?

The defendants argued that the overwhelming argument against liability to third parties was the nature of the relationship between solicitors and their clients. Lawyers are engaged to protect clients' interests. If solicitors also owed a duty to third parties

---

[32] *Hedley Byrne & Co Ltd v Heller & Partners Ltd* [1964] AC 465.
[33] *Caparo Industries Plc v Dickman and Others* [1990] 2 WLR 358.
[34] *Ross v Caunters* [1980] Ch 297.

they would have to constantly consider the risk that they may claim against them. This would lead to a grave weakening of the duty to their client. This argument did not convince the court.

Megarry VC found that the solicitors owed a duty of care since the beneficiary was someone within their direct contemplation. They could reasonably foresee that she would be injured by their acts or omissions. Accordingly, in the absence of any consideration to the contrary, the claim should succeed. The court acknowledged that the courts were traditionally concerned that such liability might weaken duties to clients.[35] Nevertheless, the judge's decision confirmed that there was no longer any rule that a solicitor who is negligent in his professional work could only be liable to his client in contract.

Hedley Byrne had pointed to the fact that solicitors and their clients, like everybody else, could be liable for financial loss resulting from reliance on a negligent misrepresentation of fact. *Ross v Caunters* exploded the assumption that solicitors owed no general duty of care to third parties. Nevertheless, that duty could still be contained. The means of limiting the case was the special facts of the case. The judge said that the solicitors' duty of care towards the testator included a duty to confer a benefit on the plaintiff. The duty to act with due care, binding the solicitor to his client, is one that could readily be extended to a third party beneficiary.

Ross v Caunters based liability to third parties on a duty to use proper care in carrying out the client's instructions to confer a third party benefit. As the judge said, '[i]f it is to be held that there is a duty that is wider than that, that will have to be determined in some other case.' In this way, he consciously avoided the possibility that defendants would be exposed 'to a liability in an indeterminate amount for an indeterminate time to an indeterminate class'.[36] 'Instead, there would be a finite obligation to a finite number of persons, in this case one'.[37]

The case of *White v Jones*[38] involves a variation of the duty to a beneficiary under a will. A solicitor negligently delayed drawing up a will and the testator died before it could be executed. As neither the testator nor the estate had a remedy against the solicitor, only the intended beneficiary could seek a remedy. The House of Lords held that the beneficiary could sue the deceased's solicitor for the value of the bequest. It was reasonably foreseeable that the negligence would cause such a loss. The remedy was provided for the beneficiary on the basis that 'the assumption of responsibility by the solicitor towards his client should be held in law to extend to the intended beneficiary'.[39] It is clear that solicitors are under a duty to expedite execution of a will, particularly when there was an imminent risk that a testator may die.[40]

In *Carr-Glynn v Frearsons*,[41] the principle in *White v Jones* was again extended. The testatrix was a joint tenant of a property with her nephew. She intended to leave her

---

[35] *Robertson v Fleming* 4 Macq 167; *Groom v Crocker* [1939] 1 KB194.
[36] The US case *Ultramares Corporation v Touche* (1931) 174 NE 441, per Cardozo CJ at 444.
[37] *Ross v Caunters* [1980] Ch 297, per Megarry VC at 309.
[38] *White v Jones* [1995] 1 All ER 691.
[39] ibid, at 710.
[40] *Hooper v Fynmore*s [2001] *Law Society Gazette*, 28 June 2001, at 45.
[41] *Carr-Glynn v Frearsons* [1998] 4 All ER 225.

share to her niece, the plaintiff, and instructed the defendant solicitors to take the necessary steps. This involved serving a notice of severance of the joint tenancy on the nephew, so as to create a tenancy in common. The solicitors negligently failed to serve notice before the testatrix died, with the result that the nephew became beneficial owner of the whole property.

The Court of Appeal noted that the nephew may have felt morally obliged to honour the testator's intention, but had not offered to do so. It therefore reversed the first instance decision and held that the intended beneficiary could recover from the deceased's solicitors. They owed a duty to intended beneficiaries under *White v Jones*. Although the failing did not involve negligence in drafting or arranging execution of the will, the task of severing the joint tenancy was a necessary part of carrying out the instructions regarding the will.

Apart from avoiding negligence, solicitors must beware substituting their own moral judgement for that of their clients. In *Feltham v Freer Bouskell*,[42] S, a solicitor with the defendant firm, received instructions to change the will of an elderly client (C) from L. L was to inherit the bulk of the estate at the expense of the former beneficiaries. S accepted the instructions subject to satisfying himself as to C's testamentary capacity. He immediately instructed a doctor, who reported favourably. Following this, S had to see C on other matters. Rather than raising the issue of the instructions transmitted via L, S decided to wait until C mentioned drawing up the will before doing anything further.

S having done nothing, C asked L to prepare her will, which C then executed. S encouraged the beneficiaries to challenge the will and L settled out of court. L then sued S for losses she suffered by making a compromise settlement. S was held liable. The court understood S' concern that C was suffering from dementia and that this might negate her testamentary capacity. This made it even more important that he establish the facts and acted on the instructions he had been given. Had he done so, any doubt as to C's capacity would not have existed and L would not have had to surrender part of her inheritance to the disaffected former beneficiaries. Further, because S had created the situation, there was no break in the chain of causation, as S had argued, when C asked L to prepare her will.

The case of *Ross v Caunters* opened the door to solicitors being liable to third parties for negligence. The courts have, however, been careful not to fling it wide. Extensions of the principle in *Ross v Caunters* have been relatively modest. The Court of Appeal has held that 'it is quite impossible to extend the principles arising from the special situation of a beneficiary under a will'.[43] There is, for example, no duty of care to a prospective beneficiary of a client's disposition in a donor's lifetime.[44] The cases are, nevertheless, cautionary. In particular, as *Feltham* shows, solicitors should never strive to achieve 'justice' in the distribution of their client's estate. Otherwise, they may find themselves compensating deprived beneficiaries.

---

[42] *Feltham v Freer Bouskell* [2013] EWHC 1952 (Ch).
[43] *Regent Leisuretime Ltd v Skerrett* [2007] PNLR 9, per Sir Peter Gibson at 33.
[44] See generally *Clark v Bruce Lance* [1988] 1 All ER 364; *Al-Kandari v Brown* [1988] 1 All ER 833; *Gran Gelato Ltd v Richcliff Ltd* [1992] 1 All ER 865; *Hemmons v Wilson Browne (a firm)* [1995] Ch 223.

c. Negligence Causing Loss to Unrepresented Third Parties

Lawyers must be careful when dealing with unrepresented parties. Any gratuitous advice offered that proves to be wrong could result in a negligence claim. In *Dean v Allin & Watts*,[45] for example, the unrepresented claimant, a car mechanic, relied on the advice of the defendant's solicitor regarding security for a loan he was making to the defendant. At the time the loan was made, both parties had a mutual interest in ensuring that it was secured. The advice was wrong and the solicitor, who knew the claimant was unrepresented, had not advised him to obtain independent legal advice. It was held that, exceptionally, a duty of care existed and the solicitors were held liable. In contrast, in *Hemmens v Wilson Browne*,[46] the solicitors escaped liability because they had advised the claimant to get independent advice.

d. Negligence Causing Loss to Witnesses

A similar duty to offer accurate advice was imposed in a 2005 County Court case. A trainee solicitor advised one his client's witnesses that he could not be sacked if, when giving his evidence, he admitted smoking at work. The witness was sacked. Damages were awarded for the loss caused by the negligent advice.[47]

e. Negligence towards Victims of Crime

A possibility that is untested in English law is whether a professional owes a duty to warn a prospective victim whom a client has threatened to harm. Such a duty has been held to exit in the US.[48] If a duty to third parties does exist, it would have to excuse a breach of a duty of confidentiality to a client. This is implicit in revealing information of this kind. It would need to cover the issue of whether disclosure can be made only to the victim or also to the authorities. It would also need to deal with the issue of whether disclosure is mandatory or permitted or whether this is dictated by the seriousness of the circumstances.

Codes have allowed breach of confidence in such circumstances. For example, the Guide included as guidance the statement that information could be revealed if it was necessary 'to prevent the client or a third party committing a criminal act that the solicitor believes on reasonable grounds is likely to result in serious bodily harm'.[49] Since this was guidance it had dubious authority. Since the language was permissive, it is doubtful that there was a positive duty to warn a potential victim. The acid test would be whether a lawyer would be liable in negligence for a failure to warn. Such a finding would then be reflected in the codes. At present, there is no mention of this situation in any of the codes.

---

[45] *Dean v Allin & Watts* [2001] All ER (D) 288; J Ross (2001) 151 *New Law Journal* 960.
[46] *Hemmens v Wilson Browne* [1995] Ch 223.
[47] See *Law Society Gazette* 1 September 2005, at 4.
[48] *Tarasoff v Regents of the University of California* [1976] 131 *Cal Rpter* 14. See further ch 10: 'Confidences'.
[49] N Taylor (ed), *The Guide to the Professional Conduct of Solicitors* (London, the Law Society, 1999) r 16.02, 'Circumstances which override confidentiality', guidance note 3.

ii. Breach of Undertakings

An undertaking is a binding promise to do something. The important feature of undertakings given by lawyers is that the promise must be carried out. This is so even if the circumstances in which the promise was made totally change. If the change of circumstance was unforeseeable, and operates to the detriment of the person giving the promise, the promise must be fulfilled.

Solicitors frequently give undertakings, usually to the other side in litigation or in relation to a transaction. They may promise to discharge mortgages, produce or return documents, hold monies to order or exchange contracts for the sale of land or facilitate some other event. Much business could not be speedily or efficiently carried out without reliance on undertakings. The courts have enforced solicitors' undertakings in different ways, for example, as a basis for creating trusts, ordering performance and awarding compensation.

a. Creation of Trusts

The role of the court arose in the rather unsatisfactory case of *Twinsectra Ltd v Yardley and others*.[50] A solicitor (S) acted for Y in connection with the purchase of land. The client needed to borrow £1m to complete the purchase. A lender (T) was found but it would only loan against a solicitor's personal undertaking to use the monies as directed. S was unwilling to give an undertaking so Y approached a second solicitor, S^2. S^2 represented himself as acting for Y and received the money on the terms of an undertaking by his firm.

The terms of the undertaking were that

> (1) The loan moneys will be retained by us until such time as they are applied in the acquisition of property on behalf of our client. (2) The loan moneys will be utilised solely for the acquisition of property on behalf of our client and for no other purposes (3) We will repay to you the said sum of £1m together with interest.

S^2 released the money to S, as instructed by Y, on assurances from Y that the money would be used for the purchase of the property.

S released the money to Y, who used part of the sum to purchase a property and nearly £358,000 for other purposes. S took no steps to ensure that the money was only applied in the acquisition of property. S^2 went bankrupt and the loan was not repaid. T commenced proceedings against S, alleging that he had dishonestly assisted in a breach of trust by S^2. The Court of Appeal held that the undertaking given by S^2 had created a trust. However, although S had deliberately shut his eyes to the implications of the undertaking given by S^2, he had not been dishonest.

The House of Lords held that S^2 held the money on trust for the lender subject to a power to apply it, by way of a loan to the client, in accordance with the undertaking. The result was that the money remained the lender's money until such time as it was applied for this purpose. The second issue was whether S was liable as an accessory to the breach of trust. To be so, he had to have acted dishonestly by the ordinary

---

[50] *Twinsectra Ltd v Yardley and others* [2002] UKHL 12.

standards of reasonable and honest people. He also had to be aware that, by those standards, he was acting dishonestly.

The House of Lords reversed the Court of Appeal finding that S was dishonest. It upheld the judge's finding that S had honestly believed that the undertaking given to the lender was not his concern and that, once in his hands, the loan money was at the free disposal of the client. Lord Hutton considered that S took a 'blinkered approach to his professional duties as a solicitor', but was not dishonest.[51] Only Lord Millett, dissenting, pointed out that S knew the terms of the undertaking given by S^2 but appeared to take the view that the breach of undertaking was solely S^2's responsibility. He considered that S was liable as an accessory to the tort of wrongful interference with the performance of S^2's fiduciary and contractual undertaking and breach of trust.

The undertaking in *Twinsectra* was unusual, rather vague in its terms and possibly unenforceable. This may explain the decision not to hold S liable. While it did not happen in this case, it illustrates the fact that, in some circumstances, courts could hold solicitors to strict standards in relation to third party interests.[52]

b. Ordering Performance and Awarding Compensation

In relation to litigation, the court can exercise its inherent supervisory jurisdiction over solicitors and order the performance of an undertaking. If this is not possible it can award compensation. An illustrative case is *Udall v Capri Lighting Ltd.*[53] A solicitor acting for the defendant company sought to adjourn appointments to hear judgment summonses against it. He gave an oral undertaking to secure charges in favour of the claimant, covering property of the directors of a company. Judgment was entered against the company, but it went into liquidation and could not be enforced. The charges had not been executed by the solicitor and could not now be executed. The plaintiff claimed that the defendant's solicitor was liable on the breach of undertaking.

The Court of Appeal held that failure to implement an undertaking was, prima facie, misconduct, even where the solicitor had not acted dishonourably or could not implement it. The court could, in the exercise of its inherent jurisdiction, either order the implementation of the undertaking, where possible, or order compensation from the solicitor where it was not.[54] The case illustrates the proposition that a solicitor's undertaking is binding even if discharging it proves to be outside his control.[55]

c. Causing Loss to Opponents

Breach of an undertaking to a third party may be actionable in negligence. An example arose in the matrimonial case of *Al-Kandari v Brown*.[56] The solicitor for the husband undertook not to release his passport to him. On this basis, the husband

---

[51]   ibid, at [22].
[52]   A similar approach was taken in the case of *Bryant & Bench v The Law Society* (2007) *Law Society Gazette* 24 January 2008, at 28.
[53]   *Udall v Capri Lighting Ltd* [1988] QB 907.
[54]   See also *Fox v Bannister* [1987] 1 All ER 737.
[55]   *Citadel Management Inc v Thompson* [1999]1 FLR 21.
[56]   *Al-Kandari v Brown* [1988] 1 All ER 833.

was granted access to the children of the family. Owing to the solicitor's lack of care, the husband obtained the passport and took his children out of the country. The wife sued in negligence and succeeded. The solicitors, in giving the undertaking, had 'stepped outside their role as solicitors for their client and accepted responsibilities towards both their client and the plaintiff and the children'.[57]

iii. Wasted Costs

Wasted costs orders were introduced to provide a remedy for parties in litigation affected by the unsatisfactory work of opposing lawyers.[58] Wasted costs are defined as costs incurred by a party as 'a result of any improper, unreasonable or negligent act or omission on the part of any legal or other representative or any employee of such representative'.[59] The court may, at the instigation of either the client or the other side to the litigation, order the lawyer to pay the whole or any part of any wasted costs.

The source of the responsibility imposed on lawyers by costs orders can be conceived as a manifestation of the obligation to uphold the proper administration of justice. Lawyers required to pay the costs of the other side are given a stark reminder that it is not only their client's interests that they need to consider. At the time that the Courts and Legal Services Act 1990 was debated, the Law Society was very concerned that wasted costs orders would be used by the opposing side to intimidate or prevent a solicitor from acting properly for his client. This is an issue that the courts have grappled with in deciding whether to make such orders. It is considered in more detail in chapter seventeen: 'Litigation'.

B. General Obligation of Fairness

Apart from giving specific remedies the courts impose a general obligation of fairness on lawyers, particularly in litigation or other situations of conflict. This tends to be when an opponent is disadvantaged in a situation and it would be unconscionable for a lawyer to take advantage. This may be because the other person lacks knowledge or skill, for example because they are acting as a litigant in person, or because the situation is unfair.

i. Other Side's Client

a. Taking Advantage of Errors

A well-established example of taking unfair advantage is where privileged papers are disclosed in error. In *Ablitt v Mills & Reeve (A Firm) and Another*,[60] a solicitor (S)

---

[57] ibid, at 836.
[58] Senior Courts Act 1981, s 51(6), as amended by the Courts and Legal Services Act 1990, ss 4, 111, 112.
[59] ibid, s 51(7).
[60] *Ablitt v Mills & Reeve (A Firm) and Another* Ch D *The Times* 24 October 1995.

received seven files containing privileged information which had been sent in error by the other side's counsel. S consulted the Guide to Professional Conduct of Solicitors (sixth edition, 1993), paragraph 16.07 of which required a solicitor in his position to stop reading, inform the other side and then return the documents. It also advised, anomalously in the view of the court, that before returning the documents, the solicitor should consider whether to seek instructions from his client about the matter. Once S realised that the documents were privileged, he stopped reading them and sought further instructions from the client. The client instructed S to read all the files and then return them to the other side. Subsequently, S's firm offered undertakings not to make use of information derived from the files. An injunction was granted restraining the firm from acting in the action. It was held that the firm could have gained an accurate perception of the view of A's advisers as to the merits of his claim. To allow it to take advantage of such information would be contrary to the requirements of fairness and justice. Parties must be free to communicate with their legal advisers without fearing that such privileged information may be used by the opposing side.

An injunction preventing the lawyer who has read privileged information from acting is not inevitable in such circumstances. The critical factor is the degree of prejudice likely to be suffered. In *English & American Insurance Co Ltd & Others v Herbert Smith*,[61] counsel's papers for P were accidentally sent to solicitors for D, whose clients instructed them to read the papers. They returned the papers having read them. P was granted an injunction restraining D from making use of any of the information. It was held that, if the privileged information had not yet been tendered in evidence, the person entitled to legal professional privilege could restrain any use by the other side, including use in pending proceedings.

b. Limited Responsibilities in Other Situations

Apart from the law of negligence, and situations where it would be unconscionable to allow someone to take advantage, the common law recognises limited professional obligations to third parties. This is illustrated by *Re Schuppan (A Bankrupt)* (1996).[62] A solicitor for a petitioning creditor acted in litigation against S, who was found guilty of fraud and dishonesty. S could not satisfy the judgment and was made bankrupt. In the aftermath, S brought an action in slander against the creditor's solicitors. The solicitor was then retained by the trustee in bankruptcy to advise him on the administration of the S's estate.

S objected to the appointment of the solicitor on the ground that, having acted for a petitioning creditor in the previous litigation, he was in a position of conflict of interest. It was quite conceivable that the solicitor might be prejudiced against S. Even without the slander action, it was likely that the solicitor's experience of S as an opponent would affect his attitude towards him as an adviser to the trustee in bankruptcy. Nevertheless, the court held that it was not unreasonable for the trustee to retain creditors' solicitors in such circumstances. They would have the advantage of knowing of the difficulties relating to the tracing the bankrupt's assets.

---

[61] *English & American Insurance Co Ltd & Others v Herbert Smith* [1988] FSR 232, ChD 1987, (1987) *New Law Journal* 148.
[62] *Re Schuppan (A Bankrupt)* [1996] 2 All ER 664.

The court proposed quite elaborate measures to overcome any disadvantage to S. It suggested that any conflict of interest that might arise from the trustee's solicitors having access to the bankrupt's litigation documents could be resolved. One solution, for example, would be for the solicitor to give an undertaking not to use those documents without leave of the court. The decision can be contrasted with the stringent requirements laid down for solicitors' own client conflicts of interest. Any obligation of fairness to an opposing third party is set considerably lower than that standard.

ii. Unrepresented Opponents

Another example of the court's willingness to impose an obligation of fairness arises when lawyers are dealing with unrepresented parties. In *Haiselden v P & O Properties*,[63] a litigant in person mistakenly set down a case for trial in the County Court when it should have been dealt with as a small claim. The claimant lost the case, which the judge commented had been brought in good faith.

The trial judge awarded costs to the defendant that could not have been recovered on a small claim. The Court of Appeal noted that the defendant did not alert either the court or the unrepresented claimant that the claimant had made a mistake. Lord Justice Thorpe thought that,

> faced with a plaintiff [claimant] in person the defendants had some obligation to draw to his attention and/or to the attention of the court the error that had been made ... and particularly to draw to the attention of the plaintiff the beneficial consequence which the defendants intended to harvest from the error.

The defendant's costs on the County Court scale were therefore disallowed.

There are situations where courts may intervene to prevent lawyers taking advantage of unrepresented parties. One is where lawyers assert untenable claims. An example of this was the practice of solicitors in Employment Tribunal cases sending letters threatening costs applications where employees brought cases against them. These letters were improper because costs are awarded in only very limited and exceptional circumstances in Employment Tribunals.

An example of pressure being improperly applied to an opponent in relation to costs occurred in one Employment Tribunal case. The tribunal had been unduly influenced by a QC's threat to seek costs against the applicant and had issued the applicant with a warning on costs. The applicant settled, but the case was remitted for re-hearing after the Court of Appeal held that this put the applicant under undue pressure.[64] In 2001, the rules were changed to prevent the intimidation of applicants.[65] This is intended to preserve the character of Employment Tribunals as accessible to all, including the unrepresented employee.

---

[63] *Haiselden v P & O Properties* [1998] All ER 180 (D).
[64] *Gee v Shell UK Ltd* [2002] EWCA Civ 1479.
[65] P Plowden, 'Employment Tribunal Costs – Some Comfort for Applicants' *Legal Action* May 2004, at 28.

iii.   Other Third Parties Affected by Proceedings

a. Children as Third Parties

Some proceedings involve third parties who may be indirectly involved but not represented. The obvious case is children who are not separately represented in proceedings that affect them, such as divorce or guardianship proceedings. The Children Act 1989 created an exception to legal privilege, whereby expert reports, and possibly other documents bearing on the welfare of children were required to be disclosed.[66] This could involve lawyers acting against the wishes of client parents or guardians and in favour of a third party, the child. This is a relatively rare example of an obligation imposed on lawyers for the benefit of third parties.

b. Other Side's Non-professional Representative

While the conduct of reserved activities by unqualified persons is strictly prohibited, there have been inroads into the idea that people can only be assisted by qualified professionals. In *McKenzie v McKenzie*,[67] it was held that an unrepresented litigant could receive support and advice from a friend.[68] Such a person, a so-called McKenzie friend, has no right to address the court unless the court allows. Lay representatives can, however, speak on behalf of a party in the Small Claims Court and in tribunals, the Lord Chancellor having granted this right under section 11 of the Courts and Legal Services Act 1990. Lay representatives can even sometimes obtain the costs of representation.

There is now a finer line between unlawful practice on the one hand and providing lawful assistance and advice. Such activity must be distinguished from acting as a solicitor. As Lord Justice Potter put it,

> [T]he words 'acting as a solicitor' are limited to the doing of acts which only a solicitor may perform and/or the doing of acts by a person pretending or holding himself out to be a solicitor. Such acts are not to be confused with the doing of acts of a kind commonly done by solicitors but which involve no representation that the actor is acting as such.[69]

This situation is quite complicated for lawyers acting against a party represented by someone who is unqualified.

c. Other Sides' Professional Representatives

The courts tend to impose a duty of fairness on lawyers acting in litigation. In *Ernst & Young v Butte Mining Co*,[70] the court had approved a consent order setting aside a judgment by default. The defendants were permitted to serve a defence and counterclaim within a set time. The plaintiff's solicitor had the carriage (ie drafting and issuing) of the order and, immediately after obtaining it, filed a notice to discontinue the

---

[66] See further ch 10: 'Confidences'.

[67] *McKenzie v McKenzie* [1970] 3 All ER 1034.

[68] *R v Leicester City Justices* [1991] 3 All ER 935; *Re H* [1997] 2 FLR 423; *R v Bow County Court, ex p Pelling* [1999] 4 All ER 751; *Noueiri v Paragon Finance Plc The Times* 4 October 2001.

[69] *Piper Double Glazing Ltd v DC Contracts (1992) Ltd.* [1994] 1 All ER 177, per Potter J at 186.

[70] *Ernst & Young v Butte Mining Co* [1997] 2 All ER 471.

action. This was intended to prevent the defendants from filing their counterclaim. It was held to be an abuse of process. The plaintiff's solicitors had misled the defendants as to their intentions. They had sought an unfair advantage by obtaining the defendant's agreement to their having the carriage of the order.

VI. Regulation of Relationships with Lay Third Parties

A. Barristers

Some of the fundamental principles appearing at the start of the Bar Code potentially support a duty to third parties. Traditionally, these principles prohibit behaviour that is dishonest or otherwise discreditable to a barrister, prejudicial to the administration of justice or likely to diminish public confidence in the legal profession or the administration of justice or otherwise bring the legal profession into disrepute.[71]

The Bar Code of Conduct itself has no particular focus on lay third parties. Any non-client focus within the rules tends to be directed toward the duties a barrister owes to the court. These duties, for example, covering the treatment of witnesses, are dealt with in the chapter on advocacy. Of course, third parties are often the beneficiaries of such duties, because they tend to support openness and fairness in the conduct of litigation.

In the new Bar Code of Conduct third parties are not mentioned in the core duties. Some core duties could affect dealings with third parties, but these are at a high level of generality. For example, acting with honesty and integrity,[72] or behaving so as not to diminish public trust and confidence in the profession[73] cover conduct towards third parties. It is not clear, however, what specific obligations they are owed. This also applies to the rules in Chapter 2: 'Behaving Ethically'.

One of the rules in Chapter 2, which provides that barristers should not knowingly, or recklessly, mislead, or attempt to mislead, anyone, imposes an obvious constraint on dealings with third parties.[74] This appears to be quite an onerous duty, yet it is not clear precisely what is intended. Not misleading is not quite a duty of candour, being open or transparent, but it is quite close. It is consistent with the duty to the court, but would be a considerable constraint in negotiation. It would mean that a barrister could, arguably, never stay silent if the opposing side has made an error. The existence of such a broad duty is not indicated by the guidance to Chapter 2 in the Code.

---

[71] BSB, *Bar Code of Conduct 2004*, 8th edn, at para 301.
[72] BSB, *Handbook 2014, Code of Conduct*, CD3.
[73] ibid, CD5.
[74] ibid, r C9.1.

B. Solicitors

i. A Brief History of the Regulation of Duties to Third Parties

a. The Evolution of Regulation of Third Parties

The Solicitors' Practice Rules 1990 contained no explicit reference to any duty to lay third parties. The nearest that Rule 1, the basic principles, came to such a notion lay in not harming the good repute of the solicitor or of the solicitors' profession and upholding the solicitor's duty to the court. This was not true of the Guide, the 1999 version of which included a wide duty to third parties.

The main principle of Chapter 17 of the Guide, relationships with third parties, provided that '[s]olicitors must not act, whether in their professional capacity or otherwise, towards anyone in a way which is fraudulent, deceitful or otherwise contrary to their position as solicitors. Nor must solicitors take unfair advantage either for themselves or another person'.[75] Of course everyone, including solicitors, has an obligation not to deceive or defraud as such acts are contrary to the law.

If solicitors could be said to be subject to professional ethical constraints as a result of Principle 17 they flowed from the obligation not to take 'unfair advantage'. Not much guidance was given on this, although, in context, the main focus was unrepresented parties. The 1999 Guide also told solicitors that they must not write 'offensive letters' to third parties, or behave offensively.[76] Good manners are required however appalling the solicitor or his client considers the other side to be.

The remainder of the chapter on third parties in the 1999 Guide was largely a ragbag of prohibitions without much guiding rationale. Thus, solicitors were warned not to stop cheques issued on client account,[77] to give opposing parties time to agree costs[78] and to ensure that they administered oaths properly.[79] One paragraph, advising solicitors to report instances where they found parties represented by unqualified persons, smacked of protectionism rather than concern for relationships.

Apart from the reference to unfairness in Rule 17.01, the 1999 Guide contained one other paragraph hinting at a more expansive notion of responsibility to third parties. This was that '[w]hen writing a letter of claim, a solicitor must not demand anything other than that recoverable under the due process of law'.[80] The example given was of a solicitor sending a letter of claim for a simple debt and demanding the cost of the letter of claim. This, it was said, would be improper because it could not be known at that stage whether such a cost would be legally recoverable.[81] An interesting feature of this paragraph was that, although the Guide did not claim the status of rules, the formulation ('must not claim') was the language of a rule.

---

[75] Taylor, *The Guide to the Professional Conduct of Solicitors* (n 49) r 17.01.
[76] ibid, r 17.01, para 6 and r 19.01.
[77] ibid, 17.02.
[78] ibid, r 17.03.
[79] ibid, rr 17.06 and 17.07.
[80] ibid, r 17.05.
[81] ibid, r 17.05, guidance note 1.

Although not writing misleading letters was a clear example of being fair to third parties, the provision of only one example suggested a very narrow compass. The creation of wasted costs orders had already imposed potential responsibility for improper and unreasonable conduct in litigation. The decision to limit prohibited unfair conduct to letters before action presumably represented a deliberate decision not to follow the law. This implied that, as far as the Law Society was concerned, solicitors could indulge in 'improper and unreasonable conduct' provided they paid for it.

b. The Solicitors' Code of Conduct 2007

The principle relating to third parties was simplified in the Solicitors' Code of Conduct 2007, which omitted the prohibition of fraud and simply provided that '[s]olicitors must not use their position to take unfair advantage of anyone either for [their] own benefit or for another person's benefit'.[82] Despite the devotion of a chapter to third party obligations the constituent rules did not really take substantive obligations to third parties much further. Rather, they related to giving undertakings, agreeing costs and not contacting parties represented by lawyers .

The guidance to the chapter was more expansive on the scope of third party duties. For example, it suggested that the duty not to take unfair advantage applied when a solicitor was involved in a road accident. It was considered a breach of the rule if the solicitor used his position 'unfairly to harass or intimidate the other motorist'.[83] This made it clear that the duty not to take unfair advantage applied beyond the workplace.

The 2007 Rules also contained a rule prohibiting letters which made claims that they knew were 'not recoverable through the proper legal process' and repeated the example of sending a letter of claim for a simple debt claiming costs.[84] This, it was said, would breach Rule 10. This guidance was a potential foundation for a rule that solicitors should not use the authority of the solicitor's role to try to intimidate or pressurise the other side to concede illegitimately. Again, however, the decision to continue to limit the principle to a single example may be significant.

The second piece of guidance to Rule 10, which was new, developed the idea of obligations owed to third parties. It advised that particular care needed to be taken when dealing with unrepresented parties to 'find a balance between fulfilling your obligations to your client and not taking unfair advantage of another person'. The guidance went on to recognise that 'this limits your duty to act in the best interests of your client'.[85] The guidance was sparse in describing the degree of limitation envisaged.

The guidance to Rule 10 gave an example of a situation where an unrepresented opponent produces badly drawn documentation. It went on to suggest, rather unhelpfully, that the solicitor should 'suggest the opponent finds legal representation'. It went on to consider the situation where the opponent did not do so and suggested, even more unhelpfully, that the solicitor would then 'need to ensure that a balance is

---

[82] SRA, *Solicitors' Code of Conduct 2007*, r 10.01.
[83] ibid, guidance to r 10.01, para 1.
[84] ibid, guidance to r 10.01, para 5.
[85] SRA, *Solicitors' Code of Conduct 2007*, guidance to r 10, para 2.

maintained between doing your best for the client and not taking unfair advantage of the opponent's lack of legal knowledge and drafting skills'.[86]

The idea of 'balancing' is the nearest that the guidance came to defining a specific obligation to third parties. At least however, it clarified that such an obligation existed. As described, it probably did not exceed by much, if at all, the standards that the courts would impose on a solicitor. They did not, for example, have to correct any mistakes made by other solicitors in litigation, and could take advantage of them,[87] provided this would not be a breach of the duty to the court.

The generally conservative approach to recognising responsibilities to third parties was maintained throughout the rules and guidance to Chapter 10 in the 2007 Code. The guidance continued with a number of obvious examples. Solicitors should not, for example, receive or keep documents subject to an express condition if they are either unable or unwilling to abide by that condition.[88] The guidance also noted that so to do would 'diminish the trust the public places in you or the profession', contrary to Core Duty 1.06. More significantly, solicitors were under no obligation to refuse representation to a client with a hopeless case. Such cases expose the opponent to a level of cost and risk that might be considered 'unfair'.

The Solicitors' Code of Conduct 2007 provided some advice on dealing with cases where it may be necessary to breach client confidentiality by disclosing expert reports affecting children. The supplement to the Code reminded solicitors of their duty to reveal expert reports commissioned for the purposes of proceedings to other parties and to tribunals. They were reminded that the position in relation to voluntary disclosure of other documents or communications between solicitors and clients was uncertain and that advocates were under a duty not to mislead the court. Consequently, solicitors were advised, as advocates with knowledge adverse to the client's case, to seek the client's agreement for full voluntary disclosure. This was said to be for three reasons:

1. the matters the client wants to hide will probably emerge anyway;
2. you will be able to do a better job for the client if all the relevant information is presented to the court; and
3. if the information is not voluntarily disclosed, you may be severely criticised by the court. The advice continued '[i]f the client refuses to give you authority to disclose the relevant information, you are entitled to refuse to continue to act for the client if to do so will place you in breach of your obligations to the court'.[89]

This reasoning, while possibly quite correct, revealed as much concern for the solicitor's interests as the client's. It revealed no concern whatever for third party interests.

c. The SRA Handbook

The SRA Handbook added nothing to substantive obligations owed to lay third parties. The first of the four outcomes in Chapter 11, 'Relations with Third Parties',

[86] ibid.
[87] *Thames Trains Ltd v Adams* [2006] EWHC 3291 (QB); and *Thompson v Arnold* [2007] EWHC 1875 (QB).
[88] SRA, *Solicitors' Code of Conduct 2007*, guidance to r 10.01, para 6(a).
[89] ibid, guidance note 15.

reflected the overarching duty not to take unfair advantage of third parties in either a professional or personal capacity.[90] The other three outcomes relate to very specific situations and only one relates to lay third parties. This is the obligation on solicitors acting for a seller of land to inform buyers immediately if the client intends to deal with more than one buyer.[91] The other two outcomes, performing undertakings on time[92] and properly administering oaths, affirmations or declarations,[93] are system-facing responsibilities.

The indicative behaviours for Chapter 11 replicate previous rules or guidance. They largely include system-facing responsibilities, for example, providing sufficient time and information to agree costs,[94] returning documents or money held subject to a condition that is not met[95] or on demand where held to the sender's order.[96] They also include one ambiguous, negative indicative behaviour: taking unfair advantage of a public office held by solicitors, members of their firm or by their families.[97] The implication of including this in Chapter 11 is that the unfair advantage taken is at the expense of an identifiable third party.

As in previous iterations of rules and guidance, indicative behaviours suggesting obligations to third parties tend to be confined to very specific situations. Therefore, solicitors are unwise to communicate with represented parties, except to get details of their lawyer, unless the other lawyer consents or in exceptional circumstances.[98] There are familiar restrictions on taking unfair advantage of an opposing party's lack of legal knowledge where they have not instructed a lawyer[99] and on a solicitor demanding anything for himself, or for a client, that is not legally recoverable.[100]

VII. Legal Responsibility to Professional Third Parties

A. Common Law

i. Other Side in Litigation

In a situation, such as that arising in *Ernst & Young v Butte Mining Co*, lay clients benefit from the court imposing a requirement of fairness in litigation. As the tenor of the judgment makes clear, however, this could be for the benefit of the opposing

---

[90] SRA, *Handbook 2011*, as amended, Outcome 11.1 and Indicative Behaviour 11.9.
[91] ibid, Outcome 11.3.
[92] ibid, Outcome 11.2.
[93] ibid, Outcome 11.4.
[94] ibid, Indicative Behaviour 11.1.
[95] ibid, Indicative Behaviour 11.2.
[96] ibid, Indicative Behaviour 11.3.
[97] ibid, Indicative Behaviour 11.10.
[98] ibid, Indicative Behaviour 11.4.
[99] ibid, Indicative Behaviour 11.7.
[100] ibid, Indicative Behaviour 11.8.

lawyers. An obvious example is where a mistake by lawyers could enable their client to sue for negligence, but the court intervenes to stop the opponent taking advantage of the mistake.

Delivering judgment in *Ernst & Young v Butte Mining Co*, Walker J said:

> Heavy, hostile commercial litigation is a serious business. It is not a form of indoor sport and litigation solicitors do not owe each other duties to be friendly (so far as that goes beyond politeness) or to be chivalrous or sportsmanlike (so far as that goes beyond being fair). Nevertheless even in the most hostile litigation ... solicitors must be scrupulously fair and not take unfair advantage of obvious mistakes ... [This duty] is intensified if the solicitor in question has been a major contributing cause of the mistake.[101]

In the context of court proceedings, such an obligation of fairness can be seen as part of the duty to uphold the administration of justice.

VIII.   Regulation of Relationship between Professional Third Parties

A. Solicitors

i. Dealings between Solicitors

a. The Underlying Relationship

The Law Society Guide 1999 required a solicitor to deal with other solicitors with 'frankness and good faith consistent with his or her overriding duty to the client.'[102] The idea of frankness between solicitors was, however, problematic because it suggested a requirement of complete candour in all circumstances. Such an obligation was inconsistent with the adversarial nature of litigation and negotiation.[103] The Solicitors' Code of Conduct 2007 did not replicate the obligation, although some level of obligation conceivably fell within the ambit of Core Duty 1.06 (not diminishing public confidence).

The SRA Code of Conduct contains no material that explicitly sets the tone of relationships between solicitors. Other solicitors are therefore presumably to be treated as third parties for the purposes of Chapter 11.01. This means that, in common with other third parties, they must not be taken unfair advantage of.

---

[101] *Vernon v Bosley (No 2)* [1997] 1 All ER 614 (CA) and ch 19: 'Advocacy'.
[102] Taylor, *The Guide to the Professional Conduct of Solicitors* (n 49) rr 17.03 and 19.01.
[103] A Boon 'Cooperation and Competition in the Handling of Disputes and Transactions' (1994) 1(1) *International Journal of the Legal Profession* 109.

ii. Undertakings

The fundamental importance of solicitors honouring their promises was apparently so obvious that the Solicitors' Practice Rules 1990 mentioned undertakings several times in, but contained no specific obligation to perform them. This was rectified in the Guide 1999 in Chapter 18, 'Professional Undertakings'. The chapter defined an undertaking as ' any unequivocal declaration of intention addressed to someone who reasonably places reliance on it' made by solicitors or their staff in the course of practice or by a solicitor not in the course of practice.[104]

The nature of an undertaking was further defined by the chapter. For example, an undertaking did not have to be a legal contract to be binding[105] and it was binding on all partners in the firm.[106] Where it was given in return for consideration, however, and the consideration failed, the undertaking would be discharged. In an undertaking on behalf of a client, a solicitor could disclaim personal responsibility.[107] Any ambiguity in the form of undertaking was to be construed against the giver.[108] The chapter stated that solicitors were under no obligation to give or accept undertakings, even where it was in a client's best interests to do so.[109]

If a solicitor gave an undertaking, however, they were obliged to carry it out even if the circumstances in which they could do so was beyond their control.[110] Therefore, before giving their undertaking, they had to be sure that they would be in a position to honour it. Unusually, the chapter reinforced the obligation by stating that '[a] solicitor who fails to honour an undertaking is *prima facie* guilty of professional misconduct'.[111] One exception was where the solicitor was in breach of an undertaking to the court. Only the court has power to enforce such undertakings and no other disciplinary action would normally be taken.[112]

The definition of undertakings changed for the purposes of the Solicitors' Code of Conduct 2007. They were defined as 'a statement made by you or your firm to someone who reasonably relies upon it, that you or your firm will do something or cause something to be done, or refrain from doing something'.[113] Other requirements remained the same. Therefore, undertakings could be given to anyone, not just to other solicitors. They could be oral or in writing. Rule 10.05 continued the requirement to fulfil an undertaking in the course of practice or outside it. Undertakings endured for as long as the solicitor remained on the roll, and could not be unilaterally withdrawn.

Among the principles in the current SRA Handbook, the second, acting with integrity, seems particularly relevant to honouring undertakings. The SRA Code of Conduct, Chapter 11, has an outcome that undertakings are performed 'within an

---

[104] ibid, r 18.01.
[105] ibid, r 18.08.
[106] ibid, r 18.10.
[107] ibid, r 18.09.
[108] ibid, r 18.07.
[109] ibid, r 18.03.
[110] ibid, r 18.04.
[111] ibid, r 18.02.
[112] ibid, r 18.16.
[113] SRA, *Solicitors' Code of Conduct 2007*, r 24.01

agreed timescale or within a reasonable amount of time'.[114] Directly relevant indicative behaviours include maintaining an effective system of recording when undertakings are given and when they have been discharged[115] and notifying the recipient when it becomes apparent that contingent undertakings, those dependent upon the happening of a future event, will not occur.[116] This text seems fairly light, given the weight of material previously developed around the rule. It is an area where considerable reliance is placed on existing norms.

Although the stern warning about breach of undertaking has been dropped from the Handbook, failure to honour an undertaking would presumably result in disciplinary proceedings against the solicitor. Compensation for losses flowing from breach may be available through the firm's insurance or the Solicitors' Insurance Fund (SIF). Compensation for broken undertakings has, in the past, been a considerable drain on the SIF. Unsurprisingly the SRA is concerned that undertakings are too easily given by solicitors, and are too vague in scope. Solicitors should ensure that any undertaking given is specific, confirmed in writing and realistic in the sense that it does not promise to do anything not in the solicitor's absolute control.

iii. Contacting a Represented Opposing Party

Restrictions on solicitors contacting opposing clients were dealt with as an issue relating to lay clients. It is also a breach of professional etiquette in that it is disrespectful to the lawyer the other party has instructed. Finally, such contact also offends the principle of representation around which the legal system is built. The Solicitors' Code of Conduct 2007 added the clients of licensed conveyancers to those who opposing solicitors should not contact, except with the consent of that solicitor.[117] The rules did not prohibit client to client communications or solicitors contacting witnesses.

The guidance clarified the exceptional circumstances that might justify solicitors contacting opposing clients. They were where the other solicitor has failed to communicate or pass on messages to their client. Solicitors were advised that, if the solicitor reasonably considered that the other lawyer or licensed conveyancer was refusing or failing to take instructions or communicate requests or correspondence to their client, then a warning should give them the opportunity to object if an incorrect conclusion had been drawn. Following this, and no objection being received, direct contact could be attempted.[118]

Guidance to the 2007 rule also covered the situation where a solicitor represented corporate clients. It suggested that, where an employee was designated by the company as the person responsible for giving instructions, a solicitor could contact other employees of the company directly. The guidance warned that such a course could be hazardous. First, it may involve a breach of client confidentiality. Second it may put

---

[114] SRA, *Handbook 2011*, as amended, Outcome 11.2.
[115] ibid, Indicative Behaviour 11.5.
[116] ibid, Indicative Behaviour 11.6.
[117] SRA, *Solicitors Code of Conduct 2007*, r 10.04.
[118] ibid, guidance to r 10, note 18.

the employee in an invidious position, such as being asked to disclose confidential information about their employer. The guidance suggested that such contact should not be made without advising the employer, or their legal representative, so that they could seek advice about whether to allow the contact.[119]

The current SRA Code of Conduct contains an indicative behaviour in Chapter 11, 'Relations with Third Parties', to the effect that solicitors meet the outcomes by not communicating with other parties who have retained lawyers, unless the lawyers consent or in exceptional circumstances.[120] It is not obvious which outcome this helps to meet, unless it is not treating third parties unfairly. A, possibly semantic, point in relation to this is that simply contacting someone does not necessarily involve treating them unfairly. Perhaps this is why 'not contacting' is an indicative behaviour.

iv. Reporting other Solicitors

Luban relates an incident in 1977 in which a partner in a firm and senior lawyer in the United States, 'an upright and courtly man', lied to an opponent to conceal discoverable documents, perjured himself to conceal the lie and, upon confessing the truth, resigned his job and spent a month in prison.[121] The relevance of this is the reaction of the associate who worked for the partner concerned. He

> saw [the partner] lie and really couldn't believe it. And he just had no idea of what to do. I mean, he ... kept thinking there must be a reason. Besides what do you do? The guy was his boss and a great guy.

Luban attributes the complicity of the associate to the ambiguity of the ABA's model rule which permitted a subordinate lawyer to defer to a senior lawyer's reasonable resolution of an arguable question of professional duty. He argues that it is also the product of working in a large organisation where lines of responsibility are confused and ambiguous, resulting in gradual desensitisation to these issues. Whereas these would once have been compelling reasons for silence on such issues, the climate is arguably more conducive to the disclosure of wrongdoing within legal organisations than it once was.

In England and Wales disciplinary 'whistle-blowing' is not only allowed under the Public Interest Disclosure Act 1998, it is encouraged. The Solicitors' Code of Conduct 2007, Rule 20.04 required a solicitor to report any serious misconduct by another solicitor including, if a principal in the firm, misconduct by an employee of the firm. Any conduct involving dishonesty, deception or amounting to a serious, arrestable offence amounts to serious misconduct. There was also a duty to report if there is 'reason to doubt the professional integrity of a solicitor' or that a firm is in serious financial difficulty which could put the public at risk. An employee could be reported to another employee, or to the principal or other director of the firm, on an anonymous basis.[122]

---

[119] ibid, guidance to r 10.04, para 21.
[120] SRA, *Handbook 2011*, as amended, Indicative Behaviour 11.4.
[121] DJ Luban, 'Milgram Revisited' (1998) 9 *Researching Law: An ABF Update* 1, at 4.
[122] SRA, *Solicitors' Code*, r 20.04, guidance para 22.

The rule was subject 'where necessary' to the reporting solicitor's client's consent. This envisaged the report involving disclosure of privileged or confidential information[123] of either the client or the other side. The client could have an objection in other circumstances. For example, he or she may well be reluctant to get involved in the unprofessional conduct of the other side's solicitor unless it impinges directly on their case. Such a report may delay matters or cause other problems to the client. There is no guidance on this.

In the current SRA Code of Conduct, solicitors have a reporting obligation. It comprises a duty to report promptly to the SRA serious misconduct by any authorised person or firm, or any employee, manager or owner.[124] The duty to consult clients about such steps has been replaced by a requirement to take into account the duty of confidentiality to clients. This, obviously, is another relaxation of the obligations to clients.

B. Relationships with Barristers

The significance of the relationship between solicitors and barristers was reflected in the Law Society Guide 1999, which devoted a chapter to relations with the Bar and professional agents. The content was, however, relatively thin, with the main principles confined to stressing the duty to pay fees, even when the solicitor was not put in funds by clients, and challenging counsel's fees.[125] There were only two specific issues dealt with. One covered situations when it was necessary to attend with counsel in court. The other specified that solicitors' obligations were not abrogated by instructing counsel.[126]

Guidance stated that solicitors had a duty to brief appropriate counsel.[127] They were advised to check that counsel's advice did not contain any 'obvious errors'. As noted above, the common law went further than this by requiring solicitors to exercise their own judgement on counsel's advice. This raised the interesting possibility of solicitor and counsel presenting differing advice to the client. This is a position that only the client can resolve by deciding whose advice to accept. It opened the way, however, to the possibility of a later action against the lawyers if something went wrong.

Relationships with barristers did not feature as such in the 2007 Rules or the SRA Code of Conduct. Some of the earlier principles were rules of etiquette that had been overtaken by events. For example, the principle that solicitors had personal responsibility to pay barristers' fees was no longer needed because it had become possible for barristers to enter binding contracts for fees. Nevertheless, a lot of abandoned advice and guidance remained good practice.

An example of still relevant guidance on managing relationships with barristers referred to attendance in court. In routine criminal cases it was not uncommon for barristers to return briefs at a late stage so that a substitute had to take over at the last

---

[123] ibid, r 20.04, guidance paras 23 and 28.
[124] SRA, *Handbook 2011*, as amended, Outcome 10.4.
[125] Taylor, *The Guide to the Professional Conduct of Solicitors* (n 49) rr 20.01 and 20.07.
[126] ibid, rr 20.04 and 20.05.
[127] ibid.

minute. While this could happen in civil cases, it appeared to be less common. In such cases it is usually desirable for a solicitor to attend court with the substitute barrister in order to protect the interests of the client. Provision of competent assistance for advocates was, however, increasingly seen as expensive 'double manning'.

The growth of solicitor advocacy and the economics of practice weakened the practice of solicitors attending court with barristers.[128] The Law Society's transitional advice in the Guide was that 'careful judgement' was required before a solicitor decided not to attend court. It suggested various situations where attendance was desirable. For example, where a client was a juvenile, or was handicapped in some way, or was a 'difficult character' or where a substantial sentence of imprisonment is likely.[129] This advice still represents good practice, particularly in situations where barristers do not know clients well.

IX. Responsibilities to Private Third Party Funders

A. Private Funders

Third party funders may support an action for a variety of reasons. They might also decide to withdraw funding, leaving lawyers with clients but no less prospect of getting paid. Lawyers must remember that, whatever the reason they decided to act for a client they should not readily relinquish the obligation, even if the funder withdraws.

An example of how obligations may accrue, and not be honoured, arose when the Labour Party announced that it was supporting councillors accused of election fraud.[130] This involved the party retaining solicitors on the councillors' behalf. The case became a political embarrassment and the party withdrew support for the councillors one week before trial. The solicitors withdrew at the same time. Whether or not this was for funding or other reasons, it created a clear impression of the clients' guilt.

When a funder withdraws financial support, a solicitor's duty is still to the client. The solicitor is, however, able to withdraw from the case where it is clear that the client can no longer cover the fees and costs. Reasonable notice of withdrawal is a minimum requirement for discharging any responsibility to the client. In the event, the councillors had to rely on a barrister, acting pro bono, who had not done any preparation for the case. The judge found the conduct of the Labour Party and the solicitors 'inexcusable'.

---

[128] J Flood, A Boon, A Whyte, E Skordaki, R Abbey and A Ash, *Reconfiguring the Market for Advocacy Services: A Case Study of London and Four Fields of Practice* (A Report for the Lord Chancellor's Committee on Legal Education and Conduct, 1996) at 101.

[129] Taylor, *The Guide to the Professional Conduct of Solicitors* (n 49) guidance to r 20.04, para 2.

[130] *Private Eye* 15 April 2005.

B. Insurance Companies

Insurance companies are the largest private funders of litigation and other legal expenses. The most basic third party motor insurance policy allows the insurance company to instruct solicitors to defend claims against the party they insured. Usually, the insured client is a purely nominal client. For all practical purposes the case is managed by the insurance company and the client has little personal involvement in its progress. Nevertheless, the theory is still that the solicitor receives instructions from the insured client and is therefore responsible to him or her.

In the modern legal services market there is a proliferation of potential third party funders of claimant litigation. Organisations providing 'before the event insurance' to help personal injury victims include insurance companies, trades unions or professional bodies, associations like the AA or RAC, charities and pressure groups. It is not unusual, in the case of personal injury for example, for household or motor insurance to cover the prospective claimant's legal costs.

i. The Operation of before the Event Legal Expenses Arrangements

The Financial Services Ombudsman states that legal expenses complaints are usually about one or more of three issues. These are whether proposed actions have reasonable prospects of success; choice of solicitor and maladministration of the policy or the claim.[131] These tend to involve the insurance company, but lawyers may also be implicated.

a. Deciding whether there is an Obligation to Cover Risks

An issue that sometimes arises is whether or not there was an 'insured event'. Insured parties may be able to claim on a legal expenses insurance policy when the event occurred before the policy was taken out. An example is where they suffer loss, as a result of negligence by another party, of which they were not aware at the time. In such circumstances, the insurance company may decide not to cover legal expenses. Whether or not the court or the regulator requires cover to be provided depends on the terms of the insurance and the behaviour of the insured. If, for example, they knew about the prior event before taking out insurance they are less likely to be entitled to claim.

Another common issue in before the event insurance claims is legal merit. There is generally a contractual clause providing that there must be a 'reasonable prospects of success', before an insurance company has to cover legal expenses. In the insurance industry this generally means that there is a *51 per cent or more* chance of winning. An even chance of success is not usually sufficient. Normal practice is for the insurer to consider whether there is a prima facie case and to then pass the file to an external

---

[131] Financial Services Ombudsman (www.financial-ombudsman.org.uk/publications/technical_notes/legal-expenses.html).

firm of solicitors on the insurer's panel. The opinion of this firm usually determines whether the insurer agrees to fund the claim or the defence.

When policyholders dispute the funding decision they usually have to produce evidence from a suitably qualified independent lawyer to support their view. This procedure creates a risk of opposing views. In such cases, it is usual practice for the insurer to obtain an opinion from a barrister specialising in the relevant area of law. Greater weight is usually placed on the barrister's opinion than that of either solicitor.

The third common issue raised in consumer complaints is prejudicial behaviour by the insured. An insurance company may be able to avoid providing legal expenses where the insured party has prejudiced the claim in some way. The most common cause is delay. This may mean that it is no longer possible to preserve evidence or trace witnesses. There may be other difficulties in launching litigation such as time limits or the risk of paying large sums in costs. These risks may have increased where proceedings have been undefended for a period of time.

b. Proportionality of Cost

Insurers can often refuse funding if, in the opinion of their lawyers, the cost of proceedings is likely to be disproportionate compared to the amount of any sums recovered. The test of whether an insurer can refuse to back a claim is whether a prudent *uninsured* person would probably fund an action in the absence of insurance. Some policies provide for the insurer simply to pay their insured the sum of money at stake. In cases of doubt, the financial services regulator may order the insurer to pay. Where the legal issue is not a money claim, but, for example, a claim for an injunction, a legal opinion as to the likelihood of the court granting the remedy is still decisive.

c. Choice of Solicitor

Solicitors cannot generally enter into agreements with insurance companies giving them the right to act for a particular client. This would restrict the client's freedom of choice of solicitor. Most insurance companies have a panel made up of solicitors' firms that they trust and they prefer to use them when they can. Insured parties often want to use their own solicitors from the start of a matter. Legal expenses policies generally allow insurers a free choice of solicitor to provide advice and assistance up to the time where legal proceedings start.

Once proceedings are issued the Insurance Companies (Legal Expenses Insurance) Regulations 1990[132], which give effect to European Directive 87/344,[133] come into play. Regulation 5(4) provides that 'The company shall ... afford the insured the right to entrust the defence of his interests from the moment that he has the right to claim from the insurer under the policy, to a lawyer of his choice'.

Regulation 6 continues, rather unnecessarily, to state that the insured shall have freedom of choice of a lawyer 'to defend, represent or serve the interests of the

---

[132] Insurance Companies (Legal Expenses Insurance) Regulations 1990 (SI 1990/1159).
[133] Council Directive 87/344/EEC of 22 June 1987 on the coordination of laws, regulations and administrative provisions relating to legal expenses insurance. *Official Journal of the European Communities* (1987): 77-80.

insured in any inquiry or proceedings'. Regulation 6(2) states that the insured has a free choice of lawyer where a conflict of interest arises. The Regulations cover legal proceedings pursued and defended in tribunals, for example, employment tribunals. This places solicitors handling claims in a potential conflict of interest situation. They have an interest in delaying the issue of proceedings. This is considered further below.

The time between the receipt of a claim for legal expenses and the start of proceedings is something of a grey area. The regulator of insurance companies usually respects the right of insurers to instruct solicitors of their choice until proceedings are commenced, except in exceptional circumstances.[134] This is a question of fact and degree in each particular case. According to case studies published on Financial Services Ombudsman's website, legal expenses policies do not generally guarantee any particular firm of solicitors, any specific location or any minimum size of firm.

The Financial Services Ombudsman takes the view that, with modern communications, panel solicitors can be located anywhere without disadvantage to the insured. He tends not to regard disputes over freedom of choice of solicitor as a conflict of interest. The Ombudsman considers that a solicitor would only be professionally embarrassed if they continued to act where, for example, they had previously acted for the policyholder's opponent, knew the policyholder personally or knew confidential information about the opponent or were guilty of an act of professional negligence.

Although the policyholder has a free choice of solicitor once proceedings begin, that solicitor has to accept the insurance company's standard terms of appointment in a separate contract. The contract does not usually specify an hourly rate for the solicitor and this is a matter usually negotiated separately. There are potential problems when insurers specify a particularly miserly hourly rate. Their panel solicitors may accept the rate because their economies of scale, handling bulk work for the insurer, make it viable. The policyholder's chosen solicitors may find the rate unacceptable.

d. Maladministration

Insurance companies are not usually responsible for delay or other default by solicitors they instruct on behalf of insured parties under their legal expenses insurance policies. This may not be the case where the insurance company intervenes in the claim. In *Chapman v Christopher*,[135] for example, the court found that the solicitor for the plaintiff was, in reality, being instructed by the insurance company. In the circumstances, it held that the insurance company was liable for the costs of the other side. Such liability could not be limited by the terms of the insurance contract with the nominal claimant.

Where solicitors are guilty of gross maladministration in relation to a claim, and the insurer was aware of this but failed to intervene, the regulator may also order that compensation be paid by the insurer to the insured party. There is also an option for the lay client to pursue a complaint with the Legal Ombudsman.

---

[134] But see C-199/08 *Eschig v UNIQA Sachversicherung AG*.
[135] *Chapman v Christopher* [1998] 2 All ER 873.

ii. General Ethical Problems

The usual rules apply when a solicitor is instructed by an insurer to act for an insured. Therefore, the solicitor is required to consider, and advise on, alternative funding sources. They must also consider whether there is a conflict of interest in the situation. It is not assumed that merely receiving third party funding is a conflict of interest, although it may create practical and ethical difficulties for the solicitor. Whoever pays solicitors' costs, their prime duty is to advance the best interests of the lay client, not those of the funder.

There are obvious ethical problems for panel solicitors in the early stages of claims. They have a primary relationship with an insurance company but are investigating a claim for a client. The interests of insurance companies, put crudely, is not to risk their funds on pursuing claims if at all possible. Therefore, solicitors may be reluctant to certify to insurers that claims have more than a 50 per cent chance of success. If the case is lost, the insurer may decide not to risk instructing the solicitor again. Although some clients may challenge the panel solicitor's opinion, there is a cost and risk attached. Balancing the interest of the lay client and the third party funder in this situation presents a classic conflict of interest.

A further ethical problem for the panel solicitor is that they have a personal interest in maximising their costs. In a matter where they are paid on an hourly basis, this means continuing to handle the claim for as long as possible. If they know that the client would prefer to instruct a solicitor they know, they have an incentive to delay issuing proceedings for as long as possible. This is because the issue of proceedings triggers the operation of the Insurance Companies (Legal Expenses Insurance) Regulations 1990 and the insured's right to their own choice of solicitor. The solicitor's interest in continuing with the claim provides an incentive not to issue proceedings, even though this may be in the lay client's interest.

Once proceedings have started there are other ethical risks posed by third party funding. The risk of conflict of interest potentially impinges on the duty to preserve the client's confidentiality. Many legal expenses funding arrangements require solicitors to inform the funder of the progress of the case. The insurance agreement normally imposes express contractual responsibility on the client to do this. This however, is essentially a matter between the insurance company and their insured.

Solicitors should not breach confidentiality by providing client information direct to the insurer, even where the client has agreed with the insurer to provide information. It is not clear where the boundary between information that the insurer is entitled to, for example, about the progress of the case, and client confidential information, actually lies.

C. Regulatory Responsibilities to Private Third Party Funders

The Solicitors Act 1974, section 71 provides that third parties can apply for assessment of costs. Beyond the general prohibition on taking unfair advantage, the Codes of Conduct have not provided any specific duties towards third party funders. They may benefit from other general requirements, such as the requirement that solicitors allow sufficient time and information for their costs to be agreed or assessed.[136] 'Information' includes the basis on which fees are calculated.

D. Regulatory Responsibilities of Private Third Party Funders

In the wake of the Jackson Report on the cost of civil litigation, the Civil Justice Council set up a committee led by Michael Napier, an eminent solicitor, to consider practical ways of implementing the reforms. This led to the publication of a code of conduct for third party funders of litigation and the formation of the Association of Litigation Funders. Members of the Association agree to abide by the code. Lord Justice Jackson said that he expected solicitors to advise their clients to only enter agreements with litigation funders who signed up to the code.[137] This falls some way short of regulation of funders, but offers a way forward on improving standards in the industry.

X. Responsibilities to Legal Aid Authorities

Legal aid has been administered by the Legal Aid Agency (LAA), an executive agency of the Ministry of Justice, since April 2013. It replaced the Legal Services Commission (LSC), an agency that was at 'arm's length' of the Ministry of Justice. This is an example of a public third party funder of litigation. Any obligation a lawyer owes to such agencies could be regarded as a duty to the administration of justice, or to society generally, rather than to the agency itself. It is dealt with in this chapter because the LSC was formerly identified, in various codes, as a party to whom duties are owed.

A. Solicitors

The circumstances of legal aid raise similar ethical issues as arise in the case of insurance, namely the possibility of a conflict of interest between the interests of the client and the interests of the LAA. Issues can arise regarding the right to free choice of solicitor and client confidentiality. Such ethical considerations were raised by opponents of legal aid when it was first introduced. Nevertheless, the best interests of the client overall lay in favour of the legal aid scheme.

There are possible breaches of client confidence when the solicitor makes reports on the progress of the case, or changes in the client's circumstances to the LAA. The

---

[136] SRA, *Handbook 2011*, as amended, Indicative Behaviour 11.1.
[137] V Wozniak, 'CJC publishes third-party funding code of conduct' *The Lawyer* 24 November 2011.

agency is also bound by client confidentiality in that they are not allowed to publish details relating to clients or use the information other than in relation to the administration of the scheme. Nevertheless they can get access to client details for research purposes and for client satisfaction surveys as well as for administrative purposes. A considerable number of people usually have access to the information both within and outside the agency.

i. Legal Aid Block Contracts

The use of block contracts between the LSC and the supplier (which can be a solicitor or a not for profit organisation like a Citizens' Advice Bureau) eroded the freedom of legal aid clients to instruct a chosen solicitor. These contracts provide for a specified number of cases (or matter starts) per year in specified areas of law (for example, family law, criminal law, welfare law). In general the provider cannot give services to the client outside these areas (though there are some accepted 'tolerances' which permit help and advice in related areas of law in certain circumstances).

The majority of the terms of the contracts are concerned with fees and their payment. Fixed fees are set for standard procedures and solicitors are expected to deal with a set number of cases for a set overall payment. Obviously this affects the standard of work that can be done for particular clients—but this is also the case for privately paying clients whose resources are limited.

Work done under the contract must meet the test of 'sufficient benefit' to the client and be 'reasonable' in the eyes of the agency, which audits the work done. The contract requires the solicitor to meet 'such level of performance, as measured by performance indicators, as we may require'. In addition the contract required both the LSC and the solicitor to 'work together in mutual trust and cooperation'. It did, however, recognise that this was 'without prejudice to ... your professional obligations in respect of clients'.

Contracts also restrict the solicitor's freedom to use, for example, experts and interpreters or to get paid for legal research. This protects the funder, potentially to the detriment of legally aided clients. They may well not be offered or receive the kind of comprehensive or holistic service that the private client would be offered. The contract also provides that the rules of the professional body must be abided by, in particular the Code of Conduct.

These provisions clearly indicated that the solicitor had a dual duty to both the client and the LSC. If he favoured the client too much in preference to the LSC then at the very least there was a risk that he would lose the contract or not get it renewed when the next round of competitive tendering came round. However, it was also advantageous to the client that the LSC required an expert standard of work and audited performance. The client could have some confidence that the solicitor had expertise in the area of law concerned and was required to reach a minimum standard.

Legally aided clients could not supplement the service received by offering private payment. The client had a free choice of solicitor, provided the solicitor has a contract in the relevant field of law, but there were restrictions on changing the solicitor once the client's case has been started. Changes needed to be approved by and usually needed to be justified. A substantial reason, such as conflict of interest, was required, not simply that the client does not get on with the solicitor or disagrees with the advice.

A solicitor acting under a legal aid contract is under a duty to report to the LAA any information that would otherwise be confidential to the client. Monthly reports on completed cases were usually sent to the LSC. Solicitors were required to report suspected abuse of the scheme by the assisted person, reasons for any doubts that the action should be continued and other information on the conduct of the assisted person. The LSC was given access to the files of clients and former clients. These reporting obligations were imposed both by law and by the contract. In theory the solicitor should have informed the client of these obligations at the start of the case and obtained client consent, for example, for disclosure of confidential information.

ii. Regulation

The 1999 Guide contained a chapter on legal aid.[138] This provided that is was unbefitting conduct not to advise a client of a right to legal aid.[139] It also provided that 'legally aided clients must be treated in the same way as privately funded clients and the same standards of care apply'.[140] The Guide contained specific obligations that put the legally aided client in a different position to a solicitor's privately funded clients.

The Guide placed solicitors under two specific obligations to report abuses of legal aid by clients. In relation to civil matters, solicitors had to report to the legal aid authorities certain information 'concerning the client that is confidential or privileged'. This obligation to report on clients had two dimensions. First, solicitors had to respond to requests for information from a senior manager in the legal aid service.[141] Secondly, they had to volunteer information to the authorities where they believed that the client was abusing legal aid. Solicitors were advised to persuade clients to convey information themselves. If they did not agree, however, the solicitor was told to stand down and report the matter himself.[142]

Specific examples of behaviour that solicitors had to report to the legal aid authorities included client breaches of provisions in the basic legislation, such as those against making false declarations about income. They could also be reported for requiring the case to be conducted in a way that was incurring unreasonable expense.[143] They had to report if the client refused a reasonable offer of settlement.[144] They also were required to provide reasons to the authority for giving up a legally aided case in which they had begun acting.[145] Solicitors had a similar statutory duty to inform the relevant court officials.[146]

---

[138] Taylor, *The Guide to the Professional Conduct of Solicitors* (n 49) ch 5.
[139] ibid, guidance to r 5.01, guidance note 2.
[140] ibid, guidance to r 5.01, guidance note 7.
[141] ibid, guidance to r 5.03, guidance note 1.
[142] Taylor, *The Guide to the Professional Conduct of Solicitors* (n 49) r 5.04.
[143] ibid, guidance to r 5.03, guidance note 2.
[144] ibid, guidance to r 5.03, guidance note 4.
[145] ibid, guidance to r 5.03, guidance note 3.
[146] Legal Aid in Criminal and Care Proceedings (General) Regulations 1989 (SI 1989/343).

No specific obligations in relation to legal aid were contained in the Solicitors' Code of Conduct 2007. The only reference was to encourage economy in the representation of multiple-defendants. Guidance to Rule 3, dealing with conflicts of interest, provided that '[i]n publicly funded cases, regulations require that one solicitor be appointed to act for all co-defendants in a legal aid case unless there is, or is likely to be, a conflict'. The rule went on to explain that '[t]he purpose of this is to ensure economy in the use of public funds by ensuring that a single solicitor represents co-defendants where it is proper to do so'.[147]

The SRA Code of Conduct makes only one oblique reference to legal aid. This is an indicative behaviour in Chapter 1, 'Client Care', which suggests that solicitors explain any limitations or conditions on what they can do for their client, for example, because of the way the matter is funded.[148]

B. Barristers

The Bar had duties to the LSC under the Access to Justice Act 1999, and related regulations, when acting for a client on legal aid.[149] The Bar Code 1981 reflected this by reminding barristers that, in supplying legally aided services, the barrister 'owes his primary duty to the lay client'. In giving an opinion on an applicant's case, a barrister has to act both for his client and the LSC. Counsel were required to set out any rival accounts of the facts so that the LSC could estimate the strength of the applicant's case. They were also required to state whether a conference had been held to estimate the applicant's reliability as a witness, and to suggest any limitations that should be imposed on the grant of funding.

In the Bar Code of Conduct 2014, guidance on the rule against discrimination[150] makes it clear that barristers must not refuse cases on the ground that they are legally aided.[151] This only requires that barristers do not discriminate against legally aided clients. They are entitled to refuse such work, even under the cab rank rule, on the ground that they have not been offered a proper fee.[152] The guidance also refers to a term in the LAA's Unified Contract Standard Terms prohibiting payment of referral fees in publicly funded work.[153]

The new Code also addresses the situation where it is clear to a barrister that a client has obtained legal aid under false pretences. In such cases, the barrister must first try and ensure that action is taken by the client to remedy the situation immediately.[154] If this fails they must promptly cease to act and return their instructions.

---

[147] SRA, *Solicitors Code of Conduct 2007*, r 3, guidance note 24.
[148] SRA, *Handbook 2011*, as amended, Indicative Behaviour 1.5.
[149] BSB, *Bar Code of Conduct*, 8th edn, as amended, at paras 303(c), 304 and Annex E.
[150] ibid, rC28.
[151] ibid, gC88.
[152] ibid, rC30.8.
[153] ibid, gC30.1.
[154] ibid, rC25.1.

XI. Conclusion

Some rules imposing obligations to third parties, such as those relating to undertakings, tend to be designed to facilitate legal transactions. Others, duties to the Legal Services Commission and the wasted cost jurisdiction, ensure the protection of public funds and prevent frivolous litigation respectively. Apart from these specific situations, there is a relative absence of obligation to third parties. This affords lawyers considerable freedom in determining what they will do for clients. Even the courts have found it difficult to limit or to police that freedom, or to set clear limits for lawyer behaviour.

One of the exceptional areas in which legal professions have created obligations is the treatment of lay third parties. There has been a longstanding and broad duty not to take unfair advantage enforced by the courts and replicated in the codes. This suggests that it is acceptable to 'merely' take advantage. This is probably defensible. It is implicit in adversarial proceedings that one side is seeking advantage. An unfair advantage implies behaviour that is not explicitly sanctioned by the rules and may be regarded as underhand.

What is considered unfair advantage may vary according to the identity of an opponent. The examples of unfair advantage in codes of conduct are narrow. They relate to litigants in person and sending unjustified letters of claim. It seems fair to conclude that the main constraints on the conduct of cases which are not vexatious or frivolous are the courts and the rules of court rather than the code of ethics. Courts tend to allow latitude for some unfairness to third parties, depending how fairness is defined. What is regarded as unfair tends to be approached on a case by case basis.

14

Collective Third Parties

'uncontrolled expansion of libertarian ideology into lawyers' common consciousness—to the point where lawyers have come to feel genuinely affronted and indignant when any authority tries to articulate a public obligation of lawyers that may end up putting them at odds with clients. We have no public obligations, they claim; we are private agents for private parties (though at the same time they claim privileges and immunities that ordinary citizens don't have); our loyalties to clients must be absolute and undivided. In this libertarian mood, they tend to characterize the framework of law as some alien other—"the government," the "cops" the "regulators"—an adversary that they are entitled to outwit and frustrate with every trick in the book'.[1]

I. Introduction

Lawyers may owe third party obligations to various groups, as opposed to identified individuals. Some obligations could, in theory, be owed to the whole of society. Consumers, for example, as potential clients, may be affected by the various ways in which lawyers are allowed to generate business. Obligations may also, for particular purposes, be owed to sections of society. Residents of an area may be affected by the impact of the operations of large corporations, facilitated by lawyers, on the environment. The extent to which duties to such collectives are recognised is one of the more contentious areas of professional ethics.

The claim of lawyers to balance self and client interests with the good of the wider community is one of the key claims of legal professionalism. Any such obligations can be seen as part of a wider ethic of public service, although it may not be expressed as such. The oldest example of an obligation to a collective entity is the duty to the court, which is well established in case law. The field is also expanding to recognise the rights of other third party collectives, such as the general public. This is often, in fact, the state. It is, for example, the duty to the state and to the rule of law that is the central justification for current rules on reporting money laundering. Such duties may also be called upon to justify lawyers acting as special advocates in immigration cases.

---

[1] RW Gordon, 'A Collective Failure of Nerve: The Bar's Response to Kaye Scholer' (1998) 23 *Law and Social Inquiry* 315.

In certain circumstances it may be possible to envisage that lawyers' duties to other collective entities might be upheld. These groups could include employees, pensioners or shareholders of companies for whom they act. Finally, it could be argued that lawyers should have an obligation to assist in dealing with large social issues. An example is where lawyers might help prevent global financial or environmental disasters precipitated by clients. An obligation to avoid such disaster could be conceived as a duty to society, or even to humankind generally.

Wider obligations are expressed in lawyers' codes of ethics in various ways. Few are obviously 'public-facing'. The public may, however, benefit from duties owed to much narrower groups. For example, duties to protect the honour of the profession, the public interest or the administration of justice, all benefit members of the public indirectly. The categories of obligation can be divided into three. First, there are duties to the profession imposed by the profession. Secondly, there are duties imposed by the state for the benefit of society. Thirdly, there is a vaguer set of obligations owed to unidentified third party collectives.

II. Duties to the Profession

A. Restrictions on Attracting Potential Clients

Personal contact and word of mouth was the traditional method of attracting clients. Other, more active methods of attracting business were regarded as unethical. There were various explanations of this position, some claiming virtuous motives. Therefore, for example, rejection of commercial methods of seeking customers signified professional disdain for the profit motive. Professionals were sought out by clients, rather than the other way round.

The less honourable explanation of advertising bans is that clients were forced to rely on reputation alone. This favoured the lawyers with established businesses, who dominated professional bodies and made the rules. Advertising bans preserved the position of lawyers with established reputations and clienteles, and worked against new lawyers and new businesses.

Historically, the legal profession maintained specific bans on general advertising, paying third parties for referring clients and approaching prospective clients direct. These prohibitions were relaxed before the Legal Services Act 2007 (LSA 2007), but the Act placed much greater importance on the interests of consumers in providing legal services. This has stimulated debate about how the interests of consumers are best served.

B. Responsibilities to Consumers

Consumers are a group including potential users of legal services. It therefore comprises the whole of society. In this section we are looking at people who have not chosen a lawyer. We do not deal here with prospective clients who have asked a lawyer to act for them. As far as a lawyer is concerned, these are identified third parties and they were covered in the last chapter. The focus here is the responsibility lawyers are under to help consumers choose legal services. For professions this raises a number of questions. One example is how to strike a proper balance between providing consumer information and maintaining professional integrity.

Lawyers have had responsibility to consumers for some time, most obviously expressed through advertising codes. The level of responsibility and accountability is, however, increasing. This is most obvious since the LSA 2007, section 1. The regulatory objectives of the Act, which are directed towards the Legal Services Board (LSB) and approved regulators, contain no mention of clients. Three of the Act's eight regulatory objectives are aimed at consumers. The first, very explicit, objective of the Act is 'protecting and promoting the interests of consumers'. The second, 'promoting competition in the provision of services', aims to benefit consumers by forcing down the price of legal assistance. The third, 'increasing public understanding of the citizen's legal rights and duties' is more ambiguous, but could be read as aiming to de-mystify law or increase the possibility of self-help.

In addition to pursuing the regulatory objectives, the LSB was required by the Act to establish a Consumer Panel.[2] The Act provided that the panel could make representations to the LSB and was entitled to be provided with reasons should the LSB disagree.[3] The LSB can also seek advice from the panel or ask it to conduct research.[4] The panel can publish any representations and responses and any advice given or research conducted. Consumer views are therefore integral to the operation of the LSB and to the policy-making process for legal services regulation.

The Act cements a distinction between prospective clients and clients. Prior to the Act, lawyers already owed obligations to non-clients, whether as consumers or citizens. The Act merely makes the expectation that the profession have regard to consumers more explicit. The precise form of any obligation is not, however, specified. Of course, the process by which a consumer becomes a lawyer's client usually impacts on the subsequent relationship. It affects expectations and the basis on which services are provided. Attracting clients potentially advances several regulatory objectives of the Act, for example, increasing access to justice, protecting the interests of consumers and promoting competition in the provision of services.

C. Regulation of Consumer Contact

i. Advertising

Advertising can be a valuable source of information for consumers, enabling them to make an informed choice of adviser. Alternatively it can be a way of concealing problems or inflating virtues. It is in the general interest of professions that some limits

---

[2] LSA 2007, s 8.
[3] ibid, s 10.
[4] ibid, s 11.

are placed on the claims their members can make. It may reduce tension between members. Complaints about solicitor advertising are generally made by other solicitors rather than members of the public. Regulators often advise that minor breaches are resolved at local level rather than being raised as disciplinary issues.

a. Barristers

Advertising legal services by barristers is permitted but controlled. Since 1989, the Bar has allowed advertising in accordance with the British Code of Advertising and Sales Promotion. This meant that fees and methods of charging could be advertised but certain other claims were banned. Barristers could not make comparisons with other barristers or advertise success rates. These controls were imposed so as not to 'diminish public confidence in the legal profession or the administration of justice' or bring the legal profession into disrepute. Under the old Bar Code, advertising was not allowed to indicate that the barrister could refuse representation, except as provided in the Code.[5]

The Bar Code 2014 provides that barristers must not mislead persons to whom they supply legal services about the nature of those services.[6] Despite relatively extensive guidance on advertising in the Code,[7] however, advertising the implications of the cab rank rule is not specifically mentioned. The emphasis has shifted, for example, towards making sure that confusion is avoided when barristers share premises with solicitors and making sure that unregistered barristers make the disadvantages of instructing them plain.

b. Solicitors

The Solicitors' Practice Rules 1990 provided that solicitors could publicise their practices provided there was no breach of the rules or of a Solicitors' Publicity Code. This was created by the Law Society and approved by the Master of the Rolls.[8] The Solicitors' Publicity Code 1990 provided that, as a matter of professional conduct, solicitors had to comply with the general law and could not be inaccurate or misleading in any way when publicising their practices.[9] Solicitors were allowed to advertise their fees, subject to very specific rules on information not being misleading.[10] They could claim to be experts in a field, provided this could be justified, but could not claim a 'success rate'.[11] Nor could they make direct comparisons with the charges or quality of service of another, identifiable solicitor.[12]

The Solicitors' Code of Conduct 2007, Rule 7, adopted many of the rules of the old publicity code. Publicity on charges had to be 'clearly expressed', making clear

---

[5] Bar Council, *Code of Conduct of the Bar of England and Wales*, (London, The General Council of the Bar of England and Wales, 2004) at paras 710.1 and 710.2.
[6] BSB, *Handbook 2014*, pt 2: *The Code of Conduct*, r C19.1 (http://handbook.barstandardsboard.org.uk/handbook/part-2/).
[7] ibid, gC53-63.
[8] Solicitors' Practice Rules 1990, r 2.
[9] Solicitors' Publicity Code 1990, rr 1(c) and (d).
[10] ibid, r 5.
[11] ibid, rr 2(b) and (c).
[12] ibid, r 2(d).

whether disbursements and VAT are included. It had to clearly state gross fees, not fees discounted by any commission.[13] Claims to expertise in a particular field had to comply with the Advertising Standards Authority (ASA) British Code of Advertising requirement that it is 'legal, decent, honest and truthful'. However a breach of this Code was not automatically a breach of Rule 7.[14]

There were also some key changes from the previous regime in the Solicitors' Code of Conduct 2007. For example, the rule that publicity could not make direct comparison with the charges of an identifiable solicitor[15] was abolished. The prohibition in the Solicitors' Publicity Code 1990 that solicitors could 'not publicise their practices in any manner which may reasonably be regarded as being in bad taste'[16] was also abandoned.

This relaxation of advertising rules may have reflected the difficulty of maintaining standards. In 2004, for example, it was quite easy to find advertising of questionable taste in any local newspaper. One solicitor's advertisement promised prospective personal injury clients £300 on account of compensation within seven days of signing up.[17] This offer was presented in an advertisement asking 'Do you need more cash this Christmas?'.

The SRA Handbook 2011 devotes a chapter to Publicity. It reveals direct links with the previous regimes. Of the five outcomes in Chapter 8 that must be achieved by regulated parties, two are directed at consumers in general. One requires that appropriate information is provided about the firm, including the approved persons within it and how it is regulated.[18] The other outcome is that letterheads, websites and emails show the words 'authorised and regulated by the Solicitors Regulation Authority' and either the firm's registered name if it is an LLP or company or, if it is a partnership or sole practitioner, the name under which it is licensed or authorised.[19] In either case it must also display the number allocated by the SRA. The outcomes maintain familiar formulae regarding accurate publicity, referring to the need for trust in the provision of legal services.[20] They demand particular care when quoting charges.[21]

ii. Personal Contacts and Referrals

a. Making Direct Contact

Attempting to make direct contact with potential clients has always been forbidden. The term 'ambulance chasing', approaching injury victims either directly or by leaving cards in hospitals, is still a term of professional abuse. The Solicitors' Code of Conduct 2007 banned 'cold calling'. Unannounced visits to old peoples' homes, with

---

[13] See SRA, *Solicitors' Code of Conduct 2007*, r 7, guidance para 8.
[14] ibid, at paras 5 and 6.
[15] Solicitors' Publicity Code 1990, at para 2(d).
[16] ibid, at para 1(b).
[17] See *Law Society Gazette* 8 April 2004, at 4.
[18] SRA, *Handbook 2011*, as amended, Outcome 8.4.
[19] ibid, Outcome 8.5.
[20] ibid, Outcome 8.1.
[21] ibid, Outcome 8.2.

offers to make their wills, were expressly prohibited. Rule 7.03 stated that 'you must not publicise your practice by making unsolicited visits or telephone calls to a member of the public'.

The SRA Handbook 2011 specifies one negative outcome in relation to publicity. It is that unsolicited approaches may not be made in person or by telephone to members of the public for publicity purposes.[22] The indicative behaviours also include a number that are negative. They include approaching people in the street, at ports of entry, in hospital or at the scene of an accident, either to conduct surveys involving collecting contact details of potential clients, or other kinds of promotion.[23]

b. Contact made through a Third Party

Paying a third party for their client contacts is problematic for several reasons. First, they may have used methods to generate contacts that a solicitor would not be allowed to use. These recruitment methods may, for example, impinge on the prospective client's right to the lawyer of their choice. Secondly, payment by the lawyers for the contact creates a motive to recoup the outlay from the client. Thirdly, the desire to keep the flow of business is an incentive for the lawyers to prioritise the introducer's interest over the client's. Paid referrals therefore create conditions for bad faith and conflict of interest.

In September 2011, despite probable incompatibility with UK and EU competition law,[24] the government announced that it would adopt Lord Justice Jackson's recommendation to limit referral fees.[25] The resulting legislation prevents regulated persons referring or being referred for payment 'prescribed legal business', which the LASPO Act currently defines as claims for personal injury and death.[26] The reasons behind this, and the regulatory regime for referral fees, are considered in more detail in chapter twelve, 'Fees'.

D. Bringing the Profession into Disrepute

Obligations not to damage the interests of professions as a whole are well established in the rules. Rule 1 of the Solicitors' Practice Rules 1990 required solicitors not to harm the 'good repute' of the profession. Similarly, the old Bar Code stated that barristers must not engage in conduct 'discreditable to a barrister' or likely to 'diminish public confidence in the legal profession or the administration of justice or otherwise bring the profession into disrepute'.[27] The last core duty in the Solicitors' Code of Conduct 2007 required that solicitors 'must not behave in a way that is likely to diminish the trust the public places in you or the profession'.

---

[22] ibid, Outcome 8.3.

[23] ibid, Indicative Behaviour 8.5.

[24] A Higgins, 'Referral Fees: The Business of Access to Justice' (2012) 32 *Legal Studies* 109.

[25] Ministry of Justice press release, 'Curbing Compensation Culture: Government to Ban Referral Fees' 9 September 2011.

[26] Legal Aid, Sentencing and Punishment of Offenders Act 2012, ss 56(1) and 56(4).

[27] Code of Conduct of the Bar of England and Wales, 8th edn (2004) as amended, paras 301 and 301(iii). See also para 710.2(b) on advertising.

Breaches of specific rules of conduct bring professions into disrepute, as does unlawful conduct, especially of a criminal nature. There is little guidance on what other behaviour is caught by general rules to protect a profession's reputation. It is unclear whether the need to 'protect' the reputation of the profession prohibits private conduct that might be regarded as odd, undesirable or unconventional although not criminal; promiscuity, belonging to a religious sect or promoting currently unacceptable political beliefs, for instance.

Presumably, it should not be the behaviour itself, but the harm to the reputation of the profession, that is the acid test. For example, some criminal conduct would not necessarily be regarded as bringing the profession into disrepute. If it were, any lawyer guilty of dropping litter, speeding or careless driving would also be subject to professional sanctions. Similarly, action short of criminal behaviour will involve a common sense evaluation of the norms of society generally. While the likelihood is that any standards set will be on the conservative side, the liberal ideal suggests that there should be tolerance of eccentric behaviour. The focus on 'reputation' does, however, run the risk that professions aspire to regulate social standards as well as workplace standards.

The codes of conduct of both solicitors and barristers have regulated members' involvement in activities that might be disreputable in themselves. The Bar warns barristers that they must not engage, either directly or indirectly, in any occupation which might affect the reputation of the Bar adversely. The Solicitors' Code of Conduct 2007 advised against behaviour 'within or outside' the profession which damages public trust in the profession. It may be assumed that a legal activity, like running a sex shop, might fall foul of such rules, but what about marginal activities, such as running a betting shop, a pawnbrokers or a high interest doorstep moneylender business?

Most of the areas of risk, like advertising, are policed by regulation. Some, like statements to the press, have also been regulated. The risk that wild or inaccurate statements will discredit the profession can be used by clients to their own advantage. An example of this situation happened in the litigation against Railtrack arising from the Ladbroke Grove rail crash. The solicitor for relatives of a deceased victim issued a press release informing the press that the closing speech of their counsel would reveal 'shocking evidence of total mismanagement and utter callous disregard for safety' by the defendants.[28]

Railtrack complained to the Law Society that these comments were a breach of the Advertising Code and brought the profession into disrepute. After an 18-month investigation, during which the relatives' solicitor incurred considerable legal costs, it was decided that the press release broke no professional rules. The implication is that wealthy parties can use professional rules to restrict opposing lawyers' statements to the press. This suppresses public knowledge of the details of legal proceedings and their wider implications.

In the SRA Handbook 2011, the core obligation from the 2007 Code, behaving so as not to diminish trust in the profession, became one of the new principles. It was, however, expressed differently, as a responsibility to maintain 'the trust the public places in

---

[28] C Dyer, *Guardian* 9 January 2002.

you and in the provision of legal services'.[29] It is not obvious why 'trust in the profession' had become trust in 'the provision of legal services'. It may have been acknowledgement of the fact that those delivering legal services were no longer all members of the profession. It may also have been an attempt to escape the connotations of professionalism in the era of 'independent regulation'. The shift of focus from 'reputation' to 'trust' suggests a slightly different test for whether lawyer conduct breaches the Code.

III. Mandatory Obligations to the State

The privileged position of the legal profession is a gift of the state which has always incurred special obligations. The earliest surviving collective obligation is the duty to the court. As society has become more complex, there is a greater perception of threats to its existence. The state has imposed more obligations on professions in an effort to suppress these threats. These measures include legislation designed to hinder the growth of large-scale criminal activity, prevent terrorism and control tax evasion.

A. Duty to the Court

The duty to the court was traditionally owed by advocates.[30] According to Lord Justice Brooke in *Copeland v Smith*,[31] the justice system of England and Wales 'has always been dependent on the quality of the assistance that advocates give to the bench'. It was also said that this permits the state to avoid 'having to incur the cost of legal assistance for judges'.[32] Clients therefore pay their lawyers to inform the state about its own laws.

The duty to the court is not an unduly onerous burden for the profession. Lord Justice Brooke said that the need to keep up to date encompassed only the material to be found in generalist law reports, such as the Weekly or All England Reports, and not specialist reports. Whether the comment is still valid must be open to question in the light of current sophisticated legal search engines and websites available.

B. Reporting on the Use and Laundering of Proceeds of Crime

In efforts to control crime the state has introduced a number of offences that attempt to disrupt serious crime, including terrorism, by limiting the movement of proceeds

---

[29] SRA, *Handbook 2011*; SRA Principles 2011, as amended, Principle 6.
[30] See further ch 19: 'Advocacy'.
[31] *Copeland v Smith* [2000] 1 All ER 457.
[32] ibid, at 462–63.

of crime. These offences involve dealing with, and being party to arrangements involving, proceeds of crime. Solicitors, and others, are required by law to disclose suspected activities to the relevant authorities. One of the main activities targeted by the legislation is money-laundering.

i. Scope of Offences

Money laundering was originally described by the Law Society as the process by which 'dirty money', the proceeds of crime, is handled so that the money appears 'to originate from a legitimate source'.[33] Concern that sophisticated criminal clients could use lawyers, and abuse the rules on confidentiality and legal privilege, to launder the proceeds of crime, proved well founded. An infamous example is of Michael Renton, a partner in a South London criminal practice, who was convicted of laundering some of the thirty million pounds stolen in the Brinks Mat gold bullion robbery. Overseas accounts were used to launder the money and produce profits from property transactions.[34]

Money laundering is an international problem. The European Council Directive 91/308/EEC[35] requires disclosure of suspicious transactions by credit and financial institutions throughout the European Union. The requirement for lawyers to break client confidentiality was challenged under Article 6 of the European Convention on Human Rights by the bars in Belgium, France and Poland.[36] The original UK legislation in the UK was the Criminal Justice Act 1988,[37] the Drug Trafficking Offences Act 1994 and the Prevention of Terrorism (Temporary Provisions) Act 1989. The current provisions are contained in the amended Proceeds of Crime Act 2002 and its associated Money Laundering Regulations 2007, which came into force at the end of 2007.

The Proceeds of Crime Act 2002 and the Terrorism Act 2000, as amended,[38] apply to all solicitors and other professionals. New Money Laundering Regulations[39] were enacted in response to an EU Directive.[40] These apply to solicitors' activities where there is a high risk of money laundering. This section provides an overview of the main provisions.[41] This excludes money laundering offences linked to terrorism, dealt with in the next section.

---

[33] *Law Society Guidance* 1993, at para 2, reproduced in JA Holland (ed), *Cordery on Solicitors* (London, Butterworths, 1995).

[34] P Lashmar, 'Grassing on the Client' *The Guardian* 29 March 1994.

[35] Council Directive 91/308/EEC of 10 June 1991 on prevention of the use of the financial system for the purpose of money laundering. *Council Act of, 29*, OJ L344.

[36] *Law Society Gazette* 21 July 2005, at 1.

[37] Criminal Justice Act 1988, s 93A (inserted by the Criminal Justice Act 1993, s 29).

[38] Terrorism Act 2000 and Proceeds of Crime Act 2002 (Amendment) Regulations 2007 (SI 2007/3398).

[39] Money Laundering Regulations 2007 (SI 2007/2157).

[40] Directive 2005/60/EC of the European Parliament and of the Council of 26 October 2005 on the prevention of the use of the financial system for the purpose of money laundering and terrorist financing, OJ L309.

[41] Law Society Practice Notes, Anti Money Laundering, ch 6: 'Legal Professional Privilege' (www.lawsociety.org.uk/advice/practice-notes/aml/legal-professional-privilege/).

a. Disclosure

The main purpose of the legislation on proceeds of crime is to secure disclosure of suspected activity to the relevant authorities. For example, a person commits an offence of failing to disclose money laundering if three conditions are satisfied.[42] The first condition is that the person knows or suspects, or has reasonable grounds for knowing or suspecting, that another person is engaged in money laundering. The second condition is that the information giving rise to the knowledge or suspicion came to him in the course of a business in the regulated sector.

The regime covers all persons, but the main offences relate to 'business in the regulated sector'. This covers a wide range of financial activity.[43] including holding property on trust, holding documents of title, managing and advising on investments, all activities undertaken by most solicitors and those authorised by the Financial Conduct Authority to undertake investment business. The third condition is that he does not make the required disclosure as soon as is practicable. This was originally to a nominated officer or a person authorised by the Director General of the National Criminal Intelligence Service (NCIS), later merged with the Serious Organised Crime Agency (SOCA) in 2006.

The Proceeds of Crime Act 2002 makes provision, under section 337, for what are known as 'protected disclosures'. Such a disclosure is 'not to be taken to breach any restriction on the disclosure of information (however imposed)'.[44] This means that solicitors who make disclosures in relation to clients are not regarded as having acted in breach of the rules relating to privilege or confidentiality. They cannot be subjected to disciplinary proceedings. Nor will they be in breach of contract and cannot be successfully sued by the client.

The circumstances for protected disclosures are that the information or other matter disclosed came to the discloser in the course of his trade, profession, business or employment. The information or other matter will have caused the discloser to know or suspect, or given reasonable grounds for knowing or suspecting, that another person was engaged in money laundering. The disclosure must then be made to a constable, a customs officer or a nominated officer as soon as is practicable.[45]

Solicitors can offer the defence of legal professional privilege to the offence of failure to disclose suspected money laundering. Section 330(6) provides that an offence is not committed if there is a reasonable excuse for not disclosing the information. Alternatively, they may claim that they are a professional legal adviser and the information or other material came to them in privileged circumstances.

The defence is set out in section 330(10) of the Proceeds of Crime Act. It is defined in a similar way to the defence in the Police and Criminal Evidence Act. Circumstances are privileged if the information is communicated to or given to the legal adviser by a client of his in connection with the giving by the adviser of legal advice to the client, or by a person seeking legal advice from the adviser, or by a person in connection with

---

[42] Proceeds of Crime Act 2002, s 330.

[43] The Proceeds of Crime Act 2002 (Business in the Regulated Sector and Supervisory Authorities) Order 2003 (2003 No 3074).

[44] Proceeds of Crime Act 2002, s 337(1).

[45] ibid, s 337(2).

legal proceedings or contemplated legal proceedings. This defence, however, is not available if the information was given to a solicitor with the intention of furthering a criminal purpose.[46]

b. Tipping off and Prejudicing an Investigation

Solicitors considering reporting a suspicion of money laundering must not inform the client. This is at the risk of committing further offences. These offences can only be committed once the solicitor knows or suspects the money laundering disclosure has been made. 'Tipping off' is committed by a person in the regulated sector disclosing to a third person that a suspicious activity report has been made or that an money laundering investigation is underway.[47] A broader class of people can commit an offence by prejudicing a confiscation, civil recovery or money laundering investigation.[48] Therefore a solicitor should be very careful before warning a client, or any other person, that money laundering is suspected. It can be done only after a disclosure has been made and it must not be done in such a way as to prejudice investigation. It is not tipping off for a lawyer to include a paragraph in a standard client care letter about the obligation to report money laundering.

c. Dealing with Criminal Property

Under the Proceeds of Crime Act 2002, section 329, a person commits an offence if he acquires criminal property, uses criminal property or has possession of criminal property. Under section 327, a person commits an offence if he conceals, disguises, converts, transfers criminal property or removes it from England and Wales, Scotland or Northern Ireland. Concealing or disguising criminal property includes concealing or disguising its nature, source, location, disposition, movement or ownership or any rights with respect to it.[49]

Offences are not committed under either section in a number of circumstances. First, there is no offence if such a person makes an authorised disclosure under section 338 and obtains the appropriate consent. Secondly, there is no offence if they intended to make such a disclosure, but had a reasonable excuse for not doing so. Thirdly, there is no offence if they perform a forbidden act in carrying out a function relating to the enforcement of the Act or any similar provision.[50]

d. Becoming Concerned in an Arrangement

Under the Proceeds of Crime Act 2002, section 328, it is a criminal offence for a person, including a solicitor, to enter into or become concerned 'in an arrangement which he knows or suspects facilitates (by whatever means) the acquisition, retention, use or control of criminal property by or on behalf of another person'.[51] Criminal

---

[46] ibid, s 330(11).
[47] ibid, s 333A (as amended by the Proceeds of Crime Act 2002 (Amendment) Regulations 2007).
[48] ibid, s 342.
[49] ibid, s 327(3).
[50] ibid, s 327(2).
[51] ibid, s 328(1).

property is broadly defined in the 2002 Act as a benefit obtained from criminal conduct.[52] Criminal conduct includes any offence in the UK, or conduct that would be an offence in the UK if it had occurred there.

As with section 327, offences are not committed under section 328 where a person makes an authorised disclosure under section 338 and obtains the appropriate consent. Nor is an offence committed where they intended to make such a disclosure but had a reasonable excuse for not doing so. An offence is not committed when they commit the act while carrying out a function they have relating to the enforcement of any provision of this Act or other relevant enactment.[53]

e. Interpretation of the Offences and Defences

It is of considerable practical importance to lawyers undertaking any, apparently normal, legal transaction to consider the possibility that they are party to illegality. Therefore, if a solicitor knows or suspects that a client is buying a house with money that originated from a criminal offence, but does the conveyancing, he or she will be guilty of the offence. In one such case, a solicitor sold a house at an undervalue for an estate agent he 'trusted'.[54] The house was owned by drug traffickers and the solicitor was jailed for six months. He claimed he was only guilty of an error of judgement but the Court of Appeal upheld the conviction, stating that 'society demands a high degree of professionalism from solicitors'.

A first decision under the Proceeds of Crime Act 2002 suggested that solicitors could easily become concerned with an 'arrangement' relating to 'criminal property' in the course of litigation. *P v P* involved a relatively minor case of tax evasion.[55] The solicitor on the other side was concerned that he was bound to report his suspicion under money laundering reporting requirements. This caused considerable consternation in the legal profession. A subsequent Court of Appeal case, *Bowman v Fels*,[56] restored some equilibrium. *Bowman* was a case on the ownership of the home on relationship breakdown. The female claimant was asserting an equitable interest in the former home of herself and her male partner. Her solicitor suspected that the defendant had included the costs of renovating his home in his business account and VAT returns. He reported this suspicion of criminal activity to the National Criminal Intelligence Service (NCIS) under section 328.

The Court of Appeal noted that the UK Government had enacted legislation that potentially went further than the EU Directive in requiring suspicions to be disclosed. The consequence for civil proceedings was the possibility of considerable disruption while any reported suspicions were considered. The court heard that, even though in 75 per cent of cases consent to proceed with the case was given in 24 hours, the NCIS could have up to five weeks to respond.

In the event, it was held that the ordinary conduct of litigation was not covered by section 328. Brooke LJ, delivering the judgment of the Court of Appeal, said

---

[52] ibid, s 340(3).
[53] ibid, s 328(2).
[54] *Law Society Gazette* 9 November 2006, at 4.
[55] *P v P* [2003] EWHC Fam 2260.
[56] *Bowman v Fels* [2005] EWCA Civ 226.

Parliament cannot have intended that proceedings or steps taken by lawyers in order to determine or secure legal rights and remedies for their clients should involve them in 'becoming concerned in an arrangement which … facilitates the acquisition, retention, use or control of criminal property', even if they suspected that the outcome of such proceedings might have such an effect.[57]

Any other decision, said the Court, would introduce the risk of unacceptable delay into all proceedings, prejudicing the right to a fair trial under Article 6 of the European Convention on Human Rights.

Following the case, the Law Society published guidance based on the assumption that a *Bowman v Fels* exemption from section 328 covered the final division of assets in accordance with a judgment or settlement, including the actual handling of the assets. The property itself is still, however, 'criminal property' and future dealings with it may require a report to SOCA.[58] It is not clear whether any exemption covers mediation or other processes ancillary to court proceedings.[59]

f. Ethical Issues

Sceptics may feel that this legislation gives solicitors the best of both worlds. Failure to disclose may be justified by legal professional privilege, but clients cannot complain about disclosure. Solicitors may, however, have an uncomfortable conflict of interest and a genuine ethical dilemma in such cases. It is arguable that, since no offence is committed where privileged circumstances exist, they should not disclose suspicions of money laundering when they are not obliged to do so. After all, if the general law does not require disclosure, the expectation that privilege applies should prevail. Arguably, they should risk possible criminal prosecution and act in the best interests of their client by refusing to disclose.

If they do decide to 'shop' their client, a further issue is whether a solicitor continues to represent that client. In ordinary circumstances this would justify the withdrawal of the solicitor from the case, but this is not possible because of the certainty of committing a tipping off offence. The tipping off requirements involve such a fundamental breach of loyalty and confidence that lawyer and client relationship is irrevocably undermined. This is a clear and irreconcilable conflict of interest between client and solicitor. In some circumstances, as in *Bowman v Fels*, solicitors might be stalling proceedings waiting for consent from SOCA to continue. They cannot say anything to the client. In due course, the client is likely to sack the solicitor anyway.

g. Money Laundering Regulations 2007

The Money Laundering Regulations 2007 implemented the Third European Money Laundering Directive requiring increased requirements on those responsible for reporting suspected money laundering.[60] The Law Society resisted the imposition

---

[57] ibid, at para 83.

[58] P Way, 'Proceeds of Crime Act 2002—The Impact of Bowman v Fels' *Family Law Week* (www. familylawweek.co.uk/site.aspx?i=ed261).

[59] 'Protecting a privileged position' *Law Society Gazette* 18 March 2005.

[60] Council Directive 2005/60/EC of the European Parliament and of the Council of 26 October 2005 on the prevention of the use of the financial system for the purpose of money laundering and terrorist financing OJ 2005 L 309.

of obligations on solicitors to investigate persons having beneficial ownership of property, under trusts and the like, on the grounds that the provisions were vague and costly to carry out. Some positive response by the government to lobbying was achieved. The Law Society also succeeded in excluding non-regulated solicitors from the tipping off criminal penalties.[61] Nevertheless, similar, and often wider, rules were introduced throughout Europe and the USA.[62] The regulations apply to a wide range of business in a more broadly defined regulated sector.[63] The regulations cover 'relevant persons', including 'independent legal professionals', firms or sole practitioners providing legal services to participants, for example, in financial or real property transactions, managing client money or creating trusts.[64]

The regulations require solicitors to ensure that their firm's employees are trained to recognise and handle suspicious transactions. This includes ensuring that client's identities, and those of certain beneficiaries of trusts, are adequately checked. Internal reporting procedures must be set up to maintain records of transactions for five years. Staff must be adequately trained in the law relating to money laundering and terrorism.[65] This enables an audit trail of transactions to be followed. The regulatory authorities have extensive supervisory and inspection powers and can also resort to various civil and criminal penalties for failure to adhere to the regulations.

The requirement that firms verify a client's identity before proceeding with any financial transaction[66] applies even to what may appear to be mundane transactions. Even a domestic house purchase is subject to standard due diligence, verification of identity using 'documentation, data or information obtained from a reliable and independent source'.[67] The obligations imposed on legal employers to detect money laundering are stringent. They render excuses based on lack of knowledge or staff failings, with which solicitors escaped responsibility in the early days of the regime,[68] increasingly unsustainable.

h. Sanctions

The maximum penalty for money laundering is 14 years' imprisonment. Various factors influence severity of sentence including the amount of money involved, number of transactions and the connection to drugs. Civil or criminal confiscation proceedings can be used to recover the proceeds of criminal activity. Someone involved in money laundering might also be convicted for contempt of court. In one case an advocate received a 15-month prison sentence for falsely representing that a £1 million payment from his father, a convicted money launderer, was for legal services.[69] Lawyers

[61] *Law Society Gazette*, 18 January 2007.
[62] A Odby, 'The European Union and Money Laundering: The Preventive Responsibilities of the Private Sector' in I Bantekas (ed), *International and European Financial Criminal Law* (London, Lexis/Nexis, Butterworths, 2006).
[63] Money Laundering Regulations 2007, reg 2(1).
[64] ibid, reg 3.
[65] ibid, reg 21.
[66] ibid, reg 7.
[67] ibid, reg 5.
[68] *Francis and Francis v Central Criminal Court* [1988] 3 WLR 989.
[69] J Harris, 'Jersey lawyer jailed for role in money laundering' *The Lawyer* 19 May 2011.

can also be subject to disciplinary proceedings, with striking off or disbarment a likely outcome.

C. Preventing Terrorism

There are various measures designed to suppress terrorism,[70] but the main provisions are in the Terrorism Act 2000 (as amended). The Act criminalises participation in terrorist activities and the provision of monetary support for terrorists. The Act creates general offences that apply to lawyers, as well as others subject to UK law, and some that apply to the regulated sector, which includes many lawyers.

i. General Criminal Offences of Dealing with Property Intended for Use in Terrorism

The principal terrorist property offences in sections 15–18 apply to all persons and therefore to all lawyers. Additionally, lawyers, by operating in the regulated sector, can commit further offences based on failing to report knowledge or suspicions that the primary offences have been committed.

The first offence is for people to be involved in raising funds that they know or have reasonable cause to suspect may be used for terrorist purposes.[71] The offence can be committed by inviting, receiving and making financial or other contributions that could be used in this way. It is no defence that the money or other property is a payment for goods and services. The second offence is using or possessing money or other property for terrorist purposes, including when there is reasonable cause to suspect such use.[72] The third property offence under the Terrorism Act is becoming involved in an arrangement which makes money or other property available to another when it is known, or reasonably suspected, that it may be used for terrorist purposes.[73]

The final offence covers money laundering. It is an offence to enter into or become concerned in an arrangement facilitating the retention or control of terrorist property by, or on behalf of, another person.[74] This includes concealing property, removing it from the jurisdiction or transferring it to nominees. It is a defence that a person did not know, and had no reasonable cause to suspect, that the arrangement related to terrorist property.

The Terrorism Act 2000 provided a number of general defences based on disclosure to and co-operation with authorities. Therefore, it is a defence for a person involved in a transaction or arrangement relating to money, or other property covered by the Act, to act with the consent of a constable or to disclose his suspicion, and the

---

[70] See eg The Al Qaida and Taliban (United Nations Measures) Order 2006 (2006 No 252) and Terrorism (United Nations Measures) Order 2009 (2009 No 2012).

[71] Terrorism Act 2000, s 15.

[72] ibid, s 16.

[73] ibid, s 17.

[74] ibid, s 18.

information on which it is based, to a constable.[75] It is also a defence where a person is in employment, and the employer has established a procedure for making disclosures, that disclosure is made under the procedure.[76]

The Terrorism Act Regulations 2007 (TACT Regulations 2007) introduced three new defences to the property offences.[77] The first was that the relevant person had made a disclosure to an authorised person before becoming involved in a transaction or an arrangement, following which, the person acts with the consent of an authorised officer. The second was where such a person was already involved in a transaction or arrangement and made a disclosure, provided there was a reasonable excuse for failure to make a disclosure in advance. The third defence was that the person intended to make a disclosure but had a reasonable excuse for failing to do so.

ii. Offences Relating only to the Regulated Sector

The regulated sector definition is similar to that used for the Proceeds of Crime Act 2002. The sector covers a wide range of activity, much of it involving lawyers in one way or another.[78] The main offence is failing to disclose. This was expanded by the TACT Regulations 2007 to cover failure to disclose an attempted offence under sections 15–18. There are two tipping off offences, applying only to persons in the regulated sector.

a. Failing to Disclose

Under the Terrorism Act 2000, section 21A a non-disclosure offence is committed if three conditions are satisfied. The first condition is that the person knows or suspects, or has reasonable grounds for knowing or suspecting, that another person has committed or attempted to commit an offence under any of sections 15–18. The second condition is that the information or other matter on which his knowledge or suspicion is based, or which gives reasonable grounds for such knowledge or suspicion, came to the recipient in the course of a business in the regulated sector. The third condition is that the person does not disclose the information or other matter to a constable, or a nominated officer, as soon as is practicable after it comes to him[79] or to an authorised member of staff of the Serious Organised Crime Agency.[80]

The section goes on to state that a person does not commit an offence if he has a reasonable excuse for not disclosing the information or other matter.[81] A lawyer has a defence if information came to him in privileged circumstances. Someone employed by a law firm to assist and support lawyers who receives privileged information can also claim such a defence.[82] This is defined, in the same way as for money laundering,

---

[75] ibid, ss 21(1) and (2).
[76] ibid, s 21(6).
[77] Terrorism Act 2000 and Proceeds of Crime Act 2002 (Amendment) Regulations 2007 (SI 2007/3398) (amending Terrorism Act 2000, s 21 by introducing s21ZA–21ZC).
[78] Terrorism Act 2000, sch 3A, pt 1.
[79] ibid, ss 21A(1)–(4).
[80] ibid, s 21A(14).
[81] ibid, s 21A(5).
[82] ibid, s 21A(5A).

as giving legal advice to a client or by a person in connection with legal proceedings or contemplated legal proceedings.[83] The defence is not available where the information is given with a view to furthering a criminal purpose.[84]

It is a defence for lawyers in firms with a reporting system to make a timely report of suspected activity. In deciding whether someone has committed an offence under section 21A, a court must consider whether he followed any relevant guidance issued, inter alia, by a supervisory authority or any other appropriate body.[85] This is defined to include a body regulating or representative of a profession, business or employment carried on by the alleged offender.[86] The Act provides that protected disclosures are not regarded as breaching any restriction on revealing information, 'however imposed'.[87]

b. Tipping off

The first tipping off offence relates to information that came to a person in the course of a business in the regulated sector. It relates to any disclosure that might prejudice investigations that might be carried out. It is an offence for a person to disclose to a third person that a report of such information has been made by any person to the police, HM Revenue and Customs, SOCA or a nominated officer.[88] The second offence is disclosing that an investigation into allegations relating to terrorist property offences is being contemplated or carried out, if that disclosure is likely to prejudice an investigation.[89] Again, the offence requires that the information disclosed came to the person in the course of business in the regulated sector.

A tipping off offence is not committed if a lawyer shares information with an employee, officer or partner of the same undertaking, including undertakings in common ownership, management or control.[90] Nor is such an offence committed in a number of other circumstances. The most relevant are where information is shared for the purpose of preventing a money laundering offence or where both parties have equivalent professional duties of confidentiality and protection of personal data.[91] Most significantly, a tipping off offence is not committed if the disclosure is part of an attempt to dissuade a client from engaging in conduct amounting to an offence.[92]

iii. Regulation

The SRA Handbook contains an outcome requiring compliance with 'with legislation applicable to your business, including anti-money laundering and data protection legislation'.[93]

---

[83] ibid, s 21A(8).
[84] ibid, s 21A(9).
[85] ibid, s 21A(6).
[86] ibid, s 21A(13).
[87] ibid, s 21B(1).
[88] ibid, s 21D(1).
[89] ibid, s 21D(3).
[90] ibid, s 21E.
[91] ibid, s 21F.
[92] ibid, s 21G(2)(b).
[93] SRA, *Handbook 2011*, ch 7: 'Management of Your Business', Outcome 7.5.

iv. Ethical Implications

As with the money laundering regime, anti-terrorism legislation undermines the foundation of a lawyer and client relationship based on loyalty and trust. When a lawyer begins to be suspicious about a client's motives and intentions, they can no longer be concerned for the client's best interests. They are immediately put in a position where they must probe for information, so as to confirm their suspicion, but without letting the client know what is happening. One of the concessions that the legislation makes to lawyers is that it is a defence to tipping off when an attempt is made to dissuade the client from an offence. This would need to be combined with a timely report if commission of the primary offence, failing to report, is to be avoided.

D. Disclosing Details of Tax Avoidance Schemes

Under the Finance Act 2004, the promoters and users of certain types of tax avoidance schemes are required to disclose details to Her Majesty's Revenue & Customs (HMRC). Under section 306, these 'notifiable arrangements' are those that 'enable, or might be expected to enable, any person to obtain an advantage in relation to any tax that is so prescribed in relation to arrangements of that description'.[94] This refers to schemes for tax avoidance, not routine tax advice.

The aim of the measures is to allow HMRC to obtain advance warning of new tax schemes being promoted by the financial services industry. The authorities can then attempt to circumvent them in advance by new regulations or litigation. The duty of disclosure is imposed on the promoters of the schemes, which includes anyone whose business or profession involves offering tax services and who designs or promotes a notifiable tax scheme. A wide range of professionals are likely to be caught. Accountants and financial advisers are clearly covered, but so, on the face of it, are lawyers, either as designers or organisers of the arrangement.[95]

Where professionals are under a duty to disclose tax avoidance schemes it overrides the normal rule of confidentiality to clients. Persons subject to legal professional privilege are not included within the definition of 'promoter' of the schemes.[96] Lawyers wishing to claim exemption from reporting a tax avoidance scheme must establish that it is covered by either advice or litigation privilege. The House of Lords decision in the *Three Rivers* case, makes establishing this less difficult than did the Court of Appeal's decision in the same case.[97] Accountants, unsurprisingly, consider that this gives lawyers an unjustified commercial advantage.

Although a lawyer claiming legal privilege does not have a duty of disclosure, the client does have a personal duty to disclose the scheme to the Revenue within five days of the first transaction forming part of the scheme. The lawyer must advise his client

---

[94] Finance Act 2004, s 306(1)(b).

[95] ibid, s 307(1)(b).

[96] ibid, s 314; Tax Avoidance Schemes (Promoters, Prescribed Circumstances and Information) Amendment Regulations 2004 (SI 2004/2613).

[97] ibid, and see *New Law Journal* 29 October 2004, at 1608.

of this. Lawyers should counsel reluctant clients to make disclosure, but, because such communications are privileged, it follows that there is no duty to report a client who fails to disclose their scheme to the authorities. It is arguable whether there is a duty to terminate the representation if the client does not disclose. This would depend on whether, by continuing to act, the lawyer might become complicit in a criminal purpose, that is, tax evasion.

IV. Obligations to the State Accepted as a Condition of Performing Work

While government has imposed exceptions to confidentiality and legal privilege for protection of the state, it has also sought to adjust professional legal ethics in other areas. Therefore, as described in the next chapter, it has raised expectations that lawyers should perform free work, *pro bono publico*. It has also imposed restrictions on how some kinds of legal work is conducted on behalf of the state, as a condition of undertaking that work. Therefore, lawyers can choose not to do the work, but, if they do it, they must accept the limitations. Restrictions on doing work for legal aid authorities were dealt with in the last chapter. Here, the example of special advocacy is considered.

A. Special Advocacy

Special advocacy is a topic connected with the handling of terrorist suspects or others, usually immigrants or asylum seekers, in respect of whom sensitive material is held. The relevant legislation is the Special Immigration Commission Appeals Act 1997 and the Procedure Rules 2003, as extended by the Anti-Terrorism, Crime and Security Act 2001 and the Nationality, Immigration and Asylum Act 2002. In order to handle such cases, lawyers have compromised their role in relation to clients in order to accommodate the needs of the state.[98] This is often alleged to be necessary in order to protect national security.

The Special Immigration Appeals Commission (SIAC), created in 1997, has rules which allow immigration hearings to be held in private, when sensitive security issues are involved. The SIAC rules provide for the appointment by the Attorney General of 'special advocates' to represent the interests of the appellant. There is a pool of about 20 such advocates, mainly barristers, who are security vetted. The role of the special advocate is one for which barristers volunteer. This procedure has been extended

---

[98] A Boon and S Nash, 'Special Advocacy: Political Necessities and Legal Roles in Modern Judicial Systems' (2006) 9 *Legal Ethics* 101.

to cases whereby foreign nationals are certified as being terrorism suspects, for the removal of citizenship, and detention pending deportation.

Hearings involve severe compromises to clients' legal rights, at least as they are conventionally conceived. Some parts of the hearing may be held in the absence of the appellant and his chosen lawyer. In this way the case is dealt with without revealing the evidence to either the appellant or his lawyer. The process provides very limited rights of cross-examination, a procedure that violates normal rules of procedural justice.

The special advocates' brief is to review sensitive evidence and make representations to the Tribunal on behalf of the appellant at the closed hearing. They are instructed to act in the interests of the appellant, but must not reveal any of this sensitive evidence to the appellant. So seriously is this instruction taken that the special advocate is even forbidden from communicating with the appellant after the information has been revealed, a precaution designed to prevent inadvertent leakage.

Special advocates therefore act for the appellant 'but without instructions and sometimes, even, consent'.[99] The advocate is a lawyer who 'cannot take full instructions from his client, nor report to his client, who is not responsible to his client and whose relationship with the client lacks the quality of confidence inherent in any ordinary lawyer-client relationship'.[100] This represents the antithesis of the conventional relationship of lawyer and client and, of course, is contrary to numerous professional conduct rules for both branches of the profession.

Special advocates are appointed by the state, 'the client' has a very limited choice restricted to members of the panel and the advocate works to detailed rules laid down by the state. The fundamental objection, however, is that the role cannot be reconciled with acting independently in the best interests of the 'client', except in the very limited sense that it may be better to have a shackled lawyer than no lawyer at all. The duty of disclosure to the client is compromised and, therefore, so is the duty to take instructions from the client.

The role of the special advocate has obviously been found useful. It has been extended in a rather ad hoc fashion to other courts and tribunals dealing with national security issues. These include the Proscribed Organisations Appeal Commission and the Pathogens Access Appeal Commission. A further extension is to the ordinary courts, using their powers to regulate their own procedures. Such extensions have been controversial, giving rise to dissenting judicial opinions.[101] The pragmatic justification of special advocacy is that it helps the state to observe due process requirements by providing a degree of legal protection to alleged enemies of the state.

Special advocacy compromises the traditional legal role in relation to clients. If use of the system continues to expand, it will surely begin to undermine the ethics of the profession in a far wider category of cases. The alternative is to recognise that special advocates are in reality agents or employees of the state and not lawyers in the conventional sense. Although the role of special advocate drives a coach and horses

[99] ibid.
[100] *R v H; R v C* [2004] UKHL 3, per Lord Bingham.
[101] *Roberts v Parole Board* [2005] UKHL 45, per Lords Bingham and Steyn.

through the Bar's Code of Conduct, the Bar Council nominates suitable candidates and makes no special provision for special advocacy in its rules.

V. Duties to the Public at Large

A. Context

Widespread anxiety over lawyers' ethics is sometimes said to have started with the Watergate scandal in the 1970s. The Republican President, Richard Nixon, was allegedly implicated in a plot to enter the offices of the Democratic Party, photograph documents and place bugs in the run up to an election. Following a cover-up when the break-in was discovered, Nixon resigned and 43 members of his staff, many senior aides, were indicted. Nixon and a number of his aides were lawyers. One of the conclusions sometimes drawn from the Watergate scandal was that lawyers over-emphasise client loyalty at the expense of wider third party obligations.

Watergate led to calls for the end to self-regulation of lawyers in the US. In response the American Bar Association (ABA) produced a new model code of professional responsibility emphasising the need for good conduct. It also required that professional responsibility be taught on ABA-approved law degrees. Indirectly, Watergate raised the issue of whether lawyers should be under explicit duties to avoid harm to the public at large, or sections of the public. This remains a hotly contested issue.

The kinds of situation where lawyers might be subject to a broader duty is where they hold client information which, if revealed, may help to prevent financial, environmental or public health disasters. Limited examples of such reporting regimes already exist. In relation to the environment, for example the Aarhus Convention imposes obligations on public authorities to disclose environmentally sensitive information.[102] The creation of such responsibilities potentially risk in-house and external lawyers advising corporations being subject to conflicts between their public duties and their duties to clients.[103]

In situations in which clients try to hide environmental activity that is obviously a public risk, lawyers cannot be involved. They must withdraw from representing the client if they persist with illegal actions. But should their responsibility end there? The reason that society places trust in professions is because their members can 'elevate the social good' above the narrow interests of their practitioner members and their clients.[104] Arguably, they should also be required to warn of environmental threats that

---

[102] Convention on Access to Information, Public Participation in Decision-Making and Access to Justice in Environmental Matters (United Nations Economic Commission for Europe, 1998).
[103] A Osborn, 'Environment law in public hands' *The Lawyer* 20 October 1998, at 11.
[104] R Abel, *The Legal Profession in England and Wales* (Oxford, Blackwell, 1988) at 27.

already exist or which clients are planning. This would compromise the strict rules on maintaining client confidence.

B. Regulation

Lawyers' codes of conduct are generally silent regarding collective third party responsibilities. The Solicitors' Code of Conduct 2007, for example, required only that solicitors act with integrity towards the courts and 'others' as well as their clients and also 'not behave in a way which damages or is likely to damage the reputation or integrity of the profession'.[105] The latter obligation is expressed negatively. There are no positive duties in the Rules to promote justice, or access to it, and no duty to consider the impact of any action on wider society.

The general outcome that opens Chapter 11, 'Relations With Third Parties', specifies that, 'you do not take unfair advantage of third parties in either your professional or personal capacity'.[106] It is arguable that this outcome envisages that the solicitor is dealing with an identifiable third party. In most circumstances it would be impossible to know whether an unfair advantage is being taken unless the other party is known. Therefore, in exploring a basis of responsibility, one is forced back to the principles underpinning the SRA Code of Conduct and the very broad duties to uphold the rule of law and the administration of justice. As discussed below, these are not a promising foundation for the kinds of obligation needed to prevent social harm.

C. Financial Risks

One of the areas in which damage to collective third party interests is most obvious is in financial and stock markets. Here, there have been repeated failings over many years. In many cases, lawyers are implicated. Before exploring some of these cases in more detail it is necessary to look at the legal position of third party collectives suffering financial loss.

i. Liability for Financial Loss at Common Law

The common law provides some context for considering the responsibility of lawyers and other professionals for financial losses caused to groups rather than individuals. The key cases often concern auditors or surveyors, who are required to prepare documents upon which a party beyond their immediate client can rely. Such 'remote' parties can sometimes suffer financial loss as a result of their reliance. Liability for economic loss due to negligent misstatement was confined to cases where the statement or advice had been given to a known recipient for a specific purpose.

---

[105] SRA, *Solicitors' Code of Conduct 2007*, Core Duties, r 1.
[106] SRA, *Handbook 2011*, as amended, Outcome 11.1.

Additionally, the maker had to be aware of this purpose and that the recipient would rely on this advice and act on it to his detriment.[107]

In 1990, the proposition that a duty might be owed to a wide class of people was tested in *Caparo Industries Plc v Dickman*.[108] A firm of accountants, TR, had prepared an auditor's report on a public company, F, as required by statute. The purpose of the document was to report on the stewardship of the company by the directors, enabling shareholders to exercise their class rights in general meeting. C had purchased shares in F as part of a takeover bid and, relying on TR's report, had then bought further shares.

The report gave a false picture of F's projected profits and C suffered a loss. C brought an action against two directors of F, alleging negligent misstatement. The Court of Appeal distinguished existing shareholders, to whom TR owed a duty, and potential investors, to whom no duty was owed. If existing shareholders held on to, or sold shares based on the accounts, and suffered loss, they should be able to sue. The House of Lords upheld an appeal by the accountants, deciding that no duty of care was owed to either group.

The House of Lords decided that, applying the three standard tests for a duty of care, proximity, foreseeability and reliance, no duty to existing shareholders, or to potential investors, arose. Auditors of public companies preparing routine company accounts, as opposed to reports for a specific purpose for an identified party, owed no duty to the public at large making investment decisions. To impose such a liability would open the floodgates to an indeterminately wide class of people. The House of Lords thereby limited liability for economic loss due to negligent misstatement. This applies only to cases where the statement or advice is given to a known recipient, for a specific purpose of which the maker was aware, and upon which the recipient had relied and acted to his detriment.

ii. Professional Responsibility for Financial Loss

a. Striking the Balance

Cases such as *Caparo v Dickman* are merely indicative of the courts' current attitude to third party liability for negligence. Lawyers are not in the same position as auditors certifying company accounts when it comes to producing information on which reliance may be placed. Nevertheless, the increasing prevalence of financial catastrophes raises questions about the preventative responsibilities of professionals. Some would wish to see more of a balance struck between duties to clients and wider duties to sections of the public, shareholders, employees and pensioners.

It has been argued that, in the USA in relation to the collapse of the Enron Corporation, traditional principles of neutrality and partisanship operated to 'sprinkle ... transactions with holy water', that were, in reality, designed to confuse the public or conceal their true nature.[109] Regulation might attempt to address this problem.

---

[107] *Hedley Byrne & Co v Heller & Partners* [1964] AC 465.
[108] *Caparo Industries Plc v Dickman* [1990] 2 AC 605.
[109] RW Gordon, 'Professionalisms Old and New' (2005) 8 *Legal Ethics* 24.

For example, it might be desirable to impose a duty on lawyers to report risk of significant financial loss or other harm to a public authority. Failure to do so might be used as a basis for legal liability.

b. Public Duty Based on Government Indemnity

Those suffering financial harm with no legal or insurance claim may be lucky. Their losses may sometimes be shouldered by government and paid for by the taxpayer. It is therefore, arguable that professionals who participate in activity that causes financial losses owe a duty to the wider public to avoid such losses occurring. These issues have been thrown into particularly sharp relief by the global financial crisis. This was pre-cipitated in 2008 by risky behaviour on the part of global financial institutions. Some of this behaviour may have been illegal or, at least, breached financial regulations. Many of the institutions involved had professionals, including lawyers, at the core of operations or took the advice of leading firms.

c. Exploring the Limits of Professional Responsibility

The next section examines three case studies of major financial calamities in which lawyers participated. All three involve US financial disasters and only the last involves an English law firm in a leading role. It is, nevertheless, useful to see how such situations unfold, what role lawyers played and what actions were taken to deal with the situation. The advantage of these case studies is that regulators tend to publish reports. The crises relate to the Savings and Loan scandal (the Kaye Scholar affair), the collapse of the Enron Corporation and the failure of Lehmann Brothers. Each case study concludes with a section considering the implications of what happened for regulation in England and Wales.

iii. The Kaye Scholer Affair

a. Context

The collapse of US Bank, Lincoln Savings and Loan, and the role of its lawyers, Kaye, Scholer, Fierman, Hays and Handler (Kaye Scholer) in the affair stimulated considerable academic debate in the US.[110] The bank was controlled by a financier, Charles Keating, who took advantage of looser banking regulation in the 1980s to use bank funds to finance real estate developments. The bank was liquidated leaving 23,000 customers with worthless bonds. Further losses of $3.4 billion had to be picked up by the United States federal banking and insurance system.

Kaye Scholer were appointed lawyers to the bank in 1986. The banking regulators were concerned that many banks were over-extended. Lincoln Savings and Loan had just been through a regulatory investigation stimulated by concerns that it was

---

[110] WH Simon, 'The Kaye Scholer Affair: The Lawyer's Duty of Candor and the Bar's Temptations of Evasion and Apology' (1998) 23 *Law and Social Inquiry* 243; GC Hazard 'Lawyer Liability in Third Party Situations: the Meaning of the Kaye Scholer Case' (1992) 26 *Akron Law Review* 395, Faculty Scholarship Series Paper 2374 (http://digitalcommons.law.yale.edu/fss_papers/2374).

engaged in 'unsafe and unsound' banking practices. One of Kaye Scholer's main tasks was to convince the regulator that the bank was viable. It assumed control of communications with the bank and resisted the regulator's attempts to uncover the true situation for several months. Eventually, the regulator closed the bank in 1989.

Management of the liquidated bank passed to a new federal government agency, the Office of Thrift Supervision (OTS). This agency had broad powers of investigation and could pursue directors of financial institutions and their accountants and lawyers. OTS charged Kaye Scholer with providing the bank with reckless advice, misstating facts to the regulator and failing to disclose information showing that the bank's practices were 'unsafe and unsound'. They sequestrated (seized) the law firm's assets.

Three days after its assets were sequestrated Kaye Scholer settled, paying $41 million and agreeing to restrictions on the practising certificates of some of its lawyers. Unsurprisingly, the circumstances of Kaye Scholer's capitulation caused anxiety among US lawyers. The power to freeze a law firm's assets for assisting a client was unheard of in 1986. There was therefore concern about what standards the OTS were applying. Because of the settlement, the formal charges against Kaye Scholer were never adjudicated.

b. The Lawyers' Role

One of the concerns generated by the Kaye Scholer case was the question of what responsibility lawyers owed to unidentified third parties when protecting client interests. The OTS, sifting through the confidential records of the defunct bank, found documents suggesting that it systematically misled the regulatory authorities for three years prior to its collapse. Simon's analysis of the pleadings in the case showed active participation by Kaye Scholer.[111] He concluded that, had the firm not provided misleading information to the regulator, numerous dubious transactions would not have happened and substantial losses would probably have been prevented.

c. Legal Liability

The fact that the firm's actions may have been a cause of financial loss to depositors and investors, losses underwritten by the government, raises the question of whether Kaye Scholer should have been liable to pay compensation. This would be controversial because it attaches substantial blame to the lawyers. While they may share some fault, the behaviour of the bank was the primary cause of the losses. It should also be noted that the government regulator might also share blame. It could have acted more decisively if it was dissatisfied with the way the bank or its lawyers responded.

Hazard suggests a tenable basis for a claim by shareholders or other individuals affected by the collapse of the bank. He argues that Kaye Scholer failed in its duty to the client (the bank) by following the instructions of a third party (Keating, the corporate management of the bank). Therefore, the case can be read as the OTS stepping into the shoes of the corporation to enforce the rights of shareholders against the directors and the bank's lawyers.

---

[111] ibid, Simon, at 247–51.

Simon suggests that the OTS proposed two possible standards for liability under the statute allowing it to seek recovery. The first was a minimal obligation not to mislead explicitly. The second, higher, standard was to fulfil the client's obligation of full disclosure under the banking regulations. The regulator's argument for the higher duty was based on two arguments. The first was that the firm had actively 'interposed' itself between the regulator and the client by insisting that the regulator should deal directly it.

The second argument for a positive duty to disclose was based on the alleged existence of a general duty to reveal regulatory evasion by clients. Simon agrees that the first argument could be the basis for responsibility to make full disclosure, but regards the second as less plausible. Even in the context of a strict regulatory regime operating in the public interest, he could see a basis for a wide obligation of disclosure.

d. Professional Responsibility

Simon saw the key ethical issue raised by the case as the lawyer's obligation to withdraw when he cannot act for a client without furthering a fraud.[112] The relevant conduct rule is unambiguous. It provides that 'a lawyer shall not counsel a client to engage, or assist a client, in conduct that the lawyer knows is criminal or fraudulent'.[113] This raises questions. Did the bank's activity meet the definition of criminal or fraudulent? If so, were the lawyers aware of this? If so, should they be liable to compensate for resulting financial losses?

On the issue of whether what happened was criminal or fraudulent, the bank's director, Keating, was convicted in the early-1990s of offences including fraud and conspiracy. He served four and a half years in prison before the convictions were overturned and lesser counts substituted. While these lesser counts still included elements of fraud, the quashing of the original convictions creates doubt about what conduct was known to Kaye Scholer's lawyers.

It is also unclear whether, if Kaye Scholer's lawyers knew about specific activity, they also knew that it was criminal or fraudulent as legally defined at the time.[114] These were issues the Bar could have pursued through disciplinary proceedings against individual Kaye Scholer lawyers, but did not do so. The New York Supreme Court, the disciplinary authority, found no grounds for professional discipline. Nevertheless, civil judgments worth billions of dollars remain outstanding against Keating and his associates.

e. Political Implications

Simon suggests that the legal establishment defended Kaye Scholer by arguing that lawyers' duty of confidentiality bound them not to disclose details of their client's actions. The duty, it was said, was more relevant and binding because the firm was instructed in anticipation of litigation by the regulator. The statements to the regulator were in the nature of arguments rather than statements of fact. Simon's critique of

---

[112] ibid, at 244.
[113] ABA, *Model Rules of Professional Conduct 2004*, r 1.2(d).
[114] DC Langevoort, 'What Was Kaye Scholer Thinking?' (1998) 23 *Law and Social Inquiry* 297.

this defence is that a key argument for confidentiality is that it encourages disclosure of planned wrongful conduct, allowing lawyers an opportunity to dissuade clients from the wrongful course of action.[115] This was patently not what the Kaye Scholer lawyers did.

The Kaye Scholer affair divided opinion among US academics on the issue of protecting collective third party interests. Simon argued that the failure of the Kaye Scholer lawyers to attempt to dissuade the bank reveals the flaw in lawyers' ethics. The legal establishment's defence of Kaye Scholer casts doubt on the US profession's capacity to regulate itself. Other academics supported the profession's position. Pepper argued that confidentiality allows clients to legitimately explore the limits of legality.[116] Macey pointed out that any expectation that Bar institutions would not defend Kaye Scholer and client confidentiality was naive.[117]

Miller argued that Simon's conclusions are based on a misinterpretation of the circumstances of the Kaye Scholer affair.[118] First, the 'onerous standard' Simon proposed was the standard that, in fact, applied. The difficulty with the case was the unproven nature of the allegations. Miller also argues that the payment by Kaye Scholer to settle the case does not prove the firm's guilt. The regulatory body had obtained an order freezing the firm's assets and effectively stopped them from trading. Settlement, he argues could therefore be seen as the only prudent course for the firm. Moreover, it was arguably an oppressive and unethical tactic by government lawyers, possibly used only because they were doubtful about their ability to prove the charges.[119]

f. Ethical Implications for England and Wales

In England and Wales, it is clear that a lawyer whose client proposes criminal or fraudulent activity, and cannot be persuaded otherwise, must withdraw from representation. Were lawyers found liable in a case on similar facts to Kaye Scholer, it would generate pressure for recognition of firmer obligations to third parties. As we have seen, ethics rules generally aspire to a higher standard than the law. A formal finding of liability would involve formulating an obligation encapsulating lawyers' responsibility to unidentified third parties when engaged in commercial work for clients.

Simon suggests that the facts of Kaye Scholer justify imposing an intermediate standard of disclosure on lawyers. Lawyers, he argues, should be prohibited from directly or indirectly misleading conduct and 'from providing any services substantially related to active unlawful client conduct'.[120] 'Unlawful' is a vague term that

---

[115] Simon, 'The Kaye Scholer Affair' (n 110) at 270–73 and 281.

[116] S Pepper, 'Why Confidentiality?' (1998) 23 *Law and Social Inquiry* 331.

[117] JR Macey, 'Professor Simon on the Kaye Scholer Affair: Shock at the Gambling at Rick's Palace in Casablanca' (1998) 23 *Law and Social Inquiry* 323.

[118] GP Miller, 'Kaye Scholer as Original Sin: The Lawyer's Duty of Candor and the Bar's Temptations of Evasions and Apology' (1998) 23 *Law and Social Inquiry* 305.

[119] KR Fisher, 'Neither Evaders nor Apologists: A Reply to Professor Simon' (1998) 23 *Law and Social Inquiry* 341 and Macey, 'Professor Simon on the Kaye Scholer Affair' (n 117) and Simon's comment, 'Further Thoughts on Kaye Scholer' (1998) 23 *Law and Social Inquiry* 365.

[120] Simon, 'The Kaye Scholer Affair' (n 110) at 255.

could be interpreted to cover civil liability. If it did not, it is not clear how Simon's proposed rule would be preferable to the model rule forbidding assistance to a client in conduct that the lawyer knows is criminal or fraudulent.

iv. The Enron Scandal

a. Context

The role of lawyers in the collapse of the energy giant, Enron, in the US in 2001 caused as much ethical soul searching as the Watergate scandal. One of the major issues that arose was whether the lawyers acting for Enron owed a duty to safeguard the interests of the shareholders, the employees and possibly the pensioners of Enron, or, even more widely, the community at large. All these groups were harmed or placed at risk in numerous ways by the collapse into bankruptcy of a mega corporation.

Enron, once one of the seven largest corporations in the world, went bankrupt in 2001 leading to the eventual dissolution of its accountant and auditors, Arthur Anderson, then one of the five leading accountancy firms in the world.[121] Enron traded in financial contracts connected with their energy assets. Enron executives managed to hide losses of billions of dollars using accounting loopholes and false financial reporting and by pressurising Arthur Andersen to ignore the issues. Many of these financial arrangements involved creating a multitude of partnership organisations, the main aim of which was to allow a sanitised version of the corporation's accounts to be presented to the public. This gave a totally false impression of the corporation's security and solvency.

The arrangements also made a lot of money for the individual executives involved in their creation, including at least one in-house lawyer employed by Enron. Much of this was clearly not only unlawful but criminally fraudulent. Many of the senior managers involved were sentenced to prison terms. An Enron insider, not a lawyer, finally revealed the fraud and the corporation collapsed, resulting in the loss of the loss of 4000 jobs and $70 billion of savings and shares. Shareholders filed a $40 billion lawsuit, but enjoyed limited success through legal actions. Arthur Anderson were charged with obstruction of justice after destroying documents, emails and files relating to Enron auditing.

b. The Lawyer's Role

Lawyers play a significant role in offering shares and securities on financial markets. They are primarily responsible for the verification of the legal requirements for the prospectus for an initial public offering. Markets depend on the integrity of information and on credible disclosure of material facts facilitating informed investment decisions. Lawyers are generally regarded as 'gatekeepers', independent professionals who

---

[121]   D Rhode and P Paton, 'Lawyers, Ethics and Enron' (2002–03) 8 *Stanford Journal of Law Business and Finance* 9; E Wald 'Lawyers and Corporate Scandals' (2004) 7 *Legal Ethics* 54.

serve investors by preparing, verifying or assessing disclosures. They are effectively, field marshals of the disclosure process.[122]

Lawyers were involved in many facets of the Enron scandal. First, 'attorneys all played an important role in the process of drafting and certifying disclosure statements, and advising whether the legal and accounting requirements governing [the partnership organizations] had been met'.[123] Secondly, senior lawyers in the corporation, presented with evidence of malpractice, failed to investigate or take any action. Thirdly, an outside firm of lawyers, Vinson & Elkins, were implicated in some of the illegality, yet also agreed to undertake, at the request of Enron itself, an investigation into the process once questions were asked about the probity of the way the company was being run.

The outside law firm was investigating its own work. It was in a position where its interest conflicted with those of other third parties. Unsurprisingly the report that resulted from the firm's investigation was short, exculpatory and dismissive. Finally, once it was clear that government investigation and litigation was likely to ensue, one of Enron's senior employed lawyers began to shred the evidence. A misleading press release was drafted on Enron's position.

c. Legal Liability

Legal action by groups like shareholders and pensioners, whose interests should have been a primary concern to lawyers acting on behalf of Enron, was a clear possibility. As in most corporations, the chief executive officer (CEO) was purporting to act on behalf of the corporation and had authority to give the lawyers instructions. The corporation was the 'real' client and its interests were different from those of the CEO.[124] It was clear, however, that the Enron lawyers, both in-house and external firms, identified with the senior executives of the organisation and were not acting independently of their interests. As Gordon noted, '[a]t best, the lawyers were closing their eyes to the risk of disaster; at worst they were helping to bring it on'.[125]

In the aftermath, 16 people pleaded guilty to charges alleging crimes committed at the company, and five others, including four former employees of Merrill Lynch, the brokerage and securities firm, were found guilty at trial. It is clear that many of the lawyers involved had broken a variety of accepted ethical norms and had also been involved in the promotion of fraud. A senior lawyer who shredded evidence had attempted to frustrate a federal investigation. Five years after Enron collapsed, two in-house lawyers were charged with civil fraud in connection with one deal each in the pre-Enron collapse.[126] In 2009 the actions were settled by payment of total fines of just

---

[122] SM Solaiman, 'The Enron Collapse and Criminal Liabilities of Auditors and Lawyers for Defective Prospectuses in the United States, Australia and Canada: A Review' (2006–07) 26(8) *Journal of Law and Commerce* 81.

[123] Rhode and Paton, 'Lawyers, Ethics and Enron' (n 121) at 15.

[124] WH Simon, 'Whom (or What) Does the Organisation's Lawyer Represent?: An Anatomy of Intra-client Conflict' (2003) 91 *California Law Review* 57; MC Regan,' Professional Responsibility and the Corporate Lawyer' (2000) 13 *Georgetown Journal of Legal Ethics* 197.

[125] R Gordon, 'A New Role for Lawyers? The Corporate Counsel after Enron' (2003) 26 *Harvard Journal of Law & Public Policy* 1185, at 1192.

[126] P Lattman, 'SEC Charges Two Enron Lawyers with Fraud' *Wall Street Journal* 29 March 2007.

over $50,000 and agreement to a suspension from appearing before the Commission for two years.[127] The settlement terms included no admission of wrongdoing.

Although civil legal action by members of third party collectives is a theoretical possibility, it can be expensive for individuals relative to the sums in issue. Civil actions are also risky because of courts may fear 'opening the floodgates of liability'. Therefore, discussion often revolves around the scope for attaching criminal liability to lawyers' acts[128] rather than civil liability for losses.

d. Professional Responsibility

If lawyers are to be effective gatekeepers of certain financial transactions, their independence and integrity must be safeguarded and it must be clear where their duty lies. The ABA's Model Rules provides a broad permission to disclose information that may have prevented some of the Enron dealings and may have given the regulator reason to take a closer look at the company. The rules provided that:

> [A] lawyer may reveal [confidential] information . . . to the extent the lawyer reasonably believes necessary 'to prevent the client from committing a crime or fraud that is reasonably certain to result in substantial injury to the financial interests or property of another and in furtherance of which the client has used or is using the lawyer's services.[129]

This is obviously permissive, allowing, but not requiring reporting.

Gordon notes that many state Bar rules go further than that, for example, by providing that 'a lawyer *shall* reveal such information to the extent the lawyer reasonably believes necessary'.[130] One view of how this changes the obligations of lawyers is that any fraud, especially one accomplished through lawyers' efforts,

> must try to get clients to correct the wrong, and that if the client does not comply, the lawyer may or must withdraw and disaffirm any documents he has helped to prepare; and if serious harm is likely to result, may or must disclose to relevant parties or authorities.[131]

As Gordon notes, an interpretation that would turn lawyers into self-regulators of financial services would be highly controversial. It is expected that lawyers should withhold consent to risky financial dealings, and entirely reasonable that they should counsel clients against them. It is something else to require that they report suspicions to the authorities because it undermines the trust relationship with clients. It would also ensure that independent law firms would be kept at the margins of financial activity as far as possible, thus depriving them of the possibility of dissuasion.

The effectiveness of Vinson & Elkins, the external law firm, as a brake on illegal dealing may have been reduced by the fact that Enron was its largest client. Many of the firm's employees had taken jobs with Enron as in-house counsel. It is difficult for an external firm to act as a gatekeeper of legality when it is in a dependent role

---

[127] US Securities and Exchange Commission, Litigation Release No 20866 26 January 2009 (www.sec.gov/litigation/litreleases/2009/lr20866.htm).

[128] Solaiman, The Enron Collapse and Criminal Liabilities of Auditors and lawyers' (n 122).

[129] ABA, *Model Rules of Professional Conduct 2004*, r 1.6(b)(2).

[130] Gordon, 'A New Role for Lawyers?' (n 125) at 1195, citing *Connecticut Rules of Professional Conduct* (2003) r 1.6(b).

[131] ibid.

in relation to clients. It is easier, and in the external firm's own interests, to look the other way.

e. Political Implications

In 2001 and 2002 there were numerous Senate committee hearings about Enron and the issues of accounting and investor protection. In 2002 Congress passed the Company Accounting Reform and Investor Protection Act, also known as the Sarbanes-Oxley Act. The provisions of the Act appear to be a direct response to Enron's governance failings. They include establishment of a Public Company Accounting Oversight Board to develop standards for auditing, provisions on independent audit and expanded financial disclosure requirements.

The Sarbanes-Oxley Act imposes specific responsibilities on lawyers.[132] It empowers the Securities Exchange Commission (SEC) to set minimum standards of professional conduct for attorneys appearing and practising before it. Attorneys are required to report material violation of securities law, or fiduciary duty or similar violation by companies or their agents to either the chief legal counsel or the CEO of the company. If the recipient of the report does not act on the evidence reported, lawyers are required to then report to the audit committee of the board of directors.[133] Failure to report could lead to the attorney facing criminal charges and civil action.

The requirements for internal audit were considerably bolstered after Enron. Audit committees had to include independent members. Attorneys could also report to another committee of the board of directors comprised solely of directors not employed directly or indirectly by the company. There was, however, no statutory obligation to alert the SEC if reports did not lead to action. In a company like Enron, where involvement was widespread, it may be that only an outside reporting requirement would be a deterrent or provide a remedy.

f. Implications for England and Wales

While the lawyers in Kaye Scholer came on the scene after the event, and concealed matters that exacerbated loss, Enron lawyers were complicit in wrongdoing. Some of these lawyers were employed in-house. This raises the issue of whether they were right to protect confidentiality and whether, had they been in England, their advice would have been privileged. The issues, including the question of 'who is the client' in a corporate context, arose in *Three Rivers v Bank of England*.[134] If it were clear that illegal activities were going on, privilege could not be claimed. The duty of confidentiality would, however, still apply. This would leave the whistle-blowing lawyer in an awkward position.

It does not appear that the lawyers advising Enron were personally motivated by greed, although keeping a well-paid job may be a good enough incentive not to rock the boat. Because the court case against them did not happen, their motivations were

---

[132] Company Accounting Reform and Investor Protection Act 2002, s 307.
[133] ibid, s 307(2).
[134] *Three Rivers District Council & Others v Governor and Company of the Bank of England (No 6)* [2005] 1 AC 610 (HL) per Baroness Hale at [63]. See ch 10: 'Confidences'.

not revealed. It may be that their perception could have been that such a powerful corporation could not be doing anything so wrong. If they had suspicions, or more, they may simply have been looking the other way.

If the Enron lawyers knew full well the scale of the problems at the corporation their inaction raises the issue of whether their perceived duty to the client ranked too highly. If so, it may be that they were not attuned to the need to protect the corporation from its own leaders. Some commentators think that their behaviour is perfectly consistent with that of large firm lawyers generally.

Nancy Rapoport blames the conduct of the Enron lawyers and similar cases to the 'eat what you kill' philosophy of large firms, the work ethic that constitutes a 'race to exhaustion, a race to sloppiness, and a race to malpractice' with no countervailing ethic within the work environment.[135] This raises the question of what can be done, through education or otherwise to change this mind-set. It is often asserted that big City solicitors' firms in England and Wales also identify more with their corporate clients than with the legal profession as a whole or the Law Society as its regulatory body.

As in the Kaye Scholer affair, the Enron Corporation did not get the benefit of their lawyers' advice against wrongdoing. The attitude of both the CEOs of Enron and its lawyers seemed to be that legal obligations were to be got round or evaded if at all possible; the law 'seen as merely an imposition and a nuisance'[136] and not as a guide to conduct. This suggests a need for a positive obligation to alert those higher up in corporate hierarchy that illegality, or suspected illegality, is being perpetrated.

One lesson to emerge from the Enron debacle was to avoid compromising the independence of the lawyers by restricting their proximity to corporate clients and other professionals. It would be sensible to require independent firms, unconnected with the transactions in question, to perform any gatekeeping functions.

An associated concern is whether the capacity of law and accountancy firms to act as effective gatekeepers would be reduced by multi-disciplinary practice. Steven Crane, President of the New York Bar Association, noted of the Enron debacle that

> [i]f such conflicts exist within the framework of an accounting firm that does not provide legal services to the public, there can no longer be any serious questions that allowing lawyers to practise under the same roof, with their duties of client confidentiality and loyalty, would be a colossal mistake.[137]

Enron may have encouraged caution in the European Court of Justice. It upheld the right of Netherlands, and therefore other European Member States, to prevent lawyers entering into MDPs with accountants, even if this restricts competition. Jonathan Goldsmith, Secretary-General of the Council of the Bars and Law Societies of the European Union, told *The Lawyer* magazine in an interview on this matter:

---

[135] NB Rapoport, 'The Curious Incident of the Law Firm that did Nothing in the Night' (2007) 10 *Legal Ethics* 98.

[136] Gordon (n 125) at 1197.

[137] B Malkin, 'Legal/Accounting Repercussions from Enron International Bar Association' (May 2002) (www.envoynews.com/iba/e_article000072235.cfm).

We're not trying to get glory out of Enron and the poor people affected, but that is exactly what we were warning. The integrity of a service, whether auditing or legal, is undermined if you've got pressure from other professions selling services across yours.[138]

v. *Lehman Brothers Holdings Inc*

a. Context

At the time that Lehman Brothers Holdings Inc (Lehman Bros) filed bankruptcy proceedings in 2008 it was the fourth largest investment bank in the US. The world financial crisis beginning in 2008 was not caused by the collapse of Lehmann Bros, but it was a precipitating event in that process.[139] The bankruptcy caused losses to large numbers of small investors. The global economic crisis continues to cause unemployment and financial hardship around the world. Unsurprisingly, reviews of regulatory systems for financial services precipitated by the crisis have paid particular attention to what went wrong at Lehman Bros. One factor examined was the role and responsibility of professional firms servicing the financial industry.

Lehman Bros was one of a number of companies that held onto a specific kind of property investment, known as sub-prime mortgages. During 2007 and 2008 the value of these investments were shown to be worth considerably less than their book values. Lehman Bros' collapse, precipitated by this fall in its value, began a period of volatility in financial markets. Congress was forced to agree a $700 billion package to stabilise the markets.

In 2010 a court-appointed examiner, Anton R Valukas, published a report showing that Lehman Bros converted assets into cash for periodic financial statements, misleading regulators and investors as to its true position.[140] This accounting treatment was known as Repo 105. Under Repo 105, short-term loans were shown as sales, reducing financial liabilities on Lehman's balance sheet. The accountancy firm Ernst & Young faced financial malpractice charges and its chief executive faced criminal charges for allowing the use of Repo 105.

b. The Role of Lawyers

In order to justify using Repo 105 Lehman Bros had to prove that the transactions shown on its balance sheet were 'sales at law'. In order to do so they needed a 'true sale' opinion letter from a law firm. No American firms would issue such a letter because, under American law, repos were not legally sales. Lehman Bros therefore obtained a true sale opinion form Linklaters, a magic circle firm in the City of London. The letter was addressed to the company's European branch, Lehman Brothers International Europe (LBIE). LBIE was based in New York and used the letter to satisfy the legal requirement.

---

[138] ibid.
[139] L Elliott and J Treanor, 'Five years on from Lehman: 'We had almost no control' *The Guardian* 13 September 2013.
[140] AR Valukas, *Lehman Brothers Holdings Inc Chapter 11 Proceedings Examiner Report* (http://jenner.com/lehman/).

Linklaters' opinion was significant in the accounting treatment. It was required by financial regulators as part of the regulatory process. It had to be available to auditors as evidence for an accounting treatment or security rating. The opinion therefore facilitated Lehman Bros adopting the approach that misled regulators and the capital markets and led to the collapse of Lehman Bros. It is not known whether Linklaters knew the exact purpose for which the opinion was provided or the implications of providing it. Nevertheless, $50 billion of debt was hidden.

c. Legal Liability

The administrators of Lehman Bros predicted payments of 33 cents on the dollar to creditors. In 2010, Mr. Valukas concluded there were credible civil claims against Lehman Bros' chief executive, its former finance chiefs and Ernst & Young. By 2011, however, the SEC doubted that it could prove that the accounting treatment was illegal.[141] Even if blame could be attached to using the controversial treatment, SEC officials were doubtful that Lehman investors could show that they had suffered loss. The SEC's position cast doubt on the possible success of criminal proceedings.

d. Professional Responsibility

Kershaw and Moorhead argue that Lehman Bros' collapse exemplifies situations in which transaction lawyers could be made subject to tighter regulation.[142] Firms in Linklaters' position could not be liable in civil law in the absence of inducement, procuration or 'knowing assistance' in a breach of trust or fiduciary duty. They could however, be constrained by the threat of misconduct charges. A request for a true sale opinion letter, they suggest, should put a corporate law firm on notice of a particular kind of risk. Kershaw and Moorhead argue that, where there is a *real, substantial and foreseeable* risk of client action that is unlawful, or probably unlawful, a finding of misconduct would be justified.

e. Implications for England and Wales

Empirical studies of the lawyer and client relationship suggest that corporate and commercial clients are usually in a position to dictate to lawyers. In a highly competitive market these clients can readily find other lawyers and will do so if they are dissatisfied. This puts lawyers under considerable pressure to satisfy clients. A requirement that lawyers suspicious of their clients' motives should refuse to act would mean that clients simply moved to other lawyers. There would be significant problems for regulators in proceeding against corporate law firms for breach of any such requirements.

It is perhaps because of the difficulty of regulating commercial transactions that the ethical codes of the legal professions in England and Wales do not address the responsibility of transaction lawyers, except in the context of conveyancing. Corporate clients did not appear at all in the index of the vast 1999 edition of the

---

[141] J Eaglesham and L Rappaport, 'Lehman Probe Stalls: Chance of No Charges' *Wall Street Journal* 12 March 2011.

[142] D Kershaw and R Moorhead, 'Consequential Responsibility for Client Wrongs: Lehman Brothers and the Regulation of the Legal Profession' (2013) 76(1) *Modern Law Review* 26.

Guide. They were only obliquely mentioned in the Solicitors' Code of Conduct 2007 in relation to conflicts of interest. The SRA Handbook 2011 does not contain any relevant outcomes. While Enron occurred under previous regulatory regimes, this hypothetical discussion proceeds as if the SRA Handbook 2011 was in force during similar circumstances.

The prospect of an expanded third party liability is not really offered by the SRA Principles. The leading contenders, upholding the rule of law and the proper administration of justice, have very specific meanings, reflected in previous codes and the current Handbook. The sparse notes to the principles suggest that upholding the rule of law and the proper administration of justice encompasses 'obligations not only to clients but also to the courts and third parties with whom you have dealings on your clients behalf'.

There is a positive reference to the broader interest in the notes to the principles. This suggests that 'where two or more come into conflict the one which takes precedence is the one which best serves the public interest in the particular circumstances, especially the public interest in the proper administration of justice.'[143] Of course, before the public interest becomes a factor, two principles must conflict. The lack of specific principles relating to collective third party financial interests means that the note will be largely irrelevant in the contexts under discussion. This means that any obligation to specific and identifiable third parties, or collective ones, is circumscribed.

In the notes accompanying the SRA Principles, acting with integrity is also interpreted narrowly. It is said to refer to 'professional dealings with clients, the court, other lawyers and the public'. This mentions third parties and the public, but not in such a way that suggests specific or wide duties. Regarding 'maintaining the trust the public places in you' the note also suggests a narrow conception, that '[m]embers of the public should be able to place their trust in you'. Nothing in the SRA Handbook, or the previous history of regulation, suggests that solicitors need have collective third parties in contemplation when they act.

Kershaw and Moorhead search for a basis for professional responsibility, in situations like Lehman Bros, lies in what they refer to as 'the core tenets of what it means for law to be a profession', specifically the professional principles of upholding the rule of law and not doing anything that undermines public trust. These, they argue, provide a basis for imposing consequential responsibility on lawyers when their actions facilitate unlawful activity. It is more likely, however, that a new principle would be needed on which to base outcomes related to third party collectives.

Kershaw and Moorhead suggest that Outcomes Focused Regulation provides too much scope to corporate transaction lawyers to ignore risk. Therefore, they argue, the SRA Handbook should include a provision requiring lawyers not to assist a client where that assistance creates a foreseeable likelihood of wrongdoing, defined as breach of criminal or civil law or regulation. This would be something like Simon's suggested rule ('you do not provide any services substantially related to active unlawful client conduct').

In order to achieve the impact that Kershaw and Moorhead intend, it would probably need to be accompanied by an outcome, such as the state Bar rule cited

---

[143] SRA, *Handbook 2011*, as amended, 'Introduction to the SRA Code of Conduct'.

by Gordon. This states that 'a lawyer *shall* reveal such information to the extent the lawyer reasonably believes necessary [to avoid unlawful client conduct]'. Even if this could be used as a basis for sanctions against transaction lawyers, it would probably be used infrequently. Kershaw and Moorhead speculate that, because of the considerable difficulty in taking action, regulators would only proceed in cases of substantial detriment to clients, third parties or the public interest.

A final implication of the Lehman Bros case study derives from the multi-jurisdictional nature of Linklaters' involvement. As discussed, Linklaters provided a 'true sale' opinion letter to Enron's European arm. If, however, they knew that it was for use in the US, they could have been caught by SRA Chapter 13A, 'Practice Overseas'. The main outcome is that 'you must be aware of the local laws and regulations governing your practice in an overseas jurisdiction'.[144] In that case they would be required to disregard an 'outcome to the extent necessary to comply with that local law or regulation'.[145] In that event law firms would be subject to the more explicit US regulation.

vi. Conclusions on Lawyers' Responsibility for Financial Risks Based on Three Case Studies

These case studies demonstrate the fact that financial regulatory authorities are struggling to control financial markets. The problem is controlling risk without unduly restricting financial institutions' freedom of action. Lawyers are not quite as exposed in these situations as accountants, but they are often involved. The more extreme examples are often crimes and punished as such. Lawyer regulation is struggling to deal with the implications of the scale of risk and the likelihood that lawyers will be implicated in financial catastrophe and regulatory recriminations. The specific problem arises where lawyers are not directly guilty of criminal conduct but might have prevented client crimes had they been required to break confidentiality.

There are a number of difficulties with a duty to report. One is the circumstances in which a duty is triggered. If it is a duty to report a suspicion, as with money laundering, it would arguably depend on fine distinctions. Such an obligation would weaken chances that lawyers would be trusted with information in the first place. An alternative is that regulation requires independent lawyers to perform a specific gatekeeping function, such as, in the Lehman Bros example, certifying a true sale. If, however, tighter regulation of specific lawyer gatekeeping functions is required, it should be specified for a particular requirement. It is more difficult to conceive of a generally appropriate regulatory formula.

D. The Environment

Although financial scandals have very serious short- and medium-term consequences, damage to the environment may be irrecoverable. Such risks pose a threat to future

---

[144] ibid, r 13A.5.
[145] ibid, r 13A.6.

generations. The main argument against imposing obligations on lawyers to protect the environment is impracticality. If an overseas government permits logging, for example, even though this may cause environmental damage, the basis for whistle-blowing in unclear. If the regime does not permit it, the English-based law firm is already required not to participate in the illegal activity. The gap in the situation is that the firm is not required to report its client's proposed activity.

Many regard it as shocking that lawyers are not obliged to report clients causing illegal pollution or planning activity that will precipitate ecological problems, such as illegal deforestation overseas. These risks could be mitigated by introducing a positive duty of whistle-blowing for certain public risks. This would, however, raise a familiar collateral issue; it would diminish the potential of the lawyer to offer wise counsel. This argument would be more persuasive if it was known that such counselling is being undertaken effectively. Since such evidence is unlikely to be produced, the duty to offer counsel to avoid harm could be made more explicit.

If a duty to prevent collective third party harms were imposed, it would be important to ensure it did not impinge on litigation privilege. Corporations charged with offences in relation to collective harms are still entitled to effective representation. To avoid conflict of interest, they should not be represented by lawyers implicated in causing the very harm that is the subject of litigation. It would be sensible, therefore, for any future rules to clarify that lawyers involved in precipitating relevant harms should not act in related litigation.

VI. The Future for an Expanded Concept of Responsibility to Collective Third Parties

Gordon blames the Kaye Scholer affair, and the US Bar's response, on the

> uncontrolled expansion of libertarian ideology into lawyers' common consciousness—to the point where lawyers have come to feel genuinely affronted and indignant when any authority tries to articulate a public obligation of lawyers that may end up putting them at odds with clients. Lawyers claim to be 'private agents for private parties' (though at the same time they claim privileges and immunities that ordinary citizens don't have); our loyalties to clients must be absolute and undivided. In this libertarian mood, they tend to characterize the framework of law as some alien other—'the government,' the 'cops' the 'regulators'—an adversary that they are entitled to outwit and frustrate with every trick in the book.[146]

Assuming that Gordon is correct in his assessment of the situation in the US, it is necessary to ask whether the situation is the same in the UK. Critics of the professional regulation of lawyers argue that

---

[146] Gordon, 'A Collective Failure of Nerve' (n 1).

the codes' silence on issues of general justice and the public interest as compared to the detailed regulation of matters such as how solicitors firms should be named, what matters can be referred to in lawyers' publicity, and the ownership and storage of documents, suggest that they are more important than questions of acting justly in regard to specific others, the general public or the environment.[147]

The conduct rules in England and Wales give no permission to break client confidence to avoid 'substantial injury to the financial interests or property of another' as does the ABA Code. Collective third party obligations regarding money laundering have not, as predicted, led to broader professional responsibilities to third parties.[148] If anything, lawyers may guard privilege more jealously. In most circumstances, legal privilege and client confidentiality prevail. Existing duties towards third parties, or representative entities such as 'the public interest' or 'justice', are weak and unenforceable.

The fact that Enron and similar scandals might have been prevented by the lawyers acting for the corporations is not by itself a clear-cut reason for imposing wider responsibilities in the professional codes. Indeed, it is doubtful that this will happen unless there is a very clear reason for impinging on client autonomy. An exception to this general proposition could be made where lawyers are required to perform a specific gatekeeping role, such as signing off on a transaction. Here, it would be possible to impose a requirement of absolute independence from the party seeking a lawyer's authorisation. In such circumstances issues of client confidentiality and privilege would be circumscribed.

Broad obligations to collective third parties present many problems for lawyers within a lawyer and client relationship. Because of this, the specific circumstances in which their duties within the relationship are abrogated should be specified and the requirements made explicit. So, for example, if a high degree of lawyer independence is necessary, it may be required that lawyers performing a gatekeeping role are unconnected with the party seeking clearance. It is likely that any such move would need to be taken by the legislature or courts. Lawyer regulations need only specify that lawyers perform such obligations faithfully, as in the case of money laundering.

VII. Conclusion

Wider duties in lawyers' codes of conduct are frequently rather vague 'catch-all' phrases that often promise more than they deliver. Examples of how principles requiring integrity or promoting public confidence are put into operation tend to be rather

[147] D Nicolson and J Webb, *Professional Legal Ethics: Critical Interrogations* (Oxford, Oxford University Press 1999) at 111.
[148] A Odby, *Lawyers as Gatekeepers': The Impact of Preventative Anti Money-Laundering Obligations on the Legal Profession in England and Wales* (PhD Thesis, University of Westminster, 2006).

restricted or anodyne. They involve complying with binding orders or requests for information from the Legal Services Ombudsman. Statutory inroads into the principle of client confidentiality have not led to increased expectations of responsibility for lawyers representing organisations, including companies. Lawyers may not participate in client frauds but duties to members, shareholders or employees of organisations are often unclear.

Large corporations have greater ability than private individuals to harm people, society and the environment. Often, they cannot achieve their occasionally dubious aims without assistance from lawyers. Lawyers can design schemes so as to make corporate activities appear legal or to conceal their illegality from the authorities. One of the most striking lessons to emerge from the corporate scandals in the US is the failure of the professional regulatory bodies to take disciplinary proceedings against lawyers. If legal professions take this attitude to breaches of their own codes, it is to be expected that the state will resort increasingly to legislative controls.

15

Service

'It is demonstrably true that today the sharpest critics of the legal profession and the administration of justice are judges, lawyers, and teachers of law. It is historically true that the great legal reforms of the twentieth century have been devised, fought for, and established by lawyers. Often they have been opposed by too many members of the profession; often they have won the day only by securing public support; but the fact remains that the constructive leadership came from within the profession itself'.[1]

'It is pretty hard to find a group less concerned with serving society and more concerned with serving themselves than the lawyers'.[2]

I. Introduction

The link between professionalism and the idea of service is well established in the literature.[3] A commitment to service is seen as a key virtue for lawyers.[4] Kronman argued that the deployment of skill without concern for the public interest makes a person a legal technician, not a good lawyer.[5] Others have argued for a conception of professional responsibility that includes serving the public good.[6] Yet others propose very specific manifestations of service, such as *pro bono publico*, or the provision of free legal services.[7] There is, therefore, no consensus on what constitutes service.

Since the introduction of the welfare state the profession in England and Wales has adopted a commitment to public service. This is somewhat consistent with a concep-

---

[1] R Pound, *The Lawyer from Antiquity to Modern Times: With Particular Reference to The Development of Bar Associations in the United States* (St Paul, MN, West Publishing, 1953) at X.

[2] F Rodell, 'Goodbye to Law Reviews' (1936) 23 *Virginia Law Review* 38, at 42.

[3] R Abel, *The Legal Profession in England and Wales* (Oxford, Blackwell, 1988) at 27.

[4] A Flores, 'What Kind Of Person Should A Professional Be' in A Flores (ed), *Professional Ideals* (Belmont, CA, Wadsworth, 1988) at 1.

[5] AT Kronman, 'Living in the Law' in D Luban (ed), *The Ethics of Lawyers* (Aldershot, Dartmouth Publishing Co, 1994) at 835.

[6] HT Edwards, 'A Lawyers' Duty to Serve the Public Good' (1990) 65 *New York University Law Review* 1148.

[7] N Strosen, 'Pro Bono Legal Work: For the Good of Not Only the Public but also the Lawyer and the Legal Profession' (1992–93) 91 *Michigan Law Review* 2122.

tion of service as eschewing self-interest, particularly making money, as the raison d'être of professional practice. Recently, providing services free of charge, or *pro bono publico*, to those who cannot afford to pay has achieved a high profile as the expression of service. This has been promoted by the profession and government alike as the new face of public service. This can be seen as a cost of continuing monopoly, making demonstrable forms of service a new overhead of professional practice.

Professional rules of conduct rarely formalise or state positively such service obligations. For example, there has never been a rule requiring provision of legal services *pro bono publico* in the codes of legal professions in England and Wales. The American Bar Association's Model Rules has, however, included an aspirational rule. This illustrates the fact that some professional norms are contested and may be difficult to specify or enforce. The fact is that considerable growth in the provision of voluntary legal services has been achieved despite this. This may be an example of the impact of culture, in this case a rediscovered and re-imagined tradition, on professional behaviour.

II. Different Conceptions of Public Service

A. Public Service

Altruism is the unselfish concern with the welfare of others. During the industrial revolution, particularly during the period between 1840 and 1880, the Victorians laid the foundations of civically minded democracy.[8] In the public schools, the likes of Thomas and Matthew Arnold urged on privileged young men the moral duty of working for the good of others. They were offered a life of serious dedication to a calling, personal generosity, self-sacrifice, characterised as public service. The idea of lawyering as an act of public service was captured by Roscoe Pound's definition of a profession as 'a group of men pursuing a learned art as a common calling in the spirit of public service—no less a public service because it may incidentally be a means of livelihood'.[9]

Implicit in Pound's notion of public service is the idea of a higher motivation than profit. Professions were a public benefit because their cultural rejection of selfishness was service. What Pound actually meant by public service was more difficult to pin down. He saw the very act of maintaining a profession, and thereby the integrity of lawyers, the legal process and the rule of law, as a public service. He observed that, whenever lawyers had been discouraged or had been weakly organised, from ancient Rome to the American frontier, abuse was rife and the public interest suffered.[10]

---

[8] S Heffer, *High Minds: The Victorians and the Birth of Modern Britain* (London, Random House, 2013).
[9] Pound, *The Lawyer from Antiquity to Modern Times* (n 1) at 5.
[10] ibid, at XXV and 40.

Pound cited three concrete examples of ways in which bar associations in the United States prioritised the public good over self-interest. First, unlike businessmen, they were not competitive with each other. Pound said that, if a lawyer discovered something 'useful to the profession and so to the administration of justice through research or experience he publishes it in legal periodicals... It is not his property'.[11] Secondly, professionals, unlike other employees, did not go on strike. Therefore, in a very clear way, they put their public obligations before their personal self-interest. Thirdly, professionals acted collegially with each other, advancing the science of jurisprudence, promoting the administration of justice, upholding the honour of the profession of law and establishing cordial relations among the members of the Bar.[12]

The notion of public service emerging in Victorian society appeared to be particularly influential on the emerging solicitors' profession. The gentlemanly veneer, aspirations to collegiality and mounting of public lectures on legal innovations, fitted well with the idea of professional work as public service.

B. Social Service

In the twentieth century, public service became more closely identified with government financing of services essential to the public. The idea of 'a public service' covered water, power and waste removal, but also health care, education and law enforcement. The advent of the welfare state after the Second World War added medicine and legal advice and assistance to the list of public services the state aspired to provide. Combined with changes in the legal services market, competitiveness between firms and threats of strike action by legal aid lawyers, legal aid threatened Pound's genteel conception of public service.

As law itself became a public service, there may have been a subtle shift in the ethos of the profession, away from wider notions of public service towards an ethic of dedicated service to individual clients.[13] The 'spirit of public service' may even have led to creation of a 'social service ethos' in those parts of the legal profession closely involved with legal aid.[14] This may even have begun to tie the idea of public service to the performance of legal aid work. It was certainly consistent with the idea that the profit motive was not the dominant reason for professional work. Legal aid rates were said to be set at 10 per cent below the market rate for the job.

It may be no coincidence that the exposure of lawyers to ordinary people since the Second World War, and the changing terms of engagement, apparently led to a fall in public esteem. A survey of respondents in three London boroughs in 1967–68 revealed a broadly positive perception of lawyers, with many thinking that they

---

[11] ibid, at 6 and 10.
[12] ibid, at 14.
[13] G Mungham and PA Thomas, 'Solicitors and Clients: Altruism or Self Interest?' in R Dingwall and P Lewis (eds), *The Sociology of the Professions: Lawyers, Doctors and Others* (Basingstoke, Macmillan Press, 1983).
[14] G Hanlon, *Lawyers, the State and the Market: Professionalism Revisited* (Basingstoke, Palgrave Macmillan, 1999).

charged fair prices, were honest, and gave both rich and poor equal attention.[15] These positive perceptions were contradicted by respondents also thinking that lawyers would do anything to help their clients and often overcharged.

Negative perceptions grew in the succeeding decades, when public service claims were increasingly queried. This may have been due to a variety of factors, from the world-wide growth of consumerism, better information or increased contact with professions by ordinary people. In the US, the President, and Chief Justice, even rebuked the profession for its low public standing, which opinion polls suggested was due to its 'greedy and self-serving' image.[16] By 1987 the Law Society's own research showed that, compared with similar occupations, solicitors were only perceived as less dishonest and avaricious than estate agents.[17]

C. Statutory Definition

The definition of service became somewhat more concrete when government tried to restrict the use to which practising certificate fees could be put.[18] The Solicitors Act 1974, section 11(3) originally stated that '[a]ll fees received by the Society under subsection (1) shall be applied in such manner as the Society may think fit for the purposes of the Society'. The Access to Justice Act 1999, section 46 restricted the purposes for which the income from practising certificates could be used to regulation, education and training.[19] These purposes were further defined by statutory instrument before reaching their current form in the Legal Services Act 2007 (LSA 2007).[20] The LSA provides that the Legal Services Board must ensure that any rules covering the use of money raised by practicing fees include regulation, including education and training, and the following purposes:

(c)   the participation by the approved regulator in law reform and the legislative process;
(d)   the provision by relevant authorised persons, and those wishing to become relevant authorised persons, of reserved legal services, immigration advice or immigration services to the public free of charge;
(e)   the promotion of the protection by law of human rights and fundamental freedoms;
(f)   the promotion of relations between the approved regulator and relevant national or international bodies, governments or the legal professions of other jurisdictions.[21]

The permission to use practicing fee income for the provision of free reserved services, and immigration advice, reflects persistent attempts by government to develop pro bono as part of a strategy for providing access to justice.

---

[15]   B Abel-Smith, M Zander and RB Ross, *Legal Problems and the Citizen: A Study in Three London Boroughs* (London, Heinemann Educational, 1973) at 249.
[16]   HC Petrowitz, 'Some Thoughts About Current Problems in Legal Ethics and Professional Responsibility' (1979) 6 *Duke Law Journal* 1275.
[17]   J Jenkins, E Skordaki and CF Willis, *Public Use and Perception of Solicitors' Services* (London, The Law Society, 1989) at 10.
[18]   See further ch 5: 'Governance'.
[19]   The Access to Justice Act 1999, s 46(2)(b), as extended under s 46(3)(a).
[20]   See, for example, The Access to Justice Act 1999 (Bar Practising Certificates) Order 2001 (2001 No 135 LSA 2007, ss 51(2) and (3).
[21]   LSA, 2007 s 51(4).

III. A Theory of Pro Bono

The English system is founded on a notion of the rule of law based on formal legality. This assumes that there is access to justice and that people are able to enforce legal rights. Some may propose that, in a society in which some people cannot afford lawyers, the performance of free work to assist potential litigants is both an obligation for lawyers and a mark of the highest professionalism. This is a contestable notion, however, particularly after the state assumed responsibility for access to justice as part of the welfare state.

An alternative theory of *pro bono publico* is that it is a manifestation of the transition of notions of public service from the kind of professional restraint advocated by Pound, to a more consumerist notion of service. This casts privileged sections of society in the role of collaborators in the provision of public goods. The professional role of lawyers hinges on providing society with the good of justice. Lawyers, as a privileged class, contribute the good that they command.

IV. History of the Provision of Free Legal Services until 1990

A. Origin of Free Legal Services

The origins of the *pro bono publico* tradition are obscure. Pound suggests it may have developed from bans on legal representatives accepting fees in ancient Rome and dark-age Europe. He notes that, as late as the Middle Ages, payment was in the form of a gift.[22] It may have been connected with the fact that both the medical and legal professions assumed responsibility for their areas of expertise from the clergy and, with them, charitable responsibility for the poor and the dispossessed.[23] There are also suggestions, perhaps more plausible, that the impetus for pro bono services came from the courts rather than lawyers.

There is evidence that, by 1300, justices on the Eyre circuits were assigning serjeants to act gratuitously. A Shropshire litigant in 1292 asked the court for the grant of a serjeant 'so that his right is not lost'.[24] This links *pro bono publico* to the right to

---

[22] Pound (n 1) at 52, 55 and 68.
[23] JA Brundage, 'Legal Aid for the Poor and the Professionalisation of Law in the Middle Ages' (1988) 9 *Journal of Legal History* 169.
[24] P Brand, *The Origins of the English Legal Profession* (Oxford, Blackwell Publishers, 1992) at 104.

sue *in forma pauperis* and court assignment of lawyers to act for litigants without a fee. A right to sue *in forma pauperis* was established by statute in 1495 but probably has earlier origins.[25] A modern survival of this kind of practice is the dock brief in criminal trials, whereby the judge asks an advocate to appear for an unrepresented defendant.[26]

The court's motive for requiring lawyers to act *pro bono publico* was not necessarily charitable, since corralling lawyers to act for litigants in person helps matters progress more swiftly and efficiently. Such practices would explain the fact that the literal translation of *pro bono publico* is 'for the good of the state', rather than 'for the good of the public' or community, as is often assumed today.[27]

There was no serious consideration of the accessibility of legal services as an issue of policy before the twentieth century. In the sixteenth and seventeenth centuries litigation among all classes was more widespread than at any time until the 1970s. It has been estimated that over 75 per cent of litigants at that time were 'non-gentlemen'.[28] Subsequently, judicial discouragement of free representation,[29] and professional disdain for 'low grade' work, caused a decline of *pro bono publico*. In civil cases, the ancient laws against maintenance, supporting litigation in which one had no legitimate interest, and champerty, sharing damages, discouraged lawyers supporting impoverished litigants.

There was a change of attitude to free work for the poor in the later-Victorian era, when the professional middle class adopted the *noblesse oblige* traditions of the aristocracy. This was manifest as an ethic of disinterested service and continuing desire to gain distance from work seen as 'money grubbing'.[30] By the beginning of the twentieth century, a confused and contradictory case law had evolved to the point where lawyers were reasonably safe acting without expecting payment, provided the proceedings were not frivolous and vexatious.[31] The volume of free work conducted by the legal profession at this time is not known, but was probably low.

B. The Poor Persons' Procedure

Attempts to introduce limited legal aid in the early-twentieth century were undermined by the professional bodies' concern to stamp out 'a black market in legal aid' conducted on a 'commission' basis.[32] This was effectively a campaign against

---

[25] JM Maguire, 'Poverty and Civil Litigation' (1923) 36 *Harvard Law Review* 361.

[26] WR Prest, *The Rise of the Barristers: A Social History of the Bar 1590–1640* (Oxford, Clarendon Press, 1986) at 22.

[27] JW Bellacosa, 'Obligatory *Pro Bono* Legal Services: Mandatory or Voluntary? Distinction without a Difference' (1991) 19 *Hofstra Law Review* 744.

[28] M Burrage, 'From a Gentleman's to a Public Profession' (1996) *International Journal of the Legal Profession* 45, at 47.

[29] T Goriely, 'Law for the Poor: The Relationship Between Advice Agencies and Solicitors in the Development of Poverty Law' (1996) 3(1/2) *International Journal of the Legal Profession* 215, at 217.

[30] H Perkin, *The Rise of Professional Society: England since 1880* (London, Routledge, 1989).

[31] J Levin, 'Solicitors Acting Speculatively and Pro Bono' (1996) 15 *Civil Justice Quarterly* 44.

[32] B Abel-Smith and R Stevens, 'Legal Services for the Poor' in *Lawyers and the Courts: A Sociological Study of the English Legal System 1750-1965* (London, Heinemann, 1967) at 135–64, 146 and 158.

contingency-based charging and speculative work by solicitors. By 1914 working class demands for the right to divorce led to the introduction of the Poor Persons' Procedure, whereby solicitors and barristers provided their services free.[33] The demand for assistance led to the establishment of a large office, but, because in some cases solicitors charged expenses, a committee was established to consider the procedure.

In 1919, the Lawrence Committee decided to drive out the profiteers and to make the procedure more inaccessible,[34] but demand continued to exceed the supply of services. The Law Society feared that anything less than a free service might result in officials being appointed to handle cases. A second Lawrence report reaffirmed the principle of free legal service. In fact, it suggested that there was a moral obligation, in return for the monopoly in the practice of law, to offer legal services to those who could not afford to pay, provided this did not place an unnecessary burden on practitioners.[35] It recommended that the Law Society administer the Poor Persons' Procedure, which it did from 1926.

Between the World Wars, a gap opened up between the professional elite in the Law Society and practitioners conducting the Poor Persons' Procedure. Elite solicitors held a conception of public service that eschewed profit and recognised a social obligation to those less fortunate, while many regional solicitors demanded that the scheme be formalised and that payment be made for their work. Meanwhile, the Bar had a relaxed attitude towards the Poor Persons' Procedure, bordering on indifference. The reason for the Bar's attitude was possibly because the scheme had marketing potential for independent advocates building a clientele.

Instructions under the Poor Persons' Scheme enabled barristers to advertise their services to solicitors and potential lay clients attending court. The Bar had objected to the presentation of divorce petitions in the County Courts because they wanted to preserve barristers' exclusive advocacy rights under the Poor Persons' Procedure. It also objected to poor persons' cases being concentrated on specific days, apparently because the barristers would not then have a wider audience.[36]

While the Bar favoured the Poor Persons' Procedure continuing to be free, solicitors' resistance, and demands for payment, particularly in Wales, laid the ground for the Rushcliffe Committee in 1945. This recommended the creation of a legal aid scheme.[37] The Law Society was aware that managing legal aid would reduce its independence from the state. In the period after the Second World War in which the welfare state was built, the Law Society resisted the establishment of state-employed, salaried lawyers. It decided to accept responsibility for the Legal Aid Scheme out of fear that something worse might be imposed.[38]

---

[33] T Goriely, 'Gratuitous Assistance to the "Ill-dressed": Debating Civil Legal Aid in England and Wales from 1924 to 1939' (2006) 13 *International Journal of the Legal Profession* 41.

[34] T Goriely, 'Civil Legal Aid in England and Wales 1914 to 1961: the Emergence of a Paid Scheme' (PhD thesis, University College London, 2003).

[35] Goriely, 'Gratuitous Assistance to the "Ill-dressed"' (n 33); AA Paterson 'Professionalism and the Legal Services Market' (1996) 1(2) *International Journal of the Legal Profession* 137, at 160.

[36] Goriely, 'Civil Legal Aid in England and Wales' (n 34).

[37] ibid.

[38] Goriely, 'Law for the Poor (n 29) at 224.

C. The Growth of the Advice Sector

The Legal Aid Scheme, as the Law Society feared, changed the legal profession's relationship with, and attitude to, low paying work. Accepting responsibility for 'poor persons' law', and doing it for profit, challenged the established ethos of doing what was seen as 'honourable' work. It also put the profession in potential conflict with the voluntary advice sector.

The Law Society was adamant that legal aid should not support advice bureaux, and the London centres only survived with support from the London County Council.[39] This ambivalence was reflected in restrictions imposed on solicitors working as volunteers for advice centres. The rationale for this restriction was that doing free work amounted to advertising and the unfair attraction of business.[40]

By the 1960s various gaps in legal aid provision were partly filled by advice agencies and Law Centres. This was particularly the case in employment and other tribunals that did not award lawyers' costs. The 'sympathetic lay advice' became more specialised and expert.[41] Then, as now, advice agencies tended to provide high level advice to low income groups on social security, housing, family and consumer law. These areas all potentially competed with local solicitors.

Solicitors' anxiety about competition with the advice sector was allayed when they saw that it provided points of access and screened out weak or unprofitable cases.[42] Solicitors often worked without payment in advice centres in evening sessions. This may have been partly because it was a good way of identifying cases suitable for them to handle with assistance from legal aid. By 1977 an agreement had been reached that, provided they did not encroach on areas such as personal injury and crime, the Law Society would grant waivers to solicitors working in Law Centres from certain practice rules.

A 1986 survey by the Advice Services Alliance recorded that, nation-wide, there were 896 Citizens' Advice Bureaux service points, 354 generalist, independent advice services, 142 generalist advice agencies serving specific groups, for example, young people, 55 independent housing advice service points, 25 money advice service points and 14 immigration advice service points.[43] Advice agencies had become important players in delivering local legal provision.[44] In 1988, the Marre Report, referring to the spread of advice agencies, acknowledged that '[i]t is no longer possible to consider only the two branches of the legal profession when considering the supply of legal services'.[45] The success of the advice sector had an apparent impact on the distribution of civil legal aid. Green form bills for areas of 'social welfare' law for 1975–76

---

[39] Goriely (n 34).

[40] M Zander, *Lawyers and the Public Interest: A Study of Restrictive Practices* (London, Weidenfeld and Nicolson, 1968) at 238.

[41] Goriely (n 34) at 220–21.

[42] ibid, at 233–37.

[43] *The Recruitment Crisis* (London, The Training Committee of the Law Society, 1988) at 17.

[44] Abel-Smith, Zander and Brooke, *Legal Problems and the Citizen* (n 15) at 217.

[45] Lady Marre CBE, *A Time for Change: Report of the Committee on the Future of the Legal Profession* (London, General Council of the Bar and Council of the Law Society, 1988) at para 5.28.

were £27,000 or 11 per cent of the total. By 1994–95 this had risen to £468,000, or 30 per cent of the total.

D. The Decline of Legal Aid since the 1990s

From the late-1980s, government tried to reduce the legal aid budget by raising the eligibility threshold.[46] A working party chaired by Lord Justice Otton in 1995 noted that, in March 1995 alone, there were 4258 litigants in person in actions in the High Court, an increase from one in ten to one in three since 1989/90.[47] They absorbed disproportionate court time and were less successful than represented parties. This was both a considerable burden on the courts and evidence of a decline in access to justice, which was becoming a political issue. The Law Society now represented a profession swollen in numbers supported by legal aid revenues. Espousing access to law as a right, it launched a campaign against legal aid cuts.

The government, criticised from all sides, actively considered ways of addressing the problem. The Thatcher Government's strategy had been to force reforms that might reduce the legal profession's market control. The Labour Government opted for encouraging the advice sector to compete with lawyers, building upon what had become recognised as superior expertise in many areas of welfare law.

By the 1980s, advice agencies of various kinds offered sophisticated and, in areas such as welfare benefits, highly specialist legal advice. Their legal surgeries often ran free sessions staffed by local solicitors, barristers and students. The sector was thriving. It was no surprise when advice agencies became a cornerstone of the government's plan for a Community Legal Service or were invited to bid for legal aid franchises. This policy was accompanied by a political campaign against lawyers, criticising them for encouraging litigation, for charging high fees and for not doing enough free work.

From the 1990s the scope of legal aid declined dramatically. This began with reduced eligibility and continued with removal of categories of case from legal aid altogether. The process may be complete with the Legal Aid, Sentencing and Punishment of Offenders Act 2012 (LASPO 2012), which came into force from April 2013. This aims to cut £350 million per annum form the £2 billion legal aid budget. For these reasons the Bill was highly controversial. It was defeated 14 times in the House of Lords, and ultimately passed only after a tied vote.

The Act imposes further limits on case type, eligibility and the kind of intervention available. Legal aid is no longer automatically available for divorce and child custody disputes, personal injury and some clinical negligence cases, employment and education law, immigration cases where the person is not detained, some debt, housing and benefit issues.[48] Family matters may be funded where abuse is involved. Some categories of case may be suitable for lawyer-funded fee agreements but, overall, the changes are expected to exacerbate significantly levels of unmet legal need. A spokesman for

---

[46] J Plotnikoff and R Woolfson, *Report of Study into Reasons for Refusal of Offers of Legal Aid* (London, Legal Aid Board, 1996).

[47] *The Times* 7 July 1995; J Ames, 'Rescuing DIY Litigants' *Law Society Gazette* 26 July 1995.

[48] LASPO 2012, sch 1.

the Ministry of Justice said that '[l]egal aid will continue to be provided to those who most need it, such as where domestic violence is involved, where life or liberty is at stake or people risk losing their home'.[49]

V. Development of Free Legal Services and Infrastructure since 1990

A. Pressure on the Legal Profession to do more Free Work

It was probably during the 1990s that the term 'pro bono' became more familiar, probably following usage in US television shows. In the early 1990s the legal profession's performance of pro bono work became a political issue within professional bodies and, briefly, for governments. The underlying reasons for this are considered below while the policy and its impact are considered here.

While in opposition the Labour Party legal affairs spokesman, Paul Boateng, had threatened wealthy law firms with a framework for them to make a contribution to 'the traditional duty and responsibility of lawyers as a profession to the proper and equitable administration of justice'. This was widely taken to mean that pro bono work would be made a condition of practice. By late 1994, however, Boateng was proposing a levy on the 'private legal profession to supplement public resources'.[50] Whilst opposing this, the Law Society established a Pro Bono Working Party, which also reported in 1994.[51]

B. The Law Society's Pro Bono Working Party

The Law Society's Pro Bono Working Party recommended that solicitors should not be subject to a mandatory professional obligation to provide free legal services. It stressed the point that the profession should not ameliorate or redress, by the provision of free services, the growing legal need created by declining legal aid budgets. It did, however, make six proposals for stimulating the involvement of solicitors in pro bono activity, including publishing a policy statement encouraging solicitors, creating

---

[49] BBC News UK, 'Legal Aid Changes' 20 March 2013 (www.bbc.co.uk/news/uk-21668005).
[50] 'Labour Suggests Levy to Support Legal Assistance' *The Lawyer* 27 September 1994, at 3; 'Labour Eyes US *Pro Bono* Model' *The Lawyer* 8 November 1994, at 2, 'Labour Creates Future Vision' *Law Society Gazette* 22 February 1995, at 68.
[51] Report of the Law Society's *Pro Bono* Working Party (1994) *The Times* 9 October 1995.

a free representation advice agency and establishing a trust fund to receive voluntary funds to support pro bono activities.[52]

In 1995, in a speech to the London Solicitors' Litigation Association, Boateng took a more conciliatory line. He suggested a mutual responsibility for access to justice, promising that Labour would invest in the 'legal infrastructure' if lawyers tackled the 'Spanish practices and customs', by which he meant abuses, that contributed to the £1.6 billion legal aid bill. The President of the Law Society criticised the policy of urging pro bono work on lawyers, suggesting that 25 per cent of small firms earned less than £10,000 a year.[53]

The pro bono issue did not subsequently gain much more traction within the Law Society. By the end of 1996, progress was reported on only one of the working party's six proposals, concerning representation at tribunals. One suggestion of the Law Society's Working Party, abandoning the term *pro bono publico* in favour of the potentially ambiguous 'voluntary legal services', was adopted, apparently because it provided scope to claim that solicitors were doing more free work.

Boateng wrote to the new President of the Law Society, Tony Girling, threatening 'alternatives of a statutory nature, if necessary'. This move might have been inspired by the example of the American Bar Association's projects in Chicago. These provided resources from private practice for specific projects, a model that had been copied in 600 locations in the USA.[54] Anticipating proposals for a levy on law firms to support pro bono in Labour's consultation paper *Justice Indeed*, Boateng wrote to the Law Society and the Bar Council offering collaboration on a 'public-private partnership'.[55]

By December 1996, the Labour Party appears to have revisited the idea of legislation to force solicitors to do more pro bono work.[56] Meanwhile, the failure to create an access to justice partnership with lawyers put the Labour Government into a combative mode. During the passage of the Woolf Reforms and the Access to Justice Bill in 1998 the Lord Chancellor, Lord Irvine, cited the profession's failings on pro bono in support of his proposals for franchising and block contracting of legal aid to advice bureaux and the proposed Community Legal Service.

C. The Solicitors' Pro Bono Group

Solicitors and others disappointed with progress on the Law Society's Pro Bono Working Party Report attended an open meeting at the Law Society in 1996. The meeting was convened by Lord Philips of Sudbury, a solicitor in a leading charities firm and a life peer, and Caroline Knighton, head of Business in the Community Professional Firms Group. The meeting resulted in the formation of the Solicitors' Pro Bono Group (SPBG), which was initially led by some of the large London firms.

---

[52] R Abbey and A Boon, 'The Provision of Free Legal Services by Solicitors: A Review of the Report of the Law Society's Pro Bono Working Party' (1995) 2 *International Journal of the Legal Profession* 261.
[53] 'Hard Labour?' *The Times* 7 November 1995, at 35.
[54] '*Pro bono* Wrangle' *Law Society Gazette* 13 December 1996, at 6.
[55] ibid.
[56] 'Boateng in Threat to Impose *Pro bono* Rules' *The Lawyer* 10 December 1996, at 1.

The aim of the SPBG was to promote pro bono work among solicitors generally,[57] while building relations with Citizens' Advice Bureaux and Law Centres and establishing a nationwide referral system.[58] It did not aspire to deliver services directly. The initial target was to increase membership of the large City firms, a number of which paid the start-up costs. By 2000 the SPBG had a full-time organiser and 130 firms and other members, including 40 per cent of the top 50 law firms.[59]

The focus on large firms was understandable because of their high levels of organisation and resources.[60] Their positive response probably reflected a concern among elite lawyers with the image and status of solicitors at the time. This was a time of contested elections for President of the Law Society, with many members feeling that a more 'trade union' focus was required. Although the SPBG's publicity materials emphasised the advantages, mainly 'business' advantages, of participation, it is clear that large firms had varying degrees of engagement with *pro bono publico*.

In 1994 a small number of firms had appointed in-house pro bono co-ordinators and begun vying for recognition as leaders in the field. This number mushroomed following creation of the SPBG, which undoubtedly increased the profile and efforts of large firms. LawWorks, adopted as its operating name, formed a partnership with the Law Centres Federation to match lawyers with advice centres.

By 2000 the atmosphere had changed in relation to solicitors' pro bono. In 2001, the SPBG reported recruiting 500 volunteers to LawWorks, mainly from large firms.[61] By 2006 it had set up 55 free clinics in Citizens' Advice Bureaux and local council buildings. It helped 26,000 clients a year in new areas, like bankruptcy, that were not supported by legal aid.[62] A new scheme, LawWorks for Community, aimed to match up senior solicitors and in-house lawyers with community groups needing commercial advice.

By 2001, 13 of the top 20 firms had pro bono co-ordinators, and many claimed to be performing thousands of hours of free work. For example, Alan and Overy claimed 12,232 hours of pro bono hours per annum and Clifford Chance 18,000 hours.[63] A survey of a thousand lawyers found 70 per cent claiming pro bono work and 38 per cent of firms having an organised programme. Firms with over 100 partners were least likely to be organised, although lawyers from these firms often contributed.[64]

In 2001, the SPBG won a £700,000 award from government to allow corporate lawyers to offer free advice by email. David Lock of the Lord Chancellor's Department said that, although it was no substitute for publicly funded assistance, pro bono work would complement the work of the Community Legal Service.[65] The SPBG also won a £350,000 grant from government to establish a website through which lawyers could

---

[57] 'Solicitors vote for boost to *Pro Bono*' *The Lawyer* 12 November 1996, at 1.

[58] The Solicitors *Pro bono* Group brochure (undated).

[59] M Swallow, 'Who is Behind *Pro bono*?' *The Lawyer* 27 September 1999.

[60] RA Katzmann (ed), 'Themes in Context' in *The Law Firm And The Public Good* (Washington, The Brookings Institute, 1995).

[61] L Hickman, 'Pro plus' 98(28) *Law Society Gazette* 12 July 2001.

[62] C Dyer, 'Win or lose, no fee: pro bono week promotes free legal services' *The Guardian* 5 June 2006, at 14.

[63] Hickman, 'Pro plus' (n 61).

[64] ibid.

[65] *Law Society Gazette* 18 January 2001.

answer questions raised by CABx and similar organisations.[66] It sponsored projects training corporate lawyers to deal with welfare type areas, providing non-litigation advice to small charities and encouraging pro bono by law students.[67] Expanding its reach beyond London, with projects in Leeds and the Midlands,[68] the College of Law promised to provide clinics at its branches in collaborations with regional firms.[69]

By 2013 LawWorks had a number of delivery modes, offering case brokerage, email advice and the network of free legal advice clinics. In 2013, 2,883 enquiries were made to LawWorks, in person, by telephone or email, an increase of 56 per cent on the previous year.[70] Telephone enquiries nearly doubled as legal aid cuts brought about by LASPO 2012 came into effect and funding cuts on advice agencies and Law Centres bit.

D. Law Student Pro Bono

Law students have been involved in live casework since at least the late-1970s, at Citizens' Advice Bureaux and Student Law Clinics.[71] At the time, their involvement was intended to enrich legal study and make it more relevant. Only a handful of law schools were involved.[72] The numbers of students working in live clinics burgeoned in the 1990s. By this time, involvement was more likely to be called student pro bono clinic.[73] In 2011 a LawWorks survey found that more than 65 per cent of all law schools in England and Wales had some form of pro bono activity. This represented an increase of over 40 per cent since similar research was conducted in 2006.[74] This percentage may, however, give a misleading impression of participation. Because of the cost of supervision, only a small number of students at each institution are likely to perform any pro bono work.

E. The Law Society's Engagement with Pro Bono

While the growth of the SPBG proved to be important for the development of solicitors' pro bono, there was a relatively slight impact on the professional body. It was not

---

[66] Hickman 'Pro plus' (n 61).

[67] S Bucknall, 'Pro bono—meeting the challenge' *New Law Journal* 16 March 2001, at 389; A Cox 'Something for Nothing' *Legal Week* 18 October 2001.

[68] N Rovnick, 'SPBG Midlands launch sparks pro bono fever' *The Lawyer* 5 November 2001; N Rovnick, 'Solicitors' pro Bono Group goes for national coverage with Leeds project' *The Lawyer* 28 January 2002, at 6.

[69] Rovnick, 'SPBG Midlands launch sparks pro bono fever' (n 68); 'Wragges and College of Law team up' *The Lawyer* 16 July 2001.

[70] J Robins (ed), *The Pro Bono Yearbook of England and Wales* (London, ProBonoUK.net, 2013).

[71] A Boon, M Jeeves and J Macfarlane, 'Clinical Anatomy: A Definition for Clinical Legal Education' (1987) 21 *The Law Teacher* 61.

[72] A Boon and M Jeeves, 'The Common Law in Action Simulation: Reversing the Burden of Proof in Skills Education' in 'What Are We Learning About Legal Education?' (1990) 24(1) *The Law Teacher* 82.

[73] S Browne, 'A Survey of Pro Bono Activity by Students in Law Schools in England and Wales' (2001) 35 *The Law Teacher* 33.

[74] http://www.lawworks.org.uk/index.php?cID=10&cType=news.

until September 1998 that the Law Society Council adopted a weak, almost grudging, motion, instigated by the SPBG, that:

> Recognises the value of solicitors providing voluntary services, and emphasises the valuable contribution which they already make to the community by providing their professional services and skills to support community and charitable projects;

> Welcomes the successful launch of the Solicitors' *Pro bono* Group and declares its support for the Group and the work which it does

> Encourages solicitors and firms to become members of the Solicitors' *Pro bono* Group and to work together and with the Solicitors' *Pro bono* Group towards greater co-ordination of *pro bono* effort; and

> Recognises clearly that voluntary legal services work is not and never can be a substitute for a properly funded legal aid scheme.[75]

Surprisingly, this period marked a high water mark of the Law Society's efforts. In 1998, the Law Society supported the creation of the Young Solicitors' Group Annual Pro Bono Awards.[76] The following year, Kamlesh Bahl, the Vice President of the Law Society, suggested the adoption of an aspirational pro bono target, possibly to be calculated as a number of hours of pro bono work per solicitor or a target calculated as a percentage of gross fees.[77] It was proposed to allow Continuing Professional Development points for pro bono work and the allocation of the whole of the Law Society's challenge fund (£50,000) to develop local pro bono projects. The Law Society trust also made a contribution of £90,000, spread over two years, to the SPBG.[78] Towards the end of 2004 the Law Society refused to support the SPBG further. This began a desperate search for support of the SPBG's operating costs.

Generally, the Law Society's ambivalence towards pro bono reflected its awareness that many members were suffering an often disastrous decline in legal aid income. This was a theme of the Law Society Working Party Report. It stated that any obligation to provide voluntary legal services to the poor had been reduced by the impact on 'high street' firms of declining income from legal aid and conveyancing. It argued that legal aid firms made a significant contribution *pro bono publico* because legal aid rates were less than the private rate for work. It was claimed 'the legal aid factor is largely responsible for the fact that there is no national pro bono scheme, even though 75 per cent of firms do pro bono work'.[79]

Some opinion in the Law Society doubted whether it should support the idea of solicitors providing free legal services at all. This attitude changed over time, particularly following the formation of the Attorney General's Pro Bono Co-ordinating Committee in 2002. Latterly, its public pronouncements have been less ambivalent and it has supported solicitor pro bono organisations, like LawWorks, financially. This included a recent, three-year project to increase student involvement in pro bono.[80]

---

[75] The Law Society Council Minutes (24 September 1998).
[76] J Ames, 'Do the Right Thing' *Law Society Gazette* 27 July 2000.
[77] *Law Society Gazette* 6 November 1999.
[78] *Law Society Gazette* 20 January 1999, at 4.
[79] A Bradbury, 'Solicitors Rally for UK *Pro Bono* Scheme' *The Lawyer* 15 October 1996, at 1.
[80] Robins, *The Pro Bono Yearbook of England and Wales* (n 70).

In 2011 it was reported that that the Law Society was establishing a pro bono committee.[81] It was promised that this would make recommendations for a more 'developed policy' on pro bono. A statement by the Law Society acknowledged that its policy, that pro bono is an adjunct to, rather than substitute for, legal aid was 'being challenged'. It anticipated 'increased demand for pro bono services in the face of severely diminished legal aid provision and local authority cuts that will hit the third sector'. The Law Society's paper linked *pro bono publico* with the government's Big Society agenda. It suggested that in a world of commoditised legal services, pro bono demonstrates the ethic of a true professional and that the legal profession had a position 'that other professions are keen to emulate'.

The issues identified for the Law Society's committee returned to some fundamental issues: Is pro bono a professional obligation? Should pro bono cover former legal aid areas?; Will pro bono help distinguish solicitors from post-Legal Services Act competitors?; Will commitment to pro bono help counter the charges of self-interest that are levelled against the Law Society in relation to defending legal aid? This list was quite revealing in terms of understanding the competing pressures the Law Society experienced regarding pro bono.

Under the new legal aid provisions introduced by LASPO 2012, the Law Society announced a scheme to test the limits of the legislation.[82] The Act provides for applications in situations where failure to provide funding would breach the client's human rights.[83] This most obviously relates to Article 6 rights to a fair trial, but could involve other articles. The arrangement, made with the Public Law Project, is to support practitioners in submitting exceptional funding applications and in identifying suitable test cases. Unsuccessful applications will not be paid for, which makes the scheme highly suitable for a co-ordinated pro bono campaign.

F. The Bar

In contrast with the Law Society, the Bar positively embraced pro bono during the 1990s. At that time, it had a close relationship with a fully-fledged pro bono service provider in the form of the Free Representation Unit (FRU). The idea for FRU was planted in 1972, by a group of Bar students wishing to represent those unable to afford legal services.[84] It started in a pub in Chancery Lane in 1972 as 'Bar Students for Legal Advice'.

The Bar Students cheekily wrote to the Council of Legal Education, 'You may know that there's a certain amount of unrest and disquiet among your charges about the education you are giving them. To assist you to make your students happy, quiet

---

[81] 'Law Society to review pro bono policy in face of legal aid cuts and Legal Services Act' *Legal Futures* 9 May 2011 (www.legalfutures.co.uk/news/law-society-to-review-pro-bono-policy-in-face-of-legal-aid-cuts-and-legal-services-act).

[82] The Law Society, 'Legal Aid Changes: Key Information and Advice' 13 March 2013 (www.lawsociety.org.uk/advice/articles/legal-aid-changes-key-information-and-advice/).

[83] LASPO 2012, s 10.

[84] FRU pamphlet (undated) at 1.

and satisfied, we offer you the following advice'.[85] At the time, the advice was not heeded, but FRU subsequently became an option on the Bar Vocational Course.[86]

Over the next 20 years the FRU's office moved from the pub to an attic at the top of Middle Temple Lane and then to a couple of rooms in Gray's Inn. Since its formation the FRU had expanded its work to embrace a range of tribunals for which legal aid was not available. It aimed to provide representation equal to that available through legal aid. Today, the FRU is authorised by the Bar Council in relation to each of the tribunals in which its representatives appear. The FRU provides more than 1500 training places annually for potential volunteers in employment and social security law.[87]

The FRU is still independent of, but close to, the Bar. Many senior barristers and judges are former FRU representatives. The Bar Council and Inns of Court are among the largest contributors to FRU's operating costs on an annual basis. FRU trustees are nominated by the chair of the Bar Council. In 1989, in response to the Green Papers, the Bar warned that the implementation of the government's proposals would diminish the public service work performed by solicitors and barristers. Nevertheless, it undertook to encourage barristers to do pro bono work and to expand the FRU both in London and in other major centres.[88]

During the early-1990s, when solicitors were under pressure to perform more pro bono work, the Bar did not seem to attract similar political attention. This was possibly because it was seen to be actively involved in promoting *pro bono publico*. It may also have been because the numbers and skills of solicitors offered a better prospect of making a dent in the growing legal aid deficit.

In 1992, 2063 cases were referred to FRU by Citizens' Advice Bureaux and Law Centres. As a result, barristers appeared in 1200 cases. In 1993, this rose to 2400 clients.[89] In 1995, there was a decline in the number of cases for which FRU representation could be found from 1682 in 1994 to 1394. The chair of the Bar, Peter Goldsmith, took cases himself to encourage more senior barristers to supplement volunteer Bar students and pupils.[90]

By 2007, the FRU's caseload fell to around 700 cases a year, comprising 300 employment, 300 social security benefits and the rest criminal injury compensation and immigration.[91] FRU remained well organised and was now geared to doing more complex cases. It employed administrators and a solicitor to help with preparation. These posts were funded by the Bar Council, the Inns of Court, covenants entered into by individual barristers, subscriptions from referral agencies and income from training days.[92]

In 1993, FRU appealed to barristers in London and the South East to assist by launching its 'Chamber Scheme', which was supported by the Bar Council. In 1996,

---

[85] H Brooke, 'Second Annual Nottingham Pro Bono Lecture' (Nottingham Law School, 15 November 2007) (www.judiciary.gov.uk/Resources/JCO/Documents/Speeches/shb_nottingham151107.pdf).

[86] N Duncan, 'FRU and the Bar Vocational Course' *New Law Journal* 5 November 1993.

[87] FRU, *Annual Report 2012*.

[88] General Council of the Bar, *The Quality of Justice: The Bar's Response* (London, Butterworths, 1999).

[89] D Conn, 'A matter of principle' *Counsel* July 1993, at 18.

[90] M Phelan, 'Effective Access to Justice' *Counsel* April 1996, at 16.

[91] C Tulloch, 'Thirty Five years of 'Poverty Law' *Independent Lawyer* November 2007, at 11.

[92] *Counsel*, 'FRU—The Bar's Contribution' *Counsel* April 1994, at 23.

the Bar Pro Bono Unit (BPBU) was formed as an independent charity.[93] This joined a number of existing schemes, especially the regional schemes run on the Northern Circuit, Western Circuit and Wales and Chester Circuit, and those run by specialist subject Bar Associations. These included the Employment Law Bar Association Scheme, the Planning Bar Association's Free Advocacy Scheme and Environmental Legal and Mediation Service.

On the launch of the BPBU, barristers were asked to donate two or three days a year to free work. A contributor to *Counsel* described this as 'far too modest'.[94] In 1996, BPBU had 282 volunteers and 171 requests for help. In 1997 it took on 44 per cent of the cases referred to it, although half just involved giving advice. It was reported that 720 barristers of differing levels of seniority, including 120 QCs, had agreed to provide at least three days a year. This represented less than 10 per cent of the practising Bar.

By 1998, the number of participating barristers had increased to 800, including 130 QCs. Assistance was provided in 400 cases.[95] Some significant cases involved more substantial assistance. One, a case brought by a pensioner against the National Grid over the use of £47 million of pension fund money to make redundancy payments, was reported in the national press.[96] In 2002, BPBU had 886 requests for assistance and 1,220 barristers registered.[97]

In 2000, Bar in the Community was launched to recruit barristers to the management committees of voluntary organisations.[98] In 2002 the BPBU set up a solicitors' panel for cases that needed a solicitor as well as barrister.[99] This comprised 11 firms, including most of the 'magic circle'. The BPBU received a major grant from the Bar in 2001 but raised some of its overheads independently. In 2005 it offered secondments to members at solicitors' firms.[100] It earned praise from the government for its work and for publishing reliable data on the BPBU's work.

The BPBU has a panel of barristers willing to do pro bono work. A senior review panel assesses all cases for merit, suitability and financial eligibility. The panel is steadily growing. In 2011, it had reported over 2000 barrister members including more than 250 QCs. In 2013, it had 3300 members, including one-third of all QCs. It currently has a full-time staff of seven administrators.[101]

The Bar operates an 'opt-out' contribution, currently £30, for barristers paying practising certificate fees, as a contribution to the BPBU. The Bar Council contributes £60,000 annually, 50 per cent of its operating costs. Formerly housed in the Bar Council administrative offices, the BPBU relocated to bespoke premises at High Holborn with the FRU in 2004.

---

[93] V Sims, 'Pro Bono at the Bar' (1998) 4 *Amicus Curiae* 21.

[94] Phelan, 'Effective Access to Justice' (n 90).

[95] S Solley and R D'Cruz, 'Deliverance from Death Row?' *Counsel* October 1998, at 22.

[96] C Dyer, 'On the Lawyers Who Work for Free' *The Guardian* 15 July 1997, at 17.

[97] S Weale and C Dyer, 'Heard the one about the lawyer who works for nothing...' *The Guardian* 11 June 2002.

[98] BPBU, *Annual Report 2000–02*.

[99] 'BPBU creates solicitor panel' *The Lawyer* 28 January 2002.

[100] BPBU, *Annual Review 2005*.

[101] www.barprobono.org.uk/overview.html.

G. The Attorney General's Pro Bono Co-ordinating Committee

In 2002 a strong lead from government saw the creation of the Attorney General's Pro Bono Co-ordinating Committee with a remit to promote, develop and co-ordinate the national effort.[102] The committee was chaired by the Attorney General, Lord Goldsmith, the founder of the Bar Pro Bono Unit. It had a membership including the Solicitor General, representatives of the profession and various pro bono interest groups. Goldsmith appointed Michael Napier, a solicitor and former President of the Law Society, pro bono envoy, with special responsibility for the provinces.

In 2001, a report by Boon and Whyte for the Nuffield Foundation was circulated to the first meeting of the Attorney General's Pro Bono Committee.[103] It proposed limiting pro bono to legal work, but expanding the traditional conception to include transaction and community work. The report also recommended that the legal profession used pro bono to 'rebuild the connection between legal professionalism and public service'.[104] It suggested that the professions explore ways of recovering costs in pro bono cases.

The Attorney General's committee produced a pro bono protocol that clarified many of the issues around pro bono. For example, paragraph 1 unambiguously declared that '[w]hen we refer to Pro Bono Legal Work we mean legal advice or representation provided by lawyers to individuals and community groups who cannot afford to pay for that advice or representation and where public funding is not available'.[105] It went on to provide that '[l]egal work is Pro Bono Legal Work only if it is free to the client, without payment to the lawyer or law firm (regardless of the outcome) and provided voluntarily either by the lawyer or his or her firm'.[106]

With the encouragement of the Attorney General's committee, the professions collaborated to launch National Pro Bono Week in 2002 to celebrate and encourage pro bono.[107] In 2003 Michael Napier announced three initiatives. The committee would publish a national protocol setting out key elements of pro bono work,[108] focus on law student activity and launch a national pro bono website.[109] The second of these initiatives met a hurdle when, in 2005, the Higher Education Funding Council for England and Wales rejected the idea of funding law schools to provide students with pro bono experience.

The committee tackled the costs issue by proposing the creation of pro bono costs orders. These were implemented by the LSA 2007, section 194, and became operative in courts in England and Wales from October 2008. The section applies to civil court proceedings in which one or both parties are represented by a legal representative free

---

[102] Press release from the Attorney General's Chambers, 23 April 2002; V MacCallum 'Lord Goldsmith unveils pro bono drive to co-ordinate work across the country' *Law Society Gazette* 25 April 2002.

[103] A Boon and A Whyte, 'Something for Nothing?: The Provision of Legal Services *Pro Bono Publico*' (London, University of Westminster, 2001).

[104] ibid, at 11.

[105] Pro Bono Protocol (www.barprobono.org.uk/pro_bono_protocol.html).

[106] ibid, at para 1.2.

[107] 'Power of pro bono' *Law Society Gazette* 25 April 2002.

[108] ibid; and see V MacCallum, 'Attorney-General unveils protocol that sets out key elements of pro bono work' *Law Society Gazette* 3 April 2003, at 4.

[109] M Napier, 'Delivering hope on pro bono' *Law Society Gazette* 3 April 2003.

of charge, in whole or in part. In these circumstances, the court may order any person to make a payment in respect of the whole of the representation or the part provided free of charge.

Under the Civil Procedure Rules, the party who received pro bono representation is able to claim costs by preparing, filing and serving a written statement of the sum equivalent to the costs that party would have claimed for that legal representation had it not been provided free of charge.[110] The court is required to have regard to whether it would have made an order for costs against a party had the person who was represented pro bono been paying for their representation. It is also required to consider on what terms it would have made such an order.

The second problem was to whom the costs were awarded. If they were given to the party aided pro bono, they received an undeserved windfall. If they were given to that party's lawyer, it would be sanctioning an unregulated speculative fee. Further, the representation would no longer be pro bono. The second innovation in the LSA 2007 was, therefore, the ability of the court to award the costs to a charity prescribed by order of the Lord Chancellor.[111]

The charity prescribed by the Lord Chancellor to receive sums raised by pro bono costs orders is the Access to Justice Foundation (AJF).[112] The AJF is a national charity providing grant funding to support pro bono and advice agencies.[113] The Foundation was established by the Advice Services Alliance, Bar Council, ILEX and Law Society. Former Attorney General Lord Goldsmith QC chairs the Foundation.

The introduction of pro bono costs orders had limited initial success. In the year after they became active, between 70 to 80 per cent of practitioners had not heard of the orders. Those that had either could not be bothered applying for a pro bono costs order or anticipated difficulties in having them agreed or taxed by the court. This suggests that such orders may need to be compulsory to generate significant funds. In the meantime the AJF launched a campaign, *It's Not Just Peanuts*, to encourage law firms to donate small, dormant client balances. Only sums over £50 are subject to permission from the SRA.

H. The National Pro Bono Centre

The National Pro Bono Centre houses the professions' national clearing houses for legal pro bono work. These are the Bar Pro Bono Unit, LawWorks (the Solicitors' Pro Bono Group) and the CILEx Pro Bono Trust (CILEx PBT). The Centre was, fortuitously, housed in a prestigious location on Chancery Lane, available for five years because of the recession. The opportunity was taken to offer space to four other related charities. These were the Access to Justice Foundation, the London Legal Support Trust, the Environmental Law Foundation and i-ProBono. The Centre is

---

[110] Civil Procedure Rules 1998, r 46.7 and Practice Direction 46—Costs Special Cases: Personal Liability of Legal Representative for Costs—Wasted Costs Orders: Rule 46.8, para 4.1.

[111] LSA 2007, ss 194(3) and (8).

[112] The Legal Services Act 2007 (Prescribed Charity) Order 2008 (SI 2008/2680).

[113] www.accesstojusticefoundation.org.uk/downloads/Access_to_Justice_Foundation_leaflet.pdf.

therefore a hub for pro bono work. It offers opportunities for forming the relationships and collaborations that are essential in building a broad-based movement.

I. Legal Executives

Membership of the National Pro Bono Centre provided a fillip to CILEx's pro bono efforts. CILEx launched the Joint ILEX Pro Bono Forum and Bar Pro Bono Unit Scheme (the JIB Scheme) for Fellows or Graduate Members of CILEx. This enables them to work with BPBU volunteer barristers in pro bono cases. In 2012, it established an independent charity to work with LawWorks and the Bar Pro Bono Unit. The aim was to increase the engagement of CILEx and other lawyers and trainees in pro bono work and raise awareness of that work. The survey of ILEX members in 2013 revealed a low level of awareness of pro bono. Fewer than one in ten legal executives were aware of pro bono bodies, the Access to Justice Foundation and pro bono costs orders.[114]

J. International Pro Bono Activity

In addition to domestic pro bono activity, a certain amount of international activity is also promoted by pro bono organisations in England and Wales.

i. The Attorney General's International Pro Bono Committee

The ambition of the Attorney General's Pro Bono Co-ordinating Committee did not stop with the national pro bono effort. The Attorney General's International Pro Bono Committee clearing house aims to support strategic development and co-ordinated delivery of pro bono work across the world. The committee jointly developed international pro bono principles providing best practice guidance and the first draft of a pro bono toolkit to share experience and good practice between Commonwealth countries. The committee is creating a database of international projects. This is aimed at encouraging closer working and information exchange between the agencies sharing strategic aims. It will help prevent duplication and reinvention and will eventually become a public resource.

ii. Independent Projects

A number of independent organisations are based in, or have offices in England and Wales. Some of these either aim to provide free services or promote pro bono activity overseas. The UK-based International Lawyers Project (ILP) merged with the International Senior Lawyers Project (ISLP), the US-based organisation

---

[114] Robins (n 70).

that originally inspired its foundation, to form ISLP-UK. It was thought that ISLP-UK would be better placed to attract 'experienced lawyers and distinguished law firms to promote the rule of law, human rights and equitable economic development worldwide'.[115] Another brokerage agency, Advocates for International Development, established in 2006 by a group of 1500 City of London lawyers, became a global organisation.

K. Summary

Pro bono publico is a legal institution that is historically linked to the provision of free representation in courts, probably at the request of judge. By the 1990s, pro bono work occurred in some sections of the legal profession. With a few exceptions, contributions were handled in an ad hoc and uncoordinated way. Whether or not lawyers participated in pro bono work was largely a matter of individual conscience.[116]

The involvement of lawyers in Law Centre work from the 1960s meant that, when the term re-emerged in the 1990s, advice work was seen as included within the scope of pro bono. During the 1990s, pro bono was reinvented to meet various contemporary needs. The Law Society Working Party tried to ditch old associations and adopt a vague and meaningless term in place of pro bono. This provided a basis for making exaggerated claims for solicitors' voluntary work.

During the 1990s, many large firms began to adopt social programmes. Some of these were corporate social responsibility (CSR) programmes, based on charity work and volunteering and some provided legal services pro bono. Sometimes the programmes were combined, so that pro bono was offered as an example of CSR. Transaction lawyers were integrated into pro bono schemes. So that the culture was inclusive, pro bono was often defined to include corporate volunteering by support staff.[117] Similar trends have been evident in other jurisdictions, for example the US.[118]

The tendency for pro bono to mean a variety of different things was arrested by the agreement of the pro bono protocol at the instigation of the Attorney General's Pro Bono Committee. This clarified that pro bono was about lawyers providing a variety of legal services, to the same standard that a paying client would be expect, and with no expectation of payment.

---

[115] ibid.

[116] A Boon and R Abbey, 'Moral Agendas?: *Pro Bono Publico* in Large Law Firms in the United Kingdom' (1997) 60 *Modern Law Review* 630; and see, considering Australia, E Nosworthy, 'Ethics and Large Law Firms' in S Parker and C Sampford (eds), *Legal Ethics and Legal Practice* (Oxford, Clarendon Press, 1995) at 70.

[117] A Boon and A Whyte, '"Charity and Beating Begins at Home": The Aetiology of the New Culture of Pro Bono Publico' (1999) 2(2) *Legal Ethics* 169.

[118] S Cummings, 'The Politics of Pro Bono' (2004) 52 *UCLA Law Review* 1.

VI. The Value of *Pro Bono Publico*

A. Solicitors

i. Data Collection

In the late-1990s, the government's attack on solicitors' record on legal aid and pro bono continued unabated. In a House of Lords debate Lord Irvine reported that barristers' and QCs' fees, and their claims on the legal aid fund were impeding access to justice. The quoted levels of legal aid payments to individual barristers, £1 million per annum, were only true of top commercial silks. Leading criminal silks specialising in fraud and child care cases could earn £200,000 to £300,000 per annum, largely from legal aid.[119] In June 1998, the clerk to the Parliaments refused to sanction legal aid bills presented by QCs for work in the House of Lords.[120] In March 1999, Andrew Dismore, solicitor and Labour MP, asked a parliamentary question about the relevance of pro bono work to appointment as Queen's Counsel.

Lord Philips of Sudbury, a leading light in the formation of the SPBG, lamented the lack of ammunition to counter the 'drip, drip of denigration from government spokesmen' in the House of Lords.[121] Neither the Bar nor the Law Society had, historically, collected data on free services provided by members.[122] Even in the US, the American Lawyers' annual survey of large firm contributions, dated only from 1990.[123]

There was some evidence for lawyers' pro bono contributions, but it was sketchy at best. In 1976, the Royal Commission on Legal Services estimated that 3,300 solicitors supported advice agencies by offering free services.[124] In 1989 an independent survey of 59 Law Centres found 369 wholly or partly qualified lawyers, less than 1 per cent of the solicitors then holding practising certificates, offering voluntary services.[125]

From the moment the Law Society began collecting data it seemed that the point of the exercise was to prove solicitors provided lots of free services. To this end, it seemed reluctant to call free legal services *pro bono publico*. In a Law Society survey

---

[119] *The Guardian* 15 July 1997, at 1; C Dyer, 'Law Chief Fires Fresh Volley on "Fat Cat" Lawyers' *The Guardian* 10 December 1997.

[120] C Dyer, 'On Trial: A System That Makes QCs Rich' *The Guardian* 3 June 1998.

[121] A Philips, 'Want of Experience' *Law Society Gazette* 28 April 1999.

[122] Even after this the Law Society's panel survey found that 68% of firms kept no record of time spent: Research and Policy Planning Unit, *Panel Study of Solicitors' Firms* (London, The Law Society, 1997).

[123] M Galanter and T Palay, 'Public Service Implications of Evolving Firm Size and Structure' in Katzmann, *The Law Firm And The Public Good* (n 60) at 41.

[124] Lord Chancellor's Department, *The Royal Commission on Legal Services Final Report* (Cmnd7648, 1979) (Benson Report) at para 2.21.

[125] L Hiscock and G Cole, 'The Motivation, Use and Future of Volunteer Lawyers in Law Centres' (1989) 6 *Journal of Social Welfare Law* 404.

of solicitors in 1989, 41 per cent claimed to carry out 'public service work for which [they did] not charge fees' but the majority performed one hour or less work a week.[126]

In 1993, the Law Society's' Pro Bono Working Party attempted a survey of 123 local Law Societies. Only 32 responses were received and none of the respondents held records or monitored free work in any way. The report claimed that many local societies were 'aware' that local practitioners were active in assisting Citizens' Advice Bureaux on a rota basis.[127]

As political pressure grew for lawyers to do more free work, the Law Society attempted a publicity offensive. In 1997 it issued a press release, based on a Law Society Research Unit study, claiming that 70 per cent of 460 surveyed firms provide legal advice to private individuals whose cases fell outside the scope of legal aid. The Law Society survey claimed that only 11 per cent of firms provided no such services.

The Law Society press release stated that solicitors in private practice contributed an annual average of 37 hours of services 'free of charge or at a rate substantially below that normally charged either during the firm's time or during [their] own'.[128] On this basis, the Law Society claimed that 'value of pro bono work by solicitors is the equivalent to a cash gift to good causes of at least £124 million a year'. This figure was based on volunteer hours claimed by solicitors in 1,113 interviewees, which was then multiplied by an unspecified charging rate.[129]

A possible explanation of the discrepancy between the Law Society's claimed free work and the data that did exist was partly due to the confusion caused by the Law Society. The working party's recommendation, to drop the term *pro bono publico* in favour of 'voluntary legal services', opened the door to dubious counting of irrecoverable fees or undercharged services, cases handled for 'a rate substantially below that normally charged', unsuccessful conditional fee cases, time spent on friends and acquaintances, loss leaders for existing clients and even bad debts.[130] These considerations, together with the fact that the Law Society's data depends on solicitors self-reporting, means that claims for the value of pro bono performed must be viewed with caution.

ii. Financial Contribution

Despite the methodological issues, the growth of pro bono activity demonstrated by the annual survey was still impressive. In 2006/07, the value claimed for solicitors' pro bono work was £338 million,[131] in 2009/10 it was £475 million,[132] in 2011/12 it was

---

[126] G Chambers and S Harwood, *Solicitors in England and Wales: Practice, Organisation and Perceptions* (London, The Law Society, 1991).

[127] Law Society, *Report of the Law Society's Pro Bono Working Party* (London, The Law Society, 1994) Annex C, at para 1.

[128] J Jenkins, *Law Society Omnibus Survey 2: Report 5: Pro Bono Activities Conducted by Private Practice Solicitors* (London, The Law Society, 1997).

[129] Law Society news release, 'Solicitors Give at Least £124 Million of Free Legal Help a Year' (27 January 1998).

[130] Boon and Whyte, 'Something for Nothing?' (n 103).

[131] N Goswami, 'Survey reveals fifty per cent slump in individual pro bono hours' *The Lawyer* 12 November 2007, at 4.

[132] Law Society, *Solicitors' pro bono work: Law society annual individual omnibus survey 2010 (Report 5)* (London, The Law Society, 2010) (http://www.lawsociety.org.uk/representation/research-trends/research-publications/solicitors-pro-bono-work---omnibus-survey-2010/).

£511m and in 2012/133l, it was £488 million. For the purpose of these surveys, 'pro bono work' was defined as the 'delivery of free legal services to individuals, organisations and communities in need'. The reported volumes typically represented between 2 and 3 per cent of the total turnover of solicitors' firms.

iii. Participation

There was an increasingly broad spread of pro bono work among layers of the profession and across sectors. In 2002, 45 per cent of solicitors had conducted pro bono work within the previous 12 months. In 2007 the figure hit 51 per cent, a 6 per cent increase on the previous year,[133] before falling back to 44 per cent in 2011/12. In 2012/13, 45 per cent of newly qualified solicitors were providing pro bono services, up from 36 per cent in 2012. An equal proportion of newly qualified and partner-level solicitors were involved. There was also a slight increase in the number of in-house solicitors providing pro bono work, but they tended to do less than private practitioners.[134]

The number of pro bono hours provided by each solicitor was generally on the rise. In 2002, solicitors performing pro bono work provided 32 hours each.[135] In 2007, this fell to 15 hours of free advice a year. This was explained by the Law Society as 'a spreading around' of the hours. In 2011/12 the average number hours was 45, a slight fall on the 47 hours reported in 2012.

B. Barristers

The Bar approached the issue of significance in a different way from solicitors. The Bar has tended to focus on the numbers of cases barristers have appeared in, or succeeded in, rather than the hours performed or monetary value on the services provided. Its pro bono organisations also refer to cases that have made a significant difference, either to individuals or to the law. FRU, for example, provided representation in a case producing useful guidance on how the EAT should handle vulnerable witnesses.[136] The public benefit of such judicial decisions is potentially huge, though difficult to measure in cash terms.

FRU arranges representation in 1,000 cases per annum, appearing in around 50–65 per cent of cases referred.[137] In 2013, the BPBU reported that it had handled 1,400 cases, reporting an 87 per cent acceptance rate. Barristers had appeared pro bono in 65 Court of Appeal cases and six Supreme Court cases.[138] The approach of Bar organisations in reporting pro bono may grab fewer headlines than seven

---

[133] Goswami, 'Survey reveals fifty per cent slump' (n 131).
[134] 'Record number of junior lawyers working pro bono' *Law Society Gazette* 7 November 2013 (www.lawgazette.co.uk/practice/record-number-of-junior-lawyers-working-pro-bono/5038629.article).
[135] Goswami (n 131).
[136] *Duffy v George* [2013] EWCA Civ 908.
[137] FRU, *Annual Report 2012*.
[138] Robins (n 70).

and eight figure sums, but it makes pro bono contributions feel more tangible and reliable.

C. CILEx

CILEx adopted the Law Society's approach to monitoring pro bono. A survey of CILEx members conducted in 2013 found that almost one-third had undertaken pro bono work in the previous 12 months, providing a total of 6000 hours of pro bono work. This was said to be worth over £1,000,000 at an average private client charging rate.

VII. Interests and Motivations

A. Context

It is difficult to decide what motivates some professionals, and perhaps especially lawyers, to work for free. The starting point must be altruism, 'the unselfish regard for the welfare of others'.[139] Many people who choose to become lawyers do so because they want to help people in trouble. This may be a vague ideal for many, but the idea of being someone's 'knight in shining armour', can be encouraged, for example, by the emphasis in the law school curriculum on 'personal plight' subjects. Torts, crime and family are popular with students, although many decide, at some point in their legal studies to pursue safer and more remunerative routes.

Pro bono work offers those with altruistic reasons for becoming lawyers the chance to fulfil their calling.[140] The precise motive may be more difficult to pin down and it could vary between people. Some volunteers may see pro bono as a way to promote social justice, others may only want to promote a particular cause. The variations in the volume of pro bono work, and the generally upward trend, suggests that there may be other factors at work besides individual propensities for altruism.

As the account of the recent growth of organised pro bono activity demonstrates, there is a strong relationship between institutional support for pro bono and levels of activity. This is not surprising since people are more likely to give up their free time if they believe that society, and their professional superiors and peers, acknowledge and value the work that is done. It is therefore necessary to consider what institutional

---

[139] C Menkel-Meadow, 'Is Altruism Possible in Lawyering' (1992) 8(2) *Georgia State University Law Review* 385, at 389.
[140] A Boon, 'From Public Service to Service Industry: the Impact of Socialisation and Work on the Motivation and Values of Lawyers' (2005) 12(2) *International Journal of the Legal Profession* 193.

and other structures may provide an impetus for the pro bono culture and support its development.

B. Globalisation and the Contracting State

During the 1980s change was driven by globalisation, the world-wide intensification of technological, economic and cultural interconnectedness between nations. Globalised economies embraced technological advances, such as the internet, and were open to the exchange of labour forces, ideas, knowledge, products and services. Increasing dependence on global trade for economic growth depended on international corporations.

In the face of globalisation, nations were faced with a stark choice; to open markets to world trade or to become relatively poor. The need to compete in world markets almost inevitably involved reducing the size of the state and compromising on state commitments.[141] The Labour Governments from the late 1990s, facing the inevitability of scaled down social welfare programmes, resuscitated the idea of private philanthropy. This was part of a so-called 'third way', between leftist welfare policies and recent experiments in rightist 'market fundamentalism'.[142] The 'third way' reflected a social philosophy built on individualism, responsibility and materialism.[143] It envisaged a strong civil society enshrining rights and responsibilities, and strong communities built upon shared responsibility and devolved power.[144] This vision placed a strong emphasis on reversing the decline of voluntary activity occurring over the previous century.[145]

The idea of volunteering was sold to the public as 'an act of citizenship'.[146] It was sold to the corporate sector as an act of self-interest. It offered a way to reduce the threat from a disenfranchised 'underclass', and an opportunity to build communities safe for business. The growth in large firm pro bono also reflected changes in the wider economic, political and social environment.

A flagship policy of the Conservative election campaign in 2010 was the so-called Big Society.[147] Like the third way, this incorporated the idea of volunteering, together with devolution of power from the state and increased emphasis on localism. There have been no direct appeals to the legal profession to participate in such an agenda, for example, in the wake of legal aid cuts. Nor has there been evidence of the pursuit of this agenda, at least in terms of building an infrastructure of support. Nevertheless, the economic and political environment, and the responding policies, undoubtedly influenced the development of pro bono culture.

---

[141] J Gray, *False Dawn: The Delusions of Global Capitalism* (London, Granta Publications, 1998).
[142] G Soros, *The Crisis of Global Capitalism: Open Society Endangered* (London, Little Brown and Co, 1998).
[143] B Jordan, *The Common Good: Citizenship Morality and Self-Interest* (Oxford and New York, Basil Blackwell Limited, 1989).
[144] T Blair, *The Third Way: New Politics for the New Century* (London, The Fabian Society, 1998) at 6.
[145] R Hoggart, *The Way We Live Now* (London, Chatto and Windus, 1995).
[146] ibid, at 2 and 14.
[147] 'The big society' *The Times* 14 April 2010.

C. Firms

i. Differences in Scale and Kinds of Engagement with Pro Bono

A survey conducted by LawWorks in 2013 found that firm size had a significant impact on how pro bono was perceived and operated.[148] Two-thirds of smaller firms identified their motive for pro bono as 'giving back to the community' and nearly one-third as business development. In medium-sized firms, 53 per cent regarded the motive for pro bono work as giving back to the community and 17 per cent saw it as business development. Only 41 per cent in small firms recorded time donated pro bono, whereas 70 per cent of those in medium-sized firms did.[149] One reason for this difference was that small firms apparently regarded pro bono as 'part of everyday delivery and not recorded separately'.[150]

The LawWorks survey found that over 50 per cent of larger organisations had a pro bono partner or committee. Almost two-thirds recognised pro bono in chargeable hours targets, and around 37 per cent recognised it in awarding bonuses. Among the largest respondents, 86 per cent actively encouraged staff to undertake pro bono work, compared with 4 per cent which discouraged participation. This contrasts with medium-sized organisations, where 81 per cent encouraged involvement. In the smallest organisations, over half reported that lawyers were left to decide for themselves whether they worked pro bono. Participation in pro bono activity was actively discouraged in 15 per cent of small organisations.

It appears that there are different levels and kinds of engagement by law firms in pro bono and different levels of encouragement to participate, depending on type of firm. This may be attributable to resources, but it also raises questions about the motivations and interests of those involved. It is speculated, for example, that the approach of many small and medium-sized firms reflects a traditional approach. On the other hand the bulk of larger firms and many medium-sized firms are departing from these traditions by becoming more proactive, organised and even directive in their pro bono activity. The reasons for this can be explored by looking further at the performance and practice of large firms.

ii. Growth in Large Firm Involvement

There was significant growth in pro bono work in large law firms from the 1990s. A study conducted between 1990 and 1994 found a contradictory picture. Large London law firms seemed to have little interest in pro bono, but several claimed substantial pro bono programmes.[151] A survey of the 100 largest national firms in 1994 also found a

---

[148] Law Works, *Pro Bono Survey 2013* (London, Law Works, 2013) at 12 (http://www.lawworks.org.uk/index.php?cID=798&cType=document).
[149] ibid, at 13.
[150] ibid.
[151] M Galanter and T Palay, 'Large Law Firms and Professional Responsibility' in R Cranston, *Legal Ethics and Professional Responsibility* (Oxford, Clarendon, 1995) 201.

mixed picture.[152] Six firms had a policy on pro bono work conducted by the firm and four assigned work to firm members. Twenty-seven firms claimed to perform work exceeding £10,000 in value per annum but eight said they undertook no pro bono work whatsoever. The same was probably true of 39 firms that did not respond.

The formation of the SPBG in 1996 marked a significant change of approach in some large firms. They began to focus more on their own firms' contributions. There were diverse reasons for this change. Large firms were affected by the changed social climate in relation to voluntary work, which affected the corporate sector generally. They were also directly affected by agencies involved in driving change and by their own clients.

iii. Influences on Large Firm Involvement

a. Volunteering Agencies

The 1990s saw an increase in agencies involved in promoting volunteering activity, developing links and providing brokerage, placing clients with volunteers. One of these agencies, Business in the Community (BITC) played a significant part in this transformation generally and in relation to lawyers. BITC was formed in 1981 following an Anglo-American conference on the private sector's role in urban regeneration. It penetrated mainstream commercial life as 'a public way to deliver socially responsible brand values'.[153]

The attempt to increase public altruism among corporations enjoyed a mixed response. Following a high profile campaign in 1990, the 100 or so leading contributors increased contributions to nearly 1 per cent of pre-tax profits. By 2002, however, the top 400 firms making community contributions were only at 0.42 per cent.[154] BITC brought the idea of employee volunteering to large firms through its Professional Firms Group. This was formed in 1989 and, by 1996, had 40 law firms among its 200-firm membership. The professional firms agreed to provide up to £5,000 worth of their professional services for specific projects at no charge. BITC was also active in the formation of the SPBG in 1996.

b. Corporate Clients and Corporate Social Responsibility

The diminution in state power caused by globalisation, combined with the growing power of corporations made it difficult for individual states to control global corporations. This focused concern on issues of regulation. One proposal was that corporations should be encouraged to regulate themselves according to public interest criteria. This would require that they looked beyond the interests of their own shareholders when forming policy and making decisions.

The idea of a wider conception of corporate responsibility grew from the notion that companies should actively consider the interests of stakeholders, all those

---

[152] A Boon and R Abbey, 'Moral Agendas: *Pro Bono Publico* in Large Law Firms in the United Kingdom' (1997) 60 *Modern Law Review* 630.
[153] N Hill, 'Market Ethics' *The Guardian* (*Society* supp) 19 May 1998, at 85, quoting Peter Mandelson.
[154] 'The Giving List: FTSE 100 givers' *The Guardian* 25 November 2002, at 4.

affected by their actions, as well as shareholders.[155] CSR is a business model building this idea into corporate self-regulation.[156] It typically involves corporations voluntarily committing to a number of values. These might include, for example, legality, compliance, ethical conduct, sustainability and social responsibility.

The increasing financial success of large corporate law firms from the late-1980s was notable. They had increasingly adopted corporate identity but, unlike many clients, had not accepted CSR as representing the firm's values. As the 1990s progressed, large law firms came under increasing pressure from some corporate clients to make a public commitment to pro bono. British Aerospace, for example, announced that:

> British Aerospace has a vision. We have five corporate values and one of those is partnership with the community. We want our law firms to be aligned to our values, to have a similar culture to our culture.[157]

When Zurich Financial Services joined the SPBG in 1999 it announced that it would be demanding a commitment to pro bono from its external lawyers.[158] One lawyer said that four other corporate clients had insisted on evidence of commitment to pro bono as part of tenders for their legal work.[159] In 2001 in-house legal departments in large corporations were committing to providing pro bono services and requiring that their external law firms did so.[160]

It is unlikely that the impact of client corporations was solely to force law firms to do pro bono. It is also likely that close relationships with clients committed to CSR led to law firms and lawyers absorbing some of the values of the volunteering culture in client corporations.[161] A recent survey showed that, in larger organisations, almost two-thirds of those responsible for the delivery of pro bono also lead on community engagement or charitable giving, and nearly 60 per cent are also responsible for Corporate Responsibility.[162]

c. US Law Firms

Another factor that may have influenced large firms was the example of US law firms in the City. US-based firms had been exposed to expectations of corporate pro bono for longer. Despite their lack of familiarity with local law, they were generally ahead of UK firms in performance.[163] In 2000, the Law Society hosted an ABA seminar on promoting pro bono in a global environment.[164] In 2001, firm leaders met to discuss provision of joint programmes. Although offering advice on English law was a

---

[155] R Freeman, *Strategic* Management: a Stakeholder Approach (Boston, Pitman, 1984).

[156] R Shamir, 'Socially Responsible Private Regulation: World Culture or World-Capitalism?' (2011) 45(2) *Law and Society Review* 313.

[157] *The Lawyer* 3 November 1998, at 13.

[158] D Jordan, 'Zurich In-House Demands Firms Commit to *Pro bono*' *The Lawyer* 4 October 1999.

[159] ibid.

[160] 'Ford Credit links up with Lovell's for Prince's Trust pro bono work' *The Lawyer* 19 February 2001.

[161] WW Powell, 'Fields of Practice: Connections between Law and Organisations' (1996) 21(4) *Law and Social Inquiry* 959.

[162] Law Works, *Pro Bono Survey 2013* (n 148).

[163] J Bartle, 'UK firms pro bono efforts put to shame by US counterparts' *The Lawyer* 4 October 2004, at 4.

[164] S Forsythe and Y Waljiee, 'UK pro bono meets US' *The Lawyer* 24 July 2000, at 14.

longer-term goal, the US law firms committed themselves to a variety of community schemes[165] and some appointed full-time pro bono officers.[166]

iii. Functions of the Pro Bono Culture in Large Firms

a. External Functions of Pro Bono

Performing pro bono work probably performs more functions than simply complying with the wishes of clients subscribing to CSR. It is also an opportunity to gain access to niche markets. For example, many large, non-governmental organisations make significant use of legal services. A spokesman for Freshfields, following the firm's selection as legal consultants to Green Globe, an environmental pressure group, said

> [w]e are happy to provide the service on a *pro bono* basis because it is a very good way of accessing a huge market which we think we are uniquely well placed to serve.[167]

It is generally accepted that CSR, and therefore, for lawyers, offering services pro bono, is a valuable marketing tool. In the US, for example, corporate charitable donations were forbidden except for the benefit of the company.[168] CSR overcame the problem of demonstrating shareholder benefit.[169] This was because cause-related marketing is an acknowledged technique for establishing a brand.[170] It demonstrates active engagement with the evolving corporate culture, potentially attracting corporations seeking new lawyers.

Such is the success of contemporary legal *pro bono publico*, it is now common to find details of activity in the marketing brochures of large firms. An active culture and high value contribution sends many potentially positive signals. It suggests that the firm is entrepreneurial, outward looking and well-organised, with good staff morale. This tends to be supported by the strong correlation between successful firms, measured by size, number of associates and gross revenue, and the high volume of *pro bono publico* work performed.[171]

Another significant audience for the pro bono efforts of large firms is government. Large firm domination of the market place may accentuate inequalities in access to justice.[172] This may seem less offensive if, occasionally, access is supported. In this way, lawyers demonstrate their social responsibility and support for progressive social forces. The profession's relationship with the state may also be eased when large firms are seen to be 'doing their bit'.[173]

---

[165] C Smith, 'US firms in London set to launch joint initiative on pro bono work' *The Lawyer* 12 February 2001.

[166] J Baxter, 'White and Case hires first pro bono officer' *Legal Week* 15 March 2001, at 2.

[167] 'Freshfields to do free work for Fresh Fields' *The Lawyer* 22 November 1994, at 3.

[168] Bowen LJ in *Hutton v West Cork Railway Company* (1883) 23 Ch D 654, at 673.

[169] CM Slaughter, 'Corporate Social Responsibility: a New Perspective' (1997) 18 *The Company Lawyer* 313.

[170] H Pringle and M Thompson, *Brand Spirit: How Cause Related Marketing Builds Brands* (Chichester, John Wiley and Sons, 1999).

[171] Galanter and Palay, Large Law Firms and Professional Responsibility' (n 151) at 43.

[172] ibid, at 40.

[173] Paterson, 'Professionalism and the Legal Services Market' (n 35) at 155.

b. Internal Functions of Pro Bono

Providing pro bono opportunities serves positive internal functions for large law firms. An obvious area to benefit could be the internal culture of the firm. Pro bono provides a measure of a firm's worth that does not depend on numbers of employees or profits generated. It provides an opportunity for younger employees to do useful work, developing skills and gaining confidence. It offers opportunities for employees from different parts of the firm to integrate. Performing pro bono work may also help to build the collective morale of the firm. A Mori survey in 2006 found that 58 per cent of employees in the UK thought that companies' social responsibility was important, apparently partly because this enhances their self-image and esteem.[174]

US research shows that the opportunity for pro bono participation is often seen as a 'life-style reward', and is used to attract and keep staff.[175] Commercial firms, including 'magic circle' firms, publish details of their pro bono activities targeted at law students.[176] The internal functions of pro bono are well recognised in large law firms. The arguments for why firms should do pro bono have been crafted by the numerous external pro bono organisations. They have been adopted by proponents of pro bono within the firms themselves to convince sceptical colleagues. They have even been reproduced for external consumption.

D. Lawyers

While large firm engagement was one of the most noticeable features of the culture of pro bono emerging in the 1990s, it was not the only change. Pro bono moved up the agenda of many lawyers, as evidenced by the data on individual involvement in providing free services. One of the interesting issues about the change of culture surrounding pro bono is why lawyers engaged in this activity in ever increasing numbers.

The 1994 survey showed that advisory work at Citizens' Advice Bureaux and Law Centres, conducted by trainees, was the major area of activity. The work of senior personnel was minor or highly specialised. For example, they might deal with appeals to the Judicial Committee of the Privy Council from countries that retained this appeal route on independence. Prisoners on death row in the Caribbean, for example, often could not afford lawyers. There was a long tradition in some London solicitors' firms and barristers' chambers of acting for free in such cases. The 2013 LawWorks survey showed that solicitors, and then trainees, were the largest participating groups, and that partners were the most difficult to engage.[177]

---

[174] S Brammer, 'Feel-good factories' *The Guardian* 21 January 2006.
[175] Galanter and Palay (n 151) at 127; E Levenson 'A Nice Package' *The Lawyer* 5 November 2001, at 31.
[176] SPBG, *A Guide to Law Firm Pro Bono Programmes in England and Wales* (London, SPBG, 2004).
[177] Law Works, *Pro Bono Survey 2013* (n 148) at 10.

i. Trainees and Pupils

It is not surprising that trainees and recently qualified lawyers are the most enthusiastic proponents of pro bono. Increasingly, many will have experienced pro bono work at some stage in their education. This may help create sympathetic attitudes to those needing free legal services.[178] They may have less work pressure and therefore better opportunities for pro bono work. Trainees' enthusiasm for it may be explained by their idealism and their motivation to help people. It may also follow from the fact that the value of work to the community is one of the least important factors in choosing employment for both males and females.[179] Pro bono work may be an outlet for altruistic feelings.

It may be that there are also less altruistic, more pragmatic, reasons for trainee involvement in pro bono. Barristers were always encouraged to do as much practical work as possible, for example, during the second six months of pupillage. When legal aid work was plentiful, pupils were paid. With the contraction of legal aid, pupils were increasingly encouraged to find alternative routes to gain experience of court work, hence the success of FRU.

Young barristers are not the only lawyers who may see pro bono as providing useful experience. Large firms often offer junior lawyers less contact with clients than do high street firms.[180] They can be well into the post-qualification period before they are trusted. Pro bono therefore provides an opportunity for large firm trainees to practise and develop their legal skills. Working for disadvantaged people with limited resources sharpens decision-making powers and increases sensitivity to the human dimension of complex problems.[181] This benefits the firm because it increases young lawyers' sense of engagement with practice.

Pro bono may also provide opportunities for young lawyers to enhance their status and self-image. It gives them an early opportunity to be admitted to the ranks of 'front-line' professionals admired by the public.[182] Pro bono work also provides scope for developing powers of creativity. The Young Solicitor Group Pro Bono Awards usually include several nominations of young lawyers in large firms who have thought of ways of improving pro bono delivery.

Because many trainees have little experience of practice, their deployment invites the criticism that they are learning at the expense of clients who cannot afford 'real lawyers'. Such criticisms may not be valid, since trainees often have recent exposure to welfare law. The pro bono protocol provides that all services have to be provided to the standard expected of paying clients. Many organisations train young lawyers from large firms so that they can give welfare advice.

---

[178] LA McCrimmon, 'Mandating a Culture of Service: ProB in the Law School Curriculum' (2003–04) 14 *Legal Education Review* 53.

[179] L Norman, *Career Choices in Law: a Survey of Law Students* Research Study 50 (London, The Law Society, 2004) at 24.

[180] Boon, 'From Public Service to Service Industry' (n 140).

[181] DW Hoagland, 'Community Service Makes Better Lawyers' in Katzmann (n 60).

[182] A Abbott, 'Status and Status Strain in the Professions' (1981) 86 *American Journal of Sociology* 819.

ii. Senior Lawyers

Senior lawyers sometimes stumble across a case that they consider important. A recent report told of a case that may not have succeeded without pro bono. It featured a long legal battle waged by a Scottish off-shore construction surveyor (D) over a £1500 laptop.[183] A shop assistant said he could return the laptop if it was not suitable. It was then purchased with a £50 deposit and a credit agreement with a bank. The laptop was returned, and the deposit eventually recovered, but the bank insisted that payments be made under the credit agreement.

Important financial transactions attempted by D subsequently failed and he discovered that he had a negative credit rating. D claimed damages for financial loss caused by the damage to his credit. Sixteen year later, and with accumulated costs of around £250,000, D was given leave to appeal to the Supreme Court in a case involving a matter of public interest.[184]

LawWorks put D in touch with a QC who agreed to represent him pro bono. The court held that D was entitled to rescind the credit agreement. The Bank then had a responsibility to adjust his credit record accordingly. D was awarded £8000 in damages. It was predicted that the case would change practice in the execution of credit agreements to the benefit of consumers generally.

Early large firm pro bono schemes built on the tradition of running sessions at local advice centres, but used trainees and junior solicitors. In the 1990s there appears to have been stronger efforts to involve large firm senior lawyers in working pro bono. Finding suitable free work for experienced transaction lawyers to do involved a shift in emphasis. Advising charitable trusts, or doing conveyancing for them, enabled older lawyers to contribute without the need to train to give welfare advice or go to Law Centres. There was an increase in organisations acting as brokers, putting together clients and pro bono lawyers.

A powerful factor in the increase in the spread of lawyers doing the work could be, simply that they were more likely to be asked. The work is often rewarding, in that clients receiving free services may be more likely to be grateful rather than complaining. Large firm lawyers, who otherwise spend all their time working for large corporations, may appreciate the opportunity to fulfil a more social role. This has been put, a little unkindly, as allowing them 'to feel a little better about themselves'.[185] Many senior lawyers may see the opportunity to work pro bono as a positive personal benefit.

E. Professional Bodies

Since the separation of the professions' regulatory and representative functions, pro bono is one of the few areas of activity that the Law Society and Bar Council can directly influence. The professional bodies have a strong incentive to support high

---

[183] *Durkin v DSG Retail Limited and another* (Scotland) [2014] UKSC 21.

[184] R Jones, 'A £250,000 16-year legal battle—over a laptop' *The Guardian* 10 January 2014.

[185] S Scheingold and A Bloom, 'Transgressive Cause Lawyering: Practice Sites and the Politicization of the Professional' (1998) 5(2/3) *International Journal of the Legal Profession* 209, at 221.

profile, public activity of this kind. A key part of the representative function of professional bodies is to promote the reputation of the profession. Public support for institutions is strongly influenced by knowledge of and respect for those institutions.[186] Pro bono is a very obvious source of acclamation.

Pro bono is also, potentially, a source of tension between different sections of professions. A former President of the Law Society expressed this in remarking that 'if a big City firm is doing a certain amount of pro bono work this has far less value for ordinary people than pro bono work by High Street practices which are geared up for everyday problems'.[187] The tension is not reduced when large firms get very positive press coverage of their efforts.[188] Lawyers from regional and high street firms might wonder why similar fuss is not made of their own contributions. They sometimes suggest that pro bono is just a marketing opportunity for their wealthier brethren.

The solicitors' and barristers' professional bodies have, to different degrees, reflected this ambivalence towards pro bono. This may be for fear of raising expectations of what a profession can or is willing to do. It might be because of concerns about standards. The Law Society's Working Party suggested that imposing a requirement for *pro bono publico* work is counter to the Law Society's role in promoting 'high standards of integrity, a high quality of work and guaranteed compensation when things go wrong'.[189] Mainly, the ambivalence seems to reflect the desire to keep alive the argument that the state should pay for access to justice, not expect lawyers to provide it for free. This argument has been made consistently since the 1990s.[190]

The link made between pro bono and reduction of legal aid provision is so familiar that it pervades the whole culture. Today, the promotional material of key pro bono institutions usually comes with a warning. It invariably states that cuts in legal aid pose threats to access to justice that pro bono cannot meet, and should not try to meet. Such fears are certainly not unfounded. In 2001, a judge in a family case told solicitors that they should act pro bono when costs limits imposed by the Legal Services Commission were exceeded.[191]

None of the professions has ever proposed a conduct rule regarding pro bono. It is very likely that such a move would be fiercely resented by sections of the memberships. Rather, the professions have settled into a supportive, if slightly detached role, in relation to pro bono. They fund external organisations, support pro bono competitions and the like. This ensures that the professional bodies cannot be directly criticised for performance. It also means that it is easier to withdraw from any commitments.

Even if lawyers are not required to provide pro bono services, there is still scope for regulation. The marketing of pro bono for the firm's benefit undermines the claim

---

[186] A Sarat, 'Support for the Legal System' in WM Evan (ed), *The Sociology of Law: A Social-Structural Perspective* (New York, Free Press, 1980) at 167.

[187] J Smerin, 'For Love Not Money' *Law Society Gazette* 25 October 1995.

[188] N Rovnick, 'Cobbetts consolidates its pro bono initiatives' *The Lawyer* 15 October 2001; J Hobson, 'Lawyers give helping hand' *The Times* 19 October 1999; C Dyer, 'A bono fide freebie' *The Guardian* 3 June 2003.

[189] The Law Society, *Pro Bono Working Party Report* (n 127) at para 22.

[190] General Council of the Bar, *The Quality of Justice* (n 88) at paras 2.28–2.32; Smerin, 'For Love Not Money' (n 188); N Maley, 'Bar and Law Society Warn *Pro Bono* Work is "No Substitute" for Legal Aid' *The Lawyer* 10 October 1995, at 2.

[191] S Allen, 'Act pro bono if cash runs out, judge tells solicitors' *Law Society Gazette* 15 February 2001.

that it is an ethical act.[192] It might be better if publicity for *pro bono publico* could be used sensitively and to promote the profession as a whole. Regulation, therefore, could aim to control references to pro bono in firm brochures and publicity, maintaining the delicate balance between ethics and commercialism.[193] There is, of course, an argument that such measures would be at odds with the minimalist regulatory strategy and not worth the effort involved in policing them.

F. Mixed Interests, Mixed Motivations

The culture of *pro bono publico* represents an interesting mixture of the various interests and motivations. A good example of this is provided by the website of Allen and Overy, one of the City of London Magic Circle firms. The site candidly identifies five drivers behind Allen and Overy's commitment to pro bono work. These are that pro bono is: the professional obligation of every lawyer; the provision of an interesting way to develop legal skills; a good marketing opportunity; a good sales window for recruitment and retention; and the means of fostering a sense of community within the firm.[194]

Whether it matters that individual lawyers are personally motivated to do pro bono work or not depends on whose perspective the issue is viewed from. Ordinary people are probably more concerned to have legal advice and help than why they receive it. Government is merely concerned that the pressure for access to justice is alleviated. Law firms may want to reach targets for pro bono for their own purposes. Lawyers would probably prefer not to be required to undertake pro bono, even if they would do it anyway. Professions would prefer not to have to make them because it is a potentially enormous task.

It might be a sign that the service ideal of legal professionalism is alive if pro bono was altruistically motivated. The plethora of reasons why pro bono seems to be more prevalent makes it tempting to adopt Menkel-Meadow's description of 'mixed motive altruism'.[195] This is not quite accurate though, since altruism is one of the many motives and pressures currently operating on lawyers who do pro bono. Arguably, the pro bono efforts of lawyers warrant praise when access to justice is the primary consideration. Others argue that motives underlying positive social behaviour do not matter. The reasons why people do good are complex and unknowable.[196] What matters is that the work is done.

[192] Nosworthy, 'Ethics and Large Law Firms' (n 116) at 71; CS Rhee, 'Pro Bono, Pro Se' (1996) 105 *Yale Law Journal* 1719, at 1724.
[193] Nosworthy (n 116) at 71.
[194] H Brooke, 'Second Annual Nottingham Pro Bono Lecture' (n 85) at 8.
[195] C Menkel-Meadow, 'The Causes of Cause Lawyering: Toward an Understanding of the Motivation and Commitment of Social Justice Lawyers' in A Sarat and S Scheingold, *Cause Lawyering: Political Commitments and Professional Responsibilities* (Oxford, Oxford University Press, 1998).
[196] M Ridley, *The Origins of Virtue* (Harmondsworth, Penguin, 1997) at 21; M Waters, 'Collegiality, Bureaucratization, and Professionalization: A Weberian Analysis' (1989) 94 *American Journal of Sociology* 945.

VIII. Regulation of Pro Bono

There is no general regulation of pro bono services, but there is regulation by the SRA of pro bono by in-house lawyers. This is imposed as a result of the LSA 2007, which requires that the provision of reserved legal services to the public is carried out through an authorised body. Therefore, the SRA regulations allow in-house solicitors to conduct pro bono work subject to three qualifications.[197] First, the work must not be a reserved legal activity which is part of the business of the organisation employing the person donating the services. Secondly, it must be covered by indemnity insurance. Thirdly, no fees can be charged, or a conditional fee agreement must be used and any fees recovered from the other side paid to a charity under a fee sharing agreement.

IX. The Future of the Service Ideal

A. Pro Bono as Service

Pro bono publico has become a key component of the modern ideology of legal professionalism and the promise to prospective lawyers. This is illustrated by the example of young lawyers at the New York office of Clifford Chance. The firm was bottom of a national league table measuring associate satisfaction. It sought the reasons from their young lawyers. The complaints outlined in a memorandum to the partners included their 'deplorable animosity' to pro bono work. Clifford Chance responded by including the performance of pro bono work as one of seven criteria for promotion.[198] Pro bono is a promise the profession may be unable to forget.

For the present, and particularly since the decline of legal aid, pro bono is the flagship for the service aspirations of lawyers. Indeed, it is rapidly becoming the defining feature of legal professionalism in common law jurisdictions[199] and beyond.[200] English lawyers even export the pro bono ideal overseas. For example, following a merger with a German firm, a City of London firm, Lovells, announced it was spreading its pro

---

[197] SRA, Practice Framework Rules 2011, r 4.10.
[198] N Rovnick, 'Clifford Chance New York puts pro bono on associates' agenda' *The Lawyer* 3 February 2003, at 3.
[199] C Arup and K Laster, *For the Public Good: Pro Bono and the Legal Profession in Australia* (Annandale, NSW, Federation Press, 2001).
[200] F Regan, 'How and Why Is Pro Bono Flourishing: A Comparison of Recent Developments in Sweden and China' in Arup and Laster, ibid, at 148.

bono practices to the Berlin office.[201] Barristers have established a panel to take cases to the European Court of Human Rights.[202]

Large firms find pro bono a convenient umbrella for a range of increasingly ambitious projects. Allen and Overy developed a European-wide child protection project with the Belgian charity Child Focus, based on its network of offices.[203] Under the banner of pro bono, law firms promote the rule of law overseas. For example, a team of associates with a US firm conducted an analysis for the International Bar Association Human Rights Institute of Zimbabwean legislation that clamped down on voting rights.[204]

The increase in pro bono activity and the use of the label for new kinds of activity suggest that pro bono will survive in some form. Lawyers have found a variety of uses for pro bono, including as a vehicle with traditional connotations for new corporate ventures. While entrants to the professions were less likely to be attracted to legal aid and similar work, interest in pro bono appears to be growing.

B. Mandatory Pro Bono

It is doubtful that the legal profession would seek to make pro bono mandatory of its own accord. This would presumably require the SRA's support. Such a move does not sit easily with its regulatory philosophy. It is possible that the government could put pressure on the profession to do pro bono in other ways. In Australia, firms bidding for government contracts are obliged to do pro bono work. The UK Solicitor General, Oliver Heald, rejected that idea, saying 'my feeling is voluntarism is the heart and soul of it'.[205] It is, however, possible that aspirational targets will be introduced as a means of encouraging activity.

C. The Legal Services Market

There are features of the legal services market that render the continuation of pro bono unpredictable. One aspect is the change in professional regulation and culture brought about by the LSA 2007. In the short term, pro bono could be a source of further tension in the relationship with government. Attempts by the state to exploit the gift of professional monopoly to extract free services from lawyers could provoke a negative reaction. On the other hand, in an era in which the state seeks evidence that

---

[201] 'Pro bono export' *Law Society Gazette* 17 August 2000.

[202] N Rovnick, 'Liberty sets up human rights pro bono unit' *The Lawyer* 22 October 2001.

[203] N Rovnick, 'A&O launches pro bono first with pan-European work for Child Focus' *The Lawyer* 25 March 2002.

[204] K Hobbs, 'Shearmans in pro bono anti-Mugabe endeavour' *The Lawyer* 25 March 2002, at 13.

[205] K Hall, 'Solicitor general discourages mandatory pro bono call' *Law Society Gazette* 7 November 2013   (www.lawgazette.co.uk/practice/record-number-of-junior-lawyers-working-pro-bono/practice/solicitor-general-discourages-mandatory-pro-bono-call/5038643.article).

institutions serve the public interest, the professions may strive hard to maintain *pro bono publico* as a symbol of their 'conscientious administration of trust'.[206]

In the long term the possibility is that, as a voluntary and unregulated activity, pro bono could be a casualty of the gradual de-professionalisation of legal services. The government's long-term strategy appears to be reduction of the scope of legal aid. LASPO 2012 will reduce assisted cases by 600,000,[207] the lowest levels of legal aid at any time since its introduction. This will lead to significant job losses in solicitors' firms and legal advice centres. It may mean that access to law can only be delivered by new methods and, probably, by new providers.

A possibility is that, in time, routine and low value matters will be handled by large organisations, like ABS, and free or cheap legal advice delivered online. In the same interview that the Solicitor General dismissed the idea of mandatory pro bono, he said '[t]he new ABS [approach] will change law in many ways'.[208] They would, he predicted, become a common feature of the high streets with non-legal businesses such as the Co-op underpinning them financially.

The idea that the provision of legal services for the poor would benefit from removing the established professions from them is not new.[209] In the eventuality that most low value legal work is done by ABS, however, elite lawyers may feel even less connection with everyday legal problems. High street lawyers may not have the capacity to deliver any more than occasional free assistance to their own clients.[210] If the structure of the profession changes, so that welfare-type work is no longer seen as the work of lawyers, there may be less enthusiasm for doing such work for nothing.

D. The Strategic View

The Nuffield Report argued that pro bono services are unlikely to make up for a lack of public funding, so the profession should focus on the quality of pro bono, not the quantity.[211] Rather than ensure that all lawyers do a little, it should make sure that what is done is genuinely useful. For example, it should concentrate on cases that will advance social welfare and rights generally by creating new law. In doing so, the profession may find itself in uncomfortable political territory, such as arguing for benefits for social groups or acting against the state.[212]

At present there are blind spots in pro bono provision that may undermine the ability to hold the state to account. Some categories of case may need legal innovations, for example class actions, before the issues can be aired. Lawyers may need to organise their pro bono effort more effectively to ensure that their role in upholding

---

[206] Boon and Whyte (n 103).
[207] N Byrom, *The State of the Sector: The Impact of Cuts to Civil Legal Aid on Practitioners and their Clients* (University of Warwick, Centre for Human Rights in Practice, 2013).
[208] Hall, 'Solicitor general discourages mandatory pro bono call' (n 205).
[209] A Southworth, 'Taking the Lawyer Out of Progressive Lawyering' (1993) 46 *Stanford Law Review* 213.
[210] LawWorks, *Pro Bono Survey 2012* (London, LawWorks, 2012).
[211] Boon and Whyte (n 103).
[212] Law Society press release, 'Undermining Human Rights across the World in the War against Terror' 15 November 2005.

the rule of law can be fulfilled. There may, however, be limits to what can be achieved in this way. Some types of case, community, environmental or social welfare cases for example, can alienate corporate clients. In the US, the conservative Federalist Society demonstrated outside the ABA's annual conference in New York to alert clients to the causes their lawyers were supporting.[213]

Using pro bono as a way of holding the state to a liberal agenda may be a useful way of interpreting the obligation to uphold the rule of law. Within the separation of powers, the judicial arm holds the executive to account. The courts need lawyers to bring cases to court in order to fulfil this role effectively. There is no lack of good causes. In the modern state, rights to privacy and confidentiality are asserted as essential social goods. Yet, as recent disclosures about the extent of government surveillance of the internet demonstrate, they are breached with impunity. Law remains the most effective way of policing the powers of the state.[214]

X. Conclusion

The notion of service has been through several transitions. *Pro bono publico* is a tradition of service that has been reinvented. It represents a small but significant proportion of law firm work. The basis for the provision of these services, and how they fit into the long-term strategy for legal services, is unclear. It may be that the profession's efforts are a bridge between legal aid and a mass legal services system operated by ABS. Free services will doubtless continue to be provided for a variety of reasons, but whether they can provide broad access to justice is doubtful.

The future for pro bono is as uncertain as it is for the professionalism on which it is built. Lawyers may desert low paid work, including legal aid and areas of law no longer covered by legal aid. Yet they would be ill-advised to surrender an institution, pro bono, that has potent ideological force. Many lawyers are highly motivated to act pro bono. They may see any attempt to end this tradition as a betrayal. If the data is reliable, the growth of pro bono activity may provide evidence that the idea of providing access to justice has meaning to many lawyers.

---

[213] Ames, 'Do the Right Thing' (n 76); and see further E Wentworth, 'Barriers to Pro Bono: Commercial Conflicts of Interest Reconsidered' in Arup and Laster (n 200) at 166.

[214] M Taylor and N Hopkins, 'Amnesty in legal challenge to surveillance by state' *The Guardian* 9 December 2013, at 4.

16

Employment

'Psychologists, organization theorists, and economists all know that the ethics of ethical decision-making change dramatically when the individual works in an organisational setting. Loyalties become tangled and personal responsibility gets diffused. Bucks are passed and guilty knowledge bypassed. Chains of command not only tie people's hands, they fetter their minds and consciences as well. Reinhold Niebuhr called one of his books *Moral Man, Immoral Society*, and I suggest for students of ethics no topic is more important than understanding whatever truth the title contains'.[1]

I. Introduction

Professional ethics often pays little attention to the employment relationship as a source of ethical obligation. This is partly because sole practice was required at the Bar and quite common among solicitors. It may also be explained by the fact that regulation, and professional ethics, was primarily directed at the individual. Following the Legal Services Act 2007 (LSA 2007), organisations have been subject to closer regulation and scrutiny than before. This may, however, be a continuation of a trend that was evident before the Act.

The recent emergence of the corporate form has changed perceptions of legal employment. The dominance of the profession by large law firms is a fairly recent phenomenon, as are Alternative Business Structures. Such organisations are more likely to rely on hierarchical employment relationships. The professions turned their attention to employment with the realisation that they needed to extend their regulatory reach in order to protect members in the workplace.[2]

Although legal employers are subject to the same legal duties as other employers, it is arguable that they are in a different position in relation to their employees than non-professional employers. They have, for example, an obligation to behave ethically, consistent with the aspirations of the profession, and to support ethical performance

---

[1] DJ Luban, 'Milgram Revisited' (1998) 9(2) *Researching Law: An ABF Update* 1, at 4.
[2] See generally P Thomas (ed), *Discriminating Lawyers* (London, Sydney, Cavendish Publishing Ltd, 2000).

of the professionals they employ. Both main legal professions have increasingly made organisations responsible for ethical performance.

The ethical responsibilities of employers arguably apply also to recruitment. The privileged position of professions carries responsibility to ensure that entry to the profession is truly open to all and can lead to a rewarding career. People will not invest time in long education and training if there are few jobs, inadequate remuneration and no support. For all these reasons it is in the interests of legal businesses to ensure that they are based on sound ethical foundations.

II.   Solicitors' Employment Pre-qualification

A.   Articles of Clerkship

From the eighteenth century, intending lawyers, attorneys, notaries and solicitors entered articles of clerkship with an established practitioner, the principal, for periods of between five and seven years. No standards of training were laid down, even for solicitors, so articled clerks' experience was variable until the Solicitors Act 1922 made one year of part-time attendance at law school compulsory.[3] Elite firm solicitors also sent their children to elite universities to befriend future captains of industry.[4]

Following the Ormrod Report in 1971, five-year articles of clerkship were phased out[5] and a university degree and two years' articles became the norm. Burrage thought that the 'hardship, drudgery and semi-servitude' of five-year articles encouraged an appreciation of membership and the time served offered thorough induction into the ethical community.[6] He suggests that subsequent preference for the university route led to declining responsibility for the 'collective honour of the profession'.[7] If this is true, training carries heavy burdens. They include translating learned principles of conduct into practice and impressing entrants with their importance.

B.   The Training Contract

The training contract replaced articles of clerkship in 1993, when the Legal Practice Course (LPC) and the Professional Skills Course (PSC) were introduced. Continuity between the LPC and the training period was improved and trainees had to work in four different departments, or 'seats', to gain broad experience. The PSC comprised

---

[3]   E Cruikshank, 'Building a Profession' (2003) 100(25) *Law Society Gazette* 32.
[4]   J Slinn, *A History of Freshfields* (London, Freshfields, 1984); J Slinn, *Linklaters and Paines—The First One Hundred and Fifty Years* (London, Longman, 1987).
[5]   The Hon Mr Justice Ormrod (chair), *Report of the Committee on Legal Education* (Cmnd 4595, 1971).
[6]   M Burrage, 'From a Gentleman's to a Public Profession' (1996) *International Journal of the Legal Profession* 45, at 68.
[7]   ibid, at 72.

further communication and advocacy skills, financial and business skills and client care,[8] together with an ethics component with minimum tuition time of 12 hours.[9] Firms were required to provide study leave and pay the course fee. A code of conduct was introduced requiring monitoring and appraisal of trainees.[10]

In the late-1960s, 5 per cent of firms still demanded payment of a premium by the articled clerk, but most paid small salaries. The Law Society recommended this be seen as an 'allowance' rather than a living wage.[11] Under the training contract, firms had to pay trainees a minimum salary, unless waiver was granted.[12] They were subject to closer monitoring[13] possibly resulting in them being prevented from taking on trainees. Small and niche firms could collaborate to provide four seats, but the bureaucratic requirements were more difficult to meet. The changes upset a delicate balance whereby first year traineeships were of equal benefit to firm and trainee, but the second year mainly benefited the firm.[14]

The new requirements resulted in training contracts becoming a bottleneck in the qualification process. In 1988, the Law Society had reported a recruitment crisis, particularly in local government, the CPS and in private practice in the North East, parts of the North West and the Midlands.[15] The report noted that 'even firms in the City of London report difficulties'.[16] In 1995 there were nearly 10,000 applications to study the LPC but only 7000 full-time and 954 part-time places. Then there were only 4063 training contracts registered with the Law Society for 7800 students studying the LPC. The demography of the profession, the potential unfairness of recruitment practices and the cost of qualification generated debates at national level.[17]

C. Barriers to Entry

i. Discrimination

During the 1980s pressure mounted for the legal profession to reflect the composition of society.[18] The Law Society appointed an equal opportunities officer and, in

---

[8] Law Society Training Regulations 1990.

[9] Originally called 'Ethics and Client Responsibilities', but renamed 'Client Care and Professional Standards' in the relaunch of the PSC in 2000.

[10] ibid.

[11] E Cruikshank, 'Surviving Hard Times' (2003) 100(32) *Law Society Gazette* 22.

[12] Law Society Education and Training Unit, *Training Trainee Solicitors: The Law Society Requirements* (July 2007) pt 3.

[13] SRA, *Annual Report 2006/07*, at 10.

[14] K Economides and J Smallcombe, *Preparatory Skills Training for Solicitors* (London, The Law Society, 1991) at 16.

[15] The Law Society, *The Recruitment Crisis, A Report by the Training committee of the Law Society* (London, The Law Society, 1988).

[16] ibid, at para 11(c).

[17] The Legal Services Consultative Panel, *Advice to the Secretary of State on The Legal Profession: Entry, Retention and Competition* (May 2005).

[18] W Twining, 'Access to Legal Education and the Legal Profession: a Commonwealth Perspective' in R Dhavan, N Kibble and W Twining (eds), *Access to Legal Education and the Legal Profession* (London, Butterworths, 1989).

1995, introduced the Solicitors Model Anti-discrimination Policy.[19] Based on the Sex Discrimination Act 1975 and Race Relations Act 1976, the model policy defined direct discrimination as treating people 'less favourably' on the grounds of sex or race. Indirect discrimination was defined as applying an unjustifiable requirement or condition equally to all groups when it has a disproportionately adverse effect on one particular group.[20]

Solicitors who did not have an anti-discrimination code of their own were deemed to have adopted the Law Society's model policy. The model policy was very relevant to recruitment. It provided that the firm subscribed to equal opportunities hiring policies, and would ensure that 'applications are attracted from both sexes and all races and from people with disabilities'.[21] It committed firms to take 'positive action to ensure greater representation of unrepresented groups'.[22] It also committed them to 'compliance with Law Society policy on targets for the employment of ethnic minorities',[23] defined as people of 'Asian, African-Caribbean, African or Chinese origin'.[24]

A schedule to the model policy noted that setting enforceable quotas was contrary to the law, but that setting targets 'to reach as good practice' was not.[25] It went on to state that small firms with between six and ten fee-earners should have at least one fee-earner of ethnic minority origin and firms with more than ten fee-earners should have at least 10 per cent trainees and 5 per cent fee earners from ethnic minorities.[26]

Solicitors introducing their own policy on anti-discrimination were bound by a new anti-discrimination rule providing that firms would not discriminate on grounds of race, sex or sexual orientation, and 'must not discriminate unfairly or unreasonably on grounds of disability, in their professional dealings with clients, staff... or other persons'.[27] The chapter went on to provide that solicitors could not discriminate in any of the proscribed ways 'in the selection, treatment or promotion of staff'.[28] In 2000, the chief executive of the Law Society claimed a good record in combatting unlawful discrimination in the legal profession,[29] but there were still significant hurdles to achieving a representative profession.

Throughout the 1990s the Law Society developed greater understanding of entry to the profession. It funded two studies of training. In the first, Goriely and Williams assessed the impact of the new training scheme, finding deep problems in the process. Following their report, the Law Society commissioned a longitudinal study of the

---

[19] The Law Society, *The Law Society's Model Anti-discrimination Policy* (London, The Law Society, 1995).

[20] ibid, at paras 3(a) and (b).

[21] ibid, at para 5.

[22] ibid, at para 4.

[23] ibid, at para 6.

[24] ibid, at para 4.

[25] ibid, at sch, para 1.

[26] ibid, at sch, paras 2 and 3.

[27] N Taylor (ed), *The Guide to the Professional Conduct of Solicitors* (London, The Law Society, 1999) r 7.01.

[28] ibid, r 7.02.

[29] 'Opinion—Janet Paraskeva' *The Lawyer* 11 March 2002, at 19.

process of entry to the legal profession. The 'Cohort Study' eventually comprised six surveys, undertaken by different academic teams, following a large group of under-graduate students into practice.[30]

Goriely and Williams reported that a key question in recruitment to solicitors' firms was 'are they one of us?'.[31] This potentially discriminated against anyone who was not male, white and middle class. Nepotism and favouritism were deeply ingrained. In 1995, at the same time as the Law Society issued its model anti-discrimination policy, a President of the Law Society wrote to the *Gazette*, defending discriminatory practices in small firms. It was acceptable, he said, if a firm, while not intending to take a trainee, made 'an exception for the son or daughter of one of its partners or valuable clients'.[32]

Surprisingly, the President's view was somewhat vindicated when, in 2001, the Lord Chancellor survived a challenge to his appointment of 'a friend', former Herbert Smith lawyer Garry Hart, to be his special adviser. The Court of Appeal held that, in the circumstances, appointment from close circles of family, friends and acquain-tances was 'not likely to constitute indirect discrimination'.[33] This gives a sense of the rather uncertain attitudes regarding discrimination at the time. The fifth cohort survey confirmed that appointment following introduction to firms by relatives or recruitment consultants was common.[34]

The Law Society's efforts on recruitment to the profession were gradually repaid. Of the 104,543 solicitors with practising certificates in 2006, 44,394 were women and 9,471 from ethnic minorities.[35] While this approached proportionate representation, the pattern of employment was a new concern. In 2008, just over one half of minority ethnic group solicitors worked in firms with four or fewer partners, compared with only 28 per cent of white Europeans.[36] The Law Society's own research had already suggested why this might be.

The third cohort study found that ethnic minorities might not get training contracts in large firms because of indirect discrimination. Large firms tended to recruit early, offering training contracts to second year undergraduates, in order to compete for 'high flyers'. Since this meant that a degree classification was not available, the firms took 'A' levels as the most reliable indicator of academic quality.[37] This was also

[30] D Halpern, *Entry Into the Legal Professions: The Law Student Cohort Study Years 1 and 2* (London, The Law Society, 1994), (first survey); M Shiner and T Newburn, *Entry Into the Legal Professions: Law Student Cohort Study Year 3* (London, The Law Society, 1995) (second survey); M Shiner *Entry into the Legal Professions: The Law Student Cohort Study Year 4* (London, The Law Society, 1997) (third survey); M Shiner, *Entry into the Legal Professions: The Law Student Cohort Study Year 5* (London, Law Society, 1999) (fourth survey); E Duff, M Shiner, A Boon, A Whyte, *Entry into the Legal Professions: The Law Student Cohort Study Year 6* (London, The Law Society, 2000) (fifth survey).

[31] T Goriely and T Williams, *The Impact of the New Training Scheme: Report on a Qualitative Study* (London, The Law Society, 1996).

[32] M Mears, letter to *Law Society Gazette* 29 November 1995.

[33] T Branigan, 'Irvine has the right to employ a friend' *The Guardian* 23 November 2001, at 14.

[34] A Boon, L Duff and M Shiner, 'Career Paths and Choices in a Highly Differentiated Profession: The Position of Newly Qualified Solicitors' (2001) 64(4) *Modern Law Review* 563.

[35] ibid; Cole, *Trends in the Solicitors' Profession* (London, Law Society, 2006).

[36] B Cole, N Fletcher, T Chittenden and J Cox, *Trends in the Solicitors' Profession Annual Statistical Report 2009* (London, Law Society, 2009) at 20.

[37] H Rolfe and T Anderson, *The Recruitment of Trainee Solicitors* (London, The Law Society, 2002).

common practice among elite, non-lawyer corporations.[38] It favoured students with social capital, from professional backgrounds, and disadvantaged those from lower social classes and ethnic minorities.[39] It may have also sent a message that elite employers did not want to attract them.[40]

As a result of the publicity generated by the research, some large firms did, apparently, adjust their recruitment practices. Many tried to recruit from a more diverse pool, using work placements to screen potential trainees with non-traditional profiles. In the wider profession, diversity continued to provoke mixed reactions. A survey in 2007 showed that nearly 70 per cent of lawyers favoured hiring former comprehensive school students, but between 30 and 40 per cent were opposed to diversity monitoring.[41]

ii. Cost

Cost proved a significant barrier to entry.[42] Large firms paid course fees and provided a living allowance to their intending trainees. Other entrants had to find around £10,000 for LPC fees plus living expenses. Many decided not to add to their undergraduate debt. In 2002, a severe shortage of trainees in legal aid work led the Legal Services Commission to sponsor solicitors working in legal aid firms, and intending barristers to work in immigration and asylum.[43] In return, they gave a commitment to work for two years post qualification in legal aid. This, it was thought, would benefit disadvantaged entrants.[44]

By 2010, 750 legal aid lawyers had been helped to qualify in the previous eight years, but the scheme had not worked quite as intended. Many recruits to the Training Contract Grant Scheme were altruistically motivated students from wealthy backgrounds.[45] The advantage lay in encouraging the many firms which claimed that they would not have been able to afford trainees without the scheme. In 2010, the Ministry of Justice announced that it was dropping the scheme immediately. It explained that 'we now have too many lawyers chasing too little work, and greater pressure to save public money, so the financial inducements no longer make economic sense'.[46]

[38] D Williams, 'Degrees of separation' *The Guardian: Rise* 21 January 2006, at 3.
[39] M Shiner, 'Young Gifted and Blocked! Entry to the Solicitor's Profession' in Thomas, *Discriminating Lawyers* (n 2) at 87.
[40] D Wilkins and G Mitu Gulati, 'Why Are There So Few Black Lawyers in Corporate Law Firms: An Institutional Analysis' (1996) 84 *California Law Review* 493.
[41] K Williams, 'Firms rail against diversity monitoring' *The Lawyer* 10 September 2007, at 21.
[42] L Norman, *Career Choices in Law: A Survey of Law Students* Research Study 50 (London, The Law Society, 2004).
[43] Legal Services Commission, *Consultation Paper: Developing Legal Aid Solicitors* (2002).
[44] ibid, at 3.
[45] S Bacquet, A Boon, L Webley and A Whyte, 'Making Legal Aid Solicitors?: The Training Contract Grant Scheme' in A Buck, P Pleasence and NJ Balmer (eds), *Reaching Further: Innovation, Access and Quality in Legal Services* (London, The Stationery Office, 2009).
[46] 'Djanogly scraps training contract grant scheme' *Solicitors Journal* 7 July 2010.

D. Quality of Training Experience

i. Differences between Large Firms and Small Firms

Research in the 1980s suggested that some trainees experienced legal work as 'a nasty shock'.[47] In the mid-1990s a survey of trainees and recently qualified lawyers found a 'considerable level of disquiet', attributable 'to debt, lack of job security and the quality of supervision and training'.[48] Goriely and Williams found that small firms often looked for a short-term return on salaries and were more likely to give trainees routine tasks, such as photocopying.[49] Large firms tended to recruit trainees with a view to their long-term development. The Law Society's longitudinal study found the differences in motivation were reflected in training experience.

Large firms increasingly tended to employ directors of education and training. Numbers increased from four to 96 between 1987 and 1990.[50] This helped improve the quality of training in-house, including PSC and Continuing Professional Development programmes, but there were some negative consequences. One was that it weakened bonds between trainees and individual partners. This combined with the effect of movement of trainees between 'seats', with the result that large firm partners spent less time in their training role.

Large firm trainees found that training replaced experience in their early development as lawyers.[51] They had inadequate exposure to clients and no work of a sufficiently low level on which to cut their teeth. In contrast, small firm trainees often had too much experience. Some complained of having to quickly manage onerous caseloads with inadequate supervision and of being expected to contribute to profitability. Others welcomed responsibility and the opportunity to develop.[52]

ii. Harassment and Bullying

Respondents in the fifth cohort survey reported a disturbingly high incidence of harassment and bullying. This was reflected in calls to the Trainee Solicitors' Group (TSG) Helpline. In 1997/98 there were 42 calls to the TSG Helpline. One trainee reported being asked to take an 'unethical short cut' at work. Having refused, the trainee claimed that he 'was subjected to such a malicious campaign that, eventually, I had to leave'.[53] The following year, there were 122 calls to

---

[47] P McDonald, 'The Class of "81"—A Glance at the Social Class Composition of Recruits to the Legal Profession' (1982) 9 *Journal of Law and Society* 267.

[48] R Moorhead and F Boyle, 'Quality of Life and Trainee Solicitors: a Survey' (1995) 2 *International Journal of the Legal Profession* 217, at 218.

[49] Goriely and Williams, *The Impact of the New Training Scheme* (n 31).

[50] EH Greenebaum, 'Development of Law Firm Training Programs: Coping with a Turbulent Environment' (1996) 3(3) *International Journal of the Legal Profession* 315, at 318–19, 331 and 345.

[51] E Levenson, 'A nice package' *The Lawyer* 5 November 2001, at 31.

[52] A Boon, 'From Public Service to Service Industry: the Impact of Socialisation and Work on the Motivation and Values of Lawyers' (2005) 12 *International Journal of the Legal Profession* 193.

[53] 'Help at hand for trainee troubles' *The Lawyer* 19 May 1998.

the Helpline in the first six months.[54] The TSG liaison officer reported also receiving 2500 calls a month, many from trainees. Some reported firms hiring para-legals on the promise of a training contract 'if we like you' and holding out para-legals as trainees.

Between 1 August 2003 and 12 March 2004, there were 1,162 calls to the helpline. Of these, 13 per cent related to bullying and harassment, including sexual harassment, or inadequate training and supervision.[55] In the year from March 2004 to March 2005, 2,241 calls were received.[56] In 2008 the TSG was replaced by the Junior Lawyers Division of The Law Society. Thereafter, trainees could ring the Law Society's other helplines or consult the list of frequently asked questions on the Law Society web-site.[57] These contained a familiar set of complaints, from failings, such as not registering training contracts, to bullying.

iii. Ethical Components of Training

In the 1990s, Goriely and Williams found little evidence of any kind of informal ethical induction within firms. Few trainee supervisors had read the Guide to the Professional Conduct of Solicitors, regarding it as a reference work rather than an integral part of working life. Trainers and trainees were dismissive of the PSC, except for the advocacy component. Trainees regarded the day spent on professional conduct as a 'token gesture'.[58]

Despite a review of the training scheme in 2000, the Law Society's guidance to trainees raised few expectations regarding ethics in the training contract.[59] Guidance issued in 2007 provided lists of skills and subjects to which the trainee was to be exposed. It provided for reviews, appraisal and 'guidance', but barely mentioned ethics, even in an extensive list of trainee responsibilities.[60] It did, however, recommend that trainees record any professional conduct issues arising in their training contract record.

E. Reform of Training

A recurrent policy issue was whether the system of training could achieve similar results in different ways,[61] including shorter and cheaper routes to qualification. In 2005, the Law Society's Training Framework Review proposed Day One outcomes

---

[54] 'Trainee Group Helpline calls hit record high' *The Lawyer* 4 May 1999.

[55] TSG, *Trainee Solicitors' Group Helpline Review, August 2003—March 2004* and see 'Bullying Concerns as pleas to TSG Helpline soar' *Law Society Gazette* 26 November 2004 (www.lawgazette.co.uk/news/bullying-concern-as-pleas-to-tsg-helpline-soar/42961.article).

[56] TSG, *Trainee Solicitors' Group Helpline Review, March 2004—March 2005.*

[57] http://juniorlawyers.lawsociety.org.uk/node/143.

[58] Goriely and Williams (n 31).

[59] Law Society, *A Trainee Solicitor's Guide to Authorisation* (Redditch, Law Society Monitoring and Training Department, 2000).

[60] Law Society, *Training Trainee Solicitors: The Law Society Requirements* (July 2007) s 4, and see s 8 for trainee responsibilities.

[61] C Thomson, 'Fairness for all' *The Lawyer* 20 May 1997 (student supp, at vi).

to be met by intending solicitors. No particular route for achieving the outcomes, was prescribed, but a two-year period of work-based learning was retained as a pre-requisite for practice. It was proposed this could be completed at a range of training organisations, without the need to provide four seats.[62]

The Training Framework Review proposed tighter procedures for monitoring and review of trainees. This included regular appraisal, completion of a reflective journal and a centrally administered test, involving ethics questions. All of these elements were to be completed before the end of the work-based learning period. This liberalisation of the training period regime allowed students to qualify through different routes, including by having previously worked for a firm as a para-legal. Trainees could have a maximum of six months removed from their two-year training contract by agreement with their employing firm. The SRA then ran a successful pilot programme to explore work-based learning as an alternative to a training contract.

The work-based learning pilot required candidates to acquire, develop, apply and evidence skills and knowledge. Eight key learning outcomes included the practical application of the law, professional communication, relationships with clients and the application of the rules and principles of professional conduct in legal practice.[63] Students could also qualify through a supervised work-based programme. An example of such a programme is an unpaid work placement at a registered firm, combined with work in a university law clinic.[64]

i. Current Training Regime

The main elements of the training regime introduced in 1993, including the training contract, survive for the present. The main thrust of policy is towards liberalising requirements for work-based learning rather than replacing them. Under the SRA's current regulations, training establishments must provide trainees with close supervision by partners, senior solicitors or others with the appropriate experience in English law.[65]

Trainees must receive regular feedback and at least three appraisals during training. They must have practical exposure to three distinct areas of English law, skills in both contentious and non-contentious work and development of practice skills meeting the practice skill standards. Trainees must maintain a training contract record linking experience to the skills developed.

Under the current SRA training regulations, a training establishment can grant a reduction in the period of the training contract of up to six months. It must be satisfied that a trainee considered for this reduction has gained equivalent experience in one or more areas of English law, and acquired one or more of the practice skill standards, in the three years immediately preceding commencement.[66] For the experience

---

[62] J Eldred, 'How to put recruits through their paces' *Law Society Gazette* 5 September 2002, at 21.
[63] J Wiseman, P Roe and E Davies, *Final Evaluation of the Work-Based Learning (WBL) Pilot* (Birmingham, BMG Research, 2012).
[64] www.northumbria.ac.uk/sd/academic/law/mlaw/faqs/.
[65] SRA Training Regulations 2011, pt 2: Training Provider Regulations, reg 6(1).
[66] ibid, reg 7.1.

to count, the prospective trainee must have been working full-time, or not less than two and a half days per week, and been adequately supervised and appraised.[67]

ii. Current Entry Patterns

In 2011/12 nearly 15,000 students graduated with a degree in Law.[68] Just over a third of these graduates are from Black and Minority Ethnic (BME) groups.[69] Around 60 per cent aim to qualify as lawyers, mainly solicitors.

a. Traineeships

In 2007/08, 6,303 traineeships were registered, the highest number since recording began in1998/99. The following year, registrations fell compared with the previous year, by 8 per cent, to 5,809.[70] In 2011/12, registrations again fell, to the lowest ever recorded level, 4,869.[71] A large component in this decline is ascribed to the general economic situation. The practice of appointing candidates for traineeship as paralegals[72] could be a contributory factor.

Of the new trainees registered in 2009, 62 per cent were women and nearly 20 per cent with known ethnicity were from minority ethnic groups. In 2012, the proportion from BME groups was up to 23 per cent.[73] Nearly 40 per cent of the training contracts were from firms located in the City of London. The next largest groups were the rest of London, at 16 per cent, the North West at 12 per cent and the South East at 7 per cent. Nearly 94 per cent of the traineeships were with private practice firms with nearly 40 per cent in firms with more than 81 partners. The intake of these firms comprised 771 men, 42 per cent of all men, and 926 women, 34 per cent of all women.[74]

b. Admissions

In 2011/12 admissions to the roll of newly qualified solicitors fell from the all-time high of 8,491 in 2008/09 to 6,350.[75] The drop of nearly 25 per cent is the largest since records began.[76] Of the total entrants, around 50 per cent were law graduates, while 16 per cent were conversion course students. The largest age group for new admissions, around 1600, was the 30 to 40 range. This reflects the fact that just over 20 per cent of admissions in 2011/12 represented members of other legal professions converting to being solicitors.

---

[67] ibid, reg 7.2.
[68] The Law Society, *Trends in the Solicitors Profession 2012* (London, The Law Society, 2013) at 35.
[69] ibid, at 34.
[70] Cole, Fletcher, Chittenden and Cox, *Trends in the Solicitors' Profession Annual Statistical Report 2009* (n 36).
[71] The Law Society, *Trends in the Solicitors Profession 2012* (n 68).
[72] IPS, BSB and SRA, *The Future of Legal Services Education and Training Regulation in England and Wales* (June 2013) at para 2.136.
[73] The Law Society, *Trends in the Solicitors Profession 2012* (n 68) at 43.
[74] ibid, at 46.
[75] ibid, at 48.
[76] ibid, at 55.

Of the converts to the solicitors' profession among new admissions, around 14 per cent were overseas lawyers, 6 per cent barristers and 2 per cent FILEX transfers.[77] Of the overseas lawyers, the largest group being admitted as solicitors were lawyers from Australia and New Zealand. The proportion of transfers into the solicitors' profession actually fell in 2011/12, from 25 per cent in 2009. This was possibly due to low levels of registration for the Qualified Lawyers Transfer Scheme, which replaced the Qualified Lawyers Transfer Test in 2010.

Since 2001/02, the admission of men as solicitors was consistently 10 to 20 per cent lower than that for women. In 2001/02 the percentage of men being admitted as solicitors was 44 per cent, whereas in 2012 it was 40 per cent.[78] In fact, the proportion of men being admitted in 2012 was at the lowest level since 1996. Around 27 per cent of new admissions were BME candidates. The proportion had risen from 16 per cent in 2002 and 20 per cent in 2007.[79]

iii. Proposed Reform

The Legal Education and Training Review considered the fitness for purpose of the system. The research report stated that firms look for good 'A' levels and 'good' universities.[80] The report presented some data on attitudes towards the training contract. On a scale ranging between 'completely agree' and 'completely disagree' only 38 per cent of solicitors 'completely disagreed' that the training contract be abolished.[81] Around 30 per cent of law students, and 27 per cent of para-legals, 'completely agreed' with abolition.[82]

The LETR Report recorded almost universal agreement among respondents that 'some element of supervised workplace training must be retained'. It argued for more flexibility in allowing trainees to work and study concurrently. It suggested that 'the burden should be on the regulator, adopting a risk-based approach, to identify why a proposed route should not be permitted if the relevant learning outcomes can be achieved'.[83] The report envisaged multiple routes to achieving the same outcomes.

The LSB responded to the LETR with a consultation setting out its own ideas for change. It stated that 'a liberalised legal services market can only function effectively for consumers if there is a significantly more flexible labour market'.[84] Regulation of education and training, it said, should be outcomes focused and risk based.[85] The

[77] ibid, at 50.
[78] ibid, at 48.
[79] ibid, at 53.
[80] IPS, BSB and SRA *The Future of Legal Services Education and Training* (n 72) at para 2.143 and Table 2.10.
[81] ibid, at para 2.62.
[82] ibid, Table 2.3.
[83] ibid, at xv and recommendations 14 and 15.
[84] LSB, *Increasing Flexibility in Legal Education and Training: Consultation on Proposals for Draft Statutory Guidance to be Issued under Section 162 of the Legal Services Act 2013* (London, Legal Services Board, 2013) at para 11.
[85] ibid, at para 20.

LSB proposed that training requirements be either role or activity specific, with some requirements applied by all regulators. An example of a common requirement was 'areas such as professional principles and ethics'.[86]

The implication of the LSB's approach was a move to activity-based regulation. Training would then focus on the skills needed by the person delivering the services, and the risk involved, rather than on preparation of people for a specific and broadly based profession.[87] Regulation would focus on whether proposed routes met desired outcomes.[88]

III. Post-qualification Practice of Solicitors

A. Workplace Regulation of Solicitors before the Legal Services Act 2007

Some regulation of employing organisations is longstanding. In 1999, for example, the *Guide* provided that a firm had to have at least one principal admitted for three years and that solicitors could only enter partnership with other solicitors.[89] There was also regulation of those persons solicitors could and could not employ. For example, the 1999 *Guide* provided that solicitors could employ '[a] non-practising barrister'.[90] They could only employ solicitors who had been struck off, however, with the permission of the Law Society. Partners were responsible for the firm, a responsibility that extended to the acts or omissions of staff.

The regulation of everyday employment by professions was relatively light. The Guide required attendance of suitably qualified lawyers for the kind of work conducted in the office.[91] Solicitors, not just partners, were responsible for 'exercising proper supervision of staff', including independent contractors employed by the firm.[92] There had to be arrangements for the supervising solicitor to see incoming mail.[93] Principals were 'responsible' for all work carried out by staff[94] and could face disciplinary action where they knew or should have known about any breaches of accounts rules by the firm.[95]

---

[86] ibid, at page 15 (Outcome 1a).
[87] ibid, at paras 52–57.
[88] ibid, at para 59.
[89] ibid, rr 3.01 and 3.02.
[90] ibid, r 20.08.
[91] ibid, r 3.08(1).
[92] ibid, r 3.07.
[93] ibid, r 3.08(2).
[94] ibid, r 3.07, note 2.
[95] ibid, r 3.06, note 2.

B. Regulation of Solicitors' Workplaces after the Legal Services Act 2007

Regulation of employment by and of solicitors has grown and has become more complex under the LSA 2007. There are three main areas, relating to type of regulated organisation, personnel and the kinds of obligation imposed.

i. Organisations

The LSA 2007 extended the potential range of organisations handling legal work to Alternative Business Structures. This potentially changed management responsibility for lawyers and the scope of employment relationships. The possibility of non-lawyer ownership and management of ABS meant that responsibility could no longer be laid solely at the door of solicitors and partners.

ii. Personnel

a. Employees

Another anticipated feature of ABS was that they would involve multi-disciplinary practice, mixing people with different professional backgrounds. There was a possibility that different people in the same workplace could be subject to different regulatory regimes. Such people could include members of all the law professions, now approved regulators, and Registered European Lawyers (RELs) and Registered Foreign Lawyers (RFLs).[96] The mixture of professional backgrounds within law firms was already a feature of many practices before the LSA 2007, so was not revolutionary. The SRA regime did, however, make specific provision by subjecting all those working within entities to the SRA Code.

A wide range of people are now subject to the SRA Code of Conduct, including non-lawyer owners of ABS or managers or employees of firms.[97] Managers and employees of an authorised firm, which the SRA does not regulate, are subject to the Code when doing work SRA-authorised work for their firm.[98] All of those subject to the SRA Code of Conduct must receive training on its requirements appropriate to their role and level of responsibility. For example, all staff must understand confidentiality but only fee earners need to manage conflicts of interest. Staff are only responsible for implementation at their own level of responsibility.[99]

b. Managers

Responsibility for businesses under the SRA Code of Conduct lies with managers. These are defined to include a member of an LLP, a director of a company, a partner

---

[96] See further ch 4.
[97] SRA, *Code of Conduct*, ch 13: 'Application, Waivers and Interpretation', at r 13.1(b)(ii).
[98] ibid, at 13.1(b)(v).
[99] ibid, at 13.8.

in a partnership or a member of the governing body of any other body.[100] The LSA 2007 imposes a duty on a non-authorised person, whether employees or managers of licensed bodies (ABS firms). The duty is not to do anything which causes or substantially contributes to a breach by the licensed body, or an authorised person in relation to a reserved legal activity, of the duties imposed on them by section 176.

c. Compliance Officers

The Act also prescribes that licensed bodies shall have a Head of Legal Practice and a Head of Finance and Administration. The Head of Legal Practice must ensure compliance with the terms of the licence, ensure that authorised persons conducting reserved legal activities comply with duties imposed by the approved regulator[101] and report to the licensing authority any failure to comply with the terms of the licence.[102] Licensed bodies must, in accordance with the LSA 2007, also report non-material breaches. The Head of Finance and Administration must ensure compliance with the SRA Accounts Rules, recording breaches and reporting any material failure to the SRA as soon as reasonably practical.

As part of its regime for managing ABS, the SRA extended these requirements to all the entities it regulates, renaming the Head of Legal Practice a Compliance Officer for Legal Practice (COLP) and the Head of Finance and Administration, Compliance Officer Finance and Administration (COFAs). Firms can decide how the COLP and COFA operate within their business structure depending on the nature of the business and business risks. Managers are responsible for ensuring that COLPs and COFAs are effective, including by providing support and, in large firms, clear reporting lines. Sole practitioners will find that that they are both COLP and COFA for their business.

Unsurprisingly, the imposition of an infrastructure designed to control complex ABS on all solicitors, caused concern. Apart from the obligation to report colleagues, there was the difficulty of deciding when a breach becomes material. In making this decision the COLP or COFA must take account of a number of factors. They include the detriment, or risk of detriment, to clients, the extent of any risk of loss of confidence in the firm or in the provision of legal services, the scale of the issue and the overall impact on the firm, its clients and third parties.[103] Firms therefore had the scope, and the incentive, to define breaches as non-material and therefore not reportable by a non-ABS entity.[104]

iii. Employer Obligations

COLPs and COFAs must ensure compliance in their areas of responsibility. Under the SRA Handbook, managers have overall responsibility for meeting the outcomes and

---

[100] SRA, *Handbook*, Definitions.
[101] LSA 2007, s 176.
[102] ibid, s 91.
[103] SRA, Authorisation Rules for Legal Services Bodies and Licensable Bodies 2011, r 8(1) guidance note x.
[104] J Hyde, 'COLPs and COFAs need help to enjoy new-found freedom' *Law Society Gazette* 17 October 2013.

for compliance generally.[105] The outcomes include a requirement to have a clear and effective governance structure and reporting lines.[106] There must be effective systems and controls in place to achieve compliance with the SRA principles.[107] Training must be provided to enable individuals to maintain a level of competence appropriate to their work and level of responsibility.[108] Employers must also ensure statutory requirements for the direction and supervision of reserved legal activities are met, for example, by ensuring that they are not outsourced to persons not qualified to conduct them.[109]

iv. Transition into Qualified Practice

Different firms tend to have different policies on retention of trainees at the end of the training period. In commercial firms, retention rates tend to be around 70–80 per cent.[110] This relatively high level is partly because of the high investment made in each trainee. In fact, special measures, including salary rises,[111] are often taken to keep staff, such as providing mentors to discuss problems with.[112] Trainees do have the protection of employment law and firms must behave cautiously and reasonably to avoid claims for unfair dismissal.[113]

The fifth phase of the cohort study found that the majority of trainees did not have much choice when accepting a training contract. Around 14 per cent were unhappy with the type of firm they were in.[114] Movement between types of firm was rare, however. Newly qualified solicitors were usually limited to the type of firm they trained in and the type of work they did.[115] This may explain why 6 per cent thought they would not be working as a solicitor or barrister in five years and a further 18 per cent were not sure.

v. Terms and Conditions

Menkel-Meadow argues that the quality of life of employees is an ethical issue for law firms.[116] The terms and conditions of lawyers' employment are different although probably more variable in high street firms. There are potentially six aspirations of those entering professional work. These are desires for adequate financial reward, for job security, for interesting work, for rewarding work, for personal autonomy in work and for career progression. Some of these areas have overlapping features. The fifth

---

[105] SRA, Authorisation Rules for Legal Services Bodies and Licensable Bodies 2011, r 8(1).

[106] SRA, *Handbook 2011*, as amended, *SRA Code of Conduct 2011*, Outcome 7.2.

[107] ibid, Outcome 7.3.

[108] ibid, Outcome 7.6.

[109] ibid, Outcomes 7.7 and 7.9.

[110] G Charles, 'Retention rates for top 50 firms promise stability for trainees' *The Lawyer* 25 October 2004, at 2.

[111] J Wilson, 'Young City lawyers pay price for salary rise' *The Guardian* 7 August 2000, at 3.

[112] J Harris, 'Herbies asks associates to stay as more jump ship' *The Lawyer* 31 October 2005, at 3.

[113] See the Employment Relations Act 1999 and A Coles 'Training contracts under the microscope' *Law Gazette* 22 September 1999.

[114] M Shiner, *The Law Student Cohort Study Year 4* (London, The Law Society, 1997) ch 6.

[115] Duff, Shiner, Boon and Whyte, *Entry into the Legal Professions* (n 30).

[116] C Menkel-Meadow, 'Portia Redux: Another Look at Gender Feminism, and Legal Ethics' in *Legal Ethics and Legal Practice: Contemporary Issues* (Oxford, Clarendon Press, 1995) at 24.

cohort study survey found high levels of job satisfaction among solicitors, but many problematic areas.

a. Salaries

Lawyers' earnings are widely diverse. The large commercial solicitors' firms generally pay the highest salaries to newly qualified staff, often higher than those of the partners in some legal aid firms. The fifth solicitors' cohort study found significant differences in newly qualified salaries, between £20,000 in high street and £50,000 in City firms.[117]

Different firms have different systems for rewarding staff. The lockstep system, where salary is based on seniority, is traditional in law firms. Such a system is beneficial in large firms because it avoids distinguishing between different levels of performance. It can, however, be a disincentive to effort. Possibly for this reason, many firms have moved to more merit-based systems. This shift may have accelerated since the financial crisis.

The use of merit-based systems raises issues within law firms. There is, for example, an issue of fairness where decisions on pay depend on the views of senior partners. Attempts to make processes more objective can involve using crude measures, such as income generated and clients attracted.[118] However pay is decided, merit systems encourage rivalry, hogging of the most profitable work and wrangles over the credit for bills.[119]

Partners share the profits of the firm after deducting the overheads, including staff salaries. Those who achieve partnership in large firms tend to be rewarded through the traditional lockstep method of dividing partnership profits rather than by merit or bonus schemes.[120] Under a lockstep system, partners move towards taking a full profit share incrementally. As with their employees, this may reduce their incentive to work. Managed lockstep systems, where progression is not automatic and where there is even the possibility of demotion, has therefore gained ground. Some British firms over recent years have also moved to more merit-based systems,[121] particularly following mergers with US firms. Most of the larger, commercial firms have adopted bonus schemes by 'top slicing' the profits and allocating them to high performing staff. Such systems can also be used to lure 'stars' from other firms.

Partnership carries the risk of receiving less from the business than employees on fixed salaries when times are hard. In smaller firms, particularly those relying on legal aid, partners allegedly struggle to earn more than £30,000 per annum. In contrast, some partners in large firms earn in excess of £1million per annum.

b. Security

Security of employment is one of the traditional benefits and expectations of professional life. In general, turnover rates for assistant solicitors are relatively low. In 2005,

[117] Duff, Shiner, Boon and Whyte (n 30).
[118] M Moore, 'Merit Marks' (2003) 147 *Solicitors Journal* 371.
[119] P Hodkinson and A Novarese, 'Fakes and Ladder' *Legal Week* 17 March 2005.
[120] M Chambers and R SenGupta, 'The Mystery of Lockstep' (2000) 39 *Commercial Lawyer* 23.
[121] A Mizzi, 'Stepping stone to revolution' (2001) 98(1) *Law Society's Gazette* 14.

for example, the average assistant solicitor turnover rate in the top 50 firms was 14 per cent.[122] Law firms do, however, reflect changes in the employment market generally, which has become more insecure since the 1980s. The trade press contains many stories of firms 'clearing out' groups of lawyers. Sometimes, leading lawyers themselves instigate moves, taking whole departments with them. The explanation for the frequency of these acts of disloyalty is that marketisation of legal services has loosened the bonds of the employment relationship, introducing instability and uncertainty.

c. Interest

Graduates may be more likely to find law work boring for a number of reasons.[123] First, it often fails to meet expectations raised by the media. Film and television series portray law work as unrealistically glamorous. Secondly, it may be because they are not working in a preferred area. Thirdly, it could be because of an acquired interest in substantive law and a relative lack of intrinsic interest in legal procedure.

Law students enjoy EU law, human rights and civil rights, but also criminal law, family law, benefits law and personal injury law.[124] There is a disproportionately high level of interest in careers in human rights and EU law compared with available jobs. 50 per cent of prospective solicitors were interested in legal aid work but only 8 per cent were likely to pursue this given the career prospects.[125] Commercial areas, including commercial property and business and commercial affairs, had low levels of interest compared with the numbers that are expected to work in them.

d. Reward

Many people distinguish between the intellectual and emotional rewards of professional work. Emotional rewards are intangible and susceptible to being disproportionately diminished by negative experiences. For example, some entrants cite the opportunity to help people as a primary motivation. Personal plight work is one of the areas offering the highest potential rewards. Commercial firms do not offer areas such as crime and family law, which involve people in crisis. Over 42 per cent of women leaving the profession were disappointed that their expectations regarding the value of the work to the community were not met.[126]

Emotional rewards may derive from a sense of achievement. Across a range of occupations intrinsic work motivation is associated with challenging tasks. Emotional exhaustion is caused by high workload and lack of social support,[127] low status, poor

---

[122] H Morris and E Quinn, 'Top 50 law firms' assistant turnover rate hits 14%' *Lawyer 2B* October 2005, at 1.

[123] J Carvel, 'Graduates find prized jobs boring, say survey' *The Guardian* 27 July 2006, at 8.

[124] Shiner, *Entry into the Legal Professions: Year 5* (n 30) at 32–33.

[125] Norman, *Career Choices in Law* (n 42) at 31.

[126] ibid, at 96.

[127] I Houkes, PPM Janssen, J de Jonge and AB Bakker, 'Specific Determinants of Intrinsic Work Motivation, Emotional Exhaustion and Turnover Intention: A Multisample Longitudinal Study' (2003) 76 *Journal of Occupational and Organisational Psychology* 427.

work life balance, stress,[128] emotional exhaustion and unmet career expectations.[129] A competitive environment exacerbates old demands, like turning over work, and adds new ones, like attracting and keeping clients. There may be workplace pressure to indulge in unethical practices, such as 'padding', inflating the hours billed.[130] These pressures potentially diminish the satisfaction found in work.

Across different kinds of legal organisation, but particularly in large firms, a culture of long hours has emerged. The cohort study found that just over a quarter in high street firms, 40 per cent in large provincial and 56 per cent in City firms worked over 50 hours a week.[131] This may be a reason why, in the 1990s, lawyers suffered from more workplace stress than other professions, including doctors.[132]

A director of the legal healthcare charity SolCare observed that, between 1997 and 1999 the subject of the majority of calls received had switched from alcohol to stress. He suggested that parts of the legal profession had adopted the attitude that 'if you aren't stressed you're not working properly' and that lawyers had been sacked for complaining about workloads. Menkel-Meadow argues that the 'long hours culture' needs to be defined as an ethical issue.[133]

Also in the 1990s, Sommerlad found relatively low levels of job satisfaction in high street firms. This was caused by declining conveyancing income and increasing commercialisation.[134] Legal aid practitioners and women were particularly affected. Funding constraints and franchise auditing mechanisms symbolised a propensity for 'denigration and distrust' in the political establishment that undermined the morale of public sector professionals. In contrast, interviews conducted for the final stages of the cohort study found that young lawyers in well-established high street practices were content, even pleased, with their experience of practice.[135] They were offered interesting professional work, the opportunity to specialise, together with good terms and conditions. Their firms tended to be traditionally organised, providing a high level of autonomy in a collegial setting.

e. Autonomy

In the European context, autonomy refers to the freedom of individual professionals to exercise discretion in their work. It is supported by the collegial form of professional organisations. In a relationship of equal professionals, each has control of their own sphere of influence. Some areas offer more autonomy than others. Clients

[128] Department for Education and Skills, *Literature Review in Relation to 'Gateways to the Professions'* (London, DfES, 2005) ch 3.

[129] Houkes, Janssen, de Jonge and Bakker 'Specific Determinants of Intrinsic Work Motivation, Emotional Exhaustion and Turnover Intention' (n 127).

[130] DR Richmond, 'The New Law Firm Economy, Billable Hours and Professional Responsibility' (2000) 29 *Hofstra Law Review* 207.

[131] Duff, Shiner, Boon and Whyte (n 30) at 41; and see H Syedain, 'Stressed out—but quids in?' *The Observer* 11 July 1999.

[132] P Goodrich, 'Law-Induced Anxiety: Legists, Anti-Lawyers and the Boredom of Legality' (2000) 9(1) *Social and Legal Studies* 143.

[133] Menkel-Meadow, 'Portia Redux' (n 116) at 55.

[134] H Sommerlad, 'Managerialism and the Legal Profession: a New Professional Paradigm' (1995) 2 *International Journal of the Legal Profession* 159.

[135] Boon, 'From Public Service to Service Industry (n 52).

in crisis tend to be 'one-shotters', unfamiliar with what is involved in legal work. This provides scope for a high degree of individual professional autonomy.

Since the 1990s there has probably been a decrease in the professional autonomy of lawyers, in England and Wales, compared with legal professions elsewhere. Lawyers of all kinds have been affected by the shift towards a consumer society. Clients are more likely to resent professional authority and to demand to be treated liked customers. This changes the emotional balance in the professional relationship. It raises expectations of client satisfaction and undermines the 'professional detachment' that is a feature of professional autonomy.

Hochschild found that workers in certain service jobs perform 'emotional labour', involving emotional display.[136] A number of studies have found a similar phenomenon among professionals.[137] The need to perform emotional labour impinges on the autonomy of young lawyers. It also potentially increases the pressure on the individual and the likelihood of emotional exhaustion. Workers in service industries with demanding and abusive customers were able to cope better by sharing problems with co-workers.[138] Declining collegiality and a more individualistic culture may exacerbate the ability of legal workplaces to provide this support. Legal specialisation has a negative impact on relationships by reducing the common work experience of employees and the ability of colleagues to provide necessary support.

f. Career Progression

Gallanter and Pallay coined the phrase 'tournament of lawyers' to describe the internal race to partnership in large US law firms.[139] The tournament is a process whereby firms recruit too many young lawyers and select potential partners from within the group. Those that are selected emerge from long and gruelling competition, working long hours, generating high income and attracting and retaining elite clients. Some large firms apparently expected associates to bill 2,420 hours per annum which, assuming four weeks' holiday, represents 10 hours of chargeable time for every working day.

A variation of the tournament model has operated in some English large law firms,[140] although the recession, combined with the high cost of training, may have reduced its prevalence. The fate of those solicitors who do not become partners is a potential ethical issue. Lee suggests that many English large firms have adopted the 'up or out' policy, which is a feature of the tournament model. Solicitors who do not achieve partnership are asked to leave, or, feeling their position untenable, choose to

---

[136] AR Hochschild, *The Managed Heart: Commercialisation of Human Feeling* (Berkeley, CA, University of California Press, 1983).

[137] CA Wellington and JR Bryson, 'At Face Value? Image Consultancy, Emotional Labour and Professional Work' (2001) 35 *Sociology* 933.

[138] M Korczynski, 'Communities of Coping: Collective Emotional Labour in Service Work' (2003) 10 *Organization* 55, at 57.

[139] M Galanter and T Palay, *Tournament of Lawyers: Growth and Transformation of the Big Law Firm* (Chicago, Chicago University Press, 1991); M Galanter, 'Old and in the Way: the Coming Demographic Transformation of the Legal Profession and its Implications for the Provision of Legal Services' (1999) *Wisconsin Law Review* 1081.

[140] Boon (n 52).

go.[141] A variation, also identified in the US, is 'two-tier partnerships', in which some lawyers remain associates and never become partners.[142]

Never making partnership may be a preferable option to 'up or out', but it challenges the collegial assumptions of the traditional law firm model.[143] Solicitors who never make partner may have their sense of agency undermined. They may be demotivated and unable to fully participate in the joint enterprise.[144] Unless the situation is clear to them, they are unable to make good career decisions. This, Lee suggests, undermines the ethical principles of individual autonomy and fairness. It offends the Kantian injunction that people are to be treated as ends rather than means.[145]

In the early-1990s a quarter of solicitors holding practising certificates were women, but many were working part-time or unemployed.[146] Women who took a career break to raise families were unlikely to make partnership.[147] When firms laid off solicitors, those affected were disproportionately women. Since 1994, more women than men have been admitted annually as solicitors. In fact, across all ethnic groups, the gender gap has increasingly widened. At present, women make up 60 per cent of new admissions.[148]

The fifth cohort study found that women's pay began to slip quite quickly compared with men.[149] This, and later research by the Law Society,[150] found that female solicitors earned less than men, were more dissatisfied about long hours and work/life balance[151] and were significantly more likely to have considered leaving the profession. Among the issues troubling many women solicitors was progression to partnership.

In 1998, women made up half of newly qualified lawyers but only 15 per cent of partners.[152] In 2011/12 there were just over 30,000 partners in solicitors' firms. Of these, around 22,000 were men and 8,000 women. There were around 3,000 male sole practitioners and under half that number of women in sole practice.[153]

It might be expected that the progress of women would be different in the large firms because of their open and meritocratic cultures. This was not so. In 2009, firms with more than 81 partners appointed 1,064 women trainees compared with 831 male trainees. This represented 32 per cent of all women traineeships and 40 per cent of

---

[141] R Lee, '"Up or Out"—Means or Ends? Staff Retention in Large Firms' in P Thomas (ed), *Discriminating Lawyers* (London, Cavendish, 2000) 183.

[142] W Henderson, 'An Empirical Study of Single-tier versus Two-tier Partnerships in the Am Law 200' (2006) 84 *North Carolina Law Review* 1691.

[143] E Lazega, *The Collegial Phenomenon: The Social Mechanisms of Cooperation Among Peers in a Corporate Law Partnership* (New York, Oxford University Press, 2001); J Flood 'Partnership and Professionalism in Global Law Firms: Resurgent Professionalism?' in D Muzio, S Ackroyd and J Chanlat, *Redirections in the Study of Expert Labour: Established Professions and New Expert Occupations* (Houndmills, Palgrave Macmillan, 2007) at 52.

[144] Lee, 'Up or Out' (n 141) at 195.

[145] ibid, at 187.

[146] H Sommerlad, 'The Myth of Feminisation: Women and Cultural Change in the Legal Profession' (1994) 1(1) *International Journal of the Legal Profession* 31.

[147] J Ames, 'Late Bloomer' *Law Society Gazette* 24 March 1993, at 10.

[148] The Law Society, *Trends in the Solicitors Profession 2012* (n 68).

[149] Duff, Shiner, Boon and Whyte (n 30).

[150] J Siems, *Equality and Diversity: Women Solicitors*, vol I (London, The Law Society, 2004); L Duff and L Webley, *Equality and Diversity: Women Solicitors*, vol II (London, The Law Society, 2004).

[151] ibid, vol 1, at 119.

[152] R Verkaik, 'Women lawyers suffer pay bias' *Independent* 6 September 1999, at 34.

[153] The Law Society, *Trends in the Solicitors Profession 2012* (n 68) at 26.

all males appointed to traineeships.[154] This willingness to recruit significant numbers of women trainees was not, however, however reflected in appointment of women to senior positions in City firms.

It was 1998 before the first woman achieved senior partner in a top 100 law firm.[155] The difficulty for women in achieving partnership was national news in 2005.[156] In fact, in 2006, there were more women partners and women associate solicitors in the large national firms than in City firms. The top firm in a 2006 Diversity League Table of the top 100 firms was Shoosmiths, with 40 per cent female partners and 59 per cent female associates. Clifford Chance was the first City firm with 19 per cent female partners, but it also had the lowest percentage of female associates at 51 per cent.[157]

The record of large firms in enabling women to achieve career progression is slowly improving. A recent diversity league table showed that two firms in the top 100 firms comprised over a third of women partners. All the top 10 firms had more female than male associates. Many had introduced measures to address disadvantage, such as mentoring support for women to encourage more to aim for partnership.[158]

There are different theories explaining these common features of women's legal careers. The fact that women partners in US law firms typically come from higher social groups than their male counterparts has been taken to indicate gender barriers to female progression.[159] This could be because there is blatant discrimination against women. It could also be due to the structure and culture of solicitors' firms and more subtle exclusionary mechanisms and gender stereotyping.[160] A recent study for the LSB found that stereotyping and perceived bias causes women and BME lawyers to abandon their careers in disproportionately high numbers.[161]

A theory of how law firm environments disadvantage women is based on Gilligan's theory of male and female moral orientations. This speculated that men's judgements are based on an ethic of rights whereas women's are based on a so-called ethic of care.[162] According to this theory, male-led organisations would have rational and legalistic cultures[163] whereas those led by women would make allowances for

---

[154] Cole, Fletcher, Chittenden and Cox (n 36) at 40.

[155] *The Lawyer* 20 October 1998, at 3.

[156] F Gibb, 'The route to the top law jobs is disturbingly familiar' *The Times: Student Law* 24 May 2005.

[157] S Hoare, 'National firms shame City giants in diversity stakes' *The Lawyer* 27 March 2006, at 1.

[158] H Begum, 'Freshfields to kick off female buddy scheme' *The Lawyer* 20 February 2006, at 1.

[159] D Rhode, 'Perspectives on Professional Women' (1988) 40 *Stanford Law Review* 1163.

[160] H Sommerlad and P Sanderson, 'The Legal Labour Market and the Training Needs of Women Returners in the United Kingdom' (1997) 49 *Journal of Vocational Education and Training* 45.

[161] H Sommerlad, L Webley, L Duff, D Muzio and J Tomlinson, *Diversity in the Legal Profession in England and Wales: a Qualitative Study of Barriers and Individual Choices* (London, University of Westminster, 2010); LSB, *Market Impacts of the Legal Services Act: Interim Baseline Report* (April 2012) at para A.1.8 (www.legalservicesboard.org.uk/what_we_do/Research/Publications/pdf/market_impacts_of_the_legal_services_act_interim_baseline_report.pdf).

[162] C Gilligan, *In a Different Voice: Psychological Theory and Women's Development* (Cambridge, MA, Harvard University Press, 1982); N Noddings, *Caring: A Feminist Approach to Ethics and Moral Education* (Berkeley, CA, University of California Press, 1999).

[163] C Menkel-Meadow, 'Portia in a Different Voice Speculation & Women's Lawyering Process' (1985) 1 *Berkeley Women's Law Journal* 39.

individuals.[164] The emphasis on working long hours and on generating business,[165] and a lack of willingness to accommodate motherhood, suggest prioritisation of male work preferences. This potentially leads to the subordination of women.[166]

An alternative set of theories suggests that male and female career paths reflect gender preferences. Men enter the high status business areas of practice for long-term salary prospects. Women prioritise intrinsic interest and the value of work to the community[167] or areas of work with demands consistent with motherhood. They are more likely to work on family and relationship problems or conveyancing and wills. These choices affect career progression. In large firms, women often decide to work in 'knowledge areas' like employment litigation, rather than in the corporate and commercial departments from which partners tended to be drawn.[168]

These are obvious generalisations and reality probably lies somewhere between these theories. Many law firms have seen working long hours as an indication of commitment and as a prerequisite of progression. This is unlikely to change.[169] There may be gradual 'feminisation' of the workplace as numbers of women increase, but organisational norms that are important to survival are likely to persist.[170] Women often have to mimic stereotypical 'male' behaviour, for example, by generating a client base, to compete for partnership on equal terms with men.

Ethnic minorities are present in smaller numbers in elite sectors and so it is more difficult to generalise about their advancement in law firms. Given the supposed difficulty for ethnic minorities in gaining training contracts in City firms, the firms perform relatively well on ethnic minority data. In the 10 most ethnically diverse firms in the top 100 solicitors' firms, ethnic minority partners usually constitute less than 5 per cent of partners and 10 per cent of associates. There are variations. Clifford Chance, for example, had 5.5 per cent ethnic minority partners and 17 per cent ethnic minority associates.[171]

Ethnic minority candidates may not have attended elite educational institutions. This may be an impediment to progression in large firms,[172] not least because they will not have had early access to social networks in key financial and business institutions.[173] If this is important to firms, they may have to help facilitate the development of such networks. Unfortunately, there is a suspicion that ethnic minorities may not

---

[164] R Auchmuty, 'The Fiction of Equity' in S Scott Hunt and H Lim (eds), *Feminist Perspectives on Equity and Trusts* (London, Cavendish, 2001) at 1.

[165] P Sanderson and H Sommerlad, 'Professionalism, Discrimination, Difference and Choice in Women's Experience in Law Jobs' in P Thomas (ed), *Discriminating Lawyers* (London, Cavendish Publishing Limited, 2000) 155, at 161.

[166] ibid, at 182.

[167] Norman (n 42) at 45.

[168] Boon (n 52).

[169] H Sommerlad and P Sanderson, *Gender, Choice and Commitment: Women Solicitors in England and the Struggle for Equal Rights* (Brookfield, VT, Ashgate Publishing Company, 1998).

[170] A Giddens, *Modernity and Self-Identity: Self and Society in the Late Modern Age* (Cambridge, Polity Press, 1991) at 229–30.

[171] Hoare, 'National firms shame City giants in diversity stakes' (n 157).

[172] See generally H Glennerster and R Pryke, 'The Contribution of the Public Schools and Oxbridge: 1 "Born to Rule"' in J Urry and J Wakeford (eds), *Power in Britain* (London, Heinemann Educational Books, 1973) at 213; V Bermingham and J Hodgson, 'Desiderata: What Lawyers Want From Their Recruits' (2000) 35 *The Law Teacher* 1.

[173] G Hanlon, *Lawyers, the State and the Market* (Hampshire, Macmillan Press Limited, 1999) at 113.

follow the usual progression routes to partnership within firms. A Department of Constitutional Affairs junior minister, David Lammy, has suggested that, like women, ethnic minority recruits are often channelled into the 'knowledge areas' that are less likely to lead to partnership.[174]

IV. Barristers

A. Patterns of Employment

In 2011, 15,581 barristers held practising certificates.[175] There were 12,674 self-employed barristers, comprising 81 per cent of this total, and 2,907 employed barristers, comprising 19 per cent.[176] There were 427 sole practitioners but the rest of the self-employed Bar were in 768 chambers. The average chambers size is therefore around 20.

B. Organisation

Chambers is nominally a mechanism for self-employed barristers to share costs. Each one is serviced by a team of clerks which, among other tasks, allocate work to barristers and negotiate the barristers' brief fees with solicitors. They are headed by a chief clerk. At one time the chief clerk took a percentage of the fees of all barristers in chambers. This is now giving way to different arrangements, including some chambers doing without a clerk. There are around 1,200 barristers' clerks and a professional association, the Institute of Barristers' Clerks. Members have a code of conduct[177] and are expected to also know the Bar Code of Conduct.

C. Obligations

Despite the unusual status of chambers as a collective of self-employed professionals, they have considerable collective responsibility. Like the previous version, the new Bar Code of Conduct contains several rules directed specifically at chambers.[178] These require that barristers ensure that their chambers are administered competently and

---

[174] M Mullally, 'A Step Forward' *Legal Director* 17 August 2004.
[175] J Sauboorah, *Bar Barometer: Trends in the Profile of the Bar* (London, Bar Standards Board/Bar Council, 2012).
[176] ibid.
[177] IBC, *Code of Conduct for Institute of Barristers' Clerks* (www.ibc.org.uk/about/code_of_conduct/).
[178] BSB, *Bar Code of Conduct 2014*, ch 5.3: Chambers rC89.

efficiently. Appropriate risk management procedures must be in place and complied with. A person must be appointed to liaise with the Bar Standards Board regarding regulatory requirements and ensure that there are proper arrangements for dealing with pupils.

Chambers are required to have 'corporate' arrangements for managing conflicts of interest and ensuring client confidentiality. They must also ensure that non-authorised persons working in chambers are competent to carry out their duties and are aware of provisions of the Handbook affecting the performance. There must be systems in place in chambers to ensure, inter alia, the independence of individual members of chambers from one another.

D. Pupillage

i. A Brief History

In 1863, the Inns of Court created consolidated regulations covering admission of students, keeping of terms, conditions of call to the Bar and the grant of practising certificates. At this time it was customary to be tutored by a senior practitioner.[179] In 1847, students were advised to spend a year with a conveyancer or equity draftsman, then six months each with a special pleader or common law barrister and a solicitor, and finally another half-year with a barrister.[180] The premium for pupillage was 200 guineas but later became 100 guineas for one year.

In 1959, a requirement for completion of 12 months' pupillage, with a qualified pupil supervisor was imposed as a requirement for practice. In 1971, following the Ormrod Committee on Legal Education recommendation, entry to the Bar was restricted to university graduates. It was not until 1975 that supervisors were stopped from charging pupillage fees. Some chambers then began offering bursaries.

In 1989, the Bar Council decided that pupils should receive a wage. Three committees then failed to settle an acceptable rate or mechanism for implementation. In 1998, a working party recommended implementation,[181] but there were then concerns that some pupils fell within the terms of the Minimum Wage Act 1998 and that the amount set by the Bar Council would be inadequate. A test case, *Edmonds v Lawson*,[182] resolved the issue by holding that pupillage is an arrangement beyond the scope of the Act. It is a binding contract for education and training and not an apprenticeship or contract of employment. Pupillage does not, therefore, require a pupil to do anything that is not conducive to his own training and development.

In 2000, it was decided to pay all pupils, although it was possible for a pupillage that was not intended to be funded to be approved by the Bar Council. In 2002, the Bar Council announced that pupils would be paid a minimum amount, initially set at £10,000 annually. There was anxiety that this, combined with increasing regulation

---

[179] D Wood, *Review of Pupillage: Report of the Working Group* (London, BSB, 2010) para 17.
[180] ibid, para 18.
[181] S Pye, 'Cash crisis and poor prospects for young bar' (1998) *The Lawyer* 20 October.
[182] *Edmonds v Lawson* (2000) QB 501, [2000] 2 WLR 1091.

of pupillage, would create disincentives for chambers thinking about taking pupils, reducing an already short supply of available pupillages.

The numbers commencing their first six in 2001–02 was 812 compared with 518 over the same period in 2003–04. In the year ending 30 September 2007, 527 first six and 563 second six pupillages were registered.[183] Funding pupillage therefore exacerbated an already short supply, but not by as much as feared in the long term. Typically there are only ever enough pupillages for about a quarter of those eligible.

At the same time as announcing funded pupillages, the Bar published regulations requiring that all pupillages commencing after 1 January 2003 should be advertised in accordance with the Bar Equality and Diversity Code. Then the Bar attempted to mitigate unfair recruitment practices by introducing a clearing system, but some chambers simply opted out of the process.

In the late-1980s, concerns about recruitment and the quality of pupillage led the Bar Council to commission a longitudinal study. The Bar cohort study was based on a survey of 822 students entering practice. It covered three years from the vocational course taken in 1989/90, through pupillage in 1991 to practice in 1993.[184] In the mid-1990s two reports led to the conclusion that the quality problems in pupillage training lay not in the structure or written guidance, but in the implementation of pupillage guidelines.[185]

As a result of the reports on pupillage, the Bar Council published a *Guide to Good Practice in Pupillage*. This rejected standardisation of practice, but recommended that chambers put in place safeguards.[186] The suggestions included pupillage committees, agreed induction procedures, policies on allocating and controlling the flow of paperwork to pupils and periodic review and feedback on performance.

ii. Prerequisites

Before commencing pupillage a barrister must sign a declaration and undertaking,[187] the Standard Declaration of Call, and be called to the Bar. No period in chambers completed before commencement counts towards the period of pupillage. The Standard Declaration of Call requires disclosure, inter alia, of criminal offences and other matters 'which might reasonably be expected to affect the mind of a Bencher of the Inn considering your application'. An applicant must also declare that 'so long as I remain a barrister I will observe the Code of Conduct'.[188] Falsification or breach of the declaration constitutes professional misconduct.[189]

[183] Data provided by Bar Standards Board Education and Training Department.
[184] J Shapland, V Johnston and R Wild, *Studying for the Bar* (Sheffield, Institute for the Study of the Legal Profession, 1993); and J Shapland and A Sorsby, *Starting Practice: Work and Training at the Junior Bar* (Sheffield, Institute for the Study of the Legal Profession, 1995) at 90.
[185] Mallins Report, *Report of the Professional Standards Committee Pupillage Working Party* (London, Bar Council, 1994); Hooper Report, *Report of the Working Group on Pupillage* (London, Bar Council, 1995).
[186] Shapland and Sorsby, *Starting Practice* (n 184).
[187] Bar Council, *The Consolidated Regulations of the Inns of Court and the General Council of the Bar* (as at 1 October 2001) (London, General Council of the Bar, 2001) at para 24(a).
[188] ibid, sch 5.
[189] ibid, at para 24(c).

iii. Structure and Content

An intending barrister's pupillage is divided into a non-practising six months, 'first six', and a practising six months, 'second six'.[190] Both or either six can be in private or employed practice. Both periods must be spent with a trained pupil supervisor approved by the Bar Council. A Pupil Master must be entered on the Bar Council's register and, unless approval is given, may only take one pupil at a time.[191] The obligations owed by the supervisor to the pupil barrister were set out in the old Bar Code and applied to employed barristers since 2003.[192] The new Handbook contains sections on diversity and pupillage funding.[193]

The first six is intended to be spent working on the supervisor's cases, reading and researching, and the second six working on one's own account. All pupillages should involve training in professional conduct and etiquette, practical experience of advocacy, conferences, negotiation and legal research.[194] Pupils must attend advocacy training and a course called Advice to Counsel. They must complete a checklist at the end of their first and second six.

Completion of the pupillage checklist must be confirmed by the pupil supervisor and retained by chambers for three years for review and monitoring by pupillage review panels. Weaknesses in advocacy must be reported to pupil supervisors and may be taken into account before signing the pupil's certification form which confirms satisfactory completion of pupillage.

iv. Terms

The current minimum rate for pupillage is £12,000 although some top sets of commercial chambers, in an effort to compete with each other and large law firms, pay pupils over £60,000 per annum. Relatively few applications to waive payment are approved. Waivers may be given to overseas students intending to return home on completion of pupillage.

v. Quality

Detailed guidance on pupillage is provided to pupils, formerly in a pupillage file.[195] This was revised by the Bar Standards Board and reissued as a pupillage handbook in 2011.[196] It brings together the regulations with a commentary. Responsibility for the quality of pupillage falls on heads of chambers.[197] They must take all reasonable steps

---

[190] ibid, pt V, at para 41.2.
[191] ibid, at paras 47 and 48.
[192] See Bar Council, *Code of Conduct of the Bar of England and Wales 1981*, as amended, at para 804.
[193] See generally BSB, *Bar Code of Conduct 2014*, s D: 'Rules Applying to Particular Groups of Regulated Persons'.
[194] Bar Council, *Pupillage File* (undated) s 2.3.
[195] Bar Council, *Pupillage File, 2008/08* (London, BSB, 2007).
[196] BSB, *Pupillage Handbook* (London, BSB, 2011).
[197] ibid, at 14.

to make proper arrangements, including drawing up a chambers pupillage policy, making an annual return to the Bar Council, and appointing a Pupillage Training Principal to take responsibility for pupils and pupillage arrangements.

vi. Entry

a. Data

During the period from 2007 to 2011, the numbers of barristers holding practising certificates grew at nearly 1 per cent per annum.[198] In 2010/11, 1,494 barristers were called to the Bar. In the same year only 446 first six pupillages were registered, a decrease of 3 per cent on 460 in 2009/10. The higher number of second six pupillages (477) was actually a decrease of nearly 4 per cent on 2009/10. In 2010/11, 191 newly qualified barristers began work as employed barristers, an increase of 12 per cent on the previous year. In 2010/11, also, 541 tenancies were registered, an increase of 16 per cent on the previous year.

Patterns of entry show a slight decrease in the proportion of women progressing at most stages. In 2010/11, of 1,414 students recruited to the BPTC, 52 per cent were women and 48 per cent men. In the same year, of the 1,494 barristers called to the Bar, 49 per cent were women and 51 per cent men. This reversed the trend of the previous four years, when women were called in larger numbers. These figures benchmark the gender profile approaching the bottlenecks of pupillage and tenancy.

Of the pupils registered in 2010/11, 41 per cent were women and 54 per cent men, while 5 per cent did not disclose their gender. In the previous four years, women had the majority of pupillages twice. When men had the majority, however, it tended to be by a larger margin.[199] In 2010/11, 52 per cent of tenants and newly employed barristers were women and 48 per cent were men. This was a reversal of the previous year, when 56 per cent of new tenants were men.

Analysing entry for BME candidates is slightly more complicated. The BPTC is recognised as an entrance qualification for lawyers in some former British Commonwealth countries, and the course has a large intake from these and other non-EU countries. Therefore, while many overseas BME students are called to the Bar on completion of the BPTC, they do not necessarily seek pupillage or tenancy.

In 2010/11, 42 per cent of students recruited to the BPTC recorded their origin as BME, while 44 per cent were recorded as white and 14 per cent did not disclose their ethnicity. Around 20 per cent of UK domiciled students were recorded as BME.[200] In the same year, 1,494 barristers were called to the Bar. Of these, 34 per cent were British and 66 per cent were non-UK nationals. In the same cohort, 44 per cent described themselves as BME, 53 per cent as white, and 3 per cent did not disclose their

---

[198] Sauboorah *Bar Barometer* (n 175).
[199] ibid, at 43.
[200] Bar Council Research Department, *An Analysis of Students Enrolled on the 2010/11 Bar Professional Training Course* (London, BSB, 2012).

ethnicity.[201] In 2010/11, 13 per cent of pupils registering and 12 per cent of tenants and new employed barristers described themselves as BME[202]

It is not possible to tell, from these data, what proportion of BME students recruited to the BPTC, and intending to practise at the Bar in England and Wales, actually gained pupillage or tenancy. Although BME and white students may enter the BPTC and receive call in roughly equal numbers, the much lower proportion in pupillage and tenancy could be explained by overseas BME students returning home. Therefore, there could be a number of explanations for underrepresentation of BME barristers, including inequality of opportunity.

Writing in the early 1990s, Glasser claimed that entry to the Bar was controlled by an 'invisible' process of selection.[203] This prioritised 'ascribed' characteristics that were irrelevant to performance. The expense of training and examinations in Latin and Greek controlled numbers effectively. This preserved the Bar as an elite haven, closed to people of lower social class and all but a few from ethnic minorities.[204] The Bar still has an image of privilege and selectivity based on class. The pattern may change when the Bar expands, but it is conceivable that it returns when there is relative contraction of available pupillages.

In 2001 the Bar's own data showed that, especially the elite chambers, controlled entry by recruiting, predominantly, from Oxbridge and Russell Group universities.[205] This may be becoming more marked. In 2009/10, 23 per cent of Bar pupils attended Oxbridge, rising to 35 per cent in 2010/11. In 2009/10, 46 per cent of pupils attended a Russell Group university, rising to 64 per cent in 2009/10.[206] This recruitment pattern tends to garner privately educated recruits. While approximately 11 per cent of the population attend a fee-paying school, 40 per cent of Bar pupils did so.[207] This has longer-term consequences. In 2005, research by the Sutton Trust showed that judges, and solicitors and barristers in leading commercial practices were overwhelmingly privately educated and from Oxbridge and Russell Group universities.[208]

Statistics can be misleading. The 2010 Wood Review of pupillage claimed that the Bar 'shows higher ethnic minority participation than the economically active population with higher qualifications'. It also suggested that the Bar shows higher female participation among new entrants than the professional employment sector at large.[209] Nevertheless, patterns of recruitment to the Bar suggest that candidates from lower social classes, including many BME candidates, suffer disadvantages.

[201] Sauboorah (n 175).

[202] ibid.

[203] C Glasser, 'The Legal Profession in the 1990s: Images of Change' (1990) 10 *Legal Studies* 1.

[204] Barrow Report (Final Report of the Committee of Inquiry into Equal Opportunities on the Bar Vocational Report), *Equal Opportunities at the Inns of Court School of Law* (1994); Shapland and Sorsby (n 184).

[205] L Twigg, *Analysis of Combined 1998/1999/2000 PACH statistics* (Education and Training Committee of the General Council of the Bar, 2001).

[206] Sauboorah (n 175) at 51.

[207] ibid, at 50.

[208] Sutton Trust, *The Educational Backgrounds of the UK's Top Solicitors, Barristers and Judges* (June 2005).

[209] BSB, *Review of Pupillage—Report of the Working Group* (London, BSB, 2010).

Potential Bar entrants from lower social classes are less likely to have attended an elite university. They rely on performance on the vocational course to demonstrate capability. The Bar's data reveals, however, that 32 per cent of pupils had an offer of pupillage before commencing their BPTC.[210] Another problem is that candidates without substantial financial support may not be able to carry the level of debt acquired through education and training. Most pupils report debt, the largest group being in the £20,000–£29,000 bracket, with a small minority owing over £50,000.[211]

b. Regulation

The Courts and Legal Services Act 1990 took the remarkable step of making it unlawful for a barrister or barrister's clerk to discriminate against a woman in making offers of pupillage or the terms on which it was offered.[212] The Bar equality and diversity code, created in 1995, was updated in 2004 to take into account of legislation and awareness of equality issues. The code was not mandatory but reflected good practice guidance.

Since 2003, all vacancies for pupillage had to be advertised on a website specified by the Bar Council.[213] The notice must contain prescribed information about the chambers and details of the appointment process. It required chambers to have a written statement of policy on equality and diversity and an equality and diversity officer. The BSB's 2009 chambers monitoring pilot study 'had not been effective as well as revealing significant areas of non-compliance with the equality provisions in the Code'.[214] The Bar Standards Board therefore proposed strengthening the requirements of the Bar Code in relation to equality and diversity.

In 2012, new rules were submitted to the LSB for approval as an addition to the Bar Code 1981, as amended. Under the amendment, each barrister was required to ensure that their chambers had a written statement or policy on equality and diversity and an equality and diversity officer.[215] Additionally, there had to be an implementation plan. From 2013, members with lead responsibility for selection of members of chambers, pupils, clerks or assessed mini-pupils had to have received recent and appropriate training in fair recruitment and selection processes. The intention was that all selection panel members were to have to receive this training by 1 July 2014.

The Code provided that chambers' selection processes must use objective and fair criteria. Chambers were required to review regularly the number and percentages of staff, barristers, pupils and assessed mini-pupils from different groups. They were also required to consider the spread of applications for assessed mini-pupillage, pupillage, staff and membership of chambers. Finally, they had to review the allocation of

---

[210] Sauboorah (n 175) at 47.

[211] Sauboorah (n 175) at 48.

[212] Courts and Legal Services Act 1990, s 64, amending the Sex Discrimination Act 1975 by adding s 35A.

[213] The Pupillage Funding and Advertising Requirements 2003, incorporated into the Bar Code of Conduct 1981, as amended, Annex R, para 4.

[214] BSB, *Amendments to the Bar Code of Conduct—Equality and Diversity Provisions* (www.legalservices-board.org.uk/what_we_do/regulation/pdf/application_final_2.pdf).

[215] Bar Council/BSB, *The Bar Code of Conduct 1981*, 8th edn, at para 408.

unassigned work. Chambers' reviews were required to include data broken down by race, disability and gender, together with reasons for any disparities in that data. The review and analysis was required to be followed by 'appropriate remedial action'.[216]

c. Process

The Bar Council introduced a clearing scheme in the 1990s to try and ensure that entry processes were open and transparent. In 2001, the paper-based Pupillage Application Clearing House scheme (PACH) was replaced by the Online Pupillage Application System (OLPAS), upgraded to OLPAS Pupillage Portal (OLPAS/PP) in 2009. Under this system, students can apply for up to 12 pupillages. It is, however, a voluntary system and around half of chambers do not participate.

The operation of the pupillage clearing system remains controversial. Critics claim that other employers are not bound by similar recruitment restrictions. Supporters of the system argue that the level of non-participation creates concerns about the fairness of the system generally. Various reports reflect some ambivalence about the scheme. The Neuberger Working Party recommended that recruiters should be subject to a common recruitment timetable, but not necessarily within the clearing system.[217] The Woods Report on pupillage agreed that participation in the clearing system should not be imposed on chambers.[218]

E. Post-qualification Practice

Entry-level indicators for the Bar Professional Training Course reflect the demography of the population of England and Wales, but there are significant career progression problems for many women and ethnic minority entrants thereafter.[219]

i. Transition into Qualified Practice

Transition from pupillage to self-employed practice can be difficult. Newly qualified barristers used to be able to rely on criminal work. Even in the 1990s, the Bar cohort study confirmed the trend noted in the Goldsmith Report of declining work levels. Attracting work was only a major problem for 16 per cent in London and for 8 per cent in the provinces. There were more tenants, less magistrates' court work and more solicitors doing minor court appearances themselves. 20 per cent of respondents reported finding it difficult to manage financially. At nearly 30 per cent, Crime remains the largest single category of pupillage specialisation.[220] There is strong competition

---

[216] ibid, at para 408.2(e).
[217] General Council of the Bar, *Entry to the Bar Working Party Final Report* (London, General Council of the Bar, 2007) rec 43.
[218] BSB, *Review of Pupillage—Report of the Working Group* (London, BSB, 2010) at para 178.
[219] LSB, *Market Impacts of the Legal Services Act* (n 161).
[220] Sauboorah (n 175) at 46.

for work. In the commercial and chancery sections of the Bar, there are often limited advocacy opportunities for newly qualified barristers.

ii. Terms and Conditions

a. Income

As self-employed practitioners, barristers' earning depends on the briefs they attract and the fees they can command. At the commercial bar, Queen's Counsel can earn more than £1 million per annum. Barristers specialising in less serious criminal defence matters argue that they cannot earn a living wage. The income of many young barristers has been adversely affected by declining rates of legal aid and competition with solicitors for the small-scale advocacy work.[221]

By 2005, legal aid payment rates had fallen to such an extent that there was a threat of strike by criminal defence barristers in the summer. A review by Lord Carter of Coles was preceded by the government publishishing figures showing that in 2004–05 one barrister had been paid £1.18 million from legal aid.[222] The next 10 barristers received more than £600,000 each from the legal aid fund. Barristers at the lower end of the scale had not seen their rates rise since 1997.

Lord Carter's detailed proposals aimed to ensure a fairer distribution of public money. They included reducing the numbers of small solicitors' firms allowed to do criminal legal aid work, cutting the fees paid to the top end of the Criminal Bar, redistributing them to barristers doing one to ten-day cases in the Crown Courts. The Carter reforms did not address the underlying problem that criminal legal aid was almost continually reducing in real terms. They are unlikely to reverse the long-term pattern of decline.

In the run up to the 2014 strikes of criminal defence barristers, the chair of the Criminal Bar Association claimed that some experienced barristers earned as little as £13,000 per annum.[223] The Ministry of Justice countered that 1,200 barristers earned £100,000 each from legal aid in 2013. Barristers responded that VAT, chambers fees, pension provision, travel and other expenses would reduce that to £50,000 of taxable income. Some, it was claimed, earned as little as £13,000.

b. Support

One of the strengths of the chambers system is the collegial support it provides to independent practitioners. In *Edmonds v Lawson*, the Court of Appeal noted that it was beneficial to chambers to have talented and hardworking members, just as it was beneficial to the pupils to prove worthy of tenancy in a flourishing set. It may be that these benefits are not always experienced by some women and ethnic minorities.

---

[221] A Gillan, 'Car mechanics overtake barristers' hourly rate' *The Guardian* 17 February 2006, at 5.

[222] C Dyer, 'Shakeup in legal aid will put end to £1m-a-year earnings' *The Guardian* 10 February 2006, at 16.

[223] O Bowcott, 'Lawyers walk out in protest against legal aid budget cuts' *The Guardian* 6 January 2014; O Bowcott, P Walker and L O'Carroll, 'Lawyers' walkout empties criminal courts' *The Guardian* 7 January 2014.

The Bar cohort study recorded that 24 per cent of barristers thought racial discrimination, and 26 per cent felt that sexual discrimination, were major problems at the Bar.[224] A surprising 40 per cent of women entering the Bar suffered sexual harassment at work[225] and 70 per cent claimed to have encountered sexual discrimination in their careers.[226] Some support for the conclusion that the Bar is not a supportive environment for female and BME barristers may be suggested by the demographic data.

Despite the majority of new tenants being women, the overall composition of the Bar is changing very slowly. It is still the case that around 65 per cent of the self-employed Bar are men and 12 per cent are from a BME group.[227] These figures do, however, include the large preponderance of senior men who entered when the Bar was almost entirely white and male. Women are not proportionately represented as senior judges or QCs, perhaps because of earlier difficulties in establishing practices.

c. Opportunity

Low representation at higher levels of the Bar may be due to some groups having unsuccessful early careers. Flood's study of barristers' clerks in 1983 found that clerks' criteria for allocating work showed 'a strong reluctance to accept women and members of ethnic minorities as tenants in chambers'.[228] Senior barristers were said to avoid tackling the problem because clerks operated in their interests.

The Courts and Legal Services Act 1990 amended the Sex Discrimination Act 1975 to make it unlawful for a barrister or barrister's clerk to discriminate against a woman in the arrangements made for determining to whom a tenancy should be offered, the terms on which it was offered or to discriminate against her in the benefits, facilities or services which are afforded or denied to her.[229]

By 1997, barristers' clerks were still being accused of depriving black pupils of work.[230] The Bar Diversity Code 2004 recommended that chambers monitor the distribution of briefs.[231] A 2007 survey of the self employed Bar suggested that female barristers do not progress as quickly as men in their careers.[232]

Gender and ethnicity appears to be a factor in the areas of specialisation practitioners gravitate towards. More recent BSB research showed that BME and female barristers are more likely to work in publicly funded work areas such as crime, where public funding supports 87 per cent of cases, and family, where it supports 58 per cent.[233] Twice as many women work in family as in any other practice area. BME barristers are most likely to work in civil law, where they make up 14 per cent of practitioners, and family, where they comprise 10 per cent.

[224] Shapland and Sorsby (n 184) at 25.
[225] ibid, table 5.3 at 71; and see B Hewson, 'A Recent Problem' *New Law Journal* 5 May 1995, at 626.
[226] Shapland and Sorsby (n 184) at 74–75.
[227] Sauboorah (n 175) at 46.
[228] JA Flood, *Barristers' Clerks: The Law's Middlemen* (Manchester, Manchester University Press, 1983) at 132.
[229] Courts and Legal Services Act 1990, s 64, inserting s 35A into the Sex Discrimination Act 1975.
[230] T Growney, 'Bar to Equal Opportunity' *The Guardian* 27 May 1997.
[231] Bar Council, *Equality and Diversity Code for the Bar* (London, Bar Council, 2004) at 103.
[232] LSB, *Market Impacts of the Legal Services Act* (n 161).
[233] ibid.

Specialisation may be reflected in the proportions of different groups billing less than £80,000. Only 21 per cent of white men were in this group. This compares with 39 per cent of BME, 44 per cent of white women and 54 per cent of BME women billing less than £80,000. Women are more likely to be billing between £80,000 and £125,000 than men. Over 80 per cent of BME women bill less than £125,000, compared with 43 per cent of white men.[234]

There are, however, some positive data in recent research studies. *The Bar Barometer* reported very low attrition of BME barristers between five years' and 15 year's call. The high number of female barristers for pupillage has not translated into better gender diversity for barristers over 12 years' call. The report stresses that this is strongly correlated with other factors such as accessibility of childcare.[235] Both women and BME barristers are well represented in junior judicial posts.

d. Autonomy

While self-employed status suggests high levels of personal autonomy, shortage of work puts pressure on young barristers to cultivate professional and lay clients.[236] Having attracted work, barristers may be less able than before to maintain an air of detachment in their professional relationships. In the Bar cohort study, a third of young barristers reported problems, for example, with poor instructions from solicitors or in their dealings with clients or their relatives.

F. Regulation

The general provisions of the old Bar Code relating to equality and diversity applied equally to pupils and tenants.[237] Problems over allocation of work were recognised explicitly by inclusion of two new paragraphs in 2012. Paragraph 305.1 provided that

> a barrister must not, in his professional practice, discriminate unlawfully against, victimise or harass any other person on the grounds of race, colour, ethnic or national origin, nationality, citizenship, sex, gender re-assignment, sexual orientation, marital or civil partnership status, disability, age, religion or belief or pregnancy and maternity.

Paragraph 408 of the old Bar Code addressed a number of problems related to the treatment of pupils and tenants. It required 'the fair distribution of work amongst pupils and members of chambers'.[238] It provided that chambers have a written anti-harassment policy, dealing with promulgation and procedures for dealing with complaints.[239] It also required chambers to have a policy on parental and adoption leave and flexible working.[240] Each chambers was also required to appoint a Diversity

---

[234] ibid, at para A.1.6.
[235] ibid, at para A.1.8.
[236] LC Harris, 'The Emotional Labour of Barristers: An Exploration of Emotional Labour by Status Professionals' (2002) 39 *Journal of Management Studies* 553.
[237] Bar Council/BSB, *The Bar Code of Conduct 1981*, 8th edn, at para 408.
[238] ibid, at para 408.2(f).
[239] ibid, at para 408.2(h).
[240] ibid, at paras 408.1(f) and (h).

Data Officer. This person was responsible for collection, processing and publication of diversity data on chambers' website, in the first instance by 31 December 2012 and thereafter every three years.

V. Legal Executives

A survey of 832 Legal Executives in 2009 found 82 per cent were from families in which parents had not gone to university.[241] A third of respondents had been legal secretaries before while others held para-legal and more general secretarial roles. Encouragement from employer or colleagues was a factor in nearly half of the respondents deciding to qualify. Just under half (44 per cent) had received financial support from their employer. Others (36 per cent) had been unable to afford to study full-time at university and some saw CILEx as the quickest route to qualifying as a lawyer (26 per cent).

Nearly three-quarters of respondents to the CILEx survey were employed full-time. Of those working in the legal sector, most (57 per cent) were fee-earners. The remainder were legal secretaries, managing other legal work or handling non-legal work. Some 35 per cent had management or supervisory responsibilities. Conveyancing was the most common practice area (31 per cent), followed by personal injury (18 per cent), probate/wills (16 per cent), family (16 per cent), general litigation (12 per cent) and debt recovery (11 per cent). These areas were followed by commercial work, employment, housing and criminal defence.

VI. Employed Lawyers

A. Entry and Composition

Around 20 per cent of barristers and a little over 20 per cent of solicitors with practising certificates work as employed lawyers, that is, as employees within corporations, public bodies or local and central government. At the employed Bar, the ratio of women to men is higher than in private practice. In 2001, the employed Bar comprised 53 per cent men (1550) and 47 per cent women (1357).[242] At just over 12 per cent, BME barristers are probably also a higher proportion of the employed workforce than

---

[241] 'Future Rights of Legal Executives' *The Chartered Legal Executive Journal: 2010 Student Supplement*.
[242] Sauboorah (n 175).

they are in private practice. It is difficult to be sure of this, however, because 21 per cent of barristers did not disclose their ethnicity.[243]

If there are higher numbers of women and BME barristers in employed positions, it may be explained by the pressure corporations are under to comply with diversity policies. It is possible that in-house law departments provide more hospitable work environments for women and ethnic minorities than those found in private practice.

B. Function

Employed lawyers may have areas of work they are engaged to conduct for their employers. They may also be involved as general legal advisors. They are often involved in the appointment of private practice firms to act for their corporate employers. A range of reports show that in-house counsel negotiate down fees, and try alternatives to traditional legal services such as Legal Process Outsourcing (LPO).[244] They may also promote diversity in private practice. In 1999, for example, the Association of Corporate Counsel, representing in-house lawyers in the US, made a statement on behalf of 300 of the largest companies. It stated that they gave weight to the promotion of diversity in the workplace in appointing outside counsel.

C. Regulation

As employed practice grew more significant in the 1990s, both professions decided to accommodate it within the code of conduct for private practitioners. Employed lawyers are subject to the usual ethical rules, but these apply to their relationship with employers. For example, in relation to confidentiality, the SRA Handbook simply says 'The outcomes listed above apply to your in-house practice'.[245] This makes it difficult for in-house lawyers to work for competing businesses because they cannot comply with past and present client confidentiality requirements.

Employed lawyers are generally allowed only to act for their employer, except in specified and circumscribed circumstances. Therefore, under the SRA Practice Framework Rules 2011, solicitors can act for a long list of clients other than their employer. These tend, however, to be people related in some way to the employment. Alternatively, the services provided must be provided in a restricted way. Thus they can, for example, act for a former work colleague, or a related company, or provide advice by telephone.[246] In such situations, employed lawyers must act within the limits of any authorisation to conduct reserved activities.[247] They must also ensure that they have appropriate indemnity insurance cover.[248]

---

[243] ibid.
[244] 'General Counsel Look for Alternatives as Law Firm Fees Continue to Soar' (2009) *Strategic Legal Advisor*; LSB, *Market Impacts of the Legal Services Act: Interim Baseline Report* (April 2012) at para B.8.3.
[245] SRA, *Code of Conduct* 2011, as amended, ch 4: 'Confidentiality and Disclosure'.
[246] SRA, *Practice Framework Rules* 2011, rr 4.1–4.26.
[247] ibid, r 4.1(b).
[248] ibid, r 4.2.

VII. Conclusion

The legal professions' relationship with employers has often been problematic. While there has been a growing need to focus regulation on organisations, the mechanisms of control have been underdeveloped. This has been demonstrated by the mixed experience of trying to ensure equal access to the professions and accommodating more diverse membership. There are also various practical issues that the profession has had to confront. One is the increasing orientation of the profession towards commerce. This has given large firms a growing role in training new lawyers. It has also seen a decline in the availability of public service legal careers. These shifts in employment patterns present challenges to the coherence of the professional framework and to the training system.

The LSA 2007, and the regulatory regime now emerging, is placing increasing emphasis on the role of organisations in educating and training lawyers. Employers may be offered opportunities to pioneer new routes to qualification in-house and to determine individual competence thereafter. The regulator's role in the qualification process is conceived to be the mere setting of standards. These may be no more specific than broad outcomes. This poses the question of whether, and if so how, professions should continue to play a role in devising and inculcating professional values and standards.

PART V

DISPUTE RESOLUTION

17

Litigation

'The one great principle of English law is, to make business for itself'.[1]

I. Introduction

Litigation, including advocacy, is one of the original activities of lawyers in England and Wales. It is now one of the relatively few activities reserved to lawyers by the Legal Services Act 2007. In a market in which legal activity could be increasingly opened up to competition, litigation is one area that is likely to remain a core and defining activity of lawyers. While many solicitors do no litigation work, and it does not provide the largest revenues, most solicitors' firms have the capacity to conduct litigation.

Together with advocacy, litigation ethics provide the template of professional legal ethics. The core of the duties to clients, on confidentiality and conflicts of interest, are defined in the context of litigation. The adversarial orientation of lawyers, even in transactions, originates in litigation. The expectation that lawyers can serve clients effectively, while preserving wider obligations of integrity and duties to other entities, derives from advocacy and litigation.

II. Authorisation

In order to conduct litigation lawyers need two forms of authorisation. First, since it is one of the six reserved activities set out in the Legal Services Act 2007 (LSA 2007), they must be authorised to conduct litigation.[2] A person may, however, be

---

[1] C Dickens, *Bleak House* (London, Bradbury and Evans, 1853) chs 1 and 39.
[2] LSA 2007, ss 12(1)(b).

exempt from being an authorised person in relation to the conduct of litigation[3] if, for example, they have been granted a right by a court in relation to specific proceedings.[4] Secondly, at common law, they need special authority to issue proceedings in the client's name[5] or to take part in proceedings on the client's behalf.[6]

Because litigation is a reserved activity, a litigator must belong to a profession that can authorise a member to conduct litigation. The Courts and Legal Services Act 1990 recognised only the Law Society's right to regulate litigators, but the door was left open for other professions to come forward.[7] Under the LSA 2007, six of the approved regulators are regulators for the conduct of litigation. These are the regulators for solicitors, barristers, legal executives, patent attorneys, trade mark attorneys and costs lawyers. However, only solicitors automatically gain rights to conduct litigation in all courts on qualification.

The Bar experimented with public access to barristers for conducting litigation in 2004. Since January 2014, however, barristers can gain an extension to their practising certificate to conduct litigation. Importantly, because it will enable them to continue to focus on advocacy, they can share premises with non-barristers for that purpose. In order to gain the extension, barristers need to convince the Bar Standards Board that they have appropriate systems to conduct litigation, the skills and knowledge of litigation to provide a competent service to clients and adequate insurance. Training courses are available for barristers wishing to develop expertise. This will avoid clients having to act as self-representing litigants as under the public access arrangements.

In order to gain authorisation to conduct litigation, barristers within the first three years of practice must confirm that they have a qualified person in their place of practice able to provide guidance on conducting litigation. A qualified person is a barrister, or other authorised person, such as a solicitor, entitled to conduct litigation.[8] They must have practised for at least six years in the previous eight years, with litigation as their primary activity in the last two years.

Other approved regulators have special arrangements for accreditation to conduct litigation. For example, ILEX Fellows can qualify as Chartered Legal Executive Litigators holding one of two certificates.[9] A Rights to Conduct Litigation (Civil Proceedings) Certificate covers all civil proceedings, excluding family proceedings, exercising rights of audience in Judge's room hearings in the County Court and High Court. A Rights to Conduct Litigation (Family Proceedings) Certificate covers litigation in all family proceedings exercising rights of audience in Judge's room hearings in the County Court and High Court in all family proceedings.[10]

---

[3] ibid, s13(1) and (2).
[4] ibid, sch 3, s 2(2)(b).
[5] *Wright v Castle* (1817) 3 Mer 12.
[6] *Wheatley v Barstow* (1855) 7 De GM & G 261.
[7] Courts and Legal Services Act, s 28(6).
[8] BSB, *Authorisation to Conduct Litigation* (2014) (www.barstandardsboard.org.uk/regulatory-requirements/for-barristers/authorisation-to-conduct-litigation/).
[9] CILEx, *Rights to Conduct Litigation and Rights of Audience Certification Rules* (2011) r 3.
[10] ibid, r 5.

III. Conduct

A. Solicitors' Conduct Rules for Litigation

Despite the importance of litigation to the solicitor's role, until recently it did not have a central role in solicitors' conduct rules. In fact, until solicitors gained access to higher courts as advocates, and adopted much of the Bar Code in relation to advocacy, litigation did not feature in the rules. The orientation of solicitors towards all activities, including litigation, was found in the core duty to act in clients' best interests.

The chapter on client relations in the SRA Code of Conduct 2011 contains one outcome specific to litigation. This concerns the provision of services to clients in a manner which protects their interests in their matter, subject to the proper administration of justice.[11] The chapter on third parties contains one outcome and three indicative behaviours that are arguably relevant to litigation.[12] The outcome is not taking unfair advantage of third parties.[13] The indicative behaviours are providing sufficient time and information to agree costs,[14] not taking unfair advantage of an opposing party's lack of legal knowledge where they have not instructed a lawyer[15] and not demanding anything for yourself or on behalf of your client, that is not legally recoverable.[16]

Chapter 5 of the SRA Code of Conduct 2011, 'Your Client and the Court', sets out the duties to clients, and to courts, of those exercising a right to conduct litigation or acting as an advocate. The eight outcomes are said to apply to both litigation and advocacy. A bundle of outcomes are, however, traditionally associated with advocacy, although they could as easily apply to litigation generally. These are complying with the duty to the court,[17] not deceiving or knowingly or recklessly misleading the court[18] or being complicit in another person doing so.[19] A related outcome is informing clients in circumstances where these duties outweigh obligations to them.[20]

A second set of outcomes more obviously relate to the conduct of litigation generally. These are not very informative about obligations in conducting litigation. In fact they appear to be statements of the blindingly obvious. They are complying with court orders placing obligations on the solicitor,[21] not being in contempt of

---

[11] SRA, *SRA Code of Conduct* 2011, ch 1: 'Client Relations' Outcome 1.2.
[12] ibid, ch 11: 'Relations with Third Parties'.
[13] ibid, Outcome 11.1.
[14] ibid, Indicative Behaviour 11.1.
[15] ibid, Indicative Behaviour 11.7.
[16] ibid, Indicative Behaviour 11.8.
[17] SRA, *SRA Code of Conduct* 2011, ch 5: 'Your Client and the Court', Outcome 5.6.
[18] ibid, Outcome 5.1.
[19] ibid, Outcome 5.2.
[20] ibid, Outcome 5.5.
[21] ibid, Outcome 5.3.

court[22] and not bribing witnesses.[23] A further outcome in this category deals with the consequences of litigation. Outcome 5.7 is ensuring that evidence relating to sensitive issues is not misused.[24] The intended scope of this outcome is particularly unclear.

There is one indicative behaviour relevant to Outcome 5.7. It is ensuring that child witness evidence is kept securely and not released to clients or third parties.[25] It is not clear whether this is intended to apply to evidence given in open court, which could be reported by the press. It is also unclear whether solicitors would fail to achieve the outcome if they pass on such information when, for example, the press was not in court. On the face of it, the outcome could prevent solicitors providing information to the press, including details emerging in the litigation about clients of the other side.

It may be that Outcome 5.7 applies whether or not the press could report the information. This is consistent with solicitors having high standards of integrity. On the other hand, there is arguably no 'misuse' of information if it has come out in open court. It may be that the outcome is only intended to apply to information which is restricted to the proceedings.

An analogous situation on disclosure is covered by the Civil Procedure Rules 1998 (CPR). These provide that parties receiving documents may use them only for the purpose of the proceedings in which they are disclosed, except where the document has been read to or by the court, or referred to, at a hearing which has been held in public.[26] If solicitors are restricted in their use of third party information produced in open court, it is unclear whether this restriction covers all situations.

Among the other indicative behaviours in Chapter 5, many are most relevant when solicitors act as advocates. An example is informing the court when the advocate has inadvertently misled it.[27] A second set of behaviours expressly relate either to advocacy or litigation generally. An example is an indicative behaviour suggesting that solicitors should not appear as advocates, or act in litigation, if it is clear that they, or anyone at their firm, will be called as a witness in the matter, unless they are satisfied that their independence, the interests of their client or the interests of justice would not be prejudiced.[28]

A third set of indicative behaviours in the SRA Code of Conduct derive from the Law Society advocacy code. This was based on provisions of the old Bar Code of Conduct. These rules related to litigation tasks more commonly, formerly at least, performed by barristers, such as drafting statements of case. Therefore, an indicative behaviour suggests that solicitors should not draft documents in proceedings containing contentions they do not consider to be properly arguable.[29] The same behaviour suggests they should not make allegations of fraud, unless they are instructed to do so and have material which they reasonably believe shows fraud. While drafting is

---

[22] ibid, Outcome 5.4.
[23] ibid, Outcome 5.8.
[24] ibid, Outcome 5.7.
[25] ibid, Indicative Behaviour 5.3.
[26] Civil Procedure Rules 1998, r 31.22.
[27] SRA, *SRA Code of Conduct* 2011, ch 5: 'Your Client and the Court', Indicative Behaviour 5.4.
[28] ibid, Indicative Behaviour 5.6.
[29] ibid, Indicative Behaviour 5.7.

obviously classified as a litigation task rather than an advocacy task, this wording is almost exactly the same as that used in the former Bar Code.[30]

The fourth and final set of indicative behaviours in the SRA Code of Conduct specifically relate to issues that are more likely to arise in relation to litigators than advocates. A positive behaviour is advising clients to comply with court orders made against them, and advising them of the consequences of failing to comply.[31] Two negative behaviours are attempting to influence a witness regarding the contents of their statement[32] or tampering with evidence or persuading a witness to change their evidence.[33]

This account of conduct rules shows that litigation is less heavily regulated by the professions than might be imagined. This may be because it is also regulated by the rules of court, enforced by the courts.

B. Barristers' Conduct Rules for Litigation

Although barristers probably had the right to accept litigation clients during the twentieth century, they rarely did so.[34] The Bar Code traditionally focused on advocacy, but did touch on litigation roles in which barristers were also instructed, for example, drafting. The rules now provide that barristers may only accept such instructions when they have been authorised to conduct litigation in accordance with the requirements of the Handbook.[35] Other amendments made as a result of the right to conduct litigation are consequential rather than substantive. Provisions formerly referring to rights of audience now refer to litigation also.

The new Code of Conduct specifies that Core Duty 1, observing the duty to the court in the administration of justice, overrides any other core duty.[36] The first outcome is that the court must be able to rely on the information provided to it by those conducting litigation and by advocates.[37] This is supported by rules, familiar from the old regime, that relate either specifically to litigation or to both litigation and advocacy. For example, barristers must not knowingly or recklessly mislead or attempt to mislead the court, must take reasonable steps to avoid wasting the court's time, and must ensure that their ability to act independently is not compromised.[38] Those requirements relating more naturally to advocacy, such as handling witnesses, are dealt with in chapter nineteen.

The new Bar Code also includes obligations that arise more naturally from litigation than from advocacy. The duty to the court covers the discovery of documents that come to light which should have been disclosed. Barristers cannot continue to

---

[30] Bar Council, *Bar Code of Conduct 1981*, as amended, at para 704.
[31] SRA, *SRA Code of Conduct* 2011, ch 5: 'Your Client and the Court', Indicative Behaviour 5.1.
[32] ibid, Indicative Behaviour 5.10.
[33] ibid, Indicative Behaviour 5.11.
[34] M Arnheim, 'Public Access—The Future of the Past' (2010) 46 *The Barrister* (www.barristermagazine.com/archive-articles/issue-46/public-access-%E2%80%93-the-future-of-the-past.html).
[35] BSB, *Handbook 2014*, pt 2: *The Code of Conduct* gC70.1.
[36] ibid, gC1.1.
[37] ibid, oC1.
[38] ibid, rC3(1) to (3).

act unless their client agrees to the disclosure of the document.[39] The duty to act with honesty and integrity includes not knowingly or recklessly misleading or attempting 'to mislead anyone'.[40] There is also an obligation to comply with any undertaking given in the course of conducting litigation within an agreed timescale or within a reasonable period of time.[41]

The old duties relating to drafting that were adopted by solicitors have also been transported into the new Bar Code. Therefore, when drafting a statement of case, witness statement, affidavit or other document, barristers must not include statements of fact or contentions not supported by their instructions, or any contention not considered to be properly arguable.

Another old rule reproduced in the new Code is that barristers must not make any allegation of fraud without clear instructions to allege fraud and reasonably credible material which establishes an arguable case of fraud. When drafting a witness statement, or affidavit, barristers must not include any statement of fact other than the evidence which they reasonably believe the witness would give orally.[42]

IV. Regulation of Litigation Lawyers by the Court

Courts have an inherent jurisdiction to secure the proper administration of justice.[43] This includes controlling the lawyers that prepare the case and appear before the courts. The jurisdiction is summary, meaning that the charge against a lawyer arises out of the case and can be dealt with immediately. For this to happen, the charge must be capable of being put to the lawyer in simple terms. Statements of case and disclosure of documents are not required and the proceedings should not be complicated or overlong.[44] A number of outcomes are possible. There may be an order for a new trial, an order for costs against one of the lawyers or a report made to the lawyer's disciplinary body.

At common law, the nature of the jurisdiction may be different for solicitors and barristers. Solicitors' historic role as officers of the court meant they could be disciplined directly.[45] Barristers were not officers of the court, but owed a duty as advocates. When the roles of advocates and litigators were more distinct, judges may have referred barristers to their Inn for discipline and exercised direct control over solicitors.

---

[39] ibid, gC13.
[40] ibid, rC9.1.
[41] ibid, rC11.
[42] ibid, rC9.2.
[43] Per Lord Wright in *Myers v Elman* [1940] AC 282, at 319.
[44] *Harley v McDonald* [2001] 2 WLR 1749.
[45] *Abraham v Jutsun* [1963] 2 All ER 402.

One of the forms of control over solicitors in litigation included an award of costs against them. This jurisdiction was codified, replacing the inherent jurisdiction, at least insofar as it relates to costs.[46] This leaves the question of whether there is anything left of the inherent jurisdiction. In a key case before codification, *Myers v Elman*,[47] the House of Lords laid down some important principles regarding the jurisdiction over solicitors as it then stood. In an action against five defendants for fraudulent conspiracy, solicitors for one of the parties filed an inadequate affidavit verifying a client's list of documents.

The Court of Appeal considered the solicitor could not be personally liable in costs because the work had been done by his managing clerk. The House of Lords reversed this decision, holding him liable for a third of the costs of the case. Lord Atkin said that a solicitor had a 'duty owed to the court to conduct litigation before it with due propriety'. Lord Maugham said that the duty of solicitors covered all those against whom they were opposed. Lord Wright said that before a solicitor can be condemned there must be a failure to fulfil a duty to aid in promoting the cause of justice.

The House of Lords also laid down five important principles regarding the inherent jurisdiction over solicitors. Their Lordships said, first, that the disciplinary jurisdiction over solicitors was separate from that required to make an order for wasted costs. Secondly, a disciplinary finding requires serious professional misconduct but a wasted costs order does not. Thirdly, the wasted costs jurisdiction derives from the duty to the court to promote justice. Fourthly, it is not necessary to find conduct justifying striking a solicitor from the roll to make a wasted costs order. Fifthly, the jurisdiction is compensatory and not merely punitive. The separation of the duty to the court and the right to make wasted costs orders is important, but they are linked by a common concern over the conduct of lawyers.

Twenty years later, the Court of Appeal considered solicitors' duties in litigation in *Wilkinson v Wilkinson*.[48] The wife in divorce proceedings was granted a decree by the court in the absence of her husband. The husband appealed on the grounds that he had not received notice of the hearing. The solicitors acting for the wife refused to answer his solicitors' letters and contested the application, even though they knew they could not prove that notice had been given. The decree was set aside and the wife's solicitors ordered to contribute to the husband's costs.

Lord Justice Ormrod thought that failing to reply to letters was discourteous, but that more was needed to justify sanctioning the solicitors. The additional element was provided by the solicitors' post book, in which all letters sent out by the firm were recorded. The entry allegedly recording the letter giving due notice to the husband's solicitors had been altered. This fact was concealed from the wife's solicitors. Discovery of the post book was given shortly before the hearing to set aside the decree. The husband's solicitors knew that they could not trace the postage clerk who was alleged to have made the entry and so could provide no explanation of the change.

---

[46] Supreme Court Act 1981 (now the Senior Courts Act), ss 51(6) and (7); CPR r 46.8 and Practice Direction 46—Costs Special Cases, at para 5.
[47] *Myers v Elman* [1940] AC 282.
[48] *Wilkinson v Wilkinson* [1963] P 1.

Without concluding that the altered entry was the result of impropriety, the trial judge found that the wife's solicitors had been 'oppressive'. The Court of Appeal found no reason to disagree. Ormrod LJ noted the House of Lords confused rationale for summary awards of costs against solicitors in *Myers v Elman*. He pointed out that Lord Maugham considered such awards to be compensatory. Lord Atkin thought they were punitive. Lord Wright, however, considered that both elements were present'.[49]

Under the CPR, wasted costs orders can only be made where a representative has acted 'improperly, unreasonably or negligently'[50] and caused the other party to incur unnecessary costs.[51] Such orders are considered below. This presumably leaves an inherent jurisdiction to sanction litigators, for serious professional misconduct, as outlined in *Myers v Elman*. Therefore,, in appropriate cases, litigators could have an award of costs made against them and be disciplined if they were guilty of serious misconduct. This might apply, for example, if a solicitor in *Wilkinson v Wilkinson* had been found to have changed the entry in the post book.

A. Statutory Duty to Act with Independence in the Interests of Justice

A statutory duty to act with independence in the interests of justice applies to litigators under the Courts and Legal Services Act 1990, section 28, as amended by the Administration of Justice Act 1999. The Courts and Legal Services Act 1990 provided that a person had the right to conduct litigation if permitted to do so by an approved authorised body. The Administration of Justice Act 1999 added section 28(A), which provided that persons exercising a right to conduct litigation have 'a duty to the court to act with independence in the interests of justice and a duty to comply with rules of conduct of the body relating to the right'.[52] It also provided that those duties overrode any obligation which the person may have (otherwise than under the criminal law) if it was inconsistent with them.[53]

The legislation did not specify how the duty related to either the inherent jurisdiction of the court to control its officers, or those appearing before it, or to the jurisdiction to impose wasted costs orders. The section was replaced by the LSA 2007, section 188, which specified that both advocates and litigators had 'a duty to the court in question to act with independence in the interests of justice' and to observe the conduct rules of their authorising body. The duty to act with independence and observe conduct rules arguably has a narrower scope than that covered by the court's inherent jurisdiction. It is therefore assumed that section 188 has not superseded or replaced that jurisdiction.

---

[49] ibid, at 13.
[50] CPR Practice Direction 46.8, para 5.5(a)
[51] ibid, 5.5(b).
[52] The Access to Justice Act 1999, s 42.
[53] Courts and Legal Services Act 1990, s 28(2A) (rights to conduct litigation).

B. Wasted Costs Orders

i. Origin

That part of the court's inherent jurisdiction to sanction solicitors by awards of costs was formalised in the Courts and Legal Services Act 1990. The Act extended the courts' general discretion to award costs in civil[54] and criminal matters[55] by making wasted costs orders. Thereafter, judges in the main civil courts could disallow, or order a legal or other representative to meet the whole of any wasted costs under what is now known as the Senior Courts Act, 1981 section 51(6).[56]

ii. Scope

In civil cases the yardstick for making such orders was the rules of court. The term 'wasted costs' applied to costs incurred by a party in two circumstances. The first was where they were incurred 'as a result of any improper, unreasonable or negligent act or omission by the opposing representative or any employee of such a representative'.[57] The second circumstance was where, 'in the light of any such act or omission occurring after they were incurred, the court considers it is unreasonable to expect that party to pay'.[58] In criminal cases, awards were made in accordance with regulations. While there are procedural differences in the process of making awards, the principles applied by the appeal courts are similar in both civil and criminal cases.

A collection of applications for wasted costs orders under the name of the first case, *Ridehalgh v Horsefield and another*, provided the Court of Appeal with an opportunity to consider the wasted costs jurisdiction.[59] Two important points emerged from the case. The first was that advocates, as well as litigators, could, in principle, be subject to a wasted costs order. The second was a three-stage test, which subsequently became the basis of a practice direction in the CPR. Following this test, the court had discretion to make a wasted costs order (i) where the legal representative has acted improperly, unreasonably or negligently; (ii) the conduct has caused a party to incur unnecessary costs; and (iii) it is just in all the circumstances to order compensation to the party for the whole or part of those costs.[60]

The CPR provide for the personal liability of a legal representative for costs in Part 46.8. This provides that the 'court will give the legal representative a reasonable opportunity to make written submissions or, if the legal representative prefers,

---

[54] ibid, s 4, amending the Supreme Court Act 1981 by substituting a new s 51.

[55] Courts and Legal Services Act 1990, s 111, amending the Prosecution of Offences Act 1985, s 19A and Magistrates' Courts Act 1980, s 145A.

[56] Supreme Court Act 1981 (now the Senior Courts Act), s 51(6).

[57] ibid, 51(7)(a).

[58] ibid, s 51(7)(b).

[59] *Ridehalgh v Horsefield and anor* [1994] Ch 205; and see *Orchard v SE Electricity Board* [1987] 1 All ER 95 under the old costs jurisdiction.

[60] CPR Practice Direction 46—Costs Special Cases: Personal Liability of Legal Representative for Costs—Wasted Costs Orders: Rule 46.8; Practice Direction 46—Costs Special Cases, para 5.5.

to attend a hearing before it makes such an order'.[61] The court can direct that the client receive notice of any proceedings under this rule, or of any order made under it against his legal representative.[62]

Another complication in the issue of causation arises because potential liability for wasted costs is not limited to parties or their lawyers. In *HB v PB*,[63] a father failed to return a child after an access visit and made serious allegations against the mother. Subsequent proceedings were delayed because of the failure by the local authority to prepare an adequate report. Cobb J found that the local authority had failed fundamentally to investigate, address or analyse the father's allegations.

The father was awarded costs against the local authority for the various hearings that could not proceed without adequate reports. This was justified by the court on the basis that the local authority's failings were sufficiently 'closely connected' with the litigation to justify the order. The decision is only consistent with the CPR if the local authority is treated as a potential party in the proceedings. Despite the decision, the possibility of an order to pay wasted costs against a non-party is likely to be exceptional.

iii. The Three-stage Test

a. Improper, Unreasonable or Negligent Acts

The Court of Appeal in *Ridehalgh v Horsefield and another* concluded that three elements of the statutory definition of the litigator's duty were intended to have their ordinary meanings. 'Improper', therefore, applied to conduct amounting to a significant breach of a substantial duty imposed by a relevant code of professional conduct. It included conduct regarded as improper by the consensus of professional opinion. 'Unreasonable' described conduct not permitting of a reasonable explanation; it was likely to be vexatious or harassing rather than intended to advance resolution of the case. 'Negligent' was to be understood to denote a failure to act with the competence reasonably to be expected of ordinary members of the profession. In practice, the distinctions seldom seem to be a significant factor in the courts' decisions.

One of the cases considered in *Ridehalgh v Horsefield and another* involved complex landlord and tenant law. Both sides' solicitors had misconstrued the legislation, as had the judge at first instance. It was held that the solicitors had not been negligent or careless in coming to their mistaken conclusions on the meaning of the legislation. Another case raised what became a recurring theme in wasted costs applications; the lawyer acting in a 'hopeless case'.

There are different kinds of hopeless case. For example, there are cases that must fail in law and those that may be very difficult to establish, either in law or fact. Lawyers presenting hopeless cases could, in theory, be sanctioned for abuse of process. For example, before the Gambling Act 2005, section 335, gambling debts were

---

[61] CPR, r 46.8(2).
[62] ibid, r 46.8(4).
[63] *HB v PB* [2013] EWHC 1956 (Fam).

irrecoverable for reasons of public policy. Claims for gambling debts, intended to embarrass a debtor, were therefore classic hopeless cases.[64]

Beyond a few exceptional cases, the courts have been reluctant to sanction lawyers for bringing claims that turn out to be unmeritorious. The rationale for this is, simply, because presenting even weak cases is central to their role, as defined by the rule of law. In *Rondel v Worsley*[65] it was said to be deplorable, and injurious to the cab rank rule, if lawyers were to be sanctioned for pursuing hopeless cases. This dicta was cited with approval by Sir Thomas Bingham MR in *Ridehalgh v Horsfield and another*.

The 'hopeless case' in *Ridehalgh v Horsefield and another* concerned a barrister who had accepted a case at short notice and had caused costs to be wasted by not proceeding expeditiously. The Court of Appeal held that, because a barrister had to obey the cab rank rule, pursuing a hopeless case with inadequate instructions was not, of itself, conduct falling within the section.

Sir Thomas Bingham said that

> [a] legal representative is not to be held to have acted improperly, unreasonably or negligently simply because he acts for a party who pursues a claim or defence which is plainly doomed to fail.[66]

He recognised that it is not always easy to distinguish the case which is hopeless from the case which is an abuse of the process of the court, but stated that any doubt should be resolved to the benefit of the legal representative.

A contemporaneous case in which a wasted costs order was made is *C v C*.[67] A divorcing husband and wife, in dispute over financial provision, both applied for a wasted costs order against the wife's solicitor. During the case, it became clear that the husband's assets were much less than originally thought. Expensive further investigations were made and information required of the husband. An offer to settle the case for £50,000 was rejected by the wife, who was eventually awarded £20,000. By that time her costs amounted to £60,000 and the husband's £70,000. A wasted costs order was made in respect of some of these costs on the grounds of unreasonableness and negligent conduct on the part of the solicitor.

Another case where a wasted costs application was successful, *Tolstoy v Aldington*,[68] followed shortly after *Ridehalgh v Horsefield and another*. A lengthy and successful libel action was brought by Lord Aldington against Count Tolstoy, who then sought to have the judgment set aside on the ground of fraud. Tolstoy had been declared bankrupt and so could not pay any costs.

Tolstoy's solicitors acted for him without fee and without applying for legal aid. This was significant because it would have provided a screening process on the merits of the case. Nor did the solicitors send a letter before action. At first instance, the court found that the case was hopeless and struck it out as an abuse of process. Aldington succeeded in an application for a wasted costs order against the solicitors. The

---

[64] See eg *R v Weisz* [1951] 2 KB 611.

[65] *Rondel v Worsley* [1969] 1 AC 19, per Lord Pearce at 275.

[66] *Ridehalgh v Horsefield* per Lord Bingham at 233F. See similarly *Locke v Camberwell HA* [1991] Med LR 249 and *C v C* [1994] 2 FLR 34.

[67] [1994] 2 FLR 34. See also *Woolwich Building Society v Fineberg* (1998) PNLR 216.

[68] *Tolstoy v Aldington* [1996] 2 All ER 556.

grounds of the judgment are that the proceedings were 'at least potentially vexatious'[69] and a collateral attack on the judgment of the court.

In the Court of Appeal, Lord Justice Rose stressed that acting without a fee, even in a hopeless case, was not sufficient to justify an order on its own. He concluded, however, that no solicitor could 'reasonably have instituted these proceedings'. Lord Justice Ward likewise thought that the 'solicitors allowed themselves to be dragged outside that broad province where their actions could reasonably be said to further the ends of justice.'[70] Although counsel had signed the statement of claim, no case against counsel was before the court. Rose LJ stressed that counsel's involvement did not exonerate the solicitors from their duty to exercise their own independent judgement in relation to the case.[71]

In *Dempsey v Johnstone*,[72] a test for deciding whether proceeding with a hopeless case invited a costs sanction was proposed. The court asked whether no reasonably competent legal adviser would have evaluated the chance of success as being such as to justify continuing with the proceedings. This of course, ignored the fact that it is often the client who wishes to proceed, sometimes against advice. This was apparently the case in *Mitchells Solicitors*,[73] where the respondents contended that the applicant's solicitors should bear their costs. They suggested that it was clear halfway through an employment case that the applicant could not succeed. They had even offered not to seek costs if she withdrew. She continued, having consulted her solicitors.

The Employment Appeal Tribunal observed that lawyers could

> advise clients of the perceived weakness of their case and of the risk of failure. But clients are free to reject advice and insist that cases be litigated. It is rarely if ever safe for a court to assume that a hopeless case is being litigated on the advice of the lawyers involved.[74]

It therefore held that, for a wasted costs order to be made, the legal representative had to lend assistance to proceedings amounting to an abuse of process or the duty to the court. Where a claim is 'doomed to fail' parties should apply to strike out the claim rather than waiting to pursue wasted costs. Moreover, the fact that a claim had been abandoned on appeal should not be taken to mean that it had been pursued negligently.[75]

The possibility that wasted costs orders may have a 'chilling effect' on lawyers' willingness to pursue hopeless cases is a consideration that the courts have probably borne in mind. In *Southcombe & Anor v One Step Beyond*,[76] for example, the Court of Appeal considered a case where solicitors (S), acting in a company liquidation, had obtained several adjournments on behalf of their client. They were invited to not to apply for their costs, of around £1000, under threat of an application for a wasted costs order against them. The court stated that S was entitled to take steps to protect their reputation and not be held to ransom by wasted cost applications. They should

---

[69] ibid, at 567c.
[70] ibid, at 572c.
[71] See also *Davy Chiesman* [1984] 1 All ER 321; *Locke v Camberwell HA* [1991] Med LR 249.
[72] *Dempsey v Johnstone* [2013] All ER (D) 515.
[73] *Mitchells Solicitors v Funkwerk Information Technologies York Ltd* [2008] PNLR 29.
[74] ibid, at 22.
[75] *Koo Golden East Mongolia v Bank of Nova Scotia* [2008] EWHC 1120 (QB).
[76] *Southcombe & Anor v One Step Beyond* [2008] EWHC 3231 (Ch).

not be criticised for not abandoning their proper claim for their own costs, even where the sums in issue were modest.

While the courts have been reluctant to penalise pursuit of hopeless cases, the threat of a wasted costs application is still a concern. It would have been helpful therefore if the Court of Appeal in *Ridehalgh v Horsefield and another* had made a general statement that bona fide actions aimed at bringing about a change in the law would not fall foul of the wasted costs jurisdiction.

b. Causation

In *Ridehalgh v Horsefield and another* it was held that orders should only be made under the Senior Courts Act, section 51(6) when the defined conduct directly caused wasted costs.[77] In the recent case of *A (A child)*,[78] the Court of Appeal affirmed the approach and commended the statement of the law in *Harrison v Harrison*.[79] The case of *A (A child)* concerned an application by parents to reopen an investigation into their child's bone damage for which they were initially held to blame. An expert report commissioned by the court did not support their case, but the parents' solicitors continued with a hopeless appeal anyway, because of an over-optimistic assessment by counsel.

In *A (A child)*, the Court of Appeal found that counsel, not the solicitors, had caused wasted costs. As the judge said, however, counsel was not 'in the frame' when the case was considered. The court decided that it would not be fair to impose liability when counsel had not had a chance to be heard. The case demonstrates that, if the court accepts that a litigator's conduct is improper, unreasonable or negligent, it is still necessary to show a causal link between the conduct complained of and the wasted costs. This involves demonstrating that, but for the conduct complained of, the applicant would not have incurred the costs in question.[80]

The application of the causation test was demonstrated in *D v H*.[81] A husband (H) involved in matrimonial proceedings brought a wasted costs application against his wife's lawyers. H later agreed to pay his wife a lump sum and forego an order for costs against his wife. He then continued with the wasted costs application. It was held that the agreement to forego costs had broken the causal link. H no longer had any recoverable loss.

In *Hedrich v Standard Bank*, the claimant disclosed emails during the trial, following which the claim was discontinued.[82] The defendant bank could not recover costs from the claimant. It then applied for wasted costs from the claimant's solicitors, because the emails were disclosed late. The Court of Appeal held that the solicitor had not been negligent and that all of the costs had been incurred when the emails were disclosed. Therefore, causation of loss had not been established.

---

[77] *Ridehalgh v Horsefield* (n 59) at 232C–233A, C–E, 237E–F.
[78] *A (A child)* [2013] EWCA Civ 43.
[79] *Harrison v Harrison* [2009] EWHC 428 (QB).
[80] *Brown & anor v Bennett and others* [2002] 2 All ER 273.
[81] *D v H* [2008] EWHC 559 (Fam).
[82] *Hedrich v Standard Bank* [2009] PNLR 3.

In *Koo Golden East Mongolia v Bank of Nova Scotia*,[83] the High Court held that part of the claim for wasted costs was misconceived. The costs in question were to be the subject of assessment and the defendant had shown no lack of willingness to pay. At the time of the application, no bill had yet been presented and no demand had been made for payment. The defendant banks could not, therefore, show that they had suffered any loss.

c. Whether it is Just in all the Circumstances to Make an Order

The wasted costs jurisdiction is always subject to the discretion of the court. Even if the first two stages of the test are met, the court must still decline to make a wasted costs order if it is not just in all the circumstances to do so. The precise circumstances are not delineated, but there are at least three types of circumstances evident in the cases. The first is where the application for an order is used for some tactical advantage. The second is where it would be procedurally unfair to the lawyer against whom costs are claimed. The third is where a wasted costs order would have a disproportionate personal impact on the lawyer.

Threatening to make an application for wasted costs orders may be seen as a form of intimidation and would therefore be seen as an improper tactic. In *Orchard v South Eastern Electricity Board*, a legally aided claimant brought a case claiming that the defendant had allowed electricity leaks that heated underground water, damaging his house.[84] Early in the case the defendants threatened to make a wasted costs order against the solicitors if they continued with the claim. The claim was shown to be spurious and the threat was pursued.

The Court of Appeal said, *per curiam*, that it was not proper to threaten to make an application for wasted costs during or prior to a hearing in order to browbeat solicitors for legally aided clients into dropping the case or procuring the revocation of the legal aid certificate. Lord Justice Dillon went so far as to say it could be a contempt of court.[85] This is obviously difficult territory for lawyers. The particular case involved a threat to make an application unless the case was dropped. Presumably, a more targeted warning, relating to specific conduct, might be more acceptable.

Another example of the tactical use of the wasted cost jurisdiction relates to the attempted recovery of costs that may not otherwise be recoverable. In *Symphony Group v Hodgson*,[86] Lord Justice Balcombe noted that wasted costs orders might be abused by successful parties trying to recover costs from impoverished litigants, legally aided parties or the legal aid administration. Such orders are only made exceptionally against lawyers for legally aided clients.[87] In *Ridehalgh v Horsefield and another*, Sir Thomas Bingham agreed, saying that it would 'subvert the benevolent purposes of [the legal aid] legislation if such representatives were subject to any unusual personal risk'.[88] This continues to be a concern of the courts.[89]

---

[83]   *Koo Golden East Mongolia v Bank of Nova Scotia* [2008] EWHC 1120 (QB).
[84]   *Orchard v South Eastern Electricity Board* [1987] QB 565.
[85]   ibid, at 581.
[86]   *Symphony Group v Hodgson* [1993] 4 All ER 143.
[87]   See eg *Kelly v South Manchester HA* [1997] 3 All ER 274.
[88]   *Ridehalgh v Horsefield* [1994] (n 59) at 234H. .
[89]   *A (A child)* (n 78) at [12].

Another concern of the judges was that arguments over costs might be used as another way of continuing an argument. In *Hedrich v Standard Bank*, for example, the court referred to the risk of 'satellite litigation' spinning off from the main case. This language may reflect concern that parties may use wasted costs applications to cause delay, put personal pressure on opposing lawyers or to create bargaining chips for later negotiations.

A procedural issue, considered by the Court of Appeal to be relevant to the issue of justice, was the summary nature of proceedings in wasted costs applications. When the House of Lords first considered the area in *Medcalf v Mardell*,[90] their Lordships expressed similar concern. The case concerned two barristers alleged to have amended a notice of appeal to allege fraud. It was claimed that the allegations had no basis in the evidence, as required by the Bar Code of Conduct. The other side to the litigation then claimed wasted costs from the barristers to cover the costs of investigating and rebutting the fraud allegations. The barristers claimed that their client was unwilling to waive professional privilege. They could not therefore demonstrate that they had credible evidence of fraud before them when drafting the appeal.

The House of Lords decided that a court should not make a wasted costs order

> unless, proceeding with extreme care, the court could say that it was satisfied that there was nothing that counsel could, if unconstrained, have said to resist the order, and that it was in all the circumstances fair to make the order.

The majority held that, since the barristers were under the disadvantage of being bound by privilege, they had to have the benefit of the doubt. Accordingly, the House of Lords reversed the Court of Appeal and quashed the wasted costs order.

The approach in *Medcalf v Mardell* suggests that courts will seek to be fair to the lawyers contesting a wasted costs application. Only exceptionally and in the clearest cases are applications apt for summary determination. Hearings to investigate the conduct of a complex action are likely to be expensive and time consuming. Lord Bingham thought that, while dealing with lawyers' unjustified conduct is 'an important public interest, it is... only one of the public interests which have to be considered'.[91] Lord Hobhouse said that the dominant interest for protection was not that of opposing parties, to whom barristers owe 'no duty', but the duty to the court.[92]

The disproportionate effect of a wasted costs order made against legal representatives was taken into account in *R (on the application of Hide) v Staffordshire County Council*.[93] The defendant local authority applied for a wasted costs order against a solicitor advocate who represented the claimant (H) in an unsuccessful action for judicial review.

The local authority submitted that the solicitor had instigated, managed and maintained the action as part of a campaign, stepping outside the role of legal representative. The court accepted that the solicitor's behaviour was unreasonable and negligent and that the action was unnecessary and doomed to failure. Nevertheless, it refused to make an order for wasted costs against the solicitor because of the significant risk

---

[90] *Medcalf v Mardell* [2002] 3 All ER 721.
[91] ibid, per Lord Bingham at 734–35. See also *Harley v McDonald* [2001] 2 WLR 1749.
[92] ibid, per Lord Hobhouse at 741.
[93] *R (on the application of Hide) v Staffordshire County Council* [2007] EWHC 2441 (Admin).

of her bankruptcy. The court considered this a disproportionate consequence, despite the solicitor's conduct.

iv. *Importance of the Wasted Costs Jurisdiction in Controlling Lawyer Conduct*

Although the courts remain willing to make wasted costs orders, the numerous court decisions have often favoured lawyers facing such applications. Taken together, the cases suggest that judges exercise their jurisdiction to grant wasted costs orders with extreme caution. While wasted costs awards are not made lightly, first instance decisions are frequently overturned because the three-part test is incorrectly applied. This may seem unduly lenient to lawyers. As noted in *Harley v McDonald*,[94] issues of negligence or professional conduct can, and possibly should in ordinary circumstances, be dealt with by court proceedings for negligence or by disciplinary proceedings rather than under the wasted costs jurisdiction.

Despite the relative lack of success of wasted costs applications, the mere existence of the jurisdiction in civil cases means that lawyers cannot simply act as hired guns. This creates an environment of some uncertainty. In considering acting in a weak case, for example, lawyers must weigh competing considerations. They must exercise their own discretion in bringing a case but are accountable to the court. They need not filter out hopeless cases, so need not only take cases with a better than even chance of success. They must advance their client's cause within reason, but are potentially liable if they get it wrong.

v. *Relationship of Wasted Costs Jurisdiction to other Control Mechanisms*

It is important to recognise that the wasted costs jurisdiction is only part of the courts' armoury for controlling lawyer behaviour in litigation. As the cases show, there may be a finding against a lawyer, but the court may refuse to make an order because there is no causal link to wasted costs or because an order would not be just in the circumstances. In such cases, the court may resort to other sanctions. In *Re A barrister*,[95] for example, it was observed that, where a court finds improper conduct but no wasted costs, it may refer the lawyer to the relevant disciplinary body, or the legal aid authorities if appropriate.

The issue of whether a reference to a professional body could be made after a wasted costs award is not clear-cut. If the jurisdiction is punitive, it would seem that to add a further sanction is unfair. If, as seems to be the case, it is primarily compensatory, the fact of an award does not necessarily wipe the disciplinary slate clean.[96]

---

[94]   *Harley v McDonald* [2001] 2 WLR 1749, at paras [49]–[54].
[95]   *Re A barrister (wasted costs order) (No 1 of 1991)* [1993] QB 293.
[96]   See further P Jones and N Armstrong, 'Living in Fear of Wasted Costs' (1994) 13 *Civil Justice Quarterly* 208 and H Evans, 'The Wasted Costs Jurisdiction' (2001) 64 *Modern Law Review* 51.

Presumably then, a reference for professional discipline could still be made, even after a wasted costs order, if the misconduct is so serious that the costs sanction is inadequate. Such an approach would appear to integrate the disciplinary and compensatory aspects of the court's inherent jurisdiction over lawyers.

V. Rules of Civil Litigation

The ethos of litigation is created by the rules governing litigation, the courts and the approach of participants in the system, including lawyers. Lord Woolf's reform of civil litigation sought to create a more co-operative ethos. This led to a comprehensive revision of the rules of court, presented in the form of the CPR 1998. It is important to understand the essential elements of the old procedures in order to understand how the ethical choices for lawyers changed after the Woolf reforms.

A. Civil Procedure before the Woolf Reforms

Before the Woolf reforms lawyers had considerably more control of the civil litigation process. Prior to the Courts and Legal Services Act 1990 the overlapping jurisdiction of the High Court or the County Courts was often exploited by lawyers seeking the quicker procedures and generous fee scales of the High Court. The Act placed responsibility on lawyers for assessing the suitability of the case for the venue, giving courts encouragement to change the venue.

The High Court process began with an originating process, a writ or other document. A statement of claim could be included with the writ or followed shortly after. The defendant was required to acknowledge service. If they did not do so, judgment could be entered in default. Having, acknowledged service, the defendant could file a defence. The statement of claim and defence constituted 'pleadings'. After a defence was filed, both sides could seek further particulars and the formal responses became part of the pleadings.

When the formal exchange of pleadings was complete, the parties provided lists of relevant documents that were or had been in their custody or control. These included those for which privilege was claimed. Inspection and exchange of documents followed. Completion of these steps meant that the case could be listed for trial. Behind the formal processes the parties would be investigating the case, lining up witnesses of fact and obtaining expert reports. The process was governed by timetables for service of documents. Automatic directions governed most County Court claims. In most personal injury cases in the High Court, standard directions also applied. Routine cases could proceed to trial be completed with little or no intervention by the court.

Where standard directions applied, the court's involvement in the preparation of cases was instigated by the parties. This might occur, if, for example, one side failed to deliver a document in the allotted time, or a claim for privilege was disputed, or an extra expert was required. In these cases, court directions tailored to the circumstances of the case were issued by a judicial officer, called a Master. In most cases, no court involvement was required. In fact, most cases were settled. The litigation process provided a backdrop to negotiation. Trial was a default option if settlement failed.

The pre-Woolf system of litigation provided ample opportunity and incentive for lawyers to deploy strategies and tactics. Litigation strategies generally involve psychological pressure on the opponent, manipulating the key variables of unpredictability, delay and cost. Repeat player defendants might slow down litigation hoping, for example, that claimants would lose interest or witnesses would disappear before trial. The approach calculated that many claimants would either give up or settle claims cheaply. They could use payment into court to increase the risk of litigation for claimants and the pressure on them to settle.

Claimants' lawyers might try to avoid the risks that their client may be pressurised into cheap settlements by proceeding rapidly with litigation, incurring as much cost as possible before payment in. This so-called 'litigation first' strategy advanced cases nearly to trial as quickly as possible. It gave claimants a good negotiating position. Defendants could not value claims accurately before medical or other evidence had been produced. This meant that they could not make offers that would put claimants at risk on costs. This rapid escalation of claimants' costs, which defendants would probably end up paying, increased pressure on them to settle. It also benefitted claimants' lawyers by running up costs in cases that would probably be settled before trial anyway.

Prior to the Woolf reforms, changes to the civil justice system often suffered from a problem of unintended consequences. An example of this was preventing costs recovery in County Court small claims. This probably reduced legal assistance in bringing small claims[97] without necessarily increasing use of courts.[98] It may have encouraged procedural compromise.[99] The absence of potential costs penalties may have encouraged 'nuisance claims' or encouraged litigation. Small businesses often find that low costs regimes encourage chronic debtors to defend claims.[100]

To avoid unintended consequences, reformers must identify clear objectives and consider how they will be achieved. The pre-Woolf litigation system was seen to suffer from particular problems of delay and cost. Despite timetables for the various stages to be completed, there was often no pressure on either side to move swiftly. Delay was common and sometimes tactical. Piecemeal reforms had tried to increase efficiency and place tighter constraints on lawyers' discretion. Lord Woolf's brief was to examine the whole civil litigation system and expand access to justice without additional public expenditure.[101]

---

[97] R Smith, 'The Changing Motive of Legal Aid' in R Smith (ed), *Shaping the Future: New Directions in Legal Services* (London, Legal Action Group, 1995) 209.

[98] J Baldwin, *Monitoring the Rise of the Small Claims Limit: Litigant's Experiences of Different Forms of Adjudication* (London, Lord Chancellor's Department, 1997) at 74.

[99] R Thomas, 'A Code of Procedure for Small Claims: A Response to the Demand for Do-It-Yourself Litigation' (1982) 1 *Civil Justice Quarterly* 52, discussing the small claims procedures of the County Courts and the extent to which they meet the demand for access to justice in relation to small claims.

[100] T Aldridge, 'Downside of Procedural Reform' *Solicitors Journal* 29 November 1996, at 1142.

[101] Lord Woolf, *Access to Justice* (Final Reports to the Lord Chancellor on the Civil Justice System in England and Wales) (London, HMSO 1996) para 3, at 5.

B. The Woolf Reforms

i. Aims

Lord Woolf's report concluded that the existing litigation system was costly and slow, and that lawyers exacerbated its faults by their behaviour.[102] It identified a substantial risk that the system undermined the competitive position of national courts in the global market for legal work. The report identified the overriding objective of the litigation system as justice, but envisioned commencing proceedings 'only as a last resort'.[103] Woolf's proposed litigation system would be 'less adversarial and more co-operative', better understood by the public and available at reasonable cost.[104]

The Woolf Report proposals, implemented in April 1999 with the CPR, were radical by the standards of its predecessors, bringing together a host of ideas in a 'big bang'. The CPR swept away the previous system, and the aims of the civil litigation system were newly articulated. Dealing with cases justly was conceived as ensuring equality of the parties, saving expense, ensuring expedition and fairness and allocating appropriate resources. Procedures were to be proportionate to the issue, decisions were to be just and predictable, litigants were to be treated fairly, appropriate procedures provided and cases processed speedily.[105]

The CPR increased the transparency of the system and tightened up a number of existing procedures. For example, claimants would have to clearly state their case, or risk having it struck out,[106] and defendants give reasons for denying liability, and either deny, admit or require proof of each allegation.[107] Revised timetables and mechanisms for information exchange, disclosure and agreeing joint experts were introduced.

ii. Measures to Control Litigant Behaviour

a. Pre-action Protocols

The scope for using a 'litigation first' strategy was reduced by the introduction of pre-action protocols. Henceforth, these would have to be completed before litigation was commenced. Lawyers would be forced to disclose information early on so that parties were better informed before litigation commenced. This enabled defendants to value claims more accurately at an early stage and prevented claimants' lawyers incurring litigation costs before settlement could be attempted. The cost of proceedings was therefore avoided where settlement was possible. This was obviously at the expense of further delay if the case was not settled.

---

[102] Lord Woolf *Access to Justice* (Interim report) (London, HMSO, 1995) at 7, 12 and 13.
[103] Lord Woolf, *Access to Justice* (Final Report) (n 101) at paras 8 and 9.
[104] ibid, at 5.
[105] Civil Procedure Rules 1998, r 1.1(2)
[106] ibid, r 3.4(2)(a).
[107] ibid, rr 16.5(1)(a)–(c).

b. Judicial Case Management

One of the key strategies of the new regime, judicial case management, shifted the responsibility for controlling bigger and more complex cases from lawyers to judges. Judges were to take a much more proactive role, forcing the pace of cases and facilitating settlement by encouraging mediation. The allocation questionnaire allows parties to seek a month's stay of the operation of the timetable to allow for settlement efforts.[108] Judges were key to implementing one of the most important principles introduced by the CPR; proportionality. This concern reflected the fact that in over 40 per cent of claims for £12,500 or less the costs exceeded the amount in dispute. Procedures were therefore matched to the sums involved, the importance of the case, the complexity of the issues and the financial positions of the parties.

In order that cases received proportionate treatment, the court structure was reconfigured, with the introduction of three tracks. A small claims track was for low value cases, currently those below £10,000, a fast track for those with higher value and multi-track, currently for cases valued over £25,000.[109] Both sides complete a directions questionnaire shortly after defence is filed, so that the court could place cases on one of the three tracks.[110]

Fast track cases were heard in the County Court. The fast track incorporated fixed timetables and a fixed cost regime. Once the case had been allocated to the small claims track or fast track the fixed timetable applied. On the fast track, the target was to reach trial within 30 weeks. Trial hearings were kept to one day by dispensing with openings by lawyers and having witness statements stand as evidence in chief. Multi-track cases were heard in the High Court only and subject to individual case management by the judge.[111]

The courts' responsibility to manage cases actively included, inter alia, encouraging the parties to co-operate in conducting the proceedings.[112] The parties, and their representatives, were obliged to 'help judges' with furthering the overriding objective.[113] Directions most suited to the particular case were made following allocation to the multi-track. Experts could only be called in the court's discretion[114] and the order was likely to be that they be jointly appointed, except for multi-track cases.[115] Joint experts owed an overriding duty to the court rather than the party paying their bill.[116]

c. Encouraging Settlement

One of the policies promoted by the CPR was promoting settlement. Particular emphasis was placed on alternative dispute resolution (ADR), particularly mediation. Courts were allowed to suspend the proceedings for a period to allow the parties to hold settlement discussions or pursue ADR. This is considered further in chapter twenty.

---

[108] ibid, r.1.4(2)(e).
[109] ibid, r 26.6.
[110] ibid, rr 26.3 and 26.5.
[111] ibid, r 29.
[112] ibid, r 14(2)(a).
[113] ibid, r 1.3.
[114] ibid, r 35.4.1.
[115] ibid, r 32.1.
[116] ibid, rr 35.7, 35.8 and 35.3.

d. Rules on Awarding Costs

The rules on costs were changed to enable the court to penalise litigants as appropriate. While the principle that costs follow the event was retained, the discretion was refined. The court was to consider the conduct of the parties and their success in different parts of the case.[117] In 2007 the requirement for formal payment into court of a sum offered in settlement was removed from Part 36. Thereafter, claimants were potentially at risk on costs when they refused a reasonable offer even in the period before commencement of litigation.[118]

Decisions in early cases showed willingness to sanction aggressive litigants, those leaving 'no stone unturned' or acting unreasonably.[119] In *MBI Incorporated v Riminex Investments*,[120] for example, a landlord's rejection of proposed terms, including rent, was found to be unreasonable. The landlord was ordered to contribute towards costs the tenant had incurred since making the settlement offer.

e. Wasted Costs Orders

The CPR specified a procedure for making wasted costs applications. It required identification of what the legal representative was alleged to have done or failed to do. It also required the applicant to specify the costs sought from the legal representative.[121] The court then considered, first, whether there was evidence or other material which, if unanswered, would be likely to lead to a wasted costs order being made and whether the wasted costs proceedings were justified, notwithstanding the likely costs involved. Then, having heard from the accused lawyer, in writing or at a hearing, the court considered whether it was appropriate to make a wasted costs order.[122] The burden of showing that a wasted costs order should be made was placed on the applicant.

iii. The Impact of the Woolf Reforms

An important goal of the Woolf reforms was to change the litigation culture. The courts were to construe the CPR in light of the overriding objective of doing justice.[123] Contemporaneously, the right to conduct litigation was subjected to duties 'to the court to act with independence in the interests of justice and to comply with the rules of conduct of the authorising body'.[124] These duties were to 'override any

---

[117] ibid, r 44.3(4)(a)–(c) and *Crouch v Kings Healthcare NHS Trust and Murry v Blackburn NHS Trust* [2004] All ER (D) 189 (CA).

[118] Civil Procedure Rules 1998, r 36.14.

[119] ibid, r 44.3(5); and see *Phonographic Performance Ltd v AEI Rediffusion Music Ltd* [1999] 2 All ER 299; *Firle Investments v Datapoint International Ltd* [2001] EWCA Civ 1106; *Mars UK Ltd v Teknowledge Ltd (No 2)* The Times 8 July 1999.

[120] *MBI Incorporated v Riminex Investments* [2002] EWHC 2856 (QB).

[121] Civil Procedure Rules 1998, Practice Direction 46—Costs Special Cases: Personal Liability of Legal Representative for Costs – Wasted Costs Orders: Rule 46.8, 5.9.

[122] ibid, at 5.7.

[123] *Totty v Snowden* [2002] 1 WLR 1384 at [34].

[124] Administration of Justice Act 1999, s 42(2) amending the Courts and Legal Services Act 1990, s 28 (rights to conduct litigation granted by an authorised body).

obligation which the person may have (otherwise than under the criminal law) if it is inconsistent with them'.[125]

Under the new ethos of 'doing justice', litigants were less likely to be denied access to the courts for technical, procedural breaches.[126] There was a higher expectation that lawyers would help the other side correct technical errors.[127] They could expect to be criticised for correspondence that might antagonise.[128] There were, however, mixed messages on the control of expense. For example, on one hand, it was decided that parties could not be prevented from hiring expensive lawyers because their opponents could not afford to.[129] On the other, some judges showed interest in limiting costs where one side had exercised restraint.[130]

The CPR was probably responsible for an immediate and dramatic reduction in the workload of the High Court by up to 80 per cent.[131] This might have been due to cases being delayed by the need to complete pre-action action protocols, earlier settlements and the transfer of business to the County Courts. This reduction in the volume of civil cases in the courts appears to be consistent and permanent. The argument that this, in fact, represents a denial of justice[132] is only one possible criticism of the Woolf reforms.

iv. Criticism of the Woolf Reforms

It was predicted that the Woolf reforms would result in a general deterioration of the court system, including less accurate judgments.[133] Some critics suggested, however, that the reforms did not go far enough. In 2003, Mr Justice Lightman argued that, if the aim was to reduce the cost of litigation, the adversarial model could not be fixed.[134] Its use makes cost inevitable. Lawyers are expensive because they have to keep abreast of voluminous case law and analyse, collect and present evidence. Lightman J proposed that the only solution was to implement the inquisitorial system, relying on the skill and training of judges rather than that of lawyers generally.

Calls for consideration to be given to the introduction of an inquisitorial system were repeated in 2014, in the light of a continued boycott of courts by barristers. Lord Thomas, the most senior judge in England and Wales, said that an inquisitorial system would be an improvement for litigants in person. Such a change would involve 'a greater degree of inquiry by the judge into the evidence being brought forward'.[135]

---

[125] ibid.
[126] *Chilton v Surrey County Council* (1999) LTL 24/6/99.
[127] *Hertsmere Primary Care Trust v Estate of Rabindra-Anandh* (2005) The Times 25 April 2005.
[128] *King v Telegraph Group Ltd* (2004) *The Times* 21 May 2004.
[129] *Maltez v Lewis* (1999) *The Times* 4 May 1999.
[130] *McPhilemy v Times Newspapers Ltd.* [1999] 3 All ER 775.
[131] R Musgrove, 'Unified Civil Jurisdiction' in *Civil Justice Council: Annual Report 2004.*
[132] O Fiss, 'Against Settlement' (1983) 93 *Yale Law Journal* 1073
[133] D O'Brien, 'Blood on the Tracks: The Woolf Report and Substantive Justice (1998) 3 *Contemporary Issues in Law* 17.
[134] Lightman J, 'The Civil Justice System and the Legal Profession—The Challenges Ahead' (2003) 22 *Civil Justice Quarterly* 235.
[135] O Bowcott, 'Lord chief justice floats rethink of adversarial hearings' *The Guardian* 4 March 2014, at 13.

The fall in the numbers of High Court cases suggested other possible, negative consequences of the Woolf reforms. Speeding up cases reduces time for preparation, favouring wealthy clients whose lawyers can mobilise resources quickly[136] and potentially increasing inequality. The front-loading of preparation imposes investigation and disclosure costs, even on cases that might have settled without.[137] Lord Woolf did not think it a problem that the pre-action protocols could be an impediment to bringing viable claims. He argued that 'the courts should not be used merely as part of the tactical equipment of a macho lawyer'.[138]

One of the aspects of Woolf's report that did not prove particularly contentious was the promotion of mediation. There were very practical reasons why it might have been so. If settlement does not follow, mediation is an additional cost of the proceedings. Even if settlement does follow, it is difficult to show that it was as a result of mediation. In fact, in some contexts, settlement rates and times may not change, except for the worse, as a result of mediation.[139]

The earlier experimentation with ADR in the USA drew a sustained and trenchant critique of mediation and settlement for other reasons.[140] The thrust of this criticism is the potential for the law to lag behind social developments when a common law system is denied the access to cases. This effect can be exaggerated if so-called 'irrational' claimants are forced to funnel their cases down a mediation route[141] and companies are able to deflect and 'buy off' claimants whose cases could set precedents.[142]

It is arguable that the Woolf reforms promoted the quick and easy determination of large numbers of cases, placing 'access to justice' over procedural justice as a priority of the system. This downgraded one of the courts' main functions in policy implementation, that of producing standards for governing society.[143] The general mistrust of lawyers that underpinned the reforms led to the imposition of tighter controls. Lawyers, wrapped in a blanket of controls, lost the flexibility to engineer settlements quickly and expeditiously.

C. The Jackson Reforms

Lord Justice Jackson's reforms continued in the direction that Woolf set, in particular by tightening judicial control over litigation. The Legal Aid, Sentencing and Punishment of Offenders Act 2012 (LASPO 2012) and the new CPR implemented most of Jackson LJ's recommendations regarding costs in civil litigation from April

---

[136] C Glasser, 'Civil Procedure a Time for Change' in R Smith (ed), *Shaping the Future: New Directions in Legal Services* (London, Legal Action Group, 1995).

[137] M Zander, 'The Government's Plans on Civil Justice' (1999) 61 *Modern Law Review* 382.

[138] J Fleming, 'Trying Woolf' *Law Society Gazette* 28 April 2000, at 18.

[139] A Boon, P Urwin and V Karuk, 'What difference Does it Make?: Facilitative Judicial Mediation in Employment Tribunals? (2011) 40(1) *Industrial Law Review* 45.

[140] See eg Fiss, 'Against Settlement' (n 132) at 1076; D Barnhizer, 'The Virtue of Ordered Conflict: A Defense of the Adversary System' (2001) 79 *Nebraska Law Review*; and see further ch 18: 'Alternative Dispute Resolution'.

[141] FB Cross, 'In Praise of Irrational Plaintiffs' (2000) 86 *Cornell Law Review* 1.

[142] J Robins, 'Food for Thought' *The Lawyer* 6 September 2004, at 19.

[143] N Armstrong, 'Making Tracks' in AAS Zuckerman and R Cranston (eds), *Reform of Civil Procedure: Essays on Access to Justice* (Oxford, Clarendon Press, 1995) at 97; O'Brien, 'Blood on the Tracks' (n 133).

2013. These are dealt with more fully in chapter twelve. LASPO 2012 introduced damages-based agreements (DBAs) and extended the requirement to use the online portal for personal injury claims. It banned referral fees for personal injury cases and ended recovery of after the event insurance premiums. Following LASPO 2012, the CPR were substantially revised. Changes included amendments to existing practice on costs and case management rules.

The Jackson reforms included many refinements in the use of costs to ensure the efficient and fair conduct of litigation. As regards efficiency, under the cost budgeting rules, litigators must make a realistic assessment of costs at the start of a case and stick to them.[144] They may lose the right to recover any costs if they do not conform to the requirements exactly.[145] As regards promoting fairness, the qualified one-way costs shifting (QOCS) regime introduced in personal injury litigation is built on the assumption of proper conduct. Personal injury claimants' protection from costs liability depends on claimants' proper behaviour, and that of their representatives.

One of the refinements introduced in the new rules is to CPR Rule 3.9. This formerly required the court consideration of nine factors when considering whether to relieve a party of costs sanctions. Under the new rules these have been reduced to two. Therefore, in considering whether to give relief from any sanction for failure to comply with any rule, practice direction or court order, the court will consider all the circumstances of the case including the need (i) for litigation to be conducted efficiently and at proportionate cost and (ii) to enforce compliance with rules, practice directions and orders.[146]

VI. Criminal Litigation

A. Context

It is arguable that the ethical orientation of lawyers in the criminal justice system should be determined by the aim, or possibly aims, of that system. This is, however, contestable. It is likely to be justice, the same overriding objective that Lord Woolf identified for civil justice. This would arguably involve a commitment to a form of procedural justice consistent with the commitment to the rule of law. This, at least, is the kind of commitment that emerges from the codes of conduct. Often, the defendant's rights seem to take precedence.

Justice is not, however, the only candidate. Young and Sanders propose that the function of the criminal justice system is to promote freedom.[147] This may

---

[144] See ch 12: 'Fees'.
[145] *Mitchell v News Group Newspapers Limited* (2013) EWHC 2355.
[146] Civil Procedure Rules 1998, r 3.9.
[147] R Young and A Sanders, 'The Ethics of Prosecution Lawyers' (2004) 7(2) *Legal Ethics* 190.

be achieved, they argue, by reducing the fear of crime, achieved by convicting wrongdoers. It is also achieved by ensuring that the innocent have nothing to fear. This suggests that the criminal justice system should seek to balance the human and civil rights of individuals and the protection of society. This is achieved by striking the right balance in the relationship between prosecution and defence.

The state arranges the terms of both prosecution and defence in criminal trials. This is an awkward relationship because of the potential for abuse of power. Under the human rights legislation, justice requires that those accused of crimes receive fair treatment, including expedition in bringing charges, processing,[148] and a 'fair and public hearing …, including an adequate defence'.[149] The right to a fair hearing does not necessarily include a right to representation by a lawyer. A person has the right 'to defend himself in person or through legal assistance of his own choosing or, if he has not sufficient means to pay for legal assistance, to be given it free when the interests of justice so require.'[150] Whether or not lawyers are provided, the state must ensure fair proceedings.

B. Criminal Procedure Rules

Part 1 of the new Criminal Procedure Rules identifies the overriding objective of criminal procedure as dealing with cases justly.[151] This involves achieving the objectives of acquitting the innocent and convicting the guilty, dealing with the prosecution and the defence fairly and recognising the rights of a defendant, particularly those under Article 6 of the European Convention on Human Rights.[152]

Dealing with cases justly also includes respecting the interests of witnesses, victims and jurors. This involves keeping them informed of the progress of the case, dealing with the case efficiently and expeditiously and ensuring that appropriate information is available to the court when bail and sentence are considered. All of this must take into account the gravity of the offence alleged, the complexity of what is in issue, the severity of the consequences for the defendant, and others affected, and the need to deal with other cases in a similar way.[153]

Participants in the conduct of cases must prepare and conduct the case in accordance with the overriding objective.[154] This involves complying with the Criminal Procedure Rules, practice directions and directions made by the court. A participant in the process should inform the court, and other parties, of any significant failure, whether or not that participant is responsible for that failure, to take any procedural step required. Anyone involved in any way with a criminal case is a participant in

---

[148] Human Rights Act 1998, sch 1, pt I, art 5 (right to liberty and security).
[149] ibid, sch 1, pt I, art 6 (right to fair trial), para 1.
[150] ibid, para 3(c).
[151] Criminal Procedure Rules 2013, r 1.1
(www.justice.gov.uk/courts/procedure-rules/criminal/docs/2012/crim-proc-rules-part-01.pdf).
[152] Criminal Procedure Rules 2013, r 2.
[153] ibid.
[154] ibid, r 1.2.

its conduct for the purpose of the rule. A failure is considered significant if it might hinder the court in furthering the overriding objective.

C. Agencies

A degree of fairness may be guaranteed by the institutional arrangements for prosecution and defence and the way in which they are controlled and monitored. Criminal prosecutions are brought by the Crown Prosecution Service (CPS), headed by the Director of Public Prosecutions (DPP). The DPP operates independently, but is under the superintendence of the Attorney General who is accountable to Parliament for the work of the CPS. The CPS services the casework of local police forces, which retain the right to caution individuals rather than refer them for prosecution. Since 2003, a Crown Prosecutor, rather than the police, decides whether to prosecute a suspect in serious cases.[155] The police and CPS often work together in Criminal Justice Units to prepare cases for court. The CPS employs many solicitors and barristers as caseworkers and advocates, and also instructs private practitioners as advocates.

The previous arrangements involved the police preparing cases and independent barristers prosecuting them. The introduction of the CPS evoked a lot of criticism, including from judges, regarding the lack of independence and competence of the CPS. These criticisms have now faded, but as state employees, prosecutors may be under pressure to meet targets that private practitioners would not. This may affect their judgement on particular issues and encourage them to cut corners in order to meet targets. Using state-employed lawyers for criminal defence creates an obvious conflict of interest, but the payment of private practice barristers through legal aid is seen to be more expensive.

In addition to the CPS, some regulatory agencies have authority to prosecute offences. These include the Her Majesty's Revenue and Customs and the Department for Work and Pensions. These agencies have different propensities to prosecute and it is not clear that they work to common criteria. This is an issue of fairness for the system and for lawyers asked to advise on prosecuting individual cases.[156]

Different concerns surround the arrangements for criminal defence, where there are recurring doubts about both the quality and cost of representation. The UK Government has sought an alternative defence organisation to mirror the CPS. The Legal Services Commission was tasked with trialling a Criminal Defence Service at a few metropolitan centres.[157] Although this is currently a network of preferred suppliers, mainly solicitors' firms, a public defender service, using directly employed lawyers, currently exists in a few centres. The benefits of the alternative system on cost were not demonstrated decisively and, at present, initial pilots are unlikely to be extended.

---

[155] Criminal Justice Act (2003), s 28 and Schedule 2.
[156] Young and Sanders 'The Ethics of Prosecution Lawyers' (n 147) at 196–99.
[157] Administration of Justice Act 1999, s 12.

D. Ethical Considerations

It may be thought that criminal trials, and the rights of the defendant, are the main justification of the lawyer's distinctive, adversarial ethic. Aspects of process are surprisingly co-operative. For example, on indictments, and in some summary cases, both sides are under duties of openness laid out in the Criminal Procedure and Investigations Act 1996. Evidence detrimental to the prosecution case, including details of adverse witnesses, must be divulged to the defence, except where public interest immunity is confirmed by the court.[158]

Criminal trials generate distinct ethical conduct dilemmas. These vary according to the nature of the system and the procedures that it allows or prohibits. An ethical issue in one jurisdiction does not arise in another. An example of this is plea bargains. These are arrangements whereby a lighter sentence can be accepted by the prosecution in return for a guilty plea, subject to approval by the judge. The subject commands a significant ethical literature in the US, where plea bargains are permitted. The official position in the UK is that plea-bargaining is not normally permitted, except in a very limited form allowed by Criminal Justice Act 2003, section 144. Therefore, the courts can take into account the timing and circumstances when guilty pleas are entered in sentencing, but must state in open court the reasons for any discounted sentence.[159] Significant discounts on sentence are usually given for guilty pleas, especially where made at the earliest opportunity.[160] The nuances of these arrangements are discussed in the next chapter, on negotiation.

i. Prosecution Ethics

Prosecutors are expected to comply with the Code of Conduct of their authorising body in relation to conduct matters. They must also follow the Code for Crown Prosecutors, issued under the Prosecution of Offences Act 1985, section 10, when deciding whether or not to prosecute.[161]

a. Decision to Prosecute

The Code for Crown Prosecutors provides that

> [p]rosecutors must be fair, independent and objective. They must not let any personal views about the ethnic or national origin, gender, disability, age, religion or belief, political views, sexual orientation, or gender identity of the suspect, victim or any witness influence their decisions. Neither must prosecutors be affected by improper or undue pressure from any source. Prosecutors must always act in the interests of justice and not solely for the purpose of obtaining a conviction.[162]

---

[158] Criminal Procedure and Investigations Act 1996, s 3(a).

[159] Powers of Criminal Courts (Sentencing) Act 2000, s 152.

[160] See further C Flood-Page and A Mackie, *Sentencing Practice: An Examination of Decisions in the Magistrates' Court in the mid-1990s* (London, Home Office, 1998).

[161] CPS, *Code for Crown Prosecutors*, 7th edn (London, CPS, 2013) (www.cps.gov.uk/publications/code_for_crown_prosecutors/decision.html).

[162] ibid, at para 2.4.

Prosecutors must apply the principles of the Human Rights Act 1998, at each stage of a case, comply with guidelines issued by the Attorney General, with the Criminal Procedure Rules, and the obligations arising from international conventions. They must also follow the policies and guidance of the CPS. The decision to prosecute is taken according to criteria in the Code for Crown Prosecutors. There is a two-stage test; whether the evidence offers a realistic prospect of conviction and, if so, whether the public interest requires a prosecution[163] as opposed, for example, to an out of court disposal.

Each charge must be justifiable on the evidential test. The guidance makes it clear that ethical factors come into play in decisions to prosecute. Prosecutors must weigh the impact of any defence, and any other information that suspects put forward or that they may rely on.[164] They must consider whether 'an objective, impartial and reasonable jury or bench of magistrates or judge hearing a case alone, properly directed and acting in accordance with the law, is more likely than not to convict the defendant of the charge alleged'.[165]

Prosecutors should proceed with prosecutions provided there is a realistic prospect of conviction, even though they are not totally convinced of the defendant's guilt. This can be justified because, to suggest otherwise, would be to pre-judge the evidence and the capacity of the trial to resolve such doubts.[166] There is a specific duty to keep the decision to prosecute under review as cases develop.[167]

In deciding whether prosecution is in the public interest, prosecutors must consider a number of issues. These are the seriousness of the offence, the culpability of the suspect, the circumstances and the harm caused to the victim,[168] whether the suspect was under 18 at the time of the offence, the impact on the community, broadly defined,[169] the proportionality of prosecution as a response to the offence and the need to protect sources of information.[170] The best interests and welfare of children or young persons must be considered. This includes any adverse impact on their future prospects that may be disproportionate to the seriousness of the offending.[171]

One or more of the considerations may outweigh others in a particular case. If, for example, the offence was motivated by the victim's ethnic or national origin, gender, disability, age, religion or belief, sexual orientation or gender identity, or the suspect demonstrated hostility towards the victim based on any of those characteristics, prosecution is more likely.[172] In deciding whether or not to prosecute, prosecutors must consider whether it is desirable for the court, rather than the prosecutor, to weigh the various factors in reaching its decision.[173]

---

[163] ibid, at para 4.1.
[164] ibid, at para 4.4.
[165] ibid, at para 4.5.
[166] Young and Sanders (n 147) at 200–03, but see D Nicolson and J Webb, *Professional Legal Ethics: Critical Interrogations* (Oxford, Oxford University Press 1999) at 228–29.
[167] CPS, *Code for Crown Prosecutors* (n 161) at para 3.6.
[168] ibid, at para 4.12c.
[169] ibid, at para 4.12e.
[170] ibid, at para 4.12g .
[171] ibid, at para 4.12d.
[172] ibid, at paras 4.12 (a) to (g).
[173] ibid, at para 4.11.

The main threats to prosecutorial independence are political considerations and other agencies. As to politics of prosecution, the Code provides that '[a] case which does not pass the evidential stage must not proceed, no matter how serious or sensitive it may be'.[174] Prosecutors are under a duty not to start or continue a prosecution which would be regarded by the courts as oppressive or unfair and an abuse of the court's process.[175]

Among the threats to prosecutorial independence from other agencies is that posed by the police service. There were suggestions that previous prosecutorial regimes paid too much attention to police views in reaching conclusions.[176] The present Code for Crown Prosecutors recognises that prosecutors and investigators work closely together, but states that the final responsibility for decisions to prosecute, or continue a case, rests with the CPS.[177] Therefore, prosecutors can advise what evidence should be collected to rectify evidential weaknesses, but must step back from involvement when making decisions on prosecution.[178]

b. Conduct Issues

The ethical orientation of prosecutors is distinctive. Rather than the partisan disposition of most litigation lawyers, prosecutors have been cast as 'ministers of justice', whose primary role is to assist in the administration of the criminal justice system.[179] The implication of this disposition is that they should not struggle to convict. This ethos is captured in the old Bar guidance, which provided that prosecutors should 'lay before the Court fairly and impartially the whole of the facts which comprise the case for the prosecution and should assist the Court on all matters of law applicable to the case'.[180] In line with the Criminal Procedure and Investigations Act 1996, mentioned in opening the section, the Annex also provided that prosecutors 'ensure that all relevant evidence is either presented by the prosecution or made available to the defence'.[181]

While prosecutors may not recommend a sentence, they have active duties to perform at the sentencing stage. They must draw the judge's attention to any victim personal statement, any statutory provisions relevant to the offender, or the offences and any aggravating or mitigating factors.[182] They may also make submissions as to the appropriate sentencing range.[183]

---

[174] ibid, at para 4.4.

[175] ibid, at para 3.5.

[176] M McConville, A Sanders and R Leng, *The Case for the Prosecution* (London, Routledge, 1991) at 147.

[177] *Code for Crown Prosecutors* (n 161) at para 3.6.

[178] ibid, at para 3.3.

[179] See eg *R v Puddick* (1865) 4 F & F 497, per Compton J at 499, approved in *R v Banks* [1916] 2 KB 621, 12 Cr App R 74, esp Avory J at 76, cited by A Sherr, 'The Ethics of Prosecution' (http://sas-space.sas.ac.uk/255/1/Ethics%20of%20Prosecution.pdf).

[180] Bar Council, *Bar Code of Conduct 1981*, as amended, Annexe H, at para 11.1.

[181] ibid, at para 11.2.

[182] *R v Cain (Alan John)* [2006] EWCA Crim 3233, [2007] 2 Cr App R (S) 25, The Times 26 December 2006.

[183] Addendum to the Attorney General's Guidelines on the Acceptance of Pleas and the Prosecutor's Role in the Sentencing Exercise 2005, New Paragraph C6.

Similar obligations are set out in the Core Quality Standards for the CPS. These outline a number of tasks that prosecuting advocates should perform in sentencing.[184] The duties include outlining the facts of the case to the court, drawing attention to any aggravating features of the offence and any mitigating factors that are apparent from the prosecution case.[185] They should also draw attention to the impact of the offender's behaviour by presenting a victim personal statement to the court, where available.[186] They may also ask the court to order the offender to pay compensation to the victim. They may provide evidence of the impact of the offending on a community. The Core Quality Standards were replaced by Casework Quality Standards from March 2014,[187] but these were expressed at a higher level of generality and were significantly less detailed.

It can be argued that the role of prosecutors as 'ministers of justice' is overstated.[188] There is still a high premium on conviction for those instructed to achieve it. Nevertheless, the Bar guidance to prosecutors underscores the point that the adversarial ethic should not infect litigation tactics. It should be manifest in the arguments constructed on the evidence, which should be available to both sides. Young and Sanders suggest that the values of the system of criminal justice are 'predominantly orientated towards crime control rather than due process, human rights or freedom'.[189] They argue that the system militates against prosecutors protecting defendants by behaving ethically. This task therefore falls to defence lawyers.

ii. Criminal Defence Ethics

Criminal defence is taken as the main justification of neutral partisanship and may be assumed to involve relatively extreme pursuit of client interests. The licence accorded the criminal defence lawyer was put at its highest by the US academic, Monroe Freedman,[190] particularly in relation to what he called the three hardest questions.[191] Freedman's questions related to three dubious practices available to defence lawyers. They were, to discredit an honest witness, not reveal perjury that produces the right verdict and to advise a client in a way that allows him to commit perjury. Freedman justified each of these practices because of the priority afforded, by the adversarial system, to individual rights and liberty.

Freedman's first two examples relate mainly to advocacy. In this context, slightly different rules may apply and these are discussed in the chapter on advocacy. The consequences of counselling that allows a client to tailor evidence could also

---

[184] CPS, *Core Quality Standards*, Standard 9: Sentencing and Confiscation, (http://www.cps.gov.uk/publications/core_quality_standards).

[185] ibid, Standard 9: Sentencing and Confiscation, at para 9(3)a.

[186] ibid, Standard 9: Sentencing and Confiscation, at para 9(4)a-c.

[187] CPS Casework Quality Standards (http://www.cps.gov.uk/publications/casework_quality_standards/index.html).

[188] Young and Sanders (n 147) at 196.

[189] ibid, at 209.

[190] MH Freedman, 'Professional Responsibility and the Criminal Defense Lawyer: The Three Hardest Questions' (1996) 64 *Michigan Law Review* 153.

[191] ibid.

have implications for an advocate, depending on circumstances. This will also be considered in more detail later. Freedman's third example, counselling the client in a way that enables them to tailor evidence, relates to the litigation process and will be dealt with here.

a. Assisting the Client in Tailoring Evidence

Freedman's third example of ethically marginal behaviour concerns a lawyer advising a client accused of murder. The issue is what he is entitled to tell the client about the legal implication of carrying a knife, before he asks him whether he usually carries a knife. Carrying a penknife, for example, may, or may not, depending on the circumstances, support the prosecution's argument on intent in a stabbing case. Freedman concludes that the lawyer is entitled to tell the client that, if he did not usually do so, carrying a knife on a particular occasion would be evidence of premeditation.

The specific situation is not touched on in the Bar Code 2014. The closest rule, in the chapter on behaving ethically, is that 'you must not encourage a witness to give evidence which is misleading or untruthful'.[192] It is doubtful that the counselling described by Freedman falls within the scope of this rule. The general attitude of the Bar Code to the counselling issue can be deduced from the balance struck regarding presenting incredible or inconsistent stories. Here, barristers should advise their clients on the wisdom of this but, ultimately, not pre-judge the court's reaction.[193] Therefore, it does not matter that a client's case is not believed, provided the barrister does not actively mislead the court.

The SRA Code of Conduct may be a little firmer on this issue. The closest relevant clue is an indicative behaviour against 'constructing facts supporting your client's case'.[194] It is not clear what 'constructing facts' means, but it could include advising clients in such a way that they can tailor their account of events to fit with the law. It is doubtful that is what was intended, particularly as the phrase appears in a sentence about drafting documents. It would be difficult to counsel a client on plea without discussion of their conduct in relation to the law. Therefore, some such discussion must be permitted, provided what is presented later is consistent with the duty to the court.

The general position on offering advice that could assist breaking the law was touched on in chapter nine. General counselling, regarding whether an offence has been committed, whether it is the same as the offence charged and the appropriate plea, falls within the broad bounds of that general discussion. This emphasised the role of lawyers in supporting personal autonomy. Clearly, a lawyer should not conspire to concoct a false story. It is, however, inconsistent with the lawyer's general role that they should try to nail down a client's account before offering any legal advice. Therefore, the line implicit in the other provisions of the Code suggests some tolerance regarding counselling on the relevant criminal law.

---

[192] BSB, *Handbook 2014*, pt 2: *The Code of Conduct*, C2: 'Behaving Ethically', rC9.3.
[193] ibid, C1: 'You and the Court' gC6 and gC7.
[194] SRA, *Handbook, Code of Conduct* 2011, as amended, ch 5: 'Your Client and the Court, Indicative Behaviour' 5.7.

b. Advice on Plea

It has been perfectly proper under the conduct rules to allow clients who admit guilt, but want to plead 'not guilty', to do so. The proviso is that the way in which CPS the case is presented must not mislead. This means that the prosecution can be required to prove its case on the evidence. This, admittedly, potentially places the lawyer in a morally ambiguous position. The justification is that this ambiguity is necessary in order to operationalise the rule of law principle. A more pragmatic justification is that it allows for a proper assessment of the facts, increasing the chances of correct verdicts and proportionate sentences.[195]

The reverse problem for criminal defence lawyers is a client, whom the lawyer believes will be convicted on the evidence, who wants to plead not guilty. Such defendants may be better served by a guilty plea. This may persuade the CPS to drop or reduce charges. An early indication of guilt may itself attract a sentence discount. Where defendants are innocent of the charges, such a rational calculation is obviously at the expense of the integrity of the client, the lawyer and the system. In the Crown Court, around 10 per cent who plead guilty are believed by defence and prosecution to be innocent.[196]

The circumstances outlined in this section relate to advice on plea where there is no interaction with the prosecution or judge. Where such interaction occurs, the situation turns into a kind of negotiation. These circumstances are therefore dealt with in the next chapter.

c. Conduct Issues

The criminal defence lawyer is not required to be as even-handed as prosecution lawyers. The need to avoid wrongful conviction justifies a more partisan approach by the defence. Therefore, for example, defence advocates need not correct prosecution errors of fact of which they have knowledge.[197] The scope that criminal defence lawyers have beyond such minor dispensations is debatable. Because of their unique position, as the accused's 'champion against all the world', particularly the potentially oppressive state, it is arguable that they should have considerable freedom in how they conduct the defence.

Nevertheless, the need for vigorous defence raises the issue of how far defence lawyers should go on behalf of their client. They have a number of legitimate tactical options in preparing and presenting the case. For example, defence lawyers can exploit the relevant provisions of the Prosecutor's Code of Conduct and 'submit evidence or information to the prosecutor via the police or other investigators, prior to charge, to help inform the prosecutor's decision'.[198] There may be opportunities in this process to influence the decision whether or not to prosecute.

---

[195] A Ashworth, 'Ethics and Criminal Justice' in R Cranston (ed), *Legal Ethics and Professional Responsibility* (Oxford, Clarendon Press, 1995) 146.

[196] M Zander and P Henderson, *The Crown Court Study Royal Commission on Justice Study No 19* (London, HMSO, 1993).

[197] M Blake and A Ashworth, 'Ethics and the Criminal Defence Lawyer' (2004) 7(2) *Legal Ethics* 167, at 178, citing Lord Diplock in *Saif Ali v* Mitchell and Co [1980] AC 198, at 220.

[198] CPS, *Code for Crown Prosecutors* (n 161) at para 3.3.

Before a case comes to trial, there are opportunities for tactical delay. This may cause a case to be dismissed, witnesses' nerves to fray or recollections to dim. Delay may also result in the victim's commitment to pursue a matter to dissipate. Deliberate use of delay by the defendant is frowned upon. Early in proceedings the accused must serve a defence statement setting out the nature of the defence, details of any alibi and those elements of the prosecution case that are contested.[199] This tends to hasten the process of defence preparation.

A review of the criminal courts by Lord Justice Auld suggests that defence lawyers are frequently not compliant with the formal requirements.[200] Auld LJ also wanted the costs of pre-trial hearings necessitated by failure to comply with timetables to be followed by public reprimands and reporting of offending lawyers to the professional body and Legal Services Commission.[201] He favoured using conduct codes, disciplinary and costs sanctions to force defence lawyers to comply exactly with the requirements.[202] Following criticism of lawyers' behaviour by the BCCI Working Party interim report as 'unattractive', the then Lord Chancellor, Lord Falconer, planned to replace legal aid lawyers who delayed cases. The plan was for the judge to report them to the Legal Services Commission, which would then ask the defendant to find another lawyer.[203]

The requirement for the defence to co-operate with the prosecution encourages early identification of issues. In *R v Gleeson*,[204] the court recognised that disclosure of defence details allowed the prosecution to plug gaps in its case. In this context, it was

> understandable why as a matter of tactics a defendant might prefer to keep his case close to his chest. But that is not a valid reason for preventing a full and fair hearing on the issues canvassed at the trial. A criminal trial is not a game under which a guilty defendant should be provided with a sporting chance. It is a search for truth in accordance with the twin principles that the prosecution must prove its case and that a defendant is not obliged to inculpate himself, the object being to convict the guilty and acquit the innocent. Requiring a defendant to indicate in advance what he disputes about the prosecution case offends neither of those principles.[205]

In *R v Chorley Justices*,[206] it was said that defendants refusing to identify the issues

> can derive no advantage from that or seek, as appears to have happened in this case, to attempt an ambush at trial. The days of ambushing and taking last-minute technical points are gone. They are not consistent with the overriding objective of deciding cases justly, acquitting the innocent and convicting the guilty.[207]

Consistent with this approach, advocates spotting a gap in the prosecution case must not wait to make a submission of no case to answer.

[199] Criminal Procedure and Investigations Act 1996, s 5.
[200] Auld LJ, *A Review of the Criminal Courts of England and Wales* (London, The Stationery Office, 2001).
[201] ibid, at para 220.
[202] ibid, at paras 115–84 and 194–205.
[203] N Goswami, 'Falconer: tardy litigators will be fired' *The Lawyer* 4 June 2007.
[204] *R v Gleeson* [2003] EWCA Crim 3357.
[205] ibid, per Auld LJ at [36].
[206] *R v Chorley Justices* [2006] EWHC 1795 (Admin).
[207] ibid, per Thomas LJ at [26].

In *R v Penner*,[208] an appeal in a case where a submission of no case to answer had been refused, Lord Justice Thomas said:

> It is no longer permissible for the ambush of the type that it might be suggested happened in this case, to be performed in the future ... The appeal fails simply because, had the true position been put before this court, leave to appeal would never have been granted.[209]

If the defence notices a remediable gap in the prosecution case but says nothing, and then makes a submission of no case to answer at the end of the prosecution case, the court may allow the prosecution to reopen their case.[210]

Despite the efforts of courts to control inappropriate zeal in criminal defence lawyers, the most serious risk is their failure to be sufficiently zealous. Studies in both the USA and UK suggest that their diligence, competence and commitment is often in doubt. One reason offered for a decline of motivation is disillusionment. Lawyers find that their clients tend to be guilty and this corrodes their determination and diligence in mounting a defence.[211] Another factor could be the financial rewards in criminal defence, which may not attract the most able or motivated lawyers. Poor profitability may also explain discontinuous representation, whereby different staff are assigned to deal with different stages of a case.

The accumulation of experience, poor rewards and poor morale undermine the individual lawyer's commitment and sense of responsibility for a client. Research in the 1990s by McConville et al found that:

> Almost all our respondents came to see criminal defence practices as geared, in co-operation with the other elements of the system, towards the routine production of guilty pleas. A minority of them found this to be a source of injustice for clients and of disillusionment for themselves, given their earlier expectations of the defence solicitors' role in an adversarial system.[212]

The lack of adversarial spirit may be manifest as deference to prosecution lawyers or lack of confidence in clients. This risk may be reduced by clear guidelines on appropriate conduct and a suitably supportive professional culture.[213]

E. Regulation of Criminal Litigation

The mechanisms of control over lawyer conduct are the same in criminal litigation as they are in civil litigation. The judge may sanction lawyers, for example, by referral to their regulator, or impose a wasted costs order. In criminal cases, the purpose of sanctions is more likely to be punitive than compensatory. Judges will take steps independently, invoking the inherent jurisdiction of the court, rather than in response to applications by the parties.

---

[208] *R v Penner* [2010] EWCA Crim 1155.
[209] ibid, at [19].
[210] *R (CPS) v Norwich Magistrates' Court* [2011] EWHC 82 (Admin).
[211] Flood-Page and Mackie, *Sentencing Practice* (n 160) at 137.
[212] M McConville, J Hodgson, L Bridges and A Pavlovic, *Standing Accused: The Organisation and Practices of Criminal Defence Lawyers in Britain* (Oxford, Clarendon Press, 1994) at 71.
[213] Blake and Ashworth, 'Ethics and the criminal defence lawyer' (n 197) at 182.

The issues that arise in criminal cases tend to be different from those arising in civil cases. There is a different emphasis because, in criminal matters, practitioners are more likely to be dealing with clients who are difficult to represent. This may lead to the practitioner's behaviour seeming unreasonable when it is the client who is being difficult. Judges must be aware of this when considering sanctions against criminal litigators, particularly wasted cost orders.

The authority for wasted costs orders in criminal cases is the Courts and Legal Services Act 1990. This provides that in any criminal proceedings in the Court of Appeal, the Crown Court or a magistrates' court, 'the court may disallow, or (as the case may be) order the legal or other representative concerned to meet, the whole of any wasted costs or such part of them as may be determined in accordance with regulations'.[214] The section covers persons exercising a right of audience, or a right to conduct litigation, on behalf of any party to the proceedings.

As in the civil field, the jurisdiction is summary and lawyers have a right to be heard. Orders may, however, be made if the lawyer had notice of the judge's intention and an opportunity to make representations.[215] Appeals lie from a magistrates' court to the Crown Court and from the Crown Court to the Court of Appeal.

When considering whether costs were incurred by a party as a result of any improper, unreasonable or negligent act or omission by any representative, or any employee of a representative, criminal courts consider the general principles set out in *Ridehalgh v Horsefield and another* and *Medcalf v Mardell* and the relevant practice direction.[216] The appeal courts have tried to maintain consistency in the application of the wasted costs jurisdiction between these different contexts.

Further guidance was given in *Re P (a Barrister)*,[217] particularly regarding the standard of proof. A barrister (P) appealed against a decision ordering him to pay £1,500 in a trial aborted because of his closing speech. In it, P erroneously asserted that his client was of good character with no previous convictions. P argued on appeal that the judge should have disqualified herself because she was both judge and witness. P also argued that the criminal standard of proof should apply. Lord Justice Kennedy, upholding the order, said that, because of the penal element, a mere mistake is not sufficient to justify an order. There must be a more serious error. If the allegation is one of serious misconduct or crime the standard of proof will be higher, but otherwise it will be the normal civil standard of proof.

In *Re a Barrister (Wasted Costs Order) (No 9 of 1999)*,[218] a defence barrister was not informed of his client's antecedents, leading to an aborted trial. The barrister had, however, sought a copy of the antecedents before trial and received an assurance from his client regarding previous convictions. The Court of Appeal held that, in the particular circumstances, the error was understandable and did not justify a wasted costs order. It was held that such an order is appropriate only where the lawyer 'gave advice or committed an act or was responsible for an omission which no member of

---

[214] Prosecution of Offences Act 1985, s 19A and Magistrates' Courts Act 1980, s 145A.

[215] Re Thomas Boyd Whyte Solicitors and Re Haskell Solicitors [2007] EWCA Crim 2740.

[216] Practice Direction (Criminal Proceedings: Costs) [2010] 1 WLR 2351, pt 4.2: 'Costs against Legal Representatives—Wasted Costs'.

[217] *Re P (a Barrister)* [2001] EWCA Crim 1728, [2002] 1 Cr App R 207.

[218] *Re a Barrister (Wasted Costs Order) (No 9 of 1999)* (2000) The Times 18 April.

the profession, who was reasonably well informed and competent, would have given or done or omitted to do'.[219]

The distinctive problems of the wasted costs jurisdiction in criminal cases was exposed in *Re Boodhoo, Solicitor*.[220] A wasted costs order was made against a solicitor acting for a defendant charged with burglary. The client rang an assistant at the solicitors' firm on the day of trial to say he would not be attending court. He left no instructions on how proceed. The judge made strenuous efforts to persuade both counsel and solicitors to continue with the case in the absence of the defendant. This included threats to make a wasted costs order against the solicitors.

In the event, both solicitor and counsel in the case declined to act and the trial was abandoned. The recorder then made a wasted costs order against the solicitor. On appeal, the order was quashed. The court found that the recorder had failed to appreciate the professional difficulties faced by the solicitor. It decided that a decision to withdraw from a case was to be respected when a solicitor genuinely believed that he could not properly represent his client.

VII. Conclusion

Lawyers' performance of the litigation role has, historically, been closely controlled by the courts. Extensive rules of court detail how every step and task in litigation should be performed. Lawyers are incentivised to obey the procedure because they may be censured, or fail to recover costs, if they do not. Maybe for these reasons, specific rules regarding litigation did not originally feature in solicitors' conduct rules. There were some in the Bar Code relating to drafting. General rules of conduct, for example, treating third parties fairly, applied in litigation as elsewhere.

Lawyers' role in civil litigation is absorbing new requirements for co-operation following the Woolf reforms. These moves accompany reduced levels of legal aid and a significant push towards mediation rather than adjudication. This might be said to mark a change from a conception of justice as legal formality to one focusing on the accessibility of dispute resolution. In the process of this transition, lawyers' control of litigation has given way to judicial control. Procedures have been introduced to increase transparency and encourage settlement. Costs sanctions are increasingly used to punish improper or incompetent conduct. The ethical landscape has changed considerably, with new procedures reducing the scope for tactical manipulation of litigation procedure.

---

[219] ibid, per Clarke LJ.
[220] *Re Boodhoo, Solicitor* [2007] EWCA Crim 14.

18

Negotiation

'Maintaining moral sensitivity and awareness is crucial to the practice of law. The profession must resist inroads on the lawyer's commitment to the truth, and take steps to correct rules that lessen this commitment. The unique role lawyers occupy in our society and their position as officers of our judicial system require that their word be trusted. More is required of a lawyer than the custom of the marketplace, than bargaining in a bazaar, or in playing poker. Lawyers must feel that theirs is a worthy role and an honourable profession'.[1]

I. Introduction

Arranging deals of various kinds is a central part of most lawyers' work, both in the context of transactions (non-contentious proceedings) or disputes (contentious proceedings). Different processes are used, including negotiating and bargaining. Negotiation, in ordinary speech, is a process of seeking agreement. Bargaining generally describes a narrower process of seeking agreement face to face.[2] In civil actions, negotiation, rather than adjudication, determines the outcome in the majority of cases. Unlike advocacy, bargaining usually occurs in private, unmonitored by the court. Clients are often unsure of what happened when their lawyers met the other side. In no other area of legal representation is the conduct of lawyers as important to clients or the ethics of lawyers more tested and difficult to verify.

When it forms part of the litigation process, bargaining may be subject to the litigator's duty to the court. Lawyers must then act with independence in the interests of justice and to comply with the rules of conduct of their professional body.[3] Otherwise, despite the practical importance of negotiation to lawyers, it is relatively unregulated. No rules of conduct expressly apply. Prospective values, fair treatment of third parties,

---

[1] RF Thurman, 'Chipping Away at Lawyer Veracity: The ABA's Turn Toward Situation Ethics in Negotiations' (1990) *Journal of Dispute Resolution* 103, at 115.

[2] DA Lax and JK Sebenius, *The Manager as Negotiator: Bargaining for Co-operation and Competitive Gain* (New York, Free Press, 1986).

[3] Courts and Legal Services Act 1990, s 28(2A) (rights to conduct litigation), as amended by the Access to Justice Act 1999, s 42; and see ch 17: 'Litigation'.

honesty, frankness and integrity, are relevant, but it is not clear how. Whether they prevail depends on the culture of negotiation and the models of bargaining in use. Whereas other important activities, litigation and advocacy for example, are subject to sophisticated rules of procedure, the 'unwritten rules' of negotiation are intuitive and obtuse. In bargaining there is a distinct possibility that ethical norms are 'violated with ... confidence that there will be no discovery and no punishment'.[4] Lawyers potentially descend into 'the swamp' of practice and progress the messy business of solving client conflicts in the real world.[5] Yet, with attempts to curb the adversarial ethic in litigation generally, there is an argument that negotiation and bargaining should be governed by norms of frankness and fairness.

II. Theories of Negotiation

There is a voluminous literature on the theory of negotiation.[6] Much of this is based on studies of lawyers.[7] The research suggests that there are generalisations that can be made about the process of negotiation and bargaining. These cover the orientation of negotiators, the importance of problem type and practices of bargaining in different contexts. Certain patterns tend to be universal in different cultures and cover both transactions and disputes.[8]

A. Orientation

Research into the practice of negotiation by lawyers has not revealed high levels of sophistication. In early research, Williams identified two styles of bargaining among lawyers; competitive and co-operative. According to Williams' typology, co-operative negotiators seek 'fair' agreements and 'communicate a sense of shared interests, values and attitudes using rational, logical persuasion as a means of co-operation'.[9]

---

[4] CB Craver, *Effective Legal Negotiation and Settlement* (Charlottesville, VA, Michie Co, 1993).

[5] DA Schon, *Educating the Reflective Practitioner: Toward a New Design for Teaching and Learning in the Professions* (London, Jossey-Bass Publishers, 1987).

[6] See summaries in GT Lowenthal, 'A General Theory of Negotiation Process, Strategy and Behaviour' (1982) 31 *Kansas Law Review* 69; C Menkel-Meadow 'Toward Another View of Legal Negotiation: The Structure of Problem Solving' (1984) 31 *UCLA Law Review* 754.

[7] HL Ross, *Settled Out of Court: the Social Process of Insurance Claims Adjustment* (Chicago, Aldine, 1970); G Williams, *Legal Negotiation and Settlement* (St Paul, MN, West Publishing Co, 1983); SR Gross and KD Syverud, 'Getting to No: A Study of Settlement Negotiations and the Selection of Cases for Trial' (1991) 90 *Michigan Law Review* 319, M Heumann and JM Hyman, 'Negotiation Methods and Litigation Settlement in New Jersey: "You Can't Always Get What You Want"' (1997) 12 *Ohio State Journal on Dispute Resolution* 253.

[8] P Gulliver, *Disputes and Negotiations: A Cross-Cultural Perspective* (New York and London, Academic Press, 1979).

[9] Williams, *Legal Negotiation and Settlement* (n 7) at 53.

Co-operative negotiators seek to build a sense of shared interests, values and attitudes, using logical persuasion to reach an agreement fair to both sides. They make concessions to build trust and seek a reasonable settlement. Williams characterised the main alternative to co-operative negotiation as the competitive or 'adversarial' style. The aim of this approach is the pursuit of one-sided gains by dominating the negotiating relationship.

Other researchers accepted the essential truth of Williams' classification and articulated the implications of his findings. Condlin, for example, observed that

> co-operative argument consists of non-coercive rational analysis in which the objective is to teach another about the truth of one's substantive claims. This effort stops when the listener understands, or when the claims have been shown to be false ... Competitive argument consists of rhetorical psychological manoeuvring designed to coerce an adversary, sometimes subtly and sometimes not, into deferring to one's view when, if fully informed he would not or should not. The objective is manipulation not understanding. Efforts to persuade stop when the adversary agrees to do as one wishes[10]

Which approach is preferable in any given situation depends on the overall context, including the type of problem. It should also depend on the client's preferences regarding outcome. However, Williams found that lawyers' bargaining orientation tended not to change according to circumstances.

B. Problem Types

The issue of problem type is fundamental to negotiation strategy.[11] Theory suggests two broad type of problem, each requiring a different approach. One problem type involves distribution of a fixed resource, such as money or goods. In this type of problem, the more of the resource one party gains, the less is available for the other. This is a distributive problem type, sometimes called a 'zero sum' game. The other kind of negotiation problem arises where parties have mutually compatible needs. Both can have exactly what they want without impinging on the other's interests. The need for negotiation arises only because it is necessary to resolve the basis of the relationship. This problem type is integrative.

C. Methods

i. Strategies and Skills

Different kinds of negotiating problems suit different processes. Finding the best solution to an integrative problem involves identifying the underlying interests of the parties, generating solutions that satisfy those interests and selecting the best solutions.

---

[10] See RJ Condlin, 'Cases on Both Sides: Patterns of Argument in Legal Dispute-Negotiation' (1985) 44 *Maryland Law Review* 65.

[11] DG Gifford, *Legal Negotiation: Theory and Applications* (St Paul, MN, West Publishing Co, 1989).

Successful resolution of a problem susceptible to integrative solutions depends upon thorough exploration of the situation, identification of a range of possible solutions revealed and a sound implementation plan. The skills and qualities that are compatible with this approach include openness, transparency, good communication, imagination and creativity, open-mindedness and effective decision-making.

The conclusion of distributive problems usually involves different aspirations, approaches and sets of skills. Since the resource is fixed, the purpose of the negotiation is for both parties to gain as much of it as they can. However, if settlement is to be possible, they know that they will have to limit their aspirations. The limit of what each party will accept creates an overlap, a 'settlement zone'. The problem for opponents in this situation is that revealing their limit leaves them in a weak bargaining position. A party is unlikely to give you what you hope for if they know you will accept less.

In the absence of precise knowledge of the other side's limits, opponents discussing shares of scarce resources usually try to shift the other side's expectations of what they can get from the negotiation. This involves a bluffing, demonstrating a degree of intransigence. A 'positional approach' is often used. This involves stating a position and explaining, convincingly, why it cannot change. If agreement is possible, the parties move towards each other, usually in small steps, until resolution is reached. The relative success of each party depends partly on the strength of their bargaining position and partly on their capacity to mislead and bluff convincingly.

ii. Choice of Approach and Strategy

While both competitive and co-operative negotiators can proceed by 'positional' bargaining they do so with very different orientations towards settlement. At the extreme, competitive negotiators pretend that they are indifferent to settlement. To the extent that they appear willing to consider it, they demand an unrealistic share of the distribution. They make few offers or counter-offers and may even deliver a 'take it or leave it' ultimatum. They run a high risk that the negotiation will break down.

Competitive positional bargaining misses the opportunity to explore the integrative potential of the situation. In situations where parties foresee a long-term business or personal relationship, a competitive exchange may harm future relationships. An extreme focus on issues of distribution may also impede exploration of other issues, including how long-term relationships could be made to work better.

Given the different orientations of competitive and co-operative bargainers, the competitive negotiator is likely to be at an advantage in a simple haggle, for example, over price. Rigid commitments at or near the other side's minimum acceptable settlement point is a basic tenet of competitive negotiation and the discovery of that point is the fundamental aim of competitive strategy.[12] The lion's share of a fixed resource is likely to go to the person making extreme demands and few, if any, concessions.

Maximising integrative potential is achieved by a problem-solving approach in which basic, underlying interests are identified, understood and explored and creative

---

[12] Lowenthal, 'A General Theory of Negotiation Process Strategy and Behaviour' (n 6).

solutions to meeting these needs proposed and tested. This process is best conducted in a constructive spirit. A co-operative approach enables parties to identify mutual best interests and optimum deployment of resources and capabilities to meet needs.[13] The problem is that the co-operative bargainer is vulnerable to exploitation by the competitor.

iii. Principled Negotiation

US academics Roger Fisher and William Ury popularised a method they called principled negotiation. The method assumes that the aim of negotiation is a fair and reasonable agreement, efficient in expression and operation, and capable of improving, or at least not harming, any continuing relationship between the parties.[14] They claimed that principled negotiation was robust enough to use in any situation against whatever approach an opposing negotiator used. They also suggested that it would produce a fair outcome on distributive issues and exploit the integrative potential of a situation.

The key elements of principled negotiation are a focus on interests, rather than positions, and the search for creative ways of satisfying those interests. Principled negotiators resolve distributive problems, not by positional bargaining, but by identifying objective criteria for valuing any limited resource. They reduce the interpersonal friction with the other negotiator by 'focusing on the problem, not the people'. They build on the potential for co-operation, encouraging attention to long-term relationships between parties. They consider the other side's interests and produce an agreement maximising the advantages for both sides. If both sides adopt a principled negotiation strategy, agreement is more likely.

D. The Ethics of Negotiation

i. Consonance of Approaches with General Ethical Principles

a. Ethical Idealism and Ethical Relativism

Research studies suggest that negotiation behaviour may reflect ethical orientation. For example, one study compared the orientation to negotiation of ethical idealists and ethical relativists. It was found that ethical idealists, those most likely to follow rules of conduct, were more assertive, more likely to be competitive and less likely to identify integrative possibilities.[15] Ethical relativists tended to bend the rules, believing that ends justify means.

---

[13] ibid.

[14] R Fisher, W Ury and B Patton, *Getting to Yes: Negotiating Agreement Without Giving In*, 2nd edn (London, Century Business, 1992).

[15] JT Bana and JM Parks, 'Lambs Among Lions? The Impact of Ethical Ideology on Negotiation Behaviors and Outcomes' (2002) 7 *International Negotiation* 235.

b. Autonomy, Beneficence, Non-maleficence and Justice

There is powerful case for saying that principled negotiation is the strategy most consistent with honesty and integrity. Principled negotiation also promotes widely accepted core ethical principles; promoting individual autonomy, beneficence, non-maleficence and justice.[16] By seeking to meet people's needs, principled negotiation respects and promotes individual autonomy; by attempting to expand the 'negotiating pie' it supports beneficence; by not taking advantage of the other side it respects the principle of non-maleficence; by identifying objective criteria for resolving distributional issues it does justice. In contrast, none of these general ethical goals are met by other methods. Positional bargaining, for example, promotes one individual at the expense of another and can therefore be said to be neither beneficent nor just. Co-operative bargaining potentially sacrifices parties' best interests for the sake of agreement.

c. The Ethical Evolution of Bargaining

It has been suggested that bargaining practices have evolved from a warrior concept based on self-interest and opportunism, through mercantile and civil styles.[17] This progression is marked by increasing recognition of the rights of the other side to expect benefits from the exchange. The most recent stage of bargaining evolution, the constructive concept, embraces willingness to explain and explore all interests on the basis of reciprocity. The development of negotiation theory is consistent with broader social theory. Habermas, for example, identifies the importance of communication exploring shared values through argumentation.[18] Kohlberg regards development towards non-arbitrary social co-operation as an advanced stage of moral development.[19]

ii. Consonance with Ethical Principles of Lawyers

a. The Adversarial Imperative

There is considerable literature in the US on whether the lawyer's duty to her client obliges her to take a partisan, and therefore competitive, stance in negotiation.[20] It is therefore necessary to consider whether English lawyers' duty to pursue each client's

---

[16] TL Beauchamp and JF Childress, *Principles of Biomedical Ethics*, 5th edn (New York and Oxford, Oxford University Press, 2001).

[17] W French, C Häßlein and R van Es, 'Constructivist Negotiation Ethics' (2002) 39 *Journal of Business Ethics* 83.

[18] See eg J Habermas, *Communication and the Evolution of Society* (T McCarthy (trans)) (Boston, MA, Beacon Press, 1991).

[19] L Kohlberg, 'Stages and Sequence: The Cognitive Development Approach to Socialisation' in DA Goslin (ed), *Handbook of Socialisation Theory and Research* (Chicago, Rand Mcnally, 1969) cited in French et al, 'Constructivist Negotiation Ethics' (n 17).

[20] RJ Condlin, 'Bargaining in the Dark' (1992) 51 *Maryland Law Review* 1; DE Rosenthal, *Lawyer and Client: Who's in Charge* (New York, Russell Sage, 1974); WH Simon 'Visions of Practice in Legal Thought' (1984) 36 *Stanford Law Review* 469; JP Heinz, 'The Power of Lawyers' (1983) *Georgia Law Review* 891; and C Fried 'The Lawyer as Friend: The Moral Foundations of the Lawyer-Client Relationship' (1976) 85 *Yale Law Journal* 1060.

best interests produces a similar conclusion. In the context of the adversarial system, a client's best interests could be interpreted as a duty to do the best deal possible using a competitive and positional approach. There are competing arguments for and against using competitive and positional bargaining or principled negotiation.

There is some doubt about whether effective competitive negotiation, while consistent with adversarial principles, requires unethical conduct. Misleading the other side regarding the 'bottom line' is a clear example. Although earlier versions of the ABA Model Rules prohibited making false statements of material fact, estimates of value were not treated as material facts.[21] Therefore, bluffing in bargaining was arguably allowed under the model rules.

There is a question mark over the issue of whether principled negotiation is consistent with adversarial principles and with professional legal ethics. Seeking an outcome that is objectively fair, which is what principled negotiation offers, may be inconsistent with an obligation to promote the best interests of each client. If a lawyer has an opportunity to take 'fair advantage' of the other side, is it a denial of the adversarial ethos not to do so?

b. Principled Negotiation

Proponents of principled negotiation argue that it offers superior outcomes to a distributional approach, because it focuses on interests not just resources. There are of course, some who doubt its claims to offer a panacea for conflict. Critics suggest that principled negotiation has less value when there are no continuing relationships to consider, or when dealing with negotiators who have the leverage to achieve their goals by the exercise of power.[22]

Fisher concedes that there are very narrow circumstances where interests are irrelevant and effective positional bargaining offers the best outcome. He says that in

> single issue negotiations among strangers where the transaction costs of exploring interests would be high and where each side is protected by competitive opportunities, haggling over positions may work better than joint problem solving. A typical case would be negotiating a sale on the New York Stock Exchange.[23]

Therefore, it may be argued that positional bargaining trumps principled negotiation in a narrow category of circumstances. This is where interests and future relationships are irrelevant and only a distribution of scarce resources is required. Conducted properly, however, problem-solving bargaining is more rigorous and resistant to exploitation than an adversarial approach based on positional strategies.

Some critics doubt the implicit claim of principled negotiation to ethical superiority.[24] It can be argued, for example, that objective criteria are persuasive rationalisations for positions and that warnings about reaching agreement are just subtle threats.

---

[21] RB McKay, 'Ethical Considerations in Alternative Dispute Resolution' (1990) 45 *The Arbitration Journal* 15, at 19.

[22] JJ White, 'The Pros and Cons of Getting to Yes' (1984) 34 *Journal of Legal Education* 115; R Fisher, in his response to this review ('Fisher's Response to Jim White' (1984) *Journal of Legal Education* 120; and Menkel-Meadow, 'Toward Another View of Legal Negotiation' (n 6) at 829.

[23] 'Fisher's response to Jim White 1984' (n 22) at 120.

[24] See eg Condlin, 'Bargaining in the Dark' (n 20).

Principled approaches to bargaining, which depend on honesty and problem solving, offer a more coherent theoretical basis for the lawyer's role in dispute resolution. Condlin argues that the strength of principled negotiation lies not in its effectiveness, but in its ability to harness the 'power of legitimacy'.[25]

Principled negotiation is an even better fit with a more co-operative litigation culture. There is research evidence, for example, that providing the other side with too much information is potentially dangerous against a competitive negotiator. However, modest information provision improves outcomes, even when unreciprocated.[26] This supports the idea that lawyers in civil dispute resolution should be required to co-operate with each other and with non-lawyer representatives of other parties.

E. Potential Influences on Bargaining Culture

i. Personal Perceptions

There is evidence that personal perceptions of performance and ethicality are affected by feedback received on performance. An experiment by Kim et al tested the reaction of negotiators to feedback.[27] Negotiators bargained with previous opponents having been told that, on a previous exercise, they had been found to be either good or poor negotiators or ethical or unethical negotiators. It was found that this feedback changed bargaining behaviour. Negotiators who received positive feedback on their effectiveness became more competitive. Those receiving negative feedback on competence not only became less competitive, but also less able to identify mutually compatible interests.

Surprisingly, in the experiment, people were significantly more likely to behave ethically having been told that they had been experienced as unethical in the previous negotiation. If they had been told that they appeared ethical, they behaved less ethically thereafter. This was attributed to the fact that, having been experienced as unethical, a negotiator is more likely to consider that their bluffing is transparent and to stick to the truth as closely as possible, and vice versa. There are a number of implications of such studies. They suggest, for example, that education and training could be at least as important as rules in building an ethical professional culture of negotiation.

ii. Bargaining Reputation

Generally, lawyers develop bargaining reputations[28] and this is particularly true in small fields of practice. It is unlikely that lawyer negotiators would consistently tolerate

---

[25] ibid, at 26.

[26] L Thompson 'Information Exchange in Negotiation' (1991) 27 *Journal of Experimental Social Psychology* 161.

[27] PH Kim, KA Diekman and AE Tenbrunsel, 'Flattery May Get you Somewhere: The Strategic Implications of Providing Positive vs. Negative Feedback about Ability vs. Ethicality in Negotiation' (2003) 90 *Organizational Behavior and Human Decision Processes* 225.

[28] M Galanter, 'Why the "Haves" Come Out Ahead: Speculations on the Limits of Legal Change' (1974) 9 *Law & Society Review* 95.

colleagues who tried to take advantage of others. Negotiators who always make unreasonable demands could find that opponents refuse to enter negotiation or do not take the process seriously. This would disadvantage clients who want their lawyers to achieve a settlement. Therefore, a lawyer may be unfair to future clients by being unreasonable on behalf of a present client. In theory, the transaction costs of lawyers with bad negotiating reputations are increased. Others may deal with them cautiously or not at all.

iii. Client Preferences

The discussion so far has assumed that lawyers have free choice in how they approach negotiation. In fact, the requirement that they act in clients' best interests suggests that the choice of negotiation strategy should reflect client goals. Therefore, if clients are more concerned with long-term relationships, principled negotiation would be an appropriate method. If they are more concerned with their share of a limited resource, effective positional bargaining may be preferred. In participatory models of the lawyer and client relationship[29] lawyers would discuss the client's preferences and the implications of particular approaches. Therefore, it is arguable that lawyers should be able to discuss the advantages of different approaches to negotiation with clients and implement them as appropriate.

In a culture in which client autonomy is promoted, the issue of whether clients should be present in negotiations is raised. With integrative bargaining their presence and participation may be necessary. Only clients can reflect on their own wants and preferences and decide that solution A is better than solution B in satisfying these interests. A lawyer may, however, feel constrained in their behaviour by the presence of a client, perhaps feeling that it limits their flexibility. Much of the guidance given to lawyers appears to assume that initial instructions are sufficient. They envisage that clear instructions are taken and advice given at the outset of a matter, but do not deal with what should happen thereafter. Clients may only hear that an offer has been made after negotiation has taken place.

Some people may be troubled by the fact that their lawyer used dubious tactics in representing them. Discovering the client's wishes may therefore extend to the means as well as the ends of negotiation. In theory, this could be an ongoing responsibility. A lawyer is in no position to know how the client values different possibilities, or to evaluate creative solutions suggested by the other side. Respecting client autonomy regarding the goals and methods of negotiation has considerable disadvantages for lawyers. One problem is that the client's preference may result in the lawyer having to use a style of negotiation she is uncomfortable with. Another is that consultation makes the process more longwinded, complicated and, potentially, costly. Subordinating the lawyer's choice of method to the client's instructions, either in general or for the specific negotiation, promotes the client's autonomy at the expense of the lawyer's.

---

[29] See further ch 9: 'Loyalty'.

iv. Professional Culture

It is arguable that the bluff and deception associated with positional bargaining sets an unfortunate precedent. If misleading others is acceptable in some situations the rationale can easily be extended. This may blur the 'bright line' between the ethical and unethical and create uncertainty, encouraging the escalation of unacceptable behaviour.[30] Principled negotiation would make it easier for legal professionals to be honest. For example, principled negotiators need not disclose all information but should make it clear that they are not doing so and why.[31] It is arguable that a professional culture that aspires to honesty and integrity should set clearer boundaries for behaviour.

It is likely that supporting and promoting principled negotiation would improve the position of clients generally. The main reason is that it would increase trust between lawyers. Co-operation between negotiators is crucial in producing the best possible outcomes to integrative bargaining. Trust is vital to co-operation and generally benefits markets by facilitating agreement and reducing transaction costs.

In a competitive bargaining environment, each interaction carries risks, encouraging caution. Protagonists are unsure what to expect, and this breeds excessive caution and results in poor solutions for clients in the long term.[32] The balance of the argument therefore seems to be to regulate to promote an environment of trust between legal professionals. Candour promotes trust most effectively when there is a perceived commitment to shared ethical norms.[33]

III. Legal Negotiation in Practice

A. Scope

Legal negotiation, perhaps more than any other activity, has a claim to be the core legal role. It arises both in the context of transactions (non-contentious proceedings) and in disputes (contentious proceedings).[34] The form of legal negotiation differs considerably according to context. In litigation the terms of settlement of an action are agreed by negotiation. In commercial matters, agreements, from the sale of goods

---

[30] DJ Luban, 'Milgram Revisited' (1998) 9 *Researching Law: An American Bar Foundation Update* 1, at 4.

[31] Fisher, Ury and Patton, *Getting to Yes* (n 14).

[32] See generally RA Johnson, *Negotiation Basics: Concepts, Skills and Exercises* (London and New Delhi, Sage Publications, 1993) at 77 and Condlin (n 20).

[33] C Provis, 'Ethics, Deception and Labor Negotiation' (2000) 28 *Journal of Business Ethics* 145; W Ross and J La Croix, 'Multiple Meanings of Trust in Negotiation Theory and Research: A Literature Review and Integrative Model' (1996) 7 *The International Journal of Conflict Management* 314.

[34] See generally Gifford, *Legal Negotiation* (n 11) at 38–42; MA Eisenburg, 'Private Ordering Through Negotiation: Dispute Settlement and Rulemaking' (1976) 89 *Harvard Law Review* 637.

to company transfer, are agreed through negotiation. In conveyancing, lawyers must agree dates for exchange of contracts or completion of the transaction.

Negotiation may be conducted by a range of communication methods, both verbal and written. A matter may be settled by a single telephone call, follow intermittent exchanges or uninterrupted discussions lasting several days. It may be based on a standard contract or follow years of formal and informal information exchange. The agreement may be bounded by well-established conventions or be completely novel.

B. Formality

Negotiation often results in a binding agreement. The outcomes of some negotiations are endorsed by third parties. For example, settlement of a dispute that has reached trial may be formally approved by the judge. Other agreements, such as those affecting parties suffering from lack of capacity, may also need some formal approval. Some negotiated settlements may not be formally recorded, but merely recorded by a lawyer in a file note. Nevertheless, as with other contracts, a verbal agreement is enforceable, subject to proof of terms, intention and other formal requirements.

C. Process

i. Choice of Method

Research presents practical legal negotiation across jurisdictions as a prosaic, routine activity.[35] In the UK, this is so for both solicitors and barristers.[36] It is often bargaining on the telephone, using a positional process and at fairly 'low intensity', particularly in low value matters. Initial attempts may lead to re-evaluation and later attempts to settle. High value matters receive more intense and focused attention. Some commercial matters, for example, need to be concluded to a schedule. They can involve negotiating teams, with different personnel responsible for different parts of the deal.

Gifford reasons that many lawyers entering a negotiation first try a competitive approach. If this is unsuccessful, they consider using either a co-operative or integrative approach.[37] The chosen strategy is adapted in response to the other side. Many accounts of legal negotiation suggest that it often take the form of co-operative positional bargaining.

Very few research studies have found evidence that lawyers make much use of problem-solving approaches to negotiation, such as principled negotiation.[38]

---

[35] M Galanter, 'The Federal Rules and the Quality of Settlements: A Comment on Rosenberg's, The Federal Rules of Civil Procedure in Action' (1989) 137 *University of Pennsylvania Law Rev* 2231, at 2236.

[36] M Murch, 'The Role of Solicitors in Divorce Proceedings' (1977) 40 *Modern Law Review* 625; J Morison and P Leith, *The Barrister's World and the Nature of Law* (Milton Keynes and Philadelphia, Open University Press, 1992).

[37] DG Gifford, 'A Context-Based Theory of Strategy Selection in Legal Negotiation' (1985) 46 *Ohio State Law Journal* 41.

[38] Heumann and Hyman, 'Negotiation Methods and Litigation Settlement in New Jersey' (n 7).

Heumann and Hyman, for example, found that US litigation lawyers used positional bargaining in 71 per cent of cases and a 'problem-solving' approach in only 16 per cent of cases. In fact, many studies suggest that co-operative positional bargaining is normal in legal negotiations, even at the Bar.[39]

ii. Possible Factors in Choice of Method

A number of factors may encourage the use of positional bargaining in legal work. For example, the use of standard form contracts reduces the scope of negotiation and may encourage positional bargaining. Use of positional bargaining may also be due to cultural factors. Practitioners frequently describe a process akin to a 'market place' haggle as a recognised way of transacting business.

a. Negotiator Competence

Lack of negotiator competence or highly complex cases produce incentives to simplify strategy. An example of this is a practitioner account of a negotiation he conducted as a novice. His supervising partner instructed him that nothing in the client's standard form agreement could be changed. He concluded a deal on the terms of the agreement, although he understood hardly any of its contents, by responding 'it's not negotiable' to every proposal by the other side.[40] Gifford suggests that claiming lack of authority to increase an offer is a tactic used by insurance companies.[41]

b. Client Engagement

Another reason behind the use of simple negotiation strategies is the limited potential for client engagement. In some circumstances, clients' aspirations are obvious and opportunities for exploring them limited.[42] In other situations, involving clients in settlement discussions would be disproportionately expensive. Clients may not want to be involved in the settlement process. An employment and pensions practitioner explained that his instructions were limited to maintaining certain positions. He represented the attitude of his corporate clients as 'This is what we want—get on and do it'. He suggested that 'If you kept calling up saying "this is where we are, what do you think?" they'd soon get fed up'.[43]

c. Profitability

One of the explanations of co-operative bargaining among lawyers is the desire to reach settlement. This may be good for business or it may be seen as a proportionate response to low level or problematic legal cases. The concern is that lawyers may not

---

[39] Morison and Leith, *The Barrister's World and the Nature of Law* (n 36) at 121.

[40] A Boon, 'Cooperation and Competition in the Handling of Disputes and Transactions' (1994) 1(1) *International Journal of the Legal Profession* 109.

[41] Gifford, 'A Context-Based Theory of Strategy Selection in Legal Negotiation' (n 37).

[42] A Boon, 'Client Decision Making in Personal Injury Schemes' (1995) 23 *International Journal of the Sociology of Law* 253.

[43] Boon, 'Cooperation and Competition in the Handling of Disputes and Transactions' (n 40).

do the best possible for clients for these reasons. Life is easier and they still get paid for less than diligent performance. Clients who are unable to judge performance, personal plight 'one-shotters', for example, are not in a position to complain. There are, therefore, particular reasons for concern when lawyers have incentives for inadequate efforts on behalf of clients.

d. Professional Relationships

A co-operative orientation to negotiation in legal practice may be encouraged where there are continuing relationships between professional 'repeat players'. Repeat interactions may lead to the development of strong professional relationships. These relationships are sometimes valued more than the duty of loyalty to clients. Therefore, in criminal cases in the US, defence lawyers recommended plea bargains for reasons that were in the lawyer's interests, not the client's.[44] These included reducing the workload and protecting their relationship with prosecutors. In personal injury settlement negotiations, also in the US, plaintiff lawyers prioritised relationships with insurance company representatives over those with their clients.[45]

e. Inequality of Arms

There is some support for the proposition that a situation of unequal resources between the parties may justify the weaker side using tactics that would otherwise be deemed unfair or unethical.[46] The argument tends to be found in literature from the US and is not a widely accepted.

IV. Criminal Practice

A. Context

Criminal work offers many potential areas for negotiation, particularly regarding plea and the sentence. In some jurisdictions the vast majority of cases are disposed of following plea bargains.[47] Such arrangements are accepted because they avoid the need for a trial and because the result seems fair. In order to ensure the integrity of the

---

[44] D Sudnow, 'Normal Crimes: Sociological Features of the Penal Code in the Public Defender's Office' (1965) 12 *Social Problems* 255; AS Blumberg, 'The Practice of Law as Confidence Game: Organizational Co-optation of a Profession' (1967) 1(2) *Law and Society Review* 15; M Heumann, 'A Note on Plea Bargaining and Case Pressure' (1975) 9 *Law and Society Review* 515.

[45] Ross, *Settled Out of Court* (n 7).

[46] WH Simon, 'Ethical Discretion in Lawyering' (1988) 101 *Harvard Law Review* 1083; Gifford (n 11) at 134.

[47] See generally AW Alschuler, 'The Prosecutor's Role in Plea Bargaining' (1968) 36(1) *The University of Chicago Law Review* 50.

process, plea bargaining is usually heavily regulated. In the US for example, the terms of any plea bargain must be approved in open court.

There is no precise definition of a plea bargain. The term might include agreements whereby a defendant agrees to plead guilty to charges if a prosecutor agrees to drop others. This happens in England and Wales, although not as a result of bargaining. Prosecutors are supposed to decide charges objectively, without entering a process of negotiation with the defendant's lawyers. The courts have also striven to control trading of guilty pleas for lighter sentences. Therefore, in the English system, the potential for lawyers to negotiate the terms of guilty pleas are, at best, heavily circumscribed.

B. Determining the Offences to be Charged

i. The Prosecutors' Discretion

In more serious or complex cases, prosecutors decide whether a person should be charged with a criminal offence and, if so, the offence to be charged.[48] Prosecutors must consider whether there is enough evidence to convict and whether prosecution is in the public interest. When considering the public interest in prosecuting any case, consideration must be given to whether an out of court disposition, such as a simple caution or a conditional caution, is appropriate.[49] This depends on the circumstances of each case. The relevant factors include the seriousness of the offence, the results of the offending behaviour, the antecedents of the offender and the likely outcome at court.

In 2004, the government issued a Victims' Charter.[50] This promised to provide a voice to victims in the criminal justice system. One of the provisions offered victims a discussion with the local office of the CPS, if they believed that the sentencing of the perpetrator in the case where they were a victim was unduly lenient. This meeting was with a view to the case being sent to the Attorney General for possible referral.[51] The current version of the Attorney General's guidelines on the acceptance of pleas emphasises the need of the criminal justice system to protect the interests of victims, as guaranteed by the Charter.[52] There is a commitment to ensure the accuracy and reasonableness of pleas and to take the views of victims into account where possible.

Prosecutors have power to accept pleas to a lesser offence or offences charged if they consider that it is in the public interest to do so. The Code for Crown Prosecutors envisages that they may consider allowing defendants to plead guilty to some, but not all, of the charges against them, or to plead guilty to a different, possibly less serious,

---

[48] DPP, *The Code for Crown Prosecutors*, at para 3.1.

[49] DPP, *The Director's Guidance On Charging 2013*, 5th edn (May 2013) (revised arrangements) at para 9.

[50] DCA, *The Victims' Charter: A Statement of Service Standards for Victims of Crime* (London, Department of Constitutional Affairs, 2004).

[51] ibid, at 15.

[52] Attorney General's Office, *The Acceptance of Pleas and the Prosecutor's Role in the Sentencing Exercise* (revised 2009) at para A1 (www.gov.uk/the-acceptance-of-pleas-and-the-prosecutors-role-in-the-sentencing-exercise).

charge.[53] They have no power to make provisional arrangements with the defendant regarding confiscation, compensation, disqualification or any other aspect of sentence. An exception is where an offender assists investigations and prosecutions under provisions in the Serious Organised Crime and Police Act 2005.

Prosecutors can only accept the defendant's plea if they think the court is able to pass a sentence that matches the seriousness of the offending,[54] particularly when the plea would enable the defendant to avoid the imposition of a mandatory minimum sentence.[55] Prosecutors must also consider the views of victims, or in appropriate cases their families, when deciding whether it is in the public interest to accept the plea.[56] It must be made clear to the court on what basis any plea is advanced and accepted.[57]

Prosecutors are required to consider various factors in selecting charges. The charges must reflect the seriousness and extent of the offending supported by the evidence, give the court adequate powers to sentence and impose appropriate post-conviction orders and enable the case to be presented in a clear and simple way.[58] Prosecutors should not to bring multiple charges with the explicit aim of dropping some as a negotiation ploy.[59] The practice of charging is usually controversial. For example, there is evidence that sexual crimes that could be charged as rape may brought to court as lesser offences. Sexual assault, or sexual activity with a child under 16, is easier to prove because consent is not an issue.[60]

ii. Defendants

Defendants may enter pleas of guilty or not guilty to charges brought against them. They have options regarding their response. They can also admit guilt, but dispute the basis of offending alleged by the prosecution. In such cases defendants can enter the basis of plea on which they are prepared to plead guilty.[61] The prosecution can accept or contradict that account and, if necessary test the defendant's evidence on those matters in a Newton hearing.[62] Such a hearing follows the normal principles of a criminal trial, but the prosecution is generally expected to leave the questioning to the judge.

iii. Scope for Negotiation

The official position is that the process of determining charges involves no 'plea bargaining', which the English system ostensibly discourages. It is supposedly a process

---

[53] DPP, *The Code for Crown Prosecutors*, at para 9.1.
[54] ibid, at para 9.2.
[55] ibid, at para 9.6.
[56] ibid, at para 9.3.
[57] ibid, at para 9.4.
[58] ibid, at para 6.1.
[59] ibid, at para 6.3.
[60] R Williams, 'Fewer rape convictions because plea bargains prevail, report suggests' *The Guardian* 20 March 2010.
[61] *R v Underwood* [2004] EWCA Crim 2256, [2005] 1 Cr App R 13.
[62] *R v Newton* (1982) 77 Cr App R 3 (1982) 4 Cr App R (S) 388.

where prosecutors decide the correct number and level of charge objectively. They can however, seek information from defendants and their lawyers. The process of deciding whether defendants can plead guilty to some of the charges, or to less serious charges, potentially involves a process of influencing. It inevitably involves communication regarding the possibilities at the very least. Officially, this does not constitute plea bargaining.

iv. *Fraud and other Economic Crimes*

a. Complex Fraud

In July 2006 the Attorney General and the Chief Secretary to the Treasury published a report on fraud cases for public consultation. It was based on the final report of the government's inter-departmental review of arrangements for the detection, investigation and prosecution of fraud. This made a number of recommendations, including establishing a national strategic authority and a national fraud reporting centre. It made proposals for the improvement of fraud trials and the possibility of establishing a 'financial court'.

b. Indicative Sentencing

The government report on fraud cases recommended that there should be a formal plea bargaining system (or 'indicative sentencing') for cases dealt with by the Serious Fraud Office, the Fraud Prosecution Service in the CPS, and for serious and complex fraud cases brought by other prosecuting authorities. It was argued that the advantages of encouraging court-sanctioned agreements at the earliest possible stage include allowing the authorities to focus on other cases, savings of public money and easing the strain on defendants, victims and witnesses. The government approved the recommendations in March 2007.

As part of the new arrangements, the Attorney General issued guidelines for handling plea agreements in serious and complex fraud cases.[63] Under the guidelines, the prosecutor may initiate plea discussions with any person who is being prosecuted or investigated with a view to prosecution in connection with a serious or complex fraud, where he or she believes it advantageous to do so.[64] It is a requirement that the person being investigated is legally represented, and the prosecutor will not initiate plea discussions with a defendant who is not. If the prosecutor receives an approach from such a defendant, he or she may enter into discussions if satisfied that it is appropriate to do so.

The Attorney General's guidelines for complex fraud cases provide that prosecutors must be ' transparent with the defendant, the victim and the court'.[65] Supplementary guidance from the Director of the CPS provides that plea discussions must be open

---

[63] Attorney General's Office *Plea Discussions in Cases of Serious or Complex Fraud* (www.gov.uk/plea-discussions-in-cases-of-serious-or-complex-fraud--8).

[64] ibid, at para C1.

[65] ibid, at para B4.

and transparent.[66] Prosecutors are required to prepare and retain a full and accurate record of negotiations. They must ensure that the defendant has sufficient information to enable him or her to play an informed part in the plea discussions.

Before accepting a reduced basis of plea, prosecutors are required to communicate with the victim and, where practicable, explain the position. Finally, they must ensure that the plea agreement placed before the court fully and fairly reflects the matters agreed. Prosecutors must not agree additional matters with the defendant which are not recorded in the plea agreement or are not made known to the court.

c. Deferred Prosecution Agreements

The Crime and Courts Act 2013 provides that a 'deferred prosecution agreement' (a DPA) can be made with companies, partnerships, and unincorporated associations[67] in common law cases of conspiracy to defraud, cheating the revenue and in a host of statutory offences.[68] It is envisaged that DPAs might apply, for example, where there is insufficient evidence to prosecute. Such agreements can only be made by designated prosecutors, the Director of Public Prosecutions, the Director of the Serious Fraud Office or prosecutors designated by the Secretary of State, or by their nominees authorised in writing.[69] A range of sanctions are available, including fines, which must be equivalent to those a court would impose for the offence.[70]

The procedures for DPAs are set out in Schedule 17 of the 2013 Act, but the Director of Public Prosecutions and the Director of the Serious Fraud Office will jointly issue a code for prosecutors. These provisions are supplemented by amendments to the new Criminal Procedure Rules. The rules require the parties to make formal declarations to the court that the information each has supplied is accurate and complete.[71] They also include provision for the court to order one party to pay the other's legal costs in proceedings for breach of the agreement.

v. Plea Bargains

a. Context

Outside of the area of economic crime, agreements not to prosecute are officially frowned upon. However, one of the practices often treated as plea bargaining, the process of determining the sentence to be charged, is not treated as such. In England and Wales, the situation that has caused problems is where a defendant is encouraged to plead guilty in return for a lighter sentence. The courts have been very wary

---

[66] CPS, *Director's Guidance to Accompany the Attorney General's Guidelines on Plea Discussions in Cases of Serious or Complex Fraud*, Conducting plea discussions. (www.cps.gov.uk/publications/directors_guidance/director_s_guidance_to_accompany_the_attorney_general_s_guidelines_on_plea_discussions_in_cases_of_serious_or_complex_fraud.html).

[67] Crime and Courts Act 2013, sch 17, pt 1, s 4.

[68] ibid, sch 17, pt 2, ss 15–16.

[69] ibid, sch 17, pt 1, ss 3(1) and 3(3).

[70] ibid, sch 17, pt 1, ss 5(3) and 5(4).

[71] Criminal Procedure (Amendment No 2) Rules 2013 (SI 2013/3183).

of judge-sanctioned sentences in return for guilty pleas. That is one reason why the approach to complex fraud is exceptional.

b. The Approach of the Courts to Sentencing

Once the charges are determined, the scope for negotiating the core issues of criminal trials, guilt and sentence, is severely constrained. The antagonism of the courts is due to the risk that the offer of a reduced sentence places pressure on an innocent defendant to accept guilt. Preventing plea bargains was intended to control a situation where an accused maintained his innocence but was convinced by his lawyer that he would be convicted. The prospect of not spending time in prison is often decisive in drawing guilty pleas.

In England and Wales, courts typically reward guilty pleas, particularly where accompanied by appropriate expression of remorse, with a discounted sentence. The Criminal Justice Act 2003, section 144 sets out the relevant factors. It provides that, in deciding what sentence to pass on offenders pleading guilty, courts are required to take into account the stage in the proceedings when the offender indicated his intention to plead guilty and the circumstances in which this indication was given. Therefore, discounted sentences are supposed to be purely in the hands of judges, not lawyers.

c. The Guidance in *R v Turner*

The indications of what reassurance defendants could be given on sentence when pleading guilty were laid down in 1970 in *R v Turner*.[72] The details of the case are instructive, both in terms of the situations that can arise and the danger that there will be perceived to be a 'plea bargain'. The defendant was accused of stealing his own car from a garage, where it had been repaired and left on the street. When the owner of the garage found it was missing, he rang the police, who interviewed the defendant. The police officers alleged that he first told them that he had not taken the car to the garage and then, the next day that he had taken it away with the consent of the garage owner.

At the Crown Court, the defendant's case was going reasonably well. The garage owner and his son had given evidence which had been neutral if not helpful. The defendant had, however, instructed his barrister to attack the police evidence. Accusing the police of lying would, however, have allowed the prosecution to bring in evidence of the defendant's character, which included a list of relatively old convictions. The barrister therefore advised the defendant that a guilty plea might tip the balance in favour of a non-custodial sentence.

Discussions with the prosecution continued well into the afternoon, when the clerk of the court was dispatched to say that the judge wished to proceed. The barrister thought that he had received an indication from the clerk that, in the event of a guilty plea, a fine would be the disposition. This was later disputed by the clerk. In any event, after a further discussion with his barrister, the defendant changed his plea to guilty and received a four-month sentence. The Court of Appeal accepted that, on

---

[72] *R v Turner (Frank Richard) (No 1)* [1970] 2 QB 321.

the facts, the defendant was resolved to plead not guilty until his barrister's advice was confirmed by what he thought was an indication from the judge. Therefore, the defendant's plea should be treated as a nullity and a new trial ordered.

Having decided the outcome of the appeal in *Turner*, the Court of Appeal turned to what it called 'the vexed question of so-called "plea-bargaining"'.[73] The Court's advice on that issue has been the benchmark for judges and lawyers since. It was that:

1. Counsel must be completely free to do what is his duty, namely to give the accused the best advice he can and if need be advice in strong terms. This will often include advice that a plea of guilty, showing an element of remorse, is a mitigating factor which may well enable the court to give a lesser sentence than would otherwise be the case. Counsel of course will emphasise that the accused must not plead guilty unless he has committed the acts constituting the offence charged.
2. The accused, having considered counsel's advice, must have a complete freedom of choice whether to plead guilty or not guilty.
3. There must be freedom of access between counsel and judge. Any discussion, however, which takes place must be between the judge and both counsel for the defence and counsel for the prosecution. If a solicitor representing the accused is in the court he should be allowed to attend the discussion if he so desires. This freedom of access is important because there may be matters calling for communication or discussion, which are of such a nature that counsel cannot in the interests of his client mention them in open court.
4. The judge should, subject to the one exception referred to hereafter, never indicate the sentence which he is minded to impose. A statement that on a plea of guilty he would impose one sentence but that on a conviction following a plea of not guilty he would impose a severer sentence is one which should never be made. This could be taken to be undue pressure on the accused, thus depriving him of that complete freedom of choice which is essential.[74]

So, if judges indicate what sentence they have in mind, they must not mention what they would do if the accused were convicted following a plea of not guilty. The only exception is where a judge is able to say that, whatever happens, whether the accused pleads guilty or not guilty, the sentence will or will not take a particular form. Therefore the judge may say, for example, that the disposition in this case will be a probation order or a fine, or a custodial sentence.

Since *Turner*, the Court of Appeal has consistently reinforced the message that the accused must have freedom to enter their plea of choice. Despite this, subsequent appeals and references by the Attorney General reveal quite different practice in lower courts. In fact, it appeared that plea bargains were routinely, if circuitously, negotiated.

In *R v Peverett* the defendant, a former school head teacher, faced multiple charges of indecent assault on schoolchildren.[75] He initially pleaded not guilty. Prosecuting counsel, in the judge's presence, offered to drop some charges in return for guilty pleas on others. Defence counsel said he would recommend this to his client provided no

[73] ibid, at 326.
[74] ibid, at 326–27.
[75] *Attorney General's Reference (No 44 of 2000) (R v Peverett)* [2001] 1 Cr App R (S) 132. See further M Blake and A Ashworth 'Ethics and the Criminal Defence Lawyer' (2004) 7(2) *Legal* Ethics 167, at 179–82.

custodial sentence was involved. Prosecuting counsel suggested a suspended sentence might be fair and would be accepted by all of the victims except one as such.

After further submissions by both counsel in his chambers the next day, the judge handed down an 18-month sentence suspended for two years. He also ordered that the defendant pay £6,500 as a contribution to prosecution costs and ordered him to register as a sex offender. The decision was reported as a surprise to victims, one of whom had apparently been led to expect imposition of a sentence of up to five years.[76]

The Attorney General referred the case to the Court of Appeal for review of sentence under powers that had existed since 1988.[77] Lord Justice Rose said that the case 'demonstrates, at almost every turn, the wisdom of the authorities in this Court which have, for many years, set their face against plea bargaining'.[78] The Court of Appeal decided, however, that it could not overturn the sentence. The Crown, by its agents, had made representations to a defendant on which he was entitled to rely and on which he acted to his detriment. He had pleaded guilty in circumstances in which he would not otherwise have pleaded guilty. This gave rise to a legitimate expectation on his part that the Crown would not subsequently act contrary to those representations. For this purpose, the Crown and its agents were to be regarded as indivisible.

Much of the explicit criticism in a judgment that was highly critical by any standard was reserved for prosecuting counsel. It focused on his seeking out the judge in chambers in what was deemed an unexceptional case, his positive encouragement of a plea bargain, together with his behaviour in suggesting acquiescence to a particular sentence. The Court emphasised that

> the anguish on all hands caused by this lamentable history of the matter could have been avoided had counsel seen fit to take note of what this Court has so often said about not seeing a judge privately with regard to sentence.[79]

The reference resulted in publication of the Attorney General's guidelines on the acceptance of guilty pleas in 2000. The thrust of the guidelines was that prosecutors should not give any indication of favouring a particular sentence. Indeed, in suitable cases, they were even required to remind the court of the possibility of review. This created considerable difficulties in being fair to defendants.[80] Additional issues arise as a result of the Victims' Charter and consequent amendments to the guidelines. It may be necessary to show that every effort has been made to take the views of victims into account when accepting a plea.

d. Indicative Sentences

There were apparent problems of fairness when, despite defendants receiving an indication of sentence from the judge before pleading guilty, sentences were still reviewed. It was thought that this problem was resolved when the Court of Appeal

---

[76] C Dyer, 'Making a pact with the devil' *The Guardian* 30 October 2000.
[77] Criminal Justice Act 1988, s 36.
[78] *Attorney General's Reference (No 44 of 2000)* (n 75) at 47.
[79] ibid.
[80] *Attorney General's Reference (Nos 86 & 87 of 1999)* (*R v Webb, R v Simpson*) [2001] 1 Cr App R (S) 141; *Attorney General's Reference (No 19 of 2004)* (*R v Charlton*) [2005] 1 Cr App R (S) 18.

allowed advance indications in *R v Goodyear*,[81] and the Attorney General guidelines were revised accordingly. This did not resolve all issues, however. The Court of Appeal subsequently reviewed a case in which there had been 'a *Goodyear* indication', because prosecuting counsel had failed to remind the Court of the possibility of referral.[82]

This decision obviously carried a significant risk of being unfair to the defendant, who had entered a plea on the basis of an indication that was later found to have been too lenient. The Court reassured itself that the defendant was not unfairly prejudiced. This was because defence lawyers had a duty to advise clients that judges' indications were subject to review, if the Attorney General considered the sentence unduly lenient. This seems to be a very peculiar conception of procedural fairness.

A further difficulty that has sometimes arisen in the acceptance of guilty pleas is where the judge has made a factual error. This may, for example, occur where there is uncertainty over when the defendant first accepted guilt. The indications are that mistakes should not be held against defendants where the Prosecution was in a position to correct the error, but did not do so.[83]

e. Summary: Criminal Practice Directions

The current state of practice is contained in recent practice directions on sentencing.[84] These provide that prosecutors can ask the judge in the case to approve a plea to a lesser charge.[85] Where they do not do so, the judge can express dissent and invite reconsideration with those instructing the prosecutor[86] and, ultimately, adjourn the case for prosecutorial review, potentially involving the Attorney General as necessary.[87] Prior to entering guilty pleas, defendants may seek an indication of sentence.

It is also possible for defendants to provide a basis of plea, limiting the scope of offending for which the defendant is to be sentenced on a guilty plea. Bases of plea fall into one of four categories. The first category is a basis of plea agreed by prosecution and defence. The second is where there is no agreement or only partial agreement by the prosecution. The third contains mitigation without contradiction of the prosecution case. The fourth involves serious or complex fraud, where the basis of plea is agreed by the prosecution and defence and accompanied by joint submissions as to the appropriate sentence.[88]

f. Negotiation of Pleas

It seems a little strange to discuss the arrangements for acceptance of guilty pleas as negotiation, since the rules do not deal with prosecution and defence discussing the terms of acceptance. As the cases illustrate, the process is supposed to follow a strict

---

[81] *R v Goodyear* [2005] 2 Cr App R 20.
[82] *Attorney General's Reference (No 48 of 2006) (R v Farrow)* [2007] 1 Cr App R (S) 558 (and see *Newman* [2011] 1 Cr App R (S) 86).
[83] *Attorney General's Reference (No 79 of 2009) (R v Haimes)* The Times 17 March 2010.
[84] Criminal Practice Direction VII: Sentencing, A–P.
[85] ibid, B: Determining the Factual Basis of Sentence, B.2.
[86] ibid, at B.3.
[87] ibid, at B.4.
[88] ibid, at B.6.

protocol that is very much at arm's length. Forms of communication do, however, take place and a kind of negotiation does occur, sometimes involving the judge. This can be characterised as a distributive negotiation in which defendants are in a weak position. They have relatively little bargaining leverage and the judge can veto whatever plea agreement has been reached.

As far as defendants are concerned the process of accepting a plea is fraught with uncertainty. They are advised by their lawyers on the consequences of their actions regarding plea and, as a result of their decisions, certain outcomes are supposed to occur. Whether or not these outcomes hold depend on whether the appeal court thinks a particular outcome reasonably reflects the gravity of the offences. The exception is in complex fraud cases, where the public policy of avoiding long and expensive trials has produced a regime aimed at reaching early, judge-approved plea agreements.

In cases of complex fraud, charges are more likely to have followed a negotiation between the prosecution and defendant or their lawyers. This is recognised to serve the public interest, particularly by saving the time and cost of trials. The charges brought by the prosecutor will reflect those agreed, rather than those that the prosecutor would necessarily have preferred if no agreement had been reached. Where a plea agreement is reached, it remains entirely a matter for the court to decide how to deal with the case.

It is considered that the risks that innocent defendants will be under pressure to accept lesser charges is acceptable. The difference in complex fraud cases from other cases is explained in the CPS Director's guidelines for such cases by reference to the fact that defendants

> are represented by solicitors experienced in commercial litigation, including negotiation. This means that the defendant is usually protected from being put under improper pressure to plead. The main danger to be guarded against in these cases is that the prosecutor is persuaded to agree to a plea or a basis that is not in the public interest and interests of justice because it does not adequately reflect the seriousness of the offending.[89]

A negotiation is also likely to have occurred where there is a Deferred Prosecution Agreement with a defendant in a case of alleged economic crime. Once negotiations between the prosecutor and the defendant have commenced, but before the terms of the DPA are agreed, they obtain confirmation from the Crown Court that the DPA is 'likely to be in the interests of justice', and that the proposed terms of the DPA are 'fair, reasonable and proportionate'. Once agreed, the Crown Court must also declare that the agreed terms are fair, reasonable and proportionate.

g. Making Plea Agreements that are Resistant to Review

Within the tightly circumscribed role allocated to lawyers in the process of determining pleas, there are measures that sensible prosecutors and criminal defence lawyers should take. These simple steps may help ensure that pleas are secure from interference, on referral, by the Court of Appeal. For example a defence lawyer should record a realistic basis of plea in writing and warn clients that sentences can be reviewed.

---

[89] CPS, *Directors' Guidance to Accompany the Attorney General's Guidelines on Plea Discussions in Cases of Serious or Complex Fraud* (n 66) Basic Principles.

Prosecutors should make appropriate representations as soon as possible, pointing out any error that might affect sentence. They should identify and agree the correct guideline and direct the judge to it, highlighting any disagreement with the defence. When an indication of sentence is given that appears lenient, prosecutors should remind the judge of the power of referral.[90]

V. Regulation of Legal Negotiation and Settlement

A. Education and Training

The course requirements for the Bar Professional Training Course provide some indication of preferred models of negotiation. Barristers must be able to select strategies and methods for conducting a negotiation that will further the client's best interests.[91] They must understand, and demonstrate, the skills needed in order to conduct such a negotiation. They must also be able to advise solicitors on steps to be taken in preparation for negotiation, for example, in terms of identifying documents and evidence. They must be aware of the possibility of invoking the aid of the court to assist the process. Although negotiation was one of the original skills that students had to be competent in to pass the Legal Practice Course, the current course outcomes do not include negotiation.

B. Negotiation in Codes of Ethics

Negotiation is rarely mentioned in lawyers' ethical codes or other guidance. Growing awareness of the gap between theory and practice has led to periodic calls for more effective regulation of negotiation in the US.[92] The gap may exist, however, because the architects of codes assume that negotiation, with its implications of bluff and deception, is an area that it is best left unregulated, opaque and ambiguous.

The absence of specific duties in relation to negotiation means that it falls to the general provisions of codes to provide the ethical framework of bargaining. This provides plenty of scope for speculation. The duty to pursue the client's best interests vies with other responsibilities. These include duties to others with whom lawyers negotiate, lawyers and non-lawyers, and protecting the reputation of the profession.

---

[90] R Bryan and L Waine, 'A Rough Guide to Avoiding an Attorney-General's Reference' *News@One* 2011 (www.onepaper.co.uk/attorney_general_references_5.pdf).

[91] BSB, *Bar Professional Training Course: Course Specification Requirements and Guidance* (2012) at para 2.2.1(c).

[92] RR Perschbacher, 'Regulating Lawyers' Negotiations' (1985) 27 *Arizona Law Review* 75–138; AR Rubin, 'A Causerie of Lawyer's Ethics in Negotiation' (1975) 35 *Louisiana Law Review* 577; WW Steele Jr, 'Deceptive Negotiating and High-Toned Morality' (1986) 39 *Vanderbilt Law Review* 1387.

Professional codes tend not to address the issue of whether lawyers should lie for their clients in negotiations.[93]

C. The Duty to Clients

The duty a lawyer owes to client in negotiation is unclear. It is arguable that solicitors have a duty to understand the potential of principled negotiation and to advise clients accordingly. Unless they do so, and used a principled approach as required, they may be failing to promote their client's best interests by ignoring and failing to exploit the potential of the situation. If, however, the client is not interested in this potential, but wants the lawyer to engage in hard bargaining, how far must the clients' wishes be respected?

If, despite a lengthy discussion of the benefits of co-operation and the advantages of harmonious family relationships, a client demands the most money achievable, must the ethical family lawyer comply? The codes are ambiguous on this issue. The formula used, acting in the client's best interests, is not the same as respecting client preferences. It could be read so as to allow lawyers to impose their own perceptions of what is in the client's interests. It could also be read as an obligation to discover clients' underlying interests before deciding how best they can be served.

The US literature on the ethics of bargaining tends to view bargaining as a partisan activity which must be carried out under the umbrella of 'zealous advocacy'.[94] Interpretation of the obligation of zeal has provoked a spectrum of positions. At one end of the spectrum, there are those who justify lying in negotiation. Proponents of this view argue that 'effectiveness in negotiations is central to the business of lawyering and a willingness to lie is central to one's effectiveness in negotiations'.[95] Less strident defenders of positional bargaining defend the practice of 'bluffing' regarding the bottom line. They treat this as part of the process of 'concession exchange' rather than deception.[96] At the other end of the spectrum, irrespective of jurisdiction, the standard obligation of 'zeal' is arguably not associated with underhand tactics.[97]

Lawyers in England and Wales are not subject to an obligation of zeal. The first edition of this book argued that the English profession's emphasis on best interests suggests a less stringent duty than 'zealous advocacy'. If this is correct, much of the US discussion becomes irrelevant. Whether or not lawyers have an obligation to pursue their clients' lawful preferences, or their best interests, their latitude as to methods is constrained by whatever duty is owed to the other side.

---

[93] Condlin (n 20); LE Fisher, 'Truth as a Double-Edged Sword: Deception, Moral Paradox, and the Ethics of Advocacy' (1989) 14 *The Journal of the Legal Profession* 89.

[94] D Luban, *Lawyers and Justice: An Ethical Study* (Princeton, Princeton University Press, 1988).

[95] GB Wetlaufer, 'The Ethics of Lying in Negotiation' (1990) 76 *Iowa Law Review* 1219.

[96] C Provis, 'Ethics, Deception and Labor Negotiation' (2000) 28 *Journal of Business Ethics* 145, at 148.

[97] T Dare, 'Mere Zeal, Hyper-Zeal and the Ethical Obligations of Lawyers' (2004) 7(1) *Legal Ethics* 24.

D. Treating the other Side Fairly

An obligation to treat the other side fairly may limit what can be achieved for clients in negotiation. Such an obligation may mean, for example, that underhand tactics cannot be used. One feature that is common in competitive positional bargaining is misleading the other side as to the 'bottom line', the maximum or minimum that will be paid or accepted in settlement. This could be regarded as deception and an underhand tactic.

More realistically, some authors justify misleading on the bottom line as 'stylistic competitiveness', ethically dubious but consistent with treating the other side fairly. This is because they are not actually misled; participants in competitive bargaining expect bluffing behaviour.[98] This still leaves the issue of whether such behaviour is consistent with lawyers' conduct rules and, particularly, the virtuous aspirations they often express.

E. Solicitors' Obligations to Third Parties in Negotiations

i. The Position in Later Editions of the Guide

a. Duties to the World at Large

Later editions of the Guide contained two rules directly relevant to the issue of bluffing in negotiation. The first, a duty to the world at large, was expressed as follows:

> Solicitors must not act, whether in their professional capacity or otherwise, towards anyone in a way which is fraudulent, deceitful or otherwise contrary to their position as solicitors. Nor must solicitors use their positions as solicitors to take unfair advantage for themselves or another person.[99]

The caution against fraud or deceit should not have been troubling since, as the Guide observed, any such conduct would 'render the offending solicitor liable to disciplinary action in addition to the possibility of civil or criminal proceedings'.[100]

It could be argued that the duty not to be fraudulent and deceitful could cover positional bargaining where a lawyer positively misled an opponent about their bottom line. It might also be thought that a duty not to take unfair advantage of others might apply if an opponent in negotiation, particularly a lay person, did not understand the 'rules of the game' of concession trading. Rude and bullying behaviour, a tactic used by some negotiators, would appear to taking unfair advantage. The other principle concerning obligations to third parties only applied to other solicitors. This was apparently much more likely to apply to deception in negotiation.

---

[98] See Lowenthal (n 6).
[99] N Taylor (ed), *Guide to the Professional Conduct of Solicitors*, 8th edn (1990) r 17.01, at 346.
[100] ibid, note 1 to r 19.01.

b. Duties to other Solicitors

Rule 19.01 of the Guide obliged solicitors to 'act towards other solicitors with frankness and good faith consistent with the overriding duty to the client'.[101] 'Frankness' is an interesting choice of word, because it means something more than honesty. To be frank implies openness, straightforwardness and sincerity, sometimes to the point of bluntness. Therefore, while someone can be honest by being truthful in response to questions, frankness, suggests a more positive transparency. The use of the term 'good faith' also had a potential application to negotiation. In the bargaining literature, 'good faith' is linked with honesty, not seeking unconscionable advantage and coming to the table with an open mind.[102]

It was unclear whether Rule 19.01 was drafted with negotiation in mind. The fact that it related to dealing with other solicitors, and negotiation is one of the most common activities that solicitors share, suggests it must have been. While an unqualified obligation of frankness and good faith imposed a potentially onerous burden for a lawyer to carry in positional negotiations, it could be consistent with a principled approach. The fact that the duty was subject to the duty to the client's 'overriding interest' also suggested that an adversarial context was considered relevant. This could be read as abrogating the need for frankness or good faith where client interests required it. Rule 19.01 was therefore contradictory and problematic in the negotiation context.

Judicial consideration of the duties of frankness and good faith in negotiation occurred in *Thames Trains Ltd v Adams*.[103] Mr Adams, a US citizen, suffered serious injuries in a train crash for which Thames Trains was liable. Its solicitors paid US $9.3 million into court. Adams' solicitor, C, then rang Thames Trains' solicitors to explore the possibility that their client would pay US $10 million, including the sum in court, to settle the case. C was told that no further monies were available. She then instructed another solicitor in her firm to send a fax to Thames Trains' solicitors accepting the US $9.3 million in court.

Thames Trains' solicitors did not see the fax from Adams' solicitors because of an internal computer problem. In the meantime, they had contacted Thames Trains, and had received instructions to offer a further US $500,000. This was communicated to C by telephone, who accepted. On discovering the earlier fax, Thames Trains sought to set aside a consent order recording the terms of settlement. They claimed that the agreement to pay the extra sum was void for mistake. They also claimed estoppel based on the unconscionable conduct by C. They argued that the failure to inform them of the earlier offer was a breach of C's duty to act towards other solicitors with frankness and good faith.

From the evidence presented it appeared that neither side had been frank or acted in good faith. C may have had instructions to accept the sum in court were the attempt to obtain an increase to fail, or at least knew she could get authority to accept. When it was put to her in cross-examination that her client had no plans to travel to England for

[101] ibid, r 19.01, at 359.
[102] HC Black, JR Nolan and JM Nolan-Haley, *Black's Law Dictionary* 'Definitions of the Terms and Phrases of American and English Jurisprudence, Ancient and Modern' (St Paul, MN, West, 1990) at 693, *Central Estates (Belgravia) Ltd v Woolgar* [1971] 3 All ER 647, per Lord Denning MR at 649.
[103] *Thames Trains Ltd v Adams* [2006] EWHC 3291.

a trial she answered 'I remain silent'.[104] Similarly, on the agreed facts, her opponent had sought instructions for an increased payment having stated that no more was available. Did a duty of frankness and good faith require C to declare the true position? Counsel for C conceded that she would have been under a duty to answer a direct question accepting the payment in. It was also argued that, even had she not been frank, the issue was one of professional misconduct rather than a reason to overturn the consent order.

Counsel for Thames Trains argued that the duty to act in the best interests of the client was counterbalanced by the solicitor's independence and integrity, his good repute and the profession's good repute and the solicitor's duty to the Court. He declared that Rule 10.01 was a solicitors' practice rule, which the judge accepted, although it appears not to have been the case. He noted that the guidance notes to Chapter 1 of the Guide stated that, where principles came into conflict, the public interest in the administration of justice must take precedence.[105]

Counsel continued by arguing that any opportunistic conduct amounting to sharp practice is not in the interests of the administration of justice and that the law should support commercial and professional probity. He proposed that solicitors should be able to rely upon their fellow members to act fairly and in a frank and straightforward manner, and that the best interests of litigants are best promoted by a transparent and fair negotiation process. Thus, he concluded, the statutory duty of a solicitor to his lay client is not absolute, but qualified by considerations of public policy.[106]

Nelson J held that, in contract law, the fax was an offer to settle that could be withdrawn at any time. C had implicitly withdrawn the earlier acceptance when accepting the higher sum. The agreement to pay the higher sum was therefore enforceable unless C's conduct was unconscionable and sufficient to upset the agreement. Therefore, it fell to consider the issue of estoppel against Adams as a result of C's conduct. An estoppel by silence or acquiescence arises where 'a reasonable man would expect' the person against whom the estoppel is raised, 'acting honestly and responsibly', to bring the true facts to the attention of the other party known by him to be under a mistake as to their respective rights and obligations.

The judge thought that C was bound by her duty to her client. It was significant that it was only after agreeing to accept the additional sum that she checked and discovered that the fax had been sent. He thought that, at that point, she would have breached her duty of confidentiality to her client had she revealed, during the conversation about an increased offer, her willingness to accept the sum in court. Nelson J therefore concluded that C's conduct

> was not deceitful nor sharp practice, nor did she take advantage of R's ignorance of the earlier offer, given that it had only been made as a result of him giving the inaccurate information that no further money was available, and that he had failed to receive the fax due to system failures within his own office.[107]

The judge felt that his decision to uphold the settlement at the higher figure was 'counter-intuitive'. He recognised that the courts should promote the duty of frankness between solicitors and litigants. In all the circumstances, however, he concluded

---

[104] ibid, at [11].
[105] Taylor, *Guide to the Professional Conduct of Solicitors* (n 99) guidance note 1.02.6
[106] *Thames Trains Ltd v Adams* [2006] EWHC 3291, at [13].
[107] ibid, at [56].

that C's duty to the administration of justice, or as an officer of the court, did not require her to correct her opponent's misapprehension. He did say, however, that, had he found that there was a duty on C to disclose the fact that the sum in court had been accepted, she would have been estopped from asserting the higher settlement.

While C's conduct did not invalidate the settlement, Nelson J suggested what a solicitor should do in the circumstances of the case. As soon as she realised that she was to be offered more money, C should have said that she had sent a fax accepting the sum in court, but that now, having realised that more money was available, that offer was withdrawn. Of course, there may then have been an argument about whether the increased offer remained on the table and capable of acceptance. This approach would, the judge argued, have been more consistent with the duty of frankness and good faith.

Thames Trains Ltd v Adams, which was subsequently followed,[108] showed the limits of frankness and good faith in negotiation. The judge concluded that there was no unconscionable conduct. It appears that, on this view, disciplinary proceedings could not have been brought on these facts. It is interesting to speculate whether, had C accepted Thames Trains' higher offer in the certain knowledge that the acceptance fax had been sent, the outcome would have been different. The judge attached importance to the fact that she did not know for sure that it had been sent. If she had known, and the same decision was reached, it is difficult to see how the third party duties in Rule 10.01 could ever supersede the duty to negotiate the best deal for the client.

c. Summary

Solicitors' duties to the other side in negotiation were, in later editions of the Guide, confused. Positive duties of frankness and good faith were owed to other solicitors whereas negative duties, not to be fraudulent or deceitful, were owed to anyone. The duty of frankness and good faith is arguably a more exacting standard. The lesser standard, not to be deceitful or take unfair advantage, apparently covered solicitors dealing with lawyers who were not solicitors or non-lawyers.

In any kind of positional bargaining, solicitors were disadvantaged. Strictly, the obligations to be frank and to act in good faith severely constrained, or even ruled out, effective positional bargaining against other solicitors. The obligations not to be deceitful or take unfair advantage arguably ruled it out against 'anyone', certainly if they did not understand the process. This appeared to be an incoherent position to adopt in relation to negotiation.[109]

ii. The Solicitors' Code of Conduct 2007

The Solicitors' Code of Conduct 2007 made a step forward in recognising an obligation to support client autonomy. It provided that solicitors must:

(a)   identify clearly the client's objectives in relation to the work to be done for the client;

---

[108]   *Thompson v Arnold* [2007] EWHC 1875 (QB).
[109]   A Boon, 'Ethics and Strategy in Personal Injury Litigation' (1995) 22(3) *Journal of Law and Society* 353.

(b) give the client a clear explanation of the issues involved and the options available to them;

(c) agree with the client the next steps to be taken; and

(d) keep the client informed of progress, unless otherwise agreed.[110]

This would certainly seem to envisage a relationship that could support meaningful principled negotiation.

The Code contained only one explicit reference to negotiation. This was a rule requiring that the other side have sufficient time and information to agree costs.[111] The new Code did not incorporate the troublesome principles from the Guide into the new rules, at least not in the previous form. The duty of frankness and good faith to solicitors disappeared. The replacement, Rule 10.01, made no distinction between dealings with solicitors or others. It stated 'you must not use your position to take unfair advantage of anyone either for your own benefit or for another person's benefit'.[112]

The formula adopted by Rule 10.01 of the new Code abandoned the different standards for dealing with solicitors and with anyone else. It also abandoned the 'overriding interest of clients' qualification when solicitors dealt with other solicitors. There was now a common standard for dealing with third parties. This does not mean, however, that none of the behaviour previously identified in the rules was relevant. It was presumably covered by the notion of not taking unfair advantage. The core duty not to damage the reputation and integrity of the profession was also still relevant. Therefore, it was at least arguable that lawyers who are not frank, do not act in good faith, or who are fraudulent and deceitful, bring the profession into disrepute.[113]

Guidance to Rule 10 suggested that 'it would be unfair to demand anything that is not recoverable through the proper legal process'.[114] It is doubtful that this applies to extra-legal solutions, a key element of integrative bargaining. First, the guidance is probably limited to letters before action. Secondly, it is doubtful that proposing an extra-legal solution would constitute a 'demand'.

iii. The SRA Code of Conduct

The current Code of Conduct, which reformulates many of the rules from the earlier publications as outcomes and behaviours, does not advance understanding of, or clarity regarding, solicitors' obligations in negotiation. The key outcome in Chapter 11, that 'you do not take unfair advantage of third parties in either your professional or personal capacity'[115] is even more opaque than previous guidance. This is balanced by the duty to promote each client's best interests. As *Thames Trains Ltd v Adams* demonstrates, conflict between these outcomes would not necessarily be resolved in favour of third parties, even bearing in mind the duty to the administration of justice.

---

[110] SRA, *Solicitors' Code of Conduct 2007*, r 2.02.

[111] ibid, r 10.02.

[112] ibid, r 10.

[113] ibid, r 1.06.

[114] ibid, Guidance to r 10 note 5.

[115] SRA, *Handbook, SRA Code of Conduct*, ch 11: 'Relations with Third Parties', Outcome 11.1.

The other Code outcome arguably relevant to negotiation is in Chapter 1, 'Client Care'. This provides that 'the service you provide to clients is competent, delivered in a timely manner and takes account of your client's needs and circumstances'.[116] The last part of this outcome appears to support the idea that solicitors need to have a good idea of client interests. This, of course, is a prerequisite of principled negotiation.

F. Barristers' Obligations to Third Parties in Negotiations

The new Bar Code of Conduct does not specifically consider negotiation. Therefore, the position of barristers is determined by the interpretation of two conflicting core duties. The first is the duty to act in the best interests of each client[117] and the second is the duty to act with honesty and integrity.[118] The rules clarify the former by providing that barristers must 'promote fearlessly and by all proper and lawful means the client's best interests'.[119] The addition of 'proper and lawful means' is not a particularly helpful guide to whether bluffing tactics are permitted. Competitive bargaining is not unlawful and 'proper' is often interpreted as meaning 'permitted by the rules'.

The duties owed to third parties are perhaps a little more revealing. In Chapter 2: 'Behaving Ethically', the rules provide that barristers must not do anything which could reasonably be seen by the public to undermine their honesty, integrity and independence.[120] The rule is said to cover 'not knowingly or recklessly mislead[ing] or attempt[ing] to mislead anyone'.[121] This would appear to apply to bluffing in negotiation, although it is not clear that this is intended. A barrister accused of breaking the rule by misleading an opponent might argue that an experienced negotiator would not be misled by such behaviour.

VI. Future Regulatory Possibilities

A. Orientation

It appears that principled negotiation is a method of bargaining most consistent with professional commitments to virtues such as honesty, integrity and fairness. It is tempting to suggest, therefore, that conduct rules should support principled negotiation

---

[116] ibid, ch 1: Client Care Outcome 1.5.
[117] BSB, *Handbook*, pt 2: The Code of Conduct, 'The Core Duties', Core Duty 2.
[118] ibid, Core Duty 3.
[119] BSB, *Handbook*, pt 2: The Code of Conduct, 'The Conduct Rules', rC15.1.
[120] ibid, rC8.
[121] ibid, rC9.1.

more explicitly. Such a step should not, therefore, be taken lightly. There are various policy issues to consider. First, for example, conducted properly, principled negotiation should produce outcomes very similar to those produced by mediation. The distinction between negotiation and mediation is one that both lawyers and their clients may wish to retain. Secondly, imposing a duty to be principled may give an advantage to those who are unprincipled. Thirdly, there may also be an increase in transaction costs, such as insurance, if more prescriptive regulation gave rise to legal actions.[122]

B. Education and Training

Both the solicitors' and barristers' vocational courses teach negotiation, but courses tend to be light on bargaining theory. They tend to conflate problem-solving methods of bargaining and more adversarial styles. Greater attention to negotiation in education and training would be a necessary part of changing the culture of bargaining for lawyers.

C. Conduct Rules

The current situation, where there are no definitive rules of bargaining for lawyers, is inimical to an environment of trust in the legal services market. It is arguable that there should be no exceptions for 'bluffing' in negotiation. Exceptions to truthfulness norms often encourage a culture of deceit.[123] The argument is that making an exception for negotiation would be likely to lead to unintended violations, compromise the position of lawyers as officers of the court and lead to lower levels of trust and co-operation.

There are various possibilities for improving the transparency of regulation of negotiation. This would involve defining what constitutes ethical behaviour in this sphere of activity given (i) different models of bargaining that may be appropriate and (ii) the large range of situations potentially subject to bargaining.

An example of how it might be possible to distinguish the standards expected in negotiation from those in other areas is provided by the ABA's model code. This distinguishes between the lawyer's role in advising and as advocate, as follows:

> As advisor, a lawyer provides a client with an informed understanding of the client's legal rights and obligations and explains their practical implications. As advocate, a lawyer zealously asserts the client's position under the rules of the adversary system.[124]

---

[122] AM Burr, 'Ethics in Negotiation: Does Getting To Yes Require Candour?' (2001) May/July *Dispute Resolution Journal* 10.

[123] See generally S Bok, *Lying: Moral Choice in Public and Private Life*, 2nd edn (New York, New York Books, 1999); Thurman, 'Chipping Away at Lawyer Veracity' (n 1).

[124] ABA, *Model Rules of Professional Conduct 2004* (Chicago, American Bar Association, 2002) preamble, at para 2.

A rule on negotiation could marry the obligations of honesty and candour in relation to material facts with:

—— an obligation to explore with clients their perceptions of their interests; and
—— to seek a settlement where that is in the client's best interests; and
—— to seek a settlement which satisfies the client's interests as far as possible and which is fair and reasonable to both sides.

Such a move would be consistent with continuing attempts to make litigation more transparent and less vulnerable to manipulation. Such proposals seem destined to fall on sceptical ears. Judged by the codes of conduct, the legal profession appears to pride itself on a pragmatic approach to conducting business in an adversarial setting.

VII. Conclusion

It is not only in England and Wales that the incoherence of the lawyer's role in litigation and settlement has been noted.[125] The existence of different kinds of negotiating problems and different defensible models of negotiation complicates the task of defining an appropriate ethic of negotiation for lawyers. To suggest that an approach may be ethical in some circumstances but not others is problematic. Distributive bargaining, with either loss or gain for each party, may produce favourable outcomes for one side. In contrast, a successful negotiation involving integrative features depends on maximising the benefit of both parties.

Serving the best interests of the client suggests that competence in different styles of negotiation is required unless, as many have suggested, lawyers commit themselves to a principled bargaining approach in all circumstances. The advantage of this is that some methods such as principled negotiation support collegial obligations and expectations of integrity more effectively than more adversarial styles. The problem arises when clients demand adversarial lawyers and one-sided gains.

If no method of negotiation is promoted as ethical, it falls to general rules of conduct to regulate the bargaining process. It can be argued that obligations not to take unfair advantage of, or not to mislead opponents, apply to some bargaining behaviour. It is doubtful that the existence of such general obligations can, without more, sustain an ethical negotiation culture, or convey to participants what to expect from others.

[125] Condlin (n 20).

19

Advocacy

'It should be remembered that if counsel fails to appear the opposing counsel will take his place and in the best of faith adduce the facts and state the law that he must meet and overcome. Here is "priesthood"'.[1]

'today we live in a consumerist society in which people have a much greater awareness of their rights. If they have suffered a wrong as a result of the provision of negligent professional services, they expect to have the right to claim redress. It tends to erode confidence in the legal system if advocates, alone among professional men, are immune from liability for negligence'.[2]

I. Introduction

Advocacy is at the heart of the legal role. In its broadest sense, advocacy involves the presentation of another's case or point of view. Lawyers are often regarded as advocates in this sense, in whatever task they perform. Advocacy, in the narrow sense, refers to the presentation of a case in court. This kind of advocacy has an impact that transcends its significance as a legal task. Certainly in contemporary society, transaction work is central to the work of more lawyers than advocacy is. It has been argued that the impact of the ethic of advocacy on lawyers' orientation to legal work generally, is harmful to professional legal ethics.

The rules of advocacy tend to be pervasive across different types of tribunal. Adversarial criminal trial is arguably the model on which other kinds of advocacy are based. The need to protect the rights of criminal defendants demands rigorous testing of evidence. Lawyers enjoy some latitude in how they approach the task of questioning, particularly in the cross-examination of opposing witnesses. This has caused some controversy in relation to how vulnerable witnesses are treated in the courts. Increasingly, there are limitations on how advocates approach the task of testing oral evidence.

---

[1] B Hollander, *The English Bar: The Tribute of an American Lawyer* (London, Bowes, 1964).
[2] *Arthur J S Hall & Co (a firm) v Simons, Barratt v Ansell and others (t/a Woolf Seddon (a firm), Harris v Schofield Roberts & Hill (a firm) and another* [2000] 3 All ER 673, per Lord Steyn.

In all courts and tribunals the advocate's power and control is offset by a duty to the court. This cuts across partisan obligations owed to clients. The duty to the court partly rests on the classical role of the judge as an umpire in a clash of champions. Advocates expose flaws in evidence and present legal arguments. Unclear of the details of the case, and the advocate's instructions, judicial intervention could be totally misconceived.[3] The quid pro quo for this detached judicial role is that the advocate must not deceive the judge as to the true position in the case, so that a just conclusion can be reached.

II. The Obligations of Advocacy

Modern theories of ethics are still predicated on the lawyers' role in constraining the state. The framework of the discussion was memorably provided in articles by Freedman and Noonan in the US in the 1970s. Freedman thought that the clash of two 'versions of the truth' provided a natural defence against oppression that is absent in civil systems. George Bernard Shaw characterised this as '[t]he theory ... that if you set two liars to exposing each other, eventually the truth will come out'.[4] Freedman argued that the adversarial system was not perfect, but was better than any alternatives. The state has massive power and resources at its disposal. Because of the potential for abuse and corruption of the state apparatus, state interests 'are not absolute, or even paramount', and should be constrained.

Freedman thought that the best way to prevent the state from overpowering the liberty of its subjects was to ensure that 'the defendant is at least afforded that one advocate, that 'champion against a hostile world', whose zealous allegiance is to him or her alone.[5] For Freedman, the word zeal is freighted with significance. 'Zealous advocacy' is a bulwark against state oppression. Willingness to advance a client's case despite public, governmental or professional disapproval is its bedrock.[6] To Freedman, a trial must be treated as a battle, with 'zealous advocacy' the right of criminal defendants.[7]

In Freedman's account, the independence of the legal profession, expressed in its alignment with individuals against the state, is the key to an effective state system of justice and a healthy democracy. He asserted that

there is only one way to keep the law "trustworthy"—only one way to keep the bureaucrats honest, and to make the law work, that is, by making sure that there is an independent

---

[3] M Frankel, 'The Search for the Truth: An Umpireal View' (1975) 123 *University of Pennsylvania Law Review* 1024.

[4] Quoted in MJ Saks, 'Accuracy v. Advocacy: Expert Testimony Before the Bench' (1987) Aug/Sept *Technology Law Review* 43.

[5] ibid, at 48.

[6] SL Jacobs, 'Legal Advocacy in a Time of Plague' (1993) 21 *Journal of Law Medicine and Ethics* 382.

[7] MH Freedman, 'Professional Responsibility of the Criminal Defence Lawyer' (1966) 64 *Michigan Law Review* 1469.

Bar, prepared to challenge governmental action and to do so as zealously and effectively as possible.[8]

Freedman controversially went further in his interpretation of 'zeal'. He claimed that the role of the criminal defence advocate justified behaviour that almost everyone else considers unethical. Under the umbrella of zealous advocacy, he argued, defence advocates must discredit witnesses known to be telling the truth, allow perjured testimony and advise clients in a way that enables them to give perjured evidence. This, unfortunately, became the version of the standard conception of the lawyers' role that later academics used as a basis for proposed alternatives.

An initial challenge to Freedman's notion of zealous advocacy came from Noonan. He criticised Freedman's conception of trials as 'battles'.[9] The advocate's duty, Noonan suggested, is to assist the judge in making an impartial, wise and informed decision and to seek to establish the truth. Noonan believed that 'the advocate plays his role well when zeal for his client's cause promotes a wise and informed decision of the case'. Justice demands proper assessment of the facts, increasing the chance of correct verdicts and, where conviction results, a sentence proportionate to the crime.[10]

The clash of views between Freedman and Noonan reflects different aspects of the advocate's torn ethical allegiance to clients and to the courts. Each emphasises one commitment, arguably at the expense of the other. In reality, certainly in England and Wales, they are in a kind of balance. A high watermark is the famous quotation from Henry Brougham, a leading advocate in Georgian England. Brougham represented the estranged wife of George IV during a messy and politically charged divorce.

In the course of Brougham's representation of the Queen he explained that

[a]n advocate, in the discharge of his duty, knows but one person in all the world, and that person is his client. To save that client by all means, and expedients, and at all hazards and costs to other persons, and among them, to himself, is his first and only duty; and in performing this duty he must not regard the alarm, the torments, the destruction which he may bring upon others. Separating the duty of a patriot from that of an advocate, he must go on reckless of consequences, though it should be his unhappy fate to involve his country in confusion.[11]

This has become a touchstone for the duty of partisanship. The 200 years since Brougham's famous defence have seen containment of the kind of advocacy with which he would have been familiar. A significant transition occurred between 1820 and 1850. Infamous cases of counsel asserting their client's innocence, while being aware of their guilt,[12] led to the rule against expressing an opinion[13] and misleading the court.[14]

---

[8] MH Freedman, 'Are There Public Interest Limits on Lawyers' Advocacy' (1977) 2 *The Journal of the Legal Profession* 47, at 54.

[9] J Noonan, 'The Purposes of Advocacy and the Limits of Confidentiality' (1966) 64 *Michigan Law Review* 1485.

[10] A Ashworth, 'Ethics and Criminal Justice' in R Cranston (ed), *Legal Ethics and Professional Responsibility* (Oxford, Clarendon Press, 1995) 146.

[11] *Trial of Queen Caroline* (J Nightingale (ed) (1821)) quoted in Frankel, 'The Search for Truth (n 3) at 1036; and GC Hazard, 'The Future of Legal Ethics' (1991) 100 *Yale Law Journal* 1239, at 1239.

[12] A Watson 'Changing Advocacy: Part One' (2001) 165 *Justice of the Peace* 743.

[13] Bar Council, *Bar Code of Conduct 1981*, as amended, at para 708(b).

[14] ibid, at para 302.

The English legal profession has never adopted the phrase 'zealous advocacy', although academic discussion usually proceeds as if it had. Dare, for example, recently proposed an obligation on advocates of 'mere zeal', diligence, rather than the 'hyper zeal' promoted by Freedman.[15] The formal position in England and Wales has tended more towards Noonan's theory of the purpose of the system than Freedman's. The rules support Noonan's interpretation of the advocate's role. The Bar, however, adheres to neutrality as an organising principle of its ethics. The obligation of representation arises whether or not the advocate is sympathetic to the client and the client's cause.[16]

III. The Advocate's Duties

For both branches of the profession the advocate's duty is no more nor less than part of the general duty to protect the client's best interests. This is balanced by the duty to the court and to the administration of justice. The duty to the administration of justice may include, but is arguably larger than, the duty to the court. Both duties may require actions conflicting with clients' interests. Before considering how these duties are presented in the codes, it is necessary to see how they have been treated by the courts. It is logical to begin by looking at the duty to the court because this circumscribes the duty to clients.

A. Advocate's Duty to the Court

The duty to the court constitutes a qualification to the proposition that lawyers can only pursue their clients' interests. The duty is owed as a matter of general law. It is not owed specifically to other litigants. It does not derive from professional codes, although it is certainly represented there. The duty covers the whole process of litigation. The parts specific to advocacy are not as onerous as may be thought. There is a duty to refer the judge to relevant authorities and points of law that may have eluded an opponent. There is also a duty to point out procedural irregularities. Finally, there is a duty not to allow the presentation of certain kinds of misleading testimony. This is arguably the most difficult and contentious area.

---

[15] T Dare, 'Mere-Zeal, Hyper Zeal and the Ethical Obligations of Lawyers' (2004) 7 *Legal Ethics* 24.
[16] See R Audi, 'The Ethics of Advocacy' (1995) 1 *Legal Theory* 251.

i. Misleading the Court

One of Freedman's 'three hardest cases' concerned advocates permitting the presentation of perjured evidence in order to achieve a just result. Hazard suggests that such conduct would have almost certainly resulted in disbarment under US state laws operative at the time.[17] The Marre Report presented the official position in England and Wales, asserting that:

> A lawyer may not, directly or indirectly, lend himself knowingly to any false story being put before the court. If he is asked to do so, he must immediately cease to act for the client.[18]

The case law is a little more ambiguous than this, although the broad statement of principle is sound. While fabricating evidence is proscribed, the position where an advocate is silent when misleading evidence is presented is less clear.

Decisions over the past 50 years indicate that the courts have moved towards more demanding standards for presentation of testimony. Towards the end of the nineteenth century, the imprecise nature of the duty not to mislead was suggested by dictum in re Mayor Cooke,[19] where it was said that

> it was a part of [a lawyer's] duty that he should not keep back from the Court any information which ought to be before it, and that he should in no way mislead the court by stating facts which were untrue ... How far a solicitor might go on behalf of his client was a question far too difficult to be capable of abstract definition, but when concrete cases arose every one could see for himself whether what had been done was fair or not[20]

The cases typically involve applications for new trials or disputes over costs. The conclusion of both types of case may not affect the advocate personally, although disciplinary sanctions may follow the court's decision. Hilbery, for example, talked of the sanction being a reprimand from the judge followed by ostracism by the advocate's peers for repeat offenders.[21] The cases therefore define the scope of the duty as perceived by judges at particular times.

The 'concrete cases' referred to in re Mayor Cooke duly appeared in the twentieth century. They revealed that the courts were prepared to extend the duty beyond the advocate 'stating facts which were untrue', although this was achieved with difficulty. Therefore, while it may be impossible to specify all the instances in which the duty to the court may be breached[22] it is possible to provide examples. From these it is possible to derive categories of case where the duty may arise.

---

[17] Hazard, 'The Future of Legal Ethics' (n 11) at 1257, citing McKissick v United States 379 F.2d 754 (5th Cir 1967), Dodd v Florida Bar 118 So 2d 17 (Fla 1960).
[18] Lady Marre CBE, A Time for Change: Report on the Committee on the Future of the Legal Profession (London, The General Council of the Bar, The Law Society, 1988) at para 6.6 (Marre Report).
[19] In re G Mayor Cooke (1889) 5 Times Law Reports 407.
[20] ibid, at 408.
[21] M Hilbery, Duty and Art in Advocacy (London, Stevens and Sons Ltd, 1946) at 21.
[22] Per Wright J in Myers v Elman [1940] AC 282, at 319.

a. Allowing a Witness to Conceal Relevant Personal Information

The first category of case is where advocates allow witnesses to give evidence while concealing relevant facts about themselves. One such case was *Tombling v Universal Bulb Company Limited*,[23] which concerned an application for a new trial based on the behaviour of the plaintiff's counsel. He had conducted an examination in chief of a witness and established his home address, his previous employment as a prison governor, and his subsequent employment. The way the questions were put allowed the witness to conceal the fact that he was serving a prison sentence for a driving offence at the time of the trial. He had actually been brought to court by prison officers.

The Court of Appeal refused to set aside the decision of the court below and order a new trial. The relevant test was that the court must be satisfied (i) that the matters would have discredited the witness, and (ii) that the decision depended on the witness's evidence. The Court of Appeal was not satisfied that, had the Court been aware of the true position, it would have affected the outcome of the trial.

Two of the Court of Appeal judges were disinclined to criticise counsel. Lord Justice Somervell felt that counsel was probably not under any duty to disclose the witness' convictions, but that it would have been better had he not led the plaintiff's evidence in the way he had. Lord Justice Denning would have been disposed to order a new trial had there been any improper conduct by the successful party. But, he said, there was nothing improper in the conduct of the plaintiff's counsel. Had the questions been put to the witness with the intention of misleading the court, it would have been a different matter. He was satisfied, however, that it had not been counsel's intention to mislead.

Lord Justice Singleton took a less forgiving line on counsel's conduct. He said that, 'in this case counsel thought only of his duty to his client to the exclusion of the duty which he owed to others, and, in particular, that which he owed to the court'.[24] The judge would have ordered a retrial on the basis that this witness' evidence was material to establishing the plaintiff's case. There was a need to see that the conduct of court proceedings was above suspicion and parties should feel that they had a fair deal.

In *Meek v Fleming*,[25] a case with broadly similar facts, a retrial was ordered because witness credibility was central. A journalist claimed damages for an uncorroborated assault by the defendant, a senior police officer. The defendant's counsel, a QC, took full responsibility for concealing the fact that his client had been demoted for deceiving another court in the course of his duty as a police officer. At the trial the defendant had been deliberately dressed in civilian clothes and was addressed as 'Mister' throughout. Yet his status and seniority had clearly been a material factor in the trial.

The Court of Appeal decided that upholding the first instance decision would be a miscarriage of justice. Lord Justice Holroyd Pearce accepted Denning LJ's argument in *Tombling* that the intention of the advocate was material. The instant case, he said, was different from *Tombling* in that the Court was deceived as a 'premeditated line of

---

[23] *Tombling v Universal Bulb Company Limited* [1951] 2 The Times Law Reports 289.
[24] ibid, at 296.
[25] *Meek v Fleming* [1961] 2 QB 366.

conduct'.[26] Wilmer LJ said that counsel's decision had 'involved insufficient regard being paid to the duty owed to the court and to the plaintiff and his advisers'.[27]

The cases on misleading the court are somewhat ambiguous. As a general proposition counsel should never 'knowingly' allow the evidence to create a false impression about the position and status of the witness, particularly where this may affect the court's assessment of their credibility. If misleading testimony is presented a new trial may be ordered where the evidence was material. Counsel may be subject to discipline where they knew the reality of the situation. The impact of these cases survived the introduction of the Civil Procedure Rules, insofar as the application of the principles furthered the overriding objective of doing justice.[28]

b. Relevant Facts not Presented in Evidence

The second category of case covered by the duty not to mislead the court involves facts known to the advocate that are not presented in evidence. In *re Mayor Cooke*, it was said that the duty to the court covered documents that might be material to the way the evidence is perceived. The judge said

> [if counsel] were to know that an affidavit had been made in the cause which had been used and which, if it were before the Judge, must affect his mind, and if he knew that the judge was ignorant of the existence of that affidavit, then if he concealed that affidavit from the Judge he would fail in his duty ... if he were to make any wilful misstatement to the judge he would be outrageously dishonourable.[29]

A practical application of this principle arose in *Vernon v Bosley (No 2)*,[30] although the relevant document only came to light after trial. The case involved similar circumstances to those described in *re Mayor Cooke*. The claimant was awarded over £1 million in damages for nervous shock resulting from witnessing the death of his two daughters caused by B's driving. B appealed, but lost the appeal. Before an order was drawn up, B's counsel received copies of a judgment in unconnected family proceedings.

The family court judgment suggested that the experts who had prepared the report in the tort action had stated in the matrimonial proceedings that the plaintiff had substantially recovered. This information was probably available by the time the judgment was delivered in the plaintiff's claim for shock and certainly before B's appeal was heard. Obviously, the damages would have been less in that case had this information been available to the court.

On an application by B to re-hear the appeal the majority of the Court of Appeal found for B, reducing the damages payable by half. Lord Justice Stuart-Smith held that there should have been disclosure of the fact that the claimant had substantially recovered. The reports, having been obtained in Children Act proceedings, were not subject to litigation privilege. The duty of litigants not to mislead the court applied until the point at which that judgment was given. Where there had been a change in

---

[26] ibid, at 379.
[27] ibid, at 383.
[28] *Hamilton v Al-Fayed (No 4)* [2001] EMLR 15.
[29] ibid, at 408.
[30] *Vernon v Bosley (No 2)* [1997] 1 All ER 614.

material circumstances essential to the case, there was no difference between actively misleading the court and passively allowing it to believe that the earlier state of affairs still existed. Counsel had a duty to advise his client to disclose the new information.

If the client refused counsel's advice to disclose relevant information 'it was not, as a rule, for counsel to make the disclosure himself, but he could no longer continue to act'. The court recognised that justice might be better served by a positive duty on the advocate to break the obligation of confidentiality to the client. Nevertheless, some protection for the integrity of the process would be achieved by the non-appearance of the party's counsel. In the present case, for example, the claimant's solicitor, the defendants' advisers, and also the judge, would be alerted to the fact that something was amiss.

Lord Justice Thorpe argued that the current reform of civil justice must include 'strengthening the duty to the court'. He argued that counsel would know instinctively or intuitively that a course of action felt wrong and that, in such cases, he should not follow it. His Lordship suggested that the correct course of action was for the claimant's counsel to make disclosure to the opposing counsel in order to avoid the likelihood that injustice would be done.[31] Thorpe LJ's judgment is notable for its appeal to 'ordinary morality' as a guide to lawyers' behaviour. This failed to recognise that advocates are guided by the specific morality of their adversarial role when confronted with a question of ethics.

Lord Justice Evans dissenting, sought to blame the claimant's expert witnesses, who had given evidence in both sets of proceedings. The claimant's counsel, he said, did not mislead the court or act improperly in any way. He was particularly concerned that expert witnesses, having given their evidence, changed their minds. *Vernon v Bosley (No 2)* is authority for the proposition that the duty to the court is not discharged until after the case is concluded. This timespan arguably includes the period in which an appeal is possible, even if one has not been launched. During this period, counsel is obliged to disclose any relevant material that is not covered by client privilege or litigation privilege. This includes material relating to the sum payable in damages.

c. Procedural or Judicial Errors

Lawyers are under an obligation to point out procedural errors. In *Haiselden v P&O Properties*,[32] a litigant in person commenced an action for damages for personal injury in the County Court. The sum involved required the court to enter the case as a small claim, where no costs would be awarded. In error, the case was put on the path to trial, where the claimant was at risk of costs if the case was lost. The error remained undetected, the claimant lost the case and costs were awarded against him.

On appeal to the Court of Appeal against the award of costs, Lord Justice Thorpe said that the defendants' advocate had

> very creditably and candidly informed us that at all stages the defendants perceived the advantage to themselves of the error of the court service ... They thought that they would win on liability; they did not want an arbitration determination; they wanted determination by

---

[31] D Pannick, 'When Counsel Should Come Clean' *The Times* 14 January 1997.
[32] *Haiselden v P&O Properties* [1998] All ER (D) 180, [1998] EWCA Civ 773.

trial so that they had the prospect of recovering the costs of their defence. Accordingly they took advantage of the judicial error and felt able to do so because they considered that it was still arguable that some administrative notice of reference to arbitration needed to be issued. They comforted themselves by saying, 'if and when such a notice is issued we will then apply to the judge *inter partes* for a ruling rescinding the reference to arbitration'.[33]

The claimant succeeded in having the order for costs set aside on the basis that there should never have been a trial. The judgment did not criticise the advocate who, realising the court's mistake, had allowed the process of trial to continue. The implication, however, is that an advocate must not allow a legal process to commence or continue on an incorrect footing, for example, where there is a misapprehension as to jurisdiction. *Haiselden v P&O Properties* may suggest the courts' greater willingness to find that they have been misled.

ii. Matters not Covered by the Duty to the Court

The decisions on the duty to the court show that advocates should not allow partial evidence to create a wrong impression. The obvious case is where the information is material to the credibility of a witness. *Tombling* and *Meek*, for example, concerned the way the witness was presented to the court, not how they gave evidence in chief. The advocate could entertain doubts about the credibility of their evidence while not being obliged to speak out. Nor is there a duty to point out to an opponent, unless perhaps it is a litigant in person, that they may have made a tactical error in running their case, even though this could affect both process and outcome.

It seems likely that there will be continuing pressure to increase obligations on advocates to assist the court.[34] This is somewhat inconsistent with the trend towards greater judicial control of cases. In jurisdictions where judges have more active responsibilities, the duties of lawyers to the court are often fewer. For example, as noted in *Hall v Simons*, continental jurisdictions, Germany for example, tend not to oblige advocates to refer the court to adverse authorities.[35]

iii. Consequences of Breach of Duty

As the cases demonstrate, it is not necessary for advocates to have known that the court was being misled before the court can act.[36] In some of the cases, the lawyers involved were found to be blameless. If, however, the lawyer knows they have a duty to take action he or she must do so, even if, ultimately, it is by withdrawing from the case. Suitable cases of breach of this duty could be punished by referral of barristers to their Inn or by summary sanction in the case of solicitors. Both barristers and solicitors could be punished by wasted costs orders in suitable cases.

---

[33] ibid.
[34] C Dyer, 'Law Chief Justice urges advice for judges on sentencing limits' *The Guardian* 15 January 2007, at 15.
[35] *Arthur J S Hall & Co (a firm) v Simons* (n 2) at 682 ff.
[36] *Visham Boodoosingh v Richard Ramnarace* [2005] UKPC 9.

B. Duties to Clients

Many see the advocate's role to be presentation of their client's case in the same way as the client would if he had the skills. This presents a potential problem where the client wishes the case to be presented in a way that puts the advocate in conflict with their duty to the court. Practice has evolved so that the advocate can fulfil both sets of duties. This is illustrated by the example of the client who admits guilt but wants to plead not 'guilty'.

An advocate can represent a client who admits something that may seem damning to his case, as long as he does not mislead the court. In practical terms, this may involve requiring the prosecution to prove its case that the offence charged has been committed. In doing so, the advocate must not do anything that could mislead the court, for example, by putting the accused's inconsistent version of events to witnesses through questions.[37] The ethical justification for this approach is that it is not the advocate's role to decide who is guilty and who innocent, but for the judge or jury. Just because an argument does not convince the advocate, it does not mean it will not convince others. A pragmatic justification is that it would be inefficient if advocates had to withdraw when they suspect clients are guilty, forcing their clients to find new representation.

i. The Scope for Fearless Protection of Clients

Regarding any conflict between the client's wishes and the duty to court, the duty to the court prevails. The English barrister is not a 'hired gun' as depicted in the standard conception of the lawyer's role. In cases where clients demand conduct the advocate believes is in breach of the duty to the court, he must explain why he must refuse and what the client's options are. These will include the option of sacking that advocate.

The Bar's notion of 'fearless' advocacy is not clearly defined. It is clear, however, that the court's will is not the same as the advocate's duty. Therefore, there may be circumstances where the advocate can legitimately defy the court. In *R v G*,[38] for example, it was held that a court could not require a barrister to give an undertaking not to disclose, to a client, information discovered in a hearing he was entitled to attend.

In some circumstances, the court may impose conditions with which the advocate may have to comply in order to serve the client's interest. In *R v Davis*,[39] for example, advocates were given the option of cross-examining concealed witnesses or being able to see the witness and not describing them to their clients. The barrister could observe the duty to both court and client by seeking instructions that would allow him to see the witness without telling the client. If the client could not accept the restriction, the witness would remain obscured from the barrister's view. Obviously, the

---

[37] *R v Webber* [2004] UKHL 1; and S Nash 'Drawing Inferences from Positive Suggestions Put to Witnesses: *R v Webber*' (2004) 9(1) *International Journal of Evidence and Proof* 50.

[38] *R v G* [2004] 1 WLR.

[39] *R v Davis* [2006] EWCA Crim 1155.

court believed that, having given such an undertaking, the advocate would not reveal anything to their client.

ii. Advocates' Discretion in Handling Cases

Fearless advocacy does not imply that the advocate is directed by the client. The advocate has a wide area of discretion in handling the client's matter that is not necessarily delineated by the need to comply with the duty to the court. Within the scope of this discretion, the barrister can ignore the client's wishes. In fact, the convention is that the barrister is responsible and accountable for strategic decisions in the presentation of the case.[40] There is, for example, arguably no breach of a legal or ethical duty if an advocate refuses to call a witness the client wants to be heard but who is likely to damage the client's case.[41]

The issue of the scope of the advocates' discretion was recently considered in *R v Farooqi*,[42] where Lord Judge CJ said:

> Something of a myth about the meaning of the client's 'instructions' has developed. As we have said, the client does not conduct the case. The advocate is not the client's mouthpiece, obliged to conduct the case in accordance with whatever the client, or when the advocate is a barrister, the solicitor 'instructs' him. In short, the advocate is bound to advance the defendant's case on the basis that what his client tells him is the truth, but save for well-established principles, like the personal responsibility of the defendant to enter his own plea, and to make his own decision whether to give evidence, and perhaps whether a witness who appears to be able to give relevant admissible evidence favourable to the defendant should or should not be called, the advocate, and the advocate alone remains responsible for the forensic decisions and strategy.

This suggests that the scope of the advocate's discretion remains considerable and the scope for client preferences relatively small.

This grey area, between the client's wishes and the barrister's discretion, is relatively uncharted, but some idea of the contours can be gleaned from the cases leading up to the abolition of advocates' immunity from suit. One of the reasons underlying the advocate's immunity from client actions was the need to preserve their independence from clients. This was seen to be necessary so that advocates would observe their duty to the court.

iii. Advocates' Immunity from Actions in Negligence

In *Rondel v Worsley*,[43] advocates' immunity from actions in negligence was confirmed by the House of Lords. The appellant was convicted of causing grievous bodily harm.

---

[40] 'Duties of an Advocate to the Court' Supplementary memorandum by the General Council of the Bar (Ev 01d) to the Joint Committee on The Draft Legal Services Bill (Minutes of Evidence), particularly no 5, 'Difficult Cases'.

[41] *Arthur J S Hall & Co (a firm) v Simons* (n 2) per Lord Steyn.

[42] *R v Farooqi* [2013] EWCA Crim 1649.

[43] *Rondel v Worsley* [1969] 1 AC 191.

The respondent, a barrister, had appeared on a 'dock brief'. The appellant then issued a writ claiming damages for professional negligence against the respondent for failings in handling the evidence. On appeal, the House of Lords confirmed that the action should be struck out as disclosing no reasonable cause of action. It held that a barrister's conduct and management of litigation could not give rise to a claim for professional negligence.

The House of Lords based its decision in *Rondel v Worsley* on three public policy grounds. The first ground was that a barrister ought to be able to carry out his duty to the court fearlessly and independently. The second was that actions for negligence against barristers would inevitably amount to retrials and thus prolong litigation, contrary to the public interest. The third was that the cab rank rule obliged barristers to accept any client if a proper fee was paid and could not refuse a client on any other ground. Removing immunity from the vindictiveness of awkward clients might well undermine their willingness to take them on.

The majority in *Rondel v Worsley* found that this immunity covered work in conducting trials, or work so intimately connected with trials that it constituted a preliminary decision on the conduct of the case. Lord Upjohn, however, thought that immunity should cover letters before action onwards. The decision was applied by the Court of Appeal with startling affect in *Saif Ali v Sydney Mitchell & Co*.[44] The claimant was injured in a motor accident. His solicitors sued the wrong defendant and the action against the true defendant became statute-barred. The claimant then sued his former solicitors for negligence and they joined a barrister as third party, alleging that he was negligent in advising as to the appropriate defendant.

The Court of Appeal held that a barrister was immune from liability for negligence for all advice given upon matters which do or may lead to litigation. Advocates' immunity from negligence claims was upheld by the courts throughout the 1980s,[45] even where advocates acted against clients' express wishes when conducting cross-examination.[46] Courts would not even grant new trials where incompetent advice caused injustice.[47] Immunity from civil actions in negligence continued to be upheld by the courts through the 1990s, although the possibility that claims may lie for 'flagrant incompetence' was aired.[48]

A case that reflected changing judicial attitudes to advocates' immunity was *Acton v Graham Pearce & Co*.[49] A solicitor (A) was charged with defrauding the Law Society by using false information in legal aid claims. A claimed that he and an employee, S, had completed the forms. S produced memoranda stating that legal aid could not be claimed on some of the files. The defendant solicitors (GP) acted for A in defending the charges.

Contrary to counsel's advice and A's instructions, GP did not instruct experts to test the memoranda. Nor did they interview S's previous employers who it was known had

---

[44] *Saif Ali v Sydney Mitchell & Co* [1978] QB 95.
[45] *Somasundaram v M Julius Melchior* [1988] 1 All ER 129; *Telfer v DPP* (1996) 160 JP 512.
[46] *R v Gantam* [1988] CLY 574.
[47] *R v Ensor* [1989] 1 WLR 497.
[48] *R v Roberts* [1990] Crim LR 122.
[49] *Acton v Graham Pearce & Co* [1997] 3 All ER 909.

dismissed her. A was convicted. The conviction was overturned on appeal. A claimed damages for GP's negligent conduct of his defence in the criminal proceedings.

The Court of Appeal found that the memoranda had been prepared later than S claimed and that S was a 'pathological liar'. It held, allowing the claim, that GP did not enjoy immunity from suit. The public interest was usually against re-hearing of criminal cases in civil courts. That interest was, however, subject to the interests of justice. Damages were ordered to be assessed on the basis that, had GP acted competently, A's chances of conviction would have been 50 per cent. By 2000, advocates' immunity from civil action had been upheld and extended to actions preparing for advocacy.

In 2000, however, in *Hall v Simons*,[50] the House of Lords abolished advocates' immunity in both criminal and civil proceedings. *Hall v Simons* came to the House of Lords as three cases of negligence against solicitors in litigation that had been struck out on grounds of public policy. Lord Steyn cited various reasons for sustaining immunity. These included the dignity of the Bar, the 'cab rank' principle, the assumption that barristers may not sue for their fees, the undesirability of re-litigating cases decided or settled, and the duty of a barrister to the court'.[51] The main reason though in their Lordships' minds in *Rondel v Worsley*, he concluded, was that barristers might not observe their duty to the court if their client could hold them to account for it. This was closely followed by the risk of collateral litigation.

Lord Steyn conducted a comprehensive review of the literature, policy considerations and practice in other countries. Australia and New Zealand had followed *Rondel v Worsley* but European countries, where the duty to the court was less extensive, did not recognise immunity. US prosecutors and defenders in a few states had immunity, but not Canada. Lord Steyn regarded Canada as important since *Rondel* was considered in *Demarco v Ungaro*.[52] The Canadian court had concluded that fears that actions against barristers would undermine the public interest were 'unnecessarily pessimistic'.[53]

Lord Steyn considered the arguments for advocates' immunity unconvincing. He dismissed the risks in removing advocates' immunity as insubstantial. He was not concerned by any threat to the cab rank rule, observing that solicitor advocates had no such rule but still claimed immunity. As to the rule itself he believed:

> [I]ts impact on the administration of justice in England is not great. In real life a barrister has a clerk whose enthusiasm for the unwanted brief may not be great, and he is free to raise the fee within limits. It is not likely that the rule often obliges barristers to undertake work which they would not otherwise accept.[54]

Lord Steyn dealt in similar fashion with other arguments against removing immunity.

---

[50] *Arthur J S Hall & Co (a firm) v Simons* (n 2).

[51] See also RF Roxburgh 'Rondel v. Worsley: The Historical Background' (1968) 84 *Law Quarterly Review* 178; and RF Roxburgh, 'Rondel v. Worsley: Immunity of the Bar' (1968) 84 *Law Quarterly Review* 513.

[52] *Demarco v Ungaro* (1979) 95 DLR (3d) 385.

[53] *Arthur J S Hall & Co (a firm) v Simons* (n 2) per Lord Steyn at 683a.

[54] ibid, at 680e.

First, Lord Steyn thought that unmeritorious claims against barristers could be summarily struck out under the Civil Procedure Rules.[55] Secondly, he was not convinced that the risk of unfounded actions might negatively affect the conduct of advocates. Thirdly, he thought exposure of isolated acts of incompetence at the Bar would strengthen the legal system. Fourthly, public confidence in the legal system would be enhanced if there was no immunity. Fifthly, it was unsatisfactory that litigants, embarking on one of the most important decisions in their lives, were not usually warned of the immunity. Sixthly, it was also unsatisfactory that conduct covered by the immunity was beyond the remit of the Legal Services Ombudsman.

In the event, Lord Steyn, and the majority of the seven Law Lords hearing the case, favoured abolishing the immunity. They argued that advocates making decisions in litigation should be in the same position as other professionals facing equivalent difficult dilemmas. He cited the difficulty for a doctor faced by an Aids-infected patient who asks that his condition is not revealed to others.[56] Their Lordships acknowledged a different and broader remit for reinvestigation in criminal proceedings, but, on balance, the majority thought that immunity should be removed for both civil and criminal proceedings. Lord Hope, Lord Hutton and Lord Hobhouse dissented by holding that immunity was still required in criminal proceedings.

The House of Lords was correct in predicting that there would not be a flood of cases, but, in a few, lawyers were subject to uncomfortable examination of their performance. In *Moy v Pettman Smith (A Firm)*,[57] the House of Lords had the opportunity to consider a marginal case and clarify the scope and limits of liability. The appellant, a barrister (C), appealed against a decision holding her liable to a personal injury claimant. A payment into court had been made. C advised and framed her advice on quantum in the hope and expectation that favourable medical reports would be admitted in evidence. The claimant decided to proceed with the case. The application to adduce further medical evidence failed and the claimant consequently accepted a reduced offer.

The claimant sued his solicitors who joined C as co-defendant. The House of Lords reversed the decision of the Court of Appeal holding C negligent and liable for a proportion of the agreed damages. C's advice fell within the range of that to be expected of reasonably competent counsel of C's seniority and purported experience. Their Lordships considered it important that the courts should not stifle advocates' independence of mind and action in the manner in which they conducted litigation and advised their clients.

C. Duties to the Administration of Justice

In addition to the duty to the court, advocates have a duty to assist in the administration of justice. This is mentioned in some of the cases, but it is not always clear whether it is the same as the duty to the court. The Legal Services Act 2007 did not

---

[55] B Malkin, 'In the firing line' *The Lawyer* 3 September 2001.
[56] *Arthur J S Hall & Co (a firm) v Simons* (n 2) at 682b.
[57] *Moy v Pettman Smith (A Firm)* [2005] UKHL 7, [2005] 1 WLR 581.

clarify the issue. It imposed 'a duty to the court in question to act with independence in the interests of justice' and a duty to 'comply with relevant conduct rules … of the authorising body'.[58] The professional principles, however, state that those exercising rights of audience should 'comply with their duty to the court to act with independence in the interests of justice'.[59] This suggests that the duty of independence is co-extensive with the duty to the court and no more.

A duty to act with independence in the interests of justice suggests that advocates should not to be driven solely by client agendas. Therefore, the advocate is obliged to consider the obligation of integrity in the way cases are presented. If, as is arguable, the obligation extends beyond the duty to the court, it presumably applies to the treatment of third parties in general and to witnesses in particular. To the extent that the duty to the court is concerned with not misleading the court, these other matters are not embraced by that general duty.

i. Duties to Third Parties Generally

The risk of collateral attacks on advocates or court decisions does not only arise in negligence or solely from the advocate's own clients. Without some kind of immunity, actions in defamation could provide ample opportunity for re-litigating. The courts have therefore denied such claims, even where the alleged defamation is vexatious. A striking case, decided in 1883, was *Munster v Lamb*.[60] Lamb, a solicitor, was sued by Munster, a barrister, over unsupported allegations made in a criminal trial. Munster's house had been burgled and, it was alleged, his servants had been drugged as part of the plan. Lamb was representing the wife of the man convicted of the crime. The wife was accused of drugging the servants. Lamb alleged that the drugs had been in the house for Munster's own, criminal purposes.

The Court of Appeal held that no action could lie against Lamb, as an advocate, for defamatory words spoken in the course of a judicial tribunal. The rule was based on public policy. The principle

> requires that a judge [or counsel], in dealing with the matter before him, a party in preferring or resisting a legal proceeding, and a witness in giving evidence, oral or written, in a court of justice, shall do so with his mind uninfluenced by the fear of an action for defamation or a prosecution for libel.[61]

Even though words were uttered by the advocate maliciously, not with the object of supporting the case of his client and with no justification or excuse, immunity could be claimed from an action in defamation.

Immunity from defamation actions arising from advocacy potentially applies to any party named in court proceedings, including, as in *Munster v Lamb*, when the slandered individual is not actually appearing in the case. This immunity must apply to witnesses who are defamed by advocacy in proceedings. There is however a possibility

---

[58] LSA 2007, s 188.
[59] ibid, s 1(3)(d).
[60] *Munster v Lamb* (1883) 11 QBD 558.
[61] ibid, per Brett MR at 605.

that a witness is owed a specific duty. This could arise from the general duty to act with independence in the interests of justice or from public policy, for example, in supporting victims.

ii. Duties to Witnesses

a. Advocates' Questioning Techniques in Adversarial Trials

If advocates are obliged to observe standards of behaviour in the treatment of opposing witnesses it is not because the court may be misled. It is intrinsic to the adversarial trial that two versions of the truth are tested to see which is correct. There are a variety of reasons why there may be differences between the versions. These might stem from misunderstandings, mistaken perceptions or deliberate lying. If a witness is allowed to merely repeat a rehearsed account the testing of testimony is inadequate. It may only be when a witness is discomfited that the truth emerges. Unfortunately, giving evidence under pressure can make truthful witnesses seem unreliable.

The handling and treatment of witnesses involves achieving a delicate balance. The process is expressly intended to test and expose flaws in witnesses' accounts, thereby indicating who is telling the truth.[62] The strategies range from limiting the impact of witnesses[63] to discrediting them completely.[64] Techniques for discrediting include questioning that sets out to attack their credentials or character to exposing inconsistencies in recollection. Achieving these purposes may be assisted by a range of tactics including confronting, flustering, confusing and entrapping a witness.

There are specific conventions governing techniques of eliciting witness evidence. Examination in chief, if and when it still occurs, requires the advocate to ask open questions. This allows a witness to tell their story in a way that lends them authenticity. In cross-examination the advocate leads the opponent's witness. One of the key skills is the use of closed and leading questions often requiring 'yes' or 'no' in answer.

The use of leading questions stems from prohibitions on defence closing speeches in criminal trials, thereby forcing counsel to explain their case to the jury through their questions.[65] This may involve repeating propositions that the witness is bound to disagree with. This allows counsel to control the witness and elicit limited responses consistent with the advocate's own 'theory of the case'.[66] This behaviour would, in any other context, be regarded as bullying.

The intimidating barrage of questions in cross-examination is often combined with other techniques for discomfiting witnesses. For example, where it is suspected that a witness has 'learnt' a set of responses to probable questions, the advocate may jump around the chronological order of events in order to maximise the witness' confusion. Inconsistencies in their account may be picked upon as a basis for suggesting that they are lying.

---

[62]   Audi, 'The Ethics of Advocacy' (n 16) at 276.
[63]   E Loftus, *Eyewitness Testimony* (Cambridge, MA, Harvard University Press, 1996).
[64]   A Boon, *Advocacy*, 2nd edn (London, Cavendish Publishing Ltd, 1999).
[65]   D Cairns, *Advocacy and the Making of the Adversarial Criminal Trial 1800–1865* (Oxford, Clarendon Press, 1998) at 31.
[66]   Boon, *Advocacy* (n 64).

Given that the adversarial trial encourages attacks on a witness' credibility, honesty and motives, it is important to consider whether there are limits to the treatment that witnesses can be expected to take. One of Freedman's three hardest questions concerned discrediting a witness 'known' to be truthful. His example, however, provides the advocate with ample excuse for such an approach.[67] Pepper argues that truthful witnesses should always be challenged if it is necessary to the client's case.

In *Rondell v Worsley*, Lord Reid expressed the advocate's duty in questioning witnesses as follows:

[E]very counsel has a duty to his client fearlessly to raise every issue, advance every argument, and ask every question, however distasteful, which he thinks will help his client's case. But ... counsel ... must not lend himself to casting aspersions on the other party or witnesses for which there is no sufficient basis in the information in his possession[68]

If, as seems likely, the information in counsel's possession is his own client's account of events, Lord Reid's limitation on the advocate's discretion is slight. It potentially allows broad scope for attacking a potentially truthful witness quite forcefully. There are, however, increasing limitations imposed on advocates with the aim of protecting witnesses. Some apply to all witnesses and others apply only to special categories.

b. Vulnerable Witnesses

There are special cases where cross-examination of witnesses has caused particular problems. Such categories include cases involving children, people with learning difficulties and rape victims.[69]

Rape Victims

The low conviction rate for alleged rape was a blot on the reputation of the courts.[70] One of the problems is the reluctance of alleged victims to enter the court system. This caused the Attorney General to mandate prosecutors to support alleged victims of rape at all stages of the case.[71]

Statistics for rape are controversial. The number of reported cases has risen dramatically, but conviction rates are based on cases that are actually instigated. On this basis, figures released by the Crown Prosecution Service for 2012/13 showed that there were 3,692 prosecutions for rape in the previous year, resulting in 2,333 convictions.[72] This, at 63 per cent, was the highest recorded conviction rate for rape prosecutions on record. To the extent that this is a reliable indicator of successful prosecution

---

[67] S Pepper, 'The Lawyers' Amoral Ethical Role: A Defense, A Problem and Some Possibilities' (1986) *American Bar Foundation Research Journal* 613.

[68] *Rondell v Worsley* [1969] 1 AC 191, per Lord Reid at 227.

[69] L Ellison, 'The Mosaic Art?: Cross Examination and the Vulnerable Witness' (2001) 21 *Legal Studies* 353.

[70] C Dyer, 'Judges try to block rape reforms' *Guardian* 23 January 2007, at 1; R Ford, '"Betrayal of Justice" as rapists walk free' *Timesonline* 30 March 2006.

[71] The Rt Hon Lord Goldsmith, *Statement by the Attorney General, The Prosecutors' Pledge* (London, Office of the Attorney General, 2006); L Ellison, 'Witness Preparation and the Prosecution of Rape' (2007) 27 *Legal Studies* 171, at 185.

[72] O Bowcott, 'Rape conviction rate at an all-time high' *The Guardian* 23 April 2013.

strategies,[73] it must be partly due to continuing efforts to reduce the intimidation effect of the court experience on victims.

Particular problems arise when victims of rape are required to give evidence. The need to balance the rights of alleged victims against those of the accused provides scope for defence tactics that are sometimes abusive. Representing a defendant on a rape charge where the defence is consent is a minefield for advocates. There is often no independent evidence to corroborate the account of either party, so it is one person's word against another. A common defence strategy is to undermine victims' credibility by focusing on their past sexual history. This may allow the defence to present a victim as promiscuous and, therefore, more likely to have consented. Alleged victims are often subject to long cross-examination by defence advocates, and by different advocates when there are multiple defendants.

In rape cases, judges sometimes ignore the fact that they demand that advocates have wide discretion in the presentation of cases. The system allows advocates to present the case as the client wants, even if the advocate's own judgement differs.[74] Advocates tend not to be blamed for the tactics that form part of this approach. In delivering convictions for a gang rape, the judge in one case said to the defendants that, 'outrageous suggestions were put to her (the victim) on your instructions. You, not your counsel, added insult to injury and heaped further humiliation on her'.[75]

The treatment of victims giving evidence was brought to a head by the former practice of allowing men accused of rape conduct their own defence. Defendants in person could 'abuse the rules in relation to relevance and repetition which apply when witnesses are questioned'.[76] Changes in the rules followed one such case. In *JM v United Kingdom*, the applicant took her case against the UK authorities to the European Court for Human Rights.[77] She had been brutally raped over a period of time. At the trial, the accused cross-examined the victim for six days, wearing the same clothes used in the attack. After this ordeal, the victim was admitted to hospital.

The claim in *JM v United Kingdom* against the UK was settled before it could be heard by the European Court for Human Rights. Subsequently, measures were introduced to prevent cross-examination of protected witnesses, including rape complainants, by the accused in person.[78] Courts were required to appoint, as advocates, lawyers chosen either by the accused or, in default, by the court, to conduct cross-examination.[79] It is often said, however, that rape victims suffer as much from the questioning of opposing lawyers as from that of the accused.

There were two legislative attempts to control the introduction of prejudicial sexual history into rape trials. The first attempt having failed,[80] the Youth Justice and Criminal Evidence Act 1999, section 41 provided that, at a trial a person charged with

---

[73] R Whiston, 'How the Panic over Rape was Orchestrated' *Straight Statistics* 2 September 2009 (http://straightstatistics.org/article/how-panic-over-rape-was-orchestrated).

[74] D Pannick, *Advocates* (Oxford, Oxford University Press 1992) 92–93.

[75] *The Guardian* 24 August 1996, at 5.

[76] *R v Milton Brown* [1998] EWCA Crim 1486.

[77] *JM v United Kingdom* App No 41518/98 Unreported 28 Sept 2000 (ECHR), *The Lawyer* 29 October 1996; and see also *R v Ralston Edwards* [1997] EWCA Crim 1679.

[78] Youth Justice and Criminal Evidence Act 1999, ss 34–35.

[79] ibid, s 38.

[80] Sexual Offences (Amendment) Act 1976.

a sexual offence, 'except with the leave of the court, no evidence may be adduced, and no question may be asked in cross-examination by or on behalf of any accused at the trial, about any sexual behaviour of the complainant'.[81] Before giving leave to admit any evidence or question, the court had to be satisfied that refusal might render a conclusion of the jury or the court unsafe on any relevant issue.

To be considered for admission as relevant, evidence of behaviour of the complainant has to be so similar to the circumstances in the case that it could not reasonably be explained as a coincidence.[82] When the issue is an issue of consent, it must take place at or about the same time as the event which is the subject matter of the charge. The behaviour sought to be admitted in evidence must be similar to the behaviour complained of in the case. No evidence or question is to be admitted if it appears to the court that the purpose for which it would be adduced or asked is to establish or elicit material for impugning the credibility of the complainant as a witness.

The Youth Justice and Criminal Evidence Act 1999 at least represented an attempt to ensure that evidence of sexual history was relevant and probative. The defence was also required to notify the prosecution that sexual history would be an issue within 28 days of committal. The notice has to provide a summary of the evidence and details of the questions to be asked. [83] It must also explain how the behaviour falls into the exceptional categories.

Research by Kelly, Temkin and Griffiths evaluated the impact of the Youth Justice and Criminal Evidence Act during a three- month period in 2003. The study examined 400 rape cases before Crown Courts in England and Wales, finding a suspiciously high level of cases where victims' sexual history was admitted into evidence.[84] Applications to introduce sexual history were made in almost one-quarter of cases and were successful in two-thirds of these. In many cases there was no application in writing before the trial.

Kelly et al found that lawyers deliberately flouted the rules by applying, at trial, to have evidence of the complainant's behaviour admitted in evidence. The defence suffered no penalty by applying late and did not have to prepare the required written notices. They were also able to put the victim under maximum pressure by delaying giving notice. The research concluded that many victims were subject to inappropriate cross-examination on their sexual history as a result of the devious tactics of defence barristers and the ignorance of some judges. Barristers admitted to poring over medical records 'for dirt-digging opportunities', one saying 'When I'm defending it's no holds barred'.[85]

A further attempt to limit the scope for introducing prejudicial evidence was made in the Criminal Justice Act 2003, sections 98–113. This updated and abolished the common law rules on admitting evidence of the bad character of non-defendants. 'Non-defendants' are not defined in the Act but probably include victims, the deceased in cases of homicide, witnesses, police officers who have been involved in the

---

[81] Youth Justice and Criminal Evidence Act 1999, ss 38 and s 41(1).
[82] ibid, s 41(3)
[83] Crown Court Rules 1982, as amended, r 23D.
[84] L Kelly, J Temkin and S Griffiths, *Section 41: An Evaluation of New Legislation Limiting Sexual History in Rape Trials* (London, Home Office, 2006).
[85] F Abrams, 'Haunted by the Past' *The Guardian* (G2) 29 May 2001, at 16.

case, third parties who are not witnesses in the case and defence witnesses. The Act provided that bad character is admissible only if it is important explanatory evidence and has substantial probative value in relation to a matter of substantial importance in the context of the case as a whole.[86]

The Youth Justice and Criminal Evidence Act 1999, section 41 continues to apply where the sexual behaviour claimed to be relevant is also 'bad character' evidence. This means that in a trial for a sexual offence, evidence of a complainant's previous sexual behaviour, which is also 'bad character' evidence, will have to satisfy both statutory tests. In the light of continuing controversy over the handling of vulnerable witnesses, the Bar introduced a training course for barristers involved in rape cases, aimed at ensuring they deal with the issues more sensitively.[87]

Children

Another category of vulnerable witnesses where lawyers' questioning techniques have excited much controversy is children.[88] There is an argument that many of the familiar techniques of cross-examination should not apply in examining child witnesses, because they can be suggestible and easily confused.[89] The suitable level of questioning is always a matter of degree, depending on the child's age and capacity. The courts have become increasingly flexible on the issue. Generally, it is expected that the level of questioning used by defence advocates is to be adapted according to a reasonable assessment of the child witness' age and capacity.

Questioning is one of the issues that should be discussed in a meeting to determine the 'judge's ground rules' for how cases involving children will run. This meeting should be scheduled before the main case begins. It will deal with issues such as use of video feeds and intermediaries to elicit children's oral testimony.

In *R v Barker*, the Court of Appeal held that a child aged four at time of trial could be a competent witness to a rape that had allegedly occurred when the child was two.[90] Obviously, there were restrictions on cross-examination in such cases because of the risk of a child acquiescing to leading questions. The Lord Chief Justice observed:

> [T]he competency test is not failed because the forensic techniques of the advocate (in particular in relation to cross-examination) ... have to be adapted to enable the child to give the best evidence of which he or she is capable ... When the issue is whether the child is lying or mistaken in claiming that the defendant behaved indecently towards him or her, it should not be over-problematic for the advocate to formulate short, simple questions which put the essential elements of the defendant's case to the witness, and fully to ventilate before the jury the areas of evidence which bear on the child's credibility. Aspects of evidence which undermine or are believed to undermine the child's credibility must, of course, be revealed to the jury, but it is not necessarily appropriate for them to form the subject matter of detailed cross-examination of the child and the advocate may have to forego much of the kind of

---

[86] Criminal Justice Act 2003, s 100.

[87] A Travis, 'Barristers and judges accused of undermining rape reform' *The Guardian* 21 June 2006.

[88] L Tickle, '"Why are you lying?" demands the barrister. Is this the way to treat a child alleging rape?' *The Observer* 19 May 2013.

[89] JR Spencer and ME Lamb (eds), *Children and Cross-Examination: Time to Change the Rules?* (Oxford, Hart Publishing, 2012).

[90] *R v Barker* [2010] EWCA Crim 4, at [40].

contemporary cross-examination which consists of no more than comment on matters which will be before the jury in any event from different sources.[91]

In *R v Wills*, the grounds of appeal were that the appellant's counsel had followed the judge's ground rules for cross-examining the young teenage witnesses whereas a co-defendant's counsel had not.[92] The Court of Appeal found no substance in that complaint, but laid down guidelines for questioning in such cases. These were that limitations on questioning must be clearly defined. The judge should explain the limitations to the jury, and reasons for them, and ensure that they are complied with. If an advocate fails to comply with limitations, the judge should give relevant directions to the jury at the time. Any inconsistencies should be commented on after, not during, cross-examination.

In the light of the practice developed by the courts, the Judicial College for England and Wales has issued a checklist for benches dealing with child cases.[93] On the issue of questioning this provides that advocates should adapt questions to a child's developmental stage, enabling each child to give their 'best evidence'. Invariably this involves asking short, simple questions, one idea at a time, and following a logical sequence. Advocates are required to speak slowly, pause and allow a child enough time to process questions. In the case of younger children, the guidance suggests allowing almost twice as much time as usual. The child must be allowed a full opportunity to answer.

The judicial guidance directs that advocates should avoid question types that may produce unreliable answers. These include 'tag' questions, for example, 'He didn't touch you, did he?'. These are said to be particularly complex for children to process. Advocates are told to put such questions more directly, for example, 'Did Jim touch you?', and, if the answer is 'yes', to continue 'How did Jim touch you?'. It is suggested that children are not asked to demonstrate intimate touching on their body, but are asked to use a body diagram instead.

Courts have developed limits on the kind of questions a victim can be asked in court and restrictions on aggressive questioning. There were, however, no limits on how long a victim could be questioned or by how many people. In 2013, the Ministry of Justice announced another review of the hostile tactics sometimes used by defence barristers. This was to consider whether victims should have to answer the same question put by more than one barrister and whether fresh guidance was needed for judges.

The Minister raised concerns about the treatment of victims of a child prostitution ring in Telford, Shropshire, in court. One girl witness was aggressively cross-examined for 12 days by seven different defence barristers. They took it in turns to accuse her of lying and left her in tears on the stand. One defence barrister walked out in protest at the conduct of cross-examination by colleagues. Pending the Minister's review, the Crown Prosecution Service produced interim guidelines addressing the issue of multi-defendant trials.

---

[91] ibid, at [42].

[92] *R v Wills* [2011] EWCA Crim 1938.

[93] Courts and Tribunals Judiciary, *Judicial College Bench Checklist: Young Witness Cases* (January 2012) (www.judiciary.gov.uk/publications-and-reports/guidance/2012/jc-bench-checklist-young-wit-cases).

The interim guidelines produced by the Crown Prosecution Service for child sexual abuse trials urge that the issue of multiple defence advocates be dealt with at the 'ground rules hearings'.[94] The defence advocates should agree who will be the lead counsel to put questions to the victim and the length of time given to the cross-examination. Where children are involved as witnesses, courts can consider applications for special measures made by the party calling the witness. The decision as to whether the special measure applied for is granted is a matter for the court.

The interim guidelines also state that

> in multi-defendant cases the judge should be asked to consider whether repeat cross-examination on similar points should be restricted. Being accused of lying, particularly if repeated, may cause the witness to give inaccurate answers, or to agree to false suggestions, simply to bring questioning to an end. It may also have a longer term damaging impact on the child or young person. If such a challenge is essential, it should be addressed separately, in simple language, at the end of cross-examination.[95]

D. Summary

Advocates owe complex duties. They are accountable to their client and to the court. They also owe a duty to act with independence in the interests of justice. This obligation is arguably large than the duty to the court and includes an obligation to treat witnesses fairly. This is always a matter of degree. Being cross-examined by an effective advocate can be a bruising and chastening experience. Care must be taken to protect vulnerable witnesses while also protecting the rights of the accused. In an adversarial system, there will always be questions about whether the rules strike the correct balance between fairness to victims and the right to a robust defence.

IV. Regulation

A. Education and Training

The vocational courses for both barristers and solicitors assess the skill of advocacy, but together with a particular focus on evidence, the Bar requires more extensive coverage.

---

[94] CPS, *Interim Guidelines on Prosecuting Cases of Child Sexual Abuse* (June 2013) at para 89 (www.cps.gov.uk/consultations/csa_consultation.html#a16).
[95] ibid, at para 92.

i. Solicitors

The Legal Practice Course (LPC) advocacy component is of equal weighting to the other skills taught on the course and is assessed on the basis of competence. There are three specific advocacy outcomes for the course, with two relating to case preparation and two for presentation.[96] The advocacy outcomes provide that students should understand the importance of preparation and the best way to undertake it, and understand the basic skills in the presentation of cases before courts and tribunals.

The case preparation element involves preparing a submission and identifying, analysing and assessing the purpose and tactics of examination, cross-examination and re-examination to adduce, rebut and clarify evidence. The two presentation outcomes are identifying, analysing and assessing the specific communication skills and techniques employed by a presenting advocate and demonstrating an understanding of the ethics, etiquette and conventions of advocacy. All of these outcomes can be achieved without performing advocacy.

The LPC outcomes only require one performance in presentation or advocacy. This is the formulation and presentation of 'a coherent submission based upon facts, general principles and legal authority in a structured, concise and persuasive manner'.[97] This is fairly slight when compared, for example, to the six elements and 22 outcomes devoted to writing and drafting, many of which require performance. Following the LPC, solicitors undertake further advocacy training in the Professional Skills Course. It is understood that trainees have to be extremely poor to fail this element.

ii. Barristers

Responding to the challenge from solicitor advocates, the Bar sought to increase the focus on advocacy training. Internal reports for the Bar prepared by the Collyear and Dutton Working Parties both suggested a revamp of advocacy training.[98] Barristers were also perceived to need more advocacy exposure than previously because of the dearth of smaller cases for pupils. Dutton noted that 3–5 per cent of pupils on subsequent advocacy training were not competent to represent clients in court.[99] The conclusion was that the Inns combine to provide training and that advocacy should be assessed on the Bar Vocational Course (BVC).

Following the Elias Working Party in 2001, significantly more hours were devoted to advocacy on the BVC, covering a greater range of trial tasks. Each BVC student had to have 50–60 hours of advocacy training delivered in 12 sessions, with two advocacy assessments covering written arguments, interventions from the bench and witness handling. Together these elements were to comprise 20 per cent of the course

---

[96] SRA, *Legal Practice Course Outcomes 2011*, at 24 (www.sra.org.uk/students/lpc.page).

[97] ibid.

[98] J Collyear, *Blueprint for the Future* (London, General Council of the Bar, 1999); T Dutton QC, *Advocacy Training at the Bar of England and Wales: Organisation, Delivery and Outcomes* (London, General Council of the Bar, 2002) (Dutton 1).

[99] Dutton 1, *Advocacy Training at the Bar of England and Wales* (n 98) at para 85.

mark.[100] The BVC also assessed all skills, including advocacy, on a graded basis, thereby identifying outstanding potential. The hours of advocacy training undertaken by pupils were increased from nine to twelve hours and assessment, leading to the award of a certificate of competence in a number of areas. The Advocacy Certificate covered case analysis, use of skeleton arguments, oral submissions, examination in chief and cross-examination.[101]

The hours of training for newly qualified barristers on the New Practitioners' Programme[102] were increased from six to nine for all barristers commencing practice after 1997, including employed lawyers. The diverse training provided by the Inns and circuits were brought together under one organisation, the Advocacy Training Council, which was to standardise materials and training of instructors. The review of the BVC conducted by the Wood Working Party did not recommend any substantial changes to the teaching of advocacy, except that all teachers and assessors passed a special training course.[103]

The BPTC learning outcomes for advocacy are far more extensive that the LPC equivalent. Students must be able to prepare a case effectively, understand the relevant law, facts and principles, observe the rules of professional conduct and plan the advocacy task in question, demonstrate basic advocacy skills in a range of civil and criminal scenarios, in applications and in trials, and before a range of tribunals.[104] They must prepare and deliver an opening speech, a closing speech, an unopposed submission and an opposed submission. They must also be able to examine, cross-examine and re-examine witnesses and meet the minimum required competency standards for Level 1 Advocates under the Quality Assurance Scheme for Advocates (QASA).

The Bar's continuing emphasis on advocacy at the vocational stage, and subsequently, gives barristers a significant lead in advocacy over solicitors at qualification. This is justification for the fact that solicitors continue to only achieve equality of access to courts by obtaining a 'higher rights' qualification.

B. Authorisation

i. Barristers

a. Initial Authorisation

The Courts and Legal Services Act 1990 preserved existing rights of audience of barristers in all courts and approved the Bar Council's arrangements for training advocates. Barristers who complete all stages of education and training are called to

---

[100] Elias J, *Report of the BVC Re-specification Working Party* (London, General Council of the Bar, 2001).

[101] T Dutton QC, *Report on the Assessment of Advocacy* (London, General Council of the Bar, 2004) (Dutton 2).

[102] The Continuing Professional Development Regulations 2001, paras 1–2.

[103] BSB, *Review of the Bar Vocational Course: Report of the Working Group* (London, BSB, 2008).

[104] BSB, *Bar Professional Training Course: Course Specification Requirements and Guidance* (2012) at para 2.2.1(c).

the Bar. They can then offer advocacy services in all courts, provided that they are working in the office of a qualified person. When they have maintained a practice for three years they can offer advocacy services in all courts.

b. Right to Undertake Criminal Advocacy

In addition to having a higher rights qualification for criminal courts, barristers can only undertake criminal advocacy if they are approved for that purpose under the QASA. This scheme began with a working group established by the Legal Services Commission. The purpose was to control the standard of criminal advocacy funded by legal aid. At the suggestion of the Legal Services Board the embryonic scheme was handed over to the BSB, SRA and ILEX to develop in 2009, and a Joint Advocacy Group (JAG) was established.

The QASA Handbook for Criminal Advocates, published by the three regulators, provides that criminal advocates must be accredited at one of four levels in order to conduct criminal advocacy. Level 1 covers magistrates' court and youth court work. The other three levels are all for Crown Court work. Level 4 covers the most serious and complex Crown Court cases, for example, serious sexual offences, substantial child abuse and murder.

Persons regulated by the three regulators are qualified to become accredited at level 1 by virtue of completing the education and training qualifications to enter their respective professions.[105] This initial accreditation expires after five years. In order to re-accredit, advocates must complete advocacy-focused, assessed CPD to satisfy level 1 requirements and prove to the regulator that they satisfy the requirements.[106] Advocates who fail to re-accredit after five years drop out of the scheme and cannot, thereafter, perform criminal advocacy. Accreditation for subsequent levels is dealt with below.

ii. Solicitors

a. Advocacy Rights on Qualification

Solicitors were given audience in the County Courts when introduced in 1834 and have automatic rights of audience in many courts and tribunals on qualification. These include the right to appear in all hearings in the County Court and Magistrates Courts and House of Lords.[107] They can also appear in all hearings in chambers in the High Court and the Court of Appeal. They may appear in formal or unopposed proceedings before a judge in open court. They can also appear before the High Court bankruptcy judge, the Companies Court registrar and in some family proceedings.

---

[105] BSB, SRA and ILEX Professional Standards, *QASA Handbook for Criminal Advocates* (September 2013) at para 2.14.
[106] ibid, at para 2.16.
[107] See further A Thornton, 'The Professional Responsibility and Ethics of the English Bar' in R Cranston (ed), *Legal Ethics and Professional Responsibility* (Oxford, Oxford University Press, 1995) at 57.

b. Higher Rights of Audience

Solicitors do not have automatic rights of audience in the higher courts, the High Court and Court of Appeal, on qualification. The initial regime for acquiring the right to appear before higher courts required three years' practical experience of advocacy.[108] Solicitors had to establish either that they had 'appropriate judicial or higher court advocacy experience' or recent, extensive and 'suitable experience'. For the second route, solicitors had to show the range, frequency, regularity and quality' of advocacy experience. This had to cover the period in the two years preceding the application.[109] The Criminal Proceedings Qualification required appearances in magistrates' court criminal work, bail applications, adjournment applications, committals, summary trials and guilty pleas, including summary offences, either way offences and indictable offences.[110] The Civil Proceedings Qualification demanded an equivalent range of County Court work, including contested trials.[111] Two references from members of the judiciary, the court service or the legal profession able to offer informed opinions were also required.[112]

This qualified them to proceed to either, the Test of Evidence and Procedure in the Higher Criminal Courts and/or the Test of Evidence and Procedure in the Higher Civil Courts. Passing the test was only the prerequisite to attending the appropriate course(s). These were the Higher Criminal Courts Advocacy Training Course and the Higher Civil Courts Advocacy Training Course.[113] Both courses were provided by authorised and monitored providers.

The course requirements, content and assessment appeared demanding.[114] Participants were required to prepare an action for trial, develop a case presentation strategy, identify admissible evidence, examine, cross-examine and re-examine witnesses, draft pleadings relevant to the conduct of proceedings in the relevant courts including applications for leave to appeal and notices of appeal. Participants were sent home if they had not completed preliminary reading, including consulting ethics sources. The minimum duration of the course was 34 hours, of which 17 hours were spent on oral and written practical exercises.[115] These formed the basis for assessment.[116]

In 2007, the SRA consulted on whether it should continue to maintain a separate qualification regime to exercise rights of audience in the higher courts. It proposed securing standards in some other way, possibly though a voluntary quality assurance mechanism. Despite receiving a majority of responses in favour of the proposals, the SRA decided not to proceed.

Rather than abolish the higher rights regime, through various iterations, it was adjusted. It is now found in the SRA Higher Rights of Audience Regulations 2011.[117]

[108] The Higher Courts Qualification Regulations 1992, reg 2 (Applications).
[109] ibid, sch 2(2).
[110] ibid, sch 2(5).
[111] ibid, sch 2(6).
[112] ibid, sch 2(1).
[113] ibid, reg 6(2).
[114] ibid, sch 4.
[115] ibid, sch 4(3).
[116] ibid, sch 4(4).
[117] SRA, Higher Rights of Audience Regulations 2011 (www.sra.org.uk/solicitors/handbook/higherrights/content.page).

These require that those seeking the higher rights qualifications must still demonstrate competence to undertake advocacy in the relevant type of proceedings by successfully completing assessments prescribed by the SRA.[118] The SRA issued detailed standards against which the competence of those applying for a qualification could be assessed.[119]

The current version of higher rights standards comprises seven standards relating to ethics. These appear to represent a strange selection of priorities, and notable omissions. For example, three standards require solicitors to advise clients on the most suitable representation for their matter, deal with issues arising from disclosure of confidential or privileged information and comply with courtroom etiquette. It is not clear why these areas have been chosen while others have not. Handling vulnerable witnesses, for example, appears as a standard for trial advocacy, but not as an ethical issue.

As regards the remaining SRA ethics standards for higher rights qualification, there seems to be some overlap. Solicitors are required to advise on situations where, as advocates, they may become a witness. This is a situation of professional embarrassment, but a separate standard requires that they recognise situations of professional embarrassment creating a need for withdrawal. Another overlap arises in relation to a standard requiring advice to clients on the need to draw unfavourable authorities to the attention of the court. Yet, another standard relates to resolving conflicts created by the advocate's duty to the court, of which disclosing unfavourable authorities is clearly an example.

Under the SRA Higher Rights of Audience Regulations 2011, any solicitor or Registered European Lawyer who wishes to exercise rights of audience in the higher courts must pass a compulsory advocacy assessment. This is administered by one from a list of approved assessing organisations. It is not clear whether the assessment has become easier since the initial higher rights regime was introduced, the details of the assessment having not been revealed. They must also include at least five hours of higher court advocacy related CPD in each of the first five years of qualification.[120]

c. Right to Undertake Criminal Advocacy

The completed version of the QASA Handbook for Criminal Advocates is now included in the SRA Handbook as the SRA Quality Assurance Scheme for Advocates (Crime) Regulations 2013.[121] The Regulations prohibit advocates from accepting work at a level for which they are not qualified. There are limited exceptions. An example of an exception to the experience requirement is that advocates may accept a case, despite not having the relevant level accreditation, where they have subject expertise not usually required for criminal work.

---

[118] ibid, reg 4.1.
[119] SRA, *Statement of Standards for Solicitor Higher Court Advocates* (www.sra.org.uk/solicitors/accreditation/higher-rights/competence-standards.page).
[120] SRA, Higher Rights of Audience Regulations 2011, reg 9.
[121] SRA, Quality Assurance Scheme for Advocates (Crime) Regulations 2013, reg 2.3.

iii. Legal Executives

ILEX Fellows can qualify as Chartered Legal Executive Advocates. Members establish eligibility based on knowledge and experience and then successfully complete the relevant skills course within 12 months.[122] ILEX Professional Standards (IPS) is responsible for accrediting course providers seeking to deliver advocacy skills courses. The accreditation process involves an assessment to ensure that courses will meet the course outcomes and assessment criteria under the scheme. IPS also monitors course provision and ensures that advocates undertake regular CPD. Successful advocates are awarded Advocacy Certificates authorising them to practise as Chartered Legal Executive Advocates in the practice area in which they hold a certificate. There are two rights of audience certificates, one relating to general civil matters and the other to family matters.[123]

A Rights of Audience (Civil Proceedings) Certificate enables the holder to appear in open court in the County Court in all actions, except family proceedings.[124] He can also appear before magistrates, District Judges (Magistrates' Court) or Justices' Legal Advisers in the Magistrates' Courts in relation to all civil and enforcement matters. Finally he can appear before any tribunal having jurisdiction in England and Wales listed in Schedule 6 of the Tribunals, Courts and Enforcement Act 2007.

A Rights of Audience (Family Proceedings) Certificate enables an ILEX Fellow to exercise rights of audience similar to those exercised by solicitors and barristers in certain courts. They may appear in all matters in all County Court family proceedings, before Justices or a District Judge (Magistrates' Court), in the Family Proceedings Courts and before Coroners' Courts.

C. Conduct Rules

i. Barristers

a. A Brief History of Conduct Rules for Advocacy

The Bar's Code of Conduct was first created in 1981. The ethical rules focused heavily on advocacy and were substantially drawn from two lectures, delivered by Sir Malcom Hilbery and subsequently published as *Duty and Art in Advocacy.*[125] A contemporary review observed that although

> the learned judge has little new to say on this topic he puts the moral code which should govern the advocate at once clearly and unflinchingly and does not hesitate to refer to the failures in this respect of lawyers as eminent as the late Lord Birkenhend.[126]

---

[122] ILEX Professional Standards, Rights to Conduct Litigation and Rights of Audience Certification Rules 2011, r 53.
[123] ibid, r 4.
[124] ibid, r 6.
[125] Hilbery, *Duty and Art in Advocacy* (n 21).
[126] Reviews (1948) 11(2) *Modern Law Review* 240.

From the review we can see that Hilbery's summary was already conventional wisdom, but more clearly conveyed than had been achieved previously. He dealt with the issue of advocacy and particularly the management of the duty to the court. The Bar Code of Conduct was considerably developed over subsequent editions, but the main changes were to regulatory material. Hilbery's ethical core was retained. The rules were supplemented by the Bar Written Standards of Work. These were somewhat repetitive of the Code, but contained much useful additional information.

b. BSB Handbook and Bar Code 2014

The new Bar Code of Conduct incorporates rules that were well established in previous versions. It also includes much relevant material from the Written Standards of Work as guidance. This makes for a more logical and convenient organisation of material, although the paragraph numbering of outcomes, rules and guidance is extremely confusing. The essence of Hilbery's analysis of the ethical core of the advocate's role is retained.

It may be significant that the first chapter of the new Bar Code is 'You and the Court'. The chapter has five outcomes. The final outcome is that the public has confidence in the administration of justice and in those who serve it.[127] This, logically, should precede the other outcomes, all of which emphasise the subsidiarity of client loyalty to the duty to the court.

The first outcome in Chapter 1 is that the court is able to rely on information provided to it by those conducting litigation and by advocates who appear before it[128] and the second that the proper administration of justice is served.[129] The third outcome is that the interests of justice are protected to the extent compatible with the previous two outcomes and the core duties.[130] The remaining outcome is that clients and others appearing before the court understand clearly the duties the advocate owes to the court and the circumstances in which client duties are overridden.[131] Chapter 1 is then divided into two parts. The first part is un-headed, and deals with the duty to the court. The second part is headed 'not abusing your role as advocate'.

The main rule in the first part of Chapter 1 provides that 'You owe a duty to the court to act with independence in the interests of justice. This duty overrides any inconsistent obligations which you may have (other than obligations under the criminal law)'.[132] The rule continues to outline three specific obligations applying to barristers acting as advocate. These are: not knowingly or recklessly misleading or attempting to mislead the court, avoiding wasting the court's time and acting independently.

The duty to act independently includes drawing to the attention of the court any decision or provision which may be adverse to the interests of the client.[133] This is said to be particularly important when appearing against a litigant who is not legally

[127] BSB, *Handbook 2014*, pt 2: *The Code of Conduct*, oC5.
[128] ibid, oC1.
[129] ibid, oC2.
[130] ibid, oC3.
[131] ibid, oC4.
[132] ibid, rC3.
[133] ibid, gC5.

represented. The core rules on the duty to the court in Chapter 1 are, first, that the duty to act in the best interests of each client is subject to duty to the court[134] and, second, that the duty to the court does not require breaching client confidentiality.[135]

The guidance to the first chapter of the new Bar Code reflects the longstanding advice on presenting cases the barrister does not believe in. The guidance makes it clear that the duty to the court does not prevent presenting a client's case 'simply because you do not believe that the facts are as your client states them to be (or as you, on your client's behalf, state them to be)', as long as any positive case put forward accords with instructions and does not involve misleading the court.[136]

Barristers are advised to draw a witness' attention to evidence conflicting with what the witness is saying and to indicate that the court may find testimony difficult to accept.[137] But, if the witness maintains that the evidence is true, having recorded the fact on the witness statement, the barrister does not mislead the court by calling the witness to confirm their witness statement. In circumstances where a conflict with the duty to the court forces a barrister to withdraw from a case, he must not disclose confidential information obtained in the course of the instructions to the court unless the client authorises disclosure.[138] This would include the reason for withdrawal.

Another issue dealt with in the guidance to Chapter 1 is a situation where the client admits to having committed the crime charged. The guidance provides that this admission must not be disclosed to the court without the client's consent. It continues by noting that the barrister does not mislead the court if, after a plea of 'not guilty' is entered, the barrister goes on to test in cross-examination the reliability of the evidence of the prosecution witnesses. The barrister may then address the jury to the effect that the prosecution had not succeeded in making them sure of the client's guilt.[139]

The guidance explains that it is improper to set up a positive case inconsistent with a confession. This could include suggesting to a prosecution witness that the client did not commit the crime, calling the client to give evidence that he did not commit the crime or submitting to the jury that the client did not commit the crime. It would also be inconsistent with the admission to suggest that anyone else had committed the crime or to put forward an alibi.[140]

Conflicts between duties to clients and to the court must be resolved in favour of the duty to the court. When the barrister learns confidential information in the course of instructions he must seek the client's permission to disclose it to the court.[141] The example provided in the guidance is where the prosecution is unaware of a client's previous convictions. In cases where mandatory sentences apply, non-disclosure will result in the court failing to pass the sentence that is required by law. If the client does

---

[134] ibid, rC4.
[135] ibid, rC5.
[136] ibid, gC7.
[137] ibid.
[138] ibid, gC8.
[139] ibid, gC9.
[140] ibid, gC10.
[141] ibid, gC11.

not consent to disclosure of the conviction, the barrister must cease to act but cannot inform the court of the convictions.

If the case is one where mandatory sentences do not apply, and a client does not consent to disclosure of previous convictions, a barrister can continue to represent provided the court is not misled. This means that the barrister is unable to say anything about previous good character in mitigation. If the court asks direct questions the barrister should withdraw rather than give an untruthful answer.[142]

The only example in the chapter not drawn from a criminal context relates to disclosure of a document that should have been disclosed, but has not been. The barrister must not continue to act unless the client agrees to the disclosure. If the client refuses the barrister must withdraw but not reveal the existence or contents of the document to the court.[143]

As regards the second part of Chapter 1, 'Not abusing your role as advocate', the main rule guards against misuse of the immunity from defamation claims and other abuses from the nineteenth century.[144] This rule comprises four prohibitions. The first prohibits making statements or asking questions merely to insult, humiliate or annoy a witness or any other person. The second prohibits making serious allegations against a cross-examined witness unless the witness was given a chance to answer the allegation in cross-examination.

The third prohibition concerns making a serious allegation against any person, or suggesting that a person is guilty of a crime with which the client is charged. This is allowed but only if there are reasonable grounds for the allegation and it is relevant to the client's case or to the credibility of a witness. Where the allegation relates to a third party, such person must not be named in open court unless this is reasonably necessary. The fourth prohibition is putting forward to the court a personal opinion of the facts or the law, unless the barrister is invited or required to do so by the court or by law.

Other provisions of the new Bar Code relating to witnesses are mainly concerned with witness integrity. The rule comprises a number of prohibitions that rather go without saying. Therefore, barristers must not encourage a witness to give misleading or untruthful evidence, or rehearse, practise with or coach a witness, or communicate with witnesses while they give evidence or pay witnesses contingent on evidence or on the outcome of the case.[145]

As can be seen, the presence of the client does not loom large in the new Bar Code. Chapter 3, 'You and Your Client', tends to focus on the mundane, receiving a competent standard of work and service[146] and understanding how to bring complaints,[147] rather than the commitment they can expect from their barrister. The strongest client-focused outcome of the new Code is that clients' best interests are protected and promoted by those acting for them.[148]

---

[142] ibid, gC12.
[143] ibid, gC13.
[144] ibid, r C7.
[145] ibid, C9.3.
[146] ibid, oC10.
[147] ibid, oC19.
[148] ibid, oC11.

Rule c15, of the new Bar Code retains the obligation to 'promote fearlessly and by all proper and lawful means the client's best interests'. The rule states this takes precedence over personal interests or the consequences to any other person. It also states that barristers must not let professional clients, employers or others limit their discretion as to how the interests of clients can be served. These 'others' may, or may not, be intended to include the state.

ii. Solicitors

a. Advocacy in The Guide and Solicitors' Code of Conduct 2007

Advocacy did not feature in the early editions of the Guide. On being granted the ability to award higher rights in 1993, the Law Society created a new code for advocacy. It was added as a supplement to the Guide.[149] In relation to the key ethical principles, the Law Society advocacy code was substantially based on the Bar Code. It even repeated the Bar's commitment to 'promote and protect fearlessly and by all proper and lawful means the client's best interests'.[150]

There was one significant difference between the Bar Code and the solicitors' advocacy code. The latter contained no equivalent to the cab rank rule. The solicitors' advocacy code did, however, contain a rule against discrimination.[151] It also contained a rule against refusing instructions on the grounds that the 'nature of the case is objectionable' or that 'the conduct, opinions or beliefs of the client' are unacceptable to the advocate or a section of the public.[152]

The solicitors' advocacy code was repealed by the Solicitors' Code of Conduct 2007,[153] which included many of its main points in Rule 11 and the guidance thereto. Some of the original requirements, such as organising practices to support advocacy, maintaining libraries and ensuring that employees are aware of obligations arising under the solicitors' advocacy code[154] were not included. The duty to accept difficult cases was retained in the same form as in the solicitors' code for advocacy.[155] There were also changes and a general reorganisation of priorities in the 2007 Code of Conduct.

The most significant change in the 2007 Code was that the advocate's duty to 'promote and protect fearlessly and by all proper and lawful means' disappeared. There was no replacement duty for advocacy. Presumably, therefore advocates owed the same duty to their clients as other solicitors, to promote their best interests. As to reorganisation, for example, the code for advocacy required solicitors to consider

---

[149] See eg N Taylor (ed), *The Guide to the Professional Conduct of Solicitors*, 8th edn (London, The Law Society, 1999) at 385.
[150] ibid, at para 2.3(a).
[151] ibid, at para 2.4.1.
[152] ibid, at paras 2.4.2(b) and (c).
[153] SRA, *Solicitors' Code of Conduct 2007*, r 25.01(g).
[154] Solicitors' Advocacy Code, at para 3.1.
[155] SRA, *Solicitors' Code of Conduct 2007*, r 11.04.

whether a particular brief was consonant with their experience,[156] and whether or not their firm was the most suitable to conduct the case. The Solicitors' Code of Conduct 2007 relegated these matters to guidance.[157]

b. SRA Code of Conduct 2011, as Amended

The SRA Code of Conduct Chapter 1, concerned with clients, contains no specific reference to advocacy. The only hint of any specific obligation arising as a result of being instructed as an advocate lies in the outcome concerning provision of services in a manner protecting their interests, subject to the proper administration of justice.[158]

All of the outcomes in Chapter 5, 'Your Client and the Court', concern restrictions on what can be done for clients by way of advocacy before the courts. They are similar to the restrictions contained in the Bar Code. Therefore, solicitor advocates must draw the court's attention to relevant cases and statutory provisions, and any material procedural irregularity.[159] They must inform the court, with the client's consent, if the court has been misled, or cease to act if the client does not consent to the solicitor advocate informing the court.[160] As with barristers, solicitors must try to persuade clients to agree to disclose the truth to the court.[161] They must not call a witness whose evidence they know is untrue.[162] There are restrictions on appearing as an advocate if anyone at the firm will be called as a witness in the matter.[163]

The indicative behaviours in Chapter 3 also represent prohibitions originally drawn from the Bar Code. These include not drafting court documents containing contentions not properly arguable or alleging fraud, unless instructed to do so, on the basis of documents showing fraud.[164]

Solicitor advocates must not suggest that a person is guilty of a crime, fraud or misconduct unless these allegations are material to the client's case and appear to the solicitor to be supported by reasonable grounds.[165] They must not name in open court any third party whose character would thereby be called into question, unless it is necessary for the proper conduct of the case.[166] They must give witnesses a chance to counter allegations in cross-examination if those allegations are later relied on.[167]

---

[156] ibid, at para 4.3.1.
[157] ibid, guidance to r 11, note 4.
[158] SRA, *Handbook, Code of Conduct 2011*, as amended, ch 5: 'Your Client and the Court', Outcome 1.2.
[159] ibid, Indicative Behaviour 5.2.
[160] ibid, Indicative Behaviour 5.4.
[161] ibid, Indicative Behaviour 5.5.
[162] ibid, Indicative Behaviour 5.9.
[163] ibid, Indicative Behaviour 5.6.
[164] ibid, Indicative Behaviour 5.7.
[165] ibid, Indicative Behaviour 5.8.
[166] ibid, Indicative Behaviour 5.12.
[167] ibid, Indicative Behaviour 5.13.

D. Judicial Regulation

i. Inherent Jurisdiction

Judges have jurisdiction to regulate barristers as advocates with a duty to the court and solicitors as officers of the court. These distinctions have substantially broken down. The tradition in relation to barristers was that judges would report serious matters to a barrister's Inn if it was considered worthy of discipline. They might have a word with a barrister's head of chambers if there was a minor issue worth addressing. Issues are more likely to be addressed formally today, for example, with a report to the approved regulator or by summary disposition, for example, imposition of a wasted costs order.

ii. Quality Assurance Scheme for Advocates (QASA)

In addition to providing an accreditation mechanism, QASA also represents an additional layer of regulation of criminal advocacy. This has three levels; initial accreditation, judicial evaluation and regulatory reporting.

a. Accreditation beyond Level 1

Accreditation for advocates at levels 2, 3 and 4 of the scheme is a two-stage process. First, advocates must register with their regulator to receive provisional accreditation at the level they are practising at. Secondly, they must apply for full accreditation within 24 months of provisional accreditation.[168] They are spot-checked to see that they are registered at the correct level for their experience. If the regulator decides that initial registration was deliberately misleading, downgrading and referral for disciplinary proceedings could result.[169]

b. Judicial Evaluation

Full accreditation at the level registered for must be applied for within two years of provisional accreditation. To obtain full accreditation, advocates must be assessed by judicial evaluation in up to three trials at their selected level. Judges participating in the scheme are trained to assess advocates. When assessing an advocate's performance they complete a complicated form, the Criminal Advocacy Evaluation Form (CAEF), for each trial.

The standards on the CAEF are calibrated for the different levels of the scheme. The completed form is usually returned to the relevant regulator, who will make the CAEF available to the advocate once it has been received. If the judge returns the form to the advocate it must be submitted by the advocate to the regulator.[170]

---

[168] BSB, SRA and ILEX Professional Standards, *QASA Handbook for Criminal Advocates* (September 2013) at para 2.21.
[169] ibid, at para 2.26.
[170] ibid, at para 2.28.

The level at which an advocate is allowed to operate is decided by the judicial evaluation. For example, to qualify at level 4 an advocate must obtain a minimum of two and a maximum of three CAEFs assessed as Very Competent at level 3 in consecutive trials to obtain provisional accreditation, valid for 12 months. Advocates can qualify for level 2 or 3 by assessment at an assessment organisation,[171] following which they must still comply with the requirements for judicial review of their performance.[172] Accreditation at all levels is valid for five years before it must be renewed.

c. Regulatory Reporting

Where a judge participating in the scheme has concerns about an advocate's competence, the CAEF will be sent to the advocate's regulator with a request for ongoing monitoring of the advocate.[173] Regulators receiving an ongoing monitoring referral will consider the seriousness of the issue identified, the history of the advocate and the source of the reference.[174] As regards seriousness the regulator will consider the consequences of the concerns identified, such as the impact of the advocate's actions on client interests. As regards the advocate's history, the regulator may consider previous evaluations and any referrals. The record of a judge making the referral may also be considered. If, on the basis of other evaluations, there is an indication that a judge may be biased against a particular group, this will be taken into account.

Independent assessors may be appointed to observe advocates who have been made subject to monitoring referrals.[175] Following independent assessment the regulator can decide to take no further action, mark the advocate's record as a potential risk or recommend the advocate undertake further training. In extreme cases the regulator may remove the advocate's full accreditation at their current level and grant provisional accreditation at their current level or at a level below.[176] The regulator may consider whether to take appropriate action under its conduct rules using evidence from one or more evaluations.[177]

The rules do not provide for immediate removal of accreditation in appropriate cases. The Handbook does note, however, that an advocate's evaluation record will be considered on application for accreditation, progression or re-accreditation under the scheme. At this stage, accreditation may presumably be refused for any of the higher levels. It is not clear whether, in that case, solicitor or barrister advocates are allowed to continue to practise at level 1. Each regulator has a separate process under which they can consider appeals under the scheme.[178]

---

[171] ibid, at paras 2.32–2.35.
[172] ibid, at para 2.37.
[173] ibid, at para 2.86.
[174] ibid, at para 2.87.
[175] ibid, at para 2.94.
[176] ibid, at para 2.95.
[177] ibid, at para 2.92.
[178] ibid, at para 2.99.

V. The Future of Advocacy

The model of advocacy reflected in the codes is criminal defence. Any reading of the professional rules would hardly excite concern that the rights of clients dominate the thoughts of the advocacy regulators. The client clearly comes second best in the conception of the advocate's role. Even the 'client's best interests' formula is capable of a paternalistic spin. The continued use of the word 'fearless' does not quite convey the true position of the Code.

The advocate's position, as portrayed in the Code of Conduct, is conservative and establishment leaning. Examples in the literature that support the standard conception of the lawyer's role are forbidden by the rules. For example, an advocate could not, following a client's confession, conduct a contradictory and brutal cross-examination of a rape victim.[179] The new codes do not convey the bold determination to defy the state that once justified the Bar's demand for institutional independence. The question is whether the failing capacity of legal aid to sustain a cadre of high quality advocates, and creeping regulation, will fatally diminish the ability of advocates to hold power to account.

In September 2013, four barristers supported by the Criminal Bar Association sought judicial review of the LSB decision to approve QASA.[180] The claimants argued that the scheme 'offends fundamental issues of justice' and threatened the independence of barristers and judges. Advocates would fear, at least subconsciously, that standing up to the judge would earn a bad evaluation. In the High Court, three judges, led by Sir Brian Leveson, President of the Queen's Bench Division, held that the scheme was proportionate and fell within the legitimate exercise of the powers of the LSB and those of the three regulators seeking approval.[181]

As to the evil of dependency on judicial goodwill, the Court noted that judges had exercised disciplinary power over advocates for centuries and often reported advocates.[182] The fear of a 'not competent' rating was said to be 'not different in kind from fear of an unjustified complaint',[183] although, clearly, it is very different. The legal aid cuts meant that the quality assurance of advocacy could not be left to market forces. In the court's view, the objective of competent advocacy was important. The scheme

---

[179] D Luban, *Lawyers and Justice: An Ethical Study* (Princeton, NJ, Princeton University Press, 1988) at 150; S Galoob, 'How do Roles Generate Reason? A Method of Legal Ethics' (2012) 15(1) *Legal Ethics* 1, at 6.

[180] N Rose, 'BSB presses ahead with QASA preparations despite judicial review' *Legal Futures* 17 September 2013 (www.legalfutures.co.uk/latest-news/bsb-presses-ahead-qasa-preparations-despite-judicial-review).

[181] *Lumsden, Taylor, Howker and Hewertson v LSB and others* [2013] EWHC 28 (Admin); D Bindman, 'QASA given green light by High Court as JR fails' *Legal Futures* 20 January 2014 (www.legalfutures.co.uk/latest-news/qasa-given-green-light-high-court-jr-fails).

[182] ibid, at [62].

[183] ibid, at [68].

was justified by concerns, expressed before QASA, of sub-standard advocacy. As to this, the Court concluded that

> [t]here are obvious risks posed both to individuals and to the criminal justice system as evidenced from the time of the Ipsos MORI survey in 2006, through the CPS review in 2009 to the large scale survey reported by ORC International in 2012. None of these were as comprehensive and as complete as one would conduct in an ideal world, but they produced significant evidence of concerns about advocacy standards from a range of sources, including the views of the judiciary[184]

Whether or not the scheme was a threat to independence could be judged from the core standards the scheme assessed. These were all concerned with basic competence:

> [N]o advocate is fulfilling his duty either to the client or to the court if he is not properly prepared, or presents obscure and rambling submissions, or conducts unfocussed questioning. If and insofar as a client seeks to persuade the advocate that he should attempt by prolonged and irrelevant questioning of witnesses to divert the jury from the real issues in the case, the advocate's duty is to refuse. [185]

Expensive advocacy is not always effective. For example, Mr Justice Tomlinson's post-BCCI Working Party's interim report singled out an 80-day opening speech in that case as 'wasted'.[186] Nevertheless, it would be a retrograde step for society if, in future, only those with deep pockets obtain the advocacy they need and desire.

VI. Conclusion

Advocacy is one of the few distinguishing activities of lawyers. It has been the source of considerable prestige and status to lawyers in England and Wales. In recent years, the elevated status of advocacy has been under considerable strain. The system is built on control by the Bar. It dominated prestigious higher court advocacy, and with it, access to judicial appointment. At the lower end, the junior Bar also controlled criminal advocacy, which was symbolically important. These factors helped to preserve an adversarial model of advocacy based on partisanship, a highly developed duty to the court and professional discretion in the presentation of cases.

A critical stage in the reform of legal services was breaking the Bar's control of advocacy and, with it, the barristers' priest-like control of the law. This was partially achieved by promoting competition for access to higher courts. The Criminal Bar was undermined by reduced levels of criminal work, competition with government lawyers and reduced income from legal aid. The long-term future of the Bar depends on its continued excellence, economy and efficiency in providing advocacy services.

---

[184] ibid, at [131].
[185] ibid, at [70].
[186] N Goswami, 'Falconer: tardy litigators will be fired' *The Lawyer* 4 June 2007.

The current arrangements may not survive sustained competitive pressure, hence the Bar's final embrace of the right to conduct litigation.

Some advocacy will continue to command high status and its practitioners will command high fees. It is open to question whether the volume of this kind of advocacy will sustain an elite and broad-based profession. Another question is whether the tension between the duty to clients and to the court will be satisfactorily maintained. There will be pressure to further temper the adversarial ethos, increase judicial control of proceedings and control advocates. It is important, if the rhetoric of the rule of law is to be meaningful, that lawyers continue to be fearless defenders of client rights.

20

Alternative Dispute Resolution

'Why ... are lawyers, in essence, such obscure men? Why do their undoubted talents yield so poor a harvest of immortality? The answer, it seems to me ... is their professional aim and function [is] not to get at the truth, but simply to carry on combats between ancient rules'.[1]

I. Introduction

The Alternative Dispute Resolution (ADR) movement can be traced to the 1960s, and particularly to the US. It is associated with dissatisfaction with the role of the state, and with the role of state institutions, in dispute resolution.[2] Legal machinery was seen as particularly inappropriate to resolving issues that are really economic, social or political problems. ADR offers parties to disputes greater autonomy by letting them decide the method, means and rules of dispute resolution. Most common law jurisdictions have placed increased emphasis on ADR, particularly mediation. In England and Wales, as elsewhere, this has been instead of, or as an adjunct to, litigation.

There may be a number of reasons why alternatives to litigation tends to develop. The first field of activity is often commercial. This may be a reaction to the fact that commercial disputes are likely to be complex and involve multiple parties. There may be higher levels of interdependency between parties and issues.[3] Conventional litigation is often considered too ritualised and slow.

ADR processes can be tailored to a variety of conflict types, disputes or parties.[4] Indeed, by the end of the 1980s, ADR was seen as part of a social and political

---

[1] HL Mencken, 'Editorial' *American Mercury* (January 1928) at 35, 36.

[2] LA Mistelis, 'ADR in England and Wales: A Successful Case of Public Private Partnership' in NM Alexander (ed), *Global Trends in Mediation* (The Netherlands, Kluwer Law International, 2006) 139, at 143.

[3] DP Emond, 'Alternative Dispute Resolution: A Conceptual Overview' in DP Emond (ed), *Commercial Dispute Resolution: Alternatives to Litigation* (Aurora, Canada Law Books Inc, 1989) 1, at 14.

[4] P Gulliver, *Disputes and Negotiations: A Cross-Cultural Perspective* (New York, Academic Press, 1979); WF Felstiner, RL Abel and A Sarat, 'The Emergence and Transformation of Disputes: Naming, Blaming, Claiming' (1980–81) 15 *Law and Society* 631, esp at 640–41.

movement towards 'informalism' and subject to a more rigorous critique.[5] During the following decade ADR was adopted by the state as a cheap alternative to litigation. Critics argue that this undermines and compromises the considerable advantages of ADR.

The growth of ADR raises many issues for legal regulators and for lawyers. If ADR represents a change in the form of legal business, lawyers must decide whether they should offer ADR services. Legal regulators then need to consider if the provision of services needs to be controlled, and if so, how. The decision may have implications for education and training and for professional ethics. One issue that needs to be considered is how far an ethic based on adversarial assumptions can accommodate a competing ethic of co-operation and conciliation.

II. Defining Alternative Dispute Resolution

A wide range of processes are embraced by the term ADR. Categorisations usually include arbitration, mediation, conciliation, mini-trial and expert-determination. These terms refer to widely different processes with different aims, varying degrees of formality and degrees of enforceability. There are a number of hybrids combining features of one or more methods. ADR processes can be divided into two groups. In the first group there is a binding and enforceable outcome. In the second, there may, but need not be, a binding or enforceable outcome.

The first group of processes often classed as ADR methods includes arbitration, mini-trial and expert-determination. Arbitration is a non-judicial proceeding in which awards tend to be binding, final and enforceable in the courts.[6] In some cases it can be almost as formal as a trial. A mini-trial is a shortened, full-trial presented to senior executives of the parties to the dispute, or a retired judge, to clarify legal and factual merits.[7] It may take place as a precursor to negotiation. Expert-determination involves instructing an expert to decide an outcome based on an agreed brief.[8] It is often agreed that the outcome of processes in which the third party is a substitute for a judge, are enforceable in the courts.[9]

---

[5] See generally RL Abel, 'The Contradictions of Informal Justice' in RL Abel (ed), *The Politics of Informal Justice: The American Experience* (New York, Academic Press, 1982).

[6] BH Goldstein, 'Alternatives for Resolving Business Transactions Disputes' (1983) 58 *St John's Law Review* 69; MP Reynolds, *Arbitration* (London, Lloyd's of London Press, 1993) pt 1; BJ Thompson, 'Commercial Dispute Resolution: A Practical Overview' in Emond, 'Alternative Dispute Resolution' (n 3) at 91.

[7] JF Davis and LJ Omlie, 'Mini Trials: The Courtroom in the Boardroom' (1985) 21 *Willamete Law Review* 531; BC Hart 'Alternative Dispute Resolution: Negotiation, Mediation and Mini-trial' (1987) *FICC Quarterly* 113; C Ervine, *Settling Consumer Disputes: A Review of Alternative Dispute Resolution* (London, National Consumer Council, 1993) at 12.

[8] J Kendall, 'Simpler Dispute Resolution' *Solicitors Journal* 29 November 1996, at 1152.

[9] *Mercury Communications Ltd v Director of Telecommunications* [1996] 1 All ER 575, [1996] 1 WLR 48.

The second group of processes, those without enforceable outcomes, includes conciliation and mediation. Conciliation is a process of bringing parties together and reconciling differences. It may be a final process in some situations, but in others it may only be a precursor to a further ADR process. Mediation is a process, facilitated by a mediator, where parties explore possible avenues to resolution of a dispute. It leads to resolution only if the parties agree a settlement.

A. In what Way is ADR Alternative?

The unifying feature of the different ADR processes is that a third party helps to resolve the dispute. This is essentially what a judge does, raising the issue of why ADR is considered 'alternative'. The simple answer is that the methods are alternatives to litigation and trial. Beyond this, any difference is mainly a question of differences between the kinds of processes used and the kinds of outcomes reached.

i. Adjudicative Processes and Outcomes

In arbitration, expert-determination or mini-trial the similarities to trial are strongest. They all involve adjudication by a neutral third party. These processes may be specified as the means of resolving disputes arising from commercial contracts. In agreeing the contract, the parties also agree a process for resolving a dispute. This will include the forum and rules of procedure.

Parties to a contract containing an arbitration clause may agree a named independent arbiter, or a means of selecting one. They agree to accept the outcome in advance and the process follows state adjudication closely, often allowing recourse to the courts. Parties to an arbitration agreement can apply for a stay of proceedings in any litigation relating to a matter covered by the agreement.[10]

The motive for using these 'alternative' judicial processes is varied. It may be to reduce litigation costs, to provide a swifter outcome to disputes or to use a specialist adjudicator of choice. There is also potential to use more flexible procedures than courts would normally allow. This group of processes are 'alternative' in that they are not litigation. Both parties opt to use them, rather than one being coerced, and they are not state sponsored.[11] They are, however, geared to producing an adjudicated outcome, just as court systems are. They are also 'alternative' in the sense that the parties choose the style and process of adjudication, usually in advance.

ii. Collaborative Processes and Outcomes

As with arbitration, an agreement to mediate or conciliate a dispute may be written into a commercial contract. However, the second set of ADR processes are more likely

---

[10] Arbitration Act 1996, s 9.
[11] GC Hazard, 'Court Delay: Toward New Premises' (1986) 5 *Civil Justice Quarterly* 236.

to be agreed following a dispute. Mediation and conciliation tend to use ad hoc or established processes that are adopted or adapted by the parties. These methods tend to aim for a more diverse set of outcomes than conventional dispute resolution or alternative adjudicative processes. In mediation and conciliation, a third party brings together the disputants aiming to facilitate understanding of differences, resolve them if possible, and create a better relationship. The outcome may be novel, or non-legal, solutions, including acceptance or accommodation of problems.[12]

Conciliation may have achieved its aim when the parties understand each other better, as when a couple with marital problems agree to continue their relationship. Mediation offers resolution of problems in a way that conciliation alone cannot. For example, the separating couple may need to divide marital property. Mediation may have purposes linked to, but not dominated by, resolving the dispute. This is considered in the next section. As regards dispute resolution, this second group of processes is 'alternative' because the parties are, generally, not committed in advance to a specific process or kind of outcome. Indeed, they may choose not to reach a formally binding conclusion.

B. Mediation

When ADR is discussed, it is often with reference to mediation. This is because, unlike the other ADR methods, mediation offers a means of settling a material dispute by a fundamentally different process to litigation. The mediation process takes many forms. It often begins with the mediator meeting both sides separately. A process of 'shuttle diplomacy' often follows, with the mediator moving backwards and forwards between the parties. In this way, the mediator can control the flow of information and limit interpersonal friction. If this initial process goes well, a joint meeting may follow. Sometimes, however, a settlement can be agreed without the parties meeting face to face. This is, however, a generalisation. Some types of mediation have different kinds of aim and work from different principles.

i. Types of Mediation

There are labels for different approaches to mediation, for example, facilitative, evaluative and transformative. Each has a distinct philosophy and method. These variations stem from facilitative mediation, which was the original format.

a. Facilitative (or Problem-solving) Mediation

In facilitative mediation a mediator helps the parties to explore underlying interests and resolve differences. This is similar to a problem-solving negotiation, the difference lying in the crucial role of the third party.[13] Mediators structure a process of

---

[12] R Young, 'Neighbour Dispute Mediation: Theory and Practice' (1989) 2 *Civil Justice Quarterly* 319.
[13] C Menkel-Meadow, 'Lawyer Negotiations: Theories and Realities: What We Learn from Mediation' (1993) 56 *Modern Law Review* 361.

information exchange, facilitate a fuller understanding by the parties of the other side's perceptions, circumstances and feelings. The third party aims to promote rational communication and negotiation.[14] They encourage the parties to clarify values and identify possible joint gains.

Facilitative mediators take a more proactive role than the parties could, seeking to maintain momentum towards agreement. They can help sustain dialogue, remind both sides of the advantages of agreement and persuade and cajole them to continue the process. Facilitative mediators help the parties to understand and value their own interests. They tend to leave parties in charge of the substantive decision-making process and try not to influence the outcome.

b. Evaluative Mediation

Evaluative mediation is a more judicial process than facilitative mediation. An evaluative mediator offers the parties an assessment of the strengths and the weaknesses of their cases. If it is a legal dispute, they may offer a prediction of the outcome based on evidence. An evaluative mediator tends to make recommendations to the parties regarding suitable outcomes. These can take in factors such as cost and convenience in a way that formal judicial processes cannot. Recommendations may take into account the parties' needs and interests, but these tend not to be central concerns. The strength of evaluative mediation is an agreement reflecting a legal notion of fairness.

c. Transformative Mediation

As developed by Bush and Folger, transformative mediation has two main aims. These are mutual recognition by the parties of the other and mutual empowerment.[15]

Recognition means acknowledging the other party's needs, interests and values. It also involves achieving a better understanding of the other party's perspective. Recognition in itself may seem to be a modest goal. In transformative mediation, however, it has substantial value. Reconciliation of the parties may not be possible, but there are other points on a continuum of outcomes that can be achieved. One outcome that can nearly always be achieved is the kind of moral growth achieved by 'recognition of the other'.

Bush and Folger's concept of recognition is given in thought, words or actions. In thought, it means adopting the other party's perspective. In words, it is making statements conveying understanding of the other party's position or view. In action, it means changing one's own conduct to accommodate the other. While recognition is a valuable part of transformative mediation in its own right, it is also a platform for achieving the other main aim, empowerment.

Empowerment relates to five key areas: goals, options, skills, resources and decision-making. Empowerment in relation to goals involves a party understanding the importance of their interests. In relation to options they understand the available

---

[14] M Roberts, 'Who is in Charge? Reflections on Recent Research on the Role of the Mediator' (1992) 14 *Journal of Social Welfare and Family Law* 372, at 374–76. See generally A Bevan, *Alternative Dispute Resolution* (London, Sweet and Maxwell, 1992) and JM Haynes, *Alternative Dispute Resolution: Fundamentals of Family Mediation* (Horsmonden, Kent, Old Bailey Press, 1993).

[15] FG Folger and RAB Bush, *The Promise of Mediation* (San Francisco, Jossey-Bass Publishers, 1994).

options and their ability to choose between them. In relation to skills, they develop conflict resolution capabilities. These include listening, communicating, analysis, argumentation, persuasion, organisation, problem-solving and decision-making. In relation to resources they learn how to gain additional resources and use their existing resources more effectively. These forms of empowerment lead parties to gain 'a greater sense of self-worth, security, self-determination and autonomy'.[16]

Transformative mediation involves three patterns of mediator conduct. Mediators first focus specifically on each party's individual contributions to the exchange. Secondly, they encourage the parties to deliberate, reflect and choose. Thirdly, they assist in framing and reframing arguments so as to lead parties to recognise the other party. This approach stands in contrast to facilitative, problem-solving mediation, where mediators tend to discourage focus on relationship issues.

The aims of transformative mediation determine the process. Mediators support the parties in choosing their own mediation process and in determining its direction. The mediator follows this lead. Unlike other forms of mediation, it is an essential part of transformative mediation that the mediator meets with the parties together. Only the parties can give each other the 'recognition' that is the main rationale of the method. Transformative mediation sees the process of mediation as more important than the outcome. The aim of the process is to transform the participants. It claims to do this by helping 'parties recognize and exploit the opportunities for moral growth inherently presented by conflict'.[17]

ii. Practical Significance

Facilitative, problem-solving mediation was the original format pioneered in the 1960s. The potential to assist parties to settle disputes led to an increasing emphasis on settlement. Transformative mediation was proffered as a means of recovering the original aspiration to empower and transform the participants. According to Bush and Folger, the processes of transformative and facilitative, problem-solving mediation, are antagonistic; they cannot be combined. Neither can use the other's methods to achieve results. Mediators must therefore choose one approach or the other and follow that one alone.

Evaluative mediation apparently sacrifices participant engagement and empowerment in favour of more accurate prediction of possible outcomes beyond the immediate mediation context. Purists would argue that evaluative mediation does not fit easily within the mediation paradigm. The focus on evaluation, rather than needs and interests, means that this approach could be classified as a form of adjudicative ADR rather than mediation. Transformative mediation treats conflict as a tool of personal growth, while the aspiration of other models is settlement via a process that minimises interpersonal conflict.

[16] ibid, at 87.
[17] ibid, at 12.

III. ADR in England and Wales

A. A Brief History of the Use of ADR Processes in England and Wales

The UK has a history of experimentation with different types of ADR. London has been a centre for arbitration since the late-1800s. Conciliation in divorce proceedings predates the Second World War and grew thereafter, with schemes set up by local professionals, lawyers, social workers and probation officers.[18] It grew in significance from the 1960s, when a six-fold increase in the rate of divorce saw unofficial annexation of conciliation schemes to some divorce County Courts and magistrates' domestic courts. Matrimonial conciliation was popular with solicitors,[19] a greater problem being lack of funding and formal structures.

Since the 1960s ADR has been part of world-wide efforts to innovate in the area of civil justice. At the earlier stages of this development, the involvement of lawyers was contentious. This was partly a reaction to fact that lawyers create litigation and settlement in their own image. Lawyers were, however, also part of the move away from the litigation paradigm, particularly in commercial sphere and in family and matrimonial matters. From the mid-1970s, conciliation was used in trade union disputes, through the Arbitration and Conciliation Advisory Service (ACAS).[20]

In construction disputes, ADR was given statutory foundation. Under a procedure established by the Housing Grants, Construction and Regeneration Act 1996, parties could seek interim or non-binding adjudications by legal or construction professionals. This was so successful that ADR became the norm in construction disputes, rather than the alternative.[21]

The success of ADR influenced court schemes. The Commercial Court was an innovator in the use of ADR. In 1993, a practice statement was issued indicating that the court's judges would not be involved in ADR processes, but would invite parties to consider whether their use might be appropriate.[22] The Commercial Court scheme, established in 1994, became increasingly committed to ADR,[23] issuing a second

[18] A Ogus, M Jones-Lee, W Cole and P McCarthy, 'Evaluating Alternative Dispute Resolution: Measuring the Impact of Family Conciliation on Costs' (1990) 53 *Modern Law Review* 57, at 59.
[19] Lady Marre CBE, *A Time for Change: Report on the Committee on the Future of the Legal Profession* (London, The General Council of the Bar, The Law Society, 1988) (Marre Report) at para 11.10.
[20] R Singh, 'Dispute Resolution in Britain: Contemporary Trends' (1995) 16 *International Journal of Manpower* 42.
[21] M O'Callaghan, 'The Best Alternative' *The Lawyer* 10 September 2001, at 39.
[22] Practice Statement (Commercial Cases, Alternative Dispute Resolution) [1994] 1 WLR 1024, per Cresswell J.
[23] Mistelis, 'ADR in England and Wales' (n 2) at 145–47.

practice statement encouraging its use in 1996.[24] In the County Courts, 'arbitration', a more relaxed judicial procedure, was used for small claims in the County Courts.

There was some evidence that ordinary people welcomed ADR. In a survey conducted by the National Consumer Council, many consumers expressed a preference for ADR over court-based dispute resolution.[25] Three-quarters of respondents would have preferred some form of ADR to the process of civil litigation they had actually experienced. In six out of ten personal injury or divorce case the parties would have preferred mediation. Less than one in ten favoured a full trial as the best means of resolving their dispute.

ADR was not universally successful. Based on the advice in a Law Commission Report, the Family Law Act 1996 proposed to introduce mediation for divorce.[26] The legislation, due to come into force in 2000, was scrapped after pilots. This was partly because ADR added an average of £150 to the cost of settling a child custody dispute.[27]

B. The Range of Private ADR Services

There are a wide variety of private ADR schemes and providers covering different processes and methods of ADR. This account is not intended to be exhaustive, but to provide an idea of the type and scale of ADR organisations and processes in England and Wales.

i. Organisations

a. Providers

The London Court of International Arbitration (LCIA) grew out of a business need for cheap and effective dispute resolution in the late-nineteenth century.[28] It is now a private organisation providing international dispute resolution expertise in arbitration and mediation in major commercial cases. The court has 35 members, drawn from eminent commercial arbitrators. No more than six can be from the UK at any one time. In 2012, a total of 265 arbitrations were referred to the LCIA, in addition to 12 requests for mediation or some other form of ADR. Over 80 per cent of the parties involved in the LCIA's pending cases are not English and, apart from the UK, where 16 per cent of the parties were from, no more than 10 per cent come from a single country or region.[29]

The LCIA publishes its own forms and rules, both of which are often used by parties even when the LCIA is not involved in a dispute. The LCIA has gained ground

---

[24] Practice Statement (Commercial Cases, Alternative Dispute Resolution) (1996) No 2 [1996] 1 WLR 14, per Waller J.
[25] National Consumer Council, *Seeking Civil Justice* (London, NCC, 1995) at 11.
[26] The Law Commission, *The Ground for Divorce* (Law Com No 192, 1990).
[27] Ogus et al, *Evaluating Alternative Dispute Resolution* (n 18) at 73.
[28] LCIA, 'History of the LCIA' (www.lcia.org//LCIA/Our_History.aspx).
[29] LCIA, 'Registrar's Report 2012' (www.lcia.org/).

on major rivals in Paris and Stockholm, but critics argue that more needs to be done. For example, international companies prefer not to have impediments to swift solutions. Therefore, it is more competitive, although probably not fairer, if rules do not provide for appeals from arbitration decisions to the courts.[30]

Lawyers were among the first groups to develop ADR services. In the first wave, IDR Europe, established in 1989, is an organisation created by solicitors. It draws mediators from a network of law firms. Another major provider is the Centre for Effective Dispute Resolution (CEDR), established in 1990. CEDR was sponsored by the Confederation of British Industry and leading law firms. Its aims were to promote ADR in general and mediation in particular.

CEDR has a particular, but not exclusive, focus on commercial work. It has worked with major national and international agencies and law firms to develop practice and train mediators. It now offers a range of services, such as early neutral evaluation, as well as mediation. It handles around 600 major mediations a year and seeks to influence the development of ADR in the international sphere.

b. Membership Organisations

Despite the size and importance of the sector, there was no membership organisation for mediation until 2003, when the Civil Mediation Council (CMC) was formed. CMC covers civil, commercial, workplace and other non-family mediation. It is an unincorporated association with around 400 members drawn from providers, academics, professional bodies and government departments. CMC accredits organisations providing mediation services, which then accredit mediators. Since providers are not obliged to seek accreditation, CMC cannot be said to regulate the sector.

ii. Areas of Work

a. Business and Commercial

The use of a country's dispute resolution fora boosts its invisible earnings and the UK, London in particular, aims to be a major international centre for dispute resolution. The UK has judges who are admired internationally for high standards, and London attracts a good share of international litigation. In a rapidly developing, competitive world market for dispute resolution, the provision of ADR is an essential complement to conventional judicial processes. International companies engage in 'forum shopping', choosing the national systems that offer the quickest and most flexible, efficient and reliable means of resolving disputes.

The UK has a patchy record as a leader in dispute resolution methodology. It was one of the last major countries to adopt the UN-sponsored model code for arbitration.[31] The Arbitration Act 1996 was introduced to revise an inadequate regulatory framework[32] for international arbitration. There were high hopes for the Act in

---

[30] 'Global Warring' *Law Society Gazette* 2 November 2000, at 32.
[31] UNCITRAL Model Law on International Commercial Arbitration 1985, as amended.
[32] 'Fair, Speedy and Cost Effective Resolutions of Disputes' *Solicitors Journal* 23 February 1996.

terms of changing the environment for international dispute resolution. Lord Justice Saville, chair of the Departmental Advisory Committee of the Department of Trade and Industry, hoped that, as a result of the legislation, the UK would 'retain pre-eminence in the field of international arbitration, a service which brings this country very substantial amounts indeed by way of invisible earnings'.[33]

The Arbitration Act contained mandatory and non-mandatory provisions.[34] Those dealing with the conduct of proceedings were mainly non-mandatory.[35] This was intended to provide the parties with the maximum flexibility to design their own process without intervention by the court, except in limited circumstances.[36]

b. Industry

Many industries have adopted ADR as a routine response to disputes. The construction industry is a good example. It provides about 10 per cent of gross domestic product and most projects involve problems of some kind. The number of major cases litigated has fallen by three-quarters since 1995, following the Civil Procedure Rules (CPR) and increased use of arbitration and mediation.[37]

c. Consumer

At the other end of the commercial scale, ADR is sometimes specified in standard contracts. For example, it may be used for handling a variety of consumer complaints. Such schemes do not necessarily have high levels of satisfaction with consumers, usually because the outcomes are perceived as unfair.[38]

C. Public ADR

ADR has entered the mainstream of dispute resolution in various areas of public dispute resolution provision. For example, in the Technology and Construction Court (formerly the Official Referee's Court), which deals with complex disputes, judges are available to act as arbitrators if the parties choose. These involve, for example, building or other construction disputes, engineering disputes, disputes involving specialised advisers relating to the services, claims by and against local authorities relating to their statutory duties concerning the development of land or the construction of buildings, and claims relating to the design, supply and installation of computers, computer software and related network systems.[39]

---

[33] M Rutherford, 'Arbitration Act Update' (1996) *Solicitors Journal* 22 November, at 1125; and see further PR Ellington, 'The New Arbitration Act 1996' (1998) 3 *Amicus Curiae* 14.

[34] Arbitration Act 1996, s 4.

[35] ibid, ss 33–95.

[36] S York, 'Privatisation of Disputes in 1997' (1996) 140 *Solicitors Journal* 1153.

[37] R Gaitskell, 'Trends in Construction Dispute Resolution' (December 2005) (www.scl.org.uk/files/129-gaitskell.pdf).

[38] National Consumer Council, *Out of Court: A Consumer View of Three Low Cost Trade Schemes* (London, NCC, 1991).

[39] *The Technology and Construction Court Guide*, 2nd edn, issued 3 October 2005 (second revision with effect from 1 October 2010) at para 1.3.1.

The adoption of ADR reflects a conscious decision by the state that can be interpreted in different ways. A benign view is that ADR expands consumers' range of choice of dispute resolution options. A more cynical view is that it reduces state responsibility for providing more conventional routes to justice through legal aid. ADR can therefore be seen as a means of expanding the state, in the form of civil society, using informal networks to replace formal institutions.[40] Through this lens, ADR is an expansion of state power using 'covert manipulation', community justice schemes and the like, depriving users of the coercive powers of courts.[41]

i. Mediation in Civil Litigation

a. Civil Procedure Rules

Lord Woolf's review of the civil justice system in 1996 proposed an increased role for ADR.[42] The CPR, introduced in 1999, contained a number of measures to ensure that the mediation option was at the forefront of dispute resolution options. The pre-action protocols required the parties to consider ADR and allowed judges to stay proceedings for up to a month for mediation to take place, even where the parties did not request it.[43] Judges were required to encourage parties to use ADR if appropriate, as part of the overriding objective of dealing with cases justly.[44] This was to be achieved through use of their powers of active case management. The CPR included provision to penalise parties through costs for unreasonable behaviour in litigation. Unreasonableness included refusing or obstructing mediation.[45]

With enthusiastic encouragement from judges, it appeared that mediation had a strong initial impact, but it did not last. Cases filed in the Queen's Bench Division dropped dramatically with the introduction of the CPR. In 1995, there were around 120,000 writs and originating proceedings issued in the district registries and just over 5000 in the Central Office.[46] In 1998 these had fallen to around 95,000 and 2000. In 2000, 20,000 cases were issued in the district registries and just over 5000 in the Central Office. They have remained just below this level since. This dramatic fall was probably not wholly attributable to mediation, but to other requirements of the CPR, such as pre-action protocols.[47] CEDR references, for example, actually dropped, from 468 in 1999 to 338, by 2001.[48]

---

[40] B de Sousa Santos, *Toward a New Legal Common Sense: Law, Globalization, and Emancipation* (London, Butterworths, 2002).

[41] Abel, 'The Contradictions of Informal Justice' (n 5).

[42] Lord Woolf, *Access to Justice* (Final Report) (London, HMSO 1996) at 4–12.

[43] Civil Procedure Rules 1998, rr 26.4(1) and (2).

[44] ibid, r 1.4.

[45] ibid, rr 44.3 (4) and (5).

[46] Ministry of Justice, *Judicial and Court Statistics 2006* (Cm 7273, 2007) at 39.

[47] R Peysner and M Seneviratne, *The Management of Civil Cases: the Courts and the post-Woolf Landscape* (London, DCA, 2005).

[48] J Ede, 'It's Good to Talk—Rather than Sue' *The Times* 26 November 2002, at 7; M Lind, 'ADR and mediation-boom or bust' *New Law Journal* 17 August 2001, at 1238; H Genn, 'Solving Civil Justice Problems: What Might be Best?' (paper for Scottish Consumer Council on Civil Justice, 19 January 2005).

b. Mediation Pilot Schemes

Anticipating the CPR, a number of mediation pilot schemes were run as adjuncts to courts, mainly the County Courts. Evaluations of a patchwork of voluntary schemes were conducted for the Central London County Court (1996) and Court of Appeal (Civil Division) (1997) and in Birmingham (2001), Leeds (2000) and Manchester (2000). These local schemes were often different in character, but the results from most were broadly similar.

Analysis of the mediation pilot schemes showed that they were relatively successful.[49] All dealt with significant volumes of cases, around a third of cases issued in the period of the studies. They varied in their remit between the different County Courts, dealing with small claims in one and fast and multi-track in others, but were similar in approach. Three-hour mediation slots were allocated to parties volunteering to mediate or directed to do so by the court. All dealt mainly with contractual claims, but some with housing repairs and personal injury.

All of the court-based mediation schemes had relatively high settlement rates and satisfaction levels from both solicitors and parties. Some parties experienced pressure to settle from mediators, but did not necessarily resent this. There were generally clear savings of court time. Two schemes, a small claims support service and a small claims mediation scheme, were effective in achieving settlements by using telephone 'shuttle diplomacy'.[50] This raises questions about the need for 'formal' mediation in all cases, and justifies interest in a more holistic approach to defining issues and dispute resolution processes.

One of the longest standing schemes continued to have mixed results. The Automatic Referral to Mediation scheme at Central London County Court evoked a high rate of objection and 'opt out' and added between £1000–£2000 to the cost of unsettled cases.[51] A parallel voluntary scheme was also relatively unpopular, particularly for personal injury cases, and settlement rates were disappointing at less than 50 per cent.

c. Other Forms of State Support for ADR

The push towards mediation received massive support from the state. A Community Legal Service Fund covering litigation and mediation costs[52] replaced legal aid, and assistance could be refused where parties had unreasonably failed to try mediation first. In March 2001, the Lord Chancellor's Department announced that ADR would be used to replace litigation wherever possible. The government also pledged to include

---

[49] L Webley, P Abrams and S Bacquet, *Evaluation of the Birmingham Court-Based Civil (Non-Family) Mediation Scheme* (London, DCA, 2006); S Prince, *An Evaluation of the Effectiveness of Court-based Mediation Processes in Non-Family Civil Proceedings at Exeter and Guildford County Courts* (London, DCA, 2006); S Prince, *An Evaluation of the Small Claims Dispute Resolution Pilot at Exeter County Court* (London, DCA, 2006).

[50] Craigforth, *Evaluation of the Small Claims Support Service Pilot at Reading County Court* (London, DCA, 2006); M Doyle, *Evaluation of the Small Claims Mediation Service at Manchester County Court* (London, DCA, 2006).

[51] H Genn, P Fenn, M Mason, A Lane, N Bechai, L Gray and D Vencappa, *Twisting Arms: Court Referred and Court Linked Mediation under Judicial Pressure* (London, Ministry of Justice, 2007).

[52] Access to Justice Act 1999.

ADR clauses in all standard government contracts.[53] In 2004, the Lord Chancellor's Department agreed with the Treasury to use ADR to reduce County Court and High Court cases by 200,000 cases, or 10 per cent, to reduce log jams and cost.[54]

ii. Mediation in Family Matters

Since 2000, those seeking legal aid to pursue family law cases were usually required to attend a mediation information and assessment meeting (MIAM) before a court application could be issued. This increased the number of family mediations from around 800 a year to 14,500.[55] In the year to 31 March 2013, more than 30,000 couples attended publicly funded MIAMs, resulting in over 13,500 mediations. Around two-thirds of those starting mediation reached an agreement without entering the court system.

The Legal Aid and Punishment of Offenders Act 2012 (LASPO 2012) cut funding for divorce, except for cases involving domestic violence. Legal aid continued to be provided for mediation. Since LASPO 2012, the number of mediations has dropped dramatically. This is possibly because parties are anxious about cost when legal aid is not normally available for divorce. It could also be because parties previously seeking legal aid for divorce are now escaping the mediation net. This means that parties that might have unexpectedly reconciled through mediation will no longer do so. Parties who are determined to divorce will, however, find it difficult to avoid mediation.

The Family Procedure Rules 2010 place a heavy emphasis on mediation.[56] Courts enquire whether a pre-action protocol requiring consideration of mediation has been followed.[57] The court can take into account failure to comply with the protocol in assessing the conduct of a party and can unilaterally refer the matter for arbitration. In proceedings involving children there is an automatic first hearing dispute resolution appointment, attended by the Children and Family Court Advisory and Support Service, to consider mediation or other processes.[58] When dealing with financial aspects of a case, the court must consider, at every stage in the proceedings, whether mediation is appropriate.[59] It can adjourn at any time for mediation to take place.[60]

---

[53] 'Government pledges to opt for ADR' *The Lawyer* 26 March 2001, at 2.
[54] B Malkin, 'LCD pledges to cut costs as Govt. pushes mediation plan' *The Lawyer* 15 March 2004, at 4.
[55] M Taddia, 'Mediation: An Acquired Taste' *Law Society Gazette* 12 August 2013 (www.lawgazette.co.uk/law/mediation-an-acquired-taste/5036957.article).
[56] Family Procedure Rules 2010, as amended by Family Procedure (Amendment) (No 5) Rules 2012.
[57] Family Procedure Rules 2010, Practice Direction 3a—Pre-application Protocol for Mediation Information and Assessment, at para 4.1.
[58] ibid, at para 3.4.
[59] Family Procedure Rules 2010, Financial Procedure Rules, pt 3, Alternative Dispute Resolution: The Court's Powers, at para 3.2.
[60] ibid, at para 3.3.

iii. Judicial Mediation in Employment Tribunals

A mediation scheme was piloted in a few Employment Tribunals between 2006 and 2007. The role of mediator was fulfilled by volunteer tribunal chairs trained by representatives of ACAS. The responsible government department commissioned detailed statistical comparison of cases undergoing mediation and those where there was no mediation.[61] This found no discernable or statistically significant impact on early resolution attributable to judicial mediation. Employers tended to be more satisfied with the process, while employees often wanted a more evaluative approach from the judge.

There were however, some ancillary benefits from the judicial mediation scheme. Notable among these were cases in which employers came to understand employees' feelings better and acknowledged that discrimination had occurred. This sometimes laid the foundation for resumption of employment. Over 30 per cent of the employers revised their employment and discrimination policies following the mediation. Judicial mediation was made available for discrimination cases at Employment Tribunal regional offices in England and Wales from January 2009.

IV. Definition of ADR Responsibilities by the Courts

Courts have had ample opportunity to define the legal responsibilities of participants in ADR. Typically, the principles they apply are ethical principles, including neutrality, fairness and confidentiality. Some of these apply to participants in ADR generally, such as those engaged as third party neutrals. Some are more likely to apply specifically to lawyers, such as those concerned with advising actual or prospective participants in ADR processes.

A. Advice

i. Lawyers Providing ADR Advice

Whether or not lawyers are actively involved in providing ADR services, the availability of such services impinge on practice in many areas. For example, lawyers may need to insert a dispute resolution clause into an agreement. This possibility requires that consideration be given to the best model and forum for the types of dispute that might arise. Lawyers might also be asked to advise on the possible outcome of mediation. Some

---

[61] A Boon, P Urwin and V Karuk, 'What Difference Does it Make?: Facilitative Judicial Mediation of Discrimination Cases in Employment Tribunals' (2011) 40(1) *Industrial Law Review* 45.

codes counsel that parties should not reach agreement without taking legal advice. Mediators may suggest this in the particular circumstances of the case.

The possibility of involvement in advising mediation participants gives rise to complicated responsibilities. Subjecting mediated outcomes to legal scrutiny may subvert the ethical principle of promoting client autonomy. Lawyers should therefore be wary of substituting their own preferences for the party's.[62] They must also be aware, however, of the possibility of liability for negligence if they do not warn a client that they may be under-settling their claim. Therefore, when lawyers are asked to review proposed mediation agreements in this way, they should be sensitive to the distinctive aims of mediation, the specific context and consider both the interests of the party and their position in law in framing their advice.

ii. Unreasonable Refusal to Mediate

a. The Overriding Objective and Costs

Inclusion in the mainstream methodologies for dispute resolution imposed different kinds of obligations on lawyers. In theory, they had to be aware of the potential of the new methods, their advantages and disadvantages and relative costs in order to offer clients comprehensive advice. This duty arose from the CPR and the obligation to achieve the overriding objective of doing justice.

The overriding objective, applied to costs, required that courts take into account all the circumstances when making and order for costs. The circumstances included the conduct of all the parties and whether a party has succeeded on part of its case. The court had to consider offers to settle under Part 36. It might also take into account admissible offers to settle not being an offer to which costs consequences under Part 36 applied.[63] The conduct of the parties was defined by the CPR to include conduct before proceedings, including following pre-action protocols. It also included the reasonableness of parties raising, pursuing or contesting particular allegations or issues, the manner of handling the claim and whether the claim was exaggerated.[64]

b. The Obligation to Mediate

The decision in *Dunnett v Railtrack*,[65] which caused considerable concern, suggested that the conduct of the parties in refusing mediation was relevant to the court's decision in awarding costs. In *Dunnett* the judge, while granting leave to appeal, had advised consideration of alternative dispute resolution. The claimant (C) approached the defendants (R) regarding the possibility. R refused to consider mediation at the time, but made an offer to settle nearer to the hearing date. R succeeded in an appeal and sought costs against the claimant. It was held that there should be no order as to costs.

---

[62] SC Grebe, 'Ethics and the Professional Family Mediator' (1992) 10 *Mediation Quarterly* 155.
[63] Civil Procedure Rules 1998, r 44.2.4.
[64] ibid, r 44.5.
[65] *Dunnett v Railtrack PLC* [2002] EWCA Civ 303.

It was said that, if a party rejected alternative dispute resolution out of hand when it had been suggested by the court, they would suffer the consequences when costs came to be decided. Parties had a duty to further the overriding objective of the CPR. In the instant case, R had refused to even contemplate alternative dispute resolution at a stage prior to the costs of the appeal escalating. It was therefore not appropriate to take into account the fact that later offers had been made to compromise the action. This was widely interpreted as indicating that mediation was, in effect, compulsory, even if not ordered by the court.

c. Factors in Determining Reasonableness of Refusal to Mediate

In subsequent cases, the harsh lesson of *Dunnett* was somewhat softened. In *Halsey v Milton Keynes General NHS Trust*,[66] the Court of Appeal demonstrated a sophisticated understanding of the issues surrounding ADR and compulsion. In the case, the claimant (H) sued for medical negligence causing the death of her husband. The defendant (M) disputed liability and refused H's invitation to take part in alternative dispute resolution. M was awarded costs at first instance. It was said that the CPR were not designed to compel parties with a good defence to settle claims that they ultimately went on to win.

Dismissing the widow's appeal against the costs order, the Court of Appeal agreed that M had not acted unreasonably by refusing to mediate. The judge had found that the claimant's offer was 'somewhat tactical'. The cost of mediation would have been disproportionately high compared with value of the claim and the prospective costs of trial. In the circumstances, H had not discharged the burden of proving that mediation had a reasonable prospect of success.

The Court of Appeal adopted a passage of the main work containing the court rules and commentary:[67]

> The hallmark of ADR procedures, and perhaps the key to their effectiveness in individual cases, is that they are processes voluntarily entered into by the parties in dispute with outcomes, if the parties so wish, which are non-binding. Consequently the court cannot direct that such methods be used but may merely encourage and facilitate.[68]

The court went on to reiterate that the court's role is to encourage, not compel. It then had the complex task of reconciling the principle that mediation should be voluntary with the idea, which it also accepted, that 'the form of encouragement may be robust'.[69]

The Court of Appeal decided that unreasonable refusal to mediate should be punishable by an order in costs, but that the burden must be on an unsuccessful party to show why there should be a departure from the general rule on costs. The fundamental principle was that the loser paid the winner's costs unless the winner was guilty of an unreasonable refusal to agree to ADR. The stronger the encouragement from the

---

[66] *Halsey v Milton Keynes General NHS Trust* [2004] EWCA Civ 576.
[67] The White Book, vol 1 (2003) s 1.4.11.
[68] *Halsey v Milton Keynes General NHS Trust* (n 66) per Dyson LJ at [9].
[69] ibid, at [11].

court to participate, the easier it will be for the unsuccessful party to discharge the burden of showing that the successful party's refusal was unreasonable.[70]

The Law Society made a successful intervention regarding the factors relevant to the question of whether a party had unreasonably refused ADR. These were: (i) the nature of the dispute; (ii) the merits of the case; (iii) the extent to which other settlement methods had been attempted; (iv) whether the costs of the ADR would be disproportionately high; (v) whether any delay in setting up and attending the ADR would have been prejudicial; and (vi) whether the ADR had a reasonable prospect of success. The Court of Appeal emphasised that in many cases no single factor would be decisive, and that the factors were not an exhaustive checklist. [71]

The conclusion drawn from *Halsey* was that ignoring a court direction to mediate would be almost certain to be punished by costs sanctions,[72] but otherwise, sanctions were less likely. In *Allen v Jones*,[73] *Dunnett* was distinguished. It was held that, as a matter of principle, a successful party should not be deprived of costs merely because he had refused to submit to mediation in an 'all or nothing' case. In the circumstances, there was no middle way between the parties to be explored and the court had not suggested that mediation should take place. Similarly, in *Cressman v Coys of Kensington (Sales) Ltd*[74] it was held that where one party did not clearly commit to mediation they could not use the other's reluctance as an argument why they should not pay costs.

d. Timing

The timing of an offer to mediate is a critical factor in its own right. Parties can be penalised for a refusal to mediate at any stage of a dispute. Therefore, when one side suggests mediation before proceedings begin, the court can scrutinise the reasons for refusal.[75] Subsequently, parties must seriously consider a recommendation by a judge to mediate. If, however, a losing party is to avoid a costs order they must show that their offer to mediate was not merely motivated by the real prospect of losing, that it was sincere and that it was timely.

Depending on the circumstances, other informal methods of dispute resolution may be preferable to mediation. This is particularly the case when an offer to mediate is made near to trial date. This proposition was amply demonstrated by *ADS Aerospace Ltd v EMS Global Tracking Ltd*.[76] The case involved a $16 million claim for the breach and repudiation of an agreement heard in the Technology & Construction Court. The contract was for the exclusive distribution of satellite-tracking devices for aeroplanes or helicopters. The defendant successfully defended the claim. It was found that it had not acted unreasonably in not wishing to participate in mediation.

---

[70] ibid, at [29].
[71] ibid, at [16].
[72] *Hurst v Leeming* [2002] EWHC 1051 (Ch); *Leicester Circuits Ltd v Coates Bros PLC* [2003] EWCA Civ 333; *Royal Bank of Canada Trust Corporation v Secretary of State for Defence* [2003] EWHC 1479 (Ch).
[73] *Allen v Jones* [2004] EWHC 1189 (QB).
[74] *Cressman v Coys of Kensington (Sales) Ltd* [2004] EWCA Civ 133.
[75] *Burchell v Bullard and others* [2005] EWCA Civ 358.
[76] *ADS Aerospace Ltd v EMS Global Tracking Ltd* [2012] EWHC 2904 (TCC).

For two months before the offer of mediation, the defendant's solicitors had tried several times to initiate settlement discussions with the plaintiff's solicitors.

An offer to mediate came from the claimant six weeks before the trial date. It was made in the light the claimant's firm assessment that it would not accept much less than $16 million. In these circumstances, the Court said, the defendants should not be penalised for refusing mediation. They were entitled to take the view that they had a strong case on liability, causation and quantum. The claimant gave every appearance that it was simply not interested in a nuisance payment. The defendant had shown willing to engage in without-prejudice discussions. There was no good reason why the defendant should not have tried that approach. With less than 20 working days before the trial, without-prejudice discussions would have been quicker, cheaper and less intrusive than mediation.

e. A Duty to Constructively Engage with Offers of Mediation

Following the Jackson review of civil litigation the signs were that the courts would continue to follow a hard line on the obligation to mediate. In *PGF II SA v OMFS Company 1 Ltd*,[77] the claimant made a thoughtful and detailed offer of mediation and, having received no response, repeated the offer three months later. The defendant made a Part 36 offer to settle which was accepted just before the hearing. Normally, this would entitle the defendant to costs from when the offer was made. The Court of Appeal noted that, since *Halsey v Milton Keynes General NHS Trust*, the court had imposed costs sanctions, usually when parties gave reasons for not participating in mediation. What, asked the court, 'should be the response of the court to a party which, when invited by its opponent to take part in a process of alternative dispute resolution ("ADR"), simply declines to respond to the invitation in any way?'.

The trial judge had found the refusal to mediate unreasonable and had denied the defendant costs that would otherwise have been recoverable by them. He did not however, order the defendant to pay the claimant's costs over the same period. Both parties appealed. The Court of Appeal agreed that a failure to respond was itself unreasonable, whether or not the defendant had reasonable grounds to refuse mediation. Lord Justice Briggs said that

> the constraints which now affect the provision of state resources for the conduct of civil litigation (and which appear likely to do so for the foreseeable future) call for an ever-increasing focus upon means of ensuring that court time, both for trial and for case management, is proportionately directed towards those disputes which really need it, with an ever-increasing responsibility thrown upon the parties to civil litigation to engage in ADR, wherever that offers a reasonable prospect of producing a just settlement at proportionate cost.[78]

The Court of Appeal found some support in precedent for treating silence as refusal to participate in ADR.[79] It found that there is a duty to 'constructively engage' with any request for ADR.[80] This may amount to no more than giving grounds for

---

[77] *PGF II SA v OMFS Company 1 Ltd* [2013] EWCA Civ 1288.

[78] ibid, at [27].

[79] *Burchell v Bullard* (n 75), per Ward LJ at [43], *Rolf v De Guerin* [2011] EWCA Civ 78, per Rix LJ at [46].

[80] *PGF II SA v OMFS Company 1 Ltd* [2013] EWCA Civ 1288, at [30].

refusal,[81] but the response must be given at the time that the offer of ADR is made.[82] In dismissing the cross-appeals, the court was aware that this seemed be a little harsh on the defendant. It would be deprived of substantial costs, despite having an offer to settle accepted late in the day. However, Briggs LJ took comfort in the thought that:

> The court's task in encouraging the more proportionate conduct of civil litigation is so important in current economic circumstances that it is appropriate to emphasise that message by a sanction which, even if a little more vigorous than I would have preferred, nonetheless operates *pour encourager les autres*.[83]

iii. Summary

The decision in *Dunnett*, and subsequent cases, had clear implications for lawyers in terms of the advice they offered to clients. In *Dunnett* it was said that it was a lawyer's duty to further the overriding objective of the CPR. That duty included an obligation to consider whether alternative dispute resolution might provide a solution. In a later case, Lord Woolf said that ADR must be considered when advising on disputes, resulting from the 'heavy obligation to resort to litigation only if it is really unavoidable'.[84]

The cases on the obligation to mediate carry clear guidelines for lawyers to consider with clients. In *Halsey* it was said that 'all members of the legal profession who conduct litigation should now routinely consider with their clients whether their disputes are suitable for ADR'.[85] Clients must also be warned that they must positively engage with offers of ADR, even where there are good reasons for not trying to resolve disputes in this way. If such an offer is made a response should always be provided, with clear reasons given if the offer is declined.

B.   Representative Responsibilities

Lawyers have complex responsibilities in acting as representatives in mediation. This starts with the issue of whether they should act at all, given the theoretical arguments for non-lawyers as representatives or for clients to represent themselves. As representatives, lawyers must demonstrate ordinary standards of competence and possess a level of appreciation and skill enabling them to participate in meeting clients' interests. In a business setting, for example, they must be aware of the commercial context of the dispute, the interests of the party in a continuing relationship, the potential for mutually beneficial agreement and so on.[86]

---

[81] ibid, at [34].
[82] ibid, at [35]–[36].
[83] ibid, at [56].
[84] Per Lord Woolf in *Cowl and Others v Plymouth City Council* Times Law Reports 8 January 2002, at [27].
[85] *Halsey v Milton Keynes General NHS Trust* (n 66) at [11].
[86] Thompson, 'Commercial Dispute Resolution' (n 6) at 90.

If they decide to act, they must be careful not to subvert the purpose of mediation, which includes finding a 'non-legal' solution to a problem, while being constantly aware of what legal solutions offer. They must be clear what their role is in the particular kind of mediation and have a clear agreement with the client about what is offered. If mediation is occurring during litigation, it will be necessary to consider issues of timing and purpose. It is unclear whether a representative in mediation has a broad discretion in handling the case, like an advocate, or whether they are more tightly bound to clients' instructions.

In the context of the CPR representatives should engage with one eye on the overriding objective of achieving justice. This involves participating, and ensuring that clients participate, in good faith. They must seek to assist the mediator in finding the best way to handle the dispute and not disrupt the process. Mindful of the costs sanction, lawyers must persist with mediation, even if they think initial proposals inadequate. They will also be bound by conventional obligations relating to litigation.

The risk on costs that flows from not engaging with mediation creates a potential for conflict between solicitors and clients. If a client is found liable for not engaging, they may argue that they were not properly advised by their lawyer on either the advantages of ADR or the risks regarding costs. They may well seek to recover costs from a lawyer in negligence. It is also possible that they could claim in negligence if they lose a claim that might have been settled, if there is evidence that they were not properly advised.

There are some aspects of lawyers' responsibilities in mediation that are less clear. One of these is whether a representative owes the mediator a duty equivalent to the duty to the court or whether the duties are more like those owed to a third party in negotiation. There are arguments both ways and their strength may vary depending on the type of process. For example, if the mediation is a judicial mediation as part of employment proceedings, the argument for a higher duty is strong. It may be less strong in other situations, particularly since representatives in mediation need not be lawyers. Such representatives are not subject to any higher duty.

C. Responsibilities as Third Party Neutrals

i. Roles and Duties

'Neutral third party' is an omnibus term covering the central role in ADR processes, whether arbitrator, mediator or conciliator. The ethical principles binding third party neutrals are clear and are reflected in legal decisions. They include general duties of honesty, integrity, neutrality, impartiality and candour with the parties. They also include more specific responsibilities such as avoidance of conflicts of interest, including over fees and fee arrangements.[87]

---

[87] T Arnold, 'Reviewing Ethics Issues in Mediation' (1995) 19 *ALI-ABA Course Material Journal* 53; JDD Smith, 'Mediator Impartiality: Banishing the Chimera' (1994) 31 *Journal of Peace Research* 445.

There are various sources of specific duties. The authority and duties of arbitrators may be found in the arbitration agreement or the law of the specified jurisdiction or the rules of the arbitrator's organisation. In international contexts they may include international codes including professional codes.[88] They may be incorporated in the contractual agreement giving rise to the claim or agreed after the dispute arises.

The rules will differ according to the type of ADR process in use. In mediation, for example, a mediator can ignore a lawyer's legal submissions when it is clear that a client is asserting an alternative agenda.[89] In arbitration it could be negligent to ignore legal submissions. In Mediation/Arbitration the position depends on the agreement. Typically, third party neutrals attempt to mediate between the parties but, in default of agreement, can make an arbitral award.[90] Therefore, there is an obligation to take account of legal argument.

The volume of rules may also differ according to the type of ADR and the involvement of the courts. Because arbitration has been operating for longer, and because of the fact that it mirrors court outcomes, a more developed case law underpins it. There are fewer cases dealing with mediation and conciliation.

Cases come to court from ADR for a variety of reasons, usually because one side does not like the outcome. In arbitration, because the parties have agreed to accept the decision, they have to attack the integrity of arbitrator or the process. The case law reflects ethical principles that should guide practice in the relevant area. Arbitrators and mediators are also subject to civil liability, for example for breach of contract, breach of fiduciary duty or professional negligence. This area of liability also produces cases relevant to the ethics of process.

The brief overview that follows is intended as a sketch of the ethical responsibilities of third party neutrals in the different ADR methods. This overview focuses on three methods, arbitration, mediation and conciliation, and four legal and ethical requirements, competence, neutrality, impartiality and confidentiality. In relation to mediation and conciliation the main focus is confidentiality.

D. Arbitration

Arbitration awards are particularly susceptible to review by courts on the grounds of the arbitrator's misconduct, lack of neutrality or partiality. It is important to distinguish neutrality from impartiality. Neutrality is not supporting or assisting either side in a dispute or conflict, whereas impartiality is not favouring one side more than another'.[91] Neutrality is consistent with a pre-existing state of non-alliance, whereas impartiality relates to later behaviour. Therefore, an arbiter can be formally neutral, yet partiality can develop during the course of a matter.

---

[88] See eg the International Bar Association, *Rules of Ethics for International Arbitrators.*
[89] L Mulcahy 'Can Leopards Change their Spots? An Evaluation of the Role of Lawyers in Medical Negligence Mediation' (2001) 8 *International Journal of the Legal Profession* 203 at 216.
[90] Thompson (n 6) at 92.
[91] *Oxford Paperback Dictionary* (Oxford, Oxford University Press, 1979).

i. Competence

The courts have determined that competence is a question of fact rather than an issue of position. Therefore, if an arbitrator loses a position which led to the initial appointment, such as a formal position in a professional association, he may still retain the competence to act.[92] Arbitrators must follow agreed procedures and apply the principles of natural justice in reaching decisions.[93] If they fail to do so they may be removed or their decisions reversed. In *Oakstead Garages Ltd v Leach Pension Scheme (Trustees) Ltd*,[94] for example, an appeal was allowed against the decision of an arbitrator in a rent review. He had told parties that he would inspect relevant comparable properties but failed to do so. In *Mabanaft GBMH v Consentino Shipping Company SA*,[95] an arbitrator's decision was based on a theory not raised with the applicants. This was potentially a reason to set aside the decision. It was held to be an issue of fact and degree whether a party should have an opportunity to respond to points affecting the decision.

ii. Neutrality

The duty of neutrality requires that any possible conflict of interest be disclosed at the outset. An objection should be made at that stage. If a party is aware of a conflict of interest and does nothing, they cannot complain later that the arbitrator was not neutral. In *Fletamentos Maritimos SA v Effjohn Internation BV*,[96] an arbitrator had, in another matter, provided a witness statement highly critical of the applicants' solicitor. He also failed to formally disclose the possible conflict. This was drawn to the applicants' attention early in the proceedings, but no objection was raised at the time. A later attempt to remove the arbitrator failed, there being no evidence of partiality in his handling of the case.

Where it is alleged that an arbitrator has a conflict of interest it must be shown that there is a proper foundation for such a claim. In *Bremerhandelsqueseuschaft mbh v ETS Soules etc cie & Anar*,[97] for example, an application by a commodity seller for removal of the director of a commodity house from a Board of Appeal was refused. Although the third party neutral was from the other side of the commodities industry, there was nothing in the individual's record suggesting bias towards buyers.

An alleged conflict of interest must also be shown to be material. An interesting application of this principle arose in *Kuwait Foreign Trading Contracting and Investment Co*.[98] In that case, a barrister was appointed arbitrator in a case in which a barrister from the same chambers was instructed by one of the parties. It was held that

---

[92] *Pan Atlantic Group Inc and Others v Hassneh Insurance Co. of Israel Ltd* (1992) *Arbitration and Dispute Resolution Law Journal* 179.
[93] HJ Kirsh, 'Arbitrating Construction Disputes' in Emond (n 3) 175, at 180.
[94] *Oakstead Garages Ltd v Leach Pension Scheme (Trustees) Ltd* [1996] 24 EG 147.
[95] *Mabanaft GBMH v Consentino Shipping Company SA* [1984] 2 Lloyd's Rep 191.
[96] *Fletamentos Maritimos SA v Effjohn Internation BV* (1996) LTL 21/2/97.
[97] *Bremerhandelsqueseuschaft mbh v ETS Soules etc cie & Anar* (1985) FTCR 4.5.85.
[98] In *Kuwait Foreign Trading Contracting and Investment Co* (Paris, Court of Appeal, 1991) (1993) *Arbitration and Dispute Resolution Law Journal* pt 3.

this was insufficient connection for a conflict of interest. There had to be 'material' or 'intellectual' connections with one of the parties. An English barrister's membership of chambers was found not to create 'common interests or any economic or intellectual interdependence among its members'. The sharing of chambers was, surprisingly, not a material connection which affected a barrister's status as a sole practitioner.

There may be circumstances where it is difficult to find an arbitrator who is seen as neutral to all sides, as in international matters.[99] Where this occurs a common solution is for a panel of three arbitrators to be appointed. One panel member is nominated by each side to interpret local laws and customs and to ensure that all arguments are heard. A neutral third is appointed by agreement or nominated by an institution, either under the arbitration agreement or otherwise.

iii. *Impartiality*

An arbitrator must not be seen to lean towards either side. A decision can be overturned and an arbitrator removed for bias if, on the evidence adduced and arguments made, the decision was unfair[100] or the arbitrator's conduct was unreasonable viewed from the perspective of a reasonable man. Most of the decisions on unreasonable conduct fall into two categories. The first is the arbitrator's failure to observe a judicial distance from the parties.[101] The second area relates to the admission of evidence.

In order to maintain judicial distance, arbitrators should not normally communicate with either party in the absence of the other except regarding purely administrative matters. If an arbitrator is observed sitting behind one party's counsel, apparently giving instructions, the reasonable man would think that the arbitrator was in the enemy's camp and that there was a real likelihood of bias.[102]

Arbitrators can suggest the parties should explore settlement, but should not participate unless this is allowed by the governing rules and agreed to by the parties. There must be substantial grounds for alleged bias, going beyond mere suspicion. In *Christopher Alan Turner v Stevenage Borough Council*, an application to remove an arbitrator for bias because one side had complied with his request for interim payment, but the other had not, was rejected.[103]

In relation to the second ground, admission of evidence, the failings must be substantial rather than mere procedural errors.[104] Arbitrators must be careful in using any power to call witnesses or using their own knowledge and experience in interpreting evidence. They must not use their experience to supply evidence that the parties have not chosen to supply themselves.

---

[99] J Epstein, H Gabriel, R Garnett and J Waincymer, *Practical Guide to International Commercial Arbitration* (Dobbs Ferry, NY, Oceana Publications, 2001).

[100] *The Ellisar* [1984] 2 Lloyds Rep 84 approved in *Town Centre Securities Plc v Leeds City Council* (1985) *Arbitration and Dispute Resolution Law Journal* 54.

[101] *Road Rejuvenating and Repair Services v Mitchell Water Board and Another* (1990) *Arbitration and Dispute Resolution Law Journal* 46.

[102] *Tracomin SA v Gibbs Nathaniel (Canada) and Anor* (1985) FTCR 1.2.85.

[103] *Christopher Alan Turner v Stevenage Borough Council* (1997) EGCS 34.

[104] In *L/S A/S Gill Brakh v Hyundai Corporation* (1987) ILR 2.11.87.

In *Top Shop Estates Ltd v C. Domino*,[105] an arbitrator's award was overturned, inter alia, on the ground that he gathered evidence without the consent or knowledge of the parties, including conducting a 'pedestrian court'. He accepted unsupported evidence without affording an opportunity to challenge his interpretations. Arbitrators must beware 'discarding the role of an impartial arbitrator and assuming the role of an advocate for the defaulting side'.[106]

In the Australian case, *Road Rejuvenating and Repair Services v Mitchell Water Board and Another*, an arbitrator managed to demonstrate partial behaviour in relation to both evidence and conduct. As to evidence, he had accepted hearsay and irrelevant material damaging to the plaintiff. As to judicial distance, he arrived for a meeting driven by an officer of the first defendant. The court called this an 'inexcusable alignment of an arbitrator with one party'. It went on to suggest that 'arbitrators are not mediators. It is not their function to deal directly with disputants where legal representatives are retained'.[107]

E. Mediation

i. Competence

There is no universally accepted description of the mediator's role or commonly agreed standards. Mediators should be capable of exploring the interests of the parties, the most suitable options for satisfying those interests and the costs and benefits of these options. Some models may require a more proactive approach, such as proposing packages or mechanisms for reaching agreement, taking steps towards 'operationalising' the agreement and evaluating and monitoring enforcement procedures.[108]

Since mediation is voluntary, and terminable at any time, it is arguable that breakdown of the process through incompetence of the mediator should not result in liability. There is, however, an argument that removal of a mediator for incompetence could result in an action for negligence or breach of contract.[109] This argument is strengthened where there are compulsory codes of mediator conduct, as there are for solicitors. The measure of damages could include costs thrown away.

ii. Impartiality

Most models of mediation stress the need for the mediator to be even-handed. They must be cautious about holding private meetings with the parties and about passing

---

[105] *Estates Ltd v C. Domino* (High Court 1984) (1992) *Arbitration and Dispute Resolution Law Journal* 47.

[106] *Fox v P.G. Wellfair Ltd* [1981] 2 Lloyds' Rep 514, per Lord Denning MR.

[107] *Road Rejuvenating and Repair Services v Mitchell Water Board and Another* Supreme Court of Victoria, per Nathan J (1990) *Arbitration and Dispute Resolution Law Journal* 46.

[108] CW Moore, *The Mediation Process: Practical Strategies for Resolving Conflict* (San Francisco, Jossey Bass, 1986) at 14.

[109] Bevan, *Alternative Dispute Resolution* (n 14) at 33.

on information discovered in such meetings.[110] Even making recommendations to avoid breakdown of the mediation, at the request of the parties, may be seen as compromising impartiality. Rather, the Law Society's Code of Practice for Civil and Commercial Mediation suggests advising parties 'as to the desirability of seeking further assistance from professional advisers such as lawyers, accountants, expert valuers or others'.[111] This generally means that mediators cannot redress inequalities between the parties.[112]

iii. Confidentiality

Confidentiality and privilege refer to two different areas of protection. Confidentiality refers to a client's expectation that anything divulged to another party will not be disclosed in any context, whereas privilege means that it cannot be produced in court. The justification for attaching confidentiality and privilege to material produced with a view to settlement is twofold.[113] First, there is a public policy interest in encouraging settlement and protecting settlement negotiations, in whatever form they take. The intention to claim this protection is usually conveyed by using the words 'without prejudice' in communications aimed at settlement. Secondly, there is the express or implied agreement of the parties that their communications for that purpose be protected. There may be circumstances where one applies but not the other.

Effective ADR is often dependent on full disclosure of oral or documentary information. Conventions as to what this involves do differ between forms of ADR. Arbitration is a formal process and disclosure requirements are similar to those in litigation. Therefore, a solicitor is bound to notify the arbitrator and other side of discovery of documents that should be disclosed, such as an order form showing the incorporation of standard terms into a contract.[114] In mediation, however, discussion and agreement are generally the means of verifying information.

Although mediation processes seldom require the parties to produce specific relevant documents, disclosure may resolve misunderstandings. The disclosure and verification process may be different in court-annexed mediation. Disclosure of documents may have already occurred or may be occurring before mediation takes place. If it has not, parties are under no specific obligation to disclose information. They may suffer in costs however, if they withhold information that later proves material.

It is important that a party's interests are protected when disclosing material against their own interests in mediation. While courts in the UK, and abroad, have asserted the importance of protecting the secrecy of settlement,[115] uncertainty surrounds the security of disclosed information. There are particular difficulties when privileged

---

[110] Arnold, 'Reviewing Ethics Issues in Mediation' (n 87) at 63.

[111] N Taylor, *The Guide to the Professional Conduct of Solicitors* (London, The Law Society, 1999) 419, at 5.4 and 5.5.

[112] Bevan (n 14) at 34.

[113] *Rush & Tompkins Ltd v GLC* [1989] AC 1280; *Cutts v Head* [1984] Ch 290; *Unilever plc v Proctor & Gamble Co* [2000] 1 WLR 2436.

[114] *Yoldings v Swann Evans (A firm)* [2000] All ER (D) 1633 (Technology and Construction Court).

[115] *Hall v Pertemps Group* [2005] All ER (D) 15.

information is disclosed for the purposes of mediation and yet privilege is claimed for the same information in later litigation.

A case illustrating the problem of information security in mediation is *Robert Aird and Karen Aird v Prime Meridian Ltd*.[116] One of the parties to a court-annexed mediation wanted to use a joint experts' report, prepared at the direction of the judge, in continuing litigation. The other party resisted this on the ground that they had understood that it would be privileged. The Court of Appeal held that the joint expert statement complied with CPR Rule 35.12, having been agreed by both sides, and was not a mediation document privileged from production.

The confidentiality and privilege from production in court enjoyed by mediation is based on the use of the 'without prejudice' formula and the mediation agreement. Suggesting that discussions are 'without prejudice' is not decisive.[117] The court is entitled to consider the purpose and nature of the discussion, and its relevance to settlement of the same dispute for which privilege is claimed.[118] The court is also entitled to consider whether it is fair and just to allow the use of material in litigation[119] and to consider whether settlement was reached.[120]

Inclusion of material gathered in mediation in a list of documents is not a waiver of privilege.[121] Continuing uncertainty regarding the security of confidential information disclosed in mediation has led to suggestions that no notes or records should be kept of confidential discussions.[122] This would not, however, prevent mediators being asked questions about what they could remember.

When mediators discover that there has been false information exchanged, or bad faith, the ethical arguments for keeping confidences are turned on their head. In such circumstances, it has been suggested that a mediator should try to persuade the parties to rectify the problem and, if this fails, to withdraw.[123] Whether this is sufficient is debatable, particularly if the process has concluded.

Mediators are legally obliged to bring some criminal activity to the attention of the authorities. The obvious risk is committing an offence under the Proceeds of Crime Act 2002, section 328.[124] This is most likely to occur where the lawyer becomes involved in an arrangement known or suspected to be facilitating 'the acquisition, retention, use or control of criminal property by or on behalf of another person'.[125] Assisting in negotiating a settlement could be treated as being 'concerned' in an arrangement for the purposes of the Act. A mediator or representative lawyer would be obliged to report suspicious activity, as discussed in chapter 14. Clients cannot be informed of this disclosure if investigations are ongoing.

---

[116] *Robert Aird and Karen Aird v Prime Meridian Ltd* [2006] EWHC 2338 (TCC), [2006] EWCA Civ 1866.
[117] Bevan (n 14) at 31.
[118] *Muller v Linsley & Mortimer* The Times 8 December 1994; *South Shropshire District Council v Amos* [1986] 1 WLR 1271; *Rediffusion Simulation v Link-Miles* [1992] FSR 196; and see J McEwan, 'Without Prejudice: Negotiating a Minefield' (1994) 13 *Civil Justice Quarterly* 133.
[119] *Smith Group plc v Weiss* [2002] All ER 356 (Ch).
[120] *Brown v Rice* [2007] All ER 252.
[121] *Smith Group plc v Weiss* [2002] All ER 356 (Ch).
[122] BE Larson and SB Hansen, 'Ethics in ADR' (1992) 22 *The Brief* 14.
[123] Bevan (n 14) at 32.
[124] *P v P (Ancillary Relief: Proceeds of Crime)* [2003] EWHC Fam 2260, [2004] 1 FLR 193.
[125] Proceeds of Crime Act 2002, s 328(1).

F. Conciliation

Conciliation does have some important similarities to, and differences from, other ADR processes. It was perceived that family conciliation, for example, should be voluntary and that for it to be compulsory may be counterproductive.[126] Nevertheless, it was anticipated that the third party neutral may have a role in counteracting attempts by a stronger party to exploit the weaker party.[127] There was a pilot family conciliation scheme in the 1980s and a practice direction issued in the early 1990s.

Privilege attaches to communications arising during the course of family conciliation[128] and to proceedings under the Children Act (1989).[129] Conciliation privilege may no longer rely on the 'without prejudice' formula, having developed into a new head based on the public interest in promoting the stability of marriage.[130] The effect is that neither advisers nor conciliators can be compelled to give evidence of what transpired in conciliation. The privilege extends from the parties, if they attempt conciliation themselves, to their advisers including lawyers[131] or other official parties, like lawyers, probation officers or priests, or even private individuals, appointed as conciliators.[132]

There are exceptions to the general principle against non-disclosure; where the process was not genuine or the parties consent to disclosure. In such cases, a third party neutral cannot themselves claim privilege.[133] Privilege may also be lost if the evidence concerns potential harm to a child, or a risk of such harm in future. Even here, however, the circumstances must be exceptional. The judge will exercise discretion in deciding whether protecting the child outweighs the public interest in preserving the confidentiality of matters raised in attempted conciliation.[134]

V. Professional Regulation of ADR

A. The Legal Profession's Early Engagement with Regulation of ADR

Many professional groups tend to be involved in ADR processes. Their level and type of engagement varies depending on the area of work. Lawyers may not be a majority of mediators in a particular area. Their participation level will depend on which

---

[126] Law Commission *Family Law: The Ground for Divorce* (n 26) at para 5.34.
[127] ibid; and see Roberts, 'Who is in Charge? (n 14) at 373.
[128] *La Roche v Armstrong* (1922) 1 KB 485.
[129] Children Act 1989, s 1(1) and see Practice Direction (Family Division: Conciliation) [1992] 1 WLR 147.
[130] See Lords Hailsham and Simon in *D v National Society for Prevention of Cruelty to Children* [1978] AC 171.
[131] *Henley v Henley* [1955] 1 All ER 590.
[132] *McTaggart v McTaggart* [1949] P 94; *Mole v Mole* [1951] P 21; and *Theodoropoulas v Theodoropoulas* [1964] P 311.
[133] *McTaggart v McTaggart*, ibid.
[134] In re *D (Minors)* [1993] Fam 231.

other groups offer services and the type of services clients in that field prefer. Whether lawyers are involved may depend on whether they offer additional value to the dispute resolution process. When firms are instructed in high value, specialist matters, multi-disciplinary teams may be formed.[135] This is particularly likely when different perspectives, for example on gender[136] or cultural issues,[137] are required.

Lawyers' interest in mediation can be traced to Solicitors in Mediation, a body formed by five family law solicitors and the former training officer for the National Family Conciliation Council in 1985.[138] This offered mediation in child and property disputes. The Bar responded to this by offering an early neutral valuation scheme. This was not widely used.

The Law Society formed a Family Mediators Association (FMA) in 1988. In 1991, reports for the Bar and Law Society considered ADR. The Bar Committee, under Lord Justice Beldam, and the Law Society report, prepared by Henry Brown, acknowledged the potential importance of ADR.[139] The Beldam Committee report recommended that facilitative mediation be offered in civil disputes, with experienced lawyers acting as mediators.[140] The Law Society report was more measured. It suggested that ADR would be inappropriate in cases where issues of principle of a public nature were involved, where there were power imbalances between parties or where ADR was used as a tactic, for example to delay litigation.[141]

Lord Woolf's proposal to extend the use of mediation precipitated an increase in numbers of mediators and providers of mediation services. The number of providers increased from less than 10 before 1999 to around 60 after.[142] The established providers continued to flourish, however. For example, the major provider of commercial ADR, the Centre for Effective Dispute Resolution, increased its caseload.

In the run-up to the introduction of the CPR, mediation pilot schemes in the Central London County and other centres reported initial signs that lawyers would be hostile to the introduction of mediation. Many apparently believed that mediation was only suited to litigants in person,[143] preferring their 'known litigation strategies' for their own clients.[144] They were reluctant to recommend mediation and the take-up was low.

A pilot for an out of court mediation scheme in Bristol, backed by the Law Society, had only 24 cases in its first year. Only two of the cases actually reached the mediation

---

[135] In family mediation, solicitors and social workers sometimes co-work on all issues (Roberts (n 14) at 373).

[136] G Davis and M Roberts, *Access to Agreement: A Consumer Study of Mediation in Family Disputes* (Milton Keynes, Open University Press, 1988).

[137] S Shah Kazemi, 'Family Mediation and the Dynamics of Culture' (1996) 6 *Family Mediation* 5.

[138] S Roberts and M Palmer, *Dispute Processes: ADR and the Primary Forms of Decision-Making* (Cambridge, Cambridge University Press, 2005) at 66.

[139] The Beldam Committee, *Report of the Committee on Alternative Dispute Resolution* (General Council of the Bar, 1991).

[140] S Roberts, 'Mediation in the Lawyers' Embrace' (1992) 55(2) *Modern Law Review* 258 at 260.

[141] H Brown, *Alternative Dispute Resolution*, prepared for the Law Society's Courts and Legal Services Committee (July 1991).

[142] G Chadwick, 'Finding its feet' *The Lawyer* 10 September 2001, at 33; A Glaister, 'ADR: Quality not Quantity' (2000) 144 *Solicitors Journal* 1024.

[143] H Genn, *The Central London County Court Pilot Mediation Scheme: Evaluation Report* (Lord Chancellor's Department, 1998).

[144] L Tsang, 'Research Finds Solicitors are Hostile to Mediation Scheme' *The Lawyer* 4 August 1998, at 2.

stage.[145] Some solicitors thought, perhaps quite reasonably, that investment in mediation was not justified by the returns, particularly in view of the fillip the Woolf reforms gave to inter-parties negotiation.[146]

Following the introduction of the CPR in 1998, the Law Society introduced a Civil and Commercial Mediation Panel in autumn 2001. Accreditation standards for the panel were worked out with the leading providers. Practitioner members were required to undergo 65 hours of experience and training over two years. The Law Society also formed a Dispute Resolution Section in 2006 to represent the common interests of litigators and mediators. This aimed to 'influence the increasingly complex legal and commercial environment'.[147] A few organisations trained mediators, including some lawyers, and undertook mediations, but numbers of mediators were disproportionate to the number of cases. The use of lawyers as representatives varied between schemes and type of case.

B. The Need for Regulation

i. The Advantages and Disadvantages of Regulation

The disparity between mediators and cases was predictable. As often happens in new markets in mediation, a group of super mediators, lawyers and male, emerged, snapping up the plum cases.[148] The apparent proliferation of services, and lack of work, led to calls for stricter regulation to control numbers and supplement the providers' kite mark quality systems. The Law Society was uninterested in regulating mediators generally, probably because this would involve regulating non-lawyers.[149] The lack of central professional organisation for mediators had some theoretical advantages, but also carried some risk.[150]

The theoretical advantage of an unregulated mediation market lay in the potential for expansion of 'the universe of recognised conflicts' to produce new groups of practitioners with new ideas, approaches and methods.[151] The problem was that, without common standards, there would be considerable scope for difference in approach, with localised approaches emerging for different areas of work.[152]

There was a further risk that an unregulated mediation market could lead to arrangements that hindered development of a free market. An example of this was an agreement between the Forum of Insurance Lawyers and the Association of Personal Injury Lawyers (APIL). These bodies agreed to co-operate to promote common

---

[145] York, 'Privatisation of Disputes in 1997' (n 36).

[146] Genn, *The Central London County Court Pilot Mediation Scheme* (n 143).

[147] Press release by Law Society, 27 February 2006.

[148] C Baar and RG Hann, 'Mandatory Mediation in Civil Cases: Purposes and Consequences' (paper for Hart workshop, Institute of Advanced Legal Studies London, 2001).

[149] D Jones, 'The men from the boys' *The Lawyer* 10 September 2001, at 37.

[150] A Boon, R Earle and A Whyte, 'Regulating Mediators?' (2007) 10(1) *Legal Ethics* 26.

[151] W Warfield, 'Some *Minor* Reflections on Conflict Resolution: The State of the Field as a Moving Target' (2000) *Negotiation Journal* 381.

[152] J Fleming, 'PI mediation boost' 97(25) *Gazette* 22 June 2000, at 5.

standards of mediation. They also sought to establish a joint panel of mediators in those personal injury cases for which mediation was suitable. Obviously, lawyers outside these arrangements were potentially unable to compete.

The proliferation of mediation schemes could lead to there being no common ethic for practice.[153] Such a field could become more and more difficult to regulate fairly. One group, for example, lawyers, might be subject to professional and court jurisdiction, while others could be outside any regulatory framework. It could also present difficulties for educating and training potential mediators, including those within professions.

ii. Potential Regulators

The difficulty inherent in one profession regulating ADR does not prevent it regulating members' participation in these fields. This would presumably involve formation of rules of conduct for participants and, possibly, requirements for education and training. The standards of non-professional providers tend to coalesce around professional standards. For example, the ADR Group, a leading ADR service provider, requires non-lawyer members to subscribe to the Law Society Civil and Commercial Panel Code.

C. Education and Training

Until recently, ADR did not feature significantly in legal education and training. ADR or one of the methods, such as arbitration or mediation, is sometimes an optional course on degrees or professional courses. Both of the vocational courses have acknowledged that there is more to dispute resolution than litigation. This has not made any radical difference to the curriculum on the LPC, which tends to be based on adversarial assumptions. The BPTC has, however, adopted an ambitious ADR component.

i. Solicitors

Despite having a proposed syllabus for an introductory course on ADR in 1992, the LPC never included a relevant compulsory or skills component. In the current version of the course, Civil Litigation became Civil Litigation and Dispute Resolution.[154] Of the nine competencies for the subject only one refers to ADR as opposed to litigation.[155] This requires that prospective solicitors 'identify the appropriate forum for the resolution of the dispute, including appropriate methods of alternative dispute

---

[153] See further, R Dingwall, 'Divorce Mediation—Market Failure and Regulatory Capture' (paper for *Liberating Professions*, Conference of the Institute for the Study of the Legal Profession, Sheffield, July 1995).

[154] SRA, *Legal Practice Course Outcomes 2011* (www.sra.org.uk/students/lpc.page).

[155] ibid, at para 17.

resolution'. Only one other is arguably relevant. That is 'identify[ing] possible cost consequences of different outcomes, the effect of the different costs rules and the impact of the likely costs orders on the conduct of litigation'.

The need for consideration of the implications of the absence of any alternative dispute resolution paradigm is highlighted by the criteria for interviewing and advice. Both elements are geared to the collection of information in preparation for advice giving in a way conventionally associated with lawyers. There are aspects of the interviewing element that are intended to develop rapport with clients. These include being able to listen actively and use appropriate questioning techniques. These are expressed to be for the purpose of establishing a professional relationship. There is no reference to a need to explore underlying interests.

The outcome concerned with advice giving envisages the lawyer assisting the client to make a decision. This is in the light of possible courses of action and the legal and non-legal consequences of a course of action. These consequences include the costs, benefits and risks. The implication of these priorities is that discussion of a course of action is a once and for all decision concerning the direction of the matter, which is then in the hands of the solicitor. Such an approach does not lead to the formation of the kind of relationship that should, in theory at least, facilitate effective ADR.

ii. Barristers

Among the more radical recommendations of the Wood Report was to omit negotiation as a separately taught and assessed subject and to introduce the Resolution of Disputes out of Court.[156] This subject includes negotiation, alternative dispute resolution and mediation. The detailed specification of the new subject in the BPTC course specification is potentially extensive.[157] It includes knowledge and understanding of the theory and processes underpinning the range of methods of dispute resolution that lie outside the normal judicial processes, including arbitration, negotiation, mediation (through a neutral third party), collaborative law and conciliation.

Students are required to develop the practical skills required to advise upon, prepare for, and represent, parties at all stages of these processes. Students should also understand the role of the mediation advocate or representative. They should understand the ethics and conduct issues arising in mediation, negotiation or other forms of dispute resolution. BPTC students are also required to use the skills of negotiation and mediation in-course. The specified outcomes include the ability to select cases appropriate for each process and to advise professional and lay clients about them. Students must be able to prepare clients for mediation and represent them. Following qualification, the Bar Council offers family mediation training to barristers in collaboration with ADR Group.

---

[156] BSB, *Review of the Bar Vocational Course: Report of the Working Group* (London, BSB, 2008) at paras 16.7, 16.8 and 111.
[157] BSB, *Bar Professional Training Course: Course Specification Requirements and Guidance* (2012) at para 2.2.1(c).

D. Conduct

The creation of conduct rules governing ADR can be problematic. If such rules are included in the profession's main code they may contradict the rules for more established activities, such as advocacy. Once the need for different rules has been conceded for one activity, it may lead to calls for other exceptions. Therefore, mediation has not tended to feature in the main codes but in ancillary codes and regulations.

The stand-alone ADR codes tend to focus on topics reflecting the consensus regarding the 'correct' form of ADR at a particular time. In England and Wales, the codes reflect academic consensus regarding the consensual nature of ADR.[158] They take positions against evaluating options or pressuring parties to accept them. Such actions tend to be seen as ethically compromising behaviour in pursuit of the 'right' result.

i. Barristers

Barristers are involved in providing a wide range of ADR services. These include arbitration, where many have international practices, but also mediation, in which some chambers specialise. Despite this, neither the old or new Bar Code of Conduct pays much attention to ADR or mediation. The old Code provided that '[a] barrister instructed to appear in a mediation must not knowingly or recklessly mislead the mediator or any party or their representative'.[159] This merely transferred one aspect of the duty to the court to mediation.

The written standards of work, issued as an annex to the old Code of Conduct, contained a provision requiring barristers to ensure that advice was 'practical, appropriate to the needs and circumstances of the particular client, and clearly and comprehensibly expressed'.[160] As the practice of the courts has developed, the provision of such advice must include consideration of the potential benefits of ADR and the risks of not reasonably engaging with any offer to participate in ADR processes.

The other provision relating to ADR in the old Code of Conduct was an exception to the rules prohibiting making payments to receive professional instructions. This provided that reasonable fees could be paid to an alternative dispute resolution body appointing persons to provide mediation, arbitration or adjudication services.[161] It also permitted reasonable fee-sharing arrangements required by such a body, provided they were similar to those entered with others providing such services through

---

[158] Abel (n 5); JS Auerbach, *Justice Without Law* (Oxford, Oxford University Press, 1983); D Greatbach and R Dingwall, 'Selective Facilitation: Some Preliminary Observation on a Strategy used by Divorce Mediators' (1990) 28 *Family and Conciliation Court Review* 1.

[159] Bar Council, *Bar Code of Conduct 1981*, as amended, at para 708.1.

[160] ibid, *Written Standards for the Conduct of Professional Work*, at para 5.7. (www.barstandardsboard. org.uk/regulatory-requirements/the-old-code-of-conduct/written-standards-for-the-conduct-of-professional-work/).

[161] ibid, at para 307(e).

the body. Only a version of this second rule was reproduced in the BSB Code of Conduct 2014.

ii. Solicitors

a. ADR Principles in the Guide

There was pressure from some sections for the Law Society to be involved in the regulation of mediation. The Law Society Family Law Committee proposed draft standards of practice for lawyer mediators.[162] They also favoured establishment of a family court, with annexed conciliation services.[163] The seventh edition of the Guide, published in 1996, tackled the increasing significance of ADR by including a new chapter.[164] This advised that solicitors could offer ADR services, that is, act as third party neutrals, as part of their practice or as a separate business.[165]

Three other principles were laid out in the ADR chapter. Solicitor mediators were required to inform clients that they would be independent and impartial and not advise either party.[166] They were told that they must avoid conflicts of interest by not acting as third party neutrals in disputes where they acted for either party.[167] Nor were they allowed to act for a party after provision of neutral service in relation to that matter. A third and final principle in the chapter recommended that solicitors follow a code of practice.[168] It also suggested that 'solicitors wishing to offer ADR services should undertake appropriate training and work with one of the bodies providing training and a regulatory framework'.[169]

b. The Law Society's Specimen Mediation Code

The ADR chapter in the seventh edition of the Guide also included a specimen code.[170] This was said to be for civil and commercial mediation, but required adaptation for family matters.[171] It provided that the mediator's role is to 'help parties to work out their own principles and terms for the resolution of the issues between them', continuing:

> [T]he mediator may meet the parties individually and/or together and may assist the parties for example: by identifying areas of agreement, narrowing and clarifying areas of disagreement; defining the issues; helping the parties to examine the issues and their available courses of action; establishing and examining alternative options for resolving any disagreement;

---

[162] Marre Report (n 19) at para 11.16.
[163] ibid, at para 11.19.
[164] N Taylor (ed), *The Guide to the Professional Conduct of Solicitors*, 7th edn (London, The Law Society, 1996) ch 22.
[165] ibid, at para 22.01.
[166] ibid, at para 22.02.
[167] ibid, at para 22.03.
[168] ibid, at para 22.04.
[169] ibid, at para 22.01.4.
[170] ibid, 'Mediation—specimen code of practice—practice information', Annex 22A at 375.
[171] ibid, note to 22.04.

considering the applicability of specialised management, legal, accounting, technical or other expertise; and generally facilitating discussion and negotiation, managing the process and helping them to try to resolve their differences.[172]

The process described by the 1996 Guide was a fair description of a facilitative mediation, self-consciously non-directive, rather than an evaluative mediation.

The Law Society's specimen code boldly claimed, on the confidentiality issue, that:

[A]ll discussions and negotiations during the mediation will be regarded as evidentially privileged and conducted on a 'without prejudice' basis, unless such privilege is waived by the parties by agreement, either generally or in relation to any specific aspect'; nor is such information to be referred to in any 'subsequent proceedings.[173]

The code optimistically stated that no party could require the mediator to give evidence, or have access to a mediator's notes.[174] A court refusing to recognise 'mediator privilege' would, however, have put a mediator relying on this at risk of contempt of court.

The codes have consistently constrained solicitors' use of legal expertise in the role of mediator. For example, the original specimen code provided that parties could be assisted in understanding the principles of law applicable and their application to their circumstances. It went on to state that parties should not be advised on their rights or how they might be translated into settlement terms.[175]

c. The Law Society's Panel Mediation Codes

In the eighth edition of the Guide the specimen mediation code was replaced by two panel codes, one for Civil and Commercial Mediation and one for Family Mediation.[176] Despite being described as codes, they were optional. Both were preceded by a recommendation that solicitors abide by the code when offering the kinds of services covered by the codes. Both codes were non-specific about the role that solicitors engaged in mediation would be fulfilling, whether third party neutral or representative. The content of the codes made it clear, however, that they addressed solicitors acting as mediators. By 2006, members of the Law Society's specialist panels had to agree to be bound by the codes when undertaking mediation.[177]

The introduction to both codes stated that '[t]he concept of not giving advice to the parties, individually or collectively, when acting as a mediator permeates this code'.[178] The facilitative tone established in the original specimen code was retained in the panel codes. Both the Law Society's panel codes stated that the primary aim of

---

[172] ibid, at 28 1.5.
[173] ibid at note 79 2.3.
[174] ibid, at para 2.3.
[175] ibid, commentary on s 1.
[176] ibid, ch 22.
[177] Civil and Commercial Mediation Panel, *Criteria and Guidance Notes* (Version 4, November 2006) at 4, *Law Society's Code of Practice for Family Mediation* (Version 2, September 2005) at 5.
[178] Law Society, *Law Society's Code of Practice for Family Mediation—Practice Information*, The Guide, 8th edn, at 428.

mediation is to help the parties to arrive at their own decisions regarding the disputed issues.[179] They acknowledged that

> resolution may not necessarily be the same as that which may be arrived at in the event of adjudication by the court. That allows the parties to explore and agree upon a wider range of options for settlement than might otherwise be the case.[180]

The Civil and Commercial Code of Practice, which despite revision in 2011 is substantially the same, is now prefaced by the statement '[m]embers of the Law Society's Civil and Commercial Mediation Scheme must agree to be bound by this code'. This is interesting, because the Law Society no longer has regulatory powers to enforce such codes. It would presumably have to refer breaches to the SRA. The Civil Code also contains a statement that solicitors are bound by the Solicitors' Code of Conduct while mediating. This, as noted above, does not deal with mediation as such.

The Law Society's panel codes reflect well-established principles governing the conduct of mediation. The Civil Code states that impartiality is a 'fundamental principle' and mentions, in commentary, that personal views relating to the substance of the negotiations must not be allowed to affect this.[181] Both the panel codes have a section on 'dealing with power imbalances', which envisage a proactive role for mediators in addressing such situations. The Family panel code states that 'if power imbalances seem likely to cause the mediation process to become unfair or ineffective, the mediator must take appropriate steps to try and prevent this'.[182] It continues by stating that, if 'power imbalances cannot be redressed adequately', the mediator must end the mediation.

The Law Society's panel codes avoided the risk courted by the former code on the issue of confidentiality. They provided that mediators will not disclose information discovered in the course of mediation except with the consent of the parties.[183] They may also disclose, however, where such matters are already public, where persons are at risk or where there is an overriding obligation in law to disclose.

d. The Solicitors' Code of Conduct 2007

The 2007 Code of Conduct provided that solicitors could act as mediator between the parties in family matters, but should not thereafter act for one of them if a dispute arose.[184] The mediator's role was conceived of as helping the parties to reach their own solution to the dispute, not to impose a solution upon them. The mediator was to be impartial and the process confidential. It was not the role of the mediator to give professional legal advice to the parties, either individually or collectively. This would be difficult to avoid in cases where one or both of the parties did not have a solicitor.

---

[179] ibid, at para 5.1 and *Law Society's Code of Practice for Civil/Commercial Mediation—Practice Information*, The Guide, 8th edn, at 419, para 5.1.

[180] N Taylor, above, *The Guide to the Professional Conduct of Solicitors* (1999) ch 22: *Code of Practice for Civil and Commercial Mediation*, at para 5.2.

[181] ibid, s 3 and commentary to s 3.

[182] *Law Society's Code of Practice for Family Mediation*, ss 6.2–6.4 (see also Civil Panel s 6).

[183] Civil and Commercial Code, s 7.2 and Family Code, s 7.1.

[184] See SRA, *Solicitors' Code of Conduct 2007*, r 3.06.

However, Rule 3.06 stated that a solicitor must not act for any party for whom the solicitor or the firm has acted as a mediator or vice versa.

The Solicitors' Code of Conduct made specific but limited provision for ADR as an issue of advice giving and as causing a potential conflict of interest. The guidance to the chapter on client care dealt with solicitors advising clients in a dispute with a third party. It advised that they should discuss whether mediation or some other ADR procedure may be more appropriate than litigation, arbitration or other formal processes.[185]

The rule on conflict of interest provided that solicitors providing ADR services could not advise, or act for, any party in respect of a dispute in three circumstances. They could not act where they, or any person in their firm, was acting, or had acted, as mediator. The second and third rules stopped them providing ADR services, which were defined as acting as a third party neutral.[186] They could not do so in a matter in which they, or any person at their firm, had acted for a party. Nor could they provide ADR services when they, or any person at their firm, had acted for any of the parties in issues not relating to the mediation. All of these prohibitions were curable. It was permissible to act where the facts had been disclosed to the parties and they had consented. [187]

e. The SRA Code of Conduct

The SRA Code of Conduct 2011, as amended, contains no outcomes specifically relating to ADR. Section 1, 'You and Your Client', does not require solicitors to advise on the availability of ADR. Solicitors are therefore left with three rather broad, non-specific outcomes as their conduct guide for mediation. The first of these is that they must provide services to clients in a manner which protects their interests.[188] The second is that clients are in a position to make informed decisions about the services they need, how their matter will be handled and the options available to them.[189] The third is that clients receive the best possible information, both at the time of engagement and when appropriate as their matter progresses, about the likely overall cost of their matter.[190]

As the approach of the courts has developed, these outcomes must include responsibility to give quite detailed advice about the benefits and costs of different forms of ADR. Such advice may well need to be reviewed as cases develop. It may be that approaches that were originally ruled out become appropriate as circumstances change, perceptions of a case change or the parties' attitude to litigation changes.

---

[185] ibid, ch 3, guidance note 15.
[186] ibid, r 3, guidance note 69.
[187] ibid, ch 3: 'Conflicts of Interest', 3.06: 'Alternative Dispute Resolution (ADR)'.
[188] SRA, *Handbook, SRA Code of Conduct*, ch 1: 'You and Your Client', Outcome 1.2.
[189] ibid, Outcome 1.12.
[190] ibid, Outcome 1.13.

VI. Future of ADR

The initial flush of enthusiasm for mediation as a solution to a variety of problems having passed, lawyers have a choice as to whether ADR will be a significant part of their legal business. There is no doubt that alternatives to litigation will remain significant in a variety of cases and for a range of reasons. It is likely that many lawyers will continue to offer a range of ADR services. It will be the main work of some. At the very least, lawyers will need to give advice on the full range of dispute resolution options including ADR. There are therefore a number of issues that may be considered in the future.

One of the main issues has been largely ignored is the model of mediation adopted by the legal profession. In the early stages of reception of ADR methods into the mainstream, lawyers subscribed fully to the facilitative model. The professional bodies followed suit, in their panel codes, without apparently considering that this is an ideological decision with quite serious consequences. In rejecting the evaluative model of mediation, the profession may have missed an opportunity. The potential for authoritative evaluation is one of the main advantages of lawyers being involved as third party neutrals.

If the legal profession were to adopt an evaluative model of mediation, it would be more consistent with their existing orientation to legal work. This would leave the operation of facilitative mediation to those with more conducive disciplinary backgrounds. It is likely that evaluative mediation would be popular with clients looking for quick, cheap and fair dispute resolution. In practice, clients are often confused by the 'remote' role of the facilitative mediator.[191] Adopting a more evaluative model could help mitigate the impact of power imbalances. It would also address criticisms of many clients who find that facilitative mediation frustrates their expectation of an authoritatively certified fair settlement.[192]

If it were to be adopted, an evaluative mediation model would require some thought. It has been suggested that lawyers' role in mediation would be enhanced by giving legal advice to both parties in each other's presence.[193] Since their expertise puts lawyer mediators in a good position to secure fair agreements, it is also suggested that they should be ethically obliged to do so, while seeking solutions maximising the benefits to the parties.

Even if lawyers continue to engage with ADR on the same terms, that is, under the facilitative model, it is unclear whether and how this will be reflected in education and training and in conduct rules, if at all. As the account of the regulation of ADR shows, the obligations of lawyers as third party neutrals are not recognised in the codes. They are, however, contained in codes published by the Law Society that have no regulatory force.

---

[191] Boon, Urwin and Karuk 'What Difference Does it Make?' (n 61) .
[192] M Simmons, 'Mediators offer little value' *The Lawyer* 13 March, at 33.
[193] LL Riskin, 'Toward New Standards for the Neutral Lawyer in Mediation' (1984) 26 *Arizona Law Review* 329.

The responsibilities of lawyer representatives in ADR have never been paid much attention. While the specimen code that originally appeared in the Guide had more general emphasis, the panel codes that replaced it focus on solicitors as mediators rather than as representatives. The codes impose no duty to consider ADR in giving dispute resolution advice, even in relation to the basic standard required by the courts. This is in marked contrast to the regulation of mediation in the US, for example.

Many state bar codes in the US contain rules regarding lawyers' responsibilities in advising on dispute resolution. These tend to oblige lawyers to identify the objectives or means of representation and advise which dispute resolution methods are most appropriate, given the client's preferences and the nature of the problem.

In both Texas and Colorado, lawyers are under specific obligations to advise clients regarding the availability and/or advisability of ADR.[194] This could be seen as a minimum obligation.[195] If ADR is taken seriously, legal representatives should be under a duty to consider explicitly a range of factors in giving dispute resolution advice. Where ADR is considered a possible option, this advice could include the qualifications and status of third party neutrals, the information on which the process will be based and the cost of gathering it.

VII. Conclusion

ADR offers solutions for dispute resolution that go beyond the traditional litigation and negotiation model. These private solutions provide access to justice in ways that did not previously exist. This opportunity comes with risks. Techniques developed to empower individuals may be co-opted and distorted to provide cheap and inadequate solutions to problems for which they are not ideally suited.

Government policy has offered lawyers a new role in dispute resolution at a time when civil litigation is in decline. Lawyers participating in ADR as neutral third parties, arbitrators, mediators, conciliators, or as representatives in such process, require different skills. The legal profession has adopted a facilitative model of mediation, with potential blurring of the adversarial and co-operative roles. Lawyers, arguably, have not had adequate preparation for this change in roles in terms of either skills or ethics. This is worrying when ADR codes of conduct are unclear, contradictory and provide dubious authority.

Lawyers representing clients in ADR processes require a good understanding of the potential of ADR. Legal education needs to change accordingly. The ethics of the work change also, with far more emphasis on co-operation and facilitation of the client's goals. It is unclear how far the traditional ethic of lawyers, based as they are on an adversarial tradition, will accommodate or survive this wave of co-operative influence.

---

[194] Arnold (n 87); MJ Breger, 'Should an Attorney be Required to Advise a Client of ADR Options?' (2000) 13 *Georgetown Journal of Legal Ethics* 427.
[195] S Widman, 'ADR and Lawyers Ethics' (1994) 82(3) *Illinois Bar Journal* 150.

Index

Introductory Note

References such as '178–9' indicate (not necessarily continuous) discussion of a topic across a range of pages. Wherever possible in the case of topics with many references, these have either been divided into sub-topics or only the most significant discussions of the topic are listed.